Warman's ANTIQUES AND COLLECTIBLES PRICE GUIDE

29th Edition

The Essential Field Guide to the Antiques and Collectibles Marketplace

Edited by
Harry L. Rinker

Completely illustrated and authenticated

Wallace-Homestead Book Company
Radnor, Pennsylvania

ISBN 0-87069-734-X
ISSN 0196-2272
Library of Congress Catalog Card No. 82-643542
Manufactured in the United States of America

1 2 3 4 5 6 7 8 9   4 3 2 1 0 9 8 7 6 5

EDITORIAL STAFF, 29TH EDITION

Wendy Hamilton Blue
Fan Assoc. of North
   America
6138 Deacon Rd.
Windermere, FL 34786
Fans

Mark R. Brown and Tim
   M. Sublette
Seekers Antiques
PO Box 10083
Columbus, OH 43201
(614) 291-2203
Staffordshire, Romantic

Lissa L. Bryan-Smith
   and Richard M. Smith
Box 208, RD 1
Danville, PA 17821
(717) 275-7796
Christmas Items

Craig Dinner
PO Box 4399
Sunnyside, NY 11104
(718) 894-4185
Doorstops

Roselyn Gerson
12 Alnwick Rd.
Malverne, NY 11565
Compacts

Ted Hake
Hake's Americana &
   Collectibles
PO Box 1444
York, PA 17405
(717) 848-1333
*Disneyana, Political
   Items*

John High
415 E. 52nd St.
New York, NY 10022
(212) 758-1692
Stevengraphs

Joan Hull
1376 Nevada
Huron, SD 57350
(605) 352-1685
Hull Pottery

David and Sue Irons
Irons Antiques
RD #4, Box 101
Northampton, PA 18067
(610) 262-9335
Irons

Lon Knickerbocker
20 William St.
Dansville, NY 14437
(716) 335-6506
Whimsies, Glass

Judy Knauer
1224 Spring Valley Lane
West Chester, PA 19380
(610) 431-3477
Toothpicks

Robert Levy
The Unique One
2802 Centre St.
Pennsauken, NJ 08109
(609) 663-2554
Coin-Operated Items

Ron Lieberman
The Family Album
RD #1, Box 42
Glen Rock, PA 17327
(717) 235-2134
Books

Robert A. Limons
RD #1, Box 162
Hellertown, PA 18055
(610) 838-8931
Pewter

Joyce Magee
7219 Auld Rd.
Bradford, OH 45308
(513) 447-7134
Children's Books

Clarence and Betty
   Maier
The Burmese Cruet
PO Box 432
Montgomeryville, PA
   18936
(610) 855-5388
*Burmese Glass, Crown
   Milano, Royal Flemish*

Norman Martinus
Nostalgia Gallery
3501 North Croyton
   Highway
Kill Devil Hills, NC
   27948
(919) 441-1881
Paper, Ephemera

James S. Maxwell, Jr.
PO Box 367
Lampeter, PA 17537
(717) 464-5573
Banks, Mechanical

Wayne McPeek
1211 Pembroke Rd.
Newark, OH 43055
(614) 344-7846
Verlys Glass

Evalene Pulati
National Valentine
   Collectors Association
PO Box 1404
Santa Ana, CA 92702
Valentines

INTRODUCTION

THE ANTIQUES AND COLLECTIBLES BIBLE

In 1994 *Warman's Antiques and Their Prices* became **Warman's Antiques and Collectibles Price Guide**. The new name more clearly reflects the broad range of coverage found in **Warman's**. However, no matter what its title, this book will be known simply as **Warman's** to those in the trade, a fitting tribute to a man of vision and his product.

Warman's, the antiques and collectibles "bible," covers objects made between 1700 and the present. It always has. Because it reflects market trends, **Warman's** has added more and more twentieth-century material to each edition. Remember, 1900 was 95 years ago—the distant past to the new generation of twentysomething and thirtysomething collectors.

The general *antiques* market consists of antiques (objects made before 1945), collectibles (objects of the post–World War II era that enjoy an established secondary market), and desirables (contemporary objects that are collected, but speculative in price). Although **Warman's** contains information on all three market segments, its greatest emphasis is on antiques and collectibles.

Also note the book's subtitle: *Essential Field Guide To The Antiques And Collectibles Marketplace*, first introduced in the 27th Edition. This indicates that **Warman's** is much more than a list of object descriptions and prices. It is a basic guide to the field as a whole, providing you with the key information you need every time you encounter a new object or collecting category.

"WARMAN'S IS THE KEY"

Warman's provides the keys needed by auctioneers, collectors, dealers, and others to understand and deal with the complexities of the antiques and collectibles market. A price list is only one of many keys needed today. **Warman's 29th Edition** contains many additional keys including: histories, reference books, periodicals, collectors' clubs, and museums. Useful buying and collecting hints also are provided. Used properly, there are few doors these keys will not open.

Warman's is designed to be your first key to the exciting world of antiques and collectibles. As you use the keys this book provides to advance further in your specialized collecting areas, **Warman's** hopes you will remember with fondness where you received your start. When you encounter items outside your area of speciality, remember **Warman's** remains your key to unlocking the information you need, just as it has for over 47 years.

ORGANIZATION

Listings: Objects are listed alphabetically by category, beginning with ABC Plates and ending with Zsolnay Pottery. If you have trouble identifying the category in which your object belongs, use the extensive index in the back of the book. It will guide you to the proper category.

We have made the listings descriptive enough so that specific objects can be identified. We also emphasized items that are actively being sold in the marketplace. Some harder–to–find objects are included to demonstrate market spread, useful information worth considering when you have not traded actively in a category recently.

Each year as the market changes, we carefully review our categories—adding, dropping, and combining to provide the most comprehensive coverage possible. **Warman's** quick response to developing trends in the marketplace is one of the prime reasons for its continued leadership in the field.

Wallace–Homestead Book Company also publishes the Warman's Encyclopedia of Antiques and Collectibles, volumes in the Warman format that concentrate on a specific collecting group, e.g., American Pottery & Porcelain, Americana & Collectibles, Coins and Currency, Country, English & Continental Pottery & Porcelain, Furniture, Glass, Jewelry, Oriental Antiques, and Paper. Several are second or subsequent editions. Their expanded coverage compliments the information found in **Warman's**.

History: Collectors and dealers enhance their appreciation of their objects by knowing something about their history. We present a capsule history for each category. In many cases this history contains collecting hints or tips to spot reproductions.

References: References are listed in each category to help you learn more about their objects. Included are author, title, publisher (if published by a small firm or individual, we have indicated "published by author"), and date of publication or most recent edition.

Finding these books may present a problem. The antiques and collectibles field is blessed with a dedicated core of book dealers who stock these specialized publications. You will find them at flea markets and antiques shows and through their advertisements in trade publications. Many dealers publish annual or semi–annual catalogs. Ask to be put on their mailing lists. Books go out–of–print quickly, yet many books printed over 25 years ago remain the standard work in a category. Used-book dealers often can locate many of these valuable reference sources.

Periodicals: The newsletter or bulletin of a collectors' club usually provides the concentrated focus sought by speciality collectors and dealers. However, there are publications, not associated with collectors' clubs, about which collectors and dealers should be aware. These are listed in their appropriate category introductions.

In addition, there are several general interest newspapers and magazines which deserve to be brought to our user's attention. These are:

Antique Review, PO Box 538, Worthington, OH 43085
Antique Trader Weekly, PO Box 1050, Dubuque, IA 52001
Antique Week, PO Box 90, Knightstown, IN 46148
Antiques (The Magazine Antiques), 551 Fifth Avenue, New York, NY 10017

Antique & The Arts Weekly, Bee Publishing Company, 5 Church Hill Road, Newton, CT 06470

Antiques & Collecting Hobbies, 1006 South Michigan Avenue, Chicago, IL 60605

Collector News & Antique Reporter, Box 156, Grundy Center, IA 50638

Collectors Journal, PO Box 601, Vinton, IA 52349

Collectors' Showcase, PO Box 837, Tulsa, OK 74101

Inside Collector, 225 Main Street, Suite 300, Northport, NY 11768

Maine Antique Digest, PO Box 358, Waldoboro, ME 04572

MidAtlantic Monthly Antiques Magazine, PO Box 908, Henderson, NC 27536

New England Antiques Journal, 4 Church Street, Ware, MA 01082

New York–Pennsylvania Collector, Drawer C, Fishers, NY 14453

Southern Antiques, PO Box 1107, Decatur, GA 30031

West Coast Peddler, PO Box 5134, Whittier, CA 90607

Yesteryear, PO Box 2, Princeton, WI 54968

Space does not permit listing all the national and regional publications in the antiques and collectibles field. The above is a sampling. See David J. Maloney, Jr.'s *Maloney's Antiques & Collectibles Resource Directory 1994–1995* (Wallace–Homestead, 1993) for a more detailed list.

Collectors' Clubs: Collectors' clubs add vitality to the antiques and collectibles field. Their publications and conventions produce knowledge which often cannot be found elsewhere. Many of these clubs are short–lived; others are so strong that they have regional and local chapters.

Museums: The best way to study a specific field is to see as many documented examples as possible. For this reason, we have listed museums where significant collections in that category are on display. Special attention must be directed to the complex of museums which make up the Smithsonian Institution in Washington, D.C.

Reproductions: Reproductions are a major concern to all collectors and dealers. Most reproductions are unmarked; the newness of their appearance is often the best clue to uncovering them. Specific objects known to be reproduced are marked within the listings with an asterisk (*).

Reproduction Archives is a new, eight page feature being introduced for the first time in this 29th Edition of *Warman's Antiques and Collectibles Price Guide.* Reproductions, copycats, fantasy items, and fakes have existed in the antiques and collectibles field for centuries. **Reproduction Archives** documents these problems of the past. The first offering is an annotated bibliography of books relating to reproductions, copycats, fantasies, and fakes. Future offerings will concentrate on specific collecting categories, e.g., brass buckles, majolica, and political pinback buttons.

The reason **Reproduction Archives** concentrates on the past rather than the present is the excellent editorial efforts found in *Antique & Collectors Reproduction News,* a monthly newsletter reporting on the latest problems in the field. It is highly recommended. Send $32 for twelve issues to: ACRN, Box 71174, Des Moines, IA 50325. This publication completed its third year of publication at the end of 1994. Consider buying all available back issues. The information they contain will be of service long into the future.

Index: A great deal of effort has been expended to make our index useful. Always begin by looking for the most specific reference. For example, if you have a piece of china, look first for the maker's name and second for the type. Remember, many objects can be classified in three or more categories. If at first you do not succeed, try, try again.

Black and White Photographs: You may encounter a piece you cannot identify well enough to use the index. Consult the photographs and marks. If you own several editions of **Warman's**, you have available a valuable photographic reference to the antiques and collectibles field. Learn to use it.

Color Photographs Sixteen pages of color photographs are one of the many new features in this 29th edition of *Warman's Antiques and Collectibles Price Guide*. Rather than just pretty pictures with captions, the photographs were carefully selected to make specific points about a collecting category or group. Read the captions closely. You will find collecting hints as well as descriptive information.

PRICE NOTES

In assigning prices we assume the object is in very good condition. If otherwise, we note this in our description. It would be ideal to suggest that mint, or unused, examples of all objects exist. The reality is that objects from the past were used, whether they be glass, china, dolls, or toys. Because of this, some normal wear must be expected. In fact, if an object such as furniture does not show wear, its origins may be more suspect than if it does show wear.

Whenever possible, we have tried to provide a broad listing of prices within a category so you have a "feel" for the market. We emphasize the middle range of prices within a category, while also listing some objects of high and low value to show market spread.

We do not use ranges because they tend to confuse rather than help the collector and dealer. How do you determine if your object is at the high or low end of the range? There is a high degree of flexibility in pricing in the antiques field. If you want to set ranges, add or subtract 10% from our prices.

One of the hardest variants with which to deal is the regional fluctuations of prices. Victorian furniture brings widely differing prices in New York, Chicago, New Orleans, or San Francisco. We have tried to strike a balance. Know your region and subject before investing heavily. If the best prices for cameo glass are in Montreal or Toronto, then be prepared to go there if you want to save money or add choice pieces to your collection. Research and patience are key factors to building a collection of merit.

Another factor that affects prices is a sale by a leading dealer or private collector. We temper both dealer and auction house figures.

PRICE RESEARCH

Everyone asks—where do we get our prices? They come from many sources. First, we rely on auctions. Auction houses and auctioneers do not always command the highest prices. If they did, why do so many dealers buy from them? The key to understanding auction prices is to know when a price is high or low in the range. We think we do this and do it well.

Second, we work closely with dealers. We screen our contacts to make certain they have full knowledge of the market. Dealers make their living from selling antiques; they cannot afford to have a price guide which is not in touch with the market.

Over 50 antiques and collectibles magazines, newspapers, and journals come into our office regularly. They are excellent barometers of what is moving and what is not. We don't hesitate to call an advertiser and ask if their listed merchandise sold.

When the editorial staff is doing field work, we identify ourselves. Our conversations with dealers and collectors around the country have enhanced this book. Teams from **Warman's** are in the field at antiques shows, malls, flea markets, and auctions recording prices and taking photographs.

Collectors work closely with us. They are specialists whose devotion to research and accurate information is inspiring. Generally, they are not dealers. Whenever we have asked them for help, they have responded willingly and admirably.

BOARD OF ADVISORS

Our Board of Advisors is made up of specialists, both dealers and collectors, who feel a commitment to accurate information. You'll find their names listed in the front of the book. Several have authored a major reference work on their subject.

Members of the Board of Advisors file lists of prices in the categories for which they are responsible. They help select and often supply the photographs used. If you wish to buy or sell an object in their field of expertise, drop them a note along with an SASE. If time or interest permits, they will respond.

BUYER'S GUIDE, NOT SELLER'S GUIDE

Warman's is designed to be a buyer's guide to what you would have to pay to purchase an object on the open market from a dealer or collector. **It is not a seller's guide to prices.** People frequently make this mistake. In doing so, they deceive themselves. If you have an object listed in this book and wish to sell it to a dealer, you should expect to receive approximately 50% of the listed value. If the object will not resell quickly, expect to receive even less.

A private collector may pay more, perhaps 70 to 80% of our list price. Your object will have to be something needed for his or her collection. If you have an extremely rare object or an object of exceptionally high value, these guidelines do not apply.

Examine your piece as objectively as possible. As an antiques and collectibles appraiser, I spend a great deal of time telling people their treasures are not "gold" at all, but items readily available in the marketplace.

In respect to buying and selling, a simple philosophy is that a good purchase occurs when the buyer and seller are happy with the price. Don't look back. Hindsight has little value in the antiques and collectibles field. Given time, things tend to balance out.

COMMENTS INVITED

Warman's Antiques And Collectibles Price Guide: The Essential Field Guide To The Antiques And Collectibles Marketplace continues to be the leader in the antiques and collectibles price guide field because we listen to our readers. Readers are encouraged to send their comments and suggestions to Harry L. Rinker, c/o Rinker Enterprises, Inc., 5093 Vera Cruz Road, Emmaus, PA 18049.

ACKNOWLEDGMENTS

1994 was a year of transition at Rinker Enterprises, Inc. Early in the year my formal consulting-editor relationship with Chilton Books ended. It was a great seven years. Rinker Enterprises, Inc., continues to provide manuscripts for several Warman and other Chilton titles; and, I still recruit authors for Wallace–Homestead and Warman titles and serve as series editor for the Warman Encyclopedia of Antiques and Collectibles. As you see, my personal relationship and that of Rinker Enterprises, Inc., with Chilton Books remains strong.

Changes bring new opportunities and responsibilities. Ellen Schroy, who many of you know as senior editor of the Warman titles that I edit as well as author of *Warman's Glass* and *Warman's Pattern Glass*, increased her supervisory role as Director of Publications and Research at Rinker Enterprises, Inc. She is my left and right hand. Bluntly put, she runs Rinker Enterprises, Inc. Her expanded responsibilities include office manager, book indexing, and logistical support for the Institute for the Study of Antiques and Collectibles. She does it all. Nothing more need be said.

In addition to her duties as Associate Editor for Warman titles, Terese Oswald has taken on the added responsibilities of financial manager for Rinker Enterprises, Inc., and in-house editor for a revision of the House of Collectibles' limited edition plate book. As Matt and Christa become increasingly more responsible as teenagers, Terese's role at Rinker Enterprises, Inc., continues to grow. I deeply appreciate Terese's steadfastness and dedication. She is one of the great unsung heroes in this trade, deserving far more credit than some clients and the field give her.

In addition to serving as Associate Editor of Warman titles and co–author of *Warman's Country*, Dana Morykan's researching and pricing expertise can be seen each month in *Collectors' News*, "Rinker's Monthly Price Index" feature. She is in continual contact with auction houses, catalog sellers, and specialized dealers throughout the nation. As if this wasn't enough responsibility, Dana also does our computer page design and layout.

Harry Jr., Rinker Enterprises, Inc.'s Art Director, had a banner year. His antiques and collectibles photographs appeared in national magazines, newspapers, and over half a dozen books and on CD–ROM discs, a line of magnets, and a jigsaw puzzle. In addition, he is one of the prime movers in Rinker Enterprises, Inc.'s first CD–ROM antiques and collectibles priced picture guide scheduled for release in early 1995.

Nancy Butt continues to make certain that the Rinker Enterprises, Inc., reference library is the best in the field. Jocelyn Mousley at the photocopy machine insures that our reference files are current. Richard Schmeltzle sees that the Rinker Enterprises, Inc., physical plant is ready for occupancy day or night—and, believe me, the night lamp burns bright and often.

The trade knows the above group as The Rinkettes. I know them as family. We are a team. I am the boss only on paper. Each Rinkette is a highly capable, skilled, independent operator. If a person is known by the company he keeps, I am blessed.

It is because of this talented group that I was able to devote 1994 to developing several new projects. These range from **Whatcha Got,** a nationally syndicated antiques and collectibles radio call–in show, to the creation of a series of CD–ROM priced picture guides. Look for several new titles listing me as author in 1995 including a book on Hopalong Cassidy collectibles. There is much more to come. I am saving the rest as surprises.

Each year I automatically thank two groups—the Board of Advisors and others who supply the information used to prepare **Warman's** and you, its users. While the thanks may be automatic, I want each group to know that I fully realize that they are as much responsible for the success of **Warman's** as are The Rinkettes and myself. **Warman's** would not exist if it were not for you. Thank you, thank you, thank you.

Jeff Day, Edna Jones, Troy Vozzella, Tony Jacobson, and a host of other individuals at Chilton Book Co., parent company of Wallace–Homestead, have contributed to **Warman's** for so many years that they are as much fixtures in respect to this book as are we of the editorial staff. All are committed to creating the best product available in the market. Their professionalism shows from edition to edition.

1995 is the year it happens at Rinker Enterprises, Inc. I have not felt this enthused or optimistic since the mid–1980s. You will find this same feeling conveyed in my *State of the Market Report*. There are good times ahead. Hallelujah, Let's All Be Happy!!!

Rinker Enterprises, Inc.   Harry L. Rinker
5093 Vera Cruz Road   Editor
Emmaus, PA 18049
January 1995

STATE OF THE MARKET

I normally write my *State of the Market* report for **Warman's Antiques and Collectibles Price Guide** in early December. This time I waited until the last possible moment, early January 1995. The reason is simple. I wanted to make absolutely certain that I was comfortable writing the following:

THE RECESSION IS OVER IN THE ANTIQUES AND COLLECTIBLES FIELD. RECOVERY HAS BEGUN.

It has been a long time coming. The antiques and collectibles market entered the doldrums in the summer of 1988. The train that was stuck near the end of the tunnel in my 1994 *State of the Market Report* gathered enough momentum to emerge into the sunlight. Do not celebrate too quickly. The back of the train still is in the tunnel. The recovery train's speed is minimal. It is a slow freight, not a speedy passenger train. However, the good news, *and it is good news*, is the train is moving forward.

Recovery is not universal. There are some collecting categories that continue to decline slightly. The recovery is much stronger in some geographic areas than others. Recovery is strongest in the Mid–Atlantic states and on the West Coast. The key word is *stronger*. Every geographic area shows evidence of recovery. The gloom and doom days of the early 1990s are definitely past.

The effects of the recession on the antiques and collectibles field will continue to be felt for a long time. The conservatism that dominated buying and selling in the early 1990s will continue through the end of the decade. Dealers are purchasing new stock very selectively. Collectors are much more demanding in respect to condition and price. Everyone shops for the best deal possible.

A new breed of collector continues to emerge. It is hard to believe that Baby Boomers no longer constitute the youngest collecting group. Baby Boomers are the establishment. They will become the traditionalists in another ten years. The stuff the Baby Boomers grew up with in the late 1940s and early 1950s is old hat. Their children and grandchildren, the first generation of 21st-century collectors, view this immediate post–World War II period as ancient.

Today's twentysomething and thirtysomething collectors are focusing on the cultural artifacts, a fancy phrase for collectibles, of the late 1960s and 1970s. It makes sense. This is the latest group of objects to achieve a viable secondary sales market. Rinker's Thirty Year Rule—*for the first 30 years of anything's life, all its value is speculative*—holds. One knows something is afoot when the *Wall Street Journal* reports: "A cult is also growing up around series such as Aaron Spelling's *Dynasty* and Steven Bochco's *Hill Street Blues*, as bootleg videotapes become collect–and–trade items. And the nearly 30–year old *Star Trek* memorabilia market shows no signs of disappearing . . ."

To the consternation of antiques aficionados, 1994 was the year of Barbie and G.I. Joe. Barbie turned 35; G.I. Joe celebrated his 30 birthday. Mattel sponsored a Barbie convention at Disney World. Hasbro sponsored a G.I. Joe convention aboard the U.S.S. *Intrepid* in New York harbor. No wonder the collectibles market is doing so well. Industry support such as this is non–existent for collecting categories in the antiques' sector.

1994 witnessed the final collapse of the baseball card market. Oversupply, unsustainable market-price manipulation, withdrawal of some major buyers, and fraud led to the decline. Many baseball card dealers have switched their allegiance to non–sport trading cards, a collecting category that has helped many comic book shops keep their doors open. Will non–sport trading cards follow the same path as baseball cards? Bet on it.

The selling of fraudulent material reared its ugly head many times during 1994. The problem is epidemic in the area of autographed baseballs. The general feeling is that over half the balls in the market are fakes. As 1994 ended, a wire service carried a story of the discovery in Florida of a hoard of baseballs with faked Roger Maris signatures.

Several trade newspapers reported on a large quantity of modern majolica being passed in the market as period. The sellers had the audacity to state publicly that they saw no problem selling modern majolica for period prices so long as the customer did not ask if the piece was old or new. Collectors and dealers in the trade rely on *Antique & Collectors Reproduction News* (Box 71174, Des Moines, IA 50325) as the best defense against being stung. The $32 yearly subscription is one of the best investments in the trade one can make.

Crazes come and go. 1994 proved no exception. Pez fell on hard times, once again due in part to a group of fake Pez containers that entered the American market from Europe. O.J. Simpson's freeway ride and arrest saw prices for O.J. Simpson collectibles triple and quadruple over night. The market quickly found its sanity. Prices are now only slightly above their pre–freeway-ride levels. At year's end, speculation in scarce Mighty Morphin Power Rangers was rampant. Fools and greed do not make strange bedfellows. They always sleep together.

The Hess Company, whose annual Christmas vehicles have been a source of speculation for toy collectors for over a decade, put an end to the madness once and for all by flooding the market with this year's offering. Instead of the vehicle selling out on Thanksgiving, the day when it is first sold publicly, it was possible to buy the Hess vehicle as late as the day before Christmas. The Hess lesson was learned by Neiman Marcus and Bloomingdales who offer special issue, series merchandise from previous years in current catalogs. Will Bandai learn this lesson? I doubt it; but others will. Manufacturers are tired of speculators making a killing on the resale of material that is less than a year old. The manufacturers, not the resellers, take the heat. Look for more manufacturers to flood a market when they encounter or anticipate speculation by modern collectors. Many fast food chains now restrict sales of fast food premiums to collectors.

The Japanese recession continues to play havoc with the American antiques and collectibles market. There is Japanese money around. However, it no longer surfaces as regularly as it did in the late 1980s and early 1990s. Further, it is more difficult to predict where it will crop up. Many antiques dealers continue to look to the Far East, and Japan in particular, as their market's savior. Their argument is that Japanese collectors eventually will discover the aesthetic qualities of 19th- and early 20th-century American antiques and invest heavily in them. Hopefully, they are not holding their breath.

The real foreign strength in the American market rests with the Europeans. The English, French, and Germans are becoming increasingly important as buyers. There is a strong possibility that they will replace the Far Eastern buyers as the major market force in 1995. A group showing a surprisingly strong influence are collectors and dealers from the Mediterranean, especially Portugal, Spain, and Italy.

Many, myself included, continue to wait for the South American buyer to impact on the American market. Every time I think it is finally ready to happen, something quiets that market sector. There is great untapped potential in South America. However, I am putting the concept on the back burner for the moment.

In 20 years, historians of the American antiques and collectibles field will look at the late–1990s as the period that produced the greatest changes in the field during the 20th century. The driving force behind these changes will be identified as the hardware and software of the information super highway. Signs of change are in the wind.

1994 saw the launch of Fox's *Personal FX*, a daily one-hour antiques and collectibles show, on Fox's FX cable channel. The Home and Garden Channel, another cable offering, launched the first week of January 1995. It boasts several shows focused on collecting. Two efforts—Arts & Antique Network and Collectors' Channel—to create a channel devoted primarily to antiques and collectibles met with failure, but not before attracting considerable attention from established cable networks.

The antiques and collectibles community remains divided over whether Home Shopping, QVC, and similar home-shopping channels have impacted positively or negatively on the trade. The one thing no one questions are the channels' selling success. Fenton has gained a host of new collectors as a result of its QVC sales. The key question for the field is how to switch buyer loyalty from the contemporary to our secondary market.

1994 witnessed the entry into the marketplace of a host of early QVC and other home-shopping material. When sold at auction, prices realized ranged between 20 and 30¢ on the original retail dollar. This proved especially true for ''collector dolls.'' Collectors wishing to add a home-shopping item to their personal collection have learned to be patient and wait for it to enter the secondary market. Many collectors take pride in not paying more than 20¢ on the dollar for any item they purchase. Kudos to them and my congratulations.

Antiques and collectibles CD–ROM catalog discs are not new. However, the current titles are expensive and highly specialized. Look for a revolution in 1995. The first CD–ROM picture price guides with a price point around $25 are scheduled for publication in the first quarter of 1995. Many major price guides will be on CD–ROM disc by the end of the year. The main delay in the latter is an adequate information-retrieval program. Several individuals and publishers are working to solve this problem. By the end of the decade, CD–ROM picture and price guides will be the field's principal reference sources.

In 1994 more and more collectors and dealers discovered the computer. Using commercial on–line services such as America On–Line, CompuServe, Delphi, Genie, or Prodigy, collectors reach the rec.antiques or rec.collecting area of Internet. Several individuals are attempting to launch antiques and collectibles bulletin boards. Previous attempts met with failure. I am betting that 1995 is the year when one or more succeed.

1994 was the year of the video. Dozens of antiques and collectibles video titles were launched in 1994. The professional production level and quality of information was significantly advanced from previous offerings. Look for more titles in 1995.

While the information super highway is establishing itself, a number of important changes are occurring in the publishing and periodical areas of the antiques and collectibles field. 1994 saw Landmark Specialty Publications, parent company of the *Antique Trader Weekly*, solidify its foothold in the antiques and collectibles sector through acquisition and the launch of several new publications and creation of its own publishing and book distribution operation. Krause, King of the Periodicals, now has a formidable challenger. Look for some head-to-head competition in 1995 as well as each attempting to gain a stranglehold on key specialty fields.

House of Collectibles has a new general manager and a new lease on life. The old warhorse is back in the race. Welcome. Competition is good for everyone. L–W Book Sales has increased its publishing efforts. Its products fill the title void created by the withdrawal of major publishers from the field of secondary titles. Congratulations to Neil Wood and his fine staff. In addition, many other publishing firms are trying an antiques or collectibles title or two. Coupled with private publishing efforts, 1994 was a banner year for good reference titles. 1995 promises to be even better.

This *State of the Market Report* has focused primarily on business developments and market analysis rather than major shifts in specific collecting trends. In 1994 most market categories remained stable, i.e., did not experience a price increase or decrease of plus or minus 5% over the previous year. As recovery takes hold in 1995, look for a number of individual categories to get hot and run.

I am pleased to end my *State of the Market Report* on such an upbeat note. **THERE IS A BRIGHT FUTURE AHEAD.** 1995 and, I suspect, 1996 will be building years. The real action will occur as the decade of the 1990s ends. These final few years promise to be the most exciting period in the antiques and collectibles trade since the early 1980s.

AUCTION HOUSES

The following auction houses cooperate with Rinker Enterprises, Inc., by providing catalogs of their auctions and price lists. This information is used to prepare *Warman's Antiques and Collectibles Price Guide*, volumes in the Warman's Encyclopedia of Antiques and Collectibles, and Wallace–Homestead Book Company publications. This support is most appreciated.

Sanford Alderfer Auction
Company
501 Fairgrounds Rd.
Hatfield, PA 19440
(610) 368-5477

Andre Ammelounx
PO Box 136
Palatine, IL 60078
(708) 991-5927

Al Anderson
PO Box 644
Troy, OH 45373
(513) 339-0850

Ark Antiques
Box 3133
New Haven, CT 06515
(203) 387-3754

Arthur Auctioneering
RD 2
Hughesville, PA 17737
(717) 584-3697

Noel Barrett Antiques
and Auctions Ltd.
PO Box 1001
Carversville, PA 18913
(610) 297-5109

Robert F. Batchelder
1 W. Butler Ave.
Ambler, PA 19002
(610) 643-1430

Biders Antiques, Inc.
241 S. Union St.
Lawrence, MA 01843
(508) 688-4347

Butterfield & Butterfield
7601 Sunset Blvd.
Los Angeles, CA 90046
(213) 850-7500

Butterfield & Butterfield
220 San Bruno Ave.
San Francisco, CA
94103
(415) 861-7500

W. E. Channing & Co.
53 Old Santa Fe Trail
Santa Fe, New Mexico
87501
(505) 988-1078

Christie's
502 Park Ave.
New York, NY 10022
(212) 546-1000

Christie's East
219 E. 67th St.
New York, NY 10021
(212) 606-0400

Christmas Morning
1850 Crown Rd. Suite
1111
Dallas, TX 75234
(817) 236-1155

Cincinnati Art Galleries
635 Main St.
Cincinnati, OH 45202
(513) 381-2128

Clinton-Ivankovich
Auction Co. Inc.
PO Box 29
Ottisville, PA 18942
(610) 847-5432

Cobb's Doll Auctions
1909 Harrison Rd. N
Johnstown, OH 43031
(614) 964-0444

Cohasco, Inc.
Postal 821
Yonkers, NY 10702
(914) 476-8500

Marvin Cohen Auctions
Box 425, Routes 20 &
22
New Lebanon, NY
12125
(518) 794-9333

Collector's Auction
Services
PO Box 13732
Seneca, PA 16346
(814) 677-6070

Marlin G. Denlinger
RR 3, Box 3775
Morrisville, VT 05661
(802) 888-2774

William Doyle Galleries,
Inc.
175 E. 87th St.
New York, NY 10128
(212) 427-2730

Dunbars Gallery
76 Haven St.
Milford, MA 01757
(508) 634-8697

Early Auction Co.
123 Main St.
Milford, OH 45150
(513) 831-4833

Ken Farmer Realty &
  Auction Co.
1122 Norwood St.
Radford, VA 24141
(703) 639-0939

Steve Finer Rare Books
PO Box 758
Greenfield, MA 01302
(413) 773-5811

William A. Fox
  Auctions, Inc.
676 Morris Ave.
Springfield, NJ 07081
(201) 467-2366

Freeman/Fine Arts Co.
  of Philadelphia, Inc.
1808 Chestnut St.
Philadelphia, PA 19103
(610) 563-9275

Garth's Auction, Inc.
2690 Stratford Rd.
PO Box 369
Delaware, OH 43015
(614) 362-4771 or 369-
  5085

Glass-Works Auctions
PO Box 187-102
  Jefferson St.
East Greenville, PA
  18041
(610) 679-5849

Grandma's Trunk
The Millards
PO Box 404
Northport, MI 49670
(616) 386-5351

Guerney's
136 E. 73rd St.
New York, NY 10021
(212) 794-2280

Hake's Americana and
  Collectibles
PO Box 1444
York, PA 17405
(717) 848-1333

Harmer Rooke
  Numismatists, Inc.
3 E. 57th St.
New York, NY 10022
(212) 751-4122

Gene Harris Antique
  Auction Center, Inc.
203 S. 18th Ave.
Marshalltown, IA 50158
(515) 752-0600

Morton M. Goldberg
  Auction Galleries
547 Baronne St.
New Orleans, LA 70113
(504) 592-2300

Norman C. Heckler &
  Company
Bradford Corner Rd.
Woodstock Valley, CT
  06282
(203) 974-1634

Leslie Hindman, Inc.
215 W. Ohio St.
Chicago, IL 60610
(312) 670-0010

Jackson Auction Co.
2227 Lincoln St.
Cedar Falls, IA 50613
(319) 277-2256

James D. Julia, Inc.
PO Box 830
Fairfield, ME 04937
(207) 453-7904

Charles E. Kirtley
PO Box 2273
Elizabeth City, NC
  27906
(919) 335-1262

Howard Lowery
3818 W. Magnolia Blvd.
Burbank, CA 91505
(818) 972-9080

Alex G. Malloy, Inc.
PO Box 38
South Salem, NY 10590
(203) 438-0396

Martin Auctioneers, Inc.
Larry L. Martin
PO Box 477
Intercourse, PA 17534
(717) 768-8108

Robert Merry Auction
  Company
5501 Milburn Rd.
St. Louis, MO 63129
(314) 487-3992

Mid-Hudson Auction
  Galleries
One Idlewild Ave.
Cornwall-On-Hudson,
  NY 12520
(214) 534-7828

Milwaukee Auction
  Galleries
318 N. Water
Milwaukee, WI 53202
(414) 271-1105

Neal Auction Company
4038 Magazine St.
New Orleans, LA 70115
(504) 899-5329

New England Auction
  Gallery
Box 2273
W. Peabody, MA 01960
(508) 535-3140

New Hampshire Book
  Auctions
Woodbury Rd.
Weare, NH 03281
(603) 529-1700

Nostalgia Publications,
  Inc.
21 S. Lake Dr.
Hackensack, NJ 07601
(201) 488-4536

Pam & Dick Oestreicher
4025 Saline St.
Pittsburgh, PA 15217
(412) 421-5230

Richard Opfer
  Auctioneers Inc.
1919 Greenspring Dr.
Timonium, MD 21093
(410) 252-5035

Pettigrew Auction
  Company
1645 S. Tejon St.
Colorado Springs, CO
  80906
(719) 633-7963

Phillips Ltd.
406 E. 79th St.
New York, NY 10021
(212) 570-4830

Postcards International
PO Box 2930
New Haven, CT 06515-
  0030
(203) 865-0814

David Rago Arts &
  Crafts
PO Box 3592 Station E
Trenton, NJ 08629
(609) 585-2546

Lloyd Ralston Toys
173 Post Rd.
Fairfield, CT 06432
(203) 255-1233 or 366-
  3399

Renzel's Auction Service
PO Box 222
Emigsville, PA 17318
(717) 764-6412

R. Niel & Elaine
  Reynolds
Box 133
Waterford, VA 22190
(703) 882-3574

Roan Bros. Auction
  Gallery
RD 3, Box 118
Cogan Station, PA 17728
(717) 494-0170

Selkirk Gallery
4166 Olive St.
Saint Louis, MO 63108
(314) 533-1700

L. H. Selman Ltd.
761 Chestnut St.
Santa Cruz, CA 95060
(408) 427-1177

Robert W. Skinner Inc.
Bolton Gallery
357 Main St.
Bolton, MA 01740
(508) 779-6241

C. G. Sloan &
  Company, Inc.
4920 Wyaconda Rd.
North Bethesda, MD
  20852
(301) 468-4911

Smith House Toy Sales
26 Adlington Rd.
Eliot, ME 03903
(207) 439-4614

Sotheby's
1334 York Ave.
New York, NY 10021
(212) 606-7000

Rex Stark
49 Wethersfield Rd.
Bellingham, MA 02019
(508) 966-0994

Swann Galleries, Inc.
104 E. 25th St.
New York, NY 10010
(212) 254-4710

Theriault's
PO Box 151
Annapolis, MD 21401
(301) 224-3655

Victorian Images
PO Box 284
Marlton, NJ 08053
(609) 985-7711

Vintage Cover Story
PO Box 975
Burlington, NC 27215
(919) 584-6990

Western Glass Auctions
1288 W. 11th St., Suite
#230
Tracy, CA 95376
(209) 832-4527

Winter Associates
21 Cooke St., Box 823
Plainville, CT 06062
(203) 793-0288

Wolf's Auctioneers
1239 W. 6th St.
Cleveland, OH 44113
(614) 362-4711

Woody Auction
Douglass, KS 67039
(316) 746-2694

Pacific Book Auction
  Galleries
139 Townsend St., Suite
  305
San Francisco, CA
  94107
(415) 896-2665

REPRODUCTION ARCHIVES

PERIOD, RECONSTRUCTED, REPRODUCTION, COPYCAT, FANTASY, OR FAKE: AN ANNOTATED BIBLIOGRAPHY

The issues involved with identifying period, reconstructed, reproduction (an exact copy), copycat (a stylistic copy), fantasy (a non-period form in a period motif), and fake objects are not new. Elsie de Wolfe's "Reproductions versus Antiques" article in a 1912 issue of *Good Housekeeping* notes: "The antiques the average American householder is most interested in are the old mahogany and oak and walnut things that stand for the oldest period of our own particular history... The native problem is the so-called colonial mahogany that is always alleged to be Chippendale, Heppelwhite (sic) or Sheraton. There must be ten thousand so-called pieces in the New York shops alone! It goes without saying that only a very small number of them can be really old. . ."

Simply put—there are 75 year old, 100 year old, and even older reconstructed, reproduction, copycat, fantasy, and fake objects that have stood the test of time and acquired age and wear characteristics that make it difficult for the vast majority of collectors and dealers to distinguish them from their period counterparts. Because of this, any reference library dealing with this issue must contain books printed throughout the 20th century. Modern collectors and dealers prefer to learn from the past, not repeat it.

Unfortunately, most books devoted to the subject of period versus reconstructed, reproduction, copycat, fantasy, and fake objects remain in-print for a very short period of time. Almost all the books on the following list are out-of-print. The principal methods to acquire them are through the purchase of a retiring collector's or dealer's reference library or through booksellers who specialize in out-of-print antiques and collectibles books.

Over half the books in this bibliography focus on furniture. While helpful, this is tragic. Furniture represents far less of a problem than do ceramics, glass, metal, and paper to the average collector and dealer.

Remember, there are general principles from mindset to examination techniques that carry over from one collecting category to another. This is the key. When reading a furniture book look for general principles that can be applied to other collecting categories in addition to specific points about furniture.

This annotated bibliography focuses only on hard- and softcover books devoted exclusively to the issues of period versus reconstructed, reproduction, copycat, fantasy, and fake items. It is not inclusive. It is limited by two factors: (1) books readily available in the out-of-print book marketplace and (2) books in the Rinker Enterprises, Inc., reference library.

In addition to these general books, many specialized books contain a chapter or two dealing with reproductions, et al, in their specific collecting category. Further, hundreds of general and trade-paper articles have been devoted to the issue. Hopefully, someday a detailed list of these sources will be compiled and made available.

Rinker Enterprises, Inc., welcomes any recommendations and opinions about the titles included in this list, additions that should be made, and any specific articles and portions of books that are especially helpful in a specific collecting area. Send your comments to: Rinker Enterprises, Inc., 5093 Vera Cruz Road, Emmaus, PA 18049.

Bly, John (ed.). *Is It Genuine?: How To Collect Antiques With Confidence.* London: Mitchell Beazley Publishers, Ltd., 1986. Distributed in the United States by Prentice Hall Press with title *The Confident Collector.* Out-of-print.

Bly asked 13 experts in America and England to write a chapter dealing with "deceptions, fakes, and not-quite-genuine pieces" in their specialty. The 16-chapter approach is topical. The quality of writing and content is inconsistent. Some writers have difficulty sticking to the focus at hand. Emphasis is decidely upscale. Despite its shortcomings, there are many useful pieces of general and specific information scattered throughout the text. Indexed.

Cescinsky, Herbert. *The Gentle Art of Faking Furniture.* London: Chapman & Hall, Ltd., 1931. Reprinted in paperback by Dover Publications, 1967. Out-of-print.

A must-read classic for anyone dealing in 18th- and early 19th-century British furniture. Cescinsky's writing style is cumbersome, and many cited pieces are from museums. The history of furniture construction and design found throughout the book is especially valuable. Indexed.

Crawley, W. *Is It Genuine?: A Guide To The Identification of Eighteenth Century English Furniture.* New York City: Copyright by W. Crawley and Maurice Michael in 1971 and Hart Publishing Company in 1972. Out-of-print.

The book is dedicated "To the anonymous person who offered me a substantial sum not to print this book." The author was a master cabinetmaker who was actively involved in producing reconstructed, reproduction, copycat, fantasy, and fake furniture. In addition to detailing the techniques he used to make these pieces, he also explains how they were marketed. Do not ignore this book because of its British origin. American copyists and fakers use the same techniques and marketing methods. No Index.

Feild, Rachael. *Macdonald Guide To Buying Antique Furniture.* London: Copyright by Brooks Stephenson Publishing Ltd., 1986. First published by Macdonald & Co. (Publishers, Ltd). in 1984. American editions distributed by Salem House Ltd. in 1986 and Wallace-Homestead, 1989. Out-of-print.

Feild created a unique approach for her Macdonald Guide series. After a strong introduction to the topic, she takes a single object form and covers its historical background, construction and materials, variations, signs of authenticity, most likely restoration and repairs, reproductions, and price. The key is to focus on the form, not where the object was made. Books in the Feild Macdonald Guide series should be read at least once a year. No one is capable of absorbing all that can be learned from a single reading. Indexed.

Feild, Rachael. *Macdonald Guide To Buying Antique Pottery & Porcelain*. London: Copyright by author, published by Macdonald & Co. (Publishers) Ltd., 1987. Distributed in the United States by Wallace-Homestead, 1989. Out-of-print.

Follows a similar format to her furniture book. Individual objects are discussed in terms of historical background, materials and decoration, variations, signs of authenticity, principal producers and products, reproductions, and price. Heavily weighted to 18th- and 19th-century English and Continental forms and decorative techniques. However, remember, many of these ceramics were exported to America and collected by American collectors. Especially helpful is the Index of Shapes by date, a date-line chart, and glossary. Indexed.

Feild, Rachael. *Macdonald Guide To Buying Antique Silver & Sheffield Plate*. London: Copyright by author, published by Macdonald Co. (Publishers) Ltd., 1988. Out-of-print.

This Feild volume never found an American distributor. The focus is primarily on English silver and silver plate made between 1600 and 1850. However, until something better is available, it should be considered a must own by anyone collecting or dealing in 18th- and 19th-century silver. Indexed.

[Note: The antiques and collectibles field suffered a tragic loss with the death of Rachael Feild in the early 1990s. She was working on a volume involving glass at the time of her death.]

Hammond, Dorothy. *Confusing Collectibles: A Guide To The Identification of Contemporary Objects*. Des Moines, IA: Copyright by author, published by Wallace-Homestead, 1969 with revised printing in 1979. Out-of-print.

Confusing Collectibles consists of reprints from the catalogs of leading manufacturers and craftspersons of antiques and collectibles reproductions, et al, in the 1960s along with comments about the products by Hammond. Many of these 1960s ''reproductions'' are highly collectible today. While the vast majority of the book deals with glass, there are chapters on furniture, cast iron banks and toys, metalware and woodenware, and a few miscellaneous topics. It is shocking to see how many of the pictured items have become respectable and are now a significant part of many mall and shop dealers' inventories. Indexed.

Hammond, Dorothy. *More Confusing Collectibles: A Guide To The Identification of Reproductions*. Wichita, KS: Copyright by author, published by C. B. P. Publishing Co., 1972. Out-of-print.

This 46 page paperback supplements the information found in *Confusing Collectibles*. The approach is better balanced. However, glass continues to dominate. Of special note are the seven pages devoted to ''Back Stamps And Trademarks Found On New Pieces of Pottery, Porcelain, Glass And Metal.'' Indexed.

Hayward, Charles H. *Antique Or Fake?* New York: Copyright by author, published by Van Nostrand Reinhold Co., 1981, paperback. Cloth edition published in 1970 by Evans Brothers Limited and St. Martin's Press. Out-of-print.

Given that Cescinsky, Crawley, Feild, Kaye, and Jenkins/Wilkinson are on this list, why include Hayward? The book deals only with 18th- and 19th-century British furniture, a subject covered by several of these other books. The reason is Hayward's strong emphasis on construction. If you know how a period piece was made and its proper aging characteristics, it is much easier to spot later pieces. A worthwhile read, but not to the exclusion of the other furniture books in this bibliography. Indexed.

Kaye, Myrna. *Fake, Fraud, Or Genuine?: Identifying Authentic American Antique Furniture*. Boston, Copyright by author, published by Little, Brown and Company, 1987. Available in paperback from Bulfinch Press, a division of Little Brown and Company.

This is a must-read book for collectors and dealers in American furniture. Each page contains another invaluable tip. The book's limitations are its almost exclusive focus on formal design furniture and coverage that ends in the mid-19th century. Like the Feild books, this book should be reread at least once a year. Indexed.

Jenkins, Emyl, and Joe E. A. Wilkinson. *Emyl Jenkins' Guide To Buying and Collecting Early American Furniture*. New York: Copyright by author, published by Crown Publishers, Inc., 1991.

A Rachael Feild copycat. When you first put the book down, you feel you learned a great deal. However, when you think about what you read, you realize that it is primarily a rehash of what appeared elsewhere and often fails to take points and discussions to their logical conclusions. The emphasis is high-end, like most of Jenkins' products.

Jenks, Bill, Jerry Luna, and Darryl Reilly. *Identifying Pattern Glass Reproductions*. Radnor, PA: Wallace-Homestead Book Company, 1993.

This book serves as a model for period versus reproduction, copycat, and fantasy specialty publications. It illustrates the scholarship required to fully document a specialized category and the cost to provide this information in printed form. Of value only if one plans to collect or deal in pattern glass. Indexed.

Lee, Ruth Webb. *Antique Fakes & Reproductions, Enlarged and Revised.* Wellesley Hills, MA: Published by author, 1938, 1950. [Note: This book went through at least eight editions. The later editions contain more information. A good rule is to buy only the 4th through the 8th edition.] Out-of-print.

Most of Ruth Webb Lee's books are classics. This is no exception. The book chronicles reproductions, copycats, fantasy, and fake items made between 1920 and 1950. The primary emphasis is on glass (nine out of fourteen specialty chapters). Other topics include American silver, ceramics, old and new mechanical banks, ironwork, and novelties. Unfortunately, Lee refused to name the manufacturers of the objects even though it is evident she was fully aware of who they were. Indexed.

Mills, John Fitz Maurice and John M. Mansfield. *The Genuine Article: The Making and Unmasking of Fakes and Forgeries.* London: Copyright by authors, published by British Broadcasting Corporation, 1979. Out-of-print.

The book expands a seven-part BBC television series that chronicles the history of fakery in a number of specific collecting categories—antiquities, ceramics, coins, documents, furniture, jewelry, paintings, prints and drawings, scientific instruments, sculpture, stamps, and miscellany. Excellent and frightening, it is a difficult book to put down once you begin to read it. It helps put modern concerns into perspective. Indexed.

Peterson, Harold L. *How Do You Know It's Old?: A Practical Handbook On The Detection Of Fakes For The Antique Collector And Curator.* New York: Copyright by author, published by Charles Scribner's Sons, 1975. Out-of-print.

In the 1970s, this book was the must-read general book on the subject. It still deserves this reputation. The book focuses primarily on two groups of material—wood and metal, the two subjects of most interest to Peterson, a firearm and sword collector. A concluding general chapter discusses ceramics, horn, scrimshaw, and stone. The book ends with an annotated bibliography that includes books on this list along more than half a dozen books published on the subject between 1900 and 1940. Indexed.

Yates, Raymond F. *Antique Fakes And Their Detection.* New York: Harper & Row, Publishers, 1950. Also available in a Gramercy Publishing Company, a division of Crown Publishers, Inc., edition.

The book begins: "This book is going to say some ugly things about the antique business that have long since needed saying." It provides an excellent perspective of the period versus reproduction, et al., issues of the 1940s and early 1950s. Full of generalities and suspicions, the book lacks specifics. Almost 50 years have passed since its publication. It is well worth reminding one's self that there were major problem pieces then and raise the haunting question of what happened to these objects in the period between 1950 and now. Indexed.

The techniques used in faking and marketing antiques are openly discussed in Jonathan Gash's Lovejoy novels. The series now contains over a dozen titles. Those unfamiliar with Gash's work are encouraged to read the early volumes first, e.g., *The Gondola Scam, The Judas Pair, The Sleepers of Erin,* and *The Vatican Rip.* Gash's recent works are written in a more abstract literary style with an emphasis much heavier on sex than antiques. They also are less believable. All titles, with the exception of one or two of the most recent, are available in paperback.

Gash's novels are the basis for "Lovejoy," an hour-long television series that airs in America on the Arts & Entertainment cable channel. While highly amusing at first glance, Lovejoy presents a highly negative portrayal of the antiques community, from auctioneer to dealer. Little wonder the general public perceives members of the antiques community as thieves and crooks.

This bibliography would not be complete without commenting on Colin Haynes' *The Complete Collector's Guide to Fakes And Forgeries* (Radnor, PA: Wallace-Homestead, 1988). I do not believe in the adage "If you cannot say something good about something, then say nothing," but rather in the premise that "If it stinks, say so." I found nothing in this book to recommend it to anyone. It is a complete waste of money. Fortunately, it is out-of-print. Hopefully, the next step will be to bury and forget it. It deserves this treatment.

Although this annotated bibliography focuses solely on books, two additional sources for information about period, reconstructed, reproduction, copycat, fantasy, and fake objects are worth mentioning. The first is collectors' club publications. Club newsletters and bulletins often contain information not found elsewhere. Hopefully, these clubs will extract this information into a single publication in the future and make it available to the general public.

The second is the *Antique & Collectors Reproduction News,* which began publication in April 1992. You cannot afford to have missed a single issue. It is an absolute must for every auctioneer, collector, and dealer. No matter when you begin your subscription, buy all available back issues. For subscription and back issue information write: *Antique & Collectors Reproduction News,* PO Box 71174, Des Moines, IA 50325.

The opinions expressed in this annotated bibliography are solely those of Harry L. Rinker, owner of Rinker Enterprises, Inc. Those individuals with additional suggestions or disagreements are encouraged to write Rinker at 5093 Vera Cruz Road, Emmaus, PA 18049.

ABBREVIATIONS

The following are standard abbreviations which we have used throughout this edition of **Warman's**.

4to	=	8 x 10″	k	=	karat
8vo	=	5 x 7″	l	=	length
12mo	=	3 x 5″	lb	=	pound
ADS	=	Autograph Document Signed	litho	=	lithograph
adv	=	advertising	ls	=	low standard
ah	=	applied handle	LS	=	Letter Signed
ALS	=	Autograph Letter Signed	mfg	=	manufactured
AQS	=	Autograph Quotation Signed	MIB	=	mint in box
C	=	century	MOP	=	mother-of-pearl
c	=	circa	NE	=	New England
circ	=	circular	No.	=	number
cov	=	cover, covered	opal	=	opalescent
CS	=	Card Signed	orig	=	original
d	=	diameter or depth	os	=	orig stopper
dec	=	decorated	oz	=	ounce
dj	=	dust jacket	pat	=	patent
DQ	=	Diamond Quilted	pcs	=	pieces
DS	=	Document Signed	pgs	=	pages
ed	=	edition	pr	=	pair
emb	=	embossed	PS	=	Photograph Signed
ext.	=	exterior	pt	=	pint
Folio	=	12 x 16″	qt	=	quart
ftd	=	footed	rect	=	rectangular
gal	=	gallon	sgd	=	signed
ground	=	background	sngl	=	single
h	=	height	SP	=	silver plated
hp	=	hand painted	SS	=	Sterling silver
hs	=	high standard	sq	=	square
illus	=	illustrated, illustration	TLS	=	Typed Letter Signed
imp	=	impressed	unp	=	unpaged
int.	=	interior	vol	=	volume
irid	=	iridescent	w	=	width
IVT	=	inverted thumbprint	yg	=	yellow gold
j	=	jewels	#	=	numbered

ABC PLATES

History: The majority of early ABC plates were manufactured in England, imported into the United States, and achieved their greatest popularity from 1780 to 1860. Since a formal education was limited in the early 19th century, the ABC plate was a method of educating the poor for a few pennies.

ABC plates are found in glass, pewter, porcelain, pottery, and tin. Porcelain plates range in diameter from 4⅜ to slightly over 9½ inches. The rim usually contains the alphabet and/or numbers; the center features animals, great men, maxims, or nursery rhymes.

References: Susan and Al Bagdade, *Warman's English & Continental Pottery & Porcelain, Second Edition,* Wallace–Homestead, 1991; Mildred L. and Joseph P. Chalala, *A Collector's Guide to ABC Plates, Mugs and Things,* Pridemark Press, 1980; Noel Riley, *Gifts For Good Children: The History of Children's China, Part I, 1790–1890,* Richard Dennis Publications, 1991.

CAST IRON

2⅞" d, two children with hoops, alphabet edge	**150.00**

GLASS

6" d, Thousand Eye, blue, clock center	**65.00**
6¼" d, Christmas Morning, frosted center, stippled alphabet border	**175.00**
6¾" d, Independence Hall, 1776– 1876	**135.00**

PORCELAIN

5¼" d
Franklin's Prov, black transfer print, polychrome enamel, Staffordshire	**65.00**
He that by the plough . . ., black transfer print, polychrome enamel, imp "J & C Meakin," minor wear	**60.00**

Silks and Satins, scarlet and velvet put out the kitchen fire, black transfer print, polychrome enamel, Staffordshire	**75.00**
5⅞" d, Drill, black transfer print, polychrome enamel, Staffordshire, stains	**90.00**

6" d
Ready for a Ride, black transfer print, polychrome enamel, Staffordshire, stains	**80.00**
That girl wants the pup away . . ., black transfer print, polychrome enamel, Staffordshire	**100.00**
6⅛" d, Resurrected Christ, black transfer print, polychrome enamel, imp "Meakin"	**85.00**
6¼" d, Football, black transfer print, polychrome enamel, imp "Meakin"	**100.00**

6⅜" d, Staffordshire
Floral, squirrel, brown transfer print, stains	**45.00**
The Soldiers, black transfer print, two children and dog, hairline and wear	**55.00**

7" d
Poor Richards Way to Wealth, red transfer print, Staffordshire	**60.00**

Ride a Cock Horse to Banbury Cross, dark blue transfer, marked "Swinnertons Hanley, Made in England," 7½" d, $65.00.

The Pet of the Village, black transfer print, polychrome enamel, Staffordshire, edge wear and chips **80.00**
7¼" d, Staffordshire
ABC rim, red transfer, red stripe, minor crazing **75.00**
Dr Franklin's Maxims, black transfer, green stripe, foliage rim, imp "BW & Co" **85.00**
7½" d, My Face is my Fortune, blue–green transfer print of bulldog, marked "CA & Sons England" **80.00**
8⅛" d, Staffordshire
Quizzing, sepia transfer print, enhanced red, yellow, and green enamels **230.00**
Snuffing, sepia transfer print, enhanced red, yellow, and green enamels **230.00**

TIN

3" d, Tom Thumb **45.00**
4¼" d, Sir Colin Campbell, emb man riding horse, alphabet border **200.00**
9" d, Hey Diddle Diddle **45.00**

ADAMS ROSE

History: Adams Rose, made c1820–40 by Adams and Son in the Staffordshire district of England, is decorated with brilliant red roses and green leaves on a white ground.
G. Jones and Son, England, made a variant known as "Late Adams Rose." The colors are not as brilliant and the ground is a "dirty" white. It commands less than the price of the early pattern.
Reference: Susan and Al Bagdade, *Warman's English & Continental Pottery & Porcelain, Second Edition,* Wallace–Homestead, 1991.

Creamer, early, 5¾" h **300.00**
Cup and Saucer, handleless
Early **200.00**
Late, rose dec on saucer, blue spatter border **75.00**

Plate, early, 7½" d, $175.00.

Demitasse Cup and Saucer, set of four, cup int. with blue band dec, saucer with black transfer printed registry mark and "Williams Adams & Co., Tunstall, England," late 19th C, 5" d saucer **110.00**
Plate
8" d, vine border, early, imp mark **225.00**
9" d, early **200.00**
9¼" d, emb scalloped rim, late . **60.00**
Platter
12" l, late **85.00**
17⅝" l, emb scalloped rim, early **435.00**
Soup Plate
10¼" d, early **200.00**
10½" d, late **55.00**
Sugar, cov, early **300.00**
Tea Bowl and Saucer, early **175.00**
Teapot, cov
Early **600.00**
Late **200.00**
Vegetable, cov, early, 12⅝" l **500.00**

ADVERTISING

History: Before the days of mass media, advertisers relied on colorful product labels and advertising giveaways to promote their products. Containers were made to appeal to the buyer by the use of stylish lithographs and bright colors. Many of the illustrations used the product in the advertisement so that even an illiterate buyer could identify a product.

Advertisements were put on almost every household object imaginable and were constant reminders to use the product or visit a certain establishment.

References: Al Bergevin, *Drugstore Tins and Their Prices,* Wallace–Homestead, 1990; Al Bergevin, *Food and Drink Containers and Their Prices,* Wallace–Homestead, 1988; A. Walker Bingham, *The Snake–Oil Syndrome: Patent Medicine Advertising,* Christopher Publishing House, 1994; Michael Bruner, *Encyclopedia of Porcelain Enamel Advertising,* Schiffer Publishing, 1994; Douglas Congdon–Martin, *America For Sale: A Collector's Guide To Antique Advertising,* Schiffer Publishing, 1991; Douglas Congdon–Martin and Robert Biondi, *Country Store Antiques,* Schiffer Publishing, 1991; Douglas Congdon–Martin and Robert Biondi, *Country Store Collectibles,* Schiffer Publishing, 1990; Douglas Congdon–Martin, *Tobacco Tins: A Collector's Guide,* Schiffer Publishing, 1992; Fred Dodge, *Antique Tins,* Collector Books, 1994; Warren Dotz, *Advertising Character Collectibles: An Identification and Value Guide,* Collector Books, 1993; Ted Hake, *Hake's Guide To Advertising Collectibles,* Wallace–Homestead, 1992; Bob and

Book, Ivory Soap, *Elizabeth Harding, Bride,* illus by Katherine Wireman, printed color cov, tinted color illus, 1900s, 5½ x 7½", $60.00.

Sharon Huxford, *Huxford's Collectible Advertising, Second Edition* Collector Books, 1994; Jerry Jankowski, *Shelf Life: Modern Package Design 1920–1945,* Chronicle Books, 1992; Vivian and Jim Karsnitz, *Oyster Cans,* Schiffer Publishing, 1993; Ray Klug, *Antique Advertising Encyclopedia,* Vol. 1 (1978, 1993 value update) and Vol. 2 (1985), L–W Books; Ralph and Terry Kovel, *Kovels' Advertising Collectibles Price List,* Crown Publishers, 1986; Norman E. Martinus and Harry L. Rinker, *Warman's Paper,* Wallace–Homestead, 1994; Patricia McDaniel, *Drugstore Collectibles,* Wallace–Homestead, 1994; Tom Morrison, *Root Beer: Advertising and Collectibles,* Schiffer Publishing, 1992; Alice L. Muncaster, Ellen Sawyer and Ken Kapson, *The Baby Made Me Buy It!,* Crown Publishers, 1991; Don and Carol Raycraft, *American Country Store,* Wallace–Homestead, 1994; Dawn E. Reno, *Advertising: Identification and Price Guide,* Avon Books, 1993; Joleen Ashman Robinson and Kay Sellers, *Advertising Dolls: Identification and Value Guide,* Collector Books, 1980, 1994 value update; James H. Stahl, *Collectors Guide To Key–Wind Coffee Tins With Price Guide,* L–W Book Sales, 1991; Bob and Beverly Strauss, *American Sporting Advertising,* Vol. 1 (1987, 1992 value update), Vol. 2 (1990, 1992 value update), published by authors, distributed by L–W Book Sales; B. J. Summers, *Value Guide To Advertising Memorabilia,* Collector Books, 1994; Robert W. and Harriet Swedberg, *Tins 'N' Bins,* Wallace–Homestead, 1985; *Westcott Price Guide To Advertising Water Jugs,* Globe Press, 1991; David L. Wilson, *General Store Collectibles: An Identification and Value Guide,* Collector Books, 1994.

Periodicals: *National Assoc of Paper and Advertising Collectors,* PO Box 500, Mount Joy, PA 17552; *Paper Collectors' Marketplace,* PO Box 128, Scandinavia, WI 54917.

Collectors' Clubs: Inner Seal Collectors Club, 6609 Billtown Rd., Louisville, KY 40299; The Antique Advertising Assoc., PO Box 1121, Morton Grove, IL 60053; The Ephemera Society of America, PO Box 37, Schoharie, NY 12157; Tin Container Collectors Assoc., PO Box 440101, Aurora, CO 80044.

Additional Listings: See *Warman's Americana & Collectibles* for more examples.

Banner

Parsons & Pools Uncle Tom's Cabin Co, theatre group adv, black lettering and illus on cloth, 12 x 13½" 25.00

Kellogg's Tasteless Castor Oil, two panels, one with baby with teething ring, other with product illus, c1921, 38½ x 30½" . 200.00

Satin Gloss Liquid Stove Polish, painted on coated cloth stock, product illus, horizontal hanging rod, 40 x 48" 200.00

Box

Spalding Baseball, official National League cork center, horse hide cov, pat. August 31, 1909, "The Official Ball of the Game Since Its Adoption By The National League in 1878" 85.00

Wild West Toilet and Bath Soap, wood, int. label on lid underside printed by Henry Seibert Bro Co Litho, NY, two cowboys on horseback lassoing longhorns, ext. end label, 16" w, 4" h, 12" d 525.00

Brochure, Harley–Davidson, 1936, 9" w, 6½" h 75.00

Cabinet, wood

Diamond Dyes, emb tin insert, children playing with Kodak camera, 22¼" w, 29¾" h, 10" d 1,000.00

Humphrey's Veterinary Remedies, tin insert with farm animals above list of products and cures, 21" w, 33" h, 10" d 3,350.00

Jacob & Co's Biscuits, oak case, glass fronts, two tiers, marble top, reverse and chipped glass display sign, 42" w, 38¼" h, 19" d 600.00

Perfection Dyes, Foxcroft, ME, multicolored tin insert, printed by Tuchfarber, 17¼" w, 24¼" h, 6¼" d 900.00

Calendar, paper

Clem L Kimmel Seeds and Hardware, OH, 1910, stock image, girl in red outfit with walking cane and dog, full pad, 12 x 26½" 475.00

Deering Ideal Binder, harvester machine manufacturer, 1907, pretty girl wearing pink skirt, "A Deer for my Dear," full pad, 12 x 23½" 175.00

De Laval Cream Separators, 1917, farm girl blowing dandelion seeds, sitting with collie dog, full pad, 12 x 24" 700.00

Harrington & Richardson Arms Co, MA, 1927, setter dog head, 9 x 16" 450.00

Peters Cartridge Co, 1910, Goodwin illus of bull moose, calendar pad missing Jan sheet, 15½ x 25½" 1,250.00

Seneca Cameras, 1927, Indian princess portrait, printed by Meek Co, full pad, 10½ x 22½" 350.00

Winchester, CT, 1913, hunters holding spirited horses, rams on hill in background, 13½ x 21½" 2,050.00

Canister, Sweet Cuba Fine Cut, metal, young woman portrait on front, cream colored product package on side, black lettering, minor paint loss and fading, 8" w, 10" d, 8" h 95.00

Catalog

Macey–Wernicke Co, Grand Rapids, MI, Supplement #21, 12 pgs, office desk patterns including single and double pedestal roll top desks, pictures 8 models, 6 x 9¼" 40.00

Pettibone Brothers Mfg Co, Cincinnati, OH, Catalog #353, c1918, 48 pgs, band uniforms and equipment, shakos, busbies, embroidered eagles, wreaths, letters, and ornaments, six colored sheets, 8 x 10¾" 54.00

Chair, folding

Page's Ice Cream, oak chair, two emb tin adv inserts in back, blue and white, 16" w, 32½" h 300.00

Piedmont Cigarettes, porcelain adv insert back, 16" w, 32" h . 115.00

Chalkboard, Atlantic Motor Oil,

pressed board, red, white, and blue, 17" w, 15" h **55.00**

Charger, Miller Beer, tin, trademark girl on crescent moon image, c1907, 24" d **200.00**

Clock

Ballantine Beer, white and blue ground, white, blue, and brown letters, gold hands, "P Ballantine & Sons, Newark, NJ P–538 B," glass cracked at bottom corner, 15" w, 15" h **60.00**

Cream Mustard, drop regulator, lacquered and veneered case, octagonal face, brass bezel, Ansonia, 16½" w, 25" h **400.00**

Iodent Tooth Paste, electric, textured dial, 15½" sq **75.00**

Display

Bull Durham Tobacco, hanger, diecut cardboard, comic black couple sitting on fence under large umbrella, reverse shows couple kissing through tear in umbrella, 7" w, 10" h **500.00**

Curtiss NRG Candies, hard rubber, figural, standing blonde boy pointing to Baby Ruth Candy bar at base, 7" w, 15" h **275.00**

Hickory Garters, standup, diecut wood, boy holding large umbrella while girl lifts her skirt above knees to reveal her garters, 13" w, 19½" h **500.00**

Display Case

Dr Calvin Crane's Quaker Remedies, wood case, glass insert in slant front lid, stork decal and "For Man, Woman and Child, In All The World, No Cure, So Sure" on three sides, 15½" w, 10" h, 10¼" d **900.00**

Rosenbloom's Linen & Rubber Collars, copper bound oak top, glass sides and front, oak back door, marble base, three int. shelves supported on brass pole, celluloid tag reads "Hunter Showcase Company," marble base cracked, replaced shelves and pole, 18" w, 63" h, 21" d **350.00**

Greeting Card, Texaco, "Greetings from Frank M Hawks," Tex-

aco No. 13 plane photo mounted on cardboard inside, 9¾" w, 7¾" h **195.00**

Ice Chest, Royal Crown Cola, steel cooler, double door lift top, four emb tin signs on sides, 31" w, 30" h, 22" d **250.00**

Invoices and Letterheads, album filled with over 100 examples from various businesses **250.00**

Jar, cov, Kis–Me Chewing Gum, emb clear glass, trademark children kissing on orig paper belly label, double neck labels, 4½" sq, 11" h **350.00**

Label, paper

Kentucky Tobacco, Holbrook Bros & Co, Louisville, KY, black man on nag outracing others at derby, printed by Calvert Lith, Detroit, 10¾ x 10¾" **450.00**

Murphy & Co Varnish, two images, one with little boy sitting on crescent moon, varnishing toy carriage, other with horses and chariot entitled "Rattle & Prattle, Merry Xmas," c1880, 13 x 8½" **50.00**

Sunny Side Tobacco, woman handing plug to gentleman, couples playing croquette on mansion lawn in background, 11 x 9½" **250.00**

Letter Folder, tin

Akron Sewer Pipe, factory vignette, yellow and black one side, reverse with company's products on red and black, printed by Somer's Rose, 3¼" w, 10½" h **150.00**

Comic Opera Co, portrait and full figure image of Thomas Q Seabrooke, printed by Sentenne & Green, NY **175.00**

Kellogg & Bulkeley Lithographers/Traveler's Insurance, Hartford, CT, two sided, dark red ground, gold lettering, 3" w, 12¾" h **225.00**

State Mutual Assurance, mansard–roofed building illus, printed by Kellogg & Bulkeley, 3" w, 12½" h **75.00**

Match Safe, Monmouth Gravel Co,

NJ, celluloid, nude sitting on rock, 1½" w, 2¾" h, ⅜" d **325.00**

Mirror, pocket, celluloid

Garrett's Rye, Baltimore, MD, oval, nude with transparent veil holding bow, "Oldest Brand In Baltimore," 1¾" w, 2¾" h **185.00**

New King Snuff, Nashville, TN, rect, crock of snuff illus, 1¾" w, 2¾" h **35.00**

Paperweight, Stoughton Wagon, glass, reverse painted, 3" d . . . **120.00**

Poster, paper, Wyandotte Cleaner and Cleanser, Indian brave drawing bow and arrow, 18 x 39" **750.00**

Box, Turkey Red Cigarettes, woman wearing fez and holding pack, two fez trademarks on front, others on sides, $25.00.

Sign

Aetna Insurance Co, Hartford, CT, paper, trademark Mt Vesuvius erupting in oval vignette, printed by Strobridge Lith Co, repaired tears, 31½ x 24½" **250.00**

Anheuser–Busch, paper, Budweiser girl wearing red dress, printed by Kaufmann & Strauss, c1907, 14 x 28" **600.00**

Ayer's Cherry Pectoral, paper, child holding cherries and product bottle, 10¼ x 13¼" . . **325.00**

Berry Bros Varnishes, celluloid coated tin, offset printed, boy wearing sailor suit, riding in dog–drawn cart made from varnish box, reining in at toy train crossing, 21 x 15" **1,300.00**

Bromo–Seltzer, cardboard, girl holding glass, "Sweet Relief for Overworked Nerves and Brain Fatigue," 16 x 18" **375.00**

Columbia Bicycle, paper, men on high wheel bicycles riding over hill, ladies waving from cupola, woman in foreground riding high wheel tricycle, 12¼ x 26½" **350.00**

Dobbins' Electric Soap, paper, woman scrubbing child, black maid watches, "The Best In The World," 17 x 22" **700.00**

Dupont Powders, paper, hunter in woods shooting at running deer, overprinted with Dupont logo and promotion in gold, 16 x 12½" **800.00**

Gayrock Clothing, Kohn Brothers, Chicago, emb tin, well–dressed gentleman, printed by Kaufmann & Strauss, 27½ x 39½" **450.00**

Gentiane–Kola, emb tin, buxom lass drinking toast, labeled bottle in foreground, 14 x 19½" **500.00**

Hubbard Oysters, paper, color litho, King Neptune offering oyster to maid on shore, sailing ships in background, 14½ x 23½" **1,750.00**

Mutual Life Assurance Co of Canada, porcelain, robed female figure holding sword and upraised scales, 14 x 20" . . . **900.00**

Nakomis Shoe, paper, Indian woman compares her shoe to modern high button shoe, 13½ x 17" **300.00**

New Home Sewing Machine, paper, humorous illus, old woman at treadle machine stitching rip in boys pants while boy is still wearing them, 25½ x 40" **1,200.00**

Old Schenley Whiskey, tin, pioneer wearing buckskins and coonskin cap, holding rifle, en-

titled "I've Struck The Trail,"
19½ x 27½" **375.00**
Pimlico Course, Baltimore, MD,
paper, horses racing past club-
house illus, 25 x 18" **650.00**
Sinclair Motor Oils, heavy paper,
dinosaur image, "From Oldest
Crudes," 28 x 42" **260.00**
Stoneware Food Containers, tin,
self framed, boy taking donut
from crock on table, various
crockery in room, "We sell all
sizes," 13 x 19" **950.00**
Tacoma Cigars, Seattle, WA, In-
dian princess portrait, 12 x 20" **650.00**
Western Coaline Co, Chicago,
IL, Electric Cleanser, vignettes
of before and after images,
printed by Cosack & Co, 21½
x 16½" **250.00**
Sign Letters, National Cash Reg-
ister Co, diecast aluminum, red
painted highlights, used on
building and delivery trucks, 70"
l **200.00**
Store Card
Rising Sun Stove Polish, MA,
larger than life Uncle Sam and
other foreign dignitaries watch
"little people" clamoring for
product, 11¼ x 7¼" **35.00**
Standard Clothing, Bangor, ME,
Grover Cleveland portrait,
overprinted adv, 7 x 10" **60.00**

**Pinback Button, We Guarantee
Favorite Stoves and Ranges, Best
in the World, orange ground, Baltimore Badge & Novelty Co., 1¼"
d, $15.00.**

**Mirror, "Graft," Universal Pic-
tures, serial adv, celluloid, White-
head & Hoag Co., Newark, NJ, 2⅛"
d, $35.00.**

Thermometer, International Tailor-
ing Co, New York and Chicago,
wood, lion logo and "King Of Tai-
lors," ruler next to thermometer
measures from five feet to six
feet five inches, 7" w, 23" h . . . **135.00**
Tin
Bull Durham Smoking Tobacco,
round, orig wood frame, brown
and white cow, girl wearing
pink, black and gold tobacco
pkgs, farmhouse in back-
ground, blue and orange let-
tering, 36" w, 38" h **2,200.00**
Express Tobacco, round, steam-
ing locomotive, early Globe tin,
8¼" d, 2¼" h **50.00**
Jim Dandies Peanuts, 10 lb,
multicolored kids playing
baseball and standing by bul-
letin board, 7½" d, 11" h **400.00**
Old Abe Chewing Tobacco,
round, Abe Lincoln portrait, orange and black, 8¼" d, 2¼" h **400.00**
Plow Boy Tobacco, paper label,
young boy sitting on plow
reading and smoking, Liggett
& Myers Tobacco Co, 5" w, 6"
h **50.00**
Tip Tray, Junket Dessert, round,
little girl with bowl of junket, souvenir of 1904 St Louis World
Fair, 4¼" d **150.00**

Tray, tin, serving
Cold Spring Brewing Co, MA, round, girl leaning on tiger's head, printed by Kaufmann & Strauss, 13½" d **225.00**
Columbia Brewing Co, Tacoma, WA, round, Columbia raising glass high, standing before eagle and barrel, wheat and hops border, 12" d **150.00**
Guggenheim Bros, Cleveland, BWOE rye, oval, girl portrait, printed by Meek & Beach, 13¾ x 16½" **200.00**
National Beer, National Brewing Co, San Francisco, oval, young man on charging horse ripping through paper background, holding upraised bottle, "The Best in the West," 13¾ x 16½" **900.00**
Patton's Ice Cream, sq, parfait glass and dish of ice cream, "Rich and Delicious," 13¼ x 13¼" **95.00**
Wieland's Beer, rect, girl wearing yellow dress, seated at desk with bowl of roses, 10½ x 13¼" **95.00**

ADVERTISING TRADE CARDS

History: Advertising trade cards are small, thin cardboard cards made to advertise the merits of a product and usually bear the name and address of a merchant.

With the invention of lithography, colorful trade cards became a popular advertising media in the late 19th and early 20th centuries. They were made especially to appeal to children. Young and old alike collected and treasured them in albums and scrapbooks. Very few are dated; 1880 to 1893 were the prime years for trade cards; 1810 to 1850 cards can be found, but rarely. By 1900 trade cards were rapidly losing their popularity. By 1910 they had all but vanished.

References: Kit Barry, *The Advertising Trade Card*, Book 1, published by author, 1981; Robert Jay, *The Trade Card In Nineteenth-Century America,* University of Missouri Press, 1987; Norman E. Martinus and Harry L. Rinker, *Warman's Paper,* Wallace–Homestead, 1994; Jim and Cathy McQuary, *Collectors Guide To Advertising Cards,* L–W Promotions, 1975, out–of–print; Murray Card (International) Ltd. (comp.), *Cigarette Card Values: 1992 Catalogue of Cigarette & Other Trade Cards,* Murray Cards (International) Ltd., 1992.

Periodical: *The Trade Card Journal,* 143 Main St., Brattleboro, VT 05301.

Collectors' Club: Trade Card Collector's Assoc., PO Box 284, Marlton, NJ 08053.

Additional Listings: See *Warman's Americana & Collectibles* for more examples.

BEAUTY

Compliments of Seely Manuf Co Perfumer's, Detroit, MI **8.00**
Dr Hedras Viola Cream, opens . . **10.00**
E W Hoyt & Co, perfumed calendar, 1893 . . . . **8.00**
Hoyt's German Cologne, children dancing around bottle, 1892 . . . **6.00**
Jap Rose Toilet Talcum Powder, figural, talcum can, Oriental woman illus **10.00**
Ricksecers Perfumes, Soaps, New Orleans Expo souvenir . . . **10.00**
Thorne's Hair Bazaar, 1881 . . . . . **10.00**

BEVERAGES

Arbuckle Coffee, pictorial US history with maps **4.00**
Hires Root Beer, girl holding glass **10.00**
Jersey Coffee, children on fence . **6.00**
Lion Coffee, Mrs President Cleveland **8.00**
Royal Garden Teas, September with birthstone **5.00**
Seal Brand Coffee, double sided **6.00**

CLOTHING & ACCESSORIES

A C Yates & Co, Clothing, Philadelphia **8.00**
A S T Co, Black tip Shoes, school teacher illus, 1880 . . . . **6.00**
Broadhead Dress Goods, litho illus **12.00**
Celluloid Waterproof Collars, Cuffs, & Shirt Bosoms, man illus **8.00**

Clothing, Marshall & Ball Clothiers, adv on back, 4⅜ x 3⅛", $3.50.

Dr Warners Coraline Corset, litho illus 20.00
Fosters, Mens Gloves, Locomotion Champion Records on back 20.00
Jackson Corset Co, adv on back 8.00
Jones Clothing House, green ... 30.00
Libby & Spier, clothing, New Year greeting, steel engraving 15.00
Reynolds Bros Fine Shoes, Utica, NY, horse, dog, and cat illus ... 8.00
Reynolds Pat Shoulder Brace, Corset, and Skirt Supporter ... 15.00
Robt Cherry, Germantown, Phila, shoes, woman looking at shoe box 10.00
Sollers & Co Shoes, child standing on chair, 1874 .... 8.00
Sorasia Shoe Co, 5½ x 6½" 3.50
Spun Glass Rusil Finish Dress Linings, litho illus 15.00
Standard Screw Fastened Boots & Shoes, litho illus 8.00
Strawbridge & Clothier, man carrying packages 6.00
Vogel Bros Shoes, boy wearing dad's shoes 10.00
Wm Broadhead & Sons, Dress Goods, girl picking flowers and woman with fan illus 8.00

FARM MACHINERY & SUPPLIES

Bickford & Huffman, Macedon, NY, farm tools, 1886 .... 25.00
Bucher & Gibbs Plow Co, Canton, OH 20.00
Buckeye Harvesting Machines,

Compliments C Aultman & Co, Canton, OH, fold out with metal rivet 35.00
Deering Implements, mower on back 12.00
Dietericks Harness Oil, horse and elves 35.00
Draft, Farm & Buggy Harness, Currier & Ives illus, 1879 ..... 45.00
Eldorado Engine Oil, Garfield Monument illus 6.00
Grand Rapids Manufacturing & Implement Co, Grand Rapids, MI 6.00
J S & M Peckham, Agricultural Furnace & Boiler, litho illus 15.00
L N Grill Seed Co, Elk Point, SD, figural, ear of corn 6.00
Michigan Manuf Co Fine Carriages & Platform Wagons, Farm Machinery, Jackson, MI, figural, leaf, multicolored 20.00
Milwaukee Harvester Co 15.00
Moline Plow Co, foldout, Flying Dutchman sulky 35.00
Plano Manufacturing Co, Chicago, IL, harvesting machinery 8.00
Russell & Co, Massillon, OH, threshers, engines, saw mills, litho illus 15.00
Studebacker Bros Mfg Co, Farm Machinery, South Bend, IN, die-cut, gold gilt dec 20.00
The Clinton Plow Co, Clinton, MI, children illus 25.00
The Worcester Buckeye Mower .. 20.00
Walter A Woods, Harvesting Machine 20.00
Wm Deering & Co, girl illus 10.00

FOOD

American Breakfast Cereals, 1883 15.00
Baltimore Oyster Co, 1884 calendar on back 35.00
Blookers Dutch Cocoa, litho illus . 16.00
Bordens Eagle Brand Condensed Milk, child and cat illus 6.00
Canby's Silver Star Baking Powder, litho illus 10.00
Cincinnati Sea, Coffee & Spice Co, flower illus 8.00
Compliments of Clark Bell, The Cash Grocers, adv on back ... 12.00

Culvers Restaurant, Oysters in Every Style, figural, oyster 12.00

E F Lauabee & Co Manufacturer of Biscuits, Albany, NY, biscuit list on back 10.00

Emmerson's Albumenoid Food, 1886 .... 5.00

Fermentum Compressed Yeast, 4¼ x 6", diecut, winter scene .. 6.00

Fleischmann & Co Yeast, litho illus 8.00

Gail Borden Eagle Brand Condensed Milk, multicolored, baby illus 6.00

Hannah Lay & Co, Traverse City, MI, opens, flour and factory scene 20.00

Kenton Baking Powder, owl and moon 8.00

Libbey's Extracts of Beef, calendar on back 20.00

Lion Compressed Yeast, girl with dog 6.00

Mellins Food, litho illus 8.00

Miles Premium Baking Powder, litho illus 8.00

Noix de Coco, For Puddings, Pies, Pastries, woman served by blacks 8.00

Ridges Food For Infants & Invalids, litho illus 10.00

Royal Hams, man with dog 15.00

St Charles Evaporated Cream, baby with dogs 10.00

Stollwercks Chocolate, Worlds Fair Chicago, chocolate statue . 8.00

Syrup of Figs, Fig Syrup Co, CA, opens 10.00

Taylor & Lazenby Confectioners, Toledo, OH 6.00

Tip Top Baking Powder, litho dog illus 12.00

Van Houtens Cocoa, trains 10.00

Wagners Infant Food, ... 12.00

We Eat Sears Crackers, New York Biscuit Co, Grand Rapids, MI, 6" l, diecut, shelves with two clowns 18.00

Wells Richardson & Co, Lactated Food 18.00

Wilsons Cooked Meats, sailor illus 12.00

Woolsen Spice, Harris litho illus . 10.00

FURNITURE

Geo W Wanamakers, Dining Rooms, "You & Me Celebrate St. Valentine Day" 35.00

Partridges Dining Rooms, multicolored, muted 18.00

Stalberg & Parks Furniture, boy with football 8.00

LAUNDRY AND SOAPS

Bogues Soap, figural, dog 20.00

B T Babbitts, 1776 Powder, Soap For All Nations 8.00

Empire Wringer, fox wedding 12.00

Gold Dust Washing Powder, figural, black boys in tub 20.00

L I Fisk & Co, Soaps, woman washing clothes 15.00

New Process Starch, double view, Chinaman and woman 10.00

R W Belle & Co Soap, buffalo illus 10.00

Sapolio, 4" l, watermelon shape with black face 15.00

Shaker Purest Laundry Soap ... 8.00

Soapine, mantel with trophies ... 6.00

Sweet Home Family Soap, Larkin & Co, 5¾ x 6½", Brownies riding bicycle 10.00

Williams Washing Crystal, gold gilt accents 20.00

MEDICAL

Ayers Cathartic Pills, black man and children, 1883 .... 8.00

Ayers Sarsaparilla, girl wearing white bonnet 6.00

Dry Goods, Boston Dry Goods House, blank back, 4½ x 3", $3.00.

Carters Little Nerve Pills, puzzle type, red and white 6.00

Dr Morses Indian Root Pills, metamorphic, Indian illus 25.00

German Corn Remover, metamorphic 18.00

Kings 25 Cent Bitters, King Bitter Co, Rochester, NY, litho illus .. 12.00

Loose's Red Clover, As A Cure For Cancer, men fighting bear 6.00

Lumbard Bros Druggist, Jackson, MI, black boy illus 6.00

Lydia Pinkham, litho illus 8.00

Mrs Winslows, Soothing Syrup, woman and child illus 3.00

Peckhams Croup Remedy, woman and girl illus 8.00

Schencks Mandrake Pills, seated black girl 15.00

Schencks Seaweed Tonic, standing black boy illus 15.00

St Jacobs Oil, Conquers Pain, woman wearing bonnet 8.00

Tarrants Seltzer Aperient, metamorphic 12.00

The National Surgical Institute of Philadelphia, children throwing crutches away 10.00

MISCELLANEOUS

C R Osborn, Leading Photographer, Coldwater, MI, dog with camera illus 15.00

Deep Sea Mess Mackerel, litho illus 6.00

Detroit Evening News Excursion from Detroit to the Sea, 6 x 9", 1881 .... 20.00

Ellis Knapp & Co, Manufacturer of Umbrellas & Parasols, eagle with flag and umbrella, gold and dark blue illus 45.00

Eliza Weathersby, Froliques, Petite Opera, litho illus 8.00

Improved Sheet Iron Roofing, building on fire 40.00

J N Martinek & Sons Jewelers, Traverse City, MI, January, beautiful woman illus 8.00

Knast Bros & Co, Cincinnati, OH, toy bazaar, Santa illus 15.00

Ocean Gem Mackerel, Austen & Nicholes & Co, fishing boats .. 15.00

Richard Schwarz Joy Emporium, Boston, litho illus of Santa 25.00

Rochester Lamps, Bridal Chamber Hotel int. view 8.00

Rockford Watch, round, opens .. 22.00

Sykes Steel Roofing, girl blowing bubbles 8.00

The Glass Front, Photographic and Tin Type Gallery, Jackson, MI, silver gild, 1881 .... 10.00

William Mann, Blank Book Maker & Stationer Lithographer, Printer, Philadelphia 40.00

Youths Companion, A National Family Paper, litho illus, opens, 1889 .... 12.00

PIANOS AND ORGANS

A B Chase Organs, The Winner . 20.00

Wheelock Piano, litho illus 8.00

STOVES AND RANGES

Dixons Stove Polish, opens 15.00

Garland Stoves and Ranges, beautiful woman illus 6.00

Gold Coin & Gold Medal Stoves & Ranges, litho illus 12.00

Golden Star Oil Stoves, gold gilt dec 8.00

Jewel Stoves, The Old Oaken Bucket.................... 20.00

Majestic Range, puzzle type 8.00

Red Cross Stoves & Ranges 8.00

Rising Sun Stove Polish, Story of Wise Man and Foolish Man ... 10.00

THREAD AND SEWING

Clarks Mile End Spool Cotton, carriage illus 25.00

Clarks ONT Thread, boy fishing illus 8.00

De Long Hook and Eye, Eclipses Everything, Columbus showing Indians eclipse 30.00

Domestic Sewing Machine Co, black family in wagon illus 10.00

Eureka Silk, girl having tea party 8.00

J & P Coats, We Never Fade, black boy sitting on spool of thread 8.00

Merrick Thread Co, diecut, 1889
calendar on back **6.00**
New Home Sewing Machine, dogs
chasing man **15.00**
Royal St John Sewing Machine . . **6.00**
Singer Sewing Machines, opens,
woman seated at sewing machine and children having tea
party, 1899 . . . . **20.00**
S S Corbin Millinery goods, Phila-
delphia, ship illus **12.00**
Standard Rotary Shuttle Sewing
Machine, man riding high wheel
bike **25.00**
Standard Sewing Machine,
woman playing croquette **12.00**
White Sewing Machine, woman
admiring sewing machine **12.00**
Williamantic Linen Co, HMS Pin-
afore **10.00**
Williamantic Thread, dog pulling
cart **6.00**

TOBACCO

Capadura Cigar, comical jockey il-
lus **10.00**
Double Six 5 Cent Cigar, diecut,
three dogs **18.00**
Geo P Lies & Co's Grand Republic
Cigarros, beautiful woman illus **15.00**
Horsehead Tobacco, Dansman
Tobacco Co, horse head illus . . **15.00**
Kelsey's Cigars, soldiers, poorly
cut **4.00**
Mussemans Boot Jack Tobacco,
figural, bootjack, multicolored . . **20.00**
Newboy Plug Tobacco, The
Peacemaker **10.00**
Old Judge Cigarettes **10.00**
Tippecanoe, Indians in canoe . . . **10.00**

AGATA GLASS

History: Agata glass was invented in
1887 by Joseph Locke of the New England
Glass Company, Cambridge, Massachusetts.

Agata glass was produced by using a
piece of peachblow glass, coating it with
metallic stain, spattering the surface with
alcohol, and firing. The result was a high
gloss, mottled appearance of oil droplets
floating on a watery surface. Shading usually ranged from opaque pink to dark rose.
Pieces are known in a pastel opaque green.
A few pieces have been found in a satin
finish.

**Tumbler, green opaque ground,
oil dec band, gold line at bottom,
3¾″ h, $625.00.**

Bowl, 8″ w, 4″ h, green opaque,
gold trim staining **1,150.00**
Celery Vase, 6½″ h, crimped top . **1,750.00**
Creamer, 3¾″ h, 5″ w, green
opaque, deep blue staining, gold
trim **1,450.00**
Lemonade, 5⅛″ h, 2½″ d top, 1⅝″
d base, peachblow shading, pro-
nounced mottling, gold tracery . **1,250.00**
Mug, 2¼″ h, green opaque, agata
stain, applied handle **300.00**
Pitcher
7½″ h, 6½″ w, deep peachblow
wild rose shading to white,
gold staining, blue spots, applied reeded shell handle with
staining **2,750.00**
8½″ h, 5″ w, deep raspberry
shading to pink, blue spots,
slight wear, staining on handle **4,450.00**
Plate, 6⅝″ d, ribbon candy fluted
rim **850.00**
Toothpick, bulbous, pinched in
scalloped rim **850.00**
Tumbler, 3½″ h, green opaque,
agata stain **350.00**

AMBERINA GLASS

History: Joseph Locke developed Amberina glass in 1883 for the New England Glass Works. "Amberina," a trade name, describes a transparent glass which shades from deep ruby to amber color. It was made by adding powdered gold to the ingredients for an amber glass batch. A portion of the glass was reheated later to produce the shading effect. Usually it was the bottom which was reheated to form the deep red; however, reverse examples have been found.

Most early Amberina is of flint quality glass, blown or pattern molded. Patterns include Diamond Quilted, Daisy and Button, Venetian Diamond, Diamond and Star, and Thumbprint.

In addition to the New England Glass Works, the Mt. Washington Glass Company of New Bedford, Massachusetts, copied the glass in the 1880s and sold it at first under the Amberina trade name and later as "Rose Amber." It is difficult to distinguish pieces from these two New England factories. Boston and Sandwich Glass Works never produced the glass.

Amberina glass also was made in the 1890s by several Midwest factories, among which was Hobbs, Brockunier & Co. Trade names included "Ruby Amber Ware" and "Watermelon." The Midwest glass shaded from cranberry to amber and resulted from a thin flashing of cranberry applied to the reheated portion. This created a sharp demarkation between the two colors. This less–expensive version caused the death knell for the New England variety.

In 1884 Edward D. Libbey was assigned the trade name "Amberina" by the New England Glass Works. Production occurred in 1900, but ceased shortly thereafter. In the 1920s Edward Libbey renewed production at his Toledo, Ohio, plant for a short period. The glass was of high quality. Amberina from this era is marked "Libbey" in script on the pontil.

Reproduction Alert: Reproductions abound.

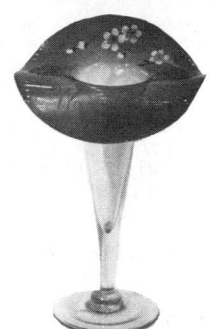

Jack-In-The Pulpit vase, gold lettering "World's Fair 1893," painted floral motif on back, 7″ h, $450.00.

Bowl
4½″ d, 2¼″ h, tri–corner, Venetian Diamond **325.00**

5½″ d, 3″ h, bulbous base, wide flaring ruffled rim, slight ribs, ground pontil, New England . **375.00**
5¾″ d, 3¾″ h, six crimped top, IVT, heavy gold floral dec, applied amber scroll feet **325.00**
8″ d, rolled turned down scalloped rim, deep ribbing, three applied amber feet, Libbey . . **820.00**
Bride's Basket, ribbed, ruffled, SP holder **650.00**
Celery
6½″ h, DQ, New England **325.00**
7½″ h, Venetian Diamond, sq top, ground pontil, New England **435.00**
Centerpiece, 14″ l, boat shape, Daisy and Button, Hobbs, Brockunier **950.00**
Champagne, 4″ h, hollow stem . . **200.00**
Cologne Bottle, 6″ h, Daisy and Button, orig stopper **2,225.00**
Compote, 5½″ d, 1¾″ h, Baccarat **85.00**
Cracker Jar, 5½″ d, 5″ h, Joseph Locke, New England, cov missing **550.00**
Creamer, 4″ h, IVT, Mt Washington **165.00**
Cruet, IVT, firing line in handle . . **175.00**
Finger Bowl, 5″ d, DQ, reverse color, attributed to Sandwich . . **165.00**
Ice Cream Set, 9¼″ w, 14½″ l tray, eight 6″ d plates, Daisy and Button, Hobbs, Brockunier **1,275.00**

Lamp, 10" h, hall, hanging, Hobnail, ornate brass trim and fittings 350.00
Lemonade, DQ, applied ring handle 275.00
Marmalade, cov, 5½" h, IVT, white metal cov, Mt Washington 175.00
Pickle Castor, IVT, SP ftd frame marked "James Tufts," matching SP cov 375.00
Pitcher
  4" h, 4½" w, IVT, deep color, applied amber rope handle, New England 925.00
  4½" h, IVT, sq top, reeded handle 425.00
  5" h, 3" w, Daisy and Button, deep fuchsia color shading to amber, fuchsia highlights on bottom, applied amber handle, Hobbs, Brockunier 550.00
  5" h, 4" w, IVT, applied amber strap handle 200.00
  5½" h, 4½" w, IVT, applied amber reeded shell handle 400.00
  7" h, 6½" d w, IVT, painted dec, applied crystal rope handle with rosettes, Hobbs, Brockunier & Co 350.00
  7½" h, IVT, sq rim, applied reeded handle 375.00
  10½" h, 5" w, tankard shape, IVT, applied amber reeded handle 350.00
Plate, 5½" d, Baccarat 40.00
Punch Cup, 2½" h, applied amber handle 85.00
Rose Bowl, 5⅛" h, paneled, ftd, Mt Washington 310.00
Salad Server, 11" l, DQ handles . 450.00
Sherbet, 5" d, sgd "Libbey," 1917 375.00
Sugar, cov, 4¼" h, IVT 350.00
Toothpick
  2" h, Baby IVT, tri–corner 275.00
  2¼" h, 1½" w, Baby IVT, sq top, New England 295.00
Tumbler
  3½" h, 2½" d, IVT, cranberry shaded to amber 45.00
  3¾" h, Honeycomb 65.00
  4" h
    Herringbone, New England .. 145.00
    Venetian Diamond, bell tone flint, New England 135.00

Vase
  6" h, lily, Mt Washington 195.00
  6" h, 4½" w, pinched in body, applied rigaree, turned in top, int. ribs, Joseph Locke, New England 550.00
  15" h, lily, deep ruby red to brilliant amber, flint, c1880 ..... 825.00

AMBERINA GLASS—PLATED

History: The New England Glass Company, Cambridge, Massachusetts, first made Plated Amberina in 1886; Edward Libbey patented the process for the company in 1889.

Plated Amberina was made by taking a gather of chartreuse or cream opalescent glass, dipping it in Amberina and working the two, often utilizing a mold. The finished product had a deep amber to deep ruby red shading, a fiery opalescent lining, and often vertical ribbing for enhancement. Designs ranged from simple forms to complex pieces with collars, feet, gilding, and etching.

A cased Wheeling glass of similar appearance had an opaque white lining, but is not opalescent and the body is not ribbed.

Bowl, 8" d, 3¼" h, melon ribbed, folded scalloped rim, purple rim shades to light and dark red ...8,000.00
Creamer, squatty, applied clear amber handle 3,300.00
Cruet, 6¼" h, deeply ribbed, trefoil

Tumbler, deep fuchsia shading to ruby to amber, opal white lining, 4" h, $800.00.

top, amber handle, amber fac-
eted stopper **3,750.00**
Pitcher, 7½" h, 6½" w, twelve ver-
tical ribs, deep ruby shading to
amber, oyster white lining, blue
highlights, applied amber handle **7,200.00**
Salt Shaker, ribbed **900.00**
Spooner, 4" h, paneled, ground
pontil **2,000.00**
Tumbler, 3¾" h, paneled **1,850.00**
Vase, 3¼" h, bulbous **2,650.00**

AMPHORA

History: The Amphora Porcelain Works
was one of several pottery companies lo-
catcd in the Teplitz–Turn region of Bohemia
in the late 19th and early 20th centuries. It
is best known for art pottery, especially Art
Nouveau and Art Deco pieces.

Several markings were used, including
the name and location of the pottery and
the Imperial mark which included a crown.
Prior to WWI, Bohemia was part of the Austro–Hungarian Empire, so the word "Austria" may appear as part of the mark. After
WWI the word "Czechoslovakia" may be
part of the mark.

Reference: Susan and Al Bagdade, *Warman's English & Continental Pottery & Porcelain, Second Edition,* Wallace–Homestead, 1991.

Additional Listings: Teplitz.

Basket, 9½" w, 5½" h, oval, roses
dec **225.00**
Bust, 12" h, 7" w, woman, 18th C
garb, brown, gold, rust, and pink,
sgd "Turn Wien Ew Depose"
and "Made in Austria," some
roughage **350.00**
Planter, 6" l, jewel type dec, mot-
tled ground, cobalt blue handles
and rim **95.00**
Plaque, 12½" h, figural, dour

maiden with flowing hair, peering
through cabbage head, cream,
green, and purple glaze, gilt
highlights, imp "Amphora, 1270/
9," red printed mark "Turn–Teplitz–Bohemia, RStK, Made in
Austria," inscribed "Ed. Stellmacher," chips to leaf edges,
c1900 . . . . **1,500.00**

**Vase, octagonal, mottled gold, tan
stripes, enameled tear drop, and
white ram's head on base, aqua
band behind head, marked "Made
in Czecho-slovakia," 10¾" h,
$220.00.**

Vase
10¼" h, two handles, pair of exotic birds glazed with fired–on
gold among stylized flowers,
gloss and matte glazes, base
stamped with crown, "Am-
phora, Austria, Imperial Amphora Turn, Campina," and
"11614/64," small nick on one
handle, 1903–18 . . . . **330.00**
20" h, bulbous ovoid body, in-
cised dec with large condor
fronting a band of intertwining
vines and pendent cluster of
grapes between geometric
borders, shades of dark blue,
medium blue, green, brown,
tan, purple, and pink, printed
mark "Czechoslovakia, Am-
phora, 813," c1925 . . . . **1,725.00**
21" h, 6¾" d, two handles,

carved polychrome birds with glossy glaze, tan and white dead matte ground, die-stamped "Amphora Czechoslovakia" **500.00**

Vide Poche, figural
11¼" h, maiden seated on furling lily pads, flowers strewn about her flowing hair, lengthy gown continues to form irregular tray at feet, blue and cream glaze, gilt highlights, imp "Amphora, 778/4," red printed mark "Turn–Teplitz–Bohemia, RStK, Made in Austria," c1900 .... **1,725.00**

19¼" h, dancing maiden, wearing flowing gown glazed in mottled ochre and green, long waving drapery forms two small trays, irid cream glaze shaded with blue and gray, gilt highlights, imp "Amphora, 776," printed "Turn–Teplitz–Bohemia, RStK, Make in Austria," c1900 .... **4,315.00**

ANIMAL COLLECTIBLES

History: The representation of animals as a theme in fine arts, decorative arts, and utilitarian products dates back to antiquity. Some religions endowed certain animals with mystical properties. Authors throughout written history embodied them with human characteristics.

Collecting by animal theme has been practiced for centuries. Until the early 1970s most collectors were of the closet variety. However, the formation of collector's clubs and marketing crazes, e.g., flamingo, pig, and penguin, brought most collectors out into the open.

Animal collectors differ from other collectors in that they care little about the date when an object was made or even its aesthetic quality. The key is that the object is in the image of their favorite animal.

References: Pauline Flick, *Cat Collectibles,* Wallace–Homestead, 1992; Marbena Jean Fyke, *Collectible Cats: An Identification and Value Guide,* Collector Books, 1993; Lee Garmon and Dick Spencer, *Glass Animals of the Depression Era,* Collector Books, 1993; Everett Grist, *Covered Animal Dishes,* Collector Books, 1988, 1993 value update; Peter Johnson, *Cats & Dogs: Phillips Collectors Guides,* Dunestyle Publishing, 1988; Alice Muncaster and Ellen Yanow, *The Cat Made Me Buy It,* Crown, 1984; Alice Muncaster and Ellen Yanow Sawyer, *The Cat Sold It!,* Crown, 1986; Herbert N. Schiffer, *Collectible Rabbits,* Schiffer Publishing, 1990; Mike Schneider, *Animal Figures,* Schiffer Publishing, 1990.

Periodicals: *Jumbo Jargon,* 1002 West 25th St., Erie, PA 16502; *MOOsletter,* 240 Wahl Ave., Evans City, PA 16033; *The Canine Collector's Companion,* PO Box 2948, Portland, OR 97208.

Collectors' Clubs: Canine Collectibles Club of America, Suite 314, 736 N. Western Ave., Lake Forest, IL 60045; Cat Collectors, 33161 Wendy Dr., Sterling Heights, MI 48310; Folk Art Society of America, PO Box 17041, Richmond, VA 23226; The Frog Pond, PO Box 193, Beech Grove, IN 46107; The National Elephant Collector's Society, 380 Medford St., Somerville, MA 02145; Wee Scots, Inc., PO Box 1512, Columbus, IN 47202.

Museums: American Kennel Club, New York, NY; American Saddle Horse Museum Assoc, Lexington, KY; Frog Fantasies Museum, Eureka Springs, AR; International Museum of the Horse, Lexington, KY; Stradling Museum of the Horse, Patagonia, AZ; The Dog Museum, St Louis, MO.

Additional Listings: See specific animal collectible categories in *Warman's Americana & Collectibles.*

BIRDS

Almanac, *Ayers American Almanac 1885,* yellow cov, black bird design **10.00**
Andirons, pr, 23" h, figural, owl, glass eyes **85.00**
Architectural Ornament, 21" h, eagle, cast iron, outstretched wings, perched on sphere, late 19th/early 20th C **700.00**
Box, 18 x 12 x 10½", American Biscuit & Mfg Co, wood, paper label with parrot illus **65.00**

Candlesticks, pr, 14¾" h, herons, brass, Oriental, turtle on base, water lily candle arm and socket . . 100.00

Christmas Ornament, 5¼" l, set of 7, blown glass, amber, angel hair tails, tin clips 200.00

Cookie Cutter, 5¾ x 3½", dove, flat back, handle 10.00

Cookie Jar
  Dove, pink, Fredericksburg Art Pottery, marked "FAPCO" . . . 40.00
  Parrot, Metlox 80.00
  Pelican, brown, baby pelican finial, California Originals 35.00

Door Knocker, 8½" h, brass 60.00

Doorstop, 10" h, penguin, cast iron, black, white chest, unsgd Hubley 250.00

Figure
  8¼" h, 11¼" l, bluejay, wood, relief carved, burl base, early 1900s 450.00
  10" h, dove, chalkware, painted dec, late 19th C 115.00
  14" h, peacock, Royal Dux 110.00
  16" h
    Cockateel, pink, Royal Dux . . 275.00
    Old Crow, black and white, molded, painted, 1950s . . . 100.00
  19" h, parrot, wood, carved, orig polychrome paint 200.00

Plaque, 12½" h, 8¼" w, oval, owl perched on quill pen, cast iron . 150.00

Post Card, Peacock illus 8.00

Tureen, 12" h, figural, cockerel, multicolored, Jacob Petit Vieux, Paris, c1850 . . . . 550.00

BOVINE

Bank, 4½" l, cow, cast iron, black finish 225.00

Cookie Jar, figural, cow, cat finial, brown, marked "W 10 Brush USA," early 1950s 65.00

Creamer, 5" h, figural, cow, spatterware, brown and black stripes, green base 450.00

Figure, 19" l, ox, chalk, wood horns and ears, red and white finish 50.00

Label, Jersey Cream, cow illus . . 10.00

Tin, 3¼" d, 5¾" h, Buttermilk and

Soda Baking Powder, round paper label, woman and cow illus . . 35.00

Vase, 11½" h, cow and calf, milkmaid seated on stool, Staffordshire 375.00

Painting on porcelain, girl with cat, 10 x 8", $1,500.00.

CATS

Andirons, 17" h, pr, cast iron, sitting, yellow glass eyes 120.00

Book, *The Little Kitten That Would Not Wash Its Face,* Edna Geoff Diehl, Samuel Gabriel & Sons, 1922, hard cov 15.00

Bottle, 7" h, Majolica, figural, wearing clothing, cork stopper, incised "7216," c1900 . . . . 145.00

Candleholder, 4 x 2 x 5" h, black cat, orange base, tail as handle, china, German 120.00

Cookie Jar, Majolica, pirate cat . . 600.00

Figure
  2¾" h, pair of Chelsea cats on pillow, porcelain, polychrome, orange, gilt dec, gold anchor mark 155.00
  3½" h, seated, porcelain, black, white, and green 35.00

3¾" l, 4¼" h, playing with ball, bronze, slate base, dark patina, G Omerth **175.00**

13¾" h, seated, brown Rockingham glaze with streaks of green, oval base with chips ..**3,300.00**

Label, White Cat, cat illus **10.00**

Music Box, Felix the Cat, litho tin, France **80.00**

Nodder, 3½" h, kitten, pine, carved wood, painted black **350.00**

Planter, 8" h, 8½" w, kitten in basket, pastel colors, glossy finish, Copley, c1950s **35.00**

String Holder, chalkware, kitten's head, holding ball of yarn, white **45.00**

DOGS

Bank
  Chalkware **50.00**
  Pottery, Scottie **23.00**
Bookends, wolfhound, Rosemeade **120.00**
Candy Container, papier mache, egg shape, litho of St Bernard and little girl, marked "Germany" **40.00**
Cookie Jar
  Alpo Dog **85.00**
  Bulldog Cafe, Treasure Craft .. **75.00**
  Calico Dog, tan, Metlox **125.00**
  Dalmatian, Treasure Craft **40.00**
  Fido Dog, Metlox **295.00**
  Scottie, black **195.00**
  Thinking Pup, McCoy **20.00**
Figure
  Boxer, 5½" l, hitched to sign post, bronze, dark patina, Emmanuel Fremiet, 19th C **225.00**
  Bulldog
    Mortens Studio **65.00**
    Ohio Pottery, 9" l, white clay, brown glaze **35.00**
  Bulldog Puppy, Mortens Studio **45.00**
  Cairn Terrier, Goebel **25.00**
  Cocker Spaniel
    Kay Finch **350.00**
    Staffordshire, 12½" h, pr, England, 19th C **285.00**
  Cocker Show Dog, Mortens Studio **45.00**
  Fox Terrier, Mortens Studio ... **45.00**
  Hunting Dogs, 14⅝" w, 11⅛" h, one standing and barking,

other sitting, bronze, dark patina, Crondeur, 19th C **1,035.00**
Pekingese, Mortens Studio **25.00**
Pointer Puppy, Mortens Studio . **45.00**
Poodle with girl, Hedi Schoop . **85.00**
Pug Puppy, Mortens Studio ... **45.00**
Scottie
  Celluloid over plaster, black .. **18.00**
  Ceramic Art Studios **35.00**
Set of 4, 3" to 10¼" l, various breeds, bronze, cold painted, Austrian, c1900 ....**1,950.00**
Whippet, 6" h, bisque, pastel polychrome **75.00**
Mobile, Scottie, Russ, orig box .. **10.00**
Napkin Ring, silver plated, two dogs begging **125.00**
Planter, dog by mailbox **24.00**
Salt and Pepper Shakers, pr
  Nipper, RCA, marked "Lenox" . **18.00**
  Scotties, Rosemeade **45.00**
Tobacco Jar, 5⅝" h, terrier, matte finish, blue stamped "R" in diamond and "N588" **175.00**
Wall Pocket, Scottie, hand carved, German **35.00**

Toy, Jumbo, litho tin windup, marked "Made in US Zone/Germany," 4¼" l, 3½" h, $90.00.

ELEPHANTS

Bottle Opener, 3½" h, worn polychrome paint **30.00**
Chocolate Mold, two pcs, circus elephant, clamp type, no hinge .. **90.00**
Figure, 14" h, rosewood, carved, ivory tusks **350.00**

Serving Plate, 12" d, twelve adults and one baby elephant on rim, blue crackle glaze, marked "Dedham" 880.00

Toy
Pull, 8¾" l, papier mache, gray, painted details, felt ears, wood base, steel wheels, Germany, early 20th C 150.00
Stuffed, 12" h, mohair, straw stuffed, glass eyes 50.00

FISH

Bottle, 11" h, fish form, Rockingham 385.00
Food Mold, 11⅝" l, figural, redware, clear glaze, brown flecks and splotches 440.00
String Holder, cast iron 60.00
Tape Measure, figural, celluloid .. 25.00

FOWL

Bank, 3½" h, turkey, cast iron, painted brown and red 125.00
Book, *Mother Goose Book of Rhymes,* Margaret Evans Price, goose illus on cov, 1916 ...... 35.00
Bottle Opener, 2⅛" h, figural, yellow, red, and green, John Wright Co 165.00
Candy Container, 4½" l, Ugly Duckling, glass, painted 45.00
Cookie Cutter, 3½ x 2¾", duck, tin, bent handle 28.00
Cookie Jar, 6 x 9 x 8", hen, ceramic, marked "USA Fapco," c1948 .... 125.00
Doorstop, 8½" h, pheasant, cast iron, sgd "Fred Everett" and "Hubley" 200.00
Figure, 4¼" h, redware, blue and white glaze, marked "Made by FTL Aug 27th 1940" 55.00
Plate, 9½" d, black transfer of pheasants and flowers, polychrome dec, price for set of 4 . 75.00
Post Card, 3½ x 5½", Best Wishes For A Pleasant Thanksgiving, two turkeys 15.00
Sauce Tureen, figural, turkey, china, multicolored 20.00
Sheet Music, *White Folks Call It*

Chanticleer But Its Just Plain Chicken To Me, Bert Williams, 1910, chicken illus on cov 15.00
Toy, chicken, litho tin, lays wood eggs, Chein 65.00
Weathervane, 22½" h, rooster, cast iron body, sheet metal tail . 800.00

FROGS

Ashtray, double, marked "Brush" 50.00
Cookie Jar, ceramic, California Original 35.00
Doorstop, 4¾" l, cast iron, traces of old green paint 55.00
Figure, metal, blue applied eyes, Salviati, paper label 175.00
Paperweight, 5¼" l, "I Croak for the Jackson Wagon," old green paint, polychrome dec 275.00
Sign, 35½" h, Buckeye Camp, Modern Cottages–Rooms, cutout plywood, frog illus, orig polychrome paint 185.00
Vase, 6" h, 5¾" d, blue quilted overlay glass body, clear frog legs around crystal tree stump, clear eyes, white lining 300.00

HORSES

Bank, 5" h, cast iron, rearing, painted gold 55.00
Cookie Cutter, 7½" l, tin 85.00
Figure, 19½" h, pottery, Ming style, grazing, wearing elaborately dec saddle cloth, stepped platform on back, green, chestnut, and cream glaze, mounted as lamp 575.00
Hitching Post, 68" h, horse head, cast iron, steel post, price for pair 90.00
Painting, 22 x 30", oil on canvas, "Up Hill Horses," American School, sgd "E Terry," 19th C . 810.00
Pinback Button
We're All Going to Hastings Races July 22–25, 1902, horse illus, cream ground ... 25.00
Wellsville Driving Park, dark brown horse, pale blue background 75.00
Print, 21 x 28", Dan Patch, chromolithograph 140.00

Tray, rect, horses pulling wagon, Success Manure Spreader adv **1,000.00**
Watch Fob, horse and horseshoe, gold filled, chain **110.00**

WILD ANIMALS

Album Card, New Year, two monkeys, S Hildesheimer & Co **8.00**
Book, *Snow White & Rose Red,* bear and two girls on cov, 12 pgs, 1929, 10 x 10½″ **40.00**
Candy Container, 3⅝″ l, rabbit, crouching, glass, painted, missing closure **50.00**
Catalog, N W School of Taxidermy, Omaha, NE, 27 pgs, 7 x 10″, moose illus **12.00**
Cookie Board, 4⅜ x 6½″, maple, bear design **225.00**
Deer Head, 22″ h, stoneware, real antlers, coleslaw collar, brown pebble glaze **880.00**
Dish, cov, 9¾″ w, Polar Bear Hunt, blue, marked "John Hall," Staffordshire **1,380.00**
Figure
  7¼″ w, 4½″ h, bear, seated, bronze, gold patina, rock crystal base **865.00**
  8¾″ l, lion, red clay, brown paint, rect base with gold paint and black detail, Ohio Pottery . . . **200.00**
  9¼″ l, lion, rect base, worn black and yellow paint, incised "CCD," Ohio Pottery **200.00**
  10¾″ h, monkey, seated, playing three tiered inro with monkey shaped netsuke, bronze, 19th C **2,525.00**
Flyer, Game of Teddy Bear adv, bear illus, 1906 . . . . **20.00**
Food Mold, 10″ l, oval, ironstone, rabbit design, marked "Copeland Spode" **45.00**
Hatpin Holder, 3½ x 4¼ x 3¼″ h, black bear standing beside green tree stump, heart shaped base, china, German **90.00**
Jar, 3¾″ h, figural, bear, amethyst **250.00**
Label, A K Grizzly Island Long Green Asparagus, bear illus . . . **8.00**
Post Card, Ringling Bros Worlds

Greatest Shows, hippo in cage, 1908 . . . . **8.00**
Tobacco Card
  Fearona, lion illus, gold gilt dec **8.00**
  Louisiana Tiger, tiger illus, gold gilt dec **8.00**

ARCHITECTURAL ELEMENTS

History: Architectural elements are those items which have been removed or salvaged from buildings, ships, or gardens. Many are hand crafted. Frequently they are carved in stone or exotic woods. Part of their desirability is due to the fact that it would be extremely costly to duplicate the items today.

The current trend of preservation and recycling architectural elements has led to the establishment and growth of organized salvage operations that specialize in removal and resale of elements. Special auctions are now held to sell architectural elements from churches, mansions, office buildings, etc. Today's decorators often design an entire room around one architectural element, such as a Victorian marble bar or mural, or use several as key accent pieces.

References: Ronald S. Barlow (comp.), *Victorian Houseware: Hardware and Kitchenware,* Windmill Publishing Co., 1991; Margaret Lindquist and Judith Wells, *The Official Price Guide To Garden Furniture and Accessories,* House of Collectibles, 1992; J. L. Mott Iron Works, *Mott's Illustrated Catalog of Victorian Plumbing Fixtures for Bathrooms and Kitchens,* Dover Publications, 1987; Alan Robertson, *Architectural Antiques,* Chronicle Books, 1987; *Stable and Barn Fixtures Manufactured by J. W. Fiske Iron Works,* Apollo Books, 1987; J. P. White's Pyghtle Works, Bedford, England, *Garden Furniture and Ornament,* Apollo Books, 1987.

Periodical: *American Bungalow,* PO Box 756, Sierre Madre, CA 91204.

Additional Listings: Stained Glass.

Arch, 96 x 206″, Eastlake, cornice, dentils, anthemion leaf brackets, incised panels, fluted columns, paneled base **500.00**

Barber Pole, wood
   72" h, side mounted type, turned ball at each end, very worn and weathered white and red repaint, age cracks, damage . **935.00**
   73" h, turned, weathered red, white, and blue repaint, age cracks, puttied repair, edge damage to base **385.00**
Bath Tub, cast iron, ball and claw feet **65.00**
Book, *The Practical House Carpenter*, Asher Benjamin, 1935, very worn, stained **130.00**
Boot Scraper, 12" w, 8½" h, cast iron, lyre shape, diamond base **150.00**
Boundary Marker, 45" h, sewer pipe, molded inscription "N.U.W. 33," from East Liverpool, OH, price for pr **550.00**
Box Lock
   Brass, 3½ x 6½", knob handles, no keeper **50.00**
   Wrought Iron, brass handle trim, brass int. handle and key . . . **150.00**
   Wrought Iron, "Y" shaped keeper and key **105.00**
Bracket Shelf, 14¾" w, 17" h, Victorian, carved walnut, old varnish finish, well detailed eagles, glass eyes, hanging fruit, price for pr **1,760.00**
Butler's Tray, 36" h, cast iron, bell boy, sheet metal fittings, old polychrome paint **450.00**
Carousel Plaque, 35" l, wood, carved faces, repainted, decal designs of eagles, orig damaged wiring, pr **495.00**
Catalog
   Acme Wire & Iron Works, Detroit, MI, 1929, 49 pgs, plain and ornamental iron, wire, brass, and bronze window guards, steel doors, gates, railings, balconies, partitions, and cages, metal grills, bronze tablets, fencing, fire escapes, and stairways, 8 x 11" **40.00**
   Adirondak Lumber Co, Wells, NY, 1932, 32 pgs, summer homes, lodges, log cabins, 52 illus, floor plans, and dimensions, 8½ x 11" **28.00**
   Berger Mfg Co, Canton, OH, Catalog #19, 1914, 148 pgs, "Classik" steel ceilings, cornices, cove and cornice moldings, rosettes, fillers, plates, corner beads, cornice mitres, and wainscots, 8 x 11" **45.00**
   Carr–Ryder & Adams Co, Dubuque, IA, c1926, 108 pgs, hard cov, Bilt–Well Mill Work Homes of Comfort, bungalows, houses, garages, barns, millwork, house plans, and dimensions, 8½ x 11¼" **45.00**
   Gordon–Van Tine Co, Davenport, IA, 1906, 26 pgs, illus price list, doors, windows, millwork, roofing, paints, gable ornaments, flooring, porches, stairways, and steps, includes envelope and two letters, 3¾ x 8¾" **20.00**
Ceiling Medallion, 31" d, plaster, acanthus leaf dec **100.00**
Chimney Pot, 29" h, sewer pipe, crown like detail **275.00**
Column
   28½" h, Corinthian, carved and painted, 19th C **1,100.00**
   58" h, composite capital, carved

Element, lion head, composition, attached to horizontal rect plinth, English, 39¼" h, $1,210.00. Photo courtesy of Butterfield & Butterfield.

and painted, labeled, American, late 19th C, losses, price for pr **375.00**

Door, 32″ w, 79¼″ h, four panel, orig yellow and brown graining, hardware removed, wear, minor damage, slight variations, set of five **275.00**

Element

27″ w, eagle, emb brass, tin back, oval label "Patented Sept 10, 1891, NY" **525.00**

72″ l, 20½″ h, fan carved, vestiges of paint, American, 19th C **635.00**

Flowerpot Holder, 22″ h, wall type, cast iron, floral lattice, ring holders at base, old white repair, price for pr **418.00**

Garden Bench, 44″ w, cast iron, foliage and berry back, griffin arms, scrollwork seat, old welded repairs, layers of white repaint **990.00**

Garden Figure, 10½″ h, rabbit, cast iron, full bodied, worn old white repaint **220.00**

Garden Fountain

27″ h, metal and copper, figural, male and female figures standing beneath umbrella, painted white, damaged **345.00**

33″ h, 42¼″ w, painted zinc, shell shaped iron basin **1,500.00**

Garden Table, 39″ d, 26¾″ h, cast iron, round reticulated top, center hole for umbrella, four foliage scroll legs **120.00**

Gate, 24″ w, 59½″ h, picket fence, paneled section in base, various sized spires, orig cast iron hardware and latch, Southern, weathered **100.00**

Hitching Post, cast iron

40″ h, horse head finial, old white repaint **360.00**

65½″ h, rope twist detail, foliage and horse head finial, pitted, white repaint, welded repair . **420.00**

Horse Trough, 12 x 20 x 72″, cast iron, rect, very worn, pitted, cracks **55.00**

Keystone, granite, carved warrior head **225.00**

Lightning Rod, 65″ h, wrought iron, tripod stand **72.00**

Mantel

56½″ l x 5½″ w shelf, 47″ h, 35½ x 44″ opening, pine cleaned down to old gray, perimeter molding **310.00**

62½″ l x 7″ w shelf, 44½″ h, 44″ w x 32″ h opening, walnut, very worn old brown grained repaint, well detailed molding . . **330.00**

Memorial Sculpture, 6½″ l, marble, carved lamb, oblong base, damaged ears, chips around base . **250.00**

Pedestal, 12¾″ d, 35½″ h, mahogany and hardwoods with mahogany finish, early 20th C **110.00**

Print Portfolio, William Woollett, Villas And Cottages, or Homes For All . . ., NY, A. J. Bicknell & Co, 1876, forty plates of Victorian home views and floor plans, adv for furnishings, building supplies, pictorial cloth, corners rubbed, 7⅜ x 12″ **115.00**

Urn, garden, cast iron

18½″ d, 26½″ h, ball finial topped by planter, smooth sphere and base, foliage detail on planter, rust pitted, damage, price for pr **440.00**

20¾″ d, 39½″ h, melon ribbed bowl, lion head handles, hexagonal plinth, round base, labeled "Wallace, Lithgow & Co, Louisville, KY 1852," rusted, crack **770.00**

21½″ d, 36″ h, white repaint, ears missing, labeled "Kramer" **440.00**

35″ d, 36″ h, fountain bowl, lacy scroll work base, made up from old parts, damage **250.00**

35″ d, 39½″ h, three part griffin stem with dolphins and foliage, round base, mismatched bowl, rebolted **1,265.00**

36″ d, 42½″ h, foliage scrolls with buffalo heads, scrolled ears with rings, sq base labeled "Mfg by the Kramer Bros. Fdy Co, Dayton, O," green repaint, some damage **2,035.00**

37″ d, 43″ h, grotesque human

faces on bowl, sq base labeled
"Mfg by the Kramer Bros. Fdy
Co, Dayton, O," damage,
cracks, loose pieces **1,320.00**
45" h, cherubs on plinths holding
oval basketweave bowls, worn
old white repaint, price for pr **5,940.00**

ART DECO

History: The Art Deco period was named
for an exhibition, "l'Exposition Internationale des Arts Décorative et Industriels Modernes," held in Paris in 1927. It is a later
period than Art Nouveau, but sometimes
the two styles overlap since they were
closely related in time.

Art Deco designs are angular with simple
lines. This was the period of skyscrapers,
movie idols, and the cubist works of Picasso
and Legras. Art Deco motifs were used for
every conceivable object being produced in
the 1920s and 1930s (ceramics, furniture,
glass, and metals) not only in Europe but in
America as well.

References: Victor Arwas, *Glass: Art
Nouveau To Art Deco*, Rizzoli, 1977; Lillian
Baker, *Art Nouveau & Art Deco Jewelry: An
Identification & Value Guide*, Collector
Books, 1981, 1994 value update; Bryan
Catley, *Art Deco And Other Figures*, Antique
Collectors' Club; Tony Fusco, *Art Deco
Identification and Price Guide*, Avon Books,
1993; Mary Gaston, *Collector's Guide To
Art Deco*, Collector Books, 1989, 1994
value update; Robert Heide and John Gil-
man, *Popular Art Deco: Depression Era
Style and Design*, Abbeville Press, 1991;
Steven Heller and Louise Fili, *Italian Art
Deco: Graphic Design Between The Wars*,
Chronicle Books, 1993; Richard J. Kilbride,
*Art Deco Chrome Book Z: A Collectors'
Guide, Industrial Design in the Chase Era*,
Jo–D Books, 1992; Katherine Morrison
McClinton, *Art Deco: A Guide For Collec-
tors*, reprint, Clarkson N. Potter, 1986; Wolf
Uecker, *Art Nouveau and Art Deco Lamps
and Candlesticks*, Abbeville Press, 1986;
Howard and Pat Watson, *Collecting Art
Deco Ceramics*, Kevin Francis, 1993.

Periodical: *The Echoes Report*, PO Box
2321, Mashpee, MA 02649.

Collectors' Club: Chase Collectors So-

ciety, 2149 W. Jibsail Loop, Mesa, AZ
85202; National Coalition of Art Deco Societies, One Murdock Terrace, Brighton, MA
02135.

Museums: Art Institute of Chicago, Chicago, IL; Corning Museum of Glass, Corning, NY; Jones Museum of Glass and Ceramics, Sebago, ME.

Additional Listings: Furniture and Jewelry. Also check glass, pottery, and metal
categories.

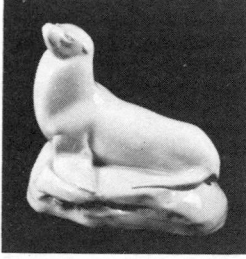

**Figurine, Sea Lion, celadon, high
glaze, marked "Skeaping, Wedgwood," c1920, 8 x 8½", $465.00.**

Bookends, bronze, nude females **95.00**
Bracelet, charm, 7" l, platinum link
bracelet with seventeen different
charms including a piano, cat,
clover, tin man, cross, elephant,
key, dancing elephant, telephone, question mark, penguin,
rabbit, flower, "I love you," lucky
number, dog, and sailboat, accented with small diamonds, colored stones, and enamel, c1925 **8,625.00**
Chairs, dining, French, set of
twelve, two armchairs and ten
side chairs, simple angular
frames, painted black, set with
Greek key brackets at juncture
of legs to seat, yellow patterned
fabric upholstery, 1940s **7,475.00**
Clock, mantel
6½" h, marble, dial marked
"Ovington, Chicago," early
20th C **315.00**
15½" h, onyx and gilt bronze,
early 20th C **285.00**

Cocktail Shaker, silver plated, milk pail design, cylindrical form, pail handle and cov, Reed and Barton, c1920 .... **160.00**

Desk Timepiece, Swiss, onyx, green clock dial, orange, black, and green base, brass numerals and hands, 20th C, 7⅜" h **150.00**

Dining Room Suite, French, mahogany, table top raised on demilune pedestals molded at center above broad ogee molded feet, 8' 5" l extended, 39" w, 29" h, six chairs with muslin upholstered seats and backs, 51" l, 18¼" d, 39¼" h sideboard, c1930 .... **14,375.00**

Dinner Service, Limoges, porcelain, bold butter yellow and black floral dec, includes two cov serving dishes, two oval serving dishes, large bowl, two cake plates, two small serving dishes, twelve bowls, twenty–four dinner plates, and twelve dessert plates **745.00**

End Table

Lacquered, 28" w, 13" d, 22" h, black rect top and lower shelf on three chrome plated tubular steel supports, by Kim Webber, c1930 .... **175.00**

Maple Veneer, split level tops on tapering X–form base, glass tops, c1940, pr **575.00**

Figure, 9½" h, girl, ivory face and hands, green marble base, artist sgd "Lorengl" **1,200.00**

Hall Rack, 83" h, 59" l, 25½" w, French, wrought iron, double sided, rect mirror plates with canted upper corners flanked by openwork sections wrought with scrolling coat hooks, lower section with umbrella compartments, raised on scrolling supports, attributed to Paul Kiss, c1925 .... **4,025.00**

Lamp

Floor

42½" h, patinated steel, vented circular shade with glass finial, rod support with medial shelf on circular base, by Kim Webber, c1925 **230.00**

70" h, French, wrought iron, standard cast with ribboning, stylized foliage, and twists, ivory parchment shade, c1925, pr **17,250.00**

Table

22" h, 14" d shade painted with Art Deco geometric designs in dark and light green, black, and purple band, orange ground, molded painted metal base with circular foot **525.00**

26" h, table, patinated metal, dancing maiden above laurel wreath with floral support, raised rect marble base ... **460.00**

Torchiere, 64½" h, circular flaring brass lamp over six wire–bound bamboo rods, circular brass base, by Russel Wright, c1960 .... **115.00**

Light Fixture, 14" d, circular chrome plated steel fixture supporting two frosted glass circular shades, pr **490.00**

Liqueur Set, crystal, black and white enamel and cut Art Deco designs, bulbous 9" h decanter, four 2¼" h shot glasses **600.00**

Living Room Suite, sofa and two chairs, tubular steel, upholstered **345.00**

Marquee Sign, 24" w, 56½" h, Greta Garbo in "The Kiss," premier at Utica Theatre, blue, yellow, white, orange, and green lettering, Garbo's face in brown, cream, orange, gray, beige, and black, framed **725.00**

Mirror, 40" h, 23" w, bronze and leaded glass, illuminated, incised architectural devices above cascading waterfall eminating from cast fountain mounted on stylized leaf border, flanked by two faceted glass sconces with white leaded glass panels, depatinated, attributed to Ferrobrandt, c1925 .... **7,475.00**

Pitcher, 12" h, chrome plated metal, Normandie, model 723, Peter Muller–Monk, mfg by Revere Copper and Brass Com-

pany, imp "Revere, Rome, N.Y.,"
c1936 ....**2,530.00**
Railing Section, 84" l, 29½" h,
French, wrought iron and
bronze, rect panel wrought with
fan–like sections of geometric
and stylized floral devices, set at
various intervals with hammered
bronze spheres, unsigned, in the
manner of Edgar Brandt, c1925 **7,765.00**
Rug, 11' 10" x 10' 2", wool, designed by George Niedecken,
beige field, off–center medallion
surrounded by ivory vine and
leaf pattern, blue fleur–de–lis
and link, salmon border **1,750.00**
Server, 72" w, 15" d, 69" h, inlaid
rosewood, two cupboards with
glazed doors and rounded inlay
joined by bowed shelf **1,600.00**
Side Board, 106¼" l, 22½" d, 39¼"
h, French, mahogany and brass,
rect top, four cabinet doors
opening to shelves and drawers,
raised on low pedestals above
extended ogee molded plinth,
c1930 ....**10,925.00**
Side Table, pr, tubular steel and
painted wood **175.00**
Tub Chair, tubular steel, upholstered **115.00**
Vase, 16" h, polychromed floral
patterns, matte and gloss
glazes, base ink stamped with
oval mark "Made in Czecho–
Slovakia Amphora," slight glaze
scratches on rim **440.00**

ART NOUVEAU

History: Art Nouveau is the French term
for the "new art" which had its beginning in
the early 1890s and continued for the next
40 years. The flowing and sensuous female
forms used in this period were popular in
Europe and America. Among the most recognized artists of this period were Gallé,
Lalique, and Tiffany.

Art Nouveau can be identified by its flowing, sensuous lines, floral forms, insects,
and the feminine form. These designs were
incorporated on almost everything pro-

duced at that time, from art glass to furniture, silver, and personal objects.

References: Victor Arwas, *Glass: Art
Nouveau To Art Deco*, Rizzoli, 1977; Lillian
Baker, *Art Nouveau & Art Deco Jewelry: An
Identification & Value Guide*, Collector
Books, 1981, 1994 value update; Giovanni
Fanelli and Ezio Godoli, *Art Nouveau Post-
cards*, Rizzoli, 1987; Albert Christian Revi,
American Art Nouveau Glass, reprint, Schif-
fer Publishing, 1981; Wolf Uecker, *Art Nou-
veau and Art Deco Lamps and Candle-
sticks*, Abbeville Press, 1986.

Additional Listings: Furniture and Jewelry. Also check glass, pottery, and metal
categories.

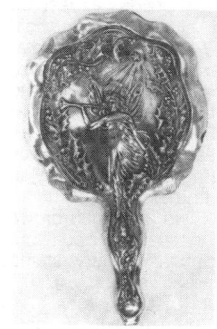

**Mirror, Christmas Angel, holly,
and star, marked "Quadruple
Plate," 10¼" l, 6" w, $95.00.**

Bowl, circular, silver plated rim and
handles **85.00**
Calling Card Tray, copper, reclining lady, feathered fan above figure **82.00**
Candlestick, 7½" h, porcelain, figural, green–gold maiden leaning
against curving stem and foliage, terminating in bud–form
candle socket, pale blue glaze
with gilt highlights, Ernst Wahliss
Alexandra, overglaze blue crown
mark, imp "Made in Austria
4693," early 20th C **225.00**
Carpet, 18' 7" x 14', signed by Victor Horta, wool, beige field

strewn with olive and tan scrolling designs, c1900 . . . . **19,550.00**

Centerpiece, 7¾" h, porcelain, figural, maiden with hair in chignon, chrysanthemums at temples, wearing long white gown and pink drape around hips, seated on water lily blossom, circular bowl molded with overlapping cream and green leaves, Ernst Wahliss Alexandra, overglaze blue crown mark, imp numbers and "Made in Austria," early 20th C **415.00**

Clock

19½" h, bronze, parcel gilt, figural, chapter ring cast with swirling clouds reserved against starry ground, held aloft by winged muse, diaphanous flower trimmed drapery extends from his hips to shaped base, triangular pierced vide poches cast in low relief with flower heads and leafage, reverse cast with clouds and stars, orig pendulum and two keys, rich brown patina, inscribed "Theo Gougon," circular foundry stamp enclosing "Louchet, Paris, Fondeur," c1900 . . . . **5,750.00**

23¾" h, bronze, figural, dark brown patina, inscribed "Marcel Debut, 98," Siot foundry stamp, dated 1898 . . . . **3,450.00**

48" h, wall, regulator, oak, grand sonnerie striking, late 19th/early 20th C **1,500.00**

Creamer and Sugar Bowl, gilt sterling silver, floral and leaf dec, vermeil int., 16 oz **275.00**

Dining Table, mahogany and marquetry, parcel gilt, top inlaid in various woods with diamond pattern, apron carved with stylized poppy blossoms and whiplash tendrils heightened in gilt, unsigned, probably Lyons, 63" l, 45" w, 30½" w, en suite with pr of carved mahogany parcel gilt armchairs with brown plush upholstery, c1900 . . . . **17,250.00**

Dresser Set, sterling silver, elaborate floral repousse with putti bearing baskets of fruit, 9" l handled brush, 7½" l comb, 7" l hand brush, 11" hand mirror, 4¼" d powder jar, Gorham **850.00**

Fire screen, 32⅝" h, silvered brass, shaped rect screen with repousse daffodil blossoms and foliage at top growing from central stem, sides with cast applied foliage, top with tendrils forming handle, raised on four short curved legs ending in leaf form feet, c1900 . . . . **1,100.00**

Jardiniere

15" h, gilt bronze, figural, obverse cast with maiden with butterfly in flowing hair, handles with berried leafy terminals, base with head of old bearded man, inscribed "G. Flamand," c1900 . . . . **1,435.00**

19¾" h, gilt bronze, figural, cast in low and medium relief, obverse with maiden clothed in diaphanous drapery reserved against foliate ground, reverse with foliage, liner, inscribed "L. Chalon, Colin," c1900 . . . . . . **4,890.00**

Lamp

Boudoir, 14½" h, nautilus shaped abalone shell, base signed "Aladdin" **125.00**

Table

13" h, patinated metal, figural, woman holding branch suspending pierced and jeweled shade, 13" h **435.00**

16¼" h, silvered bronze, figural, standing figure with upswept hair, clad in voluminous gown pierced with stars about lower section, holding shaped sphere of gray glass overlaid with cobalt blue, finely wheel carved with subtle swirls and stars, La Voie Lacree, signed "Leo Laporte–Blairsy," Susse Freres Foundry stamp, 1865–1923 **32,200.00**

21" h, patinated bronze base, cast in full relief in form of thistle plant, rubbed brown patina, inscribed "M. Bouval," cameo glass acid etched shade heightened with white and yellow enamel, signed in intaglio "Daum Nancy" with croix de Lorraine twice, c1900 . . . . **20,700.00**

23" h, 16" d four sided shade, four green slag glass triangular panels overlaid with four photographic type panels of boats and canoes, bronzed metal frame with floral design, bronzed metal molded floral candlestick base, stepped sq foot **400.00**

28" h, three bell shaped jeweled fixtures with silk fringe, molded, bronzed standard . **650.00**

32¾" h, alabaster, female figure partially draped, supporting globe overhead, 20th C **975.00**

Hammered Copper, vine shaped form, vines issuing from support surround central socket, frosted glass vase shaped shade cov with spun gilded vines **460.00**

Perfume Bottle, 6½" h, bulbous, silver overlay, green glass, marked "Alvin" **750.00**

Pitcher, Austrian, porcelain, ovoid form, gilt relief floral motif, iris dec, 15" h **315.00**

Portrait Plate, 9¾" d, hunting dog, green and pale gray ground, signed "Pirkenhammer" **200.00**

Salt, open, gilt sterling silver, sq, Oriental dec with dragonfly, Gorham and Co, late 19th/early 20th C, set of four **450.00**

Stool, 23" l, 15" w, 22" h, mahogany, green leather upholstery, unsigned, c1900 . . . . **4,600.00**

Table Fountain, 21" h, figural, lead, silver and alabaster, central merman on raised rock and shell platform supported by four mermaids kneeling on shaped base, fitted to similarly shaped mahogany replacement stand, early 20th C **6,325.00**

Tea Kettle, copper, brass warming stand, turned wood handle **110.00**

Tray

12½" d, sterling silver, poppy design, American, 20 oz **260.00**

16¼" l, porcelain, rect, modeled with head and shoulders of maiden in high relief at either end, reticulated corners, gilt highlighted cyclamen flowers, leaves, and whiplash stems in low relief, imp numbers and "Made in Austria," early 20th C **365.00**

Urn, 16" h, pewter, slender tapering form, rose dec, navy pierced handles, flaring base, c1910 . . **250.00**

Vase

6" h, black, stylized hp flowers and foliage, bright colors **38.00**

10" h, 3" d, irid glass, enameled poppies dec, signed "FH" (Fritz Heckert), numbered . . . **950.00**

12⅞" h, woman with flowers in hair on obverse, woodland scene on reverse, made at Riessner, Stellmacher & Kessel, c1898, base ink stamped with "RStK Turn–Teplitz–Bohemia, Made in Austria," and "Amphora Turn" shield mark, black rect, "1326," and "HH" painted in slip on base, "21, 580, and Amphora" in oval stamped on base **1,210.00**

17" h, porcelain and gilt metal, reserves of cupid and cupid with Aphrodite and doves, iridescent gold, signed Renard, French, late 19th/early 20th C **575.00**

20½" h, French, metal and enamel, cold painted, hammered green painted surface dec with three repousse peacock feathers inset with cloisonne enameled blue and green pea eyes, c1900 . . . . . **3,450.00**

22½" h, figural, baluster form body resembles giant calla lily bud, calla blossoms and leafage emanating from shoulder, seated maiden on shoulder clad in revealing diaphanous gown, pale green and cream glaze, gilt highlights, imp "Amphora," printed red overglaze marks and numbers, chip to one base, minor losses and repairs, c1900, pr **2,875.00**

Vide Poche, 20¼" h, figural, young maiden with flowing pale and deep blue gown, hair cascading down back, hips supporting two spade form leaves, base further cast with head of another maiden, gilt highlights, printed and imp factory marks and numbers, Amphora, c1900 . . . . **4,600.00**

ART PEWTER

History: Pewter objects produced during the Art Nouveau, Arts and Crafts, and Art Deco periods are gaining in popularity. These mostly utilitarian objects, e.g., tea sets, trays, and bowls, were elaborately decorated and produced in the Jugendstil manner by German firms, such as Kayserzinn, and Austrian companies, such as Orivit. In England, Liberty and Company marketed Tudric Pewter, which often had a hammered surface and was embellished with enameling or semi–precious stones. Most pieces of art pewter contain the maker's mark.

KAYSERZINN

Candelabra, pr, shaped rect stem, sides enhanced with differing undulating flowers, molded raised circular base with squared corners, stem issuing four bold scroll branches, circular wax pan, fluted urn form sockets, conforming central light, imp "Kayserzinn," numbered "4485" and "4486," 18¾" h **5,500.00**

Charger, four section deep plate divided by raised floral details, sgd, 14" d **110.00**

Dish, cov, sculpted foliate design, tapered feet, imp mark, designed by Hugo Leven, c1897 . **415.00**

Fish Platter, allover raised fish and other sea creatures dec, sgd, 24⅛" l **200.00**

Flagon, iris design, 15" h **245.00**

Platter, cov, oval, emb curvilinear organic motif, domed handled lid, diestamped oval mark and "4413," etched initials "JA," 21" l **440.00**

Punchbowl, cov, wedding, full form putto with harp finial on hammered and flower dec cov, conforming bulbous handled bowl with hearts and flowers design, four elaborate ball and claw feet, imp "Kayserzinn" at top border, some corrosion within, 16½" h . **470.00**

Roll Tray, lily of the valley dec, marked "Kayserzinn, 4822," 13" l **70.00**

Tea Set, 4 pcs, teapot, cov sugar, creamer, and tray, allover sinuous flowering stems design, 17" l navette shaped tray, 6½" h teapot **450.00**

LIBERTY

Ashtray, marked "Tudric" **50.00**

Centerpiece, two handled, circular dish, raised base with sinuous blossoms and stems and "And The Musk Of The Rose Is Blown And The Woodbine Spices Are Wafted Abroad," stamped "Tudric," 9¾" d **425.00**

Clock
  Desk, rect body with simple repousse dec of winding vines and berries on obverse, red, green, and blue enameled Arabic chapters on clock face, stamped "Tudric," 5½" h **500.00**
  Mantel, tapering rect body, circular face inset in central panel, mottled blue and green enamel face, surmounted by overhung domed rect top, stamped "Made In England English Pewter 0761," 8¾" h **2,420.00**

Dish, cov, circular, shallow, scalloped border, peaked cov with asymmetrical handle, design attributed to Archibald Knox, stamped "Tudric," 1903, 10" d . **770.00**

Pitcher, cov, blue enamel dec, cane wrapped handle, imp

marks, minor enamel chip, c1905, 5¾" h **195.00**

Tea and Coffee Service, teapot, coffeepot, creamer, and sugar, marked "Tudric" **495.00**

Tray, rect, shaped edge, strapwork handles, monogrammed, imp mark, 21½" l **105.00**

Vase, conical form with molded curvilinear repeating elements, three applied buttress supports, imp "Tudric 0223," 7½" h **165.00**

ORIVIT

Centerpiece, circular bowl, handled, tall cut glass liner, imp mark, c1900, 7" h, 8¼" d liner . **495.00**

Dish, figural, lady with flowing hair **195.00**

Tea Service, 4 pcs, teapot, cov sugar basin, milk jug, and tray, allover stylized overlapping flower heads raised in sinuous stems design, each piece numbered and stamped "Orivit," c1903, 6" h teapot, 18¾" l tray . **1,430.00**

ART POTTERY (GENERAL)

History: The period of art pottery reached its zenith in the late 19th and early 20th centuries. Over a hundred companies produced individually designed and often decorated wares which served a utilitarian as well as an aesthetic purpose. Artists moved about from company to company, some forming their own firms.

Quality of design, beauty in glazes, and condition are the keys in buying art pottery. This category covers companies not found elsewhere in the guide.

References: Susan and Al Bagdade, *Warman's American Pottery and Porcelain,* Wallace–Homestead, 1994; Carol and Jim Carlton, *Colorado Pottery,* Collector Books, 1994; Paul Evans, *Art Pottery of the United States, Second Edition,* Feingold & Lewis Publishing, 1987; Lucile Henzke, *Art Pottery of America,* Schiffer Publishing, 1982; Ralph and Terry Kovel, *Kovels' American Art Pottery: Collector's Guide to Makers, Marks and Factory Histories,* Crown Publishers, 1993.

Periodical: *Arts & Crafts Quarterly,* 9 Main St., Lambertville, NJ 08530.

Collectors' Clubs: American Art Pottery Assoc., 125 E. Rose Ave., St. Louis, MO 63119; Pottery Lovers Reunion, 4969 Hudson Dr., Stow, OH 44224.

Museums: Cincinnati Art Museum, Cincinnati, OH; Everson Museum of Art of Syracuse and Onondaga County, Syracuse, NY; Newcomb College Art Gallery, New Orleans, LA; Zanesville Art Center, Zanesville, OH.

Additional Listings: See Cambridge, Clewell, Clifton, Cowan, Dedham, Fulper, Grueby, Jugtown, Marblehead, Moorcroft, Newcomb, North Dakota School of Mines, Ohr, Owens, Paul Revere, Peters and Reed, Rookwood, Roseville, Van Briggle, Weller, and Zanesville.

Desert Sands, bud vase, marked "Desert Sands, Boulder City, NV," 5¼" h, $25.00.

Arequipa Pottery, (1913–18), Fairfax, CA, vase

6⅛" h, shouldered ovoid body, incised stylized meandering vine around mouth, pink and yellow glaze, matte green ground, imp tree and vase encircled by "Arequipa California, 2084," incised star mark . **1,050.00**

11⅜" h, relief dec, rim and shoulder laden with stylized wisteria trailing to base, reticulated highlighting, matte green and black glaze, attributed to Frederick H Rhead, unsigned, glaze pulls at base **495.00**

California Faience Co, (1916–30), Berkeley, CA

Jar, cov, 9½″ h, bulbous body, periwinkle blue glossy glaze, incised "California Faience" . **275.00**

Tea Tile, pr, 5¼″ d, flower basket pattern, matte and gloss glazes, marked "California Faience," mounted and framed, secured to backing with soluble silicon type adhesive **660.00**

Vase, 7½″ h, fine crystalline turquoise glaze, red clay body, imp "California Faience" **275.00**

Jervis Pottery (1908–12), Oyster Bay, NY

Bowl, 2¼″ h, low, two handled, slightly crystalline blue matte glaze, base marked with incised Jervis logo and letter "C" **165.00**

Vase, 5″ h, frieze of squares around shoulder, alternately highlighted in white and green–black glossy glaze, matte green ground, raised signature "Jervis" **2,200.00**

Kenton Hills (1939–42), Erlanger, KY

Jar, cov, 6″ h, 5½″ d, circular, orange–to–red glossy glaze, aventurine highlights, die-stamped KH mark, #87, c1941 **250.00**

Vase

9″ h, rich high gloss peachblow glaze, marked with Kenton Hills logo, #88, minor glaze scratches **275.00**

12¼″ h, stylized floral dec, painted c1940 by William Hentschel, Kenton Hills logo, #106, artist's monogram painted on side, small glaze skip at base, drilled **660.00**

Merrimac Ceramic Co (1897–1908), Newburyport, MA

Bowl, short neck, flaring to angled shoulder tapering towards base, matte green and speckled black glaze, imp "Merrimac," early 20th C **275.00**

Mug, 5¾″ h, hand thrown, flared, half–round handle, typical Merrimac green glaze with slipped color texture, imp fish and "Merrimac" mark and label **225.00**

Vase

7½″ h, white streaks, matte gray–brown glaze, red clay body, imp sturgeon mark and "Merrimac" **325.00**

8½″ h, oval body with raised rim, yellowish–gray matte glaze, blue–green striations streaking from top to bottom, paper label with sturgeon mark **450.00**

Norse (1903–13), Edgerton, WI, and Rockford, IL

Chamberstick, 5½″ h, bulbous base, buttressed handle, stamped "Norse" **185.00**

Vase, 12″ h, carved design, copper clad, slender neck, ftd, stamped "Norse," repair to foot **160.00**

Overbeck Pottery (1911–55), Cambridge City, IN

Brooch, 1¾″ h, 2″ w, molded and incised bluebird among flowers design, red, blue, green, and yellow glaze, white ground, imp "OBK," early 20th C **450.00**

Vase, 4½″ h, short rolled neck, squat bulbous form, dark mauve glaze, three bands with molded Oriental style geometric design, imp "OBK," cypher and "EH" marks, fabrication by Elizabeth, dec by Hannah Overbeck, c1915 .... **525.00**

Pewabic Pottery (1868–present), Detroit, MI

Bowl, 5″ d, 2″ h, half round, ridged, white clay with green–gray glaze, streaked blue and maroon, irid, circular "Pewabic Detroit" mark **195.00**

Box, cov, 5″ w, 3¾″ d, 1¾″ h, rect, cut corner top with imp stylized peacock dec, similarly dec base, irid blue–green glaze, imp "Pewabic, Detroit" centered by "PP," early 20th C ... **250.00**

Lamp, pr, 28½" h, bulbous body, four scrolling feet joined by ring, neck fitted with twisted iron and disc mount, light clusters with spiraling wrought iron finials, ochre glaze **4,175.00**

Vase, 15½" h, swollen vasiform, rolled arm on cylindrical neck, gold metallic and irid glaze, imp mark and paper label, drilled, c1910 .... **1,050.00**

Pisgah Forest (1913–present), Mt Pisgah, NC

Creamer and Sugar Bowl, 6" d, 3½" h, cameoware, ox–pulled covered wagon scene, dead matte white over green, Walter Stephen, stamped and artist sgd, 1953 .... **350.00**

Pitcher, 7½" d, 8" h, cameoware, ox–pulled covered wagon scene, dark green ground, glossy turquoise base, rose–pink int., raised mark, 1932 .. **600.00**

Vase, 5¼" h, cameoware, wagon train scene with dogs, trees, horses, and mountains, heavy slip painting, base marked with "Potter at the Wheel" logo and date, artist's last name is part of slip dec, Walter Stephen, 1951 ...... **550.00**

Stockton Art Pottery (1890–95, 1896–1900), Stockton, CA, ewer, 4" d, 9" h, Mariposa ware, mottled brown glossy finish, diestamped mark **275.00**

Teco (1886–1930), Terra Cotta, IL

Ashtray, 5½" l, novelty, molded in form of grumpy pottery dealer, semi–gloss green glaze, base marked with diestamped Teco logo **275.00**

Bowl, 8" d, 2½" h, scalloped edge, smooth matte green and black glaze, imp "Teco" **425.00**

Vase, 9" h, highly textured upper half, orange matte glaze, base stamped "Teco" twice, attributed to Fritz Albert, small chip on base, c1910 .... **1,975.00**

University City (1910–15), University City, MO

Jar, cov, 2" h, 1¾" d, ridged body, carved cov, high gloss white glaze, stamped mark, 1914 .... **150.00**

Vase, 6¾" h, allover honey, blue, and white crystals, base incised "UC 1912" **2,425.00**

Volkmar Pottery (1882–1903), Tremont, NY

Oil Lamp, 12" d, 17" h, squatty, green and brown flambe glaze, unmarked period red and green leaded glass shade, base marked "Volkmar" **500.00**

Tile, sq, Impressionistic landscape with trees, matte turquoise and deep green glaze, marked "V" on face, 8" sq ... **550.00**

Vase

6¼" h, 3½" d, tapering base, crackled high gloss light pink glaze, incised "Volkmar," 1942 .... **200.00**

9¾" h, variegated blue–green matte glaze, base incised "Volkmar Durant 1927, 206" **1,650.00**

Walley (1890–1917), West Sterling, MA

Bowl, 5⅝" d, 3¾" h, rolled rim on shoulder, circular ftd base, blue matte glaze, imp "WJW" **350.00**

Mug, 6" h, hand thrown, carved organic form with five repeating leaf elements, stem handle, allover green–brown glaze over red clay, imp "WJW" ... **1,425.00**

Vase, 9½" h, bulbous body, long neck, green drip glaze on brown ground, imp "WJW" .. **775.00**

Walrath Pottery (1908–21), Rochester, NY

Candleholder, 11½" h, figural, cherub sitting on tree trunk, warming his hands on heat from candle flame, Frederick Walrath, base incised "Walrath Potter" with conjoined "MI," c1915 .... **1,100.00**

Mug, 5" h, stylized leaves and berries dec, light green and red matte glaze, dark green ground, incised mark **150.00**

Vase, 4⅝" h, pink flowers dec, green matte ground, Frederick Walrath, grinding chips and blisters on base rim **1,325.00**

Wannopee Pottery, (1892–1903), New Milford, CT, candlestick, 12¾" h, dark blue irid glaze, base marked "Wannopee" in block letters, minor glaze scratches on base **165.00**

Wheatley Potter Co (1880–1936), Cincinnati, OH

Tile, 8" sq, grotesque type, emb devil mask, heavily curdled matte brown and green glaze, minor nick to front **300.00**

Vase, 9⅝" h, yellow matte glaze, base stamped with Wheatley logo, c1905 .... **875.00**

Zark Pottery, St Louis, MO, vase, 8⅝" h, variegated green matte glaze, base incised "Zark Pink KK 100," black slip painted "67," 1907–11 .... **415.00**

ARTS AND CRAFTS MOVEMENT

History: The Arts and Crafts Movement in American decorative arts took place between 1895 and 1920. Leading proponents of the movement were Elbert Hubbard and his Roycrofters, the brothers Stickley, Frank Lloyd Wright, Charles and Henry Greene, George Niedecken, and Lucia and Arthur Mathews.

The movement was marked by individualistic design (although the movement was national in scope) and re–emphasis on handcraftsmanship and appearance. A reform of industrial society was part of the long–range goal. Most pieces of furniture favored a rectilinear approach and were made of oak.

References: Steven Adams, *The Arts & Crafts Movement,* Chartwell Books, 1987; David M. Cathers, *Furniture of the American Arts and Crafts Movement,* New American Library, 1981; Donald A. Davidoff and Robert L. Zarrow (eds.) *Early L. & J. G. Stickley Furniture: From Onondaga Shops to Handcraft,* Dover Publications, 1992; Paul Evans, *Art Pottery Of The United States, 2nd Edition,* Feingold & Lewis Publishing, 1987; Malcolm Haslam, *Collector's Style Guides: Arts and Crafts,* Ballantine Books, 1988; Bruce Johnson, *The Official Identification and Price Guide To Arts And Crafts, Second Edition* House of Collectibles, 1992; Wendy Kaplan, *The Art That Is Life: The Arts and Crafts Movement In America 1875–1920,* Boston Museum of Fine Arts, 1987; Elyse Zorn Karlin, *Jewelry and Metalwork in the Arts and Crafts Tradition,* Schiffer Publishing, 1993; Coy L. Ludwig, *The Arts and Crafts Movement In New York State, 1890s–1920s,* Gallery Association of New York State, 1983; L–W Book Sales, *Furniture of the Arts & Crafts Period With Prices,* L–W Book Sales, 1992; Kevin McConnell, *Heintz Art Metal: Silver–On–Bronze Wares,* Schiffer Publishing, 1990; Mary Ann Smith, *Gustav Stickley: The Craftsman,* Dover Publications, 1983, 1992 reprint; The Roycrofters, *Roycroft Furniture Catalog, 1906,* Dover Publications, 1994; Joanna Wissinger, *Arts and Crafts: Metalwork and Silver,* Chronicle Books, 1994; Joanna Wissinger, *Arts and Crafts: Pottery and Ceramics,* Chronicle Books, 1994.

Periodicals: *American Bungalow,* PO Box 756, Sierra Madre, CA 91204; *Arts and Crafts Quarterly,* 9 Main St., Lambertville, NJ 08530.

Collectors' Clubs: Foundation For The Study Of The Arts & Crafts Movement, Roycroft Campus, 31 S. Grove St., East Aurora, NY 14052; Roycrofters–At–Large Assoc., PO Box 417, East Aurora, NY 14052; William Morris Society of Canada, Ontario, Canada.

Museums: Elbert Hubbard Library–Museum, East Aurora, NY; Museum of Modern Art, New York, NY.

Additional Listings: Roycroft Items, Stickleys, and art pottery categories.

Andirons, pr, English, copper, front emb with large stylized floral motif, unmarked, 10¼" h **200.00**

Bowl, Voulkos, stoneware, hand thrown, gray drip dec, brown satin ground, sgd, 4½" h, 12" d **900.00**

Box, Roycroft, mahogany, protruding square pulls, copper strap hardware, orig reddish finish,

some alligatoring, cov with incised Orb & Cross mark, 23" l,
12" d, 9½" h **250.00**
Brooch, Mary Gage, silver, circular design with four lily pads centering amber gemstone, silver bead highlights, imp "Mary Gage Sterling" **325.00**
Clock, mantel, L and J G Stickley, #85, slightly swollen shape with overhanging beveled top, broad, beveled base, acid etched copper face, orig finish, "Handcraft" decal, 22 x 16 x 8" **6,750.00**

Dish, lustered, winged lions, yellow and pink accents, c1888–97, "FP" mark of Fred Passenger, William DeMorgan, England, 14½" d, $1,500.00.

Furniture
Chair, Gustav Stickley, #364, riveted leather back and seat, cleaned orig finish, replaced leather, red decal, 37" h **500.00**
Crib Settee, Gustav Stickley, #208, broad slats under back and side rails, side rails mortised through front posts, orig drop–in seat cushion, enhanced orig medium dark finish, red decal, 76" l, 29" h . . . **5,500.00**
Dining Table, Stickley Brothers, round, split pedestal, flaring

base, four curved feet, recent finish to top, added varnish to base, lacks leaves, paper label "187420," copper label "Jordan Marsh Co, Boston, MA," 55" d, 29" h **1,300.00**
Library Table, Lifetime Furniture, #932, tiger oak top, small round tier held by arched crossed stretchers, recent dark finish, unmarked, 30" d, 29" h **650.00**
Office Chair, Limbert, #5335, revolving, tilting, upholstered seat and back, four splayed legs on casters, orig finish, branded mark, 39½" h **950.00**
Parlor Suite, Plail Brothers, 3 pcs, settee, armchair, and rocker, oak, barrel back, bowed crest rail, vertical slats, orig spring cushions, flared rear feet, paper label, one rocker repaired, some old refinish, edge roughness, Wayland, NY, c1910 . . . . **6,600.00**
Sewing Rocker, lady's, Gustav Stickley, #373, high back, spindled back and sides, sling seat, recent dark finish, unmarked, 39" h **700.00**
Stool, Stickley, oak, rect seat, block legs, 20" w, 16" d, 16" h **525.00**
Table, Limbert, oak, legs pierced with square cutouts, branded "Limbert's Arts Crafts Furniture, Made Grand Rapids and Holland," stenciled "146," c1915, 44" h **1,950.00**
Lamp
Floor, oak and leaded glass, flaring trapazoidal oak shade with fleur–de–lis leaded glass panels, buttressed square base over tapering square support on angled square base, c1900, 61¾" h **1,430.00**
Oil, copper and glass, owl form, 8" h **90.00**
Table
20½" h, patinated metal and glass, hexagonal shade with sloping panels over dropped border with shaped lower

rim, each panel with three slender spreading segments of striated green and white or caramel and white opaque glass, paneled baluster standard spreading to hexagonal rim, first quarter 20th C, 18½" d shade **300.00**

28½" h, attributed to Dard Hunter, two four–sided leaded glass shades with stylized pink, white, and yellow flowers on white slag glass ground, heavy four–sided hammered base, unmarked **4,750.00**

Pitcher, T C Shop, Chicago, sterling silver, oval flaring form with bracket handle, 12 oz, 7" h **980.00**

Print, Oscar Reickson, color woodblock, entitled "End Of The Day," landscape with farmhouse at twilight, dark greens and oranges, pencil signed, titled, and numbered "20/100," 6 x 6½" image **450.00**

Tea Set, K Edwin Leinonen, sterling silver **2,500.00**

Tile, depicts garden scene with fountain, green, brown, and blue matte glaze, unmarked, 4¼" sq **150.00**

Vase

Kenton Hills, porcelain, closed–in rim, stylized gray leaves and pink flowers, butterfat glaze, white ground, Dickman dec, imp mark, #188, 5" h **275.00**

Volkmar, tapering body, fine mottled green glaze, brown ground, small chip to rim, incised "V," 10¼" h **275.00**

Wheatley Pottery Co, emb and stylized floral designs, base stamped with Wheatley logo, made in Cincinnati, c1905, 3⅝" h **715.00**

Vessel, Carl Walters, Mediterranean style dec with red abstract flowers and geometric bands, hen figure, glossy white ground, imp mark, 11" h, 7½" d **300.00**

Wastebasket, Stickley Brothers, flared sides, slatted, cutout feather shaped pulls, worn orig finish, unmarked, 18" h, 14" sq **375.00**

AUSTRIAN WARE

History: Over a hundred potteries were located in the Austro–Hungarian Empire in the late 19th and early 20th centuries. Although Carlsbad was the center of the industry, the factories spread as far as modern–day Czechoslovakia.

Many of the factories were either owned or supported by Americans; hence, their wares were produced mainly for export to the United States. Responding to the 1891 law that imported products must be marked as to country of origin, many wares do not have a factory mark, but only the word "Austrian."

Reference: Susan and Al Bagdade, *Warman's English & Continental Pottery & Porcelain, Second Edition,* Wallace–Homestead, 1991.

Additional Listings: Amphora, Carlsbad, Royal Dux, and Royal Vienna.

Vase, molded leaf neck, beige and gold, red "Vienna, Austria," mark, c1900, 13" h, $7,500.00.

Cake Plate, 11½" d, deep green, maroon, beige, and gold, marked "Alhambra" **115.00**

Charger, 20¾" d, majolica, polychrome dec relief portraits of fruit sellers, imp marks, c1900, pr .. **980.00**

Compote, 8" d, porcelain, pierced gallery, blue ground body with gilt trimmed hp panels depicting classical female subjects, beehive marks, late 19th C, pr **975.00**

Decanter, 6″ h, bird, green glass
body, metal head, signed **195.00**
Finger Bowl, hp porcelain, pink
roses, gold trim, matching underplate, marked "Royal Aus-
tria," set of six **250.00**
Fish Service, porcelain, various
fish dec, oval platter, eleven
plates **325.00**
Humidor, 4½″ h, majolica, cat
head, marked "Austria" **195.00**
Pitcher
4¼″ h, 4¼″ d, china, pastel
ground, red and yellow roses,
gold trim, signed "Schreiter,"
marked "Austria" **50.00**
11″ h, porcelain, deep red
ground, raised gilt leaf designs
surrounding central hp panel
of friar sampling wines, bee-
hive mark, c1900, 11″ h **750.00**
Plate, 9½″ d, porcelain, cobalt blue
ground border, central hp dec
depicting Christopher Columbus, silver overlay, beehive
mark, late 19th C **490.00**
Stemware, 8½″ h, glass, green
hock stems, multicolored transparent enamel dec on clear
bowl, set of five **1,200.00**
Urn, 10″ h, china, two handled,
maroon field, gold trim, figural
central band, metal base, pr . . . **315.00**
Vase, 4½″ h, glass, Art Nouveau
style, irid ground, enamel floral
dec, attributed to Fritz Heckert . **150.00**

AUTOGRAPHS

History: Autographs occur in a wide variety of formats—letters, documents, photographs, books, cards, etc. Most collectors
focus on a particular person, country, or category, e.g., signers of the Declaration of
Independence.

The condition and content of letters and
documents bears significantly on value.
Collectors should know their source since
forgeries abound and copy machines compound the problem. Further, some signatures of recent presidents and movie stars
are done by machine rather than by the
persons themselves. A good dealer or advanced collector can help one spot the differences.

The leading auction sources for autographs are Swann Galleries, Sotheby's,
and Christie's, all located in New York City.

References: Mark Allen Baker, *All–Sport
Autographs,* Krause Publications, 1994;
Mary A. Benjamin, *Autographs: A Key To
Collecting,* reprint, Dover, 1986; Charles
Hamilton, *American Autographs,* University
of Oklahoma Press, 1983; George S. Lowry,
Autographs: Identification and Price Guide,
Avon Books, 1994; Norman E. Martinus and
Harry L. Rinker, *Warman's Paper,* Wallace–
Homestead, 1994; Robert W. Pelton, *Col-
lecting Autographs For Fun And Profit,* Bet-
terway Publications, 1987; George Sand-
ers, Helen Sanders, Ralph Roberts,
*Sanders Price Guide To Sports Auto-
graphs, 1994 Edition,* Scott Publishing,
1993; George Sanders, Helen Sanders,
Ralph Roberts, *The 1994 Sanders Price
Guide To Autographs, Number 3,* Alexan-
der Books, 1994.

Periodicals: *Autograph Collector's
Magazine,* 510–A S. Corona Mall, Corona,
CA 91720; *Autographs & Memorabilia,* PO
Box 224, Coffeyville, KS 67337; *Autograph
Times,* 2303 N. 44th St., No. 225, Phoenix,
AZ 85008; *The Autograph Review,* 305
Carlton Rd., Syracuse, NY 13207; *The Col-
lector,* PO Box 255, Hunter, NY 12442.

Collectors' Clubs: Manuscript Society,
350 N. Niagara St., Burbank, CA 95105;
Universal Autograph Collectors Club, PO
Box 6181, Washington, DC 20044.

Additional Listings: See *Warman's
Americana & Collectibles* for more examples.

The following abbreviations denote type
of autograph material and their sizes.

ADS	Autograph Document Signed
ALS	Autograph Letter Signed
AQS	Autograph Quotation Signed
CS	Card Signed
DS	Document Signed
FDC	First Day Cover
LS	Letter Signed
PS	Photograph Signed
TLS	Typed Letter Signed

Sizes (approximate):
Folio	12 x 16 inches
4to	8 x 10 inches
8vo	5 x 7 inches
12mo	3 x 5 inches

COLONIAL AMERICA

Lafayette, French statesman and officer, ALS, 6 x 4", in French, 1828, seal missing, minor rect stain from frame, slight foxing . **425.00**

McKean, Thomas, sgd Declaration of Independence, DS, indenture, 10 x 15", 3 pgs, 1777 land deed for land in Philadelphia, PA, fold breaks, repairs, paper seals intact **525.00**

Willett, Marinus, Sons of Liberty member, Indian fighter, DS, 8 x 3", 1782, signed "M. Willett" ... **75.00**

Yates, Robert, jurist and Chief Justice, NY, ADS, 8 x 6" inlaid legal document, undated, as attorney for the Defense **135.00**

FOREIGN

Gladstone, W E, British Prime Minister, ALS, both sides plain 4 x 7" stationery, 1878, abandoned plans for University of Scotland **125.00**

Gordon, George Hamilton, Earl of Aberdeen, British Prime Minister, free franked 5 x 3" holograph address panel with initials on lower left corner **35.00**

Leopold, Prince of Romania, ALS, 4 x 7", 2 pgs, both sides, 1869, official stationery bearing emb gold crown above red, blue, and gold initials, in Spanish to "Caro Signor Volpe" **75.00**

Mubarak, M Hosni, President of Egypt, FDC, six colorful stamps canceled 23 July 1959, fine ink signature on lower white blank . **50.00**

Pitt, William, The Younger, British Prime Minister, 5 x 3" fragment from document, large "W Pitt" signature with heading "By His Majesty's Command" **75.00**

Robinson, Frederick J, Earl of Nipon, British Prime Minister, 5 x

3" postmarked free frank holograph address panel, 1827, Robinson scratched one address and penned in another, signed "Frederick" on lower left corner **65.00**

GENERAL

Barton, Clara, founded American Red Cross, PS, "The National First Aid Association of America," 7 pgs, 5 x 7" pamphlet with 5 x 7" bust photo signed "Very Sincerely Yours, Clara Barton," tape stains **250.00**

Du Chaillu, Paul, introduced first gorillas to US, ALS, 5 x 7" plain sheet, NYC, 1897, mentions ill health, full signature at end ... **125.00**

Hotchkiss, Benjamin B, American inventor and ordnance supplier to Union Army, ALS, 8 x 10", 3 pgs, official business stationery, 1874, Paris, France, boldly signed "B.B. Hotchkiss" **1,500.00**

James, Frank, Western outlaw, 4 x 5" envelope, addressed to Mrs. Frank James, Independence, MO, 3¢ stamp, postmarked Ballatin, MO, July 7, 1883, mounted beneath 5 x 7" book photo, matted, 9 x 15" **1,950.00**

Salk, Jonas, developed polio vaccine, FDC, honoring American Medical Association's 100th anniversary, block of 3¢ stamps canceled Atlantic City, 1947, fine dark ink signature on white blank **75.00**

Scribner, Charles, publishing company founder, ADS and ALS, 8 x 10" lined ledger sheet, expense account to author W W Campbell for book **145.00**

Teller, Edward, American physicist, developed hydrogen bomb, Nobel Prize winner, FDC, Atoms For Peace, stamp and cachet canceled Washington, 1955, large blue ballpoint signature .. **55.00**

LITERATURE

Clemens, Samuel, Mark Twain, both signatures in purple ink on

small 3 x 2″ card, inscribed "Yrs
Truly," mounted to slightly larger
paper **950.00**
Grey, Zane, book, *Desert Gold,*
first edition, 1913 by Harper
Bros, signature and inscription
on first end paper, binding needs
repair **175.00**
Lee, Harper, typescript, one page,
8 x 10″ titled "To Kill A Mocking
Bird," green ink inscription lower
white border "With my best
wishes, Harper Lee" **325.00**
Runyon, Damon, TLS, 8 x 7″ "20th
Century Fox" stationery, 1942,
full black ink signature **195.00**
Seuss, Dr, 5 x 7″ card, sketch,
black ink, The Cat as the Grinch,
bust profile pose wearing orange
Santa type hat and shirt, green
border, penned black ink inscription "A Special Grinch for Sara
from Dr. Seuss" **525.00**
Wolf, Gary K, *Who Framed Roger
Rabbit?* creator and author, 8 x
10″ plain white heavy paper,
black felt tip pen full pose sketch
of Jessica Rabbitt, red ink paw
prints, signature, and inscription
"Jessica Rabbitt XXX," matted,
unframed **50.00**

MILITARY

Duncan, Hy, Civil War, ALS, 2 pgs,
7 x 12″ lined stationery, July 5,
1962, to General Ruggles,
Camp Moore, LA, discusses or-
ders **275.00**
McCarthy, Joseph J, Brigadier
General, ALS, both sides, 5 x 8″
personal stationery, eyewitness
account of flag raising on Iwo
Jima **95.00**
Montgomery of Alamein, British
General, PS, black and white,
glossy, 6 x 8″, dated 1962,
close–up portrait, wearing hat
and uniform, smiling **375.00**
Toombs, Robert, CSA General
and Secretary of State, ALS, 5 x
8″ stationery, Washington, Aug
6, 1858, to Crawford concerning
con–compliance of McElroy . . . **225.00**

Wise, Henry A, CSA General,
Governor of VA, DS, 7 x 8″,
1856, sgd as governor, emb seal **125.00**
Wright, Marcus J, CSA General,
ALS, 3 pgs, 8 x 10″, Oct 18,
1894, details resale of property
in Tennessee, full signature . . . **155.00**

MUSIC

Armstrong, Louis, band leader,
TLS, 8 x 10″, 3 plain pgs, directions to "Lose Weight The
'Satchmo Way'" by Lucille Armstrong and Louis Armstrong, humorous, signed top of first page
to "John, Louis Armstrong,
Satchmo" **250.00**
Dorsey, Tommy, bandleader, PS,
5 x 7″, sepia, personalized,
close–up bust pose, holding
trombone, CBS microphone in
background **150.00**
Gluck, Johnny, signed 1953 full
sheet music entitled "Who Put
The Devil In Evelyn's Eyes,"
Mills Brothers on cov, signed
near image **30.00**
Howe, Julia Ward, composed
"Battle Hymn of the Republic,"
ALS, 3 pgs, 5 x 8″ personal stationery, 1884, regarding appoint-
ment, folded with minor flaws . . **175.00**
Joplin, Janis, 12 x 12″ album cov,
close–up image of Joplin performing, inscribed "Love Janis
Joplin," ballpoint pen **450.00**
Parker, Frank, PS, 8 x 10″, sepia,
personalized, profile image **25.00**
Presley, Elvis, 4 x 7″ record catalog, color, 1967, 30 pgs, cov
photo inscribed "To Betty, Best
wishes, Elvis Presley," black
ballpoint pen **850.00**
Sinatra, Frank, PS, 8 x 10″, sepia,
bust pose, arms folded, wearing
tuxedo, inscribed "To Walter
who has more ups and downs
than anyone I know. The best of
everything to you, always, Sin-
cerely, Frank Sinatra, 1940" . . . **500.00**
Starr, Judy, big band singer, PS, 8
x 10″ glossy, personalized, with
NBC microphone **20.00**

The Drifters, PS, 8 x 10" black and white publicity pose, four signatures near individual images ... **75.00**

PRESIDENTS

Adams, John Quincy, DS, partly printed, 9 x 15" land grant signed as president, for property in Detroit, 1826, white paper seal intact, off white mat, mounted next to 6 x 8" engraving of Adams full formal pose, 27 x 14" overall .. **975.00**

Cleveland, Grover, autograph album, 7 x 9", approx 140 pgs, 1896, at least one signature each page, some pages with four or five, first page signatures include President Grover Cleveland, First Lady Frances F Cleveland, Vice President A E Stevenson, and Secretary of the Navy H A Herbert, album also includes signatures from Cleveland's Cabinet, the 54th Congress, Speaker Thomas Reed, Henry Cabot Lodge, John F Fitzgerald, Supreme Court Justices, and foreign ministers to US from Cuba, Argentina, Russia, Japan, and Netherlands, worn leather cover, contents very fine, at least 325 signatures **995.00**

Reagan, Ronald, campaign brochure, from first presidential term, pictures and information all sides, 4 x 9" folded size, 12 x 9" open size, blue ballpoint pen signature **225.00**

Roosevelt, Franklin D, TLS, 8 x 10" Navy Department stationery, March 15, 1919, to Senator Sheppard regarding release of Ensign Meyer C Hoffman **450.00**

Truman, Harry, PS, 5 x 8", magazine photo, dated May 8, 1945, Truman seated at desk with microphone, black ink inscription "Kind regards from Harry Truman 7/11/64" **225.00**

Wilson, Woodrow, schedule, 6 x 5", "Princeton University Schedule for Academic Special Stu-

dents, 1st term, 1903," signed as instructor of Pol. 1 class **250.00**

SHOW BUSINESS

Boyd, William, Hopalong Cassidy, ALS, 8 x 10" plain paper, boldly penned inscription "Best always, Bill Boyd, 'Hoppy'" **350.00**

Chaney, Lon Jr, DS, 8 x 12" Screen Actors Guild contract, 1956, with Universal Studios for film entitled *Money, Women and Dreams,* partly printed, typed details filled in, large black ink signature on line, 8 x 10" rider stapled on verso with initials **450.00**

Hepburn, Katherine, ADS, personal bank check, filled in and signed **450.00**

The Three Stooges, lobby photo from *The Outlaws is Coming,* 10 x 8" black and white glossy, 1965, Joe DiRita, Larry Fine, and Moe Howard, posed with guns, fine signatures on light areas **395.00**

Von Trapp, Maria, TLS, personalized card, 1974 .... **45.00**

Warhol, Andy, post card, 4 x 6", color, reproduction of work "Self Portrait," 1967, dark purplish blue bust image with purple and blond hair, pink background, large full black ink signature on lower white border **350.00**

SPORTS

Cobb, Ty, baseball, bank check, filled in and signed, 1956, cancellation holes do not touch signature **395.00**

Harlem Globetrotters, basketball, two programs, 1966, containing ten signatures including Meadowlark Lemon, Curly Neal, Bo Barnes, Bobby Jo Mason, Troy Collier, Mel Davis, Hubert Ausbie, and Hallie Bryant **45.00**

Lombardi, Vince, football, book, *Run To Daylight,* 1963, first edition, dj, inscribed "Good Luck

Baseball, Pittsburgh Pirates, team signatures, $85.00.

Vince Lombardi" in blue ink on title page 650.00

Mack, Connie, baseball, official National League baseball, 1932, with seven other signatures including Eddie Collins and Lefty Gomez 650.00

Philadelphia Phillies, baseball, 1988 yearbook with at least 20 signatures including manager Lee Elia, Kent Tekulve, Lance Parrish, Von Hayes, Mike Schmidt, and Juan Samuel 75.00

Ruth, Babe, baseball, album page, inscribed "To Paul sincerely Babe Ruth," bold ink inscription 950.00

Shoemaker, Bill, FDC honoring American horses 30.00

Tunney, Gene, boxing, TLS, 8 x 10" personal stationery, 1932, to Commander James J Lee regarding lectures for Veterans of Foreign Wars, large black ink signature 175.00

STATESMEN

Johnson, Cave, Postmaster General under Polk, began use of postage stamps, ALS, 8 x 10" plain stationery, 1939, signed as congressman, midshipman recommendation 150.00

Lincoln, Robert, son of Abraham Lincoln, Secretary of War under Arthur, ALS, 4 x 7" personal stationery, dated 24 May 1889, accepting luncheon date for his family 225.00

McLane, Lewis, Secretary of Treasury and Secretary of State, ALS, 8 x 10" plain stationery, May 2, 1832, to Hon. L Woodbury 65.00

Smith, Samuel, Revolutionary War General, Senator, ALS, 8 x 10", 1823, mentions current politics, signed "S. Smith" 95.00

Webster, Daniel, Secretary of State, ADS, 10 x 17", 4 pgs, all sides, legal, Dec 10, 1810, refers to mortgage on land in Bridgewater, NH, signed as lawyer, very large "D. Webster" signature beside paper seal 550.00

Windon, William, Secretary of Treasury under Arthur and Harrison, ALS, 5 x 7" plain stationery, 1875, regarding promotion being retroactive, signed "W. Windon" 40.00

AUTOMOBILES

History: Automobiles can be classified into several categories. In 1947 the Antique Automobile Club of America devised a system whereby any motor vehicle (car, bus, motorcycle, etc.) made prior to 1930 is an "antique" car. The Classic Car Club of America expanded the list focusing on luxury models from 1925 to 1948. The Milestone Car Society developed a list for cars in the 1948 to 1964 period.

Some states, such as Pennsylvania, have devised a dual registration system for older cars—antique and classic. Models from the 1960s and 1970s, especially convertibles and limited–production models, fall into the "classic" designation depending how they are used.

References: Quentin Craft, *Classic Old Car Value Guide, 23rd Edition,* published by author, 1989; James M. Flammang, *Standard Catalog of American Cars, 1976–1986, 2nd Edition,* Krause Publications, 1989; James M. Flammang, *Standard Catalog of Imported Cars, 1946–1990,* Krause Publications, 1992; John Gunnell, *Marques of America,* Krause Publications, 1994; John A. Gunnel (ed.), *100 Years of American Cars,* Krause Publications, 1993; John

A. Gunnel, *Standard Catalog of American Cars, 1946–1975, Third Edition,* Krause Publications, 1992; Beverly Kimes and Henry Austin Clark, Jr., *Standard Catalog of American Cars, 1805–1942, Second Edition,* Krause Publications, 1989; Jim Lenzke and Ken Buttolph, *1995 Standard Guide to Cars & Prices, Seventh Edition,* Krause Publications, 1994; Peter Sessler, *Car Collector's Handbook: A Comprehensive Guide to Collecting Rare and Historic Automobiles,* HP Books, 1992.

Periodicals: *Automobile Quarterly,* 15040 Kutztown Rd., PO Box 348, Kutztown, PA 19530; *Car Collector & Car Classics,* Suite 600, 1495 Hembree Rd., Roswell, GA 30076; *Hemmings Motor News,* PO Box 100, Bennington, VT 05201; *Old Cars Price Guide,* 700 E. State St., Iola, WI 54990; *Old Cars,* 700 E. State St., Iola, WI 54990.

Collectors' Clubs: Antique Automobile Club of America, 501 West Governor Rd., PO Box 417, Hershey, PA 17033; Classic Car Club of America, O'Hare Lake Office Plaza, 2300 E. Devon Ave., Suite 126, Des Plaines, IL 60018; Milestone Car Society, PO Box 24612, Indianapolis, IN 46224; Veteran Motor Car Club of America, PO Box 360788, Strongsville OH 44136.

Note: The prices below are based upon a car in running condition, with a high percentage of original parts, and somewhere between 60% and 80% restored. *Prices can vary by as much as 30% in either direction.*

Many older cars, especially if restored, now exceed $15,000. Their limited availability makes them difficult to price. Auctions, more than any other source, are the true determinant of value at this level. Especially helpful are the catalogs and sale bills of Kruse Auctioneers, Inc., Auburn, IN 46706.

Alpha–Romeo
1959, 750 Series, Giulietta Sprint Coupe, 4 cyl, 1290 cc, 93.7″ wheelbase **4,500.00**
1966, Giulia GTZ, 4 cyl, 1570 cc, 98.8″ wheelbase **25,500.00**
Aston–Martin
1952, DB2 Drophead Coupe, 6 cyl, 2580 cc, 99″ wheelbase **36,000.00**

Chevrolet, 1930, $7,000.00.

1961, Series 3, DB4 Saloon, 6 cyl, 3670 cc, 98″ wheelbase **12,750.00**
Auburn
1928, Model 8–88, Roadster, 8 cyl, 88 hp **17,500.00**
1936, Model 6–654, Coupe, custom dual ratio, 6 cyl **13,500.00**
Austin–Healey
1956, 100–6, 6 cyl, 102 hp, 92″ wheelbase **11,250.00**
1960, Sprite MK I, Roadster, 4 cyl, 43 hp, 80″ wheelbase ...**4,500.00**
Bentley
1952, Abbott, Fixed Head Coupe, 6 cyl, 4566 cc, 120″ wheelbase **10,250.00**
1958, S1 Type Continental, H. J. Mulliner, Flying Spur, 6 cyl, 4887 cc, 123″ wheelbase ..**18,000.00**
BMW
1959, 700, Coupe, 2 cyl, 697 cc, 83.5″ wheelbase **2,000.00**
1961, Isetta 300, Standard Sedan, one door, 1 cyl, 300 cc, 59.1″ wheelbase **3,000.00**
Buick
1916, Model D–54, Roadster, 6 cyl **9,250.00**
1924, Master Series 50, Sport Touring, 6 cyl **9,500.00**
1938, Century Series 60, Sedan, fastback, 8 cyl **5,250.00**
1942, Roadmaster Series 70, Convertible, 8 cyl **12,500.00**
1959, Invicta Series 46000, Hardtop, four door, V–8 .....**3,000.00**
Cadillac
1917, Model 55, Convertible, V–8 ....**13,500.00**

1927, Custom, Coupe, 132″ wheelbase **16,750.00**
1934, Series 452D, Convertible Sedan, Fleetwood body, modified "V" windshield, V–16, 154″ wheelbase **82,000.00**
1957, Eldorado Brougham, Hardtop, four door, V–8 . . . . **13,250.00**

Chevrolet
1926, Superior V, Touring, 4 cyl **10,000.00**
1941, Special DeLuxe, Station Wagon, 6 cyl **11,500.00**
1958, Del–Ray, Sedan, V–8 . . . **2,250.00**
1966, Corvette, Convertible, detachable hardtop **15,500.00**

Chrysler
1926, Series G–70, Sedan, leather trim, 6 cyl, 112.75″ wheelbase **4,250.00**
1935, Imperial Custom Airflow Series C–3, Sedan, four door, 8 cyl, 137″ wheelbase **11,500.00**
1956, New Yorker Series, Hardtop, St Regis, two door **7,250.00**
1964, Crown Imperial Ghia, Limousine, V–8 . . . . **6,750.00**

Crosley
1942, Station Wagon, 4 cyl, 80″ wheelbase **1,350.00**
1952, Hot Shot, Roadster, 4 cyl, 85″ wheelbase **2,500.00**

Datsun, 1960, Fairlady Roadster SPL 212, 4 cyl, 1189 cc, 87.4″ wheelbase **2,750.00**

DeSoto
1931, Model SA, Phaeton, 6 cyl **10,500.00**
1936, Airflow III S–2, Sedan, 6 cyl **4,250.00**
1948, S–11 DeLuxe, Sedan, two door, 6 cyl **2,500.00**
1956, Firedome, Convertible, V–8 . . . : **8,500.00**

Dodge
1919, Roadster, 4 cyl, 114″ wheelbase **4,500.00**
1928, Fast Four, DeLuxe Sedan, 4 cyl, 108″ wheelbase **2,500.00**
1946, DeLuxe Series D24, Coupe, 6 cyl, 119.5″ wheelbase **3,500.00**
1954, Series D50-1, Meadowbrook, Sedan, V–8, 119″ wheelbase **3,000.00**

1972, Dart, Sedan, four door . . **1,250.00**

Edsel
1958, Pacer Series, Sedan, V–8, 118″ wheelbase **3,250.00**
1960, Ranger Series, Convertible, V–8, 120″ wheelbase . . **10,000.00**

Essex, 1929, Challenger Series, Sedan, two door, 6 cyl **3,250.00**

Ford
1925, Model T, Coupe, 4 cyl . . . **2,750.00**
1942, Model 21A DeLuxe, Coupe, five passenger, V–8 . **4,250.00**
1951, F–1, Stake, light truck, ½ ton **3,000.00**
1965, Mustang, Convertible . . . **9,250.00**
1968, Thunderbird, Hardtop, 115″ wheelbase **4,500.00**

Franklin
1908, Model, G, Brougham, 4 cyl, 16 hp, 90″ wheelbase . . . **8,500.00**
1930, Model 147, Cabriolet, 6 cyl, 87 hp, 132″ wheelbase . **14,750.00**

Hudson
1922, Super Six, Cabriolet, 6 cyl **5,500.00**
1932, Major Series, Touring Sedan, 8 cyl, 132″ wheelbase . . **4,750.00**
1937, Custom Six, Series 73, Convertible Brougham, 6 cyl, 122″ wheelbase **12,750.00**

Hupmobile
1917, Model N, Year 'Round Coupe, two passenger, 4 cyl, 22 hp, 119″ wheelbase **5,250.00**
1936, Series 618–G, Sedan, six passenger, four door, 6 cyl, 101 hp, 118″ wheelbase **4,000.00**

Jaguar
1949, Mark V, Convertible Coupe, 6 cyl, 125 hp, 120″ wheelbase **27,250.00**
1961, XKE, Roadster, 6 cyl, 265 hp, 96″ wheelbase **31,250.00**
1967, 340, Sedan, four door, 6 cyl, 225 hp, 108″ wheelbase . **7,500.00**

Jeffery, 1915, Chesterfield Six, Roadster, two passenger, 48 hp, 122″ wheelbase **8,750.00**

Kaiser
1948, Custom, Sedan, 6 cyl . . . **3,750.00**
1953, Dragon, Sedan, four door, 6 cyl **4,500.00**

Lamborghini, 1966, 400 GT, 2 plus 2 Coupe, V–12, 3929 cc, 99.5″ wheelbase **38,500.00**

LaSalle
1933, Series 345C, Sedan, V–8,
130" wheelbase **13,250.00**
1940, Special Series 52 LaSalle,
Convertible Sedan, V–8, 123"
wheelbase **24,750.00**
Lincoln
1934, Series K, Convertible
Roadster, four passenger, V–
12, 136" wheelbase **43,250.00**
1953, Model BH, Cosmopolitan,
Hardtop, two door, V–8, 123"
wheelbase **5,500.00**
Mercedes–Benz
1958, 190SL, Roadster **22,000.00**
1961, 300, Hardtop, four door **20,500.00**
Mercury
1941, Series 19A, Coupe, six
passenger, V–8, 118" wheelbase **5,000.00**
1952, Mercury Custom, Hardtop,
two door, V–8, 118" wheelbase **4,250.00**
Metropolitan, 1956, Series 1500,
Nash, Convertible, 4 cyl, 52 hp,
85" wheelbase **2,000.00**
MG
1949, MG–TC, Roadster, 4 cyl,
94" wheelbase **10,000.00**
1958, MG–A, 1500 Coupe, 4 cyl,
72 hp, 94" wheelbase **7,750.00**
1968, MG Midget, Roadster, 4
cyl, 65 hp, 80" wheelbase ...**5,250.00**
Nash
1922, Series 680, Touring,
seven passenger, 6 cyl **4,750.00**
1951, Rambler, Custom Station
Wagon, two door, 6 cyl **2,000.00**
Oldsmobile
1938, L–38, Touring Sedan, 8
cyl **4,750.00**
1957, Series 88, Holiday Hardtop, two door, V–8, 122"
wheelbase **6,500.00**
Packard
1912, Model 12–48, Phaeton, 6
cyl, 36 hp **28,000.00**
1956, Clipper Executive, Hardtop **5,500.00**
Pierce–Arrow, 1915, Model 38–C,
Vestibule Brougham, 6 cyl, 38.4
hp, 134" wheelbase **22,750.00**
Plymouth
1950, Special DeLuxe, Station

Wagon, 6 cyl, 118.5" wheelbase **5,500.00**
1965, Valiant Signet, Barracuda,
V–8, 106" wheelbase **4,750.00**
Pontiac, 1951, Streamliner,
Coupe, 8 cyl **2,500.00**
Porsche
1951, Model 356, Cabriolet, 40
hp, 1100 cc **10,500.00**
1956, Model 356A, Carrera
Coupe, 1.5 liters, 100 hp ...**14,750.00**
Reo, 1918, The Fifth, Roadster,
three passenger, 4 cyl, 120"
wheelbase **5,250.00**
Rolls–Royce
1947, Freestone & Webb, Silver
Wraith, Sport Saloon, 6 cyl,
4257 cc, 127" wheelbase ..**13,250.00**
1955, Park Ward, Drophead
Coupe, 6 cyl, 4566 cc, 120"
wheelbase **22,500.00**
Studebaker
1930, President FH Model, Convertible Cabriolet **16,750.00**
1962, Lark Cruiser, Sedan, V–8,
113" wheelbase **2,000.00**
Terraplane, 1934, Major Line KU,
Coupe, two passenger, 6 cyl ..**4,250.00**
Triumph
1948, 1800, Roadster, 4 cyl, 63
hp, 100" wheelbase **7,500.00**
1958, TR–3, Hardtop Roadster,
4 cyl, 100 hp, 88" wheelbase **5,000.00**
1966, Spitfire MK II, Convertible,
4 cyl, 100 hp, 83" wheelbase **4,500.00**
Volkswagen
1946, Standard Sedan, two
door, 4 cyl, 25 hp, 94.5" wheelbase **5,500.00**
1955, Station Wagon Microbus,
4 cyl, 36 hp, 94.5" wheelbase **2,500.00**
Willys–Overland, 1928, Model 56
Willys–Knight, Touring, 6 cyl, 65
hp, 109.5" wheelbase **6,500.00**

AUTOMOBILIA

History: The amount of items related to
the automobile is endless. Collectors seem
to fit into three groups—those collecting
parts to restore a car, those collecting information about a company or certain model
for research purposes, and those trying to

use automobile items for decorative purposes. Most material changes hands at the hundreds of swap meets and auto shows around the country.

References: Gordon Gardiner and Alistair Morris, *The Price Guide and Identification of Automobilia,* Antique Collectors' Club; John A. Gunnell (ed.), *A Collector's Guide To Automobilia,* Krause Publications, 1994; Brian Jewell, *Motor Badges & Figureheads,* Midas Books, 1978; Jim and Nancy Schaut, *American Automobilia: An Illustrated History and Price Guide,* Wallace–Homestead, 1994; Dan Smith, *Accessory Mascots, The Automotive Accents of Yesteryear, 1910–1940,* published by author, 1989; Don Stewart, *Antique Classic Marque Car Keys, 2nd Edition,* Key Collectors International, 1993.

Periodicals: *Automobilia News,* PO Box 3528, Glendale, AZ 85311; *Hemmings Motor News,* PO Box 100, Bennington, VT 05201; *Mobilia,* PO Box 575, Middlebury, VT 05753.

Collectors' Clubs: Hubcap Collectors Club, PO Box 54, Buckley, MI 49620; Spark Plug Collectors of America, 14018 NE 85th St., Elk River, MN 55330.

Watch, Elgin, 8 day, 3″ d, $75.00.

Badge, 2½″ d, Plymouth, red firecracker illus, blue background, black lettering, 5″ l attached fabric ribbon, 1940 .... **25.00**
Bank, Sinclair Dino, plastic **12.00**
Book, *The Book Of The Locomobile,* 1917, 36 pgs, 9¼ x 12¼″, hard cov **100.00**

Bottle, wartime paper label
  Amalie **30.00**
  PennDrake **25.00**
  Quaker Oil **25.00**
  U–Neek, tall **35.00**
Calendar
  1913, Marble City Garage, automobiles and supplies, man and woman in open touring car, metal strips top and bottom, full pad, 15 x 20″ **95.00**
  1920, Chevrolet Motor Cars, couple in open touring car, visiting family on farm, missing most of pad, 14½ x 27½″ ... **200.00**
  1931, Pontiac, Chief Pontiac portrait above December pad, 19 x 27″ **300.00**
  1939
    Chevrolet, full color illus for each month **55.00**
    St John Motors, WA, Ford dealer, pinup, Western motif, Indian princess, full pad, 22 x 45″ **550.00**
Catalog
  Apperson Bros Auto Co, 1910, 8 pgs **30.00**
  Butler Brothers, New York, NY, 1918, 76 pgs, automotive supplies **20.00**
  Cadillac V–Eight, 1935, 12 pgs, 5½ x 7½″ **45.00**
  DeSoto, 1935, 8 pgs, Airflow and Airstream models **45.00**
  Dodge Bros, 1924, 146 pgs, 5½ x 8½″ **30.00**
  Ford Motor Co, 1916, 55 pgs, Model T **28.00**
  Globe Hoist Co, 1930, 38 pgs, automobile hoists, power cylinders, lube jacks **25.00**
  Sheldon Axle Co, 1912, 104 pgs, 6 x 9″ **30.00**
Folder, 8½ x 11″, Ford V–8, orange, black, and white, 1934 .. **25.00**
Gas Can, Texaco, red star, green "T" **25.00**
Guide Book, service station, Atlantic, 1932 .... **10.00**
Hood Ornament, chromed steel Chrysler New Yorker, 12½″ l, 4½″ h, circle with swept–back wings, 1952 .... **55.00**

Dodge, 14″ l, 3½″ h, stylized ram, charging pose, 1940s .. 75.00

Keychain/Flashlight, 3″ l, six wheeler truck form, Autolite Spark Plugs, 1950s 25.00

Kite, A–C Sparkplug, 1961 ..... 30.00

Magazine, 6½ x 9″, *Mechanics Illustrated,* "New Edsel," September 1957, 6 page article and photos 15.00

Model, 1949 Ford Tudor, orig box, unassembled, Palmer Plastics Inc 30.00

Mug, Gulf 4.00

Notepad, 2½ x 4½″, 1914 Ford, blue and white cov with "Ford The Universal Car" symbol 25.00

Paint Book, *Ford Painting Book,* 5¼ x 8¼″, Ford Motor Co, Canada, 12 pgs, 1926 .... 55.00

Pillow, Champion Spark Plugs ... 20.00

Pinback Button

Buick, 1¼″ d, cream, blue design, man and woman riding in car, c1910 .... 100.00

Chevrolet Assembly Workers Local 650 UAW, cream, dark green design, man holding pennant, 1950s 25.00

Ford V–8/America's Choice for '34, red, white, and blue 55.00

Luverne Automobile Co, black and white, white stripe, 1920s 45.00

Studebaker $665 And Up At Factory, dark blue and red litho, airplane and race car designs 30.00

Post Card, 3½ x 5½″, full color, "Studebaker Jr Wagons/Just What The Boys Want/Studebaker Bros Mfg Co/South Bend, Ind," 1910 postmark 15.00

Premium, Pep Magno–Power 1950 Ford Mystery Control Ring, white plastic ring, 3″ l blue hard plastic car, orig instruction sheet 100.00

Pump Sign

Shell, plastic, one red, one gold, 1960s, price for pair 115.00

Sinclair, 1960 .... 60.00

Quart Can

Essolube, 1930s 20.00

Havoline, Bull's Eye 15.00

Kendall, 2000 Mi, cars and planes illus 20.00

Mobiloil, aluminum, Pegasus .. 15.00

Pennzoil, DC–3 .... 40.00

Sinclair, Dino 25.00

Sign

Amoco, Pipeline Warning, porcelain 45.00

Atlantic, 9 x 13″, porcelain 60.00

Conoco, 27 x 39″, tin, 1930s .. 150.00

Goodrich Silvertown Flange, porcelain 60.00

Humble Oil, Pipeline Warning, porcelain 60.00

Shamrock Cloud Master, porcelain 125.00

Texaco Fire Chief, porcelain ... 65.00

Steering Wheel Knob, driver option clamp, silvered metal, dark tan Catalin knob, raised terrier image, 1930–40 .... 50.00

Tie Bar, 2¾″ l, Ford, brass luster, car grille, red and black logo, marked "Hickok," 1950s 25.00

Tie Tack, ½″ sq, "25 Years Ford," silver finish, three overlapping men, back marked "1/10–10K," 1960s 25.00

Token, Huskey Oil Western 6.00

Vacameter, 18″ w, 75″ h, United Service Motors, mercury, cast iron and glass, rubber wheels, minor paint chipping, wheel dry–rotted 160.00

Viewer, Chrysler Motors, car shape, 1939 World's Fair 35.00

Windshield Wipers, Anco, Laurel & Hardy sunray blocker 20.00

Yearbook, *Hot Rod Yearbook,* 8½ x 11″, 224 pgs, 1962 .... 25.00

BACCARAT GLASS

History: The Sainte–Anne glassworks at Baccarat in the Voges, France, was founded in 1764 and produced utilitarian soda glass. In 1816 Aime–Gabriel d'Artiques purchased the glassworks, and a Royal Warrant was issued in 1817 for the opening of Verrerie de Vonôche á Baccarat. The firm concentrated on lead crystal glass products. In 1824 a limited company was created.

From 1823 to 1857 Baccarat and Saint–Louis glassworks had a commercial agreement and used the same outlets. No merger occurred. Baccarat began the production of paperweights in 1846. In the late 19th century the firm achieved an international reputation for cut glass table services, chandeliers, display vases and centerpieces, and sculptures. Products eventually included all forms of glassware. The firm still is active today.

Reference: Jean–Louis Curtis, *Baccarat*, Harry N. Abrams, 1992.

Additional Listing: Paperweights.

Atomizer, amberina, 6″ h, $50.00.

Box, cov, 3″ h, 3¼″ w, sq, Rose
 Teinte, Sunburst pattern **115.00**
Candlesticks, pr, 7⅛″ h, 4″ d, Rose
 Teinte, Swirl pattern, sgd **310.00**
Candelabra, pr, 18″ h, knopped
 standard continuing to spreading
 foot, hung with beads and
 prisms **875.00**
Chandelier, 40″ h, 20″ d, gilded
 bronze gathering basket form,
 filled with glass apples, pears,
 grapes **6,850.00**
Cologne Bottle, 7″ h, 2⅝″ d, Rose
 Teinte, Swirl pattern, matching
 orig stopper **80.00**

Compote, 5½″ d, 1¾″ h, amberina,
 sgd **85.00**
Decanter
 10″ h, pr, ovoid body with
  notched cutting, faceted stopper **175.00**
 11½″ h, paneled body, mushroom stopper **185.00**
Epergne, 10¾″ h, cranberry, four
 red overlay cut to colorless crystal cones, inserted within gilt
 metal holders **550.00**
Hock Glass, set of twelve, 7½″ h,
 ruby flashed circular bowl cut
 with six ovoid facets, tapering
 hexagonal stem and foot, acid
 stamped factory mark **600.00**
Lantern, hall, 19½″ h, gilt bronze
 mounted, faceted pear form
 shade mounted with gilt bronze
 floral garlands, flame form finial,
 domed pendant molded with
 overlapping acanthus leaves terminating in an acorn **975.00**
Paperweight, 3″ w, John F Ken-
 nedy, sulphide overlay, cobalt
 blue over white **125.00**
Plate, 5½″ d, amberina, sgd **40.00**
Sculpture
 Lion, 11 x 5″, clear **495.00**
 Raven, 7″ h **115.00**
Stemware Service
 62 pcs, ten water goblets, eleven
  champagnes, eleven red
  wines, ten white wines, eight
  finger bowls, and twelve dessert plates, petal fluted pattern, faceted stems, hexagonal feet **3,225.00**
 65 pcs, fifteen tulip wines, twelve
  sherry glasses, ten white
  wines, eleven wide mouthed
  red wines, seven small
  mouthed red wines, five oversized wide mouthed red wines,
  three oversized small mouthed
  red wines, and two champagne flutes, ovoid goblets
  raised on cylindrical stem,
  spreading circular foot, acid
  stamped factory mark, 8⅜″ h
  tulips, 9⅜″ h largest red wine **990.00**
Tray, 9½ x 3½″, Absinthe green,
 sgd **35.00**

Tumbler, Rose Teinte, sgd **35.00**
Vase, pr, 16" h, gilt bronze mounted, circular domed standard headed by leaf tips supporting paneled and scalloped vase, stamped "Baccarat," Paris **4,025.00**
Wine Goblet, set of eight, 7½" h, tapering bowl with gilt rim, faceted stem, spreading foot **300.00**

BANKS, MECHANICAL

History: Banks which display some form of action while utilizing a coin are considered mechanical banks. Although mechanical banks are known which date back to ancient Greece and Rome, the majority of collectors center their interests in those made between 1867 and 1928 in Germany, England, and the United States. Recently there has been an upsurge of interest in later types, some of which date into the 1970s.

Initial research suggested that approximately 250 to 300 different or variant designs of banks were made in the early period. Today that number has been revised to 2,000–3,000 types and varieties. The field remains ripe for discovery and research.

Over 80% of all cast iron mechanical banks produced between 1869 and 1928 were made by J.E. Stevens Co., Cromwell, Connecticut. Tin banks tend to be German in origin.

While rarity is a factor in value, appeal of design, action, quality of manufacture, country of origin, and history of collector interest also are important. Radical price fluctuations may occur with an imbalance of these factors. Rare banks may sell for a few hundred dollars while one of more common design with greater appeal will sell in the thousands.

The prices on our list represent fairly what a bank sells for in the specialized collectors' market. Some banks are hard to find and establishing a price outside auction is difficult.

The prices listed are for original old mechanical banks with minor repairs, in sound operating condition, and with a majority of the original paint intact.

References: *Collectors Encyclopedia of Toys and Banks,* L–W Book Sales, 1986, 1993 value update; Al Davidson, *Penny Lane, A History Of Antique Mechanical Toy Banks,* Long's Americana, 1987; Don Duer, *A Penny Saved: Still and Mechanical Banks,* Schiffer Publishing, 1993; Bill Norman, *The Bank Book: The Encyclopedia of Mechanical Bank Collecting,* Collectors' Showcase, 1984.

Periodical: *Heuser's Quarterly Price Guide to Official Collectible Banks,* Heuser Enterprises, 508 Clapson Road, PO Box 300, West Winfield, NY 13491.

Collectors' Club: Mechanical Bank Collectors of America, PO Box 128, Allegan, MI 49010.

Reproduction Alert: Reproductions, fakes, and forgeries exist for many banks. Forgeries of some mechanical banks were made as early as 1937, so age alone is not a guarantee of authenticity. In our listing two asterisks indicate banks for which serious forgeries exist and one asterisk indicates banks for which casual reproductions have been made.

Advisor: James S. Maxwell, Jr.

Acrobats, blue base, minor wear to polychrome, 7¼" l, N1010–A **4,650.00**
Always Did 'Spise A Mule, damage, repair, old repaint, replaced bottom plate, 10" l, N2940–A . . **165.00**
Artillery Bank, eight sided block house, cannon shoots **625.00**

Sweet Thrift Bank, tin, red ground, decal, 6" h, $185.00.

Aunt Dinah and the Good Fairy .20,000.00
Automatic Coin Savings, iron 1,500.00
Baby Elephant, lead and wood . .5,750.00
Bad Accident, 10" l, N1150–A . . . 880.00
Bamboula, iron 750.00
Bank Teller, iron, tall man behind
  three sided lattice work grill . . .8,000.00
**Bear and Tree Stump, iron 675.00
**Bill E. Grin, iron 650.00
**Bird on Roof, iron 875.00
Blacksmith, lead 2,875.00
Bowling Alley, wood and iron, ball
  knocks down wooden pins and
  rings bell 16,000.00
**Boy and Bull Dog, brass 850.00
**Boy Robbing Bird's Nest, iron . . .1,350.00
Boy Scout with Tray, tin 950.00
**Bucking Mule, iron 1,050.00
**Bull and Bear, brass 5,000.00
**Bulldog Standing, coin on tongue 450.00
**Bull with Movable Horns, iron . . . 450.00
Bureau, wood, Serrill patent 975.00
**Butting Goat, tree stump 650.00
*Cabin, iron 275.00
**Called Out, iron, painted 6,000.00
Calumet with Calumet Kid, card-
  board and tin can 150.00
Calumet with Sailor, cardboard
  and tin can 350.00
Calumet with Soldier, cardboard
  and tin can 650.00
**Camera, iron 2,200.00
**Cat & Mouse, iron, cat stands on
  hands 980.00
Cat, pot metal, spring jaw 325.00
**Chief Big Moon, iron 845.00
Chinaman with Queue, tin 975.00
Circus, iron 4,450.00
Clever Dick, tin 850.00
Clown Bust with Acorn Shaped
  Hat, iron 1,650.00
Clown on Lattice Base, tin clown
  with tray on iron base, does
  flip 5,800.00
Columbian Magic Savings, iron . . 460.00
*Creedmore, worn polychrome,
  iron, 10" l 55.00
Cupola, iron, man in circular build-
  ing 1,350.00
*Darktown Battery, iron 1,150.00
Darky Fisherman, lead 11,500.00
Dinah, iron 425.00
Ding Dong Bell, tin, windup 6,375.00
Dog on Turntable, iron 400.00

Dog Standing, tin, nods head . . . 475.00
**Eagle and Eaglets, wear to poly-
  chrome, trap and glass eyes
  missing, 8¼" l, N2230–B 385.00
**Elephant, iron, Hannibal 540.00
**Elephant, iron, tusks on wheels .1,250.00
*Elephant and Three Clowns 850.00
**Elephant with Howdah, iron, pull
  tail 300.00
Feed the Kitty, pot metal 1,400.00
**Ferris Wheel, iron and tin, no
  markings (smaller than Bowen's
  Pat. model) 1,500.00
Five Cent Adding Machine, iron . 750.00
**Football, iron, boy and shed 1,900.00
Fortune Wheel, tin 875.00
Freedman, wood, pewter, cloth,
  etc., man sitting at desk 20,000.00
Frogs on Rock, iron 270.00
**Gem, iron 350.00
Giant in Tower, iron 5,500.00
**Girl Skipping Rope, iron 6,000.00
**Glutton, iron, lifts turkey 725.00
**Goat, Frog, and Old Man, iron . .2,800.00
Grenadier, iron 720.00
Guessing, lead and iron, woman's
  figure 7,800.00
Hall's Excelsior, cast iron, cashier
  missing arms, pull lever missing,
  good color polychrome paint, mi-
  nor wear, 5¼" h 275.00
Hall's Lilliput, Type I 450.00
Hall's Lilliput, Type III 350.00
Hall's Yankee Notion, iron 2,300.00
Hen and Chick, iron 1,125.00
**Hindu, iron 1,450.00
**Hold the Fort, iron, seven holes 1,500.00
Home, tin 240.00
**Horse Race, iron with tin horses,
  straight base 1,450.00
Horse Race Savings Bank, tin,
  Pat. Oct. 5, 1897 . . . . .3,500.00
Huntley and Palmers Biscuit Tin,
  pull out drawer 1,280.00
**I Always Did 'Spise A Mule, iron,
  jockey 650.00
*Indian and Bear, iron, brown bear 750.00
Indian Chief, aluminum, bust,
  black face with headdress 4,500.00
Japanese Ball Tosser, tin, windup 5,000.00
John Bull's Money Box, iron 8,000.00
**Jolly Nigger
  Aluminum
    Bar and screw side 165.00

With fez 400.00
Iron
   Butterfly tie 190.00
   Fixed eyes, minor wear to
   polychrome, one screw
   missing, 6¾" h 440.00
*Jonah and Whale, iron, rect base 950.00
**Jumbo, iron, elephant on wheels 975.00
Key, iron, Golden Gate Exposition 450.00
Leap–Frog, orig paint 440.00
Lehmann London Tower, tin 1,700.00
Lighthouse, pot metal 600.00
Lion, tin 1,150.00
**Lion and Two Monkeys, iron 575.00
Little Jack Horner, tin, windup . . . 5,000.00
Little Joe, iron 205.00
Magician Bank, orig paint 110.00
**Magic Man, iron 750.00
Magic Safe, tin 675.00
**Mama Katzenjammer, iron, dark
   blue dress painted to neck,
   1905–08 . . . . 2,750.00
Mammy and Child, red dress, mi-
   nor wear to polychrome, 7⅝" h,
   N3790–A 10,725.00
Memorial Liberty Bell, iron 750.00
**Merry–Go–Round, iron, semi–me-
   chanical version 400.00
Mickey Mouse with Accordion, tin 2,700.00
**Milking Cow, broken replaced
   fence, tail replaced, 9⅞" l,
   N3870 . . . . 2,310.00
Model Railroad Drink Dispenser,
   tin 2,200.00
Model Railroad Ticket Dispenser,
   tin 2,200.00
**Monkey, iron, drop coin in stom-
   ach 1,250.00
Monkey Bank, dark green dress,
   wear to polychrome, bottom
   plate and chain missing, 7⅝" h,
   N3960–B 330.00
Monkey Face 1,125.00
Moody and Sanky, iron and paper 700.00
Moonface, tin 1,150.00
Motor, iron, trolley car 3,750.00
Musical Savings, wood and tin,
   Regina music box 4,500.00
National, iron 1,000.00
New, iron, lever on side 400.00
North Pole, iron 5,500.00
Novelty, iron, Johnson's Pat 400.00
Old Woman in Shoe, iron 100,000.00
Organ, worn polychrome, replaced

crank handle, mismatched trap,
   7½"h 110.00
Organ Grinder and Bear, windup,
   bell, very minor wear to poly-
   chrome, trap missing, 5¼" h,
   N4350–A 4,950.00
Paddy and Pig, black coat, minor
   wear to polychrome, 8" h, N4400 1,600.00
Panorama, iron 1,800.00
Patronize the Blind Man, iron . . . 1,600.00
**Pelican with Arab, iron 900.00
**Pelican with Man Thumbing Nose,
   iron 1,125.00
**Perfection Registering, iron, girl at
   blackboard 2,900.00
**Piano, iron, modern conversion to
   musical 1,600.00
Picture Gallery Bank 1,875.00
Popeye Knockout, tin 375.00
Preacher in Pulpit, iron 15,000.00
Presto, iron, small building with
   drawer 380.00
Professor Pug Frog, iron 2,100.00
Punch and Judy, worn poly-
   chrome, replaced screw, 7⅜" h 440.00
Puss and Boots, iron 20,000.00
Queen Victoria, brass, bust 5,000.00
Rabbit, iron, small 475.00
Registering Dime Savings 475.00
Robot, aluminum 1,800.00
**Rooster, iron 315.00
Sailor Face, tin 850.00
Sambo, iron 625.00
**Santa Claus, iron 780.00
Savo, iron, rect with soldiers 275.00
Seek Him Frisk, iron, dog chases
   cat up tree 18,000.00
Sentry, tin, raises bugle 1,200.00
Shoot That Hat, iron 12,000.00
**Smyth X–Ray, iron 3,750.00
**Snap It, iron 450.00
Springing Cat, lead 4,250.00
Squirrel, lead 550.00
Starkies Aeroplane 8,500.00
Stollwerk, tin, vending 480.00
*Stump Speaker 875.00
**Tabby, iron 500.00
Tammany Bank, traces of paint,
   damage to bottom plate, wired
   repair, missing trap, 5¾" h,
   N5420 . . . . 60.00
Tank and Cannon, iron 585.00
Target Building, iron 750.00
*Teddy and the Bear 110.00

Thrifty Animal, tin 420.00
Tid–Bits Automatic Money Box, tin 1,850.00
Toad on Stump, iron 440.00
Tommy, iron 2,300.00
*Trick Dog, minor wear to poly-
  chrome, battered replaced hoop,
  replaced trap, 8¾" l 140.00
**Trick Donkey, iron 625.00
Trick Savings, wood, end drawer 285.00
**Tricky Pig, iron, risque 1,800.00
**Turtle, iron 4,000.00
Twentieth Century Savings Bank 950.00
Uncle Sam, bright polychrome,
  worn, touchup repair, 11¼"h . . . 495.00
**Uncle Tom, iron, no star 540.00
Uncle Tom, iron, no lapels 510.00
Village School Master, tin, windup 3,750.00
Watch, tin, dime disappears, sev-
  eral varieties 675.00
Watch Dog Savings, wood 950.00
*William Tell, iron, orig paint 575.00
Winner Savings, tin and glass,
  horse race 4,000.00
Wishbone, iron 12,500.00
Woodchopper, iron 810.00
Woodpecker, tin, 1940s 425.00

BANKS, STILL

History: Banks with no mechanical action are known as still banks. The first still
banks were made of wood, pottery, or from
gourds. Redware and stoneware banks,
made by America's early potters, are prized
possessions of today's collectors.

Still banks reached a "golden age" with
the arrival of the cast iron bank. Leading
manufacturing companies include Arcade
Mfg. Co., J. Chein & Co., Hubley, J. & E.
Stevens and A. C. Williams. The banks often were ornately painted to enhance their
appeal. During the cast iron era, banks and
other businesses used the still bank as a
form of advertising for attracting customers.

The tin lithograph bank, again frequently
with advertising, did not reach its zenith until
the 1930 to 1955 period. The tin bank was
an important premium, whether it be a
Pabst Blue Ribbon beer can bank or a Gerber's Orange Juice bank. Most tin advertising banks resembled the packaging shape
of the product.

Almost every substance has been used
to make a still bank—diecast white metal,
aluminum, brass, plastic, glass, etc. Many
of the early glass candy containers also
converted to a bank when the candy was
eaten. Thousands of varieties of still banks
were made, and hundreds of new varieties
appear on the market each year.

References: Savi Arbola and Marco
Onesti, *Piggy Banks,* Chronicle Books,
1992; *Collector's Encyclopedia of Toys and
Banks,* L–W Book Sales, 1986, 1993 value
update; Don Duer, *A Penny Saved: Still and
Mechanical Banks,* Schiffer Publishing,
1993; Earnest Ida and Jane Pitman, *Dictionary of Still Banks,* Long's Americana,
1980; Andy and Susan Moore, *Penny Bank
Book, Collecting Still Banks,* Schiffer Publishing, 1984, 1994 value update; Hubert B.
Whiting, *Old Iron Still Banks,* Forward's
Color Productions, 1968, out–of–print.

Periodical: *Heuser's Quarterly Price
Guide to Official Collectible Banks,* Heuser
Enterprises, 508 Clapson Rd., PO Box 300,
West Winfield, NY 13491.

Collectors' Club: Still Bank Collectors
Club of America, 1456 Carson Court,
Homewood, IL 60430.

Museum: Margaret Woodbury Strong
Museum, Rochester, NY.

CAST IRON

Animal
  Bear, worn black, 4" l 99.00
  Boston Bull Terrier, worn black
    and white, 4⅜" h 110.00
  Buffalo, brown repaint, 4⅜" l . .   72.00
  Camel, worn silver and red, 4¾"
    h 82.50
  Cat
    On tub, traces of gold, screw
      replaced, 4¼" h 27.50
    Sitting, worn black, 4¼" h . . .   33.00
  Duck, round, green, red, black,
    and yellow, slight wear, 4" h . 225.00
  Elephant
    Howdah, worn gold over black,
      3¼" l 22.00
    On tub, silver, gold, and red,
      wear, 5¼" h 99.00
    Swivel trunk, black and gold,
      wear and rust, 3⅝" l 60.00

Fido, minor wear to polychrome,
5" h **66.00**
Goose, gold, minor touchup, re-
placed screw **105.00**
Horse
On tub, black, tan, and silver,
wear, replaced screw, 5½" h **125.00**
On wheels, worn gold on
horse, gold over silver
wheels, 5" h **150.00**
Rearing, on base, gold repaint,
6¾" h **60.00**
Lion
On tub, worn blue, gold, and
red, small casting hole near
screw, 5½" h **121.00**
Standing, traces of gold, 3⅝" l **27.50**
Owl, "Be Wise Save Money,"
sand blasted, 5" h **60.00**
Pig, holding sign "The Wise Pig,"
white and pink, some wear,
6⅝" h **85.00**
Polar Bear, worn pale green re-
paint, 5¼" h **66.00**
Pup, worn black and red, light
rust, 3⅞" h **44.00**
Rabbit, gold and red, minor
wear, replaced screw, 6½" h . **188.00**
Retriever, traces of gold, 5¼" l . **50.00**
Rooster, gold with red, 4⅞" h .. **72.00**
Saint Bernard, pack, traces of
paint, light rust, 5½" l **60.00**
Stag, gold repaint, 9¼" h **72.00**
Teddy Bear, worn gold, 3⅞" h . **105.00**
Other
Aunt Jemima, worn polychrome,
6" h **150.00**
Battleship
Maine, brown japanning and
gold, 4¾" h **288.00**
Oregon, brown japanning and
gold, minor wear, 5" l **275.00**
Billiken, gold and red, some
wear, 4⅛" h **33.00**
Black Boy, two faced, worn gold
and black, 3" h **55.00**
Boy Scout, worn gold, 5⅞" h .. **38.50**
Buster Brown and Tige, dull gold
repaint, 5¼" h **77.00**
Graf Zeppelin, silver, minor
wear, 6¾" l **140.00**
I Hear A Call, worn black and
silver, int. and tongue missing,
5½" h **38.50**

Indian, worn gold, light rust, 6" h **35.00**
Liberty Bell, worn bronze finish,
3⅜" h **27.50**
Main Street, worn gold, one set
of wheels replaced, one win-
dow broken, 6⅝" l **128.00**
Safe
Arabian, worn gold, key, 4½" h **72.00**
Japanese, old polished sur-
face, key, 5⅜" h **82.00**
Royal Safe Deposit, black and
gold, black repaint, orig de-
coupage on one side, brass
dial, 6" h **72.00**
Safe Deposit, black, brass
dial, lock removed, 5¼" h .. **27.50**
Security Safe Deposit, worn
black and gold, brass dial,
hinge pin replaced, 4½" h . **72.00**
Sport, welded door, black and
gold, worn, 3" h **38.50**
Share Cropper, worn poly-
chrome, 5½" h **88.00**
Street Car, worn red and gold,
replaced twist pin, light rust,
4½" l **170.00**
Tank, worn gold, small casting
hole in one side, 5¾" l **94.00**
US Mail, green, 3½" h **50.00**
World Time, paper liner missing,
cracked bottom plate, 4⅛" h . **27.50**

CHALK

Dove, worn green, red, and yellow
ochre paint, 11" h **225.00**
Pig, old white repaint, pink ears,
7⅛" l **90.00**

GLASS

Bank of Independence Hall, clear,
tin base, chips, 7¼" h **55.00**
Dog, sitting on drum, 4⅛" h **75.00**
Liberty Bell, amber, tin base with
advertising **25.00**
Log Cabin, milk glass, paper label,
worn gold, glued lid, 3⅞" h **20.00**
Radio, clear, emb details **25.00**

PAPIER MACHE

Charlie McCarthy, "Feed Me...,"
worn polychrome **40.00**

James Bank, taffy adv on tin top,
7″ h **12.00**
Kewpie, worn polychrome **48.00**

POTTERY

Bird's Nest, four blue eggs, 3½″ d **30.00**
Cat, head, white clay, green glaze,
3″ h **95.00**
Chest of Drawers, brown glaze,
3¼″ h **110.00**
Frog
Full bodied, rect base, olive
brown glaze, minor chips,
3¾″ l **55.00**
Head, green glaze, minor chips,
3¼″ h **50.00**
Hen on nest, polychrome, 4¼″ h . **40.00**
Goat, brown glaze, 5″ l **98.00**
Pig
3⅝″ l, blue and brown sponging,
cream colored ground, small
chips, incomplete back foot .. **83.00**
4″ l, Rockingham **27.50**
6⅜″ l, marbleized olive brown,
tan, and green glaze **55.00**
6″ l, blue and brown sponging,
cream colored ground, small
flakes and chip at coin slot .. **302.00**

BARBER BOTTLES

History: Barber bottles, colorful glass
bottles found on shelves and counters in
barber shops, held the liquids barbers used
daily. A specific liquid was kept in a specific
bottle which the barber knew by color, design, or lettering.

The bulk liquids were kept in utilitarian
containers under the counter or in a storage
room.

Barber bottles are found in many types
of glass: art glass with varied decoration,
pattern glass, and commercially prepared
and labeled bottles.

References: Ronald S. Barlow, *The Vanishing American Barber Shop,* Windmill
Publishing, 1992; Richard Holiner, *Collecting Barber Bottles,* Collector Books, 1986;
Ralph & Terry Kovel, *The Kovels' Bottle
Price List, Ninth Edition,* Crown Publishers,
1992; Philip L. Krumholz, *Value Guide For*

Barberiana & Shaving Collectibles, Ad Libs
Publishing Co, 1988.
Note: Prices are for bottles without orig-
inal stoppers unless otherwise noted.

Amethyst
8⅛″ h, white enamel dec of bust
of woman, bulbous body, long
neck, tooled mouth, pontil
scar, inscribed "Vegederma" . **385.00**
8⅛″ h, white enamel floral sprig
dec, bulbous ribbed body, long
neck, tooled mouth, pontil scar **90.00**
Bristol Glass, pr, hp lettering, "Bay
Rum" and "Toilet Water" **40.00**
Cobalt Blue, 7½″ h, white and orange enameled floral dec, modified bell form, tooled mouth,
pontil scar, American **110.00**
Cranberry
7⅜″ h, opalized daisy and fern
design, segmented melon
form body, long neck, tooled
mouth, pontil scar **100.00**
7¾″ h, pr, cranberry, irid, square,
emb abstract design, ground
mouth, period closure, smooth
base **220.00**
Mary Gregory Type, 7¾″ h, amethyst, white enamel dec of boy
pointing at flying birds, bulbous
body, long neck, tooled mouth,
pontil scar **230.00**
Opalized Cranberry
6⅞″ h, coin spot design, seg-

**Blue, opalescent hobnails, 7¾″ h,
$125.00.**

mented melon form, tooled
mouth, smooth base 100.00
12" h, pr, white spatter design,
cylindrical, modified pyramid
form, tooled mouth, smooth
base, ground pontil scar 225.00
Teal Blue, 8⅜" h, coin spot design,
segmented body with long neck,
tooled mouth, smooth base ... 75.00

BAROMETERS

History: A barometer is an instrument
which measures atmospheric pressure
which, in turn, aids weather forecasting.
Low pressure indicates the coming of rain,
snow, or storm; high pressure signifies fair
weather.

Most barometers use an evacuated and
graduated glass tube which contains a column of mercury and are classified by the
shape of the case. An aneroid barometer
has no liquid and works by a needle connected to the top of a metal box in which a
partial vacuum is maintained. The movement of the top moves the needle.

Gilt Bronze and Marble, desk type,
oval barometer and clock
housed in separate molded con-

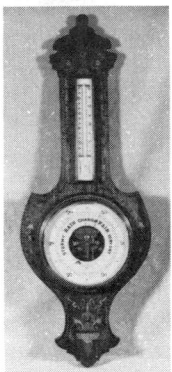

**Short, Mason, London, mahog-
any, Fahrenheit and Centigrade,
inlaid dec, 33½" l, 12½" w,
$1,250.00**

forming cylinders joined by ring
handle, lozenge form rouge
royal ft, 6½" h 700.00
Giltwood
Louis XVI, pyriform frame with
flower heads and foliage surmounted by basket, rect thermometer above circular paper
dial, dial is 19th C replacement, 46" h 2,075.00
Louis XVI Style, ornately carved
swags and foliage
Calsen, Paris, marked on
painted dial, restoration,
37½" h 2,185.00
Charpentier, Paris, central
medallion with classical figures below dial, marked on
painted dial, damage, repair,
19th C, 36½" h 1,265.00
Mahogany
English
E Bush & Co, Bradford, inlaid,
33½" h 490.00
G Introvini, 88 Georges Rd.,
Manchester, banjo type,
signed, 19th C, 37¾" h 345.00
J Watkins, Charing Cross,
stick type, broken pediment
with brass urn finial, 19th C,
41" h 1,500.00
George III
P Caminada, stick type, rect
brass plate containing thermometer and engraved ba-
rometer dial, slender waist
defined by molding and ribbon parquetry border, boss
form reservoir cov, late 18th
C, 39" h 1,100.00
Unknown Maker, split baluster
form, circular hygrometer,
arched thermometer plate,
and convex mirrored plate
above circular barometer
dial, 38" h 460.00
Neoclassical, Dutch, signed
"Jan Bekking, Rotterdam," architectural pediment, flanking
columns, early 19th C, 41" h .1,100.00
Mahogany and Ormolu, Napoleon
III, enameled face, third quarter
19th C, 17½" h 250.00
Mahogany Veneer, Hepplewhite, D

Gugeri, Boston, banjo type, inlaid sunbursts and shells, engraved silver dials and brass trim, small piece molding missing from cornice, 38¾" h **900.00**

Tin, Alvan Z Lovejoy, Boston, desk type, figural, Weather House, chalkware man and woman figures, painted dec **175.00**

BASKETS

History: Baskets were invented when man first required containers to gather, store, and transport goods. Today's collector, influenced by the country look, focuses on baskets made of splint, rye straw, or willow. Emphasis is placed on handmade examples. Nails or staples, wide splints which are thin and evenly cut, or a wire bail handle denote factory construction which can date back to the mid–19th century. Painted or woven decorated baskets rarely are handmade, unless they are American Indian in origin.

Baskets are collected by (a) type—berry, egg, or field, (b) region—Nantucket or Shaker, and (c) composition—splint, rye, or willow. Stick to examples in very good condition; damaged baskets are a poor investment even at a low price.

References: Frances Johnson, *Wallace–Homestead Price Guide To Baskets, Second Edition,* Wallace–Homestead Book Company, 1989; Don and Carol Raycraft, *Collector's Guide to Country Baskets,* Collector Books, 1985, 1994 value update; Martha Wetherbee and Nathan Taylor, *Legend of the Bushwhacker Basket,* published by author, 1986; Christoph Will, *International Basketry For Weavers and Collectors,* Schiffer Publishing, 1985.

Museums: Old Salem, Inc., Winston–Salem, NC; The Heard Museum, Phoenix, AZ.

Reproduction Alert: Modern reproductions abound, made by diverse groups ranging from craft revivalists to foreign manufacturers.

7" d, 4" h plus well shaped bentwood handle, woven splint, round, old patina **140.00**

7½" d, 10½" h, Nantucket, minor splint breaks, late 19th C **600.00**

8 x 7½", 6" h, gathering, buttocks, woven splint, bentwood handle **50.00**

9½" d, 6½" h, Nantucket, pocket type, carved whale mounted to plaque on cov, late 20th C **330.00**

9½ x 7½", 4½" h, penwork, black ground, red dec, panels of Greek figures within Neoclassical foliage borders, Greek Key bail handle, Regency period, early 19th C **825.00**

10" d, 12" h, Nantucket, early 20th C **450.00**

10¼" l, 16" h, picnic, woven natural and colored splint, bentwood handle, double hinged cov **195.00**

10½" d, 18" h, weaver's, woven splint, orange and blue watercolor design, rounded corners, divided int. **200.00**

11" d, 7" h plus bentwood handle, buttocks, woven splint, old worn patina **160.00**

11 x 10", 7" h plus bentwood handle, gathering, finely woven splint **220.00**

11½" d, 5½" h plus bentwood handle, woven splint, round, weathered two tone weaving, faded red stripe **175.00**

11½ x 12", 6¼" h plus bentwood handle, woven splint, buttocks . **105.00**

11½ x 12", 7½" h plus bentwood handle, woven splint, sq, gray weathered finish **105.00**

12 x 18½", 7" h, woven splint, swivel handles, old finish, old pencil inscription "Leesville, Ohio" on base **110.00**

13" d, Nantucket, "C W Chapin" branded on swing handle and twice on base, late 19th C **1,500.00**

13 x 14", 7½" h plus handle, woven splint, buttocks, red stripe, bentwood handle, marked "Rev Clerke," minor damage **275.00**

13½" l, splint, traces of orig cream paint, breaks, American, 19th C **330.00**

14" d, gathering, splint, painted red and green dec, imperfections, American, 19th C **725.00**

14 x 16", 9" h plus bentwood han-

Field, oak splint, damaged, 23 x
15", $90.00.

dle, woven splint, buttocks, Eye
of God design at handles, old
worn patina **225.00**
15" d, rye straw, coil work, open
handles, PA, early 20th C **80.00**
15 x 22", 10½" h plus bentwood
handles, woven splint, buttocks,
double lids, weathered finish .. **55.00**
18" h, storage, splint, breaks, 19th
C **110.00**
21" l, 12" h, egg, oval, woven
splint, radiating ribs, bentwood
handle **85.00**
21½" d, 8" h, cheese, woven splint,
gray scrubbed finish **275.00**
22" h, oval, oak splint, plaited
weaving pattern, carved hickory
handle **225.00**

BATTERSEA ENAMELS

History: Battersea enamel is a generic
term for English enamel–on–copper objects
of the 18th century.

In 1753 Stephen Theodore Janssen established a factory to produce "Trinkets and
Curiosities Enamelled on Copper" at York
House, Battersea, London. Here the new
invention of transfer printing developed a
high degree of excellence, and the resulting
trifles delighted fashionable Georgian society.

Recent research has shown that enamels
actually were being produced in London
and the Midlands several years before York
House was established. However, most
enamel trinkets still are referred to as "Battersea Enamels," even though they were
probably made in other workshops in London, Birmingham, Bilston, Wednesbury, or
Liverpool.

All manner of charming items were made,
including snuff and patch boxes bearing
mottos and memory gems. (By adding a
mirror inside the lid, a snuff box became a
patch box). Many figural whimsies, called
"toys," were created to amuse a gay and
fashionable world. Many other elaborate articles, e.g., candlesticks, salts, tea caddies,
and bonbonnieres, were made for the tables of the newly rich middle classes.

Reference: Susan Benjamin, *English
Enamel Boxes*, Merrimack Publishers Circle, 1978.

Advisors: Barbara and Melvin Alpren.

Box, 1½ x 1 x¾", "Esteem the
Giver," deep pink, scene on cov
outlined with tiny white dots, mirror in cov **275.00**
Candlesticks, pr, 9" h, baluster
shafts, late 18th/early 19th C .. **1,485.00**
Cloak Hooks, pr, 2" l, oval, rose
festooned anchors, white
ground, South Staffordshire,
c1775 .... **500.00**
Counter Box, 1½" d, ivory, fanned
playing cards top, center inscribed "Lady Luck," tortoiseshell lined, c1770 .... **950.00**
Mirror Knob, pr, 1¾" d, small brass
knob on stem with painted porcelain face, young lady leaning
on marble tombstone, painted
within wreath "Sacred to Friend-
ship," early 19th C **275.00**
Patch Box
Oval, love birds, blue field, 19th
C **325.00**
Round, 2" d, recumbent yellow
pug on grassy base, hinged
cov with vignette of similar
dog, chips and scratches ...**1,275.00**
Plaque, pr, 15" l, 12" w, gilt frames,
18th C **1,875.00**
Salt, pr **135.00**
Scent Bottle Holder, ½ x 1¼ x 2¼",
allover pink floral with trellis dec,
leafy green, Bilston, c1775 .... **350.00**
Snuff Box, cov, 2" l, oval, hinged

lid with portrait of gentleman and inscription "May All British Admirals Prove a Duncan" **100.00**
Tieback, pr **225.00**

BAVARIAN CHINA

History: Bavaria, Germany, was an important porcelain production center, similar to the Staffordshire district in England. The name Bavarian China refers to companies operating in Bavaria, among which were Hutschenreuther, Thomas, and Zeh, Scherzer & Co. (Z. S. & Co.). Very little of the production from this area was imported into the United States prior to 1870.

Reference: Susan and Al Bagdade, *Warman's English & Continental Pottery & Porcelain, Second Edition,* Wallace–Homestead, 1991.

Bridge Set, 50 pcs, Black Knight, cream ground, cobalt band, gilt dec, eight plates, ten bouillon cups and saucers, and eleven tea cups and saucers **275.00**
Chocolate Set, 5 pcs, chocolate pot and four handled cups, transfer print, grapes hanging on vine dec **65.00**

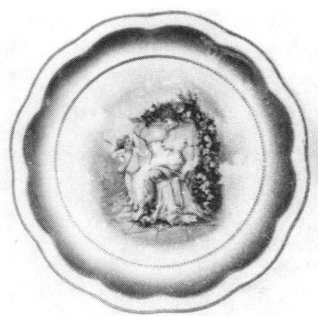

Plate, classical theme, woman being shot by Cupid's arrow, gold bands, dark blue inner band, scalloped edges, marked with crown, shield, and "Bavaria," 8¼" d, $20.00.

Cider Pitcher, 8" h, 6½" d, hp, yellow flowers, green leaves, cream ground, dull Roman gold handle, artist sgd "Lambert" **185.00**
Dinner Service, 68 pcs, hp floral dec, round two handled pedestal bowl, oval platter, oval vegetable dish, two handled rect tray, creamer, cov sugar bowl, cookie plate, eleven fruit bowls, seven salad plates, and nine dinner plates, several pieces artist sgd **575.00**
Figural Group, 5½" h, two battling goats **225.00**
Plate
  Set of five, 11" d, floral spray pattern, Schumann **45.00**
  Set of nine, 11⅛" d, service, beige ground, inner gilt trellising vine rim continuing to outer gilt dec border enclosing green shield shaped cartouches, plain outer gilt rim, Heinrich & Co, Selb, Bavaria, dec in US by Pickard **325.00**
  Set of twelve
    Dinner, emb gold bands, Royal Bavarian, orig retailed by Ovington, NY **275.00**
    Service, 11¼" d, burgundy and pale primrose–yellow banded border alternating with gilt tracery bands, second quarter 20th C **285.00**
Punch Bowl Set, 6½" h footed bowl and six 3" h cups, polychrome dec, black and red berry clusters painted on graduated green ground, punch bowl with gilt rim and gilt figural handles, sgd, c1910 .... **350.00**

BELLEEK

History: Belleek. a thin, ivory colored, almost iridescent–type porcelain, was first made in 1857 in county Fermanagh, Ireland. Production continued until World War I, was discontinued for a period of time, and then resumed. The Shamrock pattern is most familiar, but many patterns were made, including Limpet, Tridacna, and Grasses.

Irish Belleek has several identifying marks, e.g., the Harp and Hound (1865–80) and Harp, Hound, and Castle (1863–91). After 1891 the word "Ireland" or "Erie" was added. Some pieces are marked "Belleek Co., Fermanagh."

There is an Irish saying: If a newly married couple receives a gift of Belleek, their marriage will be blessed with lasting happiness.

Several American firms made a Belleek–type porcelain. The first was Ott and Brewer Co. of Trenton, New Jersey, in 1884, followed by Willets. Other firms included The Ceramic Art Co. (1889), American Art China Works (1892), Columbian Art Co. (1893), and Lenox, Inc. (1904).

References: Susan and Al Bagdade, *Warman's English & Continental Pottery & Porcelain, Second Edition,* Wallace–Homestead, 1991; Richard K. Degenhardt, *Belleek: The Complete Collector's Guide and Illustrated Reference, Second Edition,* Wallace–Homestead, 1993; Mary Frank Gaston, *American Belleek,* Collector Books, 1984, out–of–print; Timothy J. Kearns, *Knowles, Taylor & Knowles: American Bone China,* Schiffer Publishing, 1994.

Collectors' Club: The Belleek Collectors' Society, 144 W. Britannia Street, Taunton, MA 02780.

Museum: Museum of Ceramics at East Liverpool, East Liverpool, OH.

Additional Listings: Lenox.

Abbreviations: 1BM = 1st Black Mark; 2BM = 2nd Black Mark; 3BM = 3rd Black Mark; 3GM = 3rd Green Mark; 4GM = 4th Green Mark; 5GM = 5th Green Mark; 6GM = 6th Green Mark.

AMERICAN

Creamer and Sugar, 6" h, floral dec, gilt, pedestal, CAC	**175.00**
Cup and Saucer, Coxon	**40.00**
Demitasse Cup, cream int., gilt rim, sterling silver holder, Willets, brown mark	**45.00**

Humidor, 5" h, 5½" d, gold and salmon luster Art Deco design, white ground, wear to finial, CAC	**220.00**
Pitcher, silver overlay, foliate central band, #1038, Lenox	**125.00**
Salt	
Individual, set of ten, Lenox	**50.00**
Master, 2" d, 1⅛" h, three ftd, hp green and tan leaves, gold trim, CAC	**65.00**
Soup, Coxon	**100.00**
Stein, 7¼" h, hp dec with monk drinking from bottle, Lenox, green palette mark	**135.00**
Teapot	
3½" h, 7" w, silver overlay, white ground, wear to silver on spout and finial, CAC	**135.00**
6" h, aladdin shape, gilt floral motif, gilt handle, Lenox, purple mark	**385.00**
Vase	
7" h, urn form pedestal base, rose pattern, swan handles, Lenox, green wreath mark	**150.00**
11½" h, cylindrical, hp green and yellow stylized flowers, ivory field, stamped artist's palette, Lenox	**175.00**
12" h, elongated bulbous form, pedestal base, gray ground, white flashing around bottom, Lenox, green wreath mark	**175.00**
12" h, swan handles, cream ground, Armstrong, Lenox, green mark, mounted as lamp	**150.00**
17½" h, tubular shape, brown, tan, and white, white feathered birds, green mark, Willetts	**495.00**
18½" h, ovoid form with narrow cylindrical neck flaring to wide mouth, spreading circular foot, gilt dec, front painted with Madonna de la Sedia, after Raphael, within gilt and white enameled jeweled scrolling foliate and floral frame, green factory mark, Lenox, early 20th C	**935.00**

IRISH

Basket
  6" d, Erne, applied floral rim, four

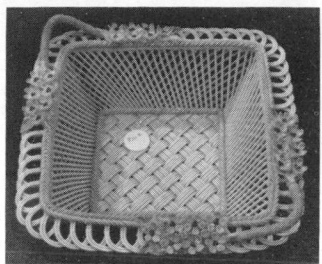

Basket, pink flowers, turquoise trim, Irish ribbon mark, 7¾" sq, $950.00.

strands, pearl finish, one pad imp "Belleek Co., Fermanagh" **475.00**

10½" d, oval, cov, handles, applied floral dec to cover, painted finish, four strands, two pads imp "Belleek R" and "Co. Fermanagh" **2,500.00**

13¼" d, Henshall's, applied center twig handle, applied floral dec on each side of handle, pearl luster, four strands, two pad imp "Belleek" and "Co. Fermanagh" **1,900.00**

Condiment Jar, 5" h, 2½" w, white ground, gold trim, RW & S SS holder **120.00**

Creamer

3" h, Echinus, tinted, 1BM **275.00**

5" h, Undine, cob luster, 3BM .. **80.00**

6" h, Ivy, painted, 1BM **100.00**

Creamer and Sugar, Neptune, 6GM **90.00**

Egg, 3¾" h, cob luster, 6GM **150.00**

Figure

Greyhound, seated, 6½" h, bisque, pearl luster, 3BM **375.00**

Swan, large, dec, 3GM **65.00**

Teapot, 3¼" h, Tridacna, pearl luster, 1BM **500.00**

Tea Set

Cloverleaf pattern, 4" h teapot, cream jug, open sugar bowl, cov honey pot, and seven cups and saucers **150.00**

Limpet pattern, teapot, two cups and saucers, and six 8" d plates **195.00**

Tobacco Box, 6½ x 3¾", Mask Tea Ware, cob luster, 3BM **275.00**

Vase

7¼" h, Aberdeen, applied floral dec, pearl luster, 2BM **550.00**

17½" h, shamrock dec, mounted as table lamp with shade **100.00**

BELLS

History: Bells have been used for centuries for many different purposes. They have been traced as far back as 2697 B.C., though at that time they did not have any true tone. One of the oldest bells is the "crotal," a tiny sphere with small holes and a ball or stone or metal inside. This type now appears as sleigh bells.

True bell making began when bronze, the mixing of tin and copper, was discovered. There are now many types of materials of which bells are made—almost as many materials as there are uses for them.

Bells of the late 19th century show a high degree of workmanship and artistic style. Glass bells from this period are examples of the glassblower's talent and the glass manufacturer's product.

Collectors' Clubs: American Bell Association, Alter Rd., Box 386, Natrona Heights, PA 15065; American Bell Association International, Inc., PO Box 19443, Indianapolis, IN 46219.

Museum: Bell Haven, Tarentum, PA.

Alarm, 8" h, brass, pull chain type, mechanical gong, mounted on wooden board **90.00**

Apparatus

6" w, from hand–tub engine, bronze, bottom mounted yoke, 19th C **175.00**

7" h, from hand–tub engine, brass, swivel mounting bracket, acorn finial, mounted on wooden base **350.00**

12" h, 12" w, chrome plated, side mounted bracket, marked "Rostand, Milford, CT" **300.00**

Brass, 8" d, iron mounting bracket **65.00**

Dairy, 24" w, 29" h, cast iron, figural, full bodied horned cow standing on black painted scroll-

Bristol Glass, white, 11½" h, $50.00.

ing foliate bracket with bell, hung at Cowneck Farm, Sands Point, NY 3,220.00

Glass, Mary Gregory, cranberry and clear 30.00

Hand, 12" h, brass, turned wood handle, 19th C 45.00

Japanese
  Bronze, raised butterfly and cursive calligraphy dec, 19th C, set of three 85.00
  Wood, carved, 12½" h, Mokugyo, dragon, tama handle, beater 145.00

Servant's, silver, double cornucopia shaped spooner holder with pointed rims, ornate etching, elaborate feet form arch where bell is suspended, sgd "Wilcox" 295.00

Sleigh, leather strap, worn
  3 2½" d bells, metal strap 28.00
  21 brass bells 50.00
  27 brass bells 65.00

Stoneware, 13" l, raised bosses and flanges, ancient bronze simulated glaze, irregular glaze, 19th C 115.00

Table
  Dutch, lobed body with recurving scroll handle entwined with two leaves, J M Van Kempen, 16.5 cm h 500.00
  English, George III, silver, bolded borders, baluster handle, marked on body and clap-

per, Peter and Ann Bateman, London, 1791, 3 oz 10 dwts, 4¼" h 1,265.00

Russian, silver gilt, formed as lady in traditional costume, clapper missing, I Sazikov, Moscow, 1847, 2¾" h 795.00

Tribal, Hemba, 11" h, three openwork metal spherical bells surmounted by wooden figure of man with hands on abdomen, enlarged head with typical crossed–coiffure, ring of feathers around waist, rich brown patina 9,775.00

BENNINGTON AND BENNINGTON-TYPE POTTERY

History: In 1845 Christopher Webber Fenton joined Julius Norton, his brother–in-law, in the manufacturing of stoneware pottery in Bennington, Vermont. Fenton sought to expand the company's products and glazes; Norton wanted to concentrate solely on stoneware. In 1847 Fenton broke away and established his own factory.

Fenton introduced the famous Rockingham glaze, developed in England and named after the Marquis of Rockingham, to America. In 1849 he patented a flint enamel glaze, "Fenton's Enamel," which added flecks, spots, or streaks of color (usually blues, greens, yellows, and oranges) to the brown Rockingham glaze. Forms included candlesticks, coachman bottles, cow creamers, poodles, sugar bowls, and toby pitchers.

Fenton produced the little–known scroddled ware, commonly called lava or agate ware. Scroddled ware is composed of different colored clays, mixed with cream colored clay, molded, turned on a potter's wheel, coated with feldspar and flint, and fired. It was not produced in quantity, as there was little demand for it.

Fenton also introduced Parian ware to America. Parian was developed in England in 1842 and known as "Statuary ware." Parian is a translucent porcelain which has no glaze and resembles marble. Bennington made the blue and white variety in the form of vases, cologne bottles, and trinkets.

Five different marks were used, with many variations. Only about twenty percent of the pieces carried any mark; some forms were almost always marked, others never. Marks: (a) 1849 mark (4 variations) for flint enamel and Rockingham; (b) E. Fenton's Works, 1845–47, on Parian and occasionally on scroddled ware; (c) U. S. Pottery Co., ribbon mark, 1852–58, on Parian and blue and white porcelain; (d) U. S. Pottery Co., lozenge mark, 1852–58, on Parian; and (e) U. S. Pottery, oval mark, 1853–58, mainly on scroddled ware.

The hound–handled pitcher is probably the best known Bennington piece. Hound–handled pitchers also were made by some 30 potteries in over 55 different variations. Rockingham glaze was used by over 150 potteries in 11 states, mainly the Midwest, between 1830 and 1900.

References: Richard Carter Barret, *How To Identify Bennington Pottery*, Stephen Greene Press, 1964; William C. Ketchum, Jr., *American Pottery and Porcelain: Identification and Price Guide*, Avon Books, 1994; Laura Woodside Watkins, *Early New England Potters And Their Wares*, Harvard University Press, 1950.

Museums: Bennington Museum, Bennington, VT; East Liverpool Museum of Ceramics, East Liverpool, OH.

Additional Listings: Stoneware.

BENNINGTON

Bottle
  7¾" h, book shape, flint enamel, marked "Kossuth," sticker with "Hammerslough–Fergenbaum Bennington Collections" **1,100.00**
  10½" h, coachman, brown, yellow, and olive Rockingham glaze, 1849 mark, professional repair to hat **1,100.00**
Figure
  9½" l, dog, standing, basket of fruit, coleslaw coat, Rock-

ingham glaze, minor damage and repairs **1,760.00**
  10" l, lion, flint enamel, coleslaw mane, repaired tail **1,265.00**
Flask
  5½" h, book shape, flint enamel, "Departed Spirits G," minor edge wear and small flakes . **415.00**
  5⅝" h, book shape, scroddleware, blue, white, and cream, applied star and molded label, "Fenton's Works, Bennington Vermont," two chipped corners, hairline along spine ...**2,585.00**
  6" h, flint enamel, imp on spine "Departed Spirits C," mid 19th C **225.00**

Cow Creamer, Rockingham glaze, $375.00.

Marbles
  Fifty–four, ⅜ to ⅞" d, blue **175.00**
  Forty, ⅜ to 1⅜" d, brown **90.00**
  Twenty–eight, ⅜ to 1⅜" d, blue **100.00**
Match Holder, 4⅜" h, parian, figural cat peering into vase shaped match holder, chip in rim of vase **260.00**
Pitcher, 11¾" h, flint enamel, paneled, 1849 mark, chips on foot **580.00**
Toby Bottle, 8½" h, "Old Tom," Rockingham glaze **360.00**
Vase, 4½" h, parian, three part, birds, chips **75.00**
Wash Bowl, 13⅞" d, flint enamel, marked "1849" **525.00**

BENNINGTON TYPE

Bottle, 11″ h, fish shape, Rock-
ingham glaze **385.00**
Figure, 7¾″ h, dog, seated, cole-
slaw coat, tooling Rockingham
glaze, chips on base and nose **935.00**
Flask, 8″ l, mermaid, Rockingham
glaze **310.00**
Toby Creamer, 5″ h, Rockingham
glaze **95.00**

BISCUIT JARS

History: The biscuit or cracker jar was
the forerunner of the cookie jar. They were
made of various materials by leading glassworks and potteries of the late 19th and
early 20th centuries.

Note: All items listed have silver–plated
mountings unless otherwise noted.

Bellaware, 10″ h, 8″ d, opal ware,
pale purple ground, red and pur-
ple lilacs, resilvered fittings **300.00**
Crown Milano, Mt Washington,
7¼″ h
Enameled floral dec, creamy
satin ground, silver plated rim,
bail handle, and cov with applied figural turtle, imp mark
and paper label **700.00**
Handpainted and enameled ex-
otic blossoms dec, burmese
color ground, silver plated bail
handle, rim, and cover, imp
mark **575.00**
Opal glass, gold outlined exotic
blossom and leaves dec, pale
satin ground, silver plated
floral rim, bail handle, and cov,
imp mark **875.00**
Cut Glass, hobstars, strawberry,
diamond, and fan, silver plated
cov, 1890s **235.00**
Opal Glass, 8½″ h, 5″ d, irid, highly
raised floral dec, relief leaves,
later cov, broken handle **125.00**
Pairpoint, 5¾″ h, blue and white
Delft dec **500.00**
Pomona Glass, 10½″ h, 5½″ w,
acanthus leaf design, 1st
ground, excellent staining, ap-

plied wishbone base, crack in
base **200.00**
Royal Bonn, 7½″ h, red roses dec,
silver plated cov **100.00**
Royal Worcester, 6¼″ h, 6½″ w, hp
flowers, cream ground, ribbed,
worn gold, chip under lid rim,
c1892 . . . . **195.00**
Smith Bros, Persian style dec, jew-
eled circles and fans, sgd **975.00**

**Wave Crest, two horizontal wavy
lines across body, green shading
to white, transfer and handpainted floral design, SP top,
$245.00.**

Wave Crest
7½″ h, hp florals, acorn finial,
beaded handle **425.00**
8″ h, pastel floral and leaf dec . **350.00**
Wedgwood, 5⅛″ d, light green jas-
per dipped body, applied yellow
trellis with white floral dec, silver
plated rim, handle, and cov, imp
mark, restored hairline **825.00**

BISQUE

History: Bisque or biscuit china is the
name given to wares that are been fired
once and are not glazed.

Bisque figurines and busts were popular
during the Victorian era, being used on fireplace mantels, dining room buffets, and end
tables. Manufacturing was centered in the
United States and Europe. By the mid–20th

century the Japanese were the principal source of bisque items, especially character related items.

References: Susan and Al Bagdade, *Warman's English & Continental Pottery & Porcelain, Second Edition,* Wallace–Homestead, 1991; Elyse Karlin, *Children Figurines of Bisque and Chinawares, 1850–1950,* Schiffer Publishing, 1990; Sharon Weintraub, *Naughties, Nudies and Bathing Beauties,* Hobby House Press, 1993.

Piano Baby, light blue dress, gray hat, brown hair, flesh-colored arms and legs, 7½" h, $255.00.

Bust, woman, portrait type, glazed
finish, sgd "Delagrange,"
France, c1900 .... **325.00**
Cigar Holder, 4¼" h, tree stump,
bird chasing insect, natural
colors, Germany, 19th C **35.00**
Fairy Lamp, figural
3¼" h, cat's head, white, amber
eyes **250.00**
3⅜" h, Pekingese dog, shades
of brown, amber eyes, blue
collar, light blue back **195.00**
3½" h, 3" d, owl's head, gray,
gold glass eyes, blue ribbon
around neck **275.00**
3⅞" h, three faces, lion, monkey,
and animal, white, colored
glass eyes **500.00**
Figure
2⅛" h, Mickey Mouse riding
Pluto, repainted, c1930 ..... **75.00**
2⅞" h, boy with football, imp "G
Kraus Germany" **110.00**
6" h, couple under umbrella, ink,

blue, lavender, peach, and
gray, wire umbrella handle .. **175.00**
Match Holder
3⅛" h, Ugly Old Woman, strikers
on both sides and rear **65.00**
3¼" h, Frowning Old Man, No.
5691 incised on back **55.00**
Nodder
Black Boy, sitting, wearing red
turban, gold cane, Germany . **50.00**
Indian Princess, 3¾" h, pale blue
robe, gold trim **125.00**
Poodle and Bulldog, 4¾" h, oval
base **145.00**
Pastille Burner, figural
3½" h, 7¼" w, cottage, polychrome dec, two chimneys .. **95.00**
5" h, bust of dog, shades of
brown, green hat, brown and
white feather, brass saucer,
built–in candle cup, finger
holder **200.00**
Plaque, pr, 10¼" d, facing pr, light
green, white relief man playing
mandolin and woman wearing
hat and long dress, scrolling and
pierced design, c1900 .... **250.00**
Shoe, 5 x 1¾ x 2" h, man's, real
shoelaces, brown and white ... **75.00**
Vase
7½" h, 5" w, woman in purple
dress standing by tree **50.00**
8¼" h, standing girl figure,
shaded blue dress and hat,
raised dots dec **115.00**

BITTERS BOTTLES

History: Bitters, a "remedy" made from natural herbs and other mixtures with an alcohol base, often was viewed as the universal cure–all. The names given to various bitter mixtures were imaginative, though the bitters seldom cured what their makers claimed.

The manufacturers of bitters needed a way to sell and advertise their products. They designed bottles in many shapes, sizes, and colors to attract the buyer. Many forms of advertising, including trade cards, billboards, signs, almanacs, and novelties proclaimed the virtues of a specific bitter.

During the Civil War a tax was levied on

alcoholic beverages. Since bitters were identified as medicines, they were exempt from this tax. The alcohol content was never mentioned. In 1907 when the Pure Foods Regulations went into effect, "an honest statement of content on every label" put most of the manufacturers out of business.

References: Carlyn Ring, *For Bitters Only,* 1980; J. H. Thompson, *Bitters Bottles,* Century House, 1947; Richard Watson, *Bitters Bottles,* Thomas Nelson and Sons, 1965.

Periodicals: *Antique Bottle and Glass Collector,* PO Box 187, East Greenville, PA 18041; *The Bitters Report,* PO Box 1253, Bunnell, FL 32110.

Mein Flussinges Kapital, German, c1920, $40.00.

Ayer Restorative Bitters, Boston, rect, aqua **170.00**
Beggs Dandelion Bitters, Chicago, IL, sq, amber **150.00**
Caroni Bitters, round, green **135.00**
Doctor Fisch's, 11⅝" h, fish form, light yellow amber, round collared mouth, smooth base **450.00**
Drake's Plantation, tall cabin form
  9¾" h, sq, olive yellow, applied sloping collared mouth, smooth base **800.00**
  10" h, strawberry puce, Arabesque lettering, applied sloping collared mouth, smooth base **150.00**
Electric Brand Bitters, H E Bucklen & Co, Chicago, IL, sq, amber .. **40.00**
Greeley's Bourbon Bitters, 9⅛" h, barrel form, smokey–gray puce,

applied sq collared mouth, smooth base **375.00**
Grenade Sauvinet Malakoff Seine, 3¾" h, natural colored pottery, emb name **25.00**
Hall Bitters, 9⅛" h, barrel form, olive yellow, applied sq collared mouth, smooth base **355.00**
Johnson's Calisaya bitters, Burlington, VT, sq, amber **85.00**
Lancaster Indian Vegetable Jaundice Bitters, twelve sided, aqua **65.00**
M G Landsberg, Chicago, 11" h, sq, corrugated corners, golden amber, applied sloping collared mouth **700.00**
National Bitters Patent 1867, figural, ear of corn, amber **200.00**
Old Sachem Bitters and Wigwam Tonic, 9¼" h, barrel form, yellow amber, applied sq collared mouth, smooth base **85.00**
Peychaud's American Aromatic bitter Cordial, New Orleans, round, amber **50.00**
Pond's Bitters, Unexcelled Laxative, sq, amber, paper label ... **30.00**
Rising Sun Bitters, John C Hurst, Philadelphia, sq amber **160.00**
Royal Italian Bitters, 13½" h, cylindrical, medium amethyst, applied sq collared mouth, smooth base **485.00**
Star Kidney and Liver Bitters, 8⅞" h, sq, amber **50.00**
The Fish Bitters, 11¾" h, fish form, reddish amber, applied round collared mouth, smooth base .. **165.00**
Tonola Bitter, J T Higby, Milford, CT, sq, amber **150.00**
Unknown, clear, sterling overlay rooster, neck, and spout **145.00**
Walker's Cocktail Bitters, round, lady's leg neck, amber **625.00**
Yochim Bros Celebrated Stomach Bitters, sq, red–amber **80.00**

BLACK MEMORABILIA

History: The term "Black memorabilia" refers to a broad range of collectibles that often overlap other collecting fields, e.g., toys, post cards, etc. It also encompasses

African artifacts, items created by slaves or related to the slavery era, modern Black cultural contributions to literature, art, etc., and material associated with the Civil Rights Movement and the Black experience throughout history.

The earliest known examples of Black memorabilia include primitive African designs and tribal artifacts. Black Americana dates back to the arrival of African natives upon American shores.

The advent of the 1900s saw an incredible amount and variety of material depicting Blacks, most often in a derogatory and dehumanizing manner that clearly reflected the stereotypical attitude held toward the Black race during this period. The popularity of Black portrayals in this unflattering fashion flourished as the century wore on.

As the growth of the Civil Rights Movement escalated and aroused public awareness to the Black plight, attitudes changed. Public outrage and pressure eventually put a halt to these offensive stereotypes during the early 1950s.

Black representations are still being produced in many forms, but no longer in the demoralizing designs of the past. These modern objects, while not as historically significant as earlier examples, will become the Black memorabilia of tomorrow.

References: Douglas Congdon–Martin, *Images in Black: 150 years of Black Collectibles,* Schiffer Publishing, 1990; Patiki Gibbs, *Black Collectibles Sold In America,* Collector Books, 1987, 1993 value update; Jan Lindenberger, *Black Memorabilia Around The House: A Handbook and Price Guide,* Schiffer Publishing, 1993; Jan Lindenberger, *Black Memorabilia For The Kitchen,* Schiffer Publishing, 1992; Myla Perkins, *Black Dolls 1820–1991: An Identification and Value Guide,* Collector Books, 1993; Myla Perkins, *Black Dolls Book II: An Identification and Value Guide,* Collector Books, 1994; Dawn Reno, *Collecting Black Americana,* Crown Publishing Co., 1986; Darrell A. Smith, *Black Americana: A Personal Collection,* Black Relics, Inc., 1988; Jean Williams Turner, *Collectible Aunt Jemima: Handbook and Price Guide,* Schiffer Publishing, 1994; Jackie Young, *Black Collectibles: Mammy and Her Friends,* Schiffer Publishing, 1988.

Periodicals: *Black Ethnic Collectibles*, 1401 Asbury Court, Hyattsville, MD 20782; *Blackin,* 559 22nd Ave., Rock Island, IL 61201

Collectors' Club: Black Memorabilia Collector's Assoc, 2482 Devoe Terrace, Bronx, NY 10468.

Museum: Museum of African American History, Detroit, MI.

Reproduction Alert. Reproductions are becoming an increasing problem, from advertising signs (Bull Durham tobacco) to mechanical banks (Jolly Nigger). If the object looks new to you, chances are that it is new.

Advertising
  Display, diecut cardboard
    Durham Smoking Tobacco, 7 x 10″, black man with wispy cotton hair holding product package, "A Full Hand!," printed by Knapp & Co, NY, c1890 . . . . **650.00**
    Gold Dust Washing Powder, ten 7½ x 15½″ connected boxes, hanging, double sided, trademark twins illus and "Gold Dust" **8,000.00**
  Poster
    Crosman Bros Seeds, 16¾ x 23½″, two black boys carrying "Peerless Water Melons" **1,800.00**
    Theater, 20 x 27″, Harlin Tarbell illus, two men in vaudeville black face make–up . . **170.00**
  Sign
    Adler's Colored Kids, 18 x 13″, three attractive black boys leaning over fence, printed by Donaldson Bros **500.00**
    Seat of North Carolina Smoking Tobacco, 10¼ x 13¼″, caricature black man on wagon loaded with huge product bag, "Look Out Dar. I Is Comin" **475.00**
Batter Bowl, Mammy, marked "Weller" **995.00**
Book, *Complete Life of Nat King Cole,* Pocket Magazines Inc, 1955 copyright, 68 pgs, color cov **25.00**

 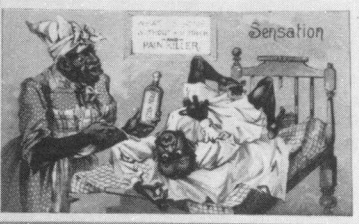

Advertising Trade Card, Perry Davis Pain Killer, three panel, titled "Anticipation," "Realization," and "Sensation," multicolored, Henderson, Achert, Krebs Litho Co., Cincinnati, $10.00.

Creamer, Mammy, marked "Weller" 495.00

Doll, 7" h, rubber, youngster, brown, molded black hair, aqua hair bow, underwear, and slippers, Irwin, 1940s 75.00

Figure
3" h, porter, lead, Barclay, 1940s 25.00
11" h, 3½" d, bisque, African woman, blue dress, pink drape, turban with colored ostrich plumes, bird perched on arm, cornucopia of flowers in other hand, gold trim, circular base, French, c1860 .... 550.00

Game, Tip The Bell Boy, game board with 8" h diecut cardboard bellboy figure, twelve wood balls, wood catapult with metal spring, orig box, All There, copyright 1929 .... 250.00

Incense Burner, 3 x 3½ x 4", bisque, painted, figural, seated man, caricature facial expression, marked "Japan," 1930s .. 125.00

Lady's Head Vase, female native 18.00

Magazine, Quick, Oct 6, 1952, Jackie Robinson article, full color cov photo 25.00

Photo
Amos N' Andy, 9 x 12", black and white, frame border design, marked "Supplement Detroit Sunday Times," 1930s 75.00
Floyd Patterson, 8½ x 11", black and white glossy, blue ink signature "To my friend, my sincere best wishes and God bless, Floyd Patterson" 50.00

Pinback Button
1" d, Equality, two hands shaking, one white, other black, 1965 .... 15.00
1¼" d
Evening World Wolligog Club, black, white, and green, c1930 .... 75.00
Shirley Chisholm, heart with bluetone photo, gold lettering, "Let's Get To the Heart Of The Problem," 1972 .... 12.00
The Hero Of Pearl Harbor, Dorie Miller, black and white photo 100.00
1¾" d, Sugar Ray Robinson, black and white, 1950s 40.00

Poster, 14 x 22", Louis–Schmeling Fight, cardboard, black and white, cartoon illus, Martin's Scotch Whiskey adv 100.00

Program, 9 x 12", Nat King Cole In Sights And Sounds, 16 pgs, orange cov with black and white photo 25.00

Puzzle Card, 3 x 4", Puzzle of Teddy And The Lions, full color, Teddy Roosevelt, lions, and black men, mechanical wheel changes image, c1909 .... 65.00

Salt and Pepper Shakers, pr

Aunt Jemima and Uncle Mose,
5" h, hard plastic, painted, F &
F Mold & Die Works, c1951 . . 75.00
Caricature, 3" h, figural, china,
base holds seated pair,
marked "Japan," 1930s 75.00
Chef, 3" h, caricature, front panel
image, white china, marked
"Japan," 1930s 55.00
Chef's heads, one black, one
white 35.00
Nude women, one black, one
white 30.00
Twins in basket 65.00
Spinner, Gold Dust Washing Pow-
der, two black boys seated in
yellow washtub, early 1900s . . . 75.00
Spoon Rest, Mammy 95.00
Syrup, Mammy
F & F Mold & Die Works, 5¼" h,
hard plastic, orig mailing box,
early 1950s 125.00
Weller, marked 595.00
Thermometer, 5½" h, composition
wood, figural, caricature youngster wearing diaper, Multi Products, 1949 copyright 55.00
Toy
Amos N' Andy Fresh Air Taxi
Cab, 3½ x 8 x 5", tin, windup,
built–in key, Marx, 1930s 400.00
Be Bop Jigger, black dancer,
graphic illus on round pedes-
tal, windup, Marx 450.00
Dance Hawaiian, windup, black
girl wearing grass skirt, built–
in key, orig box, Made In Occupied Japan, 1940s 150.00
Louis Armstrong, playing trum-
pet, windup 425.00
Mammy, 8" h, windup, litho tin,
built–in key, glossy finish, Lind-
strom 300.00
Mechanical Figure, 10½" h, car-
icature Golliwog dancer, cardboard, diecut, jointed, red,
white, blue, and black, orig envelope and instruction slip . . . 50.00
Strutting Sam, black dancer,
graphic illus on round pedes-
tal, battery operated, MIB . . . 550.00
Wall Pocket, native on tree stump 65.00
Wristwatch, stainless steel dial
with Martin Luther King Jr illus,

black strap bands, missing wind-
ing knob 55.00

BLOWN THREE MOLD

History: The Jamestown colony in Virginia introduced glassmaking into America.
The artisans used a "free blown" method.
Blowing molten glass into molds was not
introduced into America until the early
1800s. Blown three mold glass used a pre–
designed mold that consisted of two, three,
or more hinged parts. The glassmaker
placed a quantity of molten glass on the tip
of a rod or tube, inserted it into the mold,
blew air into the tube, waited until the glass
cooled, and removed the finished product.
The three part mold is the most common
and lends its name to this entire category.
The impressed decorations on blown
mold glass usually are reversed, i.e., what
is raised or convex on the outside will be
concave on the inside. This is useful in identifying the blown form.
By 1850 American–made glassware was
in relatively common usage. The increased
demand led to large factories and the creation of a technology which eliminated the
smaller companies.
Reference: George S. and Helen Mc-
Kearin, *American Glass,* reprint, Crown
Publishers, 1941, 1948.
Collectors' Club: National Early American Glass Club, PO Box 8489, Silver
Spring, MD 20907.
Museum: Sandwich Glass Museum,
Sandwich, MA.

Bottle
5½" h, medium lavender blue,
flared mouth, pontil 275.00
6" h, cobalt blue, flared mouth,
tam–o–shanter stopper 250.00
6¾" h, cobalt blue, flared mouth,
matching ribbed stopper 325.00
Castor Set, two shakers, cruet,
and cov mustard pot, clear,
tooled and ground mouths,
smooth base, pewter holder . . . 125.00
Creamer
4" h, clear, sheared rim, ribbed
applied handle 325.00

4½" h, cobalt blue, purple tones, sheared rim, solid handle ... **375.00**
Decanter, flared mouth, pontil
Barrel form, clear, matching stopper **225.00**
Diamond quilted design, brownish amethyst tint, octagonal base, qt **210.00**
Miniature, clear, matching stopper, ½ pt **375.00**
Ribbed design, grayish–blue, flared mouth, period stopper, ½ pt **935.00**
Scroll design, clear, period stopper **200.00**
Square, beveled corners, medium blue green, flared mouth, pt **825.00**
Dish, 8½" d, clear, folded rim, pontil **325.00**
Inkwell
1¼" h, drum shape, medium green, horizontal bands, disc mouth, pontil **145.00**
1½" h, deep olive amber, disc mouth, pontil **85.00**
1⁹⁄₁₆" h, cylindrical, olive green, disc mouth **75.00**
1⅝" h, drum shape, deep amber, disc mouth **285.00**
Lamp, 2⅝" d, 1⅝" h, clear, tooled mouth with burner, applied handle 1,050.00
Pitcher, 5¾" h, barrel form, clear, tooled rim, ribbed handle 1,545.00
Tumbler, 3⅛" h, barrel form, pale blue, tooled rim, pontil **285.00**
Wine Glass, 3⅞" h, clear, sheared rim, pontil **275.00**

BOEHM PORCELAINS

History: Edward Marshall Boehm was born on August 21, 1913. Boehm's childhood was spent at the McConogh School, a rural Baltimore County, Maryland, school dedicated to caring for homeless boys. He studied animal husbandry at the University of Maryland, serving as manager of Longacre Farms on the Eastern Shore of Maryland upon graduation. During World War II,

Boehm joined the Air Force and was assigned as a therapist to a convalescent center in Pawling, New York. After the war, he moved to Great Neck, Long Island, and worked as an assistant veterinarian.

In 1949 Boehm quit his job to open a pottery studio in Trenton, New Jersey. His initial sculptures consisted of Herefords, Percherons, and dogs done in hard–paste porcelain. The first five to six years were a struggle, with several partnerships beginning and ending during the period. In the early 1950s Boehm's art porcelain sculptures began appearing in major department stores. When Eisenhower presented a Boehm sculpture to Queen Elizabeth and Prince Philip during their visit to the United States in 1957, Boehm's career accelerated.

Boehm had a reputation for being opinionated, prejudiced, and unforgiving. His contributions were the image concepts and techniques used to produce the sculptures. Thousands of prototype sculptures were made, with over 400 put into actual production. The actual work was done by skilled artisans. Boehm died on January 29, 1969.

In the early 1970s a second production studio was opened in Malvern, England, as Boehm Studios. The tradition begun by Boehm continues today.

Reference: Reese Palley, *The Porcelain Art of Edward Marshall Boehm*, Harrison House, division of Crown Publishers, 1988.

Collectors' Club: Boehm Porcelain Society, PO Box 5051, Trenton, NJ 08638.

Arabian Camel and Calf, dec, 500–9, 13½ x 14" **975.00**
Barn Owl, dec, 1005, 20 x 25½" . **575.00**
Black Birds with Cherry Blossom, dec, 100–15, 22 x 12" 1,500.00
Black Capped Chickadee, dec, 400–61, 7 x 12" **575.00**
Black Eared Wheateater, dec, BJF–8, 13 x 8" **980.00**
Blue Bow, tile, dec, 16 x 10½" ... **195.00**
Cactus Wren, dec, 400–17, 13 x 9" **400.00**
Catbird, dec, 483, 14¼" h 1,035.00
Cherries, plate, dec, 12" d **125.00**
Chrysanthemum Petal Camellias, dec, 103–81, 8½ x 9½" **460.00**

Eastern Bluebirds, plaque, issued
1970, 11½ x 8", pr **1,050.00**
Goldcrest, dec, 1004, 7½" h **175.00**
Green Jays, dec, 486, 14 x 10" . . **575.00**
Green Woodpecker, dec, 100–15,
22 x 12" **2,350.00**
Lilies with Butterflies, dec, 281,
7¾" h **400.00**
Loganberries, plate, dec, 12" d . . **135.00**
Magnolia Grandi Flora with Butter-
fly, bisque, lucite base, 104, 7" h **575.00**
Mallards, pr, dec, 406, 10½ x 12" **450.00**
Meadowlark, white bisque, 435, 9"
h **115.00**
Mockingbirds, pr, dec, 459, 12" h **750.00**
Mountain Bluebirds, dec, 470,
12½ x 16" **1,735.00**
Nightingale, tile, dec, 16 x 10" . . . **375.00**
Orchid, centerpiece, dec, 400–09,
17½ x 26" **925.00**
Oriental Pheasant, white bisque,
414, 8 x 19" **315.00**
Pelargonium with Wren, dec, 100–
36, 10 x 8" **700.00**
Peregrine Falcon with Young, dec,
101, 14½ x 11" **860.00**
Queen Elizabeth Rose, dec, 161,
6½" h **425.00**
Raccoons, dec, 4002, 12 x 12" . . **285.00**
Racquet–Tail Hummingbird, dec,
40105, 9½ x 8" **975.00**
Red Fox, dec, 4003, 12½ x 13" . **285.00**
Rudolph's Bird of Paradise, tile,
dec, 14 x 11" **115.00**
Slate Colored Junco, dec, 400–12,
12 x 11" **260.00**
Snow Buntings, dec, 400–21, 7 x
13" **490.00**
Song Thrushes with Crab Apple,
dec, 100–16, 17 x 12½" **1,500.00**
Squirrels, dec, 4004, 14 x 14" . . . **575.00**
Stewart's Supreme Camellia, dec,
74, 4¼" h **60.00**
Tufted Titrice, dec, 482, 13 x 6" . **400.00**
Varied Buntings, dec, 481, 22 x 14" **2,760.00**
Western Bluebirds, dec, 400–01,
17½ x 15" **3,680.00**
Western Meadowlark, dec, 400–
15, 13¼" h **535.00**
Wood Ducks, dec, 401–62, 16 x
18" **2,750.00**
Yellow Hummers with Hawthorne,
1009, 11 x 12" **1,850.00**
Young America 1776, plate, limited

edition of 6,000, 24 k gold, dec,
13" d **95.00**

BOHEMIAN GLASS

History: The once independent country
of Bohemia, now a part of Czechoslovakia,
produced a variety of fine glassware:
etched, cut, overlay, and colored. Their
glassware was first imported into America
in the early 1820s and continues today.

Bohemia is known for its "flashed" glass
that was produced in the familiar ruby color,
as well as amber, green, blue, and black.
Common patterns include "Deer and Castle," "Deer and Pine Tree," and "Vintage."

Most of the Bohemian glass encountered
in today's market is of the 1875–1900 period. Bohemian–type glass also was made
in England, Switzerland, and Germany.

Reproduction Alert.

Bottle, 6¼" h, cranberry cut to
clear, building dec, pr **175.00**
Bowl, cov, 7" d, cranberry cut to
clear, animal and floral dec, set
of three **115.00**
Castor Set, 19" h, three colored
decanters, three matching
etched goblets, one each cranberry, emerald green, and cobalt
blue, orig stoppers, silver plated
trim, rings, handles, and base,
one stopper damaged **925.00**
Cordial, 8" h, yellow bowl etched
with flowers and bunches of
grapes, knopped stem, spread-
ing circular ft, set of twelve **140.00**
Goblet, cov, 11¼" h, gilt leaves
surrounding enamel floral me-
dallion, 20th C **345.00**
Dinner Service, amber ground,
etched landscape scenes with
elk and hounds, most initialed
"S," grouping consists of four 15"
h candlesticks, twenty–two 5" d
bowls, one 11¼" d bowl, 24" h
cov vase, twenty–three 9¼" d
plates, twelve 6⅝" h wine goblets, fifteen 4" h cordials, two 11"
h ewer–form decanters with
stoppers, two 10" d compotes,
two 8⅜" d compotes, one 7⅞" d

cov compote, one 18" h trumpet–form vase, seventeen 4¾" l
leaf–form dishes, and one damaged tiered compote, purchased
in 1857 by Sheffield Scientific
School founder **12,650.00**
Liqueur Set, crystal, amber stain,
floral cutting, 11" h Art Deco decanter, six 2¾" h pedestal
glasses, seven piece set **750.00**
Mantel Lustres, pr, 10⅛" h, clear,
green and opaque white enamel,
clear prisms, some gilt wear and
chipping, late 19th C **635.00**
Pokal
  6" h, cobalt blue cut to white to
  clear, stylized floral designs,
  ftd **70.00**
  9½" h, globular bowl, cranberry
  cut to clear, cut with eagle,
  dated 1914, faceted stem . . . **140.00**

**Tumbler, grapes, vines, and
leaves dec, 3¹¹⁄₁₆" h, $35.00.**

Tumbler, 4" h, cobalt blue cut to
white to clear, stylized floral de-
signs **65.00**
Vase
  5¼" h, emerald green cased
  over white, Moser type daffodils, gold dec, multicolored
  enamel dec **750.00**
  11½" h, cranberry cut to clear,
  bird and floral dec, set of four **165.00**
  12" h, white cut to green, hp
  flowers, gold trim **225.00**
Water Set, cranberry cut to clear,
7½" h pitcher and six glasses . **185.00**

BOOKS, ATLASES

History: America's fascination with local,
regional, state, and national history owes its
origin to the nation's centennial in 1876.
The next thirty years witnessed a prolifera-
tion of histories, atlases, genealogies, and
photographic studies.

Atlases provide a great way to study geography and the history of a region. Maps
often include natural features, place names,
railway and canal routes, as well as roads
and streets. Beautiful engraved bird's–eye
views and lithographs enhance atlases and
give the reader a feel for the scenery of the
period.

In the last quarter of the 19th century,
representatives from firms in Philadelphia,
Chicago, and elsewhere traveled the United
States preparing county atlases, often with
a sheet for each township and a sheet for
each major city or town. Although mass–
produced, they are eagerly sought by collectors. Individual sheets sell for $35 to
$100. Individual sheets should be viewed
solely as decorative and not as investment
material. When buying an entire atlas, collectors should check for completeness as
well as condition.

References: Allen Ahearn, *Book Col-
lecting: A Comprehensive Guide,* G. P. Put-
nam's Sons, 1989; Allen and Patricia
Ahearn, *Collected Books, The Guide To
Values,* G. P. Putnam's Sons, 1991; *Amer-
ican Book Prices Current,* Bancroft–Park-
man, published annually; Marjorie M. and
Donald L. Hinds, *How To Make Money
Buying & Selling Old Books,* published by
authors, 1974; *Huxford's Old Book Value
Guide, Sixth Edition* Collector Books, 1994;
Joseph Raymond LeFontaine, *The Collector's Bookshelf,* Prometheus Books, 1990;
Marie Tedford and Pat Goudey, *The Official
Price Guide To Old Books,* House of Col-
lectibles, 1994; John Wade, *Tomart's Price
Guide to 20th Century Books,* Tomart Publications, 1994; Nancy Wright, *Books: Iden-
tification and Price Guide,* Avon Books,
1993.

Periodicals: *Antique Map & Print Quarterly,* PO Box 290-681, Wethersfield, CT
06129; *Book Source Monthly,* 2007 Syossett Dr., PO Box 567, Cazenovia, NY

13035; *Rare Book Bulletin,* PO Box 201, Peoria, IL 61650.
Collectors' Club: National Book Collectors Society, 65 High Ridge Road, Suite 349, Stamford, CT 06095.
Advisor: Ron Lieberman.

A Classical Atlas, to Illustrate Ancient Geography, Alexander G Findlay, NY, c1860, 25 double page or folding engraved maps by Tegg of London, hand–colored in outline, small 4to, ½ sheep, rubbed, joints splitting, publisher's paper label, owner's inscription on front free endpaper **230.00**

A New and Authentic System of Universal Geography, Thomas Bankes, London, c1799, 113 maps and plates, 2 vol in one, folio, modern buckram **1,350.00**

A New General Atlas, Aaron Arrowsmith, Edinburgh, 1823, 52 engraved maps, small 4to, contemporary ½ sheep, front cov loose, extremities worn, scattered foxing **625.00**

A New Geographical, Historical, and Commercial Grammar..., William Guthrie, London, 1794, numerous engraved folding maps, thick 8vo, contemporary calf, front cov lacking, scattered foxing and browning **410.00**

Atlas, Designed to Illustrate the Geography of the Heavens..., Elijah H Burritt, NY, 1835, new edition, 8 maps, hand–colored, folio, orig wrappers, spine fold worn, rubbing at extremities, usual scattered foxing, minor browning to maps, orig stitching absent, remnants of gutters ... **460.00**

Atlas, Designed to Illustrate the Malte–Brun School Geography, F J Huntington & Co, NY, 1837, 5 double hand–colored maps, 7 single maps, 4 pgs of tables, folio, laid into printed wrapper, lacks stitching **200.00**

Atlas of Bergen County, New Jersey A H Walker, Reading, 1876, hand–colored litho maps, litho

view of local sites, folio, cloth with morocco tips, rebacked, endpapers renewed, title soiled, numerous small chips and tears at edges **690.00**

Atlas of Staten Island, Richmond County, New York, F W Beers, NY, 1874, 35 litho maps, most double paged, some color, folio, disbound **320.00**

Atlas of the City of Boston, Massachusetts, George and Walter Bromley, Philadelphia, 1890, 40 hand–colored litho maps, folio, ½ sheep, spine reinforced with cloth tape, defective, ex–library copy with canceled bookplate on front pastedown, small inked stamp in lower margin of title .. **150.00**

Atlas of the Philippine Islands, US Coast and Geodetic Survey, Washington, 1900, 24 pgs text, 30 color maps, folio, orig cloth, worn cov **50.00**

Atlas of the State of Rhode Island and Providence Plantations, D G Beers & Co, Philadelphia, 1870, 50 hand–colored maps, folio, cov detached **195.00**

Black's General Atlas of the World, Adam and Charles Black, Edinburgh, 1882, double page color maps, folio, ½ morocco, frontispiece defective **300.00**

Britannia: or a Chorographical Description of the Flourishing Kingdoms of England, Scotland, and Ireland, William Camden, London, 1806, engraved maps and plates, 4 vol, folio, ½ morocco gilt, needs rebinding **1,000.00**

Cary's New and Correct English Atlas, being a New Set of County Maps, John Cary, London, 1787, 46 engraved maps, hand–colored in outline, 4to, modern ½ morocco gilt, scattered minor browning **1,035.00**

Cram's Universal Atlas, Geographical, Astronomical, and Historical, Chicago, 1897, numerous color maps of US states, foreign countries, and 40 American cities, many double page and single page maps, small folio, orig binding, spine cov missing, covs detached **230.00**

Doubleday, Page & Co's Geographical Manual and New Atlas, NY, 1917, 380 pgs, 235 color maps and plates, small folio, orig full flexible leather binding, worn binding **50.00**

Geological and Geographical Atlas of Colorado and Portions of Adjacent Territory, Dept of Interior, Washington, 1877, Julius Bien Lithographer, 20 double sheet maps, 2 double sheets of panoramic view, large folio, cov detached, shabby spines, edge chips **300.00**

Illustrated Historical Atlas of the State of Minnesota, A T Andreas, 1874, 394 pgs, folio, leather backed, gilt dec cloth, heavily worn, spine loose, front cov and title page detached, some foxing, minor damage ... **325.00**

Joint Maps of the Northern Boundary of the United States, from the Lake of the Woods to the Summit of the Rocky Mountains, c1890, litho title, index map, 24 tinted litho boundary maps, linen backed, orig wrappers, letterpress cov label, some chipping and tearing at wrapper edges **230.00**

Maps of the Roads of Ireland..., George Taylor and Andrew Skinner, London, 1783, second edition, engraved maps, tall 8vo, early calf gilt **460.00**

Mitchell's New General Atlas, Samuel Augustus Mitchell, Philadelphia, 1869, hand–colored litho maps, small folio, ½ sheep, needs rebinding, contents clean **1,100.00**

New Statistical and Topographic Atlas of the United States with Maps showing the Dominion of Canada, Asher and Adams, NY, 1827, hand–colored double page maps, folio, modern buckram, scattered foxing **815.00**

Pier Map of New York Harbor Including Manhattan, Bronx, *Brooklyn, Long Island City, Staten Island, New Jersey Shore,* NY, 1928, 1 double page, 75 single page detailed maps of streets and buildings, large folio, half leather, cloth boards, spine badly chipped **380.00**

Rand, McNally & Co's Library Atlas of the World Containing Colored Maps of Every Country and Civil Division Upon The Face of the Globe, Historical, Descriptive, and Statistical Matter, Chicago and NY, c1894, 345 pgs, 100 maps, small folio, loose cov, maps set in on stubs **30.00**

The Bible Atlas, Samuel Arrowsmith, London, 1935, 19 engraved single and double page maps and charts, some hand–colored in outline, 4to, ½ sheep, worn, front board detached, publisher's page cov label, engraved title and index, occasional light offsetting, 2 adv leaves inserted at front **260.00**

The Columbian Atlas of the World, Large Scale Colored Maps of Each State and Territory in the United States, Provinces of Canada, Every Foreign Country, the Continents and Their Subdivisions, Cox Garretson, Buffalo, 1898, 159 pgs, color maps **110.00**

The Geography of the Ancients so far describ'd as it is cont'd in the Greek and Latin Classicks..., Geographia Classica, London, 1721, third edition, 29 double paged engraved maps, small 4to, contemporary ¼ sheep, spine worn **260.00**

The Illustrated Atlas and Modern History of the World, Robert Montgomery Martin, Tallis, London, c1850, 95 maps, most hand–colored, some double page, folio, contemporary boards, rebacked with gilt lettered leather **2,760.00**

The New Peerless Atlas of the World, Mast, Crowell & Kirkpatrick, Springfield, OH, 1898, 234 pgs, 74 colored maps and

plates, 4to, orig paper wrapper,
wear to spine **30.00**
*The North–American and the
West–Indian Gazetteer,* London,
1778, one folding map, 12mo,
later ¼ morocco, second edition
with half title **375.00**
*The Topographical Atlas of Sur-
veys. Bristol County Massachu-
setts, Containing Forty–Five
Double Page Maps, In Colors,
Of The Cities and
Towns...Together with a Dou-
ble Page Map of the United
States and the State of Massa-
chusetts, And A Driving Map of
Bristol County and Vicinity,
Showing All Roads In Color,*
Philadelphia, 1895, large folio,
Driving Map missing, edge wear   **200.00**
The World Described, Herman
Moll, T Bowles, London, c1720,
large engraved folding maps,
hand–colored in outline, folio,
contemporary sheep worn, map
of Asia defective, others gener-
ally clean **7,475.00**
*Zell's Descriptive Hand Atlas of
the World,* John Bartholomew,
Philadelphia, 1873, double page
color maps, 4to, later cloth **145.00**

BOOTJACKS

History: Bootjacks are metal or wooden
devices that facilitate the removal of boots.
Bootjacks are used by placing the heel of
the boot in the "U"–shaped opening, putting
a foot on the back of the bootjack, and pulling the front boot off the foot.

Advertising, cast iron
  Downs & Co **85.00**
  Musselman's Plug Tobacco . . .   **130.00**
  Try Me, emb **35.00**
Cast Iron
  Closed Loop, large **65.00**
  Double Ended, ornate design . .   **75.00**
  Scissor Action, marked "Pat
  1877" **85.00**
  Two pheasants and brush de-
  sign, 19" l **225.00**
  V Shape, ornate design **45.00**

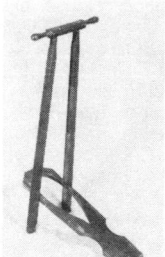

**Mixed woods, stand–up type,
19½" l, 28½" h, $60.00.**

Pine, 24" l, rosehead nails, pierced
  for hanging **40.00**
Walnut, 22" l, heart and diamond
  openwork **40.00**
Wrought Iron, 17" h, pr, rams horn
  finials, stone blades **385.00**

BOTTLES, GENERAL

History: Cosmetic bottles held special
creams, oils, and cosmetics designed to enhance the beauty of the user. Some also
claimed, especially on their colorful labels,
to cure or provide relief from common ailments.

A number of household items, e.g., cleaning fluids and polishes, required glass storage containers. Many are collected for their
fine lithograph labels.

Mineral water bottles contained water
from a natural spring. Spring water was favored by health conscious people between
the 1850s and 1900s.

Nursing bottles, used to feed the young
and sickly, were a great help to the housewife because of graduated measures, re-
placeable nipples, ease of cleaning, steril-
izing, and reuse.

References: Ralph & Terry Kovel, *The
Kovels' Bottle Price List, Ninth Edition,*
Crown Publishers, 1992; Peck and Audie
Markota, *Western Blob Top Soda and Min-
eral Bottles, Second Edition,* published by
authors, 1994; Jim Megura, *The Official
Identification and Price Guide To Bottles,*

Eleventh Edition, House of Collectibles, 1991; Diane Ostrander, *A Guide To American Nursing Bottles,* 1984, Revised Edition by American Collectors of Infant Feeders, 1992; Michael Polak, *Bottles: Identification and Price Guide,* Avon Books, 1994; Carlo & Dorothy Sellari, *The Standard Old Bottle Price Guide,* Collector Books, 1989.

Periodicals: *Antique Bottle And Glass Collector,* PO Box 187, East Greenville, PA 18041; *Bottles and Extras,* PO Box 154, Happy Camp, CA 96039.

Collectors' Clubs: American Collectors of Infant Feeders, 5161 West 59th St., Indianapolis, IN 46254; Federation of Historical Bottle Clubs, 14521 Atlantic, Riverdale, IL 60627.

Museum: National Bottle Museum, Ballston Spa, NY.

Additional Listings: Barber Bottles, Bitter Bottles, Figural Bottles, Food Bottles, Ink Bottles, Medicine Bottles, Poison Bottles, Sarsaparilla Bottles and Snuff Bottles. Also see the bottle categories in *Warman's Americana & Collectibles* for more examples.

COSMETIC

Ayers Hair Vigor, 7¼" h, peacock blue	35.00
Barry's Pearl Cream, 4¾" h, milk glass	8.00
Bush's Argentine Hair Dye, #2, aqua, open pontil	35.00
Circassian Hair Restorative, 7" h, deep amber	200.00
Fontaines Cream Of Wild Flowers, 4⅞" h, aqua, open pontil	425.00
John Fitch Co, Youngstown, OH, 5¾" h, clear	10.00
Larkin Co, 6" h, clear	5.00
Lufkin Eczema Remedy, 7" h, clear, label	8.00
Nathan Jarvis Orris Tooth Wash, 4⅞" h, aqua, open pontil	110.00
Palmolive Shampoo, B J Johnson, 4" h, paneled, aqua	8.00
Rose Hair Tonic & Dandruff Cure, 7¾" h, clear, label under glass	45.00

HOUSEHOLD

Bengal Bluing, 5¾" h, aqua	5.00
Carbona, 5" h, aqua	5.00
Electrical Bicycle Lubricating Oil, 4¼" h, oval, clear	175.00
FS Pease Sewing Machine Oil, 5⅜" h, light blue, open pontil	325.00
Liquid Stove Polish, 6¼" h, clear	3.00
Patent Gutta Percha Oil Blacking, 5½" h, amber, open pontil	1,500.00
Shulife–For Shoes, 3¾" h, olive green	5.00
Uptons Refined Liquid Glue, 2⅞" h, aqua, twelve sided, open pontil	50.00
Utility, 6½" h, rect, yellow–green, fluted corners, applied mouth	100.00

MINERAL OR SPRING WATER

Blue Lick Water Co, KY, pt, cylindrical, twelve sided, scalloped, dark olive amber, collared mouth rim, iron pontil	450.00
Blue Mountain Forest Mineral Water, 10" h, tall cylindrical, cobalt blue, emb stag's head, tooled round collared mouth	990.00
Congress & Empire Spring Co/C, qt, cylindrical, olive yellow, sloping collared mouth	325.00
Congress & Empire Spring Co/ Hotchkiss Sons, qt, cylindrical, emerald green, sloping collared mouth	100.00
Deep Rock Spring Mineral Water, cylindrical, golden amber, collared mouth with ring	275.00
Eureka Spring Co, pt, torpedo form, aquamarine, collared mouth with ring	365.00
GKW Co, qt, cylindrical, olive yellow, sloping collared mouth	525.00
Massena Spring Water, qt, cylindrical, blue–green, collared mouth with ring	90.00
Saratog/A/Spring Co, pt, cylindrical, emerald green	275.00
Saratoga/Vichy/Water, qt, cylindrical, amber, sloping collared mouth with ring	355.00

NURSING

Burr Co, Boston, MA, aqua	40.00
Happy Baby, clear, boy and girl	15.00

Little Papoose, 8" h **150.00**
Nonpareil Nurser, 5½" h, aqua .. **20.00**
Sunshine Dairy, 8 oz, picture of
  baby, orig cap **5.00**
Universal Feeder **15.00**

BRASS

History: Brass is a durable, malleable, and ductile metal alloy consisting mainly of copper and zinc. It achieved its greatest popularity for utilitarian and decorative art items in the 18th and 19th centuries.

References: Mary Frank Gaston, *Antique Brass & Copper: Identification & Value Guide,* Collector Books, 1992, 1994 value update; Dana G. Morykan and Harry L. Rinker, *Warman's Country Antiques & Collectibles, Second Edition,* Wallace–Homestead, 1994; Peter, Nancy, and Herbert Schiffer, *The Brass Book,* Schiffer Publishing, 1978.

Additional Listings: Bells, Candlesticks, Fireplace Equipment, and Scientific Instruments.

Reproduction Alert: Many modern reproductions are being made of earlier brass forms, especially in the areas of buckets, fireplace equipment, and kettles.

Andirons, pr
  13¼" h, turned stems, epoxy
    joint stem on one **55.00**

**Candlesticks, pr, Adams-type, 7"
h, $245.00.**

14¾" h, ball finials **330.00**
15½" h, polished, partial replaced pads on feet **275.00**
16½" h, belted ball finials, c1830 **450.00**
20½" h, ball and spire finials,
  early 19th C **300.00**
Bedwarmer
  36" l, floral tooled lid, turned
    wood handle **200.00**
  43" l, pierced and floral engraved
    lid, rope twist wood handle,
    polished **500.00**
  45½" l, engraved floral design
    with star, turned wood handle,
    marked "E R" and crown ... **275.00**
Bird Cage, sq, brass and copper,
  19th C **300.00**
Candelabra, 16¾" h, three candle
  arms with prisms, mid 19th C .. **175.00**
Candle Sconce
  17¾" h, pr, beveled mirrors,
    worn **85.00**
  18½" h, pr, ornate, three candle
    sockets **325.00**
  22½" h, ornate, beveled mirror
    back, two candle sockets, gilt
    dec **50.00**
  22¾" h, cast, mirror back, urn
    and dolphin dec, two candle
    sockets **75.00**
Candlestick
  6" h, pr
    Beehive detail, pushups **150.00**
    Victorian, pushups **95.00**
  6½" h, Continental, late 17th C,
    imperfections **1,100.00**
  7" h, Queen Anne, petal base,
    soldered repair **165.00**
  7¼" h, Queen Anne, octagonal
    base, soldered stem **200.00**
  7⅝" h, pr, Neoclassical, side
    pushups **385.00**
  8¾" h, pr, screw paneled stems,
    round base **55.00**
  8⅞" h, pr, Victorian, beehive and
    diamond quilted detail, push-
    ups **145.00**
  10" h, pr, Empire, gilt and eagle
    dec **475.00**
  10⅝" h, pr, Victorian, silver-
    plated traces, marked "En-
    glish" **135.00**
  11¾" h, pr, Victorian, "The Dia-
    mond Prince," pushups **165.00**

19½" h, pr, pushups, England,
late 19th C **410.00**
Coal Hod, 14" d, 19" h, decorative
detail, paw feet **145.00**
Chocolate Pot, 10½" h, Continental, 19th C **690.00**
Curtain Tiebacks, Victorian, 20
pcs **325.00**
Fire Bell, 14" h, turned wood handle, polished **175.00**
Fireplace Fender, reticulated grill
and top rail, paw feet **385.00**
Fireplace Set, Federal, 23" h andirons, urn shape finials, matching tools, c1800 .... **1,650.00**
Footman, 14½" h, England, 19th C **475.00**
Ink Stand, seated elephant centering two pineapple and leaf wells,
pen tray in front **385.00**
Kettle
11" d, cast, polished, wrought
iron bail handle **145.00**
13½" d, 6¾" h, heavy spun
brass, iron bail handle **85.00**
Lamp
Lucerne, 10½" h, double spout
font, accessories on chain ... **250.00**
Oil, 26" h, Victorian, pink and
green foliate dec shade, supported by bracket arm on standard, round foot **345.00**
Mirror, pr, 16½" h, 12" w, cast, Rococo style, two candle arms ... **255.00**
Mortar and Pestle, 5¼" h, knop-
like handles **50.00**
Muffin Bell, 10" l, turned handle,
polished **225.00**
Plant Stand, 13½" w, 32¾" h,
American Aesthetic Movement,
cast, rect top with recessed center well, 1880–85 .... **925.00**
Samovar, 17½" h, converted to
lamp, Russian hallmarks, late
19th C **45.00**
Scissor Wick Trimmers, 7½" h,
stand **275.00**
Skimmer
17¼" l, polished bowl, wrought
iron handle with cutout heart
and brass inlay **155.00**
20" l, wrought iron handle,
marked "F B S Canton, O
'86" **90.00**
Stencil, barrel label, 21" d, set of

2, one marked "Grain Alcohol,"
other "Vodka" **125.00**
Straight Edge, draftsman's, 19½"
l, polished, wood case, engraved
"Adie London" **100.00**
Surveying Instrument, 5¾" l, polished, English **115.00**
Tea Kettle, 9" h, swivel handle,
stand **60.00**
Trammel, 6" l, sawtooth **165.00**
Tray, 16¼" l, nautical design,
stamped "1910" **125.00**
Trivet
6¾ x 8", reticulated, paw feet .. **70.00**
13" l, curved reticulated top, cabriole legs **25.00**
Vase, 23½" h, lion head and ring
handles, claw foot **120.00**
Wall Sconces, pr, 12⅞" h, emb,
double arm, 20th C **285.00**
Wick Trimmer, tray **75.00**

BREAD PLATES

History: Beginning in the mid-1880s,
special trays or platters were made for serving bread and rolls. Designated by collectors as "bread plates," these small trays or
platters can be found in porcelain, glass
(especially pattern glass), and metals.

Bread plates often were part of a china
or glass set. However, many glass companies made special plates which honored national heroes, commemorated historical or
special events, offered a moral maxim, or
supported a religious attitude. The theme
on the plate could be either in a horizontal
or vertical format. The favorite shape for
these plates is oval, with a common length
being ten inches.

Reference: Anna Maude Stuart, *Bread
Plates And Platters,* published by author,
1965.

Additional Listings: Pattern Glass.

Commemorative, glass
Garfield Memorial **60.00**
Grapes, motto **45.00**
Liberty Bell, signers, handle hair-
line **95.00**
McKinley, oval **90.00**
Old State House, large, flat ... **75.00**
Teddy Roosevelt, frosted center **145.00**

McKinley, glass, clear, birth and death dates, 1901, 8 x 10½" l, $90.00.

Three Presidents	**85.00**
U S Grant	**65.00**
Milk Glass, Wheat & Barley	**60.00**
Nippon, gaudy, green and gold, pink aster dec	**225.00**
Noritake, 10" l, hp center scene and stylized flowers, wide border, gold handle	**65.00**

Pattern Glass

Actress, 7 x 12", HMS Pinafore	**90.00**
Ashman, motto	**55.00**
Barley, clear	**30.00**
Beaded Grape, emerald green .	**45.00**
Beautiful Lady, clear	**15.00**
Cape Cod, clear	**45.00**
Chain with Star, 11" l, handled .	**30.00**
Cupid and Venus, amber	**75.00**

Dahlia

Apple Green	**70.00**
Clear	**45.00**
Finecut and Panel, amber	**50.00**
Kansas, Our Daily Bread, clear	**45.00**
Lion, 12" l, frosted	**90.00**
Maryland, clear, gold dec	**25.00**
New Jersey, clear, gold dec ...	**30.00**
Question Mark, clear	**30.00**
Sprig, clear	**40.00**
Westward Ho!, clear	**175.00**

BRIDE'S BASKETS

History: A ruffled edge, glass bowl in a metal holder was a popular wedding gift in the 1880–1910 era, hence, the name of "bride's basket." The glass bowls can be found in most glass types of the period. The metal holder was generally silver plated with a bail handle, thus enhancing the basket image.

Over the years, bowls and bases became separated and married pieces resulted. When the base has been lost, the bowl is sold separately.

Reference: John Mebane, *Collecting Bride's Baskets And Other Glass Fancies,* Wallace–Homestead, 1976.

Reproduction Alert: The glass bowls have been reproduced.

Note: Items listed have silver–plated holder unless otherwise noted.

Cased, pink int., purple rim, SP base, $125.00.

Cameo Glass
  Cased white to rose–red cut back with winged griffins, floral bouquets, and swags, squared crimped edge, Mount Washington, fitted within marked "Pairpoint" SP metal mount with leaf and berry dec handle, 8" sq, 10½" h **825.00**
  Overlay, 8½ x 3½" h bowl with off–white ext. and shaded rose int., crystal ruffled edge, SP basket marked "Rogers & Bros," two small hands, chains, and fruit design on holder, 9¾" d, 11" h **285.00**
Colored Glass
  Dark Pink, gold flowers and leaves dec, ruffled edge, 10½" d **295.00**
  Raspberry ground, opalescent

seaweed dec, tightly crimped rim, 10" d **175.00**

Crown Milano, 4½" h tricorn bowl, ruffled rim, six large pansies, pale purple and orange tracery medallions, pale yellow int., orig tri–cornered ftd stand sgd "Pairpoint," numbered #2261, 11" d, 11½" h **2,750.00**

Peachblow, shaded raspberry to creamy white, emb rib pattern, ruffled, New Martinsville, SP basket holder, 10¼" d, 4" h, 12½" h overall **300.00**

Satin Glass

Blue and white 12" d x 3" h bowl, leaf type edge, resilvered holder, 13" d, 13" h **325.00**

Dark red shaded to cream, Victorian, ruffled and crimped rim, mounted in SP stand, 11½" d, 12" h **275.00**

Mother–of–Pearl 11½" w x 7" h bulbous jack–in–the–pulpit bowl, emb frieze, SP heart stand with two full figured cherubs, marked "Rogers & Brothers, Taunton, MA," 14½" h......................**1,875.00**

Pink, DQ, MOP, rect 7 x 10½ x 5" h bowl, closely ruffled, frosted binding, resilvered SP basket holder, marked "Manhattan," 12½" d, 10¾" h **795.00**

Pink shaded to opal, Victorian, floral form, floral filigree dec, 11½" d, 4" h **130.00**

Silver

German, waisted form, pierced rococo style design, glass liner, crack in liner, 30 troy oz **650.00**

Sterling

9¾" l, 16" h, cast reticulated decagonal waisted basket form frame with panel dec showing C–scrolls, flowers, cartouches with couples, and amatory trophies, lace–like openwork, swing handle centered with quiver and bow motif, gilt int., conforming clear glass liner, Louis XVI taste, pseudo hallmarks, early 20th C **1,210.00**

13½" h, pierced and engraved boat shape, Whiting, 1916, approx 28 troy oz **825.00**

BRISTOL GLASS

History: Bristol glass is a designation given to a semi–opaque glass, usually decorated with enamel and cased with another color.

Initially, the term referred only to glass made in Bristol, England, in the 17th and 18th centuries. By the Victorian era firms on the Continent and in America were copying the glass and its forms.

Vase, cream ground, green, yellow, and blue bird dec, 12¼" h, $95.00.

Cruet, 6¾" h, enameled floral design **15.00**

Decanter, 11½" h, opaque rose shading to deep rose ground, purple flowers, gilt butterfly on neck, applied handle, marbleized rose and white stopper **115.00**

Ewer, 4½" h, 2¾" d, turquoise blue, enameled pink flowers, white and green leaves, yellow scrolls, gold trim, applied turquoise handles, price for pair .. **140.00**

Goblet, 10¾" h, pedestal base, opaque blue ground, polychrome enamel floral dec, gilt trim **85.00**

Lamp
27″ h, Victorian, brass mounted, glass globe and body molded in high relief foliate and cherub's head dec, polychrome enamel painted floral reserves, electrified 470.00
32½″ h, white with blue enameled and gilt dec, white columns ending in turned heavy bases, brass finial, price for pair 250.00
Miniature Lamp, 10″ h, 4¾″ d, white shaded to soft blue, dainty enameled orange flowers, green leaves, sq ruffled shade, base with matching flowers and brown flying bird, applied opalescent shell feet, orig burner and chimney 885.00
Mug, 5⅞″ h, 1 pint, opaque white ground, romantic landscape scene, late 18th or early 19th C **1,000.00**
Patch Box, 1″ h, 1¼″ d, hinged, soft pink ground, enameled brown and white bird 100.00
Sweetmeat Jar, 5½″ h, 4½″ d, floral garlands and butterflies dec, silverplated top and bail handle 125.00
Vase
5″ h, 2½″ d, turquoise blue, bands of gold, pink enameled flowers with yellow centers, yellow leaf and dot dec, ftd, price for pr 148.00

BRITISH ROYALTY COMMEMORATIVES

History: British commemorative china, souvenirs to commemorate coronations and other royal events, dates from the 1600s, with the early pieces being rather crude in design and form. The development of transfer printing, c1780, led to a much closer likeness of the reigning monarch on the ware.

Few commemorative pieces predating Queen Victoria's reign are found today at popular prices. Items associated with Queen Elizabeth II and her children, e.g.,

the wedding of HRH Prince Andrew and Miss Sarah Ferguson and the subsequent birth of their daughter, HRH Princess Beatrice, are very common.

Some British Royalty commemoratives are easily recognized by their portraits of past or present monarchs. Some may be in silhouette profile. Other royal symbols include crowns, dragons, royal coats of arms, national flowers, swords, scepters, dates, messages, and initials.

References: Susan and Al Bagdade, *Warman's English & Continental Pottery & Porcelain, Second Edition,* Wallace–Homestead, 1991; Malcolm Davey and Doug Mannion, *50 Years of Royal Commemorative China 1887–1937,* Dayman Publications, 1988; Douglas H. Flynn and Alan R. Bolton, *British Royalty Commemoratives: 19th & 20th Century Royal Events In Britain Illustrated by Commemoratives, Value Guide with Photographs,* Schiffer Publishing, 1994; Lincoln Hallinan, *British Commemoratives: Royalty, Politics, War and Sport,* Antique Collectors' Club, 1993; Josephine Jackson, *Fired For Royalty,* Heaton Moor, 1977; Peter Johnson, *Royal Memorabilia: A Phillips Collectors Guide,* Dunestyle Publishing, 1988; Eric Knowles, *Miller's Royal Memorabilia,* Millers Publications, 1994; John May, *Victoria Remembered, A Royal History 1817–1861,* London, 1983; John and Jennifer May, *Commemorative Pottery 1780–1900, A Guide for Collectors,* Charles Scribner's Sons, 1972; David Rogers, *Coronation Souvenirs and Commemoratives,* Latimer New Dimensions, 1975; Sussex Commemorative Ware Centre, *200 Commemoratives,* Metra Print Enterprises, 1979; Geoffrey Warren, *Royal Souvenirs,* Orbis, 1977.

Collectors' Club: Commemorative Collector's Society, 25 Farndale Close, Long Eaton, Nottingham NG10 3PA England.

Advisors: Doug Flynn and Al Bolton.

Additional Listings: See *Warman's Americana & Collectibles* for more examples.

Beaker
Elizabeth II, 1953 Coronation, 3½″ h, Poole **35.00**
George VI, 1937 Coronation, 4⅝″ h **75.00**

Bust, Victoria, parian, 1897 Jubilee, imp "Turner and Wood, Jubilee," 13″ h, $225.00.

Bowl
  Elizabeth II, 1959 Canada Visit,
    1½″ h, Royal Albert 50.00
  George VI/Elizabeth, 1937 Coronation, coat of arms, 5½″ d,
    Paragon 45.00
  Victoria, 1901, In Memoriam,
    9½″ d, pressed glass 100.00
Box, Elizabeth II, 1977 Jubilee,
  raised flowers, 1⅞″ d, Crown
  Staffordshire 20.00
Cake Plate, Victoria, 1897 Jubilee,
  sepia portraits, residences, Man
  of War, 10¾″ d 130.00
Cup and Saucer
  Charles/Diana, 1981 Wedding,
    Duchess 30.00
  Edward VII/Alexandra, 1888 Silver Wedding Anniversary, coat
    of arms, oversize 175.00
  George VI/Elizabeth, 1937 Coronation, sepia portraits with
    Princess Elizabeth and Margaret, Welworth 45.00
Jar, cov, Elizabeth II, 1953 coronation 39.00
Jug
  Elizabeth II, 1953 Coronation,
    emb crowning scene, 8¼″ h,
    Burleigh Ware 240.00
  George VI/Elizabeth, 1937 Coronation, musical, sepia portraits, Princess Elizabeth/Margaret on reverse, Shelley . . . 260.00

Lithophane
  Alexandra, 1902, cup, crown,
    and cypher, 2¾″ h 190.00
  Edward VII, 1902, mug, crown,
    and cypher, 2¾″ h 95.00
  George V, 1911, mug, crown,
    and cypher, 2¾″ h 150.00
  Mary, 1911, cup, crown, and cypher, 2¾″ h 270.00
Loving Cup
  Elizabeth II, 1972 Silver Wedding Anniversary, 3″ h, Paragon 175.00
  George VI/Elizabeth, 1937 Coronation, brown portrait, 3¼″ h,
    Marcus Adams, Sampson
    Smith 135.00
  Victoria, 1897 Jubilee, brown
    portrait, 4″ h, Victoria 175.00
Miniature, Prince Charles and
  Diana, copper, hand enameled,
  gilt wood frame, wedding 25.00
Mug
  Duke/Duchess of Windsor, In
    Memoriam, black and white
    portraits, important dates, 3⅜″
    h, Dorincourt 55.00
  George VI, 1939 visit, Royal
    Winton 35.00
  Prince Charles and Diana, glass,
    enameled, wedding 35.00
  Victoria, 1887 Jubilee, color
    beaded crown and ribbon, 3¼″
    h, William Whiteley 90.00
Paperweight
  Edward VIII, 1937 Coronation,
    black and white portrait, 4¼″ l,
    1⅛″ h 20.00
  Victoria/Albert, black and white
    portraits, color and glitter, 2⅞″
    d 30.00
Pin Tray
  Edward VII/Alexandra, 1902
    Coronation, sepia portraits, 4″
    d 40.00
  George VI, 1937 Coronation, sepia portrait, 3″ sq, Royal
    Crown Derby 40.00
  Victoria, 1897 Jubilee, sepia portrait, 5″ d 45.00
Pitcher
  Elizabeth, 1953 Coronation,
    brown portrait, 6¼″ h, Royal
    Doulton 185.00

Victoria, 1887 Jubilee, black and
white portrait, 5″ h **120.00**
Plate
Charles, 1969 Investiture as
Prince of Wales, sepia portrait,
8″ d, Coronet **65.00**
Edward VII/Alexandra, 1902
Coronation, color portraits, 7″
d...................... **50.00**
Elizabeth II
5⅞″ d, 1953 coronation, Stanley China **20.00**
6½″ d, 1953 coronation, Clarice Cliff, numbered **25.00**
8⅞″ d, 1953 coronation, Staffordshire **35.00**
10″ d, 1959 Canadian visit, St
Lawrence Seaway, Eisen-
hower **50.00**
George VI
8″ d, 1939 visit, little princess,
Manitoba merchant givea-
way **45.00**
8⅞″ d, 1939 visit, Woods **35.00**
Princess Margaret, Birth, para-
keets, flowers, 6″ d, Paragon **75.00**
Victoria, 150th Anniversary of
Coronation, gold portrait, 10½″
d, limited edition 150, Caver-
swall **135.00**
Playing Cards
Edward VIII, 1919 Canada Visit,
color portrait, single deck, C
Goodall & Co **75.00**

**Coke Bottle, Prince Charles and
Lady Diana, Royal Wedding, July
29, 1981, $15.00.**

Elizabeth II, 1977 Jubilee, sepia
portrait, single deck, Wadding-
tons **25.00**
George V/Mary, 1911 Corona-
tion, color portraits, double
deck **75.00**
Shaving Mug
Edward VII/Alexandra, 1902
Coronation, color portraits,
3¾″ h.................... **100.00**
Elizabeth II, 1953 Coronation,
color portrait, 4″ h **70.00**
George VI/Elizabeth, 1937 Cor-
onation, sepia portraits, 4½″ h,
Shelley **95.00**
Teapot
Charlotte, In Memoriam, black
and white dec, 6″ h **275.00**
Edward VII/Alexandra, 1902
Coronation, color portraits,
4¾″ h **65.00**
Elizabeth II, 1953 Coronation,
relief portraits, Jasperware,
white on royal blue, 5″ h,
Wedgwood **225.00**
George V/Mary, 1911 Corona-
tion, color portraits with Prince
of Wales, 6″ h, bone china .. **255.00**
Victoria, 1897 Jubilee, color coat
of arms, 6″ h, Aynsley **250.00**
Tea Set, Elizabeth II, 1953 Coro-
nation, teapot, cream and sugar,
relief portraits, Jasperware,
white on royal blue, Wedgwood **325.00**
Tin
Edward VII/Alexandra, 1902
Coronation, color portrait, 5 x
3½″, Ridgway Ltd. Tea **95.00**
Edward VIII, 1937 Coronation,
color portrait, hinged lid, 5¾ x
3¾″, Riley's Toffee **45.00**
Elizabeth II, young image,
Trooping of the Colors **35.00**
George V/Mary, 1935 Jubilee,
color portraits, 6¾ x 4½″ **45.00**
George VI/Elizabeth, 1937 Coronation, sepia Vandyk portrait,
4½ x 3¼ x 5¾″ **50.00**
Princess Mary, 1914 Christmas,
brass, emb profile, hinged lid,
4¾ x 3 x 1″ **50.00**
Victoria, 1897 Jubilee, color dec,
accession picture on lid, 5½ x
3½ x 3½″ **100.00**

Tumbler, George VI, 3⅞" h, ceramic **65.00**

BRONZE

History: Bronze is an alloy of copper, tin, and traces of other metals. It has been used since Biblical times not only for art objects, but also for utilitarian purposes. After a slump in the Middle Ages, bronze was revived in the 17th century and continued in popularity until the early 20th century.

References: Pierre Kjellberg, *The Bronzes of the Nineteenth Century: Dictionary of Sculptors,* Schiffer Publishing, 1994; Lynne and Fritz Weber, *Jacobsen's Thirteenth Painting and Bronze Price Guide, January 1992 to January 1994,* Weber Publications, 1994.

Notes: Do not confuse a "bronzed" object with a true bronze. A bronzed object usually is made of white metal and then coated with a reddish–brown material to give it a bronze appearance. A magnet will stick to it.

A signed bronze commands a higher market price than an unsigned one. There also are "signed" reproductions on the market. It is very important to know the history of the mold and the background of the foundry.

Figurine, bull with Piccolo Pete, carrying bucket, $175.00.

Candelabra, ormolu mounted, figural, six–light, each with similarly posed boy seated on stump, one modeled with cloven feet, other with human feet, holding three–light vining trumpets in each hand, inscribed "Clodion," electrified, late 19th C, 31" h, pr **4,315.00**

Candlesticks, Louis XVI style, convertible, urn form, early 20th C, 7" h, pr **635.00**

Chenets, each with central urn flanked by pr of birds on vines, Louis XVI style, 11⅛" l, 13⅝" h, pr **635.00**

Cigarette Humidor, rect, carved figural, geometric, and fruit dec, E F Caldwell & Co, NY, 6⅛" w, 4¼" d, 2¼" h **345.00**

Clock, Charles X, gilt and patinated, figural, second quarter 19th C, 14" h **520.00**

Compote, French, Neoclassical style, circular bronze stand surmounted by lion's head masks with rings, four legs with paw feet, X–form stretcher base, polished cut glass compote insert, late 19th/early 20th C, 5¾" d, 6⅛" h **575.00**

Figural Group
   Bacchanalian, dancing baccante and baby satyr, dark patina, Claude Michel Clodion, 1738–1814, 22" h **2,750.00**
   Girl with sheep, Jean Chateignon, Paris, dark patina, 1911–24, 9¼" w, 11" h **575.00**
   Minstrel, two black boys, one playing banjo, pink marble base, dark copper and gilt patina, damaged, 20th C, 6¾" h **490.00**
   Pegasus and Perseus, inscribed "E Picault, Salon des Beaux Arts," brown patina, late 19th C, 19¼" h **635.00**
   Youth offering food to rooster, Austrian, late 19th/early 20th C, 6⅜" h **285.00**

Figure
   American Indian, "Lurking Scout," Carl Kauba, Austria, dark gilt patina, c1908, 7½" h **625.00**
   Bear, standing, repaired marble base, late 19th/early 20th C, 23½" h **1,725.00**
   Cherub, playing cello, back of cello signed "August Moreau, Paris," dark patina, rust marble base, late 19th C, 6" h **460.00**

German Industrial Miner, holding miner's pick, signed "Hasse, fer.," dark patina, red marble base, chips, 1930s, 14½" h .. **630.00**

Moroccan Soldier, cleaning rifle barrel, Jean–Didier Debut, prix de Rome, medium patina, mid 19th C, 15⅜" h **1,275.00**

Narcissus, nude, circular base, Italian foundry marks, verdigris, second half 19th C, 24½" h **1,025.00**

Setter Dog, on point, Pierre Jules Mene, dark patina, mid 19th C, 13⅛" l **800.00**

Soldier, French, inscribed "Susse Freres Editeurs, Paris," green marble base, late 19th C, 42" h **1,850.00**

Venus, F Barbedienne Fondeur, stamped "Reduction Mecanique A Collas," 19th C, 37½" h **1,150.00**

Wounded Panther, large cat with two arrows through body, Charles Valton, gold patina, 1851–1918, 17½" l, 11" h ... **450.00**

WWI Soldier, advancing, Emile Joseph Nestor Carlier, 1849–1927, gold patina, gun damaged, 11½" h **225.00**

Young girl holding a bouquet of flowers, seated, inscribed "Ruth Milles, Founder's Seal of Eug. Blot, Paris," c1900, 6½" h **490.00**

Youth emerging from lotus flower, holding bird, mounted on marble base, Egyptian, 5" h **775.00**

Lamp
Cylindrical form with raised floral medallions and archaic borders, Japanese, late 19th/early 20th C, 27½" h, pr **550.00**

Figural, oil, bird's body front and neck, single claw foot, 19th C **500.00**

Model, Napoleon's column, shaft with raised bands of military scenes, black marble base, dark patina, 19th C, 18⅛" h **1,265.00**

Pen Wiper, Austrian, painted, contoured bristles set in donkey's back, some paint wear, late 19th/early 20th C, 5⅞" l, 5⅞" h **200.00**

Plaque, Italian, classical female in relief, signed "F. Nisini–Roma," mounted to wooden frame, 19th C, 13½" h **345.00**

Table Base, Neoclassical style, verdigris, folding X–form, rect inset marble top, 28" h **4,025.00**

Trophy Plaque, game bag, hare, and pheasant hanging from nail, Pierre Jules Mene, rect board, dark patina, 1850, 6½" w, 12¼" h **450.00**

Urn
Classical dec, bright gilt and dark green patination, one damaged, 19th C, 7⅞" h, pr .**3,100.00**

Mythological subjects in relief, double handled, mounted atop cylindrical rouge marble base, damage, French, 19th C, 9½" h **90.00**

Vase
Classical subjects with greek key and stylized palmette borders, double handled, late 19th C, 21" h, pr **700.00**

Stylized raised dec, Chinese, 19th C, 15¾" h **145.00**

BUFFALO POTTERY

History: Buffalo Pottery Co., Buffalo, New York, was chartered in 1901. The first kiln was fired in October 1903. Larkin Soap Company established Buffalo Pottery to produce premiums for its extensive mail order business. Wares also were sold to the public by better department and jewelry stores. Elbert Hubbard and Frank L. Wright, who designed the Larkin Administration Building in Buffalo in 1904, were two prominent names associated with the Larkin Company.

Early production consisted mainly of dinner sets of semi–vitreous china. Buffalo was the first pottery in the United States to produce successfully the Blue Willow pattern, marked "First Old Willow Ware Mfg. in America." Buffalo also made a line of hand decorated, multicolored willow ware, called Gaudy Willow. Other early items include a series of game, fowl, and fish sets, pitchers, jugs, and a line of commemorative, historical, and advertising plates and mugs.

In 1908–09 and 1921–23, Buffalo Pottery produced the line for which it is most famous, Deldare Ware. The earliest of this olive green, semi–vitreous china depicts hand decorated scenes from English artist Cecil Aldin's Fallowfield Hunt. Hunt scenes were only done in 1908–09. English village scenes also were characteristic and found throughout the series. Most are artist signed.

In 1911 Buffalo Pottery produced Emerald Deldare, which used scenes from Goldsmith's The Three Tours of Dr. Syntax and an Art Nouveau type border. Completely decorated Art Nouveau pieces also were made.

In 1912 Abino was born. Abino was done on Deldare bodies and showed sailing, windmill, and seascape scenes. The main color was rust. All pieces are artist signed and numbered.

In 1915 the pottery was modernized, giving it the ability to produce vitrified china. Consequently, hotel and institutional ware became their main production, with hand–decorated ware de–emphasized. Buffalo china became a leader in producing and designing the most famous railroad, hotel, and restaurant patterns. These wares, especially railroad items, are eagerly sought by collectors.

In the early 1920s, fine china was made for home use, e.g., the Bluebird pattern. In 1950 Buffalo made their first Christmas plate. They were given away to customers and employees from 1950–60. Hample Equipment Co. ordered some in 1962. The Christmas plates are very scarce.

The Buffalo China Company made "Buffalo Pottery" and "Buffalo China," the difference being that one is semi–vitreous ware and the other vitrified. In 1956 the company was reorganized, and Buffalo China became the corporate name. Today Buffalo China is owned by Oneida Silver Company. The Larkin family no longer is involved.

Reference: Seymour and Violet Altman, The Book Of Buffalo Pottery, reprinted by Schiffer Publishing, 1987.

Note: Numbers in parentheses refer to plates in the Altmans' book.

Advisor: Seymour & Violet Altman.

Willow Ware, gravy boat, blue mark, dated 1911, $35.00.

ABINO WARE

Pitcher, 7" h, Portland, ME Portland Head Light, octagonal (256)	**950.00**
Plate, 6½" d, bread and butter, windmill scene (243)	**300.00**
Tea Tile, 6" d, nautical scene (259)	**700.00**

BLUE AND GAUDY WILLOW

Blue Willow

Creamer (26)	**35.00**
Cup and Saucer (26)	**25.00**
Plate, 9¼" d (26)	**25.00**
Platter, 16" l, 13" w (24)	**60.00**
Teapot, round, 6 cup	**100.00**

Gaudy Willow

Butter Pat	**25.00**
Pitcher, 8" h (C8)	**385.00**
Plate, 10½" d (28)	**140.00**

COMMERCIAL SERVICES

Bowl, 6" d, 2¼" h, matching 11¼" w handled serving plate, Roy-

croft Inn, handles dec with stylized leaves, both pieces with
Roycroft green and brick red
geometric pattern and logo, sgd,
some crackling 550.00
Cake Plate, 10" d, Roycroft Inn
(288) 200.00
Creamer and Sugar Bowl, 2¾" h
creamer, 3½" h sugar, Roycroft
logo and green and brick red
pattern, sgd "Buffalo Pottery
1926, Roycroft," hairline to
creamer, chip to sugar underside   385.00
Cup and Saucer, George Wash-
ington (276) 275.00
Plate
  9" d, Fairview Golf Club (298) .   80.00
  9½" d, dinner, set of four, Roycroft Inn, logo integrated in
  green and brick red geometric
  pattern, stamped "Buffalo Pottery, Semi–Vitreous" 470.00
Salt and Pepper Shakers, pr, 2¾"
h, Roycroft Inn, orb mark on
ivory ground, green border
around top, brick red and green
geometric designs outlined in
black, marked "Buffalo Pottery
1926, Roycroft," hairline in salt-
shaker base 275.00

DELDARE

Candlestick, 9½" h, untitled scene,
1909, sgd "WF" (156) 475.00
Cereal Bowl, set of four, 6½" d, 2"
h, Ye Olden Days, earth tones,
olive green body, indistinct artists' signatures "A. Wade,"
stamped mark on base, 1908
(154) 250.00
Creamer and Sugar, scenes of Vil-
lage Life in Ye Olden Days,
some crazing (138) 295.00
Fruit Bowl, 9" d, 3¾" h, Ye Village
Tavern, earth tones, olive green
body, artist sgd "Stiner,"
stamped mark on base, 1908
(152) 250.00
Humidor, cov, 6¾" h, octagonal, Ye
Lion Inn, L Winter artist, base
marked with "Buffalo Pottery
Deldare Ware" logo, artist's

name on side, chips on inside
rim (174) 325.00
Pitcher, 8" h, Welcome Me with
most Cordial Hospitality, To demand my annual Rent (168) . . .   425.00
Platter, 13½" l, The Fallowfield
Hunt, the Start, earth tones, olive
green body, artist sgd "L. Anna,"
1908 . . . .   195.00

EMERALD DELDARE

Cup and Saucer, Dr Syntax At Liv-
erpool (181) 400.00
Fern Dish, 8" d, butterflies and
flowers (186) 750.00
Plate, 8¼" d, Misfortune At Tulip
Hall, sgd E Miessel (213B) 600.00

GAME SETS

Deer Set, 7 pcs, oval platter and
six plates, wild game motif, sage
green border 150.00
Pitcher, 6⅜" h, buffalo calf and Indians hunting buffalo, teal blue
on white ground, solid teal blue
handle, rim with gold highlighting, stamped, wear under spout
(47) 300.00

HISTORICAL, COMMEMORATIVE, AND ADVERTISING WARE

Milk Jug, 6" h, The Whaling City
scenes, green and white, inscribed "Souvenir of New Bed-
ford, Mass." (38) 325.00
Mug, 3½" h, Beechland Farms
(112) 95.00
Plate
  7½" d
    George Washington (101) . . .   250.00
    Old Fellows Hall, Cambridge-
    port, Mass. (96) 85.00
  10" d
    New Bedford, Massachusetts–
    New Bedford Fifty Years
    Ago, green and white (85) .   65.00
    Niagara Falls (81) 60.00

MISCELLANEOUS

Cake Plate, 6" d (324) 35.00

Dinner Set, 100 pcs, Maple Leaf
(314) **400.00**
Feeding Dish, Mary Had A Little
Lamb (331) **50.00**
Pitcher, 8″ h, diamond shaped,
polychrome dec brown transfer
dec, paneled Roosevelt Bear
scenes, each titled and versed,
printed mark "Buffalo Pottery
1907 copyright Edward Stern &
Co," hairlines, staining (42) **990.00**
Plate, 9″ w, garden scene, Rouge
Lamelle body (349) **115.00**

BURMESE GLASS

History: Burmese glass is a translucent
art glass originated by Frederick Shirley and
manufactured by the Mt. Washington Glass
Co., New Bedford, Massachusetts, from
1885 to c1891.

Burmese glass shades from a soft lemon
to a salmon pink. Uranium was used to attain the yellow color and gold was added to
the batch so that on reheating one end
turned pink. Upon reheating again, the
edges would revert to the yellow coloring.
The blending of the colors was so gradual
that it was difficult to determine where one
color ended and the other began.

Although some of the glass has a surface
that is glossy, most of it is acid finished. The
majority of the items were free blown, but
some were blown molded in a ribbed, hobnail, or diamond quilted design.

American–made Burmese is quite thin,
fragile, and brittle. The only factory licensed
to make Burmese was Thos. Webb & Sons
in England. Out of deference to Queen Victoria, they called their wares "Queen's Burmese."

Reproduction Alert: Reproductions
abound in almost every form. Since uranium can no longer be used, some of the
reproductions are easy to spot. In the
1950s, Gunderson produced many pieces
in imitation of Burmese.

Abbreviations:
MW = Mount Washington
Wb = Webb
a.f. = acid finish
s.f. = shiny finish
Advisors: Clarence and Betty Maier.

**Salt Shaker, tomato shape, au-
tumn dec, 1¾″ h, $165.00.**

Biscuit Jar, 5″ w, 6″ h, 9½″ h overall, deep salmon to brilliant yellow, applied yellow base, orig SP
hardware, English hallmarks,
acorn finial, Wb **1,250.00**
Bowl
4½″ w, 5″ l, 2″ h, rect, deep color,
thin body, MW **425.00**
6″ d, 2½″ h, ruffled, Gunderson **385.00**
7¼″ d, 6″ h, ruffled and pulled
edge, three applied shell
reeded feet, large berry over
pontil, MW **1,500.00**
Ewer, 6″ h, 2½″ d, long spout, loop
handle, applied base, MW, a.f. . **950.00**
Ice Cream Dish
6¼″ d, 1″ h, DQ, thin bell tone,
MW, a.f. **225.00**
9″ d, 2¾″ h, deep salmon pink
shading to bright yellow, MW,
s.f. **950.00**
Jack–in–the–Pulpit Vase, 12½″ h,
painted and enameled pale blue
flowers, buds, and leaves, white
enamel beaded base, salmon
pink neck int., MW **1,850.00**
Juice Glass, 3½″ h, 2⅛″ d, MW,
a.f. **275.00**
Pitcher
4⅝″ h, flattened hobnail, sq top,
brilliant yellow reeded handle,
salmon pink body, MW, a.f. .. **675.00**
6″ h, Hobnail, deep color, applied
loop handle, MW, s.f. **1,450.00**
Plate
8″ d, Pairpoint, s.f., c1920 .... **225.00**
9¼″ d, salmon pink shading to
yellow, bell tone, MW, a.f. ... **375.00**
Rose Bowl
2¼″ h, 2¼″ d, 8 crimp top, Wb,
a.f. **185.00**

2¼" h, 2½" w, floral dec **285.00**
Sugar, 3¾" d, 2" h, deep color,
MW, a.f. **100.00**
Sweetmeat, dec, etched silver lid **700.00**
Toothpick Holder
Bulbous
2½" h, sq top, enameled white
and yellow mums, green and
brown leaves, MW **675.00**
2¾" h, sq top, deep salmon
pink, a.f. **295.00**
2¾" h, sq top, pale pink to yellow, enameled pink and dark
blue raspberries, MW, a.f. . **650.00**
Tri–corner, enameled white and
yellow mums, MW, a.f. **675.00**
Vase
3" h, 3½" d, bulbous, enameled
yellow daisies and leaves, MW **850.00**
3½" h, 3" d, black bands, small
blue flowers with red centers
and green leaves garland, Wb,
a.f. **285.00**
3⅞" h, 2⅞" d, ruffled, Wb, a.f. . **235.00**
5½" h, bulbous, flared rim, MW,
a.f. **550.00**
6" h, bulbous, MW, s.f. **350.00**
6½" d, 3½" w, egg shape, two
handles, allover Ginkgo tree
pattern, MW **950.00**
10¼" h, 5½" w at shoulder, 5¼"
neck, gourd, MW, a.f. **750.00**
12" h, 7" d base, gourd, allover
enameled and painted yellow,
white, and purple asters,
leaves, and vines, deep yellow
with pink shading ⅗ from top,
dec attributed to Albert Steffin,
MW **1,850.00**

BUSTS

History: The portrait bust has its origins
in pagan and Christian tradition. Greek and
Roman heroes, and later images of Christian saints, dominate the early examples.
Busts of the "ordinary man" first appeared
in the Renaissance.

Busts of the nobility, poets, and other notable persons dominated the 18th and 19th
centuries, especially those designed for use
in a home library. Because of the large number of these library busts, excellent exam-

ples can be found at reasonable prices, depending on artist, subject, and material.

Reference: Lynne and Fritz Weber, *Jacobsen's Thirteenth Painting and Bronze
Price Guide, January 1992 to January
1994,* Weber Publications, 1994.

Additional Listings: Ivory, Parian Ware,
Soapstone, and Wedgwood.

Baccarat, 10¾" h, woman, frosted,
clear octagonal base, sgd **350.00**
Bisque
15" h, pr, English nobleman and
lady, 19th C **650.00**
19" h, girl feeding bird, pastel
enameling and gilt dec **665.00**
20¼" h, queen, polychrome
enamel and gilt, marked "J 4" **675.00**
Bronze
15½" h, Neapolitan lady in Renaissance costume, sgd
"Grang Colombo, France,"
plaque on onyx base engraved
"Grand Dame Patricienne
Florentine au XIV Eme Sie-
gle," c1905 ....**2,525.00**
17¾" h, young woman, laurel
wreath, sgd "E F Frey 1937" **665.00**
18¼" h, Seneca, Roman political
leader and philosopher,
shaped red marble plinth,
damage, late 19th/early 20th C **575.00**
23" h, Michelangelo, inscribed
"Carrier–Belleuse," red marble
base, late 19th C **635.00**

**Parian Ware, Jesus Christ, un-
marked, 9" h, $115.00.**

Marble, 46" h, Joan of Arc, Continental **1,000.00**
Metal, 9" h, young woman, wearing lace cap, patina, sgd "H Muller," late 19th/early 20th C . **345.00**
Parian
   5⅞" h, Greek youth **55.00**
   10½" h, George Stephenson, English, late 19th C **230.00**
   11½" h, man, long hair and mutton chops, English, late 19th C **230.00**
   13½" h, Henry Wadsworth Longfellow, English, late 19th C .. **220.00**
Plaster, 12½" h, Michelangelo's David, bronze finish **25.00**
Porcelain
   2½" h, Laughing Child, black basalt, raised circular base, imp "Wedgwood," 19th C ... **320.00**
   3¾" h, Venus, black basalt, raised rect marble base, imp "Wedgwood," 19th C **415.00**
   4" h, black basalt, raised circular base, imp "Wedgwood," 19th C
     David Garrick **490.00**
     Shakespeare **375.00**
   5¾" h, pr, young girls, enamel and gilt dec, underglazed crossed sword mark, losses, Meissen, Germany, late 19th C **430.00**
   7" h, Burns, black basalt, raised base, imp title and "Wedgwood," mid 19th C **575.00**
   8¼" h, George Washington, Staffordshire, England, 19th C **490.00**
   11⅝" h, Napoleon, imp mark, firing imperfections, edge chips, Sevres **2,075.00**
   13½" h, Byron, black basalt, raised circular base, imp title and "Wedgwood," mid 19th C **1,150.00**
Pottery, 18½" h, Goethe, dark bronze finish, label marked "R U 1879" **90.00**
Wood
   14" h, lady, Baroque reliquary, gilded and polychromed, three–quarter length, upraised right arm, left hand resting on book, rect plinth, damaged .. **700.00**
   19½" h, female, reliquary, walnut, carved, Continental, 17th C **2,200.00**

BUTTER PRINTS

History: Butter prints divide into two categories: butter molds and butter stamps. Butter molds are generally of three piece construction—the design, the screw–in handle, and the case. Molds both shape and stamp the butter at the same time. Butter stamps are of one–piece construction, sometimes two pieces if the handle is from a separate piece of wood. Stamps decorate the top of butter after it is molded.

The earliest prints were one piece and hand carved, often thick and deeply carved. Later prints were factory made with the design forced into the wood by a metal die.

Some of the most common designs are sheaves of wheat, leaves, flowers, and pineapples. Animal designs and Germanic tulips are difficult to find. Rare prints include unusual shapes, such as half–rounded and lollipop, and those with designs on both sides.

Reference: Paul E. Kindig, *Butter Prints And Molds,* Schiffer Publishing, 1986.

Reproduction Alert: Reproductions of butter prints date as early as the 1940s.

Stamp, double heart with flower, crimped stylized edges, oval, 5½ x 3½", $415.00.

MOLDS

Pear, geometric border, round, cased, marked "Hildesheim," worn varnish, 5" d **165.00**

PRINTS

Bird, cased, turned handle, old patina, 1½" d **175.00**
Cow, turned handle, old patina, 2" d **200.00**

Eagle
Lollipop, eagle on one side, star flower on other, pine, old patina, 9″ l **990.00**
Turned handle, old patina, 3¾″ d **385.00**
Floral
Recessed design, lollipop, old dark patina, 10¼″ l **55.00**
Stylized, turned handle, 5⅛″ d . **140.00**
Two floral designs, one on each side, old patina, minor edge damage, 5¼″ d **300.00**
Four Leaf Design, turned inserted handle, old patina, 3¾″ d **95.00**
Pineapple, stylized, turned handle, old patina, 4½″ d **75.00**
Pinwheel
Lollipop, pinwheel on one side, star design on other, old patina, age cracks and edge damage, 7¼″ l **300.00**
Turned inserted handle, old patina, primitive carving, 5¼″ d . **415.00**
Star Flower, turned handle, old patina, 5″ d **165.00**
Tulip, stylized, turned handle, old patina, 4¼″ d **300.00**

CALENDAR PLATES

History: Calendar plates were first made in England in the late 1880s. They became popular in the United States after 1900, the peak years being 1909 to 1915. The majority of the advertising plates were made of porcelain or pottery with a calendar, the name of a store or business, and either a scene, portrait, animal, or flowers. Some also were made of glass or tin.

Additional Listings: See *Warman's Americana & Collectibles* for more examples.

1909
Gibson Girl **38.00**
Mercantile Co, photo center . . . **65.00**
1910
Boxer Dog, Somerville, NJ adv **35.00**
Lighthouse center **35.00**
Poppies, New York City **36.00**
Portrait, woman, large hat, calendar months, fruit, and floral border **50.00**

Calendar Plate, 1909, John Kemper, Harness Maker, Butler, PA, Mediterranean woman in center, marked "Voorey," 9″ d, $25.00.

Sailboats on water **35.00**
Scenic **35.00**
1911, Schanley Jewelers, Quakertown, PA, horse head in horseshoe, multicolored **80.00**
1912
Airplane, glider **25.00**
Hot Air Balloons **75.00**
Indian, husking corn **25.00**
1913
Rose garland and holly border, calendar months center **20.00**
Sweet Peas, pink and lavender ground **45.00**
1914, Washington's Tomb, Milford, DE, artist sgd "A Smith" **35.00**
1916, man in canoe scene center **35.00**
1919
American Flag, John J Rutgers Co, Holland, MI adv **40.00**
Walnut Grove, MN **45.00**
1921, Tabor & Pukwana, SD **60.00**
1922, game birds and hunting dog center **45.00**
1932, fish in center **45.00**

CALLING CARD CASES AND RECEIVERS

History: Calling cards, usually carried in specially designed cases, played an important social role in the United States from the period of the Civil War until the end of World War I. When making a formal visit, a caller left his card in a receiver (card dish) in the front hall. Strict rules of etiquette developed. For example, the lady in a family was expected to make calls of congratulations, visits to the ill, and condolence.

The cards themselves were small, embossed or engraved with the caller's name, and often carried a floral design. Many hand–done examples, especially in Spencerian script, can be found. The cards themselves are considered collectible and range in price from a few cents to several dollars.

Note: Don't confuse a calling card case with a match safe.

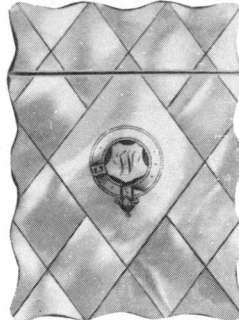

Mother of pearl and tortoise shell, monogram "W" in center, 3 x 4", $50.00.

CALLING CARD CASE

Coin Silver, American
  Capitol Building one side, Greek temple style building other side, scrolls, flowers, and foliage, stippled ground, marked "D," 3½" l, 2¼" w **275.00**
  Newstead Abbey one side, flowers, leaves and rocaille other side, unmarked, 3½" l, 2½" w **225.00**
Silver, English, flat purse form, chain handle, surface engraved with heavily scrolling foliate de-

sign, Birmingham, 1912, 3¾" l, 2½" w **95.00**
Silver Filigree and Enamel, rect, wavy bracket sides, delicate tracery border centered by blue and green enamel foliate band, conforming central plaque with filigree dragon and clouds in relief, int. with fish scale tracery and cloud shaped opening, orig cardboard box with painted court lady dec on top and goldfish, urn, and helmet on sides, unmarked, late 19th/early 20th C, 4" l, 2¾" w **450.00**
Sterling Silver
  Art Deco, 14k gold inlaid **275.00**
  Art Nouveau, raised floral design, chain handle **125.00**
Tortoiseshell
  Mother–of–pearl inlaid, 19th C . **200.00**
  Regency, molded to represent Gothic architecture, silver and ivory fittings, c1815 . . . . **325.00**

CALLING CARD RECEIVER

Stand, bronze, gilded and patinated, Charles X, variegated rouge marble base, reverse fitted with thermometer and calendar, early 19th C, 8" h **300.00**
Tray
  Porcelain, handle, Buffalo Pottery, Emerald Deldare, Dr Syntax Robbed Of His Property, 7" w **500.00**
  Sterling Silver, shell shaped, Gorham, retailed by Shreve, Crump & Low, early 20th C, 6" d, 5 troy oz **145.00**

CAMBRIDGE GLASS

History: Cambridge Glass Company, Cambridge, Ohio, was incorporated in 1901. Initially, the company made clear tableware, later expanding into colored, etched, and engraved glass. Over 40 different hues were produced in blown and pressed glass.

Five different marks were employed during the production years, but not every piece was marked.

The plant closed in 1954. Some of the molds were later sold to the Imperial Glass Company, Bellaire, Ohio.

References: Gene Florence, *Elegant Glassware Of The Depression Era, Sixth Edition*, Collector Books, 1994; National Cambridge Collectors, Inc., *The Cambridge Glass Co., Cambridge, Ohio* (reprint of 1930 catalog and supplements through 1934), Collector Books, 1976, 1991 value update; National Cambridge Collectors, Inc., *The Cambridge Glass Co., Cambridge, Ohio, 1949 Thru 1953* (catalog reprint), Collector Books, 1976, 1991 value update; National Cambridge Collectors, Inc., *Colors In Cambridge Glass*, Collector Books, 1984, 1995 value update; Mark Nye, *Cambridge Stemware*, published by author, 1985; Naomi L. Over, *Ruby Glass of the 20th Century*, Antique Publications, 1990, 1993–94 value update.

Periodical: *The Daze*, PO Box 57, Otisville, MI 48463.

Collectors' Club: National Cambridge Collectors, Inc, PO Box 416, Cambridge, OH 43725.

Museums: Cambridge Glass Museum, Cambridge, OH; Museum of the National Cambridge Collectors, Inc, Cambridge, OH.

Ashtray
Caprice, blue, 2½" d	15.00
Portia, #3500/129, sq	45.00
Terrace, red, sq	35.00

Basket, Decagon, #760, green, 7" h	35.00
Bell, Portia, dinner	150.00
Bonbon, Caprice, blue, sq, two handles, 6" d	48.00

Bowl
Rose Point, 12" l	175.00
Terrace, 5" d	12.50

Brandy, Rose Point, #3121, set of six	625.00
Butter Dish, cov, Wildflower, #3400/52	135.00
Cake Plate, Wildflower, 13½" d	32.00

Candlesticks, pr
#3400/647, Blossom Time, black, 5" h	250.00
#3900 Line, 2 lite, 6" h	35.00

Candy Dish, cov, Blossom Time, clear, Martha, ftd	95.00
Celery, Portia, handle, 14" l	95.00
Champagne, Wildflower	27.50
Cheese and Cracker, Gloria, yellow	97.50
Claret, Chantilly, 4½ oz	28.00
Coaster, Chantilly, ruffled, SS base	22.50

Cocktail
Nude, amethyst bowl	90.00
Sea horse, etch 502, red and crystal, ftd, 3 oz	35.00

Compote, ftd, etched cut florals, rubena, 8⅜" d, 3¾" h, $135.00.

Compote
Chantilly	32.00
Crown Tuscan, seashell, enamel roses	65.00

Console Bowl, Caprice, blue, 12½" d	45.00

Cordial
Apple Blossom, yellow	95.00
Tally Ho, red	65.00

Cordial Set, decanter and three 2½" tumblers, amethyst, Farberware	42.00

Creamer
Caprice, blue	20.00
Cleo, green	32.00

Cream Soup
Decagon, green	17.50
Portia, #3400, with liner	125.00

Cup and Saucer
Apple Blossom	24.00
Caprice, blue	45.00

Flower Frog
Bashful Charlotte, 6" h	135.00
Draped Lady, 8½" h	
Champagne	350.00

Dark Amber	160.00
Rose Lady, green	195.00

Goblet

Apple Blossom	25.00
Chantilly, #3600	30.00
Heirloom	7.00
Mt Vernon	8.00
Portia, #1066	35.00
Tally Ho, red	35.00
Gravy Boat, Cleo, pink, double, liner	295.00
Ice Bucket, Tally Ho	35.00
Iced Tea Tumbler, Portia, ftd	32.50
Jug, #3900/115, 76 oz, silver overlay	165.00
Juice Tumbler, Portia, ftd	32.50
Marmalade, Tantalus, Farberware, #5555, amber, 4½" h	20.00

Mayonnaise, liner

Portia, #3900/111	72.50
Wildflower, #1532	52.50
Mint Dish, Caprice, 4" sq, blue	18.00
Oyster Cocktail, Portia	37.50

Plate

Caprice, pink, 8" d	75.00
Diane, 7½" d	12.50
Hunter Scene, amber, 10½" d	85.00
Portia, 8" d	17.50
Wildflower, 6" d	15.00
Platter, Decagon, green, 10½" l	35.00

Relish Dish, divided

Elaine, 9" l	24.00
Wildflower, gold trim	37.00
Salad Plate, Wildflower	9.00
Sandwich Plate, #3900 Line, topaz, 10" d	15.00
Seafood Cocktail, Crown Tuscan, 5 oz	55.00

Sugar

Apple Blossom, pink	37.50
Caprice, blue	25.00
Swan, Crown Tuscan, 3"	28.00

Tumbler

Caprice, blue	9.00
Cascade	12.50
Farberware, #3400, cobalt blue, 6 oz, 3½" h	24.00
Portia, #3400/127, handle, 2½ oz	95.00
Vase, Caprice, milk glass, 4¼" h	85.00
Whiskey, Sea Horse, etch 502, red and crystal, ftd, 2 oz	45.00

Wine

Caprice, blue, 2½ oz	45.00

Farberware	5.00
Sandwich, dark blue	35.00

CAMBRIDGE

CAMBRIDGE POTTERY

History: The Cambridge Art Pottery was incorporated in Ohio in 1900. Between 1901 and 1909 the firm produced the usual line of jardinieres, tankards, and vases with underglazed slip decorations and glazes similar to other Ohio potteries. Line names included Terrhea, Oakwood, Otoe, and others.

In 1904 the company introduced Guernsey kitchenware. It was so well received that it became the plant's primary product. In 1909 the company's name was changed to Guernsey Earthenware Company.

All wares were marked.

Candlestick, 4" h, Terrhea, standard brown glaze	50.00
Ewer, 7½" h, Oakwood, cream,	

Bowl, four feet, matte green glaze, acorn mark, 4 imp signatures, 8½" d, 5¾" l, $115.00.

yellow, and green blended glaze,
numbered **60.00**
Flask, 10⅞" h, roughly textured repeating patterns, blue–brown matte glaze, "Cambridge Pottery" incised in base, c1900 ... **275.00**
Inkwell, acorn stopper, Terrhea .. **100.00**
Pitcher, 4" h, 5" d, Terrhea, squat bulbous body, standard brown glaze, underglaze slip dec flowers on blended brown ground, diestamped mark **135.00**
Vase
7¼" h, bud, brown streaked, molded flowers, marked "Oakwood" **150.00**
15¼" h, gold, green, and brown ground, carp and lily pond dec, rim chipped **350.00**

CAMEO GLASS

History: Cameo glass is a form of cased glass. A shell of glass was prepared; then one or more layers of glass of a different color(s) was faced to the first. A design was then cut through the outer layer(s) leaving the inner layer(s) exposed.

This type of art glass originated in Alexandria, Egypt, 100–200 A.D. The oldest and most famous example of cameo glass is the Barberini or Portland vase which was found near Rome in 1582. It contained the ashes of Emperor Alexander Serverus who was assassinated in 235 A.D.

Emile Gallé is probably one of the best–known artists of cameo glass. He established a factory at Nancy, France, in 1884. Although much of the glass bears his signature, he was primarily the designer. On many pieces, assistants did the actual work, even signing his name. Glass made after his death in 1904 has a star before the name Gallé. Other makers of French cameo glass include D'Argental, Daum Nancy, LeGras, and Delatte.

English cameo does not have as many layers of glass (colors) and cuttings as do French pieces. The outer layer is usually white, and cuttings are very fine and delicate. Most pieces are not signed. The best

known makers are Thomas Webb & Sons and Stevens and Williams.

References: Victor Arwas, *Glass Art Nouveau to Art Deco*, Rizzoli International Publications, 1977; Alastair Duncan and George DeBartha, *Glass by Galle*, Harry N. Abrams, 1984; Ray and Lee Grover, *English Cameo Glass*, Crown Publishers, 1980; Charles R. Hajdamach, *British Glass, 1800–1914,* Antique Collectors' Club, 1991; Tim Newark, *Emile Galle*, The Apple Press, 1989; Albert C. Revi, *Nineteenth Century Glass*, reprint, Schiffer Publishing, Ltd., 1981; John A. Shuman, III, *The Collector's Encyclopedia of American Art Glass,* Collector Books, 1988, 1994 value update.

AMERICAN

Durand
Box, cov, King Tut, three layer, coiled green dec on ambergris cased to opal, lined with irid gold, matching and conforming blown cov with cut star at pontil, unsigned, 5" d, 4" h .. **775.00**
Vase, 8" h, flared mouth, vertically ribbed molded design, shaded green emerald cased to opal, int. gold irid, signed "Durand 1710–8" **1,050.00**
Mount Washington, bride's basket, 8" sq, 10½" h, white cased to rose–red, cameo cut back with winged griffins, floral bouquets, and swags, squared crimped edge, fitted within marked "Pairpoint" silver plated metal mount with leaf and berry embellished handle **825.00**
Tiffany, Favrile
Cabinet Vase, brilliant yellow cased to red, finely wheel carved about base with overlapping petals, short bulbous body with flaring rim, inscribed "L.C.T. 4118D," c1909 ...... **2,590.00**
Vase, 5⅛" h, clear glass textured with dew drops, overlaid in white, finely cut with overlapping petals, edges delicately curling back upon themselves, inscribed "L.C.T. W7814," c1905 .... **4,025.00**

ENGLISH

Stevens and Williams
Basket, 11″ l, 11″ h, opaque opal cased to raspberry pink, applied amber leaves and fruits, feet and handle dec with polychrome blossoms, leaves, and gilt tracery, one cherry stem missing 650.00
Bowl, 6¼″ d, 4″ h, ftd, cased yellow ground, carved seaweed, applied glass prunt 250.00
Vase, pr, 10″ h, shaded pink cased to white, blue below white enameled flowers, yellow, lavender, and gold enhancements, applied thorn handles and feet, one foot chipped 450.00

Webb, Thomas
Biscuit Jar, cov
6″ d, 5″ h, frosted cranberry ground, carved white apple blossoms, orig SP fittings . . 950.00
7″ d, 5″ h, frosted cranberry ground, white overlay, carved apple blossoms, leaves, buds, and branches, orig SP cov, bail, and handle 2,500.00
Bowl, bright unfired Burmese yellow ground, salmon pink cameo seaweed, berry pontil, three crystal feet 1,250.00
Bowl and Underplate, 4½″ d x 2¾″ h bowl, 6″ d underplate, deep transparent cranberry, allover cut and carved cameo of prunus blossoms, leaves, branches, buds, two large butterflies, sgd "Thomas Webb and Sons" 1,250.00
Decanter, clear, three overlaid red and white oval reserves finely wheel carved with tulips and bee, apple blossoms and leafage, and hibiscus and bee, diamond patterned lower band, faceted stopper, unsigned, small chip to border of one reserve, c1900 . . . . 1,150.00
Perfume Bottle
6″ h, bulbous, frosted citron ground, white and cranberry

fuchsia design, orig SP two piece screw top 3,500.00
10″ l, lay down, frosted cranberry ground, carved white floral design, orig SP cov, orig velvet and satin carrying case stamped "Mappin & Webb, Silversmiths to the Queen, London and Sheffield" 3,850.00
Vase
4″ h, green–yellow ground, white overlay, carved floral and leaf design, center medallion, gold portrait of woman wearing hat, script sgd "Palla," full Webb sgd . 1,200.00
16″ h, amber ground, white overlay, finely cut on obverse with two acanthus skirted angels decorating large flower laden foliate mounted urn with festoon, larger foliate urn with bouquet on reverse, foliate dec borders, scrolling acanthus and other leafage dec, two handled, imp "Thomas Webb & Sons, Gem Cameo," c1890 . . . . 68,500.00

FRENCH

Arsall, hydrangea vase, 12″ h, flared flattened ovoid body, pink shaded to colorless body, double overlaid in green and amethyst, cameo etched with broad blossoms and leafy stems above dark lower border, signed "Arsall" in design 650.00
D'Argental
Goblet, 7″ h, flaring bowl, opaque ground, red landscape and ruins, grape leaf and vine dec stem, signed on base . . . 1,400.00
Lamp, table, 23½″ h, 12″ d shade, domed shade, ftd baluster base, frosted yellow ground, deep ruby red overlay, etched wooded lake scene, cameo signature "D'Argental" 8,050.00
Vase, gray shaded with pale yellow ground, caramel and

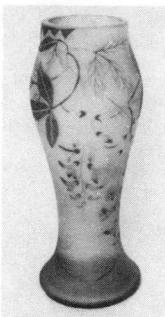

**French, Richard, vase, char-
treuse-yellow ground, amber dec,
sgd in cameo, 12½" h, $990.00.**

brown overlay, tranquil forest
and lake scene, signed in
cameo "D'Argental," c1920 . . **1,375.00**

Daum Nancy
Bowl, 13½" l handle to handle,
gray sides streaked with
strawberry and lemon yellow
ground, chocolate brown overlay, flower and garden tool–
filled baskets pendent from ribbon–tied floral festoons, gilt
bronze mounts, cast classical
motifs, signed in cameo
"Daum Nancy" with croix de
Lorraine, c1910 . . . . **2,585.00**
Inkwell, 4⅛" h, gray mottled with
pale blue ground, mottled lime
green, yellow, and purple
overlay, dragonfly, lily blossoms, and leafage, finely
wheel carved, inscribed
"Daum Nancy" with croix de
Lorraine, replaced lid, c1900 . **2,750.00**
Vase
3½" h, yellow and purple mottled ground, red currants,
leaves, and branches, internal dec and cameo carving,
ftd **3,350.00**
5" h, 5½" w, mottled purple,
yellow, and white ground,
four enameled rust and purple lady slippers, cameo spi-

der webs, carved base border, sgd with croix de
Lorraine **2,750.00**
7" h, mottled yellow and brown
ground, bright orange
cameo carved poppies,
leaves, and buds, gilt highlights, sgd "Daum Nancy" . **1,500.00**
8" h, bright yellow and red
ground, mottled and naturalistic snow scene with trees **1,600.00**
8" h, brown ground, yellow and
red overlay, river landscape **1,150.00**
23" h, pink and yellow mottled
ground, floral pond design,
scenic background, central
cameo and enamel motif of
flowers and stems, sgd
"Daum Nancy" **6,250.00**
24½" h, inverted trumpet
shape, mottled yellow and
white ground, green etched
and cameo cut scenic of
wooded lakeside, sgd
"Daum Nancy" in cameo
with croix de Lorraine **3,750.00**

Delatte
Box, cov, 3¾" h, gray mottled
pale yellow ground, raspberry
red overlay, bleeding hearts
and leafage dec, butterflies on
lid, signed in cameo "Delatte,
Nancy," c1920 . . . . **925.00**
Vase, 7⅜" h, clear sides
splashed with lime green
ground, amber overlay, wheel
carved iris blossom and leafage, signed in intaglio "De-
latte, Nancy," c1920 . . . . **575.00**

Devez, vase
3¾" h, handled tub form, blue
ground, blue and green overlay, expansive landscape centering fisherman and boat,
signed in cameo "Devez" . . . **875.00**
7¾" h, flattened oval form, fiery
opal amber ground, orange–
amber and royal blue overlay,
highly detailed desert island
landscape with mountains,
palm trees, and lagoons,
signed in cameo "Devez" . . . **925.00**
9⅞" h, bright pink ground, puce
overlay sides, Venetian lagoon

with boating, signed in cameo
"deVez," c1920 . . . . **575.00**

Galle

Bowl

7¼" d, gray sides streaked
with lemon yellow, chocolate
brown overlay, Breton seascape with a pier and boats
in foreground, signed in
cameo "Galle," c1900 . . . . . **2,015.00**

10½" d, 4" h, red ground, cut
to yellow, boat form, leaves
and berries dec **865.00**

Ewer, 5½" h, transparent lime
green walls mottled at upper
section with raspberry and amber, sides delicately enameled
with rose, lemon yellow, win-
tergreen, and white wildflower
sprays and leafage, lower section with intaglio carved leafage, gilt trim, obverse with applied cabochon enameled in
yellow and purple, signed in
enameled intaglio "Cristallerie,
d'Emile Galle, Nancy, Modele
et decor depose," minor loss
to end of trailing, c1890 . . . . . **1,275.00**

Lamp, table, 18½" h, 8" d shade,
pale yellow–green ground,
purple and clear frosted trail-
ing floral vines, orig fittings . . **8,000.00**

Miniature, vase

2½" h, yellow and white
ground, bright cherry red
cameo carved blueberries,
glossy finish **1,600.00**

3" h, frosted ground, soft pale
blue and green carving **500.00**

Scent Bottle, 3¾" h, opal gray
ground, teal blue overlay, berries and leafage, fire polished,
pale amber glass floriform
stopper, signed in cameo
"Galle," c1900 . . . . **3,175.00**

Vase

3½" h, bulbous, frosted clear
and orange ground, purple
and white hydrangea carv-
ing **600.00**

4½" h, 6¾" w, pale yellow opal
ground, blue carnations,
purple leaves and stems,
sgd **2,850.00**

5" h, baluster, frosted bright
yellow ground, brown flow-
ers **750.00**

5¼" h, 2" w, mottled bright yellow ground, brown and
green floral dec, large leafy
plants, sgd **900.00**

6" h, deep apricot ground, purple floral and leaf design,
sgd "Galle" **1,200.00**

6¾" h, banjo shape, soft yellow–orange ground, purple
floral **950.00**

7" h, banjo shape, frosted
clear ground, brown floral
and leaf design **1,200.00**

8½" h, 5½" w, pale opalescent
translucent yellow ground,
shiny purple cameo cut pond
lilies, leaves, stems, buds,
and orchid like flower, sgd
"Galle," stamped "France" . **5,250.00**

8¾" h, 3" w, yellow burgundy
opal ground, bright red wisteria dec, highly cut and
polished **1,900.00**

13" h, brown cut to yellow and
frosted, river landscape . . . **3,225.00**

14" h, 6½" w, pale pink–peach
ground, blue–gray design of
acorns and leaves on
branches, early signature
entwined in leaf **4,750.00**

15¾" h, 5½" w, brilliant yellow
ground, red and rust dog-
wood, iris, flower, and foliage
dec, highly carved **5,000.00**

19½" h, yellow ovoid body, internal red and blue swirls,
bronze trumpet foot, possibly added later cut with sea
floor scene depicting jelly
fish and sea lilies, signed in
cameo, c1910 . . . . **2,990.00**

23½" h, narrow cylindrical
neck, fattened spherical
base, pale yellow ground,
dark red overlay, iris, signed
in cameo **3,160.00**

Wall Pocket, 7¼" h, 7" w, purple,
red, and opalescent yellow
hanging fuchsia blossoms, all-
over floral cut design, sgd . . . **3,250.00**

Legras
Bowl, 7″ d, 4¾″ h, opaque opal
and amber ground, broad leaf
clusters, enameled and
polished in naturalistic green
and red amber, cameo mark
"Legras SD" **715.00**
Vase
8⅜″ h, gray ground, internally
mottled with white and yellow, acid etched, stylized
geometric band about shoulder, band enameled deep
burgundy, acid etched and
enameled "Legras," c1930 . **460.00**
21¼″ h, ovoid body, opal glass
splashed with deep umber,
cased within clear glass,
acid etched about upper
section with sea gulls in
flight, design rubbed with
dark brown stain, signed in
cameo "Legras," c1930 ...**1,035.00**
Le Verre Francais
Bowl, 14″ d, 10″ h, conical form,
circular foot, orange ground,
burgundy to orange overlay,
etched with long stems and
stylized blossoms, signed "Le
Verre Francais" and "France" **1,325.00**
Pitcher, Papillon, 12½″ h, extended pour spout, mottled
blue–yellow ground, orange
overlay, butterflies above Art
Deco border, engraved "Le
Verre Francais," small chip on
applied black–amethyst snake
handle **1,430.00**
Tazza, 5½″ h, 12¼″ w, deep rose
pink mottled ground, glossy
purple daisy–like design **850.00**
Vase, gray streaked with lemon
yellow ground, orange overlay,
stylized bearded irises, signed
in intaglio "Le Verre Francais,"
c1925 ....**1,610.00**
Lorenze Freres, jar, cov, 5¾″ h, 6″
d, frosted, clear, amethyst overlay, shallow chrysanthemum mo-
tif, elaborate cameo signature . **600.00**
Muller Croismare
Bowl, 9″ d, 4¾″ h, ftd, pale gray
ground, pink overlay, carved

poppies, engraved "Muller
Croismare, Nancy" **3,300.00**
Vase, 4½″ h, squat baluster
form, mottled green to orange
ground, brown and yellow
overlay, carved maple leaves,
two applied beetles, signed on
base, lacking one glass jewel **1,210.00**
Muller Freres
Bowl, 10″ l, gray sides streaked
with sea green and raspberry,
purple overlay, river landscape
with boating in foreground and
mountains in distance, signed
in cameo "Muller Fres, Luneville," c1920 ....**2,875.00**
Lamp, 10½″ h, opal lemon glass
mottled with orange, pale blue
and purple overlay, village, forest, and river scene complete
with crane, base and shade
each signed in cameo "Muller
Fres, Luneville," c1920 ....**10,350.00**
Vase, 6¼″ h, acid etched pump-
kin ground, cast with trees,
cream overlay, grazing sheep
above tooled lower body,
signed in intaglio "Muller Fres,
Luneville," c1920 ....**2,875.00**
Pantin, vase, 6¼″ h, irid shaded
ground, cranberry ground, grape
and leaf design **250.00**
Richard, vase, baluster form, blue
ground, allover irid floral motif,
signed "Richard," 8½″ h **450.00**
St Louis, vase, 11¾″ h, flared
cameo cut and gilded rim on
shouldered ovoid red vase, acid
etched and enameled columbine
blossoms, gilt enhancements,
price for pair **495.00**
Vessiere, vase, 6″ h, oval form,
frosted ground, amethyst overlay, acid etched freesia blossoms, signed in cameo "C. Vessiere, Nancy" **350.00**

CAMERAS

History: The collecting of cameras, except in isolated instances, started about
1970. Although photography generally is

considered to have had its beginning in 1839, it is very unusual to find a camera made before 1880. These cameras and others made before 1925 are considered to be antique cameras. Most cameras made after 1925 that are no longer in production are considered to be classic cameras. American, German, and Japanese cameras are found most often.

Value of cameras is affected by both exterior and mechanical conditions. Particular attention must be given to the condition of the bellows if cameras have them.

References: John S. Craig, *General Catalog of Photographica,* published by author, 1993; James and Joan McKeown, (eds.) *Price Guide To Antique & Classic Cameras, 1994–1995, 9th Edition,* Centennial Photo Service, 1994; *Jason Schneider On Camera Collecting, Book Three,* Wallace–Homestead, 1985; Douglas St. Denny (ed.), *The Hove International Blue Book Guide Prices for Classic and Collectable Cameras: 1992–1993,* Hove Foto Books, 1992, distributed by Wallace–Homestead; John Wade, *The Camera, From the 11th Century to the Present Day,* Jessop Specialist Publishing, 1990.

Periodicals: *Camera Shopper,* 313 N. Quaker Lane, PO Box 370279, West Hartford, CT 06137; *Shutterbug,* PO Box F, Titusville, FL 32781.

Collectors' Clubs: American Photographical Historical Society, Inc., 1150 Avenue of the Americas, New York, NY 10036; International Kodak Historical Society, PO Box 21, Flourtown, PA 19301; Leica Historical Society of America, 7611 Dornoch Lane, Dallas, TX 75248; Movie Machine Society, 50 Old Country Rd, Hudson, MA 01749; National Stereoscopic Association, PO Box 14801, Columbus, OH 43214; Nikon Historical Society, PO Box 3213, Munster, IN 46321; The Photographic Historical Society, PO Box 39563, Rochester, NY 14604; Zeiss Historical Society, PO Box 631, Clifton, NJ 07012.

Museums: Cameras & Images International, Boston, MA; George Eastman Museum, Rochester, NY; Smithsonian Institution, Washington, DC.

Additional Listings: See *Warman's Americana & Collectibles* for more examples.

Tenox, C. P. Goerg, Berlin, focusing panel with pack adapter, 4½ x 6 cm film pack, early 1900s, $115.00.

Ansco No 4, Model D, wood case	**65.00**
Bell's Straight Working Panorama camera, BG 100, horizontal format, folding bellows, 5 panoramic exposure	**250.00**
Biflex, 35mm, ¾" f2.5 Tritar lens, 200 exposure, mfg in Switzerland, made for British intelligence, c1945	**425.00**
Ciro 35T, 35mm, Wollensak Anastigmat 50mm f2.8 coated lens, Rapax shutter, c1950	**30.00**
Conley Camera Co, Rochester, NY, Folding Plate Camera, 4 x 5", red bellows	**70.00**
Devin One–Shot Color Camera, 2½ x 3½" sheet film, Goerz Dogmar 5½" f4.5 lens, Compur dial set shutter, c1940	**300.00**
Eastman Kodak	
No 2, factory loaded, sixty exposures, 1890	**225.00**
3B Quick Focus, Meniscus Achromatic lens, rotary shutter, 125 roll film, c1906–11	**125.00**
Fallowfield Hand Camera, Moroccan crocodile skin valise, c1892	**425.00**
Franke, Rollei 16S, subminiature, Tessar 25mm f2.8 lens, first Rollei with one lens, black	**75.00**
Goerz	
Minicord, 16mm, Helgro 25mm f2.0 lens, 16mm cassettes film, eye level viewing through roof prism, c1951	**150.00**
Stereo Ango, Goerz Dagor	

120mm f6.8 lens, film pack adapter, rising and sliding lens panel, c1906 .... 225.00

Jumbo Century Studio Camera, No 4A, wood, lens, hand held rubber squeeze bulb, brass hardware, orig label, made by Folmer Graphflex Corp, Rochester, NY, 12½ x 25″, 16½″ h .. 100.00

Polaroid Land Camera, Model 95B, unused 50.00

J Robinson & Sons, England, Luzo Detective Camera, Aplanat 2½″ f11 lens, variable speed sector shutter, used Eastman roll type film, first British made box camera, c1890 ....1,500.00

Ross Twin Lens Reflex, Ross Homocentric 7″ f6.3 lens, Bausch & Lomb pneumatic shutter, rotating back, c1891 ...... 575.00

Schmitz & Thienemann, Dresden, Germany, Uniflex, Unar 75mm f4.5 lens, self cocking Pronto shutter coupled to mirror, c1933 120.00

Scovill 4 x 5″ Vertical View Camera, R Morrison NY lens, rotating stops, holder and case, c1881 . 225.00

Universal Camera Corp (New York)
Iris, miniature, Ilex Vitar 50mm f7.9 lens, T B I shutter 10.00
Mercury I, 35mm half frame, Tricor 35mm f3.5 lens, rotary sector, c1947 .... 30.00

Voigtlander A G, Braunschweig, Germany, Bergheil, Heliar 4⅗″ f4.5 lens, Compur shutter, folding plate, c1930 .... 50.00

Zeiss Contraflex, Walz filter kit, wide angle and telephoto lens, instruction book and case 250.00

CAMPHOR GLASS

History: Camphor glass derives its name from its color. Most pieces have a cloudy white appearance, similar to gum camphor; the remainder have a pale colored tint. Camphor glass is made by treating the glass with hydrofluoric acid vapors.

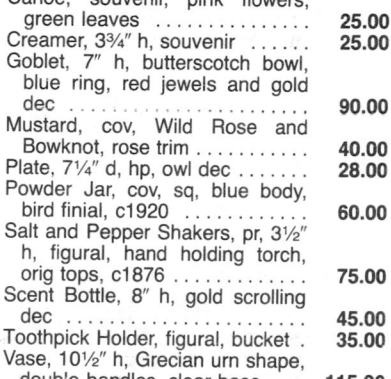

Candlesticks, pr, 7″ h, $60.00.

Bowl, 7½″ d, 3½″ h, flared, scalloped rim, ftd 75.00

Canoe, souvenir, pink flowers, green leaves 25.00

Creamer, 3¾″ h, souvenir 25.00

Goblet, 7″ h, butterscotch bowl, blue ring, red jewels and gold dec 90.00

Mustard, cov, Wild Rose and Bowknot, rose trim 40.00

Plate, 7¼″ d, hp, owl dec 28.00

Powder Jar, cov, sq, blue body, bird finial, c1920 .... 60.00

Salt and Pepper Shakers, pr, 3½″ h, figural, hand holding torch, orig tops, c1876 .... 75.00

Scent Bottle, 8″ h, gold scrolling dec 45.00

Toothpick Holder, figural, bucket . 35.00

Vase, 10½″ h, Grecian urn shape, double handles, clear base 115.00

CANDLESTICKS

History: The domestic use of candlesticks is traced to the 14th century. The earliest was a picket type, named for the sharp point used to hold the candle. The socket type was established by the mid–1660s.

From 1700 to the present, candlestick design mirrored furniture design. By the late 17th century, a baluster stem was introduced, replacing the earlier Doric or clustered column stem. After 1730 candlesticks reflected rococo ornateness. Neo-classic styles followed in the 1760s. Each new era produced a new grouping of candlesticks.

However, some styles became universal and remained in production for centuries. For this reason, it is important to examine the manufacturing techniques of the piece when attempting to date a candlestick.

References: Margaret and Douglas Archer, *The Collector's Encyclopedia Of Glass Candlesticks,* Collector Books, 1983; Tom Felt and Bob O'Grady, *Heisey Candlesticks, Candelabra, and Lamps,* Heisey Collectors of America, 1984; Ronald F. Michaelis, *Old Domestic Base–Metal Candlesticks,* Antique Collectors' Club; Wolf Uecker, *Art Nouveau and Art Deco Lamps and Candlesticks,* Abbeville Press, 1986.

Brass
  Empire, reeded nozzle, paneled standard, leaf tip molded socle, electrified, 11″ h, pr **515.00**
  Queen Anne
    Cut corner base, minor repair, 6½″ h **165.00**
    Petal base, mismatched bobeche, 9″ h **110.00**
    Scalloped base, two solder filled holes, 8¼″ h **110.00**
Brass and Crystal, George III, cut crenelated urn form nozzle above cut starburst, both draped with colorless and canary yellow prism swags, faceted pineapple form standard, gilt dec cylindrical obsidian glass pedestal, molded brass socle, 13″ h, pr **2,300.00**
Bronze
  Empire
    Gilded and patinated, figural, classically draped canephora holding twin scrolling cornucopias, leaf encrusted nozzle terminals, additional central superior urn form nozzle, molded base, applied leaves and birds dec, once electrified, early 19th C, 22½″ h, pr **6,900.00**
    Silvered, paneled standard surmounted by urn form nozzle ornamented with stiff

leaves and leaf tips, molded socle, band of flower filled urns, bellflower garlands, and pearl borders, early 19th C, 12¼″ h, pr **1,375.00**
Empire Style
  Gilded, engine turned, 12″ h, pr **1,600.00**
  Gilded and patinated, fluted and engine turned standard, similarly ornamented socle, 19th C, 12″ h, pr **800.00**
  Louis Phillippe Style, gilded and patinated, columnar, tripod hock base, fitted as lamp, 17″ h, pr **1,500.00**
  Queen Anne, scalloped base, 7⅜″ h **220.00**
Bronze and Slate, Empire style, figural, woman in classical dress, spool form column, accented bronze, slate column and base, 19th C, 12″ h, pr **1,375.00**
Crystal, William IV, complex diamond cut baluster surmounted by crenelation of strawberry leaves, circular undercut foot, first half 19th C, 6½″ h, pr **975.00**
Glass, pressed
Boston & Sandwich Glass Co, hexagonal base, minor imperfections, mid 19th C, 9¼″ h
  Canary, dolphin standard, pr . **920.00**
  Opalescent **460.00**

Porcelain, Samson, seated putti, basket of grapes, scroll molded base, gold anchor mark, late 19th C, price for pr, $500.00.

Mid–Georgian, baluster form, late 18th C, 9″ h, set of four . **1,100.00**

Porcelain

Meissen, yellow ground, gilt accents, leaf molded trim, crossed swords mark, repairs, late 19th C, 11½″ h **230.00**

Nymphenburg Type, figural, male cauldron bearer and lady's maid, each standing before tree trunk, terminal nozzle, electrified, 14″ h, pr **925.00**

Rococo Style, French, figural, seated couple, leafy column, chips and gold wear, mid 19th C, 10¾″ h, pr **290.00**

Silver

George III

Neoclassical taste, draped urn form nozzle above reeded pedestal and draped cavetto, Robert Jones and John Scofield, London, c1776, later gilding and added commemorative date and inscription, 12½″ h, pr **6,025.00**

Telescopic, plain cylindrical standard surmounted by reeded urn, molded socle, John Kay & Co, Sheffield, c1806, 9″ h, pr **1,500.00**

Mid–Georgian, Dublin, mounted as lamp, lacking maker's marks and date letters, 10″ h, pr **2,300.00**

Silver Plated

Regency Style, neoclassical taste, flattened reeded segmental standard, navette form urn nozzle, similar stepped and molded socle, 11½″ h, set of four **1,850.00**

Sheffield, push–up, baluster form, cylindrical bases, 8¾″ h, pr **115.00**

Tin, hogscraper, pushup and lip hanger, worn tin plate, 7″ h **115.00**

CANDY CONTAINERS

History: In 1876 Croft, Wilbur and Co. filled a small glass Liberty Bell with candy and sold it at the Centennial Exposition in Philadelphia. From that date until the 1960s, glass candy containers remained popular and served to outline American history, particularly transportation.

Jeannette, Pennsylvania, a center for the packaging of candy in containers, was home for J. C. Crosetti, J. H. Millstein, T. H. Stough, and Victory Glass. Other early manufacturers included: George Borgfeldt, New York, New York; Cambridge Glass, Cambridge, Ohio; Eagle Glass, Wheeling, West Virginia; L. E. Smith, Mt. Pleasant, Pennsylvania; and West Brothers, Grapeville, Pennsylvania.

Candy containers with original paint, candy, and closures command a high premium, but be aware of reproduced parts and repainting. The closure is a critical part of each container; its loss detracts significantly from the value.

Small figural perfumes and other miniatures often are sold as candy containers.

References: George Eikelberner and Serge Agadjanian, *The Complete American Glass Candy Containers Handbook,* revised and published by Adele L. Bowden, 1986; Jennie Long, *An Album Of Candy Containers,* published by author, Volume I: 1978, Volume II: 1983.

Collectors' Club: Candy Container Collectors of America, PO Box 8708, Canton, OH 44711.

Museums: Cambridge Glass Museum, Cambridge, OH; L. E. Smith Glass, Mt. Pleasant, PA.

Additional Listings: See *Warman's Americana & Collectibles* for more examples.

Automobile

Coupe, 5⅛″ l, glass and tin, black painted fenders and top, replaced wheels and closure . **60.00**

Limousine, 4″ l, glass and tin, repainted roof, West Bros **55.00**

Sedan, 5″ l, glass, painted, tin wheels, replaced closure **80.00**

Baby Chick, 3½″ h, glass, standing, painted **60.00**

Baseball Player, 3½″ h, glass, holding baseball bat, standing alongside jar, painted, metal closure **275.00**

Battleship, 5¼″ l, clear pressed

Frog and Chickens, cloth animals, oval yellow crepe paper base, 3⅞" d, $40.00.

glass, three sections, tin slide
closure 100.00
Cannon, 3¾" l, pressed glass, red
tin carriage, two pierced wheels,
tin screw–on cap 400.00
Charlie Chaplin, 3¾" h, glass,
painted, Borgfeldt 90.00
Church, 3½" h, litho tin, white brick
walls, brown door and window,
eight cutout windows 125.00
Clown, sitting on rocking horse,
blue glass 225.00
Dog
 Bulldog, 3¾" h, sitting, clear
  pressed glass, open base,
  flanged int. 30.00
 Terrier, clear pressed glass,
  open base, flanged int. 20.00
Elephant, 3¼" l, glass, emb GOP
and USA 100.00
Felix the Cat, 3⅜" h, standing
alongside barrel, glass, painted,
replaced closure 525.00
Fire Engine, 4¾" l, Little Boiler,
blue pressed glass, open base 50.00
Globe, clear glass, raised degree
lines and continents, metal
screw–on cap over North America with raised concentric circles
dec and "Our Country," metal
frame stand, marked "Pat Ap-
pli'd For" 375.00
Hat, 2" h, opaque white and

stained colors, screw–on tin
brim, cardboard closure 60.00
Hen on Nest, 4" h, bisque hen,
woven wicker base, polychrome
paint 90.00
Horn, 5½" h, milk glass, painted
dec, marked "Souvenir Sunfield" 170.00
House, 3" h, glass, painted 70.00
Jack–O'–Lantern, 2½" h, clear
pressed glass, ribbed, red intaglio nose and mouth, raised white
teeth, black ringed protruding
pop eyes, pumpkin yellow paint,
wire bail, slotted metal screw–on
cap 300.00
Jitney Bus, 4¼" l, glass, litho tin
roof closure, West Bros 160.00
Kangaroo, 5¼" h, sitting holding
cricket bat, clear pressed glass,
black paint traces, metal screw–
on cap 2,000.00
Mailbox, 3¼" h, clear pressed
glass, gilt "Souvenir–Dubua IA,"
aluminum paint, tin slide closure 125.00
Mug, 2¼" h, drum shape, painted
gold, emb eagle on one side,
slotted closure 200.00
Owl, paint traces, tin cap closure,
1920s 70.00
Phonograph, 4½" h, glass, litho tin
horn and turntable 245.00
Pipe, 4¼" h, ornate bowl, swirl
stem base 50.00
Policeman, 4½" h, glass, painted,
pumpkin head 725.00
Rabbit
 Composition, painted
  7¾" h, glass eyes, holding
   cloth flowers, Germany 120.00
  15" h, wearing glasses,
   spring–loaded ears, neck,
   and right arm, Germany ... 110.00
 Glass, painted
  3⅝" h, crouching, missing closure 50.00
  3⅞" l, pushing cart, replaced
   closure, stamped "V G Co" 340.00
  4⅜" h, eating carrot, c1947 .. 35.00
  4½" h, basket on arm,
   stamped "USA" 50.00
  5¼" h, eggshell, stamped
   "USA" 40.00
Rooster, 5" h, crowing, glass,
painted 170.00

Safe, 3" h, milk glass, painted dec,
marked "Souvenir of Mankato,"
Penny Trust Co 85.00
Safety First, 3¾" h, glass, screw
closure 200.00
Santa Claus
4½" h, standing, glass, painted,
double cuff 130.00
5" h, Santa in chimney, glass,
painted 150.00
Spark Plug, 3" h, glass, painted,
stamped "USA" 90.00
Spirit of Goodwill, 5" l, glass and
tin, painted 50.00
Tank, 4⁵⁄₁₆" l, World War I, glass,
painted, closure 110.00
Telephone, 4⅞" h, wire hanger,
wood receiver, marked "Victory
Glass Co," c1944 .... 35.00
Uncle Sam, 4" h, standing alongside jar, glass, painted, tin closure 550.00
US Mail, 3¼" h, milk glass, painted
dec 130.00
Wheelbarrow, 6" l, tin closure top 60.00

CANES

History: Canes and walking sticks were important accessories in a gentleman's wardrobe in the 18th and 19th centuries. They often served both a decorative and utilitarian function. Collectors frequently view carved canes in wood and ivory as folk art and pay higher prices for them. Glass canes and walking sticks were glass makers' whimsies, ornamental rather than practical.

References: Linda L. Beeman, *The Cane Collector's Directory,* published by author, 1993; Joyce E. Blake, *Glasshouse Whimsies,* published by author, 1984; Catherine Dike, *Cane Curiosa,* published by author, 1983; Catherine Dike, *La Canne: Objet d'Art,* published by author, 1987; George H. Meyer, *American Folk Art Canes: Personal Sculpture,* Sandringham Press, Museum of American Folk Art, and University of Washington Press, 1992; Jeffrey B. Snyder, *Canes: From The Seventeenth to the Twentieth Century,* Schiffer Publishing, 1993.

Periodicals: *Cane Collector's Chronicle,* 15 Second St. NE, Washington, DC 20002;

Walking Stick News, Suite 231, 4051 E. Olive Rd., Pensacola, FL 32514.
Museums: Essex Institute, Salem, MA; Remington Gun Museum, Ilion, NY; Valley Forge Historical Society, Valley Forge, PA.

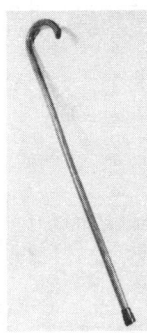

Wooden, 36¼" l, $10.00.

CANES

Ebony, 35" l, elephant head handle, ivory tusks and eyes, chip
carved staff, horn tip, India 500.00
Folk Art, 34½" l, carved and
painted pine, tapering shaft,
turned handle with elaborate relief carved dec, open hand with
silver nails centering a horseshoe, monster face with silvered
teeth, staring eyes, and serpent,
fish, bird, and names "Warren
Lawrence Mike, Orion," details
picked out in silver and gold
paint, probably PA, late 19th/
early 20th C 3,450.00
Gentleman's, gold filled handle,
ebony shaft 225.00
Glass, 46½" l, cobalt blue ext.,
white int., signed "Venini Murano
Italia" 200.00
Ivory, 33½" l, inlaid geometric dec,
incised pattern 50.00
Narwhal, 34¾" l, carved handgrip
with baleen rims, tapering shaft
dec with reeding and hatchwork
over spiral and cylindrical turn-

ings, gilt case with glass cov,
19th C **2,860.00**
Revolver, 35″ l, French, angular
staghorn handle removing to reveal six shot fluted .22 caliber
cylinder, folding trigger, marked
"Paris, Brevette," front of cylinder mounted with 5½″ triangular
blade, composition shaft with
German silver collar **2,475.00**
Scrimshaw, 36″ l, whalebone shaft,
silver collar, beautifully sculptured beast head, numerous age
cracks on back side of head, mid
19th C **800.00**
Sword
37″ l, Oriental, bamboo, intricate
carved figures with ivory inlaid
faces, ivory tooth finial, dam-
age and break in shaft **250.00**
38″ l, wood handle with gad-
rooned gilt brass mounts, slender 30″ blade of diamond section with 8″ fuller at grip,
sidelock device, wood shaft
with brass tip, light pitting on
blade, cracks in shaft **550.00**
Whale Ivory, 34″ l, whale ivory handle and ferrule, wooden shaft
with MOP inlay **140.00**
Wood
35″ l, snake, carved and painted,
initialed at handle end, Denzil
Goodpaster **350.00**
36″ l, wild animal, carved and
painted, abstracted leaf
carved globular knob with Masonic symbol on top, continuing to shaped and carved shaft
depicting snakes, rabbits,
dogs, cheetahs, elephants,
tortoises, owls, and alligators,
metal tip, third quarter 19th C **1,750.00**

HANDLE

Bone, figural lady's calf and foot
with shoe, 19th C **800.00**
Jade, 6″ l, Indian, smooth, dec with
band of stylized flowers inset
with diamond chips, terminating
in lion's head finial with finely
carved mane and ruby set eyes,
19th C **2,475.00**

Silver, 4¾″ w, Faberge, Moscow,
old man's head, dec in old Russian style, marked "K. Faberge"
in Cyrillic with Imperial warrant,
84 standard, c1900 . . . . **5,775.00**

WALKING STICKS

Commemorative, 33″ l, tin, cast
white metal knob with bust of
McKinley, 1896 . . . . **150.00**
Folk Art, 37½″ l, tattoo type, prim-
itive, pony, gazelle, fish, crane,
lizard, and snake, knob handle **30.00**
Horn, 35″ l, variegated, sterling silver top, brass tip **80.00**
Ivory, 37″ l, warped shank, slight
curve **330.00**
Lady's, wood, twisted shaft, two
grooved sides **25.00**
Walnut, 39½″ l, ivory top and tip,
tip repaired **55.00**

CANTON CHINA

History: Canton china is a type of oriental porcelain made in the Canton region
of China from the late 18th century and
early 19th century to the present and produced largely for export. Canton china is
hand decorated in light to dark blue underglaze on white. Design motifs include
houses, mountains, trees, boats, and a
bridge. A design similar to "willow china" is
the most common.

Borders on early Canton feature a rain
and cloud motif (a thick band of diagonal
lines with a scalloped bottom). Later pieces
usually have a straight line border. The
markings "Made in China" and "China" indicate wares which date after 1891.

Early, c1790–1840, plates are very heavy
and often have an unfinished bottom, while
serving pieces have an overall "orange
peel" bottom. Early covered pieces, such
as tureens, vegetable dishes, sugars, etc.,
have strawberry finials and twisted handles.
Later ones have round finials and straight,
single handles.

Reference: Gloria and Robert Mascarelli,
Warman's Oriental Antiques, Wallace–
Homestead, 1992.

Reproduction Alert: Several museum

gift shops and private manufacturers are issuing reproductions of Canton china.

Bowl
9¾" d, bird and floral dec, gold and red, c1820 .... 450.00
12¾" d, Men Riding Mice pattern, calligraphy center, brown glaze rim, unglazed foot, underglaze blue Ch'eng apocryphal seal 275.00
Brush Box, 7⁵⁄₁₆" l, 3⅝" w, 3" h, rect, divided int., glaze imperfections, 19th C 635.00
Candlesticks, pr, 7" h, trumpet shape, flat bobeche 2,400.00
Chamber Pot, cov, 8½" d, domed cov, repaired handle, 19th C .. 290.00
Charger, 24½" d, alternating shaped medallions of figures and birds, flower strewn ground 1,200.00
Creamer, 5½" h, white, rose border, gold trim 150.00

Dish, oval, water edge scene, 9 x 11¼ x 1¾", $250.00.

Fruit Bowl, undertray
9¾" l, repaired, 19th C 635.00
10¾" l, 19th C 1,035.00
Ginger Jar, cov, 8¾" h, imperfections, 19th C 260.00
Jug, 8½" h, Mandarin figures, precious artifacts, butterfly, and Famille Rose dec, early 19th C 300.00
Miniature, teapot, cov, 2⅜" h, bird and floral dec, mid to late 19th C 100.00

Plate, 8½" d, landscape scene, c1830 .... 170.00
Platter
13½" l, 10¼" w, octagonal oblong, coastal village scene, cloud border, mid to dark blue 400.00
14⅞" l, oval, shaped edge, ftd, 19th C 1,150.00
Serving Dish, 8½" w, 10¼" l, diamond shape, 19th C, price for pr 460.00
Soup Plate, 8¾" d, late 65.00
Soup Tureen, cov, 12½" l, 9½" w, 7⅝" h, stem finial, boar head handles, 19th C 865.00
Vegetable Dish, 11½" l, oval, strawberry finial, scalloped rim . 525.00

CAPO-DI-MONTE

History: In 1743 King Charles of Naples established a soft paste porcelain factory near Naples which made figures and dinnerware. In 1760 many of the workmen and most of the molds were taken to Buen Retiro, near Madrid, Spain. A new factory opened in Naples in 1771 and added hard–paste porcelains. In 1834 the Doccia factory in Florence purchased the molds and continued their production in Italy.

Capo–di–Monte was copied heavily by factories in Hungary, Germany, France, and Italy.

Reference: Susan and Al Bagdade, *Warman's English & Continental Pottery & Porcelain, Second Edition,* Wallace–Homestead, 1991.

Reproduction Alert: Many of the pieces in today's market are of recent vintage. Do not be fooled by the crown over the "N" mark; it also was copied.

Box, classical scenes with cherubs, polychrome and gilt dec, crowned "N" mark
5" l 120.00
11" l 665.00
Casket, oval form, relief dec with neoclassical figures and putti, 8" l 230.00

Cup and Saucer, cov, multicolored classical scenes, blue crowned "N" mark, 5¼" h, $80.00.

Cup and Saucer, hp figures around cup, gold trim, dragon handle 75.00
Figure, pr, peasant man and lady 275.00
Plaque, ebonized, Adam and Eve and angel, brass octagonal frame, 20" h 550.00
Platter, 22 x 14½", Christmas ... 125.00
Tray, 12½" w, 15" l, central battle scene, brilliant coloring, blue underglaze mark 1,500.00
Urn, cov, pr, domed lid surmounted by seated putto, gilt ground reserve with molded dec depicting putti at play, scrolled strap handles, circular base, 13" h 575.00

CARLSBAD CHINA

History: Because of changing European boundaries during the last 100 years, German–speaking Carlsbad has found itself located first in the Austro-Hungarian Empire, then in Germany, and currently in Czechoslovakia. Carlsbad was one of the leading pottery manufacturing centers in Bohemia.

Wares from the numerous Carlsbad potteries are lumped together under the term "Carlsbad China." Most pieces on the market are post-1891, although several potteries date to the early 19th century.

Reference: Susan and Al Bagdade, *Warman's English & Continental Pottery & Porcelain, Second Edition,* Wallace–Homestead, 1991.

Bowl, 12" sq, pale peach shading to pale blue, center transfer of five classical maidens, gold foliage, marked "Victoria–Carlsbad" 75.00
Cake Plate, 12" d, violets, pierced gold handles, marked "Victoria, Carlsbad, Austria" 45.00
Chocolate Pot, 10" h, multicolored daisies, gold trim, white ground 100.00
Dessert Set, 9½" d master bowl, twelve 5½" d bowls, scalloped and fluted, four winter scenes, apple blossom boughs, cream ground 175.00

Relish Dish, purple flowers, green leaves, cream ground, matte gold trim, red mark, 8½" l, $22.00.

Dresser Set, 5 pcs, flower petal and raised floral dec, 8½ x 11" tray, two cov jars, ring holder, and ashtray 175.00
Lamp, miniature, 8½" h, porcelain base, Bristol glass shade, orange, blue, and lavender flowers, scrolling gold trim, nutmeg burner, marked "Victoria, Carlsbad, Austria" 425.00
Mug, 4" h, decal portrait of monk, violin, marked "Victoria–Carlsbad" 75.00
Plate, 7⅝" d, scalloped, pink and yellow rose sprays, green buds and leaves, gilt trim, white ground, c1905 .... 35.00

Teapot, cov, relief scrolls, hp flowers, marked "Carlsbad, Austria 1892" **60.00**
Vase, 8½" h, monk portrait, reading newspaper, pink and gold, two handles, marked "Carlsbad Victoria" **50.00**

CARNIVAL GLASS

History: Carnival glass, an American invention, is colored pressed glass with a fired on iridescent finish. It was first manufactured about 1905 and was immensely popular both in America and abroad. Over 1,000 different patterns have been identified. Production of old carnival glass patterns ended in 1930.

Most of the popular patterns of carnival glass were produced by five companies— Dugan, Fenton, Imperial, Millersburg, and Northwood. Northwood patterns frequently are found with the "N" trademark. Dugan used a diamond trademark on several patterns.

In carnival glass, color is the most important factor in pricing. The color of a piece is determined by holding the piece to the light and looking through it.

References: Gary E. Baker et al., *Wheeling Glass: 1829–1939, Collection of the Oglebay Institute Glass Museum*, Oglebay Institute, 1994, distributed by Antique Publications; Bill Edwards, *The Standard Encyclopedia of Carnival Glass, Fourth Edition*, Collector Books, 1994; Marion T. Hartung, *First Book of Carnival Glass to Tenth Book of Carnival Glass* (series of 10 books), published by author, 1968 to 1982; William Heacock, James Measell and Berry Wiggins, *Dugan/Diamond: The Story of Indiana, Pennsylvania, Glass*, Antique Publications, 1993; William Heacock, James Measell and Berry Wiggins, *Harry Northwood, The Wheeling Years, 1901–1925*, Antique Publications, 1991; Thomas E. Sprain, *Carnival Glass Tumblers, New and Reproduced*, published by author, 1984.

Collectors' Clubs: American Carnival Glass Assoc., PO Box 235, Littlestown, PA 17340; Collectible Carnival Glass Assoc., 2360 N. Old S.R. 9, Columbus, IN 47203;

Heart of America Carnival Glass Assoc., 3048 Tamarak Drive, Manhattan, KS 66502; International Carnival Glass Assoc., Inc, RR #1, Box 14, Mentone, IN 46539; New England Carnival Glass Club, 12 Sherwood Road, West Hartford, CT 06117.

Periodicals: *The Auction Reporter*, PO Box 246, Scottsburg, IN 47170; *Encore*, PO Box 11734, Kansas City, MO 64138.

Museum: Fenton Art Glass Co., Williamstown, WV.

Pond Lily, Fenton, bonbon, 2 handles, white, 7¼" d, 3½" h, $90.00.

Acorn, Fenton
Bowl, 7½" d, cobalt blue, radium finish **85.00**
Ice Cream Bowl, green **70.00**
Acorn Burrs, Northwood
Butter Dish, cov, purple **225.00**
Creamer, marigold **55.00**
Ice Cream Bowl, marigold **35.00**
Spooner, marigold **75.00**
Tumbler, green **55.00**
April Showers, Fenton, vase, 8" h, marigold **50.00**
Basketweave, Northwood, bowl, hat shape, marigold and white . **50.00**
Big Fish, Millersburg, bowl, sq, amethyst, small base nick **950.00**
Bouquet, Fenton, pitcher, blue .. **500.00**
Bushel Basket, Northwood
Marigold **65.00**
White, chip **85.00**
Butterfly and Berry, Fenton
Bowl, 9¼" d, marigold **80.00**
Table Set, marigold, 4 pcs **400.00**
Tumbler, blue **35.00**

Cherries, Dugan, plate, 6″ d, tight crimp, purple 210.00
Cherry, Millersburg
Bowl, 10″ d, marigold, tiny flake 195.00
Vase, 9½″ h, fine rib, red 400.00
Colonial Panel, Imperial, vase, 10½″ h, purple 48.00
Cosmos & Cane, US Glass, jelly compote, white 325.00
Dahlia, Dugan or Diamond Glass Co
Bowl, 10″ d, ftd, white 195.00
Butter Dish, cov, marigold 150.00
Creamer, purple 125.00
Sauce, marigold 40.00
Tumbler, purple 185.00
Dragon & Lotus, Fenton
Bowl, 8″ d, ruffled
Amber opalescent 700.00
Blue 150.00
Ice Cream Bowl, 9″ d, collared base, blue 55.00
Fanciful, Dugan, bowl, 10″ d, ruffled, white 215.00
Fentonia, Fenton, bowl, large, blue 265.00
Fine Cut & Roses, Northwood, candy dish, 3 ftd, green 150.00
Fishnet, Dugan, epergne, peach opal 195.00
Flute, Imperial, bowl, 8″ d, teal . . 200.00
Fruits & Flowers, Northwood, bonbon, marigold 130.00
Good Luck, Northwood
Bowl
8″ d, piecrust edge, light amethyst 300.00
8½″ d, ruffled, scalloped, marigold, ribbed back 155.00
Plate, purple 300.00
Grape, Imperial
Bowl, 4¾″ d, marigold 15.00
Compote, green 20.00
Cup and Saucer, Helios Green 70.00
Goblet, marigold 25.00
Plate, marigold, 6½″ d 50.00
Tumbler
Purple 45.00
Smoke 110.00
Water Carafe, purple 220.00
Wine, purple 38.00
Grape and Cable, Northwood or Fenton
Banana Boat, marigold 175.00

Bonbon, stippled handle, dark marigold 45.00
Butter Bowl, purple 150.00
Cologne Bottle, orig stopper, purple 350.00
Dresser Tray, purple 200.00
Hatpin Holder, green 275.00
Plate, amethyst 255.00
Punch Cup, purple 30.00
Sweetmeat, purple 275.00
Grape and Gothic Arches, Northwood
Butter Bowl, electric blue 195.00
Spooner, marigold 48.00
Sugar, marigold 48.00
Water Set, dark marigold 325.00
Hearts and Flowers, Northwood
Compote, dark marigold 190.00
Plate, marigold 300.00
Holly, Fenton
Bowl, 3–n–1 edge, cobalt blue . 125.00
Compote, small, dark marigold . 35.00
Hat, ruffled, red 365.00
Plate, blue 350.00
Leaf & Beads, Northwood
Candy Dish, ftd, green 75.00
Nut Bowl, purple 65.00
Rose Bowl, blue 160.00
Leaf Rays, Dugan, nappy, blue . 250.00
Lotus & Grape, Fenton
Bonbon, ftd, marigold 40.00
Bowl, 5″ d, blue 45.00
Plate, 9″ d, blue 600.00
Mikado, Fenton, compote, marigold 400.00
Morning Glory, Millersburg, vase, 5¼″ h, flared 48.00
Mystery Peacock, Millersburg, bowl, amethyst 300.00
Orange Tree, Fenton
Bowl, 8″ d, green 65.00
Breakfast Set, individual size creamer and cov sugar, blue . 125.00
Compote, 6″ d, marigold 25.00
Creamer, marigold 35.00
Goblet, blue 60.00
Ice Cream Bowl, dark marigold 150.00
Pitcher, blue, rough feet 175.00
Plate, clambroth 215.00
Powder Jar, cov, blue 135.00
Peacock, Northwood, bowl, piecrust edge, marigold 275.00
Peacock and Dahlia, Fenton, bowl, 7¼″ d, marigold 75.00

Peacock and Urn, Millersburg
Berry Set, master bowl, five
   sauces, purple 750.00
Goblet, marigold 75.00
Ice Cream Bowl, marigold, tiny
   chip 300.00
Plate, 9″ d, marigold 172.00
Peacock and Urn, Northwood, ice
cream bowl, icy blue, tiny chip . 700.00
Peacock at the Fountain, Northwood
Berry Bowl, master, marigold .. 90.00
Butter Dish, cov, purple 300.00
Creamer, purple 90.00
Orange Bowl, blue, small air
   bubble burst on one foot 695.00
Spooner
   Purple 150.00
   White 190.00
Tumbler, purple 50.00
Peacock at the Urn, Fenton
Bowl, ruffled, blue 165.00
Compote, ruffled, aqua 195.00
Plate, blue 450.00
Persian Gardens, Dugan, plate,
7″ d, white 175.00
Plum Panels, Fenton, vase, 10½″
h, marigold 30.00
Poppy Show, Northwood, plate,
white 550.00
Raindrop, Dugan, bowl, 9″ d, ruffled, pedestal base, amethyst,
cobalt blue satin irid 110.00
Ripple, Imperial, vase, 12¼″ h,
purple 110.00
Rose Show, Northwood
Bowl, marigold 275.00
Plate, 9″ d, electric blue 1,200.00
Round Up, Dugan, bowl, white .. 150.00
Scroll Embossed, Imperial
Bowl, 9″ d, marigold 40.00
Compote, 6 x 4¼″, ruffled, green 65.00
Singing Birds, Northwood
Mug, purple 125.00
Sugar, large, satin marigold ... 130.00
Springtime, Northwood
Butter Bowl, marigold 245.00
Creamer, marigold 125.00
Spooner, purple 275.00
Sugar, cov, amethyst 200.00
Star of David, Imperial, bowl, Helios, green 200.00
Stippled Rays, Northwood
Bonbon, blue 40.00

Bowl
   5⅝″ d, marigold 40.00
   10″ d, crimped, amethyst 55.00
Creamer and Sugar, marigold . 68.00
Plate, 7″ d, amethyst 45.00
Strawberry, Millersburg
Bonbon, two handles, marigold 32.00
Bowl, plain ext., green 150.00
Swirl Hobnail, Millersburg, rose
bowl, amethyst 250.00
Ten Mums, Fenton, bowl, 10¼″ d 120.00
Thistle, Fenton
Banana Boat, marigold 175.00
Bowl, green 125.00
Three Fruits, Northwood
Bonbon, marigold 50.00
Bowl, ruffled, stippled, green .. 595.00
Plate, 7″ d, basketweave ext.,
   green 115.00
Town Pump, Northwood, purple,
repaired on bottom 125.00
Vintage, Fenton
Bowl, 8″ d, green 100.00
Card Tray, marigold 45.00
Cup, green 35.00
Epergne, amethyst 100.00
Fernery, blue 45.00
Water Lily, Fenton, bowl, 5″ d, 3
ftd, vaseline 175.00
Windflower, Dugan, bowl, marigold 95.00
Wreath of Roses, Fenton
Bonbon, 3¾″ h, 5″ d, two handles, pedestal, dark green ... 55.00
Rose Bowl, marigold 48.00
Spittoon, amber 165.00
Zig Zag, Fenton, bowl, 10″ d, amethyst, radium finish 325.00

CAROUSEL FIGURES

History: By the late 17th century, carousels were found in most capital cities of Europe. In 1867 Gustav Dentzel carved America's first carousel. Other leading American manufacturers include Charles I. D. Looff, Allan Herschell, Charles Parker, and William F. Mangels.

Original paint is not critical since figures were repainted annually. Park paint indicates layers of accumulated paint; stripped means paint removed to show carving; restored involves stripping and repainting in the original colors.

References: Charlotte Dinger, *Art Of The Carousel,* Carousel Art, 1983; Tobin Fraley, *The Carousel Animal,* Tobin Fraley Studios, 1983; Tobin Fraley, *The Great American Carousel: A Century of Master Craftmanship,* Chronicle Books, 1994; Frederick Fried, *The Pictorial History Of The Carrousel,* Vestal Press, 1964; William Manns, Peggy Shank, and Marianne Stevens, *Painted Ponies: American Carousel Art,* Zon International Publishing, 1986; Dana G. Morykan and Harry L. Rinker, *Warman's Country Antiques & Collectibles, Second Edition,* Wallace–Homestead, 1994.

Periodicals: *Carrousel Art Magazine,* PO Box 992, Garden Grove, CA 92642; *Carousel Shopper,* Zon International Publishing, PO Box 47, Millwood, NY 10546; *The Carousel News & Trader,* Suite 206, 87 Park Avenue West, Mansfield, OH 44902.

Collectors' Clubs: American Carousel Society, 3845 Telegraph Rd., Elkton, MD 21921; National Amusement Park Historical Association, PO Box 83, Mount Prospect, IL 60056; National Carousel Association, PO Box 4333, Evansville, IN 47724.

Museums: Carousel Museum of America, San Francisco, CA; Heritage Plantation of Sandwich, Sandwich, MA; Herschell Carrousel Factory Museum, North Tonawanda, NY; International Museum of Carousel Art, Portland, OR; Merry–Go–Round Museum, Sandusky, OH; New England Carousel Museum, Inc., Bristol, CT.

Cat, carved wood, American, Gustav Dent, $27,500.00.

Deer, prancing, closed mouth, eagle behind saddle, restored, Gustav Dentzel, c1885 ......**17,500.00**
Donkey, 43" l, nodding head, carved, saddle and blanket, gray, red, brown, yellow, and blue, brass handle grip, Bayol of Angers, France, c1880 ....**1,425.00**
Elephant, 26" h, 34" l, pine, carved, traces of gilding, black paint, glass eyes, black trimmed red blanket on back **3,300.00**
Horse
43" h, wood, laminated construction, white repaint, green, red, and blue accents, glass eyes, replaced horsehair tail **915.00**
50" l, laminated carved wood, good detail, glass eyes, horsehair tail, old worn repaint, old repairs, braces, attributed to Dentzel **6,050.00**
55" l, standing, wooden, laminated, glass eyes, old polychrome repaint, added steel base and brass rod **330.00**
57" h, 48" l, jumper, outside row, Armitage–Herschell, c1890 ..**2,250.00**
73" h, 64" l, standing, orig paint, iron stirrups, Stein and Goldstein, Brooklyn, NY, c1899–1900 ....**40,000.00**
Ostrich, 56" h, 58" l, running, carved feathers and saddle, hinged neck, refinished, Savages of King's Lynn, England, c1875 ....**3,300.00**
Ox, 37¼" h, laminated carved wood, old worn repaint, minor edge damage and repair, modern base and pole with finial .. **470.00**
Pig, 59" l, carved and painted, Limonaire Freres, Paris, 19th C .**1,210.00**
Rooster, 38" h, 32" l, running, 19th C **2,500.00**

CASTLEFORD

History: Castleford is a soft–paste porcelain made in Yorkshire, England, in the 1800s for the American trade. The ware has a warm, white ground, scalloped rims (resembling castle tops), and is trimmed in deep blue. Occasionally pieces are decorated further with a coat of arms, eagles, or Lady Liberty.

Bowl, 5″ d, scalloped, white ground, blue bands 185.00
Creamer, 3½″ h, three brown oval medallions, one with white applied eagle and shield, second with Lady Liberty, and third with cherubs and eagle on cloud . . . 300.00
Sugar, cov, round, mythological scenes, vertical panels, twisted rope band near top, scalloped edge with oval medallions, blue enamel lines, dome lid, floral knob 200.00

Teapot, blue dec, 9″ l, 5¼″ h, $225.00.

Teapot, cov, mythological scenes, flanked by floral panels, acanthus leaf borders top and bottom, blue enamel lines on body, lid, and handle, leaf shape spout, floret knob 225.00

CASTOR SETS

History: A castor set consists of matched condiment bottles within a frame or holder. The bottles are for condiments such as salt, pepper, oil, vinegar, and mustard. The most commonly found castor set consists of three to five glass bottles in a silver–plated frame.

Although castor sets were known as early as the 1700s, most of the sets encountered today date from the 1870 to 1915 period when they enjoyed great popularity.

2 Bottle, Quimper Pottery, blue sponge trim, shaped cupped tray base, 8″ w, 5⅜″ h 150.00
3 Bottle, Bohemian glass, one each cranberry, emerald green, and cobalt blue, orig stoppers, silver plated trim, rings, and handles, silver plated holder, three matching etched goblets, 19″ h 925.00
3 Bottle, Bristol glass, enameled flowers, silver plated holder . . . 110.00
3 Bottle, Mt Washington, salt, pepper, and mustard, figural swan feet, center handle, Wilcox frame 135.00
3 Bottle, pink luster, salt, pepper, and mustard, orig china shovel, matching ftd holder 45.00
3 Bottle, Satin Glass, white, ribbed, silver plated holder marked "Pairpoint" 225.00
4 Bottle, blown three mold, clear barrel form bottles, three applied neck rings, flared mouth, pewter holder 110.00
4 Bottle, blown three mold, cruet with solid ball stopper, mustard with ribbed cov, two shakers with orig metal caps, red painted sq tin frame 400.00
4 Bottle, clear bottles, pewter holder 75.00
4 Bottle, Fenton, opaque turquoise glass bottles, matching holder . 95.00
4 Bottle, pattern glass, Daisy and Button, blue, glass holder 125.00
5 Bottle, blown three mold, clear bottles, tooled and ground mouths, pewter holder 90.00
5 Bottle, clear bottles, 9½″ h silver plated frame 240.00
5 Bottle, cut glass bottles, lunar and geometric cutting, sterling silver mountings, sterling silver Warwick form holder with shell shaped foot, English, hallmarks, c1750, 8½″ h 600.00
5 Bottle, freeblown, turned wood holder with brass handle, five ivory finials 55.00
5 Bottle, ivory, silver plated tops, mahogany case 150.00
5 Bottle, pattern glass, Bellflower

pattern, two bottles with ribbed period stoppers, pewter stand . **300.00**

5 Bottle, pattern glass, Heavy Paneled Finecut pattern, silver plated holder **90.00**

5 Bottle, Sandwich glass, Cable pattern, pewter frame, Rufus Dunham, Westbrook, ME, 19th C **350.00**

5 Bottle, vaseline glass, fern engraving, orig tops and stoppers, handled frame sgd "Meriden" . **275.00**

Six Bottles, cut and etched, SP holder with floral medallions, 14" h, $130.00.

6 Bottle, amberina glass, metal holder marked "Aurora, 487" . . **2,000.00**

6 Bottle, cut glass bottles, 9¾" h silver plated oval holder with baluster stem, loop handle **375.00**

6 Bottle, Victorian, cut glass bottles, silver plated foliate dec stand, 17½" h **115.00**

7 Bottle, cut glass bottles with sterling silver collars and caps, 8½" h George III silver canoe shape holder with galleried dec and scroll feet, marked "Peter, Ann & William Bateman, London" . . **1,250.00**

CATALOGS

History: The first American mail order catalog was issued by Benjamin Franklin in 1744. This popular advertising tool helped to spread inventions, innovations, fashions, and other necessities of life to rural America. Catalogs were profusely illustrated and are studied today to date an object, identify its manufacturer, study its distribution, and determine its historical importance.

References: Don Fredgant, *American Trade Catalogs: Identification and Value Guide,* Collector Books, 1984; Norman E. Martinus and Harry L. Rinker, *Warman's Paper,* Wallace–Homestead, 1994; Lawrence B. Romaine, *A Guide To American Trade Catalogs 1744–1900,* R. R. Bowker, 1960, 1990 reprint.

Museum: National Museum of Health and Medicine, Walter Reed Medical Center, Washington, DC.

Additional Listings: See *Warman's Americana & Collectibles* for more examples.

A Cutler & Son, Buffalo, NY, 51 pgs, Cutler desks **45.00**

Adolph Meyer & Co, Boston, MA, 1893, 72 pgs **18.00**

Smith's Welding & Cutting Equipment, Smith's Inventions, Inc., Minneapolis, MN, Bonniwell Calvin Iron Co., Kansas City, MO, soft cov, 28 pgs, black and white illus, 4 x 8¾", $15.00.

Atlas School Supply Co, Chicago, IL, 1911, 72 pgs 25.00

Bacon & Vincent Co, Buffalo, NY, 1926, 60 pgs, school supplies . 22.00

Bausch & Lomb Optical Co, Rochester, NY, 1898, 15 pgs 15.00

Benjamin Allen & Co, Chicago, IL, 1923, 732 pgs, jewelry 90.00

Bucher & Gibbs Plow, 1931, 32 pgs 34.00

Butler Brothers, New York, NY, 1918, 76 pgs, automotive supplies 20.00

Carl Forslund Furniture, 1949, 67 pgs 30.00

Chicago Spring Butt Co, Chicago, IL, 29 pgs, spring hinges and hardware 18.00

Corgi, 1966, Bond's Aston Martin cov 45.00

Crawford Co, Reading, PA, 1916, 24 pgs, clothing 10.00

Curtis Companies, Inc, Clinton, IA, 1920, 238 pgs, architectural supplies 55.00

C W Sweetland & Son, Boston, MA, 1937, 56 pgs, International Silverware distributor 30.00

Deforest Radio Co, Jersey City, NJ, 1929, 31 pgs 20.00

Dinky Toys, c1912 .... 150.00

Eastman Kodak Co, Rochester, NY, 1929, 32 pgs 6.00

Edison Storage Battery Co, 1930, 31 pgs, $3\frac{1}{2}$ x $6\frac{1}{2}$" 15.00

Enterprise Rubber Co, Boston, MA, 1915, 44 pgs, automobile accessories 20.00

Gimbel Brothers, New York, NY, 1922, 24 pgs, lamps 28.00

Hall Mammoth Incubator Co, Utica, NY, 1910, 72 pgs 16.00

Hammerblow Tool Co, Wausau, WI, 1940, 22 pgs, automotive supplies 35.00

H H Mayhew Co, 1901, 52 pgs, tools 20.00

International Harvester, 1923, 98 pgs, $3\frac{1}{2}$ x $5\frac{1}{4}$" 45.00

John Wanamaker Co, Philadelphia, PA, No. 66, 1908, 20 pgs 12.00

Kalamazoo Stove Co, 1935, 38 pgs 22.00

Kennedy Bros Arms Co, St Paul, MN, 1930, 64 pgs, sporting goods 25.00

King Sewing Machine Co, Buffalo, NY, 1909, 56 pgs 25.00

Marshall–Wells Co, Duluth, MN, 1921, 365 pgs, plumbing and heating 35.00

Maurice Miller Co, Johnstown, PA, 1929, 12 pgs, clothing 15.00

Mermod, Jaccard & King Co, c1930, 40 pgs, jewelry 25.00

Moline Plow Co, 1918, 116 pgs, $5\frac{1}{4}$ x $7\frac{1}{2}$" 35.00

Nehi Bottling Co, Ponca City, OK, 1929, 8 pgs, premiums 15.00

Novelty Cutlery Co, Canton, OH, 29 pgs 65.00

O Ditcher & Grader Co, Owensboro, KY, 1915, 16 pgs 32.00

Olson Rug Co, Chicago, IL, 1926, 36 pgs 25.00

Peck Clothing Co, Syracuse, NY, 1905, 16 pgs 22.00

Perfection Mfg Co, St Louis, MO, 1923, 32 pgs, child's nursery accessories 25.00

Pilley Packing & Flue, 1910, 56 pgs, tool supplies 30.00

Rockford Watch Co, Rockford, IL, 1882, 12 pgs 48.00

Rush Sash & Door Co, Kansas City, MO, 1929, 48 pgs 30.00

Samuel Ward Mfg Co, Boston, MA, 1909, 68 pgs, stationery 25.00

Schmoller & Mueller Piano, 1913, 32 pgs, $8\frac{1}{2}$ x 11" 45.00

Schoenhut Toys, c1912 .... 150.00

Singer Mfg Co, 1929, 10 pgs ... 11.00

Spellman Brothers, New York, NY, 1879, 36 pgs, clothing accessories 32.00

Spiegel, Christmas, 1963, 395 pgs 40.00

Stowe Hardware & Supply, 1932, 610 pgs, $8\frac{1}{2}$ x 11" 45.00

Underwood Typewriter Co, New York, NY, 1912, 24 pgs 8.00

United Cigar Stores Premiums, 1927 .... 15.00

W A W & Reaping Machine, Hoosick, NY, 1878, 16 pgs 49.00

Winchester Repeating Arms, 1940, 76 pgs, rifles and shotguns 30.00

W M Ritter Lumber Co, 1920s, 33
pgs, oak flooring 25.00
York Manufacturing Co, York, PA,
1920, 176 pgs, ice making and
refrigerating machinery 20.00

CELADON

History: The term celadon, meaning a
pale grayish green color, is derived from the
theatrical character Celadon, who wore
costumes of varying shades of grayish
green, in Honore d'Urfe's 17th–century pastoral romance, *L'Astree*. French Jesuits living in China applied it to a specific type of
Chinese porcelain.

Celadon divides into two types. Northern
celadon, made during the Sung Dynasty up
to the 1120s, has a gray to brownish body,
relief decoration, and monochrome olive
green glaze.

Southern (Lung-ch'uan) celadon, made
during the Sung Dynasty and much later, is
paint decorated with floral and other scenic
designs and found in forms which would
appeal to the European and American export market. Many of the Southern pieces
date from 1825 to 1885. A blue square with
Chinese or pseudo-Chinese characters appears on pieces after 1850. Later pieces
also have a larger and sparser decorative
patterning.

Reproduction Alert.

Bowl
  4½" d, conical form, shallow,
    Ch'u–Chou, Sung or early
    Ming Dynasty, price for pair . . 385.00
  5" d, imp peony design in center,
    Sung or Ming Dynasty 125.00
  5¾" d
    Bell form, Sung Dynasty 185.00
    Ribbed sides, carved haw-
      thorn center, Sung Dynasty 180.00
  6" d
    Carp design, Sung Dynasty . . 300.00
    Concentric ring design, shal-
      low, Sung Dynasty 150.00
    Leaf carved ext., grass design
      int., Sung Dynasty, in fitted
      box 295.00
  7" d, flower form, incised design,
    Sung Dynasty 385.00

Brush Washer, 2" d, fluted sides,
  Sung Dynasty 75.00
Jar, miniature
  2" h, unglazed foot, Sung Dy-
    nasty 75.00
  2¾" h, crackle glaze, brown lip
    and foot, Chun, Sung Dynasty 550.00
Paste Box, cov, 3" d, dome top,
  passion flower design, Sung Dy-
  nasty 350.00
Tea Bowl, 4" d, unglazed ring foot,
  Sung Dynasty 145.00
Vase, funerary, 19½" h, relief
  dragon and figural design, Sung
  Dynasty 300.00

CELLULOID ITEMS

History: In 1869 brothers J. W. Hyatt and
I. S. Hyatt developed celluloid, the world's
first synthetic plastic, as an ivory substitute
because elephant herds were being slaugh-
tered for their ivory tusks.

Known as "Ivorine" or "French Ivory," celluloid was made of nitrocellulose and camphor. Early pieces have a creamy color with
stripes and grooves to imitate the texture of
ivory or bone. The 1897 Sears catalog featured celluloid items. Celluloid was used
widely until synthetics replaced it in the
early 1950s. Celluloid often is used as a
generic term for all early plastics.

Bowie Knife, English style, celluloid grip, coin silver mounted hilt,
  c1880, 11½" l spear point blade,
  17⅛" l 385.00
Doll, baby, Minerva, jointed hips
  and shoulders, bent limbs,
  brown glass eyes, open mouth
  with teeth and tongue, body and
  head marked, orig box and
  clothes, 15½" h 175.00
Figures, Snow White and the
  Seven Dwarfs, 6½" h Snow
  White holding small yellow bird,
  5½" h dwarfs, paper labels,
  Grumpy repaired, some very
  small cracks 150.00
Fish Service, twelve forks and
  knives, celluloid handles, engraved SP tines and blades, fitted oak case, English, c1900 . . 350.00

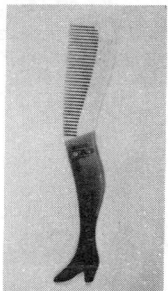

Mustache Comb, leg shape, jeweled rhinestone garter, stained gray leg, black high button boot, 5¾" l, $50.00.

Fish Serving Set, knife and fork, ivory celluloid handles, engraved SP blade and tines, fitted case, English, c1900, 12½" l **300.00**

Fruit Service, eleven forks, twelve knives, purple celluloid handles, English gilt silver blades, velvet lined leather case **120.00**

Kewpie, some mold imperfections, slight crack in leg, 21¼" h **275.00**

Letter Opener, figural, black man's head, adv on blade **25.00**

Tape Measure, Sears Roebuck Plows, multicolored, illus of David Bradley plow **75.00**

Toy
  Balancing, Donald Duck, long bill, jointed arms, standing atop orange and white weighted base, small split at neck, arms detached, 7" h . . . **450.00**
  Windup
    Mickey Mouse on Pluto, Mickey dressed as cowboy, orig box, c1932, 7¾" l **8,250.00**
    Speedy Donkey, orig box, Japan, 7½" h **450.00**

Vanity Set, 11" l, mirror, brush, powder box, nail buffer, and shoe horn, pale green, aluminum and black plastic inlays, dark semi–circular appliques, imp mark, Paul Frankl, designed for Celluloid Corp of America, produced by Rond Amerith **350.00**

CHALKWARE

History: William Hutchinson, an Englishman, invented chalkware in 1848. It was a substance used by sculptors to imitate marble. It also was used to harden plaster of paris, creating confusion between the two products.

Chalkware often copied many of the popular Staffordshire items of the 1820 to 1870 period. It was cheap, gayly decorated, and sold by vendors. The Pennsylvania German "folk art" pieces are from this period.

Carnivals, circuses, fairs, and amusement parks used chalkware pieces as prizes during the late 19th and 20th centuries. They often were poorly made and gaudy. Don't confuse them with the earlier pieces. Prices for these chalkware items range from $10 to $50.

References: Thomas G. Morris, *Carnival Chalk Prize,* Prize Publishers, 1985; Dana G. Morykan and Harry L. Rinker, *Warman's Country Antiques & Collectibles, Second Edition,* Wallace–Homestead, 1994; Ted Soufe, *Midway Mania: A Collectors Guide To Carnival Plaster Figurines, Prizes, and Equipment 1900–1950,* L–W, Inc., 1985.

Additional Listings: See Carnival Chalkware in *Warman's Americana & Collectibles.*

Dachsund Dog, sitting, black and brown, 5½" l base, 4¾" h, $25.00.

Figure
  Cat
    10" l, black and white, faded red, orig paint **175.00**

12" l, black and white, red and
blue ribbon, orig paint 175.00
12¼" l, sleeping, black stripes,
white, red, blue, and green,
orig paint 125.00
Deer, 6" h, recumbent, painted,
American 65.00
Dog
5½" h, seated, white, red and
black dec, wear, old shallow
chip on base 165.00
7¾" h, black stripes, white,
red, black, and yellow, orig
paint 165.00
8¾" h
Black spots, white, orange,
and green, orig paint 175.00
White, black, red, and green
dec, minor wear 250.00
Ox, 19" l, worn red and white
finish, wooden horns and ears 50.00
Rabbit, 10" h, white, yellow and
brown dec 50.00
Stag, 10" h, old paint, glued repair to antlers, pr 10.00
Incense Burner, 13½" l, 13½" h,
7½" d, Persian Garden Incense,
figural elephant, incense saddle
on back 25.00
Ornament, 9½" h, painted basket
of flowers, 19th C 90.00
Plaque, 13½" h, deer head, worn
old paint, oval frames, old black
repaint, edge chips, wear, glued
antlers, pr 72.00

CHARACTER AND PERSONALITY ITEMS

History: While a host of fictional characters originate from the comics, movies,
radio, and television, a group of "stars" who
retained their own identify are also a by-
product; Hopalong Cassidy is a fictional
character; Gene Autry and Roy Rogers are
real–life personalities. Real–life drama also
produces "heroes" honored for a heroic
moment or a unique personal achievement.

In many cases, toys and other products
using the image of fictional comic, movie,
and radio characters occur simultaneously
with the origin of the character. The first

Dick Tracy toy was manufactured less than
a year after the strip first appeared.

The "golden age" of character material is
the TV era of the mid–1950s through the
late 1960s. Some radio premium collectors
might argue this point. Today, television and
movie producers often have their product
licensing arranged well in advance of the
initial release.

Do not overlook the characters created
by advertising agencies, e.g., Tony the Tiger. They represent a major collecting sub-
category.

This category includes only objects related to fictional characters. Sometimes the
line can become very blurred. Bill Boyd's
portrayal of Hopalong Cassidy turned Clarence Mulford's fictional hero into a real–life
entity in the minds of many.

References: Bill Bruegman, *Cartoon
Friends Of The Baby Boom Era,* Cap'n
Penny Productions, 1993; William Crouch,
Jr. and Lawrence Doucet, *The Authorized
Guide to Dick Tracy Collectibles,* Wallace–
Homestead, 1990; Richard DeThuin, *The
Official Identification and Price Guide To
Movie Memorabilia,* House of Collectibles,
1990; Warren Dotz, *Advertising Character
Collectibles: An Identification And Value
Guide,* Collector Books, 1993; Fred Gran-
dinetti, *Popeye: The Collectible,* Krause
Publications, 1990; Ted Hake, *Hake's
Guide To Comic Character Collectibles: An
Illustrated Price Guide to 100 Years of
Comic Strip Characters,* Wallace–Home-
stead, 1993; Ted Hake, *Hake's Guide To
Cowboy Character Collectibles: An Illus-
trated Price Guide Covering 50 Years of
Movie & TV Cowboy Heroes,* Wallace–
Homestead, 1994; Ted Hake, *Hake's Guide
To TV Character Collectibles,* Wallace–
Homestead, 1990; John Hegenberger, *Col-
lector's Guide To Treasures From The Sil-
ver Screen,* Wallace–Homestead, 1991;
David Longest, *Character Toys and Collec-
tibles,* Collector Books, 1984, 1992 value
update; David Longest, *Character Toys
And Collectibles, Second Series,* Collector
Books, 1987, 1990 value update; Patrick
McCarver, *A Gone With The Wind Collec-
tor's Price Guide,* Collector's Originals,
1990; Richard O'Brien, *Collecting Toys: A
Collector's Identification & Value Guide,
Sixth Edition,* Books Americana, 1993;

Jerry Osborne, *The Official Price Guide To Elvis Presley Records and Memorabilia,* House of Collectibles, 1994; Brian Paquette and Paul Howley, *The Toys From U.N.C.L.E.: Memorabilia and Collectors Guide,* Entertainment Publishing, 1990; Edward R. Pardella, *Shirley Temple Dolls and Fashions,* Schiffer Publishing, 1992; Jay Scarfone and William Stillman, *The Wizard of Oz Collector's Treasure,* Schiffer Publishing, 1992; Patricia Smith, *Shirley Temple Dolls and Collectibles* (1977, 1992 value update), *Second Series* (1979, 1992 value update); John R. Warren, *Warren's Movie Poster Price Guide,* American Collectors Exchange, 1993; Dian Zillner, *Hollywood Collectibles,* Schiffer Publishing, 1991; Dian Zillner, *Hollywood Collectibles: The Sequel,* Schiffer Publishing, 1994.

Periodicals: *Autograph Times,* 2303 N. 44th St., No. 225, Phoenix, AZ 85008; *Big Reel,* PO Box 83, Madison, NC 27025; *Classic Images,* PO Box 809, Muscatine, IA 52761; *Gone With The Wind Collector's Newsletter,* 1347 Greenmoss Dr., Richmond, VA 23225; *Hollywood Collectibles,* 2900 N. Meade St., Suite #4, Appleton, WI 54911; *Movie Advertising Collector,* PO Box 28587, Philadelphia, PA 19149; *Movie Collectors' World,* PO Box 309, Fraser, MI 48026; *Television History Magazine,* 700 E. Macoupin St., Stanton, IL 62088; *The TV Collector Magazine,* PO Box 1088, Easton, MA 02334.

Additional Listings: See *Warman's Americana & Collectibles* for expanded listings in Cartoon Characters, Cowboy Collectibles, Movie Personalities and Memorabilia, Radio Characters and Personalities, Shirley Temple, Space Adventurers, and TV Personalities and Memorabilia.

CHARACTERS

Alfred E. Neuman, model kit, plastic pieces, instruction sheet, and uncut sign sheet, orig box, 1965 E C Publications copyright **225.00**

Andy Gump, sheet music, 9¼ x 12¼", full color images on front cov, 1923 copyright **35.00**

Aunt Jemima, sign, 9½" w, 17½" h, hanging, diecut cardboard, Aunt Jemima Pancake Flour, "I'se In Town, Honey," figural, Aunt Jemima on swing, flour box on either side, plate of pancakes on lap **5,400.00**

Batman, lamp, Batman standing in front of Bat Cave, figural **95.00**

Betty Boop
 Nodder, 7" h, celluloid, orig box, Made in Japan, copyright Fleischer Studios **1,500.00**
 Perfume Bottle, 3½" h, glass, clear, figural, painted facial features, dark red plastic cap, c1930 .... **50.00**
 Rattle, 6" h, celluloid, movable arms, orig crib string **500.00**

Buster Brown
 Dessert Dish, 5½" d, china, full color illus, German, c1905 ... **75.00**
 Game, Pin The Tie On Buster, sgd "Outcault" **125.00**
 Hatchet, 13¼" l, emb metal head, trademark Buster Brown and Tige image, wood handle **35.00**

Captain America, shield, brass, red and blue, 1941–42 ...... **350.00**

Captain Kangaroo, cup, 3½" h, soft plastic, dark reddish–brown, copyright Robert Keeshan, 1950s **25.00**

Captain Midnight
 Member Kit, Secret Squadron, 8 pg manual and code book, membership card, and chrome and plastic decoder, orig mailing envelope, 1955–56 ..... **400.00**
 Mug, 3¼" h, Ovaltine, plastic, red, full color decal, c1953 .. **25.00**

Charlie McCarthy and Mortimer Snerd Coupe, Louis Marx Toys, litho tin car, orig box, $4,840.00.

Patch, 2¼" d, Secret Squadron, black, white, and orange, unopened cellophane packet ... **35.00**

Charlie McCarthy

Bank, 7½" h, metal, painted, figural, posed with brown suitcase, 1938–39 .... **150.00**

Radio Game Premium, Chase & Sanborn, 1938, orig mailer .. **70.00**

Soap, figural, orig box with illus of E Bergen, 1940s **120.00**

Toy, 8½" h, windup, litho tin, Marx Toys, c1939 .... **200.00**

Cisco Kid

Clicker Gun, 10" l, diecut cardboard, Tip Top Bread premium, early 1950s **50.00**

Mask, 3¼ x 7", diecut, Cisco and Pancho portraits with gold outline and red accents, titled "See Us On Television," elastic string band, orig mailing envelope, Dolly Madison Ice Cream and Aristocrat Ice Cream products premium, c1950 .... **100.00**

Dagwood, paper lunch bag, waxed paper, colorful Bumstead image, 1952, KFS, unused **25.00**

Davy Crockett

Bank, 5" h, metal, copper colored, bust, front of base marked "Crockett," reverse with Ohio bank imprint, mid 1950s **50.00**

Ring, adjustable, brass, portrait dec, name on band, c1950 .. **45.00**

Dick Tracy

Big Little Book, *Dick Tracy And The Man With No Face,* Whitman, #1491, 1938 .... **60.00**

Puppet, 10½" h, fabric body, painted soft vinyl head **75.00**

Thermos, 6½" h, steel, red plastic cup, full color, Aladdin, 1967 copyright **55.00**

Felix

Cigarette Lighter, 2" l, figural, 1930s **225.00**

Figure, 3" h, celluloid, painted, black and white, 1930s **100.00**

Sand Toy, 6¾" d handled tin tray, wire mesh bottom, includes tin sand scoop and molding figures, 1930s **225.00**

Flash Gordon, puzzle, 12" l, set of 3, Milton Bradley, 1951 .... **80.00**

Foxy Grandpa

Doll, 16" h, cloth, stuffed, printed image, 1902 .... **125.00**

Toy, 4" h, cast iron, catapult lever, painted **225.00**

Green Hornet

Costume, Ben Cooper, MIB ... **250.00**

Pinback Button, 1¼" d, red, blue, and black hornet center, yellow ground, green rim with yellow lettering **250.00**

Hopalong Cassidy

Badge, 3" d, bank employee, "Savings Club," litho tin, red, white, and blue, 1950 copyright **55.00**

Birthday Card, 5¼ x 6¼", mechanical, full color illus, orig envelope, Buzza Cardozo, c1950 .... **25.00**

Camera, 2 x 2½ x 5", metal, black, black and silver title plate with Hopper and Topper images, Galter Products Co, late 1940s **85.00**

Coloring Book, 10½ x 14¾", full color cov, 20 unused pgs, Abbott **50.00**

Pennant, 20" l, black felt, white inscription and trim, c1950 .. **25.00**

Press Book, 9½ x 14½", *Renegade Trail,* black and white photo on cov **75.00**

Sweater, cream, black, and red,

Howdy Doody, mug, red plastic, decal, $35.00.

Hoppy illus on front, Topper illus on back **100.00**

Howdy Doody

Cake Decoration, six pink plastic character candle holders, blue plastic Howdy figure with "Happy Birthday," orig red, white, and blue diecut birthday cake shape package, Kagran, 1951–56 .... **75.00**

Doll, 12½" h, wood, composition head, jointed body, fabric neckerchief, decal on chest, Bob Smith copyright, 1948–51 **400.00**

Game, Howdy Doody's 3–Ring Circus, electric, Harett–Gilmar Co, Kagran copyright, 1951– 56 .... **85.00**

Little Golden Book, *Howdy Doody And The Princess,* 6½ x 8", 28 pgs, 1952 .... **20.00**

Puzzle, 9¼ x 11½", frame tray, titled "Skiing With Clarabell," Whitman, Kagran copyright, 1951–56 .... **40.00**

Wall Lamp, Howdy and Santa . **175.00**

Kayo

Bottle, 5½" h, china, figural, painted, removable head, marked "Germany," 1930s .. **75.00**

Doll, 12½" h, composition, movable head and mouth, painted, decal "Kayo By Willard/Licensed By F.A.S.," 1930s ... **250.00**

Toothbrush Holder, 5" h, china, figural, painted, marked "Made In Japan," 1930s **100.00**

Li'l Abner

Glass, 6¼" h, Daisy Mae, clear, full color portrait, weighted bottom **20.00**

Handbook, 4½ x 7¼", *Li'l Abner Square Dance Handbook,* Fred Liefer, Toby Press, 130 pgs, full color cov illus **45.00**

Toy, 7½" l, windup, Li'l Abner & Dogpatch Band, litho tin, orig box, Unique Art **650.00**

Little Lulu

Bracelet, link, charms, gold finished metal, orig blister card . **25.00**

Glass, 4¾" h, clear, black and white illus, 1950s **75.00**

Little Orphan Annie

Better Little Book, *Little Orphan Annie And The Underground Hideout,* Whitman, #1461, 1945 .... **55.00**

Doll, 9¾" h, cloth, stuffed, printed "Harold Gray," 1930s **125.00**

Game, Treasure Hunt, cardboard folder opens to full color game map, metal spinner, and four cardboard sailing boats, orig mailing envelope, Ovaltine premium, c1933 .... **75.00**

Mug, 3" h, plastic, Ovaltine **30.00**

Lone Ranger, magazine tear sheet, *Boys Life,* Sept., 1958, Savings Bond adv, "The Lone Ranger Peace Patrol" comic strip, 10½ x 13½", $10.00.

Lone Ranger

Clothing Tag, 3½ x 6½", cardboard, full color illus for Lone Ranger double knee denim blue jeans, 1950s **50.00**

Pedometer, 2¾" d, aluminum, Cheerios premium, c1948 ... **30.00**

Sheet Music, 9 x 12", *Hi–Yo Silver,* copyright 1938 .... **25.00**

Toothbrush Holder, 4" h, plaster, figural, Lone Ranger on rearing horse, painted, 1938 copyright 75.00

Mutt and Jeff
Ink Blotter, 4 x 9", black, white, and red, "The Musical Comedy Sensation Of The Age," unused 25.00
Movie Poster, 28 x 41", one sheet, *A Tropical Eggspedition,* 1920s 425.00

Popeye
Game, ring toss, standing Popeye and Olive Oyl, orig box dated 1919–33 .... 145.00
Greeting Card, Christmas, Hallmark, 1934 .... 28.00

Reddy Kilowatt
First Aid Book, 4¼ x 6", PA Power & Light Co, 1949, 52 pgs 25.00
Food Saver Set, 7½ x 10½" plastic bag holds set of five vinyl food covers, elastic strap, red, 1950s 40.00
Visor, "Vote For Reddy," diecut cardboard, red, white, and blue, unused, 1950s 15.00

Red Ryder
Better Little Book, *Red Ryder And Circus Luck,* Whitman, #1466, 1949 .... 50.00
Flashlight 35.00
Game, Red Ryder's 3 Game Set, 11" sq hinged playing board printed on both sides, die, unpunched playing pcs, Built–Rite, 1956 copyright ... 75.00
Skeezix, pinback button, "I Like Skeezix Sweaters," image of Skeezix in center, celluloid 75.00
Straight Shooter, badge, silver, inset red, blue, and silver foil checkerboard 75.00

Tarzan
Advertising Poster, 5 x 18", "Delicious Ice Cream In Tarzan Cups," full color illus, 1930s . 110.00
Better Little Book, *The Son Of Tarzan,* Whitman, #1477, Edgar Rice Burroughs 1939 copyright 55.00
Movie Poster, 78 x 78", *Tarzan And The Huntress,* six sheet,

color jungle scene, RKO Radio Pictures, 1947 .... 150.00
Thermos, 6½" h, metal, color illus, green cup, Aladdin Industries, 1966 copyright 40.00

Tom Corbett
Badge, 2" d, silvered brass, diecut, emb design 35.00
Ring, blue plastic, inset celluloid space suit disk, c1952 ...... 15.00
Wild Bill Hickok, lunch box, 7 x 8 x 4", steel, color illus, Aladdin Industries, copyright 1955 ... 125.00
Wizard of Oz, pillowcase, movie characters and names 125.00

Yellow Kid
Cap Bomb, 1½" h, cast iron, figural, head, c1896 .... 100.00
Gum Card, 2¾ x 4½", Adam's Yellow Kid Chewing Gum, #11, full color, 1896 Outcault copyright 50.00

PERSONALITIES

Allen, Jimmie, member certificate, 8 x 11", "Full Fledged Pilot Member," parchment paper, green border design, red seal, Richfield Oil issue, c1934 .... 40.00
Anka, Paul, pinback button, 1¾" d, black and white photo, light blue background, 1950s 25.00

Armstrong, Jack
Flashlight, 4½" l, cardboard, black, tube shape, metal cap ends, c1939 .... 15.00
Pedometer, 2¾" d, dark blue outer rim, General Mills premium, 1935 .... 30.00

Autry, Gene
Cap Pistol, 9" l, gold finished metal, ivory plastic grips, raised horse head dec, orig box, Leslie–Henry Co 250.00
Poster, 27 x 41", *Wagon Team,* full color, Columbia Pictures, 1952 .... 75.00
Puzzle, 9½ x 11½", frame tray, full color photo, Whitman, 1950 copyright 35.00
Wristwatch, chrome metal case, orig brown leather bands, en-

graved "Always Your Pal" and "Gene Autry" on back of case **125.00**

Bogart, Humphrey

Post Card, 3½ x 5½", black and white glossy photo, 1945 postmark **25.00**

Sheet Music, *Someday, I'll Meet You Again,* black and white photo cov, pink montage background, 4 pgs, 1944 copyright **25.00**

Cantor, Eddie, game, Tell It To The Judge, 20" sq playing board, portrait image center, orig box, c1940 .... **50.00**

Chan, Charlie

Autographed Photo, matted ... **175.00**

Game, The Great Charlie Chan Detective Mystery Game, Milton Bradley, 1937 .... **125.00**

Chaplin, Charlie

Pencil Box, 1 x 2¼ x 8", litho tin, color portrait illus on lid, 1920s **55.00**

Sheet Music, 11 x 13½", *Those Charlie Chaplin Feet,* 1915 copyright **30.00**

Coogan, Jackie, tag, 3½" h, "Near East Relief," diecut cardboard, milk bottle shape **25.00**

Crosby, Bing

Lobby Card, *Sing, Sing, Sing,* 1933 .... **45.00**

Ring, gold plastic, black and white photo on top, c1940 ... **15.00**

Davis, Bette, banner, 54 x 40", silk, *The Letter,* Warner Bros, Davis holding smoking gun image, 1940 ....**1,725.00**

Day, Doris, paper doll album, 10½ x 12", Whitman, #1952, full color cov photo, two 9½" h diecut cardboard dolls, thirty neatly cut paper outfits, copyright 1955 .. **40.00**

Dionne Quintuplets

Calendar, 8¼ x 11¾", 1938, full color illus, Brown & Bigelow Co **30.00**

Cereal Bowl, 5⅞" d, chrome plated metal, Quaker Oats premium, late 1935 .... **35.00**

Photo, 10 x 12", color, framed, 1935 NEA Service copyright . **25.00**

Plate, 7¼" d, china, three individual tinted color photos, red accent line trim, 1935–36 ... **75.00**

Durante, Jimmy

Charm, gold plastic frame, inset black and white glossy photo, c1940 .... **20.00**

Pinback Button, 1⅛" d, "Gimme Jimmy! the Candidate," red, white, and blue, 1952 ...... **25.00**

Fields, W. C., cookie jar, 22" h, figural, ceramic, marked "USA" and "153" **25.00**

Flynn, Errol, sheet music, 9 x 12", *Some Sunday Morning,* Warner Bros, copyright 1945 .... **25.00**

Garland, Judy, paperdoll, 10½ x 13" book, #996, front and back cov with 10½" h unpunched doll, 8 pgs uncut clothing, Whitman . **275.00**

Gleason, Jackie, pinback button, 1¼" d, "MMMM! Boy/Jackie Gleason," black and white photo **25.00**

Grable, Betty, paper doll, Merrill, #1558, three dolls, 65 pieces of clothing, 1951 .... **45.00**

Hayes, Gabby

Hat, black felt, upturned front brim with name in white letters, 1950s **100.00**

Nodder, 6½" h, composition, painted, 1950s **75.00**

Hope, Bob, autograph, fly leaf of *They Got Me Covered,* illus by Bing Crosby, 1st edition, 1941, orig clear dust jacket **125.00**

Kelly, Grace, magazine, *Life,* April 26, 1954, black and white photo cover, three page article **20.00**

Laurel & Hardy

Game, Laurel and Hardy Game of Monkey Business, 17" sq playing board, figures, 58 cards, four orig wood sliding pieces, Transogram, 1962 copyright **55.00**

Salt and Pepper Shakers, pr, china, figural, head, white base with black bow tie accents, Beswick China, 1960s **250.00**

Lennon Sisters, coloring book, 8½ x 11", Whitman, full color photo cov front and back, some colored pages,1959 .... **15.00**

Mansfield, Jayne

Calendar, 10 x 17", cardboard,

full color glossy photo, missing calendar pad, 1965 copyright **150.00**

Hot Water Bottle, 22" h, soft vinyl, figural, painted black bra and panties, black metal threaded cap, marked "Poynter Products copyright 1957" **100.00**

Movie Poster, 27 x 41", *The Burglar*, one sheet, full color image, wearing red outfit and matching shoes, Columbia Picture 1957 . . . . **75.00**

Mix, Tom
Belt Buckle, 2¼" l, brass, red, blue, and silver foil insert, 1936 . . . . **100.00**

Big Little Book, *Tom Mix And The Stranger From The South*, Whitman, #1183, 1936 . . . . . **30.00**

Booklet, 3 x 5½", *Secret Writing Manual*, 4 pgs, Ralston premium, c1938 . . . . **75.00**

Decoder, 2¾" d, cardboard, red, white, and blue, Ralston premium, c1938 . . . . **75.00**

Monroe, Marilyn
Book, 6 x 8½", *Will Acting Spoil Marilyn Monroe?*, Pete Martin, 1956, first edition, 128 pgs, text and 43 black and white photos, dj with full color photo **40.00**

Calendar, sample, 8½ x 14", 1956, spiral bound, four full color photos, orig envelope . . **400.00**

Sheet Music, 9 x 12", *My Heart Belongs To Daddy*, sepia photo on cov, 1938 copyright **25.00**

Pinky Lee, coloring book, 80 pgs, health and safety tips **25.00**

Presley, Elvis, Pinback Button
7/8" d, "Always Yours Elvis," litho, blue tone photo, 1956 copyright **25.00**

2½" sq, full color photo, cardboard back with inkstamped "1956 Elvis Presley Enterprises copyright" **125.00**

Rogers, Roy
Bank, 5½" h, metal, copper–bronze finish, figural, boot, horseshoe base, raised image of Roy and Trigger, script inscription, Alma Metal Arts, c1950 . . . . **75.00**

Better Little Book, *Roy Rogers And The Snowbound Outlaws*, Whitman, 1949 . . . . . . **30.00**

Little Golden Book, *Dale Evans And The Lost Gold Mine*, 28 pgs, copyright 1954 . . . . **20.00**

Plate, 6" d, white china, full color illus of Roy on Trigger, gold beaded border, marked "Rodeo By Universal," 1950s . . . **40.00**

Tablet, 8 x 10", full color cov, unused, early 1950s **25.00**

Sinatra, Frank, charm, 1" h, brown plastic, black and white inset photo, c1950 . . . . **20.00**

Temple, Shirley
Handbag, 4½ x 7½", fabric, brown oilcloth, matching strap, attached tag with photo, 1930s **125.00**

Handkerchief, 8½" sq, white, red and blue design, inscribed "To My Friend/Shirley Temple" . . **35.00**

Jewelry Set, adjustable ring, link bracelet, and pendant locket, gold colored metal, heart shape symbols, mounted on orig card, mid 1930s **55.00**

Pen, 4¼" l, plastic, red, incised "Shirley Temple," 1930s **75.00**

Sewing Cards, set of 12, yarn outline, neatly colored, orig box, Saalfield, 1936 . . . . **100.00**

Sheet Music, 9 x 12", *Oh, My Goodness*, copyright 1936 . . **25.00**

Valentino, Rudolph
Candy Container, 7½" d, 2½" h, tin, black, color litho portrait . **50.00**

Medal, 1¼" d, brass, emb image of him in costume, reverse with heraldic symbol and "Lincoln Theater/Lincoln, Nebr/ Fashion Show March 2–3–4" **30.00**

Withers, Jane, coloring book, 11 x 15", #607, sepia cover photo with full color image border, Whitman, copyright 1941 . . . . . **25.00**

CHELSEA

History: Chelsea is a fine English porcelain designed to compete with Meissen.

The factory began operating in the Chelsea area of London, England, in the 1740s. Chelsea products are divided into four periods: (1) Early period, 1740s, with incised triangle and raised anchor mark; (2) The 1750s, with red raised anchor mark; (3) The 1760s, the gold anchor period; and (4) The Derby period from 1770–1783. In 1924 a large number of the molds and models of figurines were found at the Spode–Copeland Works, and many items were brought back into circulation.

Reference: Susan and Al Bagdade, *Warman's English & Continental Pottery & Porcelain, Second Edition,* Wallace–Homestead, 1991.

Pastille Burner, purple ground, red, pink, blue, yellow flowers, gold outlines, gold anchor mark, 5½" h, 4½" w, $225.00.

Box, cov, painted floral sprays, molded floral finial, c1760, 2" h	200.00
Cachepot, floral band top	225.00
Candlesticks, pr, 8" h, floral birds, and small dogs dec, gold anchor mark, restorations and damage, 1760s	360.00
Coffee Cup and Saucer, enameled puce ribbon panels and green floral sprays, gold scalloped roundel centering small foliate medallion, gilt dentil rim, 2⅝" h cup marked with gold "CD" and anchor mark, 4¾" d saucer	415.00
Cream Jug, 3⅜" h, outward tapering fluted sides, painted floral and foliate sprays, chocolate brown rim, applied double scroll handle, red anchor mark	990.00
Cup and Saucer, 2¼" h cup, 5⅛" d saucer, fluted, cup well and saucer center enameled with orange floral sprig and green leaves, cup ext. and saucer with gold cisele floral garlands pendant from gilt dentil rim, alternating white panels enameled en grisaille with trophies suspended from puce ribbon tied below rim, underglaze blue bands with gilt dentil line rim, gold anchor mark	650.00
Dish, 9½" l, leaf form, lettuce green border, pale magenta veins holding flower heads, price for pair	1,210.00
Figure	
6½" h, ice skater, gold anchor mark, 1760s	195.00
8" h, pr, hunter with hunting horn and dog and huntress with rifle and dog, damaged rifle end, gold anchor mark, 1760s	300.00
9¼" h, seated piper with dog at feet and seated woman holding mandolin with lamb at feet, some damage to bocage on both figures, gold anchor mark, 1760s	575.00
Sauceboats and Stand, two 7⅞" w sauceboats with fluted sides and floral bouquets, 8¼" w stand with exotic birds strutting in landscape, shaped brown rim, red anchor mark, c1756	235.00
Strawberry Basket, 7" l, oval cross section, vine handle, lattice border with rosettes enclosing oval reserve with polychrome summer flowers, mid 18th C	990.00
Tea Bowl and Saucer, 2" h bowl, 5" d saucer, scalloped, enameled royal blue border with gilt highlighting, flower heads centering scalloped dentil rim, C–scroll and lambrequin border, bowl ext. and saucer with three small floral sprays, int. and saucer center with smaller spray, gold "CD" and anchor mark	300.00

"CHELSEA" GRANDMOTHER'S WARE

History: "Chelsea" Grandmother's ware identifies a group of tableware with raised reliefs of either grapes, sprigs of flowers, or thistles on a white ground. Some examples are lustered.

The ware was made in the first half of the 19th century in England's Staffordshire district by a large number of manufacturers. The "Chelsea" label is a misnomer, but commonly accepted in the antiques field.

Sauceboat and Underplate, Grape pattern, $60.00.

Butter Pat, Thistle	15.00
Coffeepot, Grape	185.00
Creamer and Sugar, cov, Grape .	150.00
Cup and Saucer	
Grape, handleless	35.00
Sprig, wishbone handle	40.00
Plate	
7¼" d, Grape	30.00
8" d, Sprig	40.00
Sauceboat, Grape	40.00
Teapot, cov, Thistle	150.00
Tea Set, Sprig, teapot, five cups, six saucers, sugar bowl, waste bowl, seven luncheon plates, and two service plates	185.00

CHILDREN'S BOOKS

History: Because there is a bit of the child in all of us, collectors always have been attracted to children's books. In the 19th century, books were popular gifts for children, with most of the children's classics written and published during this time. These books were treasured and often kept throughout a lifetime.

Developments in printing made it possible to include more attractive black–and–white illustrations and color plates. The work of artists and illustrators has added value beyond the text itself.

References: Barbara Bader, *American Picture Books From Noah's Ark To The Beast Within,* Macmillan, 1976; E. Lee Baumgarten, *Price Guide For Children's & Illustrated Books For The Years 1880–1950, 1993 Edition, Sorted by Author,* published by author, 1993; Margery Fisher, *Who's Who In Children's Books: A Treasury of the Familiar Characters of Childhood,* Holt, Rinehart and Winston, 1975; Virginia Haviland, *Children's Literature, A Guide To Reference Sources,* Library of Congress, 1966, first supplement 1972, second supplement 1977, third supplement 1982; Bettina Hurlimann, *Three Centuries Of Children's Books In Europe,* tr. and ed. by Brian W. Alderson, World, 1968; Cornelia L. Meigs (ed.), *A Critical History of Children's Literature, Second Edition,* Macmillan, 1969; Steve Santi, *Collecting Little Golden Books: A Collector's Identification and Value Guide, Second Edition,* Books Americana, 1994.

Periodicals: *Book Source Monthly,* 2007 Syossett Dr., PO Box 567, Cazenovia, NY 13035; *Martha's KidLit Newsletter,* PO Box 1488, Ames, IA 50010.

Libraries: Free Library of Philadelphia, PA; Library of Congress, Washington, D.C.; Pierpont Morgan Library, New York, NY; Toronto Public Library, Toronto, Ontario, Canada.

Advisor: Joyce Magee.

Additional Listings: See *Warman's Americana & Collectibles* for more examples and an extensive listing of collectors' clubs.

Note: dj = dust jacket; wraps = paper covers; pgs = pages; unp = unpaged; n.d. = no date; teg = top edges gilt

Alger, Horatio, *Ragged Dick; or, Street Life In New York,* serialized in *Student and Schoolmate,*

Arthur S. Maxwell, *Uncle Arthur's Bedtime Stories,* **Review and Herald Publishing, Tacoma, WA, black and white photos and sketches, 96 pgs, 5¼ x 7½", 1941, $8.00.**

Vol XIX, No. 1, Vol XX, No. 6, Jan–Dec 1867, 8vo, half leather, marbled boards, worn, foxing .. **155.00**

Austin, Margot, *Trumpet,* Dutton, c1943, 4th printing, orange pictorial boards, chipped and worn dj **20.00**

Bannerman, Helen, *Little Black Sambo,* illus by Cobb H Shinn, Whitman, 6¼ x 9¼", 64 pgs, light soiling, dark brown cloth boards, pictorial paste–down **110.00**

Baring–Gould, William S and Cecil, *The Annotated Mother Goose, Nursery Rhymes Old and New, Arranged and Explained,* NY, c1962, folio, cloth, slightly worn dj **20.00**

Baum, L Frank
Rinkitink in Oz, illus by John R Neill, Reilly & Lee, c1916, later 1935 Hanff & Green X printing, orig tan cloth, pictorial past down on cov, dj, light edge chipping **35.00**
The Lost Princess of Oz, illus by John R Neill, Reilly & Britton, Chicago, 1917, Hanff & Green XI, 1st printing, 12 color plates, paste–down on front cov, orig

blue cloth, inner hinges broken, cov worn **120.00**
The Wonderful Wizard of Oz, illus by W W Denslow, Geo M Hill Co, Chicago & NY, 1900, 1st ed, 1st state, Hanff & Greene I, 261 pgs, 18 good plates, title page and 6 color plates missing, heavily soiled and stained cov **300.00**

Bedford, A N, *Susie's New Stove,* illus by Corinne Malvern, Little Golden Book, Little Chef toy stove, Pixie's Delight recipe ... **20.00**

Burgess, Thornton, *The Adventures of Grandfather Frog,* illus by Harrison Cady, Little Brown, 1946, yellow cov, 8 color illus, back hinge reinforced, Bedtime Story–Book Series **30.00**

Carroll, Lewis, *The Annotated Alice. Alice's Adventures in Wonderland & Through the Looking Glass,* NY, c1960, folio, cloth, very good, slightly worn dj **20.00**

Disney, Walt, *The Golden Touch,* Racine, WI, Whitman, c1937, 4to, 212 pgs, cloth backed pictorial boards, worn dj, 6 color plates **45.00**

Disney, Walt and Caroline D Emerson, *Mickey Sees The USA,* Boston, Heath, c1944, 138 pgs, pictorial cloth, slightly worn and soiled **50.00**

Disney, Walt and Robin Palmer, *Mickey Never Fails,* Boston, Heath, c1939, 102 pgs, pictorial cloth **40.00**

Field, Eugene, *Lullaby Land,* black and white illus by Charles Robinson, 1923, Schribner's Children's Classics, 5 x 7½", 232 pgs, maroon cloth, gilt design, light overall wear **20.00**

Jackson, K & B, *The Little Trapper,* illus by Gustaf Tenggren, Little Golden Book **12.00**

Kunitz, Stanley and Howard Haycraft, *Junior Book of Authors,* NY, 1934, 4to, 30 pgs, pictorial cloth, slight wear **15.00**

Neill, John R, *The Wonder City of Oz,* illus by author, Reilly & Lee,

Chicago, c1940, Hanff & Greene XXXIV 1st printing, orig emerald green cloth, color paste–down on front cov, worn dj **180.00**

Paine, Albert B, *The Hollow Tree Snowed–In Book,* Harpers, 1912, c1910, ex–library, rebound in red cloth, 5¼ x 8", 286 pgs **24.00**

Parley, Peter, *The Balloon Travels of Robert Merry and His Young Friends Over Various Countries in Europe,* NY, 1860, 12mo, orig cloth, pictorial spine, engraved plates and title page, cov loose **50.00**

Peat, Fern Bisel (illus), *Mother Goose,* Saalfield, No. 883, c1932, 9½ x 13", heavy card stock, lightly worn edges **30.00**

Piper, Watty (Mabel C Bragg), *The Little Engine That Could,* illus by Lois Lenski, Platt & Munk, c1930, orange cloth, blue design, lightly soiled dj **50.00**

Thayer, Jane, *The Puppy Nobody Wanted,* illus by Sid Fleishman, Weekly Reader Club, 1961, 6¾ x 8¾", tan boards, orig dj **12.00**

Thompson, Ruth Plumly, *Grampa in Oz,* illus by John R Neill, Reilly & Lee, Chicago, c1924, Hanff & Greene XVIII 1st printing, 12 color plates, color paste–down on front cov, orig light brick red cloth **120.00**

Wehr, Julian, *Snow White,* Dunewald, 1949, four pop–up animations, spiral bound **48.00**

Wilkin, Eloise, *Prayers for Children,* Big Golden Book, 1975, 9½ x 12½", 20 pgs **12.00**

CHILDREN'S FEEDING DISHES

History: Unlike toy dishes meant for play, children's feeding dishes are the items actually used in the feeding of a child. Their colorful designs of animals, nursery rhymes, and children's activities are meant to appeal to the child and make meal times fun. Many plates have a unit to hold hot water, thus keeping the food warm.

Although glass and porcelain examples from the late 19th and early 20th centuries are most popular, collectors are beginning to seek some of the plastic examples from the 1920s to 1940s, especially those with Disney designs on them.

References: Doris Lechler, *Children's Glass Dishes, China and Furniture, Vol. I* (1983), *Vol. II* (1986, 1993 value update), Collector Books, 1983; Dana G. Morykan and Harry L. Rinker, *Warman's Country Antiques & Collectibles, Second Edition,* Wallace–Homestead, 1994; Noel Riley, *Gifts For Good Children: The History of Children's China, Part I, 1790–1890,* Richard Dennis Publications, 1991; Margaret and Kenn Whitmyer, *Collector's Encyclopedia of Children's Dishes: An Illustrated Value Guide,* Collector Books, 1993.

Feeding Dish, decal of girls feeding teddy bear, verse on each handle to teach placement of fork and spoon, marked "Salem China Co," 9" w, $60.00.

Baby
Kewpies, 7¾" d, sgd "Rose O'Neill, Royal Rudolstadt" . . . **235.00**
Nursery Rhyme, 8½" d, cobalt blue **18.00**
See Saw Margery Daw, 9" d, divided, green glass, scene of children, two dogs, cat, and pig on rim **25.00**
Bowl
Dollie Dimples and Sammy, 7½" d, gold rim, marked "Buffalo Pottery" **75.00**

Nursery Rhyme, 6¼" d, cobalt blue **15.00**

Cereal Set, cereal bowl, mug, and plate Bunnykins, marked "Royal Doulton" **100.00**

Jack and Jill, 6" d plate, marked "Royal Bayreuth" **125.00**

Snowbabies, two children and dog sledding, marked "Royal Bayreuth" **150.00**

Creamer, rabbit dressed in red jacket, green band, marked "Roseville" **35.00**

Dish, 6½" d, 1½" h, Beatrix Potter, Peter Rabbit and Farmer, Wedgwood **32.00**

Mug
Faith and Hope, 2¼" h, black transfer, pink luster border ... **50.00**

Nursery Rhyme, 3½" h, cobalt blue **18.00**

Staffordshire, multicolored, four children, VWX, "W" is for whipping **110.00**

Plate, 6" d, polychrome transfer of sleeping girls and angels **60.00**

CHILDREN'S NURSERY ITEMS

History: The nursery is a place where children live in a miniature world. Things come in two sizes. Child scale designates items actually used for the care, housing, and feeding of the child. Toy or doll scale denotes items used by the child in play and for creating a fantasy environment which copies that of an adult or his own.

Cheap labor and building costs during the Victorian era enabled the nursery to reach a high level of popularity. Most collectors focus on items from the 1880 to 1930 period.

References: Marguerite Fawdry, *An International Survey of Rocking Horse Manufacture,* New Cavendish Books, 1992; Gene Florence, *The Collector's Encyclopedia of Akro Agate Glassware, Revised Edition,* Collector Books, 1975, 1992 value update; Roger and Claudia Hardy, *The Complete Line of Akro Agate: Marbles, General Line and Children's Dishes, With Prices,* published by authors, 1992; Doris Lechler, *Children's Glass Dishes, China and Furniture,* Vol. I (1983), Vol. II (1986, 1993 value update), Collector Books; Doris Lechler, *English Toy China,* Antique Publications, 1989; Doris Lechler, *French and German Dolls, Dishes and Accessories,* Antique Publications, 1991; Doris Lechler, *Toy Glass,* Antique Publications, 1989; Anthony and Peter Miall, *The Victorian Nursery Book,* Pantheon Books, 1980; Patricia Mullins, *The Rocking Horse: A History of Moving Toy Horses,* New Cavendish Books, 1992; Lorraine May Punchard, *Child's Play,* published by author, 1982, out–of–print; Lorraine May Punchard, *Playtime Kitchen Items and Table Accessories,* published by author, 1993; Tony Stevenson and Eva Marsden, *Rocking Horses: The Collector's Guide To Selecting, Restoring, and Enjoying New and Vintage Rocking Horses,* Courage Books, 1993; Margaret and Kenn Whitmyer, *Collector's Encyclopedia of Children's Dishes,* Collector Books, 1993.

Additional Listings: Children's Books, Children's Feeding Dishes, Children's Toy Dishes, Dolls, Games, Miniatures, and Toys.

Bassinet, 68" l, swinging type, hooded, white iron and wire mesh, brass finial, includes bedding **250.00**

Carriage, wicker, mfg by Kumfy–Kab, La Porte, IA, c1925 ..... **200.00**

Chair, Louis XVI style, ivory painted, straight crest rail, rect upholstered back and seat covered in beige floral silk, reeded tapering legs, price for pair **775.00**

Cradle, 39" l, mahogany, bonnet top, rocking, 19th C **250.00**

Doll Carriage, 25½" h, wood, steel spoke wheels **250.00**

Doll Cradle, 27½" l, pine, orig red paint, white and yellow striping, foliage scrolls, name "Lucy," age cracks, old repaired break, worn black painted int. **165.00**

Go Cart, 44" l, 18½" w, 26" h, wicker, scrolling sleigh form,

Bowl and pitcher set, transfer, alternating brown and green vines, red and green fruit, raised English registry mark, 10¾" d bowl, 7¾" h pitcher, $75.00.

metal plaque stamped "Block," early 20th C **1,500.00**
High Chair
  Camphor Wood, 37" h, Anglo/ Indian, restoration, second half 19th C **175.00**
  Primitive, 39" h, ladderback, three slats, turned finials, splint seat, old red repaint ... **615.00**
  Softwood, caned seat, Chinese **225.00**
  Windsor, painted, spindle inset back, U–shaped arms, saddle seat, elongated turned legs joined by stretchers, American, late 18th/early 19th C ..**1,850.00**
Push Cart, 65" l, wood and wicker, steel spoke and rim wheels, laminated and carved wood dapple gray horse that rocks when pushed, worn orig varnish, black and gold striping, worn harness and saddle, mane missing, tail needs reattachment, wear **2,810.00**
Quilt, 50 x 73", nine patch, colorful pink, green, red, goldenrod, and blue calicoes, black on gray print, worn, stains, fabric backing in tatters, machine sewn binding **50.00**
Rattle, 7½" l, twisted wire, six bells, blue glass beads, wood handle **145.00**
Rocker
  Adirondack, 25" h, orig medium

blue paint, yellow and silver trim **60.00**
  Hardwood and Rattan, shaped back and seat, curved arms, Chinese, late 19th C **115.00**
  Oak, slat back, rush seat, Stickley **95.00**
  Wicker, 27¾" h, late 19th C ... **375.00**
Rocking Horse
  32" l, carved wood, old worn white repaint, old saddle, incomplete harness, mane, and tail, rockers removed **412.00**
  34" l, glider frame, two cutout wooden silhouettes of white horses, red and black trim, worn **55.00**
  39" h, spring mounted base, wood, very worn hide covering, deteriorated harness and saddle, glass eyes, mane, tail, and wheels missing **550.00**
  49½" l, wood, laminated body, very worn orig dapple gray paint, red base, traces of saddle and harness, mane and tail missing **385.00**
Rug, 18½ x 37", hooked rag, Little Bo Peep, three sheep, faded colors, some wear **220.00**
Sled, all wood
  33½" l
    Old natural finish, worn red, yellow striping, black stenciled design, sheet metal tipped runners, age cracks in top **195.00**
    Orig red paint, natural finish, stenciled and freehand flowers, underside marked in pencil "Enola M Brownell, Feb 5, 1909," sheet metal tipped runners **395.00**
  35¼" l, old natural finish, blue stain, worn black stenciled design with hunting dog, sheet metal tipped runners, front dowel replaced **60.00**
  38" l, worn red paint, stenciled design, underside labeled "Paris Mfg Co," sheet metal tipped runners, well executed repair **250.00**
  38¼" l, orig natural finish, black

striping, stenciled yellow, black, and green tiger, steel rod tipped runners **385.00**
Toy, 36" l, rocking, sleigh shape, two figural horse dec on front, carved detail, orig red and black paint, yellow striping **660.00**
Wheelbarrow, 34½" l, worn orig red paint, white striping, black stenciled horse **412.00**

CHILDREN'S TOY DISHES

History: Dishes made for children often served a dual purpose—playthings and a means of learning social graces. Dish sets came in two sizes. The first was for actual use by the child when entertaining friends. The second, a smaller size than the first, was for use with dolls.

Children's dish sets often were made as a side line to a major manufacturing line either as a complement to the family service or as a way to use up the last of the day's batch of materials. The artwork of famous illustrators, such as Palmer Cox, Kate Greenaway, and Rose O'Neill, can be found on porcelain sets.

References: Gene Florence, *The Collector's Encyclopedia of Akro Agate Glassware, Revised Edition,* Collector Books, 1975, 1992 value update; Roger and Claudia Hardy, *The Complete Line of Akro Agate: Marbles, General Line and Children's Dishes, With Prices,* published by authors, 1992; Doris Lechler, *Children's Glass Dishes, China and Furniture, Vol. I* (1983), *Vol. II* (1986, 1993 value update), Collector Books, 1983; Doris Lechler, *English Toy China,* Antique Publications, 1989; Doris Lechler, *French and German Dolls, Dishes, and Accessories,* Antique Publications, 1991; Doris Lechler, *Toy Glass,* Antique Publications, 1989; Lorraine May Punchard, *Child's Play,* published by author, 1982, out-of-print; Lorraine May Punchard, *Playtime Kitchen Items and Table Accessories,* published by author, 1993; Margaret and Kenn Whitmyer, *Collector's Encyclopedia of Children's Dishes,* Collector Books, 1993.

Collectors' Club: Toy Dish Collectors, PO Box 351, Camilus, NY 13031.

Plate, 6½" d, black transfer, orange and yellow accents, raised flowerhead border, unmarked English or Continental china, $115.00.

Akro Agate, tea set, Concentric Ring, small, blue creamer, sugar, and teapot, pumpkin cups, purple plates, yellow saucers, orig box **250.00**
China and Porcelain
Coffee Service, French, porcelain, 4¾" h cov coffeepot, 2⅜" h creamer, six cups, saucers, and 3¼" d plates, 2¼" h cov sugar, hp, leaf and floral dec, gilt trim, orig box, c1900 .... **260.00**
Cup and Saucer, Wedgwood, Caneware, engine turned body, red enamel trim, imp mark, England, late 19th C .. **435.00**
Dinner Service, partial
Rogers Longport, 4" l ladle, five 2¾" d plates, six 3¼" d plates, fourteen 3¾" d plates, three oval platters with handles, two 3" l sauce boats, 3½" sq ftd serving bowl, three cov tureens, two 4⅝" cov vegetable platter with handles, blue transfer printed floral and foliate design, minor rim nicks, imp marks, England, early 19th C **1,500.00**
Staffordshire, two 2¾" d plates, three 3" d plates, four

3¼" d plates, three oval platters, eight 3⅜" d soup plates, earthenware, black transfer printed rural landscapes, England, c1840, light staining **435.00**

Wedgwood, earthenware, partial, 2¾" l gravy boat with stand, six 3½" d plates, two oval platters, six 3½" soup plates, 4½" d oval cov soup tureen, 2½" l round cov tureen and stand, 4" l oval cov vegetable bowl, blue–green transfer printed Temple pattern, imp and printed marks, c1895, chips and damage . **375.00**

Tea and Coffee Service, partial, Wedgwood, Caneware, two 1½" h coffee cups, cov coffeepot, 3¼" d saucer, two 2" d teabowls, 3½" h cov tea kettle, engine turned bodies, imp marks, c1790, staining **1,035.00**

Teapot, cov, 3½" h, bulbous, Staffordshire, England, c1760, chips, hairlines, restorations . **195.00**

Pattern Glass

Banana Stand, Fine Cut and Star **45.00**

Butter Dish, cov, Michigan **60.00**

Creamer, Pennsylvania **60.00**

Dish, 3½" d, Rooster, spider in base, rim flaking **38.00**

Sugar, Menagerie, blue **275.00**

Table Setting, Lamb, minor roughness, price for 4 pcs . . . **350.00**

Tin, tea set, cats and dogs, red, blue, and white, marked "Germany," price for 9 pcs **85.00**

CHRISTMAS ITEMS

History: The celebration of Christmas dates back to Roman times. Several customs associated with modern Christmas celebrations are traced back to early pagan rituals.

Father Christmas, believed to have evolved in Europe in the 7th century, was a combination of the pagan god Thor, who judged and punished the good and bad, and St. Nicholas, the generous Bishop of Myra. Kris Kringle originated in Germany and was brought to America by the Germans and Swiss who settled in Pennsylvania in the late 18th century.

In 1822 Clement C. Moore wrote "A Visit From St. Nicholas" and developed the character of Santa Claus into what we know today. Thomas Nast did a series of drawings for *Harper's Weekly* from 1863 until 1886 and further solidified the character and appearance of Santa Claus.

References: Robert Brenner, *Christmas Past,* Schiffer Publishing, 1986; Robert Brenner, *Christmas Through The Decades,* Schiffer Publishing, 1993; Lissa Bryan–Smith and Richard Smith, *Christmas Collectibles: A Guide To Selecting, Collecting, and Enjoying The Treasures of Christmas Past,* Chartwell Books, 1993; Helaine Fendelman and Jeri Schwartz, *The Official Price Guide To Holiday Collectibles,* House of Collectibles, 1991; George Johnson, *Christmas Ornaments, Lights & Decorations,* Collector Books, 1987, 1990 value update; Polly and Pam Judd, *Santa Dolls & Figurines Price Guide: Antique to Contemporary,* Hobby House Press, 1992; Chris Kirk, *The Joy Of Christmas Collecting,* L–W Book Sales, 1994; Robert M. Merck, *Deck The Halls,* Abbeville Press, 1992; Mary Morrison, *Snow Babies, Santas and Elves: Collecting Christmas Bisque Figures,* Schiffer Publishing, 1993; Dana G. Morykan and Harry L. Rinker, *Warman's Country Antiques & Collectibles, Second Edition,* Wallace–Homestead, 1994; Margaret and Kenn Whitmyer, *Christmas Collectibles: Identification and Value Guide, Second Edition,* Collector Books, 1994.

Periodicals: *Golden Glow of Christmas Past,* 6401 Winsdale St., Golden Valley, MN 55427; *I Love Christmas,* PO Box 5708, Coralville, IA 52241; *Ornament Collector,* RR #1, Canton, IL 61520.

Additional Listings: See *Warman's Americana & Collectibles* for more examples.

Advisor: Lissa L. Bryan–Smith and Richard M. Smith.

Candy Box, 3 x 5", stockings hanging over hearth, string handle, 1940–50 . . . . **5.00**

Catalog

Georgia Manufacturing Co, 1929, Chicago, IL, 48 pgs, 5½ x 8½", novelties, favors, decorations **40.00**

Kirkman & Son, Inc, Kirkman Products, Brooklyn, NY, "For A Merry Christmas Save Your Kirkman Coupons, They Will Bring You Joy and Happiness to the Kiddies," 1920s, 8 pgs, illus, children's toys and novelties **15.00**

Montgomery Ward Co, Christmas Book, Kansas City, MO, 1949, 214 pgs, illus, pictorial wrappers **25.00**

United Merchandise Co, c1920, Tyrone, PA, 64 pages, 7½ x 10½", store type decorations, novelties **40.00**

Children's Book

Dennis The Menace Waits for Santa Claus, Carl Memling, Al White, Norm McGary, and Bill Lorencz illus, Little Golden Book, 1962 .... **10.00**

Night Before Christmas or a Visit from St Nicholas, McLoughlin Bros, 1896 .... **20.00**

Old Saint Nicholas, Chicago, Homewood Publishing Co ... **15.00**

The Chipmunks' Merry Christmas, David Corwin, Richard Scarry illus, Little Golden Book #375, 24 pgs, 1959 .... **6.00**

The Christmas Angel, Katherine Pyle, Little, Brown, 1900, 136 pgs, 1st ed **40.00**

Christmas Tree Base, 14" d, windup, musical, nickel plated sheet metal, cast iron cup to hold tree, plays four tunes, particle board base, worn orig box, marked "Made in Germany," 1956 date on orig shipping label **105.00**

Christmas Tree Fence, ten 11½" l segments, four 8" l segments with gate posts, cast iron, worn old green and gold paint **440.00**

Coloring Book, *The Christmas That Almost Wasn't,* Saalfield, #9540, 1970 .... **5.00**

Cookbook, *Christmas–Time Cook-*

book, Better Homes & Gardens, 1974, 216 pgs **10.00**

Diecut

Angel, blue clothes, tree, store adv on back **65.00**

Christmas Girl, 6½" h, garland of roses, glitter dec **15.00**

Santa

Feather beard, Norcross, 1940s, 8 x 11" **12.00**

Paper costume and boots, German, 1920 .... **75.00**

Tambourine, 9½" d, "Merry Christmas," woman, Meilink, Small & Co, Toledo, OH **10.00**

Ephemera

Advertising Trade Card, Dundee Smart Clothes, Allentown, PA, Santa with pack on back **4.00**

Menu, *SS City of Omaha,* 1950 **5.00**

Program, Annual Christmas Dinner, Bank of California, Fairmont Hotel, Dec 15, 1927 ... **8.00**

Stereograph, children and Santa peeking at each other thru keyhole, Keystone View Co, 1899 .... **10.00**

Figure

Deer, 4½" h, composition, brown, wood legs, metal antlers, Germany **45.00**

Santa, 18" h, wood, painted red and white **250.00**

Greeting Card

A Merry Christmas To You All, family strolling thru snowy woodland, c1880 .... **8.00**

Christmas Greetings In My House, house shape, Santa with tree inside, 1930s **3.00**

Hail, Day of Joy, angel kneeling, dove on finger, L Prang & Co, 1870s **15.00**

Merry Christmas and Happy New Year, children playing in snow, church background, c1860 .... **5.00**

With A Thousand Good Wishes, May Christmas Bring Happiness and Sweet Content, country churchyard and women wearing colonial dress, c1900 .... **1.50**

With Best Christmas Wishes, girl

holding flowers, Raphael Tuck
and Sons, late 1800s 15.00
Light Bulb
House, 2½" h, pink and blue, Ja-
pan 10.00
Santa, 3" h, one leg in chimney,
Japan 35.00
Magazine Cover
Harper's Weekly, Edward Pen-
field illus, Dec 1898, woman
wearing red coat, black muff,
walking dog, 13 x 7" 35.00
Ladies' Home Journal, Rose
O'Neill illus, Dec 1910 ...... 35.00
St Nicholas, Dec 1913, Will
Bradley illus, The Wonderbox
story illus 15.00
Ornament
Basket, 3" h, metal 35.00
Boy, 4" h, cotton batting, white,
composition face, brown cotton shoes, Germany 120.00
Girl, 4" h, Kewpie type, composition face, white legs, orange
dress 150.00
Kugel, blown, silvered, German
2¾" d, blue 220.00
3½" l, silver, grapes 115.00
3¾" d
Blue 135.00
Green 50.00
4" l, blue, grapes 225.00
4¾" d, blue 175.00
5½" l, silver, grapes, worn ... 125.00
5¾" l, green, teardrop 205.00
Parrot, glass, blue, red, and silver 45.00
Slipper, 5" h, flat, gold, netting
and tinsel trim, Dresden 40.00
Post Card
Christmas Greetings, Father
Christmas, putting toys thru
window, German 7.00
Kewpies, Rose O'Neill illus 25.00
Photographic, children under
tree 10.00
Santa, German, highly emb ... 15.00
Puzzle
Rudolph the Red–Nose Rein-
deer, Jaymar, frame tray, 1950
copyright, 11 x 14" 15.00
Santa Claus Puzzle Box, Milton
Bradley, c1924, three multicol-
ored litho puzzles, orig box .. 95.00

Sheet Music, *Silver Sleigh Bells,*
E T Paull, 1906, color illus 30.00

**Toy, Santa in sleigh, litho tin
windup, marked "Santee Claus,
Strauss Mechanical Toys, Known
the World Over, Reg. U. S. Pat.
Off., Ferdinand Strauss Corp.,
New York, U.S.A., U.S. Pat. Oct 18,
1921, U. S. Pat. Dec 11, 1923," 11"
l, 5" h, $1,250.00.**

Toy, roly poly, 6" h, Santa, red,
green belt 250.00
Tree
8" h, paper, green, USA 18.00
50" h, feather, painted wood
base, mounted on clockwork
revolving platform, stenciled
"Hohner Harmonicas" on each
side 200.00
57" h, green, collapsible, red
berries on branch tips, two
section trunk, stenciled red
and green bells and wreath on
orig white painted base,
marked "Germany" 360.00

CIGAR CUTTERS

History: Counter and pocket cigar cutters were used at the end of the 19th and
the beginning of the 20th centuries. They
were a popular form of advertising. Pocket-
type cigar cutters often were a fine piece of
jewelry that was attached to a watch chain.

COUNTER TOP

Advertising
Havana Cigars, "Tas Amantes,"
wood base, glass top **150.00**
King Alfred 10¢ Cigar, cast iron,
ornate Waterbury clock on top,
mechanical, 1901 . . . . **575.00**
Horse, cast iron, mounted on
wood base, American, 19th C, 6"
h, 11½" l **525.00**
Horse Head, flowing mane, silver
plated, 5¾" h **100.00**
Military Figure, standing, cast iron,
marked "Continental Cigar" . . . **450.00**
Pelican, brass and copper, rect
form hammered copper ashtray
with riveted corners, brass pelican figure with cigar cutter neck,
unmarked, 6½" h, 4⅞" w **65.00**
Walrus Tusk **165.00**

POCKET

Advertising
Dexter and National **15.00**
Morel's Fine Hams **25.00**
Figural
Boy on potty, chrome **130.00**
Monkey, riding tricycle, swing
action **120.00**
Tennis Racket, ivory and metal,
2" h **95.00**
Gold, 14k, hung from 14k gold
watch chain, 21.1 dwt **275.00**
Pendant, yellow gold set with oval
cabochon ruby and two old
mine–cut diamonds, monogram
on reverse **190.00**

CIGAR STORE FIGURES

History: Cigar store figures were familiar sights in front of cigar stores and tobacco shops from about 1840. Figural themes included Sir Walter Raleigh, sailors, Punch figures, and ladies, with Indians being the most popular.

Most figures were carved in wood, although figures also were made in metal and papier–mâché for a short time. Most carvings were life size or slightly smaller and brightly painted. A coating of tar acted as a preservative against the weather. Of the few surviving figures, only a small number have their original bases. Most replacements are due to years of wear and usage by dogs.

Use of figures declined when local ordinances were passed requiring shop keepers to move the figures inside at night. This soon became too much trouble, and other forms of advertising developed.

Reference: A.W. Pendergast and W. Porter Ware, *Cigar Store Figures*, The Lightner Publishing Corp., 1953.

Warrior, polychrome, American, 107" h, $11,100.00.

Chief, 66" h, wood, carved and
polychrome painted, red, green,
and black feathered headdress,
wearing feather and gold necklace, feather skirt, red drape
over one shoulder, and yellow
and brown shoes, repainted sq
plinth base, late 19th C **4,500.00**
Indian, wood
29½" h, carved and polychrome
painted **3,300.00**
54" h, pine, painted, standing,
wearing feathered headdress,
gold cloak, and boots with red
painted fringe, holding cigar

bundle and block of tobacco, orig base with iron handles inscribed "Cigars and Tobacco," set on pine box with iron wheels **3,000.00**

68" h, carved and painted, base inscribed "Louis J. Lord Co Cigars Tobacco," replaced feathers at headdress, old repairs and bracing, American, late 19th C **5,000.00**

68" h, carved and painted, full figure, standing on dec drum, wearing yellow, green, and red full headdress, tunic with star dec at neck and applied disc dec to sleeves, cuffs, matching leggings, and moccasins, cigar bundle applied to front, chip at hands, Dutchess County, NY, c1900 .... **2,300.00**

Princess

36" h, cast iron, polychrome painted, holding tobacco leaf bundles in both hands, red, yellow, and green, mounted on cast iron trapezoidal base, minor paint loss to headpiece, mid 19th C **2,200.00**

72½" h, wood, carved and polychrome painted, long groove–carved black hair, wearing dress and cape, gold feathered headdress and earrings, grasping knife and cigar bundle, standing on tapering box base inscribed "HPB & Co., NABOB, 5¢ Segars," some paint restoration, late 19th C **13,200.00**

Santa Claus, 60½" h, wood, carved, worn and flaked polychrome paint, deep age cracks **650.00**

Squaw, 35" h, wood, carved and polychrome painted, late 19th C **19,800.00**

CINNABAR

History: Cinnabar is a ware made of numerous layers of a heavy mercuric sulfide and often referred to as vermillion, the red hue in which it is most commonly found. It was carved into boxes, buttons, snuff bottles, and vases. The best examples were made in China.

Reference: Gloria and Robert Mascarelli, *Warman's Oriental Antiques,* Wallace–Homestead, 1992.

Bangle Bracelet, figural landscape design **40.00**

Box, Art Deco style, cinnabar and black lacquer, 18k gold and coral details, gray agate platform, coral bead feet, carved jade animal pulls, Wintz, French hallmark, orig fitted leather case .. **5,500.00**

Dish, 8" d, carved phoenix, dragon, and floral reserves, Chinese **325.00**

Platter, 11" l, oval, floriform, high relief dragon and tama in clouds design, Ch'ien Lung mark **2,200.00**

Snuff Bottle

2½" in, flattened shield shape, carved both sides with dragons chasing flaming pearls on sq diaper pattern, ruyi larger collar around neck, keyfret band around foot, gilded metal base and collar, orig stopper, Qianlong mark **1,635.00**

3½" h, spade shape, children on balcony one side, children playing tag on reverse, amethyst stopper, 19th C **600.00**

Sweetmeat Box, 13½" d, red, celadon jade mounts depicting five bats in cloud surrounding Oriental shou center, sectioned int. **745.00**

Utensil Set, pair chopsticks and knife, cloisonne dec, Chinese .. **140.00**

CLAMBROTH GLASS

History: Clambroth glass is a semi–opaque, grayish white glass which resembles the color of the broth from clams. Pieces are found in both a smooth finish and a rough sandy finish. The Sandwich Glass Co. and other manufacturers made clambroth glass.

Candlesticks, pr

8¼" h **65.00**

9¾" h, crucifix, pinpoint flakes . **55.00**

Dish, cov, matching underplate, 8″
l, 5¾″ w, 5¾″ h, melon shaped
hobnailed body and cov, base
with polished pontil, jade green
stem on cov and underplate ... **775.00**
Ewer, 7½″ h, Victorian, gilt handle,
ftd, enamel insects on bulbous
stopper **75.00**
Lamp, 11″ h, Star and Punty, Boston and Sandwich, c1850, minor
chips, price for pair **920.00**
Spill Holder, 4¾″ h, Diamond and
Thumbprint, int. wear, Ruth W
Lee, plate 210 .... **44.00**
Sugar Bowl, cov, Gothic Arch, lacy,
slight edge roughage to lid **215.00**

CLARICE CLIFF

History: Clarice Cliff, born on January
20, 1899, in Tunstall, Staffordshire, England, was one of the major pottery designers of the 20th century. At the age of thirteen, she left school and went to Lingard,
Webster & Company where she learned
free–hand painting. In 1916 Cliff was employed at A. J. Wilkinson's Royal Staffordshire Pottery, Burslem. She supplemented
her in–house training by attending a local
school of art in the evening.

In 1927 her employer sent her to study
sculpture for a few months at the Royal
College of Art in London. Upon returning,
she was placed in charge of a small team
of paintresses at the Newport Pottery, taken
over by Wilkinson in 1920. Cliff designed a
series of decorative motifs which were marketed as "Bizarre Ware" at the 1928 British
Industries Fair.

Throughout the 1930s Cliff added new
shapes and designs to the line. Her inspi-
ration came from art magazines, books on
gardening, and plants and flowers. Cliff and
her Bizarre Girls gave painting demonstra-
tions in stores of leading English retailers.
The popularity of the line increased.

World War II halted production. When the
war ended, the hand painting of china was
not renewed. In 1964 Midwinter bought the
Wilkinson and Newport firms.

The original pattern names for some patterns have not survived. It is safe to rely on
the handwritten or transfer printed name on
the base. The Newport Pattern books in the
Wilkinson's archives at the Hanley Library
also are helpful.

Bizarre and Fantasque are not patterns.
Rather they are range names, Bizarre being
used from 1928 to 1937 and Fantasque
used from 1929 to 1934.

References: Susan and Al Bagdade,
*Warman's English & Continental Pottery &
Porcelain, 2nd Edition,* Wallace–Home-
stead, 1991; Leonard R. Griffin and Susan
Pear Meisel, *Clarice Cliff: The Bizarre Af-
fair,* Harry N. Abrams, 1994; Howard Wat-
son, *Collecting Clarice Cliff,* Kevin Francis
Publishing, 1988; Howard and Pat Watson,
The Colourful World of Clarice Cliff, Kevin
Francis Publishing, 1991.

Collectors' Club: Clarice Cliff Collectors
Club, Fantasque House, Tennis Drive, The
Park, Nottingham, NG7 1AE, England.

Reproduction Alert: In 1986 fake *Lotus*
vases appeared in London and quickly
spread worldwide. Very poor painting and
patchy, uneven toffee–colored Honeyglaze
are the clues to spotting them. Collectors
also must be alert to patterns being added
to plain items bearing the "Clarice Cliff"
backstamp.

In the summer of 1985, Midwinters produced a series of limited edition reproductions to honor Clarice Cliff. They are clearly
dated 1985 and contain a special amalga-
mated backstamp.

Butter, cov, 2¾″ h, Bizarre, Crocus
pattern, lid with purple, blue, and
orange crocuses on ivory field . **275.00**
Figures, 5⅝″ h, set of four, Age of
Jazz, two groups of musicians
and two groups of dancing couples, red–orange, yellow, lime
green, cream, and black, printed
factory marks "Bizarre by Clarice Cliff, A. J. Wilkinson Ltd.,
Newport Pottery, England" ...**18,400.00**
Jug, 7″ h, Bizarre, Coral Firs pattern, Lotus shape, brown and orange trees, yellow, brown, and
gray hills, ivory field, diestamped
"Bizarre by Clarice Cliff" **700.00**
Pitcher
5¾″ h, Fantasque, Melon pattern, Conical shape, ink
stamped "Handpainted Fant-

asque by Clarice Cliff Wilkinson Ltd. England" and "Registration Applied For," tiny glaze nick at rim and base, faint scratch in orange band at base **715.00**

7" h, Bizarre, Rhodanthe pattern, brown, yellow, orange, and powder blue flowers, ivory ground, broad tapering neck, bulbous base **450.00**

7⅛" h, Fantasque, Lily Orange pattern, Athens shape, ink stamped "Hand Painted Fantasque by Clarice Cliff Wilkinson Ltd. England," incised "30" and "17," small chip at base **775.00**

Plate, Bizarre Ware, Newport Pottery, England, cobalt blue rim and center, green eyes, separated by yellows and reds, 9¾" d, $185.00.

Plate, 9¾" d, Forest Glen pattern, orange and ivory house on green hill, diestamped "Clarice Cliff, Newport Pottery, England" . . . **500.00**

Rose Bowl, 5¾" h, Fantasque, Blue Chintz pattern, Conical shape, ink stamped "Fantasque, Bizarre, Hand Painted, Newport Pottery England" on bottoms of legs, ink stamped "Clarice Cliff" on side near base, small glaze nicks on rim **465.00**

Vase
6¼" h, Fantasque, Trees and

House pattern, black, orange, and green trees, ivory field, flaring neck, #196, diestamped "Fantasque by Clarice Cliff" **800.00**

6⅝" h, Bizarre, Green Japan pattern, Bonjour shape, base ink stamped "Hand Painted Bizarre by Clarice Cliff Wilkinson Ltd. England" and "Made in England" **450.00**

8" h, Fantasque Bizarre, Secrets pattern, yellow, green, and brown trees in hilly landscape, ivory field, bulbous body, #358, diestamped "Fantasque, Bizarre by Clarice Cliff" **800.00**

9⅝" h, Fantasque, Umbrella and Rain pattern, Isis shape, leaves in each panel rather than alternating with diagonal lined panels, ink stamped "Handpainted Fantasque by Clarice Cliff Wilkinson Ltd. England," incised "Isis," three small glaze nicks at rim **2,525.00**

10" h, Fantasque, Gayday pattern, Isis shape, orange, purple, red, and blue flowers and green foliage, ivory field, diestamped "Fantasque by Clarice Cliff, Lawley's Regent Street" **1,100.00**

CLEWELL POTTERY

History: Charles Walter Clewell was first a metalworker and second a potter. In the early 1900s he opened a small shop in Canton, Ohio, to produce metal overlay pottery.

Metal on pottery was not a new idea, but Clewell was perhaps the first to completely mask the ceramic body with copper, brass, and "silvered" and "bronzed" metals. One result was a product whose patina added to the character of the piece over time.

Most of the wares are marked with a simple incised "CLEWELL" along with a code number. Because Clewell used pottery blanks from other firms, the names "Owens" or "Weller" are sometimes found.

Since Clewell operated on a small scale with little outside assistance, only a limited quantity of his artwork exists. He retired at the age of 79 in 1955, choosing not to reveal his technique to anyone else.

References: Paul Evans, *Art Pottery of the United States, 2nd Edition,* Feingold & Lewis Publishing Corp., 1987; Ralph and Terry Kovel, *Kovels' American Art Pottery: The Collector's Guide To Makers, Marks and Factory Histories,* Crown Publishers, 1993.

Tankard Set, tankard and five matching mugs, riveted metal design, marked "Clewell, Canton, OH," price for set, $775.00.

Bowl, 3⅛" h, low, copper clad, good patina, marked "Clewell 422–2–6," minor rub wear, first half 20th C **250.00**
Tankard Set, 10" h tankard and four mugs, copper clad, patina, each piece stamped "Clewell Canton Ohio," one mug with tear in copper jacket, c1910 .... **715.00**
Vase
   5⅛" h, ovoid, shouldered, waisted neck, flaring lip, three angular handles from lip to shoulder, copper clad, mottled green patina **400.00**
   6" h, faceted, raised dec, brown and green, copper clad, fine patina, copper peeling on int., unmarked **450.00**
   11⅜" h, copper clad, good patina, base incised "Clewell, 302–2–6," c1940 .... **600.00**

12¾" h, long flared neck, bulbous shoulder tapering towards foot, blue patina, incised "Clewell, 454–2–6," some scratches, early 20th C **1,000.00**
16" h, copper clad, strong patina, base marked with stylus "Clewell 277–6," ceramic blank from Weller Pottery, minor scratches and abrasions . **1,550.00**

CLIFTON

CLIFTON POTTERY

History: The Clifton Art Pottery, Newark, New Jersey, was established by William A. Long, once associated with Lonhuna Pottery, and Fred Tschirner, a chemist.

Production consisted of two major lines: Crystal Patina, which resembled true porcelain with a subdued crystal-like glaze, and Indian Ware or Western Influence, an adaptation of the American Indians' unglazed and decorated pottery with a high–glazed black interior. Other lines included Robin's–Egg Blue and Tirrube. Robin's–Egg Blue is a variation of the Crystal Patina line but in blue-green instead of straw colored hues and with a less prominent "crushed crystal" effect in the glaze. Tirrube is on a terracotta ground; features brightly colored, slip decorated flowers; and is often artist signed.

Marks are incised or impressed. Early pieces may be dated and shape numbers impressed. Indian Ware pieces are identified by tribes.

References: Paul Evans, *Art Pottery Of The United States, 2nd Edition,* Feingold & Lewis Publishing Corp., 1987; Ralph and Terry Kovel, *Kovels' American Art Pottery: The Collector's Guide To Makers, Marks and Factory Histories,* Crown Publishers, 1993.

Bowl, 3½" d, 2½" h, spherical, stylized lily pads in relief, ftd, matte green glaze, incised "Clifton, 146" **350.00**

Teapot, cov
3⅜" h, Crystal Patina, base and lid stamped "271–30," c1910 **165.00**
5⅜" h, Crystal Patina, base marked with logo "Clifton Pottery Newark, NJ" inside elongated "C" and diestamped "272–42," c1910 .... **300.00**

Humidor, Indian Ware, brown, 4½" w, 4¼" h, $45.00.

Vase
3¾" h, two handles, base incised with "Clifton," date, and "113," 1905 .... **165.00**
6¾" h, Crystal Patina, silver overlay, light crystalline glaze, base marked with Electrolytic of Trenton, NJ, logo and incised "Clifton," Clifton logo, date, and shape number "171," 1906 .... **875.00**
10" h, tall cylindrical neck, protruding shoulder, crystalline celadon glaze, incised mark and "163," 1906 .... **350.00**

CLOCKS

History: The sundial was the first man–made device for measuring time. Its basic disadvantage is well expressed in the saying: "Do like the sundial, count only the sunny days."

With need for greater dependability, man developed the water clock, oil clock, and the sand clock respectively. All these clocks worked on the same principle—time was measured by the amount of material passing from one container to another.

The wheel clock was the next major step. These clocks can be traced back to the 13th century. Many improvements on the basic wheel clock were made and continue to be made. In 1934 the quartz crystal movement was introduced.

Recently an atomic clock has been invented that measures time by the frequency of radiation and only varies one second in a thousand years.

Identifying the proper model name for a clock is critical in establishing price. Condition of works also is a critical factor. Examine the works to see how many original parts remain. If repairs are needed, try to include this in your estimate of purchase price. Few clocks are purchased purely for decorative value.

References: Robert W. D. Ball, *American Shelf and Wall Clocks: A Pictorial History for Collectors,* Schiffer Publishing, 1992; Philip Collins, *Pastime: Telling Time From 1879 to 1969,* Chronicle Books, 1993; Roy Ehrhardt, *Clock Identification And Price Guide: Book I,* rev. ed., Heart of America Press, 1979; Roy Ehrhardt, *Clock Identification And Price Guide: Book II,* Heart of America Press, 1979; Roy Ehrhardt (ed.), *The Official Price Guide To Antique Clocks,* House of Collectibles, Third Edition, 1985; Brian Loomes, *Painted Dial Clocks,* Antique Collector's Club, 1994; Tran Duy Ly, *American Clocks: A Guide To Identification and Prices,* Arlington Book Co., 1989, 1991 value update; Rick Ortenburger, *Vienna Regulators And Factory Clocks,* Schiffer Publishing, 1990; Derek Roberts, *Carriage and Other Traveling Clocks,* Schiffer Publishing, 1993; Robert W. & Harriett Swedberg, *American Clocks and Clockmakers,* Wallace–Homestead, 1989.

Collectors' Club: National Association of Watch and Clock Collectors, Inc., 514 Poplar St., Columbia, PA 17512.

Museums: American Clock & Watch Museum, Bristol, CT; Museum of National Association of Watch and Clock Collectors, Columbia, PA.

MISCELLANEOUS

Advertising
    Ever–Ready Safety Razor, wood, classic decal of man shaving foamy beard, orig pendulum inscribed "12 'Radio' Steel Blades $1," 28" h, 18" w 675.00
    Spanish Blacking, Edw P Baird & Co, NY and Montreal, figure eight regulator, wood, emb lettering and dec around dial, open glass pendulum window, 27" h, 16" w, 5" d 850.00
Alarm
    Herman Miller Co, chrome metal and glass, circular wood frame, rect foot supported by chromed side bracket, black dots for numerals, c1933, 8⅛" l 3,675.00
    Seth Thomas, shelf, mahogany veneer case, brass works, worn painted metal face, reverse painted glass panel, 15½" h 250.00
    Unknown Maker, desk, eight day, gilt metal, drum form case, gilt metal dial, Arabic numerals, subsidiary dials calibrated for 24 hours, blued steel lozenge hands, singing bird box case with basketweave design and fluted columns, late 19th C, 6¼" h 3,450.00
Atmos, Le Coultre & Cie, Switzerland, mantel, brass and glass, cut corner rect form, 20th C, 9¼" h, 8⅛" w, 6⅜" d 575.00
Automaton, unknown maker, mantel
    Empire, gilt metal, boy on dog, tree and clock tower, dog rings bell, early 19th C, some restoration, 11¼" h 2,075.00
    Empire style, gilt bronze, Napoleon and British ship, some restoration, mid 19th C, 16¼" h 2,175.00
Desk, unknown maker, English, brass, gravity drive, 10½" h ... 120.00
Garniture, 3 pcs

Kreisser, Paris, Empire style, parcel gilt porcelain, marked enameled dial, late 19th C, 12" h 1,725.00
Lemerle–Charpentier, Louis XVI style, ormolu, figural, pair of classical ladies holding upraised clock surmounted by cherub, round enamel dial marked "Lemerle–Charpentier, Bronzier, Paris, Rue Charlot, 8," pair urn form eight–light candelabra, formerly electrified, second quarter 19th C, 32" h clock 10,350.00
Lepine, Paris, Baccarat crystal, ormolu mounted, marked enamel dial, flanked by pillars, pair urn form candlesticks, 19th C, 21½" h clock 8,625.00
Unknown Maker
    Classical Revival, bronze and marble, clock with casket base with lion's head handle surmounted by seated Egyptian maid, pair male and female attendant statues, retailed by Tiffany & Co, 19th C, 22" h clock 5,465.00
    French
        Gilt bronze, onyx, and champleve enamel, pair four–socket candlesticks, retailed by Tiffany & Co, 14¾" h clock 4,300.00
        Slate and antico verde marble, late 19th C, 17" h clock, pair 11" h tazzas .. 430.00
        White marble and brass, enameled dial, pair single candlesticks, sold by Bigelow, Kennard & Co, Inc, clock 6½" h, candlesticks 5⅛" h 350.00
    French Empire style, glass, gilt bronze mounted, mottled paneled round case centering Roman numeral dial, raised on baluster stand, flanked by dolphins, paneled oval base with lion feet, pair urns with paneled bodies and double swan handles, 18" h clock 6,675.00

Louis XV Style, gilt and patinated bronze and white marble, cherubs, enameled dial marked "Robin RR du Roy," pair two socket candlesticks, late 19th C, clock 12" h ...**2,875.00**

Gravity, unknown maker

American, brass case, 24 hour movement, marked "Patented 8/2/21" **195.00**

French, mahogany case, brass finials, turned columns, porcelain dial, polished stone drum, 30 hour movement, c1940 .... **875.00**

Industry, Merden & Forster, NY, red marble and brass, sgd dial, barometer and centigrade and Fahrenheit thermometers, late 19th C, 14" h **1,725.00**

Ivory, Gubelin, miniature painting, rect gilt metal case, openwork doors, fitted leather case **495.00**

Lantern, unknown maker

Charles II, brass, urn finial above pierced frets with lion and unicorn supports, circular dial, Roman chapter ring enclosing tulip dec border engraved "Charles Fox At the Fox in Lothbury Londini Fecit," alarm disc, floral engraved center, c1670, 14½" h **5,500.00**

Japanese, gilt brass, deep bell, day and night merge escapements, thread suspended foliots with adjustable weights, alarm train behind dial plate, fixed chapter ring, single calendar aperture, hinged side and back panels, etched leaves and scrolls dec, 19th C, 12¾" h **1,425.00**

Travel

Movado, 18K gold cushion form case with basketweave dec, center opening, rect white dial, Arabic and baton markers, sweep seconds and alarm hands, hinged back frame, dial sgd "Movado, Ermetophon," case serial #28995–1 ......**1,850.00**

Unknown Maker, circular, jade wheel border, mother-of-pearl center, carved carnelian ball feet, 4" h **495.00**

SHELF

Acorn, Forestville Manufacturing Co, Bristol, CT, fuse movement, c1850, 24" h **4,125.00**

Art Deco, unknown maker, ormolu and onyx, fan form, minor chips, early 20th C, 18½" w, 11½" h . **750.00**

Beehive

Brewster & Ingraham, Bristol, CT, rosewood veneered case, cut glass tablet, paper label, eight day time and strike movement, orig brass springs and strike mechanism advance by raising hammer, movement and painted zinc dial inscribed by maker, missing key, screws added to bottom for leveling, case refinished, 1850, 19" h **450.00**

Seth Thomas, Thomaston, CT, mahogany case, painted dial, eight day tone and strike movement, orig pendulum, 1920, 10" h **100.00**

Boulle, unknown maker, Second Empire style, gilt bronze, cupid finial over cartouche form case, enameled dial with Roman numerals, allover scrolled foliate dec, C–scrolled feet, 28" h **3,000.00**

Bracket

Bertrand, Paris, brass inlaid, sur-

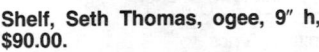

Shelf, Seth Thomas, ogee, 9" h, $90.00.

mounted by classical figure, marked enamel dial, orig bracket, restored, 18th C, 46" h 3,225.00

Fuch, Phillip, Seckau, French, gilt highlighted and painted dec, time and strike movement, repeating mechanism, possibly restored, 19th C, 18⅞" h 1,150.00

Partington, London, George III, mahogany, acorn finials, late 18th C, 18½" h 3,450.00

Robinson, George, London, mahogany, time and strike movement, mechanism with nest of bells, silvered brass dial, pendulum, key missing, 19th C, 17" h 1,100.00

Unknown Maker
Gothic Style, French, retailed by Shreve, Crump & Low Co, late 19th C, 15" h 450.00
Mahogany, round painted enamel dial, dome top rect case, retailed by Tiffany & Co, 19th C, 12¾" h 575.00
Napoleon III, boulle, brass and enamel dial, damage, 61" h 4,025.00

Washborne, John, Gloucester, George II, japanned, marked dial, bail handle, repaired, late 18th C, 21" h 3,000.00

Willard, Aaron, Boston, MA, Federal, inlaid mahogany, stepback top with painted dial within tombstone shaped arch, molded waist, bracket feet, refinished, c1800, 12½" w, 5½" d, 29½" h 9,200.00

Calendar
Ithaca Calendar Clock Co, mahogany case, ebonized carvings, silver trim, bottom glass face with tarnished silver dial labeled "Ithaca Calendar Clock Co, Ithaca, NY, H. B. Horton's Patents...," minor repairs to case, 20¼" h 1,980.00

Southern Calendar Clock Co, refinished walnut case, gilt lettered "Fashion" on glass, double dials, "Southern Calendar Clock Co, St Louis, MO," pat-

ent dates 1875, 1878, and 1879, 32" h 1,265.00

Carriage, French, brass and glass
Jaeger–Le Coultre, enameled brass, faux lapis enamel, 20th C, minor chips, 4¾" h 500.00
Vrard, L & Co, Shanghai, marked dial, hour repeating, alarm, late 19th C, 7¼" h . . .1,150.00

Unknown Maker
3" h, oval, face, sides, and back with painted enamel panels by Janetti Padre and Jigli 2,300.00
6" h, reeded handle, repeating movement 600.00
8" h, faux bamboo form, late 19th C 550.00

Cartel, Benoist, J Bte, Paris, Louis XV style, ormolu, circular enamel dial, sgd on dial and movement backplate, 19th C, 34¼" h 4,890.00

Cottage
Sperry, Henry & Co, NY, grain painted rect case, glazed reverse painted door, painted dial, 30 hour spring movement, c1850, 12" h, 8" w, 4" d 195.00
Terry, S B, Terryville, CT, poplar case, blue and gold glass tablet, painted zinc dial, paper label, 30 hour time ladder movement with gears in direct line mounted between plates, case refinished, minor touch up to dial, period key and pendulum, c1855, 10½" h 600.00

Dome, unknown maker
French, brass, glass dome, dial marked "Gaston Jolly," late 19th C, 17½" h 865.00
George III Style, inlaid mahogany, chiming, bracket base, two feet replaced, 19th C, 14½" h 550.00

Frame, unknown maker, French, brass and glass, round painted enameled dial encased in rect frame, molded onyx top, 19th C, 12¾" h 350.00

Figural
Brasseur, Paris, Empire style, malachite and bronze, seated

woman, marked dial, late 19th C, 27½" h **3,675.00**

Maniere, Paris, Louis XVI style, ormolu and white marble, classical woman and cherub, marked enamel dial, time and strike movement, pendulum, 19th C, 14½" h **1,600.00**

Marti, Samuel, Louis XVI style, gilt bronze and sienna marble, maiden seated on shell, holding wind–blown shawl, retailed by Tiffany & Co, regilded, c1900 .... **625.00**

Moreau, L & F, French, Empire style, gilded, woman and child on rockery, marble plinth, sgd enameled dial, late 19th C, 24¼" h **575.00**

Mourey, P H, gilt metal and painted porcelain, gilded wood plinth, damage, late 19th C, 19" h **350.00**

Raingo Fres, Paris, Louis XVI style, bronze, ormolu, and marble, reclining child, sgd enameled dial, 19th C, 27" l, 17" h **2,750.00**

Unknown Maker

Empire Style, bronze and ormolu, winged angel playing harp, rect base, four feet, retailed by J E Caldwell & Co, missing pendulum and key, late 19th C, 9½" w, 13½" h **1,500.00**

Louis XV Style

Dore Bronze, cupid mounted on spherical dial, raised on clouds issuing rays of light supported by neoclassical figures in repose, serpentine base mounted with floral garlands, acanthus scrolled apron, toupie feet, 19th C, 32" w, 29" h **9,425.00**

Gilt Bronze, cherub driving chariot, enameled dial, chips, late 19th C, 13" h .**2,185.00**

Louis XVI style

Gilt bronze and white marble, painted enamel dial surrounded by cherub with doves and cornucopia, late 19th C, 17" h **1,725.00**

Ormolu and white and black marble, pillared arch surmounted by foliage, enamel dial marked "Paris," 19th C, 18" h ...**1,750.00**

Neoclassical, Austrian

Fruitwood, gilt metal and gesso mounted, seated soldier, second quarter 19th C, 15" h, 15¼" l **1,150.00**

Painted and parcel gilt, replaced works, mid 19th C, 18" h **750.00**

Gallery, unknown maker, Victorian, mahogany, thirty day, painted round dial, late 19th C, 37" h .. **865.00**

German Black Forest, unknown maker, carved walnut, figural, two stags set on rocaille form base centering a clock above two pheasants and oak leaves, shaped base, 19th C, 43" h ...**3,450.00**

Gingerbread

New Haven Clock Co, pressed oak case, gold dec door glass, eight day time, strike, and alarm movement, paper label "Our Pride 8 day Striking Alarm," sgd movement and paper label on back, case refinished, dial flaking, 1875, 25" h **195.00**

Welch, E N, Forestville, CT, cast iron case front marked "N.M.S. New York #173," dec glass tablet, eight day time and strike movement, paper dial, orig pendulum, missing key, restorations include replaced dial paper and tablet and refinished case, mismatched hands, 1880, 22" h . **225.00**

Lyre, Camus, Paris, ormolu and white marble, marked enamel dial, 19th C, 22" h **3,735.00**

Mantel

Gaydamour, Paris, Louis XVI style, gilt bronze and marble, sgd circular white enamel dial, drum form case surmounted by obelisk flanked by twin pedestals with scrolling spires and bird form finials, stepped oval socle, toupie feet, late 18th C, 22" h **3,450.00**

Idrac–Le–Roy, Paris, Napoleon III, red marble, face inscribed "Idrac–Le–Roy, Rue du Bouloi 22, Paris," late 19th C, 8½" h **500.00**

P Lesperut Fils, Paris, Directoire style, gilt and patinated bronze, shield form case surmounted by turtle finial, circular enamel dial with Gothic ornamented hands, molded base with engine turned bun ft, mid 19th C, 14" h **750.00**

Raingo Fres, Paris, Louis XV style, dore bronze, figural, floral basket finial above C–scrolled case, marked enameled Roman numeral dial, flanked by putto one side, floral swag with bird other side, plinth base with anthemion and drapery mounts, toupie feet, 19th C, 25" w, 8½" d, 24" h **6,675.00**

Unknown Maker

Austrian, painted and parcel gilt, circular enamel dial within boldly carved bezel of bellflowers and mantel of grape leaves, surmounted by flowering urn, stepped base with pendulum aperture, late 18th/early 19th C, 31" h **3,100.00**

Continental, porcelain and gilt bronze mounted, baluster form with putti surrounding Roman numeral dial, raised on gilt bronze pedestal base, pair of five–light candelabra, 19½" h clock **1,725.00**

Empire Style, mahogany, rect top, molded cornice supported by four Corinthian columns with gilt metal mounts, enameled dial with Roman numerals surrounded by gilt bronze shell border, plinth base, pad feet, 19" h **490.00**

French

Brass and Glass, rect case, circular face, mercury pen-

dulum, sold by Bigelow, Kennard & Co, Boston, 14¼" h **550.00**

Ormolu, urn finial on circular case supported by two slender urn columns, rect rouge marble base, cast ormolu feet, 19th C, 16¼" h **1,000.00**

White Marble, obelisk form, round enamel face, time and strike movement, mercury pendulum, key, 19th C, 20" h **500.00**

French Empire, gilt and patinated bronze, pharaoh above enameled Roman numeral dial on lion mask, square base with ball feet, 19th C, 13" h **2,750.00**

Louis Phillipe

Gilt bronze, figural, mother and child above Roman numeral dial, rect base with scrolling foliate dec, scrolled feet, 3rd quarter 19th C, 15" w, 6" d, 19" h **2,075.00**

Gilt bronze and marble, obelisk form surmounted by putto, violet marble column holding arrow form thermometer, gilt bronze angled paw feet, block form breche d'Alep base with circular enameled clock dial and bronze bezel, first half 19th C, 34½" h **3,675.00**

Louis XIV Style, gilt bronze mounted, late 19th C **1,500.00**

Louis XV Style

Gilt bronze, putto above C–scroll and acanthus case, centering an enameled Roman numeral dial above latticework panel on scrolled supports, acanthus scrolled base, late 19th C, 18" h **1,500.00**

Tortoiseshell, ormolu mounted, gilt bronze face with white and black enameled Roman numerals, asymmetrical case dec with scrolling foliate ormolu mounted, scrolled ormolu feet, 19th C, 27" h **3,680.00**

Louis XVI Style, bronze and brass, cupid finial above arched foliate dec case, enameled dial with Roman numerals, inverted acorn feet, 20½" h **1,265.00**

Modified Tambour, variegated marble and ormolu, cupid and swan dec, 14½" h **650.00**

Renaissance Revival, NY, ormolu mounted red and black marble, surmounted by classical bust of bearded man, name on dial obscured, third quarter 19th C, 22½" h **225.00**

Second Empire, silvered metal and porcelain, urn finial porcelain Roman numeral dial, shaped case with porcelain panel, mask and scroll feet, 14" h **315.00**

Miniature, unknown maker
Rococo style, gilt metal and enamel, formed as three–fold screen, early 20th C, 6¾" h . **700.00**

Tall Case form, Continental, silver, figural and landscape repousse bombe case with figural finials, American Watch Co movement, key, 7½" h ... **465.00**

Pillar
Roberts, T M, mahogany, gilt and painted, portrait panel below painted dial, gilt pillars and ball feet, labeled "Manufactured by T. M. Roberts for Henry Hart, Bristol, Connecticut," replaced movement, 33" h **316.00**

Unknown Maker, Classical Revival, black and white marble, 19th C, 22" h **1,725.00**

Pillar and Scroll
Atkins Clock Co, Bristol, CT, rosewood, cove molded top, circular dial flanked by turned columns, fuse movement, refinished, c1840 ....**2,300.00**

Terry, Samuel, Plymouth, CT, Federal, mahogany, broken arch pediment, urn finials, dial

above panel with landscape scene, minor imperfections, c1825, 17½" w, 4½" d, 30" h .**3,000.00**

Portico, unknown maker
Charles V, ormolu and ebonized, 19th C, 20" h **375.00**

Empire Style
Ormolu and malachite, French, enameled dial, late 19th C, 24½" h **2,750.00**

Silver plated, enameled dial, 20½" h **865.00**

Ship's Bell, brass, striking
Chelsea, round dial supported by rect base, ball feet, late 19th C, 9" h **575.00**

Waterbury Clock Co, jeweled movement, 8" h **350.00**

Skeleton, brass
Unknown Maker, Victorian Gothic style, white marble base, late 19th C, 24" h **2,300.00**

Wherly, M & S Clock & Watch Makers, Sunderland, English, glass dome, white marble base, paper label, 19th C, 15½" h **975.00**

Steeple
Ansonia Clock Co, mahogany veneer, eight day, urn shape finials, quarter columns, eglomise paneled door with "The Constitution," two clasped hands, stars, and floral wreath dec, painted dial, Roman numerals, plinth base, 19th C, 19½" h, 9¾" w, 4½" d **195.00**

Birge and Fuller, Bristol, CT, Gothic, double steeple, c1840, 27½" h **1,210.00**

Brewster & Ingraham, Bristol, CT, Charles Kirk's patent cast iron back plate for 30 hour time and strike movement, mahogany veneered case, painted beehive tablet, painted dial inscribed by maker, paper label, case refinished, replaced door lock and beehive tablet, 1845, 20" h **385.00**

Smith & Goodrich, Bristol, CT, brass double fusee works, mahogany veneer, "Presidents House" dec on reverse

painted glass, loose door, 20″
h **300.00**
Unknown Maker, brass works,
mahogany veneer, worn
painted metal face, paper label, reverse painted "Washington's Rock, NJ" dec, some
veneer damage, 20″ h **150.00**
Table, unknown maker
Cut Glass, French, ten green
glass lustres with portraits and
floral medallions and painted
gilt highlights, brass base, 78″
h **375.00**
Gilt Bronze, Empire, circular en-
gine turned dial within conforming leaf clad drum, resting
on plinth cast with classical figures centering lyre, early 19th
C, 11″ h **860.00**
Gilt Metal, pink enamel, Classi-
cal urn shape, Roman numerals on time band, octagonal
marble base, 5″ h **1,265.00**
Gilt Metal and Porcelain,
painted, floor screen form,
small circular clock face and
figures in landscape on front,
ruins in landscape on reverse,
3½ x 4¼″ **495.00**
Silver, enameled and jeweled,
"steps to the forum" design
with angel, maiden, and sleeping lion on lapis lazuli steps,
circular clock above two rams'
heads, 8″ h **5,775.00**

TALL CASE

Alke, Christopher, Amsterdam, inlaid walnut case, arched scroll
frieze supported by plain columns, arched dial with moon
face aperture, engraved pastoral
scene, silvered chapter ring,
subsidiary seconds dial, date aperture, day of week sector, scroll
hands, Dutch striking movement
with anchor escapement, bird
and flower marquetry on shaped
door, glazed lenticle mounted
with ormolu C–scrolls and basket of flowers, stringing and applied ogee molding on canted

corner plinth, claw and ball feet,
alarm mechanism removed,
19th C, 92½″ h **3,300.00**
Allen, country, refinished curly
birch, bonnet with freestanding
columns, arched cornice, turned
finials, applied edge door, applied moldings, bracket feet,
mismatched brass works,
painted steel face with ghost
mark signature, worn, 86″ h . . .   **770.00**
Alston, Wm, Dundee, William IV,
mahogany, scrolled crest above
drum, glazed hood, marked
brass Roman numeral dial, flaring fluted case, paneled rect
base, bun feet, third quarter 19th
C, 80″ h, 15″ w, 10″ d **5,300.00**
Armagh, Duncan, George III Pro-
vincial, bleached pine, maker's
mark on arched painted dial,
subsidiary dial and calendar aperture, dial repainted, early 19th
C, 81″ h **975.00**
Bailey, John, Hanover, MA, Fed-
eral inlaid mahogany, arched
bonnet with cast brass ball finials, painted dial with moon
phases, pendulum door flanked
by fluted columns, French feet,
refinished, repainted dial, c1795,
94½″ h **9,200.00**
Bancher, Jas, Attleboro, George
III, Chinoiserie decorated, dial
marked "Jas Bancher, Attle-
boro," late 18th C, 87″ h **2,300.00**
Brokaw, Isaac, Bridgetown, NJ,
mahogany, inlaid, swan neck pediment with brass rosettes centering brass sphere form finial,
arched bird and floral dec calendar face, shaped rect pendulum door flanked by quarter
reeded column sides, French
bracket feet, works attributed to
Isaac Brokaw, Bridgetown, NJ,
1790–1815, 95″ h, 21½″ w, 10″
d **3,950.00**
Brookfield, inlaid cherry, broken
pediment with ball finials, arched
polychrome dial with bird and
flowers, inscribed with maker's
mark, French ft, refinished, imperfections, c1810, 92″ h **5,750.00**

Caldwell, J E & Co, carved mahogany, shield cartouche over floral and scroll carved arched bonnet, brass and steel face depicting moon phases, beveled glass pendulum door flanked by cylindrical column sides, paw feet, tubular chiming, c1900, 96" h, 24" w, 17" d 3,750.00

Fazakerley, Thomas, London, George III, chinoiserie decorated, marked dial, late 18th C, 94" h 4,900.00

Herschede, mahogany, shaped sq pediment, rect clock face with lunar and solar phases and Roman numerals set in pewter within pierced brass field, window case pane with canted corners carved with pilasters, sq molded base, bracket feet, 85½" h, 19" w, 14" d 1,850.00

Higgs, Roberto and Pedro, Londres, George III, chinoiserie lacquer, alarm, pagoda hood, plain columns flanking sgd arched dial, silvered chapter ring enclosing date aperture, seconds dial and alarm setting disc in matted center, movement with anchor escapement, hour strike, separately wound alarm train, arched trunk door with scenes of ships and travelers in exotic landscape, molded plinth, c1770, 94½" h 3,525.00

Hoadley, S, Plymouth, cherry, orig finish, bonnet with free standing front columns, gooseneck pediment, door with scalloped top edge, wide cove moldings, chamfered corners with lambs' tongues, paneled base, cutout feet, wooden works, painted wood face, gilt masonic designs, polychrome name, damaged pewter hands, old repairs and breaks, 87½" h 4,625.00

Laing, J R, Glasgow, Victorian, mahogany, sgd round dial painted black and gold, two subsidiary dials, late 19th C, 80" h 2,525.00

Lambert, Berwick, George III, mahogany, swan's neck pediment, arched brass dial marked "Lambert, Berwick," two subsidiary dials, late 18th C, 85" h 3,225.00

Lane, Aaron, Elizabethtown, NJ, Chippendale, walnut, swan's neck crest centering three brass ball and steeple finials, arched glazed door, engraved brass dial with calendar date mechanism inscribed with maker's name, waisted case with hinged door flanked by fluted quarter columns, molded paneled base, bracket feet, c1780, 93½" h, 17¾" w, 10" d 8,050.00

Maillet, Alexis, Louis XV Provincial style, oak, enameled dial, marked "Alexis Maillet a St Amande," damaged dial, 76" h . 2,175.00

Moore, John, Warminster, George III, walnut, swan neck cresting above arched door, flanked by columnar stiles, face with etched steel plate and brass spaniels, case with shaped door above similarly paneled lower section, ogee bracket feet, works by John Moore, Warminster, c1750, 92½" h 4,600.00

Morris, Benjamin, New Britain, mahogany, maker's name on brass dial, painted arch with rocking ship, subsidiary dial and calendar aperture, late 18th C, 106" h 3,450.00

Parr & Son, London, William IV, walnut, arched bonnet, large circular steel sweep minute dial with hour window, inset arched pendulum door, molded base, raised feet, 1830, 75" h, 19½" w, 11" d 1,875.00

Paterson, James, Banff, George III, chinoiserie decorated, marked dial late 18th C, 90" h . 2,185.00

Smith Paterson Co, Whittington and Westminster chimes, Victorian, mahogany, bonnet top, full columns with capitals, subsidiary dial, 94" h 2,875.00

Stier, W, Bath, George III, mahogany, broken arch pediment centering brass finial, glazed hood flanked by engaged columns with gilt Corinthian capitals, painted Roman numeral dial with dual automaton dial depicting Adam and Eve, signed "W. Stier, Bath," crossbanded rect case flanked by fluted corner columns, rect base, French feet, second quarter 19th C **2,750.00**

Taber, Elnathan, Roxbury, MA, Federal, inlaid mahogany, pierced fretwork crest surmounted by three brass ball and steeple finials, arched glazed door, white painted dial with moon phases, calendar date, and seconds registers, inscribed with makers name, flanked by brass stop fluted colonettes, waisted case with fan inlaid door flanked by brass stop fluted quarter columns, fan inlaid and crossbanded base, shaped skirt, flared bracket feet, c1800, 88½" h, 18½" w, 9¾" d **33,350.00**

Unknown Maker
Country, pine, blue repaint, dovetailed bonnet with broken arch pediment, molded edge door, standing front columns, simple bracket feet, brass works, painted steel face with touchup, worn label "Pembroke," restoration, 84" h **660.00**

Federal, cherry, swan neck pediment with carved rosettes flanked by urn finials, arched floral painted face, arched thumbmolded pendulum door, ogival bracket feet, early 19th C, 89" h, 22" w, 12" d **2,100.00**

Federal, NY or NJ, inlaid cherry, swan's neck crest surmounted by three brass ball and steeple finials, arched hinged door, white painted dial with seconds and calendar date registers and moon phases, waisted bookend inlaid case with line inlaid door flanked by reeded quarter columns, inlaid base with shaped skirt, lacks front feet, c1805, 95" h, 18⅓" w, 9" d **9,200.00**

George III, oak, arched painted dial, two subsidiary dials, dial partially repainted, early 19th C, 85" h **800.00**

Napoleon III, mahogany, enameled and brass round dial, molded cornice and acanthus carved support, glass fronted molded plinth base, late 19th C, 89½" h **1,500.00**

Pennsylvania, cherry, swan neck pediment with carved rosettes and center flame finial, arched wood floral painted face, fan carved pendulum door flanked by quarter reeded columns, ogival bracket ft, c1770, 93" h, 22½" w, 11" d **4,500.00**

Scottish, mahogany and oak, broken pediment, carved florets, swags, and leaves, arched painted dials, two subsidiary dials, raised central door panel with carved man, shaped apron, bracket feet, late 18th/early 19th C, 95" h . **1,725.00**

Willard, Aaron, Roxbury, MA, Federal, mahogany, pierced fretwork hood surmounted by three brass ball and steeple finials, arched glazed door, sgd white painted dial with moon phases, calendar date, and seconds register, waisted case with arched hinged door flanked by brass stop fluted quarter columns, molded base, ogee bracket feet, replaced fretwork, some repainting to dial, c1800, 94½" h, 18½" w, 9" d . **11,500.00**

Willard, Simon, Roxbury, MA, Federal, inlaid mahogany, three brass ball and steeple finials, pierced fretwork over arched glazed door with patterned inlay, sgd white painted dial, Roman and Arabic chapter rings, sweep second and calendar day dial, central panel painted with bird, polychrome painted spandrels with "Four Seasons" dec, flanking brass stop fluted quarter colonettes, waisted case with arched molded cupboard flanked by brass stop fluted quarter columns with brass capitals, barber pole inlaid plinths, molded box base, 1792–96, 105¾" h, 25½" w, 10½" d **77,000.00**

Wood, David, Newburyport, MA, cherry, repainted rocking ship dial, restored, c1790, 92" h **6,325.00**

Wall, Ingraham, Mosaic, calendar, rosewood case, 30" l, $695.00.

WALL

American, maple veneer and oak, rect case with leaded beveled clear glass door, time and strike movement, weight driven, late 19th/early 20th C, 37¾" h **750.00**

Anglo/American, inlaid mahogany, trunk dial, eight day movement, late 19th C, 27" h **345.00**

Banjo
  Curtis & Dunning, Burlington, VT, Federal, mahogany, giltwood, and eglomise, brass ball and steeple finial, glazed door, white painted dial inscribed "Warranted by Curtis & Dunning, Burlington, VT," eglomise throat panel with polychrome stylized leaves dec, brass side arms, lower hinged door with polychrome eglomise panel depicting seated woman holding book, talking to young girl, lower door later replacement, c1830, 34¾" h, 10" w **575.00**

Simon Willard, Federal, acorn finial, circular brass bezel, white painted dial, Arabic chapter ring, tapering throat with eglomise panel inscribed "Patent," thermometer above box base with eglomise panel, c1805, 33½" h **5,275.00**

Unknown Origin, mahogany and gilt, gilt metal eagle finial, leaf and scroll eglomised neck panel with Zeus in horse–drawn chariot, late 19th/early 20th C, 40" h **900.00**

Cuckoo
  Black Forest, German, time and quarter hour strike mechanism, cuckoo and quail, heavily carved wood case, game birds, animals, oak leaves, and acorns dec, surmounted by stag head and rifles, 19th C, 55" h, 49" w, 21" d **7,150.00**

  German, 30 hour time and strike movement, carved case, eagle and fox dec, pinecone weights, carved pendulum, case enhanced with paint, minute hand replaced, bellows replaced, c1900, 24" h **195.00**

Dutch, mahogany case, arched crest with painted face depicting moon phases, pendulum trunk, 19th C, 51½" h **825.00**

English, oak case, painted round dial marked "J B Yabsley, 72 Ludgate Hill, London," flaking, 19th C, 12¾" d **175.00**

French, ormolu, cartouche shape, 14½" h **525.00**

Louis XV Style, ormolu, starburst motif, surmounted by cherub with torch, enameled dial marked "Planchon, Paris," late 19th C, 25½" h **2,175.00**

Mirror, giltwood and ebonized, round Roman numeral dial above mirror panel, wood turned column frame, Joseph Chadwick Boscawen, NH, minor imperfections, c1820, 14" w, 30" h **4,600.00**

Tole, polygonal case, rosewood grained ground, circular enamel

dial surrounded by flower dec, 16½" d **975.00**
William IV, Parliament, oak, dial marked "Thos Shaw, Wellington," mid 19th C, 21¼" h **865.00**

CLOISONNÉ

History: Cloisonné is the art of enameling on metal. The design is drawn on the metal body. Wires, which follow the design, are glued or soldered on the body. The cells thus created are packed with enamel and fired; this step is repeated several times until the level of enamel is higher than the wires. A buffing and polishing process brings the level of enamels flush to the surface of the wires.

This art form has been practiced in various countries since 1300 B.C. and in the Orient since the early 15th century. Most cloisonné found today is from the late Victorian era, 1870–1900, and was made in China and Japan.

Collectors' Club: Cloisonne Collectors Club, PO Box 96, Rockport, MA 01966.

Bowl, cov, 3½" h, Japanese **20.00**
Box, oval **125.00**
Charger, 12" d, floral and bird dec cavetto **125.00**
Compote, 9⅜" d, 5¾" h, polychrome floral design and butterflies, blue and rust ground **80.00**
Dish, cov, 7" d, 4½" h, allover green and red floral motif, rosewood stand, Chinese, pr **20.00**
Figure, Chinese
　Girl, 12" h, holding lotus blossom and leaf in one hand, carnelian bottle in other, tinted ivory head and hands, shaped teak base with silver wire inlay, fitted case, minor enamel imperfections, 20th C **315.00**
　Lady with flowers, hoe, and small table, 13" h, carved and tinted ivory head and hands, shaped teak base with silver wire details, fitted case, 20th C **230.00**
　Woman, reclining, 15⅛" l, 11⅜" h, ivory head, hands, and foot, cloisonne costume, shaped

wooden base, fitted case, minor enamel imperfections, 20th C **345.00**
Humidor, cov, 8" h, multicolored flowers, double T fret design, light blue border, brick red ground, brass Foo dog finial, ornate teakwood base **225.00**
Jar, 5¼" d, black, polychrome floral dec, Foo dog finial, marked "Made in China" **35.00**
Planter, 8½" h, allover blue floral motif, brass stand, Chinese, pr **275.00**
Salt, Russian **50.00**
Scholars Vase, 10¼" h, allover scholarly pursuit motif, rosewood base, Chinese, pr **85.00**
Spoon, silver and cloisonne, Russian **65.00**

Vase, black ground, pastel flowers, metallic base, Japanese, 5" h, $115.00

Vase
　6¼" h, bulbous body with bird and floral reserves, flared square neck with abstract reserves **130.00**
　8¾" h, 3¼" d, white and lavender mums, green leaves, small brick red flowers, blue ground, green int., facing pr **600.00**
　9¹¹⁄₁₆" h, wisteria dec, opaque gray–green ground, minor enamel imperfections, Japanese, late 19th C **285.00**

10½" h, square form, allover blue and green dragon motif, rosewood stand, Chinese, pr   80.00

12" h, baluster form, long tapered neck, bulbous lower portion, translucent enamel and cloisonne dec, bird and floral design, Chinese 150.00

12¼" h, floral motif, brass overlay, rosewood base, Chinese, pr 95.00

12½" h, allover blue and green fire lily motif, rosewood stand, Chinese, pr 75.00

15" h, allover beige cherry blossom motif, rosewood stand, Chinese, pr 70.00

15" h, allover blue and white peony motif, rosewood stand, Chinese, pr 95.00

15¼" h, allover blue and yellow torch motif, rosewood stand, Chinese, pr 50.00

15½" h, allover brown and beige scroll motif, rosewood base, brass handles, Chinese 50.00

15½" h, hexagonal form, allover cherry blossom, peony, bird, and butterfly motif, rosewood stand, Chinese, pr 70.00

23½" h, floral dec, cobalt blue field, mounted as lamp, minor enamel repair, pr 495.00

46" h, monumental, allover bird and floral dec, royal blue ground, Japanese 300.00

CLOTHING

History: While museums and a few private individuals have collected clothing for decades, it is only recently that collecting clothing has achieved a widespread popularity. Clothing reflects the social attitudes of a historical period.

Christening and wedding gowns abound and, hence, are not in large demand. Among the hardest items to find are men's clothing from the 19th and early 20th centuries. The most sought after clothing is by designers, such as Fortuny, Poirret, and Vionnet.

Note: Condition, size, age, and completeness are critical factors in purchasing clothing. Collectors divide into two groups: those collecting for aesthetic and historic value and those desiring to wear the garment. Prices are higher on the West Coast; major auction houses focus on designer clothes and high–fashion items.

References: C. Willett Cunnington, *English Women's Clothing in the Nineteenth Century,* Dover Publications, 1990 (reprint of 1937 book); C. Willett and Phillis Cunnington, *The History of Underclothes,* Dover Publications, 1992; Dover Publications, Inc., *Women's Fashions of the Early 1900s,* Dover Publications, 1992; *Gimbel's Illustrated 1915 Fashion Catalog, Gimbel Brothers,* Dover, 1994; Carol Belanger Grafton, *Fashions of the Thirties,* Dover Publications, 1993; Tina Irick–Nauer, *The First Price Guide to Antique and Vintage Clothes,* E. P. Dutton, 1983; Terry McCormick, *The Consumer's Guide To Vintage Clothing,* Dembner Books, 1987; Diane McGee, *A Passion For Fashion: Antique, Collectible, and Retro Clothes,* Simmons–Boardman Books, 1987; Jo Anne Olian (ed.), *Children's Fashions 1860–1912: Costume Designs from "La Mode Illustree,"* Dover, 1994; Jo Anne Olian (ed.) *Everyday Fashions of the Forties As Pictured in Sears Catalogs,* Dover Publications, 1992; Franklin Simon & Co, *Franklin Simon Fashion Catalog for 1923,* Dover, 1993; Merideth Wright, *Everyday Dress of Rural America: 1783–1800,* Dover Publications, 1992.

Periodicals: *Lady's Gallery,* PO Box 1761, Independence, MO 64055; *Lill's Vintage Clothing Newsletter,* 19 Jamestown Dr., Cincinnati, OH 45241; *The Vintage Gazette,* 194 Amity St, Amherst, MA 01002; *Vintage Clothing Newsletter*, PO Box 1422, Corvallis, OR 97339.

Collectors' Club: The Costume Society of America, 55 Edgewater Dr., PO Box 73, Earleville, MD 21919.

Museums: Bata Shoe Museum, Toronto, Canada; Los Angeles County Museum (Costume and Textile Dept.), Los Angeles, CA; Metropolitan Museum of Art, New York, NY; Museum of Costume, Bath, England; Philadelphia Museum of Art, Philadelphia, PA; Smithsonian Institution (Inaugural Gown Collection), Washington, D.C.

Additional Listings: See *Warman's Americana & Collectibles* for more examples.

Baby Dress, Edwardian, white, lace, embroidery **82.00**
Baby Gown, string tie at neck ... **6.00**
Blouse
  Lace, gray, size 8 .... **15.00**
  Lace and sequins, beige, orig tag, size 10 .... **25.00**
  Silk chiffon, beaded front, c1915 **25.00**
Camisole, cotton, white, lace, Victorian **60.00**
Coat
  Broadtail, double breasted, taupe **125.00**
  Evening, silk velvet, black **50.00**
  Multicolored leather, belted, curly lamb front, collar, cuffs, and hem band **85.00**
Dress
  Chiffon, evening, black, bloused bodice, floating lace panels to waist, black velvet cummerbund, sheer long sleeves, lace cuffs, elegant pleated skirt, two lace tiers, Worth, Paris, c1913 .... **675.00**
  French cloth, evening, gold, poiret–esque roses and spots, ten pleated panels, weighted waistline, cov leather belt, wine lining, Molyneux, c1928 **1,100.00**
  Lace, white, lily embroidery, Edwardian, 26" w **88.00**
  Linen, white, satin stitched embroidery, ¾ sleeves, Edwardian style **65.00**
  Satin, evening, apricot, rhinestone straps, c1930 .... **85.00**
  Silk
    Flapper, black, drop waist, belt, MOP buckle, ecru neck inset, c1920 .... **25.00**
    Tea, golden yellow, sleeveless, Venetian beads on sides, Fortuny Die label ... **770.00**
Dressing Gown, beige, moire, size 10 .... **35.00**
Evening Dress, beaded
  Blue, silk, size 12 .... **45.00**
  Yellow, silk shantung, matching jacket, size 8 .... **65.00**

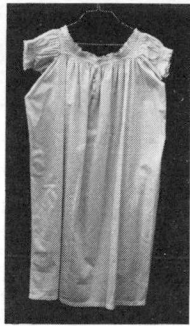

Nightgown, cotton, white, c1870, $40.00.

Fur Coat, mink, fitted, beige, large fox collar and cuffs **400.00**
Jacket
  Embroidered, Chinese silk, floral collar and hem **55.00**
  Silk, blue, stamped gold floral dec, cord trimmed neckline ending with single bead, Venetian bead hemline, Fortuny label, early 1900s **990.00**
Nightgown
  Cotton, white crocheted bodice **30.00**
  Silk, pink, Saks 5th Ave label, large **25.00**
Pajamas
  Child's, Nitey–Nite, ftd, size 4 . **5.50**
  Lady's
    Silk, pink, ribbon rosettes, crochet trim, c1920 .... **100.00**
    Taffeta, long jacket, harem pants, web motif, c1940 ... **35.00**
  Man's, flannel, medium, Harwick **16.00**
Petticoat
  Cotton, black, hand quilted **20.00**
  Flannel, small **15.00**
Robe
  Cotton, green print, medium, c1890 .... **40.00**
  Silk brocade, summer weight, blue, dragon pattern, metal buttons, Chinese, early 20th C **375.00**
Shawl
  Kashmir, patchwork, small octagonal black center, sgd,

slight loss, mid 19th C, 77½"
sq **800.00**
Victorian, paisley, red ground,
stylized geometric dec, 120 x
57" **185.00**
Shirt, man's
Cotton, Hawaiian Aloha
Long sleeve, Campus label,
cornflower blue, multicolored botanical motif, palm
buttons, double pockets ... **175.00**
Short sleeve
California label, cappuccino
brown, multicolored leaf
motif, border print, coconut
buttons, single pocket,
c1940 .... **150.00**
Kamehameha Hawaii label,
yellow, gray, and coral bor-
der print, single pocket .. **185.00**
Vana's Hawaii label, dark
blue ground, green, yel-
low, and coral floral motif,
coconut buttons **195.00**
Homespun, c1890 .... **45.00**
Skirt, felt, circular, brown, appliqued poodle, flowers, and
beads, c1950 .... **15.00**
Suit, tweed, gray, double breasted
jacket with six buttons, below
knee skirt, France, c1963 ..... **90.00**
Waistcoat, gentleman's, satin
weave silk, embroidered with silk
and metallic threads, spangles,
late 18th C, some fiber loss, minor discoloration **625.00**

CLOTHING ACCESSORIES

References: Joanne Dubbs Ball and
Dorothy Hehl Torem, *The Art of Fashion
Accessories,* Schiffer Publishing, 1993;
Adele Campione, *Women's Hats,* Chronicle
Books, 1994; Kate E. Dooner, *A Century of
Handbags,* Schiffer Publishing, 1993; Kate
E. Dooner, *Plastic Handbags,* Schiffer Pub-
lishing, 1992; Rod Dyer and Ron Spark, *Fit
To Be Tied: Vintage Ties Of The Forties
And Early Fifties,* Abbeville, 1987; Roseann
Ettinger, *Handbags,* Schiffer Publishing,
1991; Roselyn Gerson, *Vintage Vanity Bags
and Purses: An Identification and Value
Guide,* Collector Books, 1994; Evelyn Hae-

tig, *Antique Combs & Purses,* Gallery
Graphics Press, 1983; Richard Holiner, *An-
tique Purses,* Second Edition, Collector
Books, 1987, 1994 value update; Mary
Trasko, *Heavenly Soles: Extraordinary
Twentieth–Century Shoes,* Abbeville Press,
1989.

Additional Listings: See *Warman's
Americana & Collectibles* for more examples.

Apron, cotton, white, embroidered
flowers **45.00**
Baby Pants, Playtex Waterproof
Dress–eez, snap, orig box **6.00**
Boa, ostrich feathers, white, 70" l **50.00**
Bonnet, Amish type, deep blue,
c1880 .... **45.00**
Collar, satin, peach, gold thread,
pearl trim, c1920 .... **20.00**
Garters, child's, Lord Milford, orig
card **5.00**
Gloves
Kidskin, white, full length, but-
tons at wrist, c1950 .... **18.00**
Leather, white, opera length ... **15.00**

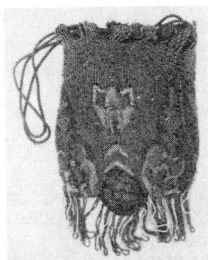

**Handbag, metal mesh, enameled,
white ground, blue and green Art
Deco floral pattern, white metal
clasp, 1⅞" fringe, marked "Mandalian Mfg Co," 6½ x 3½", $120.00.**

Handbag
Alligator
9½" w, 7" h, wedge shape,
strap handle, black, "American Designer Award Lesco
Lona" label **85.00**
17" w, 9½" h, large tortoise-

shell type handles, "JR of
Florida" label **85.00**
Beaded
Celluloid compact top, chain . **225.00**
Metallic bullion thread, curved
gilt metal frame, jeweled . . **85.00**
Victorian, exotic bird and ani-
mal dec, jeweled gilt metal
clasp **110.00**
Enameled, Mandalian **95.00**
Great Pony, orig tab **75.00**
Lucite and brass, tortoiseshell
mottling, suitcase type,
marked "France," 8 x 4¼ x
5¾" **40.00**
Petit Point, landscape design,
gilt metal, faux jade bar, green
enamel and marcasite frame . **60.00**
Hat
Baby's, lace, corded, wide brim **65.00**
Boy's, military style, early 1900s **15.00**
Lady's, Christian Dior **25.00**
Man's, derby, black **35.00**
Muff, mink fur, hanging tails, c1940 **115.00**
Panties, satin, Biltrite, size me-
dium **6.50**
Parasol, bamboo handle, ivory silk
shade, woven with pink, laven-
der, and green flowers, leaves,
and scrolls, ivory patterned silk
gauze ruffles, SS tip, marked
"Tiffany & Co," orig box, c1905 **350.00**
Roller Skates, child's, strap–on . . **12.00**
Shoes
Child's, Birth–Right, white, strap,
hard sole, size 6, orig box . . . **12.00**
Man's
Bowling, black, high top,
matching bowling bag **20.00**
Canvas, 1880s **75.00**
Woman's
Alligator
Platform, size 7 . . . . **65.00**
Pumps, 2" heel, Emilio of
Milan label, size 7 . . . . . . **85.00**
Leather, high button **85.00**
Snow Shoes, military style, 54" l,
10" toe curl, complete with boot
harness **110.00**
Socks, man's, wool, tan, blue geo-
metric border **45.00**
Stockings, BV May, May Hosiery
Mills, unused **6.50**
Stole, mink fur **125.00**

COALPORT

History: In the mid–1750s Ambrose Gal-
limore established a pottery at Caughley in
the Severn Gorge, Shropshire, England.
Several other potteries, e.g., Jackfield, developed in the area.

About 1795 John Rose and Edward
Blakeway built a pottery at Coalport, a new
town founded along the right–of–way of the
Shropshire Canal. Other potteries located
adjacent to the canal were those of Walter
Bradley and Anstice, Horton, and Rose. In
1799 Rose and Blakeway bought the
"Royal Salopian China Manufactory" at
Caughley. In 1814 this operation was
moved to Coalport.

A bankruptcy in 1803 led to refinancing
and a new name, John Rose and Company.
In 1814 Anstice, Horton, and Rose was acquired. The South Wales potteries at Swansea and Nantgarw were added. The expanded firm made fine–quality, highly
decorated ware. The plant enjoyed a renaissance in the 1888 to 1900 period.

World War I, decline in trade, and shift of
the pottery industry away from the Severn
Gorge brought hard times to Coalport. In
1926 the firm, now owned by Cauldon Potteries, moved from Coalport to Shelton.
Later owners included Crescent Potteries,
Brain & Co., Ltd., and finally, in 1967, Wedgwood.

References: Susan and Al Bagdade,
*Warman's English & Continental Pottery &
Porcelain, 2nd Edition,* Wallace–Home-
stead, 1991; Michael Messenger, *Coalport
1795–1926,* Antique Collectors' Club, 1990.
Additional Listings: Indian Tree Pattern.

Demitasse Cup and Saucer
Flowerpot pattern **40.00**
Shamrocks, wine and gold dec **85.00**
Dessert Service, twelve 9" d dessert plates and two compotes,
apple green border interspersed
by and enclosing vignettes of
woodland fowl, gilt borders **875.00**

Plate, stoneware, Canton pattern, yellow, red, and green, marked "Kingsware, Canton," 8¼" d, $75.00.

Plate

8" d, floral dec, scalloped **38.00**

9" d, luncheon, set of ten, gilt gadrooned rim with scrolled foliate and shell border **260.00**

9½" d, hp, central cartouche enamel with different castle landscapes, wide borders, gilt trim with raised pineapple and floral designs, artist sgd "A Bowdler," titled on reverse, printed marks, late 19th C, small rim chips, hairline, price for set of 16 ....**1,380.00**

10½" d, wide pink banding, raised gilt border, scrolled leaf designs, printed marks, mid 20th C, price for set of 16 ... **870.00**

Service Plate, floral centers, gilt and blue panel borders, price for set of 11 .... **465.00**

Tea and Coffee Service, cov teapot with stand, cov sugar bowl, milk jug, waste bowl, two cake plates, five coffee cups, and two saucers, spiraled shape, small gilt floral sprigs beneath cobalt blue border dec with gilt foliate vine, John Rose, repairs, wear to gilding, c1800, price for 26 piece set **550.00**

Tea Set, miniature, Willow, bone china, green transfers, gilt trim,

cup and saucer, 1¾" h creamer, 3" d plate, 1⅝" h cov sugar, 2" h cov teapot, printed marks, c1970 **60.00**

Vase, 8⅝" h, baluster shape, satyr mask beneath scrolled handles, jeweled, allover turquoise beading on gilt ground between wide yellow borders, canted sq base, green printed mark, c1900 .... **345.00**

COCA–COLA ITEMS

History: The originator of Coca–Cola was John Pemberton, a pharmacist from Atlanta, Georgia. In 1886 Dr. Pemberton introduced a patent medicine to relieve headaches, stomach disorders, and other minor maladies. Unfortunately, his failing health and meager finances forced him to sell his interest.

In 1888 Asa G. Candler became the sole owner of Coca–Cola. Candler improved the formula, increased the advertising budget, and widened the distribution. Accidentally, a "patient" was given a dose of the syrup mixed with carbonated water instead of still water. The result was a tastier, more refreshing drink.

As sales increased in the 1890s, Candler recognized that the product was more suitable for the soft drink market and began advertising it as such. From these beginnings a myriad of advertising items have been issued to invite all to "Drink Coca–Cola."

Dates of interest: "Coke" was first used in advertising in 1941. The distinctively shaped bottle was registered as a trademark on April 12, 1960.

References: Gael de Courtivron, *Collectible Coca–Cola Toy Trucks,* Collector Books, 1994; Shelly Goldstein, *Goldstein's Coca–Cola Collectibles,* Collector Books, 1991, 1993 value update; Deborah Goldstein Hill, *Price Guide to Coca–Cola Collectibles,* Wallace–Homestead, 1991; Allan Petretti, *Petretti's Coca-Cola Collectibles Price Guide, 9th Edition,* Nostalgia Publications, Wallace–Homestead, 1994; Al and Helen Wilson, *Coca–Cola: The Real Price Guide,* Schiffer Publishing, 1994; Al Wilson, *Collectors Guide To Coca–Cola Items, Vol I* (revised: 1987, 1993 value update) and

Vol II (1987, 1993 value update), L–W Book Sales.

Collectors' Club: The Coca–Cola Collectors Club International, PO Box 49166, Atlanta, GA 30359.

Museum: Coca–Cola Memorabilia Museum of Elizabethtown, Inc., Elizabethtown, KY.

Additional Listings: See *Warman's Americana & Collectibles* for more examples.

**Serving Tray, 1928, 10½ x 13¼",
$375.00.**

Book Cover, used	**12.50**
Bookmark, Hilda Clark illus, 1903	**250.00**
Bottle, New Mexico	**35.00**
Calendar, 1917, young lady seated by table, palm tree in background, full pad, matted, framed	**1,300.00**
Clock, regulator, printed dial, Ingraham Co, 32" h	**650.00**
Complimentary Card, "Have A Coke," illus of glass and character, c1942	**22.00**
Door Push, porcelain, white letters, red ground	**75.00**
Fan, cardboard, Quality Carries On Drink Coca–Cola, Ft Myers, FL, 1950s	**20.00**
Ice Chest, Art Deco style, "Please Pay Cashier, Drink Coca–Cola, Thank You," polished brass hasp, restored, repainted, 30" w, 24" d, 53" h	**600.00**
Ice Pick, wood handle, 1930s	**15.00**
Knife, ivory colored handle, "Drink Coca–Cola"	**35.00**

Mirror, early 1950s	**55.00**
Notebook, cardboard cov, red, white lettering, 1943 calendar inside cov	**25.00**
Paperweight, mirrored, celluloid and glass	**475.00**
Playing Cards, 1943	**40.00**
Play Set, soccer, MIP	**20.00**
Radio, Coca–Cola vending machine shape, battery operated, red, white, and black, c1970	**50.00**

Sign
Boy eating hotdog, holding bottle, "That taste–good feeling," paper, metal strips top and bottom, 1928, 14 x 20"	**200.00**
Flapper holding bottle, paper, metal strips top and bottom, 1928, 12 x 20"	**175.00**
"Fountain Service, Drink Coca–Cola," diecut, porcelain, red, yellow, and green, 23 x 25½"	**500.00**
Girl holding bottle, lower panel with shoppers and "Pause a minute, Refresh yourself," paper, metal strips top and bottom, 12 x 20"	**450.00**
Man with sandwich plate, popping cap from bottle, "Treat Yourself Right," paper, metal strips top and bottom, 12 x 20"	**300.00**

String Holder, "Take Home Coca–Cola in Cartons," six–pack in center	**325.00**
Syrup Dispenser, urn, Wheeling Pottery, orig spigot, "Delicious and Exhilarating, Refreshing and Invigorating," chipped lid rim, top handle broken, bowl darkened with age, hairline crack to skirt, overall wear to gold leaf trim, 11" d, 20" h	**2,000.00**
Thermometer, metal, cigar shape, "Drink Coca–Cola, Sign of Good Taste," red and white, 30" h	**95.00**
Tip Tray, 1903, Hilda Clark holding early Coca–Cola glass, ornate flowered border, 6" d	**750.00**
Token, brass	**20.00**

Tray, tin, serving
1905, oval, girl drinking from glass, "Delicious, Refreshing, In Bottles 5¢, At Fountains 5¢,"

cocoa beans and leaves border, 10¾ x 13¼" **2,050.00**
1908, round, seated long–haired nude, holding bottle, outer rim inscription "Drink Coca–Cola High Balls, Gin Rickies," inner rim inscription "Wherever Ginger Ale, Seltzer or Soda is Good, Coca–Cola is Better— Try It", distributed by Western Coca–Cola Bottling, Chicago, 12¼" d **12,000.00**
1934, rect, man and woman wearing swim suits, sitting back–to–back, holding bottles, 13¼ x 10½" **75.00**
Writing Tablet, 1950s **6.00**

COFFEE MILLS

History: Coffee mills or grinders are utilitarian objects designed to grind fresh coffee beans. Before the advent of stay-fresh packaging, coffee mills were a necessity.

The first home–size coffee grinders were introduced about 1890. The large commercial grinders designed for use in stores, restaurants, and hotels often bear an earlier patent date.

Reference: Terry Friend, *Coffee Mills*, Collector Books, 1982, out–of–print.

Enterprise Coffee Mill, cast iron, pine base, marked "Oct 21, 1873," 11½" h, $140.00.

COUNTERTOP (COMMERCIAL)

Enterprise Manufacturing Co, Philadelphia, PA, white wheels, wood base, orig red paint, 24" h **175.00**
Fairbanks–Morse, two wheels, brass finial, white paint, 38" h . **350.00**
Golden Rule, cast iron **195.00**
Parker, Charles Co, Meriden, CT, wood base, orig red and blue paint, some orig stenciling, 12" h **200.00**
Swift, cast iron, 12" d wheels **200.00**

FLOOR MODEL (COMMERCIAL)

Dell, John C. & Sons, brass hopper, sand blasted and primed cast iron, 33" d wheels, 66" h . . **900.00**
Enterprise, 72" h **400.00**

LAP (DOMESTIC)

C. P. Company, 6" w, sq **35.00**
Imperial, dovetailed box, 5½" sq . **25.00**
Logan & Strobridge, machine dovetailed, cast iron hopper and handle, oak base **70.00**

TABLE (DOMESTIC)

Arcade, sliding filler lid, replaced decal, Pat June 5, 1884 ...... **75.00**
Enterprise No. 0, clamp–on style, cast iron, 11½" h **40.00**
Landers, Frary & Clark, metal ... **65.00**
Parker, Charles Co, cast iron handle and crank, tin top and filler, 14¼" h **80.00**
Unmarked, emb cast iron top, slide open hopper, 13" h **70.00**

WALL (DOMESTIC)

Arcade, glass top, all orig **75.00**
Brighton, cast iron, mounted on wood board **65.00**
Golden Rule, cast iron and wood, glass insert, 5½ x 4 x 17" **115.00**
Koffie, red glass canister, crank handle, measuring cup at base, mounted on board **75.00**
Steinfield #17, lacy iron grinder, glass canister **35.00**

COIN-OPERATED ITEMS / 155

COIN-OPERATED ITEMS

History: Coin–operated items include amusement games, pinball machines, jukeboxes, slot machines, vending machines, cash registers, and other items operated by coins.

The first jukebox was developed about 1934 and played 78 RPM records. Jukeboxes were important parts of teenage life before the advent of portable radios and television.

The first pinball machine was introduced in 1931 by Gottlieb. Pinball machines continued to be popular until the advent of solid–state games in 1977 and advanced electronic video games.

The first three–reel slot machine, the Liberty Bell, was invented in 1905 by Charles Fey in San Francisco. In 1910, Mills Novelty Company copyrighted the classic fruit symbols. Improvements and advancements have led to the sophisticated machines of today.

Vending machines for candy, gum, and peanuts were popular from 1910 until 1940 and can be found in a wide range of sizes and shapes.

Because of the heavy usage these coin–operated items received, many are restored and at the very least have been repainted by either the operator or manufacturer. Using reproduced mechanisms to restore pieces is acceptable in many cases, especially when the restored piece will be able to perform as originally intended.

References: Jerry Ayliffe, *American Premium Guide To Jukeboxes And Slot Machines, Gumballs, Trade Stimulators, Arcade*, 3rd Edition, Books Americana, 1991; Richard Bueschel, *Pinball I: Illustrated Historical Guide To Pinball Machines, Vol I*, Hoflin Publishing, 1988; Richard Bueschel, *Slots 1: Illustrated Guide to 100 Collectible Slot Machines, Vol 1*, Hoflin Publishing, 1989; Richard Bueschel and Steve Gronowski, *Arcade 1, Illustrated Historical Guide to Arcade Machines, Vol I*, Hoflin Publishing, 1993; Nic Costa, *Automatic Pleasures: The History Of The Coin Machine*, Kevin Francis Publishing, 1988; Heirbert Eiden and Jurgen Lukas, *Pinball Machines*, Schiffer Publishing, 1992; Bill Enes, *Silent Salesmen: An Encyclopedia Of Col-

lectible Gum, Candy & Nut Machines*, published by author, 1987; Eric Hatchell and Dick Bueschell, *Coin-Ops On Location*, published by authors, 1993; Bill Kurtz, *Slot Machines and Coin–Op Games*, Chartwell Books, 1991; Stephen K. Loots, *The Official Victory Glass Price Guide To Antique Jukeboxes, 1988 (Third) Edition*, Jukebox Collector Newsletter, 1988; Vincent Lynch, *American Jukebox The Classic Years*, Chronicle Books, 1990; Christopher Pearce, *Vintage Jukeboxes: The Hall of Fame*, Chartwell Books, 1988; Scott Wood, *A Blast From the Past Jukeboxes: A Pictorial Price Guide*, L–W Book Sales, 1992.

Periodicals: *Always Jukin'*, 221 Yesler Way, Seattle, WA 98104; *Around the Vending Wheel*, 5417 Castana Ave., Lakewood, CA 90712; *Coin Machine Trader*, 569 Kansas SE, PO Box 602, Huron, SD 57350; *Coin–Op Classics*, 17844 Toiyable St., Fountain Valley, CA 92708; *Coin–Op Newsletter*, 909 26th St., NW, Washington, DC 20037; *Gameroom Magazine*, 1014 Mt. Tabor Rd., New Albany, IN 47150; *Jukebox Collector*, 2545 SE 60th St., Des Moines, IA 50317; *Loose Change*, 1515 S. Commerce St., Las Vegas, NV 89102; *Pin Game Journal*, 31937 Olde Franklin Dr., Farmington Hills, MI, 48334; *Pinball Trader*, PO Box 1795, Campbell, CA 95009; *The Coin Slot*, 4401 Zephyr St., Wheat Ridge, CO 80033; *The Scopitone Newsletter*, 810 Courtland Dr., Manchester, MO 63021.

Museum: Liberty Belle Saloon and Slot Machine Collection, Reno, NV.

Additional Listings: See *Warman's Americana & Collectibles* for separate categories for Jukeboxes, Pinball Machines, Slot Machines, and Vending Machines.

Advisor: Bob Levy.

Arcade Game, Kicker and Catcher, five balls for 5¢, two football players, one kicks, one catches, some mechanism parts missing, case cracked, handles replaced, coin slide casting broken, missing back door, working on free play **180.00**
Cash Register
National
   No. 317, candy store, ex-

tended base, tape dispenser, ornately emb, orig marquee, 17¼" w, 21" h, 15½" d **550.00**

No. IV, nickel plated brass, tape dispenser, extended oak base, 20" w, 20½" h, 16½" d **150.00**

Western, Verdic–Corbin Co, Detroit, barbershop, plated cast iron, heavily emb, .05 to 1.00, restored, castings replated, marquee and number tabs replaced, 9" w, 21" h, 15" d ... **750.00**

Collar Button Dispenser, 10¢, sq glass dome, cast iron base with six columns, restored, base repainted, top polished, 5½" w, 10½" h **400.00**

Combination Vendor, gum ball and bulk vendors, 1¢, cast metal and glass, center column with Scoopy figure who opens door and scoops gum ball out chute, flanked by bulk candy columns, 19" w, 49½" h **1,150.00**

Dixie Cup Dispenser, Dixie–Fortex Co, 1¢, tall glass dome, cast metal base, orig stenciled decal, keys, and cardboard box, 4" d dome, 36" h **650.00**

Fan, General Electric, iron base, brass blades, wired fan guard, working, coin door locked, coin mechanism not working, 14" d guard, 19" h **300.00**

Gum Vendor

Columbus, Model L, 1¢, cast iron, cast figural mask face on front, orig "Lehman & Son Company Boston" decal, 6¾" w, 16½" h, 7½" d **6,500.00**

Masters Gum Ball, vertical square, cast mechanism, orig condition, 8" w, 16" h **200.00**

Peerless Bluebird Gum Ball, 1¢, glass globe, cast metal base, replaced decal, restored, mid 1920s, 7" d globe, 14" h **110.00**

Pulver Chewing Gum, 1¢, porcelain over metal, "Pulver Chewing Gum In Popular Flavors, One Cent Delivers A Tasty Chew," painted black

professor automatically feeds gum at bottom, 10½" w, 24" h **650.00**

Topper Gum Ball, 1¢, sq glass globe, plated metal base, 6½" sq globe, 15" h **55.00**

Zeno Gum, 1¢, emb oak case, clockwork, restored and refinished, 10" w, 17" h, 8½" d ... **400.00**

Jukebox, Seaburg 100, working, cabinet refinished, some cracks to orig plastics, rotary tubes intact, new motor for chain drive, coin mechanism removed, coin door replaced with wood panel, 35" w, 54" h, 26" d **1,100.00**

Match Vendor

Advance, 1¢, ornate cast iron base, glass dome cover, four column dispenser, iron retainer ring missing from glass dome, early green paint, 8½" w, 18" h **500.00**

Safety Matches, 1¢, glass dome, sq oak base with cigar cutter attachment, cloth fringe over carousel missing, one marquee card missing, locking cash door front missing, 11" w, 18" h **150.00**

Mechanical Elephant Ride, metal,

Radio, Westinghouse, Jukebox Model 1, Model 34X475, white case, gold center band, purple fabric across speaker, carrying handle, 6 x 5½ x 9", $95.00.

gray body, red and gold saddle,
black base with wheels and handles, 58″ l **2,475.00**

Peanut Vendor

Hance, 1¢, glass globe, porcelain over cast iron ftd base,
iron mechanism with aluminum coin entrance and pull
slide, remnants of orig decal,
back door missing, repainted,
8″ w, 18″ h **650.00**

Jennings, 1¢, glass globe,
pressed metal and iron base,
orig marquee reads "Vended
In A Bag," mechanism bags
loose peanuts prior to vending,
8¼″ w, 25½″ h **200.00**

Planter's, Canadian, 10¢, red,
white, and blue sheet metal
case, coin slide selection lever, orig packing box, 12½″ w,
28¼″ h **350.00**

Penny Drop, 1¢, cast iron, tin segmented cash drawer, working,
12″ w, 16½″ h **175.00**

Pinball Machine

Sportsman Payout, ornate metal
castings, play field with hunter
and game, O D Jennings, 23″
w, 42″ h, 43″ d **325.00**

The Empire Billiard Machine,
English, vertical case, wood,
ornate gallery, orig play card at
bottom, chute and cup miss-
ing, 14½″ w, 48″ h, 6½″ d ... **135.00**

Postage Stamp Vendor, 5¢, Scher-
mack Corp, Detroit, iron base
and front, glass panels, orig emb
tin marquee with Uncle Sam
holding shield inscribed "Guard
Your Health, Use Clean Postage
Stamps, Direct from Gov't rolls,
The Only Sanitary Way," missing
top glass panel and back door,
one side panel cracked, base
corroded and pitted, plating
worn, 11½″ w, 21″ h **375.00**

Slot Machine, single wheel, floor
model

Caille, The New Century Musical
Detroit, 5¢, quartered oak
case with nickel plated castings, tin wheel, replaced marquee casting, back door, and
tin wheel, mechanism re-
stored, 26″ w, 64″ h, 17″ d ...**9,500.00**

Watling, The Owl, 5¢, quartered
oak case, replated iron castings, tin wheel with multiple
owl images, working, restored,
locks replaced, 24″ w, 66″ h,
16″ d **8,000.00**

COMIC BOOKS

History: Shortly after comics first appeared in newspapers of the 1890s, they
were reprinted in book format and often
used as promotional giveaways by manufacturers, movie theaters, candy stores, and
stationery stores. The first modern format
comic was issued in 1933.

The magic date is June 1938, when DC
issued Action Comics No. 1, marking the
first appearance of Superman. Thus began
comics' "Golden Age," which lasted until the
mid–1950s and witnessed the birth of the
major comic book publishers, titles, and
characters.

In 1954 Fredric Wertham authored *Se-
duction of the Innocent*, a book which
pointed a guilt–laden finger at the comic
industry for corrupting youth, causing juve-
nile delinquency and undermining American
values. Many publishers were forced out of
business, while others established a "comics code" to assure parents that their comics were compliant with morality and de-
cency censures upheld by the code
authority.

Comics' "Silver Age," mid–1950s through
the end of the 1960s, witnessed the revival
of many of the characters from the Golden
Age in new comic formats. The era began
with *Showcase No. 4* in October 1956,
which marked the origin and first appearance of the Silver–Age Flash.

While comics survived in the 1970s, it
was a low point for the genre. In the early
1980s a revival occurred. In 1983 comic
book publishers, aside from Marvel and DC,
issued more titles than existed in the past
forty years. The mid and late 1980s were a
boom time, a trend which appears to be
continuing into the 1990s.

References: Mike Benton, *Crime Com-*

ics: The Illustrated History, Taylor Publishing, 1992; Mike Benton, Superhero Comics of the Golden Age: The Illustrated History, Taylor Publishing, 1992; Mike Benton, The Comic Book In America, An Illustrated History, Taylor Publishing, 1989; Mike Benton, Science Fiction Comics: The Illus History, Taylor Publishing, 1992; Mike Benton, Superhero Comics of the Silver Age: The Illus History, Taylor Publishing, 1992; Comic Buyer's Guide 1995 Annual, Krause Publications, 1994; Comic Buyer's Guide, 1995 Comic Book Checklist & Price Guide: 1961–Present, Krause Publications, 1994; Ernst and Mary Gerber (compilers), Photo–Journal Guide To Comics, Volume One (A–J) and Volume 2 (K–Z), Gerber Publishing, 1990; John Hegenberger, Collector's Guide To Comic Books, Wallace–Homestead, 1990; D. W. Howard, Investing in Comics, The World of Yesterday, 1988; Duncan McAlpine (comp.), The Official Comic Book Price Guide For Great Britain, Price Guide Productions, 1992; Alex G. Malloy (ed.), Comic Book Artists, Wallace–Homestead, 1993; Alex G. Malloy and Stuart Wells, Comic Values Annual: 1994–95, The Comic Books Price Guide, Wallace–Homestead, 1994; Robert Overstreet, The Overstreet Comic Book Price Guide, 24th Edition, Avon Books, 1994; Robert M. Overstreet, The Overstreet Comics and Cards Price Guide, Avon Books, 1993; Robert Overstreet and Gary M. Carter, The Overstreet Comic Book Grading Guide, Avon Books, 1993; Don and Maggie Thompson (eds.), Comic Book Superstars: Who is Who Among Comics Creators, Krause Publications, 1993; Don and Maggie Thompson (eds.), Marvel Comics Checklist & Price Guide: 1961 to Present, Krause Publications, 1993; Jerry Weist, Original Comic Art: Identification and Price Guide, Avon Books, 1992.

Periodicals: Comic Book Market Place, PO Box 180900, Coronado, CA 92178; Comic Values Monthly, Attic Books, 15 Danbury Road, Ridgefield, CT 06877; Duckburg Times, 3010 Wilshire Blvd. #362, Los Angeles, CA 90010; Overstreet Comic Book Marketplace, 801 220th St., NW, Suite 3, Cleveland, TN 37311; The Comics Buyer's Guide, 700 E. State St., Iola, WI 54990; The Comics Buyer's Guide Price

Guide, 700 E. State St., Iola, WI 54990; Western Comics Journal, 143 Milton St., Brooklyn, NY 11222; Wizard: The Guide To Comics, PO Box 6782, Syracuse, NY 13217.

Collectors' Club: Fawcett Collectors of America & Magazine Enterprise, too!, 301 E. Buena Vista Ave., North Augusta, SC 29841.

Museums: International Museum of Cartoon Art, 300 SE 5th Ave., #5150, Boca Raton, FL 33432; Museum of Cartoon Art, Rye, NY.

Reproduction Alert: Publishers frequently reprint popular stories, even complete books, so the buyer must pay strict attention to the title, not just the portion printed in outsized letters on the front cover. If there is any doubt, look inside at the fine print on the bottom of the inside cover or first page. The correct title will be printed there in capital letters.

Also pay attention to the size of the comic. Reprints often differ in size from the original.

Note: The comics listed below are in near mint condition, meaning they have a flat, clean shiny cover that has no wear, only tiny corner creases; no subscription creases, writing, yellowing at margins, or tape repairs; staples are straight and rust free; pages are supple and like new; generally just off the shelf quality.

PRE–GOLDEN AGE

Ace Comics, No. 4, David McKay Publications	**125.00**
Famous Funnies, No. 3, Buck Rogers strip reprints begin, Eastern Color	**500.00**
King Comics, No. 12, strip reprint, David McKay Publications	**80.00**
Star Comics, No. 5, Little Nemo, Ultem Publishing	**100.00**
Western Picture Stories, No. 1, Comics Magazine Company . . .	**300.00**

GOLDEN AGE

Adventure Comics, No. 271, origin of Luthor, DC	**35.00**
Adventures of Bob Hope, No. 22, National Periodical Publications	**15.00**

Frosty The Snowman, **Dell Publishing, No. 435, copyright 1952, $3.50.**

All Star Western, No. 67, Johnny Thunder, National Periodical Publications 30.00
Batman, No. 140, Joker story ... 30.00
Bride Romances, No. 8, Quality Comics Group 5.00
Cisco Kid Comics, No. 2, Dell Publishing 20.00
Dark Mysteries, No. 20, Master–Merit Publications 25.00
Dennis The Menace, No. 11, Giant Christmas issue, Winter 1962 . 10.00
Donald Duck, No. 134, Gold Key 3.50
Falling In Love, No. 22 .... 5.00
Flash Comics, No. 35, origin of Shade, National Periodical Publications 150.00
Four Color, No. 88, Bugs Bunny's Great Adventure, Dell 35.00
GI Combat, No. 33, Quality Comics Group 10.00
Gunsmoke, No. 18, Dell 15.00
Howdy Doody, No. 8, Dell 15.00
Jungle Comics, No.57, Fiction House Magazines 50.00
Little Iodine, No. 9, Dell 5.00
Looney Tunes and Merrie Melodies Comics, No. 80, Dell 10.00
Love Romances, No. 57, Matt Baker artist, Marvel 7.50
The Lucy Show, No. 2, Gold Key 15.00
March of Comics, Western Publishing No. 95, Oswald Rabbit 8.00

No. 116, Roy Rogers 20.00
No. 166, Santa and His Reindeer 5.00
No. 282, Mister Ed 8.00
No. 423, Little Monsters 1.50
Mickey Mouse, No.68, Dell 2.50
National Velvet, 4–Color 1312, Dell 8.00
Perfect Love, No. 7, Ziff–Davis .. 8.00
Porky Pig, No. 42, Gold Key 2.00
Rawhide Kid, No. 1, Atlas 70.00
Richie Rich, No. 47, Harvey Publications 6.00
Rod Cameron Western, No. 2, Fawcett Publications 45.00
Romantic Love, No. 19, Realistic 15.00
Sheena, Queen of the Jungle, No. 12, Fiction House Magazine ... 40.00
Smiley Burnette Western, No. 3, Fawcett Publications 30.00
77 Sunset Strip, 4–Color 1106, Gold Key 18.00
Star Spangled War Stories, No. 22, National Periodical Publications 14.00
Space Patrol, No. 2, Ziff–Davis Publishing Co 100.00
Straight Arrow, No. 33, Magazine Enterprises 8.00
Superboy, No.122, DC 2.00
Terrors of the Jungle, No. 8, Star Publications 27.50
Tessie The Typist, No. 3 .... 15.00
Uncle Milty, No. 1, Victoria Publications 60.00
Uncle Scrooge, No. 55, Gold Key 12.00
Walt Disney Comics, No. 37, Donald Duck, Dell 65.00
Weird Mysteries, No. 7, Gillmore Publications 75.00
Wonder Woman, No. 35, National Periodical Publications 55.00

SILVER AGE

Action Comics, No. 269, DC 20.00
The Amazing Spiderman, No. 290, Marvel 2.00
Aquaman, No. 2, DC 60.00
Avengers, No. 88, Marvel 4.00
Captain America, No. 255, 40th Anniversary, Marvel 3.00
Captain Atom, No. 11, Millennium, DC 2.00

Casper, The Friendly Ghost, No. 48, Harvey Publications	7.50
Daredevil, No. 25, Marvel	10.00
Doom Patrol, No. 4, DC	2.00
Fantastic Four, Marvel	
No. 1	3,000.00
No. 23	50.00
No. 198	1.50
No. 320, Thing vs. Hulk	1.50
House of Mystery, No. 180, DC	2.50
Huckleberry Hound, No. 33, Gold Key	2.50
Incredible Hulk, No. 175, Marvel	2.00
Justice League, No. 3, DC	7.50
MAD, No. 105, EC Comics	2.50
Marvel Team Up, No. 18, Torch and Hulk, Marvel	3.00
New Teen Titans, No. 16, DC	3.00
Strange Tales, No. 128, Marvel	10.00
Thor, No. 185, Marvel	1.75
Top Cat, No. 14, Gold Key	3.00
Warlord, No. 31, DC	3.00
X–Men, No. 39, Marvel	12.50

POST-SILVER AGE

Adolescent Radioactive Black Belt Hamsters, No. 1, Eclipse	2.00
Airboy, No. 8, Eclipse	3.00
Battlestar Galactica, No. 4, Marvel	.30
Blood Sword, No. 7, JAD	1.50
Conan, The Barbarian, No. 23, Marvel	6.00
Dagar The Invincible, No. 3, Gold Key	2.00
Dick Tracy in 3–D, No. 1, Blackthorne	2.00
Dragonforce, No. 3, Aircel	2.00
Elfquest, No. 2, 2nd printing, $1.25 cover, WARP Graphics	2.50
Further Adventures of Indiana Jones, No. 8, Marvel	.75
Mai, The Psychic Girl, No. 2, 1st printing, Eclipse	2.00
Mighty Mites, No. 2, Eternity	2.00
Omaha The Cat Dancer, No. 2, Steeldragon	2.00
The Saga of the Swamp Thing, No. 27, DC	3.00
Star Trek, No. 5, DC	2.50
Strontium Dog, No. 10, Quagmire	1.50
Sun Runners, No. 1, Pacific	1.50
Teenage Mutant Ninja Turtles, No. 1, Mirage, 1st Printing	125.00

COMPACTS

History: In the first quarter of the 20th century, attitudes regarding cosmetics changed drastically. The use of make–up during the day was no longer looked upon with disdain. As women became "liberated" and as more and more of them entered the business world, the use of cosmetics became a routine and necessary part of a woman's grooming. Portable containers for cosmetics became a necessity.

Compacts were made in a myriad of shapes, styles, combinations, and motifs, all reflecting the mood of the times. Every conceivable natural or man–made medium was used in the manufacture of compacts. Commemorative, premium, souvenir, patriotic, figural, combination compacts, Art Deco, and enamel compacts are a few examples of the compacts that were made in the United States and abroad. Compacts combined with cigarette cases, music boxes, watches, hatpins, canes, lighters, etc., also were very popular.

Compacts were made and used until the late 1950s when women opted for the "Au Naturel" look. The term "vintage" is used to distinguish the compacts from the first half of the 20th century from contemporary examples.

References: Roseann Ettinger, *Compacts and Smoking Accessories,* Schiffer Publishing, 1991; Roselyn Gerson, *Ladies' Compacts of the 19th and 20th Centuries*, Wallace–Homestead, 1989; Roselyn Gerson, *Vintage Vanity Bags and Purses: An Identification and Value Guide,* Collector Books, 1994; Laura M. Mueller, *Collector's Encyclopedia of Compacts, Carryalls & Face Powder Boxes,* Collector Books, 1994.

Collectors' Club: Compact Collectors Club, PO Box Letter S, Lynbrook, NY 11563.

Advisor: Roselyn Gerson.

Additional Listings: See *Warman's Americana & Collectibles* for more examples.

Art Deco
    Combination compact and lipstick case, modified circular shape, mottled green jade, lip-

Engine turned, gold toned metal, orig contents and felt bag, $25.00.

stick case connected by chain of three jade beads, gold mounts, platinum and rose–cut diamond fan shape motif dec, c1920 .... **9,775.00**

Combination compact and watch, shell form, enameled black and gold dec, offset rect clock, marked "Weldwood" and "Illinois Watch Case Co" **475.00**

Compact, black and green guilloche enameled dec, diamond set floral and circle motif on lid **1,265.00**

Art Nouveau, SS, combination compact and locket, leaf and berry design on front, monogrammed powder puff on back . **75.00**

Boucheron, 14K gold and silver, cutout and engraved dec, birds amid flowers, five cabochon cut ruby accents **385.00**

Bulgari

3¼" l, oval, gold, fluted design, diamond set clasp, sgd "Bulgari" **3,750.00**

8 x 5 cm, 18K gold, rounded rect, reeded design, blue enameled dec, diamond set thumbpiece, sgd "Bulgari" **3,175.00**

Cartier

14K gold, combination compact and lipstick case, diamond set thumbpiece, sgd "Cartier," numbered "5890," c1940 .... **1,250.00**

18K gold, rect, applied black enamel dec and mother–of–pearl crane and landscape dec, bands of old European cut diamond borders, engraved hinged panel "Mrs Andrew J Miller, New York," sgd "Cartier, Londres, New York," numbered "15918," fitted box **28,750.00**

18K polished gold and black onyx, Oriental design with diamonds, rubies and polychrome panel dec, sgd "Cartier, Paris," c1920 .... **3,525.00**

Elgin, gold tone, musical design, black case **20.00**

Georg Jensen, 2⅝" d, SS, stylized singing bird on branch, engraved "Georg Jensen" and oval with "Denmark HN 231F" **200.00**

Gilt, unknown maker, filigree dec, center yellow rhinestone **75.00**

Richard Hudnut

Metal, portrait panel, red and yellow enameled dec **40.00**

Silver, aqua enameled dec, marked "Deauville" **35.00**

Sterling Silver, unknown maker

Abalone shell dec **25.00**

Engraved bamboo design, 3¾" sq, .970 dwt **65.00**

Engraved dec, 3" d, Continental **55.00**

Oval, engraved linear diamond design, enameled dec, two section int., c1900 .... **150.00**

Rectangular, openwork plaque with floral design set with various gems, int. with mirror and chased foliate motif, fitted royal blue satin and velvet box **1,100.00**

Tiffany and Company

14K gold, rect, engraved fluted design, stylized thumbpiece with four rect sapphires, int. with mirror and gold and metal mesh powder screen, red leather case **810.00**

18K yellow gold, basketweave style, diamond set thumbpiece **1,600.00**

Van Cleef & Arpels, 3½ x 2¼", 18K gold, rect, engine turned woven design, gold braiding, white enamel borders, rose diamond

thumbpiece, sgd "Van Cleef & Arpels," numbered "21864" ... **3,175.00**
Yard, 14K gold, rect, basketweave design, sapphire set thumbpiece, gold framed mirror int. engraved "G W W–S B W 7–6–60," sgd "Yard," fitted black leather case stamped "Yard" **925.00**

CONSOLIDATED GLASS COMPANY

History: The Consolidated Lamp and Glass Company resulted from the 1893 merger of the Wallace and McAfee Company, glass and lamp jobbers of Pittsburgh, and the Fostoria Shade & Lamp Company of Fostoria, Ohio. When the Fostoria, Ohio, plant burned down in 1895, Corapolis, Pennsylvania, donated a seven–acre tract of land near the center of town for a new factory. In 1911 the company was the largest lamp, globe, and shade works in the United States, employing over 400 workers.

In 1925 Reuben Haley, owner of an independent design firm, convinced John Lewis, president of Consolidated, to enter the giftware field utilizing a series of designs inspired by the 1925 Paris Exposition Internationale des Arts Decoratifs et Industriels Modernes and the work of Rene Lalique. Initially, the glass was marketed by Howard Selden through his showroom at 225 Fifth Avenue, New York, New York. The first two lines were Catalonian and Martele.

Additional patterns were added in the late 1920s: Florentine (January 1927), Chintz (January 1927), Ruba Rombic (January 1928), and Line 700 (January 1929). On April 2, 1932, Consolidated closed it doors. Kenneth Harley moved thirty–five to forty molds to Phoenix. In March 1936 Consolidated reopened under new management. The "Harley" molds were returned. During this period the famous Dancing Nymph line, based on an 8-inch salad plate in the 1926 Martele series, was introduced.

In August 1962 Consolidated was sold to Dietz Brothers. A major fire damaged the plant during a 1963 labor dispute. In 1964 the company closed its doors for good.

References: Ann Gilbert McDonald, *Evolution of the Night Lamp*, Wallace–Homestead, 1979; Jack D. Wilson, *Phoenix & Consolidated Art Glass, 1926–1980*, Antique Publications, 1989.

Collectors' Club: Phoenix and Consolidated Glass Collectors, PO Box 81974, Chicago, IL 60681.

Bowl, 8" d, Criss Cross, cranberry opal **155.00**
Box, cov, Roses and Bird, blue, round **110.00**
Candlesticks, pr, Dancing Girls, French Crystal **175.00**
Cigarette Box, cov, Santa Maria, opaque milk white, gold sailing ship on lid, emb dolphins on sides **125.00**
Compote, 7" d, Ruba Rombic, smokey topaz **200.00**
Condiment Set, Coreopsis **395.00**
Console Bowl, Martelle Cockatoo, gold traces, 13" d **95.00**
Creamer and Sugar, Catalonia, amethyst **45.00**
Lamp, 11¼" h, Florette, cased pink font, Plume & Atwood base, c1890 .... **385.00**
Miniature Lamp
  Coreopsis **250.00**
  Cosmos, 7⅝" h, opaque white, polychrome dec, c1890, shade broken and repaired **165.00**
Night Light, 10½" h, Lovebirds, orig black glass base **400.00**
Parlor Lamp, Coreopsis **350.00**
Saltshaker
  Cone, green **70.00**
  Cosmos, pink dec **65.00**
  Guttate, pink satin **100.00**

Saltshaker, pigeon blood, 2½" h, $90.00.

Sauce Dish, Criss Cross, cranberry opal	60.00
Sherbet, Fruits, green, ftd	15.00
Spooner, Florette, pink, metal rim and handles	70.00
Sugar Bowl, open, Coreopsis	65.00
Sugar Shaker, Cone, pink	135.00
Syrup, Guttate, tapering cylindrical form, salmon pink cased on white, molded vertical bands of overlapping lobes separated by beaded bands, clear handle, silverplated top	175.00
Table Set, Coreopsis	450.00
Toothpick, Florette, pink	65.00

Tumbler

Cosmos, pink band	75.00
Five Fruits, green ftd	30.00
Umbrella Stand, Blackberry, amber	375.00

Vase

10½" h, Fairy, ovoid, cobalt blue frosted	250.00
11" h, Fairy, ovoid, crystal, ruby flashed accents	70.00
Water Set, Coreopsis, 7 pcs	450.00

CONTINENTAL CHINA AND PORCELAIN (GENERAL)

History: By 1700, porcelain factories existed in large numbers throughout Europe. In the mid–18th century the German factories at Meissen and Nymphenburg were dominant. As the century ended, French potteries assumed the leadership role. The "golden age" of Continental china and porcelains was from the 1740s to the 1840s.

Americans living in the last half of the 19th century eagerly sought the masterpieces of the European porcelain factories. In the early 20th century this style of china and porcelain was a "blue chip" among the antiques collectors.

References: Susan and Al Bagdade, *Warman's English & Continental Pottery & Porcelain, 2nd Edition,* Wallace–Homestead, 1991; Rachael Feild, *Macdonald Guide To Buying Antique Pottery & Porcelain,* Wallace–Homestead, 1987; Geoffrey Godden, *Godden's Guide To European Porcelain,* Random House, 1993; Judith and Martin Miller (eds.), *Miller's Antiques Checklist: Porcelain,* Viking Studio Books, 1991.

Additional Listings: France—Haviland, Limoges, Old Paris, Sarreguemines, and Sevres; Germany—Austrian Ware, Bavarian China, Carlsbad China, Dresden/Meissen, Rosenthal, Royal Bayreuth, Royal Bonn, Royal Rudolstadt, Royal Vienna, Schlegelmilch, and Villeroy and Boch; Italy—Capo–di–Monte.

Basket, soft paste, multicolored center florals, cream ground, green trim, rope handles with floral terminals, 11" l, price for pair, $360.00.

Candlesticks, pr, baluster form, enameled floral reserves, blue field, minor damage to bobeches, French, 19th C, 9¾" h	600.00

Children's Dishes

Coffee Service

14 pcs, red ground, gilt dec with figural landscape scenes, 2" h cov coffeepot, creamer, sugar bowl, three cups and saucers, three spoons, 4" l oval tray, French, 19th C	865.00
23 pcs, gilt band dec, 4¾" h cov coffeepot, 2¾" h creamer, 2⅝" h cov sugar, six 1½" h coffee cups, six 3" d saucers, six 3¼" d plates, French, c1900	115.00
Dinner Service, 10 pcs, earthenware, green transfer, humorous painted characters, 4⅜" l oval fruit bowl with attached underplate, two 3¼" d plates,	

three 3¾" d plates, 2⅝ x 4¾" oval platter, three 3⅞" d soup plates, printed marks "St. Amand et (Nord) Hamage," French, late 19th C **115.00**

Tea and Coffee Service, 15 pcs, puce enamel floral dec, 2⅛" h cov teapot, 3" h cov tea caddy, 3" h cov coffeepot, 4¼" h cov hot water pitcher, five 2⅝" d teacups, two 2⅛" l spoons, chips, repairs, all marks ground, German, late 19th C **345.00**

Tea Service, 8 pcs, red/brown enamel ground, polychrome enamels, gilt bird and floral dec, 1¾" h cov teapot, 1¾" d sugar, two 1⅝" d teacups, two 2¾" d saucers, 2¾" d restored waste bowl, underglazed marks, Popov Factory, Russian, mid 19th C **1,150.00**

Chocolate Pot, cov, polychrome bas–relief Roman scene, late 19th C, 10⅝" h **285.00**

Compote
12" h, 14" l, oval pierced bowl and base, floral dec, gilt trim, German **495.00**
18½" h, figural, pierced basket, base supported by two classical female figures, applied flowers to basket and base, chips, repairs, mid 19th C ... **260.00**

Deep Dish, hp dec, Durytus attempting to carry off Hippodamia, putti and floral border, mid 19th C, 12⅝" d **350.00**

Demitasse Cups and Saucers, set of twelve, shaded blue, floral dec, Kuznetsov, Russia **115.00**

Dinner Service, 152 pcs, white ground, cobalt blue bands, polychrome floral sprays, cov tureen, two sauceboats, forty–one dinner plates, five rim soup plates, nineteen luncheon plates, eleven dessert plates, two cov butter dishes, three double open salts, four cake plates, two small cov sauce dishes, nine cups and saucers, two sauce stands, cov teapot, creamer, cov sugar, four compotes, oblong

cov sugar box, serving bowl, fruit bowl, oval centerpiece, two graduated round platters, ten various shapes graduated platters, open sq vegetable dish, two cov sq vegetable dishes, four condiment dishes, bowl, and small vase, mid 19th C **2,185.00**

Figural Group
Four children playing with goat, free–form base, white, painted mark, 19th C, 14¼" h **865.00**
Grape pickers with grapes and wine glasses, polychrome, damaged, French, mid 19th C, 11½" h **115.00**

Figure, pr, male and female French, faience, polychrome dec, 19th C, 6½" and 7" h ... **145.00**
Italian, Capo–di–monte style, enamel and gilt dec, marked, chips, late 19th C, 10" h **115.00**

Fruit Bowl, round, low form, gilt reserves of Oriental figures and houses, sold by Tiffany and Co **100.00**

Jardiniere, Paris
6⅞" h, under dish, hexagonal form with paneled sides, polychrome enamel dec on alternating black and white ground, 19th C **450.00**
11⅝" h, 13¾" d, bell form, hp garden and field flowers dec, some wear, 19th C **1,050.00**

Palace Vase, cov, hp enamel and gilt dec with pink luster trim, champleve finial, collar, socle, and base, French, late 19th C, 29½" h **2,750.00**

Panel, painted
5½ x 4", seated nymph, gilt metal frame **690.00**
6 x 4⅜", boy with gold locket, jeweled and enameled, oval, framed **715.00**

Pitcher, gilt lattice work background, raised bead work, central hp child's portrait, beehive mark, late 19th C, 5" h **575.00**

Plate
Chinoisserie center, floral and blue border, Samson, French, pr **415.00**
Polychrome enamel bird dec,

possibly French, late 19th C,
8¼" d, set of eleven **175.00**

Soup Tureen, cov, stand, armorial
crest dec, Chinese export style,
Samson, French, 11" w **1,265.00**

Stein, silver mounted, enameled
classical figural and landscape
subjects, French, 19th C, 4½" h,
pr **1,275.00**

Tea and Coffee Service, 20 pcs,
wide gold banded border, central
hp coastal marine landscape,
10" h cov coffeepot, cov teapot,
cream pitcher, sugar bowl, waste
bowl, five cups, eight saucers,
damage, Paris, early 19th C . . .**3,000.00**

Tea Cup and Saucer, crest, floral
and vine dec, Samson, French,
set of four **230.00**

Urns, pr
10" h
German, each with landscape
panel dec, one entitled
"Mainz," other "Coblenz,"
one base repaired, mid 19th
C **1,150.00**

Paris, powdered pink mid
band, neoclassical grisaille
devices, dolphin form crest,
gilded throat and socle,
mounted as lamps, bases
imperfect, early 19th C **375.00**

24¾" h, cov, Sevres style, metal
mounts, double mask handles,
octagonal base, enamel floral
dec, cobalt blue ground,
French, late 19th C **2,425.00**

Vase
8" h, polychrome dec, tropical
birds in shaped cartouches,
blue ground, French, possibly
Samson, late 19th C, pr **345.00**

11½" h, octagonal pear shape,
floral and crest dec, pr **630.00**

13½" h, paneled baluster form,
two handled, reticulated rim
and base, cerulean blue, rect
reserve, hp scene with children, gold accents, raised sunburst 633 in oval mark, some
rubbing, Paris, late 19th C . . . **490.00**

14½" h, figural, tree–trunk form
with encrusted base, figural

birds, flowers, and hound,
chips, repairs, 19th C **225.00**

26" h, bronze mounts, ceramic,
bird and leafy scrollwork dec,
blue ground, electrified, 19th
C, pr **575.00**

Vessel, allover crazed white glaze
with blue enamel dec "Bovani
Oglio 1698" below spout, Italian
Faience, late 17th C, 15" h **345.00**

Wash Set, cornflower spray dec,
lozenge form toothbrush holder,
small bowl, and large bowl and
pitcher, Paris, 19th C, 8" h
pitcher, price for 4 pcs **860.00**

COOKIE JARS

History: Cookie jars, colorful and often
whimsical, are now an established collecting category in their own right. Do not be
misled by the high prices released at the
1988 Andy Warhol auction. Many of the
same cookie jars that sold for over $1,000
each can be found in the field for less than
$100.

Many cookie jar forms were manufactured by more than one company and, as a
result, can be found with different marks.
This resulted from mergers or splits by manufacturers, e.g., Brush–McCoy which is now
Nelson McCoy. Molds also were traded and
sold among companies.

Cookie jars often were redesigned to reflect newer tastes. Hence, the same jar may
be found in several different style variations.

References: Mary Jane Giacomini,
*American Bisque: A Collector's Guide with
Prices,* Schiffer Publishing, 1994; John W.
Humphries, *Humphries Price Guide To
Cookie Jars,* published by author, 1992;
Dana G. Morykan and Harry L. Rinker, *War-
man's Country Antiques & Collectibles,
Second Edition,* Wallace–Homestead,
1994; Harold Nichols, *McCoy Cookie Jars:
From The First To The Last, Second Edi-
tion*, Nichols Publishing, 1991; Fred and
Joyce Roerig, *Collector's Encyclopedia of
Cookie Jars,* Book I (1991, 1993 value up-
date), Book II (1994), Collector Books; Mike
Schneider, *The Complete Cookie Jar Book,*
Schiffer Publishing, 1991; Ermagene West-
fall, *An Illustrated Value Guide To Cookie*

Jars, Book I (1983, 1993 value update), Book II (1993), Collector Books.

Periodicals: *Cookie Jarrin',* RR 2, Box 504, Walterboro, SC 29488; *Crazed Over Cookie Jars,* PO Box 254, Savanna, IL 61074.

Collectors' Club: The Cookie Jar Collector's Club, 595 Cross River Rd., Katonah, NY 10536.

Morton Pottery Co., poodle, white ground, red and black dec, $25.00.

Advertising, Kellogg's, Tony Tiger, plastic	85.00
American Bisque	
Davy Crockett	450.00
Majorette	315.00
Pennsylvania Dutch Boy	375.00
Avon	
Bear	55.00
House, basket at door	75.00
Brush	
Bunny, gray	315.00
Covered Wagon	625.00
Elephant with ice cream cone	495.00
Granny, green dress	350.00
Hobbie Horse, reglued tail	1,100.00
Squirrel, gold trim	575.00
California Originals	
Airplane and Pilot	325.00
Christmas Tree	595.00
Fire Truck, red	395.00
Girl	225.00
Scarecrow	185.00
Deforest, Buddha	135.00
Hirsch, Pinocchio	675.00

Lefton	
Lovebirds on birdhouse	175.00
Winking Santa	225.00
McCoy	
Circus Horse	200.00
Snoopy on doghouse	225.00
Stagecoach	1,250.00
Metlox	
Ballerina Bear	135.00
Beulah	455.00
Black Scotty	150.00
Broccoli	295.00
Bucky Beaver	275.00
Clown, black and white	245.00
Corn	20.00
Cow	
Purple	725.00
Yellow	375.00
Frog	185.00
Gingham Dog	
Beige	125.00
Blue	425.00
Humpty Dumpty	235.00
Koala Bear	125.00
Little Piggy	375.00
Lucy Goose	165.00
Mother Goose	495.00
Panda	135.00
Pear, yellow	225.00
Penguin	145.00
Pineapple	95.00
Rabbit on cabbage	125.00
Raccoon	155.00
Squirrel on pinecone	95.00
Strawberry	65.00
Wheat	125.00
Regal China	
Churn Boy	245.00
Dutch Girl	925.00
Goldilocks	375.00
Little Miss Muffet	325.00
Shawnee	
Dutch Boy	450.00
Jo Jo clown	425.00
Owl, gold	345.00
Puss 'N Boots, plain	165.00
Shamrocks	275.00
Winnie, clover bud	585.00
Sigma, Kliban Cat	375.00
Treasure Craft, Katrina	700.00
Twin Winton	
Elf on stump	225.00
Owl	165.00
Vallona Star, Peter Pumpkin Eater	365.00

Vandor
Betty Boop **675.00**
Cowboy **75.00**
Jukebox **295.00**

COPELAND

COPELAND AND SPODE

History: In 1749 Josiah Spode was apprenticed to Thomas Whieldon and in 1754 worked for William Banks in Stoke–on–Trent. In the early 1760s Spode started his own pottery, making cream colored earthenware and blue printed whiteware. In 1770 he returned to Banks' factory as master, purchasing it in 1776.

Spode pioneered the use of steam–powered pottery making machinery and mastered the art of transfer printing from copper plates. Spode opened a London shop in 1778 and sent William Copeland there circa 1784. A number of larger London locations followed. At the turn of the century Spode introduced bone china. In 1805 Josiah Spode II and William Copeland entered into a partnership for the London business. A series of partnerships between Josiah Spode II, Josiah Spode III, and William Taylor Copeland resulted.

In 1833 Copeland acquired Spode's London operations and the Stoke plants seven years later. William Taylor Copeland managed the business until his death in 1868. The business remained in the hands of Copeland heirs. In 1923 the plant was electrified; other modernizations followed.

In 1976 Spode merged with Worcester Royal Porcelain to become Royal Worcester Spode, Ltd.

References: Susan and Al Bagdade, *Warman's English & Continental Pottery & Porcelain, 2nd Edition,* Wallace–Homestead, 1991; D. Drakard & P. Holdway,

Spode Printed Wares, Longmans, 1983; L. Whiter, *Spode: A History Of The Family, Factory, And Wares, 1733–1833,* Barrie & Jenkins, 1970.

Game Set, stoneware, transfer game print, enameled floral border, 20½" l platter, twelve 10" d plates, price for set, $2,450.00.

Basin, 12" d, Italian pattern, marked "Spode" **195.00**
Bust, 11" h, woman, parian ware, John Hancock sculptor, dated 1863, imp Copeland marks **375.00**
Dinner Service
   Chinese Rose pattern, #629599, complete eight place servings, Copeland Spode **475.00**
   Gilt scroll design, eleven dinner plates, six soup plates, and eleven bread and butter plates, Copeland Spode **500.00**
   Luneville pattern, 98 pcs, twelve dinner, salad, bread and butter, bone, and dessert plates, twelve bouillon cups, eleven saucers, four eggcups, two tea cups and saucers, two cereal bowls, and seven serving pieces, Copeland Spode **650.00**
   Peacock pattern, #2118, 33 pcs, stone china, polychrome dec, deep dishes, plates, platters, shrimp dishes, imp and printed Spode marks, c1810, minor surface wear **1,100.00**

Spode's Aster pattern, 107 pcs, twelve dinner plates, twelve luncheon plates, twelve bread and butter plates, 15 dessert plates, 16 cups, twelve saucers, twelve demitasse cups and saucers, one rect condiment dish, and one 15″ d circular tray with inset condiment dishes, Copeland Spode **450.00**

Tower pattern, 136 pcs, blue and white, transfer printed, nine bouillon cups, three breakfast cups, fourteen tea cups, five demitasse cups, twenty–nine saucers, twelve bread and butter plates, nine dessert plates, eight soup plates, twenty–four dinner plates, two rect trays, sq tray, four rect graduated platters, large circular platter, large circular dish, cov vegetable dish, cov soup tureen, two large bowls, two sauce boats on stands, cov teapot with stand, sugar bowl, cream jug, two milk jugs, and three fan shaped dishes, blue printed mark, Copeland Spode **700.00**

Figure, 18½″ h, nude female, parian ware, shackled wrists attached by chain, imp Copeland marks, mid 19th C, foot rim, chip **750.00**

Mantel Urns, pr, 6⅜″ h, 6¾″ d, central black ground medallion encompassing dancing classical maidens, yellow–gold ground with trellising orange vines, birds, and cameo medallion, surmounted by rim with Greek Key stylized flowers and scroll dec, base marked with green interlacing C scroll, Copeland, mid 19th C **1,210.00**

Plate

9½″ d, dinner, shaped circular form, gilded border set at intervals with lunettes and floral sprays, price for set of twelve **425.00**

10¼″ d

Iron red border, gadrooned rim, gilt scrolls and garlands, Copeland, price for set of thirteen **925.00**

Mazarin blue border, gadrooned rim, gilt beaded and scrolled bands, Copeland, price for set of twelve **635.00**

10¾″ d, hp fruit, blossom, and vine dec, each plate different, Copeland Spode, price for set of twelve **275.00**

Platter, 18½″ l, 14″ w, ironstone, Imari pattern, octagonal, floral central dec, red, blue, and gold floral border, Copeland, mid 19th C **375.00**

Service Plate, Blackbird pattern, price for set of twelve, Copeland **192.00**

Spoon Warmer, 5″ h, shell form, Majolica, Nautilus pattern, Copeland, 19th C **350.00**

Tile, 8″ sq, white glazed, relief molded cherubs, Copeland, price for pair **110.00**

Tureen and Underplate, Jefferson pattern, Copeland Spode **225.00**

Urn, cov, 9″ h, parian ware, lacy pierced lid and bottom molded with classical motifs, tripartite base, imp "Copeland," restoration to finial and one support, 1860–70 .... **465.00**

COPPER

History: Copper objects, such as kettles, tea kettles, warming pans, measures, etc., played an important part in the 19th century household. Outdoors, the apple butter kettle and still were the two principal copper items. Copper culinary objects were lined with a thin protective coating of tin to prevent poisoning. They were relined as needed.

Great emphasis is placed by collectors on signed pieces, especially those by American craftsmen. Since copper objects were made abroad as well, it is hard to identify unsigned examples.

References: Mary Frank Gaston, *Antique Brass & Copper: Identification & Value Guide,* Collector Books, 1992, 1994 value update; Henry J. Kauffman, *Early American Copper, Tin, and Brass,* Medill McBride Co., 1950.

Additional Listings: Arts and Crafts Movement and Roycroft.
Reproduction Alert: Many modern reproductions also exist.

Chafing Dish, lobster legs, orig burner, black handle, $75.00.

Bedwarmer
   36½" l, tooled floral pinwheel dec on lid, turned wood handle, worn black paint **175.00**
   43" l, tooled lid, replaced turned handle **165.00**
Candlesticks, pr, 5½ x 4½", brass handle, 19th C **45.00**
Candy Kettle, dovetailed, round bottom
   14" d, 8½" h, steel rim handles **95.00**
   19½" d, 15" h, iron handles . . . **105.00**
   23¼" d, iron handles **140.00**
Coal Scuttle, 22" l **100.00**
Egg Warmer, 10" h, Victorian, pewter trim **145.00**
Food Mold
   10" d, turk's head, geometric design **85.00**
   10¾" l, fish, curved, good detail, marked "Made in Germany" . **27.50**
Hot Water Bottle, 8½" h, marked "WAFAX" **65.00**
Letter Opener, Arts & Crafts, hammered, strap handle **20.00**
Measure, set of 3, excise marks for New York, c1869 . . . . **880.00**
Pan, 10" d, dovetailed construction, applied strap handle **90.00**

Pitcher, 12" h, dovetailed, classic design **110.00**
Roasting Pan, 27 x 20 x 7", diamond shape, English, 19th C . . **360.00**
Spittoon, 14½" h, turtle, marked "Golden & Jackson's...Chicago pat'd 1891" **275.00**
Straw Holder, cov, 5" w, 11" h, soda fountain type, octagonal frame, glass panels **230.00**
Teakettle
   8½" h, dovetailed, spout flap, marked "Konrad Jonsson" . . **85.00**
   9" h, dovetailed, gooseneck spout, polished **175.00**
   11" h, dovetailed, gooseneck spout, acorn finial, brass trim, maker's mark on bottom **190.00**
Tray, 11¾" l, hammered, silver dec, Gorham & Co **650.00**
Weather Vane
   18" l, eagle, wood ball, replaced metal feet, gold repaint **75.00**
   30½" l, horse, molded, orig packing crate, Snow Iron Works, Boston, late 19th C . . **925.00**

CORALENE

History: Coralene is a glass or china object which has the design painted on the surface of the piece and tiny glass colorless beads applied with a fixative. The piece is placed in a muffle which fixes the enamel and sets the beads.

Several American and English companies made glass coralene in the 1880s. Seaweed or coral was the most common design. Other motifs were "Wheat Sheaf" and "Fleur–de–Lis." Most of the base glass was satin finished.

China and pottery coralene, made from the late 1890s to the post–WWII era, is referred to as Japanese coralene. The beading is opaque and inserted into the soft clay. Hence, it is only half to three–quarters visible.

Reproduction Alert: Reproductions are on the market, some using an old glass base. The beaded decoration on new coralene has been glued and can be scraped off.

Tumbler, satin glass, medium pink shading to light pink, cased white int., gold rim, gold coralene, 3¾" h, $235.00.

CHINA

Box, cov, 1½ x 2 x 3", copper matte ground, pink, lavender, and green thistle, marked "Kinran Pat. 16132 Japan" **125.00**
Sugar Shaker, white ground, orange coralene seaweed dec, orig top **175.00**
Vase, 8" h, bulbous, scalloped and fluted rim, shaded lavender to light blue ground, multicolored snapdragons dec, c1909 ...... **225.00**

GLASS

Bowl, 4½" d, blue, flowers and leaves, SP holder **150.00**
Pitcher, 3¼" h, 2⅝" d, orange, beaded coralene cov enameled fruit and leaves, applied amber glass handle, enameled "Patent" on base **250.00**
Tumbler, white satin ground, acorns and leaves outlined in coralene **40.00**
Vase
  4½" h, 3⅜" d, DQ, MOP, shaded pink, yellow beaded coralene stars in centers of diamonds, white enamel dot beading around top edge **475.00**
  4½" h, 3⅞" d, bulbous, round gold trimmed top, blue satin overlay, white lining, yellow beaded coralene pattern **410.00**

5" h, waisted, crimped, ruffled, yellow and green floral coralene beading, pale yellow ground, crystal rim, gold trim, some loss to beading, price for pr **325.00**
5⅜" h, golden yellow snowflake MOP satin ground, white int., yellow wheat coralene dec .. **500.00**
7½" h, peachblow, satin finish, shading from deep rose to pale pink, yellow crystal beads, seaweed design, gold trim, white casing, polished pontil, incised "PATENT" on base, c1870, Wheeling **675.00**

CORKSCREWS

History: The corkscrew is composed of three parts: (1) handle, (2) shaft, and (3) worm or screw. The earliest known reference to "a Steele Worme used for drawing corks out of bottles" is 1681. Samuel Henshall, an Englishman, was granted the first patent in 1795.

Elaborate mechanisms were invented and patented from the early 1800s onward, especially in England. However, three basic types emerged: "T" handle (the most basic, simple form), lever, and mechanism. Variations on these three types run into the hundreds. Miniature corkscrews, employed for drawing corks from perfume and medicine bottles between 1750 and 1920, are among the most eagerly sought by collectors.

Nationalistic preferences were found in corkscrews. The English favored the helix worm and tended to coppertone their steel products. By the mid–18th century English and Irish silversmiths were making handles noted for their clean lines and practicality. Most English silver handles were hallmarked.

The Germans preferred the center worm and nickel plate. The Italians used chrome plate or massive solid brass. In the early 1800s the Dutch and French developed elaborately artistic silver handles.

Americans did not begin to manufacture quality corkscrews until the late 19th century. They favored the center worm and specialized in silver mounted tusks and carved staghorn for handles.

Collectors' Clubs: Canadian Corkscrew Collectors Club, 670 Meadow Wood Rd., Mississaugua, Ontario, L5J 2S6 Canada; Just For Openers, 605 Windsong Lane, Durham, NC 27713.

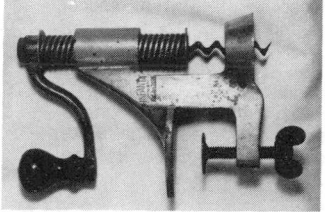

Infanta, No. 8, patented 1845, table clamp, cast iron, nickel plating, double action, American, $325.00.

Lever
Brass, rack and pinion type, double, steel shaft, center screw, cap lifter in handle, Italian, c1920 .... 30.00
Bronzed Steel, helical screw, double lever patent, Heeley "A1" 60.00
Chrome, zig–zag design, 10½" extended, French 60.00
Mechanism
Bronze Frame, rosewood handle with brush, marked "G Twigg's Patent," c1868 .... 400.00
Chrome Frame, cylindrical ebony wood handle, steel, cyphered screw, marked "Swiss Made, 2908A3" 130.00
Steel Frame, scrolling floral and leaf dec, clamp handles on base, raised steel arms, cyphered screw, marked "Yankee No 7," c1913 .... 160.00
Miniature
Crescent shape, chromed turned steel shaft wire helix, ivory handle, 1790–1820 .... 70.00
Elephant, chrome, screw trunk . 40.00

Meissen, Johann Von Schiller head handle, uncyphered center screw, underglaze crossed swords mark, c1870 .... 375.00
Mother of Pearl, carved palmette handle, helical screw 20.00
Novelty, figural
Cat, brass, tail screw, 3¾" l ... 45.00
Mermaid, celluloid, brown, steel cyphered screw, H H & S Express 300.00
Triton, blowing a shell, pewter, steel cyphered screw, 19th C 90.00
Gaucho and Horse, silver, oblong platform handle, seal from sheath with scrolling, Archimedean screw 800.00
T–Handle
Brass, Thomason type, bone handle with brush, helical screw 150.00
Steel, "The Surprise," cage frame, marked "Registered by George Willetts, Birmingham, England," 1884 .... 95.00
Wood, shaped and turned handle, cyphered center screw, bell and wire cutter, cap lifter, "Williamson" on shaft, marked "Ptd 13 Dec 1898" 30.00

COWAN POTTERY

History: R. Guy Cowan founded the Cowan Pottery in 1913 in Cleveland, Ohio. The establishment remained in almost continuous operation until 1931 when financial difficulties forced closure.

Early production was redware pottery. Later a porcelain–like finish was perfected with special emphasis placed on glazes. Lustreware is one of the most common types. Commercial wares marked "Lakeware" were produced from 1927 to 1931.

Early marks include an incised "Cowan Pottery" on the redware (1913–17), an impressed "Cowan," and an impressed "Lakewood." The imprinted stylized semicircle, with or without the initials R. G., came later.

References: Paul Evans, *Art Pottery of the United States, 2nd Edition*, Feingold & Lewis Publishing Corp., 1987; Ralph and Terry Kovel, *Kovels' American Art Pottery: The Collector's Guide To Makers, Marks and Factory Histories*, Crown Publishers, 1993; Tim and Jamie Saloff, *The Collector's Encyclopedia of Cowan Pottery: Identification and Values*, Collector Books, 1994.

Museums: Cowan Pottery Museum, Rocky River Public Library, Rocky River, OH; Everson Museum of Art, Syracuse, NY.

Bowl
 7" d, 3" h, irid gold, crackled celadon glaze, marked "R G Cowan" and "RC" **300.00**
 13⅝" d, 8¼" h, Jazz Bowl, blue and black high glazes, base diestamped "Cowan," artist's name on side, designed by Viktor Schreckengost, c1931 **16,500.00**
Bust, 15" h, woman, head and base cast as one piece, metallic charcoal and bronze glazes, inscribed "W. Gregory," imp "Cowan" **1,750.00**
Charger, 11⅜" d, Fox Hunt, poly-

Trivet, Louis Mora bust of lady, blue ground, rose and yellow flowers, green and aqua leaves, 6½" d, $200.00.

chromed figures, clear crackle glaze, designed by Viktor Schreckengost, back stamped with logo and "Cowan," artist's initials cast in design, c1930 . . . **825.00**
Lamp Base, 25½" h, stylized orchid motif, blue and green high glaze, silvered metal lamp fittings, platform base **475.00**
Strawberry Pot, 6½" h, saucer, pink and green glaze **160.00**
Vase
 9" h, beehive shape, apricot and peach **275.00**
 11⅛" h, figural, Oriental pheasant, frothy green high glaze, diestamped R G Cowan logo, c1929 . . . . **325.00**

CRANBERRY GLASS

History: Cranberry glass is transparent and named for its color, achieved by adding powdered gold to a molten batch of amber glass which then is reheated at a low temperature to develop the cranberry or ruby color. The glass color first appeared in the last half of the 17th century, but was not made in American glass factories until the last half of the 19th century.

Cranberry glass was blown, mold blown, or pressed. Examples often are decorated with gold or enamel. Less expensive cranberry glass was made by substituting copper for gold and can be identified by its bluish–purple tint.

Reference: William Heacock and William Gamble, *Encyclopedia Of Victorian Colored Pattern Glass: Book 9, Cranberry Opalescent from A to Z*, Antique Publications, 1987.

Additional Listings: See specific categories, such as Bride's Baskets, Cruets, Jack–in–the–Pulpit Vases, etc.

Reproduction Alert: Reproductions abound. These pieces are heavier, off–color, and lack the quality of older examples.

Bottle
 8½" h, 2¾" d, pink, blue, yellow, and white enameled flowers, green and gold leaves, white

enameled dots, clear bubble stopper **172.00**

8¾" h, 3" d, tiny gold dot center band, daisy like gold flowers, gold top and bottom bands, clear cut faceted stopper **115.00**

10¼" h, 3¾" d, cut to clear, matching mushroom bubble stopper **245.00**

10¼" h, 4¾" d, small gold stars dec, gold trim, clear cut stopper **175.00**

Bowl

5" d, Hobnail, ruffled edge, polished pontil, Hobbs Brockunier **40.00**

5½" h, 6⅛" d, six applied crystal berry prunts around top edge, three applied crystal fancy reeded fan shaped designs, three applied crystal scroll reeded feet, crystal berry pontil, Webb **275.00**

Box, cov, 4½" h, 2¾" d, white outlined sanded gold designs, white and gold flowers, clear finial ... **140.00**

Candlesticks, pr, 3" h, 4" d, optic diamond, bobeche top, polished pontil **295.00**

Cologne Bottle

5¾" h, 3⅛" d, white enameled flowers and leaves on front, orig cranberry bubble stopper **200.00**

8⅝" h, 2⅜" d, gold scrolls, small gold flowers, matching sq cranberry bubble stopper **175.00**

9½" h, Icicle, applied overshot icicles around neck extend down body, applied clear shell feet, orig overshot stopper, Sandwich **475.00**

Creamer and Sugar, 2" d x 3½" h creamer, 4" d x 2½" h open sugar, fancy applied clear rim trim, applied clear handle, clear wafer foot, price for set **175.00**

Cruet, 8½" h, 3" d, metal base, handle, and neck band, clear cut faceted stopper **172.00**

Decanter

10½" h, 4½" d, silver flowers, gold leaves and band, gold bands on matching cranberry bubble stopper **175.00**

11½" h, 5" d, pedestal foot, lacy white enameled dec, orig clear bubble stopper **230.00**

12½" h, 5" d, deep color, applied crystal handle, clear hollow blown stopper, price for pr ... **325.00**

Epergne, 22" h, 9½" w, large ruffled bowl, two small trumpet vases, large center trumpet vase, two crystal rope canes with hanging baskets, applied clear glass rigaree on trumpets and baskets, metal mounts **600.00**

Fairy Lamp

3¾" h, 3¼" d, Verre Moire, dome shade, opaque white loopings on frosted ground, cream pottery base marked "S Clarke's Patent Trademark Fairy Pyramid" **150.00**

4" d, 5" h, frosted, ruffled cup base, clear marked "Clarke" insert **310.00**

4¼" d, applied clear hand tooled petals, clear marked "Clarke" insert, petaled shade holder . **350.00**

Lamp

Hall, 33" h, 10" d ribbed ball shade, hanging, red brass frame, electrified **250.00**

Table, 14" h, 5½" d, ruffled shade, gold floral dec, brass foot, orig chimney and brass burner **575.00**

Liqueur Set, 8½" d round tray, 8¼" h, 3¼" d wine cruet, orig clear

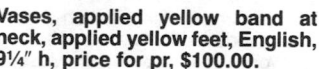

Vases, applied yellow band at neck, applied yellow feet, English, 9¼" h, price for pr, $100.00.

bubble stopper, six 1¾" h, 1⅜" d
mugs, dainty blue flowers, gold
leaves **460.00**
Pickle Castor, 10½" h, 4⅜" d, IVT,
resilvered SP frame, lid, claw
tongs **270.00**
Pitcher, 8½" h, 4" d, opaque light
green zipper design, applied
clear handle, clear wafer foot . .   **300.00**
Sugar Shaker, paneled, North-
wood **250.00**
Tumbler
3¼" h, 2¾" d, Delaware pattern,
barrel shape, gold trim **40.00**
4¼" h, 2¾" d, acid cut back band
at top, rose sprays **35.00**
Vase
4½" h, 3¾" d, applied crystal ruf-
fled top, DQ **145.00**
5" h, 4" d, triangular top, three
clear applied flowers,
branches, and leaves, clear
wafer foot **200.00**
5¾" h, 3" d, sanded enamel
white scallops, grapes, and
leaves, gold ormolu feet, pr . .   **225.00**
7⅝" h, 2½" d, blown, hobnail,
ruffled, applied clear foot **90.00**
8¼" h, 4½" d, swirl, lip on each
side of top **135.00**
9" h, 3½" d, enameled white
daisies and leaves, facing pr .   **250.00**
9⅜" h, 4⅜" d, applied clear up-
right leaves, applied clear rigaree trim at top and base,
clear pedestal foot **175.00**
9½" h, 6" d, white, green, and
blue enameled flowers, gold
fan and leaves, clear wafer
foot and handles **485.00**
13⅛" h, 5¼" d, enameled dainty
white flowers, gold berries,
scrolls, and leaves, applied
clear shell trim **225.00**

CROWN MILANO

History: Crown Milano is an American
art glass produced by the Mt. Washington
Glass Works, New Bedford, Massachusetts. The original patent was issued in
1886 to Frederick Shirley and Albert Steffin.

Normally it is an opaque white satin glass
finished with light beige or ivory color
ground embellished with fancy florals, decorations, and elaborate heavy raised gold.
When marked, pieces carry an entwined
CM with crown in purple enamel on the
base. Sometimes paper labels were used.
The silver–plated mounts often have "MW"
impressed or a Pairpoint mark as both
Mount Washington and Pairpoint supplied
mountings.

Advisors: Clarence and Betty Maier.

**Sweet Meat Jar, Diamond pattern,
swirls of taupe and gold, emerald
leaves, red bead berries, metal
top with flowers, 4" h, $625.00.**

Biscuit Jar, pale blue to pale yellow
ground, stylized iris dec, four
heavily raised gold circles of
elaborate designs **1,200.00**
Bowl
8¼" d, hp autumn leaf design,
gold accents, purple "CM"
crown and "598" mark **1,100.00**
9½" d, 3¼" h, tricorner, hp pan-
sies, roses, and forget–me-
nots, white and yellow–green
ground, cut and folded gold
rim, purple "CM" crown mark   **460.00**
Cracker Jar
6" h, Bamboo pattern, green,
gold, and brown enamel dec,
painted Burmese ground, sil-
ver hardware **900.00**
6¾" h, 6½" w, melon ribbed,
painted pink ground, raspber-

ries, leaves, flowers, and vines, cov sgd "MW 4413," numbered base **425.00**

Creamer and Sugar, 11" d x 4¼" h creamer, 12½" d x 4¾" h cov sugar, petticoat shape, blue cornflowers, purple asters, pink and yellow roses, red wild roses, beige ground, heavy gold dec, applied leaf handles on sugar .**5,250.00**

Dresser Box, cov, 7" d, 4" h, spiral twist opal, stylized dancing white herons on cov, SP rim and clasp **1,610.00**

Humidor, 6¾" h, 5½" w, pale beige ground, gold and purple spider mums, sgd "Pairpoint 2769" on base, sgd "Pairpoint" on metal mount, cracked on side to base **65.00**

Jewel Box, cov, 1¾" h, 4" w, hinged, gold wild rose dec, shaded pink and white ground, tracery, sgd in metal "Pairpoint Manufacturing Company, 980" . **250.00**

Pitcher, 8½" h, 8" w, gold pond lilies and leaves, silver highlights, pale cream ground, bright green trim, gold serpent handle with scales, eyes, and mouth, monogram and number on base ...**2,100.00**

Portrait Vase, 7¼" h, opal body, delicate lattice work dec, center scenic medallion with dancing children, handled, purple "CM" crown mark **1,380.00**

Rose Bowl, 5" h, beige–yellow satin ground, hp blue and lavender pansies, purple "CM" crown mark **690.00**

Vase

4½" h, 16" d, bulbous, eight pulled up ribs, deep beige tracery, heavy raised gold enameled petit point stylized iris, leaves, and scroll dec **875.00**

10¼" h, satin scroll, gold enameled foliate dec, applied brown handles **1,610.00**

CRUETS

History: Cruets are small glass bottles used to hold oil, vinegar, wine, etc., for the table. The high point of cruet use was during the Victorian era when a myriad of glass manufacturers made cruets in a wide assortment of patterns, colors, and sizes. All cruets had stoppers; most had handles.

References: Elaine Ezell and George Newhouse, *Cruets, Cruets, Cruets, Volume I,* Antique Publications, 1991; William Heacock, *Encyclopedia of Victorian Colored Pattern Glass: Book 6, Oil Cruets From A To Z,* Antique Publications, 1981.

Additional Listings: Pattern Glass and specific glass categories such as Amberina, Cranberry, and Satin.

Amberina, bulbous, pulled in base, flares to form pedestal base, polished pontil, amber handle, clear cut faceted stopper **125.00**

Cranberry, 8½" h, 3" d, metal base, handle, and neck band, clear cut faceted stopper **172.00**

Lime Green

7¾" h, 3¼" d, white daisies, green leaves, applied green handle, green bubble stopper **115.00**

10" h, 3½" d, lavender florals, green leaves, gold bird, applied green handle, orig green bubble stopper **115.00**

Mary Gregory, 8¾" h, 3½" d, bulbous, amber, detailed white enameled young girl, applied amber handle, orig matching amber stopper **250.00**

Opalescent

Hobnail, white, pontil, stopper

Opalescent, Bubble Lattice, blue ground, applied clear handle, 5¾" h, $225.00.

missing, Hobbs Brockunier, one bad hob **50.00**

Iris with Meander, white, orig stopper **225.00**

Orange, 8½" h, 3" d, white enameled flowers with yellow center, branches, applied clear handle, orig clear stopper **170.00**

Pattern Glass

Amazon, orig stopper **85.00**

Block and Triple Bars, orig stopper **45.00**

Esther, green, gold trim, orig stopper **225.00**

Medallion Sunburst, orig stopper **55.00**

Portland, orig stopper **75.00**

Serrated Prism, no stopper **45.00**

Sapphire Blue

8½" h, 3" d, light sapphire, white enameled flowers and foliage, yellow centers, gold trim, applied amber handle, amber ball stopper **172.00**

9" h, 4" d, bulbous, round top, lavender flowers, green leaves, gold trim, applied clear handle, clear bubble stopper . **175.00**

CUP PLATES

History: Many early cups and saucers were handleless, with deep saucers. The hot liquid was poured into the saucer and sipped from it. This necessitated another plate for the cup, the "cup plate."

The first cup plates made of pottery were of the Staffordshire variety. In the mid–1830s to 1840s, glass cup plates were favored. The Boston and Sandwich Glass Company was one of the main contributors to the lacy glass type.

It is extremely difficult to find glass cup plates in outstanding (mint) condition. Collectors expect some marks of usage, such as slight rim roughness, minor chipping (best if under rim), and in rarer patterns a portion of a scallop missing.

Reference: Ruth Webb Lee and James H. Rose, *American Glass Cup Plates*, published by author, 1948, reprinted by Charles E. Tuttle Co., in 1985.

Collectors' Club: Pairpoint Cup Plate Collectors of America, PO Box 890052, East Weymouth, MA 02189.

Notes: The numbers used are from the Lee–Rose book in which all plates are illustrated.

Prices are based on plates in "average" condition.

LR 82, acorn and leaves, silver opaque blue, fiery opalescent, $575.00.

GLASS

LR 28, 3¼" d, clear, seventeen even scallops, New England or Sandwich origin **30.00**

LR 36, 3¼" d, opal opaque, seventeen even scallops **475.00**

LR 46, 3½" d, lavender, fifteen even scallops, strawberry diamond pattern, eastern origin .. **125.00**

LR 52, 3¾" d, opalescent, fifteen scallops with points between, eastern origin **200.00**

LR 70, 3⁷⁄₁₆" d, clear, plain rope, midwestern origin **125.00**

LR 79, 3¾" d, pink tint, rope top and bottom, New England origin **50.00**

LR 82, 3⅝" d, opaque blue, plain rim, five pointed star center, attributed to New England **275.00**

LR 95, 3⅝" d, opal opaque, ten sided, rope top and bottom, one tiny under rim nick **150.00**

LR 120, 3¹⁄₁₆" d, clear, thirty even scallops, midwestern origin **165.00**

LR 135, 3⁷⁄₁₆" d, clear, twenty-four

bull's eyes, points between, attributed to midwestern origin .. **75.00**
LR 148–C, 2⅞" d, seventeen scallops, points between, clear, one point and one scallop missing . **75.00**
LR 150–B, 2¹⁵⁄₁₆" d, clear, plain, robe on bottom, midwestern origin **50.00**
LR 163, 3¼" d, light green, thirty–four scallops, radial lines between, midwestern origin **65.00**
LR 179, 3⁷⁄₁₆" d, lavender, ten scallop, rope top and bottom, attributed to Philadelphia area **125.00**
LR 183–B, 3½" d, deep blue, octagonal rim, seven scallops between corners, midwestern origin **90.00**
LR 200, 3⅛" d, clear, ninety–six sawtooth scallops, midwestern origin **35.00**
LR 225–A, 3½" d, clear, twelve large scallops, 4 small scallops between, attributed to Philadelphia area **50.00**
LR 311, 3⅝" d, twenty–three bead scallops, pairs of smaller scallops between each, Sandwich origin, amber stain on center design and border triangles, two scallops missing **300.00**
LR 343–B, 3⁷⁄₁₆" d, clear, plain, dotted below **45.00**
LR 388, 3⁵⁄₁₆" d, opaque white, plain, central star, attributed to Philadelphia area **35.00**
LR 412, 3³⁄₁₆" d, clear, ten sided, star center, Sandwich origin ... **95.00**
LR 425, 3⅜" d, deep amethyst, unlisted color, nine large scallops with hearts between on rim, trace of mold roughness **1,600.00**
LR 455, 3⅞" d, opal, forty–eight even scallops, Sandwich origin **265.00**

GLASS, HISTORICAL

LR 576, 3⁹⁄₁₆" d, medium blue, twenty–five large scallops, two smaller scallops between, Sandwich origin **85.00**
LR 580, 3¾" d, clear, Victoria and Albert, fifty–six even scallops, English origin **250.00**

LR 605–A, 3½" d, clear, octagonal, ship, three scallops lightly tipped **275.00**
LR 643, 3⁹⁄₁₆" d, clear, Bunker Hill Monument, fifty–three even scallops, drape pattern shoulders, Sandwich origin **35.00**
LR 653, 3" d, clear, plain, eagle, laurel wreath, large chip **125.00**
LR 668, 3⅛" d, clear, fifty–six even scallops, attributed to midwestern origin **100.00**
LR 676, 3¹¹⁄₁₆" d, clear, sixty even scallops, Curling's Ft Pitt Glass Works **65.00**

PORCELAIN OR POTTERY

Davenport, 3⅞" d, pink luster, imp mark **30.00**
Leeds, 3⅜" d, raised polychrome floral dec **50.00**
Staffordshire, Historical
Battersea Park, NY, 3⅝" d, dark blue transfer **360.00**
Conway, N Hampshire, 4⅛" d, light colors, marked "American Scenery" **75.00**
Oriental Scene Series, Fakeer's Rock, 4¼" d, dark blue, L Hall & Sons **120.00**
Valley Of The Sanandoch From Jefferson's Rock, light colors **75.00**
Worcester Cathedral, 4" d, tiny rub on rim, Hall **40.00**
Staffordshire, Romantic
California, Podmore Walker & Co **75.00**
Corinth, James Edwards **40.00**
Damacus, Wm Adams and Sons, blue and white **50.00**
Errand Boy, 3½" d, dark blue, imp "Clews" **310.00**
Garden Scenery, Mayer, pink, twelve sided **30.00**
Lozere, Edward Challinor **65.00**

CUSTARD GLASS

History: Custard glass was developed in England in the early 1880s. Harry Northwood made the first American custard glass at his Indiana, Pennsylvania, factory in 1898.

From 1898 until 1915, many manufacturers produced custard glass patterns, e.g., Dugan Glass, Fenton, A. H. Heisey Glass Co., Jefferson Glass, Northwood, Tarentum Glass, and U.S. Glass. Cambridge and McKee continued the production of custard glass into the Depression.

The ivory or creamy yellow custard color is achieved by adding uranium salts to the molten hot glass. The chemical content makes the glass glow when held under a black light. The higher the amount of uranium, the more luminous the color. Northwood's custard glass has the smallest amount of uranium, creating an ivory color; Heisey used more, creating a deep yellow color.

Custard glass was made in patterned tableware pieces. It also was made as souvenir items and novelty pieces. Souvenir pieces are marked with place names or hand–painted decorations, e.g., flowers. Patterns of custard glass often were highlighted in gold, enamel colors, and stains.

References: Gary E. Baker et al., *Wheeling Glass 1829–1939, Collection of the Oglebay Institute Glass Museum,* Oglebay Institute, 1994, distributed by Antique Publications; William Heacock, *Encyclopedia Of Victorian Colored Pattern Glass, Book IV: Custard Glass From A to Z,* Peacock Publications, 1980; William Heacock, James Measell and Berry Wiggins, *Harry Northwood: The Early Years 1881–1900,* Antique Publications, 1990.

Reproduction Alert: L. G. Wright Glass Co. has reproduced pieces in the Argonaut Shell and Grape and Cable patterns. It also introduced new patterns, such as Floral and Grape and Vintage Band. Moser reproduced toothpicks in Argonaut Shell, Chrysanthemum Sprig, and Inverted Fan & Feather.

Additional Listings: Pattern Glass.

Berry Bowl, master
Beaded Circle 185.00
Diamond with Peg 225.00
Ring Band 225.00
Berry Set, Chrysanthemum Sprig, sgd "Northwood" in script, 7 pcs 450.00
Butter Dish, cov
Argonaut Shell 260.00
Cherry and Scale 250.00

Intaglio, green and gold dec . . . 265.00
Louis XV 145.00
Winged Scroll 195.00
Celery Vase
Victoria, gold dec 195.00
Winged Scroll 325.00
Cologne Bottle, Northwood Grape, nutmeg stain, orig stopper, marked "N" 400.00

Creamer, Chrysanthemum Sprig, gold dec, 4½" h, $175.00.

Creamer
Chrysanthemum Sprig, sgd "Northwood" in script 100.00
Delaware, rose dec 75.00
Heart with Thumbprint 85.00
Jefferson Optic 125.00
Cruet
Geneva, undecorated 225.00
Intaglio, green dec 400.00
Goblet
Beaded Swag 50.00
Gothic Arches, nutmeg stain . . 56.00
Ice Cream Platter, Peacock & Urn, nutmeg stain, sgd "Northwood" 95.00
Jelly Compote, Inverted Fan and Feather 315.00
Lamp, Heart, green, No. 2 burner and chimney, 9¼" h 200.00
Mug, Punty Band 55.00
Nappy, Prayer Rug 50.00
Pitcher, water
Argonaut Shell, Northwood, gold trim, script sgd 425.00
Everglades 600.00
Inverted Fan and Feather 400.00
Maple Leaf 350.00

Plate, Grape and Cable, North-
wood, nutmeg stain, 7" d 25.00
Powder Jar, Ivorina Verde 65.00
Punch Cup, Grape and Cable ... 50.00
Rose Bowl, Grape and Gothic
Arches 75.00
Salt and Pepper Shakers, pr
Carnelian 450.00
Chrysanthemum Sprig, orig tops 150.00
Fluted Scrolls 125.00
Heart 155.00
Ribbed Drape 185.00
Sauce Dish
Beaded Circle 50.00
Cane Insert 30.00
Fan 40.00
Intaglio 35.00
Jefferson Optic 20.00
Peacock and Urn 40.00
Wild Bouquet 50.00
Spooner
Chrysanthemum Sprig, sgd
"Northwood" in script 100.00
Everglades 135.00
Intaglio 85.00
Sugar, cov
Argonaut Shell 165.00
Cherry and Scale 135.00
Chrysanthemum Sprig, sgd
"Northwood" in script 125.00
Geneva 85.00
Inverted Fan and Feather 185.00
Ribbed Grape 150.00
Toothpick
Argonaut Shell 275.00
Bees on Basket 48.00
Geneva 70.00
Punty Band 75.00
Ring Band 55.00
Vermont, green dec 135.00
Tumbler
Argonaut Shell 80.00
Cherry and Scale 45.00
Chrysanthemum Sprig, gold
flowers, gold, green, and pink
trim 50.00
Fan 50.00
Intaglio, blue dec 95.00
Louis XV 50.00
Northwood's Grape, nutmeg
stain 45.00
Vase, Diamond Peg, 8" h 110.00
Wine, Beaded Swag, enameled
adv 75.00

CUT GLASS, AMERICAN

History: Glass is cut by the process of grinding decoration into the glass by means of abrasive–carrying metal wheels or stone wheels. A very ancient craft, it was revived in 1600 by Bohemians and spread through Europe to Great Britain and to America.

American cut glass came of age at the Centennial Exposition in 1876 and the World Columbian Exposition in 1893. The American public recognized American cut glass to be exceptional in quality and work-manship. America's most significant output of this high–quality glass occurred from 1880 to 1917, a period now known as the "Brilliant Period."

About the 1890s some companies began adding an acid–etched "signature" to their glass. This signature may be the actual company name, its logo, or chosen symbol. Today, signed pieces can command a pre-mium over unsigned pieces since the sig-nature clearly establishes the origin.

However, caution should be exercised in regard to signature identification. Objects with forged signatures have been in exis-tence for some time. To check for authen-ticity, run your finger tip or finger nail lightly over the area with the signature. As a gen-eral rule, a genuine signature cannot be felt; a forged signature exhibits a raised surface.

Many companies never used the acid–etched signature on the glass and may or may not have affixed paper labels to the items originally. Dorflinger Glass and the Meriden Glass Co. made cut glass of the highest quality yet never acid–etched a sig-nature on the glass. Furthermore, cut glass made before the 1890s was not signed. Many of these wood–polished items, cut on blown blanks, were of excellent quality and often won awards at exhibitions.

Consequently, if collectors restrict them-selves to signed pieces only, many beautiful pieces of the highest quality glass and workmanship will be missed.

References: Bill and Louis Boggess, *Collecting American Brilliant Cut Glass, 1876–1916,* Schiffer Publishing, 1992; Bill and Louis Boggess, *Identifying American Brilliant Cut Glass, Revised,* Schiffer Pub-lishing, 1991; E. S. Farrar & J. S. Spillman, *The Complete Cut & Engraved Glass Of*

Corning, Crown Publishers (Corning Museum of Glass monograph), 1979; John Feller, *Dorflinger: America's Finest Glass, 1852–1921,* Antique Publications, 1988; J. Michael Pearson, *Encyclopedia Of American Cut & Engraved Glass,* Vol I to III, published by author, 1975; Albert C. Revi, *American Cut & Engraved Glass,* Schiffer Publishing, 1965; Martha Louise Swan, *American Cut and Engraved Glass: The Brilliant Period In Historic Perspective,* Wallace–Homestead, 1986, 1994 value update; H. Weiner & F. Lipkowitz, *Rarities In American Cut Glass,* Collectors House of Books, 1975.

Collectors' Club: American Cut Glass Association, 36 Crosstie Lane, Batesville, IN 47006.

Museums: The Corning Museum of Glass, Corning, NY; High Museum of Art, Atlanta, GA; Huntington Galleries, Huntington, WV; Lightner Museum, St. Augustine, FL; Toledo Museum of Art, Toledo, OH.

Ashtray, 5½" w, triangular, slanted cut 2" h sides, large hobstar and stars	165.00
Atomizer, 8" h, Harvard pattern, gold washed atomizer	120.00
Basket, 6" h, 8" w, Propeller pattern, Harvard, hobstars, and cane	895.00
Bell, 6¾" h, strawberry diamond and fan, pattern on knob at end of stem	550.00
Berry Set, Regis pattern, Libbey saber mark, price for eleven pc set	575.00
Beverage Set, 10¼" h ftd pitcher, six 4" h tumblers, Garland pattern, Pairpoint, price for seven pc set	1,000.00
Biscuit Jar, 5½" h, Persian pattern, silver rim, acanthus leaf bail, leaf emb lid	200.00
Bonbon, 8" d, 2" h, Broadway pattern, Huntly, minor flakes	130.00

Bowl

7" sq, Russian pattern, rayed center	600.00
7¾ x 11¼", oval, low, Brilliant Period	300.00
8" d, Gladys pattern, sgd "Hawkes", price for pr	450.00

8" d, 4" h, heavy cut, sgd "Libbey," Brilliant Period	200.00
8¾" d, prismatic motif sides, chain of hobstars rim, 32 point hobstar base	215.00

9" d

Deep cut intricate hobstars connected by vesicas, cane, and nailhead	285.00
Harvard bars, wheel cut border flowers, roughness on sawtooth rim	80.00
Hobstars and strawberry diamonds, shallow, Brilliant Period	100.00
9" d, 4¼" h, Harvard, hobstars and strawberry diamonds, Brilliant Period	300.00
9¼" d, deep miter cuts, shallow, Brilliant Period	110.00

10" d

Kohinoor pattern, blown out type blank, swirled pattern, sgd "Hawkes"	1,250.00
Waterford pattern, turned in rim, blue handles, Pairpoint	135.00
11½" d, 5½" h, hobstar with notched prism Brilliant Period design, repousse floral border, monogrammed	1,950.00
Box, cov, 8" d, hinged, round, Florence hobstar lid, miter cut sides	325.00
Bread Tray, 13" l, Holly and Snowflake pattern, Sinclaire	600.00
Bride's Basket, 9¼" d, 9" h, four hobstars, encircled by bars, vesicas of hobnails, diamond fields of cane, marked "Meriden" holder with four angels and bearded masks	320.00
Butter Dish, cov, 5" h, 8" d plate, hobstar chain, figured blank	325.00
Butter Pat, Cypress pattern, Laurel Cut Glass Co	35.00
Candelabra, 5½" h, double bowl, Hawkes, faint mark, price for pr	165.00
Candlesticks, pr, 6" h, rayed cut bottom, large teardrop in stem, Meriden, Brilliant Period	500.00
Carafe, 8" h, Wreath pattern, hobstars in vesicas surrounded by beading and flashed fans, notched and fluted neck, Laurel Cut Glass Co	90.00

Celery Dish
11" l, Brilliant Period design, minor edge flaking **125.00**
11½" l, 2" h, allover Brilliant Period pattern, sgd "Libbey" . . . **175.00**
Cheese Dish, cov, 6" h dome, 9" d, plate, cobalt blue cut to clear, bull's eye and panel, large miter splints on bottom of plate **200.00**
Cider Pitcher, 9½" h, allover Brilliant Period design with hobstars and notched prisms, sterling silver rim and spout **1,150.00**
Cologne Bottle, 7" h, bulbous, Cane pattern, long slim flute cut neck, pointed stopper **135.00**
Compote
6" d, intaglio florals, sgd "Tuthill" **215.00**
6" d, 7½" h, teardrop, notched prism stems, hobstars, fans, matched pr **550.00**
7" d, 4½" h, sgd "Clark" **140.00**
7" d, 7" h, hobstars and strawberry diamonds, notched pedestal, Brilliant Period **100.00**
7" d, 9" h, hobstars, fans, honeycomb band on teardrop stem **345.00**
8" d, 7" h, Monarch pattern, scalloped base, teardrop stem, Hoare **375.00**
Cordial, 4¾" h, 2" d, emerald green cut to clear, bull's eye, clear panel cut stems, rayed base, price for set of three **110.00**
Cracker Box, cov, 9 x 2¼ x 2½", allover cutting, hobstar, fan, crosshatching, cut rayed star in base, Brilliant Period **195.00**
Creamer and Sugar
2½" h and 4" h, sgd "Hawkes," Brilliant Period **165.00**
2¾" h and 3½" h, pinwheel design, Brilliant Period **200.00**
Cruet
5½" h, bell shaped, prism, Pitkin & Brooks, roughage **85.00**
6¾" h, ship's, Brilliant Period, chips **85.00**
7¼" h, Russian pattern, Brilliant Period, chips **75.00**
Decanter
7" h, 6½" d, Gladys pattern, handle, sgd "Hawkes," pattern cut stopper **795.00**

9½" h, Persian and Pillar pattern, repousse sterling silver cov, attributed to Dorflinger or Hawkes **1,300.00**
11" h, Gladys pattern, sgd "Hawkes," faceted stopper . . **495.00**
12½" h, Kimberly pattern, Libbey, double gooseneck, pattern cut stopper **895.00**
Dish, 9" d, Heart pattern, attributed to Strauss, Brilliant Period, rim roughage **300.00**
Dresser Box, 4½" d, 2¼" h, circular, hinged cov, wheel cut flowers, leafy stems **115.00**
Flower Center
6½" d, 7" h, allover Brilliant Period design, notched prism neck **450.00**
8" d, 8¼" h, Cosmos pattern, notched step cut neck, Brilliant Period **400.00**
8½" d, 3" h, deep cut flowers and leaves, Brilliant Period **110.00**
9" d, step cut neck, various cutting motifs **825.00**
Fruit Bowl, 8 x 11⅝", scalloped rim, Brilliant Period **325.00**
Glove Box, cov, 10½" l, Murrillo pattern, orig silverplated rim, Pairpoint **1,000.00**
Goblet, water
6" h, Rayed Button Russian pattern, teardrop stem, sgd "Hawkes," price for nine pc set **1,200.00**
6½" h, strawberry diamond and fans, double teardrop stems, polished, price for twelve pc set **850.00**
Humidor, cov, 4½" h, Brilliant Period cutting, sterling silver repousse mounting **200.00**
Ice Bucket
5¼ x 5¼", tub shape, hobstars and strawberry diamonds, Brilliant Period **150.00**
6" d, 6" h, hobstar and cross cut panels, tab handles **350.00**
Ice Cream Plate, 10" d, allover Brilliant cutting, floral panels of carnations, sgd "Sinclaire," some rim roughage **850.00**
Ice Cream Tray
7¾ x 10¾" l, Russian type pat-

tern with crossed fluted bands, Brilliant Period **325.00**

8½ x 13¾" l, cut daisies, Brilliant Period **225.00**

Jar, cov, 6" h, Holland pattern, hobstar lid, sgd "Hawkes" **300.00**

Lamp Shade, 5" d fitter ring, 4" h, mushroom shape, butterflies and florals, Pairpoint **200.00**

Loving Cup, 7" h, Brilliant Period zipper type cuttings, three notch cut handles, elaborate SS rim with emb grape design, sgd "Tiffany & Co" **1,500.00**

Mayonnaise Set, 6¼" d bowl, 7" d plate, Propeller pattern, Harvard, hobstars, and cane **525.00**

Milk Pitcher, 6" h, floral, hobstars, and cane **265.00**

Miniature Vase, 4" h, cherry blossoms, flared rim, sgd "Libbey" . **50.00**

Mustard Jar, cov, cane, buttons, and florals, cut knob finial **115.00**

Nappy, 7½" w, hobstars, feathered leaves, other cuttings, scalloped and serrated rim, double thumbprint handle **100.00**

Orange Bowl, 10" d, pinwheel, notched prism and hobstar in vesicas **175.00**

Paperweight, 3 x 2½", book shape, large cut diamond on front cut again into four small diamonds

with flowers, allover diamond point cutting on back **165.00**

Perfume Bottle, 7" h, oval cut column, hinged sterling sivler cov, polychrome portrait under glass **250.00**

Pitcher

7" h, Clifton pattern, 32 ray cut base **325.00**

15½" h, cylindrical, leaf, floral, and thumbprints motif **125.00**

Plate

6½" sq, buzz stars **85.00**

8½" d, allover chrysanthemum and scroll cutting **48.00**

Hindoo pattern, Hoare **115.00**

Pokal, 12" h, flutes and diamond point band, Waterford **195.00**

Powder Jar, cov, 5½" h, 7½" d, 32 point expanding star on cov, Brilliant cut base, sgd "Hawkes," Brilliant Period **875.00**

Punch Bowl and Base, 9¾" d, 10¾" h, two pc, Harvard pattern **900.00**

Punch Cup, hobstars, pedestal, handle **80.00**

Relish, 6" d, triform, cane bar, wheel cut flowers **45.00**

Rose Bowl, 7" d, Clear Button Russian pattern **525.00**

Salad Bowl, 12½" d, 4¾" h, alternating hobstar and expanding stars Brilliant Period pattern, elaborate repousse sterling silver border in floral design, sgd "Jacobi & Jenkins Makers, Baltimore, Sterling" **1,650.00**

Saltshaker, 4" h, Garland pattern, sterling silver lid **60.00**

Sherbet, allover Brilliant Period cutting, sgd "Eggington" **40.00**

Tankard Pitcher

10" h, zipper handle, repousse sterling silver rim, dated "1896," Brilliant Period **650.00**

11½" h, combination pinwheel, fan, crosshatch, and zipper, thumbprint handle, 32 rayed base **275.00**

12½" h, allover Brilliant Period cutting with sunflower design, notched cut handle **500.00**

13¼" h, floral cutting, crystal engraving, sterling silver top, sgd "Hawkes" **1,000.00**

Serving Plate, Kensington pattern, Hawkes, sgd, 13" d, $715.00. Photo courtesy of Skinner, Inc.

Tray, 12" l, 8" w, oval, Anita, sgd "Libbey" in circle **385.00**

Tumbler, 3½" h, Wreath pattern, hobstars in vesicas surrounded by beading and flashed fans, Laurel Cut Glass Co, price for set of six **120.00**

Vase

10¼" h, rim pulled into three large scallops, allover floral and geometric cut, ball teardrop stem, notched star base, sgd "Libbey" **235.00**

11" h

Cane cut and notched prism Brilliant Period design, monogrammed, elaborate silver repousse rim, sgd "Sterling" **800.00**

Intaglio cut, bulbous, sgd "Hawkes" **145.00**

14" h, corset form, hobstars, flashed fan, bull's eye **400.00**

14¾" h, green shading to clear, intaglio cut iris, sprays of cosmos, leaves, cut and scalloped rim **575.00**

19" h, Brilliant Period and floral rock crystal, sterling silver rim **1,500.00**

Whiskey Shot Glass, Russian pattern **75.00**

Wine, 5" h, Brazilian pattern, teardrop stem, fully cut foot, Hawkes **330.00**

CUT VELVET

History: Several glass manufacturers made cut velvet during the late Victorian era, c1870–1900. An outer layer of pastel color was applied over a white casing. The piece then was molded or cut in a ribbed or diamond shape in high relief, exposing portions of the casing. The finish had a satin velvety feel, hence the name "cut velvet."

Celery Vase, 6½" h, deep blue over white, DQ, box pleated top **725.00**

Creamer, 5¼" h, raised ribbed pattern, butterscotch over white . . **165.00**

Pitcher

8½" h, 6½" w, deep rose shading to pale rose over white, applied crystal reeded shell handle, sq top, glossy finish **1,100.00**

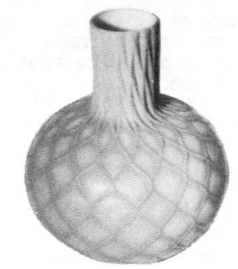

Vase, bottle neck, blue, 6" h, $245.00.

9" h, 7" w, deep rose over white, glossy, applied clear reeded handle **1,200.00**

Rose Bowl, 3½" d, 4½" h, rose over white, DQ, three crimp top **175.00**

Vase

6½" h, 4½" w, deep pink, yellow, and blue rainbow satin over white, Vertical Pinwheel Swirl pattern, sq top, bulbous base **750.00**

9" h, deeply ruffled, deep orange, DQ **675.00**

13½" h, 6" w at base, double gourd, long pumpkin stem neck, pale gold over white, DQ **650.00**

CZECHOSLOVAKIAN ITEMS

History: Objects marked "Made in Czechoslovakia" were produced after 1918 when the country claimed its independence from the Austro–Hungarian Empire. The people became more cosmopolitan, liberated, and expanded their scope of life. Their porcelains, pottery, and glassware reflect many influences.

A specific manufacturer's mark may be identified as being much earlier than 1918, but this only indicates the factory existed in the Bohemian or Austro–Hungarian Empire period.

References: Dale and Diane Barta and Helen M. Rose, *Czechoslovakian Glass & Collectibles,* Collector Books, 1992; Ruth A. Forsythe, *Made in Czechoslovakia,* Richardson Printing Corp., 1982; Ruth A. Forsythe, *Made in Czechoslovakia, Book 2,* Antique Publications, 1993; Jacquelyne Y. Jones–North, *Czechoslovakian Perfume Bottles and Boudoir Accessories,* Antique Publications, 1990.

Basket, 5" h, pottery, brown, Art Deco panels, colored balls **48.00**
Bowl, pottery, flowing black and green **145.00**
Candlestick, 8½" h, glass, multicolored, cased, sgd **80.00**
Console Bowl, glass, ftd, black, orange trim, sgd **100.00**
Jardiniere, 5" d, 4¼" h, pottery, cattails on side, figural kingfisher perched on edge **115.00**
Perfume Bottle, glass, cut
Blue, sq filigree stopper set with blue stones **225.00**
Crystal, cut feather stopper ... **130.00**

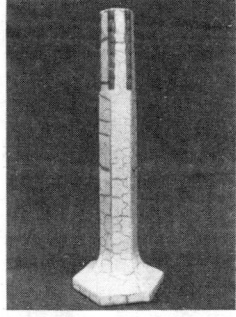

Vase, green veining on yellow ground, orange stripes at neck, c1930, 12" h, $185.00.

Vase
6½" h, glass, yellow, black handles, pink flower, gold bow knot trim **30.00**
7" h, glass, bright orange, black threading **75.00**
7½" h, glass, multicolored, cased, blue **70.00**
8" h, glass
Multicolored, predominately blue and orange, cased, sgd **80.00**
White, amber handles **35.00**

Yellow, blue oil spot dec, sgd **1,375.00**
Yellow, cased, black treading **40.00**
8¼"h, pottery, orange and beige, sgd **90.00**

DAVENPORT

History: John Davenport opened a pottery in Longport, Staffordshire, England in 1793. His ware was of high quality, light weight, and cream colored with a beautiful velvety texture.

The firm made soft–paste (Old Blue), luster trimmed ware, and pink luster with black transfer. There have been pieces of Gaudy Dutch and Spatterware found with the Davenport mark. Later, Davenport became a leading maker of ironstone and early flow blue. His famous "Cyprus" pattern in mulberry became very popular. His heirs continued the business until the factory closed in 1886.

Reference: Susan and Al Bagdade, *Warman's English & Continental Pottery & Porcelain, 2nd Edition,* Wallace–Homestead, 1991.

Bowl, cov, 6¾" d bowl, 8¾" d underplate, pink luster, allover

Tankard, blue transfer, figures in landscape, c1835, 6½" h, $200.00.

black transfer dec rural landscape scene, imp and printed marks, c1825, int. wear, hairlines **290.00**

Children's Dinner Service

Blue and red enamel, center sprigs, wide banded borders, 3⅜" d raised circular dish, two oval deep dishes, oval 3¼" l fruit cooler, eight 3" d plates, twelve each 3⅝" d and 4¼" d plates, four oval platters, two 4" l cov sauce tureens with underdishes, two oval 3⅛" serving dishes, six 4⅛" d soup plates, 5" l cov soup tureen, two 5" l cov vegetable dishes, chips, hairlines **920.00**

Green transfer printed landscape scenes, two 3¼ x 4¼" oval deep dishes, two 3" l gravy boats, four 3" d plates, five 3¼" d plates, ten 3¾" d plates, five oval platters, six 3⅝" d soup plates, 4½" l soup tureen, cov, and underdish, two 4¾" cov vegetable dishes, small chips, some imp marks, c1856 . . . . **1,265.00**

DECOYS

History: Carved wooden decoys, used to lure ducks and geese to the hunter, have become widely recognized as an indigenous American folk art form in the past several years.

Many decoys are from the 1880–1930 period when commercial gunners commonly hunted using rigs of several hundred decoys. Many fine carvers also worked through the 1930s and 1940s.

The value of a decoy is based on several factors: (1) fame of the carver, (2) quality of the carving, (3) species of wild fowl—the most desirable are herons, swans, mergansers, and shorebirds, and (4) condition of the original paint (o.p.).

The inexperienced collector should be aware of several facts. The age of a decoy, per se, is usually of no importance in determining value. Since very few decoys were ever signed, it will be quite difficult to attribute most decoys to known carvers.

Anyone who has not examined a known carver's work will be hard pressed to determine if the paint on one of his decoys is indeed original.

Repainting severely decreases a decoy's value. In addition, there are many fakes and reproductions on the market and even experienced collectors are occasionally fooled.

Decoys listed below are of average wear unless otherwise noted.

References: Joe Engers (general editor), *The Great Book of Wildfowl Decoys,* Thunder Bay Press, 1990; Henry A. Fleckenstein, Jr., *American Factory Decoys,* Schiffer Publishing, 1981; Ronald J. Fritz, *Michigan's Master Carver Oscar W. Peterson, 1887–1951,* Aardvark Publications, 1988; Bob and Sharon Huxford, *Collector's Guide To Decoys, Volume II,* Collector Books, 1992; Gene and Linda Kangas, *Decoys,* Collector Books, 1992; Linda and Gene Kangas, *Collector's Guide To Decoys,* Wallace–Homestead, 1992; Art, Brad and Scott Kimball, *The Fish Decoy, Vol. III,* Aardvark Publications, 1993; Carl F. Luckey, *Collecting Antique Bird Decoys and Duck Calls: An Identification & Value Guide, Second Edition,* Books Americana, 1992.

Periodicals: *Decoy Geographer,* 4532 Old Leeds Rd., Birmingham, AL 21673; *Decoy Hunter Magazine,* 901 North 9th, Clinton, IN 47842; *Decoy Magazine,* PO Box 277, Burtonsville, MD 20866; *Decoy World,* RFD 1, Box 5, Trappe, MD 21673; *North American Decoys,* PO Box 246, Spanish Fork, UT 84660; *Sporting Collector's Monthly,* RW Publishing, PO Box 305, Camden, DE 19934; *Wildfowl Art,* Ward Foundation, 909 South Schumaker Dr., Salisbury, MD 21801; *Wildfowl Carving & Collecting,* PO Box 1831, Harrisburg, PA 17105.

Collectors' Clubs: Minnesota Decoy Collectors Assoc., PO Box 130084, St. Paul, MN 55113; New England Decoy Collectors Assoc., 2320 Main St., West Barnstable, MA 02668; Ohio Decoy Collectors & Carvers Assoc., PO Box 499, Richfield, OH 44286.

Museums: Harve de Grace Decoy Museum, Harve de Grace, MD; Museum at Stony Brook, Stony Brook, NY; Peabody

Museum of Salem, Salem, MA; Refuge Waterfowl Museum, Chincoteague, VA; Shelburne Museum, Inc., Shelburne, VT; Ward Museum of Wildfowl Art, Salisbury, MD.

Shorebird, Bl. Bellied Plover, Cape May, NJ, $325.00.

Black–Breasted Plover
Burr, Elisha, carved wing outline and wishbone tail, black glass eyes, orig paint **1,700.00**
Dilley, John, Long Island, painted feather detail **3,750.00**
Black Duck
Crowell, A Elmer, slightly turned head, orig paint **550.00**
Harris, Ken, mated pair, Woodville, NY, glass eyes, orig paint, one sgd **350.00**
Shourds, Harry, Tuckertown, NJ, hollow carved, repainted repaired neck **250.00**
Truax, Rhoades, hollow carved, orig paint, branded "H W Cain" on back **475.00**
Bluebill Drake
Fulcher, Mitchell, Eastern Shore, VA, old repaint, carved initials **500.00**
Hudson, Ira, orig paint **1,500.00**
Schmidt, Ben, Detroit, 14¾" l, carved detail, glass eyes **250.00**
Bluebill Hen
Hayes Decoy Factory, orig paint, age split **130.00**

Schmidt, Frank, Detroit, 15" l, glass eyes, repainted and repair **300.00**
Shourds, Harry, hollow carved, old paint, restored bill **350.00**
Blue–Breasted Plover, unknown maker, Long Island, carved wings, split tail, old paint **300.00**
Blue–Wing Teal Drake, attributed to John Blair, solid body, branded "C H G C," worn mostly to natural wood **1,600.00**
Brant
Cobb, Nathan, VA, hollow carved, slightly turned and cocked down head, "V" detail, c1860 . . . .**5,500.00**
Maxwell, Roy, hollow carved, orig paint **1,600.00**
Parker, Lloyd, hollow carved, old repaint **800.00**
Bufflehead Drake, unknown maker, 10½" l, carved and painted **110.00**
Canada Goose
Hudson, Ira, Chincoteaque, VA, missing weight, age split **1,700.00**
Paul, Joe, Manahawkin, NJ, c1900, hollow carved, repainted **350.00**
Unknown Maker, 25" l, folk art, carved and painted **600.00**
Ward Brothers, Crisfield, MD, c1930, painted **1,550.00**
Canvasback Drake
Gibson, Paul, MD, sgd and dated 1952, paint wear, age cracks **125.00**
McGaw, Bob, MD, stripped to natural wood, black paint traces on breast and tail, branded "AJC" **75.00**
Curlew
Crowell, A Elmer, Cape Cod, MA, carved feathers, wire legs, orig paint, oval brand on bottom, restored wing tips . . .**9,000.00**
McNair, carved, raised wing tips, sgd, age split **800.00**
Dowitcher, William Bowman, Long Island, carved wings, raised wing tips, split tail, slightly cocked head, muscled detail, orig paint, replaced bill **7,500.00**

Eider Drake, unknown maker, ME sway back style, carved bill, inlet neck, patina, white worn paint, chip of wood missing on neck . **1,100.00**

Eider Hen, unknown maker, ME carved bill, inlet neck, orig paint, minor wear **900.00**

Goldeneye Drake

Glover, Tom, paperweight glass eyes, orig paint **150.00**

Shourds, Harry, hollow carved, orig paint **500.00**

Herring Gull, unknown maker, carved wings, detailed feather carving back and tail area, c1900 .... **2,400.00**

Kingfisher, Thomas Carlock, carved feathers **250.00**

Mallard Duck

Drake, Ira Hudson, flying, carved, scratch feather painting **4,600.00**

Hen, unknown maker, premiere grade, swirl feather painting, branded "Fuller" on bottom, orig paint, minor wear and age splits **850.00**

Merganser, unknown maker, New England, late 19th C, 6½" h, 17½" l, groove carved bill, glass eyes, tapered body, orig weathered paint **990.00**

Pintail Drake

Blair, John, hollow carved, repainted **2,600.00**

Gibian, William C, VA, preening, card on bottom incised "This is my best pintail to date!/ Praise the Lord!" and signature **550.00**

Shourds, Harry, hollow carved, repainted **1,000.00**

Pintail Hen

Crowell, A Elmer, East Harwich, MA, early 20th C, drake, 7½" h, 18" l, carved and painted, rect stamp **1,760.00**

Mason Factory, standard grade, mated pair, glass eyes, orig paint **600.00**

Plover

Morton, W S, Quincy, MA, 1809–71, carved wing tips, tack eyes, orig paint, age split ... **1,500.00**

Unknown Maker, South Shore, MA, last half 19th C, tack eyes **900.00**

Red–Breasted Merganser, Daniel Horn, old paint, age split **1,650.00**

Redhead Drake, Mitchell Fulcher, repaired neck, old paint, carved initials **500.00**

Robin Snipe, unknown maker, carved, worn finish, tail damage, unidentifiable name **475.00**

Ruddy Turnstone, John Horn, orig paint **800.00**

Snowy Egret, H Conklin, branded on bottom **400.00**

Swan

Mitchell, Madison, MD, hollow carved, unweighted **1,300.00**

Unknown Maker, 22" l, carved and painted **450.00**

Widgeon Hen, attributed to John Blair, hollow carved, branded "W P Patton" on bottom, orig paint **4,500.00**

Yellowlegs

Burr, Elisha, carved wings and tail feathers, old paint **725.00**

Crowell, A Elmer, 11" h, carved wings and tail **3,500.00**

DEDHAM POTTERY

History: Alexander W. Robertson established the Chelsea Pottery in Chelsea, Massachusetts, in 1860. In 1872 it was known as the Chelsea Keramic Art Works.

In 1895 the pottery moved to Dedham, and the name was changed to Dedham Pottery. Their principal product was gray crackleware dinnerware with a blue decoration, the rabbit pattern being the most popular. The factory closed in 1943.

The following marks help determine the approximate age of items: (1) Chelsea Keramic Art Works, "Robertson" impressed, 1876–1889; (2) C.P.U.S. impressed in a cloverleaf, 1891–1895; (3) Foreshortened rabbit, 1895–1896; (4) Conventional rabbit with "Dedham Pottery" stamped in blue, 1897; (5) Rabbit mark with "Registered," 1929–1943.

References: Lloyd E. Hawes, *The Dedham Pottery And The Earlier Robertson's Chelsea Potteries,* Dedham Historical Society, 1968; Dana G. Morykan and Harry L. Rinker, *Warman's Country Antiques & Collectibles, Second Edition,* Wallace–Homestead, 1994.

Periodical: *The Dedham Pottery Collectors Society Newsletter,* 248 Highland St., Dedham, MA 02026.

Reproduction Alert: Several rabbit pattern pieces have been reproduced.

Bowl, Rabbit pattern, inscribed mark, dated 1898, 9″ d, 3½″ h, $850.00.

Ashtray, 4″ d, Elephant pattern, stamped mark 350.00
Bowl
  4½″ d
    Grape pattern, blue mark . . . 125.00
    Turtle pattern 330.00
  12″ d, Rabbit pattern, double blue stamp and incised "Dedham Pottery" mark 460.00
Celery Tray, 9½″ l, Duck pattern, registered blue stamp and double imp rabbit mark 135.00
Cereal Dish, 5¾″ d, Azalea pattern, blue mark 125.00
Coaster, 4″ d, Rabbit pattern, blue stamp mark 225.00
Consomme Cup, Rabbit pattern, one with blue mark, price for pair 125.00
Creamer, 2¾″ h, Rabbit pattern, No. 13, blue stamp mark 275.00

Creamer and Sugar, Rabbit pattern, blue stamp 250.00
Dinner Service, Rabbit pattern, 22 pcs, four 10″ d plates, two 8″ d plates, six 6″ d plates, two cups, three saucers, two bowls, two fruit cups, and 9½″ l bacon rasher, minor chips 775.00
Dish, cov, 11″ d, Rabbit pattern, blue stamped mark and "B" . . . 500.00
Jar, cov, 5″ h, Elephant pattern, Crackleware, blue, ink mark . . . 475.00
Mug, 4¾″ h, Rabbit pattern, tankard form, incised mark, small chip on handle 365.00
Pitcher, 4⅞″ h, Morning and Night pattern, Crackleware, rooster and owl dec, two blue stamped logos, c1920 . . . . 500.00
Plate
  6″ d, Turtle pattern, double image border 330.00
  8¼″ d, Landscape pattern, stylized central scene, corn crib house border, glaze slips, minimal crackle 425.00
  8½″ d, set of 3, Rabbit pattern, blue stamp, imp rabbit mark, sgd "Maud Davenport" 345.00
  10″ d
    Dolphin and Mask pattern, "CPUS" clover mark 2,425.00
    Poppy pattern 610.00
    Turtle pattern, blue stamp and imp rabbit mark 810.00
Platter, 9½″ l, 6¼″ w, Rabbit pattern, blue mark 250.00
Rice Bowl, 3⅛″ d, Chick pattern, blue stamp 1,265.00
Serving Platter, 12″ d, Elephant pattern, blue 880.00
Tea Set, Rabbit pattern, 12 pcs, teapot, sugar, creamer, milk pitcher, four cups and saucers, minor chips, milk pitcher repaired at spout, price for 12 piece set 525.00
Vase
  5⅝″ h, experimental, white stoneware, mottled green glaze with blue traces, Hugh Robertson, imp "Dedham Pottery HCR" 330.00
  8½″ h, ovoid, glossy mottled

glaze, brown earth tones, green, and blue, imp "Dedham Pottery/BW" **825.00**
10" h, experimental, Dragon's Blood, red, green, and blue striations, imp "Dedham Pottery/BW/R," minor glaze chip **1,775.00**

DELFTWARE

History: Delftware is pottery of a soft red clay body with tin enamel glaze. The white, dense, opaque color came from adding tin ash to lead glaze. The first examples had blue designs on a white ground. Polychrome examples followed.

The name originally applied to pottery made in the region around Delft, Holland, beginning in the 16th century and ending in the late 18th century. Tin came from the Cornish mines in England. By the 17th and 18th centuries, English potters in London, Bristol, and Liverpool were copying the glaze and designs. Some designs unique to English potters also developed.

In Germany and France the ware is known as Faience and in Italy as Majolica.

Reference: Susan and Al Bagdade, *Warman's English & Continental Pottery & Porcelain, Second Edition,* Wallace–Homestead, 1991.

Reproduction Alert: Much souvenir Delft–type material has been produced in the late 19th and 20th centuries to appeal to the foreign traveler. Don't confuse these modern pieces with the older examples.

Bottle
9⅝" h, blue and white, floral landscape with fence, Irish, c1760, rim chip and repairs, glaze wear **230.00**
10¼" h, blue and white, floral dec, Liverpool, England, c1760, glaze wear to rim **470.00**
Bowl, 9" d, polychrome floral dec, Fazackerly, England, c1760, rim repairs **260.00**
Charger
13" d, blue and white Chinese fisherman in landscape, English, c1740, rim chips and wear **375.00**

Pitcher, Art Nouveau style brown leaf, tan ground, Dutch, 3⅜" h, 6" d, $375.00.

13¾" h, blue and white, central dragon figure, leafy branches, floral and trellis border, illegible marks, Dutch, early 18th C, rim wear and chips **635.00**
Deep Dish
12¼" d, blue and white, allover berry and floral dec, Dutch, c1770, rim glaze wear **490.00**
13⅞" d, blue dec, yellow and black accents, central portrait of Prince Wm of Orange, wide lobed and scalloped border with fruit and flowers garland, Dutch, late 17th C, rim chips .**1,955.00**
Dish
10⅛" d, blue dec landscape of houses by river, Chinese fishermen and boatmen, white floral relief border, Bianco Sopra Bianco, Bristol, England, c1760, glaze wear to rim **260.00**
11" d, blue and white central floral landscape, floral and berry border, Irish, c1760, glaze wear to rim **260.00**
11¾" d, blue and white, central floral design, scalloped line and scrolled leafy border, Dutch, c1750, rim glaze wear **375.00**
12½" d, polychrome, central floral baskets surrounded by flying insects, fruits and flowers border, Dutch, mid 18th C, rim chips, price for pr **1,150.00**
13½" d, manganese "ice," blue

dec Chinese house under weeping tree, three border reserves, Bristol, c1760, rim glaze wear 635.00

Flower Brick, 5" l, blue and white, floral panels, English, 1750, chips, rim glaze 865.00

Plate

7½" d, polychrome dec, floral landscapes with birds, Bristol, England, mid 18th C, rim chips and glaze wear, price for pr .. 290.00

8⅝" d, blue and white, central "FL" monogram, crown above, crossed branches, paneled lattice border, Dutch, c1740, rim chip, glaze wear 345.00

8¾" d

Blue and white, coastal landscape with houses, Bristol, mid 18th C, rim chips and glaze wear 150.00

Polychrome, Oriental landscapes with birds and wild animals, motif borders, Dutch, mid 18th C, rim glaze wear, price for pr 575.00

8⅞" d

Blue and white, scalloped edge, Oriental coastal landscape scene, floral border, Irish, mid 18th C, rim glaze wear 200.00

Polychrome fence and floral

dec, Fazackerly, Liverpool, England, c1760, rim chips and wear, price for pr 375.00

Scalloped rims, yellow, blue, and manganese dec Oriental figural scenes, Bianco Sopra Bianco, Bristol, England, c1760, rim chips and wear, price for pr 435.00

9" d

Blue and white, verse on front and back sides, floral border, Dutch, c1760, rim chips and glaze wear 375.00

Blue dec, central pillow–form cartouche of flowers, powder manganese border, English, mid 18th C 335.00

Polychrome, floral and insect borders, central and coastal landscape with houses, Dutch, c1760, rim chips and glaze wear 215.00

9⅛" d, floral, Bristol, England, c1760, rim chips 275.00

Tankard, 4¾" h, mottled blue ground, green, yellow, and manganese, dog and houses dec, hinged pewter lid, Continental, 19th C, damaged 230.00

Vase, 10" h, cov, blue and white, floral dec, mid 18th C, chips, glaze wear 325.00

DEPRESSION GLASS

History: Depression glass is a glassware made during the period of 1920–40. It was an inexpensive machine–made glass, produced by several companies in various patterns and colors. The number of pieces within a pattern also varied.

Depression glass was sold through variety stores, given as premiums, or packaged with certain products. Movie houses gave it away from 1935 until well into the 1940s.

Like pattern glass, knowing the proper name of a pattern is the key to collecting. Collectors should be prepared to do research.

References: Gene Florence, *Collectible Glassware from the 40's, 50's, 60's: An Illustrated Value Guide, Second Edition,* Collector Books, 1994; Gene Florence, *The Collector's Encyclopedia of Depression Glass, Eleventh Edition,* Collector Books, 1994; Gene Florence, *Elegant Glassware of the Depression Era, Sixth Edition,* Collector Books, 1994; Gene Florence, *Very Rare Glassware of the Depression Era,* First Series (1988, 1991 value update), Second Series (1991), Third Series (1993), Collector Books; Carl F. Luckey and Mary Burris, *An Identification & Value Guide to Depression Era Glassware, Third Edition,* Books Americana, 1994; Naomi L. Over, *Ruby Glass of the 20th Century,* Antique Publications, 1990, 1993–94 value update; Hazel Marie Weatherman, *1984 Supplement*

& Price Trends for Colored Glassware Of The Depression Era, Book 1, published by author, 1984; Hazel Marie Weatherman, Colored Glassware Of The Depression Era, Book 2, published by author, 1974, available in reprint.

Periodical: *The Daze,* 10271 State Rd., Box 57, Otisville, MI 48463.

Videotape: *Living Glass: Popular Patterns of the Depression Era,* Ro Cliff Communications, 2 vols., 1993.

Collectors' Clubs: National Depression Glass Assoc., Inc., PO Box 69843, Odessa, TX 79769; 20–30–40 Society, Inc., PO Box 856, LaGrange, IL 60525.

Reproduction Alert: Send a self–addressed stamped business envelope to *The Daze* and request a copy of their glass reproduction list. It is one of the best bargains in the antiques business.

Additional Listings: See *Warman's Americana & Collectibles* for more examples.

AMERICAN SWEETHEART, MacBeth–Evans Glass Co, 1930–36. Made in blue, cremax, monax, pink, red, and smoke.

	Blue	Monax	Pink	Smoke
Bowl				
3¾" d, berry.........	—	—	30.00	—
6" d, cereal..........	—	14.00	12.00	35.00
11" l, oval, vegetable..	—	65.00	50.00	—
Cake Plate, 12" d	165.00	15.00	20.00	85.00
Creamer, ftd..........	900.00	10.00	12.00	75.00
Cup and Saucer	120.00	14.50	16.00	80.00
Plate				
8" d, salad	65.00	9.00	15.00	25.00
9¾" d, dinner........	165.00	20.00	35.00	65.00
Platter, 13" l, oval	—	50.00	40.00	150.00
Salt and Pepper Shakers, pr..............	—	310.00	375.00	—
Sherbet, 4¼" d, ftd	—	18.00	15.00	65.00
Sugar, open, ftd........	90.00	12.00	15.00	75.00
Tid-bit, 2 tier	225.00	50.00	55.00	—

BLOCK OPTIC, Hocking Glass Co, 1929–33. Made in blue, crystal, green, pink, and yellow.

	Green	Pink	Yellow
Bowl			
5¼" d, cereal.................	10.00	6.00	—
7" d, salad	20.00	—	—
8¼" d, berry.................	14.00	—	—
Butter Dish, cov.................	45.00	—	—
Candy Jar, cov, 2¼" h	50.00	45.00	55.00
Creamer.....................	14.00	12.00	10.00
Cup and Saucer	12.00	10.00	12.00
Goblet, 4½" h	30.00	28.00	—
Ice Bucket	35.00	40.00	—
Mug	35.00	—	—
Pitcher, 8½" h, 54 oz	30.00	27.50	—

	Green	Pink	Yellow
Plate			
6″ d, sherbet	3.00	3.00	3.00
8″ d, luncheon	5.00	5.50	4.75
9″ d, dinner	20.00	30.00	32.00
9″ d, grill.	12.00	18.00	35.00
Salt and Pepper Shakers, pr, ftd . . .	35.00	65.00	65.00
Sandwich Tray, center handle	60.00	45.00	—
Sherbet, 3¼″ d	6.50	7.50	9.00
Tumbler, 9 oz, ftd	16.00	14.00	20.00
Tumble–Up	60.00	—	—
Whiskey, 2¼″ h, 2 oz	25.00	25.00	—

CHERRYBERRY, US Glass Co, early 1930s. Made in crystal, green, and pink, limited iridized production.

	Crystal	Green	Pink
Berry Bowl			
4″ d.	6.50	8.50	8.50
7½″ d	18.00	20.00	20.00
Bowl			
6¼″ d, 2″ h.	37.50	50.00	50.00
6½″ d	16.00	18.00	20.00
Butter Dish, cov	145.00	150.00	150.00
Compote, 5¾″ d	17.50	25.00	25.00
Creamer, 4⅝″ h.	15.00	35.00	35.00
Olive Dish, 5″ l, handle.	10.00	15.00	15.00
Pickle Dish, 8¼″ l, oval.	9.00	15.00	15.00
Pitcher, 7¾″ h	150.00	150.00	150.00
Plate			
6″ d, sherbet	6.00	9.00	9.00
7½″ d, salad.	8.00	15.00	15.00
Sherbet	7.50	10.00	10.00

Left: Dogwood, tumbler, green, 10 oz, 4″ h, $75.00. Center: Queen Mary, tumbler, pink, 9 oz, 4″ h, $12.00. Right: Royal Lace, juice tumbler, cobalt blue, 5 oz, 3½″ h, $28.00.

	Crystal	Green	Pink
Sugar, large....................	15.00	17.50	17.50
Tumbler, 3⅝" h	17.50	30.00	30.00

DOGWOOD, Apple Blossom and Wild Rose, MacBeth–Evans, 1929–32. Made in cremax, crystal, green, monax, pink, and yellow.

	Cremax	Green	Monax	Pink	Yellow
Berry Bowl, 8½" d	36.00	95.00	50.00	36.00	—
Bowl					
5½" d	5.00	25.00	5.00	25.00	55.00
10¼" d	70 00	180.00	70.00	300.00	—
Cake Plate, 13" d	165.00	85.00	160.00	90.00	—
Creamer, 2½" h, thin....	—	45.00	—	16.00	—
Cup and Saucer	55.00	45.00	55.00	25.00	—
Pitcher, 8" h, 80 oz	—	475.00	—	160.00	—
Plate					
6" d, bread and butter .	21.00	9.00	21.00	8.00	—
8" d, luncheon	—	8.00	—	7.50	55.00
9¼" d, dinner	—	—	—	30.00	—
10½" d, grill	—	20.00	—	20.00	—
Sherbet..............	—	90.00	—	35.00	—
Sugar, 2½" h, thin	—	45.00	—	18.00	—
Tumbler, 4" h, 10 oz, dec	—	75.00	—	35.00	—

ENGLISH HOBNAIL, Westmoreland Glass Co, 1920s–40s. Made in amber, cobalt blue, crystal, green, ice blue, pink, red, turquoise. Production was limited in cobalt blue and red. Colors vary with two distinct shades of pink, three greens.

	Amber	Crystal	Green	Ice Blue	Pink
Ashtray, 4½" d	7.00	7.00	22.50	21.00	22.50
Bonbon, 6½" d	12.50	12.00	25.00	35.00	25.00
Bowl					
6" d, crimped	12.50	12.00	16.00	—	16.00
7" d	13.00	12.50	20.00	—	18.00
8" d, ftd...........	25.00	25.00	45.00	—	45.00
10" d, flared	27.50	27.50	37.50	—	40.00
11" d, rolled edge	27.50	27.50	37.50	75.00	37.50
Candlestick, 3½" d	9.00	8.00	17.50	30.00	17.50
Candy Dish, cov	24.00	22.50	37.50	75.00	40.00
Cigarette Box, cov......	17.50	17.50	30.00	45.00	30.00
Cocktail..............	9.00	8.00	20.00	35.00	20.00
Compote, 5" d, round, ftd	12.00	12.00	25.00	—	25.00
Console Bowl, 12" d	27.50	27.50	37.50	—	37.50
Creamer, hexagonal, ftd .	8.50	9.00	24.00	45.00	25.00
Cup and Saucer	8.00	8.00	24.00	25.00	24.00
Demitasse Cup and					
Saucer	50.00	50.00	60.00	—	65.00

	Amber	Crystal	Green	Ice Blue	Pink
Finger Bowl, 4½" d	9.00	10.00	15.00	—	15.00
Goblet, 8 oz, ftd	10.00	12.00	30.00	48.00	30.00
Ice Tub, 5½" d	35.00	35.00	65.00	100.00	65.00
Lamp, 6¼" h	30.00	28.00	50.00	—	50.00
Marmalade, cov	15.00	15.00	35.00	55.00	35.00
Nappy					
5" d, round	9.50	9.00	15.00	35.00	15.00
6" d, sq	10.00	10.00	17.50	—	17.50
7" d, round	13.50	13.00	20.00	—	20.00
8" d, cupped	20.00	20.00	30.00	—	28.00
Oyster Cocktail	9.00	9.00	17.50	—	17.50
Pitcher, 32 oz, straight					
sides	50.00	50.00	150.00	—	150.00
Plate					
5½" d, sherbet	4.50	4.50	8.00	—	8.50
6½" d, bread and					
butter	6.00	6.00	10.00	—	10.00
8½" d, luncheon	8.00	8.00	12.00	25.00	12.00
10" d, dinner	12.50	12.50	12.50	65.00	12.50
Puff Box, cov, 6" d	17.50	17.50	25.00	75.00	25.00
Rose Bowl, 4" d	17.50	17.50	45.00	—	45.00
Salt and Pepper Shakers,					
pr, ftd	18.00	20.00	75.00	—	75.00
Sherbet, sq, ftd	9.00	9.00	15.00	35.00	15.00
Sugar, hexagonal, ftd . . .	9.00	8.50	24.00	48.00	20.00
Sweetmeat, 8" h, ball					
stem	20.00	20.00	55.00	—	55.00
Tidbit, 2 tier	22.50	22.50	45.00	65.00	45.00
Toilet Bottle, 5 oz	17.50	17.50	22.50	45.00	24.00
Tumbler, 8 oz	10.00	10.00	20.00	—	20.00
Vase, 8½" d, flared	35.00	35.00	115.00	200.00	115.00

FLORENTINE #1, Old Florentine and Poppy No. 1, Hazel Atlas Glass Co, 1932–35. Made in cobalt blue, crystal, green, pink, and yellow. Salt and pepper shakers have been reproduced.

	Cobalt Blue	Crystal	Green	Pink	Yellow
Ashtray, 5½" d	—	22.00	22.00	26.00	26.00
Berry Bowl					
5" d	15.00	11.00	11.00	12.00	14.50
8½" d	—	20.00	21.00	26.00	26.00
Bowl, 6" d	—	21.00	21.00	20.00	22.00
Butter Dish, cov	—	120.00	120.00	150.00	155.00
Coaster, 3¾" d	—	16.00	16.50	23.00	18.00
Compote, 3½" d, ruffled .	55.00	20.00	21.00	21.00	—
Creamer, ruffled	60.00	35.00	35.00	35.00	—
Cream Soup, 5" d	50.00	18.00	18.00	15.00	—

	Cobalt Blue	Crystal	Green	Pink	Yellow
Cup and Saucer	90.00	12.00	12.50	15.00	14.00
Pitcher, 6½" h, 36 oz....	800.00	40.00	40.00	45.00	48.00
Plate					
6" d, sherbet.........	—	6.00	6.50	6.00	7.00
8½" d, salad.........	—	7.50	7.50	12.00	12.50
10" d, dinner.........	—	15.00	15.00	21.00	20.00
Sherbet..............	—	10.00	10.00	10.00	11.00
Sugar, cov	—	22.00	24.00	34.00	36.00
Sugar, ruffled	50.00	32.50	32.50	32.50	—
Tumbler					
4¾" h, 10 oz, ftd	—	21.00	21.00	22.00	20.00
5¼" h, 12 oz, ftd	—	27.50	27.50	30.00	30.00

HOBNAIL, Hocking Glass Co, 1934–36. Made in crystal and pink. Some crystal pieces were edge trimmed in red.

	Crystal	Pink		Crystal	Pink
Bowl			Pitcher, 67 oz	25.00	—
5½" d, cereal.......	4.00	—	Plate		
7" d, salad	4.75	—	6" d, sherbet	2.00	2.00
Cordial, 5 oz, ftd	5.75	—	8½" d, luncheon	3.50	3.75
Cup and Saucer	6.50	6.00	Sherbet	3.00	3.50
Creamer, ftd..........	3.50	—	Sugar, ftd.............	4.00	—
Decanter, stopper, 32 oz	25.00	—	Tumbler, 9 oz	6.00	—
Goblet, 10 oz..........	6.50	—	Whiskey, 1½ oz........	6.25	—
Iced Tea Tumbler, 15 oz	7.00	—	Wine, 3 oz, ftd.........	6.00	—
Juice Tumbler, 5 oz	4.00	—			

IRIS, Jeannette Glass Co, 1928–1932; 1950s, 1970s. Made in crystal, iridescent, pink, recently in bi–colored red/yellow and blue/green, as well as white.

	Crystal	Irides-cent		Crystal	Irides-cent
Bowl			Goblet, 5½" h, 8 oz.....	24.00	150.00
5" d, sauce, ruffled ...	9.00	22.00	Pitcher, 9½" h, ftd	37.50	40.00
7½" d, soup	145.00	55.00	Plate		
11½" d, fruit, ruffled ..	15.00	14.00	5½" d, sherbet.......	14.50	13.50
Butter Dish, cov........	48.00	40.00	8" d, luncheon	95.00	—
Candlesticks, pr........	40.00	45.00	9" d, dinner	50.00	37.50
Candy Jar, cov	125.00	—	Sherbet, 2½", ftd.......	24.00	15.00
Coaster	90.00	—	Sugar, cov	24.00	24.00
Cocktail, 4½" h	24.00	—	Tumbler, 6" h, ftd.......	18.00	17.50
Creamer, ftd..........	12.00	14.00	Vase, 9" h	25.00	20.00
Cup and Saucer	28.00	25.00	Wine, 4" h	—	30.00

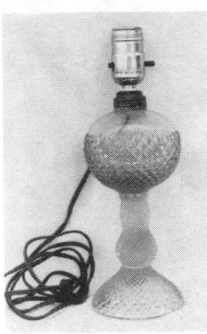

Left: English Hobnail, lamp, pink, 6¼" h, $50.00. Right: Windsor, pitcher, pink, 16 oz, 4½" h, $100.00.

MOONDROPS, New Martinsville Glass Co, 1932–40. Made in amber, amethyst, black, cobalt blue, crystal, dark green, green, ice blue, jadite, light green, pink, red, and smoke. Pricing for blue and red are quite specific, while other colors all seem to be about equal.

	Blue	Most Colors	Red
Ashtray..........................	32.00	17.50	32.00
Berry Bowl			
5¼" d	12.50	6.50	12.00
9¼" d, ruffled................	45.00	—	45.00
Bowl			
6¾" d	72.00	—	70.00
7½" d	22.00	15.00	24.00
Butter Dish, cov................	425.00	250.00	425.00
Candlesticks, pr, 5" h, ruffled......	35.00	22.00	35.00
Casserole, cov, 9¾" d...........	140.00	98.00	145.00
Celery, 11" l, boat shape	32.00	24.00	32.00
Cocktail Shaker, metal top........	60.00	35.00	60.00
Cordial, 2⅞" h	38.00	25.00	35.00
Creamer, 3¾" h.................	17.50	10.00	17.50
Cup and Saucer	24.00	15.00	24.00
Decanter, 8½" h	70.00	45.00	72.00
Goblet, 5¾" h	32.00	20.00	32.00
Gravy Boat.....................	120.00	90.00	120.00
Mayonnaise, 5¼" d..............	50.00	30.00	55.00
Perfume Bottle	200.00	150.00	200.00
Pitcher, 8" h, 50 oz, lip...........	200.00	120.00	200.00
Plate			
6⅛" d, sherbet...............	8.00	5.00	8.50
7⅛" d, salad.................	14.00	10.00	14.50
8½" d, luncheon	15.00	12.00	15.00
9½" d, dinner................	25.00	17.50	25.00

	Blue	Most Colors	Red
Platter, 12″ l, oval	35.00	20.00	35.00
Sandwich Plate, 14″ d, handles. . . .	45.00	24.00	45.00
Sherbet, 2¾″ h	17.50	12.00	17.00
Sugar, 3½″ h	16.00	10.00	16.00
Tumbler, 4⅜″ h	16.00	11.00	16.50
Vase, 8½″ h, bud	235.00	165.00	240.00
Vegetable, 9¾″ l, oval.	33.00	24.00	30.00

OLD ENGLISH, Threading, Indiana Glass Co. Made in amber, crystal, forest green, green, and pink.

	Amber	Green	Pink
Bowl			
4″ d.	15.00	15.00	16.00
9″ d, ftd.	25.00	26.00	25.00
Candlesticks, pr, 4″ h	30.00	30.00	30.00
Candy Dish, cov	48.00	50.00	48.00
Compote, 3½″ h, 2 handles	20.00	20.00	20.00
Creamer.	17.50	17.50	17.50
Fruit Stand, 11″ d	38.00	38.00	38.00
Goblet, 5¾″ h, 8 oz.	30.00	30.00	30.00
Pitcher, cov	115.00	115.00	120.00
Plate.	18.00	18.00	18.00
Sandwich Server, center handle . . .	50.00	50.00	50.00
Sherbet	18.00	19.00	18.00
Sugar, cov	45.00	45.00	45.00
Tumbler, 5½″ h, ftd	32.00	32.00	32.00
Vase, 5⅜″ h, fan	48.00	45.00	48.00

ORCHID, Paden City Glass Co, early 1930s. Made in amber, black, cobalt blue, green, pink, red, and yellow.

	Black	Cobalt Blue	Other Colors	Red
Bowl				
4⅞″ sq	32.00	32.00	16.00	35.00
8½″ d, 2 handles.	75.00	75.00	40.00	75.00
8¾″ sq	60.00	60.00	32.00	65.00
10″ d, ftd.	95.00	95.00	45.00	95.00
11″ sq	70.00	80.00	40.00	70.00
Candlesticks, pr, 5¾″ h. .	100.00	110.00	50.00	110.00
Candy, cov, 6½″ sq	95.00	95.00	50.00	95.00
Creamer.	48.00	48.00	30.00	48.00
Compote, 6⅝″ h	55.00	55.00	25.00	55.00
Ice Bucket, 6″ h	110.00	115.00	60.00	110.00
Mayonnaise, 3 pcs	100.00	100.00	55.00	100.00
Plate, 8½″ sq.	50.00	48.00	—	45.00

	Black	Cobalt Blue	Other Colors	Red
Sandwich Server.......	68.00	65.00	40.00	68.00
Sugar................	50.00	48.00	40.00	48.00
Vase, 10″ h	110.00	110.00	50.00	110.00

PATRICK, Lancaster Glass Co, early 1930s. Made in pink and yellow.

	Pink	Yellow		Pink	Yellow
Bowl, 9″ d	125.00	50.00	Mayonnaise, 3 pcs	190.00	125.00
Candy Dish	115.00	75.00	Plate		
Cheese and Cracker Set	140.00	95.00	7″ d, sherbet	20.00	15.00
Cocktail, 4″ h.........	90.00	48.00	7½″ d, salad.........	25.00	20.00
Creamer..............	75.00	40.00	8″ d, luncheon	45.00	30.00
Cup and Saucer	95.00	52.00	Sherbet	60.00	45.00
Goblet, 6″ h	100.00	68.00	Sugar...............	75.00	40.00
Juice Goblet, 4¾″ h	90.00	48.00	Tray, 11″ d, two handles.	75.00	60.00

QUEEN MARY, Prismatic Line, Vertical Ribbed, Hocking Glass Co, 1936–49. Made in crystal, pink, and limited production in ruby red.

	Crystal	Pink		Crystal	Pink
Ashtray, 3½″ d........	3.00	—	Cup and Saucer	8.50	10.00
Berry Bowl			Juice Tumbler, 3½″ h ...	4.00	9.00
4½″ d..............	4.00	6.00	Plate		
5″ d..............	6.00	10.00	6″ d, bread and butter.	4.00	5.00
8¾″ d	10.00	15.00	6⅝″ d, sherbet.......	4.00	5.00
Bowl			8¾″ d, salad........	5.50	—
4″ d...............	3.50	5.00	9¾″ d, dinner........	14.00	40.00
6″ d...............	6.50	22.00	Relish Tray, 12″ l, 3 part.	10.00	15.00
7″ d...............	10.00	12.00	Salt and Pepper Shak-		
Butter Dish, cov........	25.00	95.00	ers, pr..............	20.00	—
Candy Dish, cov	20.00	35.00	Sandwich Plate, 12″ d ..	10.00	15.00
Celery, 5 x 10″........	10.00	20.00	Sherbet, ftd	5.00	6.50
Cigarette Jar, 2 x 3″ oval	5.00	7.50	Sugar, oval...........	4.50	7.50
Coaster, 3½″ d	2.50	4.00	Tumbler, 4″ h, 9 oz	6.00	12.00
Creamer, oval	5.50	7.50			

ROYAL LACE, Hazel Atlas Co, 1934–41. Made in amethyst, cobalt blue, crystal, green, and pink.

	Cobalt Blue	Crystal	Green	Pink
Berry Bowl				
5″ d................	45.00	15.00	22.00	25.00
10″ d................	45.00	18.00	24.00	28.00
Candlesticks, pr, ruffled .	185.00	30.00	55.00	50.00

	Cobalt Blue	Crystal	Green	Pink
Console Bowl, 10" d, ruffled..............	425.00	25.00	60.00	55.00
Cookie jar, cov.........	350.00	30.00	75.00	50.00
Creamer..............	55.00	18.00	25.00	15.00
Cream Soup, 4¾" d	37.00	12.00	28.00	22.50
Cup and Saucer	38.50	11.00	35.00	18.50
Jug, 64 oz	235.00	48.00	100.00	65.00
Juice Tumbler, 3½" h, 5 oz	42.50	13.50	25.00	24.00
Pitcher, 8½" h, lip	225.00	60.00	85.00	135.00
Plate				
6" d, sherbet	12.00	5.00	10.00	9.00
8½" d, luncheon	45.00	9.00	22.50	14.50
9⅞" d, dinner........	40.00	12.00	25.00	18.00
Sherbet, metal holder...	25.00	3.50	—	—
Sugar, cov	185.00	22.00	65.00	48.00
Tumbler, 4⅛" h	37.50	12.50	27.50	17.50
Vegetable, 11" l, oval ...	70.00	20.00	25.00	20.00

ROYAL RUBY, Anchor Hocking Glass Co, 1938–40. Made only in ruby red. A limited number of pieces were made in Royal Ruby. Collectors often mix other ruby patterns, such as Old Cafe, Coronation, and Oyster & Pearl to complete the pattern. Boxes are found with crystal bases.

	Ruby Red		Ruby Red
Bonbon, 6½" d	9.00	Plate, 9⅛" d................	12.00
Cigarette Box, cov, 6⅛ x 4"....	50.00	Puff Box, cov, 4⅝" d..........	10.00
Creamer, ftd................	10.00	Sugar, cov, ftd	18.00
Cup and Saucer	8.50	Tray, 6 x 4½"................	12.50
Goblet	10.00	Vase, 9" h	17.50
Marmalade, cov, 5⅛" d........	7.50		

WINDSOR, Windsor Diamond, Jeannette Glass Co, 1936–46. Made in crystal, green, pink, with lesser quantities made in amberina red, delphite and ice blue.

	Crystal	Green	Ice Blue	Pink
Ashtray, 5¾" d.........	13.00	44.00	—	36.00
Berry Bowl				
4¾" d	4.00	10.00	—	8.50
8½" d	6.50	17.50	—	16.50
Bowl				
5" d, pointed	5.00	—	—	17.50
10½" d, pointed......	24.00	—	—	110.00
Butter Dish, cov......	26.00	80.00	—	48.00
Cake Plate, 10¾" d, ftd .	8.50	21.00	—	20.00
Candlesticks, pr, 3" h ...	20.00	—	—	85.00

	Crystal	Green	Ice Blue	Pink
Coaster, 3¼" d	3.50	16.50	—	12.50
Console Bowl, 12½" d . .	24.00	—	—	95.00
Creamer.	5.00	12.00	55.00	10.00
Cup and Saucer	6.00	17.00	75.00	15.00
Pitcher, 4½" h, 16 oz . . .	20.00	—	—	100.00
Plate				
6" d, sherbet	2.50	8.00	—	5.00
7" d, salad	4.50	18.50	—	16.50
9" d, dinner	5.00	20.00	50.00	22.00
Relish, 11½" d, divided. .	10.00	—	—	175.00
Sandwich Plate, 10¼" d .	6.50	16.00	—	16.00
Sherbet	4.00	14.00	—	12.00
Sugar, cov	8.00	30.00	—	25.00
Tumbler				
4" h, 9 oz	6.00	28.00	55.00	19.00
5" h, 12 oz	8.00	45.00	—	25.00

DISNEYANA

History: Walt Disney and the creations of the famous Disney Studios hold a place of fondness and enchantment in the hearts of people throughout the world. The release of "Steamboat Willie" featuring Mickey Mouse in 1928 heralded an entertainment empire.

Walt and his brother, Roy, showed shrewd business acumen. From the beginning they licensed the reproduction of Disney characters in products ranging from wristwatches to clothing. In 1984 Donald Duck celebrated his 50th birthday, and collectors took a renewed interest in material related to him.

The market in Disneyana has been established by a few determined dealers and auction houses. Hake's Americana and Collectibles of York, PA, offers several hundred Disneyana items in each of their bimonthly mail and phone bid auctions. Sotheby's and Christie's New York auctions offer original art and cels several times each year.

References: David Longest and Michael Stern, *The Collector's Encyclopedia of Disneyana*, Collector Books, 1992; Walton Rawls, *Disney Dons Dogtags: The Best of Disney Military Insignia From World War II*, Abbeville Press, 1992; Richard Schickel, *The Disney Version: The Life, Times, Art and Commerce of Walt Disney*, Avon Books, 1968; Michael Stern, *Stern's Guide to Disney Collectibles, First Series* (1989, 1992 value update), *Second Series* (1990, 1993 value update), Collector Books; Tom Tumbusch, *Tomart's Illustrated Disneyana Catalog and Price Guide*, Vols. 1, 2, 3, and 4, Tomart Publications, 1985; Tom Tumbusch, *Tomart's Illustrated Disneyana Catalog and Price Guide, Condensed Edition,* Wallace–Homestead, 1989.

Periodicals: *Mouse Rap Monthly,* PO Box 1724, Ojai, CA 93024; *Tomart's Disneyana Digest,* 3300 Encrete Ln., West Carrollton, OH 45439.

Collectors' Clubs: Mouse Club East, PO Box 3195, Wakefield, MA 01880; National Fantasy Fan Club for Disneyana Collectors and Enthusiasts, PO Box 19212, Irvine, CA 92713; The Mouse Club, 2056 Cirone Way, San Jose, CA 95124.

Archives/Museum: Walt Disney Archives, 500 South Buena Vista Street, Burbank, CA 91521.

Additional Listings: See *Warman's Americana & Collectibles* for more examples.

Advisor: Ted Hake.

Alice In Wonderland
  Book, *Adventures From The Original Alice In Wonderland,* 1951, 32 pgs, color illus **12.50**
  Dinner Set, 8" d plate, 6" d bowl,

Celluloid, Snow White and the Seven Dwarfs, autographed by Walt Disney, $4,400.00.

and 3″ h cup, ceramic, painted and glazed, marked "Alice In Wonderland Made In England by Johnson Bros," 1950s **75.00**
Little Golden Book, *Mad Hatter's Tea Party From Walt Disney's Alice In Wonderland,* Simon & Schuster, 1951, 28 pgs **15.00**
Bambi
Bowl, 5″ d, ceramic, white, color image int., two flower design on ext., American Pottery, c1949 .... **25.00**
Comic Book, 7¼ x 10¼″, Dell Four Color Series, #186, copyright 1948 .... **15.00**
Figure, 2½″ h, ceramic, attached metal fly on tail, Goebel, 1950s **75.00**
Planter
3 x 4 x 3½″, ceramic, Bambi and Thumper, marked "S1545C," 1950s **50.00**
3 x 6 x 5″, Bambi, figural, ceramic, painted and glazed, "Enesco" foil label, 1960s . **55.00**
Cinderella
Sheet Music, 9 x 12″, *Oh Sing Sweet Nightingale,* 3 pgs, color cov, copyright 1949 .... **15.00**

Wristwatch, silvered metal case, pink leather straps, Timex, c1958 .... **40.00**
Davy Crockett
Charm Bracelet, gold metal links, seven charms with painted accents, orig card and metal picture frame, c1955 .. **60.00**
Wallet, 3½ x 4¼″, "Davy Crockett Indian Fighter," brown vinyl, black trim, Walt Disney copyright, c1955 .... **30.00**
Disneyland
Bracelet, souvenir, gold colored metal chain, gold colored metal booklet charm with mother–of–pearl covers, opens to 7″ l cardboard strip with ten color photos of park attractions, 1950s **50.00**
Guide Book, 8 x 11½″, *Disneyland 1957 Guide,* 26 glossy pgs **65.00**
Plate, 9¼″ d, china, full color images, marked "Japan," 1950s **50.00**
Puzzle, 11 x 15″, "Disneyland Frontierland," frame tray, Whitman, 1955 copyright **25.00**
Record, 45 rpm, *It's A Small World,* orig cardboard sleeve, four different languages, 1964 **15.00**
Thermos, 6½″ h, "Disneyland It's A Small World," metal, color illus, white plastic cup, Aladdin Industries, 1964 copyright **50.00**
Donald Duck
Bank, 7″ h, figural, soft vinyl, uncut coin slot, marked "Walter J Jamieson Inc," 1950s **25.00**
Book, *Donald Duck In The High Andes,* Grosset & Dunlap, 1943, 32 pgs, dj, illus **75.00**
Box, 4 x 7 x 1″, "The New Donald Duck Wristwatch," US Time, c1947 .... **110.00**
Figure
3½″ h, ceramic, painted and glazed, lying down pose, angry expression, Brayton Laguna, c1940 .... **125.00**
4″ h, playing mandolin, bisque, 1930s **300.00**
Paint Box, 2 x 8½″, tin litho, color

illus, red ground, cardboard insert with attached paint, Transogram, 1939 .... 25.00

Projector, 3 x 3½ x 8″, hard plastic, gray, four films, instruction sheet, and orig box, Stephens Products, 1950s 75.00

Roly Poly, 5¼″ h, celluloid, movable arms, marked "Japan," mid 1930s 400.00

Sign, 9 x 10½″, Donald Duck Cola, cardboard, easel back, diecut, color illus of bottle cap and bottle, marked "Printed In Canada," 1950s 150.00

Soaky Bottle, 7½″ h, soft plastic, 1960s 25.00

Soda Bottle, 10″ h, clear glass, raised portrait image, 1950s . 50.00

Straw, Donald Duck Sunshine Straws, orig unopened box, American Seal–Cap Corp, 1950s 25.00

Dumbo
Book, *Walt Disney's Dumbo Of The Circus,* Garden City, copyright 1941, 52 pgs, 10 x 11″ . 75.00

Card Game, complete deck of 2¼ x 3½″ cards, different color illus of Dumbo and Timothy on each card, instruction booklet, 1940s 50.00

Figure, 4″ h, ceramic, Dumbo on green base with foil sticker, Goebel bee marks and incised "53," 1950s 350.00

Fantasia
Book, *Fantasia,* Simon & Schuster, copyright 1940, 10 x 13″, hardcover 200.00

Cup and Saucer, 2″ h cup, 6¼″ d saucer, ceramic, painted and glazed, marked "Flower Ballet Designed by Walt Disney/ copyright 1940 Vernon Kilns" 150.00

Figure, 3¾″ h, Sprite, ceramic, painted and glazed, Vernon Kilns, 1940 copyright 250.00

Ferdinand, book, *Ferdinand The Bull,* linen type, 8 pgs, full color, Whitman, copyright 1938 ..... 20.00

Goofy, figure, 1⅞″ h, bisque, painted, 1930s 75.00

Mary Poppins
Photo Album, 10½ x 13″, white vinyl covered cardboard covers, color illus, unused sheets, 1964 copyright 25.00

Song Book, 8½ x 11″, *Songs from Walt Disney's Mary Poppins,* Hansen Publications Inc, 1965 .... 15.00

View–Master Reels, set of 3, orig envelope, booklet, and catalog, unused, 1964 copyright 15.00

Mickey Mouse
Better Little Book, *Mickey Mouse and the Desert Palace,* Whitman, #1451, copyright 1948 .... 50.00

Book, *Mickey Mouse Adventures,* The Musson Book Co, Ltd, Toronto, 1933 copyright, 64 pgs 200.00

Box
Alarm Clock, 4½ x 5 x 3″, illus side panels, Ingersoll, c1949 75.00

Cookies, 2¾ x 5″, orange character images, Nabisco, 1940s 50.00

Brush, 2 x 3½″, wood, aluminum strip on top with Mickey image, 1930s 75.00

Bubble Gum Wrapper, 5 x 7″, waxed paper, "Save the wrappers and get a Mickey Mouse album" text, Gum Inc 200.00

Composition Book, 6½ x 8¼″, color illus on front, Powers Paper Co, copyright 1930s 75.00

Figure
3½″ h, rubber, black, red and white accents, missing tail, Seiberling, 1930s 75.00

4¼″ h, bisque, wearing gold hat, silver walking stick, incised "S33" 100.00

Little Golden Book, *Mickey Mouse Goes Christmas Shopping,* Simon & Schuster, 1953, 28 pgs 15.00

Magazine, *Mickey Mouse,* 8¼ x 11½″, Vol 3, #4, 36 pgs, 1938 25.00

Pencil Case, 4½ x 8½ x 1½″, cardboard, red, snap closure, 1950s 25.00

Puppet, 7 x 9" unpunched sheet, detailed instructions, unused, 1950s **25.00**

Snow Boots, pr, soft rubber, red and white, color illus, strap and buckle, fabric lining, 1970–80 **30.00**

Telephone, 5 x 9 x 11½", hard plastic, figural, bright yellow receiver and base, marked "Unisonic," early 1980s **90.00**

Thermos, 6½" h, school bus, metal, color illus, yellow plastic cup **25.00**

Toy
8½" h, trapeze, wood frame, wood figure with paper label on each side suspended by string, Marks, Boston, 1930s **50.00**

9" h, diecut cardboard, metal rod construction and tail, attached string with metal finger loops, marked "The Dolly Toy Co," copyright 1930s **700.00**

Wristwatch, silvered metal case, orig black leather band, orig cardboard box, Ingersoll, c1968 . . . . **100.00**

Minnie Mouse
Ashtray, 3½ x 5 x 3", china, painted and glazed, marked "Made In Japan," 1930s **200.00**

Figure
4⅛" h, bisque, wearing silver hat, holding blue umbrella and brown handbag, incised "S34," 1930s **75.00**

6" h, ceramic, painted and glazed, orig foil label, American Pottery, c1947 . . . . **200.00**

Peter Pan
Doll, 13" h, Tinkerbell, soft rubber, translucent plastic diecut wings with gold sparkles, olive green dress, c1955 . . . . **25.00**

Movie Poster, 22 x 28", half sheet, paper, full color illus, copyright RKO Radio Pictures Ltd **110.00**

Newspaper Advertisement, 11 x 15", Weatherbird Shoes adv, color illus of Peter Pan characters, copyright 1953 . . . . . . **30.00**

Pinocchio
Cordial Bottle, 3½" h, ceramic, painted and glazed, orig foil sticker, National Porcelain Co, c1940 . . . . **55.00**

Figure, 6¼" h, holding book slung over shoulder, ceramic, painted and glazed **200.00**

Paint Book, 8¼ x 11", Collins, London, copyright 1940 . . . . . **50.00**

Puzzle, 11 x 14", frame tray, Jaymar, copyright 1950s **20.00**

Pluto, salt and pepper shakers, 3¼" h, ceramic, glazed, Leeds, c1947 . . . . **40.00**

Snow White
Big Little Book, *Snow White and the Seven Dwarfs,* Whitman, #1460, copyright 1938 . . . . . **25.00**

Display, 31 x 34½", "Snow White and The Seven Dwarfs/Armour's Star Ham," cardboard, color design of Snow White cutting ham, dwarfs, and forest animals, 1938 copyright **250.00**

Glass, 4¾" h, "1939 Walt Disney All Star Parade," Snow White and Dwarfs illus, light blue title around rim **35.00**

Ironing Board, 8½ x 27 x 21", tin litho, color illus of Snow White, Dwarfs, Wicked Queen, and cottage, Wolverine Toy Co, 1970s **25.00**

Marionette, 15" h, Dopey, composition, "I Am Dopey" tag attached to front, black cardboard control unit with attached strings, 1950s **150.00**

Planter, 2 x 3½ x 3¼", ceramic, painted and glazed, Doc standing beside cottage, marked "Made In Japan," 1950s **25.00**

Sewing Set, "Snow White's Sewing Set," doily and four handkerchiefs, some orig thread, additional thread, scissors, and thimble, one handkerchief partially embroidered, others unused, orig box, Ontex **100.00**

Sheet Music, 9 x 12", *Heigh Ho,* Irving Berlin Inc, copyright 1938 . . . . **20.00**

Three Little Pigs, dish, 8" d, china, divided, color image, gold rim, reverse marked "Compliments Parker Furniture Co/West Court Square La Grange Ga," Patriot China, 1930s 100.00

Winnie The Pooh, coloring book, 8 x 11", Whitman, copyright 1965 15.00

Zorro

Costume, dry cleaning bag, white paper, Zorro image, uncut, marked with dry cleaner adv and "Walt Disney Studios Presents Zorro On ABC–TV," 1950s 50.00

Dart Game, two cardboard targets, one with diecut circles, other with point values, two vinyl beanbags, two darts, and instruction sheet, orig box, Gardner, copyright 1950s ... 100.00

Periodicals: *Doll Castle News,* PO Box 247, Washington, NJ 07882; *International Dolls' House News,* PO Box 79, Southampton S09 7EZ England; *Miniature Collector,* PO Box 631, Boiling Springs, PA 17007; *Miniatures Showcase,* PO Box 1612, Waukesha, WI 53187.

Collectors' Clubs: National Assoc. of Miniature Enthusiasts, PO Box 69, Carmel, IN 46032; National Organization of Miniaturists and Dollers, 1300 Schroder, Normal, IL 61761.

Museums: Art Institute of Chicago, Chicago, IL; Margaret Woodbury Strong Museum, Rochester, NY; The Museums at Stony Brook, Stony Brook, NY; Toy and Miniature Museum of Kansas City, Kansas City, MO; Washington Dolls' House and Toy Museum, Washington, DC.

DOLL HOUSES

History: Doll houses date from the 18th century to modern times. Early doll houses often were handmade, sometimes with only one room. The most common type was made for a young girl to fill with replicas of furniture scaled especially to fit into a doll house. Specially sized dolls also were made for doll houses. All types of accessories and styles allowed a doll house to portray any historical period.

References: Caroline Clifton–Mogg, *The Dollhouse Sourcebook,* Abbeville Press, 1993; Nora Earnshaw, *Collecting Dolls' Houses and Miniatures,* Pincushion Press, 1993; Caroline Hamilton, *Decorative Dollhouses,* Clarkson Potter, 1990; Flora Bill Jacobs, *Dolls' Houses in America: Historic Preservation in Miniature,* Charles Scribner's Sons, 1974; Donald and Helene Mitchell, *Dollhouses, Past and Present,* Collector Books, 1980, out of print; Eva Stille, *Doll Kitchens 1800–1980,* Schiffer Publishing, 1988; Margaret Towner, *Dollhouse Furniture: The Collector's Guide To Selecting and Enjoying Miniature Masterpieces,* Courage Books, 1993; Blair Whitton (ed.), *Bliss Toys And Dollhouses,* Dover, 1979.

R. Bliss, litho on board, hinged, two int. rooms, rural house style, 7½ x 11½ x 16¼", $675.00.

Bliss

11" h, 7½" w, 4¾" d, litho paper on wood, cottage, off–center front door, front opening, two floors, two rooms, some wear 550.00

12¾" h, litho paper on wood, front opening, two rooms, unmarked, very fine condition .. 465.00

16" h, keyhole type, printed paper on wood, two floors, ext. with white stone lower floor and white clapboard with yellow details, front porch with turned wood corner supports, balcony on upper level, steeply pitched roof, two room int., blue stained wood, front steps, some int. paper replaced, some paper loss to ext., American, early 20th C . **805.00**

16⅛" h, paper on wood, front porch, opening door, tiled roof, yellow shingle and blue clapboard ext., hinged front, orig int. wallpaper, some paper loss at sides, American, late 19th C **460.00**

17½" h, 10" w, Victorian, litho wood, red and yellow, front opening, arched second floor with cellophane windows, lace curtains and hinged porch door, lower floor with similar windows and curtains, balustraded porch, machine rug–lined int., section of molding and chimney missing, paper flaking, c1908 . . . . **467.50**

17¾" h, 11½" w, 9" d, litho paper on wood, front opening, two floors, good condition, some damage, late 19th/early 20th C **1,210.00**

Hacker, Christian, 20" w, butcher's shop, painted wood, transfer dec, marbleized slabs, two orig tablets, plaster joints, carcasses, butcher and customers, stamped "CH Schutzmarke" on base, inscribed in pencil "155/2," c1895 . . . . **9,675.00**

Reed, 13¼" h, litho paper on wood, cottage, two room front steps, twin chimneys, good condition, includes seven pieces of lacquered wood furniture and metal vase, ½-inch scale **350.00**

Schoenhut, 27½" h, 23" w, 22⅞" d, cottage, painted wood, fiberboard, and cardboard, two story, porch, six rooms, two hallways, lift off roof, chimney, electrified chandelier, orig litho wallpaper, orig condition, nameplate, 1920 **1,050.00**

Unknown Maker

10½" h, 6¾" w, front opening, two floors, two rooms, orig wallpaper, door hook missing, Pawtucket, RI, early 20th C . . **605.00**

14½" h, heavy paper over wood, three story, three rooms and three halls, red mansard roof, ext. painted light green with cream edging and details, sq bay window on lower floor, upper floor balcony with opening door, int. with contemporary wallpaper, borders, and floor coverings, attic floor access through hinged roof, manually powered elevator operates with side crank handle, later crudely wired for electric light, German, 1920s–30s **690.00**

29½" h, wood, two story, ext. and int. painted gray with maroon trim, green and white accents, int. accessed through three hinged panels, left side has two large rooms, right side has large hall and stairway, dark stained walls, large glazed windows, small side yard with low wall, roof terrace, later crudely wired for electricity, American, early 20th C **345.00**

30" h, 28" w, 15½" d, wood, Victorian, four rooms, front opening, brick papered ext., Art Deco wooden furniture, 1 in. scale, England, late 19th C . . **550.00**

39" h, 39" w, wood, two story, eight rooms and hallways, simulated asphalt roof and stone foundation, rain gutters and flashing, applied cream painted individual clapboards, brown trim, picture, casement, working sash windows, opening stained wood door flanked by triple casement windows, front porch with railing, stairs at front and back doors, simulated brick chimney, painted paper and canvas wall coverings, two upstairs bedrooms with closets, oak stairway, kitchen with built–in sink and cupboard, bathroom with built–in toilet, sink, and tub, living room with fireplace and tiled hearth, solid wood floors, paneled internal doors with working hardware, dark stained moldings and window surrounds, basement windows, sheer curtains or roller blinds at most windows, good condition, some damage, American, early 20th C **3,450.00**

DOLLS

History: Dolls have been children's play toys for centuries. Dolls also have served other functions. During the 14th through 18th centuries doll making was centered in Europe, mainly in Germany and France. The French dolls produced in this era represented adults and were dressed in the latest couturier designs. They were not children's toys.

During the mid–19th century, child and baby dolls, made in wax, cloth, bisque, and porcelain, were introduced. Facial features were hand painted; wigs were made of mohair and human hair. They were dressed in baby or children's fashions.

Marks from the various manufacturers are found on the back of the head, neck, or back area. These marks are very important in identifying the doll and date of manufacture.

Doll making in the United States began to flourish in the 1900s with names like Effanbee, Madame Alexander, Ideal, and others.

References: Johana Gast Anderton, *More Twentieth Century Dolls From Bisque to Vinyl, Volumes A–H, Volumes I–Z, Revised Edition,* Wallace–Homestead, 1974; John Axe, *The Encyclopedia of Celebrity Dolls,* Hobby House Press Inc., 1983; Julie Collier, *The Official Identification And Price Guide To Antique & Modern Dolls, Fourth Edition,* House of Collectibles, 1989; Carol Corson, *Schoenhut Dolls: A Collector's Encyclopedia,* Hobby House Press, 1993; Nora Earnshaw, *Collecting Dolls,* Pincushion Press, 1992; Jan Foulke, *11th Blue Book Dolls and Values,* Hobby House Press, 1993; Caroline Goodfellow, *The Ultimate Doll Book,* Hobby House Press, 1993; R. Lane Herron, *Herron's Price Guide To Dolls,* Wallace–Homestead, 1990; Judith Izen, *A Collector's Guide To Ideal Dolls,* Collector Books, 1994; Polly Judd, *Cloth Dolls: Identification and Price Guide,* Hobby House Press, 1990; Polly and Pam Judd, *Composition Dolls: 1928–1955,* Hobby House Press, 1991; Polly and Pam Judd, *Glamour Dolls of the 1950s & 1960s Identification and Values, Revised Edition,* Hobby House Press, 1993; Polly and Pam Judd, *Hard Plastic Dolls: Identification and Price Guide, Third Revised Edition,* Hobby House Press, 1993; Wendy Lavitt, *American Folk Dolls,* Alfred Knopf, 1982; Wendy Lavitt, *Dolls,* Alfred A. Knopf, 1983; A. Glenn Mandeville, *A. Glenn Mandeville's Madame Alexander Dolls Value Guide,* Hobby House Press, 1994; A. Glenn Mandeville, *Doll Fashion Anthology and Price Guide, 4th Revised Edition,* Hobby House Press, 1993; A. Glenn Mandeville, *Ginny: An American Toddler Doll, 2nd Revised Edition,* Hobby House Press, 1994; Edward R. Pardella, *Shirley Temple Dolls and Fashion: A Collector's Guide To The World's Darling,* Schiffer Publishing, 1992; Sabine Reinelt, *Magic of Character Dolls,* Hobby House Press, 1993; Lydia and Joachim F. Richter, *Bru Dolls,* Hobby House Press, 1989; Lydia Richter and Karin Schmelcher, *Heubach Character Dolls and Figurines,* Hobby House Press, 1992; Lydia Richter, *China, Parian, and Bisque German Dolls,* Hobby House Press, 1993; Mildred Seeley, *For The Love Of Dolls And Roses: A Story of the Author, Her Life, Her Successes and Failures,* Scott Publications, 1994; Patricia R. Smith, *Antique Collector's Dolls,* Vol. I (1975, 1991 value update), Vol. II (1976, 1991 Value update), Collector Books; Patricia R. Smith, *Madame Alexander Collector's Dolls Price Guide #19,* Collector Books, 1994; Patricia R. Smith, *Madame Alexander Dolls 1965–1990,* Collector Books, 1991; Patricia R. Smith, *Modern Collector's Dolls,* Volumes I, II, III, IV, V, Collector Books, 1973, 1975, 1976, 1979, 1984, 1995 value updates; Patricia R. Smith, *Modern Collector's Dolls, Sixth Series,* Collector Books, 1994, 1995 value update; Patricia R. Smith, *Patricia Smith's Doll Values Antique to Modern, Tenth Series,* Collector Books, 1994; Patricia R. Smith,

Shirley Temple Dolls and Collectibles, Vol. I (1977, 1992 value update), Vol. II (1979, 1992 value update), Collector Books; Florence Theriault, *More Dolls: The Early Years 1780–1910*, Gold Horse Publishing, 1992; Sharon Weintraub, *Naughties, Nudies and Bathing Beauties*, Hobby House Press, 1993.

Periodicals: *Antique Doll World*, 225 Main St., Suite 300, Northport, NY 11768; *Costume Quarterly for Doll Collectors*, 118-01 Sutter Ave., Jamaica, NY 11420-2407; *Doll Castle News*, PO Box 247, Washington, NJ 07882; *Doll Collector's Price Guide*, 306 East Parr Rd., Berne, IN 46711; *Doll Reader*, 6405 Flank Dr., Harrisburg, PA 17112; *Dolls–The Collector's Magazine*, 170 Fifth Ave., 12th Floor, New York, NY 10010; *Doll World*, 306 East Parr Rd., Berne, IN 46711; *Fabric of Life*, PO Box 1212, Bellevue, WA 98009-1212; *National Doll & Teddy Bear Collector*, PO Box 4032, Portland, OR 97208; *The Cloth Doll Magazine*, PO Box 1089, Mt. Shasta, CA 96067; *The Doll Times*, 218 W. Woodin Blvd., Dallas, TX 75224.

Videotape: *The Extraordinary World of Doll Collecting*, Cinebar Productions, 1994.

Collectors' Clubs: Doll Collector International, PO Box 2761, Oshkosh, WI 54903; Madame Alexander Fan Club, PO Box 330, Mundeline, IL 60060; United Federation of Doll Clubs, 10920 N. Ambassador, Kansas City, MO 64153.

Museums: Aunt Len's Doll House, Inc., New York, NY; Children's Museum, Detroit, MI; Doll Castle Doll Museum, Washington, NJ; Gay Nineties Button & Doll Museum, Eureka Springs, AR; Margaret Woodbury Strong Museum, Rochester, NY; Mary Merritt Doll Museum, Douglassville, PA; Mary Miller Doll Museum, Brunswick, GA; Prarie Museum of Art & History, Colby, KS; The Doll Museum, Newport, RI; Toy and Miniature Museum of Kansas City, Kansas City, MO; Washington Dolls' House & Toy Museum, Washington, DC; Yesteryears Museum, Sandwich, MA.

Additional Listings: See *Warman's Americana & Collectibles* for more examples.

Alt, Beck & Gottschalck
27″ h, five piece composition

Jules Steiner, A-13 Bebe Le Parisien, bisque socket head, French jointed composition body, pull string voice box, orig mohair wig and pate, blue lever operates sleep eyes, closed mouth, pierced ears, bisque hands with some restoration, orig clothes, 22″ h, $8,750.00. Photo courtesy of Cobb's Doll Auction.

body, bisque head, blue sleep eyes, open mouth, upper teeth, orig brown mohair wig, white gown, marks: 1367 .... **700.00**

28″ h, ball jointed composition body, bisque socket head, blue sleep eyes, open mouth, upper teeth, brown mohair wig, earrings, long coat, marks: 1362 .... **375.00**

Bahr & Proschild, 10″ h, five piece straight limb composition body, bisque head, brown paperweight eyes, slightly smiling closed mouth, brown mohair wig, orig printed gauze dress, pleated front, lace and ribbon trim, peach silk bonnet, socks, brown leather shoes, c1915, marks: incised 686 3/0 ....**1,955.00**

Bierschenk, Fritz, 13″ h, five piece composition body, bisque head, blue intaglio eyes, open/closed mouth, molded and painted upper teeth, brown human hair wig, peach pink satin and net gown with ribbon trim, underwear,

white leather laced ankle boots,
c1910, marks: incised FB 616 . **2,875.00**

Bru

11½" h, kid body, bisque head
and lower arms, blue paperweight eyes, closed mouth,
pierced ears, blonde mohair
wig, maroon and cream satin
frock, underwear, socks,
brown leather shoes, hat,
1880s, marks: incised 2 on
shoulderplate **6,325.00**

14½" h, gusset kid body, bisque
swivel head, pale blue eyes,
smiling closed mouth, pierced
ears, blonde mohair wig, orig
two piece dress, underwear,
hoop bustle, straw hat, socks,
light brown leather laced ankle
boots, c1875, marks: incised D **4,025.00**

16" h, jointed kid body, bisque
head and lower arms, composition lower legs, brown paperweight eyes, closed mouth,
pierced ears, blonde mohair
wig, pale green satin frock with
lace trim, furry hat with feather
plume, socks, brown leather
shoes, metal mesh bag, and
parasol with blue satin canopy,
marks: incised Bru Jne 5 . . . **13,800.00**

Cuno & Otto, 14" h, jointed composition body, molded bust, bisque head, blue paperweight
eyes, closed mouth, brown mohair wig, floral printed dress with
chiffon trim, white leather low
heeled shoes, 1920s, marks: in-
cised 1469 . . . . **1,725.00**

Effanbee

18" h, Little Lady, jointed composition, glass sleep eyes, orig
wig, dress, and shoes **75.00**

21" h, Anne Shirley, jointed composition, glass sleep eyes, repainted arms, dressed **40.00**

26" h, Lovums, cloth body, composition head and limbs, glass
sleep eyes, molded hair,
dressed **175.00**

Gaultier, Francois, 16½" h

Bebe, jointed wood and composition body, bisque head, blue
paperweight eyes, painted

lips, pierced ears, replaced
blonde wig, red wool drop
waist dress, flannel and cotton
underwear, black socks,
brown leather laced boots with
brown silk rosettes, c1880,
marks: incised F 1 G **4,025.00**

Character, gusset fabric body,
bisque swivel head, kid arms,
blue paperweight eyes, closed
mouth, pierced ears, blonde
mohair wig, red knitted shirt,
black satin skirt, white cotton
pinafore and bonnet, red button leather boots, c1875,
marks: incised 5, FG **1,265.00**

Handwerck, Heinrich, 18" h, ball
jointed composition body, bisque
head, blue sleep eyes, open
mouth, upper teeth, pierced
ears, brown wig, marks: 109,
sgd Handwerck on body **125.00**

Heubach, Gebruder

9" h

Baby Stuart, five piece curved
limb composition body, bisque head, blue intaglio eyes,
closed mouth, molded bon-
net with transfer flower dec,
white cotton baby gown,
c1912, marks: incised 7977 **810.00**

Character, bisque, intaglio
brown eyes, open/closed
mouth, two painted teeth,
molded brown hair and blue
hair ribbons, orig cotton
dress with ribbon trim,
molded painted white socks
and brown shoes, c1925,
marks: incised 104090/3 . . **2,075.00**

10¾" h, jointed wood and composition body, bisque head,
blue paperweight eyes, closed
mouth, replaced wig, blue cotton sailor color dress, underwear, straw hat, c1912, marks:
incised 7246, sun mark **1,625.00**

14" h, fabric body, composition
lower limbs, blue intaglio eyes,
open singing mouth, two
molded upper teeth, molded
blonde hair, pink hair ribbon,
orig cotton dress with lace and
ribbon trim, socks, white

leather shoes, cotton underwear, c1912, marks: incised 7851, square mark **1,385.00**

14½" h, boy, bisque head, blue intaglio eyes, pensive facial expression, closed mouth, flocked hair, red felt pants, blue felt coat with gold button and black belt, blue wool cap, black shoes, attached toy trumpet and tin drum, c1912, marks: incised 7602, sun mark **1,050.00**

17" h, jointed wood and composition body, bisque head, blue intaglio eyes, smiling open/closed mouth, molded teeth, dimpled cheeks, molded hair, blue hair ribbon, white dress with pleated skirt, cotton and flannel underwear, socks, white shoes, c1912, marks: incised 7768 . . . . **1,955.00**

Jumeau

11" h, eight ball jointed wood and composition body, bisque head, blue paperweight eyes, closed mouth, pierced ears, blonde mohair wig, purple satin dress, pink ribbon and lace trim, cotton underwear, pink silk hat, black socks, brown leather shoes, c1880, marks: incised red ink Depose E 3 J and H **4,600.00**

13¾" h, jointed wood and composition body, poured bisque head, brown glass eyes, closed painted mouth, pierced ears, blonde mohair wig, light green and cream silk and satin dress with lace trim, cotton underwear, socks, brown leather shoes, c1880, marks: incised Depose Jumeau 5, red ink check marks and 9; shoes marked EJ **1,495.00**

15¾" h, eight ball jointed wood body, bisque head, brown paperweight eyes, closed mouth, pierced ears, blonde mohair wig, pink silk and net dress, ribbon trim socks, brown leather shoes, matching bonnet, c1890, marks: incised 7 at neck socket, oval paper label on body, shoes with Depose mark **5,175.00**

19½" h, eight ball jointed wood and composition body, bisque head, brown glass eyes, closed mouth, applied pierced ears, brown mohair wig, maroon velvet and silk double–breasted frock, matching cap and bag, black socks, brown shoes, watch pendant, marks: incised 9 . . . . **5,175.00**

19¾" h, eight ball jointed wood and composition body, bisque head, blue paperweight eyes, painted mouth, applied pierced ears, blonde mohair wig, maroon silk frock with lace trim, socks, brown leather shoes, red straw hat, marks: incised 8 at neck socket, Jumeau stamp on body **2,875.00**

20" h, jointed wood and composition body, bisque head, brown glass eyes, closed mouth, applied pierced ears, blonde mohair wig, maroon velvet coat, underwear, brown leather shoes with maroon rosettes, lace trim bonnet, marks: stamped red Depose Tete Jumeau Bte SGDG 9 . . **4,325.00**

Kammer & Reinhardt

11¾" h, jointed wood and composition body, bisque head, painted blue eyes, closed mouth, molded and painted brown hair, later clothing, c1909, marks: incised 102/30 **24,150.00**

16½" h, jointed wood and composition body, bisque head, blue painted eyes, closed painted mouth, blonde mohair wig, white cotton dress with lace trim, cotton underwear, white knee socks, white laced ankle boots, holds Armand Marseille baby doll, c1909, marks: 101/43 . . . . **2,875.00**

22" h, five piece composition body, bisque head, blue sleep eyes, open mouth, upper teeth, mohair wig, white gown and bonnet with ribbon trim, marks: 121 . . . . **1,250.00**

25″ h, five piece composition body, bisque socket head, brown sleep eyes, open/closed mouth, upper teeth, human hair wig, white gown and bonnet with lace and blue ribbon trim, marks: 116A **3,500.00**

32″ h, ball jointed composition body, bisque head, blue sleep eyes, painted closed mouth, reddish human hair wig with large white bow, white dress, marks: 117A **7,500.00**

Kestner

10″ h, Gibson Girl, fabric body with bisque lower arms and legs, bisque head, blue paperweight eyes, closed mouth, auburn mohair wig, cream satin and lace gown, painted black boots, c1900, marks: incised 172 . . . . **810.00**

11″ h, jointed wood and composition body, brown paperweight google eyes, closed smiling mouth, orig brown mohair wig, orig side button cotton jacket with white belt, short pants, socks, silk shoes, straw hat with brown grosgrain ribbon, c1913, marks: incised 221 . . . . **4,900.00**

13″ h, jointed wood and composition body, bisque head, brown glass eyes, open mouth, two upper teeth, blonde mohair wig, red cotton dress, white pinafore, socks, pink leather shoes, straw hat, c1914, marks: incised F 10/237 . . . . **925.00**

14½″ h, Wunderkind, bisque, three interchangeable heads, doll and head, brown paperweight eyes, closed mouth, orig brown mohair wig, floral print cream gauze dress, lace and pink ribbon trim, socks and shoes, marks: incised 182; first head: blue paperweight eyes, open/closed mouth, molded tongue, orig blonde mohair wig, marks: incised 179; second head: blue paperweight eyes, open/closed mouth, molded teeth, orig blonde mohair wig, marks: incised 183; third head: blue paperweight eyes, open mouth, upper teeth, brown mohair wig, marks: incised 171; orig maroon box with litho label, c1910 . . . . **12,650.00**

15″ h, jointed wood and composition body, bisque head, brown glass eyes, open/closed mouth, molded and painted upper teeth, blonde mohair wig, pink and cream satin frock, cotton underwear, socks, old brown leather shoes, holds bisque baby, c1890, marks: incised 10 . . . . **3,450.00**

19″ h, Hilda, five piece composition body, bisque socket head, blue sleep eyes, open/closed mouth, upper teeth, blonde wig, cream gown and bonnet with lace and ribbon trim, marks: 245 . . . . **4,000.00**

Kley & Hahn, ball jointed composition body, bisque head, blue sleep eyes, open mouth, upper teeth, orig blonde mohair wig, printed dress with ribbon trim, ribbons in hair, marks: 250 . . . . **375.00**

Koppelsdorf, Heubach, 17″ h, five piece composition toddler body, bisque head, gray sleep eyes, open mouth, upper teeth, dressed, marks: 320 . . . . **475.00**

Madame Alexander

13″ h, Shirley, composition jointed body, glass sleep eyes, orig mohair wig, red polka dot dress, underwear, socks, and shoes **275.00**

21″ h, Bridesmaid, jointed composition, glass sleep eyes, orig mohair wig, orig dress with tag **200.00**

24″ h, Princess Elizabeth, jointed composition, glass sleep eyes, orig mohair wig, orig dress . . **50.00**

Marseille, Armand

9″ h, five piece straight limb composition body, bisque head, blue paperweight google eyes, slightly smiling closed mouth, replaced brown human hair wig, white gauze dress, matching hat, socks, and shoes, c1915, marks: incised 323 4/0 ....**1,150.00**

9½" h, composition five piece body, bisque head, blue glass google eyes, closed mouth, chine silk dress, shoes, socks, and straw hat, c1929, marks: incised Just Me 310 7/0 .....**1,150.00**

9¾" h, Oriental, fabric and composition body, bisque head, brown paperweight eyes, closed mouth, dark painted hair, tan satin pants, black brocade tunic, gold silk vest, 1920s, marks: incised 353/10 **810.00**

11½" h, five piece composition body, bisque head, blue glass google eyes, closed smiling mouth, blonde mohair wig, orig white gauze dress, socks, and white shoes, underwear, c1920, marks: incised 323 3/0 **1,035.00**

Schmidt, Bruno
11" h, jointed wood and compo-

Bruno Schmidt, #2033, Character Wendy, bisque socket head, French jointed composition body, orig mohair wig and pate, brown sleep eyes, closed mouth, pierced ears, 16″ h, $17,500.00. Photo courtesy of Cobb's Doll Auction.

sition body, bisque head, brown paperweight eyes, closed mouth, brown mohair wig, floral print dress, socks, pink shoes, and straw hat, c1912, marks: incised 2033 BSW in heart **3,450.00**

Schwab, Hertel, 8½" h, Our Fairy, bisque, straight limbs, jointed legs, brown google eyes, smiling open/closed mouth, molded upper teeth, light brown mohair wig, blue silk belted jacket and puff skirt, c1915, marks: incised 222/22 ....**1,850.00**

Simon & Halbig
9" h, jointed wood and composition body, bisque head, blue glass eyes, open mouth, upper teeth, pierced ears, replaced red wig, old cream silk gown, underwear, and bonnet, c1887, marks: incised 979 ... **920.00**

16" h, lady, ball jointed composition body, bisque socket head, blue sleep eyes, open mouth, upper teeth, human hair wig, white long dress, marks: 1159 ....**1,050.00**

18" h, jointed wood and composition body, bisque head, blue glass eyes, closed mouth, pierced ears, light brown human hair wig, white embroidery trimmed dress, underwear, and straw hat, c1910, marks: incised IV **19,550.00**

Societe Francaise de Bebes et Jouets
20" h, toddler, ball jointed composition, bisque socket head, blue sleep eyes, laughing open/closed mouth, upper teeth, French human hair wig, pink stripe dress with lace trim, hat with pink ribbon and flower trim, marks: 236 ....**1,700.00**

27" h, jointed composition body, bisque socket head, blue sleep eyes, open mouth, upper teeth, molded brows, pierced ears, orig brown wig, wearing light pink and cream French style dress, bonnet, at-

SFBJ, left: #283 Character Lady, bisque socket head, French jointed composition body, orig mohair wig and pate, blue set eyes, open mouth and teeth, repainted hands, orig tagged outfit, small upper eyelid flake, 18″ h, $5,000.00; right: #235 Character Boy, solid dome bisque socket head, French jointed composition toddler body, molded hair, blue set eyes, open closed mouth, molded teeth and tongue, wool plaid suit, velvet trim, 15″ h, $1,350.00. Photo courtesy of Cobb's Doll Auction.

tached orig dress, underwear, orig shoes, orig box, marks: 301 Bebe 12, shoes with 12 and sgd Jumeau **2,700.00**

Steiner, Jules, 35″ h, ball jointed composition body, bisque socket head and hands, blue paperweight eyes, closed mouth, pierced ears, brown human hair wig, red pin stripe dress with lace trim and red ribbon bow, Series C #7 Bourgoin Bebe **12,500.00**

DOOR KNOCKERS

History: Before the advent of the mechanical bell or electrical buzzer and chime, a door knocker was considered an essential door ornament to announce the arrival of visitors. Metal was used to cast or forge the various forms; many cast iron examples were painted. Collectors like to find knockers with English registry marks.

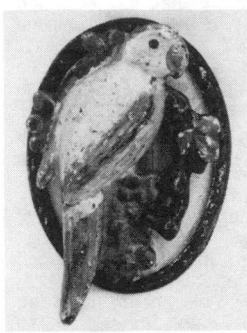

Cast Iron, parrot on branch, pink and rose body, 4″ oval base, 4½″ l overall, $35.00.

Amish Man, cast iron, movable eyes	**25.00**
Butterfly, cast iron	**65.00**
Cat, brass, arched back	**50.00**
Couple, 10½″ l, bronze, kissing . .	**40.00**
Devil, brass, Belgium	**35.00**
Dog's Head, 7″ l, brass	**65.00**
Dolphin, 11″ l, bronze	**275.00**
Eagle, 8½″ l, brass	**60.00**
Federal Style, 10½″ l, brass	**230.00**
Fruit Cluster, cast iron	**25.00**
Grecian Head, 4½″ l, bronze	**80.00**
Grecian Urn, 7″ l, brass	**30.00**
Hand, lady's, 6″ l, cast iron, holding ball, ruffled cuff, ring on finger	**70.00**
Horse's Head, 5½″ l, brass	**130.00**
Jenny Jones, brass	**75.00**
Lion's Head, 4″ l, brass, ring knocker, c1880	**75.00**
Owl, 3½″ l, brass	**35.00**
Parrot, 4½″ l, cast iron, polychrome paint	**65.00**
Renaissance Style, 11½″ l, bronze, open lyre form, maiden center, inverted lion on each side, shell shape basin, green patina, Continental, late 19th C	**880.00**
Sea Horse and Shell, brass	**80.00**

Spider, 3½" l, cast iron, hanging
from web, bee caught in web .. **95.00**
Woman, brass, holding mirror ... **35.00**

DOORSTOPS

History: Doorstops became popular in the late 19th century. They can be found flat or three dimensional and were made in cast iron, bronze, wood, and other material. Hubley, a leading toy manufacturer, made many examples.

References: Jeanne Bertoia, *Doorstops: Identification And Values*, Collector Books, 1985; Douglas Congdon–Martin, *Figurative Cast Iron: A Collector's Guide,* Schiffer Publishing, 1994; Marilyn Hamburger and Beverly Lloyd, *Collecting Figural Doorstops*, A. S. Barnes and Company, 1978.

Videotape: *Off The Ground & Off the Wall,* Gary Roma, Iron Frog Productions.

Collectors' Club: Doorstop Collectors of America, 2413 Madison Ave., Vineland, NJ 08630.

Reproduction Alert: Reproductions are proliferating as prices on genuine doorstops continue to rise. There is usually a slight reduction in size in a reproduced piece unless an original mold is used, at which time size remains the same. Reproductions have less detail, lack of smoothness to the overall casting, and lack of detail in the paint. If there is any bright orange rusting, this is strongly indicative of a new piece. Beware. If it looks too good to be true, it usually is.

Notes: Pieces described below contain at least 80% or more of the original paint and are in very good condition. Repainting drastically reduces price and desirability. Poor original paint is preferred over repaint.

All listings are cast iron and flatback castings unless otherwise noted.

Doorstops marked with an asterisk are currently being reproduced.

B + H = Bradley and Hubbard.

Advisor: Craig Dinner.

Basket, 11" h, rose, ivory wicker basket, natural flowers, handle with bow, sgd "Hubley 121" ... **135.00**
Bear, 15" h, holding and looking at honey pot, brown fur, black highlights **1,000.00**

Bellhop, black, 7½" h, carrying satchel, facing sideways, orange–red uniform and cap **385.00**
Bowl, 7 x 7", green–blue, natural colored fruit, sgd "Hubley, 456" **100.00**
Boy
9⅜" h, "The Tiger," hands at side, riding outfit, cartoon like eyes, "FISH" on front, sgd "Hubley 269" **895.00**
10⅝" h, wearing diapers directing traffic, police hat, red scarf, brown dog at side **500.00**
11" h, full figure, Dutch, hands in pocket, blue jump suit and hat, red belt and collar, brown shoes, blonde hair **445.00**
12¾" h, native wearing turban and leopard skin, one hand extended **750.00**
*Caddie, 8" h, carrying brown and tan bag, white, brown knickers, red jacket **500.00**
Cat
*7" h, male and female holding each other's waist, dressed .. **175.00**
*8" h, black, red ribbon and bow around neck, on pillow **125.00**
9½" h, 7" w, full figure, Persian, sitting, gray, light markings, sgd "Hubley" inside casting . **145.00**
10½" l, fireside, full figure, gray, light markings, sgd "Hubley" inside casting **145.00**
Child, 17" h, reaching, naked, flesh color, short curly brown hair ... **800.00**

Rabbit, B & H, orig paint, 8⅜" w, 15⅜" h, $875.00.

Clown, 10" h, full figure, 2 sided, red suit, white collar, blue hat, black shoes 725.00

Cottage
6⅜" h, three dimensional garden, tan roof, 3 red chimneys, flowers, 2 pc casting, Ann Hathaway 300.00
8⅝" l, 5¾" h, Cape type, blue roof, flowers, fenced garden, path, sgd "Eastern Speciality Mfg Co 14" 135.00

Dancer
8⅞" h, Art Deco couple doing Charleston, pink dress, black tux, red and black base, "FISH" on front, sgd "Hubley 270" 625.00
11⅛" h, black woman doing rhumba, red, yellow, and blue dress, red kerchief 400.00

Dog
Boston Bull
9" h, full figure, facing left, black, tan markings 100.00
10½" h, facing right, black, white markings 55.00
Boxer, 8½ x 9", full figure, facing forward, brown, tan markings 200.00
Japanese Spaniel, 9" h, black and white, long curly hair, sgd "1267" 185.00
Pekingese, 14½" l, 9" h, full figure, life-like size and color, brown, sgd "Hubley" 1,000.00
*Puppies, 7" h, three puppies in basket, natural colors, sgd "Copyright 1932 M Rosenstein, Lancaster, PA, USA" .. 325.00
Wire Haired Fox Terrier, 9 x 8", full figure, facing sideways, tan, brown markings 110.00

Drum Major, 12⅝" h, full figure, ivory pants, red hat with feather, yellow baton in right hand, left hand on waist, sq base 285.00
Duck, 7½" h, white, green bush and grass 285.00
Elephant, 14" h, pulling coconut out of palm tree, natural color . 175.00
Fish, 9¾" h, three, fantail, orig paint, sgd "Hubley 464" 135.00
Fisherman, 6¼" h, standing at

wheel, hand blocking sun over eyes, rain gear 145.00

Flower
Goldenrods, 7⅛" h, natural color, sgd "Hubley 268" 225.00
Jonquil, 7" h, yellow flowers, red and orange cups, sgd "Hubley 453" 185.00
Zinnias, 11⅝" h, multicolored flowers, blue and black vase, detailed casting, two rubber stoppers, sgd "B & H" 200.00

Frog, 3" h, full figure, sitting, yellow and green 40.00

Giraffe, 20¼" h, tan, brown spots, squared off lines to casting 1,200.00

Girl
8¾" h, dark blue outfit and beanie, high white collar, black shoes, red hair, incised "663" 450.00
9" h
French, holding skirt out at sides, hat, sgd "Hubley 23" 140.00
Sunbonnet, blue hat, pink dress 285.00
10⅞" h, two bathers, yellow and red swimsuits, green and yellow bathing caps under umbrella, "FISH" on front, sgd "Hubley 250" 500.00
*13¾" h, 9¾" l, white hat, flowing cape, holding orange jack–o–lantern with red cutout eyes, nose, and mouth 1,500.00

*Golfer, 10" h, overhead swing, hat and ball on ground, Hubley 425.00

Grandpa Rabbit, 8⅝" h, crouched down, sitting with hands on knees, brown skin, red jacket, white shirt, cream colored pants and collar, watch hanging out of vest 675.00

Guitar Player, 11⅞" h, flat back, yellow hat and pants, red jacket with green trim and waist band, brown guitar 350.00

Horse, 7⅞" h, jumping fence, jockey, sgd "Eastern Spec Co #790" 250.00

House
5½" h, 8¼" l, two story, attic, path to door, shutters, sgd "Sophia Smith House" 275.00
6" h, woman walking up front

stairs, grapevines, sgd "Eastern Spec Co" **165.00**

Indian Chief, 9¾" h, flatback, orange and tan headdress, yellow pants with blue stripes and red patches at ankles, green grass, sgd "A A Richardson," copyright 1927 . . . . **575.00**

*Kitten, 7" h, three kittens in wicker basket, sgd "M Rosenstein, c1932, Lancaster, PA" **350.00**

Lighthouse, 14" h, flat back, green rocks, black path, white lighthouse, red window and door trim **300.00**

*Mammy
  8½" h, full figure, red dress, white apron, blue kerchief with white spots, sgd inside "Hubley 327" **175.00**
  10" h, white scarf and apron, very dark blue dress, red kerchief on head, full figure, one pc casting **350.00**
  12" h, full figure, blue dress, white apron, red kerchief with white spots, sgd "copyright Hubley" inside **485.00**

Messenger Boy, 10" h, bouquet in hand, cap, rosy checks, front sgd "FISH" **350.00**

Monkey, 14⅜" h, hand reaching up, brown, tan, and white **750.00**

Musician, 6⅞" h
  Black man playing saxophone, white pants, red jacket **600.00**
  Black man playing drums, black paint **500.00**

Old Mill, 6¼" h, brown log mill, tan roof, white path, green bushes . **315.00**

Owl, 9½" h, sits on books, sgd "Eastern Spec Co" **235.00**

Parrot, 13¾" h, in ring, two sided, heavy gold base, sgd "B & H" . **185.00**

Penguin, 10" h, full figure, facing sideways, black, white chest, top hat and bow tie, yellow feet and beak, unsigned, Hubley **285.00**

*Pheasant, 8½" h, brown, bright markings, green grass, sgd "Fred Everett" front, sgd "Hubley" back **285.00**

Policeman, 9½" h, leaning on red fire hydrant, blue uniform and

tilted hat, comic character face, tan base, "Safety First" on front **725.00**

Popeye, 9" h, full figure, pipe in mouth, white hat, blue pants, black and red shirt, sgd "Hubley, 1929 King Features Syndicate, Made in USA" **1,000.00**

*Quail, 7¼" h, 2 brown, tan, and yellow birds, green, white, and yellow grass, Fred Everett on front, sgd "Hubley 459" **335.00**

Rabbit
  8⅛" h, eating carrot, red sweater, brown pants **300.00**
  15¼" h, sits on hind paws, tan, green grass, detailed casting, sgd "B & H 7800" **875.00**

Ringmaster, 10½" h, full figure, hands clasped behind back, red jacket, green pants, top hat . . . **1,500.00**

Rooster
  7" h, standing, black, colorful detail **135.00**
  12" h, full figure, black, red comb, yellow claws and beak **345.00**
  13" h, red comb, black and brown tail and chest, yellow stomach **325.00**

Ship
  5¼" h, clipper, full sails, American flag on top mast, wave base, two rubber stoppers, sgd "CJO" **50.00**
  11¼" h, three masts, full sail . . **25.00**

Skier, 12½" h, full figure, woman, red scarf, gloves, and belt, blue ski suit and beret, wood skis at side **385.00**

Squirrel, 9" h, sitting on stump eating nut, brown and tan **245.00**

Stork, 13¾" h, white, yellow beak, orange feet, black markings, flowers and grass **275.00**

Storybook
  Huckleberry Finn, 12½" h, floppy hat, pail, stick, Littco Products label **425.00**
  Humpty Dumpty, 4½" h, full figure, sgd "661" inside **300.00**
  Little Miss Muffet, 7¾" h, sitting on mushroom, blue dress, blonde hair **140.00**
  Little Red Riding Hood 7½" h, 9½" w, sgd "NUYDEA" **485.00**

9½" h, basket at side, red cape, tan dress with blue pattern, blonde hair, sgd "Hubley" **400.00**

Mary Quite Contrary, 11⅜" h, blue hat, yellow dress and socks, green watering can, "Littco Products" label **600.00**

Puss in Boots, flat back, head sticking out of boot, sgd "Creations Co 1930" **400.00**

Tiger, 8½" h, tan, black stripes, baseball bat on shoulder, black base **500.00**

Whistler, 20¼" h, flat back, boy, hands in tan knickers, yellow striped baggy shirt, lips rounded as if to whistle, two rubber stoppers, sgd "B & H" **2,250.00**

*Windmill, 6¾" h, 6⅞" w, ivory, red roof, house at side, green base **95.00**

Woman

8" h, Colonial, sgd "Hubley" ... **125.00**

8½" h, minuet, one hand on hip **210.00**

8¾" h, peasant, blue dress, black hair, fruit basket on head **135.00**

*11" h, flowers and shawl **135.00**

12" h, carrying parasol and hat box in left hand, satchel with "Phoebe" in right hand, flowered hat **315.00**

1727

Dresden

1883-93

Dresden

MODERN MARK

DRESDEN/MEISSEN

History: Augustus II, Elector of Saxony and King of Poland, founded the Royal Saxon Porcelain Manufactory in the Albrechtsburg, Meissen, in 1710. Johann Frederick Boettger, an alchemist, and Tschirnhaus, a nobleman, experimented with kaolin clay from the Dresden area to produce porcelain. By 1720 the factory produced a whiter hard–paste porcelain than that from the Far East. The factory experienced its golden age in the 1730–50s period under the leadership of Samuel Stolzel, kiln master, and Johann Gregor Herold, enameler.

Many marks were used by the Meissen factory. The first was a pseudo–Oriental mark in a square. The famous crossed swords mark was adopted in 1724. A small dot between the hilts was used from 1763 to 1774 and a star between the hilts from 1774 to 1814. Two modern marks are swords with a hammer and sickle and swords with a crown.

The Meissen factory was destroyed and looted by forces of Frederick the Great during the Seven Years' War (1756–1763). It was reopened, but never achieved its former greatness.

In the 19th century, the factory reissued some of its earlier forms. These later wares are called "Dresden" to differentiate them from the earlier examples. Further, there were several other porcelain factories in the Dresden region and their products also are grouped under the "Dresden" designation of collectors.

Reference: Susan and Al Bagdade, *Warman's English & Continental Pottery & Porcelain, 2nd Edition,* Wallace–Homestead, 1991.

DRESDEN

Candelabra, pr, triple arm, floral applique, couple base, 19th C, 17" h **470.00**

Centerpiece Bowl

13" d, round, six lobed, floral spray dec **350.00**

14" l, oval, scroll ends with floral painted reserves, fruit and floral applique **715.00**

Chocolate Set, polychrome cream and gold stripes, floral dec, pot, twelve cups and saucers, bowl, and plate, one saucer damaged, late 19th C **575.00**

Demitasse Set, polychrome enamel floral dec, gilt trim, six cups and 4¼" d saucers, fitted case, late 19th C **550.00**

Lamp Base, 29¼" h, enameled floral dec framed with applied fruits and flowers, Thieme factory marks, late 19th C **200.00**

Plate, service, set of twelve, cream and ornate gold borders **300.00**

Sauceboat, cov, 5¼" l, late 19th C **175.00**

Vase
10¾" h, green gilt and pansy dec **150.00**
34" h, cov and stand, body with painted Bacchanalian scene, figural cherub handles, cov with figural cherubs and crown finial, damage, late 19th C ..**1,265.00**

Vase, shaded brown and tan scene, monk holding candle, tankard, and jug, gold trim, blue "Donath & Co" mark, c1916, 9½" h, $385.00.

MEISSEN

Bowl
7⅝" d, reticulated, polychrome floral dec, underglazed blue crossed swords mark, firing imperfections, 19th C **400.00**

11¼" d, serving, shaped round form, white ground, allover raised gold morning glory dec, gilding wear, 19th C, pr **125.00**

Candelabra, pr, 14½" h, five–light, molded leaf bodies, gilt trim, crossed swords marks, damages, late 19th C **430.00**

Centerpiece, 14" h, two tiers, figural finial, crossed swords mark, c1900 .... **575.00**

Cup and Saucer, set of twelve, puce floral dec with gilt rims, late 19th C **1,375.00**

Figure
Boy, sitting with basket, underglazed blue crossed swords mark, chips and repairs, 19th C, 4¾" h **375.00**

Chocolate Maker, cherub, seated beside low table set with chocolate cup, enamel dec, crossed swords mark, late 19th C, 4¼" h **860.00**

Gardener, standing, holding watering can, leaning on shovel, enamel dec, crossed swords mark, repairs, late 19th C, 7½" h **690.00**

Girl, sitting with music box, underglazed blue crossed swords mark, damaged, 19th C, 5¾" h **175.00**

Mongolians, pr, male and female, enamel and gilt dec, free–form scrolled bases, crossed swords marks, chips, arm damage to male, 19th C, 13" h, price for pair **1,150.00**

Tailor riding goat, enamel and gilt dec, underglazed crossed swords mark, losses, late 19th C, 8¾" h **1,150.00**

Young Girl, standing by partial marbleized column, holding doll, underglazed crossed swords mark, losses, late 19th C, 5¾" h **520.00**

Grouping
Baby satyr holding bird and girl with bird cage, restoration, underglazed blue crossed swords mark, 19th C, 6" l, 6¼" h **290.00**

Girl with goats, marked "O. Pilz," underglazed blue mark, restoration, late 19th C, 15½" l, 9¾" h **450.00**

Girl with kitten, boy with dog, underglazed Mareolini star mark, restoration on boy, late 18th/early 19th C, 4½" w, 4⅜" h, price for pair **400.00**

Lady, holding Bible, seated beside table with spinning wheel, underglazed crossed swords mark, losses, 19th C, 6" h ... **400.00**

Male suitor kissing the hand of seated female, satyr boy and trunk by his side, crossed swords mark, chips, late 19th C, 5¾" h **1,100.00**

Pan, maiden, and satyr child with pan pipes, underglazed crossed swords mark, restoration, 19th C, 12⅜" h **1,375.00**

Young Man, wearing colonial dress, reading book, dog at side, underglazed crossed swords mark, restorations, 19th C, 8⅝" h **1,100.00**

Luncheon Service, partial, enamel dec birds and insects, molded basketweave borders, nine coffee cups, twelve saucers, twenty–three 9⅞" d plates, damages, late 19th C **3,900.00**

Plate
Bird dec, scalloped ring, pierced borders, enamel and gilt dec bird subjects, crossed swords marks, chips, late 19th C, 9¼" d **3,450.00**

Fruit dec, gilt ring, crossed swords marks, late 19th C, 9¾" d, set of twelve **2,300.00**

Teapot and Saucer, cov, pear shaped, floral sprays, floral finial, gilt trim **145.00**

Vase, cov
12½" h, insects between applied leaves and florets enamel dec, underglazed crossed swords mark, losses, 19th C **285.00**

16" h, gold foliage dec, underglazed blue crossed swords mark, cov repaired, 19th C .. **225.00**

DUNCAN AND MILLER

History: George Duncan, Harry B. and James B., his sons, and Augustus Heisey, his son–in–law, formed George Duncan & Sons in Pittsburgh, Pennsylvania, in 1865. The factory was located just two blocks from the Monongahela River, providing easy and cheap access by barge for materials needed to produce glass. The men, from Pittsburgh's southside, were descendants of generations of skilled glass makers.

The plant burned to the ground in 1892. James E. Duncan, Sr., selected a site for a new factory in Washington, Pennsylvania, where operations began on February 9, 1893. The plant prospered, producing fine glassware and table services for many years.

John E. Miller, one of the stockholders, was responsible for designing many fine patterns, the most famous being "Three Face." The firm incorporated, using the name The Duncan and Miller Glass Company until its plant closed in 1955. The company's slogan was "The Loveliest Glassware in America." The U.S. Glass Co. purchased the molds, equipment, and machinery in 1956.

References: Gene Florence, *Elegant Glassware Of The Depression Era, Sixth Edition,* Collector Books, 1994; Gail Krause, *The Encyclopedia Of Duncan Glass,* published by author, 1984; Gail Krause, *A Pictorial History Of Duncan & Miller Glass,* published by author, 1976; Gail Krause, *The Years Of Duncan,* published by author, 1980; Naomi L. Over, *Ruby Glass of the 20th Century,* Antique Publications, 1990, 1993–94 value update.

Collectors' Club: National Duncan Glass Society, PO Box 965, Washington, PA 15301.

Additional Listings: Pattern Glass.

Ashtray, duck, 4" d **10.00**
Bowl
Beaded Swirl, disc band, 8½" d **55.00**
Canterbury
Clear, 10" d, flared **10.00**
Ruby, 12" d, crimped **60.00**
Candlesticks, pr, American Way, blue opalescent **35.00**

Plaque, light green, sailing ship motif, 14″ d, $20.00.

Candy Dish, Canterbury, chartreuse **32.00**
Centerpiece Dish, Sanibel, pink opalescent, turned up sides, 13 x 7″ **45.00**
Champagne, Mardi Gras, straight stem **20.00**
Cocktail, First Love, 3 oz **15.00**
Compote
 Carolina, cov, 13½″ h **135.00**
 Crystal Wedding, 8″ h **65.00**
 Fago–Vera, 7½″ h **45.00**
Cornucopia, Three Feathers, blue opalescent, enamel and gold trim, 8″ l **90.00**
Creamer, Teardrop **20.00**
Decanter, First Love, 32 oz, orig stopper **110.00**
Dessert, Purinton, pink, 6½″ d ... **7.00**
Goblet
 Hobnail **8.00**
 Spiral Flutes **10.00**
Iced Tea Set, Hobnail, blue opalescent, 7 pcs **300.00**
Ivy Bowl, Hobnail, 6″ h
 Pink opalescent **35.00**
 Yellow opalescent **35.00**
Mint Tray, Sanibel, yellow opalescent, 7″ l **21.00**
Nappy, handle
 Sandwich, 4½″ d **8.00**
 Sylvan, clear, green handle, 7½″ d **16.00**
Pitcher, Spiral Flutes, green **85.00**
Plate
 Mardi Gras, 7″ d **7.00**

Spiral Flutes, crystal, etch, 8½″ d **7.00**
Punch Bowl Set, Hobnail, clear, punch bowl, ladle, underplate, twelve punch cups with various color handles, 15 pcs **210.00**
Punch Cup, Mardi Gras **7.00**
Relish, divided
 Canterbury, pink **12.00**
 Sanibel, 8½″ l
  Pink opalescent **35.00**
  Yellow opalescent **40.00**
 Teardrop, 11½″ l **22.00**
Salt and Pepper Shakers, Hobnail, aqua opalescent, orig top **35.00**
Sherbet, Hobnail **5.00**
Sugar
 Bleeding Heart, pedestal, open, purpling **35.00**
 Teardrop **20.00**
Swan
 5″ h, Pall Mall **28.00**
 7″ h
  Chartreuse **30.00**
  Ruby **35.00**
 8″ h, open, silver overlay flowers, frosted highlights **40.00**
 10″ h
  Biscayne Green **65.00**
  Ruby **75.00**
Tumbler, Spiral Flutes **7.00**
Vase
 Canterbury, pink opalescent, flared, 4″ h **21.00**
 Hobnail, flip, blue opalescent, 7″ h **55.00**
 Three Feathers, hand dec, 4″ h **20.00**

DURAND

History: Victor Durand (1870–1931), born in Baccarat, France, apprenticed at the Baccarat glass works where several generations of his family worked. In 1884 Victor came to America to join his father at Whitall–Tatum & Co. in New Jersey. In 1897 father and son leased the Vineland Glass Manufacturing Company in Vineland, New Jersey. Products included inexpensive bottles, jars, and glass for scientific and medical purposes. By 1920 four separate companies existed.

When Quezal Art Glass and Decorating

Company failed, Victor Durand recruited Martin Bach, Jr., Emil J. Larsen, William Wiedebine, and other Quezal men and opened an art glass shop at Vineland in December 1924. Quezal–style iridescent pieces were made. New innovations included cameo and intaglio designs, geometric Art Deco shapes, Venetian Lace, and oriental style pieces. In 1928 crackled glass, called Moorish Crackle and Egyptian Crackle, was made.

Much of Durand glass is not marked. Some bear a sticker labeled "Durand Art Glass," some have the name "Durand" scratched on the pontil, or "Durand" inside a large "V." Etched numbers may be part of the marking.

Durand died in 1931. The Vineland Flint Glass Works was merged with Kimble Glass Company a year later, and the art glass line was discontinued.

Vase, irid blue, white webbing, 7″ h, $350.00.

Bowl, 4¾″ d, 2½″ h, deep cranberry, ftd **100.00**
Box, cov, 5″ d, 4″ h, King Tut, three layers, coiled green dec on ambergris cased to opal, lined with irid gold, matching and conforming blown cov with cut star at pontil, unsgd **770.00**
Center Bowl, 14″ d, 7¾″ h, Peacock Feather, broad flared trumpet form, brilliant ruby color with pink and white pulled feather motif, wide border with Bridgeton Rose pattern, designed and cut by Charles Link **880.00**

Lamp
11½″ h, boudoir, King Tut, irid silver blue with opal white swirling coil design, gilt metal fittings, orig silk shade **275.00**
13¼″ h
Mantel, flared trumpet form, gold irid, green heart and vine design, gilt metal socket fixture **300.00**
Table, inverted trumpet form, leaf and spider web dec, domed shade, minor losses to webbing **2,000.00**
24″ h, King Tut, bulbous form, rainbow irid and applied glass stringing design, bronze mounts **700.00**
67″ h, floor, torcheres, pr, 8″ d crackle glass shade, opal white and irid gold with ruffled blue rim, elaborate gilt metal lamp bases molded with floral swags, knights in armor, and heraldic elements, stepped onyx base **2,300.00**
Rose Bowl, 4″ h, blown clear crystal, paperweight, trapped bubble symmetrical design, inscribed "Durand V 1995–4" **225.00**
Rose Jar, cov, 6″ h, 6″ w, irid deep gold, blue and purple highlights, matching cov with finial, sgd "V Durand & 1964–6" **650.00**
Stemware, crystal, Orleans pattern, twenty water goblets, sixteen champagne glasses (one chip), and thirteen wine glasses (two chips), price for 49 pcs ... **100.00**
Vase
4″ h, flared ovoid body, ambergris with allover blue irid luster, stark white pulled hearts and vines dec, marked "Durand V 1710–4" **990.00**
5¾″ h, flattened flared body, amber luster with allover irid, green heart and vine dec ... **522.50**
6″ h, 6½″ w, bulbous, wide rim, irid, threading, some loss of threading **150.00**
6½″ h, King Tut, flared baluster form, ambergris with dark blue and purple luster, allover irid,

pulled and hooked white–gold swirls **925.00**

6⅝" h, Lady Gay Rose, baluster form, pink cased to opal, gold irid King Tut swirling dec, gold int. rim, sgd in script "Durand" across pontil **875.00**

7" h
Irid blue, opaque heart and vine dec, sgd "Victor Durand 1812–7" **1,200.00**
Irid gold over opaque yellow, allover random threading, some loss of threading **125.00**

8" h
Deep amethyst, bulbous, optic ribbed, sgd "Victor Durand 1987–8" **400.00**
Irid blue, allover random threading, gold irid foot, sgd "V Durand 2028–1/2–8," slight loss of threading **900.00**
Shaded emerald green cased to opal, int. gold irid, flared form, vertically ribbed, sgd "Durand 1710–8" **1,045.00**

8½" h
Ambergris, red and white overlay, allover crackle and irid, oval body **475.00**
Ruby red cased in opal and amber, gold irid int., flared rim, ten ribbed body, unsgd **1,550.00**

9½" h, 10" d, King Tut, oval body, peach ground, irid, green scrolling lines dec, enameled "Durand 1964–10" **1,750.00**

9¾" h, beehive form, ambergris, gold irid, sgd "V. Durand 10–8" **825.00**

9¾" h, 5½" w, King Tut, deep blue, silver and gold irid **1,100.00**

10¼" h, broad oval body, amber, irid blue luster surface, dark acid mark at base edge **600.00**

10½" h
Ambergris, irid pale yellow, green pulled feathers **500.00**
Opal ground, blue and irid green pulled string pattern, inverted baluster form **358.00**

12" h, flared vasiform, ambergris, smooth cobalt blue and peacock purple irid luster, in-

scribed across pontil "Durand 1982–12" **875.00**

14" h, pr, trumpet form, transparent ruby red, opaque white and pink pulled feather design, Bridgeton Rose border designed and cut by Charles Link **995.00**

25¼" h, shouldered ovoid body, flaring mouth, white ground, green and irid gold leaf dec, gold threading, losses to threading, mounted as lamp on gilt metal stand, first quarter 20th C **300.00**

ENGLISH CHINA AND PORCELAIN (GENERAL)

History: The manufacture of china and porcelain was scattered throughout England, with the majority of the factories located in the Staffordshire district. The number of potteries was more than one thousand.

By the 19th century English china and porcelain had achieved a worldwide reputation for excellence. American stores imported large amounts for their customers. The special production English pieces of the 18th and early 19th centuries held a position of great importance among early American antiques collectors.

References: Susan and Al Bagdade, *Warman's English & Continental Pottery & Porcelain, 2nd Edition,* Wallace–Homestead, 1991; John A. Bartlett, *British Ceramic Art: 1870–1940,* Schiffer Publishing, 1993; John Bartlett, *English Decorative Ceramics,* Kevin Francis Publishing, 1989; David Battie and Michael Turner, *19th and 20th Century British Porcelain Price Guide,* Antique Collectors' Club, 1994; Peter Bradshaw, *18th Century English Porcelain Figures, 1745–1795,* Antique Collectors' Club; John and Margaret Cushion, *A Collector's History of British Porcelain,* Antique Collectors' Club, 1992; Rachael Feild, *Macdonald Guide To Buying Antique Pottery & Porcelain,* Wallace–Homestead, 1987; Geoffrey A. Godden, *Godden's Guide To English Porcelain,* Wallace–Homestead, 1992; Geoffrey A. Godden, *Godden's Guide To Mason's China And The Ironstone Wares,*

Antique Collectors' Club, 1991; Pat Halfpenny, *English Earthenware Figures 1740–1840*, Antique Collectors' Club, 1992; R. K. Henrywood, *Relief Molded Jugs, 1820–1900*, Antique Collectors' Club, 1985; Kathy Hughes, *A Collector's Guide to Nine-teenth–Century Jugs*, Routledge & Kegan Paul, 1985; Kathy Hughes, *A Collector's Guide to Nineteenth–Century Jugs, Volume II*, Taylor Publishing, 1991; Llewellyn Jewitt, *The Ceramic Art of Great Britain*, Sterling Publishing, 1985 (reprint of 1883 classic); Griselda Lewis, *A Collector's History Of English Pottery*, Antique Collectors' Club, 1987; Donald C. Peirce, *English Ceramics: The Frances and Emory Cocke Collection*, High Museum of Art, 1988.

Additional Listings: Castleford, Chelsea, Coalport, Copeland and Spode, Liverpool, Royal Crown Derby, Royal Doulton, Royal Worcester, Historical Staffordshire, Romantic Staffordshire, Wedgwood, and Whieldon.

BOW

Cup and Saucer, 3⅝" h cup, 5¼" d saucer, Blanc–de–Chine, applied blossoming prunus sprays, two handles, slight glaze chip on cup rim, third quarter 18th C .. **715.00**

Dish, 7¼" l, octagonal, Quail pattern, kakiemon style and palette, iron–red, blue, green, and gold, center painted with two quail, flowering prunus tree, floral sprigs and blossoms, flowering plant, and three insects, shaped molded border, gold trifid band, iron–red scroll rim, unmarked, third quarter 18th C **600.00**

Miniature, tea service, partial, nine 1¼" h coffee cups, 1⅞" h creamer, eight 3" saucers, eight 1¾" d teabowls, 3¼" h cov teapot, 3½" d waste bowl, allover underglazed blue grape and scrolled vinework, c1765 ....**1,850.00**

Plate, 9¼" d, Blanc–de–Chine, flat border, five applied blossoming prunus sprays, unmarked, third quarter 18th C **330.00**

Wall Pocket, 9" l, cornucopia, underglaze blue chinoiserie, white ground, man walking in garden, scroll molded borders, rim, and ribbed end with blue highlights, flat pierced back, unmarked, third quarter 18th C, slight rim chip and cracks **1,210.00**

CAUGHLEY

Cream Boat, 3¾" l, Cannonball pattern, gadrooned boat form, underglaze blue chinoiserie landscape, undulating rim with gadroon and rib molding, blue edging, underglaze crescent mark and imp star mark, last quarter 18th C **250.00**

Egg Drainer, 3¾" l, Fisherman pattern, transfer printed underglaze blue, two fishermen, one standing in junk, other sitting on rocky shore, cell diaper and cup and ball borders, applied white leaf handle, unmarked, third quarter 18th C **220.00**

Miniature

Coffee Set, two 1¼" h coffee cups, 3¼" h cov coffeepot, 2" h creamer, two 2¾" d saucers, 2⅜" h cov sugar, 1⅝" d waste bowl, blue Chinese landscape designs, underglaze marks, late 18th C **980.00**

Tea and Coffee Service, six 1⅜" h coffee cups, 3½" h cov coffeepot, 1⅞" h creamer, six 2¾" d saucers, six 1¾" d teabowls, 2¾" cov teapot, 2⅝" d waste bowl, gilt trim, floret dec, late 18th C **920.00**

Tea Set, four 1⅛" h coffee cups, 2" h creamer, five 2⅞" d saucers, 2½" h cov sugar, three 1¾" d teabowls, 2⅞" h cov teapot, Chinese figural coastal landscape scenes, cell borders, underglaze marks, late 18th C **1,840.00**

Mustard Pot, 3" h, Travelers pattern, transfer printed, underglaze blue vignettes of travelers on a road, double rim lines, underglaze blue "S" mark, last quarter 18th C **525.00**

DERBY

Centerpiece, 4½" h, three radiating scallop shells, underglaze blue floral spray, shell centered dentil border, shell form center handle, shell encrusted pierced trefoil shaped base, incised "BL" mark, third quarter 18th C small chips to rim and encrusted shell edges 1,870.00

Figure, 5¾" w, 4¼" h, biscuit, Cupid sleeping, lying on side, head resting on arm, oval rockwork mound base, applied cluster of flowers, unmarked, c1790 ... 425.00

Jug, 3½" h, Boy on a Buffalo pattern, transfer print, boy riding buffalo in landscape, reverse with buffalo by river with two sailboats, int. trellis border, sparrow beak, unmarked, third quarter 18th C 770.00

Tea and Dinner Service, assembled, Japan pattern and palette, peony and prunus between foliate and scrolled borders, creamer, cups and saucers, plates, platters, serving bowls, shrimp bowls, soup plates, sugar, teapot, cov tureens, tray, vegetable dishes, 19th and 20th C, stains, surface wear, hairlines, nicks, price for 144 pcs .. 8,050.00

Tea Service, peach ground, banding, scrolled gilt leaf designs, bowls, coffee canns and saucers, creamer, cov sugar, teacups and saucers, teapot, teapot stand, red painted marks, early 19th C, stains, gilt wear, and repairs, price for 48 pcs 1,035.00

JACKFIELD

Coffeepot, 12½" h, black, glazed, camel spout, ring handle with attached chain, metal mounted make–do urn and bird finial, 18th C, small rim chips 375.00

Creamer, 4¼" h, black, glazed, traces of gilt floral dec, 18th C, rim chips 195.00

Teapot
7" l, black, glazed, ftd, crabstock spout and handle, bird finial, traces of gilt dec, 18th C, chips 275.00
8¼" l, black, glazed, crabstock handle, make–do metal acorn finial, spout and handle ring with attached chain, 18th C, rim nicks 250.00

LOWESTOFT

Basket, 7⅞" l, oval, Pine Cone pattern, underglaze blue transfer print, white ground, fruiting floral spray, int. with band of flower head sprays, scroll and trellis diaper border, ext. with blue centered florets, blue and white rope handles, flower head cluster terminals, reticulated, unmarked, third quarter 18th C, one handle restored, chips 660.00

Jug, 3" h, underglaze blue chinoiserie garden scenes, house on river bank, pagoda, int. trellis diaper border interrupted by flower head at sparrow beak, unmarked, third quarter 18th C .. 385.00

Patty Pan, 4⅜" d, flat center, underglaze blue butterfly, blue line band, two floral sprays and insects, scalloped rim band, ext. with floral sprays and insects, base line border, unmarked, third quarter 18th C 200.00

Teabowl and Saucer, 1¾" h teabowl, 4⅝" d saucer, underglaze blue chinoiserie vignettes, pavilions, pagodas in gardens, trellis, and floral paneled borders, unmarked, third quarter 18th C .. 250.00

NEW HALL

Coffee Cann, 2½" h, Tobacco Leaf pattern, polychrome dec, underglaze blue, red, and green flower heads and scrolling leafage,

New Hall, sugar bowl, small pink flowers, dark pink outline, cream ground, c1810, unmarked, 6¾" h, 6½" l, $240.00.

floral vine borders, gilt highlights and ext. border, last quarter 18th C **175.00**

Teabowl and Saucer, Tobacco Leaf pattern, polychrome dec, underglaze blue, red, and green flower heads and scrolling leafage, floral vine borders, gilt highlights and ext. border, last quarter 18th C, crack in teabowl ... **200.00**

VAUXHALL

Milk Jug, 3¾" h, lightly ribbed and relief molded, flowering vines, two birds, large cartouche, underglaze blue dec, diaperwork panel, int. rim with trellis diaper and zig–zag border, applied triple scroll handle, two blue florets, unmarked, third quarter 18th C, minute rim chip **4,125.00**

Teabowl and Saucer, 1⅜" h teabowl, 4½" d saucer, Cormorant pattern, underglaze blue chinoiserie garden scene with bird and man, unmarked, third quarter 18th C **1,100.00**

ENGLISH SOFTPASTE

History: Between 1820 and 1860 a large number of potteries in England's Staffordshire district produced decorative wares with a soft earthenware (creamware) base and a plain white or yellow glazed ground.

Design or "stick" spatterware was created by a cut–sponge (stamp), hand painting, or transfer. Blue was the dominant color. The earliest patterns were carefully arranged geometrics and generally covered the entire piece. Later pieces had a decorative border with a center motif, usually a tulip. In the 1850s Elsmore and Foster developed the Holly Leaf pattern.

King's Rose features a large, cabbage–type rose in red, pale red, or pink. The pink rose often is called "Queen's Rose." Secondary colors are pastels of yellow, pink, and occasionally green. The borders vary: a solid band, vined, lined, or sectional. The King's Rose exists in an oyster motif.

Strawberry China ware comes in three types: strawberries and strawberry leaves (often called strawberry luster), green featherlike leaves with pink flowers (often called cut–strawberry, primrose, or old strawberry), and a third type with the decoration in relief. The first two types are characterized by rust red moldings. Most pieces have a creamware ground. Davenport was one of the many potteries that made this ware.

Yellow–glazed earthenware (canary luster) has a canary yellow ground, transfer design which is usually in black, and occasional luster decoration. The earliest pieces date from the 1780s and have a fine creamware base. A few hand–painted pieces are known. Not every piece has luster decoration.

Marked pieces are uncommon. Because the ground is softpaste, the ware is subject to cracking and chipping. Enamel colors and other types of decoration do not hold well. It is not unusual to see a piece with the decoration worn off.

Reference: Susan and Al Bagdade, *Warman's English & Continental Pottery & Porcelain, 2nd Edition,* Wallace–Homestead, 1991.

Additional Listings: Adams Rose, Gaudy Dutch, Salopian Ware, Staffordshire Items.

DESIGN SPATTERWARE

Coffeepot, 10" h, thistle and lily of the valley design, red spatter

loops, emb grape finial, mismatched lid **175.00**
Creamer, 4¼" h, open flower, green, yellow, black, and purple on sides, red spatter band of flower heads on rim, blue line edge **90.00**
Cup and Saucer, handleless
Floral, blue, green, ochre, and red **150.00**
Primrose, red, green, and black, blue spatter flower heads band **220.00**
Mug
4" h, geometric dec, red, green, and brown **90.00**
6" h, rosettes, blue, green bands **90.00**
Plate
6½" d, columbine, rose bud, and thistle, red, green, blue, black, and purple, green spatter flower heads border chain, red rim stripe **75.00**
8⅜" d, green stick spatter, gaudy four color floral center, red rim stripes **125.00**
8¾" d, red concentric center circles, narrow red line border with stars circled in blue **125.00**
9" d, stars in center, pinwheels around narrow red line border **125.00**
9¼" d, green flowers, red stick spatter center **125.00**
10½" d, tulip, purple and blue spatter, marked "Cotton & Barlow" **325.00**
Platter, 14⅜" l, large green, yellow, black, and purple open flower, blue open flower heads chain border, red rim stripe **165.00**
Sugar, cov, 5" h, white, blue, and red flowers, green leaves, closed ring and shell handles .. **175.00**
Teapot, cov, rosettes, blue **225.00**
Waste Bowl, 5½" d, gaudy floral polychrome enamel dec, marked "Adams Tunstall, England" **100.00**

KING'S ROSE

Coffeepot, 12" h, pink, green, yellow, and red dec, dome lid, c1825, minor restoration **1,200.00**
Creamer, 4" h, squatty, iron–red design, vine border **100.00**

Cup and Saucer, handleless, iron–red design, segmented pink border **160.00**
Plate
6½" d, vine border, yellow puff balls **140.00**
7½" d, pink border **145.00**
Platter, 13" l **300.00**
Sauce Boat, 6¾" l **150.00**
Soup Plate, 9" d **160.00**
Sugar, cov, pink rose **175.00**
Tea Set, cov teapot, four handleless cups and saucers, brick red rose, imp "Wood," price for six piece set **600.00**
Teapot, 6½" h, iron–red design, multicolored flowers, solid border, age lines **250.00**

Strawberry China, plate, pink luster band, vine dec, 8" d, $40.00.

STRAWBERRY CHINA

Bowl, 6¼" d, pink luster, red and green enamel, wide strawberry border, c1820 .... **175.00**
Coffeepot, 11¼" h, strawberry luster, dome cov, strawberry finial . **475.00**
Creamer, 3½" h, vine border, figural dolphin type handle, four small feet **350.00**
Cup and Saucer, handleless, red strawberries, yellow seed dots, green leaves, iron–red border, dark floral dec on cup, c1820 .. **185.00**

Dish, 6½" d, Strawberry pattern, solid border **35.00**
Mug, 2½" h, applied handle **90.00**
Plate
  6½" d, strawberries and morning glories, pink luster border ... **185.00**
  8¼" d, Cut Strawberry pattern . **185.00**
Relish, 8¾" d, shell shape **115.00**
Sugar, cov, 6⅝" h, vine border, ruffled rim, small double scroll handles **120.00**
Teapot, 6⅞" h, vine border, cream ground, flowers and strawberries, repairs **165.00**
Vegetable Dish, cov, octagonal .. **375.00**

YELLOW GLAZED EARTHENWARE

Bowl, 5" d, ftd, green and red flowers, brown berries and stems, brown outlined serrated rim ... **875.00**
Creamer, 3⅞" h, fluted body, iron—red and green flowers and leaves **420.00**
Cup and Saucer, 3" d handleless cup, 4¾" d saucer, brown transfer, couple at tea **300.00**
Jug, 4½" h, brown printed side commemorating death of Lord Nelson, 1805, reverse portrait of Duke of Wellington, canary ground **425.00**
Mug, child's, 2" d, brown transfer, silver luster rim, boys flying kite, inscribed "For a Favorite" **250.00**
Pitcher, 3¾" h, red and orange flowers, wine dec on neck **625.00**
Plate, 8¼" d, black transfers of history of Rome, stylized vine borders, canary ground, Montreau, c1810, price for set of eight ... **1,150.00**
Potpourri Vase, 7½" d, six classical figures outlined in black enamel, flaming brazier, inscribed "Sacrifice A L'Hymen," silver luster lion's head handles **425.00**
Sauce Tureen, cov, matching stand, 8⅛" h, oval, trailing red outlined foliage, silver resist foliage, lustered handles, canary yellow ground, early 19th C, price for pair **4,600.00**
Vase, 5" h, 4½" w, moon shaped, multicolored bird and flower dec,

gilt and white handles, round gilt feet, crown printed and incised marks, 1878, restoration to rim **2,250.00**

FAIRINGS, MATCH-STRIKERS, AND TRINKET BOXES

History: Fairings are small, charming china objects which were purchased or given away as prizes at English fairs in the 19th century. Although fairings are generally identified with England, they actually were manufactured in Germany by Conte and Boehme of Possneck.

Fairings depicted an amusing scene either of courtship and marriage, politics, war, children, or animals behaving as children. Over four hundred varieties have been identified. Most fairings bore a caption. Early examples, 1860–70, were of better quality than later ones. After 1890 the colors became more garish, and gilding was introduced.

The manufacturers of fairings also made match–strikers and trinket boxes. Some were captioned. The figures on the lids were identical to those of the fairings. The market for the match–strikers and trinket boxes was identical to that for the fairings.

Reference: Susan and Al Bagdade, *Warman's English & Continental Pottery & Porcelain, Second Edition.* Wallace–Homestead, 1991.

Advisors: Barbara and Melvin Alprea.

FAIRINGS

Ben Franklin, red vest, light black hair, grass pedestal base, Staffordshire, 3" h **75.00**
Home Run, couple by bed **250.00**
Let's Do Business Together, two boys sitting on chamber pots, green, gold, flesh, and red, 4½" h **150.00**
Looking Down on His Luck, young man and wife looking down at twins, purple, blue, and red, marked "Made in Germany," 3½" h **100.00**
Returning at One O'Clock in the Morning, wife spanking hus-

Box, gold mirror frame, child with light brown hair, white dress with green florals, blue shoes, brown dog, marked "Conta & Boehme Thuringia Germany," 5½" h, $345.00.

band, blue, red, and brown, marked "Made in Germany," 3¼" h **125.00**

MATCH–STRIKERS

Crown and scepter, oval, applied flower borders **250.00**
Drum and drumsticks, red, white, and blue, gilt accents **250.00**
Tea Party, three ladies around tea table **300.00**

TRINKET BOXES

Black Cat, blue cushion, pitcher, and book, gilt trim, 2½" h **175.00**
Fireplace with mirror, small boy, chicken on mantle, gold, red, orange, and tan, 4¾" h **165.00**
King and Queen, white, matte finish, 4" h **175.00**
Piano with mirror, open book, gilt trim, 4¾" h **125.00**

FAIRY LAMPS

History: Fairy lamps, originating in England in the 1840s, are candle–burning night lamps. They were used in nurseries, hallways, and dim corners of the home.

Two leading candle manufacturers, the Price Candle Company and the Samuel Clarke Company, promoted fairy lamps as a means to sell candles. Both contracted with other manufacturers of glass, porcelain, and metal to produce the needed shades and cups. For example, Clarke used Worcester Royal Porcelain Company, Stuart & Sons, and Red House Glass Works in England, plus firms in France and Germany. Clarke's trademark was a small fairy with a wand surrounded by the words "Clarke Fairy Pyramid, Trade Mark."

Fittings were produced in a wide variety of styles. Shades ranged from pressed to cut glass, from Burmese to Nailsea. Cups are found in glass, porcelain, brass, nickel, and silver plate.

American firms selling fairy lamps included Diamond Candle Company of Brooklyn, Blue Cross Safety Candle Co., and Hobbs–Brockunier of Wheeling, West Virginia.

Fairy lamps are found in two pieces (cup and shade) and three pieces (cup with matching shade and saucer). Married pieces are common.

Reference: John F. Solverson (comp.), *Those Fascinating Little Lamps: Miniature Lamps Value Guide,* Antique Publications, 1988.

Periodicals: *Light Revival,* 35 West Elm Ave., Quincy, MA 02170; *Night Light Newsletter,* 38619 Wakefield Ct., Northville, MI 48167.

Reproduction Alert: Reproductions abound.

Baccarat, 4⅛" h, peacock blue, molded pinwheel swirl design, marked "Baccarat Depose," price for pair **250.00**
Bisque, figural
  3¼", cat's head, white, amber eyes **250.00**
  3⅜", Pekingese dog, shades of brown, amber eyes, blue collar, light blue back **195.00**
  3⅞", three faces, lion, monkey, and other animal, white, colored glass eyes **500.00**
Brass, 4⅝" h, jeweled dec, finger holder **80.00**
Burmese
  3¾" h, clear sgd Clarke base .. **145.00**

4½" h, 5" w, pleated skirt, marked "Thos Webb & Sons Queens Burmeseware Patent" and "S Clark Fairy Patent Trade Mark," clear candle cup marked · "S Clark Pyramid Fairy Trade Mark" 1,150.00

Cranberry, 4¼" h, applied clear hand tooled petals dec, clear petal dec holder, clear sgd candle cup **350.00**

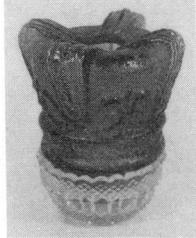

Overshot, "Crown," blue, Clarke base, $145.00.

Overshot, 4½" h, sapphire blue, clear Clarke pyramid cup **75.00**

Peachblow, 6½" h, metal base sgd "Bernard Rice's Sons Inc et al" **165.00**

Satin
  3⅞" h, blue, crimped top and bottom, ruffled blue mica cased base **55.00**
  4" h, pink, crimped top and bottom, crystal pyramid style base, orig Clarke candle, emb "RD No 92571" **110.00**
  4½" h, amber, white enameled dec, orig Clarke candle **220.00**
  4⅝" h, blue, white int., clear Clarke base **85.00**
  4¾" h, pink, crimped top, clear Clarke base **65.00**
  5" h, pale blue, ruffled top and base, clear Clarke candle cup **330.00**
  5⅝" h, peacock blue, 6" d ruffled base, shade with white flowers and leaves dec, clear Clarke candle cup **550.00**

Spangle, 5½" h, green, sgd Clarke porcelain cup, metal base, sgd "Bernard Rice's Sons Inc et al" and "Made in Germany" **55.00**

Vaseline, 5½" h, clear **185.00**

FAMILLE ROSE

History: Famille Rose is Chinese export enameled porcelain in which the pink color predominates. It was made primarily in the 18th and 19th centuries. Other porcelains in the same group are Famille Jaune (yellow), Famille Noire (black), and Famille Verte (green).

Decorations include courtyard and home scenes, birds, and insects. Secondary colors are yellow, green, blue, aubergine, and black.

Mid to late 19th–century Chinese export wares similar to Famille Rose are identified as Rose Canton, Rose Mandarin, and Rose Medallion.

Reference: Gloria and Robert Mascarelli, *Warman's Oriental Antiques,* Wallace–Homestead, 1992.

Bowl
  6½" d, fish and bat dec, Ch'ing dynasty **80.00**
  7" d, deep, turquoise ground, rounded sides with lotus flowers, insects, and butterflies, foliated edge with gilded highlights, iron red enameled foot with six character Jiaqing seal mark, 18th C **520.00**

Butter Plate, 6" d, Chinese, 19th C, minor imperfections **425.00**

Center bowl, 16½" d, well dec with duck and lotus medallion encircled by elaborately dressed noblemen and ladies alternating with flower clusters, precious symbols and scholar's table implements repeated on cavetto, flattened rim painted with dense butterflies, blossoms, and precious symbols border, ext. dec with three evenly spaced peony blossoms, star crack to base, wear to enamel, 19th C **450.00**

Charger, 13½" d, foliate edge with gilded highlights, famille rose enamels with flowering blossoms and garlands, 19th C ...**1,500.00**

Deep Dish, 8" d, chips, 19th C, set of sixteen **700.00**

Dinner Service, 20 pcs, plates, household objects design, eleven 9¾" d dinner, nine 8" d luncheon, 19th C, damage **800.00**

Dish, ogee shaped, heron, peaches, symbols of longevity, immortality, central peach medallion, gold rim, Tongzhi seal mark, 6½" d, $175.00.

Dish
9¼" l, scalloped rim, 19th C, price for pair **800.00**
11" l, oval, enameled courtesans in garden, key fret border, 19th C **320.00**

Funnel, 4¼" h, attributed to Worcester, painted rose, yellow, and blue chinoiserie garden scene, reddish–brown pierced foot, reverse with garden vignette, two painted flowering vines on rim int., two slight rim chips **26,500.00**

Jar, cov, vertical ribs, waisted neck, flared mouth, bouquets of flowers, diaper and swag borders, Chinese, mid 18th C, mounted as lamp **1,430.00**

Plate, dinner
9" d, damages, late 18th C, set of ten **450.00**
9⅛" d, chips, 19th C, set of twelve **520.00**
9¾" d, rim chips, 19th C, set of ten **430.00**

Punch Bowl, 16½" d, gently rounded sides dec with panels of European figures hunting, interspersed with stylized patterned ground, int. with single hunter and dogs, late 19th C ..**3,750.00**

Tankard, 6¼" h, pear shape, ladies and children at play vignette, gilt scroll ground, Chinese, late 18th C, price for pair **550.00**

Tea Caddy, 6" h, rect, figural dec, Chinese, pr **150.00**

Teapot, cov, 7½" h, faux burl wood handle and spout, sides dec with famille rose enamels, gilt figures in landscape framed by molded bamboo, bamboo shoot finial, 18th C **3,000.00**

Vase
13½" h, relief sprigs, flowers, fruit, and objects, red and gilt ground, Chinese, 19th C, mounted as lamp **1,430.00**
20½" h, baluster form, figures and horse in landscape setting, drilled and mounted as lamp, 19th C **400.00**
25½" h, baluster form, panels with figural dec, applied lizard dec on shoulder, crane handles, China, 19th C **690.00**

FANS

History: Today, people tend to think of fans as fragile, frivolous accessories wielded by women, yet the origin of the fan was no doubt highly practical. Early man may have used it to winnow his grain, shoo flies, and cool his brow. This simple tool eventually became a symbol of power: ancient lore maintains that Emperor Hsien Yuan (c2697 B.C.) used fans; the tomb of Egypt's Tutankhamen (1350 B.C.) yielded two ostrich feather fans with gold mounts. Fans also began to assume religious significance and were used to whisk flies from altars. Early Christians recognized the practicality of this practice and included a flabellum, or fixed fly–whisk, in their early services. Meanwhile, the Chinese and Japanese continued to use fans in their courts, often incorporating precious materials such as ivory, gold, and jade.

Until the seventh century A.D., fans were non–folding. Then, according to Japanese legend, Emperor Jen–ji noticed the logic of a bat's folded wings and applied his insight to a new fan design. Later, European traders returned from the East with samples of these wonders. By the sixteenth century sophisticated Italian women had appropriated the fans, which soon became de rigueur throughout Europe. Now primarily feminine fashion accessories, their styles changed to complement the ever–changing dress styles. Fans' popularity led to experimentation in their production and merchandising. They also became popular as a way for artists to test their skills—a fan leaf's curved, folding surface offered challenges in perspective.

World War I was the end of slower eras; the 1920s raced at a frenetic pace. The modern woman set aside her ubiquitous fan, freeing both hands to drive her roadster or carry her political banner. Fans became more an advertising tool than a fashion statement.

Some basic guidelines are:

—19th C artisans copied 18th C styles. True Georgian figures should have gray hair; if the wigs are white, the fan is more recent. The later fans will often have a "heavier" appearance, and anachronistic costuming.

—Empire fans were also copied. The period ones have sequins made by flattening circles of wire; a tiny line shows where the wire ends meet. Later sequins were stamped whole out of sheet metal and have no joining line.

—Ivory, bone, celluloid, and plastic may look somewhat alike. Ivory often has a subtle, textureless graining pattern and may feel smooth and buttery; bone frequently reveals channels. Look for mold marks in plastic.

—Many leaves became damaged with wear and were replaced. These "marriage" fans can still be delightful collectibles, but beware of dating a fan merely based on one component.

—Loops are rarely found on fans before 1830.

—Framing a fan often causes its sticks to warp, its leaf to lose its elasticity and ability to fold. It is also difficult to tell if a fan has been sewn or glued to its backing, making its removal difficult.

—The number of degrees a folding fan opens is a key to dating.

—Handle fans gently, unfolding from left to right.

Fan Terminology:

Brisé—fan with no leaf, but made of rigid, overlapping sticks held together at base by a rivet and at the other end by a ribbon.

Cockade—pleated fan opening to form complete circle.

Folding fan—fan with a flexible, pleated leaf mounted on sticks.

Fontange—shape of folding fans c1890–1935, with center of leaf longer than guards.

Guard—the outermost sticks, usually the height of fan.

Leaf or mount—flexible, pleated material which unites the upper parts of a folding fan's sticks.

Lithograph—printing process invented in 1797, often subsequently hand–colored.

Loop—often "u" shaped finger holder attached to rivet at base of fan; rare before 1830.

Medallion—pictorial representation, usually circular or oval, in leaf.

Piqué–point—decorative small gold or silver points or pins set flush with surface of sticks or guards.

Reserve—small oval or shield background for monogram or scene.

Rivet—pin about which sticks of a folding fan pivot.

Sticks—rigid framework of a folding fan.

Studs—exposed end of rivet, sometimes shaped as decorative paste "gem."

Washer—small disk to prevent friction between end of rivet and fan.

References: Helene Alexander, *Fans,* Batsford, 1984; Nancy Armstrong, *A Collector's History of Fans,* Clarkson N. Potter, 1974; Nancy Armstrong, *Fans: A Collector's Guide,* Souvenir Press, 1984; Nancy Armstrong, *The Book of Fans,* Mayflower Books, Inc.; Anna Gray Bennett, *Fans In Fashion,* San Francisco Art Museum, 1981; Anna Gray Bennett, *Unfolding Beauty,* Thames and Hudson, 1988; Braintree Historical Society, *Hunt and Allen Fans,* Braintree Historical Society, 1988; Reiko Chiba,

Painted Fans of Japan, Charles E. Tuttle Co, 1962; Debrett's Peerage, *Fans From The East,* Debrett's Peerage, Ltd, 1978; Francoise DePerthuis and Vincent Meylan, *Eventails,* Hermé, 1989; Tseng Yu–ho Ecke, *Poetry on the Wind,* Honolulu Academy of Arts, 1981; M. A. Flory, *A Book About Fans,* Macmillan, 1895; Bertha DeVere Green, *A Collector's Guide To Fans Over The Ages,* Frederick Muller Ltd, London, 1975; Julia Hutt and Helene Alexander, *Ogi,* Dauphin Publishing, 1992; Neville John Irons, *Fans of Imperial China,* Kaiserreich Ltd, 1981; Neville John Irons, *Fans of Imperial Japan,* Kaiserreich Ltd, 1981; Christl Kammerel, *Der Facher,* Himmer Verlag, Munich, 1989; Susan Mayor, *A Collector's Guide To Fans,* Wellfleet Books, 1990; Susan Mayor, *Collecting Fans,* Mayflower Books, 1980; Susan Mayor, *Fans,* Vancouver Museum, 1983; Musee de la Mode et du Costome, *L'Eventail,* 1985; McIver Percival, *The Fan Book,* T. Fisher Unwin Ltd, London, 1920; G. W. Woolliscroft Rhead, *The History Of The Fan,* Kegan Paul, Trench, Trubner & Co, London, 1910; Mary E. G. Rhoads, *The Fan Directory,* Fan Collectors Press, 1993; Maryse Volet, *L'Imagination au Service de L'Eventail,* 1986.

Collectors' Club: FANA, Fan Association of North America, 6138 Deacon Rd., Windermere, FL 34786.

Advisor: Wendy Hamilton Blue.

Note: Abbreviations:
gl–Guard Length
hp–handpainted
MOP–mother-of-pearl
op–width when opened
#/#–number of sticks/number of guards

Wedding, silk, ivory, lace, seed pearl floral applique, 12¼" radius, $65.00.

AMERICAN AND EUROPEAN

Mid 18th C, paper, bone, probably English, double leaf, paper, hp in gouache, 3 garden scene vignettes on front, each bordered by orange circles and four black dots, left: woman with body angled towards left guard, head turned to look at man in center, orange breeches, white stockings, blue coat, carrying walking stick, looking to woman on right in pink gown, green under skirt, hand extended to man, floral sprays on reserves, musical instruments with ribbons on either side of central vignette, blue border; reverse: plain, 12/2, front of sticks painted with flowers, some gold gilt, guards roughly carved, painted with birds and flowers, brass rivet, 10⅜" gl, 18" op, 150 degrees **200.00**

Early 19th C
"Imperceptible" arrow, ivory brisé, c1820, each stick carved in shape of arrow, point at rivet, notched fletches at top, each stick and guard ornately pierced and painted in bands, gilt and red flowers across fletches, gilded, cross-hatched ribbon with flowers, green ground, leaves near contemporary, actual green ribbon, gilt foliage, red flowers slightly below fan's middle, 25/2, 6½" gl, 11¼" op, clear paste stud **200.00**

"Imperceptible" horn brisé, c1810–25, translucent green-horn sticks, ornate finials alternating with Gothic arch designs, alternate sticks dec with cut steels piqué point at finial base, piqué point flowers below contemporary ribbon, ornately gilded floral sprays, 23/2, 7⁷⁄₁₆" gl, 14" op, 165 degrees **145.00**

Paper, bone, early lithograph, front: central 2¾ x 3¾" vignette, man in 18th C costume of brown breeches, white hose, gold coat, white vest, shepherd's crook, leading sheep, talking with 2 women, one in blue, yellow, and white dress, carrying basket of flowers, other in pink and white dress, rest of leaf dec in silver gilt, shepherdess on left, dancing woman on right, ornate urns, flowers in surround; reverse: silver gilt central musical instruments, flowers, draped garlands in reserves, 16/2, pierced in simple vine motif, 9⁹⁄₁₆" gl, 17¾" op, brass rivet, MOP washer, 160 degrees **165.00**

Mid 19th C

Ivory brisé, possibly Russian, plain sticks, 3 slots for white silk ribbon, 15/2, right guard: high relief intricate carving of woman in swirling drapes, crown, carrying banner, pointing over right shoulder, man climbing ship's rigging, crowned double–headed eagle, standing man in dinghy, masted ship in background, lower, masted ship sails waves, space for monogram at base, left guard: carved, entwined initials "EC," silver rivet, ivory loop, 8¹³⁄₁₆" gl, 13" op. 160 degrees **300.00**

Leather brisé, 15/2, red–brown leather gold edged sticks, braided silk ring to hold fan closed, 8¾" gl, 16" op, 175 degrees, brass rivet, MOP button, brass loop, 16½" l tassel **125.00**

Paper, bone, double leaf, lithograph, hp in gouache, front: 16 people approaching inn and host, floral reserves; reverse: 3 women in 18th C dress listen to man playing flute, buildings in background, pale green reserves, silver ferns, 12/2, sticks ornately pierced in floral vine motif, silver foil inserts, 10¾" gl, 20½" op, 170 degrees, brass rivet, loop, MOP button **160.00**

Paper, MOP, c1850, double leaf, lithograph, hp in gouache, front: man pushes young woman on swing, two other women sitting nearby, pastoral setting with stream, ornately dec French style floral motif reserves; reverse: seven overlapping scenes, hunter on either side, couples courting, playing, or reading music, carved, silver and gold foil appliqué floral motif, painted floral band at bottom, guards with animal under palm tree, 11⁵⁄₈" gl, 22" op, 170 degrees, red paste stud, ornate gold tone loop **195.00**

Silk, bone, c1860, "Jenny Lind flirting," double leaf, cream silk cut to resemble feathers, front: 3 floral groups painted in pink, blue, and purple, silver gilt painted top edges, silver foil appliqué on sticks, simply pierced vine motif, flirting mirror on right guard, 12/2, 6⅜" gl, 11¼" op, brass rivet and loop, MOP washer, 7½" l silk tassel **50.00**

Late 19th C

Gauze, wood, c1890, golden–brown double glazed leaf, hp, 12 small birds, dogwood sprays, green–gold machine lace top edge which varies from 1¼ to 3¼", 16/2, machine made wood sticks, eight grouped ornately pierced and carved leaf motif pairs in front of leaf, gilded accents, 13½" gl, 26" op, 170 degrees, brass rivet, button, and loop, orig box **150.00**

Linen, wood, single fabric leaf, painted, shaded from deep gray bottom to light top, gray, white, black, and gold gilt flowers, painting continues to top of machine stamped pierced sticks, gilded with circles, expanded motif on guards, top sections painted deep gray, 16/2, 13⁹⁄₁₆" gl, 26" op, 170 degrees, black metal loop, brass rivet and washer, 11½″ l knotted silk tassel **145.00**

Satin, wood, c1890, double leaf, black satin leaf, front: finely hp on front with two couples in 18th C court dress, young man playing violin, girl carrying bouquet; reverse: plain, 16/2, plain dark wood sticks, guards, 14⅞″ gl, 28½″ op, 180 degrees, black metal loop **150.00**

Silk, net, bone, single, cream silk leaf, seven 3 x ¾″ net inserts, alternating blue and pink outlines, paint, and sequins, alternating blue and pink draped banner, flowers above, top and bottom edged with cream looped rickrack, 14/2, pierced and carved sticks with simple flowers, painted silver, gold, and green, small circular steels set piqué point, 10⅞″ gl, 19½″ op, 160 degrees, 4¼″ l silk tassel, satin ribbon **150.00**

Early 20th C, Regency replica, paper with linen finish, wood, metal, single heavy paper leaf, central vignette of man leaning over stone wall talking to 2 women in early 19th C rural dress watching 2 doves on ground, small thatched building in background, pale silver paper printed with pale pink roses surrounds, 14/2, lacquered deep reddish brown sticks, stamped gilt with floral motif, guards emb stamped gold tone metal, right guard marked "Duvelleroy," 6⁷⁄₁₆″ gl, 12¼″ op, 160 degrees, brass rivet, washer, contemporary flora satin tapestry cov shaped box **155.00**

AMERICAN AND EUROPEAN SOUVENIR, COMMEMORATIVE, AND ADVERTISING

Late 19th C

Advertising, American, cardboard, handscreen, front: chromolithograph, Buffalo Bill standing with horse, red bordered diecut edges; reverse: adv for Maryland "Temple of Music," 8⅜″ h, 8″ w, slotted 11″ wood stick **135.00**

Souvenir, Italian, linen, wood, cockade, shaped wood frame inset with mirror, tab at top lifts linen cockade, rough machine made lace edge, beige leaf printed with gold suns, putti, 6 ovals with roses and other flowers, one side holds mirror, other is painted with bird and "Ricordo," 9⅞″ l x 2″ w frame, extends to 9½″ dia, 360 degrees **45.00**

Early 20th C, advertising

American

1904, cardboard, handscreen, front: chromolithograph, 27 little girls, caption "Have you a little 'fairy' in your home? FAIRY SOAP of course," American Lithographic Co, NY; reverse: 2 young black children sit with backs to viewer, overlooking aerial prospect of World's Fair, "The Gold Dust Twins at the World's Fair, St Louis, USA 1904," 7⅞″ h, 7½″ w, slotted 7¼″ l wood stick **200.00**

1910–20, cardboard, wood, black and white head shots of "Moving Picture Stars" Kathlyn Williams, Blanche Sweet, Warren Kerrigan, Bessie Eyton, Irving Cummings, pale gray toned drawers of generic film scenes, copyright by G A Schneider; reverse: adv for VA general store, Fort Bedfort P–Nut Butter, scalloped edges, 7⅞″ h, 7⅞″ w, 9¹³⁄₁₆″ slotted wood stick **55.00**

French

1910, paper, bone, double leaf, cloth, front: 2 vignettes, man in 18th C breeches approaches woman as fiddler plays, 2 men and woman in 18th C dress play blind man's bluff, gold printed flower baskets, garlands as surrounds, ornamental top and bottom borders; reverse: "Hotel Knickerbocker and Restaurant, James B Ragan, Eventails Duvelleroy, Paris," 14/bone sticks, simple incised and painted floral motif, 8" gl, 15" op, 170 degrees, brass rivet, washer **115.00**

1910, paper, wood, double paper leaf, chromolithograph, front: woman in stylish hat, trailing chiffon ribbons reaches as if to help man, goggles and brown leather coat, steer yellow racing car around bend of fan's bottom arc, "Souvenir Cafe Martin, New York," artist sgd in print "S. Montaut"; reverse: beige paper printed with intertwined floral garlands surrounding center "Perfumed with Floramye L. T. Piver, Paris," 14/2, plain wood sticks, 9⁹⁄₁₆" gl, 17½" op, 170 degrees, brass rivet, washer **170.00**

1930, paper, wood, double paper leaf, printed in color, front: 3 vignettes, each framed by palm trees, left: scene of two people in North African dress, mosque and ship in background, center: young couple admire North American city skyline from deck of ship, right: people in Caribbean dress dance on shore as ship passes in background; reverse: simple, multicolored map of trans–Atlantic routes sailed by French line, artist sgd in print "Edouard Collin," 8 plain darkly stained 7⅞" l wood sticks, 15" op, 160 degrees **60.00**

1935, paper, wood, double paper leaf, printed in color, same on both sides, stylized caricature seated at cafe table, adding seltzer to wine

glass, French adv, artist sgd and dated in print "d'aprés A. M. Cassandre, '35," leaf scalloped at top, 4 plain widely spaced 9¼" l sticks, 14" op, 140 degrees, nail-head rivet, washer **90.00**

Japanese, paper, bamboo, translucent "oil" paper, single leaf, garlands printed in gold and green, red and white hp flowers, "SINGER" in large blue letters across center, stamped in gold on each guard, 21/2, machine made sticks, stamped with gold flowers, 8½" gl, 15½" op, 180 degrees, steel rivet, thin brass loop **20.00**

ORIENTAL, PACIFIC

Late 18th C, ivory brisé, Chinese, c1790, single side carved, figures engaged in dragon dance; one figure carries large ceremonial fan with "Taiping" or "peace" in Chinese characters, carved birds and flowers finials, gorge carved with flowers and central "CW" monogram, later silk ribbon, 25/2, intricately carved small flowers on 10½" l guards, 16½" op, 155 degrees, brass rivet, MOP washer **500.00**

Early 19th C, goosefeather, bone, Chinese, red, green, and blue painted flowers, marabou tips, 20/2, pierced vine motif stylized bone sticks, 8¾" gl, 18" op, 165 degrees, brass rivet, MOP washer **70.00**

Mid 19th C, paper, lacquered wood, Mandarin or "Thousand Faces," Canton, double paper leaf, hp, front: broadly painted scene of people on tiled terrace, 15 figures, appliqued silk clothing, ivory faces; reverse: nearly identical, 14/2, dark reddish brown lacquered sticks, painted with family sitting in garden, both guards painted in gold, gray–red figure carrying large flower over-head, other flowers below, 11¹/₁₆" gl, 21" op, 180 degrees, brass rivet and loop, 7½" l double silk tassel with blue and purple glass beads **125.00**

Late 19th C

Chinese, paper, wood, double paper leaf, front: printed scene of bearded elder holding fan, standing behind flat stringed musical instrument, woman standing on either side, below, 2 men sweep path near stone gateway, warriors approaching on horseback, 9/2, plain stained brown wood sticks, simple elliptical carving on guards, 11½" gl, 18½" op, 150 degrees, dark metal nailhead rivet **55.00**

Japanese

Paper, Mai Ogi, wood, folding, dance type, thin, widely spaced black lacquered wood sticks support black double paper leaf, scraps of letterheads, monograms, etc. from over 200 clubs, ho-tels, schools, and individu-als, 6/2, each guard is single at bottom, separating mid-way into 3 parts to reinforce and support leaf, crisscross banded with black braided cord, 13" gl, 25¼" op, 175 degrees, brass rivet **50.00**

Silk, wood, telescoping, plain silk leaf, simple grained dark sticks, 13/2, butterfly and flowers carved guards, sticks slide into ribs to shorten length of fan when it is not in use, 7⅜ extending to 9½" gl, 14" extending to 16" op, 175 degrees, steel rivet, 4¼" l silk tassel, ornate knot ....·...... **40.00**

Late 19th or early 20th C, Japa-nese, silk, ivory, Ogi, stiff double silk leaf, hp, front: large hanging basket of flowers on right, 3 small birds fly across leaf to left; reverse: brown bird perched on

slender branch near yellow and white floral sprays, 18/2, plain ivory sticks, guards carved with birds and flowers, 11⁵/₁₆" gl, 20½" op, 160 degrees, brass loop **150.00**

Early to mid 20th C, Shanghai, silk, bone, cabriolet, single leaf, upper section hp red, white, and pink flowers, lower leaf painted with large blue, pink, purple, and orange flowers, green leaves, 28/2, pierced bone sticks, 7¹/₁₆" gl, 12¼" op, brass rivet, loop, pale yellow silk tassel, contem-porary box with glass top **35.00**

FENTON GLASS

History: The Fenton Art Glass Company began as a cutting shop in Martins Ferry, Ohio, in 1905. In 1906 Frank L. Fenton started to build a plant in Williamstown, West Virginia, and produced the first piece of glass in 1907. Early production included carnival, chocolate, custard, and pressed plus mold blown opalescent glass. In the 1920s stretch glass, Fenton dolphins, jade green, ruby, and art glass were added.

In the 1930s boudoir lamps, "Dancing La-dies," and various slags were produced. The 1940s saw crests of different colors being added to each piece by hand. Hob-nail, opalescent, and two–color overlay pieces were popular items. Handles were added to different shapes, making the bas-kets they created as popular today as then.

Through the years Fenton has added beauty to their glass by decorating it with hand painting, acid etching, color staining, and copper wheel cutting. Several different paper labels have been used. In 1970 an oval raised trademark also was adopted.

References: Shirley Griffith, *A Pictorial Review Of Fenton White Hobnail Milk Glass,* published by author, 1984; William Heacock, *Fenton Glass: The First Twenty–Five Years,* O–Val Advertising Corp, 1978; William Heacock, *Fenton Glass: The Sec-ond Twenty–Five Years,* O–Val Advertising Corp, 1980; William Heacock, *Fenton Glass: The Third Twenty–Five Years,* O–Val

Advertising Corp, 1989; Naomi L. Over, *Ruby Glass of the 20th Century,* Antique Publications, 1990, 1993–94 value update; Ferill J. Rice (ed.), *Caught In the Butterfly Net,* Fenton Art Glass Collectors of America, Inc., 1991.

Collectors' Clubs: Fenton Art Glass Collectors Of America, Inc., PO Box 384, Williamstown, WV 26187; National Fenton Glass Society, PO Box 4008, Marietta, OH 45750.

Museum: Fenton Art Glass Co., Williamstown, WV.

Additional Listings: Carnival Glass.

Advisor: Ferill J. Rice.

Epergne, Diamond Lace, French opalescent, applied aqua rim, three lily vases, 9½" h, 12" d, $175.00.

Ashtray, Lincoln Inn, cobalt blue .	17.00
Basket	
4" h, Hobnail French Opalescent	45.00
6½" h, Silver Crest	37.50
7" h, Hobnail Blue Opalescent .	60.00
8½" h, red carnival, dated 1994, sgd "Tom Fenton"	55.00
Bonbon	
5" d, Hobnail French Opalescent, handle	17.00
8" d, Silver Crest	11.00
Bowl	
5" d, Lincoln Inn, green	8.00
8" d, Thistle, carnival, marigold, ruffled edge	90.00
11" d, Silver Crest	48.00
Cake Plate, 13" h, Silver Crest, ftd	48.00
Candlesticks, pr	
Hobnail Blue Opalescent, 3½" h, cornucopia	42.00
Silver Crest, low, ruffled	20.00
Candy Dish, Lincoln Inn, ftd, oval, black	25.00
Champagne, Hobnail French Opalescent	18.00
Compote, ftd	
6" d, Emerald Crest	38.00
7" d, Apple Blossom Crest, dec	45.00
Condiment Set, Hobnail Blue Opalescent, individual size creamer, sugar, and mustard	37.00
Creamer	
Hobnail Blue Opalescent	22.00
Lincoln Inn, pink	15.00
Silver Crest, clear reeded handle	17.50
Turquoise Crest	50.00
Cruet, Hobnail Blue Opalescent, orig stopper	32.00
Cup and Saucer, Emerald Crest .	48.00
Epergne Set, Silver Crest, bowl and three horn vases	120.00
Figure, Happiness Bird, black satin	25.00
Flowerpot, Emerald Crest, attached saucer	70.00
Hat	
3½" h, Hobnail Blue Opalescent	22.00
4" h, Polka Dot French Opalescent	95.00
4½" h, Spiral Snow Crest, emerald green	80.00
Jack–in–the–Pulpit Vase, Black Rose	120.00
Juice Set, 5¼" h squatty jug, six 5 oz juice tumblers, Hobnail French Opalescent	110.00
Juice Tumbler, Hobnail Blue Opalescent	13.00
Jug, 6" h, Hobnail Blue Opalescent, handle	37.00
Lamp Base, 9" h, Dancing Lady, Mongolian green	375.00
Mayonnaise and Liner, Hobnail Blue Opalescent	75.00
Mustard, orig lid	
Emerald Crest, orig spoon	75.00
Hobnail French Opalescent . . .	24.00
Plate	
Lincoln Inn, 8" d, amethyst	7.00

Silver Crest, 6" d **6.50**
Puff Jar, cov, Hobnail French Opalescent **37.00**
Punch Cup, Silver Crest **12.00**
Relish Dish, Silver Crest, heart shaped, handle **25.00**
Rose Bowl, Waffle, green opalescent **37.00**
Salt and Pepper Shakers, pr
Cactus **85.00**
Hobnail Blue Opalescent **45.00**
Sherbet, Emerald Crest **24.00**
Shoe, Hobnail Blue Opalescent . . **24.00**
Sugar
Hobnail Blue Opalescent **22.00**
Silver Crest, ruffled top **45.00**
Tidbit Tray, Silver Crest, 3 tier . . . **48.00**
Tumbler
Hobnail Blue Opalescent **24.00**
Lincoln Inn, red **25.00**
Vase
3¾" h, fan, Hobnail French Opalescent **30.00**
4" h, Apple Blossom Crest, dec **40.00**
4¼" h, Waffle, green opalescent **40.00**
4½" h, Silver Crest, fan **12.00**
6¼" h, Jade, ebony vase, hand dec **425.00**
8" h
Black, ftd, orig paper label . . . **50.00**
Emerald Crest, bulbous **60.00**
10" h, Apple Tree, white milk glass **125.00**
11" h, custard, melon shape, daisy dec **45.00**
12" h, Lincoln Inn, amber **85.00**

MADE IN
U.S.A.

FIESTA

History: The Homer Laughlin China Company introduced Fiesta dinnerware in January 1936, at the Pottery and Glass Show in Pittsburgh, Pennsylvania. Fredrick Rhead designed the pattern; Arthur Kraft and Bill Bensford molded it. Dr. A. V. Bleininger and H. W. Thiemecke developed the glazes.

The original five colors were red, dark blue, light green (with a trace of blue), brilliant yellow, and ivory. A vigorous marketing campaign took place between 1939 and 1943. In mid–1937 turquoise was added; red was removed in 1943 because of the war effort and did not reappear until 1959. In 1951 light green, dark blue, and ivory were retired and forest green, rose, chartreuse, and gray were added to the line. Other color changes took place in the late 1950s, including the addition of a medium green.

Fiesta ware was redesigned in 1969 and discontinued in 1972–73. In 1986 Fiesta was reintroduced by Homer Laughlin China Company. The new china body shrinks more than the old semi–vitreous and ironstone pieces, thus making the new pieces slightly smaller than the earlier pieces. The modern colors are also different in tone or hue. The cobalt blue is darker than the old blue. Other modern colors are black, white, apricot, and rose.

References: Susan and Al Bagdade, *Warman's American Pottery and Porcelain,* Wallace–Homestead, 1994; Linda D. Farmer, *The Farmer's Wife Fiesta Inventory and Price Guide,* published by author, 1984; Sharon and Bob Huxford, *The Collector's Encyclopedia of Fiesta, Revised Seventh Edition,* Collector Books, 1992; Dana G. Morykan and Harry L. Rinker, *Warman's Country Antiques & Collectibles, Second Edition,* Wallace–Homestead, 1994.

Periodical: *Fiesta Collectors Quarterly,* 19238 Dorchester Circle, Strongsville, OH 44136.

Collectors' Club: Fiesta Club of America, PO Box 15383, Loves Park, IL 61115.

Reproduction Alert.

Additional Listings: See *Warman's Americana & Collectibles* for more examples.

Ashtray, dark green **90.00**
Bowl
4½" d
Chartreuse **22.00**
Turquoise **18.00**

Utility Tray, turquoise, $25.00.

4¾" d
Cobalt Blue	18.00
Green	15.00

5½" d, green	15.00
Bud Vase, red	95.00

Casserole, cov
Dark Green	325.00
Medium Green	650.00

Chop Plate
13" d
Light Green	25.00
Yellow	20.00
15" d, dark green	125.00

Coffeepot, cov
Chartreuse	450.00
Gray	475.00
Ivory	150.00
Rose	475.00
Compote, large, light green	165.00

Creamer
Light Green, stick handle	40.00
Turquoise	15.00
Cream Soup, gray	75.00
Cup and Saucer, cobalt blue	25.00

Deep Plate
Cobalt Blue	30.00
Medium Green	75.00
Yellow	24.00
Demitasse Coffeepot, light green	325.00

Demitasse Cup and Saucer
Chartreuse	390.00
Cobalt Blue	80.00
Dark Green	390.00
Ivory	55.00
Light Green	55.00
Red	80.00
Rose	390.00
Turquoise	55.00
Yellow	55.00

Eggcup
Chartreuse	165.00

Light Green	45.00
Jug, 2 pint, dark green	135.00

Mixing Bowl Lid
#1
Red	800.00
Yellow	700.00
#4, light green	700.00

Mug
Ivory, Tom & Jerry, gold letters	40.00
Yellow	35.00

Nappy
5½" d, medium green	70.00

8½" d
Medium Green	125.00
Red	65.00
9½" d, light green	75.00

Pitcher, disc
Chartreuse	165.00
Cobalt Blue, water	105.00
Dark Green	185.00

Plate
6" d, bread and butter
Green	2.50
Ivory	7.00

9" d, lunch
Ivory	16.00
Turquoise	15.00
Yellow	15.00

10" d, dinner
Ivory	38.00
Light Green, divided	40.00
Medium Green	100.00
Red	40.00

10½" d
Chartreuse, divided	75.00
Light Green	18.00
12" d, light green, divided	45.00

15" d, grill
Green	22.00
Turquoise	22.00

Platter
Cobalt Blue	25.00
Medium Green	165.00
Salad, individual, medium green	110.00

Sauce Boat
Chartreuse	45.00
Dark Green	95.00
Gray	85.00
Medium Green	160.00
Turquoise	40.00

Shaker
Green, Kitchen Kraft	35.00
Red	12.00
Sugar, cov, chartreuse	50.00

Syrup
Cobalt Blue	375.00
Ivory	325.00
Light Green	325.00
Red	375.00
Turquoise	325.00
Yellow	325.00
Teacup, light green	15.00

Teapot, cov, medium size
Light Green	75.00
Medium Green	650.00

Tumbler, juice
Turquoise	20.00
Yellow	28.00

FIGURAL BOTTLES

History: Figural bottles, made of porcelain, either in glaze or bisque form, achieved popularity in the late 1800s and remained popular to the 1930s. The majority of figural bottles were made in Germany, with Austria and Japan accounting for the balance. They averaged in size from three to eight inches.

Figural bottles were shipped to the United States empty and filled upon arrival. They were then given away to customers by brothels, dance halls, hotels, liquor stores, and taverns. Some were lettered with the names and addresses of the establishment; others had paper labels. Many were used for holidays, e.g., Christmas and New Year.

Figural bottles also were made in glass and other materials. The glass bottles held perfumes, foods, or beverages.

References: Ralph & Terry Kovel, *The Kovels' Bottles Price List, 9th Edition,* Crown Publishers, 1992; Otha D. Wearin, *Statues That Pour,* Wallace–Homestead, 1965, out–of–print.

Periodicals: *Antique Bottle And Glass Collector,* PO Box 187, East Greenville, PA 18041; *Bottles & Extras,* PO Box 154, Happy Camp, CA 96039.

Collectors' Clubs: Federation of Historical Bottle Clubs, 14521 Atlantic Ave., Riverdale, IL 60627; New England Antique Bottle Club, 120 Commonwealth Rd., Lynn, MA 01904.

Museums: National Bottle Museum, Ballston Spa, NY; National Bottle Museum, Barnsley, S. Yorkshire, England.

Sailor, high gloss front, white pants, blue blouse and hat, marked "Made in Germany," 6½" h, $15.00.

GLASS

Baby, 6" h, clear, crying	50.00
Barrel, 9⅜" h, yellow, "Old Sachem Bitters And Wigwam Tonic"	1,870.00
Boot, lady's, 3¾" h, clear	15.00
Bust, soldier, 10½" h, clear	20.00
Cat, 8" h, clear	10.00
Coachman, dark amber, Van Duncks Genever	125.00
Fish, 11½" h, reddish amber, irregular round collared mouth, "The Fish Bitters"	155.00
Golf Bag, 3¼" h, clear, orig painted dec	35.00
Hand Grenade, 4" w, 6¼" h, clear, "American Fire Extinguisher Co," tooled mouth	200.00
Indian Maiden, 12¼" h, light yellow amber, "Brown's Celebrated Indian Herb Bitters"	550.00
Lighthouse, 5½" h, clear, tin cap	55.00
Marie Antoinette, 11¾" h, clear	175.00
Pickle, 4½" h, green	110.00
Policeman, 9" h, black	75.00
Sailor, 8⅓" h, orange, standing smoking pipe	170.00
Skull, 3⅜" h, cobalt blue, emb "Poison"	1,050.00
Spanish Woman, 12" h, red, green, and gold enameled dec	45.00
Submarine, 2⅜" h, cobalt blue,	

marked "Registered" and "Poison" 725.00

POTTERY AND PORCELAIN

Barrel, 15½" h, spigot hole, Coat of Arms dec 125.00
Book
  4⅞" h, "Coming Thru The Rye," blue glaze 255.00
  7⅞" h, Bennington type, brown and white mottled glaze 110.00
Coachman, tan and brown mottled glaze
  9¼" h 155.00
  10⅝" h 110.00
  10¾" h, Bennington mark 225.00
Pig, 7" l, "Chester Idol," incised letters and seated Chinaman, dark brown glaze, Anna Pottery, c1879 .... 4,625.00
Queen, 8⅞" h, tan and light brown glaze, marked "Fulton & Water 16 High Street Lambeth" 385.00
Sweet Potato, 7" h 55.00
Windmill, 9½" h, blue dec 15.00

FINDLAY ONYX GLASS

History: Findlay onyx glass, produced by Dalzell, Gilmore & Leighton Company, Findlay, Ohio, was patented in 1889 for the firm by George W. Leighton. Due to high production costs resulting from a complex manufacturing process, the glass was made only for a short time.

Layers of glass were plated to a bulb of opalescent glass through repeated dippings into a glass pot. Each layer was cooled and reheated to develop opalescent qualities. A pattern mold then was used to produce raised decorations of flowers and leaves. A second mold gave the glass bulb its full shape and form.

A platinum luster paint, producing pieces identified as silver or platinum onyx, was applied to the raised decorations. The color was fixed in a muffle kiln. Other colors such as cinnamon, cranberry, cream, raspberry, and rose were achieved by using an outer glass plating which reacted strongly to reheating. For example, a purple or orchid color came from the addition of manganese and cobalt to the glass mixture.

Reference: James Measell and Don E. Smith, *Findlay Glass: The Glass Tableware Manufacturers, 1886–1902,* Antique Publications, 1986.

Collectors' Club: Collectors of Findlay Glass, PO Box 256, Findlay, OH 45839.

Jar, creamy white, gold dec, 3⅞" d, $310.00.

Butter Dish, cov, 5½" d, silver onyx 800.00
Creamer, 4½" h, cream onyx 525.00
Mustard, 3" h, cream onyx 275.00
Pitcher, 8" h, silver onyx, applied white opalescent handle 935.00
Spooner, 4¼" h, raspberry onyx . 600.00
Sugar, cov, 5½" h, raspberry onyx 650.00
Sugar Shaker, 5½" h, silver flowers, orig bright and shiny lid .. 545.00
Syrup, silver luster, orig metal cov, opalescent handle 1,150.00
Tumbler, 3⅝" h, platinum onyx .. 350.00

FINE ARTS

Notes: There is no way a listing of a hundred paintings or less can accurately represent the breadth and depth of the examples sold over the last year. To attempt to make such a list would be ludicrous.

In any calendar year, tens, if not hundreds of thousands of paintings are sold. Prices range from a few dollars to millions. Since each painting is essentially a unique creation, it is difficult to establish comparability.

Since an essential purpose of *Warman's Antiques and Their Prices* is to assist its users in finding information about a cate-

View of Perkiomen Mill, Bucks County, PA, oil on canvas, Walter E. Baum, $19,250.00. Photograph courtesy of Sanford Alderfer Auction Co.

gory, this "Fine Arts" introduction has been written primarily to identify the reference books that you will need to find out more about a painting in your possession.

Artist Dictionaries: Emmanuel Benezit, *Dictionnaire Critique et Documentaire des Peintres, Sculpteurs, Dessinateurs et Graveurs,* 10 volumes, Third Edition, Grund, 1976; Peter Hastings Falk, *Dictionary of Signatures & Monograms of American Artists,* Sound View Press, 1988; Mantle Fielding, *Dictionary of American Painters, Sculptors and Engravers,* Apollo Books, 1983; J. Johnson and A. Greutzner, *Dictionary of British Artists, 1880–1940: An Antique Collector's Club Research Project Listing 41,000 Artists,* Antique Collector's Club, 1976; Les Krantz, *American Artists,* Facts on File, 1985.

Introduction: Alan Bamberger, *Buy Art Smart,* Wallace–Homestead Book Company, 1990; Alan S. Bamberger, *Art for All,* Wallace–Homestead, 1994.

Price Guide References, Basic: *Art At Auction in America, 1994 Edition,* Krexpress, 1994; William T. Currier (comp.), *Currier's Price Guide To American Artists 1645–1945 at Auction, Sixth Edition,* Currier Publications, 1994; William T. Currier (comp.), *Currier's Price Guide To European Artists 1545–1945 at Auction, Fourth Edition,* Currier Publications, 1994; Huxford's

Fine Art Value Guide, Vol. II (1991), Vol. III (1992), Collector Books; Rosemary and Michael McKittrick, *The Official Price Guide To Fine Art, Second Edition,* House of Collectibles, 1993; Susan Theran, *Fine Art: Identification and Price Guide, Second Edition,* Avon Books, 1992.

Price Guide References, Advanced: Peter Hastings Falk (ed.), *Art Price Index International '95,* Sound View Press, 1994; Richard Hislop (ed.), *The Annual Art Sales Index,* Weybridge, Surrey, England, Art Sales Index, since 1969; Enrique Mayer, *International Auction Record: Engravings, Drawings, Watercolors, Paintings, Sculpture,* Paris, Editions Enrique Mayer, since 1967; Judith and Martin Miller (comps. & eds.), *Miller's Picture Price Guide, 1995,* Millers Publications, 1994; Susan Theran (ed.), *Leonard's Price Index of Art Auctions,* Auction Index, since 1980.

Museum Directories: *American Art Directory,* R. R. Bowker Co; American Association of Museums, *The Official Museum Directory; United States and Canada,* publisher updated periodically.

FIREARM ACCESSORIES

History: Muzzle loading weapons of the 18th and early 19th centuries varied in caliber and required the owner to carry a variety of equipment with him, including a powder horn or flask, patches, flints or percussion caps, bullets, and bullet molds. In addition, military personnel were responsible for bayonets, slings, and miscellaneous cleaning equipment and spare parts.

In the mid-19th century, cartridge weapons replaced their black powder ancestors. Collectors seek anything associated with early ammunition from the cartridges themselves to advertising material. Handling old ammunition can be extremely dangerous due to decomposition of compounds. Seek advice from an experienced collector before becoming involved in this area.

Military–related firearm accessories generally are worth more than their civilian counterparts. See "Militaria" for additional listings.

References: John Delph, *Firearms and Tackle Memorabilia,* Schiffer Publishing,

1991; Jim and Vivian Karsnitz, *Sporting Collectibles*, Schiffer Publishing, 1992.

Periodical: *Military Trader*, PO Box 1050, Dubuque, IA 52004.

Reproduction Alert: The amount of reproduction and fake powder horns is large. Be very cautious!

Powder Horn, engraved dec, inscribed "W. Carr, 1789," 12" l, $650.00.

Book
Sutherland, Robert Q., and R. L. Wilson, *The Book Of Colt Firearms,* dust jacket **700.00**
Wilson, R. L.
The Book Of Colt Engraving, first edition, dust jacket **250.00**
The Book Of Winchester Engraving, first edition, dust jacket **500.00**
Bullet Mold
American, brass, 12⅝" overall, 4½" turned wooden handles, casts 9 balls, bottom of mold engraved "A. Gladding," the left side engraved "Shot Mould 1 of 16 to a Pound,/6 of 18 and 2 of 20 to ditto," with intertwined initials "AG," the left side engraved "Providence December 18th, 1798," crude spread winged Federal eagle, handles with minor stress or grain cracks, nicks and dents **3,200.00**
Colt Navy Gang, steel, walnut handles, brass ferrules, casting 6 conical bullets, cavities fine, outer surfaces moderately pitted **200.00**
Cartridge Belt, western, brown

leather, 3" wide, made of doubled–over leather stitched on one edge, other edge slightly tooled to give stitched effect, fitted with 40 leather loops for 44 caliber or 45 caliber cartridges, 34" without closing strap, heavy square 2¼" nickel plated buckle, late 19th or early 20th C **225.00**
Charger, Colt Paterson shotgun, 8" overall, brass plunger nozzle, collar stamped "PATENT," lacquered copper body with 4 carrying rings, 75% orig lacquer finish, bottom seam split **1,800.00**
Flask, powder
Brass
8" overall, emb on both sides in an Art Nouveau style fluted pattern **50.00**
11½", emb fluted pattern body, lacquered finish, nickel plated top dispensing loader, adjustable to 6 "Drams," collar marked "PATENT APPLIED FOR" **150.00**
Brass and Horn, 8½" overall, pressed horn body, brass mounts, early 18th C, bottle design body **150.00**
Copper
8½" overall, emb on both sides with oak leaves and acorns, stag's head at top and face of fox at bottom, brass top stamped "G. & J. W. HAWKSLEY/SHEFFIELD" **100.00**
Batty Peace Flask, top marked "BATTY," dated "1848" and inspected "JAG," complete and orig throughout **250.00**
Horn, flattened, 11¼" overall, turned nozzle and hand carved rect wood plug, base cov with horn, fitted with 2 flattened iron carrying rings, old leather strap **75.00**
Rubber, pistol, 4⅝" overall, brass top, hard rubber body marked "GOOD–YEARS PATENT May.6.1851," exceptionally clear markings **100.00**
Flask, shot, leather
8¼", emb on both sides with

large panel depicting setter in woods, one side marked "4 lbs brass," top marked "AM. FLASK & CAP CO," near mint condition 60.00

8½", emb on both sides with Highland scene showing Scottish hunter alongside fallen stag, 2 hounds, brass top ... 45.00

Grips, pair
Colt Navy, ivory, antique one–piece style with wooden filler 250.00
Colt Root, one piece antique checkered ivory 425.00
Colt Root, solid ivory, high relief carving, American eagle standing on shield clutching arrows and olive branches, relief branches on grip, shield over a "LIBERTY" scroll, missing tiny chips at rear toe on each side 650.00

Holster
Colt Model 1849, 6" pocket, brown leather, sparse leaf tooled pattern covering the front and flap coming over top of the pistol, loop missing ... 25.00
Colt Model 1851 KM, made for the Austrian Kreigs Marine Colt Navies, designed for pistol with pouch for spare cylinder to side and another pouch in front for capper, brown leather, dry leather, both closure straps broken 175.00
Western style, brown, 10½" overall, tooled dec around the pistol shape only, c1900, remnants of orig red wool flannel lining 250.00

Horn, powder
9", relief carved ivory, body with scene of man with boar spear surrounded by dogs attacking massive wild boar, spout with open mouth, highly stylized monster's head, low grade silver base with scalloped edges, bottom engraved "1746/Prael Colod," minor age cracks ... 750.00
11", engraved large country house, smaller house on each side, orchard scene and river

below, trees with birds, scene showing 6 very stylized running dogs, round wooden base with wrought iron strap loop, 1st half of 19th C 350.00
13", PA, early 19th C, engraved spread winged American eagle, shield on its breast, grasping olive leaves and arrows, banner in beak inscribed "E Pluribus Unum," fully rigged sailing ship, interlacing hearts, figure of mermaid inscribed "Neptune," soldier on back of seahorse, compasses, horse, large fort–like building with mounted guns, faceted spout, raised ring 1,750.00
17", military, wooden base with screw out filling plug, fitted with heavy brass rings at nozzle and base with brass sling swivel fittings, broken orig 1⅜" wide dark brown leather carrying strap with iron buckle, typical of horns used by US and militia troops in early 19th C 300.00

Padlock, W. F. Ames & Co., solid brass, 3⅛" overall, stamped "W.F. & CO." on one side of hasp, other side stamped "AMES SWORD Co. CHICOPEE MASS. U.S.A./PAT. SEPT. 19, 1882," orig key 425.00

Signal Cannon, Winchester, Deluxe, serial number D113, deluxe chrome finish overall, 10 gauge, orig pine shipping crate 325.00

Tool, combination, military, 3 fittings for attachment to ramrod, screwdriver, nipple pick, and mainspring vise 80.00

FIREARMS

History: The 15th–century Matchlock Harquebus was the forerunner of the modern firearm. The Germans refined the wheel lock firing mechanism during the 16th and 17th centuries. English settlers arrived in America with the smoothbore musket;

German settlers had rifled arms. Both used the new flintlock firing mechanism.

A major advance was achieved when Whitney introduced interchangeable parts into the manufacturing of rifles. The warfare of the 19th century brought continued refinements in firearms. The percussion ignition system was developed by the 1840s. Minie, a French military officer, produced a viable projectile. By the end of the 19th century cartridge weapons dominated the field.

Two factors control pricing firearms—condition and rarity. The value of any particular antique firearm covers a very wide range. For instance, a Colt 1849 pocket model revolver with a 5-inch barrel can be priced from $100 to $700 depending on whether or not all the component parts are original, whether some are missing, how much of the original finish (bluing) remains on the barrel and frame, how much silver plating remains on the brass trigger guard and back strap, and the condition and finish of the walnut grips. Be careful to note any weapon's negative qualities. A Colt Paterson belt revolver in fair condition will command a much higher price than the Colt pocket model in very fine condition. Know the production run of a firearm before buying it.

References: Ralf Coykendall, Jr., *Coykendall's Second Sporting Collectibles Price Guide,* Lyons & Burford, 1992; Ralf Coykendall, Jr., *Coykendall's Sporting Collectibles Price Guide,* Lyons & Burford, 1991; Norman Flayderman, *Flayderman's Guide To Antique American Firearms And Their Values, Fifth Edition,* DBI Books, 1990; *Gun Trader's Guide, Fifteenth Edition,* Stoeger Publishing, 1992; Herbert G. Houze, *History of Winchester Repeating Arms Company,* Krause Publications, 1994; Joseph Kindig, Jr., *Thoughts On The Kentucky Rifle In Its Golden Age,* 1960, available in reprint; Russell and Steve Quetermous, *Modern Guns Identification & Values, Revised Tenth Edition,* Collector Books, 1994; Ned Schwing and Herbert Houze, *Standard Catalog of Firearms, 4th Edition,* Krause Publications, 1994; L. Gordon Stetser, Jr, *The Compleat Muzzleloader,* Mountain Press, 1992; *The Official Price Guide To Antique And Modern Firearms, Seventh Edition,* House of Collecti-

bles, 1994; Paul Wahl (comp.), *Paul Wahl's Big Gun Catalog, Volume One, A to L,* Paul Wahl Corporation, 1988; Paul Wahl (comp.), *Paul Wahl's Big Gun Catalog, Volume Two, M to Z,* Paul Wahl Corporation, 1988; Frederick Wilkinson, *Handguns: A Collector's Guide To Pistols And Revolvers From 1850 To The Present,* New Burlington Books, 1993.

Periodicals: *Gun List,* 700 E. State St., Iola, WI 54990; *Historic Weapons & Relics,* 2650 Palmyra Rd., Palmyra, TN 37142; *Man at Arms,* PO Box 460, Lincoln, RI 02865; *Military Trader,* PO Box 1050, Dubuque, IA 52004; *Sporting Gun,* PO Box 301369, Escondido, CA 92030; *The Gun Report,* PO Box 38, Aledo, IL 61231.

Collectors' Clubs: American Society of Military History, Los Angeles Patriotic Hall, 1816 S. Figuerora, Los Angeles, CA 90015; Winchester Arms Collectors Assoc., Inc., PO Box 6754, Great Falls, MT 59406.

Museums: Battlefield Military Museum, Gettysburg, PA; National Firearms Museum, Washington, DC; Remington Gun Museum, Ilion, NY; Winchester Mystery House, Historic Firearms Museum, San Jose, CA.

FLINTLOCK PISTOLS—SINGLE SHOT

English
  Blunderbuss, 29½" overall, 14" round iron barrel with Birmingham proofs, fitted with 12½" triangular snap bayonet, walnut full stock with lightly engraved brass furniture, 2 ramrod pipes, butt plate, trigger guard, small shield shaped wrist plate, and 2 lockplate screw escutcheons, attributed to John Whitehouse, early 19th C, metal parts complete and orig throughout, missing sliver of wood along right side at muzzle **900.00**
  Queen Anne, center hammer, 12¼", 7" round brass barrel with Birmingham proofs, cannon turned muzzle, brass box lock with floral engraving, walnut grip with floral emb hall-

marked silver butt cap, inlaid silver dec **1,400.00**
Halbach & Sons, Baltimore, MD, holster pistol, c1785–1800, 9″ brass part round/part octagonal barrel, 65 caliber, lock marked "HALBACH & SONS," large brass butt cap with massive spread wing eagle (primitive) in high relief surrounded by cluster of 13 stars, large relief shell carving around tang of barrel, full walnut stock, pin–fastened **1,650.00**
Kentucky, 10″ octagonal iron barrel, 48 caliber, full curly maple stock with brass forend cap, brass trigger guard and ramrod pipes, lock marked "Ashmore/ Warranted" **3,000.00**
U.S.
Model 1808, Navy, Simeon North, Berlin, CT, c1808–10, 10⅛″ round barrel, 64 caliber, smoothbore, unmarked barrel, lock marked with spread wing eagle above "U. STATES" ahead of hammer and vertically at rear "S. NORTH/BERLIN/CON.," hickory ramrod with swelled tip, full walnut stock, pin–fastened, iron belt hook attached to left side of stock **3,000.00**
Model 1813, Army and Navy, Simeon North of Middletown, CT, c1813–15, 9¹/₁₆″ round barrel, 69 caliber, smoothbore, breech of barrel marked "P/ US" on left side and inspector marking "H.H.P." above touchhole, lock marked ahead of hammer "S. NORTH" over an American eagle motif with letters U and S at either side over bottom line "MIDLN CON.," hickory ramrod with swelled tip at one end and metal ferrule at other, iron mountings **1,750.00**

PERCUSSION PISTOLS—SINGLE SHOT

Note: Conversion of flintlock pistols to percussion was common practice. Most English and U.S. military flintlock pistols listed

above can be found in percussion. Values for these percussion–converted pistols are from 40 to 60% of the flintlock values as given.

Percussion Pistol, multi–shot, Sharps Pepperbox No. 1, 22 cal., rim fire, 4 shot, 2.5″ round barrels, marked "C. Sharps/Patent 1859" and "C. Sharps & Co. Philada PA," spur trigger, $145.00.

Blunt & Syms side hammer, Blunt & Syms, New York, NY, c1840–50, 6″ octagonal barrel, 44 caliber, barrel marked "B & S NEW YORK," dec broad scroll engraving on frame, iron forend, ramrod mounted beneath, bag shaped handle, walnut grips **300.00**
John Dickson & Son, cased set, breech loading, underlever target pistols, Serial Numbers 4230 and 4231, 17¼″ overall, 11″ round barrel, 45 caliber, flat matted ribs, sgd "John Dickson & Sons, 63 Princess Street, Edinburgh," English scroll engraved steel butt caps, actions, trigger guards, and locks fitted with sliding half cock safeties and sgd "John Dickson & Son," well grained walnut stocks checkered at wrists, forends also checkered and fitted with horn tips, orig oak case 20¼ x 11½ x 3″, heavy brass trimmed corners, orig accessories, complete with outer leather carrying case **5,500.00**
Mule Ear, 9¼″ overall, 5⅛″ octag-

onal rifled barrel, 44 caliber, large dovetailed brass front sight, open rear sight, simple mule ear lock with external mainspring, tiger striped full stock with simple brass forend cap and trigger guard, sear and corresponding notch of hammer restored, two small cracks in stock **500.00**

U.S. Model 1842, Henry Aston, Middletown, CT (also by Ira N. Johnson of Middletown, CT, and Palmeto Armory of Columbia, SC), c1845–52, 8½" round barrel, 54 caliber, smoothbore, proof stamps on breech of barrel beneath which are inspector's initials, date stamping on barrel tang, lockplate marked "US/H. ASTON" forward of hammer, marked vertically at rear "MIDDTN/CONN.," swivel type steel ramrod, all brass mountings, brass blade front sight ... **575.00**

Waters, A. H. Waters & C., Millbury, MA, mid–1840s to 1849, round barrel, 54 caliber, smoothbore, flat flush fitted lockplate, marked "A. H. WATERS & Co./ MILLBURY MASS." in center of lock, side lug nipple, iron furniture, brass blade front sight, oval shaped rear sight on tang **475.00**

PERCUSSION PISTOLS—MULTI-SHOT

Colt
Dragoon, second model, 7½" part round, part octagonal barrel, 44 caliber, 6 shot, barrel stamped "ADDRESS SAML COLT NEW–YORK. COLT'S/ PATENT" with "U.S." centered beneath, one–piece walnut grip, square–back trigger guard and rect cylinder stop slots, Texas Ranger and Indian fight scene engraved on cylinders **4,600.00**

Navy, Model 1861, 7½" round barrel, 36 caliber, 6 shot, creeping style loading lever, barrel stamped "ADDRESS

COL. SAML COLT NEW– YORK, U.S. AMERICA – .36 CAL," cylinder roll scene depicts battle between Texas Navy and that of Mexico, one– piece walnut grip **1,450.00**

Paterson Belt Model, No. 2, 5½" octagonal barrel, 31 caliber, 5 shot, barrel stamped "Patent Arms M'g Co Paterson N:J Colt's Pt.," engraved cylinder, disappearing trigger, no trigger guard, flared walnut grips ...**4,500.00**

Other
Deringer and Deringer Type
Deringer, Henry, Philadelphia, PA, 1830–60, medium pocket model, 3½" barrel, 41 caliber, barrel stamped "DERINGER/PHILADELA," identical marking appears on lockplate, checkered walnut stock, German silver trigger guard and butt cap (Flayderman 7D–002) **800.00**

Robertson, Philadelphia, PA, pocket, 4½" barrel, approx. 41 caliber, barrel stamped "ROBERTSON, PHILA.," forends have double wedges and escutcheons and double ramrod pipes (Flayderman 7D–022) **525.00**

Pepperbox
Bacon, Thomas K., Norwich, CT, c1852–58, 4" ribbed barrel, 31 caliber, 6 shot, barrel stamped "BACON & CO., NORWICH, CT" and "CAST STEEL," single action, underhammer, engraved nipple shield, blued finish, walnut grips (Flayderman 7B–001) **350.00**

Stocking & Co., Worcester, MA, late 1840s to early 1850s, 31 caliber, 6" barrel cluster, barrel stamped "STOCKING & CO., WORCESTER" and "CAST STEEL WARRANTED," dec scroll engraving on iron frame and nipple shield, trigger spur guard (Flayderman 7B– 017) **350.00**

Remington
Belt, New Model, 6½" octagonal barrel, 36 caliber, 6 shot, barrel stamped "PATENTED SEPT. 14, 1856/E. REMINGTON 7 SONS, ILION, NEW YORK U.S.A./NEW MODEL," round cylinder, threads visible at breech end, safety notches on cylinder shoulders between nipples **550.00**

Navy, 1861, 7⅜" octagonal barrel, 36 caliber, 6 shot, barrel stamped "PATENTED DEC 17, 1861/MANUFACTURED BY REMINGTON'S ILION, N.Y.," round cylinder, walnut grips **650.00**

Revolver
Alsop, C. R., Middletown, CT, Navy Model, c1862–63, 6½" octagonal barrel, 36 caliber, 5 shot, barrel stamped "C.R. ALSOP MIDDLETOWN CONN." and patent date, round cylinder, wooden grips (Flayderman 7A–002) **1,150.00**

Nichols and Childs, Conway, MA, Belt Model, late 1830s, approx 6" barrel, approx 34 caliber, 6 shot, frame stamped "NICHOLS & CHILDS/PATENT/CONWAY/MASS.," bag shaped walnut grips, only about 25 known (Flayderman 7A–073) **5,000.00**

Walch, John, New York, NY, Pocket Model, early 1860s, 3¼" octagonal barrel, 31 caliber, 10–shot cylinder with five chambers, barrel stamped "WALCH–FIRE-ARMS CO.NEW–YORK/PAT'D FEB. 8, 1859," brass frame, two–piece walnut grips (Flayderman 7A–117)   **750.00**

REVOLVERS (CARTRIDGE)

Colt
Camp Perry, four digit serial number, 22 caliber long rifle, 8" barrel, double action, one–shot chamber, old but non–factory 13 x 7 x 2½" walnut case, fitted with custom carved wooden grips, 97–98% orig blue, excellent to mint bore (Flayderman 5B–210) **750.00**

Cloverleaf, House Model, four digit serial number, 41RF caliber, 1½" octagonal barrel stamped "COLT" on left side, 4–shot cylinder, walnut grips, hammer, trigger, and barrel all with 98% orig blue, brass frame very sharp and crisp with 97–98% orig light silver plate (Flayderman 5B–151) ..**2,300.00**

Model 1878, "Alaskan," five digit serial number, 45 caliber, stamped with U.S. inspection mark, dated 1902, most of the lightly age browned re–blue finish overall, Rampant Colt grips (Flayderman 5B–189) .. **450.00**

Woodsman, six digit serial number, 22LR caliber, 4½" barrel, 99.5% orig pre–War blue finish, orig carton missing one–half of end label **550.00**

Harrington & Richardson, Blue Jacket No. 2, three digit serial number, 32RF caliber, full factory engraved, deeper cuts highlighted with black paint or enamel, checkered hard rubber grips with head of dog at top, 99% plus orig nickel plate **175.00**

High Standard, Supermatic Trophy Auto, six digit serial number, 22LR caliber, 7¼" barrel, spare 5½" barrel, orig foam plastic carton, blued, 99.9% brand new .. **400.00**

Hopkins & Allen XL Navy, three digit serial number, 38RF caliber, 6½" round barrel, varnished grips, orig brown leather holster, leather flap replaced during period with a piece of black oil cloth, cylinder with 80% nickel, blued trigger and case colored hammer (Flayderman 8A–065) . **625.00**

Mauser, Model 1914 Auto, six digit serial number, 32 caliber, slide dated 1920, forestrap stamped with issue marks "L.Hi.116,"

one–piece wood grip, 90% plus
orig blue **200.00**
Smith & Wesson, Model 1½ Old,
six digit serial number, caliber
32RF, 5–shot non–fluted cylinder, rosewood grips, 80% orig
blue, left grip missing a small
chip at rim (Flayderman 5G–
027) **350.00**
Walther Air Pistol MDL. LP3, five
digit serial number, .177 caliber,
orig foam carton, tools and instructions, brand new **225.00**

FLINTLOCK LONG ARMS

French, Model 1766 Charlesville
Musket, orig barrel length 44¾",
lockplate only partially legible
"Charlesville," etc. markings,
correct period and matching
ramrod very slightly too short,
top jaw and screw period replacements, otherwise complete
and orig throughout **1,100.00**
Kentucky, N. Beyer, 50 caliber,
original smooth bore, 58½" overall, 42½" part round barrel, orig
front sight mounted on light engraved brass oval, sgd in script
"N. Beyer" on top flat and secured to stock with incised carving on the forend to the faceted
brass tailpipe, 2 faceted brass
ramrod pipes and brass forend
cap, beveled brass sideplate,
raised scroll carving about tang
with lightly engraved silver oval
wrist escutcheon, incise carving
at wrist on right side, left side
with raised carved scrolls, a
large raised carved scroll to rear
of cheekpiece, engraved brass
patch box with bird finial, typical
Beyer beveled brass trigger
guard, reconverted barrel and
lock **3,500.00**
U.S.
  Model 1803, Harpers Ferry Armory, later production, c1814–
  20, 54 caliber, single shot,
  muzzle–loader, 33" part octagonal and part round 36" barrel,
  blade front sight, open rear

sight, lock with integral forged
iron flashpan with fence at
rear, brass mountings, walnut
half stock of 30½" with small
cheek rest, brass patch box on
right side of butt (Flayderman
9A–114) **2,750.00**
Model 1819, Hall, breech load-
ing, second production type,
Harpers Ferry Armory, John
Hall's patents, 52 caliber, single shot, 32⅝" round barrel,
three barrel bands, breech-
block deeply stamped "J. H.
HALL/H.FERRY/1836" (Flay-
derman (A–249) **900.00**

PERCUSSION LONG ARMS

Note: Conversion of flintlock long arms to
percussion was common practice. Most English, French, and U.S. military flintlock
model long arms listed in the previous section can be found in percussion. Values for
these percussion converted long arms are
from 40 to 60% of the flintlock values previously noted.

English, 577 Rifled Musket, 39¼"
barrel fitted with folding leaf long
range sight, lockplate stamped
with crown and "1863/TOWER,"
walnut full stock with brass forend cap, trigger guard, and butt
plate, orig nipple protector, complete with correct style English
bayonet, excellent to mint con-
dition **1,200.00**
Kentucky Rifle, swivel breech, 51"
overall, deeply rifled 38 caliber
octagonal barrels, sgd "JOHN .
SHULER/LIVERPOOL. PA" on
both top flats, one side of the
barrel group a flat piece of steel,
the other with four brass ramrod
pipes, tiger striped butt stock
with engraved brass sideplate,
light engraved brass trigger
guard with double set triggers,
engraved brass patch box and
toe plate, lightly engraved German silver escutcheon at right,
2" inlay on left side, back action

lock sgd "N. ASHMORE," old ramrod probably not orig **1,000.00**

Merrill, James H., Baltimore, MD, c1862–65, Serial No. 8100, 54 caliber, breechloader with action identical to carbine, 33" round barrel, stamped "J. H. MERRILL BALTO./PAT. JULY 1858/APL. 9 MAY 21–28–61" forward of hammer, brass mountings and patchbox, full walnut stock, lug on right side of barrel at muzzle end for attaching saber type bayonet, complete and orig throughout, barrel with 95% of orig glossy brown finish (Flayderman 9B–077) **3,600.00**

Model 1863, Rifle Musket, Type II (a.k.a. Model 1864), Springfield Armory, c1864–65, 58 caliber, single shot, muzzle–loader, 40" round barrel, three barrel bands, lock stamped with eagle motif to right of hammer, "U.S./SPRINGFIELD" beneath nipple bolster, "1864" at angle at rear section of lock, single leaf rear sight, walnut stock (Flayderman 9A–341) **800.00**

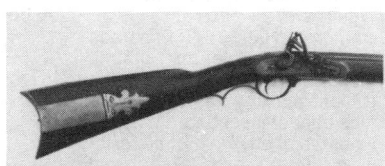

Rifle, Pennsylvania Long, marked "Peter Moll, Hellertown, Warranted No. 58," artificially striped stock, c1830, 55½" I, $1,500.00.

RIFLES

BSA Model 12, 22 long rifle, single shot, 29" blued barrel, Martini–type action, match sights, checkered walnut straight grip stock and forearm **200.00**

Harrington & Richardson Reising 60, semi–automatic, 45 caliber, blued 18¼" barrel, open rear

sight, blade front sight, 12–shot detachable box, painted wood one–piece semi–pistol grip stock and forearm **350.00**

Marlin Model 100S Tom Mix Special, 22 short, long rifle, single shot, 24" round barrel, hooded front sight, peep rear sight, plain pistol grip stock and forearm ..**90.00**

Military, United States

Model 1903, Springfield, caliber 30–06, 24" barrel, bolt action, repeating, manual thumb safety at rear of bolt, 5–shot box magazine, blade front sight, leaf with aperture, notched battle rear sight, plain one–piece stock and forearm, wood hand guard over barrel, cleaning rod–type bayonet ..**200.00**

M1 Carbine, caliber 30 M1, semi–automatic, gas operated, 18" barrel, 30–shot magazine, blade front sight with protective ears, flip–down rear sight, one–piece wood stock and forearm, wood hand guard on top of barrel **325.00**

Remington No. 4S Boy Scout Model, 22 short, single shot, 28" medium round barrel, No. 4 rolling–block action, visible hammer, blade front sight, open "v" notch rear sight adjustable for elevation, musket–style, oiled walnut, one–piece full–length stock and forearm with steel butt plate **275.00**

SHOTGUNS

Bernardelli Holland, 12 gauge, double barrel, 32" barrel, top lever break–open, hammerless, double trigger, automatic rejector, blued, straight stock **1,500.00**

Fox Sterlingworth, 16 gauge, double barrel, 26" barrel, full & full choke, top lever break–open, hammerless, double trigger, blued, checkered walnut pistol grip stock and forearm **350.00**

Savage Model 720, 12 gauge, 4–shot tubular, 30" cylinder bore, full choke, Browing patent, semi–automatic, hammerless, blued, checkered walnut pistol grip stock and forearm, plain receiver **175.00**

Stevens, Model No. 970, 12 gauge, single shot, round barrel with octagonal breech, 32" long, top lever break–open, hammerless, automatic shell ejector, automatic safety, blued, case hardened frame, checkered walnut pistol grip stock and forearm .. **65.00**

FIREHOUSE COLLECTIBLES

History: The volunteer fire company has played a vital role in the protection and social growth of many towns and rural areas. Paid professional firemen usually are found only in large metropolitan areas. Each fire company prided itself on equipment and uniforms. Conventions and parades gave the fire companies a chance to show off their equipment. These events produced a wealth of firehouse–related memorabilia.

References: Chuck Deluca, *Firehouse Memorabilia: A Collectors Reference,* Maritime Antique Auctions, 1989; Andrew G. Gurka, *Hot Stuff! Firefighting Collectibles,* L-W Book Sales, 1994; James Piatti, *Firehouse Memorabilia: Identification and Price Guide,* Avon Books, 1994; Mary Jane and James Piatti, *Firehouse Collectibles,* The Engine House, 1979.

Periodical: *Fire Apparatus Journal,* PO Box 141205, Staten Island, NY 10314.

Collectors' Clubs: Fire Collectors Club, PO Box 992, Milwaukee, WI 53201; The Fire Mark Circle of the Americas, 2859 Marlin Dr., Chamblee, GA 30341.

Museums: American Museum of Fire Fighting, Corton Falls, NY; Fire Museum of Maryland, Lutherville, MD; Hall of Flame, Scottsdale, AZ; Insurance Company of North America (INA) Museum, Philadelphia, PA; New England Fire & History Museum, Brewster, MA; New York City Fire Museum, Inc., New York, NY; Oklahoma State Fireman's Association Museum, Oklahoma City, OK; San Francisco Fire Dept. Memorial Museum, San Francisco, CA.

Additional Listings: See *Warman's Americana & Collectibles* for more examples.

Badge
Franklin Steam Fire Engine Co No 1, South Easton, PA, Instituted 1852, brass hanger bar, purple ribbon **30.00**
Reading, PA, hose, hat, openwork steamer within wreath suspended below coiled hose **165.00**
Bell, 10" d, Edwards, 1872, D C transformer **25.00**
Belt, 47" l, leather, black, red and white trim, marked "31" and "South Penn" **110.00**
Booklet, American Fire Extinguisher Co, Boston, 1967, 60 pgs **45.00**
Bucket, 12" h, leather, black, red, gold, and black circle and number one **275.00**
Catalog
Byron Jackson Co, 1930, pumps, fire truck, and fire boats, 36 pgs **10.00**
The Babcock Improved Self–Acting Chemical Fire Apparatus, Babcock Mfg Co, NY, c1885, fire engines and extinguishers, 24 pgs **200.00**
Ceremonial Hat, 6¾" h, parade type, top hat style, front portrait medallion of General Lafayette, gilt leaf scrolling frame, sapphire blue banner inscribed "Lafayette Hose Company" in gilt letters, initials "F A" and "P V," red ground, painted blue–green under brim, c1840 .... **5,500.00**
Coat, parade type, tan, navy blue trim and piping, two rows of silver buttons **65.00**
Fire Extinguisher, Badger's Pony, copper and brass, 1¼ gal **90.00**
Fire Grenade
Harden's Hand, cobalt blue, ftd, ½ pt **165.00**
Imperial, 6½" h, yellow green .. **350.00**
Rockford Hand, 10¾" h, cobalt blue **330.00**
Helmet, leather, high eagle, black, front piece with "Eureka Hose 14" **225.00**

Note Paper, 4 x 5" folder, engraved
black and white portrait on cov,
"Chief Engineer Of The New
York Fire department/Henry Se-
ward," unused, late 1800s **25.00**
Pinback Button
American Fireman, bust of fire-
man, colorful, c1900 . . . .   **20.00**
Fireman's Celebration, red,
white, and blue, bust of fire-
man, 1930–40 . . . .   **12.00**
Housing Of The Paulsboro and
Billingsport Fire Auto Trucks
Dec 4th, 1915, Paulsboro, NJ,
black and white building and
fire truck **15.00**
Post Card, Central Fire Station,
Glens Falls, NY, multicolored,
1915 . . . .   **3.00**

**Helmet, black leather, gold eagle,
red and white letters, Made by
Cairns & Bros., NY, size 7¼",
$165.00**

Ribbon, Good Will Steam Fire Eng
Co, East York, PA, Sesquicentennial, 1899, red, white, blue,
and gold **50.00**
Watch Fob
Franklin Fire Insurance, brass,
emb, bust of Benjamin Frank-
lin and fire pumper **40.00**
West Penna Volunteer Fire-
men's Assn 1926, reverse with
"33rd Annual Convention/The
Aluminum City/Aug 1926,"
ship's tiller wheel and fire-
house **45.00**

FIREPLACE EQUIPMENT

History: The fireplace was a gathering
point in the colonial home for heat, meals,
and social interaction. It maintained its dominant position until the introduction of central
heating in the mid–19th century.

Because of the continued popularity of
the fireplace, accessories still are manufactured, usually in an Early American motif.

References: Dana G. Morykan and
Harry L. Rinker, *Warman's Country Antiques & Collectibles, Second Edition,* Wallace–Homestead, 1994; George C. Neumann, *Early American Antique Country
Furnishings: Northeastern America, 1650–
1880's,* L–W Book Sales, 1984, 1993 reprint.

Reproduction Alert: Modern black-
smiths are reproducing many old iron implements.

Additional Listings: Brass and Iron.

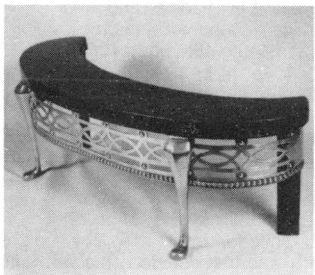

**Fender, brass and iron, 20" l, 6½"
h, $100.00.**

Andirons, pr
Brass
19" h, George III, urn finial
raised on turned standard,
spurred legs, ball feet **260.00**
21" h, geometric and floral mo-
tifs, attributed to Ernest Gim-
son, c1905 . . . .**2,415.00**
22½" h, bulbous shafts, bust
and dolphin base **220.00**
23" h, urn form finials, Ameri-
can, late 18th C **550.00**
24" h
Continental, floral top, taper-

ing acanthus dec shaft, dolphin feet, early 19th C **185.00**

Louis XVI style, torchere form, baluster support with reeded and ribbon tied tapering stem, shaped base, laurel wreath and scrolled feet **550.00**

25½" h, 17th C style mask head dec triple gourd form, triangular base, wrought iron scroll ft, Continental, 19th C **900.00**

Cast Iron, 14½" h, figural, Scottish chieftains, missing fire dogs, 19th C **200.00**

Copper, 36½" h, Caroque, ball finial above cartouche draped with chairs, out–scrolling hook above semicircular ftd base, Continental **980.00**

Coal Bucket

13" w, 10½" d, 13" h, George III, mahogany, navette form, brass bail handle and liner, staved coopered sides, brass bands, late 18th/early 19th C **1,275.00**

14" w, 15" h, Empire style, tole, painted yellow and black **515.00**

Coal Grate, 27" l, George III style, steel and brass, serpentine . . . **700.00**

Coal Hod, Victorian, brass **345.00**

Fireback, cast iron

Aesthetic Movement, stylized floral motif, third quarter 19th C, price for set of three **175.00**

Floral and fruit dec, four–piece . **85.00**

Fire Bucket, 12" d, 10" h, leather **295.00**

Fire Fender

52" l, 12" h, brass and wire, early 19th C **975.00**

68" l, brass, pierced floral etched panels, 19th C **500.00**

Fireplace Surround, 49½" w, 48" h, cast bronze, Aesthetic Movement, geometric and stylized floral motifs, fourth quarter 19th C **350.00**

Firescreen

28¾" d, 30½" h, Louis XV style, brass and gilt metal, shaped square form with egg and dart border, swag dec at bottom centered with trophy, claw feet **750.00**

34½" w, 47½" h, Louis XVI, gilt-

wood, tapestry panel, lacking supports, tapestry distressed, **925.00**

43" h, Renaissance Revival, ebonized, gros point and petit point panel, third quarter 19th C **375.00**

Rosewood

30" w, 57" h, Renaissance Revival, woolwork panel, late 19th C **550.00**

37" h, Chinese silkwork panel, distressed, mid 19th C **315.00**

Footman, 11" h, late Georgian, brass, rect form, cabriole legs, early 19th C **435.00**

Mantel, 55½" w, 9½" d, 52¾" h, George III, carved pine, elaborately carved and molded cornice above foliate carved frieze, borders similarly carved, black and white photo of Lord Spencer in front of mantel, inscribed and initialed on reverse, and letter of authenticity **2,750.00**

Tool Set, brass

2 pcs, 38" h, shovel and tongs, brass handles, 19th C **800.00**

5 pcs, 33½" h, Federal style, ring turned round top, consists of brush, poker, hearth shovel and tongs, and stand with tripod spurred legs and ball feet **550.00**

11 pcs, two pr andirons, pr bellows, bucket, four tools, and firescreen, late 19th/early 20th C **630.00**

FISCHER J. BUDAPEST. ♛

FISCHER CHINA

History: In 1893 Moritz Fischer founded his factory in Herend, Hungary, a center of porcelain production from the 1790s.

Confusion exists about Fischer china because of its resemblance to the wares of Meissen, Sevres, and Oriental export. It often was bought and sold as the product of these firms. Forged marks of other potteries are found on Herend pieces. The mark "MF," often joined, is the mark of Moritz Fischer's pottery.

Fischer's Herend is hard–paste ware with luminosity and exquisite decoration. Pieces are designated by pattern names, the best known being Chantilly Fruit, Rothschild Bird, Chinese Bouquet, Victoria Butterfly, and Parsley.

Fischer also made figural birds and animal groups, Magyar figures (individually and in groups), and Herend eagles poised for flight.

Reference: Susan and Al Bagdade, *Warman's English & Continental Pottery & Porcelain, Second Edition,* Wallace–Homestead, 1991.

Vase, triangular shape, multicolored florals, protruding reticulated roundels, blue "Fischer Budapest" mark, 14½" h, $250.00.

Bowl, 10" d, reticulated, figural butterfly **225.00**
Eggcup, gold trim **125.00**
Ewer, 15¾" h, bold multicolored florals, gold trim, long spout and handle **350.00**
Figure
  5¼" h, rooster, multicolored, dated 1943, Herend **50.00**
  14½" h, Madonna and child, hp, multicolored, Herend **350.00**
Plate
  9½" d, allover reticulated medallions, gold, rose, and tur-

quoise, marked "Budapest Hungary," price for pair **300.00**
  10½" d, Parsley pattern **115.00**
Puzzle Jug, 13" h, brown transfer, three gentlemen, polychrome and gilt accents, marked "Fischer, Budapest" **135.00**
Sauce Boat, underplate, matching ladle, Victorian Butterfly pattern, price for set **250.00**
Urn, 12" h, blue floral dec, reticulated, shield mark **325.00**
Vase, 10½" h, red, blue, and yellow stylized flowers, gold accents on neck and base, marked "Fischer, Budapest," price for pair **325.00**

FITZHUGH

History: Fitzhugh, one of the most recognized Chinese Export porcelain patterns, was named for the Fitzhugh family for whom the first dinner service was made. The peak period of production was from 1780 to 1850.

Fitzhugh features an oval center medallion or monogram surrounded by four groups of flowers or emblems. The border is similar to that on Nanking china. Occasional border variations are found. Butterfly and honeycomb are among the rarest.

Blue is the common color. Color is a key factor in pricing with rarity in ascending order of orange, green, sepia, mulberry, yellow, black, and gold. Combinations of colors are scarce.

Reference: Gloria and Robert Mascarelli, *Warman's Oriental Antiques,* Wallace–Homestead, 1992.

Reproduction Alert: Spode Porcelain Company, England, and Vista Alegre, Portugal, currently are producing copies of the Fitzhugh pattern. Oriental copies also are available.

Deep Dish
  7¾" d, bronze dec, Chinese, late 18th C **700.00**
  9½" d, blue dec, Chinese, 19th C **110.00**
Dish, 8" l, quatrefoil shape, blue dec, 19th C **750.00**

Platter, blue, 15¾" l, $450.00.

Gravy Boat, 7¾" l, blue dec, Chinese, late 19th C **150.00**

Hot Water Dish, 10⅝" d, underglaze blue, center pinecone and beast medallion, four clusters of flowers and precious objects in trellis diaper border, spearhead and dumbbell border, blue spouts, c1840 . . . . **400.00**

Plate
  Dessert, 7⅞" d, orange, center floral sprig medallion, butterflies, diaper, and scalework panels border, key fret and floral sprigs on gilt edge rim, c1820, price for pair **350.00**
  Dinner, 9½" d, green dec, price for set of four **200.00**
  Platter, 16" d, blue dec, hairline and small rim chip **550.00**
Tureen, cov, 7½" l, blue dec, shallow inner rim, Chinese, late 19th C **450.00**
Vegetable Dish, cov, design centers monogram, brown, glaze wear, 19th C, 9½" l **975.00**

FLASKS

History: A flask is a container for liquids, usually having a narrow neck. Early American glass companies frequently formed them in molds which left a relief design on the front and/or back. Historical flasks with a portrait, building, scene, or name are the most desired.

A chestnut is hand blown, small, and has a flattened bulbous body. The pitkin has a blown globular body with vertical ribs with a spiral rib overlay. Teardrop flasks are generally fiddle shaped and have a scroll or geometric design.

Dimensions can differ for the same flask because of variations in the molding process. Color is important, with scarcer colors demanding more money. Aqua and amber are the most common colors. Bottles with "sickness," an opalescent scaling which eliminates clarity, are worth much less.

Reference: George L. and Helen McKearin, *American Glass,* Crown Publishers, 1941 and 1948.

Periodicals: *Antique Bottle & Glass Collector,* PO Box 187, East Greenville, PA 18041; *Bottles & Extras,* PO Box 154, Happy Camp, CA 96039.

Collectors' Clubs: Federation of Historical Bottle Clubs, 14521 Atlantic Ave., Riverdale, IL, 60627; The National Early American Glass Club, PO Box 8489, Silver Spring, MD 20907.

Blown Three Mold, chestnut form, clear, sheared mouth, pontil, McKearin GIII–23 . . . . **2,530.00**

Historical
  Baltimore Monument, yellow olive, applied mouth with ring, iron pontil, qt, McKearin GVI–4 . . . . **150.00**
  Double Eagle, light yellow green, sheared mouth, pontil, McKearin GII–25 . . . . **475.00**
  Eagle, golden amber, vertical ribbed body, applied double collared mouth, smooth base, McKearin GII–33 . . . . **1,320.00**
  Eagle–Clasped Hands, light yellow, olive tone, applied sq collared mouth, smooth base, McKearin GXII–2 . . . . **850.00**
  Eagle–Cornucopia, aquamarine, sheared mouth, pontil, ½ pt, McKearin GII–15a **625.00**
  Eagle–Oak Tree, deep golden amber, sheared mouth, pontil, ½ pt, McKearin GII–60 . . . . . **660.00**
  General Jackson, deep aqua-

marine, floral medallion, sheared mouth, McKearin GI–68 ....**1,155.00**

General Taylor, aquamarine, sheared mouth, pontil, pt, McKearin GI–73 .... **150.00**

Jenny Lind Lyre, aquamarine, sheared mouth, pontil, pt, McKearin GI–108 .... **550.00**

Lafayette–DeWitt Clinton, yellow olive, sheared mouth, pontil, ½ pt, McKearin GI–81 .... **650.00**

Lafayette–Liberty cap, yellow olive, sheared mouth, pontil, ½ pt, McKearin GI–86 .... **660.00**

Lafayette–Masonic, yellow olive, sheared mouth, ½ pt, McKearin GI–89 ....**1,500.00**

Liberty, aquamarine, sheaf of rye, sheared mouth, pontil, pt, McKearin GX–10 .... **625.00**

Scroll, two stars, green, open pontil, McKearin GIX-12, c1850, $225.00.

Masonic

Eye in star, yellow olive, sheared mouth, pontil, pt, McKearin GIV–43 .... **175.00**

"HS" Eagle, yellowish–olive, applied sloping collared mouth, McKearin GIV–2 ...**2,750.00**

Steamboat, "The American System" and "Use Me But Do Not Abuse Me," yellowish green, sheared mouth, pontil, pt, McKearin GX–21 ....**4,180.00**

Success to the Railroad, yellow olive, sheared mouth, pontil, pt, McKearin GV–1 ....**2,100.00**

Washington, classical bust portrait, light green, sheared mouth, pontil, McKearin GI–22 **375.00**

Washington–Eagle, vaseline, sheared mouth, pontil, qt, McKearin GI–26 ....**2,750.00**

Washington–Jackson, aquamarine, sheared mouth, pontil, pt, McKearin GI–32 .... **225.00**

Washington–Taylor, copper, sheared mouth, smooth base, Dyottville Glass Works, McKearin GI–37 .... **950.00**

Zachary Taylor, aquamarine, cornstalk, sheared mouth, pontil, pt, McKearin GI–74 ... **90.00**

Pictorial

Anchor–Cabin, yellow, pale olive tone, applied double collared mouth, smooth base, McKearin GXIII–58 .... **880.00**

Anchor–Sheaf of Wheat, golden amber, applied double collared mouth, smooth base, qt **330.00**

Beads and Pearls, yellow olive diamond diapering, sheared mouth, pontil, pt, McKearin GX–26 .... **660.00**

Cornucopia–Urn, yellowish–olive, sheared mouth, McKearin GIII–4 .... **75.00**

Fairview Works, bluish–green, building, sheared mouth, pontil, pt, McKearin GI–116 ..... **725.00**

Horse and Cart, deep yellow olive, sheared mouth, pontil, pt, McKearin GV–7 .... **725.00**

Hunter–Fisherman, golden amber, applied sloping collared mouth, iron pontil, qt, McKearin GXIII–4 .... **150.00**

Sheaf of Wheat

Deep yellow olive, applied double collared mouth, smooth base, pt, McKearin GXIII–35 .... **150.00**

Reddish amber, applied round collared mouth, smooth base, McKearin GXIII–37 .. **90.00**

Star, Travelers Companion, deep aquamarine, sheared

mouth, iron pontil, McKearin
GXIV–7 . . . . **225.00**

Summer Tree, green, applied
sloping collared mouth, pontil,
qt, McKearin GX–18 . . . . **450.00**

Scroll

Aqua, 8⅞″ h, qt, iron pontil, ap-
plied lip **155.00**

Blue green, sheared mouth,
pontil, pt, McKearin GIX–10c **350.00**

Citron, sheared mouth, pint, ·
McKearin GIX–20 . . . . **825.00**

Cobalt blue, shared mouth,
McKearin GIX–10 . . . .**2,530.00**

Golden amber, sheared mouth,
pontil, pt, McKearin GIX–11 . **325.00**

Greenish–aquamarine, waisted,
sheared mouth, qt, McKearin
GIX–46 . . . . **850.00**

Light sapphire blue, sheared
mouth, pontil, pt, McKearin
GIX–11 . . . . **475.00**

Olive yellow, shared mouth, pon-
til, qt, McKearin GIX–3 . . . . . . **700.00**

Pale green, 7″ h, iron pontil,
sheared lip, GIX–II **95.00**

Pale milky lavender, sheared
mouth, pontil, pt, McKearin
GIX–10 . . . . **660.00**

Yellowish–green, sheared
mouth, iron pontil, McKearin
GIX–6 . . . . **275.00**

Sunburst

Blue green, tooled mouth, pontil,
½ pt, McKearin GVIII–29 . . . . **325.00**

Clear, sheared mouth, pontil, ½
pt, McKearin GVIII–28 . . . . . . **125.00**

Medium yellow green, sheared
mouth, pontil, pt **1,980.00**

Yellow olive, sheared mouth,
pontil, pt, McKearin GVIII–3 . **625.00**

Waisted, light sea green, sheared
mouth, pontil, pt, McKearin GIX–
44 . . . . **625.00**

FLOW BLUE

History: Flow blue or flowing blue is the
name applied to china of cobalt and white
whose color, when fired in a kiln, produced
a flowing or smudged effect. The blue varies in color from dark cobalt to a grayish or
steel blue. The flow varies from very slight
to a heavy blur where the pattern cannot be

easily recognized. The blue color does not
permeate through the china.

Flow blue was first produced around
1835 in the Staffordshire district of England
by a large number of potters including Alcock, Davenport, J. Wedgwood, Grindley,
New Wharf, Johnson Brothers, and many
others. The early flow blue, 1830s to 1870s,
was usually of the ironstone variety. The
late patterns, 1880s to 1910s, and modern
patterns, after 1910, usually were made of
the more delicate semi–porcelain variety.
Approximately 95% of the flow blue was
made in England, with the remaining 5%
made in Germany, Holland, France, and
Belgium. A few patterns also were made in
the United States by Mercer, Warwick, and
Wheeling Pottery companies.

References: Susan and Al Bagdade,
*Warman's English & Continental Pottery &
Porcelain, 2nd Edition,* Wallace–Home-
stead, 1991; Mary F. Gaston, *The Collec-
tor's Encyclopedia Of Flow Blue China,*
Collector Books, 1983, 1993 value update;
Mary F. Gaston, *The Collector's Encyclo-
pedia Of Flow Blue China, Second
Series* Collector Books, 1994; Ellen R. Hill,
*Mulberry Ironstone: Flow Blue's Best Kept
Little Secret,* published by author, 1993;
Dana G. Morykan and Harry L. Rinker, *War-
man's Country Antiques & Collectibles, 2nd
Edition,* Wallace–Homestead, 1994;
Thomas Nix, *Abbie's Flow Blue Price
Guide Survey,* Centennial Publishing, 1992;
Jeffrey Snyder, *Flow Blue: A Collector's
Guide to Pattern, History and Values,* Schif-
fer Publishing, 1992; Jeffrey B. Snyder, *His-
toric Flow Blue,* Schiffer Publishing, 1994;
Petra Williams, *Flow Blue China: An Aid To
Identification, Revised Edition,* Fountain
House East, 1981; Petra Williams, *Flow
Blue China II, Revised Edition,* Fountain
House East, 1981; Petra Williams, *Flow
Blue China and Mulberry Ware: Similarity
and Value Guide, Revised Edition,* Fountain
House East, 1993.

Collectors' Club: Flow Blue International Collectors' Club, PO Box 205, Rockford, IL 61105.

EARLY PATTERNS: c1825–1850

Berry Bowl, Whampoa, Mellor &
Venables, c1840 . . . . **80.00**

Bowl, Scinde, Thomas Walker, c1847, pedestal, handle **375.00**
Butter Dish, cov, Hong Kong, Charles Meigh, c1845, 7" d, 4" h **650.00**
Cup and Saucer, handleless cup
 Pelew, E Challinor, c1840 ..... **80.00**
 Tonquin, Heath, c1850 .... **145.00**
Cup Plate, Tivoli, Thomas Furnival, c1845, 4" d **70.00**

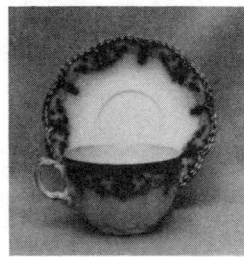

Cup and Saucer, Jewel pattern, Johnson Bros., England, $55.00.

Milk Pitcher, Rhine, Thomas Dimmock, c1844, 7" h **250.00**
Plate
 Chapoo, John Wedgwood, c1850, 9" d **150.00**
 Formosa, Thomas, John & Joseph Mayer, c1850, 10" d ... **150.00**
 Gothic, Jacob Furnival, c1850, 9" d **100.00**
 Singan, Thomas Goodfellow, c1840, 8¼" d **65.00**
 Whampoa, Mellor & Venables, c1840, 7½" d **60.00**
Platter, Hong Kong, Charles Meigh, c1845, 10½" l **225.00**
Sauce Dish, Oregon, T J & J Mayer, c1845, 5" d **50.00**
Sauce Tureen, cov, underplate, Lobelia, G Phillips, c1845 ..... **350.00**
Saucer
 Chapoo, John Wedgwood, c1850, rim chip **29.00**
 Scinde, Thomas Walker, c1847 **39.00**
Teapot
 Amoy, Davenport, c1844 ...... **900.00**
 Lobelia, G Phillips, c1845 ..... **200.00**

Vegetable Bowl, cov, Jeddo, W Adams & Son, c1845 .... **260.00**
Waste Bowl, Troy, Charles Meigh, c1840, two outer rim chips **118.00**

MIDDLE PATTERNS: c1850–1870

Creamer, Canton, John Maddock, c1850 .... **295.00**
Cup and Saucer, handleless, Tonquin, Joseph Heath, c1850 .... **250.00**
Milk Pitcher, Cashmere, Francis Morley, c1850, 7⅝" h **625.00**
Plate
 Excelsior, Thomas Fell, c1850, 10½" d **125.00**
 Japan, Thomas Fell, c1860, 9" d **75.00**
 Kyber, John Mier & Son, c1870, 8" d **75.00**
 Temple, Podmore Walker, c1850, 8¾" d **115.00**
 Tonquin, Joseph Heath, c1850, dinner **500.00**
 Yeddo, Ashworth, c1862, 8⅜" d **65.00**
Platter
 Carlton, Samuel Alcock, c1850, 15½" d, 12" w **225.00**
 Coburg, John Edwards, c1860, 17⅞" l **350.00**
 Excelsior, Thomas Fell, c1850, 11" l **250.00**
 Hindustan, Petrus Regout, 1860, 18" l **400.00**
 Kin Shan, Edward Challinor, c1855, 15½" l **400.00**
 Rock, Challinor, c1850, 12½" l . **365.00**
Soup Plate, Canton, John Maddock, c1850, 10½" d **145.00**
Sugar, Shapoo, Thomas Hughes, c1860, 9¼" d **225.00**
Waste Bowl, Timor, Petrus Regout, c1875 .... **75.00**

LATE PATTERNS: c1880–1900s

Berry Set, Oregon, Johnson Bros, c1900, master bowl, four serving bowls **175.00**
Bowl
 Mongolia, Johnson Bros, c1900, 8½" d **75.00**
 Waldorf, New Wharf Pottery, c1892, 9" d **90.00**

Butter Dish, cov
Lotus, W H Grindley, c1910, orig
drainer, gold trim **145.00**
Non Pariel, Burgess & Leigh,
c1891 . . . . **275.00**
Butter Pat
Clarence, W H Grindley, c1900 **30.00**
LaBelle, Wheeling Pottery,
c1900 . . . . **50.00**
Normandy, Johnson Bros, c1900 **285.00**
Vermont, Burgess & Leigh,
c1895 . . . . **30.00**
Chocolate Cup and Saucer, Kyber,
W Adams & Co, c1891 . . . . **135.00**
Coffeepot, LaBelle, Wheeling Pot-
tery, c1900 . . . . **875.00**
Creamer and Sugar, Argyle, W H
Grindley, c1896 . . . . **400.00**
Cup and Saucer
Argyle, W H Grindley, c1896 . . **95.00**
Chain of States, also known as
Martha Washington, Unknown
English Maker, c1900 . . . . **75.00**
Colonial, J & G Meakin, c1891 . **65.00**
Oregon, Johnson Bros, c1900 . **95.00**
Demitasse Cup and Saucer, Ar-
gyle, W H Grindley, c1896 . . . . **140.00**
Gravy Boat, Lorne, W H Grindley,
c1900 . . . . **85.00**
Ice Cream Dish, Warwick China
Co, c1900 . . . . **75.00**
Ladle Rest, Non Pariel, Burgess &
Leigh, c1891 . . . . **230.00**
Pickle Dish, Verona, Ridgways,
c1910, 8½" l **50.00**
Pitcher
Haddon, W H Grindley, c1891,
8" h **300.00**
Melton, Sampson Hancock,
c1910, 7" h **135.00**
Milan, W H Grindley, c1893, 5½"
h **170.00**
Plate
Arcadia, Arthur Wilkinson,
marked "Royal Staffordshire
Pottery," c1907, 10" d **70.00**
Duchess, Dunn Bennett, c1900
8" d **35.00**
10" d **40.00**
Eclipse, Johnson Bros, c1891,
10" d **85.00**
Lorne, W H Grindley, c1900 . . . **75.00**
Madras, Doulton & Co, c1900,
10" d **95.00**

Neapolitan, Johnson Bros,
c1900, 10" d **50.00**
Non Pareil, Burgess & Leigh,
c1891
Bread and Butter **50.00**
Dinner **110.00**
Waverly, John Maddock & Son,
c1891, 8" d **52.00**
Platter
Argyle, W H Grindley, c1896,
19" l **250.00**
Daisy, Burgess & Leigh, c1897,
16" l **198.00**
Duchess, Dunn Bennett, c1900,
12" l **235.00**
Lorne, W H Grindley, c1900,
14" l **235.00**
Normandy, Johnson Bros,
c1900, large **285.00**
Touraine, Henry Alcock, c1898,
12½" l **170.00**
Watteau, Doulton, c1900 . . . . . . **300.00**
Waverly, John Maddock & Son,
c1891, 17" l, tiny back flake . **340.00**
Relish Dish, Jeddo, W Adams &
Co, c1893, 7½" l **50.00**
Sauce Dish, Normandy, Johnson
Bros, c1900 . . . . **285.00**
Soup Plate
Duchess, Dunn Bennett, c1900 **35.00**
Lancaster, New Wharf Pottery,
c1891, 9" d, flange rim **50.00**
Waverly, John Maddock & Son,
c1891, 8" d **55.00**
Soup Tureen, Cov, Underplate,
Watteau, Doulton, c1900 . . . . . . **900.00**
Syrup, LaBelle, Wheeling Pottery,
c1900 . . . . **850.00**
Teapot, Argyle, W H Grindley,
c1896 . . . . **950.00**
Tea Tile
Atlas, W H Grindley, c1891 . . . **125.00**
Tower, Spode, c1900 . . . . **95.00**
Vegetable Bowl, cov
Blue Danube, Johnson Bros,
c1900 . . . . **200.00**
Togo, F Winkle, c1900, 16" d . . **135.00**
Vegetable Bowl, open
Savoy, Johnson Bros, c1900,
11" l **80.00**
Watteau, Doulton, c1900, 10" l . **150.00**
Waste Bowl, Touraine, Stanley
Pottery, c1898 . . . . **250.00**

FOLK ART

History: The definition of what constitutes folk art is still being vigorously debated among collectors, dealers, museum curators, and scholars. Some want to confine folk art to non–academic, handmade objects. Others are willing to include manufactured material. In truth, the term is used to cover objects ranging from crude drawings by obviously untalented children to academically trained artists' paintings of "common" people and scenery.

The folk art market is subject to hype and manipulation. Neophyte collectors are encouraged to read Edie Clark's "What Really Is Folk Art?" in the December 1986 *Yankee.* Clark's article provides a refreshingly honest look at the folk art market.

Finally, the folk art market is extremely trendy and fickle. What is hot today can become cool and passé tomorrow. Collecting folk art is not for the weak–of–heart or the cautious investor.

References: Kenneth L. Ames, *Beyond Necessity: Art In The Folk Tradition,* W. W. Norton, 1978; Robert Bishop and Judith Rieter Weissman, *Folk Art: The Knopf Collectors' Guides To American Antiques,* Alfred A. Knopf, 1983; Country Living Magazine, *Living With Folk Art,* Hearst Books, 1994; George H. Meyer, *American Folk Art Canes: Personal Sculpture,* Sandringham Press, Museum of American Folk Art and University of Washington Press, 1992; Dana G. Morykan and Harry L. Rinker, *Warman's Country Antiques & Collectibles, 2nd Edition,* Wallace–Homestead, 1994; Henry Niemann and Helaine Fendelman, *The Official Identification and Price Guide To American Folk Art,* House of Collectibles, 1988; Beatrix T. Rumford and Carolyn J. Weekley, *Treasures of American Folk Art from The Abby Aldrich Rockefeller Folk Art Center,* Little, Brown and Company, 1989; Shenandoah Valley Folklore Society, *Folk and Decorate Art of the Shenandoah Valley,* Shenandoah Valley Folklore Society, 1993.

Periodical: *Folk Art,* 61 W. 62nd St., New York, NY 10023.

Museums: Abby Aldrich Rockefeller Folk Art Center, Williamsburg, VA; Daughters of the American Revolution Museum, Washington, DC; Landis Valley Farm Museum, Lancaster, PA; Museum of American Folk Art, New York, NY; Museum of Early Southern Decorative Arts, Winston–Salem, NC; Museum of International Folk Art, Sante Fe, NM.

Train Station, painted wood, c1900, roof decorated with balustrade above two central arched entranceways each flanked by elongated and rounded windows, gold painted pilasters, maroon, gold, and green highlights, 16½" l, 13" d, 17" h, $700.00. Photograph courtesy of Sotheby's.

Bust, 8¼" h, Lincoln, pine, carved, brown finish **75.00**
Carving, American eagle, attributed to John Hales Bellamy (1836–1914), Kittery Point, ME, painted, holding banner inscribed "Don't Give Up The Ship," 25¼" l **16,000.00**
Decoy, 14" l, fish, wood, tin fins, orig brown and yellow paint, white, red, and black, spots ... **150.00**
Figure
   8½" l, acrobat on horse, whittled wood, painted, blue acrobat with adjustable arms and legs, hinge and tack joints, standing on white horse with brown leather ears, blue wedge shaped base, c1880 .... **385.00**
   9" l, reclining cat, sewer tile, yellow slip facial dec, tooled detail **235.00**

Jug
6" h, grotesque, redware, ash glazed grimacing face bulging eyes, prominent ears, broken porcelain bits for teeth, pulled handle, North Carolina **3,850.00**
13¾" h, grotesque, green ash glaze, incised inscription "Gertrude Nelson's Husband" **275.00**
Model, Fiske Farm, Lexington, MA, early 19th C, carved and painted wood, 25 pcs including animals, figures, farmhouse, and outbuildings, cut and painted heavy paper plants and trees, wooden crate, some losses, 3¾" h farmhouse **1,500.00**
Needlepoint Panel, 10¾" w, 18¾" h, dog on cushion, shades of brown, blue, white, olive, orange, and yellow, framed, sgd and dated "H 1885" **475.00**
Painting
Gray Horse in Landscape with Stable Flying an American Flag Beyond, American School, 19th C, unsigned, watercolor on paper, framed, laid down, 5½ x 7¼" **1,035.00**
Memorial, American School, 19th C, watercolor and ink on silk, monument inscribed with names and death dates of daughters of Samuel and Mary Smith of Fryeburg, ME, scattered staining, framed, 11¼ x 17" **400.00**
Portrait, 4¾ x 3¼" h, miniature, pencil on paper, lady in eyelet cap and collar, gentleman in black frock coat, sgd and dated on verso "J M Crowley, Delineator, Valatie, May 28, 1836," American School, 19th C **1,325.00**
Rug, 29 x 40", stitched loop, multicolored, worn and faded **100.00**
Sampler, 12¼" w, 12¾" h, green dyed linen homespun, alphabets and inscription "The Rule to Mark Napkins," sgd and dated "Lydia Mitchell Nine Partners 1810," framed, 1810 . . . . **2,550.00**
Show Towel, 60" l, linen, pink embroidered stars, flowerheads,

birds, reindeer, dogs, and potted flowering shrubs, zigzag crochet panel, fringed bottom, sgd and dated "Anna Marie Nies, 1816" **350.00**
Theorem
5½ x 6", basket of fruit, American School, 19th C, unsigned, watercolor on velvet, framed, 5½ x 6" **300.00**
17½ x 21", memorial, American School, 19th C, Lucy M Vilas, watercolor on velvet, "This tribute of affection, inscribed by Lucy M. Vilas, and presented to Mr. E. & Mrs. R. Carleton, in memory of their brother, Capt. George Carleton....1821," framed **635.00**
19¼" h, 23¼" w, still life, fruit, sgd "T J Graham," watercolor, painted frame **610.00**
Weather vane, 29" l, 11½" h, foxhound, running, molded copper, swell–bodied figure, rod mounting **8,250.00**
Whirligig, 32" l, horse cart and old man, wood, masonite, wire, and sheet metal, orig polychrome paint, Everette Brittingham, Gibson Co, Indiana, 1932–36 . . . . **550.00**
Wood Carving, sea gull, pine, painted, mounted on turned base, 20th C, 21" l, 19" h **800.00**

FOOD BOTTLES

History: Food bottles were made in many sizes, shapes, and colors. Manufacturers tried to make an attractive bottle that would ship well and allow the purchaser to see the product, thus assuring him that the product was as good and as well made as home preserves.

Reference: Ralph & Terry Kovel, *The Kovels' Bottles Price List, 9th Edition,* Crown Publishers, Inc., 1992.

Periodicals: *Antique Bottle and Glass Collector,* PO Box 187, East Greenville, PA 18041; *Bottles & Extras,* PO Box 154, Happy Camp, CA 96039.

Catsup, Shriver's Oyster Ketshup, 7" h, olive green **1,150.00**

Extract

Burnetts Standard Flavoring,
6¾" h, light green **6.00**

Dills Family Extract, 6¼" h, clear **2.00**

Dr Price Delicious Flavoring Extract, 6¾" h, clear **5.00**

Forbes Delicious Flavoring, 5" h,
clear **5.00**

Kings Flavoring, 6¾" h, clear . . **4.00**

Sauers, 6" h, clear **4.00**

Teitchell Champlin Co, 4½" h,
clear **5.00**

Thompson & Taylor Root Beer
Flavoring, 4" h, clear **4.00**

Grape Juice, Welch's, 1½ pt,
Howdy Doody illus, dated 1946 **100.00**

Honey

G L W B Verampshire Brand
Pure Honey **10.00**

Golden Tree Pure Honey, 4 oz,
clear **2.00**

**Horseradish Bottle, dark green,
$50.00.**

Horseradish, 7" h, aqua, "Pure
Horse Radish HD Geer" **15.00**

Mayonnaise, Mrs Chapins, pt,
clear **5.00**

Milk

A G Smalley, qt, clear, tin handle
and cap **55.00**

Big Elm Dairy, qt, green **150.00**

Clinton Milk Co, qt, smokey
beige **20.00**

Crescent Creamery, qt, round,
red pyro, nursery rhyme dec . **25.00**

Elmhurst Cream Co, ½ pt,
smokey beige **12.00**

Fikes Dairy Farm, qt, round, emb
slug plate **30.00**

Hollywood Western Dairy Co, qt,
round, emb **15.00**

Margrove Inc Cream Craft Products, qt, sq, red pyro **5.00**

North Shore Dairy Co, Chicago,
pt, round, emb **5.00**

Quality Dairy, round red pyro . . **8.00**

Superior Dairy, qt, round, orange
pyro, man and cow's head illus **15.00**

Weber Dairy Co, IL, ¼ pt, round,
emb slug plate **15.00**

Mustard

Bunte Mustard, Chicago, 4¾" h **15.00**

French's Medford Brand Prepared Mustard, pt, clear **4.00**

Olives, Bridal Brand, stoneware . **50.00**

Pepper Sauce

Cathedral, 8¾" h, aqua, six
sided **45.00**

Corbyn Cooks & Co, London, 7"
h, aqua, open pontil **30.00**

S & P Pat App For, 8" h, green,
spiral design **40.00**

Wells, Miller & Provost, 8" h,
green, fluted **175.00**

Pickle

East India Pickles, qt, aqua . . . **15.00**

Skilton Foote & Co, Bunker Hill
Pickles, 5¼" h, clear **5.00**

Syrup

Golden Crown Table Syrup . . . **8.00**

Rock Maple Vermont Syrup,
¼ pt, round, paper label **15.00**

Tomato Sauce, TA Bryan & Cos
Perfection, 8¼" h, yellow–amber **175.00**

FOOD MOLDS

History: Food molds were used both commercially and in the home. For the most part, pewter ice cream molds and candy molds were used on a commercial basis; pottery and copper molds were used in homes. Today, both types are collected largely for decorative purposes.

Pewter ice cream molds were made primarily by two American companies: Eppelsheimer & Co. [molds marked E & Co., N.Y.] and Schall & Co. [molds marked S & Co.]. Both companies used a numbering system for their molds. The Krauss Co. bought out Schall & Co., removed the S & Co. from some, but not all the molds, and added more designs [marked K or Krauss].

The majority of pewter ice cream molds are individual serving molds. When used, one quart of ice cream would make eight to ten pieces. Scarcer, but still available, are banquet molds which used two to four pints of ice cream per example. European pewter molds [CC is a French mold mark] are available.

Chocolate mold makers are more difficult to determine. Unlike the pewter ice cream molds, maker's marks were not always on the mold or were covered by frames. Eppelsheimer & Co. of New York marked many of their molds, either with their name or with a design resembling a child's toy top with "Trade Mark" and "NY." Many chocolate molds were imported from Germany and Holland and were marked with the country of origin and, in some cases, the mold maker's name.

Reference: Judene Divone, *Chocolate Moulds: A History & Encyclopedia,* Oakton Hills Publications, 1987.

Museum: Wilbur's Americana Candy Museum, Lititz, PA.

Additional Listings: Butter Prints.

Ice Cream, pewter, flag, marked "Krauss, NY 292," $60.00.

Butter, round, cased, gray scrubbed finish
3¾" d, strawberries and leaves design	80.00
4½" d, flower design	70.00
Cake, 8¾" l, lamb, two part	40.00

Candy
15" l, wood, five hearts with cross and one circular floral design	325.00
30" l, five geometric carved designs	125.00

Chocolate, tin
4" h, Snowman, two part clamp type, no hinge	45.00
4⅛" h, love birds, two part, hinged, marked	25.00
4½ x 8", Christmas scene, book type	30.00
5¾" h, rabbit, two part	35.00
6 x 15", coin, "Rosemarie de Paris," tray type, marked "Epplesheimer & Co, NY, Feb 1944"	20.00
6½ x 6", hearts, book type, two cavities	30.00
9" h, clown, two part clamp type, no hinge, marked "15262"	75.00
11 x 17", chickens and rabbits, tray type, six rows, marked "2215.S"	95.00

Cookie Board
Pewter, 3⅛ x 7⅛", eight designs, wood backing	85.00
Redware, 5¾ x 8½", six different designs	440.00

Wood
3⅜ x 12⅜", hardwood, twelve designs	200.00
6⅛ x 10", walnut, fifteen designs	175.00
7⅛ x 10¼", hardwood, three carved coiled snakes, tin border	125.00

Ice Cream, pewter
Chrysanthemum, marked "313"	55.00
Football Player, marked "S–491"	55.00
Grape Leaf, marked "E–256"	40.00
King of Hearts, marked "E–920"	35.00
Otter, 5¼" h, marked "E & Co NY"	30.00
Morning Glory, marked "S–239"	40.00
Rose Cluster, worn mark	35.00
Santa and Reindeer	65.00
Turkey, marked "E & Co, NY," number worn	40.00

Jelly, stoneware, English, late 19th
C	40.00

Maple Sugar, cherry wood box, acorn and leaf imprints	75.00

Pudding, tin
   6¾" d, 8" h, cone shape, spiral
     design **25.00**
   8" w, five point star **50.00**

FOSTORIA GLASS

FOSTORIA

History: Fostoria Glass Co. began operations at Fostoria, Ohio, in 1887, and moved to Moundsville, West Virginia, its present location, in 1891. By 1925 Fostoria had five furnaces and a variety of special shops. In 1924 a line of colored tableware was introduced. Fostoria was purchased by Lancaster Colony in 1983, and continues to operate under the Fostoria name.

References: Gene Florence, *Elegant Glassware Of The Depression Era, Revised Fifth Edition,* Collector Books, 1993; Robert E. Foster, *Fostoria American Pattern,* published by author, 1984; Ann Kerr, *Fostoria: An Identification and Value Guide of Pressed, Blown, & Hand Molded Shapes,* Collector Books, 1994; Milbra Long and Emily Seate, *Fostoria Stemware: The Crystal For America,* Collector Books, 1994; JoAnn Schleismann, *Price Guide To Fostoria, The Popular Years, Third Edition,* Park Avenue Publications; Ellen T. Schroy, *Warman's Glass,* Wallace–Homestead, 1992; Sidney P. Seligson, *Fostoria American, A Complete Guide,* published by author, 1992; Hazel M. Weatherman, *Fostoria, Its First Fifty Years,* published by author, 1972.

Collectors' Clubs: Fostoria Glass Collectors, 2109 Lassen St., #112, Chatsworth, CA 91311; Fostoria Glass Society of America, PO Box 826, Moundsville, WV 26041.

Periodical: *The Daze,* 10271 State Rd., Box 57, Otisville, MI 48463.

Museums: Fostoria Glass Museum, Moundsville, WV; Huntington Galleries, Huntington, WV.

Ashtray
   Century, crystal, individual **8.50**
   Pioneer, amber **8.00**
Basket
   American, crystal, reed handle . **95.00**
   Century, crystal, 10" oval **100.00**

Pitcher, American pattern, straight sides, ice lip, 8¼" h, $115.00.

Bonbon
   Chintz, crystal, 7⅜" d **25.00**
   Fairfax, pink **14.00**
Bowl
   American, crystal, shallow, 13" d **47.00**
   Baroque, yellow, flared, 11" d .. **35.00**
   June, yellow, ftd, 12" d **55.00**
Cake Stand, Century, crystal **50.00**
Candlesticks, pr
   Fairfax, orchid, low **50.00**
   Meadow Rose, crystal, 2 lite .. **32.00**
   Royal, black **85.00**
Candy Dish, cov, ftd, Century,
   crystal, bouquet dec **50.00**
Celery Tray, Midnight Rose, crystal, 11½" l **25.00**
Champagne, Buttercup, crystal .. **19.95**
Coach Lamp, Coin, amber **80.00**
Coaster, Fairfax, green **6.00**
Cocktail
   American, crystal, cone shape . **9.00**
   Colony, Line #2412, crystal ... **14.00**
   Holly, crystal, 5¼" h **15.00**
Commemorative Plate, Our American State Series, crystal
   California **30.00**
   Florida **30.00**
   Hawaii **30.00**
   Massachusetts **30.00**
   Michigan **30.00**
   New York **30.00**
   Ohio **30.00**
Compote, Baroque, yellow, high
   standard **85.00**
Cordial, Chintz, crystal **45.00**
Creamer and Sugar
   Century, crystal **30.00**
   Chintz, crystal, small size **35.00**

Cream Soup, Fairfax, green	18.00
Cup and Saucer	
American, crystal	12.00
Baroque, blue	47.50
Pioneer, burgundy	20.00
Demitasse Cup and Saucer	
Fairfax, pink	25.00
Royal, amber	22.00
Figurine, St Francis, frosted	225.00
Fruit Bowl, Colony, Line #2412,	
crystal, 14″ d	65.00
Goblet	
American, crystal, luncheon size	10.00
Century, crystal, 10 oz	20.00
June, yellow	35.00
Minuet, topaz	28.00
Vesper, amber	30.00
Iced Tea Tumbler	
American, crystal	20.00
Corsage, crystal	32.00
Juice Tumbler	
American, crystal, 3¾″ h	13.00
Colony, Line #2412, crystal, ftd	13.00
Mayonnaise, Camelia, crystal, divided	45.00
Muffin Tray, Colony, Line #2412, crystal	38.00
Nappy, Baroque, yellow, handle, 4″	14.00
Nut Bowl, Fairfax, azure	40.00
Oyster Cocktail, Holly, crystal ...	11.50
Pitcher	
Colony, Line #2412, blown, 2 qt	95.00
Hermitage, yellow, 3 pint	65.00
Jamestown, amber	55.00
Rambler, ftd, crystal	90.00
Plate	
American, crystal, 7¾″ d	9.00
Baroque, yellow, 8″ d	12.50
Fairfax, yellow, 10″ d	20.00
Royal, green, 10″ d	30.00
Seville, amber, 10″ d	18.00
Willow, crystal, 7½″ d	10.00
Relish, Century, crystal, three part, handle	35.00
Salt and Pepper Shakers, pr, Heather, Line #6037, crystal ..	50.00
Server, center handle, Colony, Line #2412, crystal	30.00
Sherbet	
Camelia, crystal, low	10.00
Chintz, crystal, tall	15.00
Toothpick Holder, American, crystal	25.00
Torte Plate, Chintz, crystal, 14″ d	27.50

Tumbler	
Ingrid, crystal	15.00
Rose, crystal, 12 oz, ftd	16.00
Vesper, amber, 5¼″ h	22.00
Urn, Century, crystal, bouquet dec, two handles	85.00
Vase, Colony, Line #2412, crystal, flared, 7½″ h	38.00
Vegetable, Century, crystal, oval, 9½″ l	40.00
Wine	
American, crystal, hexagonal base	14.00
Corsage, crystal, 3½ oz	24.00

FRAKTUR

History: Fraktur, the calligraphy associated with the Pennsylvania Germans, is named for the elaborate first letter found in many of the hand drawn examples. Throughout its history printed, partially printed–hand drawn, and fully hand drawn works existed side by side. Frakturs often were made by the school teachers or ministers living in rural areas of Pennsylvania, Maryland, and Virginia. Many artists are unknown.

Frakturs exist in several forms—geburts and taufschein (birth and baptismal certificates), vorschrift (writing example, often with alphabet), haus sagen (house blessing), bookplates and marks, rewards of merit, illuminated religious text, valentines, and drawings. Although collected for decoration, the key element in frakturs is the text.

Fraktur prices rise and fall along with the American folk art market. The key marketplace is Pennsylvania and the Middle Atlantic states.

References: Dana G. Morykan and Harry L. Rinker, *Warman's Country Antiques & Collectibles, Second Edition*, Wallace–Homestead, 1994; Donald A. Shelley, *The Fraktur–Writings Or Illuminated Manuscripts Of The Pennsylvania Germans*, Pennsylvania German Society, 1961; Frederick S. Weiser and Howell J. Heaney (comps.), *The Pennsylvania German Fraktur Of The Free Library Of Philadelphia*, Pennsylvania German Society, 1976, two volumes.

Museum: The Free Library of Philadelphia, Philadelphia, PA.

HAND DRAWN

Anchor Artist, birth and baptismal, Centre County, 1843, 12 x 15¼", pen and ink and watercolor, maidens and architectural details, blue, red, brown, yellow, and black, creases, minor stains, short tears, frame 14½ x 18½" . **2,500.00**

Blousey (Flying) Angel Artist, birth and baptismal, Northampton County, PA, c1795, low central text panel, angel in each of upper quadrants, pomegranate flower beneath each angel and flanking panel, birth of Maria Barbara Hunsicker, fold indications, tape stains, and some attachments on reverse, 13 x 8" . **1,600.00**

Flat Parrot Artist, birth and baptismal, Berks County, PA, c1810, 13¾ x 16½", central heart with text, two mermaids, two parrots, two distlefinks, floral rosettes in top corners, and numerous flowers throughout, initials "I.T.W." at base of text, birth of Sarah Ohmacht, 13¾ x 16½" **4,000.00**

Lykens Valley Artist, baptismal record for Johann Frederick Lupold, June 6, 1789, pen and ink and watercolor, framed, 8¼ x 13¼" **2,500.00**

Moore, Thomas C., pair of illus romantic verses, 1828, watercolor and ink on paper, discoloration, framed, one 6½" sq, other 6½ x 8¾" **350.00**

Unknown Artist
Birth and baptismal, pen, ink, and watercolor, lined paper, architectural design, two women, red, yellow, blue, and black, framed, 19¼" h, 15¼" w **825.00**
Birth Record, Northampton County, PA, 1807, pen, ink, and watercolor, flying angel, black, red, yellow, and dark brown, framed, minor stains, slight tears, 16¾" h, 19¾" w . **2,695.00**
Book Plate, PA, pen, ink, and watercolor
Laid Paper
Bird and floral design, circle

with text and "Susanna Lappin 1798," stains, bleeding, edge damage and tears, second wove paper attached to book cover, bird design, wear, fading, and damage, matted and framed together in shadowbox frame, 18½" h, 21" h **440.00**

Birth Record, 1828 birth of Maria Ziegler, red and black, red, black, blue, and yellow sawtooth border, stains, framed, 8½" h, 6" w **550.00**

Spangenberg, Johann Ernst, Lebanon County Bible artist, double page, pen, ink, and watercolor, "Johannes Jungten," single sheet with "Abraham Jungten 1788," stylized floral design, red, blue, yellow, brown, and black, stains and bleeding color, old rebacking and repair, matted and framed together in shadowbox frame, 17¼" h, 21¾" h . . **500.00**

Wove Paper
Birth Record, 1810, "Anna Maria Emig was born the 30th day of March 1810," red and black, very damaged and stained, old reeded frame, 10¾" h, 8¾" w **385.00**
Colorful flowers and verse, red, green, blue, and yellow, backing marked "purchased...from Levi Yoder, Bucks Co, on Oct 27, 1941...", 4" h, 3⅛" w **250.00**

Reward of Merit, PA, bird in floral bush with one stylized tulip and one daisy above heart reserve reading "Das Hertze mein ist dir allein," signed "Anna/1827/Tier" in script on bottom, 4¼ x 3¼" **350.00**

Valentine, pen and ink and watercolor, 1835, cutout heart, interlaced with red ribbon, text translated reads "Being acquainted, I want to send you greetings and to add that I am of nobody fonder. Since I have sat with thee I cannot forget thee...," 5¼ x 5½" **5,600.00**

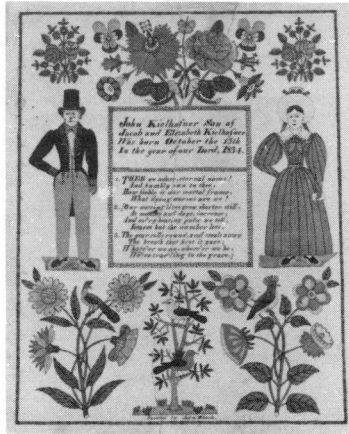

Birth Certificate, John Kiel Lafner, Oct. 15, 1834, John Zinck artist, 7¹⁵⁄₁₆ x 10⅛", $3,600.00.

HAND DRAWN–PRINTED

Brechall, Martin, birth and baptismal, Bethlehem Township, Northampton County, PA, 1811, laid paper, pen and ink and watercolor, stylized tulips and other flowers, red, blue, yellow, green, and black, minor wear, stains, and creases, 13 x 16", frame 15¾ x 16¼" **3,500.00**

Dulheuer, Henrich, birth record, Lancaster County, 1758, Christian Erb, block printed birds and flowers, hand drawn watercolor, pen and ink flowers, red, green, yellow, and blue, framed, stains, fold line damage, 16" h, 20" w . **2,750.00**

Otto, Heinrich, birth and baptismal, Lancaster County, PA, 1774, bird blocks on sides, hand drawn horizontal floral designs between text, birth of John Adam Bassler, 16½ x 13⅜" **2,500.00**

Pseudo–Otto Artist, birth and baptismal, Frederick County, MD, 1807, reverse border block motif from Otto form, hand drawn floral motif between text, birth of Catherina Konig, 16 x 13" **2,000.00**

Unknown Artist, birth and baptismal, 1805, laid paper, printed formal, three hearts, watercolor, pen, and ink dec of flowers and three birds, green, yellow, red, blue, and black, stains, minor paper damage, 15½" h, 18½" w   **385.00**

PRINTED

Baumann, birth and baptismal, 1812 Dolphin County, PA, hand colored, printed in Ephrata, good color, minor creases, framed, 15⅜" h, 18⅛" w **315.00**

Blummer & Busch, birth and baptismal, 1832 Lecha County, PA, hand colored, printed in Allentown, good color, minor stains, taped edge tears, framed, 17¾" h, 15¼" h **85.00**

Eagle Bookstore, Reading, PA, birth and baptismal **75.00**

Ebner, Henrich, Allentown, PA, 1817, Luzerne County, PA, birth and baptismal, artist sgd, minor wear, short tear, edge damage, frame 17 x 20" **250.00**

Kessler, Charles, Reading, PA, 1846, Berks County, PA, birth and baptismal, faded colors, frame 17½ x 20½" **75.00**

Peters, birth and baptismal, 1805 Lancaster County, PA, block printed color, printed in Harrisburg, stains, minor paper damage, framed, 19½" h, 16½" w . .   **115.00**

Ritter, Johann, Reading, PA, birth and baptismal, late form **70.00**

Ville, H. W., Lancaster County, Adam and Eve **500.00**

FRANKART

History: Arthur Von Frankenberg, artist and sculptor, founded Frankart, Inc., in New York City in the mid–1920s. Frankart, Inc., mass–produced practical "art objects" in the Art Deco style into the 1930s. Pieces include aquariums, ashtrays, bookends, flower vases, lamps, etc. Although Von Frankenberg used live female models as his subjects, his figures are characterized by their form and style rather than specific features. Nudes are the most collectible; caricatured animals and other human figures were also produced, no doubt, to increase sales.

With few exceptions, pieces were marked Frankart, Inc., with a patent number or "pat. appl. for."

Pieces were cast in a white metal composition in the following finishes: cream—a pale iridescent white; bronzoid—oxidized copper, silver, or gold; french—a medium brown with green in the crevices; gun metal—art iridescent gray; jap—a very dark brown, almost black, with green in the crevices; pearl green—pale iridescent green; and verde—a dull light green. Cream and bronzoid were used primarily in the 1930s.

Note: All pieces listed are all original in very good condition unless otherwise indicated.

Bookends, pr
6" h, lions, seated, stylized chip
carved **120.00**

Ashtray, kneeling nude female holding green custard glass ashtray, Roman green finish, 9¼" l, $245.00.

7½" h, golfers in baggy pants . **150.00**
9½" h, Indian chief and squaw
with papoose **175.00**
Centerpiece Bowl, 15" d dish, 8½"
h nude, flower frog **275.00**
Clock, 10½" h, two nudes, rect
glass case **975.00**
Incense Burner, 5" h, female head
on burner base, leaning back to
blow smoke through her mouth **185.00**
Lamp
7" h, two nudes, legs outstretched, sitting back to back,
5" sq crackle glass globe **425.00**
9" h, two kneeling nudes, em-
bracing 8" d crackle glass
globe **485.00**
12" h, two nudes standing face
to face, amber rods **825.00**
13" h, two nudes, dancing back
to back, geometric stacked
base, crackle glass sq shade **525.00**
23" h, two feminine figures, clad
in pajamas and wide brimmed
hats, strolling across base, silk
shade **425.00**
Smoker's Set, 7" h, nude, seated
and leaning back, geometric
base, arms resting on removable
glass cigarette box, 3" d remov-
able glass ashtray at feet **285.00**
Wall Plaque, 6" h, seated nude,
floral framework **275.00**

FRANKOMA POTTERY

History: John N. Frank founded a ceramic art department at Oklahoma University in Norman and taught there for several years. In 1933 he established his own business and began making Oklahoma's first commercial pottery. Frankoma moved from Norman to Sapulpa, Oklahoma, in 1938.

A fire completely destroyed the new plant later the same year, but rebuilding began almost immediately. The company remained in Sapulpa and continued to grow. Frankoma is the only American pottery to be permanently exhibited at the International Ceramic Museum of Italy.

In September 1983 a disastrous fire

struck once again, destroying 97% of Frankoma's facilities. The rebuilt Frankoma Pottery reopened on July 2, 1984. Production has been limited to 1983 production molds only. All other molds were lost in the fire.

Prior to 1954 all Frankoma pottery was made with a honey–tan colored clay from Ada, Oklahoma. Since 1954 Frankoma has used a brick red clay from Sapulpa. During the early 1970s the clay became lighter and is now pink in color.

There were a number of early marks. One most eagerly sought is the leopard pacing on the FRANKOMA name. Since the 1938 fire, all pieces have carried only the name FRANKOMA.

References: Susan and Al Bagdade, *Warman's Americana Pottery and Porcelain,* Wallace–Homestead, 1994; Phyllis and Tom Bess, *Frankoma Treasures,* published by authors, 1983, 1990 value update; Susan N. Cox, *Collectors Guide To Frankoma Pottery,* Book I (1979), Book II (1982), published by author.

Vase, bulbous shape, green mottled glaze, cloud-like design along incised line, imp mark "Frankoma," 5½" d, $35.00.

Bank
Boot, Ada clay **15.00**
Elephant **12.00**
Bookends, pr
Clydesdale Horse, rearing, No. 431 . . . .   **125.00**
Nude, seated, hair cascading over face, green, early clay, #425 . . . .   **135.00**

Ocelot, walking, logo **250.00**
Bowl, 9" l, 2½" h, oval, Prairie Green, panther mark **45.00**
Candlesticks, pr, 7" h, swirl pattern, double, glossy **30.00**
Cider Set, 8" h pitcher, six mugs, green and brown, price for seven piece set **75.00**
Cup and Saucer, brown and yellow, mottled **28.00**
Figure
Dreamer Girl, black glaze **125.00**
Fan Dancer, green and brown .   **100.00**
Indian Bowl Maker, bright orange glaze **85.00**
Jewelry
Bolo tie **20.00**
Earrings, pr
Bowling ball and pin **18.00**
Tepee, orig card **25.00**
Pin, Cacti, orig card **45.00**
Tie Tac **20.00**
Magazine Rack, Serva–Tray **45.00**
Mask, Indian Chief, two feather headdress, Indian Maiden with headband, dark blue glaze, price for pair **75.00**
Medallion
Woman, white, pacing leopard logo **85.00**
World's Fair **25.00**
Mug
American Airlines, eagle, advertising **25.00**
Political
1970, elephant, blue glaze . .   **30.00**
1977, donkey, pink glaze **10.00**
Planter
Cactus, oblong, Ada clay **25.00**
Madonna of Grace **45.00**
Mallard **7.00**
Plate
Early Plainsman, 6½" d **3.50**
Easter, 1972, 6" d, white **12.00**
Madonna, bisque finish, 8½" d, 1977 . . . .   **18.00**
Salt and Pepper Shakers, pr
Bulls, 1942 . . . .   **45.00**
First National Bank of Tulsa . . .   **20.00**
Sculpture
Buffalo, 6½ x 3½", #119 . . . . .   **225.00**
Swan, brown, open tail, #229 .   **20.00**
Vase, Flying Goose, pillow shape, #60B **15.00**

FRATERNAL ORGANIZATIONS

History: Benevolent and secret societies played an important part in American society from the late 18th to the mid–20th centuries. Initially the societies were organized to aid members and their families in times of distress or death. They evolved from this purpose into important social clubs by the late 19th century.

In the 1950s, with the arrival of civil rights, an attack occurred on the secretiveness and often discriminatory practices of these societies. The fraternal movement, with the exception of the Masonic organizations, suffered serious membership loss. Many local chapters closed and sold their lodge halls. This resulted in many fraternal items arriving on the antiques market.

Museums: Knights of Columbus Headquarters Museum, New Haven, CT; Museum of Our National Heritage, Lexington, MA; Odd Fellows Historical Society, Caldwell, ID 83661.

Additional Listings: See *Warman's Americana & Collectibles* for more examples.

Masonic, celluloid apron tube, 16⅜" l, $25.00.

MASONIC

Apron, 17 x 17", cotton, white, blue design, applied green and yellow braid borders **75.00**
Belt Buckle, silverplated **22.00**
Box, cov, 5" w, 2" h, brass, engraved Masonic symbols, moon and stars, inscribed "Work while it is day," 19th C **70.00**
Certificate, 14 x 17", membership, vellum, etched copper plate,

Grand Lodge of State of New York seal, orig tin sleeve **225.00**
Goblet, 6" h, clear, engraved, early 19th C **185.00**
Lapel Pin, 14K gold, sword shape **20.00**
Medal, 3¼" h, silver, bar with suspended circle and Masonic symbols, engraved "Ira E Finfrock 1893" **125.00**
Pendant, 2⅞" h, silver, engraved insignia and "Wm Faulkner Genevea, Royal Arch Chapt No 36" **500.00**
Plate, 6" d, flower dec, Los Angeles, 1905 .... **40.00**
Rug, 16 x 23", hooked, red, green, yellow, and blue, striped geometric patterns, Masonic compass, house, cow, ducks, three entwined circles, and cross compasses, initials "B F," early 20th C **1,385.00**
Shelf, 16½" h, walnut, wire nail construction, cutout Masonic symbols, cutout design in lower bracket **40.00**
Stickpin, 14K gold, pearl setting **30.00**
Tumbler, milk glass, inscribed "Landmark Lodge No 127, Baltimore, 1866–1916" **40.00**

OTHERS

Benevolent & Protective Order of the Elks, B.P.O.E.
Bookmark, SS, emb elk's head **18.00**
Cigarette Case, brass, Elks emblem **20.00**
Pitcher, 12" h, china, white, purple elk's head and clock symbols, National Art China, Trenton, NJ **100.00**
Shaving Mug, white, Elk emblem, gold dec **40.00**
Eastern Star
Cup and Saucer, symbol dec .. **15.00**
Lapel Pin, gold, gold–filled, and seed pearls, star with cross and staff, engraved on reverse "BE Tinkham" **30.00**
Plate, Indiana Grand Chapter, 1949 .... **25.00**
Independent Order of Odd Fellows
Box, 11½" w, 21¼" h, pin, painted and gilded, pierced

backplate with carved gilt tassel, applied moon, stars, and eye, front carved with three rings, book, heart, and hand, initials "F L T," late 19th C . . . **3,745.00**
Dish, 5¾" l, pink luster, c1840 . **65.00**
Teaspoon, SS, 1915 . . . . **25.00**
Trivet, 8¼" l, cast iron, heart in hand within laurel wreath **25.00**
Knights of Columbus
Accessory Set, 3 pcs, hat, sash, and sword belt, 1920s **150.00**
Matchsafe, pocket type, 1919 . **40.00**
Sword, scabbard, detailed blade, McLilley Co, Columbus, OH **45.00**
Shrine
Fez, felt **20.00**
Goblet, 5¼" h, molded glass, ruby stained, bell form, tree trunk form stem, gold and white emblem, black swirl molded foot **95.00**
Humidor, cov, clear glass, paneled, metal Art Nouveau cov, ornate emblems finial, Yaarab Temple, Atlanta **75.00**
Plate, 10½" d, comical Shrine center, desert and palms, camel border **55.00**
Wine, clear, sword symbol, gold trim, inscribed "1900, Washington, DC" **110.00**

FRUIT JARS

History: Fruit jars are canning jars used to preserve food. Thomas W. Dyott, one of Philadelphia's earliest and most innovative glassmakers, was promoting his glass canning jars in 1829. John Landis Mason patented his screw–type canning jar on November 30, 1858. This date refers to the patent date, not the age of the jar. There are thousands of types of jars in many colors, types of closures, sizes, and embossings.

References: Douglas M. Leybourne, Jr., *The Red Book No. 7: The Collector's Guide To Old Fruit Jars*, published by author, 1993; Dick Roller, *Standard Fruit Jar Reference*, published by author, 1987; Dick Roller, *Supplementary Price Guide To Standard Fruit Jar Reference*, published by author, 1987; Bill Schroeder, *1000 Fruit Jars: Priced And Illustrated, 5th Edition*, Collector Books, 1987, 1994 value update.

Periodicals: *Bottles & Extras*, PO Box 154, Happy Camp, CA 96039; *Fruit Jar Newsletter*, 364 Gregory Ave., West Orange, NJ 07052.

Collectors' Clubs: Ball Collectors Club, 22203 Doncaster, Riverview, MI 48192; Midwest Antique Fruit Jar & Bottle Club, PO Box 38, Flat Rock, IN 47234.

Additional Listings: See *Warman's Americana & Collectibles* for more examples.

Mason's Patent Nov. 30th, 1858, 1½ qt., $8.50.

Acme, clear, shield, stars, and stripes, ½ gal **8.00**
A Kline, Patd Oct 27 1863, aqua, pt **35.00**
A Stone & Co, Philadelphia, 8⅝" h, aquamarine, applied collared mouth, threaded glass stopper, qt **350.00**
Atlas
E–Z Seal, amber, qt **20.00**
Masons Patent, Nov 30th, 1858, medium green, ½ gal **10.00**
Whole Fruit, clear, qt **2.50**
Ball
Ideal, clear, qt **3.00**
Perfect Mason, olive green, qt . **30.00**
Sanitary Sure Seal, aqua, qt . . **8.00**
Standard, clear, qt **12.00**

Banner, Patd Feb 9th, 1864, aqua, pt 140.00

Bennett's No 1, aquamarine, applied collared mouth, smooth base, qt 400.00

Best Fruit Keeper, aqua, qt 25.00

Boyd Perfect Mason, aqua, qt ... 6.00

Calcutts Patent Apr 11th, clear, qt 35.00

Cassidy, clear, ground mouth, wire bail, smooth base 725.00

Champion Pat Aug 31st, 1869, aqua, qt 90.00

C K Halle & Co, 121 Water St, Cleveland O, cylindrical, aquamarine, applied collared mouth, smooth base 225.00

Crystal Mason, clear, pt 20.00

Diamond Fruit Jar Improved Trademark, clear, pt 2.50

Doolittle, aqua, block letters, qt .. 35.00

Drey Improved Ever Seal, Patd, clear, pt 6.00

Eagle, aqua, orig lid and yoke, qt 80.00

EGC Imperial, aqua, qt 20.00

Exwaco, emerald green, pt 20.00

Franklin, clear, qt 55.00

Fruit Commonwealth Jar, clear, qt 90.00

Gem, aqua, reverse with hourglass, qt 20.00

Genuine Mason, aqua, qt 12.00

Green Mountain C–A–Co, clear, ½ gal 20.00

Hamilton, clear, qt 55.00

Hero, deep aqua, emb cross, qt . 40.00

Hilton's Pat Mar 10th, 1868, aquamarine, tooled and ground mouth, smooth base, qt 225.00

HW Pettit, Westville, NJ, aqua, 2 qt 15.00

Improved, Keystone, aqua, qt ... 25.00

Kerr Self Sealing Mason, 65th Anniversary, clear, blue streak, qt . 30.00

Knowlton Vacuum, aqua, 2 qt ... 35.00

Lafayette, clear, script letters, pt . 120.00

Longlife Mason, amber, qt 15.00

Marian Jar Masons patent 1858, aqua, pt 20.00

Mason
  CFJ Improved, aqua, ½ gal 15.00
  KBGCo patent Nov 30, 1858, aqua, pt 18.00
  Masons III Patent Nov 30, 1858, aqua, qt 20.00

Millville Atmospheric, aqua, qt ... 20.00

Moores Patent Dec 3D, 1861, aqua, qt 75.00

Newman's Patent Dec 20th, 1859, 5⅝" h, deep aquamarine, ground mouth, smooth base ... 850.00

Non Pareil, Patented July 17, 1866, aquamarine, ground mouth, smooth base, qt 330.00

Pearl, aqua, qt 35.00

Potter & Bodine's/Patented/Air–Tight, barrel form, aquamarine, tooled wax seal groove mouth, iron pontil 325.00

Protector, aqua, recessed panels, orig tin lid, pt 135.00

Puritan Trademark, aqua, qt 150.00

Quick Seal, aqua, pt 8.00

Rex, No 3, clear, qt 8.00

Robert Arthurs Patent, pottery, pt 225.00

Safety Valve, aqua, Greek Key design 25.00

Superior AG Co, aqua, pt 15.00

Sure Seal Made For L Bamberger, blue, qt 12.00

The Family Fruit Jar, clear, ground mouth, wire bail, smooth base . 550.00

The Reservoir, aquamarine, applied collared mouth, ½ gal 350.00

Tight Seal, aqua, qt 5.00

Trues Imperial Brand, clear, pt .. 10.00

Union No 1, aqua, qt 250.00

Valve jar Philadelphia, aqua, ½ gal 75.00

Victor Patented 1899, aqua, pt .. 55.00

Wears, blue tint, pt 12.00

Weir Patd Mar 1st 1892, pottery, qt 20.00

Wilcox, qt 55.00

Winslow Patented 1870, Pat 1873, aqua, pt 90.00

Wm L Haller, Carlisle, PA, aquamarine, applied collared mouth, smooth base, ½ gal 325.00

Woodbury, aqua, "WGW" monogram, 2 qt 30.00

Woods, 7½" h, aquamarine, rolled collared mouth, smooth base .. 330.00

FRY GLASS

History: The H. C. Fry Glass Co. of Rochester, Pennsylvania, began operating in 1901 and continued until 1933. Their first products were brilliant period cut glass.

They later produced Depression tablewares. In 1922 they patented heat–resisting ovenware in an opalescent color. This "Pearl Oven Glass" was produced in a variety of oven and table pieces including casseroles, meat trays, pie and cake pans, etc. Most of these pieces are marked "Fry" with model numbers and sizes.

Fry's beautiful art line, Foval, was produced only in 1926-27. It is pearly opalescent, with jade green or delft blue trim. It is rarely signed, except for occasional silver overlay pieces marked "Rockwell." Foval is always evenly opalescent, never striped like Fenton's opalescent line.

Reference: Fry Glass Society, *Collector's Encyclopedia of Fry Glass,* Collector Books, 1989, 1990 value update.

Collectors' Club: H. C. Fry Glass Society, PO Box 41, Beaver, PA 15009.

Reproduction Alert: In the 1970s, reproductions of Foval were made in abundance in Murano, Italy. These pieces, including candlesticks, toothpicks, etc., have teal blue transparent trim.

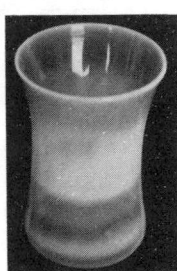

Tumbler, Foval, waisted, 3⅞″ h, $30.00.

Bowl, 9¼″ d, Foval, white opalescent sides, applied jade green band on rim and foot **140.00**
Bouillon Cup and Saucer, Foval, blue Delft handles **70.00**
Cake Plate, 10″ d, 7″ h, Foval, loop handle, jade green, opalescent white pearl, three applied ball feet **475.00**
Candlesticks, pr, 16″ h, Foval, twisted stem with threaded blue

design, bell form socket, blue connectors **495.00**
Casserole Dish, cov, 8″ d, marked "Pearl Oven Ware" **30.00**
Compote, 5¾″ d, 7″ h, Foval, jade green, white opalescent pearl . **275.00**
Cup and Saucer, Foval, applied green handle **55.00**
Lemonade Mug, tall, opal, green applied handle **65.00**
Pitcher, 9½″ h, Diamond Optic, clear, green applied handle . . . **125.00**
Punch Cup, clear crackle finish, deep blue handle **28.50**
Reamer, opaque green, marked "F4/133/2/4" **30.00**
Toothpick, Foval, blue Delft handle **70.00**
Vase
  7½″ h, Diamond Optic, clear, azure blue trim **150.00**
  12″ h, opal, pink loopings **200.00**

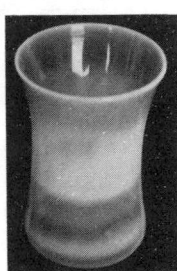

FULPER POTTERY

History: The American Pottery Company of Flemington, New Jersey, made pottery jugs and housewares from the early 1800s. They made Fulper Art Pottery from approximately 1910 to 1930.

Their first line of art pottery was called Vasekraft. The shapes were primarily either rigid and controlled, being influenced by the Arts and Crafts movement, or of Chinese influence. Equal concern was given to the glazes which showed an incredible diversity.

Pieces made between 1910 and 1920 were of the best quality, because less emphasis was put on production output. Almost all pieces are molded.

References: Susan and Al Bagdade, *Warman's Americana Pottery and Porcelain,* Wallace–Homestead, 1994; Robert

Blassberg, *Fulper Art Pottery: An Aesthetic Appreciation,* Art Lithographers, 1979; John Hibel et al., *The Fulper Book,* published by authors, n.d; Ralph and Terry Kovel, *Kovels' American Art Pottery: The Collector's Guide To Makers, Marks and Factory Histories,* Crown Publishers, 1993.

Bowl, mustard matte glaze, white overglaze drippings, stamped black mark in rect cartouche, 9⅜" d, $220.00.

Bookends, pr, figural, faces, blue glaze **425.00**
Bottle, 7¾" h, three sided, pinched form **210.00**
Bowl
  7" d, 4" h, matte blue, applied rose and leaves dec **235.00**
  8" d, 3½" h, four ftd, flaring, blue flambé glaze, rect ink mark . . **125.00**
  9½" d, 3½" h, scalloped edge, green crystalline glaze, vertical stamp mark **50.00**
Bud Vase, 8½" h, Eiffel Tower shape, light blue glaze, green top, vertical stamp mark **100.00**
Jar, 9" h, green shading to blue, pedestal base **400.00**
Musical Jug, 12½" h, handle, dark green shading to light blue glaze **75.00**
Pitcher, 4" h, gray, brown, and blue high glaze **50.00**
Powder Jar, Art Deco lady **160.00**
Rose Bowl, 4¼" d, medium green, blue, and gunmetal gray streaks **400.00**
Vase
  4¾" h, straight neck, globular body tapering to circular foot, stamped "Fulper" **175.00**
  7¼" h, classic form, two handles, pedestal, green, beige, and blue striped glaze, dye mark, dye stamp "#1018" **150.00**

8" h, bulbous, two handles Cat's eye brown glaze, vertical stamp mark **175.00**
Red/purple wisteria glaze, horizontal dye stamped, dye "#643" **125.00**
8½" h, glossy pale green glaze, double handles **215.00**
11⅞" h, glossy pale green glaze, crystalline highlights, imp mark, c1920 . . . . **375.00**
13" h, two handles, mirror black crystalline glaze **500.00**
Water Cooler, #5, marked "Ice Water," old rim chip, no lid **125.00**

FURNITURE

History: Two major currents dominate the American furniture marketplace—furniture made in Great Britain and furniture made in the United States. American buyers continue to show a strong prejudice for objects manufactured in the United States. They will pay a premium for such pieces and accept them above technically superior and more aesthetic English examples.

Until the last half of the 19th century formal American styles were dictated by English examples and design books. Regional furniture, such as the Hudson River Valley [Dutch] and the Pennsylvania German styles, did develop. A less formal furniture, often designated as the "country" or vernacular style, developed throughout the 19th and early 20th centuries. These country pieces deviated from the accepted formal styles and have a genre charm that many collectors find irresistible.

America did contribute a number of unique decorative elements to English styles. The American Federal period is a reaction to the English Hepplewhite period. American designers created furniture which influenced, rather than reacted to, world taste in the Gothic Revival style, Arts and Crafts Furniture, Art Deco, and Modern International movement.

FURNITURE STYLES [APPROX. DATES]

William and Mary	**1690–1730**
Queen Anne	**1720–1760**

Chippendale 1755–1790
Federal [Hepplewhite] 1790–1815
Sheraton 1790–1810
Empire [Classical] 1805–1830
Victorian
   French Restauration 1830–1850
   Gothic Revival 1840–1860
   Rococo Revival 1845–1870
   Elizabethan 1850–1915
   Louis XIV 1850–1914
   Naturalistic 1850–1914
   Renaissance Revival 1850–1880
   Neo-Greek 1855–1885
   Eastlake 1870–1890
Art Furniture 1880–1914
Arts and Crafts 1895–1915
Art Nouveau 1896–1914
Art Deco 1920–1945
International Movement ... 1940–Present

Furniture is one of the few antiques fields where regional preferences are a factor in pricing. Victorian furniture is popular in New Orleans and unpopular in New England. Oak is in demand in the Northwest, not so much in the Middle Atlantic states.

Prices vary considerably on furniture. Shop around. Furniture is plentiful unless you are after a truly rare example. Examine all pieces thoroughly. Too many furniture pieces are bought on impulse. Turn furniture upside down; take it apart. The amount of repairs and restoration to a piece has a strong influence on price. Make certain you know about all repairs and changes before buying.

Beware of the large number of reproductions. During the 25 years following the American Centennial of 1876, there was a great revival in copying furniture styles and manufacturing techniques of earlier eras. These centennial pieces now are over 100 years old. They confuse many dealers and collectors.

The prices listed below are "average" prices. They are only a guide. High and low prices are given to show market range.

References: Henri Algoud, Leon Le-Clerc, and Paul Baneat, *Authentic French Provincial Furniture From Provence, Normandy, and Brittany,* Dover Publications, 1993; *American Manufactured Furniture, Furniture Dealers' Reference Book,* reprint by Schiffer Publishing, 1988; John An-drews, *Victorian and Edwardian Furniture Reference and Price Guide,* Antique Collectors' Club, 1992; *Antique Wicker From The Heywood-Wakefield Catalog,* Schiffer Publishing, 1994; Sam Burchell, *A History Of Furniture: Celebrating Baker Furniture 100 Years Of Fine Reproductions,* Harry N. Abrams, 1991; Joseph T. Butler, *Field Guide To American Furniture,* Facts on File Publications, 1985; Robert Judson Clark et al., *Design In America: The Cranbrook Vision, 1925–1950,* Harry N. Abrams, Detroit Institute of Arts and The Metropolitan Museum of Art, 1983; Wendy Cooper, *Classical Taste In America: 1800–1840,* Abbeville Press, 1993; Eileen and Richard Dubrow, *American Furniture of the 19th Century, 1840–1880,* Schiffer Publishing, 1983; Eileen and Richard Dubrow *Furniture, Made In America, 1875–1905,* Schiffer Publishing, 1982, 1994 value update; Rachael Feild, *Macdonald Guide To Buying Antique Furniture,* Wallace–Homestead, 1989; Benno M. Forman, *American Seating Furniture, 1630–1730,* Winterthur Museum, W. W. Norton & Company, 1988; Phillipe Garner, *Twentieth–Century Furniture,* Van Nostrand Reinhold, 1980; Jennifer George, *Collector's Guide To Oak Furniture,* Collector Books, 1995; Katherine S. Howe et al., *Herter Brothers: Furniture and Interiors For A Gilded Age,* Harry N. Abrams, 1994; Myrna Kaye, *Fake, Fraud, Or Genuine, Identifying Authentic American Antique Furniture,* New York Graphic Society Book, 1987; Constance King, *Country Pine Furniture,* Chartwell Books, 1989; *Knopf Collectors' Guides To American Antiques: Furniture,* 2 vols., Alfred A. Knopf, 1982; Ralph Kylloe, *Rustic Traditions,* Gibbs-Smith, 1993; Lew Larason, *Buying Antique Furniture: An Advisory,* Scorpio Publications, 1992; David P. Lindquist and Caroline C. Warren, *Colonial Revival Furniture With Prices,* Wallace–Homestead, 1993; David P. Lindquist and Caroline C. Warren, *English & Continental Furniture With Prices,* Wallace–Homestead, 1994; L–W Book Sales (ed.), *Furniture Of The Arts & Crafts Period,* L–W Book Sales, 1992; Karl Mang, *History of Modern Furniture,* Harry N. Abrams, 1978; Robert F. McGiffin, *Furniture Care and Conservation, Revised Third Edition,* AASLH, 1992; Kathryn McNerney,

American Oak Furniture Book I (1984, 1994 value update), Book II (1994), Collector Books; Kathryn McNerney *Pine Furniture, Our American Heritage,* Collector Books, 1989; Kathryn McNerney *Victorian Furniture, Our American Heritage,* Book I (1981, 1994 value update), Book II (1994), Collector Books; Dana G. Morykan and Harry L. Rinker, *Warman's Country Antiques & Collectibles, 2nd Edition* Wallace–Homestead, 1994; Milo M. Naeve, *Identifying American Furniture: A Pictorial Guide To Styles and Terms, Colonial to Contemporary, 2nd Edition,* American Association for State and Local History, 1989; George C. Neumann, *Early American Antique Country Furnishings: Northeastern America, 1650–1880's,* L–W Book Sales, 1984, 1993 reprint; Peter Philip, Gillian Walkling, and John Bly, *Field Guide To Antique Furniture,* Houghton Mifflin, 1992; Ellen M. Plante, *Country Furniture,* Wallace–Homestead, 1993; Don and Carol Raycraft, *Collector's Guide To Country Furniture,* Book I (1984, 1991 value update), Book II (1988), Collector Books; Harry L. Rinker (ed.), *Warman's Furniture,* Wallace–Homestead, 1993; Steve and Roger Rouland, *Heywood-Wakefield Modern Furniture,* Collector Books, 1994; Charles Santore, *The Windsor Style in America, 1730–1830, Revised,* Volumes I and II, Running Press, 1992; Tim Scott, *Fine Wicker Furniture, 1870–1930,* Schiffer Publishing, 1990; Dominic R. Stone, *The Art of Biedermeir,* Chartwell Books, 1990; Robert W. and Harriett Swedberg, *American Oak Furniture Styles and Prices,* Book I, 3rd Edition (1992), Book II, 2nd Edition (1991), Book III, 2nd Edition (1991), Wallace–Homestead; Robert W. and Harriett Swedberg *Collector's Encyclopedia of American Furniture,* Vol. 1 (1990, 1993 value update), Vol. 2 (1992), Vol. 3 (1994), Collector Books; Robert W. and Harriett Swedberg *Furniture of the Depression Era,* Collector Books, 1987, 1994 value update; Robert W. and Harriett Swedberg *Swedberg's Price Guide To Antique Oak Furniture, First Series,* Collector Books, 1994; Robert W. and Harriett Swedberg *Victorian Furniture,* Book III, Wallace–Homestead, 1985; Norman Vandal, *Queen Anne Furniture,* The Taunton Press, 1990; Gerald W. R. Ward, *American Case Furniture,* Yale University Art Gallery, 1988; Velma Susanne Warren, *Golden Oak Furniture,* Schiffer Publishing, 1992; Christopher Wilk, *Marcel Breuer: Furniture and Interiors,* The Museum of Modern Art and Harry N. Abrams, 1981; Derita Coleman Williams and Nathan Harsh, *The Art and Mystery of Tennessee Furniture,* Tennessee Historical Society, 1988; Ghenete Zelleke, Eva B. Ottillinger, and Nina Stritzler, *Against The Grain: Bentwood Furniture From The Collection Of Fern And Manfield Steinfield,* The Art Institute of Chicago, 1993.

There are hundreds of specialized books on individual furniture forms and styles. Two examples of note are: Monroe H. Fabian, *The Pennsylvania–German Decorated Chest,* Universe Books, 1978, and Charles Santore, *The Windsor Style In America, 1730–1830, Revised,* Vols. I and II, Running Press, 1992.

Videotape: BBC Enterprises Ltd, *The Story of English Furniture,* 2 vols, Home Vision, 1981.

Additional Listings: Arts and Crafts Movement, Art Deco, Art Nouveau, Children's Nursery Items, Orientalia, Shaker Items, and Stickley.

BEDS

American Vernacular, oak, applied
  feather and fan dec on shaped
  top of paneled headboard, flat
  rect top on paneled footboard,
  sq legs, 75″ l, 40″ w **300.00**
Art Deco, French, mahogany,
  headboards, matching foot-
  boards, price for pair **1,000.00**
Chippendale, tall post, curly ma-
  ple, turned posts, scrolled headboard, poplar panel, orig side
  rails, old mellow refinishing, minor repairs to posts, 72″ l, 60″ w,
  80″ h **3,000.00**
Country Formal, American, early
  19th C
  Poster, curly maple, sq posts
    with turned detail, paneled
    headboard with scrolled crest
    edge, sq blanket rail foot-
    board, side rails, mattress, re-
    finished, 70″ l, 53″ w, 84″ h .. **3,575.00**
  Tester, mahogany, everted

Bed, Sheraton, mahogany, canopy, turned posts, fulled fluted and detailed carving, $5,000.00.

headboard and footboard, baluster turned posts with stylized rope shafts, four American eagle emb brass plates, coiled and brass covered ball feet, 47¾" w, 100½" h **5,225.00**

Eastlake, 1870, walnut and burl walnut veneer, spoon carving, incised lines, applied roundels, 83" l, 58" w **1,500.00**

Empire [Classical], New York State, c1835, tiger maple, low post, paneled headboard, conforming footboard, rails fitted with angle irons, refinished, some loss, 43¾" w, 78" l, 47" h **1,380.00**

Federal
American, 19th C, butternut, tester, arched headboards, tapering posts, turned tapering legs, twin size, 67" h, price for pair **600.00**
New England, c1800, mahogany, carved and inlaid, tall post, orig rails, replaced testers, refinished, restoration, 54" w, 87" h **2,645.00**

Federal Style, carved mahogany,

four poster, arched headboard, leaf carved posts, double size, damaged **700.00**

French Restauration, 1830–45, rope, painted, red paint on poplar, bold deeply scrolled headboard, high cannonball posts, turned legs, orig side rails, 70" l, 60" w, 51½" h **1,000.00**

Greco–Roman, NY, c1805–15, mahogany, carved, four poster, baluster turned and tapered head posts, ring turned leafage and drapery swags, arched headboard, sq tapering legs, restored Marlborough feet, 87½" h **3,575.00**

Iron and Brass, scrolling welded steel rods, brass ball finials, 74" w, 65" h, headboard only **280.00**

Renaissance Revival, third quarter 19th C, walnut and burl walnut, full size, 57" w, 89" h **1,500.00**

Rococo, New Orleans, mid–19th C, half tester, mahogany, shaped tester with beaded carved frieze, shell carved scalloped headboard with center cabochon medallion above rect panel, scroll carved side rails, columned footboard with gadrooned urn form finials, 81" l, 60" w, 100" h **7,750.00**

Rococo Style, Italian, giltwood, crest with openwork carved C–scrolls centered by acanthus, king size, headboard only, 84" w **275.00**

Shaker, mid–19th C, rope, maple, shaped headboard, sq tapered legs, wooden wheel casters, painted green, 74" l, 35½" w .. **1,400.00**

Sheraton
Poster, 19th C, mahogany, tapered turned and reeded acanthus carved posts with urn finials, headboard with twist turned crest rail scrolling down to acanthus carved rosettes and beveled raised panel, plain side rails, reeded legs, 78" l, 52" w, 95" h **4,125.00**
Tester, c1810, mahogany, crotch veneered and corner blocked tester, grained scalloped headboard, reeded tapered

posts with bulbous acanthus carved urns on turned plinth, royal blue drape and bed accessories **4,675.00**

BENCHES

Arts and Crafts, Charles P Limbert Co, Grand Rapids, MI, 1907, No. 243, window, oak, canted flat sides with four sq cutouts each centering seat, leather cushion, branded mark, dark color, shellac finish, 24" l, 19" d, 24" h . . .**4,500.00**
Country
Bucket, New England, early 19th C, painted pine, shaped ends with traces of red paint, imperfections, 47½" w, 22½" h shelf, 30½" h **1,725.00**
Settle
Pine, curved high back, shaped one board ends, mortised seat, two dovetailed drawers below, base molding, 61" l, 17" d, 60" h **1,875.00**
Stenciled, shaped two part crest rail, turned half spindle back, shaped arms, rolled plank seat, turned legs and front stretchers, polychrome stenciled birds and fruit on crest rail, white and yellow striping on arms, seat, and turnings, dark ground, striping may be old repaint, 73" l **900.00**

Bench, single board top, 36" w, 11½" d, 18" h, $75.00.

Water, pine, two shelves, shaped sides, cutout feet, old worn blue paint, 30½" l, 10½" d, 46" h **2,150.00**
Duncan Phyfe, early 19th C, window, mahogany, carved, X–form slats, reeded stiles, openwork armrests, upholstered rect seat raised on reeded saber legs, brass feet, casters, 38¾" l, 28¾" h **950.00**
George II, mid–18th C, walnut, needlepoint upholstered seat, 18½" l, 16" d, 15½" h **1,265.00**
George III, Provincial, late 18th C, settle, oak, cupboard, iron hooks over shaped arms, hinged seat, plain base, 25" l, 16½" d, 59½" h **875.00**
George III Style, late 19th C
Mahogany
Needlepoint and velvet upholstered seat, cabriole legs, 21½" l, 17" d, 16"h **300.00**
Upholstered seat, leaf carved knees, ball and claw feet, 41" l, 26" d, 22½" h **1,100.00**
Queen Anne Style, mahogany, needlepoint over upholstered seat, cabriole legs, pad feet, 23" l, 18" d, 12" h **175.00**
Regency, first quarter 19th C
Ebonized, parcel gilt, caned seat, upturned scrolling rails, downswept outcurving legs, restoration, flaking, 38" l, 22" h, price for pair **9,200.00**
Giltwood, ecru silk upholstered seat, rails stamped "T.G." three times, flaking, 26¼" l, 18" d, 19" h **5,750.00**
Renaissance Revival, third quarter 19th C, satinwood, marquetry, and gilt incised, upholstered seat**6,900.00**
Shaker, Enfield, CT, water, oblong top, lead lined drain, straight sides, bootjack feet, orig brown stain finish, 49" l, 17½" d, 33" h **850.00**
Windsor, New England, early 19th C
Maple, refinished, 78" l, 33½" h **1,150.00**
Rosewood, paint grained, green and gold stenciling, 58" l, 33" h **810.00**

Chair, Gebruder Thonet, rect back panel, surrounded by diamond form panel continuing to form back legs, surrounded by rect panel continuing to form front legs, paper label, $425.00. Photograph courtesy of Leslie Hindman Auctioneers.

BENTWOOD

In 1856, Michael Thonet of Vienna perfected the process of bending wood by using steam. Shortly after, Bentwood furniture became popular. Other manufacturers of Bentwood furniture were Jacob and Joseph Kohn, Phillip Strobel and Son, Sheboygan Chair Co., and Tidoute Chair Co. Bentwood furniture is still being produced today by the Thonet firm and others.

Bed, Art Nouveau, late 19th C, arched headboard and footboard, tightly scrolling designs, oval caned panel, side rails ...**2,425.00**
Candlestand, Josef Hoffman, c1905, round top, rim with spheres dec, 21¼" h **400.00**
Chair
  Arm
    J & J Kohn, c1930, rect bentwood back continuing to open arms, sq upholstered seat, cylindrical legs, arched stretchers, price for pair ... **750.00**
    Thonet, c1900, scrolled back and arms, cane seat, splayed legs, orig label and stamp **300.00**
  Desk, c1890, arched crest rail, tightly woven cane back, scrolled bentwood arms, round woven cane seat, adjustable pedestal, X–form base **475.00**
  Side
    J & J Kohn, c1900, oak, pressed wood seat insert, branded, orig paper label, 36" h **125.00**
    Josef Hoffman, first quarter 20th C, U–form back rail over three cross bars continuing to a shaped rect upholstered seat, four cylindrical legs, U–form base **1,250.00**
Coat Rack, Thonet Style, shaft with clustered hooks, four down curved legs, 96" h **675.00**
Cradle, Thonet, c1904, suspended type, rect cradle, arched fronts, inverted U–shape bands, curved hood, U–shape support, two legs, 41" l, 43" h **275.00**
Rocker
  Austria, c1900, arched upholstered back, rect upholstered seat, curved arms, scrolling supports and runners, adjustable footrest **3,850.00**
  Thonet Style, oval caned back, scrolling arms and rocker supports, caned seat **100.00**
Screen, Thonet, c1904, Spanish Wand model, three sections, laminated panels, cut geometric designs, green glass insets above **3,000.00**
Settee, J & J Kohn, three part scrolled cane back, scrolled arms, cane seat, splayed legs . **700.00**
Table, J & J Kohn, c1900, rect top, scrolled supports and stretchers, imp mark "J J Kohn," 37" w, 21" d, 30" h **300.00**

BLANKET CHESTS

Chippendale, northern New England, late 18th C, pine, old

Blanket Chest, tulipwood, dovetailed, Ohio legs, 31½" w, 17½" d, 19¼" h, $325.00.

black paint, scalloped apron, bracket feet, old brasses, 24" w, 12" d, 23" h **5,750.00**
Country
Ohio, walnut, dovetailed case, front panel with chip carved floral design, traces of red, green, and yellow paint, old replaced turned feet, 41½" w, 20¼" d, 26½" h **5,395.00**
Massachusetts, 18th C, pine, lift top, two faux drawers above two long drawers, bracket feet, refinished, 36" w, 20" d, 43½" h **925.00**
Federal, American, c1810, hinged rect molded edged lid, storage well with till, single long thumb molded drawer, molded bracket base, repair to back edge of lid and lock, 45⅛" w, 32" h **945.00**
George III, English, c1815, mahogany, hinged rect top, storage well, two faux drawers over deep working drawer, ogee bracket feet, 37½" w, 33" h **1,975.00**
Grain Painted
New England, 18th C, pine, early red paint, scrubbed lift top, three graduated faux drawers over long drawer, teardrop pulls, restored, 26" w, 15½" d, 30" h **1,265.00**
New Jersey, early 19th C, poplar, applied black, subtle red amber mottled, amber faux marble veining, minor imperfections, 32" w, 14" d, 21½" h .. **635.00**
Jacobean, early 18th C, walnut, rect hinged top opening to well, conforming case, foliate carved frieze and panels, block feet, 62" w, 24" d, 31" h **800.00**
Queen Anne, New England, 18th C, maple, four aligned drawers, frame of scalloped apron, cabriole legs, pad feet, old refinish, replaced brasses, 36" w, 18" d, 50½" h **6,900.00**
William and Mary
Boston or Coastal Massachusetts, 1770–1820, pine top, oak six board chest, fielded side pine panels, single drawer, painted panels and drawer outlined with black applied moldings, center yellow painted panel with black dec, flanked by black tree–like images, bun feet, restored, 44¾" w, 19" d, 30¼" h **2,415.00**
Connecticut Valley, 1670–1710, joined oak and pine, carved, "S. K." on center panel, two drawers, old refinish, replaced top, 41" w, 17½" d, 45" h ... **19,550.00**
Rhode Island, early 18th C, tiger maple, rect top, two faux drawers, two working drawers, onion shaped front feet, some orig brass, refinished, minor imperfections, 37" w, 18" d, 38¾" h **4,600.00**

BOOKCASES AND BREAKFRONTS

Edwardian, English, c1910, mahogany, inlaid, triple section, inlaid ribbons and wheat sheaves, bowed center with curved glass between two glazed doors, fluted columns with acanthus carved capitols, 30½" w, 20" d, 69" h **1,500.00**
Empire [Classical], English, c1825, rosewood, stepped front, four columns, gilt and grain painted ormolu dec, turned feet, 42" w, 14½" d, 34⅛" h **2,425.00**
Federal, late, mahogany and

cherry, rect top, projecting cornice, glass paneled doors, rect case, long drawer above cupboard doors, 47½" w, 23" d, 79" h **1,000.00**

George III, mahogany, satinwood inlaid, two sections, upper: carved pediment above molded cornice, four glazed doors, circular and triangular mullions; lower: two aligned drawers over two graduated drawers flanked by pair of inlaid doors, 91" w, 24" d, 93" h **6,000.00**

George III Style, 19th C, mahogany

Pierced swan's neck cresting, flame finial, three glazed doors opening to shelves, lower section with three paneled doors, 60" w, 24" d, 93" h **1,800.00**

Rect top, four glass paneled doors, shaped crest case, three aligned drawers over three graduated drawers, flanked by cupboard doors, 60" w, 30½" d, 81½" h **1,400.00**

Triangular pediment, pr of glazed doors flanked by another pr of doors, lower part with projecting center section fitted with drawers flanked by pr of cabinet doors, conforming plinth, 75" w, 11¼" d, 92" h **5,175.00**

Hepplewhite Style, mahogany, shaped rect top, central drawer flanked by two graduated drawers, sq tapering legs, 66½" w, 25" d, 38¼" h **3,300.00**

Louis XIV, Continental, third quarter 19th C, fruitwood, pierced pediment over glass cupboard door, flanked by niches, two aligned drawers, paneled cupboard doors flanked by pilasters, plinth base, bun feet, 56½" w, 25¼" d, 97" h **950.00**

Louis XVI, 19th C, fruitwood parquetry, rect marble top, two doors mounted with ormolu trim, grille panels, tambour slide, plain int., turned legs, 25" w, 13" d, 53" h **2,400.00**

Breakfront, Aesthetic Movement, American, brass mounted mahogany, two sections, upper: projecting cornice, three mullioned beveled glazed doors flanked by fluted flat columns, shelved int.; lower: similar columns flanking three aligned drawers over three carved doors, shelved int., turned feet, 69" w, 20" d, 88¾" h, $2,8670.00. Photograph courtesy of C. G. Sloan & Co., Inc.

Provincial, French, 19th C, oak

Arched crest, two glazed doors, lower paneled cupboard doors, scrolled feet, 56" w, 19½" d, 92" h **2,000.00**

Molded cornice, two heavily carved doors, beveled glass panels, paneled side, sq feet, 54" w, 21½" d, 71" h **1,500.00**

Projecting molded cornice, four wirework doors in upper section, lower section with four paneled cupboard doors, molded base, 104" w, 22" d, 97" h **5,200.00**

Victorian, American, carved walnut, arched cornice, center carved Shakespeare mask, two arched glass cupboard doors, shelved int., cartouches on lower panels, plinth base **1,900.00**

Knife Box, inlaid mahogany, brass escutcheons, twenty slots, 9″ w, 6″ d, 13″ h, $750.00.

BOXES

Ballot, walnut, wide drawers, carved wooden handles, 7½″ w, 7″ d, 18½″ h **125.00**
Bible, Jacobean, English, 17th C, carved oak, rect hinged cov, cleats, carved stylized floral front, plain sides, 29″ w, 9″ h .. **500.00**
Bonnet, PA, late 18th C, oval, bentwood, fitted lid, dower chest type dec, green ground, large central red, yellow, black, and white stellate device, two large sprouting dark green feathered leaf forms, foliage, and vines on lid, 21″ w, 11¾″ h **5,775.00**
Bride's, Northern Europe, early 19th C, oval, full–length portrait of lady on lid, trailing tulips dec on sides, polychrome dec, 18″ w, 11″ d, 6½″ h **485.00**
Candle, 1858, pine, sliding lid, old green paint, sgd and dated "G.M.D., 1858" in white on front, old touch–up to initials and date, 11½″ w **150.00**
Cigar, mahogany, striped inlay on lid and base, zinc lined, nickel

plated hardware, 7½″ w, 4″ d, 12″ h **165.00**
Cobblers, New England, early 19th C, wall type, pine, lift slant lid, compartmented int. five ext. drawers, remnants of red wash, 18″ w, 9¼″ d, 17½″ h **920.00**
Coffer, Baroque, German, late 17th C, olivewood, hinged lid, rosewood veneered int., fall front, two int. drawers, brass mounts, losses, 14¼″ w, 8¼″ h **2,415.00**
Document, painted, 19th C, alligatored black paint, gold pinstriping and floral dec on lid, 11½″ w, 3″ d, 4″ h **125.00**
Game, late 19th C, rosewood, brassbound, retailed by Tiffany & Co, Union Sq, chess, checkers, backgammon, and cribbage boards and playing pieces, minor loss, 12¾″ w, 6½″ h **865.00**
Glove, Victorian, 19th C, rosewood, mother–of–pearl and brass inlaid, rect, hinged top, fall front, monogram, 9⅝″ l **80.00**
Letter, Victorian, 19th C, burl walnut, leather inset slant writing surface, fitted int., 14½″ w, 14¾″ h **775.00**
Pen, Persian, 19th C, lacquer, rounded oblong, painted allover, birds and trees dec, inkwell inside, 8⅞″ l **115.00**
Rug, George III Style, English, elm and mahogany, rect hinged top, molded surrounds, straight sides, bracket feet, 42½″ w, 23″ h **675.00**
Sewing, Empire, American, mid 19th C, mahogany, serpentine edge, int. fitted with well, divided tray, 11½″ w, 8″ d, 4¼″ h **60.00**
Shadow, late 19th/early 20th C, ebonized, black and white marbleized liners, 14″ w, 16″ h, price for pair **230.00**
Spice, Provincial, French, 19th C, carved walnut, rect, hinged slant top, foliate carving, 19″ h **225.00**
Writing
  Chinese, chinoiserie papier–mache, slant front with elaborate courting scene and gilt

dec, fitted int., incised ivory
pulls, 10½" l, 8¼" w **275.00**
English, 19th C
  Black lacquer, gilt chinoiserie
  dec, book form, damages,
  13¼" l, 14" w, 3¼" h **175.00**
  Rosewood veneer, brass
  mounts, fitted int., 10¾" w,
  12¾" h **575.00**
Work, German Rococo, late 18th/
early 19th C, inlaid walnut, lift
top, fitted int., single drawer,
15¾" w, 5¾" h **435.00**

**Cabinet, Directoire, French,
c1800, table de chevet, mahogany,
brass mounts, white marble
top, pierced brass gallery, three
drawer front concealing cupboard
door, white marble int., fluted circular
tapering legs, medial shelf,
16" w, 12½" d, 31½" h, $770.00.
Photograph courtesy of Leslie
Hindman Auctioneers.**

CABINETS

Corner, Federal, late 18th C,
cherry, two glazed doors, two
cupboard doors, 55" w, 24" d,
108" h **1,400.00**
Credenza, Dutch Baroque Style,
19th C, oak, heavily carved cornice,
dentil molding, acorn pendants
above three–quarter gal-

leried rect shelf, single door
carved with rosettes surrounding
panel with Dutch farmers, single
drawer, bun feet, 25½" w, 16" d,
67" h **1,500.00**
Curio
  Ming Style, Chinese, red lacquered,
  parcel gilt, pr of cabinet
  doors, carved panels, two
  short drawers, molded base,
  31½" w, 15" d, 51¼" h **460.00**
  Louis XV Style, glazed serpentine
  door with painted armorial
  panel, ormolu mounted dec,
  cabriole legs, sabot feet, 26"
  w, 15" d, 57" h **1,825.00**
  Regency, early 19th C, chinoiserie
  dec, black lacquered,
  later ebonized stand, 63" h . . **1,265.00**
  Regency Style, ebonized wood,
  projecting molded cornice
  above glass cabinet door,
  shelves on incurved lower
  case inlaid with anthemion and
  paterae, over cupboard doors,
  brass trelliswork, sq tapering
  feet, 55¾" w, 23½" d, 80¼" h **1,300.00**
Display
  Aesthetic Movement, American,
  fourth quarter 19th C, rosewood
  and marquetry, two sections,
  upper: galleried top, pr
  of glazed doors; lower: floral
  carved panels over pr of
  glazed cupboard doors, turned
  feet, 54½" w, 20½" d, 109" h **2,415.00**
  Edwardian, c1900
    Mahogany, mirrored back,
    molded and dentiled cornice,
    glazed doors and sides,
    sq tapering legs, 36" w, 15"
    d, 72" h, price for pair **1,100.00**
    Satinwood, rect top, two short
    drawers, three long graduated
    drawers, rect base,
    15½" w, 13" h **490.00**
  Federal Style, cherry, rect top,
  glass case, blown glass
  panes, twelve reverse graduated
  drawers, curved crest,
  bracket feet, 36" w, 15" d, 82"
  h **1,300.00**
  George III Style
    Early 20th C, mahogany, Irving

& Cassons, A H Davenport Co, finials missing, 44" w, 18½" d, 85" h **2,645.00**
Late 19th C, satinwood, calamander, and marquetry, arched cornice over pr of glazed doors, shelved int., two drawers, sq tapering legs, 27¾" w, 20" d, 68" h .**4,025.00**
Regency Style, late 19th C, mahogany, parcel gilt, bowfront, architectural roof type cornice surmounted by gilded lion, urn finials with suspended gilt braid, center oval medallion, paneled and reeded frieze, four arched mullioned glass panels with center oval medallion over scrolled, molded paneled doors, plain apron, short tapered legs, minor losses, 59" w, 18" d, 75" h, price for pair **31,100.00**
Victorian, oak, single glazed door, int. shelves, bracket feet, 28" w, 12" d, 39" h **195.00**
Pie Safe, American, pine, shaped rect top, single drawer, two screened cabinet doors, 42" w, 17½"˙d, 57" h **350.00**
Side
Aesthetic Movement, American, fourth quarter 19th C, ebonized and marquetry, mirrored, 40¼" l, 16½" d, 62¼" h **1,840.00**
Napoleon III, third quarter 19th C, gilt metal mounted tulipwood and parquetry, rect verde antico marble, conforming case, glazed doors, plinth base, 34" l, 15" d, 43" h **345.00**
Renaissance Revival, late 19th C
Walnut and marble top, molded rect top, three drawers, cabinet doors, shaped plinth base, 53" l, 18½" d, 39" h **1,150.00**
Walnut and marquetry, rect top, center cupboard door with large center medallion flanked by pr of cupboard doors, acanthus leaf mold-

ing, teardrop hardware, 65" l, 19½" d, 43" h **1,725.00**
Vitrine, Louis XV Style, late 19th C
Fruitwood and marquetry, demilune glazed case, cabriole legs, floral inlay, 25" w, 14" d, 63" h **800.00**
Kingwood, breche violette top, glass door and sides with bronze mounted foliate scroll, shelf and gold silk damask int., cabriole legs with incurved lower shelf, 24¼" w, 12¾" d, 62½" h **1,325.00**

Candlestand, cherry, eight-sided top, 17¾" w, 14¾" d, 27½" h, $550.00.

CANDLESTANDS

Chippendale
Cherry, country, two board serpentine shape top, slender turned column, tripod base, snake feet, 16¾ x 17", 28" h .**2,035.00**
Walnut, two board dish top, turned column, tripod base, snake feet, old repair, 21" d, 28½" h **5,390.00**
Federal
Connecticut, c1795, cherry, ovolo cut corners on sq top, turned column, center ball and lower urn turnings, arched tripod base, snake feet, 18" w, 28¼" h **1,000.00**

New England, early 19th C, hexagonal top, turned pedestal, old finish with some stains, 27½" h 375.00

Unknown Origin, early 19th C, cherry, sq tilt top, rounded corners, vasiform standard, tripod legs, 19" w, 19" d, 28" h 425.00

George III, English, c1790, yew and mulberry, circular top, central panel veneered in radiating triangular panels about circular central medallions, narrow and separate border inlaid with stringing to inner and outer edges, slender faceted elongated baluster standard veneer panels, conforming arched tripod base, 23¼" d, 28½" h 2,750.00

George III Style, 19th C, mahogany, circular dish shape tilt top, vasiform standard, tripod cabriole legs, snake head feet, 21" d, 28" h 550.00

CHAIRS

Aesthetic Movement, English, c1880, dining, ebonized, 33½" h, price for set of four 300.00

Art Nouveau, c1910, bergere, carved giltwood, undulating form, upholstered back with carved cartouche centering crest rail, scrolled arms on partially closed upholstered sides, over upholstered seat, scroll, and cartouche carved seat rail, cabriole legs, scroll feet 1,200.00

Arts and Crafts, Handcraft, Morris, oak, slant back, leather seat and back cushions, six vertical slats on each side, orig rect label on back, 32" w, 26" d, 39½" h, price for pair 2,850.00

Biedermeier, second half 19th C, side, fruitwood, restorations, price for set of four, 37½" h ...1,725.00

Centennial, late 19th C, corner, walnut, carved lion's–head mask crest rail, two pierced splats, rush slip seat, straight legs, paw feet 225.00

Chinese, late 19th C, teak, pierced high back, dragon form arms, plank seat, pierced leaf carved apron, claw and ball feet 475.00

Chippendale
Corner, walnut, low crest rail, vase shaped splat, scrolled arms, turned arm supports, yellow velvet upholstered slip seat, sq legs, box stretcher, refinished, 30" h 445.00

Ladderback
American, late 18th C, mahogany, pierced crest rail, serpentine pierced slats, slip

Chairs, Egyptian Revival, late 19th C, armchairs, mahogany, back and embracing arms in form of Sphinx-headed bird, outstretched carved wings, human head and lower bird-like torso inlaid with ivory and mother of pearl, upholstered seat depicting court scene, lion form legs and feet, price for pr, $8,800.00. Photograph courtesy of Morton M. Goldberg Auction Galleries.

seat, Marlborough legs, price for pair **750.00**
Connecticut, c1780, mahogany, scrolled pierced slats, name "Shipley" incised on underside of rear seat rail, refinished, restoration, 18½" h seat, 37" h back, price for set of six **5,750.00**

Side

Connecticut, late 18th C, cherry, serpentine crest, pierced vasiform splat, rush seat, molded legs, box stretcher, price for set of six **2,600.00**

Massachusetts, c1790, shaped crest rail, pierced splat, rush slip seat, straight legs, box stretcher, old brown finish, 39½" h **475.00**

Chippendale Style, American

Arm, mahogany, carved crest, pierced splat, needlepoint seat, cabriole legs, claw and ball feet **475.00**

Dining

Cherry, arched crest, vasiform pierced splat, slip seat, sq legs, price for set of eight . .**1,600.00**

Mahogany, arched scrolling crest rail, pierced interlaced splat, slip seat, Marlborough legs, stretchers, price for set of four **1,600.00**

Veneered, one with arms, pierced splat, slip seat, cabriole legs, paw feet, price for set of six **750.00**

Side, mahogany

Owl's–eye splat, upholstered seat, acanthus carved cabriole legs, claw and ball feet **200.00**

Scroll carved crest rail, pierced vasiform splat, upholstered seat, Marlborough legs **325.00**

Shell carved crest rail, pierced vasiform splat, scrolled arms, upholstered seat, Marlborough legs **200.00**

Colonial Revival, American, late 19th C, legislator's armchair, mahogany, from the MA State House **385.00**

Directoire, early 19th C, side, wal-

nut, pierced lattice crest rail, crossed horizontal back splat with inset brass medallion, cane seat, saber legs, price for pair . **175.00**

Edwardian, English, c1900, side, rosewood marquetry, pierced curved tablet crest rail with center inlaid fan, spindle back, flanked by downswept stiles, bowed green leather upholstered seat, sq tapering supports, spade feet, price for pair **1,760.00**

Empire [Classical]

Dining, mid Atlantic states, c1820, mahogany, wide crest rail with out–scrolled ends, outswept front legs, needlepoint seat, 17" h seat, 33" h back, price for set of four . . . **690.00**

Fauteuil de Bureau, French, first quarter 19th C, mahogany, ormolu mounts, shaped crested back, ornate mask on arms, rosettes and scrolled mounts, four circular supports, caned round seat, down curving legs with shell carving at knees, restoration, 32½" h **3,150.00**

Side, c1830, grain painted, slightly down curved crest rail and splat, replaced cane seat, sq tapered legs, stretchers, grain painted and gold striping dec, 34" h, price for set of six **550.00**

Empire [Classical] Style, American, early 19th C, side, mahogany, out curved molded crest rail, highly carved laurel and medallion splat, anthemion upholstered slip seat, saber legs, 18" w, 31½" h, price for pair . . .**1,250.00**

Federal, Newburyport, MA, c1790, lolling, open arm, mahogany inlaid, old surface, minor imperfections, worn upholstery, Joseph Short, Newburyport label, 17" h seat, 44½" h back **16,100.00**

Federal, late, dining, stained beech, tablet crest rail, pierced foliate splat, caned seat, saber legs, price for set of six **1,800.00**

George II Style, side, walnut, open arm, caned crest rail, center scallop shell and foliate caned

Chairs, Louis XV Style, bergeres, cream painted and parcel gilt, foliate carved and upholstered backrest continuing to form armrests, loose cushion seat, foliate carved scalloped apron, foliate carved cabriole legs, cream striped damask upholstery, price for pr, $2,475.00. Photograph courtesy of Butterfield & Butterfield.

fan over vasiform splat, leather slip seat, cabriole legs, floral and foliate carved knees and hoof feet, price for set of eight **8,000.00**

George III, mid 18th C, side, oak, spindle back, ring turned supports, plank seat, double shaped stretchers **175.00**

George III Style

Arm, shield shaped back with carved rosettes, yellow striped silk upholstered seat and arm pads, sq tapered reeded legs **445.00**

Corner, mahogany, pierced interlaced splats, slip seat, cabriole legs, stretchers, claw and ball feet **650.00**

Dining, mahogany

Ladderback, slip seat, channeled legs, H–stretcher, price for set of six **850.00**

Pierced lattice back, early 20th C, attributed to Irving & Cassons, A H Davenport Co, arched crest, upholstered seats, sq banded legs, stretcher, one armchair, seven side chairs, 38" h, price for set of eight **5,175.00**

Side, mahogany, shaped crest rail with volute ears, pierced vasiform splat, upholstered seat, chamfered legs, H–form stretcher, price for set of eight **3,410.00**

Wing, mahogany, out turned wings, rolled arms, molded legs, H–form stretcher **250.00**

Georgian Style

Arm, mahogany, shaped crest rail with scrolled ears, four splats, out curved armrests, rect seat, cabriole legs with acanthus scrolls, claw and ball feet **175.00**

Side, mahogany, vasiform splat, slip seat, gadrooned apron, cabriole legs, claw and ball feet, price for set of four **600.00**

Jacobean Revival, late 19th C, dining, oak, attributed to Gillows, 38" h, price for set of six **345.00**

Louis XIV Style

Bergere, 19th C, arched floral carved crest, curved silk upholstered back and seat, cabriole legs, price for pair **3,000.00**

Fauteuil, sq back and seat, heavily carved down curving arms, scrolled legs and stretchers, sateen striped upholstery **400.00**

Louis XV Style, dining, oak, upholstered back, shaped crest rail, upholstered seat, foliate carved apron, cabriole legs, price for set of six **600.00**

Louis XVI/Directorie, side, fruitwood, tablet crest rail above

ebonized back splat, gilt painted
Roman figures, rush seat, sq tapering legs, stretchers, price for
pair **1,500.00**
Modernism, Frank Lloyd Wright,
manufactured by Henredon, mahogany, upholstered back and
seat, carved Greek key pattern
trim, two with arms, set of six . .**1,000.00**
Neoclassical, Dutch, late 19th C,
side, walnut and marquetry, 37"
h **300.00**
Provincial
Danish, dining, oak, rect crest,
C–scrolled carved splat, slip
seat, cabriole legs, price for
set of six **2,000.00**
French, 19th C, arm, fruitwood,
arched crest rail with acorn
stiles, pierced lyre form splat,
rush seat, reeded tapered
legs, shaped stretcher **175.00**
Queen Anne
Arm, Massachusetts, mid 18th
C, maple, shaped crest rail,
vasiform splat, scrolled arm
rests, rush seat, turned legs,
Spanish feet, turned front
stretcher, old refinish, 42" h . .**2,775.00**
Corner, New England, late 18th
C, old red paint, repairs and
surface imperfection, rush
seat badly deteriorated, 17" h
seat, 30" h back **1,840.00**
Side
New England, c1750, walnut,
arched crest rail with volutes, vasiform splat, slip
seat, cabriole legs, shell
carved knees, pad feet **1,450.00**
Newport, RI, 1740–60, walnut,
shaped crest rail, vasiform
splat, upholstered seat, refinished, repairs, 17" h seat,
42" h back **1,955.00**
Queen Anne Style
Corner, fruitwood, heart shaped
splats, crewelwork seat, cab-
riole legs, pointed pad feet . . **200.00**
Side, walnut, shaped uphol-
stered back and seats, front
cabriole legs, saber rear legs
set on slipper feet, 39½" h,
price for pair **200.00**

Regency, 19th C
Armchair
Ebonized, rope carved crest,
ormolu mounted splat,
caned seat, turned legs,
needs recaning, 33" h, price
for pair **2,185.00**
Mahogany, arched caned tub
back and seat, turned arm
supports, tapering legs **750.00**
Dining, ebonized and parcel gilt,
caned seats, restoration, two
with arms, 33¼" h, price for set
of eight **12,650.00**
Renaissance, 19th C, walnut, fruit
and berries frieze dec crest rails,
gold damask upholstered back
and seat, fluted tapered legs,
19½" w, 17½" d, 37" h, price for
set of eleven **6,100.00**
Renaissance Revival, American,
c1870
Arm, rosewood, carved and incised gilt back, inset bronze
maiden plaque crest, carved
female head arms, turned incised carved legs, casters, 29"
w, 25" d, 43½" h **775.00**
Side, walnut, spindle inset back-
rest, foliate incised frame,
caned seat, turned legs **70.00**
Rococo Revival, mid 19th C, arm,
inset bronze classical plaques,
green wool upholstery, price for
pair **1,100.00**
Sheraton, country, side, curly ma-
ple, slightly curved crest rail,
slightly curved splat, rush seat,
turned legs, 34¾" h **200.00**
Sheraton Style, arm, arched crest
rail with carved block rosettes,
pierced floral dec vasiform splat,
sq tapered legs with line inlaid
dec **475.00**
Victorian, American
Dining, walnut, rect crest, carved
back splat, damask uphol-
stered seat, saber legs, price
for set of four **250.00**
Side
Mahogany, shaped crest, vasiform splat, slip seat, curved
legs **90.00**
Rosewood, pierced carved

rose crest, arched upholstered back and seat, scrolled legs, price for pair . **550.00**
Walnut, balloon back, c1850
Foliate and cabochon carved backrest, serpentine seat, cabriole legs .. **150.00**
Kidney shape scroll carved back, paisley upholstered slip seat, rocaille carved serpentine skirt, 37″ h ... **150.00**
William and Mary, side
Massachusetts, c1700, turned oak and maple, upholstered back and seat, old finish, 19″ w, 15″ d, 36″ h **5,465.00**
New England, 18th C, maple, banister back, refinished, repairs, 45½″ h **450.00**
William and Mary Style, side, walnut, pierced carved fan and floral crest rail, floral velvet upholstered seat, inverted trumpet form legs, shaped stretcher, bun feet **350.00**
William IV, mid 19th C, dining, mahogany, six side chairs, two arm chairs, upholstered seats, 34¼″ h, price for set of eight **1,955.00**
Windsor
Bow Back
Arm, spindle back, turned arm supports, shaped arms, saddle seat, turned H–form stretcher, 35½″ h **400.00**
Side, c1795, nine spindle back, shaped seat, turned legs, H–form stretcher **550.00**
Fan Back
Arm, late 19th C, mixed wood, shaped crest rail with volutes, saddle seat, ring turned splayed legs, H–form stretcher **425.00**
Side, Connecticut River Valley, 1790–1810, curved yoke crest rail, spindle back, saddle seat, shaped legs, H–form stretcher, Spanish brown finish, 36″ h **750.00**
Hoop Back, I Caldwell, late 18th/early 19th C, side, mixed wood, saddle seat, ring turned splayed legs, H–form stretcher **550.00**

Rod Back, New Hampshire, 1800–20, rosewood graining, 17½″ h seat, 34″ h, price for set of four **2,425.00**

Chest of Drawers, Federal (Hepplewhite), first quarter 19th C, cherry, rect top, bowed front, conforming case, four graduated cockbeaded long drawers, lozenge form lining, shaped skirt, French feet, 40¾″ w, 12″ d, 36½″ h, $3,960.00. Photograph courtesy of William Doyle Galleries.

CHESTS OF DRAWERS

Aesthetic Movement, fourth quarter 19th C, maple, triangular cornice over open archwork over rect mirror plate, flanked by flat molded columns, galleried candle brackets, rect marble top over three graduated drawers, elaborate pulls, casters, 50¼″ w, 22½″ d, 84″ h **1,725.00**
Arts and Crafts, Gustav Stickley, 1902, Model No. 622, oak, four long graduated drawers, two short drawers, panel construction sides, large red Gustav Stickley decal with "Stickley" outlined, 41″ w, 22½″ d, 50″ h .**4,500.00**
Biedermeier, fruitwood, molded

rect top, frieze drawer, two drawers flanked by ebonized wood, gilt bronze pilasters, ebonized wood apron, toupie feet, repairs, 38¾" w, 21½" d, 32" h **2,200.00**

Chippendale

American, early 19th C, Cherry, rect top, projecting cornice, three aligned drawers, five graduated drawers, bracket feet, 46½" w, 21" d, 63½" h . . **800.00**

Country, maple, projected top, four dovetailed drawers, orig brass pull handles, applied cutout feet, refinished, 35¾" w, 32¾" h **825.00**

New England, c1790, mahogany and mahogany veneer, bow front, slightly projected top, four graduated drawers, ogee bracket feet, brass handles and escutcheons, restoration, 38¼" w, 20" d, 33" h **2,990.00**

Newport, RI, attributed to Townsend–Goddard School, 1770–80, mahogany, serpentine, four graduated drawers, bracket feet, early surface, orig brass pulls, minor surface imperfections, 39" w, 20¾" d, 34½" h **20,700.00**

Pennsylvania

Cherry, c1770, cove molded cornice, five small and four long graduated thumb molded drawers, brass bail handles, escutcheons, and lock plates, bracket feet, 47" w, 23" d, 70" h **5,400.00**

Walnut, poplar secondary wood, molded cornice, seven graduated dovetailed drawers, fluted quarter columns, molded base, ogee bracket feet, refinished, replaced brass handles and escutcheons, 38" w, 60" h .**5,500.00**

Walnut, poplar and chestnut secondary wood, molded cornice, five small and five long dovetailed drawers, ogee bracket feet, 40¼" w, 70½" h **6,875.00**

Colonial Revival, Hepplewhite

Style, 1920, solid mahogany, inlay on drawers and back rail, two small drawers over two long drawers, eagle brasses, 42" w, 19" d, 38" h **350.00**

Empire [Classical]

Massachusetts

c1820, mahogany and mahogany veneer, bow front, four small drawers, two long drawers, fluted quarter columns, turned legs, refinished, 44" w, 23¾" d, 39½" h **810.00**

North Shore, c1825, mahogany veneer, shaped back, two small drawers over four aligned long drawers, spooled and spiral carved posts, glass knobs, scalloped apron, short turned legs, old brass, refinished, minor imperfections, 38½" w, 19½" d, 49½" h **1,150.00**

Empire Style, mahogany and ebonized, rect top, four drawers flanked by pilasters, down curving feet, 46" w, 22" d, 42" h ... **850.00**

Federal [Hepplewhite]

American, country

Cherry and curly maple, chestnut secondary wood, top with reeded edge and scalloped gallery, deep top drawer, three dovetailed drawers with cockbeaded edge, turned and rope carved pilasters, paneled ends, refinished, 41" w, 53" h **935.00**

Curly Maple, poplar and chestnut secondary wood, molded edge top, four dovetailed drawers with applied beaded edge, paneled ends, replaced brass pull handles, turned feet, 41" w, 21" d, 48¾" h **990.00**

Mahogany and mahogany veneer, rect top, outset corners, four long drawers, compressed spherical carved capital over reeded column, turned feet, plain frieze, refinished, replaced brasses, 41" w, 21½" d, 43" h **920.00**

Massachusetts, 1805–13, attributed to Alden Spooner and George Fitch, cherry and bird's–eye maple veneer, bow front, four graduated drawers, shaped apron, turned legs, orig brass handles, refinished, 38" w, 20" d, 42" h **4,900.00**

New York, early 19th C, mahogany and mahogany veneer, crossbanded top, four drawers with brass pulls, French feet, 46¼" w, 23" d, 44½" h **2,100.00**

Virginia, walnut, pine secondary wood, molded edge top, four dovetailed drawers with cockbeading, splayed feet, replaced brass handles, refinished, 39¾" w, 43¼" h **610.00**

George III, c1800, inlaid mahogany

Bow front

Conforming top, three graduated drawers, French feet, restorations, 37¼" h **1,150.00**

Detailed top with fruitwood string inlay, three graduated drawers, serpentine apron, short cabriole front legs ... **935.00**

Rect top, four aligned drawers, bracket feet, 42½" w, 20½" d, 37" h **550.00**

Georgian, Late, early 19th C, mahogany, rect line inlaid top, two aligned and three graduated drawers, bracket feet, 37" w, 19" d, 36" h **400.00**

Jacobean, early 17th C, two pieces, carved and molded top, four drawers with two faux–drawer facade, applied ring turned dec, ring turned stiles, ball feet, 39" w, 22" d, 39" h ... **1,550.00**

Louis XV Style

Fruitwood, marble kidney shaped top, brass gallery top, three drawers, cabriole legs, gilt metal mounts, 20" l, 14" d, 29" h **375.00**

Mahogany, shaped marble top, three drawers, cabriole legs,

22½" w, 15" d, 76" h, price for pair **900.00**

Louis XV/Louis XVI Transitional Style, fruitwood parquetry, rect marble top, three veneered drawers, ormolu escutcheons, chamfered corners, ram's–head mounts, sq tapering legs, 25" w, 15½" d, 34½" h **500.00**

Neoclassical

Burl Walnut, early 19th C, rect top with ebonized banding, torus molded small drawer, three graduated drawers, serpentine skirt, bracket feet, 33½" w, 17¾" d, 32¼" h **935.00**

Maple, early 19th C, mahogany, projected rect top, two small and three long molded drawers, tapered sq legs, 51¾" w, 21" d, 44¾" h **880.00**

Walnut, 19th C, rect top with molded beveled edge, two short and three long drawers, satinwood circular marquetry inlaid dec, molded skirt, short down curved legs, 48½" w, 24½" d, 40" h **1,875.00**

Provincial, French, second quarter 19th C, walnut, rect top, seven graduated drawers, 72" w, 18" d, 30" h **2,000.00**

Queen Anne, New England, c1760, maple, slightly projected top, four graduated drawers, shaped skirt, short cabriole legs, pad feet, brass handles, refinished, 38½" w, 20" d, 38½" h .. **1,150.00**

Renaissance, c1870, walnut and burl walnut, gray veined marble top, stepped base, two small drawers and three long drawers with paneled fronts, brass strapwork pulls, intricate carved mirror frame back with four candleholders, molded plinth base with inset paneled sides, casters, 46¼" w, 22½" d, 37¾" h **950.00**

Rococo

Dutch, third quarter 18th C, walnut and marquetry, serpentine, extended sides, extended scalloped apron with carving, claw and ball feet, restoration,

some veneer loss, 37" w, 20¾"
d, 33" h **10,350.00**
Italian, burl walnut, serpentine,
three long drawers, scalloped
apron, cabriole legs, restoration, some veneer loss, 46½"
w, 22½" d, 36¼" h **5,750.00**
Swedish, third quarter 18th C,
ormolu mounted kingwood,
serpentine marble top, bombe
case, three drawers, splayed
legs, minor veneer loss, marble cracked, 41" w, 23" d, 32¾"
h **6,325.00**
William and Mary, walnut, rect,
four graduated drawers, replaced brasses, bulbous onion
feet, restoration, 36½" w, 24¼"
d, 36" h **2,185.00**

**Commode, Second Empire Style,
French, mahogany and gilt brass
mounted, shaped marble top, two
aligned drawers over two cupboard doors, fluted columns, claw
and ball feet, 57" w, 21½" d, 38" h,
$2,200.00. Photograph courtesy
of Leslie Hindman Auctioneers.**

CHESTS, OTHER

Bachelor, Georgian Style, late 19th
C, mahogany, shaped top with
molded edge, five graduated
drawers, scalloped skirt, bracket
feet, 24¼" w, 17¼" d, 36" h ... **385.00**
Bonnetiere, French Provincial,
19th C
Oak and Fruitwood, molded
cornice, two single paneled
doors, foliate carving separated by diaper carved drawer,
paneled sides, short curved
legs, 23" w, 17½" d, 60" h ... **600.00**
Walnut, molded cornice over single door carved with cartouche
shaped panels, paneled sides
and base, 29½" w, 17½" d, 86"
h **1,700.00**
Cellaret, Biedermeier, first quarter
19th C, walnut, down curving
hinged top, rect front, fine parquetry, bun feet, 26" w, 17" d, 25"
h **1,600.00**
Chest on Chest
George III, third quarter 18th C,
mahogany, two sections, upper: projecting molded cornice
over two drawers over three
graduated drawers; lower:
three graduated drawers,
bracket feet, losses, carving
(possibly later), 44¾" w, 23" d,
70" h **4,600.00**
Regency, 19th C, mahogany,
bow front, two sections, upper:
arched molded cornice with
two palmetto carved capitals,
reeded and carved columns,
two short and three long drawers; lower: spiral twist carved
columns, three long drawers,
reeded skirt, tapered palmetto
carved legs, brass hairy paw
feet, 46¾" w, 23" d, 83" h ...**6,100.00**
Commode
Empire [Classical], mid Atlantic
States, c1830, mahogany veneer, marble top with splashboard, single drawer, medial
shelf, refinished, 24½" w, 17"
d, 33" h **575.00**
French Style, late 19th C, possibly English, bleached oak,
rouge royal marble top, locks
marked "White & Sons Oxford
St London," 60" w, 24½" d, 35"
h **2,300.00**
Louis XV Style, 19th C, bombe
form
Faux painted, serpentine top,
three fitted drawers, splayed
feet, losses, repainted, 68¼"
w, 24¼" d, 37" h **1,265.00**

Satinwood marquetry inlay, two drawers, oval painted porcelain medallion dec, Rococo brass pull handles, ormolu mounted dec, cabriole legs, sabot feet, 34" w, 17" d, 30½" h **880.00**

Provincial, French, 19th C, walnut, serpentine front, three drawers, brass bail handles, cabriole legs, 34½" w, 17¾" d, 32½" h **1,325.00**

Rococo, Italian, mid 18th C, rouge variegated marble top, two small and two long drawers, brass pull handles and lock plates, recessed brass reeded column sides, bracket feet, 44½" w, 24½" d, 32" h . .**4,185.00**

Rococo Style, Dutch, late 19th C, walnut and marquetry, bombe shape, shaped tops, two aligned drawers, out swept legs, 29" w, 16¼" d, 29¾" h, price for pair **4,315.00**

Victorian, American

Mahogany, marble top, carved dec and crest, S–curved legs, casters, 29" w, 18" d, 29½" h **275.00**

Oak, arched crest, rect top, one long drawer above cupboard doors, 29½" w, 16" d, 29" h **125.00**

Dresser, Renaissance Revival, American, third quarter 19th C, walnut and burl walnut, marble tops, shaped pediment, side mounted candleholder supports, center drop well flanked by two aligned drawers over two long drawers, teardrop pulls, casters, 50⅛" w, 17½" d, 93" h **1,035.00**

Highboy

Chippendale, New England, c1770–90, maple, two sections, upper: flat top with molded cornice, top drawer faced to simulate five drawers with pinwheel carved center drawers; lower: two long drawers, one long drawer faced to simulate three short drawers, angular cabriole legs, claw

and ball feet, 37½" w, 18½" d, 70" h **8,250.00**

Queen Anne

Massachusetts, c1760, maple, molded cornice, two small and four long graduated drawers, three small drawers in base, shaped apron with two drop pendants, cabriole legs, pad feet, refinished, 35¾" w, 22" d, 69½" h **8,625.00**

New England

c1750, cherry, two sections, upper: flat molded cornice, two small over three long graduated thumb molded drawers; lower: one long over three small drawers, shaped apron, cabriole legs, pad feet, 37" w, 19" d, 66" h **3,750.00**

c1760, tiger maple, rect molded top, five graduated drawers over long drawer over three small drawers, scalloped apron, cabriole legs, spoon feet, replaced glass pulls, refinished, restored, 37¼" w, 17¼" d, 73" h **4,600.00**

Queen Anne Style, Kindel Furniture, cherry, two sections, upper: swan neck pediment, center fan cut drawer flanked by two drawers, four graduated drawers; lower: long drawer above center fan cut drawer, two drawers, 36" w, 20" d, 77" h **1,000.00**

Lowboy

George I Style, English, second half 19th C, walnut, feather and crossbanded quarter veneered top, arched and scalloped kneehole, three crossbanded drawers, molded sq cabriole supports, drake feet, 31¼" w, 28¼" h **3,500.00**

Queen Anne

Massachusetts, c1750, walnut and maple, rect top, single long drawer over three drawers, drop pendants, cabriole legs, old brasses, old refinish, minor imperfections, 30″ w, 20½″ d, 31″ h **10,350.00**

New England, c1750, rect molded top, three small thumb molded drawers, shaped apron with maple banding, cabriole legs, hoof feet, 35½″ w, 21¼″ d, 27½″ h **5,000.00**

Rhode Island, c1760, mahogany, rect molded top, notched corners, one long and three small drawers, shaped apron with turned drop pendant, cabriole legs, pointed slipper feet, 34½″ w, 21½″ d, 30½″ h **2,975.00**

William and Mary Style, oak, projected top, shaped apron with drawer, turned inverted cup legs, X–form stretcher, 23″ w, 29″ h **1,980.00**

Mule, pine, slant front lift lid, fitted int., one board ends, five dovetailed drawers and pullout shelf, scrolled apron, cutout feet, replaced brass handles, refinished, 35½″ w, 20″ d, 50¼″ h .. **1,430.00**

CRADLES

Chippendale, birch, canted sides, scalloped headboard, turned posts and rails, refinished, 37½″ l **300.00**

Cradle, bonnet top, spindles, 38″ l, 27¼″ h, $375.00.

Country

Curly Maple, fiddle back, figured cherry panels, sq posts, turned finials, mortised and pinned rails, cutout designs in rails, oak rockers, 38¾″ l **200.00**

Poplar, old worn green paint, dovetailed, shaped rockers and scalloped ends with heart cutouts, wear and edge damage, 39″ l **250.00**

Grain Painted, New England, early 19th C, pine, yellow ochre and burnt umber painting simulating tiger maple, 37½″ l, 19¼″ w, 25½″ h **375.00**

Victorian, walnut, sausage turned spindles **300.00**

Windsor, New England, c1800–20, bamboo turned spindles, worn finish **800.00**

CUPBOARDS

Armoire

Empire [Classical], Philadelphia, early 19th C, mahogany, reeded cavetto molded cornice, Gothic arched frieze, paneled and acanthus carved doors, four carved and turned columns, dolphin carved front feet, 72″ w, 25″ d, 96″ h **12,100.00**

Louis XVI, late 19th C, mahogany, molded cornice top, mirrored door, satinwood int., paneled sides, one long drawer, bronze mount dec stamped "P E Guerin, NY," block feet **1,550.00**

Naturalistic Revival, American, New Orleans, c1850, attributed to Prudent Mallard, mahogany, shaped crest with two finials, mirror door, shelves and drawers int., satinwood inlay, scrolled skirt **11,000.00**

Provincial, French

19th C, walnut, molded cornice over foliate carved panel, two paneled doors, shaped apron, cabriole legs, 72″ w, 21¼″ d, 78″ h **1,500.00**

Late 18th/early 19th C, cherry,

projecting molded corners, two paneled cupboard doors, bun feet, 53″ w, 25″ d, 90″ h **4,000.00**

Late 19th C, oak, molded cornice, two paneled doors, carved leaves and flowers over shell and S–scroll carved apron, curved feet, 53″ w, 21″ d, 81″ h **3,200.00**

Renaissance Revival, American, c1860, rosewood, arched molded cornice, rect mirrored door, long drawer, flattened bun feet, 51″ w, 23″ d, 98″ h . **3,425.00**

Victorian, c1840, mahogany, molded cornice with carved crest, ogee molded and mirrored door, fitted int. with three string banded shelves, one drawer in molded plinth base, bracket feet, 35¼″ w, 15½″ d, 70″ h **2,100.00**

Chiffonier, Louis XV Style, late 19th C, kingwood and tulipwood, parquetry dec, galleried rouge marble top, 23¾″ w, 14″ d, 32¾″ h **700.00**

Corner

Country, OH, late 19th C, curly maple, pine and poplar secondary wood, cove molded cornice, four paneled doors with applied butternut cutout dec, two small dovetailed drawers, orig cast iron thumb latches with porcelain knobs, wire nail construction, 45½″ w, 81″ h **3,300.00**

Federal

American, c1800, pine, flat cornice top, two glazed doors and two paneled doors, step molded base, 45½″ w, 15″ d, 69½″ h **1,210.00**

Mid–Atlantic States, 1790–1820, walnut, three painted shaped shelves, single glazed arched door, single shelf behind recessed paneled door flanked by fluted columns, old darkened surface, replaced hardware, imperfections,

some restoration, repairs, 48″ w, 22½″ d, 88″ h **2,415.00**

New England, late 18th C, pine, molded projecting cornice, long paneled door over paneled base door, applied moldings, shaped int. shelves, old finish, minor imperfections, 40″ w, 22″ d, 83″ h **2,530.00**

Court, George III, English, early 19th C, oak, projecting rect cornice with teardrop pendants, pr of arched cupboard doors flanked by single arched cupboard door, three drawers of two recessed panel cupboard doors flanking center recessed panel section, ebony escutcheons, bracket feet, 54¼″ w, 22½″ d, 74¼″ h . . **3,335.00**

Hanging, Continental, 19th C, walnut, glazed pierce carved frame door, brass female bust mount, 14½″ w, 7½″ d, 15¾″ h **150.00**

Jelly, country, walnut, molded cornice, one board door with beaded edge, simple cutout feet, 29″ w, 16″ d, 51¾″ h **990.00**

Kas, William and Mary, NY state, 1730–80, gumwood, paneled doors open to three shelved int., underhung divided drawer over single drawer, applied moldings, turned pull, front turned ball feet, old refinish, restoration, repair, 60¾″ w case, 75½″ w projecting cornice, 18¼″ d, 77½″ h **3,450.00**

Linen Press, Neoclassical Style, mahogany, 19th C, molded cornice, two paneled doors, three graduated drawers, block feet . **1,575.00**

Pewter, country

Pine, molded cornice, open shelves, shaped sides, two paneled doors, cutout feet, mellow refinishing, 53¾″ w, 80″ h **3,750.00**

Poplar, stepback, open top with perimeter molding, four shelves, base with two raised paneled doors, cutout feet, 39″ w, 16″ d, 79″ h **385.00**

Stepback

Country, New England, early

Stepback Cupboard, Chippendale, late 19th C, painted and dec, pine and poplar, two sections, upper: molded cornice, two doors, shelved int., shaped bracket support sides; lower: three small drawers, two molded cupboard doors, shelved int., ogee bracket feet, painted green, ochre, and brown, multicolored floral panels on cupboard doors, repaired feet, 59″ w, 88″ h, $2,750.00. Photograph courtesy of Butterfield & Butterfield.

19th C, molded cornice, two paneled doors on top, molded waist, two small paneled doors in base, old refinish, old red paint traces, 57″ w, 17½″ d, 89″ h **1,955.00**
Federal, American, 19th C, cherry, projecting cornice, glass doors, three aligned paneled drawers over pr of cupboard doors, bracket feet, 63″ w, 19″ d, 84″ h **2,200.00**
Wall
  Biedermeier, c1840, fruitwood and ebonized, two bow front

mullion glazed doors, shelved int., tapering block feet, 36″ w, 22″ d, 75″ h **2,400.00**
Country, Ohio, walnut, two sections, upper: molded cornice and frieze, two glass paned doors, perimeter molding; lower: paneled doors, perimeter molding, 59¾″ w, 18″ d, 90″ h........................ **550.00**
Grain Painted, New England, 18th C, yellow pine, painted red, upper and lower doors, shelved int., wooden latches, molded cornice, midsection, and base, turned bulbous feet, butterfly hinges, 41¼″ w, 20″ d, 63½″ h **6,900.00**
Jacobean Style, mahogany, rect top, two cupboard doors, one drawer, turned legs, 41″ w, 17″ d, 62″ h **110.00**
Renaissance Revival, Italian, 19th C, ebonized, two sections, upper: arched molded pediment over ivory gallery, central arched cupboard door flanked by pr of doors, central rosetted and scrolled ivory mounts, ivory inlaid scrolling foliage; lower: three aligned drawers over pr of cupboard doors inlaid with serpent and figural masks amidst scrolling foliage, bracket feet, 43″ w, 20″ d, 78″ h **3,000.00**
Wardrobe, Biedermeier, first quarter 19th C, walnut, molded rect cornice, serpentine paneled doors, block feet, 49″ w, 20″ d, 76″ h **5,400.00**

DAYBEDS

Art Deco, Jules Leleu, 1925, walnut, two high scrolling ends, rect plinth, tapered everted feet ending with scrolls, upholstered cushion and rolled pillows **4,000.00**
Classical
  c1820, NY, rosewood, painted and molded crest rail with stenciled acanthus dec, dolphin carved gilded and verde

Daybed, Queen Anne, Rhode Island, c1740, walnut, adjustable backrest, vasiform splat, outward curving molded stiles, elongated shaped seat frame, cabriole legs, pad feet, block and ball turned stretchers, restorations to splat shoe and feet, 68″ l, $3,850.00. Photograph courtesy of Butterfield & Butterfield.

antico arms, torus molded seat rail, dark green worsted wool upholstery with brass tack dec, carved cornucopia gilded verde antico brackets, carved hairy paw feet with casters .. **6,875.00**

c1825, Philadelphia, mahogany, low incurvate crest rail, rounded flowing shell carved armrests, acanthus and beaded dec legs, ball feet with casters, 72″ l, 20″ d, 28″ h ... **2,875.00**

Eastlake, walnut, machine carved dec on frame, orig upholstered, turned legs, casters **250.00**

Restauration, c1840, mahogany, down scrolled serpentine crest rail, plain seat rail, champagne colored silk upholstery, scalloped bracket feet with casters, 79″ l, 27″ w, 27″ h **1,375.00**

Rococo Revival, attributed to John Henry Belter, laminated rosewood pierced and carved frame, lacy vines, grapes, and leaf design, looping and undulating arabesques, crest carved with roses, grapes, foliage, and cornucopia, rose carved apron and knees, tufted back, blue velvet upholstery, four new metal casters, 68″ l, 43″ h **10,000.00**

Victorian, late 19th C, upholstered, modern floral tapestry upholstery, four turned walnut feet, 70″ l **175.00**

William IV, c1840, mahogany, scrolled end, serpentine arm-

rest, loose cushion seat, bulbous turned legs, casters, 82½″ l, 27″ w, 31″ h **1,500.00**

DESKS

Aesthetic Movement, American, 1885, lady's, ebonized cherry, Oriental influenced fretwork panels and carving, three small aligned drawers over inset writing surface, three graduated drawers, 30″ w, 20¼″ d, 48″ h . **1,150.00**

Chippendale
Massachusetts, mahogany, slant lid, fitted int., pullout supports, four graduated drawers, short cabriole legs, claw and ball feet, replaced hardware, refinished, 39″ w, 20″ d, 44¾″ h **2,530.00**

Rhode Island, c1780, tiger maple, slant lid, fitted int., three graduated drawers, brass handles, ogee bracket feet, 35″ w, 18¼″ d, 41″ h **4,025.00**

Chippendale Style
Cherry, slant front, graduated drawers, cabriole legs, 29″ w, 15″ d, 40″ l **325.00**

Mahogany, block front, kneehole, 36″ w, 20″ d, 29″ h **650.00**

Country
Plantation, walnut, two sections, upper: crown molded cornice, two dovetailed drawers, two glass paned doors, fall front horizontal door with fitted int.;

Desk, Chippendale, slant front, walnut, rect top, hinged slant front writing surface, fitted int., secret drawers, pull-out slides, four graduated long drawers, fluted corner columns, ogee bracket feet, 39″ w, 22¼″ d, 42¼″ h, $3,575.00. Photograph courtesy of William Doyle Galleries.

lower: lift lid with thumb molded edge, turned legs, 38″ w, 85″ h **1,430.00**

Schoolmaster's, pine, chestnut secondary wood, slanted lift top, fitted int., one drawer, turned legs, missing handles on drawer, 33½″ w, 20½″ d, 36¾″ h **610.00**

Directorie Style, French, mahogany, rect top, central drawer flanked by three drawers, central kneehole, tapering sq legs, 49½″ w, 29″ d, 29½″ h **1,000.00**

Edwardian

Early 20th C, mahogany and satinwood inlaid, tambour, rect top, fitted int., two pedestals with four graduated drawers, brass pulls, 47½″ w, 26½″ d, 48″ h **1,725.00**

Late 19th C, painted dec, satinwood, rect leather top, long

drawer flanked by pr of drawers, sq tapering legs, 53″ w, 28″ d, 31″ h **2,645.00**

Federal

American

c1790, mahogany, slant lid, fitted int. with eight small drawers over valanced pigeonholes, center prospect with shell carving flanked by columns, four graduated long drawers, scalloped apron, bracket feet, old finish, sgd "Sam Kline," inscribed on rear of small int. drawer, restoration, 40½″ w, 19½″ d, 44″ h **1,595.00**

c1820, cherry, slant front, fitted int., four graduated thumb molded drawers, circular brass pull handles, ring turned bun feet, 39¾″ w, 19½″ d, 45¼″ h **2,100.00**

New England, c1825, mahogany, two glazed doors with four arched openings, shelved int., two small drawers over three aligned long drawers, glass knobs, brass escutcheons, turned feet, old refinish, replaced brasses, imperfections, 37½″ w, 18″ d, 64″ h **1,495.00**

Federal, Late, 19th C, lap, mahogany, rect hinged lid, brass corners, center brass crest, fitted int., leather writing surface, 13½″ w, 7½″ d, 5″ h **225.00**

George I Style, late 19th C, kneehole, yewwood, rect top, slide and long drawer, central recessed cupboard door, flanked by drawers, bracket feet, 40″ w, 16½″ d, 29¼″ h **990.00**

George III, English

Mid 18th C, mahogany, slant front, fitted int., four long graduated thumb molded drawers, brass bail handles and bust and floral dec escutcheons and lock plates, bracket feet, 38″ w, 20½″ d, 41¼″ h **1,925.00**

Third–quarter 18th C, slant front, walnut, fold down writing surface, cubby holes and drawers int., four graduated drawers, bracket feet, 36" w, 19½" d, 43½" h **980.00**

George III Style, 19th C, double pedestal, mahogany, rect top, inset brown tooled leather, two pedestals fitted with drawers, 55¾" w, 31¼" d, 31" h **3,335.00**

Georgian, c1800, mahogany, dovetailed case, slant front, fitted int., four graduated drawers, French feet, 37½" w, 19" d, 42" h **880.00**

Georgian Style, late 19th C, mahogany

Rect top, double pedestal, Greek Key carved frieze containing three aligned drawers over pedestals, three drawers flanked by beading, molded plinth bases, 72¼" w, 38¼" d, 30¾" h **700.00**

Shaped top, curved front center drawer, two short drawers, two cabinet doors with arched panels, beaded carved borders, conforming plinth bases, 66¼" w, 16¾" d, 35¾" h **1,550.00**

Louis XV Style, Bureau Rognon, kingwood, ormolu mounts, four shaped drawers in rect back, shaped sides extend to rect top, scalloped apron with shaped drawers, tapered legs, 43½" w, 27" d, 37¼" h **3,750.00**

Provincial, French, early 19th C, walnut, rect top, fitted galleried int., one long over two short drawers, center kneehole with scalloped sides, sq tapered legs, 37½" w, 19¾" d, 31½" h **1,050.00**

Queen Anne, walnut, slant front

American, banded slant front, fitted int., faux frieze drawer, four drawers, bracket feet, 37" w, 22" d, 40" h **2,650.00**

New England, c1750, valanced fitted int., two drawers over two graduated drawers, center apron pediment, bracket feet, old refinish, imperfections, 34½" w, 19½" d, 39" h **5,500.00**

Renaissance Style, late 19th C, partner's, oak, paneled cup-

board doors on pedestals, 59" w, 35" d, 30" h **865.00**

Rococo, Dutch, third–quarter 18th C, walnut and marquetry, slant lid, shaped extended sides, three graduated long drawers, acanthus carved feet, paper label on back reads "J. A. Butt & Son, Fine Art Collectors and Dealers in Articles of Virtue, 7 Queen Street, Edinburgh," shrinkage, 44¼" w, 21" d, 40¼" h **9,200.00**

Rococo Style

Dutch, late 19th C, mahogany and marquetry, slant lid, shaped extended sides, three graduated long drawers, scalloped shaped apron, claw and ball feet, 50" w, 22" d, 42½" h **4,900.00**

Italian, walnut, shaped top, five drawers, cabriole legs, 54" w, 26" d, 31" h **1,300.00**

Sheraton, 19th C, rect top, one long drawer, two aligned drawers, legs, ball feet, 42½" w, 21" d, 30½" h **375.00**

Sheraton Style, lady's, mahogany, rect top, brown leather writing surface, satinwood string inlay dec, two drawers, sq tapered legs, 42¼" w, 22" d, 28¼" h ... **525.00**

Victorian, English, late 19th C, oak, pedestal, 48" w, 22¼" h, 28" h **575.00**

DOUGH TROUGHS

Decorated, pine, one board top, scrolled apron, splat base, turned legs, 25½" l, 44¾" w, 28¼" h **500.00**

Maple, dovetailed, board and batten top, scalloped apron, rect legs, 35" l, 22" w, 30" h **275.00**

Pine

American, 19th C, rect top, tapering rect case, sq splayed legs, 50" l, 25" w, 29" h **300.00**

English, old dark finish, minor insect damage, 38" l, 17½" w, 30" h **150.00**

Poplar, orig lid, orig red paint, 34" l **115.00**

Walnut, Louis XV, Provincial, mid
18th C, oblong molded top with
serpentine front, canted dough
box, conforming valanced skirt
carved with flowering urn, turned
supports and box stretcher,
40½" l, 22" w, 37" h **2,125.00**

DRY SINKS

Butternut, two doors, one int. shelf,
orig stippling and finish, 35" l, 20"
w, 42" h **500.00**
Curly Maple, rect well, work surface to right with short drawer,
two poplar wood cupboard
doors, short bracket feet, hardwood edge stripes, minor re-
pairs, refinished, 55" w, 34½" h **2,200.00**
Grain Painted, American, mid 19th
C, simulated oak graining, cupboard top with two paneled
doors, hood opening over dry
sink, base with four graduated
drawers and two cupboard
doors, cast iron hardware, 54" w,
21¼" d, 78" h **1,400.00**
Pine, country, top with well on one
side and low crest rail back, one
small drawer, paneled doors, 49"
l, 17¾" d, 30½" h **990.00**
Pine and Poplar, old mustard yellow graining, turned feet,
paneled doors with orig cast iron
latches, one dovetailed drawer,
well with lift lid, backboard crest
with vertical seam, 49" w, 21½"
d, 33" h **1,150.00**
Poplar
Crest, off–center door with swing
out attached shelf, orig cast
iron thumb latch, simple cutout
feet, stripped finish, 33 x 18½
x 26" **350.00**
Paneled doors, one small
drawer, porcelain pull, simple
cutout feet, worn layers of old
green paint, plugged hole in
side, 42" w, 19¾" d, 34" h ... **550.00**
Walnut and Poplar, pr of paneled
doors, one drawer, old finish,
dark green paint on int. of hutch
top, orig cast iron latches with
brass knobs, bottom end dam-

age on feet, 52" w, 18½" d, 49"
h **800.00**

HAT RACKS AND HALL TREES

Aesthetic Movement, American,
fourth quarter 19th C, ebonized,
wall mounted, center mirror,
painted panels, 30" h **290.00**
Art Deco, French, c1925, wrought
iron, rect, top set with shallow
open hat shelf above octagonal
mirror, shallow verde antico shelf
on angled support wrought with
straight bands and coils, two rect
sections set with three coat
hooks, outset rect umbrella
stands, scrolls and imp geomet-
ric devices, 51¾" w, 75" h ...**12,100.00**
Arts and Crafts, Gustav Stickley,
c1904, Model No. 53, four iron
hooks on two tapering posts, two
hooks on rect exposed tenon
cross brace, 22" w, 65½" h **1,700.00**
Civil War, American, c1870, cast
iron, painted and gilded, cast in
half–round, uprights form s bayonets, crisscrossed by pr of ea-

**Hall Tree, Renaissance Revival,
walnut, beveled mirror, brown
marble insert, 80" h, $2,225.00.**

gle headed sabres, two other sabres flanking hung with rope twists and tassels, olive branches crossbar hung with rope twists and tassels, small United States shield, shield shaped mirror plate, base with U S mail pouches, acorns, tassels, and ribbons, rope twist hooks, 26" w, 73" h **5,000.00**

Victorian, American, late 19th C
Cast Iron, faux bamboo, central mirror, 72" h **500.00**
Wood, reticulated bamboo back, center rect mirror plate, bamboo legs, 27" w, 12" d, 72" h . **180.00**

Windsor, pine, bamboo turned, six knoblike hooks, orig yellow varnish, black striping, 33¾" l **150.00**

MAGAZINE RACKS

Arts and Crafts
American, early 20th C, four squared posts joined by inverted V shaped side rail, over two vertical slats, five shelves, 54⅝" h **325.00**
Limbert, Michigan, c1910, four open shelves centered by flat sides with cutout circles at base, branded, refinished, 20" w, 14" d, 36½" h **600.00**
Michigan Chair Co, c1912, panel sided, rect top, five shelves each with six V–grooved boards, projecting pins, dark finish, 19¾" w, 11¾" d, 45½" h **700.00**

George III Style, late 19th C, mahogany, rect shelf above drawer, lower shelf raised on turned legs, casters, 18" w, 14½" d, 41" h **950.00**

Georgian Style, mahogany, four slot lattice top, single drawer, turned legs, casters **300.00**

Regency, mahogany, five open manganese splats, ring turned corner supports, case fitted with drawer, ring turned tapering legs, brass caps and casters, 19¼" w, 14" d, 20" h **1,650.00**

Victorian, walnut, three shelves,

turned supports, 21" w, 14" d, 31" h **150.00**

William IV, early 19th C, rosewood, twin bows form end crest rails, scrolling supports, joined by turned divider rails, two compartments, rect dais, C scroll legs, paw feet, 19½" w, 17½" d, 19" h **1,600.00**

Mirror, Chippendale, late, American, bull's eye, carved giltwood parcel ebonized, circular convex mirror plate, molded surround, foliate and shell crest, foliate pendant, 28" w, 48" h, $1,760.00. Photograph courtesy of C. G. Sloan & Co., Inc.

MIRRORS

Adams, late 18th/early 19th C, gilt gesso, crest with oval painted medallion of classical figures and floral basket cartouche, painted urn and figural reserve border, rosette corner blocks, 23" w, 57½" h **4,625.00**

Baroque Style
Continental, 19th C
Ebonized and gilt metal mounted, arched rect, foliate pierced and pressed gilt metal borders, damage, 37½" d, 57" h **1,495.00**

Giltwood, oval, surmounted by putti, two hoof feet, repairs, 15¼" h, price for pr **575.00**
Flemish, late 19th C, ebonized and faux painted, rect form, flaking, 28½" w, 34½" h **275.00**
Chippendale
American, hardwood, scroll work and bird's–heads design, orig black paint, gilt dec, label on back with "1911" and family history **685.00**
Rhode Island, late 18th C, mahogany and gilt gesso, imperfections, 14" w, 8" d, 23" h . .**3,450.00**
Chippendale Style, mahogany, scrolled crest, pendant centering beveled mirror plate, 18½" w, 35" h **50.00**
Classical Revival, gesso on wood, urn shape finial, vining dec, discolored glass, some damage and repairs, 14¼" w, 26½" h . . **225.00**
Empire [Classical], American
Giltwood carved, rect, turned borders with acanthus leaf dec, 47" w, 24" h **300.00**
Mahogany, c1850
Gilded slip, angled frame, 23½" w, 16¾" h **120.00**
Mahogany surround, reverse painted landscape above rect mirror plate **50.00**
Federal, American, second quarter 19th C
Giltwood, cornice with spherical dec, reverse painted tablet flanked by reeded columns, rect mirror plate, labeled "Edward Lothrop, 53 Marlborough Street, Boston," imperfections, 13½" w, 30" h **980.00**
Grain painted, reverse painted glass panel over rect mirror plate flanked by fluted pilasters, 13½" w, 22" h **150.00**
Wood and gilded gesso, attributed to Salem, MA, c1825, cornice with spherical dec, inset plaque with carved basket of flowers flanked by turned and combed columns, rect mirror plate, 18½" w, 36" h . .**1,265.00**
Federal Style, giltwood, round

molded frame, convex mirror plate, surmounted by spread winged eagle, 31" h **70.00**
French Style, gilt and gesso, shell and rocaille dec frame, ornate, rect beveled plate, 32½" w, 38" h **385.00**
George II Style, burled walnut and giltwood, shaped rect, arched broken pediment, ho ho bird cresting, acanthus leaves carved sides, rect mirror plate .**1,000.00**
George III Style, late 19th C, pier, giltwood, minor losses, some flaking, 56" w, 83" h **7,475.00**
Japanned, Continental, 19th C, rect form, ebonized carved foliage and floral cresting over scrolling floral and foliate japanned border, later mirror plate, restorations, 27¼" w, 37¾" h . .**1,100.00**
Louis XV Style, carved giltwood, 26" w, 43" h **200.00**
Louis XVI, mid 19th C, giltwood, floral crest, rocaille scroll and floral branches, 35" w, 76" h . . .**1,430.00**
Queen Anne, English, 18th C, walnut and gilt gesso, carved center medallion, old refinish, imperfections, 23¾" w, 48½" h **4,100.00**
Renaissance Revival, third quarter 19th C, hall, walnut, parcel gilt, rect mirror plate, 31½" w, 72" h **345.00**
Rococo, 19th C, giltwood, rocaille and floral dec crest, tongue and dart molded frame, gilt edge and beaded border **2,750.00**
Victorian
Giltwood and gesso, ornate, scrolled and leaf dec, elaborate carved crest **1,325.00**
Giltwood, carved and ebonized, shaped rect form, pierced floral cresting, sides set with carved paterae, yellow glass plates flanking central mirror plate, 27" w, 41½" h **425.00**
Mahogany and ebonized, molded frame, rect mirror plate, 23" w, 30" h **50.00**

ROCKERS

Arrow Back, orig ink graining,

scrolled arms, widely splayed back **200.00**

Art Deco, Louis Sognot, c1930, chromed metal, upholstered seat and back, 36" h **1,200.00**

Art Furniture, American, c1850, wrought iron and brass, scrolled stiles form downward curving arm supports, joined by transverse at rear, mounted upholstered leather cushion and arm pads **4,675.00**

Arts and Crafts, American

Morris, Model No. 413, oak, four horizontal back slats, orig cushions in poor condition, branded "L & J G Stickley," 29" w, 34½" d, 36" h **935.00**

Stickley, Gustav, Model No. 303, c1904, sewing, oak, four horizontal back slats, canvas seat, wide seat rail, orig paper label, 14" w, 16" d, 33" h **375.00**

Country, decorated, painted

Plank Seat, attributed to NY state, c1825, crest rail painted with red flowers, arrow form uprights, shaped arms and turned legs, light green ground **2,100.00**

Writing Arm, worn orig red and black paint, white striping, black stenciled detail, damaged woven splint seat, wear and minor age cracks in writing arm **200.00**

Grained and Stencil Dec, New England, c1830, rosewood grained, olive green stenciled crest, thumb back, yellow striping, 15¼" h seat, 32¼" h **350.00**

Ladder Back, arm, country, turned arms and posts, rabbit's–ear back posts, four slats, paper rush seat, refinished **85.00**

Shaker Style, American, maple, four serpentine slats, rush seat, turned supports **100.00**

Sheraton, country, maple, rush seat, refinished **80.00**

Victorian, American, platform, mahogany, upholstered seat and back, carved and turned arms . **135.00**

Windsor, New Ipswich, New Hampshire, early 19th C, comb back, old Spanish brown paint, natural arms, sgd "J Wilder," restoration, 13½" h, 44" h back ... **750.00**

SECRETARIES

Art Nouveau, mahogany, projecting molded cornice, pr of leaded glass doors over lower cabinet, slant front writing surface, small drawers and pigeonholes int., three drawers, turned legs, bun feet, 36¼" w, 17½" d, 83½" h .. **1,100.00**

Biedermeier, second half 19th C, birch and part ebonized, rect top, short drawer over fall front writing surface, three graduated long drawers, 43" w, 18" d, 52" h **3,750.00**

Secretary, Federal (Hepplewhite), MA, c1790–1810, inlaid mahogany, two sections, upper: hinged molded rect top opening to well, two cupboard doors with line and column inlaid panels, fitted int.; lower: hinged and baize-lined folding writing surface, four graduated long drawers, repaired French feet, 40¼" w, 48" h, $4,400.00. Photograph courtesy of Butterfield & Butterfield.

Empire [Classical], Massachusetts, c1830, mahogany veneer, molded cornice, two glass doors, two small drawers below, foldout writing surface, two long drawers in base, shaped front feet, turned back feet, refinished, 39" w, 18¾" d, 72" h **810.00**

Federal, New England, 1830s, mahogany veneer, molded cornice with scroll shape pediment, two short glazed doors with rounded arches, two small drawers below with pull handles, base with foldout lined writing surface, three drawers, twist turned columns, turned legs, old refinish, 37½" w, 18½" d, 68" h **1,500.00**

George I, early 18th C, walnut, two parts, upper: projecting cornice above pr of mirrored doors, shelved int.; lower: fall front writing surface, small drawers int., two aligned drawers over three graduated drawers, bracket feet, 38½" w, 21" d, 86" h **5,800.00**

George III, mid–18th C, mahogany, flat cove molded and dentil molded cornice, two glazed lattice doors, slant front, fitted int., four graduated cockbeaded drawers, brass bail handles, escutcheons, and lock plates, bracket feet, 42½" w, 24" d, 85¼" h **5,830.00**

George III, Late, early 19th C, satinwood and mahogany, arched pediment with center rect plinth, ogee molding over two glazed cupboard doors, fall front writing surface, pr of cupboard doors, scalloped apron, splayed feet, 36½" w, 19½" d, 81" h **6,100.00**

Georgian Style, mahogany, top with cavetto molding, two glazed doors, shelf int., slant front with fitted tiger maple and mahogany int., three drawers, inlaid dec, bracket feet, 29½" w, 15½" d, 78½" h **880.00**

Louis XV Style
   Fruitwood parquetry, shaped marble top, ogee cornice, seven drawers with foliage or-

molu mounts, shaped base, bracket feet, 27" w, 17½" d, 49" h **2,500.00**

Mahogany, shaped marble top, single frieze drawer, fall front writing surface, fitted int., three drawers with foliate ormolu mounts, splayed feet with sabots, 37" w, 17½" d, 59" h ... **2,500.00**

Louis XV/Louis XVI Transitional Style, 19th C, fruitwood parquetry, rect marble top, tambour slide, fitted int., central drawer opens to writing surface, two doors with flowering urn motifs, curved feet with sabots, 39½" w, 16½" d, 56" h **5,000.00**

Second Empire, ebony, burled walnut, and fruitwood marquetry, rect marble top, frieze drawer above fall front writing surface over three drawers, bun feet, gilt bronze mounts, 28" w, 16" d, 54" h **1,400.00**

Victorian, American
   Cherry, arched pediment, scrolled carving over glass doors, six drawers, slant front desk over two aligned drawers over two long drawers, bracket feet, 40½" w, 22" d, 88" h ... **1,100.00**

   Mahogany
      c1840, two sections, upper: ogee cornice surmounting carved frieze, arched glass doors with applied foliate carved dec; lower: slant front with fitted int., one serpentine and two large drawers with applied foliate carved dec, shaped skirt with applied foliate dec, bracket feet, 44½" w, 20" d, 94½" h **3,525.00**

      19th C, cavetto molded platform top, leaf carved edge, ogee molded drop front, fitted rosewood veneered int. with marquetry floral scrollwork inlay, three graduated drawers, rocaille carved skirt, short cabriole legs, upturned feet, 39" w, 22" d, 65½" h **2,425.00**

   Maple and cherry, rect top, projecting cornice, sq case, glazed doors, slant front desk with carving, three long drawers, turned knobs, bracket feet, 39" w, 22" d, 84" h **500.00**

Settee, Revivale, second quarter 19th C, walnut, molded crest, upholstered back, arms, and seat, straight legs, 40" l, $2,250.00. Photograph courtesy of Leslie Hindman Auctioneers.

SETTEES

Biedermeier Style, early 20th C, birch, rect form, arched back ending in scrolls, 61" l **690.00**

Chippendale Style, mahogany, camel back **450.00**

Classical, mid–Atlantic states, tiger maple and bird's–eye maple, caned shaped back and seat, scrolled arms, scalloped apron, refinished, 55¾" l, 14½" h seat, 34½" h back **3,450.00**

Empire Revival, late 19th C, arched high back with down scrolled ears, down curved armrests, straight seat rail, cabriole legs, claw and ball feet, 51½" l, 21" d, 44" h **725.00**

Empire Style, American, mahogany, scroll arms, bracket feet, floral upholstery, 83" l, 27½" d, 34" h **1,000.00**

Federal Style, mahogany, camel-back, 81" h **650.00**

George III, late 18th C, mahogany, sq back over conforming arms, sq tapering legs, casters, 65" l, 28" d, 35" h **345.00**

George III Style, late 19th C, walnut, carved crest, pierced fretwork on back and sides, caned seat, Marlborough legs, stretcher base, 40" l, 34" h, price for pair **2,550.00**

Georgian Style, rect upholstered back, seat, and arms, walnut parcel gilt cabriole legs, 71" l .. **200.00**

Louis XVI Style

Giltwood, tapestry upholstered oval back, reeded and leaf carved crest rail, beaded carved armrests, upholstered seat, skirt with carved roundel, fluted and turned legs, 44" l, 26" d, 41" h **1,100.00**

Walnut, late 19th C, bow tied laurel crest rail, ribbon and bead carved frame, out curved armrests with acanthus dec, bow front seat rail, toupie feet, 49¾" l, 23" d, 37¾" h **880.00**

Neoclassical

Baltic, second half 19th C, fruitwood, gilt metal mounted, part ebonized, 71" l, 28¼" d, 43" h **3,450.00**

Continental, 19th C, two rect upholstered backrests divided by wheat sheath and rosette carved vasiform splat, padded armrests, upholstered cushion seat, round tapered fluted legs, 57½" w, 27" d, 41¼" h . **775.00**

Italian Provincial, c1800, suite of settee and two side chairs, red painted, 29¾" h **1,725.00**

Neoclassical Style, late 19th C, walnut, aqua velvet upholstery, 54½" w, 22½" d, 36¾" h **750.00**

Renaissance Revival, third quarter 19th C, ormolu mounted rosewood and marquetry, incised gilt dec, applied painted medallions, fuchsia upholstery, center loveseat sized section flanked by two rounded chairlike sections, scalloped skirt with tassels, 95" l, 40" d, 40" h **3,450.00**

Rococo, Italian, third quarter 18th

C, cream painted frame, arched crest, outscrolled arms, serpentine seat, cabriole legs, upholstery removed, damage, 92" l, 42½" h **3,800.00**

SIDEBOARDS

Federal
Attributed to Massachusetts, c1790, mahogany inlaid, shaped top, center long drawer over pair of cupboard doors, flanked by shaped drawer over single cupboard door, sq tapered legs, old refinish, minor imperfections, 59½" w, 25½" d, 43" h **8,625.00**
Attributed to middle Atlantic states, c1815, mahogany inlaid, shaped top, conforming case with long center drawer over recessed pair of cupboard doors, flanked by small drawer over door, pedestal with drawer over cupboard door with arched inlay, turned reeded legs, ball feet, old refinish, minor imperfections, 78½" w, 25¾" d, 45" h **4,025.00**
New York, c1800, mahogany,

Sideboard, Sheraton, American, first quarter 19th C, mahogany, bowed crossbanded top, center drawer and tambour door flanked by satinwood line and fan inlaid cupboards, sq tapering legs, spade feet, 63" w, 24" d, 35" h, $4,620.00. Photograph courtesy of Leslie Hindman Auctioneers.

drop center, raised cavetto molded plinth sides with cockbeaded drawer and cupboard doors, bow front with long drawer and two cupboard doors, two compartmented bottle drawers, turned and reeded legs, brass capped feet, 78" w, 27" d, 51½" h ... **5,775.00**
French Gothic Style, 19th C, oak, molded cornice, two heavily carved doors, wrought iron mounts, two carved and paneled doors, paneled sides, 37½" w, 21¼" d, 73" h **1,400.00**
George III, mahogany, bowed top, frieze drawer, flanked by two deep drawers, sq tapering legs **650.00**
George III Style, late 19th C, mahogany, inlaid
Banded top, ribbon carved center panel, four rosettes dec between fluted drawers, two cupboard doors, tapered sq legs, spade feet, 78" w, 37½" h ... **1,320.00**
Bowed top, inlaid satinwood, conforming fluted case, sq tapering legs, 61" w, 36½" h .. **1,610.00**
Crested back, conforming top, slightly bowed drawers flanking long center drawer, floral inlay with minor loss, tapering legs with conforming inlay, spade feet, 72½" w, 29" d, 43" h **3,800.00**
Georgian Style, late 19th C
Burled walnut, rect top, three aligned drawers over cupboard doors, sq tapering legs, 48¼" w, 16" d, 39¾" h **750.00**
Mahogany, inlaid serpentine top, brass gallery, center long drawer flanked by pedestals with two aligned drawers, tapered legs, losses, 60" w, 25" d, 40½" h **2,875.00**
Georgian Style, Late, mahogany, bowed case, single drawer over serpentine top, center drawer flanked by two banks of three drawers, satinwood stringing, sq tapering legs, spade feet, 78" w, 28" d, 41" h **1,680.00**
Gothic Revival, American, c1840,

mahogany, carved scrolled gallery top, two torus molded drawers, two cupboard doors, twist reeded columns, paw feet, 51½" w, 23" d, 52½" h 825.00

Hepplewhite, c1780, mahogany, serpentine front, three drawers, two cupboard doors, one decanter drawer, sq tapered legs, banded feet, 61" w, 25¾" d, 39½" h 4,400.00

Hepplewhite Style, Landstrom, mahogany, bow front, two graduated drawers flanked by cupboard doors, sq tapering legs, spade feet, 72" w, 23" d, 37¼" h 1,200.00

Modernism, Frank Lloyd Wright, manufactured by Henredon, mahogany, one cabinet, eight drawers, Greek Key trim, 66" w, 20" d, 35" h 1,000.00

Provincial, French
19th C, oak, two sections, upper: arched molded crest centering relief carved floral base, galleried plate rack, pair of cupboards; lower: rect top over three aligned drawers, center niche with central drawers, flanked by foliate carved cupboard doors, cabriole legs, 74" w, 20" d, 72" h 2,000.00

Late 18th/early 19th C, cherry, rect top, two aligned drawers, paneled cupboard doors, serpentine apron, scrolled feet, 63" w, 21" d, 42" h 2,400.00

Renaissance Revival, American, c1870, mahogany
Shaped rect top, three aligned drawers, two cabinet doors, heavily carved acanthus leaves and shell form dec, 46" w, 27" d, 99" h 1,500.00

Winged lion, mask head, and putti cartouche pediment, two open shelves with carved putti reserves, ram and winged lion supports, five drawers, two paneled doors, mask head feet, 74" w, 27" d, 89" h 10,175.00

Renaissance Style, Italian, late 19th C, walnut, shaped back, center long drawer, applied con-

vex moldings, pedestals with obelisks, columns with scrolling capitals, compressed reeded bun feet, 30¼" w, 17½" d, 41" h 635.00

Sheraton, country, curly maple, poplar secondary wood, scalloped edge gallery top, five dovetailed drawers with applied beading, two paneled doors, turned and reeded pilasters, turned feet, replaced wood pull handles, 48" w, 20¾" d, 43" h . 4,625.00

SOFAS

Art Nouveau, Carlo Bugatti, c1900, ebonized wood, rect back and mechanical seat, slightly scrolling rect arms, parchment upholstery, painted swallows and leafy branches, hammered brass trim, four block form feet, 66⅜" l 1,750.00

Biedermeier, fruitwood and ebonized wood, upholstered central flat top back, rounded corners, cornucopia form scrolled ends with foliated capitals supporting broad flattened domed armrests, cylindrical bolsters, broad seat rail above reeded flattened triangular frieze, broad sq front supports, bottle green mohair upholstery, 72" l 3,850.00

Chippendale, attributed to New England, c1780, mahogany, upholstered back, arms, and loose cushion seat, some repairs, 74" l, 24" d, 37" h 2,415.00

Duncan Phyfe Style, mahogany, carved, yellow geometric upholstery, 82½" l 300.00

Empire [Classical]
American, early 19th C, mahogany, fluted and scrolled pediment form crest rail, out curved armrests, fluted and scrolled lyre shape seat rail, olive colored velvet upholstery, carved saber feet, 80" l, 24¾" d, 32½" h 675.00

Philadelphia, c1830, mahogany, scrolled pediment form crest rail with brass string inlay, cy-

Sofa, French Restauration, Ch. Munier, early 19th C, painted and parcel gilt, paneled and molded crestrail carved with rosettes within bellflowers and palm leaves, padded back, rolled arms, loose cushion seat, slightly boat form frame, S–scroll arm supports carved with lotus and honeysuckle, slightly bowed seat rail, scrolling bracket feet, 77″ l, $2,420.00. Photograph courtesy of William Doyle Galleries.

lindrical armrests with carved anthemion dec and upholstery, molded gadrooned seat rail, highly carved scrolled and leaf dec paw feet with casters, striped polychromed silk upholstery, 79″ l, 30″ d, 33″ h . . **1,430.00**

Federal, mahogany
New England, early 19th C, slightly curved back, baluster turned arm supports, ivory upholstered back and seat, baluster turned legs, old refinish, 75½″ l, 36″ h **2,775.00**

North Shore, MA, c1815, upholstered back, arms, and seat, reeded scrolled arms, supports, and turned legs, casters, 74½″ l, 16″ h seat, 34½″ h back **1,725.00**

George III, c1800, carved mahogany, channel molded frame, arched back, high down swept arms, curved seat rail, four front ring turned tapering supports, outer supports headed by oval carved paterae below stiff leaf carved arm supports, brass caps and casters, striped yellow satin upholstery **3,200.00**

George III Style, Neoclassical taste, carved beech, slightly arched back continuing to rounded down swept sides with center pad arms, bowed seat, four fluted turned tapering front supports, four molded outset rear supports, flowered gold damask upholstery, pr, one 19th C, other later **13,200.00**

Georgian Style, mahogany, camelback, ivory damask upholstery, Marlborough legs, 84″ l **425.00**

Louis XV Style, late 19th C, giltwood, rocaille and foliate carved frame, needlepoint upholstery, horsehair stuffed, cabriole legs, foliate carved feet **825.00**

Napoleon III, Aubusson tapestry, giltwood, serpentine crest rail, padded arms, volute supports, cabriole legs, 72″ l **2,750.00**

Renaissance Revival, American, c1830, mahogany, veneered crest rail with scrolling ears, S–shape leaf carved armrests, carved leaf and fruit brackets below seat rail, paw feet with casters, 78″ l, 22″ d, 36″ h **1,775.00**

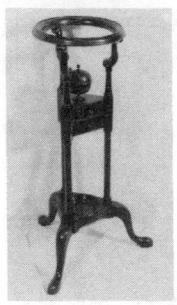

Shaving Stand, Queen Anne Style, mahogany, soap bowl, two drawers, tripod feet, $375.00.

STANDS

Boot Rack, English, late 19th C, mahogany, rect top rail, brass handle, sq supports, bracket feet, 22" w, 12" d, 26" h **350.00**

Dumbwaiter, George III Style, mahogany, graduated tiers, baluster stem, cabriole legs, 41" h .. **250.00**

Etagere
Rococo, mid 19th C, rosewood, pierced carved crest with C–scroll and S–scroll leaf dec and center cabochon, arched mirror back, reeded and carved stiles, carved serpentine base with marble top, cabriole legs, curled feet, 50" w, 20" d, 97" h **8,800.00**

Victorian, mid 19th C, mahogany, top with pierced carved gallery and two shelves, scroll carved supports, base with single drawer and two shelves, vasiform reeded posts, flattened ball feet, 37" w, 15½" d, 67" h **990.00**

Kettle, Georgian Style, 19th C, mahogany, sq recessed top, shaped apron, inlaid dec, sq flaring legs, X–form stretcher, Marlborough feet, 13" w, 13" d, 29¾" h **500.00**

Newspaper, Victorian, carved walnut, relief carved urn and flower dec, tripod base, carved lion's–paw feet, 24" h **400.00**

Night
Federal
American, c1800, bird's–eye maple, rect top, single drawer frieze, round brass pull handles, ring turned tapered legs, 20½" w, 14¾" d, 28" h **1,375.00**

New England, c1810, tiger maple, rect top, drawer, sq tapered legs, old refinish, imperfections, 18½" w, 15" d, 23¾" h **1,265.00**

Georgian Style, 19th C, mahogany, rect top, single drawer, brass bail handles and escutcheons, chamfered legs, shaped stretcher shelf, 15½" w, 13¾" d, 26¾" h **475.00**

Sheraton, early 19th C, mahogany, stepped rect top, open shelf, sq tapered legs, spade feet, 15" w, 12" d, 36" h **500.00**

Plant
Chinese Export, carved hardwood, marble top, inset top, deeply carved frieze, cabriole legs, 19" d, 17¾" h **200.00**

Empire Style, mahogany, octagonal top, carved standard, four splayed saber legs, 48½" h, price for pair **350.00**

Reading
George III Style, late 19th C, mahogany, adjustable **1,900.00**

Regency Style, faux bamboo, manufactured by Baker **285.00**

Sewing
Continental, mahogany, leather, and tole **110.00**

English, 19th C, satinwood, hinged octagonal top, sq tapering legs, 12" w, 10" d, 28" h **325.00**

Shaving, Victorian, late 19th C, circular mirror, round surface with drawers, carved support, three leaf carved feet, 56" h **345.00**

Shoeshine, Victorian, mahogany, sq hinged top, int. compartment, pierced carved legs, 14½" w, 14" h **40.00**

Tea, Chippendale, coastal North Eastern U S, c1820, tiger maple, sq tilt top, inlaid bone star and other devices, turned vasiform standard, downswept tripod base, 18″ w, 27¼″ h 1,150.00

Umbrella, Victoria, shaped and carved crest, molded marble top, single drawer flanked by two circular openings, turned feet, 34″ w, 13″ d, 35″ h 90.00

Urn, George III, late 18th C, mahogany, restoration, 11½″ d, 25″ h 435.00

Wash

Country

Cherry, replaced three board top, one dovetailed drawer, mahogany veneer, turned legs, 18″ w, 19¾″ h 275.00

Pine, galleried top, hinged fall front door, simple cabriole legs, old brown repaint, 33″ w, 19½″ d, 38″ h 225.00

Gothic Revival, American, late 19th C, walnut, marble top, incised carved blocked panels, splashboard, drop pulls, 31″ w, 17″ d, 37″ h 500.00

Jacobean Style, oak, rect marble backsplash over rect top, two cupboard doors, barley twist legs joined by stretcher 200.00

Sheraton, early 19th C

Mahogany, rect top with splashboard, baluster shape turned rear supports and scrolled front supports, bottom shelf with fitted drawer, four turned legs, 22″ w, 15¾″ d, 36″ h 400.00

Pine, top with gallery and bowl cutout, one dovetailed drawer, turned supports and legs, old mellow refinishing, old replaced gallery, 17¾″ w, 16¾″ d, 30″ h 225.00

Whatnot, single drawer, painted black, gilt classical designs and pinstriping, turned legs, minor imperfections, 19″ w, 17¾″ d, 54″ h 865.00

Work

Federal, c1830, bird's–eye ma-

ple, rect top with mahogany inlay, two drawers, circular brass pull handles, ring turned tapered legs, brass casters, 22¼″ w, 15¼″ d, 28″ h 1,375.00

Sheraton Style, mid 19th C, bird's–eye maple, rect top, single drawer frieze, brass lion's–head mask ring pull handles, shaped terminal supports joined by stretcher, flaring legs, brass paw casters, 20½″ w, 18½″ d, 29″ h 1,375.00

STEPS

Bed, Federal, 19th C, inlaid mahogany, 26″ h 400.00

Library

Georgian Style, mahogany, turned standard, lamp, four spiral steps 200.00

Victorian, late 19th C, mahogany, tooled inset leather

Baluster feet, 17″ w, 27½″ d, 26″ h 1,000.00

Bracket feet, 66¾″ h 2,760.00

STOOLS

Foot

Decorated, rect top with gold stenciled hunt scene, orig black paint, gold and yellow striping dec, turned legs 325.00

Empire, American, mahogany, ogee molded frame, round legs, 17″ w, 23″ d, 10″ h 50.00

Queen Anne, American, rosewood, mid–19th C, needlepoint seat, cabriole legs, 17″ w, 17″ d, 14″ h 425.00

Rococo Style, mahogany, cabriole legs, white cotton upholstery, 21″ l 50.00

Victorian, late 19th C

Gilt brass, needlepoint upholstery, lion's–head legs, paw feet 110.00

Mahogany, floral needlepoint upholstery, 17½″ h 100.00

Piano

Venetian Style, carved and painted wood, scallop shell

swivel seat, serpentine apron, tripod base, paw feet **40.00**

Victorian, mahogany, round upholstered swivel seat, turned baluster standard, round base, scrolled feet, 20" h **100.00**

TABLES

Breakfast

Chippendale, New England, late 18th C, mahogany, top with two drop leaves, single drawer in apron, sq legs, X–form stretcher, old refinish, repair to top, 29" w, 19¾" d, 28" h **550.00**

Classical, Philadelphia, early 19th C, hinged top, skirt with drawer, carved pedestal base, carved paw feet, 46¾" w, 28" h **1,650.00**

Federal, New England, c1800, mahogany inlaid, single

Card Table, Centennial, American, in the Salem manner, late 19th C, mahogany and satinwood, oblong top, serpentine sides and front, outset ovolu corners, conforming frieze, satinwood panels defined by rosewood crossbanding, turned tapered fluted legs, 34½" w, 18" d, 29½" h, price for matched pr, $2,640.00. Photograph courtesy of William Doyle Galleries.

drawer, "D" shaped leaves, sq tapered legs, old refinish, minor imperfections, 21½" w, 35" d, 29" h **1,840.00**

Georgian Style, mahogany, shaped rect top, painted black banding, baluster turned support, reeded down curving legs, castors, 53¾" w, 35" d, 30" h **900.00**

Bridge, Modernism, Postwar, Baker, oak, shaped top, cabriole legs, hoofed feet, 32" w, 32" d, 29" h **225.00**

Card

Chippendale Style, mahogany, rect top, rounded corners, shaped apron, acanthus carved cabriole legs, claw and ball feet, 37" w, 17¼" d, 29" h **550.00**

Empire [Classical], New York, 1830, veneer, fold over top, canted corners, carved pedestal, animal type legs, paw feet, casters, old refinish, 35¾" w, 18½" d, 29¾" h **925.00**

Federal

Massachusetts

c1790, attributed to Jacob Forster, mahogany, rounded fold over top, straight apron with inlaid dec, sq tapered legs, 36" w, 18" d, 29" h **2,300.00**

c1800, mahogany veneer, shaped hinged top, reeded tapering legs, old refinish, imperfections, 36" w, 16¾" d, 29¾" h **1,610.00**

New Hampshire, c1800, mahogany, rect hinged top, geometric banding inlay and stringing, sq tapered legs, refinished, 35½" w, 18" d, 28¾" h **1,725.00**

Federal, Late, early 19th C, mahogany inlaid, refinished, minor imperfections, one labeled "Jacob Forster, Charlestown, MA," 35¼" w, 17½" d, 29⅛" h, price for pair **16,100.00**

George III, 19th C, mahogany, rect hinged top, frieze drawer, sq legs, 28½" w, 16" d, 30" h **450.00**

Victorian, NY, c1850, rosewood, circular hinged top, carved molded edge, inset felt playing surface, carved central cabochon skirt, turned and fluted standard, plinth base, two carved S–scroll legs, 36″ w, 30″ h **1,875.00**

Center

Aesthetic Movement, American, last quarter 19th C

Giltwood

Alabaster columns and plaques, galleried shelf, 29¼″ w, 18½″ d, 31½″ h . **1,500.00**

Inset onyx rect top, painted and gilded Renaissance style frieze, loss, 55″ w, 35″ d, 30½″ h **2,415.00**

Walnut, inset onyx rect top, carved spoke like devices on side, sq tapered legs, turned stretcher, 24″ w, 16″ d, 29¼″ h **460.00**

Baroque, German, oysterwood and fruitwood marquetry, rect top, spiral turned legs, shaped stretcher, losses, 30¾″ w, 23″ d, 27″ h **2,185.00**

Biedermeier, second half 19th C, fruitwood and ebonized wood, 40″ d, 31½″ h **1,610.00**

Classical, 19th C, mahogany, variegated green and white marble top, veneered skirt, acanthus carved and turned standard, four acanthus carved paw feet, 43″ d, 29″ h **2,200.00**

Empire Style, mahogany, circular gray marble top, plain frieze, ormolu mounts, three circular legs ending in irregular shaped base, 32½″ d, 26½″ h **1,840.00**

French Empire, 19th C, mahogany, marble top with beveled edge, mounted foliage and rosette dec skirt, four bronze Egyptian caryatid supports, H–shape stretcher base, 46½″ w, 27″ d, 31″ h **5,075.00**

Louis Philippe, 19th C, boullework, serpentine shaped top with cartouche scene and gadrooned and foliate ormolu

mounts, conforming drawer, four goddess dec on skirt, cabriole legs with female mask mounts, cast sabots **1,650.00**

Napoleon III

c1860, Paris, boullework, shaped top, leaf cast border, inlaid brass and tortoiseshell dec, satyr's–head mounts, cabriole legs with female terms, rocaille sabots, 59″ w, 36″ d, 30″ h **880.00**

Late 19th C, gilt metal mounted thuywood, ebonized and marquetry, oval top, dec frieze, shaped fluted tapered legs, shaped X–stretcher with urn finial, 40½″ w, 23″ d, 30″ h **2,415.00**

Third quarter 19th C, walnut, shaped inset carrara marble top (cracked), plain frieze, turned support, four scrolled legs, 45″ w, 29½″ d, 29″ h . **865.00**

Regency Style, mahogany, circular tilt top, reeded standard, four splayed legs, sq brass feet, 39½″ d, 29″ h **375.00**

Rococo, mid 19th C, serpentine shape marble top, plain skirt, carved cabriole voluted legs, shaped stretcher with turned finial, brass casters, 41″ w, 21½″ d, 29″ h **1,325.00**

Victorian, mid 19th C, walnut, shaped veined marble top, carved skirt with mythological masque and floral leaf dec, cabriole legs with carved floral knees, leaf carved stretcher with leaf carved bulbous finial, 30½″ w, 30½″ d, 30″ h **1,980.00**

Coffee

Empire, American, mahogany and marble, circular top, tapering support, three scrolling feet, 18″ h **275.00**

Georgian Style, burled walnut, rect top, carved scrolling apron, cabriole legs, pad feet, 40″ w, 40″ d, 17″ h **200.00**

Modernism, Frank Lloyd Wright, manufactured by Henredon, mahogany, hexagonal, Greek

Key trim along sides of top and stretcher, 22" w, 22" l, 17" h . **750.00**

Queen Anne Style, Continental, mahogany, rect scalloped handled tray top, shaped apron, cabriole legs, pad feet, 27¼" w, 16½" d, 21¼" h **275.00**

Console

Adam Style, shaped top, painted diamond shape paterae surrounded by scrollwork, one drawer, faux cameos, laurel wreaths, and bellflower dec skirt, fluted sq tapered legs, 44" w, 17" d, 29½" h **775.00**

George III Style, crossbanded mahogany, frieze drawer, sq molded legs, 40" w, 15" d, 32½" h **275.00**

Louis XV Style, shaped marble top, foliate carved frieze with central heraldic device, scrolled supports, center urn with scrolled handles, 30" w, 17½" d, 29½" h **2,000.00**

Louis XVI Style, painted and giltwood, demilune marble top, beaded and guilloche carved frieze, giltwood garlands, reeded round tapering legs, surmounted by framed print and mirror plate, 16½" w, 8½" d, 64" h **500.00**

Oriental, late 19th C, black lacquer, chinoiserie gold landscape and floral reserve dec, fretwork apron, sq legs, 50½" w, 32" h **575.00**

Rococo

American, New York, 1850–60, rosewood, molded shaped top, relief carved cattail fronds and bird central medallion on skirt, cabriole legs with carved dec, cyma shape stretcher with gadrooned urn finial, 55½" w, 19" d, 35½" h **3,750.00**

Continental, mid 19th C, giltwood, faux gris marble top, rocaille carved and pierced serpentine skirt surmounting mirror back, foliate carved cabriole legs, animal paw feet, rocaille carved stretcher, 46" w, 17¾" d, 35½" h **2,200.00**

Italian, demilune, painted, restoration, worming, 45" w, 19¼" d, 32" h **3,800.00**

Dining

Chippendale Style, mahogany, oval top, gadrooned molding, two acanthus carved vasiform standards, cabriole legs with acanthus carved dec, claw and ball feet, four leaves, 110" l extended, 43" w **1,980.00**

Directorie Style, mahogany, oval top, turned tapering legs, brass feet, two 21½" w leaves, 86" w, 29" h **800.00**

Federal, North Shore Massachusetts, 1815–20, mahogany veneer, top with two D–shaped drop leaves, single drawer in apron, reeded legs, casters, refinished, replaced brass pull handle on drawer, 47" l extended, 28¾" h **975.00**

Federal Style

Cherry, rect top, turned double pedestals, two leaves, down curving legs ending in brass caps, 66" l, 42" w, 28" h ... **750.00**

Mahogany, two vasiform standards, splayed legs, brass paw casters, one table board, 101" l extended, 56" w, 28¼" h **1,650.00**

George II, mahogany, oval top, two 15¼" w drop leaves, circular tapering legs, pad feet, 40" l, 15½" w, 27¾" h **1,100.00**

George III Style, attributed to Irving & Casson, A H Davenport Co, early 20th C, mahogany, blindfret carved legs, 72" l, 48" w, 30" h **1,840.00**

Hepplewhite, early 19th C, mahogany, two D–form ends, rect drop leaves, sq tapering legs, spade feet, 95" l, 56" w, 28" h **1,200.00**

Hepplewhite Style, country, drop leaf, cherry, top with rounded corners on leaves, sq tapered legs, old red paint traces, 36" l, 17¾" w, 27½" h **335.00**

Jacobean Style, oak, rect top with demilune drop leaves, block and ring turned standard, stretcher, 78" l, 29½" h . **1,775.00**

Louis XV Style, mahogany veneered, round top, conforming frieze, four legs, 32" d, 31" h . **475.00**

Modernism, Frank Lloyd Wright, manufactured by Henredon, mahogany, rect top, two leaves, Greek Key trim, 63" w, 42" l, 29½" h **700.00**

Provincial, Danish, late 19th C, oak, rect top, four slightly tapering cabriole legs, two 20" w leaves, 69" l, 41½" w, 29½" h **300.00**

Queen Anne
New England, 18th C, orig blue–green paint, rect top, single long drawer, tapered legs, pad feet, early turned pull, minor repairs, 43" w, 24¼" d, 26½" h **14,950.00**

Philadelphia, c1760, walnut, rect top with drop leaves, cabriole legs, trifid feet, 51½" l extended, 42" w, 27½" h **3,850.00**

Queen Anne Style, American, oval, two leaves, circular legs, pad feet, 60" l, 42" w, 28½" h **300.00**

Regency, mahogany, rect top with band inlay dec, sq reeded tapered legs, brass spade feet, 56" l, 46¾" w, 30" h **990.00**

Regency Style, mahogany
Double Pedestal, baluster supports, reeded tapering legs, brass casters, 66" l, 38¾" w, 29" h **1,500.00**

Drop Leaf, rect top, two 22" w rect drop leaves, fluted apron, carved acanthus leaf, fluted, and beaded legs, casters, 49" l, 25" w, 31" h . **300.00**

Shaped rect top, inlaid banding, four splayed legs, central pr joined by stretcher, brass casters, 91" l, 42" w, 30" h **500.00**

Victorian, American, walnut, two 10" l drop leaves, 34" l, 10" w, 29" h **325.00**

William IV, c1830, mahogany,

rect top, brass bail handles on side, ring turned tapered legs, brass casters, 129" l extended, 51" w, 28¾" h **4,845.00**

Dressing
Georgian Style, late 19th/early 20th C, japanned, 42½" w, 14¾" d, 37" h table, 29" w, 57" h mirror **2,760.00**

Victorian, mid 19th C, walnut, gray veined white marble top with splashboard, rect mirror with molded carved foliate frame, serpentine skirt with long drawer, towel holder on each side, slender cabriole legs, 35½" w, 57" h **500.00**

Folding, Renaissance Revival, Gates Manufacturing Co, Philadelphia, patent 1877, cherry, rotary, adjustable sliding top, two drawers, adjustable support, four paw feet, each drawer with paper label **460.00**

Game
Empire (Classical)
Boston, early 19th C, mahogany, hinged top with molded edge, scrolled skirt, pedestal with carved leaf dec, stepped plinth base, scrolled feet with casters, 34¾" w, 35½" d, 27½" h **1,100.00**

New York, c1815, mahogany, shaped top, brass classical figural dec apron, lyre form standard, four acanthus carved flaring legs, brass paw feet and casters, 35¾" w, 18" d, 29" h **11,000.00**

Empire Style, mahogany, hinged top, acanthus carved standard, platform base, paw feet, 30" h **685.00**

Federal, c1810, mahogany, serpentine top, reeded tapered legs, ball feet, 35" w, 17¼" d, 30" h **935.00**

Federal Style, mahogany, demilune form top, pin–line inlay dec apron, eagle and bellflowers inlay, sq tapered legs, 36" w, 17½" d, 30" h **750.00**

George III, late 18th C, mahogany
Demilune, inlaid, four tapering legs, 24" w, 11¾" d, 28½" h **635.00**
Rect top, four sq tapering legs, 35" w, 17" d, 28" h **1,100.00**
Hepplewhite, late 18th C, satinwood, leather inset top, sq tapering legs, 35" w, 35" d, 28" h......................**1,700.00**
Louis XV Style, kingwood, hinged sq shaped top, leather inlay, cabriole legs, 35½" w, 30" h **2,800.00**
Napoleon III, third quarter 19th C, ebonized
Serpentine molded hinged top, carved frieze, cabriole legs, 31½" w, 15¼" d, 28½" h ... **300.00**
Shaped hinged top, plain frieze, fluted tapering legs, brass inlay throughout, losses, 32½" w, 16" d, 29½" h **460.00**
Neoclassical, American, mahogany, angular top, leaf carved standard, down swept legs, brass paw casters, 34¾" w, 17" d, 28¾" h **375.00**
Regency
c1815, rosewood, brass inlaid, felt lined playing surface, shaped standard, down swept legs, brass claw casters, 35½" w, 17¾" d, 28½" h **2,000.00**
First quarter 19th C, mahogany and ebony inlay, rounded rect hinged top, plain frieze, ring turned legs, ball feet, 34" w, 16½" d, 29¼" h **575.00**
Rococo, New York, mid 19th C, rosewood, serpentine shaped top, sq projected corners with felt lined and gold Greek Key tooled int., gadrooned frieze edge, cabriole legs with scrollwork and carved husks knees, stylized claw and ball feet, 34" w, 17¼" d, 28¼" h **3,850.00**
Victorian, late 19th C
Walnut and burl walnut, hinged reel top, rounded edges, felt lined int., shaped supports

joined by turned stretcher, scrolled feet, casters, 36" w, 17½" d, 28¾" h **460.00**
Walnut and yewwood, inset chess and checkerboard, 36" w, 19½" d, 26" h **575.00**
Harvest, probably Massachusetts, c1800, pine and maple, long rect top with two drop leaves, sq tapered legs, old refinish, 114" l, 35½" w, 26½" h **3,750.00**
Hutch
Country, pine, one board ends, shelf, simple cutout feet, old worn dark reddish–brown finish, 43" w, 36½" d, 27½" h ..**1,765.00**
New England, 18th C, scrubbed pine rect top, old color above old red base, locking compartment in base, minor imperfections, 44¼" w, 35¾" d, 29" h .**4,600.00**
New England, late 18th C, scrubbed pine circular top, early red paint, imperfections, shoe feet, stretcher, 53" w, 37" d, 28¼" h **4,025.00**
Northern New York state, late 18th C, painted, scrubbed circular top over old red base, shaped sliding stretcher type key, shoe feet, imperfections, 43½" w, 32" d, 26" h **3,740.00**
Library
Jacobean Style, carved oak, rect top, dec molding above frieze with three drawers, carved supports, trestle base, 47" w, 31½" d, 32" h **850.00**
Victorian, late 19th C, oak, octagonal faux marbleized top, molded rim with foliate and hammered motif, inset drawer with egg and dart border, support with turned finial center, lion's–head scroll feet with casters, 53" w, 31½" h **2,200.00**
William IV, 2nd quarter 19th C, mahogany, rect top, shaped side pedestals with molding, turned stretchers, brass feet and casters, 29¼" w, 17¼" d, 29" h **2,300.00**
Occasional, French Provincial, 19th C, walnut, reticulated mar-

ble top, molded serpentine skirt, fluted cabriole legs, carved doe's feet, 26½" w, 18½" d, 27¼" h .. **935.00**

Parlor, Neoclassical, c1865, rosewood, variegated marble top, incised carved molded edge, burled skirt with applied medallions and shield, central stylized urn standard, plinth base, four scrolling gilt dec palmetto legs, flattened ball feet, 24" d, 29" h . **5,500.00**

Pembroke

Federal, c1800, cherry, rect top with demilune drop leaves, single drawer frieze, sq tapered legs, 43" l extended, 34¼" d, 28" h **500.00**

George III

c1760, mahogany, drop leaf top, apron with drawer, Marlborough legs, X–form stretcher, 35½" w, 27" d, 27" h **945.00**

Fourth quarter 18th C, satinwood and rosewood, banded, minor restoration, 30¼" l extended, 27¾" h .. **1,150.00**

George III, Late, early 19th C, mahogany and boxwood inlaid, 38¼" l extended, 32¼" d, 28¾" h **2,185.00**

Hepplewhite, cherry, one board top, mortised and pinned apron, one dovetailed drawer, cross stretcher, sq tapered legs, 31" w, 18¼" d, 28½" h . **500.00**

Sheraton, c1810, mahogany, rect top with demilune drop leaves, single drawer frieze, reeded tapered legs, brass casters, 41" l extended, 36" d, 29¾" h **1,275.00**

Sheraton Style, early 19th C, walnut, two shaped drop leaves, single drawer frieze, ring turned tapered legs, 40½" w, 29" h **550.00**

Victorian, American, maple, rect top, two 10" w leaves, two aligned frieze drawers, baluster turned legs, 17½" w, 28" h **130.00**

Pier, Empire [Classical]

c1840, mahogany, marble top, ogee molded skirt, S–scroll

supports with concentric oval veneered panels, scalloped shelf, down scrolled feet **2,860.00**

Early 19th C, New York, rect white marble top, gilt stenciled frieze, white marble columnar supports, shaped shelf with gilt stenciled frieze, parcel gilt gadrooned circular feet, 17¾" w, 41½" d, 37" h **7,975.00**

Side

Arts and Crafts, Mission, oak, three–quarter gallery, two open shelves, slat form supports, sq legs, 15¾" w, 12¼" d, 31" h **550.00**

George II, mid 18th C, walnut and oak, plank rect top, plain frieze, plank legs, stretchers, 45¼" w, 24¾" d, 29¼" h **700.00**

Georgian Style, nesting, mahogany, rect top, allover floral marquetry, sq tapering legs, price for set of three **400.00**

Louis XV Style, inlaid walnut, oval brass galleried top, two drawers, applied brass pulls, wreath and swag motif, cabriole legs, 31½" h **700.00**

Napoleon III, walnut, marquetry, shaped veneered hinged top, conforming frieze, turned and fluted legs, shaped medial shelf, 17" w, 13" d, 30" h **200.00**

Renaissance Style, Italian, late 19th C, walnut

Black slate top inset with hardstone and gilt incising, central pietra dura medallion of birds, butterflies, and flowers surrounded by band of triangles, central reeded shaft, three columns, three scrolling splayed legs, 31½" h ..**1,495.00**

Rect molded top, plain frieze with drawer, shaped trestle support, turned stretcher, paw feet, 26½" w, 18" d, 24½" h **520.00**

Victorian, carved mahogany, shaped marble top, foliate carved apron, cabriole legs joined by X–stretcher with center finial, 31" w, 22" d, 29" h . **275.00**

Sofa

Regency, early 19th C, mahogany, rect molded top, two shaped drop leaves, two veneered drawers, two faux drawers, ring turned pedestal, four molded scrolling legs with brass capped ends, 55" w, 24½" d, 28½" h **1,250.00**

Regency Style

Inlaid mahogany, galleried oval top, frieze drawer, lyre form base, splayed legs, 40" w, 20" d, 28½" d **325.00**

Mahogany, molded rect top, two 11½" leaves, two frieze drawers, fluted baluster turned supports, down curving legs, fluted baluster turned stretcher, 40" w, 19½" d, 30¼" h **425.00**

Tavern

Federal, c1800, pine, rect plank top, green painted stand, one drawer, sq tapered legs, 39½" l, 24" w, 27½" h **750.00**

Hepplewhite, country, pine, rect

Tavern Table, Queen Anne, New England, 18th C, maple, single sq board top, shaped undulating frieze, splayed ring-turned tapered legs, repairs to pad feet, 28" w, 25¼" h, $3,300.00. Photograph courtesy of Butterfield & Butterfield.

two board projected top, plain apron with drawer, sq tapered legs, refinished, 47½" l, 23¼" w, 43" h **1,325.00**

Queen Anne, country, cherry and ash, two board top with rounded corners, breadboard ends, apron with drawer, brass pull handle, turned legs, mortised stretcher, 41" l, 26¼" w, 28" h **3,410.00**

Queen Anne Style, late 18th C, maple, oval top, cylindrical tapered legs, pad feet, 25" w, 32½" d, 25½" h **1,275.00**

William and Mary, New England, c1750, maple and pine, round top, plain apron, turned legs, box stretcher, varnish over old red paint, 31⅛" d, 25½" h . . . **6,325.00**

Tea

Chippendale, attributed to Massachusetts, c1780, mahogany, carved

Circular top, down curving tripod legs, old refinish, 31½" d, 27½" h **1,100.00**

Shaped tilt top, down curving tripod legs, old refinish, 33" x 33½" top, 28½" h **7,475.00**

Chippendale Style, mahogany

Scalloped tilt top, down curving tripod legs, 26" d top . . **225.00**

Shaped circular top, carved baluster support, down curving legs, paw feet, 31" d, 27" h **225.00**

Empire [Classical], New York, early 19th C, mahogany, rect scalloped edge top, molded skirt, vasiform support with lotus leaf motifs, acanthus carved legs, hairy paw feet, 30" w, 21" d, 28" h **990.00**

Federal, mahogany, sq tilt top, turned standard, tripod base, ball feet, 23" w, 29" h **350.00**

George III, late 18th C, mahogany, folding demilune hinged top, fan paterae and line satinwood inlay, conforming apron, sq tapering legs, 32" w, 19½" d, 30" h **1,000.00**

George III Style, mahogany, piecrust circular tilt top, reeded and acanthus carved standard, tripod cabriole legs, snake's–head feet, one damaged brace, 22" d, 27" h **750.00**

Victorian, late 19th C, papier–mache, tilt top, chips, 23½" d, 28½" h **260.00**

Tuck–A–Way, William and Mary, New England, 18th C, maple, turned legs, imperfections, 30" w, 28½" d, 26" h **6,900.00**

Work

Empire [Classical], American, mahogany, rect top, two 11" w D–form drop leaves, two serpentine drawers, turned legs, casters, 19" w, 25" d, 29" h . . **100.00**

Louis XV Style, late 19th C, ormolu mounted kingwood, shaped hinged top, slide drawer, cabriole legs, sabots, 23" l, 16" d, 29¼" h **550.00**

Writing

Federal, Philadelphia, c1815, mahogany, fitted top, compartmented int., fluted tapered legs, casters, old finish, 24" w, 17½" d, 28¾" h **6,325.00**

Regency, first quarter 19th C, ebonized and parcel gilt, rect leather inset top, pr of drawers opposed by faux drawers, legs ending in casters, 34¾" w, 20¼" d, 27¾" h **4,315.00**

Regency Style, walnut, two frieze drawers, trestle support, 40" w, 22" d, 29" h **550.00**

Victorian, late 19th C, mahogany, rect green gilt tooled leather top with beveled edge, gadrooned molding, two drawers, baluster turned carved legs, 46" w, 29½" h **1,100.00**

WICKER

Bench, painted white, upturned sides, crescent moon support, tendrils and curliques, tightly woven seat, 24¾" w, 16½" d, 33½" h **425.00**

Chair

Arm, matching lady's and gentle-man's chair, oval back medallion surrounded by curliques, looped arms, painted white, 45½" h, price for pair **575.00**

Photographer's, Heywood Bros & Co, Gardner, MA, late 19th C, orig label, 34½" h **690.00**

Reception, lady's, late 19th C, openweave crest over horseshoe shaped splat with center woven diamond, curliques, scrolls, braided trim, initialed "CW" on apron, 38½" h, price for set of four **5,175.00**

Side

Heywood Brothers & Co, Gardner, MA, late 19th C, orig label, 40" h **575.00**

Wakefield, late 19th C, No. 3612, paint dec, minor loss, one bearing paper label of Wakefield Rattan Co, 40" h, price for pair **1,150.00**

Music Stand, late 19th C, ornate scrolled top, three tightly woven shelves, 48½" h **920.00**

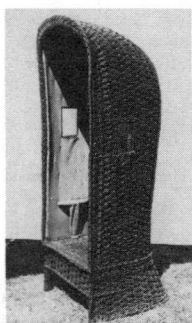

Porter's Chair, painted dark green, 24¾" w, 28" d, 69¾" h, $550.00.

Rocker

Heywood & Morrill Rattan Co, late 19th C, No. 2889B, scrolling arms, paper labels for Heywood & Morrill Rattan Co, Chicago, 44" h **575.00**

Unidentified American Maker, late 19th C

Adult's

Tight bulb shaped center lacy caned panel, three tightly woven outscrolled handles, shaped scrolling arms, 41″ h **635.00**

Ram's horn shape crest rail, reeded and basketweave design back, braided armrests, petal shape seat . . **550.00**

Child's, minor damage, 27¾″ h **375.00**

Saloon Doors, inset leaded glass panels, mirrored panels, 60″ h, price for pair **2,300.00**

Settee, painted white, alternating green and white painted beadwork, 49½″ l, 39½″ h **690.00**

Stand, late 19th C

Basket top, tight weave, painted white, deep basket type top with slightly flaring sides, tray base shelf with braided edges, 30″ h **265.00**

Octagonal top, 30½″ h **185.00**

Square top, 22¾″ h **175.00**

Suite, Regency Style, tight weave, painted white, two settees, bench, and armchair with scrolling arms, backs, and legs, 63″ l x 32″ h settees, price for four piece set **1,000.00**

Table

Center, tight weave, painted white, round dished top, scalloped apron, vasiform pedestal, sq pedestal base, 29″ h . . **300.00**

Occasional

Early 20th C, rect oak top, reeded frame with looped skirt, lyre scrolled ends, galleried shelf with braided trim, wrapped legs, 28½″ l, 23″ w, 29½″ h **1,380.00**

Late 19th C

Oval oak top, 31½″ l, 25″ w, 30″ h **2,415.00**

Round oak top, fern type frond pendant, outscrolled legs, round oak lower shelf, 21″ d, 27¾″ h, price for pair **2,415.00**

GAME PLATES

History: Game plates, popular between 1870 and 1915, are specially decorated plates used to serve fish and game. Sets originally included a platter, serving plates, and a sauce or gravy boat. Many sets have been divided. Today, individual plates are used for wall hangings.

Reference: Susan and Al Bagdade, *Warman's English & Continental Pottery & Porcelain, 2nd Edition,* Wallace–Homestead, 1991.

BIRDS

Plate

8¾″ d, pheasant, gold edge, A S & Co, Bavaria **75.00**

9½″ d

Maastricht Ware, deep rust edge **30.00**

Pate–Sur–Pate, birds on branches, turquoise, sgd "D Leroy, Minton" **450.00**

Platter

18¼ x 12″, bird flying over grass, purple flowers, daisies, shaded lavender to shrimp ground, scalloped gold rim, rococo border, marked "Limoges" **175.00**

20″ l, wild turkey, autumn sunset, curled corners, printed eagle mark, marked "Haviland & Co, Aug 10, 1880" **800.00**

Set

7 pcs, platter and six plates, artist sgd, marked "Limoges" . . **700.00**

13 pcs, platter and twelve plates, gold leaf dec, France **900.00**

66 pcs, dinner service, hp birds, blue, gray, and yellow ground, marked "Paul Mueller, Selb, Bavaria" **250.00**

ELK

Plate

9″ d, natural colors, scalloped edge **40.00**

9¼″ d, two elk standing by brook, marked "Dresden Semi–Porcelain" **35.00**

Ducks, burgundy, gold border, Limoges, sgd "Vitet," $125.00.

FISH

Plate
  10½" d, trout, cobalt blue border,
    marked "M Z Austria" **65.00**
  15" d, hp fish, artist sgd **145.00**
Platter
  14" l, bass on lure, artist sgd "R
    K Beck" **100.00**
  16½" l, bass, water lilies, emb,
    artist sgd "Max," marked "Li-
    moges" **165.00**
Set
  7 pcs, 24" l platter, six 9½" d,
    plates, Limoges **500.00**
  9 pcs, 25" l platter, eight 8½" d,
    plates, Austria **375.00**
  11 pcs, platter and ten plates,
    artist sgd "Muville," marked
    "Limoges" **550.00**
  13 pcs, 25" l platter, twelve
    plates, different fish on each,
    peach ground **450.00**
  15 pcs, oblong platter, twelve
    plates, and sauceboat with un-
    derplate, hp fish and leafage
    design, gilt dec, scalloped
    rims, Limoges **525.00**

GAMES

History: Mass production of board games did not take place until after the Civil War. Firms like McLoughlin Brothers, Milton Bradley, and Selchow and Righter were active in the 1860s, followed by Parker Brothers, who began in 1883. Parker Brothers bought out the rights to the W. & S. B. Ives Co., which had produced some very early games in the 1840s, including the "first" American board game, The Mansion of Happiness. All except McLoughlin Brothers are giants in the game industry today.

McLoughlin Brothers's games are a challenge to find. Not only does the company no longer exist [Milton Bradley bought them out in 1920], but the lithography on their games was the best of its era. Most board games are collected because of the bright, colorful lithography on their box covers. In addition to spectacular covers, the large McLoughlin games often had lead playing pieces and fancy block spinners, thus making them even more desirable.

Common games like Anagrams, Authors, Jackstraws, Lotto, Tiddledy Winks, and Peter Coddles do not command high prices, nor do the games of Flinch, Pit, and Rook, which still are being produced.

Games, with the exception of the common ones stated above, generally are rising in price. However, interesting to note is the fact that certain games with good graphics dealing with popular subject matter, e.g. trains, planes, baseball, Christmas and others, often bring higher prices because they are also sought by collectors in those particular fields.

Condition is everything when buying. Do not buy games that have been taped or that have price tags stickered on the face of their covers. Also, beware of buying games at outdoor flea markets where weather elements can cause fading and warping.

References: Avedon and Sutton–Smith, *The Study of Games,* Wiley & Son, 1971; R. C. Bell, *The Board Game Book,* The Knapp Press, 1979; Lee Dennis, *Warman's Antique American Games, 1840–1940,* Wallace–Homestead, 1991; Caroline Goodfellow, *A Collector's Guide To Games and Puzzles,* The Apple Press, 1991; Brian Love, *Great Board Games, 1895–1935,* Macmillan Publishing Co., 1979; Brian Love, *Play The Game: Over 40 Games From The Golden Age Of Board Games,* Reed Books, 1978; L-W Book Sales, *Board Games of the 50's, 60's & 70's With Prices,*

L-W Books, 1994; Norman E. Martinus and Harry L. Rinker, *Warman's Paper*, Wallace–Homestead, 1994; Rick Polizzi and Fred Schaefer, *Spin Again: Board Games from the Fifties and Sixties*, Chronicle Books, 1991; Harry L. Rinker, *Collector's Guide To Toys, Games, and Puzzles*, Wallace–Homestead, 1991; Bruce Whitehill, *Games: American Boxed Games and Their Makers, 1822–1992*, Wallace–Homestead, 1992.

Periodicals: *Toy Shop*, 700 E. State St., Iola, WI 54990; *Toy Trader*, PO Box 1050, Dubuque, IA 52004.

Collectors' Clubs: American Game Collectors Association, 49 Brooks Ave., Lewiston, ME 04240; American Toy Collectors of America, Inc., c/o Carter, Ledyard & Milburn, Two Wall St., 13th Floor, New York, NY 10005; Gamers Alliance, PO Box 197, East Meadow, NY 11554.

Museums: Checkers Hall of Fame, Petal, MS; Essex Institute, Salem, MA; University of Waterloo Museum & Archive of Games, Waterloo, Ontario, Canada; Washington Dolls' House and Toy Museum, Washington, D.C.

Additional Listings: See *Warman's Americana & Collectibles*.

Auto Race, Gorham Pressed Steel
    Corp, c1930, 10¾ x 22", multi-
    colored litho metal board, 5 col-
    ored metal cars **175.00**

Crusade, Sam'l Gabriel Sons & Co., New York, NY, c1930, 14½" sq, $17.50.

Bagatelle, early push–type, 1⅛ x
    9¹⁵⁄₁₆ x 19¼", wooden, multicol-
    ored litho pasted to face marking
    points, wooden stick with
    wooden block to push ball, one
    wooden and one clay ball, in-
    structions pasted on back **150.00**
Barney Google & Spark Plug
    Game, Milton Bradley, © 1923,
    17 x 9", colorful cardboard cutout
    comic figure tokens, ex–The Sie-
    gel Collection, taped aprons . . . **200.00**
Brownie Blocks, McLoughlin Bros,
    © 1891, 13 x 11", twenty puzzle
    cubes, makes six scenes, orig
    guide sheet booklet, ex–The
    Siegel Collection, slight wear on
    block edges, booklet taped **775.00**
Buster Brown Hurdle Race, Ott-
    man, 16 x 12", comic graphics
    on cov and board, ex–The Sie-
    gel Collection, taped aprons and
    box bottom **525.00**
Christmas Mail, Ottman, 13 x 13",
    box cov with colorful Santa car-
    rying mail sack image, board
    with city map, letter mail playing
    pieces, ex–The Siegel Collec-
    tion, taped lid corners **700.00**
Excuse Me!, Parker Bros, card
    game, © 1923, 7½ x 4¾", 124
    printed pink and white cards and
    instruction sheet, no illus **15.00**
Flap Jacks, Alderman–Fairchild,
    (All–Fair), © 1931, 15½ x 12½",
    boxed board game of skill, in-
    structions on back of box cov, 10
    flap jacks, beige, blue, and red
    board with 5 numbered round
    holes **80.00**
Game of Balloon, R Bliss Manu-
    facturing Co, c1889, 31 x 10½",
    wooden standard and hoop, 2
    hand tied racquets, 4 balloons,
    inflator, game counter, 4 score
    pins, instruction booklet, adv
    sheet, wooden dovetailed,
    hinged box **575.00**
Game of Department Store, Mc-
    Loughlin Bros, 23 x 15", large
    format game, colorful lid and
    board, inset spinner, ex–The
    Siegel Collection, some apron
    loss and tape replacement **775.00**

Game of Goose, Spear Works, 10 pcs, multicolored litho game board, 67 painted goose tokens, 2 wooden dice, wooden dice cup .. **150.00**

Game of Politics or Race for the Presidency, W. S. Reed, © 1887, 23 x 24" board, colorful board pictures Presidents through Cleveland, cards, instruction booklet, ex–The Siegel Collection, spine taped **300.00**

Game of Tortoise and the Hare, Russell Mfg Co, © 1927, 5⅞ x 9⅞", 4 pcs (folded, multicolored litho paper board with directions insert, 2 round counters, 1 wooden die) **30.00**

Game of Travel, The, Parker Bros, © 1894, eight lead tokens, implement drawer in board base, instructions, ex–The Siegel Collection, taped aprons and box bottom **525.00**

Hop Scotch Tiddledy Winks, Parker Bros, game of skill, 1891, 10¼ x 6¾", 25 pcs (1 cup, 20 winks, 2 felt pads, advertising sheet, instruction sheet), 1 felt is red and yellow with bull's–eye, other is hopscotch court **60.00**

Johnny Get Your Gun, Parker Bros, Inc, boxed board game, © 1928, 13½ x 11½", instructions on back of box cov, 16 round colored wooden counters, multicolored litho board showing various animals in circles, spinner in center is in shape of rifle and made of wood and metal **75.00**

Lindy Hop–Off, Parker Bros, c1927, 14½ x 13⅜", 25 pcs, 2 dice cups, 2 dice, 16 cards, 4 painted metal planes, instruction sheet, lift out folding multicolored litho board **375.00**

Master Rodbury and His Pupils, card game, 1844, W. & S. B. Ives Co, 2⅝ x 3¾", 18 cards and 1 instruction card, all cards hp, game invented by Anne Abbot . **150.00**

Movie Inn, W.G. Young & Co, Inc, © 1917, 10⅞ x 7¼", multicolored litho board with 5 steel balls and instructions printed at bottom, a skill game invented by Willis G. Young **75.00**

Pussy Cat 5 Pins, Milton Bradley, 11 x 10", three wood balls, ex–The Siegel Collection **500.00**

Redskin & Cowboy, Smith Kline & French, 24 x 12", colorful game board, cardboard cutout cowboy and Indian tokens on metal stands, folding board with four attached spinners, ex–The Siegel Collection **170.00**

Ring My Nose, Milton Bradley Co, target game, c1927, 8¼ x 12¼", 8 cardboard rings and metal screw for clown's nose, multicolored litho clown image on board and cov **45.00**

Siege of Havana, Parker Bros, c1898, 22½ x 16¼", wooden box, instructions on back of box cov, 9 pcs, multicolored litho board **425.00**

Steeple–Chase, unknown manufacturer, triangular trademark, c1890–95, 18 x 11½", directions on back of cov, 16 pcs, 6 numbered cards, 6 lead horses on stands, 3 dice, folding board, multicolored litho pictures **125.00**

Tally–Ho, Snow, Woodman & Co, c1880, 11¼" sq, 74 pcs (36 white wooden pegs, 36 black wooden pegs, lift out board, and instruction sheet), multicolored litho board with red star in center **75.00**

Trades or Knowledge is Power, R. H. Pease, Albany, NY, hand colored box cov and cards, orig instruction sheet with adv, ex–The Siegel Collection, box and instructions taped **1,000.00**

"White House," Thompson's Old Homestead Series, Thompson & Co., © 1905, 5½ x 3¾", 45 cards with instructions, card backs have green and white litho of White House **30.00**

World War Game, United States Soldier Company, NY, 11 x 8", shooting game, artillery battery, cutout soldiers, ex–The Siegel Collection, box taped **500.00**

GAUDY DUTCH

History: Gaudy Dutch is an opaque, soft–paste ware made between 1790 and 1825 in England's Staffordshire district. Most pieces are unmarked; marks of various potters, including the impressed marks of Riley and Wood, have been found on pieces.

The pieces first were hand decorated in an underglaze blue, fired, and then received additional decoration over the glaze. Many pieces today have extensively worn over–glaze decoration. Gaudy Dutch found a ready market within the Pennsylvania German community because it was inexpensive and intense with color. It had little appeal in England.

References: Susan and Al Bagdade, *Warman's English & Continental Pottery & Porcelain, 2nd Edition,* Wallace–Homestead, 1991; Eleanor and Edward Fox, *Gaudy Dutch,* published by author, 1970, out–of–print; John A. Shuman, III, *The Collector's Encyclopedia of Gaudy Dutch & Welsh,* Collector Books, 1990, 1991 value update, out–of–print.

Reproduction Alert: Cup plates, bearing the impressed mark "CYBRIS," have been reproduced and are collectible in their own right. The Henry Ford Museum has issued pieces in the single rose pattern, although they are of porcelain and not soft–paste.

Advisor: John D. Querry.

Teabowl and Saucer, Single Rose pattern, blue, rust, yellow, and green florals, yellow leaves, blue border, $525.00.

Butterfly
- Bowl, 11″ d 3,900.00
- Coffeepot, 11″ h 3,750.00
- Cup and Saucer, handleless ... 325.00
- Plate
  - 6½″ d 650.00
  - 9¾″ d 1,500.00
- Sugar 900.00
- Teapot, 5″ h, squat baluster form 1,400.00
- Waste Bowl 1,275.00

Carnation
- Bowl
  - 5½″ d 625.00
  - 6¼″ d 450.00
- Creamer, 4¾″ h 600.00
- Pitcher, 6″ h 510.00
- Plate
  - 5¾″ d 415.00
  - 8″ d 575.00
  - 9¾″ d 475.00
- Teabowl and Saucer 495.00
- Teapot 1,275.00
- Toddy Plate 525.00
- Waste Bowl 200.00

Dahlia
- Bowl, 6¼″ d 360.00
- Plate, 8″ d 775.00
- Sugar 850.00
- Teabowl and Saucer 700.00

Double Rose
- Bowl, 6¼″ d 400.00
- Creamer 400.00
- Gravy Boat 300.00
- Plate
  - 7″ d 425.00
  - 10″ d 370.00
- Sugar, cov 775.00
- Teapot 675.00
- Toddy Plate, 4½″ d 150.00
- Waste Bowl, 6½″ d, 3″ h 275.00

Dove
- Creamer 675.00
- Plate, 10″ d 450.00
- Waste Bowl 650.00

Flower Basket, Plate, 6½″ d 185.00

Grape
- Bowl, 6½″ d, lustered rim 385.00
- Plate
  - 6″ d 390.00
  - 7⅛″ d 225.00
- Sugar, cov 450.00
- Teabowl and Saucer 325.00
- Toddy Plate, 5″ d 375.00

Oyster
- Bowl, 5½″ d 300.00

Coffeepot, 12" h 550.00
Plate
    8¾" d 425.00
    9½" d 400.00
Soup Plate, 8½" d 450.00
Teabowl and Saucer 395.00
Toddy Plate, 5½" d 425.00
Single Rose
Bowl, 6" d 275.00
Coffeepot, 10¾" h, double gourd
    form 850.00
Cup and Saucer 75.00
Plate
    7" d 410.00
    8¼" d 450.00
Quill Holder, cov 2,500.00
Sugar, cov 675.00
Toddy Plate, 5¼" d 250.00
Sunflower
Bowl, 6½" d 425.00
Coffeepot, 9½" h 1,650.00
Creamer 475.00
Plate, 5½" d 375.00
Teabowl and Saucer 775.00
Urn
Creamer 325.00
Plate, 8¼" d 425.00
Sugar, cov, 6½" h, round, lip and
    base restored 275.00
War Bonnet
Bowl, cov 210.00
Coffeepot 3,900.00
Plate
    7" d 475.00
    8¼" d 325.00
Teapot 975.00
Toddy Plate, 4½" d 400.00

GAUDY IRONSTONE

History: Gaudy Ironstone was made in England around 1850. Most pieces are impressed "Ironstone" and bear a registry mark. Ironstone is an opaque, heavy–body earthenware which contains large proportions of flint and slag. Gaudy Ironstone is decorated in patterns and colors similar to Gaudy Welsh.

Reference: Susan and Al Bagdade, *Warman's English & Continental Pottery & Porcelain, 2nd Edition,* Wallace–Homestead, 1991.

Cup and Saucer, Morning Glory,
    underglaze blue, polychrome
    enamels, hairline crack 85.00
Jug, 7½" h, yellow, red, white, and
    blue tulips on sides, light blue
    pebble ground, luster trim, rim
    outline 300.00
Pitcher, 8" h, emb roses and flow-
    ers, underglaze blue, blue, red,
    and green enameling, some
    edge flakes 225.00
Plate
    7⅞" d, Urn pattern 60.00
    8⅜" d, copper luster highlights,
        shaped rim 85.00
    8½" d, Strawberry pattern, red
        enamel wear 30.00
    9¼" d, Blackberry pattern, 1850s 165.00
    9⅜" d, Rose pattern, red, blue,
        green, and black 85.00

Teapot, Strawberry pattern, green and cobalt blue leaves, rust strawberries, luster trim, 10¼" h, $200.00.

Platter
    12½" l, Urn pattern 600.00
    15¾" l, Strawberry pattern 785.00
Soup Plate, 9½" d, Blackberry pat-
    tern, mid 19th C 185.00
Sugar Bowl, 7⅜" h, Urn pattern,
    mismatched lid 500.00
Toddy Plate, 4¾" d, Urn pattern,
    underglaze blue, polychrome
    enamel and luster 175.00
Vegetable Dish, 10" l, Strawberry
    pattern 385.00

GAUDY WELSH

History: Gaudy Welsh is a translucent porcelain that was originally made in the Swansea area of England from 1830 to 1845. Although the designs resemble Gaudy Dutch, the body texture and weight differ. One of the characteristics is the gold luster on top of the glaze.

In 1890, Allerton made a similar ware. These wares are heavier opaque porcelain and usually bear the export mark.

References: Susan and Al Bagdade, *Warman's English & Continental Pottery & Porcelain, 2nd Edition,* Wallace–Homestead, 1991; John A. Shuman, III, *The Collector's Encyclopedia of Gaudy Dutch and Welsh,* Collector Books, 1990, 1991 value update, out–of–print; Howard Y. Williams, *Gaudy Welsh China,* Wallace–Homestead, out–of–print.

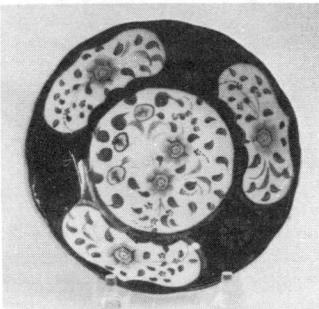

Dish, Floret pattern, 5½" d, $20.00.

Bowl	
5¼" d, Grape	40.00
6¼" d, Tulip	40.00
10½" d, Flower Basket	175.00
Compote, 10¼" d, Morning Glory	235.00
Creamer, 4" h, serpent handle, marked "Davenport Stone China"	125.00
Cup and Saucer	
Blinking Eye	55.00
Floral design	120.00
Oyster	70.00
Tulip	60.00

Dish, 8¼" sq, marked "Mason's England"	135.00
Ewer, 4" h, Tulip	100.00
Mug	
3" h, Oyster	60.00
4" h, Flower Basket	65.00
4⅛" h, Strawberry	125.00
Pitcher	
5⅝" h, marked "Stone China"	95.00
6" h, Dogwood, English registry mark	100.00
Plate	
5¼" d, Grape	50.00
5½" d, Wagon Wheel	35.00
8¼" d, Strawberry	135.00
8½" d, sq, Flower Basket	50.00
8¾" d, marked "Burleigh Ware, England," price for set of 8	100.00
9" d, crown mark	90.00
Platter	
Morning Glory, 11" l	75.00
Wagon Wheel	100.00
Sauce Bowl, cov, 8½" l, matching ladle, marked "Wedgwood"	150.00
Soup Plate	
9" d, Strawberry	100.00
10" d, Oyster, flange rim	75.00
Sugar, cov	
Flower Basket	100.00
Tulip, 6¾" h	100.00
Teapot, Daisy and Chain	180.00
Tea Set, four pcs, teapot, coffeepot, and creamer and sugar, marked "Made in England"	250.00
Wash Bowl and Pitcher, miniature, tulip design	360.00

GEISHA GIRL PORCELAIN

History: Geisha Girl porcelain is a Japanese export ware whose production commenced during the last quarter of the 19th century and continued heavily until World War II. The ware features kimono–clad Japanese ladies and children amidst Japanese gardens and temples. There are over 125 brightly colored scenes depicting the pre-modern Japanese lifestyle. Over 140 marks and almost 200 patterns and variations have been identified on pieces.

Geisha Girl ware may be totally hand painted, hand painted over a stenciled design, or occasionally decaled. The stenciled underlying design is usually red–orange, but also is found in brown, black, and green (rare).

All Geisha Girl items are bordered by one or a combination of blues, reds, greens, rhubarb, yellow, black, browns, or gold. The most common is red–orange. Borders may be wavy, scalloped, or banded and range from 1/16 inch to 1/4 inch. The borders themselves often are further decorated with gold, white or yellow lacings, flowers, dots, or stripes. Some examples even display interior frames of butterflies or flowers.

Geisha Girl is found in many forms including tea, cocoa, lunch, and children's sets, dresser items, vases, serving dishes, etc. Large plates or platters, candlesticks, miniatures, and mugs are hardest to locate. Geisha Girl advertising items add to a collection.

Reference: Elyce Litts, *The Collectors Encyclopedia Of Geisha Girl Porcelain,* Collector Books, 1988.

Additional Listings: See *Warman's Americana & Collectibles* for more examples.

Reproduction Alert: Geisha Girl porcelain's popularity continued after World War II and it is being reproduced today. Chief reproduction characteristics are a red–orange border, very white and smooth porcelain, and sparse coloring and detail. Reproduced items include dresser, tea and sake sets, toothpick holders, small vases, table plates, and salt and pepper shakers.

Biscuit Jar, Gardening, ornate cobalt blue wavy and circle border, ftd **40.00**
Bowl, 10" d, Chinese Coin motif, ruffled, pierced handle **85.00**
Butter Pat, cherry blossom shape reserve geisha, red line int. frame, flower and butterfly ground **10.00**
Calling Card Tray, 8" l, 6" w, Parasol F, free–form, cobalt blue with gold **35.00**
Children's Dishes
Bowl, 2¼" d, 1" h, red, Flower Gathering **10.00**
Demitasse Set, demitasse pot, creamer, sugar, six cups and

saucers, Parasol C, price for fifteen piece set **65.00**
Creamer, 4" h, Feeding The Carp, ribbed, hourglass shape, red with gold **20.00**
Cup and Saucer
Garden Bench B, pedestal, lobed, scalloped saucer, red with gold, tea **25.00**

Mustache Cup, Rendezvous pattern, melon ribbed, hp, two reserves, red-orange border, beige ground, cherry blossoms, gold stylized waves and crowns, sgd "Kutani," $65.00.

Lady In Rickshaw B, ribbed cup, scalloped saucer, red, demitasse **18.00**
Eggcup, child reaching for butterfly, red with gold **15.00**
Gravy Boat, underplate, Rice Harvesters A, leaf shape, mint green, deep green, and red, gold border **25.00**
Hair Receiver, Garden Bench B, red, maple leaf base **22.00**
Humidor, Battledore pattern, blue scallop, gold line **70.00**
Mustard Jar, Circle Dance, red, gold lacing, spoon **25.00**
Nappy, Temple A, underlying design, hand fluted edge, sea green border, handle **45.00**
Plate
6" d, boy with scythe, cobalt blue with gold **10.00**
7⅜" d, Porch, cobalt blue with gold, fluted swirl, scalloped edge **15.00**
8½" d, children in boat, swirl,

fluted, cobalt blue, gold lacing,
scalloped edge 30.00
Relish Dish, Picnic B, red–orange
with gold, floret edge, reserves 25.00
Rose Bowl, cobalt trim 45.00
Salad Set, red, gold buds, price for
seven piece set 110.00
Salt and Pepper Shakers, pr, 2" h,
Garden Bench F, red–orange
and gold top, cobalt shoulders . 18.00
Tea Set, teapot, sugar, creamer,
five cups and saucers, Geisha In
Sampan B, pink ground, price for
thirteen piece set 50.00
Tray, 5" l, heart shape, oversized
irises, red 15.00
Vase, 9½" h, Foo dog handles . . 130.00

GIRANDOLES AND MANTEL LUSTRES

History: A girandole is a highly elaborate branched candleholder, often featuring cut glass prisms surrounding the mountings. A mantel lustre is a glass vase with attached cut glass prisms.

Girandoles and mantel lustres usually are found in pairs. It is not uncommon for girandoles to be part of a large garniture set. Girandoles and mantel lustres achieved their greatest popularity in the last half of the 19th century both in the United States and Europe.

Brass, eight glass prisms around each candle cup, ten prisms across back, 10½" w, 17" h, price for pair, $350.00.

GIRANDOLES, PR

12" h, bronze, three light, Roman
Centurion form support, missing
some prisms, American, c1855 70.00
14¾" h, figural, peg leg soldier and
child, brass stem, cut glass
prisms 125.00
17¾" h, cast, standing Indian, leaf
and scroll standard, three scrolling candle arms, block base,
19th C 935.00
18" h
Three pcs, white marble base,
gilt brass stem with birds and
flowers, clear cut prisms 395.00
Brass, three arms with prisms . 100.00
21" h, Louis Philippe style, gilt
metal, three candle arms, fac-
eted glass prisms 450.00

MANTEL LUSTERS, PR

12¼" h, cased glass, white ext.,
rose int., painted pink roses,
green leaves 350.00
13" h, gilt bronze and crystal, faceted collar, beaded molded and
engine turned base, ball feet,
late 18th/early 19th C, price for
pair 22,000.00
14" h, ruby glass, enameled for-
get–me–not dec 800.00
20" h, Napoleon III style, gilt
bronze and cranberry glass, hurricane shades . . . .
24½" h, Baccarat style, clear, baluster stem, scalloped dished
drip pan, five ribbed glass
branches, joined by faceted
bead chains with tear shape
drops, swirl molded base, 19th
C 1,325.00

GLASS ANIMALS

History: It did not take glass manufacturers long to realize that there was a ready market for glass novelties. In the early 19th century, walking sticks and witch balls were two dominant forms. As the century ended, glass covered dishes with an animal theme were featured.

In the period between World War I and II, glass manufacturers such as Fostoria Glass Company and A. H. Heisey & Company created a number of glass animal figures for the novelty and decorative–accessory markets. In the 1950s and early 1960s a second glass animal craze swept America led by companies such as Duncan & Miller Glass Company and New Martinsville–Viking Glass Company. A third craze struck in the early 1980s when companies such as Boyd Crystal Art Glass, Guernsey Glass, Pisello Art Glass, and Summit Art Glass began offering the same animal figure in a wide variety of collectible glass colors, with some colors in limited production.

There are two major approaches to glass animal collecting: (a) animal type and (b) manufacturer. Most collectors concentrate on one or more manufacturer, grouping their collections accordingly.

References: *Boyd's Crystal Art Glass: The Tradition Continues,* Boyd's Crystal Art Glass, n.d.; Lee Garmon and Dick Spencer, *Glass Animals of the Depression Era,* Collector Books, 1993; Everett Grist, *Covered Animal Dishes,* Collector Books, 1988, 1993 value update; Frank L. Hahn and Paul Kikeli, *Collector's Guide to Heisey and Heisey By Imperial Glass Animals,* Golden Era Publications, 1991; Todd Holmes, *Boyd Glass Workbook,* published by author, 1992; Evelyn Zemel, *American Glass Animals A to Z,* A to Z Productions, 1978.

Periodical: *Boyd Crystal Art Glass,* PO Box 127, 1203 Morton Ave., Cambridge, OH 43725.

Collectors' Club: Boyd Art Glass Collectors Guild, PO Box 52, Hatboro, PA 19040.

Price Note: Prices are for animal figures in clear (crystal) glass unless otherwise noted.

Bear, sitting, Moser Glass, amber	**40.00**
Bulldog	
Imperial, clear	**30.00**
Tiffin, green	**400.00**
Cat, sitting, Moser Glass, chocolate	**6.00**
Chick, New Martinsville, crystal	**20.00**
Clydesdale Horse, Heisey	**350.00**
Colt	
Balking, Heisey, clear, 3½″ h	**175.00**
Kicking, Heisey, amber, 4″ h	**195.00**

Standing	
Heisey, clear	**80.00**
Imperial, caramel slag	**45.00**
Doe, lily pad base, Tiffin Glass	**125.00**
Dolphin, Baccarat, sgd	**75.00**
Donkey	
Duncan Miller	**165.00**
Heisey, crystal	**225.00**
Imperial, caramel slag	**55.00**
Duck, Viking, 5″ h, brown, amber, green, blue	**15.00**
Elephant, Heisey	**240.00**
Frog, Co–Op Glass Co, green	**85.00**
Gazelle, Heisey	**1,500.00**
Giraffe, Heisey	**200.00**
Goose, Heisey	
Wings down	**400.00**
Wings up	**95.00**
Hen, Heisey	**350.00**
Heron, Duncan Miller	**90.00**
Horse Head, Federal	**10.00**
Jumping Horse, bookends, American	**80.00**
Nautilus, bookend, New Martinsville	**20.00**
Owl	
Degenhart, jade green	**45.00**
Fostoria, clear	**200.00**
Viking, orange	**100.00**
Pelican, Fostoria	**95.00**
Plug Horse, Imperial, Heisey mold, pink, 1978	**35.00**
Scottie	
Heisey	**90.00**
Imperial	**45.00**
Sea Horse, Fostoria	**90.00**
Seal, baby, New Martinsville	**40.00**
Signet, caramel slag, Imperial, Heisey mold	**45.00**
Squirrel, New Martinsville, base missing	**30.00**

Robin, crystal, Westmoreland, $12.00.

Swan
    Cambridge, emerald green, 3" h,
        orig label **25.00**
    Imperial
        Caramel slag **40.00**
        Purple slag **40.00**
    Opalescent
        3½ × 2 x 4", clear and white,
          pressed, English **70.00**
        4¾" × 3 x 6", blue, pressed,
          English, c1880 .... **135.00**
    Terrier, Imperial, Heisey mold, #4,
        doeskin white **52.00**
    Tiger
        Imperial, jade green **15.00**
        New Martinsville **150.00**

GLASS, EARLY AMERICAN

History: Early American glass covers glass made in America from the colonial period through the mid–19th century. As such it includes the early pressed glass and lacy glass made between 1827 and 1840.

Major glass producing centers prior to 1850 were Massachusetts with the New England Glass Company and the Boston and Sandwich Glass Company, South Jersey, Pennsylvania with Stiegel's Manheim factory and Pittsburgh, and Ohio with Kent, Mantua, and Zanesville.

Early American glass was collected heavily during the 1920 to 1950 period. It has now regained some of its earlier popularity. Leading sources for the sale of early American glass are the auctions of Early Auction Company, Garth's, Glass–Works, Heckler & Company, James D. Julia, and Skinner, Inc.

References: William E. Covill, *Ink Bottles and Inkwells*, 1971; Lowell Inness, *Pittsburgh Glass: 1797–1891*, Houghton Mifflin Company, 1976; George and Helen Mc-Kearin, *American Glass*, Crown, 1975; George and Helen McKearin, *Two Hundred Years of American Blown Glass*, Doubleday and Company, 1950; Helen McKearin and Kenneth Wilson, *American Bottles And Flasks*, Crown, 1978; Adeline Pepper, *Glass Gaffers of New Jersey*, Scribners, 1971; Jane S. Spillman, *American and European Pressed Glass*, Corning Museum of Glass, 1981; Kenneth Wilson, *New England Glass And Glassmaking*, Crowell, 1972.

Periodicals: *Antique Bottle & Glass Collector,* PO Box 187, East Greenville, PA 18041; *Glass Collector's Digest,* Antique Publications, PO Box 553, Marietta, OH 45750.

Collectors' Clubs: Early American Glass Traders, RD 5, Box 638, Milford, DE 19963; Glass Research Society of New Jersey, Wheaton Village, Glasstown Rd., Millville, NJ 08332; The National Early American Glass Club, PO Box 8489, Silver Spring, MD 20907.

Museums: Bennington Museum, Bennington, VT; Chrysler Museum, Norfolk, VA; Corning Museum of Glass, Corning, NY; Glass Museum, Dunkirk, IN; Glass Museum Foundation, Redlands, CA; New Bedford Glass Museum, New Bedford, MA; Sandwich Glass Museum, Sandwich, MA; Toledo Museum of Art, Toledo, OH; Wheaton Historical Village Assoc. Museum of Glass, Millville, NJ.

Additional Listings: Blown Three Mold, Cup Plates, Flasks, Sandwich Glass, and Stiegel Type Glass.

Amelung (New Bremen Glass),
   wine, colorless, blown, applied
   dome foot, folded rim, hollow

Whale Oil Lamp, attributed to Boston & Sandwich, Loop pattern, peacock blue, sq base, 8½" h, $990.00.

stem, small bubble in thick solid base, 6⅜" h **275.00**

American Flint Glass Works, Manheim, PA, 1763–74, salt cellar, cobalt blue, fourteen diamonds, double ogee bowl, short stem of same gather, applied circular foot, tooled rim, pontil scar, normal ext. wear, 2" d bowl, 3⅛" h **310.00**

Coventry Glass Works, Coventry, CT, 1820–40, inkwell, dense olive amber, blown three mold, cylindrical, disc mouth, pontil scar, GII-16, 2¼" d, 1⅝" h **130.00**

Ellenville, NY, creamer, brilliant yellow amber. 3¾" h **500.00**

Kent, OH, smelling salts bottle, peacock blue, ovoid, twenty–six vertical molded ribs, sheared mouth and pontil, 3" h **250.00**

Lacy, colorless
Dish, 8¼ x 6¼", rect, Leaf and Gothic Arch, McKearin Pl 150 #5 . . . . **155.00**
Salt
Neal CD5, fiery opal, cov missing, unfilled mold upper edge **80.00**
Neal SD, Strawberry Diamond, flint **145.00**
Neal 002, octagonal, oblong, flint, base chip **65.00**

Mantua
Pan, pale green, sixteen ribs, fold over rim, 16" d **375.00**
Toilet Bottle, deep purple amethyst, ¼ pint, flared, flanged lip, pontil, 4½" h **425.00**

Marlboro Street Glassworks, Keene, NH
Bowl, 1820–40, colorless, blown three mold, inward folded rim, pontil scar, 2⅛" d, 5⅛" w, GIII-20 . . . . **240.00**
Decanter, 1820–40, yellow olive, blown three mold, tooled mouth, pontil scar, pint, ⅛" flake on mouth, GIII-16 . . . . . **375.00**
Dish, 1820–40, colorless, blown three mold, folded rim, pontil scar, 6" d, 1½" h, GIII-20 . . . . **120.00**
Flask
Ribbed, 1815–30, yellow olive, melon form, twenty vertical ribs, applied collared mouth, pontil scar, mint. haze, 1" hairline crack, 7" h **175.00**
Sunburst, 1815–30, medium green, sheared mouth, pontil scar, pint, GVIII-2 . . . . **670.00**

Midwest
Flask, 1820–40, deep orange amber, pattern molded, twenty–four vertical ribs, flattened chestnut form, sheared mouth, pontil scar, some faint int. haze, 5⅛" h **240.00**
Salt Cellar, 1820–50, cobalt blue, pattern molded, twenty–six vertical ribs, ribbed double ogee bowl and stem, applied circular foot, tooled rim, pontil scar, some minor int. haze, 2⅞" h **160.00**

New England
Blacking Bottle, 1830–60, sq, tooled mouth, pontil scar
Olive amber, 4⅝" h **70.00**
Yellow olive, 5" h **70.00**
Bottle, 1780–1830, freeblown, globular
Dark olive green, applied collared mouth, pontil scar, some minor ext. scratches, 8¼" h **390.00**
Light green, applied mouth, pontil scar, some faint int. haze, 4½" d, 7" h **250.00**
Chestnut Bottle, 1780–1830, bright yellow olive, applied mouth, pontil scar, 5¼" h **190.00**
Gin Bottle, 1800–30, deep yellow olive, freeblown, sq tapered form, applied mouth, pontil scar, some int. residue, 16¼" h **700.00**

New Jersey, South
Bank, blown, colorless, applied rigaree and prunts, arch of four applied struts, applied chicken finial, solid ball stem attached to thick round base, 10⅜" h . **1,200.00**
Creamer, cobalt blue, applied foot, handle, ring, and gadrooning, threaded lip, 4⅛" h **575.00**

New York, compote, colorless, freeblown, thick applied base, polished pontil **75.00**

Pitkin Glass Works, Manchester, CT, 1783–1830, inkwell, medium yellow olive, thirty–six ribs swirled to left, sq, disc mouth, pontil scar, minor damage, repairs, 2⅜" l, 1⅝" h **250.00**

Pittsburgh
Lamp, colorless, pressed base, blown hollow stem and font, wafers, cut foliage, panels, strawberry diamonds, and fans, pewter collar, minor chips on base, 12¼" h **575.00**

Sugar, colorless, applied domed foot with blue rim, blue looping on bowl and domed cov, clear finial, shallow flake on foot, 9⅞" h, ...**1,150.00**

Tumbler, 1860–80, cobalt blue, pressed, hexagonal, tooled rim, smooth base, 3¼" d, 3⅝" h **90.00**

Stoddard, NH
Ink Bottle, 1845–60, deep olive amber, Farleys, octagonal, tooled mouth, pontil scar, 1⅞" d, 1¾" h **475.00**

Pickle Jar, golden amber, 1860–80, cloverleaf, rolled mouth, smooth base, 8⅛" h **450.00**

Unknown
Freeblown
Bowl, 1840–60, sapphire blue, cylindrical, applied pedestal foot, folded rim, pontil scar, 4" d, 3" h **325.00**

Flip Glass, colorless, matching cov with finial, sheared rim, pontil scar, flat chip on cov finial, 5" d, 8¾" h **80.00**

Jar, yellow olive, tapered gin form, expanded mouth, tooled flared mouth, pontil scar, some ext. wear, burst bubble on int. of mouth, 9⅝" h **700.00**

Saddle Flask, 1750–60, bright yellow olive, flattened oval, long neck, sheared mouth, smooth base, 13⅛" h **200.00**

Witch Ball, 1840–60, bright sapphire blue, faint cobalt striations, sheared mouth, smooth base, 6" d **180.00**

Pattern Molded
Inkwell, 1840–60, cobalt blue, cylindrical, twelve vertical ribs, sheared mouth, matching lid, delicately applied knob, pontil scar, ⅜" bruise on lid, 2⅝" d, 2¼" h **150.00**

Pomade Jar, 1840–60, cobalt blue, cylindrical, twelve vertical ribs, sheared rim, matching lid, delicately applied knob, pontil scar, 3¼" h **150.00**

Spirits Bottle, 1800–40, light green, fourteen vertical ribs, flask form, half post construction method, tooled mouth, pontil scar, some ext. scratches, 6½" h **150.00**

Pillar Molded, decanter, colorless, eight ribs, flint, rare matching orig stopper with air trap, polished pontil, fire polished, c1850, 13" h **195.00**

Westford, CT, flask, 1860–72, olive amber, pictorial, sheaf of wheat, applied double collared mouth, smooth base, pint, GXIII-36 . . . **130.00**

Zanesville, OH, bottle, 1820–40, golden amber, twenty–four swirled ribs, globular, rolled mouth, pontil scar, three shallow bubble bursts, 7⅜" h **260.00**

GOLDSCHEIDER

History: Friedrich Goldscheider founded a porcelain and faience factory in Vienna, Austria, in 1885. Upon his death, his widow carried on operations. In 1920 Walter and Marcell, Friedrich's sons, gained control. During the Art Deco period, the firm commissioned several artists to create figural statues, among which were Pierrettes and sleek wolfhounds. During the 1930s, the company's products were mostly traditional.

In the early 1940s, the Goldscheiders fled to the United States and re-established operations in Trenton, New Jersey. The Goldscheider Everlast Corporation was listed in Trenton city directories between 1943 and 1950. Goldscheider Ceramics, located at

1441 Heath Avenue, Trenton, New Jersey, was listed in the *1952 Crockery and Glass Journal Directory.* The firm was not listed in 1954.

Bust, 5¾" h, gray and blue, USA and Everlast mark **15.00**
Figure
  8¾" h, dancer, one arm extended holding floral skirt, stamped "Lorenzl" and numbered **1,500.00**
  9" h, Madonna, sgd **65.00**
  10" h, exotic girl holding fan, wearing flowing gown, c1930 **700.00**
  10¾" h, woman seated on Empire style chair, wearing elaborate tiered gown and dancing slippers, holding mask in one hand, inscribed "Padola," printed figural factory mark with "Goldscheider Wien," imp 4684 . . . . **475.00**
  20¼" h, Moroccan woman, bronze, greenish–brown patina, inscribed "Celine Lepage," stamped "4" and "Made in France," imp "Goldscheider/LaStele" exhibition seal **17,600.00**
Lamp Base, 32" h, figural, standing bare breasted female, long lavender gown, holding garland of fruit and grains, column standard, stepped base, printed and imp marks, matching silk beaded shade, minor restoration to base **2,200.00**
Plaque, 13½" w, 25⅛" h, earthenware, rect, molded, maiden in profile, garland of blossoms and berries in hair, large blossom and cluster on left, earth tones, designer sgd "Lamassi," Goldscheider mark, c1900 . . . . **1,000.00**

GONDER POTTERY

History: Lawton Gonder established Gonder Ceramic Arts, Inc., at Zanesville, Ohio, in 1941. He had gained experience while working for other factories in the area. Gonder experimented with glazes, including Chinese crackle, gold crackle, and flambé. Lamp bases were manufactured under the name "Eglee" at a second plant location.

Gonder pieces are clearly marked. The company ceased operation in 1957.

References: Susan and Al Bagdade, *Warman's American Pottery and Porcelain,* Wallace–Homestead, 1994; Ron Hoppes, *The Collector's Guide and History of Gonder Pottery,* L–W Book Sales, 1992.

Periodical: *Gonder Pottery Collectors' Newsletter,* PO Box 3174, Shawnee, KS 66203.

Collectors' Club: Gonder Collectors, PO Box 21, Crooksville, OH 43731.

Bowl
  6" d, 2½" h, turquoise ext., brown int. **10.00**
  7¾" d, 7" h, blue and brown glossy glaze, swirl, flower frog **20.00**
Cornucopia, 7" h, turquoise and brown, marked "E5" **15.00**
Ewer
  6" h, gray, fluted **10.00**
  12" h, figural swan **30.00**
Figure
  Oriental man and woman, price for pr **55.00**
  Panther, 18¼" l, jade green . . . **85.00**
Planter, gondola **25.00**
Tea Set, cov teapot, creamer, and

Figure, green dress, rose ribbon, tan base, marked "F. G. Wien," 9″ h, $20.00.

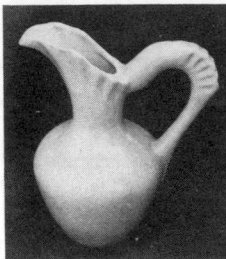

Ewer, light green, matte finish, marked "Gonder USA H34," 9" h, $30.00.

cov sugar, brown mottled, price
for three piece set **25.00**
Vase, 9" h, mottled turquoise and
brown, pink int. **20.00**

GOOFUS GLASS

History: Goofus glass, also known as Mexican Ware, Hooligan glass, and Pickle glass, is a pressed glass with relief designs. The back or front was painted. The designs are usually in red and green with a metallic gold ground. It was popular from 1890 to 1920 and was used as a premium at carnivals.

It was produced by several companies: Cresent Glass Company, Wellsburg, West Virginia; Imperial Glass Corporation, Bellaire, Ohio; LaBelle Glass Works, Bridgeport, Ohio; and Northwood Glass Co., Indiana, Pennsylvania, Wheeling, West Virginia, and Bridgeport, Ohio. Northwood marks include "N," "N" in one circle, "N" in two circles, and one or two circles without the "N."

Goofus glass lost its popularity when people found the paint tarnished or scaled off after repeated washings and wear. No record of its manufacture has been found after 1920.

References: Carolyn McKinley, *Goofus Glass,* Collector Books, 1984, out–of–print; Ellen T. Schroy, *Warman's Glass,* Wallace-Homestead, 1992.

Periodical: *Goofus Glass Gazette,* 9 Linewood Ct., Sterling, VA 20165.

Bowl, relief molded
  9" d, red roses, ruffled rim **20.00**
  10¾" d, red roses **40.00**
  11" d, red cherries, ruffled rim . **25.00**
Bread Plate, relief molded, Last
  Supper scene **50.00**
Compote, 10¼" d, relief molded,
  red fruit **65.00**
Dish, 7¼" d, fluted, green, floral
  dec **12.00**

Plate, Old Rose Distilling Co., Chicago, 8¼" h, $65.00.

Plate, relief molded
  5¾" d, red rose, lattice dec . . . **20.00**
  6" d, red sunflower center **8.00**
  7" d, red thistle, adv **125.00**
  8" d, red apples **15.00**
Saltshaker, 4" h, Grape and Leaf
  pattern **20.00**
Tray, 11" l, bronze and red, chry-
  santhemum **35.00**
Vase
  7½" h, relief molded, red grapes **20.00**
  8" h, purple, Grape pattern **20.00**
  9" h, Cockatoo **55.00**
  10½" h, Peacock pattern **75.00**
Wall Pocket, 7¾" h, relief molded,
  bird and grapes dec **55.00**

MARK

W H GOSS

GOSS CHINA AND CRESTED WARE

History: In 1858 William H. Goss opened his Henley factory and produced terra–cotta ware. A year later he moved to Stoke–on–Trent and added Parian ware to his line. In 1883 Adolphus, William's son, expanded on his father's idea of decorating small ivory pots and vases, with the coat of arms of schools, hospitals, colleges [especially Oxford and Cambridge], and other motifs to appeal to the souvenir–seeking English "day–tripper." The forms used were copied from ancient artifacts in museums.

William died in 1906, his son in 1913. Following business setbacks, the firm was sold in 1929 to Geo. Jones & Sons Ltd., who had previously acquired Arcadian, Swan, and other firms that made crested wares. As late as 1931 the Goss name was still being used. In 1936–37 Cauldon Potteries purchased the Goss assets. Production ceased in 1940. In 1954 Ridgeway and Adderley acquired all Goss assets [molds, patterns, designs, and right to use the Goss name and trademark].

From 1883 to 1931 pieces carried the mark of "GOSHAWK", with "W. H. Goss" beneath and "England" on later pieces. Many early examples carry an impressed "W. H. Goss," either with or without the printed mark.

Other manufacturers of crested ware in England were: Arcadian, Carlton China, Grafton China, Savoy China, Shelley, and Willow Art. Gemma in Germany also made crested wares.

Crests are of little value unless they match, e.g., Shakespeare's jug with Shakespeare's crest. Collectors tend to collect one form (vase, ewer, jug, etc.), one particular crest, or one type of object (boat, cat, dog, etc.). Price is determined not by crest, but size, condition, and bottom mark.

References: Sandy Andrews, *Crested China: The History of Heraldic Souvenir Ware,* Milestone Publications [England]; John Galpin, *A Handbook Of Goss China,* Milestone Publications; Nicholas Pine, *The 1984 Price Guide To Goss China,* Milestone Publications, 1984; Nicholas Pine and Sandy Andrews, *The 1984 Price Guide To Crested China* (including revisions to *Crested China*), Milestone Publications; Roland Ward, *The Price Guide To The Models Of W. H. Goss,* Antiques Collectors' Club.

Collectors' Clubs: Crested Circle, 75 Cannon Grove, Fetcham, Leatherhead Surrey KT22 9LP England; Goss Collectors Club, 4 Khasiaberry, Walnut Tree, Milton Keynes MK7 7DP England.

Vase, model of Roman vase found at Walmar Lodge, 2⅝" h, $25.00.

GOSS

Basket, 2⅔" h, Craignez Honte crest, gilt trim, center handle, ftd	**15.00**
Bottle, Swiss Vinegar, Wymondham	**20.00**
Building	
Huers House	**200.00**
Manx Cottage	**100.00**
Shakespeare's House	**100.00**
Carafe, Goodwin Sands, Hastings crest	**15.00**
Creamer, 2¼" h, City Arms London crest, white, rust, and gilt	**15.00**
Ewer	
Arundel	**20.00**

Herne Bay, Sea of York crest .. 18.00
Jar, Basingstoke crest 18.00
Jug
    Dorchester, Fowey crest 15.00
    Litchfield, Warwick 30.00
    Night–Light, 6″ h, Robert Burns .. 150.00
Pitcher, Devon Oak, Warwick crest 15.00
Porringer, Deconport 35.00
Vase
    Colchester Famous, Walton
      Naze crest 18.00
    Glastonbury, Tonbridge Wells
      crest 15.00
    Lewes Roman, Ramsgate crest 10.00
    Pineapple, City of Edinburgh .. 30.00

**OTHER CRESTED WARE
MANUFACTURERS**

Arcadian
    Bathing Wagon, Stockbridge .. 30.00
    Building, 5½″ l, Worcester Ca-
      thedral with crest 100.00
Carlton, vase, Keswick 20.00
Clifton, toothpick, 2″ h, St Asaph
    crest 22.00
Coronet Ware, pourer, 2¾″ h,
    green, orange, and green crest,
    gilt trim, crown mark 25.00
Florentine
    Seashell, 4″ l, Sea crest, orange,
      blue, and yellow, molded body,
      gilt trim, marked 25.00
    Tower, Blackpool 25.00
Foley China, bowl, 2″ d, Arms of
    Stratford on Avon, Shakespeare
    crest 30.00
Gemma
    Pot, 1⅝″ h, multicolored Margate
      crest, ribbed alternating pan-
      els, marked 12.00
    Teapot, cov, Salesbury 30.00
Shelley
    Creamer, Hawick crest 15.00
    Cup and Saucer, Braemer crest 30.00
    Hatpin holder, Turnridge Wells
      crest 50.00
    Olive Jar, Sussex 25.00
    Tea Caddy, Abbey of Glaston-
      bury 25.00
Wildman, sugar bowl, Quebec
    crest 8.00

MADE IN

Zuid Holland

GOUDA POTTERY

History: Gouda and its surrounding area in Holland has been one of the principle Dutch pottery centers for centuries. Originally the potteries produced a simple utilitarian Delft–type earthenware with a tin glaze and the famous clay smoker's pipes.

When the pipe making portion declined in the early 1900s, the Gouda potteries turned to art pottery. Influenced by the Art Nouveau and Art Deco movements, artists expressed themselves with free–form and stylized designs in bold colors.

Reference: Susan and Al Bagdade, *Warman's English & Continental Pottery & Porcelain, Second Edition,* Wallace–Homestead, 1991.

Periodical: *The Dutch Potter,* 47 London Terrace, New Rochelle, NY 10804.

Reproduction Alert: With the Art Nouveau and Art Deco revivals of recent years, modern reproductions of Gouda pottery currently are on the market. They are difficult to distinguish from the originals.

Basket, 6″ d, 7¾″ h, high gloss
    glaze, floral dec 150.00
Biscuit Jar, cov, 8″ h, multicolored 130.00
Bowl, 5½″ d, 3½″ h, Damascus
    mark 50.00
Candlesticks, pr, 7⅛″ h, 4⅛″ d,
    Spino pattern, yellow flowers,
    green leaves, black ground,
    satin finish, house mark 165.00
Charger, 12″ d, multicolored flow-
    ers, rope border, black rim 150.00
Compote, 7⅝″ h, black ground,
    geometric design, multicolored
    scroll int. 165.00
Dish, 8″ d, 4″ h, three sections,
    handle, brick, cream, blue, and
    gold dec, black ground, satin fin-
    ish, crown mark and "Regina" . 85.00
Ewer, 11½″ h, extended bark neck,
    twig handle, scenic, windmill on

obverse, lake on reverse, marked "Springer & Co/Elfangen, Germany," c1890 .... 150.00

Humidor, 6″ h, white high gloss glaze, floral dec, Jilliana Gouda house mark 250.00

Incense Burner, 8″ h, Roba pattern, flowers and geometrics, green ground 100.00

Inkwell, 8″ w, attached pen tray, matte finish, blue, Purdah Gouda, orange and black house mark 200.00

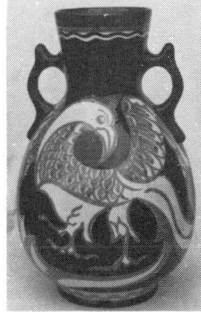

Vase, black ground, white Phoenix bird dec, 10½″ h, $235.00

Jug, 10″ h, orig stopper, multicolored dec, black matte ground .. 175.00

Pitcher, 6½″ h 125.00

Planter, 12″ l, 7″ w, 4″ h, rect, Yssel pattern 150.00

Plate, 10½″ d, matte finish, multicolored dec 100.00

Potpourri Jar, 4″ h, high gloss glaze, multicolored dec, black base 85.00

Tray, 10½″ l, leaf dec, autumn colors 150.00

Tumbler, 4⅜″ h, 3⅝″ d, multicolored flowers, green leaves, black ground, satin finish, marked "Nerf" and house mark 55.00

Vase
2½″ h, matte, starburst floral, black, Arnhem 35.00
5¼″ h, 6″ w across handles,

black matte finish, wide cobalt and multicolored band, Blareth house mark 60.00

11″ h, high glaze, Art Nouveau design, Zuid, c1896 .... 650.00

GRANITEWARE

History: Graniteware is the name commonly given to iron or steel kitchenware covered with enamel coating.

The first graniteware was made in Germany in the 1830s. Graniteware was not produced in the United States until the 1860s. At the start of World War I, when European manufacturers turned to the making of war weapons, American producers took over the market.

Colors commonly marketed were white and gray. Each company made their own special color, including shades of blue, green, brown, violet, cream, and red.

Older graniteware is heavier than new graniteware. Pieces with cast iron handles date from 1870 to 1890; wood handles date from 1900 to 1910. Other dating clues are seams, wood knobs, and tin lids.

References: Helen Greguire, *The Collector's Encyclopedia of Granite Ware: Colors Shapes and Values,* Book 1 (1990, 1994 value update), Book 2 (1993), Collector Books; Dana G. Morykan and Harry L. Rinker, *Warman's Country Antiques & Collectibles, Second Edition* Wallace–Homestead, 1994.

Collectors' Club: National Graniteware Society, PO Box 10013, Cedar Rapids, IA 52410–0013.

Reproduction Alert: Graniteware still is manufactured in many of the traditional forms and colors.

Additional Listings: See *Warman's Americana & Collectibles* for more examples.

Baking Pan, blue and gray mottled 20.00

Bread Pan, 16½″ d, 12″ h, perforated domed lid, ftd 35.00

Butter, cov, cobalt blue and white mottle 195.00

Candleholder, red, leaf shape ... 55.00

Casserole, cov, cobalt blue and white swirl 45.00

Coffee Boiler, gray	25.00
Coffeepot, gray	45.00
Colander, blue and white swirl, large	175.00
Cream Pail, white, red trim	30.00
Cuspidor, gray mottled, marked "Agate Ware"	20.00
Custard Cup, blue and white swirl, large	65.00
Dipper, red and white	15.00
Double Boiler, blue and white swirl	300.00
Funnel, blue and gray mottle	45.00
Iron, base, blue, orig box	60.00
Kettle	
Cobalt blue swirl	75.00
Green swirl	75.00

Berry Pail, gray and black, 7" d, 4¾" h, $35.00.

Ladle, 12" l, gray mottle	25.00
Measure, gray, pint	25.00
Milk Pan, 11 x 2½", gray mottled	20.00
Mold, gray	45.00
Muffin Tin, 8 cup	45.00
Pie Pan, 8¾" d, Crystolite	25.00
Pitcher and Bowl Set, white, blue trim	48.00
Platter, blue and white mottled, large	70.00
Roaster, cov, 22 x 10", blue and white	20.00
Salt Box, hanging, white, German	95.00
Sieve, gray, pan style	15.00
Skimmer, blue and purple mottle	35.00
Tea Strainer, 3" d, white, handle	10.00

Teapot, cov, blue, pewter trim, marked "Manning–Bowman"	45.00
Tray, 18" d, red and white swirl	35.00
Washboard, blue	55.00

K.G.

GREENAWAY, KATE

History: Kate Greenaway, or "K.G." as she initialed her famous drawings, was born in 1846 in London. Her father was a prominent wood engraver. Kate's natural talent for drawing soon was evident, and she began art classes at the age of 12. In 1868 she had her first public exhibition.

Her talents were used primarily in illustrating. She did cards for Marcus Ward, which are largely unsigned. China and pottery companies soon had her drawings of children appearing on many of their wares. By the 1880s she was one of the foremost children's book illustrators in England.

Reference: Ina Taylor, *The Art of Kate Greenaway: A Nostalgic Portrait of Childhood,* Pelican Publishing, 1991.

Collectors' Club: Kate Greenaway Society, PO Box 8, Norwood, PA 19074.

Reproduction Alert: Some Greenaway buttons have been reproduced in Europe and sold in the United States.

Almanac, 1881, George Routledge & Sons, $115.00.

Biscuit Jar, cov, boy, pastel dec .. 150.00
Book
Birthday Book For Children, 1st
ed, 1880, George Routledge &
Sons 95.00
The Language of Flowers, Kate
Greenaway, illus, 1887, Fred-
erick Warne & Co, Ltd 65.00
The Pied Piper of Hamelin, Rob-
ert Browning, Kate Greena-
way, illus, George Routledge &
Sons 125.00
Bowl, amber, Daisy and Button
pattern, figural girl and dog,
Reed and Barton SP holder ... 500.00
Children's Dishes, cup, saucer,
and 6" plate, price for three piece
set 100.00
Cup and Saucer, Minton 47.50
Figure
7" h, girl holding pug dog, sgd . 175.00
9½" h, children jumping rope, pr 600.00
Match Holder, girl helping little sister over log, place for matches
and striker 85.00
Mug, SS, engraved "Bessie 1882" 60.00
Plate, 9" d, children playing, oversized fruit, birds, and flowers .. 95.00
Print, *Outdoor Tea Party*, fifteen
girls, sgd 85.00
Salt and Pepper Shakers, pr, 4" h,
boy and girl in long coats, girl
with muff 80.00
Sugar Shaker, boy in long coat,
porcelain 95.00
Tea Set, floral motif, marked
"Semi–Porcelain," price for three
piece set 60.00
Thimble Holder, girl holds SS thim-
ble 125.00
Tile, Pipe Thee High, small boy
with horn, Wedgwood 75.00
Toothpick Holder, SP, ornate, girl,
standing, marked "Tufts" 175.00

GREENTOWN GLASS

History: The Indiana Tumbler and Goblet
Co., Greentown, Indiana, produced its first
clear, pressed glass table and bar wares in
late 1894. Initial success led to a doubling
of plant size in 1895 and other subsequent
expansions, one in 1897 to allow for the
manufacture of colored glass. In 1899 the
firm joined the combine known as the National Glass Company.

In 1900, just before arriving in Greentown, Jacob Rosenthal developed an
opaque brown glass, called "chocolate,"
which ranged in color from a dark, rich
chocolate to a lighter "cream" coffee hue.
Production of chocolate glass saved the fi-
nancially pressed Indiana Tumbler and
Goblet Works. The Cactus and Leaf Bracket
patterns were made almost exclusively in
chocolate glass. Other popular chocolate
patterns are Austrian, Dewey, Shuttle, and
Teardrop and Tassel. In 1902 National
Glass Company bought Rosenthal's chocolate glass formula so other plants in the
combine could use the color.

In 1902 Rosenthal developed the Golden
Agate and Rose Agate colors. All work
ceased on June 13, 1903, when a fire of
suspicious origin destroyed the Indiana
Tumbler and Goblet Company Works.

After the fire, other companies, e.g.,
McKee and Brothers, produced chocolate
glass in the same pattern design used in
Greentown. Later reproductions also have
taken place, with Cactus among the most
heavily copied pattern.

References: Brenda Measell and James
Measell, *A Guide To Reproductions of
Greentown Glass*, 2nd ed., The Printing
Press, 1974; James Measell, *Greentown
Glass: The Indiana Tumbler & Goblet Co.*,
Grand Rapids Public Museum, 1979, 1992–
93 value update, distributed by Antique
Publications.

Collectors' Club: National Greentown
Glass Assoc, 19596 Glendale Ave., South
Bend, IN 46637.

Museums: Grand Rapids Public Museum, Ruth Herrick Greentown Glass Collection, Grand Rapids, MI; Greentown
Glass Museum, Greentown, IN.

Additional Listings: Holly Amber and
Pattern Glass.

Berry Bowl, Beaded Grape, green,
gold trim 42.00
Berry Set
Cactus, chocolate, 8¼" d bowl,
six sauces, price for seven
piece set 420.00

Tumbler, Shuttle pattern, choco-late, 3⅞" h, $50.00.

Leaf Bracket, chocolate, price
for nine piece set **250.00**
Bowl
   Geneva, chocolate, 8¼ x 15" .. **160.00**
   Six Fluted, chocolate **150.00**
Butter, cov, Geneva, chocolate .. **450.00**
Children's Set, Wild Rose and
   Bowknot, white **295.00**
Creamer
   Cactus, chocolate **110.00**
   Dewey, amber, 5" h **25.00**
   Indian Head, Nile green **475.00**
Cruet
   Geneva, chocolate **1,000.00**
   Wild Rose & Bowknot, chocolate **300.00**
Dolphin
   Chocolate, sawtooth, no lid,
     some damage **50.00**
   Golden agate, red agate lid ...**1,100.00**
Goblet
   Beehive **60.00**
   Diamond Prisms **65.00**
Iced Tea Tumbler, Leaf Bracket,
   chocolate, minor flaws **35.00**
Jelly Compote, Cactus, chocolate **100.00**
Mug, cov, Troubadour, milk glass **60.00**
Nappy, Leaf Bracket, chocolate .. **50.00**
Pitcher
   Dewey, sun turned amethyst .. **50.00**
   Ruffled Eye, chocolate **500.00**
Relish, Leaf & Bracket, chocolate **70.00**
Sauce, chocolate
   Six Fluted **225.00**
   Water Lily and Cattail **90.00**
Spooner, Wild Rose and Bowknot,
   chocolate **135.00**
Sugar, cov, Geneva, chocolate .. **250.00**

Syrup, Cord Drapery, chocolate . **225.00**
Tray, Venetian, chocolate **275.00**
Tumbler, chocolate
   Cactus **65.00**
   Geneva **95.00**
   Icicle **125.00**
Wine, Shuttle, clear **15.00**

GRUEBY POTTERY

History: William Grueby was active in the
ceramic industry for several years before
he developed his own method of producing
matte–glazed pottery and founded the
Grueby Faience Company in Boston, Massachusetts, in 1897.

The art pottery was hand thrown in natural shapes, hand molded, and hand tooled.
A variety of colored glazes, singly or in combinations, were produced with green being
the most prominent. In 1908 the firm was
divided into the Grueby Pottery Company
and the Grueby Faience and Tile Co., the
latter making art pottery until bankruptcy
forced closure shortly after 1908.

References: Paul Evans, *Art Pottery of
the United States, 2nd Edition,* Feingold &
Lewis Publishing, 1987; Ralph and Terry
Kovel, *Kovels' American Art Pottery: The
Collector's Guide To Makers, Marks and
Factory Histories,* Crown Publishers, 1993.

Candleholder, 6" d, 2" h, double
   handled dish, dark matte blue
   glaze, imp mark, orig paper label **360.00**
Jardiniere, 7" h, carved leaf and
   white matte enameled flower
   dec, textured butterscotch yellow matte glaze, imp mark, artist's initials **4,400.00**
Paperweight, 2¾" d, blue disk,

carved spread wing scarab, matte yellow glaze, imp mark .. **250.00**

Tile, Faience

3" l, 6" w, rect, ivory ground, black outlines, matte green glaze, imp "Grueby Tile Boston" and artist's initials, price for set of 6 .... **375.00**

6⅛" l, ivory capped blue wave and sailing ship dec, matte blue glaze, sgd initials "M D" **695.00**

Vase, bulbous body, tapered neck, oatmeal glaze, marked "Grueby Pottery/Boston/USA" in circle, 6" h, $235.00.

Vase

5½" h, low relief leaves and bud stems dec, matte green glaze, imp mark **810.00**

8" h, alternating leaf panels, six yellow buds dec, dark green matte glaze, Ruth Erickson potter **1,320.00**

11½" h, ovoid, three hand molded yellow jonquil blossoms, spike leaf cluster, green matte glaze, imp mark and label **3,025.00**

12" h, relief leaves and bud stems dec, matte green glaze, imp mark **2,075.00**

13¼" h, ovoid body molded with overlapping leaf tips with flower stalks and buds growing up shoulder, cylindrical neck, avocado green glaze, imp factory mark, incised artist's monogram, designed by Marie Seaman, early 20th C **3,300.00**

HAIR ORNAMENTS

History: Hair ornaments, one of the first accessories developed by primitive man, were used to remove tangles and keep hair out of one's face. Remnants of early combs have been found in many archaeological excavations.

As fashion styles changed through the centuries, hair ornaments kept pace through design and use changes. Hair combs and other hair ornaments are made in a wide variety of materials, e.g., precious metals, ivory, tortoiseshell, plastics, and wood.

Combs were first made in America during the Revolution when imports from England were restricted. Early American combs were made of horn and treasured as valued toiletry articles.

Reference: Evelyn Haetig, *Antique Combs and Purses,* Gallery Graphics Press, 1983.

Collectors' Clubs: Antique Fancy Comb Collectors Club, 4901 Grandview, Ypsilanti, MI 48197; National Antique Comb Collectors Club, 3748 Sunray Dr., Holiday, FL 34691.

Museums: Leominster Historical Society, Field School Museum, Leominster, MA; Miller's Museum of Antique Combs, Homer, AK.

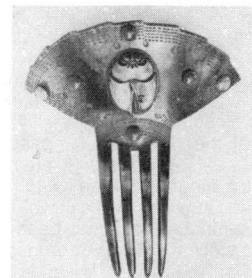

Comb, Bakelite, fan-shaped, olive, black stripes, applied blue and red plastic ovals, center scarab beetle, punched line work, 5" l, $40.00.

Back Comb
Bakelite, coral and gold wash fil-
igree, Victorian, c1890 . . . . . . 250.00
Celluloid, Spanish, Art Nouveau,
c1910 . . . . 85.00
Clip, rhinestone dec, c1930, price
for pair 20.00
Comb, sterling silver, French, Vic-
torian, c1860 . . . . 225.00
Hairpin
Amber, Art Deco, c1925 . . . . . . 45.00
Tortoiseshell, sterling filigree,
English, Victorian, c1890 . . . . 65.00
Headband, Edwardian, 14K yellow
gold, double band, engraved
scroll and leaf dec, gold hairpins 425.00
Ornament
Celluloid
French, Art Nouveau, c1910 . 55.00
Victorian, c1900 . . . . 35.00
Tortoiseshell, Art Nouveau,
c1910 . . . . 65.00
Side Comb, celluloid, Victorian,
c1890 . . . . 25.00

HALL CHINA COMPANY

History: Robert Hall founded the Hall
China Company in 1903 in East Liverpool,
Ohio. He died in 1904 and was succeeded
by his son, Robert Taggart Hall. After years
of experimentation, Robert T. Hall developed a leadless glaze in 1911, opening the
way for production of glazed household
products.

The Hall China Company made many
types of kitchenware, refrigerator sets, and
dinnerware in a wide variety of patterns.
Some patterns were exclusive, such as
Heather Rose for Sears.

One of the most popular patterns was
Autumn Leaf, an exclusive premium designed by Arden Richards in 1933 for the
Jewel Tea Company. Still a Jewel Tea property, Autumn Leaf has not been listed in
catalogs since 1978 but is produced on a
replacement basis with the date stamped
on the back.

References: Susan and Al Bagdade,
Warman's American Pottery and Porcelain,
Wallace–Homestead, 1994; Harvey Duke,
Hall: Price Guide Update, ELO Books,
1992; Harvey Duke, *Hall 2,* ELO Books,

1985; Harvey Duke, *Superior Quality Hall
China,* ELO Books, 1977; Harvey Duke,
*The Official Price Guide To Pottery And
Porcelain, Eighth Edition,* House of Collect-
ibles, 1994; C. L. Miller, *The Jewel Tea
Company: Its History and Products,* Schif-
fer Publishing, 1994; Dana G. Morykan and
Harry L. Rinker, *Warman's Country An-
tiques & Collectibles, 2nd Edition,* Wallace–
Homestead, 1994; Margaret and Kenn
Whitmyer, *The Collector's Encyclopedia of
Hall China, 2nd Edition,* Collector Books,
1994.

Periodicals: *The Daze,* PO Box 57, Otisville, MI 48463; *The Hall China Encore,* 317
N. Pleasant St., Oberlin, OH 44074.

Collectors' Clubs: Autumn Leaf Reis-
sues Assoc., 19238 Dorchester Circle,
Strongsville, OH 44136; National Autumn
Leaf Collectors Club, 7346 Shamrock Dr.,
Indianapolis, IN 46217.

Additional Listings: See *Warman's
Americana & Collectibles* for more examples.

MISCELLANEOUS

Bean Pot, cov, New England,
Chinese Red 40.00
Candlestick, Palmer House, green 25.00
Casserole, cov, 8½" d, General
Electric, round, gray, yellow lid . 20.00
Coffee Server, Flare–Ware, brass
warmer, 15 cup 25.00
Leftover, cov
General Electric, gray, yellow lid,
6" d, round 15.00
Hotpoint, 7½" d, round, maroon 30.00
Punch Set, Old Crow, punch bowl,
ladle, nine cups 165.00
Roaster, cov, Queen, delf 20.00
Water Server, General Electric,
gray, yellow lid 25.00

PATTERNS

Autumn Leaf. Premium for Jewel
Tea Co. Produced from 1933 until 1978.

Bean Pot, two handles 200.00
Butter, ¼ lb 200.00
Cream Soup 30.00
French Baker, 6¼" 125.00

Marmalade, 3 pcs	**85.00**
Plate	
6½" d	**6.00**
8" d	**9.50**
Platter, 9" l	**12.00**
Vegetable, oval	**20.00**
Warmer, round	**100.00**

Heather Rose. Produced during the 1940s.

Bowl, 6" d	**3.50**
Creamer and Sugar, cov	**12.00**
Cup and Saucer	**4.50**
Gravy Boat and Underplate	**10.00**
Plate, 10" d	**4.00**
Tureen, cov	**18.00**

Orange Poppy. Premium for Great American Tea Co. Produced from 1933 through 1950s.

Baker, fluted	**12.00**
Casserole, cov, oval	**30.00**
Creamer and Sugar	**24.00**
Cup and Saucer	**7.00**
Jug, 6½" h	**15.00**
Plate, 9" d	**7.50**
Water Server, green	**20.00**

Springtime. Premium for Standard Tea Co. Limited production.

Cake Plate	**12.00**
Creamer and Sugar, cov	**15.00**
Cup and Saucer	**5.00**
Gravy	**8.00**
Pie Baker	**22.00**
Plate	
6¼" d	**1.00**
9" d	**4.50**
Platter, 13" l	**15.00**

Teapot, blue, gold trim, $30.00.

Soup Plate	**5.25**
Teapot, cov	**40.00**

TEAPOTS

Aladdin, yellow, gold dec, round infuser	**40.00**
Basket, yellow	**75.00**
Boston, Addison, gold dec, 6 cup	**35.00**
Globe, inverted spout, lemon	**60.00**
Nautilus, yellow, gold dec	**65.00**
New York, brown, gold dec	**25.00**
Philadelphia, ivory, gold dec, 6 cup	**35.00**
Sanigrid, Chinese Red, 6 cup	**35.00**
Windshield, maroon, gold flowers	**20.00**

HAMPSHIRE POTTERY

History: In 1871 James S. Taft founded the Hampshire Pottery Company in Keene, New Hampshire. Production began with redwares and stonewares, followed by majolica decorated wares in 1879. A semi-porcelain, with the recognizable matte glazes plus the Royal Worcester glaze, was introduced in 1883.

Until World War I the factory made an extensive line of utilitarian and art wares including souvenir items. After the war the firm resumed operations, but only made hotel dinnerware and tiles. The company was dissolved in 1923.

References: Susan and Al Bagdade, *Warman's American Pottery and Porcelain,* Wallace–Homestead, 1994; Ralph and Terry Kovel, *Kovels' American Art Pottery: The Collector's Guide To Makers, Marks and Factory Histories,* Crown Publishers, 1993; Joan Pappas and A. Harold Kendall, *Hampshire Pottery Manufactured by J. S. Taft & Company, Keene, New Hampshire,* published by author, 1971.

Bowl, 6¾" d, 2½" h, emb Indian luck sign, green matte	**225.00**
Candle Sconce, hooded, green matte	**200.00**
Chocolate Pot, 9½" h, dark green glaze, raised leaf dec	**125.00**
Ewer	
8¼" h, striated matte green glaze, fancy loop handle	**165.00**
9" h, 9" w, green matte	**250.00**

11" h, green matte, glaze flake
on base 130.00
Lamp Base, 11" h, #0015, green
matte 850.00
Mug, 7" h, dark green glaze shading to red, relief borders 90.00
Pitcher, 4½" h, tan, high glaze,
marked "Hampshire Pottery" .. 85.00

Vase, green matte glaze, 6" w, $70.00.

Umbrella Stand, 17⅝" h, deep
matte green, high relief dec of
trailing ivy, textured ground 200.00
Vase, green matte
Artichoke, rim chip 65.00
Maize 130.00
Snake, high glaze 145.00

HAND-PAINTED CHINA

History: Hand painting on china began
in the Victorian era and remained popular
through the 1920s. It was considered an
accomplished art form for women in the upper and upper middle class households. It
developed first in England, but spread rapidly to the Continent and America.

China factories in Europe, America, and
the Orient made the blanks. Belleek, Haviland, Limoges, and Rosenthal are among
the European firms. American firms include
A. H. Hews Co., Cambridge, Massachusetts; Willetts Mfg. Co., Trenton, New Jersey; and Knowles, Taylor and Knowles,
East Liverpool, Ohio. Nippon blanks from
Japan were used heavily during the early
20th century.

The quality and design of the blank is a
key factor in pricing. Some blanks were very

elaborate. Many pieces were signed and
dated by the artist.

Aesthetics is critical. Value is added to a
piece when a decorator goes beyond the
standard forms and creates a unique and
pleasing design.

Collectors' Club: World Organization of
China Painters, 2641 N.W. 10th St., Oklahoma City, OK 73107.

Museum: World Organization of China
Painters, Oklahoma City, OK.

Vase, white mums, green foliage, yellow, and maroon, highlights, sgd "C Carthurst," Belleek blank, 11¼" h, $395.00.

Bowl, cov, English, porcelain, hp
floral and river landscape, gilt
trim, applied florets throughout,
molded branch handles, titled
"View near Ballschmyle Ayr-
shire," chips, 19th C, 6½" h ... 375.00
Box, cov, German, porcelain, hp
floral dec, Von Schierholz, Thuringia mark, c1900, 9" d 90.00
Dessert Plates, set of 10, Vienna
porcelain, classical and mythological scenes, various artists,
8¼" d 1,100.00
Dinner Service, Paris porcelain, hp
scrollwork and enameled floral
dec, gold band borders, two
round fruit bowls, center dish,
oval fish platter, large serving
bowl, cov sauce tureens, two

small cov tureens, large cov tureen, oval fruit basket, two gravy boats, two water pitchers, twelve various sized oval platters, compote, six various sized serving dishes, four cov vegetable dishes, sixteen cov pot de cremes, twelve coffee cups, one teacup, five 5″ d saucers, five 6″ d saucers, twenty–eight 7¼″ d plates, fourteen 7″ d shallow bowls, nineteen 8¼″ d plates, twenty–eight 9⅝″ d soup plates, nine 9″ d plates, wear, damages, 19th C **6,900.00**

Pitcher, Austrian, porcelain, deep red ground, raised gilt leaf designs surrounding central hp panel of friar sampling wines, beehive mark, c1900, 11″ h ... **750.00**

. Plaque

Earthenware, French, hp enamel dec with Renaissance male in full armor, rim chips, restoration, 19th C, 15½ x 31¼″ **350.00**

Porcelain, floral study, giltwood frame, late 19th C, 9¾″ w, 12¼″ h **260.00**

Plate, French, porcelain, hp floral dec with gilt and blue enamel feather edge to scalloped rims, 19th C, 9″ d, set of eleven **630.00**

Tea Service, Paris porcelain, banded gilt borders, hp landscape scenes, 7½″ h cov teapot, cov sugar, creamer, 8″ d waste bowl, seven teacups, seven coffee cups, seventeen saucers, damages, mid 19th C **2,300.00**

Urn, pr, Royal Vienna style, ormolu and porcelain, figural and floral reserves, royal blue ground, missing covers and some jewel accents, 10¼″ h **750.00**

Vase, French

Cornucopia form, porcelain, rect plinth, mauve, white, and parcel gilt, hp floral sprays, Jacob Petit, Paris, chips, 19th C, 9″ l, 11¼″ h, pr **860.00**

Flowers and tropical birds, polychrome enamel dec, late 19th C, 10″ h **230.00**

HATPINS AND HATPIN HOLDERS

History: When the vogue for oversized hats developed around 1850, hatpins became popular. Designers used a variety of materials to decorate the pin ends, including china, crystal, enamel, gem stones, precious metals, and shells. Decorative subjects ranged from commemorative designs to insects.

Hatpin holders are porcelain containers which sit on a dresser to hold these pins. The holders were produced by major manufacturers, among which were Meissen, Nippon, R. S. Germany, R. S. Prussia, and Wedgwood.

Reference: Lillian Baker, *Hatpins & Hatpin Holders: An Illustrated Value Guide,* Collector Books, 1983, 1994 value update.

Collectors' Clubs: American Hatpin Society, 28227 Paseo El Siena, Laguna Niguel, CA 92677; International Club for Collectors of Hatpins and Hatpin Holders, 15237 Chanera Avenue, Gardena, CA, 90249.

Museum: Los Angeles Art Museum, Costume Dept., Los Angeles, CA.

HATPINS

Art Nouveau, half clamshell shape, detailed woman in center, marked "Sterling Front," 7¾″ l, c1905 .... **75.00**

Austrian, triangular frame, rhinestones dec, filigree border, 12¼″ l **135.00**

Brass, lacy openwork, dome top with large rhinestones, 10½″ l . **30.00**

Crystal, hand cut, blown teardrop shape, 10½″ l **125.00**

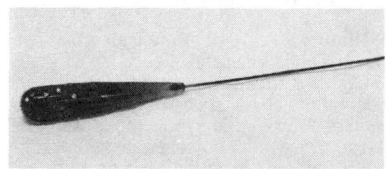

Art Deco, amber, plastic, 10½″ l, $15.00.

Garnet, gold filled, oval openwork,
9½" l **75.00**
Ivory, elephant, hand carved **90.00**
Mother–of–Pearl, 2" d **15.00**
Porcelain
  Hand Painted, Victorian motif,
  heavy gold overlay, baroque
  sleeved dec, 7½" l, c1890 ... **90.00**
  Pink relief molded flowers **35.00**
Snoqualmie Falls, Seattle, WA,
souvenir, sterling, 10¼" l **65.00**
Sterling Silver, figural, cherub ... **50.00**

HATPIN HOLDERS

Austrian, hp rose dec, gold top .. **55.00**
Belleek, hp floral dec and "E," Willets **65.00**
Carnival Glass, Grape and Cable
pattern, marigold, Northwood .. **150.00**
Limoges, gold emb border, cream
ground **30.00**
Royal Bayreuth, Art Nouveau lady,
saucer base, blue mark, 4½" h **450.00**
Royal Doulton, 6" h, Dickensware,
figural, Sam Weller, earth tone
colors **110.00**
Schlegelmilch, RS Prussia, attached rect open trinket box,
fancy emb shape, pink roses,
powder blue and gold trim, red
mark **125.00**
Silver, etched and engraved dec,
sixteen holes, 5½" h, c1880 ... **120.00**

HAVILAND CHINA

History: In 1842, American china importer David Haviland moved to Limoges,
France, where he began manufacturing and
decorating china specifically for the U.S.
market. Haviland is synonymous with fine,
white, translucent porcelain, although early
hand–painted patterns were generally
larger and darker colored on heavier whiteware blanks than on later ones.

David revolutionized French china factories by both manufacturing the whiteware
blank and decorating it at the same site. In
addition, Haviland and Company pioneered
the use of decals in decorating china.

David's sons, Charles Edward and Theodore, split the company in 1892. Theodore
opened an American division in 1936 which
continues until today. In 1941 Theodore
bought out Charles Edward's heirs and re-
combined both companies under the original name of H. and Co. The Haviland family
sold its interests in 1981.

Charles Field Haviland, cousin of Charles
Edward and Theodore, worked for, and then
ran, the Casseaux Works after his marriage
in 1857 until 1882. Items continued to carry
his name as decorator until 1941.

Haviland patterns were not consistently
named until after 1926. Pattern identification is difficult because of the similarity
found in the over 66,000 patterns that have
been made. Numbers assigned by Arlene
Schleiger and illustrated in her books have
become the identification standard for
matching.

References: Susan and Al Bagdade,
Warman's American Pottery and Porcelain,
Wallace–Homestead, 1994; Mary Frank
Gaston, *Haviland Collectibles & Art Ob-
jects,* Collector Books, 1984, out–of–print;
Arlene Schleiger, *Two Hundred Patterns of
Haviland China, Books I–V,* published by
author, 1950–1977.

Collectors' Club: Haviland Collectors Internationale Foundation, PO Box 423,
Boone, IA 50036.

Bowl, 5½" d, Greek Key design,
black and yellow **15.00**
Butter Dish, cov, gold and white,

**Cup and Saucer, Delaware pat-
tern, $12.00.**

scalloped edge, bow forms handle **40.00**
Cake Plate, 10″ d, blue flower spray, gold handles **40.00**
Commemorative Plate, La Chasse a la Licorne, limited edition, issued 1973, set of six **172.00**
Compote, 9″ d, blue and pink flowers, gold scalloped edge **55.00**
Cup and Saucer, Moss Rose, 1885 mark **40.00**
Demitasse Cup and Saucer, white, gold trim, c1900 . . . . **25.00**
Demitasse Set, 10″ h pot, six cups and saucers, pink flowers, damage to lid and one cup **145.00**
Dinner Service, partial
Blue chrysanthemums, green leaves, c1880, price for 21 pc set **175.00**
Rosalinde pattern, twelve butter dishes, seventeen coffee cups, twelve dinner plates, eleven dessert plates, eleven salad plates, twelve saucers, twelve two handled cups, twelve undertrays, price for 99 pc set **475.00**
Game Bird Set, rect platter, ten sq plates, game birds transfer, royal blue and gold border, Haviland Limoges mark, edge chips, late 19th C **1,025.00**
Gravy Boat, round, white, gold band, attached underplate **35.00**
Oyster Plate, 9″ d, white, gold starburst in center, gold rim dec, price for set of six **425.00**
Plate
7½″ d, bread and butter, Clover pattern **15.00**
8½″ d, salad, pink flowers, green scroll border **14.00**
9″ d, luncheon, rose flowered border, cream edge **15.00**
Platter
16″ l, blue flowers, gold scalloped edge **55.00**
22″ l, turquoise flowers, gold scalloped edge **65.00**
Relish, white, scattered pink flowers, gold scalloped edge **30.00**
Soup Set, 7 x 14″ tureen, ten soup plates, light green, hp pastel

flowers, tureen with gold finial and handles **1,100.00**
Teacup and Saucer, pink roses, blue ribbon dec **35.00**
Vegetable Bowl, cov, 11″ l, ftd, pink roses, scalloped **115.00**

HEISEY GLASS

History: The A. H. Heisey Glass Co. began producing glasswares in April 1896, in Newark, Ohio. Heisey was not a newcomer to the field, having been associated with the craft since his youth.

Many blown and molded patterns were produced in crystal, colored, milk (opalescent), and Ivorina Verde (custard) glass. Decorative techniques of cutting, etching, and silver deposit were employed. Glass figurines were introduced in 1933 and continued until 1957 when the factory ceased production. All Heisey glass is notable for its clarity. Not all Heisey glassware is marked with the familiar "H" within a diamond.

References: Neila Bredehoft, *The Collector's Encyclopedia of Heisey Glass, 1925–1938,* Collector Books, 1986, 1993 value update; Neila M. and Thomas H. Bredehoft, *Handbook of Heisey Production Cuttings,* Cherry Hill Publications, 1991; Mary Louise Burns, *Heisey's Glassware of Distinction,* 2nd edition, published by author, 1983; Lyle Conder, *Collector's Guide To Heisey's Glassware for Your Table*, L–W Books, 1984, 1993–94 value update; Tom Felt and Bob O'Grady, *Heisey Candlesticks, Candelabra, and Lamps*, Heisey Collectors of America, Inc., 1984; Gene Florence, *Elegant Glassware Of The Depression Era, Revised Fifth Edition,* Collector Books, 1993; Frank L. Hahn and Paul Kikeli, *Collector's Guide to Heisey and Heisey by Imperial Glass Animals,* Golden Era Publications, 1991; Ellen T. Schroy, *Warman's Glass,* Wallace–Homestead, 1992.

Collectors' Clubs: Heisey Collectors of America, 169 W. Church St., Newark, OH, 43055; National Capital Heisey Collectors, PO Box 23, Clinton, MD 20735.

Museum: National Heisey Glass Museum, Newark, OH.

Reproduction Alert: Some Heisey molds were sold to Imperial Glass of Bellaire, Ohio, and certain items were reissued. These pieces may be mistaken for the original Heisey. Some of the reproductions were produced in colors which were never made by Heisey and have become collectible in their own right.

Examples include: the Colt family in Crystal, Carmel Slag, Ultra Blue, and Horizon Blue; the mallard with wings up in Carmel Slag; Whirlpool (Provincial) in crystal and colors; and Waverly, 7–inch oval footed compote in Carmel Slag.

Powder Box, Crystolite pattern, 5″ d, $48.00.

Animal
Asiatic Pheasant	295.00
Donkey	225.00
Elephant	240.00

Goose
Wings back	95.00
Wings down	400.00
Mallard, wings up	135.00
Sparrow	67.50
Swan, large	950.00

Ashtray
Empress, #1401	295.00
Ridgeleigh, diamond shape	10.00

Basket
#461, banded picket, flamingo, 7″ h	395.00
#463, bonnet, cut dec, 9″ h	295.00

#480, daisy and leaves dec	295.00

Bowl, #1252, Alexandrite, twist, round ... 595.00

Butter, cov
Orchid	175.00
Plantation, #1567	135.00
Ring Band, custard, rose dec	245.00
#1951, cabochon, orchid	295.00

Candelabra, pr, Old Williamsburg, low base, 3 lite, pr ... 425.00

Candlesticks, pr
Lariat, #1540, Moonglow cut, 3 lite	125.00
Trident, #134, Sahara, 2 lite	125.00

Champagne
Orchid, #5025	30.00
Plantation, #5067	22.50
Victorian, #1425	13.50

Cherry Jar, cov, Greek Key, #433 195.00

Cocktail, steeplechase, Moongleam base ... 70.00

Cocktail Shaker
Hunter cutting	75.00
Rooster	125.00

Compote
Empress, yellow, 6″ d	50.00
Orchid, low foot, 6″ d	45.00

Convention Souvenir, HCA, Oscar, 1979 ... 40.00

Creamer and Sugar
Continental, #339, large, c1905, 5″ h	140.00
Empress, #1401, individual size, matching tray, Sahara	65.00
Octagon, Sahara, #500	60.00
Old Sandwich, #1404, round	135.00

Cup and Saucer, Empress, yellow 42.00
Epergne, Orchid ... 690.00
Fishbowl, 9″ d ... 435.00

French Dressing Bowl, underplate, Narrow Flute ... 57.00

Goblet
Empress, tall, etched, pink	70.00
Ipswich, 10 oz	22.50
Orchid, #5025, 10 oz	42.00
Yeoman, Flamingo, 8 oz	17.50

Iced Tea Tumbler
Donna, #3484, Orchid	57.50
Empress, etched, pink	55.00
Orchid, #5025, 12 oz	65.00
Pied Piper	39.00
Rose	35.00

Ice Tub
Fancy Loop, #1205	195.00

Pillows, #325 .... **495.00**
Ridgeleigh **65.00**
#1252, twist, handle and tongs **595.00**
Jelly, Greek Key, ftd, 5" h **150.00**
Mayonnaise, Orchid, #1519, ftd . **45.00**
Molasses Can, Punty & Diamond
Point, #305 .... **125.00**
Nappy, Queen Ann **5.00**
Nut Cup, Twist, Moongleam **29.00**
Pitcher
Banded Flute, #150, pint **130.00**
Empress, Sahara, minor nicks . **95.00**
Plate
6" d, Twist, Flamingo **14.50**
7" d, Empress, green **23.00**
8" d, Empress, Sahara **16.00**
9" d, Colonial, #1150 .... **45.00**
Puff Box, #25, large **135.00**
Punch Bowl Set
Crystolite, bowl, twelve cups, la-
dle, 20" d underplate **300.00**
Lariat, bowl, eight cups, ladle .. **115.00**
Plantation, bowl, seven cups, la-
dle, underplate **750.00**
Ridgeleigh, bowl and ten cups . **165.00**
Punch Cup
Greek Key, Flamingo **30.00**
Ridgeleigh **9.00**
Relish, Waverly, two parts, three
toes **20.00**
Rye Bottle, Victorian, #1425, 27
oz, chrome stand **125.00**
Salt and Pepper Shakers, pr
Pineapple and Fan, emerald
green, gold trim **195.00**
#57, Cohasset cut **75.00**
#1567, Plantation **75.00**
Salver, Waverly, #1519, Orchid,
low, ftd, 14" d **295.00**
Sandwich Plate, center handle
Lariat, 14" d **45.00**
Rose **185.00**
Sherbet, Minuet **29.00**
Soda Tumbler
Crystolite, #5003, 12 oz **37.00**
Donna, #3484, Orchid **57.50**
Syrup, Plantation, #1567 .... **135.00**
Tankard, Beaded Swag, opal,
cornflower dec **160.00**
Tumbler
Crystolite, #5003, 10 oz **42.00**
Saturn, 10 oz **15.00**
Vase
Moongleam, #142, high low ... **595.00**

Rooster **135.00**
Tulip, #1575, floral bowl **45.00**
#4045, ball
4" h **550.00**
6" h **695.00**
Whipped Cream Bowl, Saturn,
Limelight **140.00**
Whiskey, Ridgeleigh, 2½" h **22.50**
Wine, Duquesne, 2½ oz **25.00**

HOLLY AMBER

History: Holly Amber, originally called Golden Agate, was produced by the Indiana Tumbler and Goblet Works of the National Glass Co., Greentown, Indiana. Jacob Rosenthal created the color in 1902. Holly Amber is a gold–colored glass with a marbleized onyx color on raised parts.

A new pattern, Holly [No. 450], was designed by Frank Jackson for Golden Agate. Between January 1903 and June 1903, more than 35 items were made in this pattern; the factory was destroyed by fire in June.

References: Brenda Measell and James Measell, *A Guide To Reproductions of Greentown Glass, 2nd Edition,* The Printing Press, 1974; James Measell, *Greentown Glass, The Indiana Tumbler & Goblet Co.,* Grand Rapids Public Museum, 1979, 1992–93 value update, distributed by Antique Publications.

Collectors' Club: National Greentown Glass Assoc., 19596 Glendale Ave., South Bend, IN 46637.

Museums: Grand Rapids Public Museum, Ruth Herrick Greentown Glass Collection, Grand Rapids, MI; Greentown Glass Museum, Greentown, IN.

Additional Listing: Greentown Glass.

Bowl
7½" l, 4½" w, 2" h, oval **360.00**
8" d **450.00**
Butter Dish, cov, 7¼" d, 6¼" h . . **1,200.00**
Compote, cov, 12" d, 8½" h **1,800.00**
Creamer, 4½" h **600.00**
Cruet, 6½" h **2,100.00**
Mug, 4½" h, ring handle **535.00**
Nappy **375.00**
Sauce Dish **225.00**
Spooner **425.00**

Tumbler, 3⅞" h, $550.00.

Sugar, open 425.00
Syrup, 5¾" h, SP hinged lid 2,000.00
Tray, water, round 600.00
Tumbler 385.00
Vase, 6" h 425.00

HORN

History: For centuries horns from animals have been used for various items, e.g., drinking cups, spoons, powder horns, and small dishes. Some pieces of horn have designs scratched in them. Around 1880 furniture made from the horns of Texas longhorn steers was popular in Texas and the southwestern United States.
Additional Listing: Firearm Accessories.

Box, cov, 3½" w, 2⅞" h, tooled
  geometric designs, iron finial .. **220.00**
Chair, arm, U–shaped cowhide
  back connected with small
  horns, longhorn splat, cowhide
  seat, twelve horns form legs and
  base, price for pair **2,000.00**
Cup
  3½" h, engraved Masonic sym-
    bols and initials "WA" **195.00**
  5" h, scratch carved hunting
    scene, applied handle **75.00**
Footstool, velvet upholstered seat,
  horn legs **150.00**
Hat Rack, wall type, four horn
  hooks **25.00**
Mirror, 56 x 35", rect, applied horns
  on frame, beveled mirror, Anthony Redmile, London **140.00**

Tablespoon, tapered handle, $18.00.

Snuff Box, 1¾" d, ring handle,
  wood plug **50.00**
Spoon, 9¾" l, cow horn, carved,
  dark patina **30.00**
Tumbler, 2½" h **20.00**
Wall Decoration, 72" l, Texas longhorn steer, mounted bound
  leather, wood base **125.00**

HULL POTTERY

History: In 1905 Addis E. Hull purchased the Acme Pottery Company, Crooksville, Ohio. In 1917 the A. E. Hull Pottery Company began making a line of art pottery, novelties, stoneware, and kitchenware, later including the famous Little Red Riding Hood line. Most items had a matte finish with shades of pink and blue or brown predominating.

After a disastrous flood and fire in 1950, J. Brandon Hull reopened the factory in 1952 as the Hull Pottery Company. New, more modern style molds, mostly with glossy finish, were produced. The company currently produces pieces, e.g. the Regal and Floraline lines, for sale to florists.

Hull pottery molds and patterns are easily identified. Pre–1950 vases are marked "Hull USA" or "Hull Art USA" on the bottom. Many also retain their paper labels. Post–1950 pieces are marked "Hull" in large script or "HULL" in block letters.

Each pattern has a distinctive number, e.g., Wildflower with a "W" and number, Waterlily with an "L" and number, Poppy with 600 numbers, Orchid with 300 numbers, etc. Early stone pieces have an H.

References: Susan and Al Bagdade, *Warman's American Pottery and Porcelain,* Wallace–Homestead, 1994; Barbara Loveless Gick–Burke, *Collector's Guide To Hull Pottery: The Dinnerware Lines: Identification & Values,* Collector Books, 1993; Joan Hull, *Hull: The Heavenly Pottery, Fourth Edition,* published by author, 1995; Brenda Roberts, *The Collectors Encyclopedia Of Hull Pottery,* Collector Books, 1980, 1993 value update; Brenda Roberts, *Roberts' Ultimate Encyclopedia of Hull Pottery,* Walsworth Publishing Co, 1992; Brenda Roberts, *The Companion Guide to Roberts' Ultimate Encyclopedia of Hull Pottery,* Walsworth Publishing, 1992.

Periodicals: *Hull Pottery Newsletter,* 11023 Tunnel Hill N.E., New Lexington, OH 43764; *The Hull Pottery News,* 466 Foreston Place, St Louis, MO 63119.

Additional Listings: See *Warman's Americana & Collectibles* for more examples.

Advisor: Joan Hull.

PRE–1950 (MATTE)

Bow Knot
   Pitcher, B–15, 13½" **1,300.00**
   Vase
      B–4, 5½" **165.00**
      B–8, 8½" **200.00**

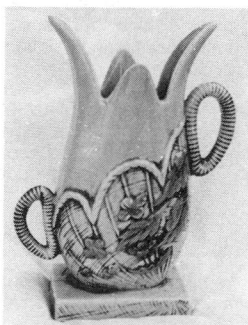

Vase, pink ground, stylized rope handles and wicker basket, yellow, red, and purple flowers, high gloss, marked "Hull/USA/T7/ copyright '55," 10¾" h, $40.00.

Wall Planter Pitcher, B–26, 6" . . **225.00**
Dogwood (Wild Rose)
   Pitcher, 505, 7" **250.00**
   Vase
      504, 8½" **100.00**
      516, 4¾" **65.00**
Iris (Narcissus), vase
   402, 4¾" **65.00**
   404, 8½" **150.00**
   405, 10½" **325.00**
Jack–In–The–Pulpit (Calla Lily)
   Bowl, 500/32, 10" **175.00**
   Vase
      520/33, 6" **100.00**
      530/33, 9" **325.00**
Magnolia (Glossy), tea set, H–20,
   H–21, H–22 . . . . **250.00**
Magnolia (Matte)
   Floor Vase, 16, 15" **425.00**
   Vase
      7, 8½" **100.00**
      14, 4¾" **45.00**
Open Rose (Camelia)
   Basket, 107, 6" **300.00**
   Pitcher, 105, 7" **200.00**
   Swan Vase, 118, 6½" **125.00**
   Vase, 124, 12" **325.00**
Orchid
   Console Bowl, 314, 13" **325.00**
   Vase
      301, 4¾" **75.00**
      304, 6" **125.00**
      309, 8½" **175.00**
Poppy
   Basket, 601, 9" **600.00**
   Vase, 612, 6½" **100.00**
Rosella
   Hanging Planter, R–10, 6½" . . . **85.00**
   Vase
      R–8, 6½" **75.00**
      R–15, 8½" **85.00**
Stoneware
   Flower Pot, 6" **60.00**
   Stein, 492, 6½" **40.00**
Thistle, 51, 52, 53, 54 . . . . **150.00**
Tulip
   Pitcher, 115–33–13" **400.00**
   Vase
      101–33–9" **200.00**
      108–33–6" **100.00**
Water Lily
   Basket, L–14–10½" **325.00**
   Cornucopia, L–7–6½" **75.00**
   Vase, L–16–12½" **325.00**

Wildflower
Basket
  W–16–10½" **375.00**
  66, 10½" **1,500.00**
Vase
  W–5–6½" **65.00**
  W–9–8½" **125.00**
  51, 8½" **250.00**
  61, 6½" **135.00**
Woodland (Matte)
  Vase, W–8–7½" **100.00**
  Window Box, W–19–10½" **135.00**
  Double Cornucopia, W–23–14" **475.00**

POST–1950

Blossom Flite
  Basket, T2, 6" **65.00**
  Console and Candleholders,
    T10, T11 . . . . **225.00**
  Flower Boat, T12, 10½" **95.00**
Butterfly
  Basket, B17, 10½" **325.00**
  Pitcher, B15, 13½" **185.00**
  B14, 10½" **95.00**
Capri
  Leaf Dish, C52, 10" **65.00**
  Llama Planter, C80 . . . . **95.00**
Continental
  Candy Dish, C62, 8¼" w **50.00**
  Vase, C29, 12" **95.00**
Ebb Tide
  Ashtray, mermaid, E–8 . . . . **175.00**
  Cornucopia, E–9, 11¾" **150.00**
Figural Planters
  Clown, 82 . . . . **50.00**
  Twin Geese, 95 . . . . **50.00**
  Unicorn Vase, 98, 12" **75.00**
Parchment & Pine
  Console and Candleholders, S9,
    S10 . . . . **175.00**
  Tea Set, S–11, S–12, S–13 . . . **200.00**
Serenade (Birds)
  Pitcher, S13, 13½" **375.00**
  Vase, S12, 14" **125.00**
Sunglow (Kitchenware)
  Vase
    88, 5½" **35.00**
    95, 8½" **50.00**
  Wall Pocket, whiskbroom, 82 . . **85.00**
Tokay/Tuscany
  Moon Basket, 11, 10¼" **125.00**
  Pitcher, 21, 14" **225.00**
  Vase, 4, 8¼" **95.00**

Tropicana
  Basket, T55, 12¾" **700.00**
  Vase, T53, 8½" **400.00**
Woodland (Glossy)
  Jardiniere, W21, 9½" **275.00**
  Vase, W1, 5½" **40.00**
  Window Box, W14 . . . . **65.00**

HUMMEL ITEMS

History: Hummel items are the original creations of Berta Hummel, born in 1909 in Massing, Bavaria, Germany. At age 18, she was enrolled in the Academy of Fine Arts in Munich to further her mastery of drawing and the palette. Berta entered the Convent of Siessen and became Sister Maria Innocentia in 1934. In this Franciscan cloister, she continued drawing and painting images of her childhood friends.

In 1935 W. Goebel Co. in Rodental, Germany, began reproducing Sister Maria Innocentia's sketches into three–dimensional bisque figurines. The Schmid Brothers of Randolph, Massachusetts, introduced the figurines to America and became Goebel's U.S. distributor.

In 1967 Goebel began distributing Hummel items in the U.S. A controversy developed between the two companies involving the Hummel family and the convent. Law suits and countersuits ensued. The German courts finally effected a compromise. The convent held legal rights to all works produced by Sister Maria Innocentia from 1934 until her death in 1946 and licensed Goebel to reproduce these works. Schmid was to deal directly with the Hummel family for permission to reproduce any pre–convent art.

All authentic Hummels bear both the signature M. I. Hummel and a Goebel trademark. Various trademarks were used to identify the year of production. The Crown Mark (trademark 1) was used from 1935 until 1949; Full Bee (trademark 2), 1950–1959; Stylized Bee (trademark 3), 1957–1972; Three Line Mark (trademark 4), 1964–1972; Last Bee Mark (trademark 5), 1972–1979; Missing Bee Mark (trademark 6), 1979–1990; and the Current Mark or New Crown Mark (trademark 7), from 1991 to the present.

References: Ken Armke, *Hummel: An Illustrated Handbook and Price Guide,* Wallace–Homestead, 1995; Carl F. Luckey, *Luckey's Hummel Figurines and Plates: A Collector's Identification and Value Guide, 10th Edition,* Books Americana, 1994; Robert L. Miller, *The No. 1 Price Guide to M. I. Hummel: Figurines, Plates, More...,* Fifth Edition, Portfolio Press, 1992; Wolfgang Schwalto, *M. I. Hummel Collector's Handbook, Part I: Rarities and Collector Pieces,* Schwalto, GMBH, 1994; Lawrence L. Wonsch, *Hummel Copycats With Values,* Wallace–Homestead, 1987, out–of–print.

Collectors' Clubs: Hummel Collector's Club, Inc., PO Box 257, Yardley, PA 19067; M. I. Hummel Club, Goebel Plaza, Rte. 31, PO Box 11, Pennington, NJ 08534.

Museum: The Hummel Museum, New Braunfels, TX.

Additional Listings: See *Warman's Americana & Collectibles* for more examples.

Ashtray, Singing Lesson, #34, trademark 4	**145.00**
Bell, Annual, 1978	**40.00**
Bookends, pr, Playmates, #61/A, trademark 3	**300.00**
Candleholder	
A Gentle Glow, #439, trademark 6	**190.00**
Birthday Cake, #338, trademark 6	**130.00**
Little Band, #388, trademark 6	**220.00**
Candy Box, Happy Pastime, #III/69, trademark 3	**275.00**
Clock, Call To Worship, #441, trademark 6	**900.00**

Figure, #111-1, Wayside Harmony, full bee mark, 5½" h, $225.00.

Figurine	
Apple Tree Boy, #142/3/0, trademark 3	**75.00**
Baker, #128, trademark 2	**275.00**
Be Patient, #197/1, trademark 4	**140.00**
Bird Watcher, #300, trademark 5	**150.00**
Builder, #305, trademark 4	**175.00**
Carnival, #3328, trademark 6	**120.00**
Chimney Sweep, #12/2/0, trademark 4	**120.00**
Congratulations, #17/0, trademark 4	**225.00**
Crossroads, #331, trademark 5	**190.00**
Doctor, #127, trademark 3	**150.00**
Duet, #130, trademark 6	**250.00**
Farm Boy, #66, trademark 3	**155.00**
Feeding Time, #199/0, trademark 2	**150.00**
Friends, #136/1, trademark 3	**165.00**
Girl With Sheet Music, #389, trademark 5	**45.00**
Goose Girl, #47/3/0, trademark 3	**120.00**
Happy Birthday, #176/0, trademark 3	**135.00**
Happy Traveler, #109/0, trademark 5, flake	**70.00**
Heavenly Angel, #21/0, trademark 3	**110.00**
Heavenly Protection, #88/1, trademark 3	**635.00**
Holy Water Font, #75, trademark 3	**95.00**
Latest News, #184, trademark 5	**135.00**

Little Cellist, #89/I, trademark 3 **130.00**
Little Sweeper, #171, trademark
3 . . . . **75.00**
Little Thrifty, #118, trademark 1 **300.00**
Mountaineer, #315, trademark 4 **140.00**
Out of Danger, #56B, trademark
6 . . . . **175.00**
Photographer, #178, trademark
4 . . . . **220.00**
Postman, #119, trademark 2 . . **180.00**
Puppy Love, #1, trademark 3 . . **250.00**
Prayer Before Battle, #20,
trademark 3 . . . . **200.00**
She Loves Me, She Loves Me
Not, #174, trademark 2 . . . . . **200.00**
Signs of Spring, #203/2/9,
trademark 2, flake **125.00**
Star Gazer, #132, trademark 4 **225.00**
Village Boy, #351/2/0, trade-
mark 4 . . . . **45.00**
Font
Angel at Prayer, #91/A&B,
trademark 3 . . . . **130.00**
Child Jesus, #26/0, trademark 1 **100.00**
The Good Shepherd, #35/0,
trademark 2 . . . . **55.00**
Lamp, Culprit, #44/A, trademark 4 **225.00**
Necklace, Valentine Gift, #387 . . **305.00**
Wall Plaque
Child In Bed, #137/B, trademark
2 . . . . **150.00**
Madonna, #48/0, trademark 2 . **125.00**
Quartet, #134, trademark 5 . . . **250.00**

IMARI

History: Imari derives its name from a
Japanese port city. Although Imari ware was
manufactured in the 17th century, the wares
most commonly encountered are those
made between 1770 and 1900.

Early Imari was decorated simply, quite
unlike the later heavily decorated brocade
pattern commonly associated with Imari.
Most of the decorative patterns are an underglaze blue and overglaze "seal wax" red
supported by turquoise and yellow.

The Chinese copied Imari ware. Important differences of the Japanese type include grayer clay, thicker glaze, runny and
darker blue, and deep red opaque hues.

The pattern and colors of Imari inspired
many English and European potteries, such
as Derby and Meissen, to adopt a similar
style of decoration for their wares.

Reference: Gloria and Robert Mascarelli,
Warman's Oriental Antiques, Wallace–
Homestead, 1992.

Reproduction Alert: Reproductions
abound, and many manufacturers continue
to produce pieces in the traditional style.

**Bowl, blue, orange, and yellow
marine motif, c1870, 10″ d,
$450.00.**

Bowl
5⅝″ d, blue and white dec, scal-
loped rim, price for pair **225.00**
6½″ d, center potted flowers dec,
scalloped rim **275.00**
7¼″ d, scalloped rim, price for
pair **175.00**
9″ d, paneled dec, seal mark . . **165.00**
10¼″ d, shallow, vase of flowers
dec **500.00**
11″ d, octagonal, paneled floral
dec **1,400.00**
15″ d, deep floriform, int. and ext.
with naturalistic floral design
separated by scrolling floral
panels, underglaze blue, iron
red, green, and gold, late 19th
C **925.00**
Charger
10″ d, scrolling panels, fish and
floral groupings, late 19th C,
price for pr, one repaired **230.00**
15⅝″ d, garden scene, gold ac-
cented traditional colors, 19th
C **315.00**

17½" d, scalloped rim **500.00**
Dish
10½" d, hexagonal, shallow, long handled vessel in center surrounded by flowering prunus and chrysanthemum, 19th C **450.00**
17¾" d, dragon motif, serpentine rim **80.00**
Fruit Bowl, round, floral and bird reserves, 19th C, 9½" d **415.00**
Ginger Jar, cov, 9¼" h **240.00**
Jar, 6" h, bird dec **100.00**
Plate
8¼" d, dinner, scalloped rim, price for set of 7 .... **700.00**
10¾" d, price for pair **200.00**
Platter
14¾" l, oval, red, blue, green, and yellow floral dec, 19th C . **325.00**
23" l, fish form, small edge chips, late 19th C **460.00**
Punch Bowl, 10¼" d, scalloped rim, bird and floral dec, Japanese, 19th C **290.00**
Soup Bowl, cov, lotus design, price for set of 4 .... **300.00**
Vase
6½" h, bottle shape, ribbed, floral dec, price for pair **175.00**
8" h, fluted, blue and white dec, price for pair **110.00**
9⅞" h, fluted sides, simple dec **85.00**
11" h, tree and foliage dec **475.00**
12" h, overlapping vertical panels with designs **275.00**

IMPERIAL GLASS

History: Imperial Glass Co., Bellaire, Ohio, was organized in 1901. Its primary product was pattern (pressed) glass. Soon other lines were added including carnival glass, NUART, NUCUT, and NEAR CUT. In 1916 the company introduced "Free-Hand," a lustered art glass line, and "Imperial Jewels," an iridescent stretch glass that carried the Imperial cross trademark. In the 1930s the company was reorganized into the Imperial Glass Corporation and continues to produce a great variety of wares.

Imperial recently has acquired the molds and equipment of several other glass companies—Central, Cambridge and Heisey. Many of the "retired" molds of these companies are once again in use. The resulting reissues are marked to distinguish them from the originals.

References: Margaret and Douglas Archer, *Imperial Glass,* Collector Books, 1978, 1993 value update; Gene Florence, *Elegant Glassware Of The Depression Era, Sixth Edition,* Collector Books, 1994; Frank L. Hahn and Paul Kikeli, *Collector's Guide to Heisey and Heisey by Imperial Glass Animals,* Golden Era Publications, 1991; National Imperial Glass Collector's Society, *Imperial Glass 1966 Catalog,* reprint, 1991 price guide, Antique Publications; Ellen T. Schroy, *Warman's Glass,* Wallace–Homestead, 1992; Mary M. Wetzel, *Candlewick: The Jewel of Imperial,* published by author, 1981; Mary M. Wetzel, *Candlewick: The Jewel of Imperial Price Guide II, Revised 2nd Edition,* published by author, 1993.

Videotape: National Imperial Glass Collectors Society, *Candlewick, At Home, In Any Home, Volume I, Imperial Beauty, Volume II, Virginia and Mary,* National Imperial Glass Collectors Society, RoCliff Communications, 1993; *Glass of Yesteryears, The Renaissance of Slag Glass by Imperial,* RoCliff Communications, 1994.

Collectors' Club: National Imperial Glass Collectors Society, PO Box 534, Bellaire, OH 43906.

Additional Listings: See Carnival Glass, Pattern Glass, and *Warman's Americana & Collectibles* for more examples of Candlewick.

ENGRAVED OR HAND CUT

Bowl, 9½" d, 3 floral sprays, molded star base **30.00**

Ivy Ball, blue opalescent hobnail, 1940s, 6⅛" h, $25.00.

Celery Vase, 3 side stars, cut star base	25.00
Pitcher, 6" h, daisies, molded star base	40.00
Tumbler, buzz star dec	15.00

JEWELS

Bowl, 9" d, irid amber	75.00
Compote, 7½" d, irid teal blue	50.00
Creamer, amethyst, pearl, and green luster	65.00
Vase, 8" h, flared rim, irid silver, mulberry ground	120.00

LUSTERED (FREE HAND)

Candlesticks, pr, 10¾" h, cobalt, white vine and leaf dec	325.00
Lamp Shade, 5" h, Art Nouveau, irid ivory, gold, and green feather pattern, colored threading, sgd	175.00
Rose Bowl, 6" d, irid orange, white floral cutting	65.00
Vase	
7" h, allover swirls, blue and white, white int.	150.00
8¼" h, 4½" d, deep cobalt blue and white swirl	
Matte finish, highly irid dark blue int.	425.00
Orig glossy finish, highly irid orange int. neck	400.00
11" h, irid emerald green, embedded white hearts and vines, orange luster throat, label	300.00

NUART

Ashtray, marked "Nuart"	20.00
Lamp Shade, crystal, frosted int., cluster electric type, flower etching	25.00

NUCUT

Berry Bowl, 7½" d	20.00
Compote, 5½" d	22.00
Creamer	12.00
Fern Dish, 8" l	35.00
Nappy, 6" w, heart shape	20.00
Salad Bowl, 10¾" d	32.00
Tumbler	15.00

PRESSED

Animal, lion, purple slag, purple base, orig paper tags	118.00
Bowl, 9" d, milk glass, Roses pattern	15.00
Candlesticks, pr, dolphin, blue	30.00
Cologne Bottle, milk glass, Hobnail, blue, ruffled, stopper, price for pair	30.00
Goblet, 5½" h, Tradition, crystal	10.00
Mug, red slag, robin	18.00
Pitcher, Windmill, red slag, pint	40.00
Plate, 7½" d, Fancy Colonial, pink	10.00
Rose Bowl, Lace Edge, amber opal	25.00
Sherbet, Mt Vernon, ruby	5.00
Sugar, cov, Lace Edge, green opal	20.00
Swan, 4¾" h, amethyst	20.00
Toothpick, ivory, orig label	20.00

INDIAN ARTIFACTS, AMERICAN

History: During the historic period there were approximately 350 tribes of Indians grouped into the following regions: Eskimo, Northeast and Woodland, Northwest Coast, Plains, and West and Southwest.

American Indian artifacts are quite popular. Currently the market is in a period of stability following a rapid increase of prices during the 1970s.

References: Susan and Al Bagdade, *Warman's American Pottery and Porcelain,* Wallace–Homestead, 1994; John W. Barry,

American Indian Pottery, 2nd Edition, Books Americana, 1984, out–of–print; C. J. Brafford and Laine Thom (comps.), Dancing Colors: Paths of Native American Women, Chronicle Books, 1992; Harold S. Colton, Hopi Kachina Dolls, Revised Edition, University of New Mexico Press, 1959, 1990 reprint; Robert Edler, Early Archaic Indian Points & Knives, Collector Books, 1990; Gary L. Fogelman, An Identification and Price Guide For Indian Artifacts of the Northeast, Fogelman Publishing, 1994; Larry Frank, Indian Silver Jewelry of the Southwest, 1868–1930, Schiffer Publishing, 1989; Lar Hothem, Arrowheads & Projectile Points, Collector Books, 1983, 1995 value update; Lar Hothem, Indian Artifacts of the Midwest, Book I (1992, 1994 value update), Book II (1994), Collector Books; Lar Hothem, North American Indian Artifacts, 5th Edition, Books Americana, 1994; Noel D. Justice, Stone Age Spear And Arrow Points Of the Midcontinental and Eastern United States, Indiana University Press, 1987; Robert W Kapoun and Charles J Lohrmann, Language of The Robe: American Indian Trade Blankets, Peregrine Smith Books, 1992; Allan Lobb, Indian Baskets Of The Pacific Northwest and Alaska, Graphic Arts Center Publishing Co., 1990; Evan M. Maurer, Visions Of The People: A Pictorial History Of Plains Indian Life, University of Washington Press, 1992; Robert M. Overstreet and Howard Peake, The Official Overstreet Price Guide to Indian Arrowheads, Second Edition, House of Collectibles, 1991; Robert M. Overstreet and Howard Peake, The Overstreet Indian Arrowheads Identification and Price Guide, Third Edition, Avon Books, 1993; Dawn E. Reno, Native American Collectibles: Identification and Price Guide, Avon Books, 1994; John L. Stivers, The Official Identification and Price Guide To American Indian Arrowheads, House of Collectibles, 1994; Laine Thom, Becoming Brave: The Path To Native American Manhood, Chronicle Books, 1992; Sarah and William Turnbaugh, Indian Baskets, Schiffer Publishing, 1986.

Periodicals: *American Indian Art Magazine*, 7314 E. Osborn Dr., Scottsdale, AZ 85251; *American Indian Basketry Magazine*, PO Box 66124, Portland, OR 97266; *Indian–Artifact Magazine*, RD #1 Box 240, Turbotville, PA 17772; *Prehistoric Antiquities & Archaeological News*, PO Box 88, Sunbury, OH 43074; *The Indian Trader*, PO Box 1421, Gallup, NM 87305.

Collectors' Club: Indian Arts & Crafts Assoc., Suite B, 122 Laveta N.E., Albuquerque, NM 87108.

Museums: Colorado River Indian Tribes Museum, Parker, AZ; Indian Center Museum, Wichita, KS; Maryhill Museum of Art, Goldendale, WA; Museum of Classical Antiquities & Primitive Arts, Medford Lakes, NJ; Museum of the American Indian, Heye Foundation, New York, NY; U.S. Dept. of the Interior Museum, Washington, DC; Wheelwright Museum of the American Indian, Sante Fe, NM.

Note: American Indian artifacts listed below are objects made on the North American continent during the pre–historic and historic periods.

Moccasins, Cheyenne, tan, hard sole, blue, green, white, and yellow beads, 1930s–40s, $225.00.

ESKIMO

Basket
   3⅜″ h, 2⅞″ d, cov, grass, coiled, faded red and green cross design **115.00**
   6¼″ h, 5½″ d, coiled, dyed grass dec **55.00**
Cribbage Board, 16¼″ l, ivory, black pigment engravings, yellowed patina **1,050.00**
Figure, carved stone, bottom sgd
   4″ l, walrus, green jadeite band **55.00**

9" l, goose 55.00
9¾" l, seal, Pangurtang 75.00
Model, 20½" l, Kayak, wood frame,
gut–sewn fish skin 375.00
Needlecase, ivory, stylized seal
form, carved, inlaid ivory, engraved details 325.00
Walrus Tusk, 10" l, carved, detailed diorama scene 175.00

NORTHEAST AND WOODLANDS

Basket, cov, 4¾" w, birch bark and
coiled sweetgrass, quill and
black cotton thread stitching dec,
beaver finial 100.00
Box, cov, 2¾" h, 7" d, quilled birch-
bark, red and purple aniline
thunderbird on lid 125.00
Cuffs, 7¼" l, pr, black cotton velvet, beaded, floral motif, silk ribbon trim, Ojibwa 250.00
Doorpost, 16½" h, totem style,
carved raven and bulldog, polychrome paint, Seneca 165.00
Ladle, 6" l, wood, clamshell shape
bowl, tapered handle with stylized animal head, patina 145.00
Moccasins, pr, 9¼" l, red, blue, yellow, green, and orange beads . 85.00
Pouch
5" l, cloth, brown cotton velvet,
beaded, ribbon edge, Micmac 485.00
5½" l, dark brown cotton velvet,
beaded, floral and concentric
curved designs, Micmac 410.00
8" l, cloth, beaded pictorial dec,
Iroquois 110.00
Spoon, 5" l, wood, carved and incised tapered handle mounted
with perched bird, reddish–
brown patina 1,150.00
Wall Pocket, 10" h, high button
shoe shape, gold velvet, multicolored beading, Iroquois 100.00

NORTHWEST COAST

Bowl, 7¼" l, wood, red cedar,
carved seal form, incised octopus image on each side, abalone shell, bone, and glass bead
dec, black pigment 1,380.00
Pipe, 8¼" l, wood, carved, two op-

posing bears form, cylindrical
brass bowl, pierced stem, reddish–brown patina 200.00
Spoon, cow horn, incised and
carved cone shape handle 230.00
Staff, 34" l, wood, cylindrical, high
relief carved and incised totem
figures 750.00
Trinket Basket
3⅝" d, 2⅞" h, aniline orange and
brown embroidery design, rattle top, Tlinglit 330.00
6½" l, 4¾" h, twined, cedar bark
base, Nootka 575.00

PLAINS

Amulet, 7" l, hide, lizard form,
beaded, throng attachment 635.00
Bag, 14" l, flared rect, hide, sinew
sewn, beaded, banded bar and
stepped geometric design, fringe
dec 550.00
Book Cover, 8 x 11¾", faded blue
suede leather, spot stitched
blue, red, and white beads 55.00
Bridle, horsehair, woven multicolored geometric designs, yellow
ground, candy striped reins,
trade glass rosettes, Ute/Sho-
shone 1,150.00
Cuffs, pr, 12" l, woman's, blue, red,
and gold faceted beads, white
ground, c1900, Sioux 225.00
Drum, 17½" d, hoop construction,
skin cov on one side with green
and faded star design 275.00
Knife Case, 10" l, hide, sinew
sewn, beaded front, parfleche
back with painted dec, wood
handle knife 450.00
Leggings, pr
25" l, 2¾" w, beaded, mountain
and cross design, cut metallic
green, red, yellow, and blue,
blue and white ground 425.00
32" l, hide and cloth, sinew
stitched beaded dec 750.00
36½" l, hide and cloth, sinew
stitched beadwork, red silk ribbon and brass button trim,
Sioux 550.00
Moccasins, pr
5½" l, child's, hide, hard soles,

beaded, sinew stitched, royal
blue edge cuffs **550.00**
7" l, child's, hide, sewn stitched,
beaded dec, Santee Sioux .. **695.00**
9½" l, yellow ochre leather,
beaded floral designs, sinew
sewn with brass button closures **475.00**
10" l, rubbed hide, sinew
stitched, beaded, banded and
stepped geometric and cross
dec, tin cone fringe **2,990.00**
Pipe Bag
15½" l, smoked tanned hide,
beaded floral motif, silk ribbon
edge, Cree **525.00**
21" l, hide, sinew sewn, beaded
and dyed porcupine quill dec,
twisted fringe, Sioux **810.00**
Pipe Bowl, 5½" h, 9¼" l, red, elbow
form, carved and incised heart
and banded dec **375.00**
Pipe Stem, 25½" h, wood, carved
pierced panels, red pigment,
brass tack and plaited wrapped
porcupine quillwork dec **1,265.00**
Pouch
4" l, hide, sq, sinew stitched,
beaded, tin cone fringe dec .. **1,265.00**
4 x 5½", beaded maroon horse
and white bull's head, reverse
with multicolored floral design,
geometric edge, Sioux **250.00**
4½ x 5¾", sinew sewn, smoked
buckskin, clear, red, blue,
white, and orange beads **200.00**

WEST AND SOUTHWEST

Basket
3⅜" h, 8¾" l, yucca and martynia
geometric design **145.00**
5" h, cov, twined overlay, knotted
and indented base, Karok ... **325.00**
15½" d, 10¾" h, two simple geometric band designs **825.00**
Blanket, 4' 4" x 6' 7", wool, stylized
Navaho chief pattern, gold, red,
and green, dark gray ground,
fringed ends, Chimayo **225.00**
Bowl
2½" d, blackware, gun metal finish, inscribed "Rose," San Ildefonso Pueblo **175.00**

2¾" d, blackware, matted
painted dec, banded feather
motif, inscribed "Blue Corn,
San Ildefonso Pueblo" **345.00**
4¼" h, basketry, half twist overlay, Hupa/Yurok **325.00**
6" d, blackware, matte painted
serpent image, inscribed
"Marie," San Ildefonso **1,035.00**
10¼" d, orange clay, flared rim,
black and red painted int.,
Hopi **325.00**
14¾" d, coiled basketry, willow
and blackened devil's claw,
flared sides, checkered bands,
Apache **410.00**
Box, 1½ x 4½ x 3", silver and turquoise, rect, stone set hinged
cover, stamped and repousse
dec, ftd, Navaho **1,150.00**
Bracelet, silver
Navaho, five turquoises with russet matrix **75.00**
Zuni, thunderbird, inlaid coral,
jet, mother-of-pearl, and turquoise dec, stamped "R B" .. **90.00**
Canteen, 10¼" h, 24" d, pottery,
polychrome dec, Acoma **410.00**
Concho Belt
Black leather strap, eleven sand
cast conchos, turquoise dec,
Navaho **375.00**
Silver, seven scalloped edged
oval conchos dec and eight
butterflies, stamped and repousse dec **750.00**
Drum, 22¾" d, rawhide cov with
blue and orange design **275.00**
Jar
3¾" h, 5⅞" d, blackware, sgd
"Marie," San Ildefonso **275.00**
3¾" h, 7⅜" d, blackware, carved,
polished figure dec, sgd
"Juanita Wo Peen," Santa
Clara **195.00**
6" h
Blackware, wing feather design, sgd "Marie," San Ildefonso **610.00**
Polychrome Pottery, dark
brown and red dec, white
slip, Zuni **250.00**
6¼" h, polished buff slip, red
ochre umber bird dec, Zia ... **140.00**

7" h, blackware, matte painted dec, inscribed "Rose," San Ildefonso Pueblo **690.00**

8¼" h, blackware, relief figure dec, Santa Clara **330.00**

9" h, red clay body, orange slip, black and orange painted dec, indented base, Zia **450.00**

10½" h, pink clay body, grayish–white slip, black painted dec, indented base, weighted bottom, Cochiti **1,450.00**

Kachina Doll
11¼" h, green case mask with red yarn dec, black body with white spots, wedding sash and fox pelt, Hopi **110.00**

12" h, green–blue case mask with feather dec, painted canvas ceremonial robe, Hopi ... **225.00**

Necklace
Santo Domingo
24" l, turquoise nugget, shell ends **55.00**

16¾" l, jet, turquoise, gypsum, and red and white plastic, thunderbird form **175.00**

Zuni, silver squash, bird design, turquoise and coral chip inlay, marked "S D" **250.00**

Olla
9" h, buff slip pottery, black and red ochre flowers and bird dec, red slip base, Santo Domingo **220.00**

10" h, buff slip pottery, black design, red ochre band, concave bottom, Santo Domingo, c1925 .... **770.00**

11" h, blackware, flared sides, indented base, tapered neck, dimpled rim, four bear paw pattern around neck **2,185.00**

Rug, Navaho
3' 9" x 5' 5", natural wool, dark brown and indigo blue stripes **325.00**

4' 5" x 6' 7", wool, red and dark brown, carded brown and natural triangular stripe design .. **625.00**

4' 5" x 7' 2", diamond design, carded red, purple, and orange with dark brown and natural, red selvage cord, c1900 **775.00**

Saddle Blanket, 24 x 28", wool, hand carded dark brown and natural design, carded tan ground, Navaho **30.00**

Tapestry
1' 11" x 2' 2", woven, dark brown and red cross dec, natural ground, Navaho **200.00**

2' 4" x 3' 4", woven, two eagles, natural, gold, lavender, and brown, gray ground, turquoise and brown border, Navaho .. **450.00**

Tray, 11½" h, basketry, coiled, willow and blackened devil's claw, whirling stepped and checkered radiants, Apache **475.00**

Vase, 8" h, blackware, imp bear paw dec, Santa Clara **175.00**

Wedding Vase, 11½" h, blackware, carved image of serpent, inscribed "Severa," Santa Clara Pueblo **690.00**

INDIAN TREE PATTERN

History: The Indian Tree pattern is a popular pattern of porcelain made from the last half of the 19th century until the present. The pattern consisting of an Oriental crooked tree branch, landscape, exotic flowers, and foliage is found in predominantly greens, pinks, blues, and oranges on a white ground. Several English potteries, including Burgess and Leigh, Coalport, and Maddock, made wares with the Indian Tree pattern.

Reference: Susan and Al Bagdade, *Warman's English & Continental Pottery & Porcelain, 2nd Edition,* Wallace–Homestead, 1991.

Bowl, 10" d, 5½" h, ftd, scalloped, marked "Copeland and Spode" **135.00**

Cake Plate, 10½" d, marked "Coalport" **30.00**

Chocolate Set, cov, chocolate pot, six cups and saucers, marked "Copeland and Spode," price for fourteen piece set **180.00**

Compote, 8" d, ftd, marked "Coalport" **60.00**

Cup and Saucer, marked "Coalport" **25.00**

Eggcup, marked "Coalport" **15.00**

Gravy Tureen, cov, ladle, English **85.00**

Plate, chamfered corners, Johnson Bros., 8″ d, $12.00.

Pitcher, 6″ h, marked "Maddox & Sons"	40.00
Plate, 8″ d, fluted, marked "Coalport"	15.00
Platter, 18½″ l, marked "Spode"	100.00
Salt and Pepper Shakers, pr, beehive shape	50.00
Sauce Boat, 8″ l, matching underplate, marked "Coalport"	100.00
Sugar, cov, marked "Minton"	50.00
Teapot, marked "Johnson Bros"	45.00
Vegetable Dish, cov, English	75.00

INK BOTTLES

History: Ink was sold in glass or pottery bottles in the early 1700s in England. Retailers mixed their own formula and bottled it. The commercial production of ink did not begin in England until the late 18th century and in America until the early 19th century.

Initially, ink was supplied in pint or quart bottles, often of poor manufacture, from which smaller bottles could be filled. By the mid–19th century when writing implements were improved, emphasis was placed on making an "untippable" bottle. Shapes ranging from umbrella style to turtles were tried. Since ink bottles were displayed, shaped or molded bottles became popular.

The advent of the fountain pen relegated the ink bottle to the back drawer. Bottles lost their decorative design and became merely functional items.

References: Ralph & Terry Kovel, *The Kovels' Bottles Price List, Ninth Edition,* Crown Publishers, 1992; Carlo & Dot Sellari, *The Standard Old Bottle Price Guide,* Collector Books, 1989.

Periodical: *Antique Bottle and Glass Collector,* PO Box 187, East Greenville, PA 18041.

Additional Listings: See *Warman's Americana & Collectibles* for more examples.

Caw's Ink, New York, sq, 2¼ x 1⅞″, $18.00.

Butler, 2³⁄₁₆″ h, sq, aqua, open pontil	75.00
C Chandler & Co, 2⅝″ h, greenish–aqua	145.00
Drapers Improved Patent, clear	125.00
Estes, NY, 4⅛″ h, aqua, eight sided, open pontil	525.00
Figural, barrel, aquamarine, emb "Pat Oct 17 1865"	
4″ h, sheared mouth	310.00
5″ h, ground mouth	300.00
F Kidder, Improved Indelible Ink, sq, aquamarine	100.00
G & RS American Writing Fluid, 2⅝″ h, aqua, open pontil	275.00
Harrison's Columbian, 4¼″ h, sapphire blue, applied mouth, partial label	575.00
Hauthaways Lynn Furnishing Ink, 9″ h, green, open pontil	75.00
J K Palmer Chemist Boston Master Ink, 9⅛″ h, cylindrical, yellowish–olive, applied mouth, iron pontil	285.00

Josiah Johnsons Japan Writing Fluid, 2½" h, pottery 150.00
Laughlins and Bushfield, 2⅞" h, aqua, eight sided 80.00
Opdyke Bros Ink, 2½" h, barrel shape, aqua 125.00
Pattersons Excelsior, 2½" h, aqua, eight sided 350.00
Petroleum Writing Fluid, 2⅝" h, aqua 125.00
Shephard & Allens Writing Fluid, 6⅜" h, gold amber 75.00
SO Dunbar, Taunton, MA, 2⅛" h, aqua, twelve sided, open pontil 145.00
Thaddeus Davids & Co Steel Pen Ink, 6" h, blue–green 75.00
W E Bonney, 5¾" h, barrel form, aquamarine, collared mouth .. 230.00
Willistons Superior Indelible Ink, 2⅜" h, aqua, open pontil 250.00

INKWELLS

History: The majority of commonly found inkwells were produced in the United States and Europe from the early 1800s to the 1930s. The most popular materials were glass and pottery because these substances resisted the corrosive effects of ink.

Inkwells were a sign of the office or a wealthy individual. The common man tended to dip his ink directly from the bottle. The period from 1870 to 1920 represented a "golden age" when inkwells in elaborate designs were produced.

References: William E. Covill, Jr., *Inkbottles and Inkwells,* William S. Sullwold Publishing, 1971; Betty and Ted Rivera, *Inkstands and Inkwells: A Collector's Guide, Second Edition,* Crown Publishers, 1973.

Collectors' Club: The Society of Inkwell Collectors, 5136 Thomas Avenue So., Minneapolis, MN 55410.

Additional Listings: See *Warman's Americana & Collectibles* for more examples.

Annular, 1⅝" h, 2¹³⁄₁₆" d, olive green, sheared mouth 800.00
Bakelite, 12 x 7", double inkwells, two pen troughs, dark marbleized base 175.00

Bennington Type, 1⅝" h, 2¼" d, petal form, brown and yellow glaze 245.00
Blown Three Mold
  1½" h, 2" d, olive amber, disc mouth 185.00
  1½" h, 2⅜" d, olive green, disc mouth, Coventry Glass Works 100.00
  1⅝" h, 1⅞" d, yellow olive, disc mouth, Keene Marlboro Street Glassworks 165.00
  1¾" h, 2⅝" d, yellow olive, disc mouth, Coventry Glass Works 135.00
  1⅞" h, 2½" d, medium green, disc mouth, Mt Vernon Glass Works 2,530.00

Cast metal, rect, double snail swivel bottles, $95.00.

Cast Iron, 5½" h, stag's head, clear glass well 135.00
Cut Glass, cov, 2⅜" h, turquoise blue, six cut facets 150.00
Figural, glass
  Boot, 2⅞ x 3", turquoise blue .. 150.00
  Teakettle, 2¾" h, 3¼" l, lime sherbet clambroth, six lobed body, sheared mouth, brass cap 1,050.00
  Turtle, 1⅞" h, 3¾" l, clear, sheared mouth, smooth base 385.00
Free Blown, cov, 2 x 2½", cobalt, open pontil 225.00
Mechanical, 3" h, revolving wheelbarrow, milk glass snail shape bottle 275.00

Pitkin Type, thirty–six swirled ribs, funnel mouth

1½" h, 2" d, olive green, chip and mouth flake **145.00**

1⅞" h, 2¼" d, yellow olive **475.00**

Porcelain

3⅛" h, floral design, red, green, and blue **55.00**

5¼" sq, girl playing with cat, multicolored **125.00**

Redware, 1¼ x 2¼", coggled edge **145.00**

Tiffany Type, cov, 2¼ x 3¾", purple ground, irid blue and pink dec, brass lid **275.00**

Wood, 3⅞ x 5¾", hand carved cat in shoe **125.00**

IRONS

History: Ironing devices have been used for many centuries, with the earliest references dating from 1100. Irons from the Medieval, Renaissance, and early industrial eras can be found in Europe, but are rare. Fine brass engraved irons and hand–wrought irons dominated the period prior to 1850. After 1850 irons began a series of rapid evolutionary changes.

Between 1850 and 1910 irons were heated in four ways: 1) a hot metal slug was inserted into the body, 2) a burning solid, e.g., coal or charcoal, was placed in the body, 3) a liquid or gas, e.g., alcohol, gasoline, or natural gas, was fed from an external tank and burned in the body, and 4) conduction heating, usually drawing heat from a stove top.

Electric irons are just beginning to find favor among iron collectors.

References: Esther S. Berney, *A Collectors Guide To Pressing Irons And Trivets*, Crown Publishers, 1977; A. H. Glissman, *The Evolution Of The Sad Iron*, published by author, 1970; Dave Irons, *Pressing Iron Patents: A Pictorial Presentation of Patent Briefs, 1876-1912*, published by author, 1994; Brian Jewell, *Smoothing Irons, A History And Collector's Guide*, Wallace–Homestead, 1977, out–of–print; Judy (author) and Frank (illustrator) Politzer, *Early Tuesday Morning: More Little Irons and Trivets*, published by author, 1986; Judy and Frank Politzer, *Tuesday's Children*, published by authors, 1977.

Collectors' Clubs: Club of the Friends of Ancient Smoothing Irons, PO Box 215, Carlsbad, CA 92008; Midwest Sad Iron Collectors Club, 2828 West Ave., Burlington, IA 52601.

Museums: Henry Ford Museum, Dearborn, MI; Shelburne Museum, Shelburne, VT; Sturbridge Village, Sturbridge, MA.

Additional Listings: See *Warman's Americana & Collectibles* for more examples.

Advisors: David and Sue Irons.

Charcoal, double spout, marked "New Plus Ultra/Pat'd July 29, 02," iron body, wood handle, $115.00.

Billiard Table Iron, English, 6 x 12" base **175.00**

Charcoal, Bless/Drake, face of bearded man on rear, damper, high chimney **75.00**

Electric

Deco, Sauders, "Silver Streak," Pyrex, red or blue **700.00**

Universal Travel, curling iron insert **40.00**

Fluter

Gribs, wrought fluting scissors . **200.00**

Knox, machine type, oval on base, enclosed picture of Susan R Knox, 1870 .... **225.00**

Fluting board with flat steel clips . **45.00**

Goffering

Queen Anne style, 3¾" l barrel, all iron, no heater **375.00**

Wrought single barrel, 4" l, spider with three or four legs, no heater **400.00**

Miniature
Double point, sad iron, cylinder
grip, all iron, 2½" to 3" 40.00
Geneva, hand fluter, 1866 .... 200.00
Kenrick Co, sad iron, 3" l, all iron,
oval base 60.00
Polisher Troy, grid design to bot-
tom, round front 45.00

IRONWARE

History: Iron, a metallic element that occurs abundantly in combined forms, has
been known for centuries. Items made from
iron range from the utilitarian to the decorative. Early hand–forged ironwares are of
considerable interest to Americana collectors.

References: Frank T. Barnes, *Hooks,
Rings & Other Things: An Illustrated Index
of New England Iron, 1600–1860,* The
Christopher Publishing House, 1988; Doug-
las Congdon–Martin, *Figurative Cast Iron:
A Collector's Guide,* Schiffer Publishing,
1994; *Griswold Cast Iron: A Price Guide,*
L–W Book Sales, 1993; Kathryn McNerney,
Antique Iron Identification and Values, Col-
lector Books, 1984, 1993 value update;
Dana G. Morykan and Harry L. Rinker, *War-
man's Country Antiques & Collectibles,
Second Edition,* Wallace–Homestead,
1994; George C. Neumann, *Early American
Antique Country Furnishings: Northeastern
America, 1650–1880's,* L–W Book Sales,
1984, 1993 reprint; Herbert, Peter, and
Nancy Schiffer, *Antique Iron,* Schiffer Pub-
lishing, 1979; Diane Stoneback, *Kitchen
Collectibles: The Essential Buyer's Guide,*
Wallace–Homestead, 1994.

Periodicals: *Cast Iron Cookware News,*
28 Angela Ave., San Anselmo, CA 94960;
*Griswold Cast Iron Collectors' News &
Marketplace,* PO Box 521, North East, PA
16428; *Kettles 'n Cookware,* Drawer B, Perrysburg, NY 14129.

Collectors' Club: Griswold & Cast Iron
Cookware Assoc., 54 Macon Ave., Asheville, NC 28801.

Additional Listings: Banks, Boot Jacks,
Doorstops, Fireplace Equipment, Food
Molds, Irons, Kitchen Collectibles, Lamps,
and Tools.

Andirons, pr
9¼" h, cast, detailed bust of
man, plumed hat, plinths with
"P B" 175.00
13" h, wrought, goose neck,
penny feet, faceted finials ... 125.00
Architectural Fittings, pr, 35" w,
69½" h, painted and parcel gilt,
circular apertures, pierced and
scrolled surrounds 925.00
Basin, 11¼" d, cast, pitted, pinhole 40.00
Boot Scraper, 20½" l, cast, figural,
dachshund, painted black, red
accents 85.00
Candelabra
11½" h, pr, painted, jesters on
spheres with twin light balancing bar 825.00
59" h, wrought, 20th C 145.00

Skeleton Key, 5½" l, $17.50.

Candleholder, wrought
14" l, sticking tommy, pitted ... 145.00
20½" h, hanging type, twisted
stem with hook and three
sockets, black finish 500.00
Candle Stand, 63" h, wrought,
twisted stem, adjustable arm,
two brass sockets, tripod base . 330.00
Charger, 18¾" d, cast, classical
dec, dark patina, late 19th/early
20th C 175.00
Cookie Board, cast
3 x 4⅞", rect, oval center with
bird on branch 175.00
4½ x 6", oval, pineapple dec .. 155.00
4¾ x 5¾", oval, swan in circle . 175.00
Cuspidor, 13½" l, cast, turtle
shape, painted black, missing
int. pan 95.00

Doorstop, cast
   10" h, police dog, dark bronze
     finish **55.00**
   13¾" h, dog, seated, black and
     white, red collar **250.00**
Factory Torch, 7¼" h, cast,
   marked "Strength & Durability,
   Well's Unbreakable A G Wells &
   Co" **145.00**
Figure, 5½" l, cast, frog **70.00**
Fireback, cast, 18th C
   15½" h, mask, dated 1763 .... **200.00**
   24" h
     Caricatured figure, repaired
      crack **575.00**
     Horse and rider **810.00**
     Tombstone form, from Plymp-
      ton, MA, home **230.00**
   33" h, heraldic lion **575.00**
Firedogs, 9" h, pr, cast, brass finials, late 19th C **30.00**
Garden Ornament, 12" h, cast, figural, rabbit, white repaint **225.00**
Garden Urn, 29¼" h, cast, bowl
   rebolted to stem **110.00**
Gate, pr, Italian, wrought, arched
   form with dec allover, scrolls and
   foliage dec, late 19th C **2,300.00**
Hinges, pr, wrought
   7½" l, ram's horn scroll, pins .. **125.00**
   16" l, ram's horn scroll **145.00**
   16½" l, bird's head ends **110.00**
   20" l, openwork design **275.00**
   31" l, scroll ends **200.00**
Hitching Post, 48½" h, cast, tree
   branch form, concrete base ... **350.00**
Ladder, 53½" h, wrought, steps on
   both sides **250.00**
Lamp, Betty, wrought
   3½" h, hanger, missing wick pick **175.00**
   4" h, twisted hanger, old black
     paint **210.00**
   4½" h, brass spade shaped or-
     nament, engraved border,
     marked "J J" **325.00**
Mirror Frame, 16" h, cast, painted
   dec, American, mid 19th C **432.00**
Mortar and Pestle, cast
   6¼" h **85.00**
   6¾" h, flared foot **55.00**
Nutcracker, 6¼" h, cast, fits over
   knee, Minerva head ornament . **110.00**
Peel, wrought
   43" l, ram's horn handle **145.00**

   46½" l, ram's horn handle, pitted
     blade **110.00**
Pencil Holder, bulldog, painted,
   medallion around neck, 1933
   Chicago World's Fair **37.50**
Pipe Drying Rack, 16" l, wrought **325.00**
Plaque, 21½" l, 17" h, cast, oval,
   medieval dec, dark patina, late
   19th/early 20th C **175.00**
Rushlight Holder
   9½" h, tripod base, tooled brass
     wafer at bottom stem **375.00**
   10¼" h, mushroom top counter-
     weight, wood base **275.00**
   16½" h, wrought, candle socket
     counterweight, twisted detail . **475.00**
Scale, cast, oval brass pan
   marked "Fairbanks" **145.00**
Sugar Nippers, 9" l, wrought, simple tooled detail **200.00**
Terrace Railings, four 54½" l, 14"
   h sections, Victorian, late 19th C **520.00**
Toaster, 14½" l, wrought, adjusta-
   ble handle **55.00**
Toy, 4" h, stove, "A1," orig gilt fin-
   ish, attributed to J & E Stevens **235.00**
Trammel, sawtooth, wrought
   14" l, fleur–de–lis finials, pitted . **250.00**
   21½" h, dec crest **245.00**
   35" l, lollipop finial **175.00**
Trivet, cast
   Eagle, horseshoe with "God
     Bless Our Home," 10" l **100.00**
   Floral, star handle, 9" l **75.00**
   George Washington, 9½" l **75.00**
   Lyre, 7¼" l **40.00**
   Pinwheel, 7½" l **90.00**
   Round, leaf center, 6" d **115.00**
   Tulip, 8" l, marked "S B Miller" **55.00**
Umbrella Stand, 29" h, Victorian,
   cast, nautical motif, central an-
   chor supporting ropes over shell
   form base **575.00**
Wall Ornament, 31½" l, two birds,
   compote of fruit, and scrolls dec,
   white and black repaint **225.00**

IVORY

History: Ivory, a yellowish–white organic
material, comes from the teeth or tusks of
animals and lends itself well to carving. It

has been used for centuries by many cultures for artistic and utilitarian items.

Ivory from elephants shows a reticulated criss–cross pattern in a cross section. Hippopotamus teeth, walrus tusks, whale teeth, narwhal tusks, and boar tusks also are ivory sources. Vegetable ivory, bone, stag horn, and plastic are ivory substitutes which often confuse collectors.

For information on how to identify real ivory, see Bernard Rosett's "Is It Genuine Ivory?" in Sandra Andacht's *Oriental Antiques & Art: An Identification and Value Guide* (Wallace–Homestead, 1987).

Reference: Gloria and Robert Mascarelli, *Oriental Antiques,* Wallace–Homestead, 1992.

Periodical: *Netsuke & Ivory Carving Newsletter, 3203 Adams Way, Ambler, PA 19002.*

Note: Dealers and collectors should be familiar with The Endangered Species Act of 1973, amended in 1978, which limits the importation and sale of antique ivory and tortoiseshell items.

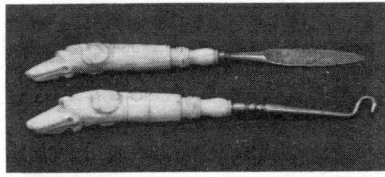

Button Hook and Manicure Item, dog head handles, price for pair, $48.00.

Box
  Ball form
    Chinese, relief carved lid and sides, intricate dragons, scrolls, 3¾" d **165.00**
    Continental, stone carved ext. with center hinge separating two carved figural scenes, late 18th/early 19th C, 1¾" d **550.00**
  Book form, carved and inscribed ivory paneled covers, Biblical subjects, wood frame, Continental, 18th C, 3⅞" l **300.00**
  Rectangular, chamfered lid, ve-

neered ivory and bone panels, red and green incised bellflowers, blind fret bands, Anglo–Indian, 19th C, 9" w, 6½" d, 4½" h **800.00**
Shell shaped, hinged allover carved lid, Continental, late 18th C, 3" l **750.00**
Chess Set, fitted case, one pawn missing **200.00**
Cup, cov, European, highly carved, scrolled leaves surrounding figureheads and fruits, painted metal and mother–of–pearl finial figure, 19th C, 13¾" h **2,750.00**
Figural Group
  Ancient with staff, boy on goat, 12" h **450.00**
  Figures on hillside, teak stand, Chinese **200.00**
Figure
  Boy wearing classical costume, ivory trimmed walnut pedestal, Continental, 18th C, 7½" h . .**1,600.00**
  Infant
    Reclining, rect base, Continental, fine age lines, 19th C, 5⅛" l **375.00**
    Sitting, oval base, European, age cracks, late 17th/early 18th C, 4¼" h **450.00**
  Maiden, holding scroll and pen, teak stand, Chinese, 12½" h . **250.00**
  Man, holding fan, mask, and bells, painted, signed, Chinese, 6¾" h **650.00**
  Woman, praying, possibly Colonial, 18th C, 7" h **520.00**
Handle, carved male head, mounted on wood stand, stem damage, late 18th/early 19th C, 4" h **375.00**
Knife and Fork, Continental, ivory handles carved with female figures in suggestive poses, steel blade and fork, fitted case, 18th C, 7" l fork, 8" l knife **1,325.00**
Miniature Portrait, lady wearing fur hat, oval, signed "Rochat," gilt metal frame, 19th C, 3½ x 2¼" **210.00**
Model, Taj Mahal, presented to American Ambassador to India from Indian government, fitted

case, minor imperfections, c1910, 9¼" sq base, 6½" h ... **860.00**
Mystery Ball, stand, Chinese, 2¼" d **120.00**
Painting
Indian image on oval ivory medallion set in wooden floral carved standing frame, late 19th C, 5¼" h **285.00**
Youth dressed as harlequin, three–quarter length view, signed "IBM & PEL," label on back "la petite Girand au theatre la cigale, Paris July 1917," framed, 4⅛ x 2½" **750.00**
Plaque
George Washington, round, set in wood frame, 19th C, 2¼" d **700.00**
Queen, high relief carving, rect, Continental, 19th C, 2¾ x 3¼" **865.00**
Snuff Bottle, sides carved with floral and figural design, brown stone stopper, signed, Chinese, late 19th/early 20th C, 2¼" h .. **135.00**
Stein, German, carved Roman subjects in high relief, silver and silver–gilt mounted, 19th C, 8⅝" h **4,725.00**
Vase, carved and pierced, oval cylindrical form, dragon and cloud design, Oriental, 5¼" h **85.00**

JACK-IN-THE-PULPIT VASES

History: Jack-in-the-Pulpit glass vases, made in the trumpet form, were in vogue during the late 19th and early 20th centuries. The vases were made in a wide variety of patterns, colors, and sizes.

Additional Listings: See specific glass categories.

Cranberry, 10" h, applied crystal rigaree dec and feet **200.00**
Loetz
13¾" h, gold spotted iridescent, calla lily form top, bulbous base, Austrian **1,200.00**
15½" h, irid gold and purple, applied leaves and vines dec .. **485.00**
Mt Washington
Burmese, 6¾" h **300.00**
Satin, 12½" h, ruffled rim, white

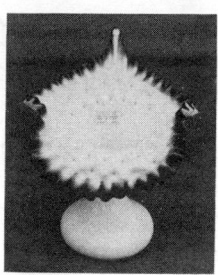

White opaline body, ruby red trim around ruffles, pleated and dimpled, 9¼" h, $150.00.

ground, lavender and white flowers, green leaves **325.00**
Opalescent, 5⅜" h, flower petal top, pink and yellow stripes ... **85.00**
Spatter, 7¼" h, green, peach, yellow, and white spatter top, green Diamond Quilted pattern body . **65.00**
Steuben, 6" h, Aurene, irid glass, broad undulating rim over tapering stem, circular foot **865.00**
Tiffany
11" h, irid, ruffled flower form rim, round foot, marked "9166 L C Tiffany–Favrile" **2,000.00**
17" h, gold, floriform, slender stem with ribbed int., bulb base, luster finish, inscribed "LCT 2198B" **5,465.00**
18¼" h, gold irid, pink–blue luster, folded ruffled rim, amber stem, bulb shape foot, marked "L C T 1302B" **3,200.00**

JADE

History: Jade is the generic name for two distinct minerals, nephrite and jadeite. Nephrite, an amphibole mineral from Central Asia and used in pre–18th century pieces, has a waxy surface and ranges in hues from white to almost a black green. Jadeite, a pyroxene mineral found in Burma and used from 1700 to the present, has a glassy appearance and comes in various shades of white, green, yellow–brown, and violet.

Jade cannot be carved because of its hardness. Shapes are achieved through sawing and grinding with wet abrasives, such as quartz, crushed garnets, and carborundum.

Prior to 1800 few pieces were signed or dated. Stylistic considerations are used for dating. The Ch'ien Lung period (1736–95) is considered the "golden age" of Jade.

Reference: Gloria and Robert Mascarelli, *Warman's Oriental Antiques,* Wallace–Homestead, 1992.

Periodical: Bulletin of the Friends of Jade, 5004 Ensign St., San Diego, CA 92117.

Museum: Avery Brundage Collection, de Young Museum, San Francisco, CA.

Bangle Bracelet
   3″ d, carved, Chinese, 19th C . **100.00**
   3½″ d, yellow, russet inclusions **275.00**
Belt Hook, carved in form of foo
   lion, 5″ h **25.00**
Bi, archaistic green and russet,
   carved bosses and calcification,
   6″ d **770.00**
Bowl, nephrite, quatrefoil form,
   carved with birds and flowers, 9″
   l **275.00**
Brush Washer, carved in form of
   lotus leaf, silver rim, hardwood
   stand, 5″ l **345.00**
Cabinet Vase, floral form with bird
   and rooster beside, teak stand,
   5¾″ h **325.00**
Cong, archaistic, well carved geo-
   metric designs, 5″ h **440.00**

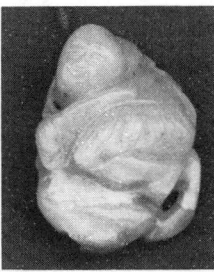

Burial Tomb Pendant, $115.00.

Figure
   Qilin, archaistic yellow, black
     markings, 18th C, 4″ l **330.00**
   Quan Yin with lotus blossom,
     teak stand, 9″ h **415.00**
   Recumbent Buffalo, green, fully
     carved figure, finely carved
     stand, 17th/18th C, 8″ l **5,500.00**
Hand Ax, russet, finely carved in
   Chou dynasty style, 19th C, 5″ l **358.00**
Model, citron, grayish–white, 18th
   C, 4½″ l **2,310.00**
Plaque, greenish–white, carved
   peaches and bats, 19th C, 4¾″ l **220.00**
Snuff Bottle, nephrite, ovoid form,
   dragon in relief, well–hollowed
   stopper, 19th C, 2¾″ l **192.00**
Sword Hilt–Facings, pr, Turkey,
   spinach colored sections, flat
   back, convex front, carved with
   pointed cusped pommel, pierced
   three times, 17th C, 4⅞″ l **2,400.00**
Urn, carved in form of foo dragon,
   carved wood stand, price for pair **115.00**

JAPANESE AND CHINESE CERAMICS

History: The Chinese pottery tradition has existed for thousands of years. By the 16th century, Chinese ceramic wares were being exported to India, Persia, and Egypt. The Ming dynasty (1368–1643) saw the strong development of glazed earthenwares and shapes. During the Ch'ing dynasty, the Ch'ien Lung period (1736–95) marked the golden age of interchange with the West.

Trade between China and the West began in the 16th century when the Portuguese established Macao. The Dutch entered the trade early in the 17th century. With the establishment of the English East India Company, all of Europe was seeking Chinese–made pottery and porcelain. Styles, shapes, and colors were developed to suit Western tastes. The tradition continued until the late 19th century.

Like the Chinese, the Japanese spent centuries developing their ceramic arts. Each region established its own forms, designs, and glazes. Individual artists added to the uniqueness.

Japanese ceramics began to be exported to the West in the mid–19th century. Their beauty quickly made them a favorite of the patrician class.

The ceramic tradition continues into the 20th century. Modern artists enjoy equal fame with older counterparts.

References: Christopher Dresser, *Traditional Arts and Crafts of Japan,* Dover Publications, 1994; Gloria and Robert Mascarelli, *Warman's Oriental Antiques,* Wallace–Homestead, 1992.

Periodical: *Orientalia Journal,* PO Box 94, Little Neck, NY 11363.

Museums: Art Institute of Chicago, Chicago, IL; Asian Art Museum of San Francisco, San Francisco, CA; George Walter Vincent Smith Art Museum, Springfield, MA.

Additional Listings: Canton, Fitzhugh, Imari, Kutani, Nanking, Rose Medallion, and Satsuma.

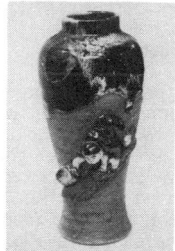

Vase, Sumida Guwa, child and pitcher, green robe, redware ground, black glaze top, sgd, cartouche mark, 7″ h, $175.00.

CHINESE

Bowl
 6¾″ d, hexagonal, turquoise, yellow, and orange dec, ftd .. **55.00**
 7″ d, green, pink, orange, and yellow dec **225.00**
 9″ d, blue and white lake, bridge, figures, and mountain scene, four character mark **80.00**
Charger, 19½″ d, octagonal, blue and white figures in landscape scene, paneled border with different designs **250.00**
Compote, 6¾″ d, 5″ h, dragon dec, yellow ground **225.00**
Cup, 1½″ h, white glazed, quatrefoil form, bas–relief floral and vase design, Qing Dynasty, damage, price for pair **330.00**
Dish
 7″ l, shaped, orange, green, brown, and rose floral dec ... **80.00**
 10¼″ w, square, blue and white landscape dec, paneled border with different designs ... **325.00**
Figure
 6¼″ h, parrots, rose, gilt beaks, price for pair **1,900.00**
 8″ h, female, seated, wearing robe, multicolored, 19th C ... **110.00**
 8½″ h, pigsty, green glaze, tower and rect pen enclosing pig, Han Dynasty **1,540.00**
Hat Stand, 11″ h, maroon and white mountain landscape scene **250.00**
Jar, cov, 10″ h, rose and green peony and foliage design, lime green ground, price for pair ... **600.00**
Planter, 27″ h, 18″ d, bird and floral dec, wood stand **275.00**
Plaque, 17½″ d, cloisonne enamel foliate and peacock feather designs, 19th C **715.00**
Plate
 9¼″ d, flowers, insects, and bird dec, price for pair **145.00**
 10¼″ d, blue and white landscape scene, hairline on rim . **75.00**
Platter, 14″ l, blue and white landscape scene **200.00**
Shaving Bowl, 10½″ d, blue and white floral dec **1,300.00**
Snuff Bottle, 2⅜″ h, blue and white dec **750.00**
Storage Jar, 9″ h, blue and white dragons and flowering plants dec **175.00**
Teapot, cov
 2¾″ h, Blanc–de–Chine, pomegranate form, six–pointed star shaped foot, applied handle spreading to leafy branches molded in relief on shoulder, leaf branches circling tapering cylindrical pouring spout, low

domical lid, c1700, firing crack to body, twig finial missing, crack to pouring spout, unmarked **990.00**

6¾" h, Mandarin pattern, late 18th/early 19th C, replaced mahogany lid **220.00**

Urn, 46¼" h, waterfront procession, battle scene with warriors, boats, and spectators in pavilion scene, dragon handles, wood stands, price for pair **600.00**

Vase

6" h, baluster form, panels with Dutch type figures, two love birds, blue flowery branches, rouge–de–fer and green ground, 18th C **220.00**

7½" h, bottle shape, blue and white dec, label "Bluett & Sons," Kang Shi **325.00**

7¾" h, cylindrical, crackleware, blue and white dec, hairline cracks, price for pair **40.00**

8" h, blue and white Hawthorn pattern, four character mark, price for pair **120.00**

9" h, gourd form, blue and white birds and insects dec, Kang Shi **150.00**

9⅝" h, floral panels, green ground, late 19th C **1,200.00**

11" h, dragon dec, turquoise ground, wood stand, price for pair **225.00**

12" h, cylindrical, blue and white village scene, Kang Shi **275.00**

12¼" h, cylindrical, blue and white dec, Kang Shi, four character mark **225.00**

13½" h, bottle form, blue and white dec **250.00**

14" h, cov, dragon dec, yellow ground, price for pair **950.00**

15½" h, cov, blue and white dec, price for pair **375.00**

17½" h, bottle form, incised dragon dec, yellow/brown glaze **220.00**

19" h, cov, multicolored floral dec, turquoise ground **130.00**

20½" h, pink and white exotic birds and flower dec, green ground **3,000.00**

24" h, allover multicolored figure vignettes, two handles **3,000.00**

25" h, dragon dec, celadon ground with cloud motif, stand, price for pair **700.00**

CHINESE EXPORT

Bowl, 9" d, figures in landscape dec, stand, 18th C **2,750.00**

Charger, 11½" d, armorial, int. finely penciled in iron–red and gilt, elegant peony and lotus sprays enclosed in gilt medallion, elaborate chrysanthemum and lotus border band at cavetto, modified egg and dart garland under wide border band, gilt peony and seasonal flower branches, blue enamel highlights surrounding arms of husbands, motto "In Ardua Virtus," gilt rim, Yongzheng Period, c1730, minor chips and restorations to rim, hairline cracks **1,540.00**

Cup and Saucer, floral dec **70.00**

Dish

7¼" d, cov, pomegranate form . **1,600.00**

8¹³⁄₁₆" d, armorial, central well dec with two cupids holding coronet, central coat of arms of Antonio de Araujo de Azevado, garland motto "ad Araujo," rose and blue diaper trellis at cavetto, grisalle landscape reserves, brilliant blue scalloped borders, blue and gilt rim, Qianlong Period, extensive surface wear **1,210.00**

Plate

8⅜" d, nine dec roundels encircling center fish dec, orange, green, blue, and yellow, price for pair **5,000.00**

9" d, bird on branch and leaf and floral dec, vine type border, price for pair **220.00**

Platter

12⅞" l, armorial, octagonal, wide blue enamel band, gold husks, gilt stippled band, blue cell diaper border, small modified floral band at cavetto, arms of Morgan, reindeer head with inscription "Elias Morgan," Qianlong Period, c1795, minor wear, rubbed **1,540.00**

13⅛" l, central field of garland urn, gilt starp surround, blue ground, cavetto painted with sawtooth band of gilt enamel and stars, gilt chain, concave border penciled with elaborate gilt garland on blue field, Jiaqing Period, c1821–49, very minor rim chips **660.00**

Punch Bowl, 11½" d, gilt, iron–red, and rich blue overglaze enamels, floral bands, festoon borders, int. rim, blue and gilt floral spray in well center, ext. banded en suite, floral sprays, framed oval sepia monochrome reserves, large house in park–like setting, river view, ships under sail, c1810, hairline crack, wear to enamels **1,320.00**

Sauce Dish, 5½" d, Famille Verte, shallow well, painted free interpretation of Boucher composition "Les Amours Pastorales," shepherdess guarding her flock, attended by lover, floral garland band at gilt rim, Qianlong Period, rim chips, hairline crack **550.00**

Soup Plate, 8¾" d, summer house with figures, blue, green, pink, rust, and gilt **220.00**

Tankard, 4¾" h, figural panels, rim chips **275.00**

Teapot, cov, 4⅞" h, globular, all-over pattern of grapevines, central arms of Hanbury with Comyn in Pretence, wide handle, extended spout, knob finial, Yonzheng Period, c1735, extensive wear to gilt **825.00**

Warming Dish, 9" d, blue and white dec, c1800 . . . . **125.00**

JAPANESE

Bowl, Kozan Pottery, calligraphic and landscape dec, light gray crackleware ground, 5" d, 4" h, price for pair **35.00**

Charger
15" d, unusual design and cart with flowering vase, large green seal mark **220.00**
15½" d, woman playing instrument, large green seal mark . **250.00**

Creamer, 4½" h, figural, seated figure, extended mouth forms spout, hair braid forms handle, black robe, blue garment, unglazed face, Sumida Guma . . . **150.00**

Dish, 14½" d, circular, blue and white dec, seal mark **150.00**

Ewer, 13½" h, cylindrical body, burnt red enamel dec, mottled brown glaze around neck and handle, applied raised figures of elder and seal, Sumida **115.00**

Figure, 17" h, cat, seated **700.00**

Incense Burner, 3½" h, Shishi form, green glaze, Oribe **375.00**

Pitcher, 4¾" h, figural, Chinaman blowing on conch shell, Sumida **44.00**

Plate
7¾" d, zodiac, scalloped edge, twelve signs in circular medallions, four variant stylized diaper ground, blossoming prunus blossoms on ext., chocolate rim, Arita, 19th C . . **225.00**
7⅝" d, blue and white dec **600.00**

Teabowl, 4¾" d, hand molded, irregular straight sides, small recessed ring foot, central well of flower head, peach glaze, double crackle pattern, Raku **150.00**

Teapot, 5½" h, gray ware, polychrome, seven gods of wisdom, partially glazed, Banko **410.00**

Vase, 12" h, hexagonal form, short flaring neck, creamy ash glaze, green flashes, Sansho, Shigaraki, late 18th C **500.00**

KOREAN

Bowl, cov, 7" h, Three Kingdoms, red stoneware, price for pair . . **50.00**

Figure, 8" h
Gray Stoneware, figure wearing hat, holding scepter, Old Silla **85.00**
Red Stoneware, figure wearing hat and bead necklace, Old Silla **65.00**

Lamp, 8" l, duck, gray stoneware,

Kaya States, punch motif relief
wings **100.00**
Vase, 8½" h, baluster form, Yore
Dynasty **110.00**

JASPERWARE

History: Jasperware is a hard, unglazed
porcelain with a colored ground, varying
from the most common blues and greens
to lavender, yellow, red, or black. The white
designs are applied in relief and often reflect a classical motif. Jasperware was first
produced at Wedgwood's Etruria Works in
1775. Josiah Wedgwood described it as "a
fine terra–cotta of great beauty and delicacy
proper for cameos."

Many other English potters, in addition to
Wedgwood, produced jasperware. Two of
the leaders were Adams and Copeland and
Spode. Several continental potters, e.g.,
Heubach, also produced the ware.

References: Susan and Al Bagdade,
*Warman's English & Continental Pottery &
Porcelain, 2nd Edition,* Wallace–Home-
stead, 1991; R. K. Henrywood, *Relief–
Moulded Jugs, 1820–1900,* Antique Collec-
tors' Club.

Reproduction Alert: Jasperware still is
made today, especially by Wedgwood.

Note: This category includes all pieces
of jasperware which were made by companies other than Wedgwood. Wedgwood
jasperware is found in the Wedgwood listing.

Biscuit Jar, 6" d, 6" h, bulbous,
white hunting scene, dark blue
ground, SP cover, rim, and handle, marked "Adams, England" **135.00**
Bookends, pr, 6" h, white figural
colonial man with cane, woman
with basket, blue ground, German **120.00**
Bowl, 7" d, white classical figures,
dark blue ground **225.00**
Box, cov
3⅞" l, 2½" w, 2⅛" h, white
winged lady, flowers, garlands
and cherubs, blue ground,
marked "Germany" **60.00**
5" l, oval, white cherub and

nymph, blue ground, marked
"Schafer & Vater, Germany" . **40.00**
Chamberstick, black and white,
snuffer **265.00**
Clock, 9⅛" h, white cherubs, foliage and flowers, sage green
ground, clock not working **150.00**
Coffeepot, 10" h, white classical
figures, green ground **185.00**
Creamer, blue, Kewpie, sgd **165.00**
Cup and Saucer, white classical
figures, formal foliage and engine turning, blue ground,
marked "Turner, England,"
c1800 .... **175.00**

**Clock, blue, marked "Swiss
Made," 6" h, $550.00.**

Hair Receiver, 3⅜" d, 3½" h, white
classical ladies and flowers, cu-
pids on lid, blue ground, marked
"Germany" **65.00**
Jardiniere, 7½" h, white Columbus
landing scene, light blue ground,
marked "Copeland" **195.00**
Jug, 8" h, white fox hunting scene,
green ground, c1820 .... **175.00**
Match Box, cov
Blue and white **85.00**
Lilac Dip **115.00**
Medallion, group of forty, various
Greek and Roman statesmen,
poets, and philosophers, blue
and white, imp lower case

marks, mounted in three gilt-wood frames, one cracked, one chipped **17,600.00**
Perfume Bottle, blue and white, hallmarked SS top **275.00**
Pin Dish, white Indian chief dec, holding bow and arrow, green ground, marked "Heubach" . . . **65.00**
Plaque
4" d, Judgment of Paris, blue and white, imp "Wedgwood," giltwood frame, first half 19th C **250.00**
5" d, white floral arrangement on marble style plinth, blue ground, 8 x 8" frame, glass dome **330.00**
7" h, robed maiden and child, framed, marked "Limoges," 19th C, price for pair **165.00**
Saltshaker, white classical figures, dark blue ground **60.00**
Sugar, cov, 6" h, two handles, white sacrifice scene, swan finial, blue ground, marked "Adams," c1800 . . . . **1,150.00**
Urn, 8" h, white hunting scene, cobalt blue ground, marked "Adams, Tunstall, England" **200.00**
Vase, 7" h, Lincoln portrait on front, eagle on reverse, white cameo relief, dark brown ground, unmarked, numbered "12" **132.00**
Wall Pocket, 5¼" h, cameo of two maidens dancing, hanging pendants, green ground **50.00**

JEWEL BOXES

History: The evolution of jewelry was paralleled by the development of boxes in which to store it. Jewel box design followed the fashion trends dictated by furniture styles. Many jewel boxes are lined.

Brass, 9" w, 4½" h, oblong, pink porcelain inserts, enameled flowers, musical instruments, beaded mounts, velvet lined, engraved "Maison Boisser" **450.00**
Cast Iron and Brass, 9" w, 7" d, 6" h, Napoleon III, relief scroll work,

birds, and emperor silhouette on cov, paw feet **75.00**
Cinnabar, Art Deco, black lacquer, 18K gold and coral details, carved jade animal pulls, gray agate platform, coral bead feet, orig fitted leather case, Wintz, French hallmark **5,500.00**
Glass
4½" d, 5½" w, sapphire blue, Mary Gregory dec of boy and girl, brass mounts and handles **600.00**
5" d, 5¾" w, cranberry, gold enamel floral dec, brass mounts and ring, key **425.00**
7" d, round, frosted and clear light blue glass, delicate enamel floral dec, brass colored ormolu feet **300.00**

Bronze, village scenes, French, 8 x 6¼" oval, 5" h, $265.00.

Gold, 3¼" w, ½" h, miniature, gold, encased hair cov, central miniature eye dec **1,500.00**
Porcelain, 3" d, 8" w, raised design collar, mottled green, pink, and white flowers, blue and beige leaves, pink silk lining, hinged lid, Wavecrest, c1904 . . . . **675.00**
Wood
6½" w, rect, Regency, satinwood, oval panel with dried flowers under glass dome on cov, ftd, early 19th C **350.00**
13" w, 10" d, 21" h, Victorian, rosewood, hinged brass line inlaid top, fitted int., drawer, later stand, English, mid 19th C **500.00**

JEWELRY

History: Jewelry has been a part of every culture. It was a way of displaying wealth, power, or love of beauty. In the current antiques marketplace, it is easiest to find jewelry dating after 1830.

Jewelry items were treasured and handed down as heirlooms from generation to generation. In the United States, antique jewelry is any jewelry at least 100 years old, a definition linked to U.S. Customs law. "Period," or "Heirloom/Estate" jewelry, i.e., jewelry at least 25 years old and acquired new, used, or through inheritance, is the term used for old jewelry that does not meet the "antique" definition.

The jewelry found in this listing is antique, period or heirloom/estate fine jewelry (i.e., made from gemstones and/or precious metals). The list contains no new reproduction pieces. Inexpensive and mass-produced costume jewelry is covered in *Warman's Americana & Collectibles*.

The value of a piece of old jewelry is derived from several criteria, including craftsmanship and scarcity, in addition to the current value of precious metals and gemstones. Note that antique and period pieces should be set with old cuts of stones that were in use at the time the piece was made. Antique jewelry is not comparable to contemporary pieces set with modern cut stones, and should not be appraised with the same standards. Nor should old mine, old European, or rose cut stones be replaced with modern brilliant cuts.

Several major auction houses, especially Christie's, Doyle's, Sotheby's, Skinner's, and Butterfield & Butterfield hold specialized jewelry auctions several times each year.

References: Lillian Baker, *Art Nouveau & Art Deco Jewelry: An Identification & Value Guide,* Collector Books, 1981, 1994 value update; Lillian Baker, *Fifty Years of Collectible Fashion Jewelry, 1925–1975,* Collector Books, 1986, 1992 value update; Lillian Baker, *100 Years of Collectible Jewelry, 1850–1950,* Collector Books, 1978, 1993 value update; Lillian Baker, *Twentieth Century Fashionable Plastic Jewelry,* Collector Books, 1992; Vivienne Becker, *Antique & Twentieth Century Jewellery, Sec-* ond Edition, N.A.G. Press, 1987; Vivienne Becker, *Fabulous Costume Jewelry: History of Fantasy and Fashion in Jewels,* Schiffer Pubilshing, 1993; Jeanenne Bell, *Answers to Questions About 1840–1950 Old Jewelry, Third Edition,* Books Americana, 1992; David Bennett and Daniela Mascetti, *Understanding Jewellery, Revised Edition,* Antique Collectors' Club, 1994; Matthew L. Burkholz and Linda Lichtenberg Kaplan, *Copper Art Jewelry: A Different Lustre,* Schiffer Publishing, 1993; Shirley Bury, *Jewellery 1789–1910: The International Era,* Antique Collectors' Club, 1991; Deanna Farnetti Cera (ed.), *Jewels of Fantasy: Costume Jewelry of the 20th Century,* Harry N. Abrams, 1992; Franco Cologni and Ettore Mocchetti, *Made By Cartier: 150 Years of Tradition and Innovation,* Abbeville Press, 1993; Genevieve Cummins and Neryvalle Taunton, *Chatelaines: Utility to Glorious Extravagance,* Antique Collectors' Club, 1994; Ginny Redington Dawes and Corinne Davidov, *Victorian Jewelry: Unexplored Treasures,* Abbeville Press, 1991; Lodovica Rizzoli Eleuteri, *Twentieth–Century Jewelry: Art Nouveau to Modern Design,* Electa, Abbeville, 1994; Roseann Ettinger, *Forties & Fifties Popular Jewelry,* Schiffer Publishing, 1994; Roseann Ettinger, *Popular Jewelry, 1840–1940,* Schiffer Publishing, 1990; Gabriele Greindl, *Gems of Costume Jewelry,* Abbeville Press, 1991; Sibyelle Jargstorf, *Baubles, Buttons and Beads: The Heritage of Bohemia,* Schiffer Publishing, 1994; Susan Jonas and Marilyn Nissensor, *Cuff Links,* Harry N. Abrams, 1991; Arthur Guy Kaplan, *The Official Identification and Price Guide To Antique Jewelry, Sixth Edition,* House of Collectibles, 1990, reprinted 1994; Elyse Zorn Karlin, *Jewelry and Metalwork in the Arts and Crafts Tradition,* Schiffer Publishing, 1993; J. J. Kellner, *The First Complete Reference Guide To Siam Sterling Nielloware,* published by author, 1993; Jack and Pet Kerins, *Collecting Antique Stickpins: Identification and Value Guide,* Collector Books, 1994; Antoinette Matlins and A. C. Bonanno, *Jewelry & Gems: The Buying Guide,* Gemstone Press, 1987; Patrick Mauries, *Jewelry By Chanel,* Bulfinch Press, 1993; Anna M. Miller, *Cameos Old and New,* Van Nostrand Reinhold, 1991; Harrice Simons Miller, *Costume Jewelry: Identification and*

Price Guide, 2nd Edition, Avon Books, 1994; Penny Chittim Morrill and Carol A. Beck, *Mexican Silver: 20th Century Handwrought Jewelry and Metalwork,* Schiffer Publishing, 1994; Michael Poynder, *The Price Guide to Jewellery 3000 BC– 1950 AD,* Antique Collectors' Club, 1990 reprint; Penny Proddow, Debra Healy, and Marion Fasel, *Hollywood Jewels: Movies, Jewelry, Stars,* Harry L. Abrams, 1992; Dorothy T. Rainwater, *American Jewelry Manufacturers,* Schiffer Publishing, 1988; Christie Romero, *Warman's Jewelry,* Wallace-Homestead, 1995; Nancy N. Schiffer, *Rhinestones! A Collector's Handbook & Price Guide,* Schiffer Publishing, 1993; Nancy N. Schiffer, *Silver Jewelry Treasures,* Schiffer Publishing, 1993; Walter Schumann, *Gemstones of the World,* Sterling Publishing Co., 1988; Sheryl Gross Shatz, *What's It Made Of? A Jewelry Materials Identification Guide,* published by author, 1991; Doris J. Snell, *Antique Jewelry With Prices, Updated Edition,* Wallace-Homestead, 1991; Ulrike vonHase–Schmundt et al., *Theodor Fahrner, Jewelry...between Avant–Garde and Tradition,* Schiffer Publishing, 1991; Janet Zapata, *The Jewelry and Enamels of Louis Comfort Tiffany,* Harry N. Abrams, 1993.

Periodicals: *Auction Market Resource For Gems & Jewelry,* PO Box 7683, Rego Park, NY 11374; *Gems & Gemology* Gemological Institute of America, 1660 Stewart St., Santa Monica, CA 90404; *Jewelers' Circular Keystone/Heritage,* PO Box 2085, Radnor, PA 19080-9485.

Videotape: *Hidden Treasures,* Venture Entertainment, Leigh Leshner and Christie Romero, 1992.

Collectors' Clubs: National Cuff Link Society, PO Box 346, Prospect Heights, IL 60070; The Society of Jewelry Historians, U.S.A., Jewelry Design Resource, E–312, Fashion Institute of Technology, 227 West 27th St., New York, N.Y. 10001.

Advisor: Christie Romero.

Dates:

Georgian	**1714–1830**
Victorian	**1837–1901**
Edwardian	**1890–1920**
Arts and Crafts	**1890–1920**
Art Nouveau	**1895–1910**
Art Deco	**1920–1935**
Retro Modern	**1935–1945**
Post-War Modern	**1945–1965**

Bracelet
Art Deco
Flexible, platinum, a straight line of 55 old European–cut diamonds, approx 6.00 cts tw, 55 sq–cut sapphires, approx 11.00 cts tw, set in alternating rows of 5 stones each, forming a checkerboard pattern, several sapphires replaced, 7" x ⅜" ...**5,750.00**
Link
Nine oval black onyx links joined by platinum horizontal bar links, each set with 4 circ–cut diamonds, sgd "Tiffany & Co.," 7¼" × ⅜" **2,990.00**
Two openwork notched rect plaques, each set with a center marquise–shaped diamond, approx .55 ct each, set throughout with circ–cut and baguette diamonds, joined by opposed D–shaped links set with circ–cut and baguette diamonds, approx 10.00 cts tw, 6⅞" × ¾" **7,475.00**
Art Nouveau, link, yg, 6 oval opals, each prong and bezel–set within an open scrolled yg wire frame joined with an old European–cut diamond–set link, repair evident, 7¼ × ¾" **3,910.00**
Arts and Crafts, link, silver, links of alternating grape clusters and leaves terminating in an oval clasp set with amber cabochon, approx 25.00 × 16.80 mm, imp "830," "GJ" for Georg Jensen, c1915–30 mark, 7" × 1" **1,380.00**
Post–War Modern, cuff, SS, freeform band, curved edge tapering from 1¾" at one end to 1" at the other, lengths of applied square wire curving over surface, sgd "ed wiener", 2⅝" dia **1,495.00**

Retro Modern

Bangle, 14k, rose gold, wide stepped–shoulder, center prong–set circ–cut 38.75 mm citrine, flanked by 2 horizontal rows of channel–set synthetic ruby baguettes, 2⁷⁄₈" dia, 1½" **2,990.00**

Flexible, 14k, yg, brickwork mesh strap terminating in buckle clasp set with 12 sq–cut sapphires and 22 circ–cut diamonds, 8" × ¾" **3,450.00**

Link, 14k rose and yg, open round–wire eccentric circ within oval bicolor gold links, 7¼" x ⅝", 18.06 dwts **412.50**

Victorian

Bangle

Enamel, pink enameled yg, front half of bangle set with clusters of 4 seed pearls with rose–cut diamond centers alternating with trefoiled silver tapered bars of rose–cut diamonds, enamel slightly chipped, 2½" dia, ½" w . . **3,220.00**

Etruscan Revival, hinged, 15k yg, scrolled foliate granulation and wirework, raised wirework borders, 2½" dia, ⁷⁄₈" w, pair **6,060.00**

Link

14k yg, Scottish, grad circ

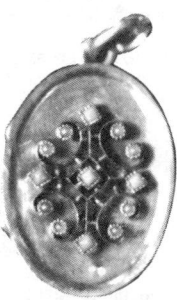

Locket, Victorian, 18K yg, oval, turquoise and pearl dec center design, $850.00.

links, three center links set with lg circ–cut citrines encircled by inlaid jasper and agate, domed links inlaid with agate and jasper quatrefoils, engraved yg mounts, fitted box, 7⁵⁄₈" x 1" **2,875.00**

Silver, square openwork links set throughout with rose–cut Bohemian (pyrope) garnets, "souvenjr" (Czech for "souvenir") spelled out in smaller garnets, one capital letter within each link, silver mount, 7" x ¾" **345.00**

Brooch/Pin

Art Deco

Bar pin, platinum

Geometric pierced tapered bar, cusped terminals, bezel–set approx .90 ct center emerald–cut emerald, set throughout with 94 old European–cut diamonds, approx 2.35 cts tw, fitted box, 2½" w x ⁷⁄₈" **4,025.00**

Horizontal row of 16 French–cut sapphires flanking center old European–cut diamond, flared terminals set with 12 old European and circ–cut diamonds, 2¼" w x ⅜" . . **1,495.00**

Openwork annular elliptical frame with graduated rows of 7 old European–cut diamonds within black enameled borders above and below open center, approx 3.00 cts tw, terminating in pierced platinum cusped sides set throughout with 30 smaller old European–cut diamonds, J.E. Caldwell & Co., Philadelphia, sgd "J.E.C. & Co.," #4599, enamel chipped, 2⅜" w x ⁷⁄₈" **4,887.00**

Oval carved and pierced floral and foliate motif, jadeite plaque, 42.5 x 22 x 3.08 mm, prong–set, platinum frame, opposed C–scroll terminals set throughout with 27 old European–cut and 8 baguette diamonds, 2″ w x ⅞″ **3,460.00**

18k white gold, etched rock crystal bow shape bordered by small old European and single–cut diamonds, with a center prong–set old European–cut diamond, approx .50 ct, encircled by small diamonds, French hallmarks, sgd "Cartier London," #6170, in box, 2½″ w x ⅜″ **7,150.00**

Art Nouveau

14k yg, yellow enameled daisy, green enameled leaves within a C–scrolled diamond–set frame, mkd "Krementz," ⅞″ w x 1⅛″ . . . **1,380.00**

18k yg, oval opal cabochon, 17.02 x 11.17 x 6.87 mm, asymmetrically scrolling foliate frame, applied yg daisies set with 6 small old European–cut diamonds, translucent green enameled leaves, suspending a baroque pearl drop, 6 x 4 mm, sgd "T.B. Starr," small amount of loss to enamel, 1⅜″ w x 1⅞″ total l **3,450.00**

Arts and Crafts

18k yg, platinum, openwork domed circ wire frame, plique–a–jour enameled stylized foliate motifs in shades of green and purple, center circ–cut amethyst bezel–set, sgd "Tiffany & Co.," 1⅛″ dia **6,440.00**

Silver, oval labradorite cabochon bezel–set within scrolling wire frame flanked on three sides by stylized flower heads, each set with three small opals, imp "Georg Jensen" "830," #90, c1909–14, converted from a buckle, some solder, 2″ w x 1⅜″ . . . **460.00**

Edwardian

Bar, scroll and foliate motif pierced platinum bar, spade–shaped terminals set with horizontal row of 7 slightly graduated old European–cut diamonds in millegrained bezels, 3.0 cts tw, 3″ w x ⅜″ **2,185.00**

Rounded lozenge–shaped plaque set throughout with 109 old European–cut diamonds, 6.50 cts tw, pierced platinum mount, yg pin stem, 2⅜″ x 1″ **4,312.50**

Retro Modern

14k yg

Dancing ballerina, rose–cut diamond head, holding circ–cut ruby–set ribbon overhead, skirt set with small rubies, sapphires, diamonds in star–cut mounts, row of rubies bordering bottom edge, 1½″ w x 2½″ **1,495.00**

Stylized figure of Aquarius pouring water from vessel, curling yg ribbon "stream" set with 4 small diamonds, sgd "Trabert & Hoeffer–Mauboussin," 1½″ w x 2¼″ **1,380.00**

Musical staff, treble clef and 6 eighth notes, 3 set with circ–cut rubies, 3 set with circ–cut sapphires, 1¾″ w x 1⅛″ **330.00**

Tricolor gold stylized floral spray, scrolling ribbon, 5 circ–cut citrines, prong–set, gold wires, 3 small single–cut diamonds set at base of scrolled ribbon, 1½″ w x 3⅛″ **632.50**

Victorian

Bar

14k yg, rubies, graduated row of five yg swallows, old mine–cut diamond, 2 ruby and 2 sapphire heads, mounted on a slightly curved yg round wire bar, 2⅞″ w x ⅝″ **978.00**

Yg, Etruscan Revival, bead–edged bar, bead and wire twist dec, ram's heads within circ disk terminals, 1⅞″ w x ½″ **522.50**

10k yg, delicate floral spray,

pink, yellow and green enameled flower heads, 3 flower centers set with old mine–cut diamonds, some enamel loss, 2½″ w x 1″ ... **220.00**

18k yg, bat shape, cabochon ruby eyes, platinum wire accents, 2″ w x ⅝″ **1,870.00**

Micromosaic, 18k yg, Pantheon, shades of brown, oval yg wire twist frame, 1¾″ x 1½″ **770.00**

Silver–topped yg, five–petaled flower, head mounted en tremblant, old mine–cut diamond center, approx .20 ct, petals, leaves, and stem set throughout with 46 small rose–cut diamonds, ⅞″ w x 2″ **1,035.00**

Cameo

Onyx, yg, Etruscan Revival, oval black and white onyx cameo, carved mischievous putto about to grasp butterfly, circ beaded and wirework frame surmounting horizontally opposed C–scrolls, balustered finial terminals, sgd "Pierret," engraved "C.E.C. 1877," 2½″ x 1⅜″ **5,750.00**

Shell, yg, oval cameo, profile of woman wearing headdress, very good detail, bead and wirework yg frame, 1⅞″ w x 3⅜″ **546.25**

Chain

Art Nouveau, 14k yg, cable link yg chain interspersed with scrolled foliate links alternating with oval turquoise cabochons bezel–set within scrolled foliate frames, 54″ l, 25.2 dwt .. **1,495.00**

Edwardian, twisted bar and cable link platinum vest chain interspersed with 3 spectacle–set old European–cut diamonds, 14″ l x ⅛″ **275.00**

Victorian

Alternating blue and red enameled yg cylinder links, white enameled dots, interspersed with seed pearls, 61″ l **3,450.00**

Loop–in–loop long chain terminating in swivel hook, 14k yg, large fancy–shaped engraved slide with black enamel (taille d'epargne) accents, surmounted by a cusped bow set with 5 rose–cut diamonds, 59″ l, slide 1″ w x 1¼″, 48.4 dwt **2,070.00**

Clip, Art Deco, rock crystal, platinum, carved crystal semi–circ fan–shaped plaque, 15 center circ–cut pave–set diamonds, outlined by 11 calibre–cut rubies, flat–backed hinged clip on reverse, sgd "Boucheron, Paris," sgd pouch, 1½″ w x ⅞″ **3,737.50**

Cuff Links, pr

Art Deco, yg, pharoah's head, calibre–cut synthetic rubies headband, joined by cable links to navette–shaped backs, ¾″ x ½″ **253.00**

Art Nouveau, 18k yg, griffin, ruby eyes, circ scrolled foliate frame, joined by cable links to pierced foliate elliptical backs, French hallmarks, ⅝″ dia **632.50**

Victorian, 18k yg, theatrical masks, one male, one female, joined by cable links to entwined snake backs, leather box mkd "Federico Fasoli, Roma," ½″ x ½″ **990.00**

Dress Set, Art Deco, yg, pair of double cuff links and 3 studs, platinum squares with stepped borders and central horizontal rows of circ–cut or single–cut diamonds, studs mounted on yg bars, sgd "Cartier," #11879, cuff links ½″ x ½″, studs ¼″ **2,450.00**

Earrings, pr

Art Deco, platinum, suspended round black opal cabochon, approx 8.0 mm, encircled by old European–cut diamonds, vertical row of old European–cut diamonds, bezel–set round opal surmount, approx 5.0 mm, screw backs, 1½″ l x ⅝″ **2,875.00**

Edwardian

Platinum, suspended pear–shaped diamond surrounded

by 8 circ–cut diamonds, open beaded wire frames, suspended from row of 3 articulated circ–cut diamonds, bow motif surmount set with 14 circ–cut diamonds, fitted box, 1½" l x ½" **3,450.00**

Silver–topped yg, suspended teardrop–shaped jade cabochon surmounted by diamond–set cap, suspended from a vertical row of collet–set diamonds on knife–edge bar, collet–set diamond surmount, ear wires, 2" l x ¼" .**2,875.00**

Retro Modern
14k yg, graduated fringe of flat honeycomb links suspended from domed comma–shaped surmount, sgd "OHB" for Oscar Heyman & Bros., clip backs, 1⅞" l x ⅞" **345.00**

18k yg, multiple looped ribbon bow set with 3 rect–cut topazes, sgd "Boucheron, Paris," clip backs, 1" x 1" ..**1,840.00**

Victorian
14k yg, pendant suspending teardrop–shaped lapis lazuli cabochon from yg wire twist chain and beaded surmount set with square lapis cabochon, screw backs, 1⅞" l x ⅜" **467.50**

18k yg, Etruscan Revival, round coral cabochon, circ beaded frame suspending seed pearl–set fringe, coral bead surmount, 2" l x ⅝" .. **690.00**

Silver–topped yg, rose–cut diamond rosette suspended from small paired foliate motif and collet–set rose–cut diamond surmount, ear wires, 1¼" l x ½" **690.00**

Locket, Victorian, 15k yg, convex oval, diagonal raised letters spelling "Mizpah" surrounded by engraved scrollwork, surmounted by pendant bail, 1¼" w x 2⅛" **345.00**

Locket and Chain
Art Nouveau, 14k yg, quatrefoil

locket, woman's profile, foliate ground, small diamonds and ruby in hair, suspended from fine chain, Austrian hallmarks, 1⅛" w, 1¼" **575.00**

Victorian, sterling silver, oval locket, allover engraved geometric and foliate design, pink and green foliate overlay across center, suspended from engraved flat oval and scalloped 15" l link chain, locket 1⅛" w x 2⅜" **345.00**

Lorgnette, Art Nouveau, 14k yg, repousse case, laurel leaves, reeded dec, 4¾" l, 1¼", 19.87 dwts **770.00**

Necklace
Art Nouveau, dog collar, 14k yg, 8 openwork curvilinear yg plaques, each set with octagonal cut amethyst, alternating with fine chain sections forming X–pattern with freshwater pearl center, plunger pin closure, #A9520, 14⅝" l x 1¼", 46.30 dwts **3,162.50**

Arts and Crafts, 14k green gold, 3 geometric plaques, sq–cut green tourmalines in millegrained mounts flanked by applied scroll and foliate motifs, alternating with 4 smaller plaques, jointed to fancy link chain, mkd "585" and maker's mark, spring ring clasp, 16½" l x ⅜" **800.00**

Edwardian
Dog Collar, silver–topped yg, 18 strands of seed pearls attached at intervals to 5 rect openwork silver–topped yg plaques, vertical row of 4 petal flower heads within each frame set throughout with small rubies and rose–cut diamonds, approx 2¾" w x 14" l **3,850.00**

Yg, lobed swags set throughout with diamonds, suspended diamond and pearl drop, platinum–topped yg mounts, platinum chain, 14" l **2,760.00**

Retro Modern, 14k yg, snake chain or "gas pipe" of uniform width

Three applied flower head ruby clusters with 6 circ diamond centers evenly spaced across center front, group of 4 prong–set circ sapphires flanking each cluster, Forstner Jewelry Mfg Corp, Irvington, NY, sgd "Forstner," 15" l x ⅜", 48 dwts **3,450.00**

16½" l x ⅜", 45.0 dwts **880.00**

Victorian

Cameo, 14k yg, nine oval carved shell cameos of graduated size, mythological scenes, plain bezels, linked with two lengths of fine chain between each cameo, fitted box, some damage, 15" l x ⅞" **2,185.00**

Coral, graduated row of fancy spool–shaped curved coral beads suspending carved winged cherub's head, pendant drop, terminating in round coral beads, hidden coral clasp, 16" l **805.00**

18k yg, Etruscan Revival, alternating lotus and palmette motifs collar, textured yg, granulation and wire twist dec, 14⅝" l x ¾", 34 dwts **20,900.00**

Flexible graduated yg links suspending engraved snake's head, engraved heart–shaped locket suspended from its mouth, large oval cabochon garnet surmounting snake's head and in center of heart, small round cabochon garnet eyes, 15¼" l, 11.1 dwts ... **1,093.00**

Pendant

Art Nouveau, 18k yg, lobed oval, foliated C–scroll design framing 3 collet–set oval opals, suspending collet–set pear–shaped opal drop, fleur–de–lis bail, 2¾" l x 1¾" **1,100.00**

Arts and Crafts

Silver, oval turquoise cabochon with matrix, cast grapevine dec frame, gold–plated leaves, freshwater pearl drop, 1⅝" w x 1¾" l **450.00**

Yg, openwork scrolled heart–shaped yg frame, large bezel–set center oval opal, flanked by two oval–cut bezel–set peridots, small circ–cut peridots above and below, suspended bezel–cut oval opal drop, sgd "F. G. Hale," 1⅛" w, 2⅝" l **2,875.00**

Edwardian

Articulated pear–shaped sapphire drop, independent rose and old mine–cut diamond wreath suspended within circ rose–cut diamond and calibre–cut sapphire ribbon–twist frame, platinum pendant loop, 1⅛" dia **4,600.00**

Cross, openwork platinum frame, pearl center, set throughout with old mine–cut and circ–cut diamonds, fan–shaped terminals, arched row of calibre–cut simulated sapphires, row of collet–set diamonds, 1¾" w x 2⅞" **4,025.00**

Victorian, cross

14k yg, trefoiled terminals, wire twist and beadwork, central faceted yg dome, 1⅞" x 3⅛" **690.00**

Pietra Dura, 14k yg, black stone Latin cross, inlaid pink rose and lily of the valley motifs, green leaves, yg pendant bail with wire twist dec, 1⅞" w x 3" **575.00**

Pendant and Chain

Art Deco

Knotted, draped, and folded scarf shape, pave–set, circ–cut diamonds, calibre–cut sapphire borders, small pierced foliate designs scattered throughout, large pear–shaped suspended diamond, pierced foliate pear–shaped frame pave–set with circ–cut diamonds, attached to fine baton link

15" l platinum chain, ¾" x 3⅛" l pendant **6,670.00**

Three–dimensional oval jadeite plaque, approx 47.0 mm x 31.0 mm, pierced and carved asymmetrical foliate motif, suspended from black enameled and open lozenge and kite–shaped diamondset links, attached with swivel clasp to chain of diamond–set navette–shaped platinum filigree links, 24" l **7,150.00**

Art Nouveau, inverted triangular openwork pendant, stylized foliate design, green and yellow plique–a–jour enamel accents, small rose–cut diamonds, central oval amethyst cabochon, suspended freshwater pearl, trace link chain, butterfly motif maker's mark, 1⅞" w x 2¼" pendant, 21" l chain **690.00**

Arts and Crafts, 18k yg, openwork mushroom–shaped plaque set with cluster of 18 freshwater pearls, irregularlyshaped bezels, three suspended pearl drops with bell caps, 20" l trace link neck chain, T–bar clasp, 1¼" w x 2⅞" l **1,500.00**

Edwardian, 14k yg, large truncated lozenge–cut kunzite flanked by smaller octagoncut kunzites, applied yg foliate motifs, large pear–shaped kunzite suspended drop, each encircled by seed pearls and black enameled borders, double strand seed pearl and yg chain, 2¼" w x 2" top to bottom pendant **1,380.00**

Pendant/Brooch and Chain

Art Deco, white gold, openwork chamfered corner rect tapering up to detachable pendant ball, pierced geometric and scrolled design set throughout with old European–cut diamonds accented by two vertical rows of calibre–cut simu

lated emeralds, 21" l fancy link platinum chain, 1⅛" w x 2¾" .**3,220.00**

Art Nouveau, 14k yg, openwork curvilinear circ frame, central bezel–set oval turquoise cabochon, pear–shaped turquoise cabochon suspended drop, surmounted by opposed Cscrolls and seed pearl, fine chain caught by round turquoise cabochon knot, Bippart, Griscom & Osborn, Newark, NJ maker's mark, 1" w x 2" l **517.50**

Ring

Art Deco

14k white gold, sq top, central large old European–cut diamond, 1.10 cts, framed by 2 concentric sq of small circ diamonds, 1.75 cts tw, tapered shank, size 6, ⅝" x ⅝", 3.0 dwts **2,200.00**

Platinum

Central rect step–cut sapphire, approx 10.8 mm x 6.3 mm, flanked by 2 channel–set baguette–cut diamonds, line of four sq channel–set French–cut diamonds on shoulders, sgd "Tiffany & Co," repaired shank, size 5¼, 2.4 dwts **9,625.00**

Tapering domed mount, central collet–set old European–cut diamond, .60 ct, topped and bottomed with diamond–set crescent, framed by quatrefoil of 20–calibre sapphires, shoulders set with additional diamonds, pierced and engraved gallery and shank, slight nick on central diamond, 2.8 dwts . . .**5,775.00**

Art Nouveau, 14k yg, sea monster shape, scaled undulating shank, 1897 American patent date, engraved "MLE Easter 1908," size 7, ⅞" x ½", 4.4 dwts **1,100.00**

Arts and Crafts, 18k yg, large circ moonstone cabochon set in shaped bezel in sq foliate frame, circ–cut Montana blue sapphire in each corner, tapering shank, attributed to Edward Oakes, Boston, ¾" x ¾" **2,990.00**

Edwardian, platinum
18k yg, 39 old European–cut 1.30 cts tw diamonds, pierced, scallop–edge navette–shaped platinum–topped yg mount, central six–petaled flower head design, 1" l x ¾" w **2,300.00**

Openwork top, center row of 3 old European–cut diamonds, 1.90 cts tw, octagonal mounts outlined in single–cut diamonds, center stone flanked by diamond baguettes set vertically, polished platinum shank, bent, ½" x ⅞" **1,300.00**

Retro Modern
Aquamarine, yg, prong–set rect–cut aquamarine, approx 15.57 ct, flanked by vertical rows of cabochon rubies at shoulders, tapered shank, sgd "Seaman Schepps," ¾" w x ⅞" **2,530.00**

14k rose gold, ten circ–cut rubies, 7 circ–cut diamonds set in scallop–edge scrolled shell motif, tapered shank, 1" w x ¾" **633.00**

Victorian, yg
Cameo, oval, carved flower bouquet, bezel set, yg rope–twist border, 1¼" x 1⅛" ... **300.00**

Oval multicolored enamel miniature portrait of young Queen Victoria, yg bezel, rose–cut diamond frame, flanked on one side by rose–cut diamond cipher "V" and "R" on opposite side, light blue enameled yg mount, slightly chipped, ¾" w x ⅞" **8,050.00**

Row of 5 slightly graduated oval–cut demantoid garnets, two small rose–cut diamonds set between, engraved yg shank, ⅞" x ¼" . **3,450.00**

Scarf Pin/Stickpin
Art Nouveau

14k yg, collet–set sapphire as center of oval yg frame surmounted by trefoil between 2 Greek key motifs curving into foliate motif at base, Whiteside & Blank, Newark, NJ, mark of arrow bisecting crescent, ½" x ¾" head, 2½" l **358.00**

Yg, profiled woman's head, flowing hair, enameled face, green enameled headdress set with 8 small rose–cut diamonds and circ–cut emerald, yg pin stem, French hallmarks, 2¾" l x ½" **805.00**

Arts and Crafts, 14k yg, mushroom–shaped head, center collet–set sapphire, blue enamel, yg mount, ½" x ½", 2½" l **220.00**

Edwardian, platinum
Pave–set diamond rooster head, red enameled combs, yg pin stem, 2½" x ½" **690.00**

Rose gold stem topped with crowned openwork old European, rose–cut, and single–cut diamond–set shield, border of calibre–cut rubies mounted in yg, fitted box stamped "Cartier," 2¾" x ½" **770.00**

Victorian, yg
Round reverse painted rock crystal intaglio of dog's head, bezel set, yg frame, twisted wire and beaded edges, orig box, 3" x ⅞" ... **770.00**

Scottish, bloodstone disk, yg frame, pierced and beaded border, quadrate cross set with agates, engraved yg, yg pin stem, ⅞" d, 2¾" l **450.00**

Suite
Post–War Modern, brooch/pin and earrings, 14k white gold, boomerang–shaped brooch, large prong–set sq–cut amethyst, small pearl mounted on projecting round and flat angled wires, matching pr of earrings, each with sq cut amethyst suspended below open wire boomerang shape, wire

mounted pearl, marked "de patta 14k wg," maker's mark of Margaret de Patta, San Francisco, 3¼" x 1¼" brooch, ½" w x 1¼" earrings **1,840.00**

Retro Modern, clip and earrings, 14k yg, starburst motif clip, polished yg spikes, approx 33 diamonds and 80 circ rubies center, double–pronged hinged clip on reverse, matching clipback earrings, all sgd "Tiffany & Co," one ruby missing, 1⅞" w x 1¾" brooch, 1⅛" w x 1⅛" earrings **3,738.00**

Victorian, brooch/pin and earrings

14k yg, curved and shaped plaque brooch, applied scrolled wire and beading, textured engraving, suspended flat oval link and bead encircled by beaded–edge ring, black enamel tracery, matching pendant earrings suspended from heart–shaped surmounts, fishhook earwires, 1½" w x 2" brooch, 1⅞" l x ⅞" w **920.00**

18k yg, horizontal cylindrical malachite bar, central overlaid shaped yg plaque, wirework and granulation suspending a swagged chain, 2 large elongated malachite drops, yg caps, matching pendent earrings, single malachite drop, 1½" w x 2" brooch, ⅝" w x 2" earrings . **1,210.00**

Yg

Domed disk brooch, applied wirework, center cabochon (carbunkle) garnet, seed pearl border, suspended bellcap coiled wirework tassel, two lengths of chain, 1⅜" dia x 2¼" l with tassel, matching drop earrings ⅝" dia x 1⅜" l tassels **990.00**

Shield–shaped yg plaque surmounted by textured yg floral and foliate motifs, round coral cabochon

flower head center mount, matching pendant earrings, flower head surmounts, 1⅜" w x 1⅞" l brooch, 2" x ¾" earrings . **358.00**

Watch Fob, Art Nouveau, 14k yg, four linked curvilinear scrolled wirework plaques, central lion's head motif, short cable link chain, swivel hook, 1" w x 5⅜", 16.20 dwts **632.50**

JUDAICA

History: Throughout history, Jews have expressed themselves artistically in both the religious and secular spheres. Most Jewish art objects were created as part of the concept of "Hiddur Mitzva," i.e., adornment of implements involved in performing rituals both in the synagogue and home.

For almost 2,000 years, since the destruction of the Jerusalem Temple in 70 AD, Jews have lived in many lands. The widely differing environments gave traditional Jewish life and art a multifaceted character. Unlike Greek, Byzantine, or Roman art which have definite territorial and historical boundaries, Jewish art is found throughout Europe, the Middle East, North Africa, and other areas.

Ceremonial objects incorporated not only liturgical appurtenances, but also ethnographic artifacts such as amulets and ritual costumes. The style of each ceremonial object responded to the artistic and cultural milieu in which it was created. Although diverse stylistically, ceremonial objects, whether for Sabbath, holidays, or the life cycle, still possess a unity of purpose.

Judaica has been crafted in all media, though silver is the most collectible. Sotheby's, Christie's, and Swann's hold several Judaica auctions in the United States, England, Amsterdam, and Israel.

References: Abraham Kanof, *Jewish Ceremonial Art,* Harry N. Abrams, n.d.; Cecil Roth, *Jewish Art—An Illustrated History,* Graphic Society of New York, 1971; Geoffrey Wigoder (ed.), *Jewish Art and Civilization,* Chartwell Books, 1972.

Museums: B'nai B'rith Klutznick Museum, Washington, DC; H.U.C., Skirball

Museum, Los Angeles, CA; Judah L. Magnes Museum, Berkeley, CA; Judaic Museum, Rockville, MD; Spertus Museum of Judaica, Chicago, IL; Morton B. Weiss Museum of Judaica, Chicago, IL; National Museum of American Jewish History, Philadelphia, PA; Plotkin Judaica Museum of Greater Phoenix, Phoenix, AZ; The Jewish Museum, New York, NY; Yeshiva University Museum, New York, NY.

Diecut, Procession Carrying Palms, 4⅛" w, 2¾" h, $5.00.

Beaker Cup, 2½" h, silver, incised "shtetel scenes" dec, Russian, c1870 . . . . **250.00**
Book, *Service for the First Nights of Passover,* Jos Schlesinger, Vienna, 1927, folio, 96 pgs, cloth backed dec paper over flexible boards, slight wear, bilingual edition, Hebrew and English texts, translated and annotated by Joseph Loewy and Joseph Guens, several color plates by M Kunstadt **85.00**
Candelabra, 15" h, five branch, baluster stem, pierced and chased lions amidst foliage upper section, domed circular base, Polish, mid 19th C **300.00**
Candlesticks, pr
  9" h, brass, bulbous, chased, sq base, Polish, sgd "Warsaw," 19th C **400.00**
  12½" h, brass, bulbous, sq base, Polish, sgd "Warsaw," 19th C **475.00**
  14½" h, sterling silver, detacha-

ble bobeches, Russian, hallmarked, 19th C **2,400.00**
Etrog Container, 4" w, 7" l, box, octagonal, olivewood, hinged lid, attached carved etrog on top, Palestine, c1940 . . . . **550.00**
Lamp, Hanukkah, 10" h, silvered brass, Baroque foliage design on back plate, surmounted by repousse crown, two rampant lions on either side of menorah, Polish, sgd "Warsaw," mid 19th C**1,200.00**
Mezuzah, 5½ x 1½", replicated Chagall lithograph, 24 karat gold plated over bronze, 20th C **600.00**
Mezuzah Case, 3½ x 5", silver, sgd "L. Wolpert," 20th C **550.00**
Noisemaker, Purim, ivory, incised "Hamen" and "Esther," German, 19th C **900.00**
Prayer Shawl Bag, velvet and silver thread, Moroccan, early 20th C **250.00**
Rosewater Spice Container, 11½" h, silver, rounded bulbous container, incised foliage dec, long tapering top, ftd base, Middle East **325.00**
Seder Plate, 12" d, ceramic, luster finish, Hebrew calligraphy in recessed compartments, Czechoslovakian, c1920 . . . .**1,500.00**
Seder Tray, 12" l, pewter, Hebrew inscriptions, German, dated 1811 . . . .**1,200.00**
Shofar, 10" l, molded ram's horn, German, 19th C **100.00**
Spice Tower, 10" h, German silver, steeple form, molded circular base, repousse motifs, triple tier filigree rounded upper section, surmounted by flag, hallmarked**1,500.00**
Torah Finials, pr
  14" h, German silver and gilt, sgd "Posen" at base **3,000.00**
  15" h, tiered, Moroccan style, stylized Menorah dec, French hallmarks, Moroccan, 19th C **6,000.00**
Torah Pointer
  8" l, silver, incised dec, Moroccan, early 20th C **700.00**
  9" l, wood, Polish, 20th C **300.00**
Wine Cup, silver, stemmed
  5¾" h, American, tulip form, pre-

sentation inscription, dated
1866 .... **475.00**
6" h, Irish, Hebrew inscription,
dated 1973 .... **550.00**

Bowl, turquoise, maroon, Oriental style, pedestal, 6½" d, 4" h, $165.00.

JUGTOWN POTTERY

History: In 1920 Jacques and Julianna Busbee left their cosmopolitan environs and returned to North Carolina to revive the state's dying craft of pottery making. Jugtown Pottery, a colorful and somewhat off–beat operation, was located in Moore County, miles away from any large city and accessible only "if mud permits."

Ben Owens, a talented young potter, turned the wares. Jacques Busbee did most of the designing and glazing. Julianna handled promotion.

Utilitarian and decorative items were produced. Although many colorful glazes were used, orange predominated. A Chinese blue glaze that ranged from light blue to deep turquoise was a prized glaze reserved for the very finest pieces.

Jacques Busbee died in 1947. Julianna, with the help of Owens, ran the pottery until 1958 when it was closed. After long legal battles, the pottery was reopened in 1960. It now is owned by Country Roads, Inc., a non–profit organization. The pottery still is operating and using the old mark.

Reference: Susan and Al Bagdade, *Warman's American Pottery and Porcelain,* Wallace–Homestead, 1994.

Bowl, 10⅝" d, Chinese blue glaze,
honey brown stain, marked ... **175.00**
Candlesticks, pr, 7" h, orange
glaze **50.00**
Jar, 10½" h, ovoid, four pinched

strap handles, brown–olive green
glaze, marked "Jugtown Ware" **45.00**
Pitcher
  3½" h, frogskin, pinched spout . **35.00**
  6¼" h, tan, incised dec **100.00**
Pot, 4" h, orange glaze, marked . **50.00**
Sugar, cov, Chinese blue glaze .. **120.00**
Vase
  5" h, handled, sgd "Pamela
    Owens" **32.00**
  6" h, ovoid body, Chinese
    Blue glaze, stamped "Jugtown
    Ware" **625.00**
  6 x 7", Chinese Blue **600.00**
  8½" h, Chinese blue, sgd Vernon
    Owens, 1985 .... **225.00**

K.P.M

KPM

History: The mark, KPM, has been used separately and in conjunction with other symbols by many German porcelain manufacturers, among whom are the Königliche Porzellan Manufaktur in Meissen, 1720s; Königliche Porzellan Manufaktur in Berlin, 1832–1847; and Krister Porzellan Manufaktur in Waldenburg, mid 19th century.

Collectors now use the term "KPM" to refer to the high–quality porcelain produced in the Berlin area in the 18th and 19th centuries.

Reference: Susan and Al Bagdade, *Warman's English & Continental Pottery & Porcelain, 2nd Edition,* Wallace–Homestead, 1991.

Bowl, 13″ l, hp flowers and butterflies, gold trim, scepter and "KPM" mark 95.00

Candlesticks, pr, figural, late 19th C, 8½″ h 400.00

Coffeepot, 10½″ h, cream ground, rust flowers, blue leaves, rust trim, green crown and "KPM" mark 50.00

Compote, figural, polychrome nautilus shell mounted with putti, maiden head, and various crustacean, supported by mermaid emerging from sea, base mounted with winged sea horses, some restoration, 19th C, 11½″ h 385.00

Cup and Saucer, 4″ h, angel and gilt floral dec, 19th C 75.00

Figure
7½″ h, white bear, standing . . . 65.00
9″ h, woman, holding baskets of flowers, multicolored 595.00
18″ h, nude classical maiden standing beside seated warrior, pedestal draped with a lion, late 19th/early 20th C . . 2,075.00

Fruit Basket, oval, double handled, openwork sides, floral painted center, gold trim, 13″ l 1,150.00

Plate, blue band, apple with plum, gold trim, 8¼″ d, $35.00.

Jar, cov, 26½″ h, faience, baluster, black and white painted Oriental scene, red ground, cock bird finial, early 19th C 1,320.00

Painting, Yum–Yum, from the Mikado, signed at lower left "E Wagner Wien," gilt frame, 12½ x 8½″ 6,875.00

Plaque, portrait
Christopher Columbus in chains, signed "C.F. Deininger Mohn," imp KPM and scepter marks, late 19th C, 11 x 8⅞″ 4,025.00
Young Woman
8½ x 10¾″, signed "F. Bauer," late 19th C 3,000.00
10⅛ x 12½″, bust length, dark hair, holding pink rose, signed "J. J. Heinz" on reverse, 1908 . . . . 3,900.00

Plate
9½″ d, painted roses and forget–me–not floral center, burnished gold ground, gilt etched rim, blue scepter, brown eagle, and "KPM" marks, c1825 . . . 5,100.00
10⅛″ d, dinner, underglazed blue floral dec with gilt leaf and scalework borders, printed marks, chips, early 20th C, price for 21 pc set 975.00

Platter
14 x 13″, floral reserve surrounded by gilt border, gilt frame, 19th C 1,950.00
15 x 13″, figures in mountainous landscape surrounded by gilt scrolling foliate border, gilt frame, 19th C 1,850.00

Salt, 5⅛″ h, oval, painted birds on branches, pink, turquoise, and gilt scroll base, draped putto dec, blue scepter mark, late 19th C 485.00

Teapot, cov, 5½″ h, globular shape, pink, yellow, blue, and purple flowers, basketweave border, white and gilt spout, rosebud finial, 1770–80 . . . . 850.00

Tureen, cov, 13″ h, paneled garden banquet scene, floral dec osier molded rim, Bacchic putto finial, c1880 . . . . 1,900.00

Vase
  8" h, two floral reserves, gold encrusted field **685.00**
  13" h, inverted baluster form, mauve and flambe mottled and streaked glazes, tear finial, scepter mark, 1885–95 . . **1,875.00**

KAUFFMANN, ANGELICA

History: Marie Angelique Catherine Kauffmann was a Swiss artist who lived from 1741 until 1807. Her paintings were copied by many artists who hand decorated porcelain during the 19th century. The majority of the paintings are neo–classical in style.

References: Susan and Al Bagdade, *Warman's English & Continental Pottery & Porcelain, 2nd Edition,* Wallace–Homestead, 1991; Wendy Wassying Roworth (ed.), *Angelica Kauffman: A Continental Artist in Georgian England,* Reaktion Books, 1993, distributed by University of Washington Press.

Clock, multicolored decal of classical scene, blue, red, and brown accents, cream ground, sgd "Chelsea, England," 14¾" h, $220.00.

Bowl, 9¼" d, multicolored transfer of classical maidens, sgd, hairline crack **65.00**
Condensed Milk Can Holder, cov,

matching underplate, classical maiden, green ground, gold tracery **85.00**
Cup and Saucer, classical scene, royal blue ground, beehive mark **100.00**
Demitasse Cup and Saucer, ftd, classical ladies scene, fruit on gold band, beehive mark **55.00**
Demitasse Service, demitasse pot, six cups and saucers, tray, classical scenes, sgd, price for fourteen piece set **950.00**
Marmalade Jar, cov, scene of Three Graces **60.00**
Plate
  6¼" d, flowers, gold trim, sgd . . **60.00**
  10" d, four classical maidens with cupid, beehive mark **150.00**
  10½" d, two ladies, green border, gold trim **70.00**
Tobacco Jar, 7½" h, dark green muted with orange and yellow, SP rim and lid **300.00**
Urn, 12" h, multicolored classical scenes, sgd "Kauffmann" **275.00**
Vase, 10½" h, multicolored classical scene, blue pearlized ground **95.00**

XEW-BLAS

KEW BLAS

History: Amory and Francis Houghton established the Union Glass Company, Somerville, Massachusetts, in 1851. The company went bankrupt in 1860, but was reorganized. Between 1870 and 1885 the Union Glass Company made pressed glass and blanks for cut glass.

Art glass production began in 1893 under the direction of William S. Blake and Julian de Cordova. Two styles were introduced. A Venetian style consisted of graceful shapes in colored glass, often flecked with gold. An iridescent glass, labeled Kew Blas, was made in plain and decorated forms. The pieces are close in design and form to Quezel products, but lack the subtlety of Tiffany items.

The company ceased production in 1924.

Museum: Sandwich Glass Museum, Sandwich, MA.

Bowl, 8½" d, ruffled edge, blue int., dark green ext., sgd **800.00**
Candlesticks, pr, 8½" h, twisted stem, irid gold **725.00**
Compote, 7" d, twisted stem, ribbed cup, irid gold, pink highlights **375.00**
Decanter, 14" h, green–gold irid, spherical long stemmed stopper, sgd **275.00**
Goblet, 6" h, irid gold, knob stem **350.00**

Bowl, green dec, cream ground, irid int., pedestal base, sgd, 4⅞" d, 4¼" h, $475.00.

Pitcher, 5" h, King Tut, white, green, and gold, blue handle, irid blue lining, sgd **1,900.00**
Plate, 6" d, irid gold, sgd **180.00**
Rose Bowl, 3½" d, green and gold hooked dec, butterscotch ground, gold lining, sgd **525.00**
Salt, open, irid gold **225.00**
Tumbler, 4" h, pinched sides, gold luster, sgd **235.00**
Vase
4¾" h, bud, baluster, irid peach, dark peach feathering **375.00**
6" h, irid apricot, gold pulled feathers, tooled prunts **825.00**

KITCHEN COLLECTIBLES

History: The kitchen was a central focal point in a family's environment until the 1960s. Many early kitchen utensils were handmade and prized by their owners. Next came a period of utilitarian products made of tin and other metals. When the housewife no longer wished to work in a sterile environment, color was added through enamel and plastic and design served both an aesthetic and functional purpose.

The advent of home electricity changed the type and style of kitchen products. Many items went through fads. The high–technology field already has made inroads into the kitchen, and another revolution seems at hand.

References: Ronald S. Barlow, *Victorian Houseware: Hardware and Kitchenware,* Windmill Publishing, 1992; Gene Florence, *Kitchen Glassware of the Depression Years, 5th Edition,* Collector Books, 1994; Linda Campbell Franklin, *300 Years of Housekeeping Collectibles,* Books Americana, 1992; Linda Campbell Franklin, *300 Hundred Years of Kitchen Collectibles, 3rd Edition,,* Books Americana, 1991; Mary Jane Giacomini, *American Bisque: A Collector's Guide with Prices,* Schiffer Publishing, 1994; *Griswold Cast Iron: A Price Guide,* L–W Book Sales, 1993; Garry Kilgo et. al, *A Collectors Guide To Anchor Hockings "Fire–King" Glassware,* K & W Collectibles Publisher, 1991; Jan Lindenberger, *The 50s & 60s Kitchen: A Handbook & Price Guide,* Schiffer Publishing, 1994; Kathryn McNerney, *Kitchen Antiques 1790–1940,* Collector Books, 1991, 1993 value update; Gary Miller and K. M. Mitchell, *Price Guide To Collectible Kitchen Appliances,* Wallace–Homestead, 1991; Dana G. Morykan and Harry L. Rinker, *Warman's Country Antiques & Collectibles, 2nd Edition* Wallace–Homestead, 1994; Ellen M. Plante, *Kitchen Collectibles: An Illustrated Price Guide,* Wallace–Homestead, 1991; Susan Tobier Rogove and Marcia Buan Steinhauer, *Pyrex By Corning: A Collector's Guide,* Antique Publications, 1993; Diane Stoneback, *Kitchen Collectibles: The Essential Buyer's Guide,* Wallace–Homestead, 1994; Don Thornton, *Beat This: The Eggbeater Chronicles,* Off Beat Books, 1994; Jean Williams Turner, *Collectible Aunt Jemima: Handbook & Price Guide,* Schiffer Publishing, 1994; April M. Tvorak, *A History And Price Guide To Mothers–In–The–Kitchen,* published by author, 1994;

April M. Tvorak, *Fire–King II,* published by author, 1993; April M. Tvorak, *History & Price Guide To Fire–King,* AL Enterprises, 1992; April M. Tvorak, *Pyrex Price Guide,* published by author, 1992.

Periodicals: *Cast Iron Cookware News,* 28 Angela Ave., San Anselmo, CA 94960; *Kettles 'n' Cookware,* PO Box B, Perrysburg, NY 14129; *Kitchen Antiques & Collectible News,* 4645 Laurel Ridge Drive, Harrisburg, PA 17110.

Collectors' Clubs: Cookie Cutter Collectors Club, 1167 Teal Rd., S.W., Dellroy, OH 44620; Fire–King Collectors Club, 2156 Carlmont Dr. #6, Belmont, CA 94002; Griswold & Cast Iron Cookware Assoc., 54 Macon Ave., Asheville, NC 28801; International Society for Apple Parer Enthusiasts, 3911 Morgan Center Rd., Utica, OH 43080; National Reamer Collectors Assoc., 405 Benson Rd. N., Frederic, WI 54837–8943; The Glass Knife Collectors Club, PO Box 342, Los Alamitos, CA 90720.

Museums: Corning Glass Museum, Corning, NY; Kern County Museum, Bakersfield, CA; Landis Valley Farm Museum, Lancaster, PA.

Additional Listings: Baskets, Brass, Butter Prints, Copper, Fruit Jars, Food Molds, Graniteware, Ironware, Tinware, and Woodenware. See *Warman's Americana & Collectibles* for more examples including electrical appliances.

Butter Mold, 7½" d, lollipop type,
   cut fluted edge floral design ... **175.00**

Bacon Slicer, marked "Arcadia Manufacturing Co., Newark, New York, Pat'd 1885–1891," adjustable blade, iron handle, fold-down locking legs, 9¾ x 21¾", $85.00.

Butter Print, 4⅞" d, leaf on one
   side, rose spray and "A L" on
   other, brass tack dec **330.00**
Butter Scoop, 8½" l, bird's–eye
   maple, worn refinishing **50.00**
Cake Mold
   Lamb, #866, Griswold **95.00**
   Santa, Griswold **550.00**
Canister, jadeite, round
   Coffee **96.00**
   Sugar **110.00**
   Tea **60.00**
Casserole, red and white, Pyrex . **14.00**
Cheese Basket, 9½" d, 5" h,
   woven splint, old patina **85.00**
Cheese Sieve, 25" d, woven splint,
   minor damage **550.00**
Cookie Board
   4¾" x 22½", chestnut, fourteen
     designs and animals **275.00**
   10 x 12½", hardwood, relief
     carved boy on rocking horse
     on one side, other with angel
     on swan, dark finish **1,760.00**
Corn Sheller, hand
   Brothers, gray **275.00**
   Decker, Keokuk, IA **50.00**
Dough Bowl, 27¼" l, rect, pine, red
   ext., scrubbed int., branded
   "AAS" **385.00**
Dutch Oven, cast iron
   Diamond 8 .... **25.00**
   Griswold, #10, Chuckwagon .. **150.00**
Food Chopper, round, wooden
   handle, 3" h plus metal blade .. **17.00**
Food Grinder Display Stand, Griswold **650.00**
Herb Drying Basket, 23 x 25½",
   woven splint, openwork bottom,
   bentwood handle **225.00**
Ice Box, Eddy & Sons Refrigerator,
   Boston, 1905, chest top, locking
   lid, two inner doors, orig wood
   grain paint, turned wood screw
   feet, 24 x 48 x 32" h **1,295.00**
Meat Grinder, Griswold, cast iron **13.00**
Mixing Bowls, nested set, Cinderella, Pyrex **20.00**
Muffin Pan, Russell–Ervin, cast
   iron **35.00**
Pie Birds
   Blackbird, blue and black **30.00**
   Bird
     Blue and white, stoneware .. **55.00**

Pink, green, and yellow	60.00
White	20.00
Chick, yellow	60.00

Duck
Pink and yellow	50.00
Yellow	60.00

Elephant
Holding shamrock	100.00
White	100.00
Shawnee	30.00
Popover Pan, #10, Griswold, marked "U.S.N."	150.00
Roaster, oval, #5, Griswold, aluminum	75.00
Rolling Pin, ceramic, floral dec ..	90.00
Salesman's Sample, Royal Super Ware, aluminum cooking pan, 1½" d, 3" l, information about waterless cooking inside	135.00

Scoop
8" l, brass, wood handle	28.00
12" l, oval, brass on copper, ring base	45.00
22" l, brass, ring base	75.00

Skillet, cast iron, Griswold
#12	75.00
#13 ....1,000.00
#14	150.00
#80, double	60.00
#90, double	65.00
Spatula, 15¼" l, wrought iron, two brass inlays	355.00
Spice Set, Griffith's, milk glass, orig rack, 12 pcs	65.00
Stuffing Spoon, Greighty Co, Toledo, OH, 1948, heavy plate ...	45.00

Tea Canister, glass
Delphinium blue, round	195.00
Jadeite, sq	48.00

Trivet, cast iron
8" d, star and braid	75.00
10" l, floral scrolls	100.00
11" l, lacy, child, dog, and hat dec	145.00
Waffle, heart and star, Griswold .	150.00
Wheat Stick Pan, cast iron, #272, Griswold	150.00

KUTANI

History: In the mid–1600s Kutani originated in the Kaga province of Japan. Kutani comes in a variety of color patterns, one of the most popular being Ao Kutani, a green glaze with colors such as green, yellow, and purple enclosed in a black outline. Wares made since the 1870s for export are enameled in a wide variety of colors and styles.

Reference: Gloria and Robert Mascarelli, *Warman's Oriental Antiques,* Wallace–Homestead, 1992.

Bottle, cov, red ground, gold dec, figures in garden, boy playing flute finial	900.00
Bowl, nesting, set of three, landscape dec, largest 9" d, Taisho period, price for set	300.00
Brush Pot, 7¼" h	35.00
Charger, 14" d, landscape scene, multicolored, gilt border	225.00
Chocolate Pot, 8½" h, red, orange, and gold, reserve panels of peonies, birds, and figures in garden scene	125.00
Creamer and Sugar, cov, 5¼" creamer, 7½" h sugar, hp scenes, gold tracery, bamboo handles, burnt orange ground, ftd, sgd Oriental character, 19th C	250.00
Cup and Saucer, eggshell	25.00
Dish, 6½" d, Ko, shallow decagonal form, green, yellow, and blue enameled dec, large central medallion of long tailed phoenix, iron red details, yellow and aubergine foliate scroll border, undersides painted iron red and black, scattered pine needles, chocolate brown rims, short foot encircled by single and double outer ring, iron red fuku mark encircled by double ring, Edo period, late 17th C, price for pair .6,050.00
Ewer, 8¼" h, duck on floral base, key fret band, green, yellow, aubergine, and blue enamel	150.00
Figure, 7½" l, crouching hare, clear white glaze finished with high sheen transparent glaze, stamped "Kutani" on base, Edo/Meiji period, 19th C 1,100.00
Ginger Jar, cov, 5" h, blue, green, and carmine enamel dec, Foo dog finial	100.00

CERAMICS

In the last twenty years ceramic collecting has experienced a number of significant changes. In the period immediately following World War II (1945 through 1970), eighteenth and nineteenth century English and Continental pottery and porcelain, e.g., Amphora, Staffordshire, and R. S. Prussia, dominated the category. In the 1970s and 1980s, many collecting categories within this group lost favor among American collectors, e.g., Luster wares and Lowestoft. A select revival in the traditionalist categories is taking place in the mid-1990s. Romantic Staffordshire and KPM are at record pricing levels.

American redware and stoneware reached record prices during the Bicentennial-driven folk art craze. Both markets experienced strong price declines in middle market and common pieces during the 1980s and 1990s. Art Pottery, the darling of the 1980s, is stable in price. Activity centers primarily around top quality pieces.

American dinnerware and utilitarian ware from the 1930s through the 1960s is one of the strongest market segments. California pottery, Watt, and Purinton had major market runs. Many collectors keep their collections regionally focused. Red Wing continues strong in the upper Midwest.

Collectors rediscovered topical collecting. While the cookie jar, lady head planter, and figural salt and pepper crazes are winding down, there appears to be a growing interest once again in cup and saucer sets and teapots. Of course, crossover collectors, e.g., World's Fair, continue as a major market influence.

Jar, redware, slip decorated, attr. to Bucks Co., PA, late 18th or early 19th century, **$4,500.00.**

Cookie Jar, Doranne, Farmyard Follies, mkd "CJ-100 of U.S.A. Doranne" on bottom, 10 3/4" h, **$30.00.**

The collecting of teapots, a strong mid-century ceramic collecting category, is undergoing a revival. Collectors are attracted by the variety of shapes and decorative motifs. Some concentrate on the products of a single country or era.

Top left: Romantic Staffordshire, English, R. S. Adams, Palestine pattern, **$350.00**; *top right:* Nippon, Japanese, mkd "Imperial Nippon, Hand Painted," 5 1/2" h, **$95.00**; *center right:* Spatterware, English, peafowl pattern, unmkd, c1830–50, 6" h, **$250.00**; *bottom right:* Leeds, soft paste, English, imp. "L Wood" in bottom, c1820–40, 7 1/2" h, **$275.00**.

In the 1990s American collectors exhibit a decided preference for American manufactured products, whether Art Pottery or utilitarian wares. Manufacturer, pattern, association with a recognized designer, and stylist shape are some of the major collecting emphases.

Top left: Purinton, Apple pattern, ink stamped "Purinton Slip Ware," six cup, 6 1/2" h, **$70.00;** *center left:* Hall, Autumn Leaf pattern, Aladdin shape, gold stamped "Hall's Superior Quality Kitchenware, Tested and Approved by Mary Dunbar, Jewel Homemakers Institute," 6 1/2" h, **$45.00;** *bottom left:* Art Pottery, Pisagh Forest, part of set, **$375.00;** *top right:* Unidentified maker, Rebekah At The Well, emb design, unmkd, 7 1/4" h, **$35.00.**

Ceramic drinking mugs with pewter tops were common souvenirs from World's Fairs at the turn of the century. Value: **$150.00**. *Rolfes collection.*

This Satsuma vase from the 1893 Columbian Exposition, Chicago World's Fair, pictures the Fisheries Building. Value: **$900.00**. *Rolfes collection.*

The Trylon and Perisphere of the 1939–40 New York World's Fair are among the most recognizable World's Fair symbols. This Lenox jasperware was sold in vast quantities. Value relates to availability of form. Cigarette box, **$65.00**; vase, **$35.00**; cigarette cup, **$50.00**. *Rolfes collection.*

PAPER COLLECTIBLES

Paper collectibles are one of the hottest antiques and collectibles collecting categories of the 1990s. Availability, affordability, displayability, nostalgic appeal, and an "everything and anything is fine" attitude are the primary reasons.

The paper market is driven by two distinct groups of collectors—those who collect by topic, e.g., broadsides, letterhead, and sheet music, and those who collect by subject, e.g., cat, golfing, or tobacco material. The latter group constitutes the crossover collectors, i.e., collectors from other collecting categories who seek paper items that relate to their specific collecting interest.

A large amount of paper is purchased by individuals who want to mat, frame, and display it, rather than actually collect it. It is a favorite among decorators wishing to create a period ambience.

Collecting by illustrator is one of the hottest trends in paper collectibles. Previous favorites such as Fisher and Flagg are being replaced by Fox and Thompson. Parrish prints remain strong, while Rockwell illustrations are waning. Women illustrators such as Bessie Pease Gutmann and Jessie Wilcox Smith are *hot, hot, hot.*

This card appeals to the iron and cat collector as well as the trade card collector. Value: **$8.00.**

New York World's Fair poster. Value: **$1,500.00.**

Top left: Post cards from the Golden Age, 1898–1918, feature highly colorful images. Value: **$10.00.** *Top right:* Linen cards (named for their surface texture) from the 1920s through the 1950s and glosses (glossy surface cards) often featured photographic images. Value: **$4.00.** *Bottom left:* Souvenir cards from the 1950s and later are approaching values ranging from $1.00 to $5.00. Value: **$.75.** *Bottom right:* The post card is an excellent example of the multi-faceted collectibles, i.e., a single item that can appeal to more than one collector. How many collectors can you identify for this card? There are more than six. Value: **$3.00.**

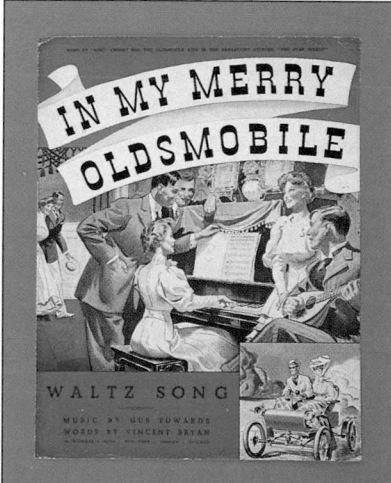

Top left: Gene Autry's "Here Comes Santa Claus" made the 1948 Hit Parade. Value: **$4.00** to a sheet music collector; **$10.00** to a Gene Autry collector. *Top right:* Cover art by many famous illustrators graced sheet music covers. Value: **$8.00** to a sheet music collector; **$20.00** to a collector of this illustrator. *Bottom left:* A single song often can be found with a dozen or more different covers. Value: **$3.00** to a sheet music collector; **$10.00** to an automobile collector; **$15.00** to an Oldsmobile collector. *Bottom right:* At the moment, this sheet's primary value is to an astronaut collector. Value: **$2.00** to a sheet music collector; **$10.00** to an astronaut collector.

Paper doll books have existed as a major doll collecting category since the 1960s. A major collection could be built by focusing only on paper doll books featuring movies and movie stars. "Gone with the Wind" material is so popular that it is a stand alone category. Value: **$95.00.**

Magazine tear sheets became a staple in the paper marketplace in the 1970s. When buying a matted example, remember that most of the value is in the matting. Initially selling for a dollar or two, magazine tear sheets with strong graphics now command prices in the $8.00 to $15.00 range. Value: **$5.00.**

TOY CARS

The difference between men and boys is the price of their toys. Based on prices seen in the 1990s toy car marketplace, toy cars are a collecting category for men, not boys.

Toy collecting is generation driven. The collectors who grew up with the great cast-iron and lithograph tin toys of the first quarter of the twentieth century are dying off. In some categories, values declined, not increased in the 1990s. The hottest toy car categories of the moment are the lithograph tin wind-up and battery operated cars of the 1930s through the 1950s. However, a casual reader of *Toy Shop* might easily get the impression that the toy market of the 1990s is dominated by cars and other toys made between 1960 and the present. It's closer to the truth than most collectors will admit.

Germany, Japan, and the United States were the leading producers of lithograph tin toy cars of the 1930s and 1940s. These cars are becoming pricey, ranging between $100 and $750 for most models. Tin Lizzy, wind-up, Arnold, West Germany, 9 3/4" l, **$375.00.** *Bausch collection.*

Marx introduced the lithograph tin wind-up Amos 'n Andy Fresh Air Taxi in 1930. It rolls forward for a short distance and then shakes its occupants. Toy collectors in general have made the original box a major component in having the "complete" toy. Box art often is more graphic and appealing than the toy inside. The original box can double the value of a toy. **$850.00.**

Cast-iron cars were the king of the toy collectibles from the 1930s through the late 1960s. They survived because they were well made and designed for heavy play use. Original paint and parts are the two key collecting criteria. Wilkins touring car, combination cast iron and sheet metal, 9" l, **$1,200.00.** *Bausch collection.*

Reproduction cast-iron cars are a problem. Spot them by looking for loose fits, unfinished castings, and incorrect paint. Period paint develops a mellow appearance. Arcade Mack truck, #223L, mechanical action, 12" l, **$750.00.** *Bausch collection.*

Restoration is an accepted practice for older cast iron. American firms, such as the Tin Toy Works in Allentown, Pennsylvania, are known throughout the world. It is a common practice when restoring to add age to replacement parts. Check any car carefully. Dent, touring car, 8 3/4" l, **$1,000.00.** *Bausch collection.*

Lithograph tin finishes a close second in the contest for most favorite type of toy car from the first quarter of the 20th century. Most lithograph tin made during this period came from Europe, with England, France, and Germany the leading manufacturing countries. Paint is critical. Collectors talk about these cars in terms of percent of original paint remaining. Lehmann, autobus, double decker, German, wind-up, 4 1/2" l, **$1,500.00.** *Bausch collection.*

Automobile racing captured the public's fascination in the first decades of the 20th century. Racers were one of the most popular toy car forms of the period. Mors Racer, European model, rubber wheels, 17 1/2" l, **$600.00.** *Bausch collection.*

Although nautical, collectors of early 20th century lithograph tin always include several ships among their prized possessions. This German, possibly Gunterman, key wound, amphibious auto, has dual appeal. Note the paint flaking, a common problem with early lithograph tin cars or any toy. Value: **$3,000.00.** *Bausch collection.*

Matchbox cars were first manufactured by Lesney Products, an English company founded in 1947 by Leslie Smith and Rodney Smith. Their first diecast cars were made in 1953 on a scale of 1:75. The trademark "Matchbox" was registered in 1953. In 1979 Lesney Products Corp. made over 5.5 million toys a week. Matchbox currently is a division of Tyco.

Top: The large and elaborate gold-colored Coronation Coach with the King and Queen inside is the hardest of the variations to find, **$800.00;** *middle:* The Aveling Barford Road Roller No. 1 was the first vehicle in the Matchbox 1-75 series of miniatures, **$50.00,** *Marshall collection; bottom:* The Lesney Toy milk float (cart) was the first model to be packed in its own individual box, **$200.00.**

COUNTRY

Country is a decorating style that has become a collecting category in its own right. While all Country objects are either antiques, collectibles, or desirables, they are simply referred to as Country by most collectors. What makes an object Country? The broad answer is use in rural and small town America from the period of settlement to the late 1930s. An object does not necessarily have to be farm related to be considered Country. Not all Country items are inexpensive, as seen by some of the objects that follow.

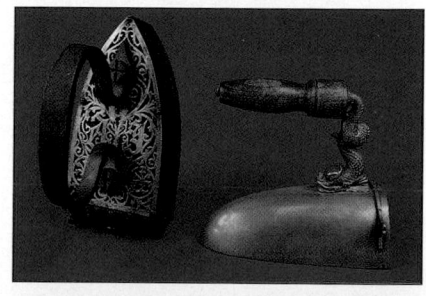

Top right. Slug Iron, *(left)* European, cutwork initials "A.I.," hinged gate, late 1800s, 7 5/8" l, **$750.00.** Slug, *(right)* ox tongue, European, all brass with detailed dolphin post, hinged gate, late 1800s, 7 3/4" l, **$575.00.** *Above:* Machine fluter, Knox Standard, A-1, AM Fluting Machine, Rudolph Felder, Machinists, New York, picture of woman in oval, about 1875, 5 3/4" l, **$500.00.** *Right:* Companion trivet for French slug, wrought and pierced construction, 9" l slug, early 1800s, extremely scarce, **$1,250.00.** *All irons from the collection of David and Sue Irons.*

Copper played a major role in Country collecting in the period between 1930 and 1970. It lost favor in the early 1970s due largely to the numerous reproductions that flooded the market. New copper can be easily aged. Inexperienced collectors have difficulty distinguishing modern from period pieces. Measure, one gallon, **$85.00**.

Pewter, especially examples made in America in the late eighteenth and early nineteenth centuries, was a focal point of any Country collection. Today, English, Irish, and Continental pewter compete actively with American examples for collector favor. Teapot, mass produced, mid-19th C, **$115.00**.

Although the use of butter pats and stamps continued on farms well into the twentieth century, they are most often associated with the late eighteenth and nineteenth centuries. A large number of reproductions flooded the market in the 1950s and 1960s. Butter print, wheat pattern, **$100.00**.

Like copper, tin ware and tole (painted tin ware) were popular favorites of Country decorators from the 1930s through the late 1960s. As tin wares rapidly escalated in price, individuals seeking the "Country look" turned to modern reproductions, many of which are difficult to distinguish from period pieces. Candle mold, tin, six candle, **$60.00**.

Kerosene lanterns similar to this hung on barns and in the front of locomotives. This particular example was used aboard a canalboat during the mule drawn canalboat era of the nineteenth and early twentieth centuries. Value: **$150.00**.

Cobalt blue decorated stoneware combines subdued background colors and bright decorative motifs well. Jug, bird decoration, late 19th C, **$275.00**.

Apples are a popular Country decorating motif. Watt Pottery, largely utilitarian in nature, experienced a major market run in the early 1990s. Watt Pottery, mixing bowl, open apple pattern, 7" d, **$100.00**.

Regionalism plays a major role in Country collecting. *Top:* Although there is Pennsylvania German formal (high-style) unpainted furniture, this ethnic group is best known for its painted examples. This blanket chest is attributed to the Mertztown area of Berks County, Pennsylvania, and was made between 1800 and 1820. Value: **$15,000.00;** *Right:* Although the Windsor chair is generic in nature, collectors spend a great deal of research time attempting to attribute eighteenth and early nineteenth century examples to a particular region or maker. Sampson Barnet of Wilmington, Delaware, made this comb back Windsor in the early 1800s, **$7,500.00.**

Lamp, 15 x 8¼ x 8½", underglaze blue and colored glazes and enamels dec, kiri designs on honeycomb pattern, reticulated slightly domed rect cov, stand set on four cabriole legs, Meiji period, late 19th C **3,300.00**
Sake Cup, 1⅞" h, floriform rim, short ring foot, enamel and gilt dec, patterned rim band, gilt scrolling flower and trellis dec . **100.00**

Plate, 8½" d, $40.00.

Teapot, 6" h, pair of falcons dec . **100.00**
Umbrella Stand, 28" h, multicolored butterflies, flowers, foliage, and medallions **500.00**
Vase
  7" h
    Allover floral and bird dec . . . **50.00**
    One Thousand Faces, sgd . . **175.00**
  7¼" h, baluster form, floral dec, artist sgd, price for pair **400.00**
  9½" h, courting scene **75.00**
  12" h
    Peacock dec, three character mark **150.00**
    Village scene, handles, three character mark **200.00**
  12⅜" h and 11½" h, baluster form, late 19th C, converted to table lamp, one cut down, price for pair **290.00**

LALIQUE

LALIQUE

History: Rene Lalique (1860–1945) first gained prominence as a jewelry designer. Around 1900 he began experimenting with molded glass brooches and pendants, often embellishing them with semiprecious stones. By 1905 he was devoting himself exclusively to the manufacture of glass articles.

In 1908 Lalique began designing packaging for the French cosmetic houses. He also produced many objects, especially vases, bowls, and figurines, in the Art Noveau style in the 1910s. The full scope of Lalique's genius was seen at the 1925 Paris International Exhibition of Decorative Arts. He later moved to the Art Deco form.

The mark "R. LALIQUE FRANCE" in block letters is found on pressed articles, tableware, vases, paperweights, and mascots. The script signature, with or without "France," is found on hand–blown objects. Occasionally a design number is included. The word "France" in any form indicates a piece made after 1926.

The post–1945 mark is "Lalique France" without the "R"; there are exceptions to this rule.

References: Hugh D. Guinn (ed.), *The Glass of Rene Lalique At Auction,* Guindex Publications, 1992; Katherine Morrison McClinton, *Introduction to Lalique Glass,* Wallace–Homestead, 1978, out–of–print; Tony L. Mortimer, *Lalique,* Chartwell Books, 1989; Ellen T. Schroy, *Warman's Glass,* Wallace–Homestead, 1992.

Periodical: *Lalique Magazine,* 400 Veterans Blvd., Carlstadt, NJ 07072.

Videotape: *The World of Lalique Glass,* Nicholas M. Dawes, Award Video and Film Distributors, 1993.

Collectors' Club: Lalique Society of America, 400 Veterans Blvd., Carlstadt, NJ 07072.

Reproduction Alert: Much faking of the Lalique signature occurs, the most common being the addition of an "R" to the post–1945 mark.

Bookends, pr, 6½" h, thoroughbred horse's head, mounted on black glass platform base, molded mark "R Lalique France" **7,475.00**

Bottle, molded, cylindrical form, butterflies dec, relief signed "R. Lalique," etched "France," c1940, 5½" h **460.00**

Bowl

8" w, 3¾" h, allover frosted leaf motif, signed "Lalique France," pr **575.00**

9" d, opalescent, Perruches, molded with parrots against foliate and branch ground, acid etched "R. Lalique France" **2,525.00**

9½" d, molded, opalescent, swirling sea nymphs, Rene Lalique, c1945 .... **630.00**

14½" d, molded opal, center nude woman dec, raised mold mark "R Lalique" **5,465.00**

Box, cov, oval, brass fittings depicting roses in relief, signed "Lalique France 500," 3½" h .. **475.00**

Center Bowl

7½" h, oak leaf shape, clear oval base, signed "Lalique France 500" **1,085.00**

10" d, 4" h, dark sepia ground, press molded rows of daisies, black enamel accents, molded "R Lalique France" mark **1,045.00**

Figure

Bull, signed, 4" h **125.00**

Plate, fish, 10¼" d, $395.00.

Nude Woman, 3⅜" h, frosted, seated on platform disk above black sq base, marked "Lalique France" **265.00**

Partridge, frosted and molded, signed "Lalique France," set of three **460.00**

Finial, etched, circular form depicting two maidens amidst floral sprays, signed "R. Lalique France," 2½" h **1,150.00**

Goblet, 5⅛" h, bulbous frosted stems, Langeais, price for set of 6 .... **175.00**

Jar, cov, frosted, molded, circular form depicting three moths, relief signed "R. Lalique," inscribed "France," c1930, one cover missing, 2" h, pr **575.00**

Paperweight, Thistle, intaglio, frosted and clear, signed "Lalique France" **45.00**

Plate, 8" d, salad, crescent form, frosted molded thistle pods and thorny branches dec, marked "Lalique France" **345.00**

Urn, 13¾" h, spreading rim with egg and dart border, bowl dec with flowers and leaves above lobed vase, spreading circular foot etched with acanthus leaves, sq base, signed "Lalique France" **2,525.00**

Vase

5⅝" h, frosted, molded leafy trees and polished blossoms, pale blue patina, engraved "R Lalique France, No 940" **1,265.00**

6½" h, octahedral shape, plain sides, base with lion masks at sides and pierced center, signed "Lalique France" **800.00**

6¾" h, crystal, brown holly berry dec, etched signature on base **1,265.00**

8" h, entitled "The Love Birds," depicting two entwined lovebirds on shaped oval base, signed "Lalique France" **475.00**

9⅛" h, fiery blue opal body, molded peacock heads dec, gray wash accents, engraved "R Lalique France" **4,315.00**

9⅜" h, press molded, frosted, flared, bulb shape border with

lilac leaf design, engraved "R Lalique France" **1,380.00**
9½" h

Baccantes, tapering cylindrical form, field carved with bas relief of female nudes **1,950.00**

Thistle motif, tapering form, signed "Lalique France" . . . **185.00**

LAMPS AND LIGHTING

History: Lighting devices have evolved from simple stone–age oil lamps to the popular electrified models of today. Aimé Argand patented the first oil lamp in 1784. Around 1850 kerosene became a popular lamp–burning fluid, replacing whale oil and other fluids. In 1879 Thomas A. Edison invented the electric light bulb, causing fluid lamps to lose favor and creating a new field for lamp manufacturers to develop. Companies like Tiffany and Handel developed skills in the manufacture of electric lamps, having their decorators produce beautiful aesthetic bases and shades.

References: James Edward Black (ed.), *Electric Lighting of the 20s–30s,* L–W Book Sales, 1988, 1993 value update; James Edward Black (ed.), *Electric Lighting of the 20s & 30s, Volume 2 with Price Guide,* L–W Book Sales, 1990, 1993 value update; J. W. Courter, *Aladdin Collectors Manual & Price Guide #2,* published by author, 1993; J. W. Courter, *Aladdin Collectors Manual & Price Guide #14,* published by author, 1992; J. W. Courter, *Aladdin Collectors Manual & Price Guide #15, Kerosene Mantel Lamps* published by author, 1994; J. W. Courter, *Aladdin Electric Lamps,* published by author, 1987; J. W. Courter, *Aladdin Electric Lamps Price Guide #1,* published by author, 1989; J. W. Courter, *Aladdin, The Magic Name in Lamps,* Wallace–Homestead, 1980; J. W. Courter, *Angle Lamps: Collectors Manual & Price Guide,* published by author, 1992; Robert De Falco, Carole Goldman Hibel and John Hibel, *Handel Lamps,* H & D Press, 1986; Larry Freeman, *New Light on Old Lamps,* American Life Foundation, 1984; L–W Book Sales (ed.), *Quality Electric Lamps: A Pictorial Price Guide,* L–W Book Sales, 1992; Ed-

ward and Sheila Malakoff, *Pairpoint Lamps,* Schiffer Publishing, 1990; Nadja Maril, *American Lighting: 1840–1940,* Schiffer Publishing, 1989; Richard Miller and John Solverson, *Student Lamps of the Victorian Era,* Antique Publications, 1992, 1992–93 value guide; Bill and Linda Montgomery, *Animated Motion Lamps 1920s To Present,* L–W Book Sales, 1991; Leland & Crystal Payton, *Turned On: Decorative Lamps of the 'Fifties,* Abbeville Press, 1989; *Quality Electric Lamps,* L–W Book Sales, 1992; Catherine M. V. Thuro, *Oil Lamps,* Wallace–Homestead, 1976, 1992 value update; Catherine M. V. Thuro, *Oil Lamps II,* Collector Books, 1983, 1994 value update.

Periodical: *Light Revival,* 35 West Elm Ave., Quincy, MA 02170.

Collectors' Clubs: Aladdin Knights of the Mystic Light, 3935 Kelley Rd., Kevil, KY 42053; Historical Lighting Society of Canada, 9013 Oxbow Rd., North East, PA 16428; The Incandescent Lamp Collectors Assoc., Museum of Lighting, 717 Washington Place, Baltimore, MD 21201; The Rushlight Club, Inc., Suite 196, 1657 The Fairway, Jenkintown, PA 19046.

Museums: Kerosene Lamp Museum, Winchester Center, CT; Pairpoint Lamp Museum, River Edge, NJ.

AMERICAN, EARLY

Argand, pr

18¾" h, Clark and Cargill, NY, patinated bronze, single arm, missing shades **1,320.00**

21" h, unknown maker, single arm, orig prisms, shade, electrified, early 19th C **1,200.00**

Astral, 21½" h, brass, fluted column, white marble base, wheel cut and frosted shade, 19th C . **250.00**

Baker's, tin

7" l, rect, four brass burners . . . **110.00**

8½" l, cylindrical, orig bronze finish **225.00**

9¾" l, 5¼" h, cylindrical, five wicks **450.00**

Betty

12" h, tin, stand, repaired bottom **160.00**

26" h, standing, brass faced lamp mount and spade feet,

adjustable, worn faceted knob
on top and clamp **900.00**
Chamber, 5¼" h, lemon shape
font, saucer base, missing
burner **80.00**
Gimbal, 3½" h, pewter, Yale & Cur-
tis, New York City, 1858–67 . . . **550.00**
Hand
3¾" h, pewter, bell shape, Capen & Molineaux, New York
City, 1848–54 . . . . **225.00**
6" h, tin, saucer base, unusual
lift–out burner **150.00**
Kettle, 10" h, brass, mounted on
circular iron foot, Continental . . **150.00**
Miner's, 18" h, iron hook, French,
19th C **75.00**
Sparking, 3¾" h, blown glass,
clear, period burner **275.00**
Witch's, 9" l, iron, missing cov,
Salem, MA **300.00**

BOUDOIR

Art Deco, 17" h, brass tapered
standard, molded and frosted
shade, sgd "SE V B 243" **1,000.00**
Candlestick, crystal, hexagonal
base, price for pair **65.00**
Handel, 14" h, bronze metal stan-
dard, frosted hexagonal shade
with sailing vessel and tropical
bay scene **2,000.00**
Pairpoint
14" h, Art Deco, reverse painted,
brass double handled vasiform
standard, hexagonal shade
with floral dec **750.00**
16" h, nickel plated candlestick
form standard, Copley shade
with painted forest scenes int.,
frosted ground **1,200.00**

CANDELABRA, pr

Brass and Cut Crystal, 15½" h,
twin arm brass candleholders,
crystal urn above and below,
suspended with prisms, electri-
fied **900.00**
Empire, bronze
18" h, tapering cylindrical standard with masks surmounted
by shuttle form vessel holding

three C–scroll arms, engine
turned nozzles, cast stylized
anthemion socle, gilded and
patinated, mounted as lamp,
pr **5,175.00**
21" h, flaming orb within three
swan–form candle arms ending in urn form nozzles, complex column with plain and engine turned bands, engine
turned pedestal, stepped
base, gilded and patinated,
19th C, pr **2,750.00**
23" h, winged classical figure
holding aloft bowl with three
scrolling candle arms, figure
resting on orb mounted on
cast and reeded pedestal,
gilded and patinated, 19th C,
pr **4,885.00**
36" h, draped classical figure
holding bouquet of four scrolling candle arms modeled as
leaves and tendrils, fluted nozzles, pale black and gray marble truncated columns with sq
bronze bases, pr **4,885.00**
Empire Style, 27⅛" h, bronze and
ormolu, figural, four light, marble
base, marble chips, late 19th C **3,740.00**
Louis XV Style, 18½" h, porcelain,
gilt bronze mounted, three light,
apple green vases with foliate
branch mounts, flanked by putti
in scrolling handles, loss, late
19th C **975.00**
Louis XVI Style, 15¼" h, white
marble, ormolu mounted, three
light, urn form, holding branches
with buds, flanked by satyr
masks, square base with four ft,
slight damage, 19th C **800.00**
Regency Style, 22½" h, faceted
crystal baluster–form standard
surmounted by a brass lyre and
Appoline mask, two scrolling
branches with faceted crystal
urn–form nozzles **1,035.00**

CHANDELIER

Baccarat
36" h, crystal and opaline glass,
ten scrolled candle arms with

etched hurricane shades, hung with bells and prisms . . **5,300.00**
43" h, crystal and gilt bronze, twelve scrolled candle arms draped with faceted prism swags and pendant drops . . . **3,675.00**
Baroque Style, 27" h, iron, skeletal eccentric baluster form, twelve light **975.00**
Continental
31½" h, twelve light, brass and crystal, two tiers of scrolled candle arms hung with cut crystal drops **2,300.00**
40" h, cut crystal, faceted baluster standard draped with prism swags, suspending six scrolled candle arms mounted with bobeche, hung with faceted prisms **1,850.00**
64½" h, twelve light, cut and molded glass, baluster glass standard, two tiers of scrolling candle arms, electrified **1,850.00**
Daum Nancy, 21" h, 15" d shade, patinated metal, circular concave orange glass shade, etched circles and rays pattern, patinated cast metal roses and leaves mount **2,990.00**
Delft, 42" h, brass and pottery, six arm, bell form centering blue and white dome shade, issuing six scrolled candle arms, 20th C . . **860.00**
Empire Style
9" h, gilded and patinated bronze, five light **1,100.00**
14½" h, ormolu, flower and leaf dec, pinecone and flame finials, scrolling foliate branches, six light, 19th C **2,415.00**
27" h, gilded bronze, everted corona suspending chains with brilliant encrusted links, molded and floral cast ring centering horn–form arms, basal tier with slender prisms, twelve light, 19th C **6,050.00**
George III Style, 36" h, gilded brass and crystal, massive swirling faceted baluster beneath corona of prism swags and valances, central disk radiating S scroll arms, pierced bronze noz-

zles, inverted acorn–form hurricane shades, six light **19,550.00**
Italian Baroque Style, 22" h, gilded iron, bead encrusted, skeletal baluster form, pyriform pendants, six light **2,075.00**
Louis XV Style
27" h, gilded bronze and crystal, skeletal baluster form, multiple rock crystal pyriform drops, four light **1,850.00**
31" h, silvered and gilded iron, skeletal baluster form, multiple faceted pendants, eight light . **1,950.00**
Louis XVI Style, 26" h, gilded bronze and crystal, modeled as two concentric tiers of Vitruvian scrolls separated by links of rods and rings, eight light **2,175.00**
Maria Theresa Style, Continental, 90" h, bronze and crystal, six scrolled candle arms hung with cut crystal pendant drops **1,600.00**
Neoclassical Style, 34" h, painted iron, open scrolling baluster with wrought flower heads above nine S–scrolling candle arms . . **1,500.00**
Steuben, irid glass, ceiling fixture, three light, silvered metal fixture supporting three irid glass

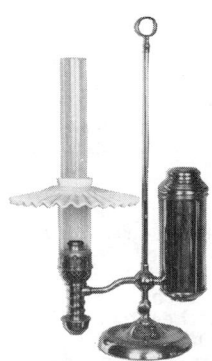

Student, Manhattan Brass Co., nickel-plated brass, sgd, 20¼" h, $855.00. Photograph courtesy of James D. Julia, Inc.

shades with pulled feather design, each shade marked "Steuben" **575.00**

Tiffany, 23½" d, gilt metal and favrile glass, five light, center urn favrile glass shaft, five scroll arms **300.00**

Tin, 15½" h, baluster–form standard, eight arms, imperfections **925.00**

Victorian

32" h, ormolu and brass, brass fonts and swags, wheel etched frosted shades, cherry to white cased glass smoke bells, clear prisms, three light, electrified, some glass imperfections, one bell repaired, mid 19th C **2,650.00**

40" h, tinted glass, faceted baluster column, swags, and prisms, six light, formerly electrified, repaired, late 19th C .. **2,875.00**

DESK

Charles X, 23½" h, ormolu and tole peinte, adjustable green painted shade, mid 19th C **6,900.00**

Handel, 15" h, cameo glass and bronze, oval shaped dome glass shade with berry cov curving green stems ending in cluster of green shading to orange leaves, signed "Handel 7186" on bronzed base with molded woven straw motif, impressed "Handel" **2,075.00**

Student, brass, twin arm, twin serpent loop center handle, two ribbed white glass shades, electrified **325.00**

Tiffany

11½" h, bronze, harp shape, opalescent and reddish–brown pulled feather bell shape globe, sgd "LCT" on shade, base marked "Tiffany Studios, New York 416" **2,000.00**

16" h, bronze, twelve paneled green linen–folded shade, imp "Tiffany Studios, New York 1837" on shade and "Tiffany Studios New York 612" on base **2,700.00**

FLOOR

Charles X Style, 82" h, torchere, pr, ormolu, patinated bronze, and giltwood, six light, lion paw ft **6,325.00**

Greek Revival, 53" h, bronze, three sockets, circular dished base with intricate cutout floral dec, verdigris, late 19th C **925.00**

Louis XVI Style, 68" h, gilt brass, tapering reeded standard, lion's–paw feet, pr **1,150.00**

Renaissance Revival Style, 32" h, torchere, gilt and patinated metal, standard molded with masks and entwined scrolling foliage **100.00**

Rococo Style, 60" h, torchere, painted white, late 19th C, pr .. **430.00**

FLUID

Banquet, Colonial Revival, 21" h, silver plated and crystal, compressed globular font surmounted by Hinks burner, resting on Corinthian columnar standard, molded and cast base ornamented with rams' heads, electrified, late 19th C **1,275.00**

Boston and Sandwich Glass Co, 10" h, pressed glass, cobalt blue, hexagonal font, stepped base, minor imperfections, c1850, pr **1,725.00**

Glass Overlay

12" h, font cut white to pink, punty, brass and marble stepped base, imperfections, 19th C **450.00**

12½" h, font with starburst pattern cut white to cobalt, opaque white base, imperfections, 19th C **315.00**

Mappin and Webb, 9" l, kerosene, silver plated, Grecian form, ram's head details, 20th C **430.00**

TABLE

Bradley & Hubbard, 23" h, gilt metal, circular base, octagonal

Table, Dufner and Kimberly, domed stained glass shade with lotus flower border, 24″ h, 21½″ d shade, c1910, $2,600.00. Photograph courtesy of William Doyle Galleries.

opal glass shade, one lower
  panel cracked **575.00**
Charles X Style, gilt metal and cut
  crystal, urn shaped, scroll and
  mask handles, sq base, shade . **415.00**
Chinese, 18¾″ h, cov jar form,
  malachite and rose quartz, patinated metal fittings, early 20th C **625.00**
Continental, porcelain
  26″ h, vasiform, light blue
    ground, central pink floral mo-
    tif, bronze base, pr **425.00**
  29″ h, bird and floral reserves
    dec, pink ground, gilt high-
    lights **550.00**
Daum Nancy, 8″ h, cameo glass,
  landscape with trees dec, later
  mounts added, signed on bottom **550.00**
Empire Style, 17″ h, crystal and
  bronze, classical urn with swan's
  neck handles, sq stepped base **1,150.00**
Figural
  16″ h, porcelain and gilt metal,
    parrots with flowers in beaks,
    twin light, pr **1,875.00**
  17″ h, pottery, baluster form with
    applied three dimensional
    Chinese dragon, turquoise
    glaze, electrified, early 20th C **175.00**

19½″ h, carved and gilded griffin,
  wood base, drilled for fixture . **400.00**
25½″ h, Baroque style, giltwood,
  young man holding candle,
  electrified, gilding loss, late
  19th/early 20th C **225.00**
Galle, 18½″ h, 7″ d, pink lotus
  flower shade, patinated bronze
  light green stem–form standard
  overlaid with burgundy highlights, lily pad molded base,
  signed "Galle," c1910 . . . . . . **27,600.00**
Handel, 9½″ h, black metal candle-
  stick base, globe with winter
  scene, sgd "Handel 5895 0389" **1,050.00**
Italian, 15″ h, alabaster, vasiform,
  carved floral and leaf dec, late
  19th C, pr **490.00**
Middle Eastern Style, 23″ h, brass,
  star and crescent finial on circular shade, amber glass bead
  tassels **300.00**
Neoclassical Style, 25″ h, patin-
  ated metal and marble, molded
  with frieze of classical figures
  and masks, pr **1,100.00**
Oriental, 21½″ h, bronze, figural,
  Buddha seated on lotus blossom, green and white opaline
  glass lotus blossom shade **450.00**
Pairpoint, 21″ h, reverse painted
  glass bell shaped shade dec
  with roses, daisies, and poppies
  against black ground with C–
  scrolled and acanthus leaf border, brass tone urn–form base
  with curled handles on shaped
  sq foot, shade signed "Pair-
  point" **2,875.00**
Rose Quartz, 29″ h, vasiform,
  snuff bottle finial, late 19th C . . **345.00**

WALL

Louis XVI Style, bronze
  13″ h, acanthus–form wall plate
    with three reeded scrolling
    candle arms, plain cylindrical
    nozzles, set of four **2,750.00**
  16″ h, athenienne–form back-
    plate holding reeded loop with
    three cast nozzles, gilded and
    patinated, pr **1,600.00**
Rococo, 32″ h, giltwood, modeled

as abundantly filled foliate–form vase centering beaded reliquary aperture, later added six wire candle arms, pr **1,375.00**

Sconces, pr

Empire Style, 16" h, bronze, horn shape with four S–scroll candle branches and central superior light **925.00**

Italian Neoclassical, 47" h, giltwood and metal, nine light, foliate standard issuing three tiers of scrolling candle branches, applied metal leaf dec **350.00**

Louis XV Style, 17" h, dore bronze, foliate scrolled backplate issuing five acanthus scrolled candle arms mounted with foliate candle sockets, 19th C **2,075.00**

Neoclassical Style, 7⅞" h, gilded bronze, double arm, ram's head finial, electric, 20th C . . **260.00**

Victorian, 15" h, gilt brass, mirrored, Bacchus mask crest above shaped mirror plate, two foliate candle arms **525.00**

LAMP SHADES

History: Lamp shades were made to diffuse the harsh light produced by early gas lighting fixtures. These early shades were made by popular Art Nouveau manufacturers including Durand, Quezal, Steuben, Tiffany, and others. Many shades are not marked.

References: Dr. Larry Freeman, *New Lights on Old Lamps,* American Life Foundation, 1984; Jo Ann Thomas, *Early Twentieth Century Lighting Fixtures,* Collector Books, 1980, out–of–print.

Arts and Crafts, 27" d, leaded, mottled yellow amber glass panels, irid green, yellow, and olive amber Prairie School triangular and rect segment borders, imp "Linden Glass Co, Chicago, Ill" **3,575.00**

Burmese, 8¾" d, birds, butterflies, and floral dec **265.00**

Custard, brown dec, 2" fitter ring, $35.00.

Cameo Glass, 13½" d, Regas, blue cut to frosted glass, bird and flowering branch dec **460.00**

Carnival Glass, 2" d, forest scene, price for pair **110.00**

Durand, 3½" d, candle type, irid gold **125.00**

Fostoria, 5" h, gold, green leaves and vines, white luster ground . **125.00**

Handel, 22" d, slag glass, paneled **1,500.00**

Leaded Glass, 14" h, 24" d, crown cap, pink rose blossoms border, red cherries **440.00**

Loetz, 5" h, irid gold spotting, deep blue feather and red dot design **400.00**

Northwood, 8¼" d, light pink frosted, etched flowers, ruffled rim **115.00**

Quezal

6½" h, gold, irid deep green hooked and pulled feather design, price for set of four **4,500.00**

8" d, white, green luster feather design, sgd **275.00**

16" d, white frosted, gold design **800.00**

Steuben

5" h, acid cutback, bows, leaves, and flower design, price for set of five **300.00**

7" h, gold aurene, swirled oval, flared ruffled rim, fleur–de–lis mark **250.00**

Tiffany

3¾" h, irid and opalescent, hooked feather and wave design **450.00**

4¼" h, 6¼" w, irid gold and green, hooked feather design, sgd "L C Tiffany" **900.00**

4½″ h, gold, irid silvery blue King Tut design, sgd "L C T" **525.00**

5″ h, oyster white, deep green pulled feather design, gold highlights **900.00**

5¼″ h, irid gold, green pulled feather design, sgd "L C T" . **500.00**

6″ h, 5¾″ w, irid opalescent, deep green pulled feather leaves, sgd **700.00**

18″ d, leaded glass, swirling leaf design **5,250.00**

Tiffany Style, 23″ d, 10″ h, stained and leaded glass, pink and red roses **2,190.00**

LANTERNS

History: A lantern is an enclosed, portable light source, hand carried or attached to a bracket or pole to illuminate an area. Many lanterns can be used both indoors and outdoors and have a protected flame. Fuels used in early lanterns included candles, kerosene, whale oil, coal oil, and later gasoline, natural gas, and batteries.

References: Anthony Hobson, *Lanterns That Lit Our World,* published by author, 1991; Dana G. Morykan and Harry L. Rinker, *Warman's Country Antiques & Collectibles, Second Edition,* Wallace–Homestead, 1994.

Barn, 11″ h, wood and glass, chamfer edge corner post, tin

Candle, black painted tole frame, four glass panels, New York State, mid 19th C, 12½″ h, $100.00.

arched cap and wire bail handle, tin socket, 19th C **525.00**

Bicycle, 7″ h, nickel plated brass, marked "Solar–The Badger Brass Mfg Co, Kenosha, Wis, USA" **65.00**

Candle

6″ h, tin, conical body and pierced top, glass door, strap handle **240.00**

11¼″ h, tin, peaked top, ruffled air vent, ring handle, old black paint **220.00**

16″ h, tin and glass, triangular shape, pierced chimney, ring handle, painted red, 19th C . . **550.00**

Conductor's, 14½″ h, brass, stamped "Blake's Patent 1852," globe etched "A Carter," imperfections **990.00**

Dietz, 22″ h, Station #60, cone shape, clear globe, wire bail and hanging hook, white reflector int., painted black **200.00**

Hall, Gothic Revival, late 19th C . **470.00**

Hand, tin

10½″ h, orig burner, patent date April 14, 1874 . . . . **225.00**

11″ h, bull's–eye lens, Peter Gray & Sons, Boston, MA . . . **225.00**

13″ h, orig burner and brass cap, shade marked "Woodwards Patent April 1864" **150.00**

Hanging, 18″ h, 12″ d, brass and slag glass, chain suspension, square hipped roof, slag glass box, latticework frame, early 20th C **250.00**

Kerosene, 20½″ h, tin, painted black, orig burner, emb brass label "Tubular Square Lamp," 1867 and 1878 patent dates . . **100.00**

Miner's, 23″ h, iron, hooks and tools, rooster finial, stamped signature on front **110.00**

Railroad, presentation, 16″ h, nickel plated, globe etched "J. D. Carr," base marked "S. T. Louis R. W. Supplies" **385.00**

Revere Type, tin, punched dec

12½″ h, conical top, ring handle **185.00**

13″ h, painted green, ring handle **175.00**

Signal, ship's, copper and brass, side holding handles, brass

press–down lever at front con-
trols internal open/close shutter,
oil reservoir, two brass labels,
one inscribed "Davey & Co, 88
West India Dock Road, London,"
other "ACDL Davey's Patent
Windproof Ship Lamp" **520.00**
Skater's, 7" h, tin and glass,
domed pierced vent cap, wire
bail handle **75.00**
Tole
13½" h, orig oil font and burner,
redecorated, slightly dented
top **80.00**
25" h, hanging, French Empire
style, gilt bronze mounted dec,
six–light, price for pair **1,095.00**
Wall, 18" h, 9½" d, copper, domical
cov, banded lattice cylindrical
shade, textured amber glass
liner supported by rect wall
bracket, c1905 .... **330.00**
Whale Oil
12" h, pierced tin, brass cap, orig
tin whale oil lamp **175.00**
13½" h, tin, pierced cap, ovoid
globe with pierced star and
diamond design cap, ring handle, orig worn brown japanning, removable burner, mid–
19th C **195.00**
16" h, glass and tin, American,
chimney inscribed "Police,"
early 19th C **600.00**

LEEDS CHINA

History: The Leeds Pottery in Yorkshire,
England, began production about 1758.
Among its products was creamware that
was competitive with that of Wedgwood.
The initial factory closed in 1820, but various subsequent owners continued until
1880. They made exceptional cream–colored ware, either plain, salt–glazed, or
painted with colored enamels, and glazed
and unglazed redware.

Early wares are unmarked. Later pieces
bear marks of "Leeds Pottery," sometimes
followed by "Hartley–Green and Co." or the
letters "LP." Reproductions also have these
marks.
Reference: Susan and Al Bagdade, *Warman's English & Continental Pottery & Porcelain, 2nd Edition,* Wallace–Homestead,
1991.

**Bud Vase, creamware, multicol-
ored florals, blue feathered edge,
molded rect foot, c1790, repaired,
price for pair, $600.00.**

Charger, 15½" d, multicolored,
floral spray, blue feathered edge **450.00**
Creamer, 3⅜" h, brown, yellow dec **125.00**
Cup and Saucer, multicolored,
floral and crosshatched dec ... **100.00**
Jug, 8¾" h, mask, men and
women figures, molded bead
work border, floral terminals on
handle, iron–red, yellow, green,
brown, and black enamel, gilt
dec, c1775 .... **575.00**
Loving Cup, 4⅞" h, flower dec, two
handles with leaf terminals, inscribed "Robert Hill 1791" **400.00**
Pitcher
6⅛" h, ovoid, pearlware, hp blue
and orange gaudy swirl stylized blossoms and leafy
scrolls, pointed spout, C–form
handle, early 19th C **330.00**
8½" h, ovoid, pearlware, hp blue
leaf sprig, stylized flowers, and
leaf sprigs, pointed spout,
strap handle, early 19th C ... **715.00**

Plate

    7" d, American eagle, scalloped green border, 19th C **475.00**

    7¼" d, brown, yellow, and green, eagle dec, underglaze blue .. **240.00**

    8¼" w, octagonal, pearlware, hp polychrome American eagle and shield, blue feather edge design **660.00**

    9½" d, Chinese landscape dec, underglaze blue, c1780 ..... **465.00**

Platter, 16½" l, creamware, blue feather edge **165.00**

Sugar Bowl, cov, pearlware, hp yellow, green, brown, and orange, stylized tulip blossom and leaves, early 19th C **415.00**

Tea Caddy, 6" h, ribbed body, floral dec, chips and cracks **125.00**

Teapot, 5" h, octagonal, white, emb feathers dec, c1780 ..... **415.00**

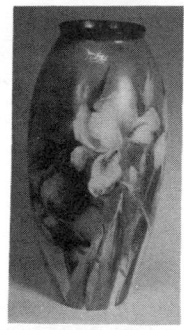

Vase, large iris florals, 18" h, $625.00. Photograph courtesy of Jacksons Auction Co.

LENOX CHINA

History: In 1889 Jonathan Cox and Walter Scott Lenox established The Ceramic Art Co. at Trenton, New Jersey. By 1906 Lenox formed his own company, Lenox, Inc. Using potters lured from Belleek, Lenox began making an American version of this famous ware.

Older Lenox china has two marks: a green wreath and a palette. The palette mark appears on blanks supplied to amateurs who hand painted china as a hobby. The Lenox Company still exists and currently uses a gold stamped mark.

Reference: Susan and Al Bagdade, *Warman's American Pottery and Porcelain,* Wallace–Homestead, 1994.

Additional Listings: Belleek.

Bowl, Yale, souvenir, underside inscribed, green wreath mark ... **120.00**

Bust

    Art Deco man and woman, 8" h, heads, cylinder base, green wreath marks, price for pair .. **550.00**

    Baby, white, green wreath mark **200.00**

Chocolate Cup, pedestal, ivory, gold handle, blue dots, CAC mark **40.00**

Coaster, 4" d, adv for Otis Elevator, US and Canadian symbols, c1970, price for set of 15 ..... **85.00**

Cup and Plate, US Merchant Marine Academy seal, gold trim and handle, price for two piece set . **40.00**

Cup and Saucer, Lenox Rose pattern **22.00**

Desk Set, pheasants, double pen holder **175.00**

Dinner Service

    Rose Pattern

        Service for ten, 8 pc place settings, early pink mark **1,500.00**

        Service for twelve, 6 pc place settings, gold mark **1,200.00**

    Wheat pattern, service for eight **295.00**

Figure

    Schnauzer, sitting **175.00**

    Swan, pink, green wreath mark **35.00**

    The Reader, minor ruffle damage, green wreath mark **125.00**

Gravy Boat, Lenox Rose pattern . **65.00**

Lamp, ivory, swan handles, green wreath mark **65.00**

Pitcher, cov, 8½" h, deep cobalt blue ground, Art Nouveau style

silver overlay, monogram,
printed mark, late 19th C **230.00**
Planter, bird, pink and gray **95.00**
Sugar, cov, two handles, factory
dec, red rooster crowing good
morning, calligraphed verse on
back, transition CAC mark **165.00**
Vase, 18½" h, handles, gold paste
work, hp flowers, gold trim, pale
green and white body, CAC
Lenox wreath mark **1,200.00**

LIBBEY GLASS

History: In 1888 Edward Libbey established the Libbey Glass Company in Toledo, Ohio, after the closing of the New England Glass Works of W. L. Libbey and Son
in East Cambridge, Massachusetts. The
new Libbey company produced quality cut
glass for the "Brilliant Period."

In 1930 Libbey's interest in art glass production was renewed. A. Douglas Nash was
employed as a designer in 1931.

The factory continues production today
as Libbey Glass Co.

References: Carl U. Fauster, *Libbey
Glass Since 1818: Pictorial History & Col-
lector's Guide,* Len Beach Press, 1979;
Ellen T. Schroy, *Warman's Glass,* Wallace–
Homestead, 1992.

Additional Listings: Amberina Glass
and Cut Glass.

Bowl
8" d, brilliant and heavy cut, sgd **200.00**
11½" d, clear, oval, pale blue
net–like design, ftd, etched
mark **400.00**
Candlestick, pr, 6" h, acid marked
"Libbey" **700.00**
Celery Dish, 11½" l, allover cut
brilliant pattern, sgd **175.00**
Champagne, 6½" h, green con-
centric circles design, twisted
stem **125.00**
Compote, 7" h, turquoise, Zipper
pattern, twisted stem **275.00**
Cordial, clear, Concord pattern .. **45.00**
Decanter, 13" h, engraved wheat
and grass motif, elaborate monogram, teardrop stopper,
marked "Libbey" **575.00**

**Condiment Set, salt and pepper
shakers, mustard, glass base,
Maize pattern, clear, 5¾" h, 6" w,
$195.00.**

Pitcher, 8¾" h, Maize, irid amber,
blue husks, applied strap han-
dle, Joseph Locke patent **585.00**
Sherbet, 5" d, 5" h, amberina, sgd,
1917 .... **365.00**
Sugar, cov, 2¾" h, pale blue opal,
Optic Rib pattern, gold enamel
"World's Fair 1893," satin finish **150.00**
Toothpick, peachblow, pink shad-
ing to soft white, shiny finish, fine
ribs **425.00**

LIMITED EDITION
COLLECTOR PLATES

History: Bing and Grondahl made the
first collector plate in 1895. Royal Copenhagen issued their first Christmas plate in
1908.

In the late 1960s and early 1970s, several
potteries, glass factories, mints, and artists
began issuing plates commemorating people, animals, events, etc. Christmas plates
were supplemented by Mother's Day plates,
Easter plates, etc. A sense of speculation
swept the field, fostered in part by flamboy-
ant ads in newspapers and flashy direct–
mail promotions.

Collectors often favor the first plate issued in a series above all others. Condition
is a prime factor. Having the original box
also increases price.

Limited edition collector plates, more than
any other object in this guide, should be

collected for design and pleasure and only secondarily as an investment.

References: Susan Elliott and K. Samara, *The Official Price Guide To Limited Edition Collectibles,* House of Collectibles, 1993; Diane Carnevale Jones, *Collectors' Information Bureau's Collectibles Market Guide & Price Index, 12th Edition,* Collectors' Information Bureau, 1995, distributed by Wallace–Homestead; Diane Carnevale Jones, *Collectors' Information Bureau's Collectibles Price Guide 1994, Fourth Edition,* Collectors' Information Bureau, 1994, distributed by Wallace–Homestead; Diane Carnevale Jones, *Collectors' Information Bureau's Directory To Limited Edition Collectible Stores,* Collectors' Information Bureau, 1993, distributed by Wallace–Homestead; Diane Carnevale Jones, *Collectors' Information Bureau's Directory To Secondary Market Retailers: Buying And Selling Limited Edition Artwork,* Collectors' Information Bureau, 1992, distributed by Wallace–Homestead; Carl Luckey, *Luckey's Hummel Figurines & Plates: A Collector's Identification and Value Guide, 10th Edition,* Books Americana, 1994; Paul Stark, *Limited Edition Collectibles, Everything You May Ever Need To Know,* New Gallery Press, 1988.

Periodicals: *Collector Editions,* 170 Fifth Ave., 12th Floor, New York, NY 10010; *Collector's Mart Magazine,* 700 E. State St., Iola, WI 54990; *Collectors News,* 506 Second St., PO Box 156, Grundy Center, IA 50638; *Insight On Collectibles,* 103 Lakeshore Rd., Suite 202, St Catharines, Ontario L2N 2T6 Canada; *International Collectible Showcase,* One Westminster Place, Lake Forest, IL 60045; *Plate World,* 9200 N. Maryland Ave., Niles, IL 60648; *Toybox Magazine,* 8393 East Holly Rd., Holly MI 48442.

Collectors' Clubs: Franklin Mint Collectors Society, The Franklin Mint, U.S. Route 1, Franklin Center, PA 19091; Hummel Collector's Club, Inc., PO Box 257, Yardley, PA 19067; International Plate Collectors Guild, PO Box 487, Artesia, CA 90702; M. I. Hummel Club, Goebel Plaza, Rte. 31, PO Box 11, Pennington, NJ 08534.

Museum: Bradford Museum, Niles, IL.

Additional Listings: See *Warman's Americana & Collectibles* for more exam-

ples of collector plates plus many other limited edition collectibles.

BAREUTHER (Germany)

Christmas Plates, Hans Mueller artist, 8″ d

1967 Stiftskirche, FE	**100.00**
1968 Kapplkirche	**35.00**
1970 Chapel in Oberndorf	**18.00**
1972 Christmas in Munich	**35.00**
1974 Church In The Black Forest	**20.00**
1976 Chapel in the Hills	**25.00**
1978 Mittenwald	**30.00**
1980 Miltenberg	**38.00**
1982 Bad Wimpfen	**40.00**
1984 Zeil on the River Main	**42.00**
1986 Christmas in Forchheim	**42.00**
1988 St Coloman Church	**65.00**
1990 The Old Forge in Rothenburg	**52.00**
1992 Market Place in Heppenheim	**56.00**
1993 Market Fun	**60.00**
1994 Coming Home For Christmas	**60.00**

Father's Day Series, Hans Mueller artist, 8″ d

1969 Castle Neuschwanstein	**48.00**
1970 Castle Pfalz	**15.00**
1972 Castle Hohenschwangau	**30.00**
1974 Wurzburg Castle	**45.00**
1976 Castle Hohenzollern	**25.00**
1978 Castle Falkenstein	**30.00**
1980 Castle Cochum	**35.00**
1982 Castle Zwingenberg	**40.00**
1984 Castle Neuenstein	**42.00**

Mother's Day

1969 Mother & Children, FE	**75.00**
1970 Mother & Children	**30.00**
1972 Mother & Children	**22.00**
1974 Musical Children	**35.00**
1976 Rocking The Cradle	**28.00**
1978 Blind Man's Bluff	**28.00**
1980 The First Cherries	**35.00**
1982 Suppertime	**40.00**
1984 Village Children	**42.00**

BERLIN (Germany)

Christmas Plates, various artists, 7¾″ d

1970 Christmas In Bernkastel	**130.00**

1972 Christmas In Michelstadt .	**50.00**
1974 Christmas In Bremen	**25.00**
1976 Christmas Eve In Augsburg	**30.00**
1978 Christmas Market At The Berlin Cathedral	**55.00**
1980 Christmas Eve in Mittenberg	**55.00**
1982 Christmas Eve In Wasserburg	**55.00**
1984 Christmas in Ramsau . . .	**50.00**
1986 Christmas Eve in Gelnhaus	**65.00**
1988 Christmas Eve in Ruhpolding	**90.00**
1990 Christmas Eve in Partenkirchen	**80.00**

Bing and Grondahl, 1928, Eskimo Looking At Village Church in Greenland, 7″ d, $60.00.

BING AND GRONDAHL (Denmark)

Christmas Plates, various artists, 7″ d

1895 Behind The Frozen Window	**3,600.00**
1896 New Moon Over Snow Covered Trees	**1,475.00**
1897 Christmas Meal Of The Sparrows	**1,100.00**
1898 Christmas Roses And Christmas Star	**600.00**
1899 The Crows Enjoying Christmas	**900.00**

1900 Church Bells Chiming In Christmas	**800.00**
1901 The Three Wise Men From The East	**485.00**
1902 Interior Of A Gothic Church	**285.00**
1903 Happy Expectation of Children	**150.00**
1904 View of Copenhagen From Frederiksberg Hill	**125.00**
1905 Anxiety Of The Coming Christmas Night	**130.00**
1906 Sleighing To Church On Christmas Eve	**100.00**
1907 The Little Match Girl	**125.00**
1908 St. Petri Church of Copenhagen	**85.00**
1909 Happiness Over The Yule Tree	**100.00**
1910 The Old Organist	**90.00**
1911 First It Was Sung By Angels To Shepherds In The Fields	**80.00**
1912 Going To Church On Christmas Eve	**80.00**
1913 Bringing Home The Yule Tree	**85.00**
1914 Royal Castle of Amalienborg, Copenhagen	**75.00**
1915 Chained Dog Getting Double Meal On Christmas Eve .	**120.00**
1916 Christmas Prayer of the Sparrows	**85.00**
1917 Arrival Of The Christmas Boat	**75.00**
1918 Fishing Boat Returning Home For Christmas	**85.00**
1919 Outside The Lighted Window	**80.00**
1920 Hare In The Snow	**75.00**
1921 Pigeons In The Castle Court	**55.00**
1922 Star Of Bethlehem	**60.00**
1923 Royal Hunting Castle, The Hermitage	**55.00**
1924 Lighthouse In Danish Waters	**65.00**
1925 The Child's Christmas . . .	**70.00**
1926 Churchgoers On Christmas Day	**65.00**
1927 Skating Couple	**110.00**
1928 Eskimo Looking At Village Church In Greenland	**60.00**
1929 Fox Outside Farm On Christmas Eve	**75.00**

1930 Yule Tree In Town Hall Square Of Copenhagen **85.00**
1932 Lifeboat At Work **90.00**
1934 Church Bell In Tower **75.00**
1936 Royal Guard Outside Amalienborg Castle In Copenhagen **70.00**
1938 Lighting The Candles **110.00**
1940 Delivering Christmas Letters **170.00**
1942 Danish Farm On Christmas Night **150.00**
1944 Sorgenfri Castle **120.00**
1946 Commemoration Cross In Honor Of Danish Sailors Who Lost Their Lives In World War II....................... **85.00**
1948 Watchman, Sculpture Of Town Hall, Copenhagen **80.00**
1950 Kronborg Castle At Elsinore **150.00**
1952 Old Copenhagen Canals At Wintertime With Thorvaldsen Museum In Background . **85.00**
1954 Birthplace Of Hans Christian Andersen, With Snowman **100.00**
1956 Christmas In Copenhagen **140.00**
1958 Santa Claus **100.00**
1960 Danish Village Church ... **180.00**
1962 Winter Night **80.00**
1964 The Fir Tree And Hare .. **50.00**
1966 Home For Christmas **50.00**
1968 Christmas In Church **45.00**
1970 Pheasants In The Snow At Christmas **20.00**
1972 Christmas In Greenland . **20.00**
1974 Christmas In The Village . **20.00**
1976 Christmas Welcome **25.00**
1978 A Christmas Tale **30.00**
1980 Christmas In The Woods . **42.00**
1982 The Christmas Tree **55.00**
1984 Christmas Letter **55.00**
1986 Silent Night, Holy Night .. **55.00**
1988 In the Kings Garden **65.00**
1990 Changing of the Guards . **64.00**
1992 Christmas at the Rectory . **70.00**
1994 A Day At The Deer Park . **72.00**
Jubilee, various artists
1915 Frozen Window **225.00**
1920 Church Bells **65.00**
1925 Dog Outside Window **285.00**
1930 The Old Organist **225.00**
1935 Little Match Girl **900.00**
1940 Three Wise Men **1,950.00**

1945 Amalienborg Castle **150.00**
1950 Eskimos **175.00**
1955 Dybbol Mill **200.00**
1960 Kronborg Castle **100.00**
1965 Churchgoers **40.00**
1970 Amalienborg Castle **35.00**
1975 Horses Enjoying Meal ... **50.00**
1980 Yule Tree **60.00**
1985 Lifeboat at Work **65.00**
1990 The Royal Yacht Dannebrog **95.00**

HAVILAND & PARLON (France)

Christmas Series, various artists, 10″ d
1972 Madonna And Child, Raphael, FE **80.00**
1973 Madonnina, Feruzzi **100.00**
1975 Madonna And Child, Murillo **45.00**
1977 Madonna And Child, Bellini **40.00**
1979 Madonna Of The Eucharist, Botticelli **150.00**
Lady And The Unicorn Series, artist unknown, 10″ d
1977 To My Only Desire, FE .. **60.00**
1979 Sound **50.00**
1981 Scent **60.00**
1982 Taste **65.00**
Tapestry Series, artist unknown, 10″ d
1971 The Unicorn In Captivity . **145.00**
1973 Chase Of The Unicorn .. **120.00**
1975 The Unicorn Surrounded .. **75.00**
1976 Brought to the Castle **42.00**

LALIQUE (France)

Annual Series, lead crystal, Marie—Claude Lalique, artist, 8½″ d
1965 Deux Oiseaux (Two Birds), FE **800.00**
1967 Ballet de Poisson (Fish Ballet) **200.00**
1969 Papillon (Butterfly) **80.00**
1971 Hibou (Owl) **60.00**
1973 Petit Geai (Jayling) **60.00**
1975 Due de Poisson (Fish Duet) **75.00**
1976 Aigle (Eagle) **100.00**

LENOX (United States)

Boehm Bird Series, Edward Marshall Boehm, artist, 10½" d

1970 Wood Thrush, FE	225.00
1971 Goldfinch	65.00
1973 Meadowlark	60.00
1975 American Redstart	50.00
1977 Robins	55.00
1979 Golden–Crowned Kinglets	65.00
1981 Eastern Phoebes	100.00

Boehm Woodland Wildlife Series, Edward Marshall Boehm, artist, 10½" d

1973 Raccoons, FE	80.00
1975 Cottontail Rabbits	60.00
1977 Beaver	60.00
1979 Squirrels	75.00
1981 Martens	100.00
1982 River Otters	180.00

RECO INTERNATIONAL (United States)

Christmas Series, Royale, various artists

1969 Christmas Fair, FE	125.00
1970 Vigil Mass	100.00
1971 Christmas Night	50.00
1972 Elks	40.00
1973 Christmas Down	35.00
1974 Village Christmas	60.00
1975 Feeding Time	35.00
1976 Seaport Christmas	30.00
1977 Sledding	30.00

REED & BARTON (United States)

Audubon Series, various artists

1970 Pine Siskin, FE	175.00
1971 Red–Shouldered Hawk	75.00
1972 Stilt Sandpiper	70.00
1973 Red Cardinal	70.00
1974 Boreal Chickadee	60.00
1975 Yellow–Breasted Chat	60.00
1976 Bay–Breasted Warbler	60.00
1977 Purple Finch	65.00

ROSENTHAL (Germany)

Christmas Plates, various artists, 8½" d

1910 Winter Peace	550.00
1911 The Three Wise Men	325.00
1912 Shooting Stars	250.00
1913 Christmas Lights	235.00
1914 Christmas Song	350.00
1915 Walking To Church	180.00
1916 Christmas During War	235.00
1918 Peace On Earth	210.00
1920 The Manger In Bethlehem	325.00
1922 Advent Branch	200.00
1924 Deer In The Woods	200.00
1926 Christmas In The Mountains	175.00
1928 Chalet Christmas	175.00
1930 Group Of Deer Under The Pines	225.00
1932 Christ Child	200.00
1934 Christmas Peace	200.00
1936 Nucrnberg Angel	185.00
1938 Christmas In The Alps	190.00
1940 Marien Church in Danzig	250.00
1942 Marianburg Castle	300.00
1944 Wood Scape	275.00
1946 Christmas In An Alpine Valley	250.00
1948 Message To The Shepherds	875.00
1950 Christmas In The Forest	185.00
1952 Christmas In The Alps	190.00
1954 Christmas Eve	185.00
1956 Christmas In The Alps	190.00
1958 Christmas Eve	190.00
1960 Christmas In Small Village	200.00
1962 Christmas Eve	185.00
1964 Christmas Market In Nucrnberg	225.00
1966 Christmas In Ulm	250.00
1968 Christmas In Bremen	195.00
1970 Christmas In Cologne	165.00
1972 Christmas Celebration In Franconia	90.00
1974 Christmas In Wurzburg	100.00

ROYAL COPENHAGEN

Christmas Plates, various artists, 6" d 1908, 1909, 1910; 7" 1911 to present

1908 Madonna And Child	1,775.00
1909 Danish Landscape	150.00
1910 The Magi	120.00
1911 Danish Landscape	135.00
1912 Elderly Couple By Christmas Tree	120.00
1913 Spire Of Frederik's Church, Copenhagen	125.00
1914 Sparrows In Tree At	

Church Of The Holy Spirit, Copenhagen 100.00
1915 Danish Landscape 150.00
1916 Shepherd In The Field On
Christmas Night 85.00
1917. Tower Of Our Savior's
Church, Copenhagen 90.00
1918 Sheep and Shepherds ... 80.00
1919 In The Park 80.00
1920 Mary With The Child Jesus 75.00
1921 Aabenraa Marketplace .. 75.00
1922 Three Singing Angels ... 70.00
1923 Danish Landscape 70.00
1924 Christmas Star Over The
Sea And Sailing Ship 100.00
1925 Street Scene From Chris-
tianshavn, Copenhagen 85.00
1926 View of Christmas Canal,
Copenhagen 75.00
1927 Ship's Boy At The Tiller On
Christmas Night 140.00
1928 Vicar's Family On Way To
Church 75.00
1929 Grundtvig Church, Copenhagen 100.00
1930 Fishing Boats On The Way
To The Harbor 80.00
1932 Frederiksberg Gardens
With Statue Of Frederik VI .. 90.00
1934 The Hermitage Castle ... 115.00
1936 Roskilde Cathedral 130.00
1938 Round Church In Osterlars
On Bornholm 200.00
1940 The Good Shepherd 300.00
1942 Bell Tower of Old Church
In Jutland 300.00
1944 Typical Danish Winter
Scene 160.00
1946 Zealand Village Church .. 150.00
1948 Nodebo Church At Christmastime 150.00
1950 Boeslunde Church, Zealand 175.00
1952 Christmas In The Forest . 120.00
1954 Amalienborg Palace, Copenhagen 150.00
1956 Rosenborg Castle, Copenhagen 160.00
1958 Sunshine Over Greenland 140.00
1960 The Stag 140.00
1962 The Little Mermaid At Wintertime 200.00
1964 Fetching The Christmas
Tree 75.00

1966 Blackbird At Christmastime 55.00
1968 The Last Umiak 40.00
1970 Christmas Rose And Cat . 100.00
1972 In The Desert 85.00
1974 Winter Twilight 80.00
1976 Danish Watermill 80.00
1978 Greenland Scenery 80.00
1980 Bringing Home The Christmas Tree 60.00
1982 Waiting For Christmas ... 65.00
1984 Jingle Bells 55.00
1986 Christmas Vacation 55.00
1988 Christmas Eve in Copenhagen 60.00
1990 Christmas at Tivoli 76.00
**Mother's Day Plates, various
artists, 6¼″ d**
1971 American Mother 125.00
1972 Oriental Mother 60.00
1974 Greenland Mother 55.00
1976 Mermaids 50.00
1978 Mother And Child 25.00
1980 An Outing With Mother .. 35.00
1982 The Children's Hour 45.00

ROYAL DOULTON (Great Britain)

**Beswick Christmas Series, var-
ious artists, earthenware in
hand–cast bas–relief, 8″ sq**
1972 Christmas In England, FE 40.00
1974 Christmas In Bulgaria ... 40.00
1976 Christmas In Holland 45.00
1978 Christmas In America 45.00
1980 Bringing Home The Tree . 50.00
1982 Waiting for Christmas ... 60.00
1984 Jingle Bells 54.00
1986 Christmas Vacation 58.00
1988 Christmas Eve in Copenhagen 60.00
1990 Christmas at Tivoli 70.00
1992 The Queen's Carriage ... 70.00
1994 Christmas Shopping 72.00
**Mother And Child Series, Edna
Hibel artist, 8¼″ d**
1973 Colette And Child, FE ... 450.00
1974 Sayuri And Child 150.00
1976 Marilyn And Child 120.00
1978 Kathleen And Child 100.00

WEDGWOOD (Great Britain)

**Christmas Series, jasper stone-
ware, 8″ d**

1969 Windsor Castle, FE	**225.00**
1971 Piccadilly Circus, London	**40.00**
1973 The Tower Of London ...	**45.00**
1975 Tower Bridge	**40.00**
1977 Westminster Abbey	**48.00**
1979 Buckingham Palace	**55.00**
1981 Marble Arch	**75.00**
1983 All Souls, Langham Palace	**80.00**
1985 The Tate Gallery	**80.00**
1987 Guildhall	**80.00**

Mother's Day, jasper stoneware, 6½" d

1971 Sportive Love, FE	**25.00**
1973 The Baptism Of Achilles .	**20.00**
1975 Mother And Child	**35.00**
1977 Leisure Time	**30.00**
1979 Deer and Fawn	**35.00**
1981 Mare And Foal	**50.00**
1983 Cupid And Butterfly	**55.00**
1985 Cupids and Doves	**55.00**
1987 Tiger Lily	**55.00**

LIMOGES

History: Limoges porcelain has been produced in Limoges, France, for over a century by numerous factories other than the famed Haviland. One of the most frequently encountered marks is "T. & V. Limoges" which is on the ware made by Tressman and Vought. Other identifiable Limoges marks are A. L. (A. Lanternier), J. P. L. (J. Pouyat, Limoges), M. R. (M. Reddon), Elite and Coronet.

References: Susan and Al Bagdade, *Warman's English & Continental Pottery & Porcelain, Second Edition*, Wallace–Homestead, 1991; Mary Frank Gaston, *The Collector's Encyclopedia Of Limoges Porcelain, 2nd Edition*, Collector Books, 1992, 1994 value update.

Additional Listings: Haviland China.

Bud Vase, 5¹³⁄₁₆" h, enamel and brass, baluster form, floral dec, royal blue ground, some damage, early 20th C **175.00**
Butter, cov, soft pink flowers, gold beading around scalloped rim . **65.00**
Cabinet Vase
  6" h, enameled, maiden in landscape holding fan, signed "Cotti" **275.00**
  7" h, enameled, double winged griffin handles, romantic couples and cupid dec, 19th C .. **850.00**
Celery, 12½" l, hp, artist signed "Jerah" **125.00**
Chop Plate, 13½" d, Grape Cluster **275.00**
Dinner Service
  Over 70 pcs, including twelve dinner plates, twelve luncheon plates, twelve fruit plates, ten dessert plates, twelve compote dishes, and twelve saucers **3,000.00**
  Approx. 450 pcs, L Bernardaud & Co, gold and sepia European figural landscape motifs, white ground, includes dessert, bread and butter, luncheon, and dinner plates, tea, coffee, and demitasse cups and saucers, bowls, sauces, serving dishes, platters, coffee and teapots, creamers, cov sugars, and handled tray, some imperfections, late 19th C **2,300.00**
Dish, 10¼" w, triangular, lobed, hp flowers, gold trim, rococo rim .. **120.00**
Dresser Tray, 10½ x 8¼", rect, blue flowers, pink buds, pastel ground, artist signed **65.00**
Ewer, 6" h, cream ground, pink and gold flowers, gold ribbing and handle, 1892 .... **150.00**
Fish Plate, variant fish center, rich gilt border, M Lalane, 19th C, price for set of twelve **465.00**
Fish Set
  15 pcs, various fish dec, large platter, small platter, sauceboat, bowl, tray, and ten plates, chip on large platter .. **650.00**
  50 pcs, twenty–four 9⁹⁄₁₆" d plates, twenty–four 8" d plates, two sauce dishes with attached trays, platter missing, sold by L Bernardaud & Co, Limoges, c1900 ....**1,025.00**
Fruit Plate, 10¼" d, hp, artist signed "Dubois" **295.00**
Mug, grapes and vines, pastel ground **85.00**
Pin Tray, hp, floral dec, gold rim, marked "Pouyat," c1900 ...... **25.00**

Plaque

2⅞ x 2⅛", oval portraits, profiles of Roman emperors, enamel, Laudin Grisaille, custom matted and framed as one unit, possibly 17th C, price for set of twelve . **4,890.00**

5¼ x 4", enameled 16th C man and lady, framed, price for pair **1,700.00**

5½ x 7", rect, enamel dec Biblical scene, chips, 19th C **490.00**

Plate, 9¼" d, hp, artist signed "Jerah" **125.00**

Platter, 16¾" l, pink forget–me–nots **120.00**

Portrait Plaque, 3¾" h, miniature, mineral enamel, oval, waist length view of young woman in Renaissance costume, illegibly signed, paper label on reverse "Mde de Contad," minor stress cracks and scratches, late 19th/early 20th C **400.00**

Punch Bowl, 15" d, hp grapes and leaf dec, ftd base, Linda Smith, Feb 1908 .... **250.00**

Salt, 1" d, 1" h, hp, roses, gold trim, marked "B & D," price for pair . **85.00**

Shaving Mug, eagle, flags, shield, world globe, name in gold, marked "T.V. Limoges" **110.00**

Soup Tureen, cov, underplate, floral dec, green ground, gilt highlights **630.00**

Tankard, hand dec iris florals, 18" h, $950.00. Photograph courtesy of Jacksons Auction Co.

Tankard

14" h, hp floral dec, artist signed "Gutret" **300.00**

14½" h, hp, monk drinking, red fruit, white flowers **395.00**

Tureen, cov, pink forget–me–nots **145.00**

Urn, 13½" h, pink, French fashion scene **350.00**

Vase, 9" h, reticulated cov, gold floral dec, cobalt blue ground, Redon, professional repair to one cov, matched pr **750.00**

Vegetable, cov, 7½" l, 5" h, blue and white flowers **65.00**

LINENS

History: The term linen now has become a generic designation for household dressings for table, bed, or bath, whether made of linen, cotton, lace, or other fabrics.

Linen, as a table cover, is mentioned in the Bible and other writings of an early age. We see "borde cloths," with their creases pressed in sharply, in early drawings and paintings. It was a sign of wealth and social standing to present such elegance.

During the period before the general use of forks, when fingers were the accepted means of dining, napkins were important. They usually were rectangular and large in size. In the early 18th century, napkins lost their popularity. The fork had become the tool of the upper classes who apparently wished to show off their new–found expertise in the use of the fork. After diners did much damage to tablecloths, finicky hostesses decided that the napkin was a necessity. It soon reappeared on the table.

The Victorian era gave us the greatest variety of household linens. The lady of the house had time to sit and sew a fine seam. Sewing became a social activity. Afternoon callers brought their handwork with them when they came to gossip and take tea. Every young girl was expected to fill her hope chest with fine examples of her prowess. In the late 19th century these ladies made some very beautiful "white work," using white embroidery of delicate stitchery, lace insertions, and ruffles on white fabrics. These pieces are highly sought after today.

The 20th century saw a decline in that

type of fine stitchery. The social pace quickened. Household linens of that period show more bright colors in the embroidery, the designs become more light–hearted and frivolous, and inexpensive machine–made lace was used. Kitchen towels were decorated with animals or pots and pans. Vanity sets dominated the bedroom; the bridge craze put emphasis on tablecloths and napkin sets. To fill the desire for less–expensive lace cloths and bedspreads, women of the Depression started crocheting. Many examples of this craft are available.

With the advent of World War II, more women went to work. The last remnant of fine stitchery quickly diminished. Technological advances in production and fibers lessened the interest in hand–made linens.

Collecting And Use Tips: Most old linens are fragile, some are age stained from being stored improperly for years. Unless you have a secret for removing these stains without damaging the fabric, look for those items in very good or better condition.

Linens which are not used frequently are best stored unpressed, rolled Boy Scout style, and tucked away in an old pillowcase out of bright light. Be sure the linens and pillowcases have been rinsed several times to remove all residue of detergent.

For laundered pieces which are used often, wrap in acid–free white tissue or muslin folders. If the tissue is not acid free, it will cause the folded edges to discolor. If possible, store on rollers to prevent creasing. Creased areas become weak and disintegrate in laundering. Acid–free wrapping material can be purchased from Talas, 104 Fifth Avenue, New York, NY 10011.

References: Virginia Churchill Bath, *Lace*, Henry Regnery Co, 1974; Francoise de Bonneville, *The Book of Fine Linen*, Flammarion, 1994; Maryanne Dolan *Old Lace & Linens Including Crochet: An Identification and Value Guide*, Books Americana, 1989; Alda Horner, *The Official Price Guide Linens, Lace and Other Fabrics*, House of Collectibles, 1991; Frances Johnson, *Collecting Antique Linens, Lace, and Needlework*, Wallace–Homestead, 1991; Lois Markrich and Heinz Edgar Kiewe, *Victorian Fancywork*, Henry Regnery Co., 1974; *McCall's Needlework Treasury*, Random House, 1963; Francis M. Montgomery,

Textiles In America, 1650–1870, W. W. Norton & Co. (A Winterthur/Barra Book); Dana G. Morykan and Harry L. Rinker, *Warman's Country Antiques & Collectibles, 2nd Edition*, Wallace–Homestead, 1994; Elisa Ricci, *Italian Lace Designs: 243 Classic Examples*, Dover Publications, 1993; Patricia Esterbrook Roberts, *Table Settings: Entertaining And Etiquette, A History And Guide*, Viking Press, 1967.

Periodical: *The Lace Collector*, PO Box 222, Plainwell, MI 49080.

Collectors' Club: International Old Lacers, PO Box 481223, Denver, CO 80248.

Museums: Metropolitan Museum of Art, New York, NY; Museum of Early Southern Decorative Arts (MESDA) Winston–Salem, NC; Museum Of Fine Arts, Boston, MA; Rockwood Museum, Wilmington, DE; Shelburne Museum, Shelburne, VT; Smithsonian Institution, Washington, DC.

Antimacassar Set
  Filet crochet, nautical motif, ship
    center, anchors on arm pcs,
    c1930 . . . . **18.50**
  Linen, white, satin stitch mono-
    gram center, scalloped edges,
    c1890 . . . . **35.00**
Bedspread
  Appliqued, baby, cotton, white,
    animals and flowers, pastel
    shades, bound and backed
    blue print cotton **45.00**
  Battenberg, white, allover de-
    sign, double size, c1890–1900 **375.00**
  Muslin, bleached, two green
    bower peacock design, motif
    bolster end, twin size, 1930s
    kit **85.00**
Blanket Cover, seersucker, white,
    machine bound, double size,
    c1935 . . . . **18.00**
Bolster Cover, pr
  Button back, linen, white, small
    tuck edge ruffles, heavy satin
    stitch floral design center **95.00**
  Throw type, cotton, white, lace
    edged ruffles around sides,
    center of one red embroidery
    "Sweet," other "Dreams,"
    Pennsylvania, c1880–90 . . . . **85.00**
Bridge Set
  34 x 34", organdy, light yellow,

linen appliqued flowers outer edge, hemstitched around appliques and border, four matching napkins **50.00**

35 x 35", linen, white, rose motif filet crocheted inserts on corners, crocheted edge, four matching napkins **35.00**

Curtain Panel, pr, 36" w, 108" l, white net, overall floral design, machine tambour stitch, scalloped edges, pocket top, c1920 **85.00**

Doily

25" d, two hand tatted rows of medallions, white linen center, c1920 .... **35.00**

28" d, Battenberg lace, white linen center, c1900 .... **45.00**

Dresser Scarf

Alencon lace, 14" w, 48" l, floral and medallion designs, ecru, machine made, c1930 ...... **40.00**

Chantilly lace, 15" w, 40" l, white, floral design, machine made . **15.00**

Handkerchief

Cotton, white, bright colored printed flowers, set of 3, c1935 **10.00**

Linen, 12 x 12", white, Apenzell embroidery and drawn work, c1920 .... **20.00**

Swiss embroidery, 12½ x 12½", white, delicate lace border, maple framed under glass, early 20th C **65.00**

Napkin

Cocktail

6" sq, linen, white, crocheted edge and one corner motif, set of 6 .... **15.00**

6 x 8", linen, lavender and green, bunch of grapes form, handmade, set of 6 .. **30.00**

Dinner

24" sq, linen, double damask, white, chrysanthemum pattern, hand rolled edges, set of 6 .... **25.00**

28 x 29", linen, damask, white, satin stripe design, satin stitch "E" center, hand rolled edges, set of 8 .... **80.00**

Luncheon, 15" sq, Madeira, linen, white, pale blue embroi-

dery and cut work corner, set of 8 .... **45.00**

Pillow Cases, pr

Linen, white, satin stitch monogram, hemstitched, c1900 ... **45.00**

Muslin, white, embroidered girl with full skirt and flowers, crocheted edge, made from stamped kit, c1930 .... **18.50**

Percale, French blue, satin stitch "L," wide white crocheted border, c1935–40 .... **22.50**

Sheet

Linen, hand turned hem top and bottom, double size, c1920 .. **25.00**

Muslin, white, 3" w filet crochet rose motif insert, double size, c1920 .... **15.00**

Tablecloth

53 x 72", linen, hand loomed, seamed center, woven heavy corded design, hand turned ends, one corner embroidered in red cross–stitch "D.F" and "1870" **45.00**

54 x 54", tea cloth, linen, natural, Battenberg lace center motif and corners, four matching napkins, price for set **45.00**

54 x 56", luncheon, cotton, white, colorful linen flower appliques, crochet edges, six matching napkins, c1930–35, price for set **35.00**

68 x 98", dinner, linen, natural, cut work and embroidered floral and leaf pattern center and border, 8 matching napkins, price for set **195.00**

72 x 101", Chinese rice cloth, white, four sections hemstitched together, drawn work and embroidered floral design, deep borders **65.00**

144 x 86", banquet size, Pointe de Venise, ecru, allover cupids, urns and floral spray design, 12 linen napkins with lace border and corner motif, handmade in China, orig wrapping, unused, c1935–40, price for set **1,200.00**

Tête–A–Tête Set, 1 mat, 2 matching napkins, linen, light blue, two

corners with embroidered pink
roses and vines, c1940 . . . .   **25.00**
Towel, linen
  16 x 38", damask, red woven
    grape leaves and vines border,
    fringe on each end, c1900 . . .   **25.00**
  18" w, 36" l, hand loomed, each
    end with crocheted lace, finely
    stitched side hems, dated and
    sgd in black ink "1830" **65.00**
Vanity Set, 3 pcs, muslin, white,
  embroidered cross–stitch floral
  design, white machine made
  Cluny type lace border, c1920–
  30 . . . .   **25.00**

LITHOPHANES

History: Lithophanes are highly translucent porcelain panels with impressed designs. The design is formed by the difference in thickness of the plaque. Thin parts
transmit an abundance of light while thicker
parts represent shadows.

Lithophanes were first made by the Royal
Berlin Porcelain Works in 1828. Other factories in Germany, France, and England
later produced them. The majority of lithophanes on the market today were made
between 1850 and 1900.

Collectors' Club: Lithophane Collectors
Club, 2030 Robinwood Ave., PO Box 4557,
Toledo, OH 43620.

Museum: Blair Museum of Lithophanes
and Carved Waxes, Toledo, OH.

Candle Shield, 9" h, bronze collar,
  rococo frame, two country boys
  on grass, goat and castle in
  background **250.00**
Cup and Saucer, 3" d, gilt floral
  motif, peach ground, lithophane
  bottom depicting young girl,
  looped snake handle, KMP, sec-
  ond quarter 19th C **500.00**
Fairy Lamp, lady leaning from
  tower window, two panels, rural
  romantic scene **1,200.00**
Lamp, 23½" h, double student
  type, four scenes, brass base,
  marked "Germany" **1,850.00**

**Fairy Lamp, lady in tower, three
lithophane panels, 9" h, $1,200.00.**

Lamp Shade
  8" d, five panels, people in dif-
    ferent poses, pressed metal
    frame **525.00**
  10" d, 5¼" h, five panels, child-
    hood scenes, emb brass
    frame, marked "PPM" **550.00**
  13" d, seven panels, European
    and American scenic views,
    panel of woman carrying
    mousetrap upstairs, copper
    frame **700.00**
Panel
  KK, 8 x 16", General Zachary
    Taylor, holding telescope in
    left arm, men fighting battle in
    background, wreath, eagle,
    and two flags above, leaded
    frame, ruby flashed **675.00**
  PPM, 6½ x 8", elderly lady
    teaching girl to knit, lead
    mounted edge **150.00**
  PR Sickle, 4⅛ x 5", cupid and
    girl fishing **150.00**
  Unknown Maker, 6½ x 8", Christ
    holding orb with cross, incised
    "Inri/Die" **185.00**
Portrait, oval, 7⅛ x 5¾", Samuel
  Colt, sitting at table, revolver in
  right hand, pair of dividers in left
  hand **875.00**
Stein, 7½" h, German, half liter,
  porcelain, transfer print panel of
  gentleman and mistress, lithophane depicts tavern scene of

gentleman and barmaid, pewter
lid, thumbpiece **65.00**
Tea Set, teapot, creamer, cov
sugar, six cups and saucers,
price for fifteen piece set **150.00**
Tea Warmer, 6 x 6", four panels
Romantic, Sheffield SS holder,
orig burner **275.00**
Scenic, pierced top, metal
frame, molded ftd base, Germany **165.00**

LIVERPOOL CHINA

History: Liverpool is the name given to
products made at several potteries in Liverpool, England, between 1750 and 1840.
Among the early potters who made tin
enameled earthenwares were Seth and
James Pennington and Richard Chaffers.
By the 1780s tin–glazed earthenware
gave way to cream–colored wares decorated with cobalt, enamel colors, and blue
or black transfers.

The Liverpool glaze is characterized by
bubbles, and most often there is clouding
under the foot rims. By 1800 about 80 potteries were working in the town producing
not only creamware, but soft paste, soapstone, and bone porcelain.

Reference: Susan and Al Bagdade, *Warman's English & Continental Pottery & Porcelain, 2nd Edition,* Wallace–Homestead,
1991.

Bottle, 10¼" h, Delft, blue and
white, floral dec, glaze wear to
rim, c1760 .... **470.00**
Mug, 5" h, creamware, transfer
dec, hairlines, glaze loss along
rim, early 19th C **430.00**
Pitcher
7" h, creamware, transfer dec,
obverse with tavern scene

**Jug, Ring of States, eagle dec,
c1805, 6⅝" h, $450.00.**

above verse "From night till
morn I take my glass, in hopes
to forget my Chloe...," reverse
with flutist serenading lady
above verse "The softest ones
his flute can give...," hairlines,
19th C **375.00**
7½" h, creamware, transfer of
ship flying American flag, reverse with "the farmers arms,"
flower motif under spout, enhanced polychrome enamel
and gilt, 19th C **575.00**
8" h, creamware, transfer hunting scene inscribed "death of
the fox from a much admired
painting in the exhibition at the
Royal Academy," reverse with
sly gentleman inscribed
"twenty thousand I've got–how
lucky's my lot," sgd below
"Thos Fletcher Shelton," early
19th C **925.00**
9" h, creamware, transfer of
Washington map, reverse with
battle scene enclosed by ribbon, inscribed "Our country,
extended our commerce, and
laid the foundation of a great
empire," early 19th C **1,725.00**
9½" h, transfer dec, obverse with
"Washington Monument," reverse with "Washington in
Glory," "America in Tears"
profile portrait facing right under spout with American eagle, rim and body with gilt dec,

chip at spout and base, early
19th C **1,725.00**
10¾" h, Masonic presentation,
obverse with design of pillars,
pavement, and other Masonic
symbols, reverse with wreath
of symbols centering verse
"The world is in pain our secrets to gain...," wreath of symbols and inscription "Nath. L
Otis" under spout, base
cracks, early 19th C **1,150.00**
11½" h, creamware, transfer
with "Faith, Hope, and Char-
ity," monogram and date under
spout, restored, 1792 .... **550.00**
Plate
8⅞" d, Delft, polychrome fence
and floral dec, Fazackerly, rim
chips and wear, c1760, price
for pair **375.00**
9¾" d, creamware, transfer
printed and enamel dec,
seated Hope figure and ship,
England, early 19th C **125.00**
10" d, transfer dec of three–
masted ship, 19th C **85.00**
Teabowl and Saucer, creamware,
portrait medallions of Washington and LaFayette, saucer with
"Washington His Country's
Father," star crack, early 19th C **400.00**

LOETZ

History: Loetz is a type of iridescent art
glass made in Austria by J. Loetz Witwe in
the late 1890s. Loetz was a contemporary
of L. C. Tiffany and worked in the Tiffany
factory before establishing his own operation; therefore, much of the wares are similar in appearance to Tiffany. Some pieces
are signed "Loetz," "Loetz, Austria," or
"Austria." The Loetz factory also produced
ware with fine cameos on cased glass.

Bowl, 7" h, deep orange gold,
three applied blue irid prunts
dec, applied blue edge and ftd
base **500.00**
Jack–In–The–Pulpit Vase, 11½" h,
4½" w, irid gold, blue highlights,
gooseneck **1,250.00**

**Sweetmeat, green base, maroon
striping, sq handle, sterling silver
top, sgd "Loetz, Austria," 5¼" h,
4¾" w, $150.00.**

Loving Cup, 5" h, deep blue, Art
Nouveau floral design, irid blue
raindrop `pattern, SS overlay,
three handles **2,100.00**
Pitcher, 7" h, frosted, applied
reeded handle **175.00**
Rose Bowl, 6" h, amber, tooled
crimped rim, gold irid dec, polished pontil **410.00**
Urns, pr, baluster form, striated
blue irid on plum ground,
mounted with white metal Egyptian style bracket handles raised
on eagles with spread wings,
paw feet, 16" h **750.00**
Vase
3¾" h, squat bulbous form, ruby
red, blue irid dec, inscribed
"Austria" and arrow and star
mark **2,300.00**
4" h
Free–form body with irregular
rim, applied branch dec, allover yellow irid **185.00**
Transparent brilliant blue, SS
stylized overlay **125.00**
4½" h, yellow, green waves and
gold irid spots dec **1,700.00**
4¾" h, transparent olive green,
Art Nouveau floral daisy SS
overlay **125.00**
5" h, flared rim, green snakeskin **285.00**
5½"
Highly irid green raindrop surface **250.00**
Pinched trefoil rim, dimpled

body with swirling red and
yellow irid **125.00**
6" h, twisted body, green, filigree **275.00**
8" h
Gold snakeskin, matching underplate **500.00**
Irid purple, blue, green, and
rose **350.00**
Pinched trefoil rim, tapering
cylindrical body with allover
vine shaped lattice dec,
translucent purple **105.00**
8¼" h, ovoid form, allover applied fern lattice dec, translucent purple **95.00**
8¾" h, cylindrical form, cobalt,
green, and rust translucence . **75.00**
9" h, irid amber **150.00**
10" h, deep rose, clear overlay
threading **650.00**
11" h, ruffled rim, baluster
shape, mottled irid sheen in
blue, purple, and gold **115.00**
12½" h, gold irid ground, blue
hooked design, Art Nouveau
bronze holder of grapes,
leaves, and owls' heads **650.00**
16½" h, torch form, red–amethyst irid, elaborate cast
bronze Art Nouveau holder .. **1,610.00**

LOTUS WARE CHINA

History: Knowles, Taylor and Knowles
Co., East Liverpool, Ohio, made a translucent, thinly potted china between 1891 and
1898. It compared favorably to Belleek. It
first was marked "KTK." After being exhibited at the 1893 Columbian Exposition in
Chicago, Col. John T. Taylor, company
president, changed the marking to "Lotus
Ware" because the body resembled the petals of the lotus blossom.

Blanks also were sold to amateurs who
hand painted them. Most artist–signed
pieces fit this category.

References: Susan and Al Bagdade,
Warman's American Pottery and Porcelain,
Wallace–Homestead, 1994; Timothy J.
Kearns, *Knowles, Taylor & Knowles: Amer-
ican Bone China,* Schiffer Publishing, 1994.

**Vase, green vine dec, gold insect,
8" h, $675.00.**

Bowl, 6" d, creamware, blue transfer print of landscape **125.00**
Candy Dish, 7½" w, 5½" h, sea-
weed dec, coral feet **285.00**
Chocolate Pot, sunflowers, hp ... **375.00**
Creamer, 3⅞" h, floral dec, pale
green neck, gold striping **90.00**
Cup and Saucer, blue flowers ... **70.00**
Ewer, 10" h, floral sprays, garlands
of raised blue forget–me–nots . **700.00**
Pitcher
6½" h, cream, gold dec **385.00**
11" h, white, multicolored flowers, green leaves, gold trim .. **400.00**
Rose Bowl, 5" d, 4½" h, white, gold
flowers, leaves and branches,
KTK **375.00**
Sugar, cov, white, hp flowers **175.00**
Syrup, cream, hp flowers, brass
top and spout, KTK **325.00**
Tea Set, teapot, creamer, and
sugar, gold leaf design, price for
three piece set **600.00**
Vase, 8" h, ftd cylinder, gold netting, ball panels alternating with
foliate designs, minor gold loss,
green KTK Lotus Ware circular
mark **295.00**

LUSTER WARE

History: Lustering on a piece of pottery creates a metallic, sometimes iridescent, appearance. Josiah Wedgwood experimented with the technique in the 1790s. Between 1805 and 1840 luster earthenware pieces were created in England by makers such as Adams, Bailey and Batkin, Copeland and Garrett, Wedgwood, and Enoch Wood.

Luster decorations often were used in conjunction with enamels and transfers. Transfers used for luster decoration covered a wide range of public and domestic subjects. They frequently were accompanied by pious or sentimental doggerel as well as the humors of everyday life.

Copper luster was created by the addition of a copper compound to the glaze. It was very popular in America during the 19th century and experienced a collecting vogue from the 1920s to the 1950s. Today it has a limited market. The market stagnation can partially be attributed to the large number of reproductions, especially creamers and the "polka" jug, which fool many new buyers. Reproductions are heavier in appearance and weight than the earlier pieces.

Pink luster was made by using a gold mixture. Silver luster was first covered completely with a thin coating of a "steel luster" mixture containing a small quantity of platinum oxide. An additional coating of platinum, worked in water, was applied before firing.

Sunderland is a coarse type of cream—colored earthenware with a marbled or spotted pink luster decoration which shades from pink to purple. A solution of gold compound applied to the white body developed the many shades of pink.

The development of electroplating in 1840 created a sharp decline in the demands for metal–surfaced earthenware.

Reference: Susan and Al Bagdade, *Warman's English & Continental Pottery & Porcelain, 2nd Edition,* Wallace–Homestead, 1991.

Additional Listings: English Softpaste.

COPPER

Creamer, 4½" h, transfer of Gen-
eral Lafayette and surrender of Cornwallis, canary luster band . 150.00
Cup and Saucer, stylized flower dec, highlighted copper luster . 55.00
Jug, 5⅝" h, woman and two children transfer, canary luster band 200.00
Pitcher
  6¾" h, tapered body, black transfer printed bust of Andrew Jackson, titled "General Jackson–The Hero of New Orleans," raised beaded band on rim, sq handle 1,100.00
  7¼" h, cylindrical, flared top, polychrome floral enameled dec 145.00
  11½" h, clock dec, England, 19th C 210.00
Shaving Mug, 4" h, blue with copper diagonal stripes, pink int. rim 55.00
Teapot, cov, copper luster body, floral enamels 75.00

PINK

Bowl, 6½" d, House pattern 90.00
Demitasse Cup and Saucer, House pattern 45.00
Mug, 2½" h, red transfer of man and woman, pink luster bands . 85.00
Pitcher, 11½" h, black ship *Caroline* transfer, pink luster rim . . . 145.00
Plaque, 9¼ x 8", polychrome transfer titled "Retribution Steamer," pink border 125.00
Vase, 4¼" h, floral sprays, oval panel with butterfly, wigglework border, Leeds, 1810, price for pair 250.00

Creamer, silver luster, vertical ribbing, raised dots at waist, 5" l, 3½" h, $95.00.

SILVER

Bowl, 9¼" d, wavy band and grape
   clusters dec, early 19th C **165.00**
Creamer, 5¾" h, garland design
   around top, pedestal base, silver
   luster body **85.00**
Mug, 2" h, brown transfer, boys
   flying kite, silver luster rim, inscribed "For a favorite" **230.00**
Pitcher, 5½" h, bulbous ovoid
   body, farmer's arms design,
   neck band with grapevines,
   pinched spout, angled handle . **140.00**
Saltshaker, 4" h, bulbous, beaded
   dec, pedestal foot **80.00**
Teapot, cov, 6" h, ribbed design,
   ftd **120.00**

SUNDERLAND

Cake Plate, 10" d, pink, mottled . **145.00**
Plaque, 7⅞ x 8½", black transfer
   scene, polychrome enameled
   highlights, pink luster trim, scroll
   molded shaped rim, marked
   "Waverley, S Moore & Co, Sunderland" **255.00**

LUTZ–TYPE GLASS

History: Lutz–type glass is an art glass
attributed to Nicholas Lutz. He made this
type of glass while at the Boston and Sandwich Glass Co. from 1869 until 1888. Since
Lutz–type glass was popular, copied by
many capable glass makers, and unsigned,
it is nearly impossible to distinguish genuine
Lutz products.

Lutz is believed to have made two distinct
types of glass—striped and threaded. This
style often is confused with a similar style
Venetian glass. The striped glass was made
by using threaded glass rods in the Venetian manner. Threaded glass was blown and
decorated by winding threads of glass
around the piece.

Compote, 7" h, lavender, pink, and
   opalescent swirl design, entwined serpent stem **250.00**
Dish, 6" d, round, white lattice,

**Bowl, fluted edge, clear, pink and
gold thread design, broken pontil,
6" d, $115.00.**

   goldstone, blue, and white swirl
   design, pedestal base **125.00**
Glass
   3" h, clear, pink and white swirl
     design, sheared rim **310.00**
   3¼" h, clear, yellow, white, and
     gold speckled swirl design, ap-
     plied red rim **325.00**
Plate, 6¼" d, goldstone, threaded,
   rose center shading to amber,
   scalloped rim **90.00**
Toothpick, bulbous, white lattice,
   goldstone, blue, and white swirl
   design, ruffled edge **95.00**
Whimsey, 6⅜" h, clear glass tube
   with doll, bulbous finial, knob
   stem, latticinio rings dec foot .. **300.00**

MAASTRICHT WARE

History: Maastricht, Holland, is where
Petrus Regout founded the De Sphinx Pottery in 1836. The firm specialized in transfer
printed earthenwares. Other factories also
were established in the area, many employing English workmen and their techniques.

Maastricht china was exported to the United States in competition with English products.

Reference: Susan and Al Bagdade, *Warman's English & Continental Pottery & Porcelain, Second Edition,* Wallace–Homestead, 1991.

Periodical: *The Dutch Potter,* 47 London Terrace, New Rochelle, NY 10804.

Plate, Sana pattern, black and white, salmon border, marked "Petrous Regout Maastricht," 8¼" d, $18.00.

Bowl
8" d, Pajong pattern, black and tan transfer, white ground ... **35.00**
8" d, 4¼" h, Oriental motif, multicolored **70.00**
9½" d, blue and white florals, wreaths, and medallions, marked "Maastricht–Holland" **20.00**
Charger, 14½" d, blue and white, children skating, cottages, windmill, marked "J Sonnerville, Maastricht" **65.00**
Cup and Saucer, handleless, deep saucer, flow blue, pale blue ground, tulip, feather inside cup, marked "Maastricht–Regout, Holland" **25.00**
Game Plate, 9½" d, bird, deep rust edge **30.00**
Plate
7" d, stick spatter and floral dec, red and blue, stamped "So-

ciete Ceramique Maastricht, Made In Holland" **35.00**
8" d, Abbey pattern, blue and white **20.00**
9" d, Willow pattern, pink **18.00**
Tureen, cov, matching ladle, white **45.00**

MAJOLICA

History: Majolica, an opaque, tin glazed pottery, has been produced by many countries for centuries. It originally took its name from the Spanish Island of Majorca, where figuline (a potter's clay) is found. Today majolica denotes a type of pottery which was made during the last half of the 19th century in Europe and America.

Majolica frequently depicted elements in nature: leaves, flowers, birds, and fish. Human figures were rare. Designs were painted on the soft clay body using vitreous colors and were fired under a clear lead glaze to impart the rich color and brilliance characteristic of majolica.

Among English majolica manufacturers who marked their works were Wedgwood, George Jones, Holdcraft, and Minton. Most of their pieces can be identified through the English Registry mark and/or the potter–designer's mark. Sarreguemines in France and Villeroy and Boch in Baden, Germany, produced majolica that compared favorably with the finer English majolica. Most Continental pieces had an incised number on the base.

Although more than 600 American potteries produced majolica between 1850 and 1900, only a handful chose to identify their wares. Among these manufacturers were George Morely, Edwin Bennett, the Chesapeake Pottery Company, the New Milford–Wannoppee Pottery Company, and the firm of Griffen, Smith, and Hill. The others hoped their unmarked pieces would be taken for English examples.

References: Susan and Al Bagdade, *Warman's American Pottery and Porcelain,* Wallace–Homestead, 1994; Susan and Al Bagdade, *Warman's English & Continental Pottery & Porcelain, Second Edition,* Wallace–Homestead, 1991; Nicholas M. Dawes, *Majolica,* Crown Publishers, 1990; Marilyn G. Karmason and Joan B. Stacke,

Majolica: A Complete History And Illustrated Survey, Harry N. Abrams, 1989; Mariann Katz–Marks, *The Collector's Encyclopedia of Majolica,* Collector Books, 1992, 1994 value update; William C. Ketchum, Jr., *American Pottery and Porcelain,* Avon Books, 1994; Mike Schneider, *Majolica,* Schiffer Publishing, 1990; Jefrey B. Snyder and Leslie J. Bockol, *Majolica: European and American Wares,* Schiffer Publishing, 1994.

Collectors' Club: Majolica International Society, 1275 First Ave., Suite 103, New York, NY 10021.

Basket, 7″ l, 6½″ h, green double twisted rope handles, blue and plum sides, fruit dec, damage .	65.00
Candle Holder, 8″ h, elephant standing on rear legs, dressed in coat with tails, holds top hat with trunk	310.00
Center Bowl, 11½″ d, green lily pad and white water lilies, ftd, incised "J Holdcroft"	475.00
Charger, 20″ d, Renaissance style	860.00
Compote, 15¾″ h, shell form, winged griffin base, animal head handle, W S & Sons, No. 4961	625.00
Creamer	
Bird and Iris, two chips	110.00
Etruscan, shell and seaweed pattern, 3¼″ h, imp marks . . .	290.00
Dessert Set, platter and twelve plates, lilies of the valley dec . .	525.00
Dish, 9″ l, leaf shape, green, pink dogwood blossoms, open handle	160.00
Figure, pr, 39½″ h, dolphins, raised tails, polychrome dec, Continental, late 19th C	1,100.00
Jardiniere, 10″ h, leaf and scroll dec, royal blue ground, dragon handles, late 19th C	285.00
Oyster Plate, 10″ d, set of 8	525.00
Pedestal, 46″ h, Neoclassical style, sq top, doric capital, female masks, sq tapering column ending in paw feet, sq plinth . .	700.00
Pitcher	
7″ h, strawberry dec, incised bird design	150.00
7¼″ h, stork with fish at top, bamboo base	265.00

9¾″ h, figural, monkey, brown, black, and red	665.00
11″ h, blue and white, allover scrolled leaf dec	460.00
Planter, 9½″ l, rect, ram's head ends, fawn and fruit sides, blue field, hoofed feet	600.00
Plaque	
8½″ d, set of 4, polychrome biblical scenes, wood frame, Italian, early 19th C	5,175.00
12½″ d, turquoise border, red poppies, man's head in relief on one, woman's head on other, imp mark, price for pr .	450.00

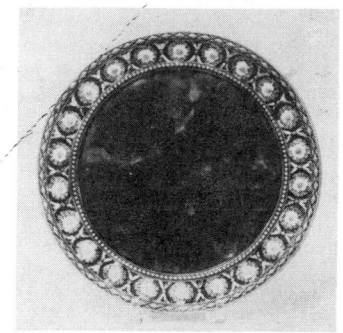

Plate, green and brown splashed center, raised floral border with yellow centers, impressed "Wedgwood," 8″ d, $145.00.

Plate	
7½″ d, raised strawberries and leaves, Portuguese	110.00
8½″ d, mermaid riding dolphins in center, shells and lobsters on rim, albino	225.00
10″ d, Basketweave and Blackberry, brown ground	135.00
Platter, 17″ l, oval, nine raised pilgrim figures, floral border	3,200.00
Portrait Plate, 12″ d, raised portraits of young men, Renaissance period costumes, European, price for pr	295.00
Sardine Box, cov, brown and	

green mottled dec, pink int., attached underplate **350.00**
Teapot, 5¼″ h, Etruscan, shell and seaweed pattern, imp marks .. **400.00**
Tea Set
3 pcs, cream, basketweave design, pink flowers, Banks & Thorley, English, registry mark **600.00**
4 pcs, cov teapot, cream pitcher, and two cups, cabbage form, serpent handles and spouts, cups damaged **745.00**
Tobacco Jar, Arab sheik, turban as lid **175.00**
Umbrella Stand, 22″ h, cylindrical, molded scroll and floral dec, pierced serpentine collar, damaged **50.00**
Vase
8¾″ h, polychrome leaf dec, blue dot ground, Italian, 19th C ... **230.00**
27¾″ h, cobalt blue, polychrome clouds and dragon, tail encircling base, c1880 .... **690.00**

MAPS

History: Maps provide one of the best ways to study the growth of a country or region. From the 16th to the early 20th centuries, maps were both informative and decorative. Engravers provided ornamental detailing which often took the form of bird's-eye views, city maps, and ornate calligraphy and scrolling. Many maps were hand colored to enhance their beauty.

Maps generally were published in plate books. Many of the maps available today result from these books being cut apart and sheets sold separately.

In the last quarter of the 19th century, representatives from firms in Philadelphia, Chicago, and elsewhere traveled the United States preparing county atlases, often with a sheet for each township and a sheet for each major city or town. Although mass–produced, they are eagerly sought by collectors. Individual sheets sell for $25 to $75. The atlases themselves can usually be purchased in the $200 to $400 range. Individual sheets should be viewed solely as decorative and not as investment material.

References: Norman E. Martinus and Harry L. Rinker, *Warman's Paper,* Wallace–Homestead, 1994; Carl Morland and David Bannister, *Antique Maps,* Phaidon Press, 1993; Dana G. Morykan and Harry L. Rinker, *Warman's Country Antiques & Collectibles, Second Edition,* Wallace–Homestead, 1994.

Periodical: *Antique Map & Print Quarterly,* PO Box 290–681, Wethersfield, CT 06129.

Collectors' Clubs: The Association of Map Memorabilia Collectors, 8 Amherst Rd., Pelham, MA 01002; The Chicago Map Society, 60 West Walton St., Chicago, IL 60610.

Museum: Hermon Dunlap Smith Center for the History of Cartography, Newberry Library, Chicago, IL.

Africa
Africa ex magna orbis terre, Gerhardus Mercator, Amsterdam, c1630, double page, engraved, hand–colored in outline, wide margins, French text on verso, small stains on image, 385 x 470 mm **750.00**
Carta do Curso de Rio Zaire, Capello and Ivens, Portugal, 1883, litho, folding, sectional map, 40 sections, linen backed, 700 x 1165 mm **320.00**
Guillaume Delisle, Augsburg, c1775, engraved, folding, hand–colored in outline, minor browning, small hole, 455 x 585 mm **345.00**
Celestial, Andreas Cellarius, Amsterdam, 1660, double page, engraved, wide margins, hand–colored.
Haemisphaeria Sphaerarum, gold highlights, 435 x 515 mm **865.00**
Planisphaerium Arateum, shows planetary arrangement according to Greek astronomer Aratos, 445 x 530 mm **1,610.00**
India, Improved Map of India, Aaron Arrowsmith, London, 1820–21, large 7 part, engraved, 128 sections, hand–colored in outline, some scattered browning and soiling, linen backed .. **260.00**
Italy, Plan of Rome, Jan Blaeu,

Amsterdam, 1663, double page, engraved city map, wide margins, Latin text on verso, hand–colored, extensive repairs, 380 x 505 mm **290.00**

Polar, Regiones sub Polo Arctico, Jan Blaeu, Amsterdam, 1635, double page, engraved, wide margins, hand–colored in outline, slight soiling, 410 x 530 mm **690.00**

United States

A Map of the Most Inhabited Part of New England, Thomas Jeffreys, London, 1774, four sheet map, hand–colored in outline, orig margins, joined as two sheets, some damp staining and browning, 1040 x 975 mm **1,955.00**

A Plan of the Town, Bar, Harbour and Environs, of Charlestown in South Carolina, William Faden, London, 1780, double page, engraved, hand–colored, wide margins, four expertly closed repairs on verso, central reinforced fold, 520 x 690 mm **1,380.00**

A Township Map of the State of Iowa, Fairfield, IA, and Philadelphia, PA, 1854, folding, litho, hand–colored, orig 16mo cloth case, 540 x 870 mm sheet size **345.00**

Floridae Americae Provinciae, Charles Hubert Alexis Jaillot, Paris, c1690, double page, engraved, trimmed margins, several small areas of damage, 370 x 450 mm **2,990.00**

Map of the State of New York, David H Burr, NY, 1849, engraved, 24 sections, hand–colored in outline, linen back, orig ½ morocco folio case, 1190 x 1430 mm **2,070.00**

Map of the United States, A Keith Johnston, London, 1857, four part, engraved sectional, each part with 20 sections, hand–colored in outline, linen back, orig worn morocco slipcase, 1460 x 1800 mm **1,725.00**

Sectional and Geological Map of Iowa, N H Parker, Colton, NY, 1856, folding, litho, hand–colored, orig 16mo cloth case, 820 x 1215 mm **420.00**

Virginia, Marylandia et Carolina, Johann Baptist Homann, Nuremburg, c1730, double page, engraved, hand–colored in outline, wide margins, 490 x 580 mm **920.00**

World, double page, engraved, double–hemispheric

Le Globe Terrestre, Jean Nicolas Du Trallage, hand–colored, wide margins with few chips and tears, slight separation along vertical fold, slight expert repair, 460 x 605 mm ... **1,955.00**

Mappemonde, Philippe Bauche and Guillaume Delisle, Paris, 1755, hand–colored in outline, margins slightly trimmed, 450 x 685 mm **1,100.00**

MARBLEHEAD POTTERY

History: This hand–thrown pottery had its beginning in 1905 as a result of a therapeutic program introduced by Dr. J. Hall for the patients confined to a sanitarium located in Marblehead, Massachusetts. In 1916 production was removed from the hospital to another site. The factory continued under the directorship of Arthur E. Baggs until it closed in 1936.

Most pieces found today are glazed with a smooth, porous, even finish in a single color. The most desirable pieces are decorated with a conventional design in one or more subordinate colors.

Reference: Susan and Al Bagdade, *Warman's American Pottery and Porcelain,* Wallace–Homestead, 1994.

Bowl

6″ d, 3″ h, matte brown glaze, yellow and dark brown specks **200.00**

Vase, tapered cylinder, lavender, 5¼" h, $135.00.

9" d, 4" h, dark blue ext., light
blue gloss int., imp mark **465.00**
Cider Cup, 4" h, dark blue designs,
dark green band **185.00**
Pitcher, 8¼" h, matte green body,
black handle, incised black band
at rim, c1904, repaired spout .. **250.00**
Urn, 6¾" h, 4½" w, bulging cylindrical form, wide mouth, sharply
painted design, thin brown
branches, green leaves, large
pomegranates, brown linear border, soft black outlines, grainy
gray ground, dec by Hanna Tutt,
die stamped mark **2,700.00**
Vase
4" h, gray ground, blue floral, sea
gull mark **1,100.00**
5½" h, blue oval body, green
modeled leaves border, red
berries, green rim band, imp
ship mark **700.00**
6¾" h, black outlined stylized
trees, green leaves, red berries, brown trunks, blue
ground **1,100.00**
7" h, bud, gray glaze **275.00**
9" h, Arts and Crafts dec, gray
painted design, matte gray
glaze, brown and gray specks,
sgd "H. T." **3,500.00**
Wall Pocket **350.00**

MARY GREGORY TYPE GLASS

History: The use of enameled decoration
on glass, an inexpensive imitation of cameo
glass, developed in Bohemia in the late
19th century. The Boston and Sandwich
Glass Co. copied this process in the late
1880s.

Mary Gregory (1856–1908) was employed for two years at the Boston and
Sandwich Glass Co. factory when the
enameled decorated glass was being manufactured. Some collectors argue that Gregory was inspired to paint her white enamel
figures on glass by the work of Kate Greenaway and a desire to imitate pate–sur–pate.
However, evidence for these assertions is
very weak. Further, a question can be
raised whether or not Mary Gregory even
decorated glass as part of her job at Sandwich.

The result is that "Mary Gregory Type" is
a better term to describe this glass. Collectors should recognize that most examples
are either European or modern reproductions.

Reference: R. and D. Truitt, *Mary Gregory Glassware: 1880–1990,* published by
author, 1992.

Museum: Sandwich Glass Museum,
Sandwich, MA.

Barber Bottle
7⅝" h, Vegederma, yellow green **600.00**
7¾" h, bulbous, amethyst, white
enamel boy and flying birds
dec **230.00**
8" h, white enamel dec, ribbed . **265.00**
Bottle, 9½" h, 3½" d, sapphire
blue, white enameled young girl,
blue bubble stopper **215.00**
Box, 4" w, 3½" h, paneled sides,
coppery amber, hp boy with
flower sprig on lid, foliage and
fence ground **435.00**
Cheese Dish, 9" h, high dome,
cranberry, white enameled two
girls and boy, clear base, clear
fancy finial **365.00**
Cruet
8" h, sapphire, IVT, white enameled figures **225.00**
8¾" h, 3½" d, amber, detailed
white enameled young girl,
bulbous base, applied amber
handle, orig matching amber
stopper **250.00**

Decanter, cranberry, flat sides, boy
and girl playing **300.00**
Ewer, 5¼" h, 3⅜" d, turquoise blue
opaque satin, white enameled
young girl, applied blue satin
handle **175.00**
Jewel Box, cov
5" d, blue, white enameled girl
with basket **325.00**
5½" d, 5" h, round, cranberry,
white enameled girl blowing
bubbles, ftd ormolu base **275.00**
Liqueur Mug, facing pr, 1⅞" h, 1⅜"
d, barrel shape, amber optic pattern body, white enameled boy
on one, girl on other, applied am-
ber handle **115.00**

**Tumblers, honey amber, cobalt
blue base, white enameled children, 6¾" h, price for pr, $185.00.**

Match Holder, 2¼" h, 2¼" d, cranberry, white enameled boy **85.00**
Patch Box, 1" h, 2" d, cobalt blue,
white enameled girl on cov,
white enameled dots around
base, hinged **230.00**
Perfume Bottle, 4¾" h, bulbous,
sapphire blue, white enameled
girl holding branch, silver snow-
flakes dec **165.00**
Pitcher
9" h, hp dec, ruffled edge **75.00**
12¼" h, pale amethyst and gold,
white enamel dec of girl hold-
ing butterfly net **450.00**
Powder Jar, 5¾" h, boy and foliate
landscape, 19th C **55.00**
Stein, 6½" h, IVT, sapphire blue,

white enameled boy wearing
pink suit, pewter lid with clear
inset **300.00**
Sugar, cov, 3½" d, 5" h, golden
amber, white enameled little boy,
white enamel trim on lid **200.00**
Tumbler, 4" h, 2⅞" d, golden am-
ber optic pattern ground, de-
tailed white enameled young girl **70.00**
Vase
3⅞" h, 2" d, cranberry, white
enameled girl **130.00**
6" h, 2¼" d, orange, white enam-
eled boy **115.00**
8¼" h, cranberry, white enam-
eled boy with cane **200.00**
11 " h, 3⅜" d, lime green, white
enameled boy in suit, round
top **90.00**
12" h, matched pair, green
ground, white enameled
woman on one, man on other,
white tree in background, clear
rigaree sides **475.00**
Whiskey Glass, 2¼" h, 2⅛" d, bul-
bous, cranberry, white enameled
girl **85.00**

MATCH HOLDERS

History: After 1850 the friction match
achieved popular usage. The early matches
were packaged and sold in sliding cardboard boxes. To facilitate storage and to
eliminate the clumsiness of using the box,
match holders were developed.

The first examples were cast iron or tin,
the latter often having advertising on them.
A patent for a wall hanging match holder
was issued in 1849. By 1880 match holders
also were being made from glass and china.
Match holders lost popularity in the late
1930s and 1940s with the advent of gas
and electric heat and ranges.

Reference: Denis B. Alsford, *Match
Holders,* Schiffer Publishing, 1994.

Advertising
Barker Brand Clothing Collar, silvered brass, emb dog holding
a man's collar, hinged lid, early
1900s **60.00**
Hood Rubber Company, boot

shape, black, rubber, removable top, "Compliments of Hood Rubber Company/Boston, USA," c1800, unused **150.00**

Schlitz Beer, litho, cardboard . . **325.00**

The Fashion Clothing Store, silvered metal, 1902 calendar on reverse **75.00**

Art Deco, 4¾" d, 6⅛" h, nasturtium pattern, orange and yellow flowers, spattered brown **140.00**

Brass, pocket type, figural, pig . . **110.00**

Cast Iron

Hunting scene, Germany **60.00**

Open scroll work, dated 1867 . **55.00**

China, wall type

Bust, Edwardian girl **75.00**

Holly dec, two pockets **85.00**

**Mahogany, tulip shaped, 3¾ x 5",
$40.00.**

Glass

Amber, 2⅝" d, 2⅝" h, oaken bucket, wire bail handle **20.00**

Apple Green, Indian head **40.00**

Clear, Jumbo **40.00**

Custard, Winged Scroll pattern, Heisey **100.00**

Light Blue, Indian head **50.00**

Milk Glass, 3¼" h, Indian, orig gold dec **175.00**

Quimper, standing **75.00**

Royal Bayreuth, hanging

Cavalier musicians dec **395.00**

Devil and Cards **195.00**

Poppy, red **110.00**

Silver

Plated, man riding horse, pocket type **85.00**

Sterling, 2½" h, Victorian, repousse, hinged lid **70.00**

MATCH SAFES

History: Match safes are small containers used to safely carry matches in one's pocket. They were first used in the 1850s. Match safes are often figural with a hinged lid and striking surface.

Reference: Audrey G. Sullivan, *A History of Match Safes In The United States,* published by author, 1978.

Note: While not all match safes have a striking surface, this is one test, besides size, to distinguish a match safe from a calling card case.

Advertising

Anheuser–Busch, 2¾" l, eagle, silver plated, c1900 . . . . **40.00**

Bamberger's Shoe Store, silvered brass, black and white horse illus on one side, "Mens Shoe Annex" on other, early 1900s **50.00**

Fan Tan Cigars, silvered brass, black and white illus on one side, 1902 calendar on reverse **60.00**

Fleischmann's Restaurant/Bakery, silvered brass and celluloid, early 1900s **60.00**

Monitor Works, blue and white design, Monitor iron warship, "Use Monitor" on reverse, early 1900s **75.00**

Number Five Cigar, brass, engraved floral pattern, lid **75.00**

Rochester Composite Brick Co, silvered brass, black and white brick, company address on reverse, early 1900s **70.00**

Turtle, tortoise shell top, nickel-plated brass body, 2⅜" l, $275.00.

Brass, Art Nouveau style, raised relief lady in pearl panel on one side, raised hunting dog and rider's crop on other, late 1890s/ early 1900s **75.00**

Cast Iron, hanging, figural
Bacchus Head, open pocket, grapes and leaves back plate **85.00**
Monks Head, cathedral spires on reverse **85.00**

Glass, hanging
Amber, boot shape **20.00**
Clear, 4½" h, Miss Liberty's head **80.00**
Milk Glass, 3⅞" h, blue, mottled, flag shield form, marked "America" and "1492–1892" . **175.00**

Silver, sterling, Art Nouveau, floral design, blue enameled center, "Y" and "99" on one side, engraved "PRB" initials on reverse **65.00**

Souvenir, Mount Vernon, silvered brass, Washington's Mansion and Tomb photos **45.00**

Tin, hanging, 2 x 3 x 5½", open crimped shell red pocket, painted, triangular green back, asphalt center striking surface . **65.00**

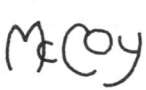

McCOY POTTERY

History: The J. W. McCoy Pottery Co. was established in Roseville, Ohio, in September 1899. The early McCoy Co. produced both stoneware and some art pottery lines, including Rosewood. In October 1911, three potteries merged creating the Brush-McCoy Pottery Co. This company continued to produce the original McCoy lines and added several new art lines. Much early pottery is not marked.

In 1910, Nelson McCoy and his father, J. W. McCoy, founded the Nelson McCoy Sanitary Stoneware Co. In 1925, the McCoy family sold their interest in the Brush-McCoy Pottery Co. and started to expand and improve the Nelson McCoy Co. The new company produced stoneware, earthenware specialties, and artware. Most of

the pottery marked "McCoy" was made by the Nelson McCoy Co.

References: Susan and Al Bagdade, *Warman's American Pottery and Porcelain,* Wallace–Homestead, 1994; Sharon and Bob Huxford, *The Collectors Encyclopedia of McCoy Pottery,* Collector Books, 1980, 1995 value update; Dana G. Morykan and Harry L. Rinker, *Warman's Country Antiques & Collectibles, Second Edition,* Wallace–Homestead, 1994; Harold Nichols, *McCoy Cookie Jars: From The First To The Last, Second Edition,* Nichols Publishing, 1991; Steve and Martha Sanford, *The Guide To Brush–McCoy Pottery,* published by authors, 1992.

Periodical: *Our McCoy Matters,* PO Box 14255, Parkville, MO 64152.

Additional Listings: See *Warman's Americana & Collectibles* for more examples.

Vase, white ground, pink flowers, green leaves, brown twigs, 6¼" h, $17.50.

Ashtray, leaf **15.00**
Birdbath, 27" h, Greystone finish . **65.00**
Bowl, Amaryllis pattern, pastel .. **20.00**
Cookie Jar, cov
Frontier **65.00**
Lamb, basketweave base **65.00**
Rooster **120.00**
Snoopy, doghouse **225.00**
Woodsey Owl **295.00**
Ewer, 10" h, emb grapes and leaves, dark brown glaze, marked "Rosewood, McCoy," c1905 .... **185.00**
Flowerpot, 2½ x 4", Rockraft, 1931 **45.00**

Garden Dish, 5½ x 12", hunter,
1955 .... **44.00**
Jardiniere, 12" h, Florastone **95.00**
Mug
Corn pattern, pale yellow ker-
nels, green husk, c1910 .... **60.00**
Little Red Riding Hood, marked
"Brush–McCoy" **40.00**
Pitcher, 9½" h, emb reserve of
grapes and leaves, green and
brown wood grain ground, c1920 **50.00**
Planter, figural
Carriage with parasol, c1955 .. **38.00**
Duck with umbrella **35.00**
Spinning Wheel **24.00**
Pretzel Jar, cov, emb buccaneer
and parrot, green glaze, marked
"Nelson McCoy Sanitary Stone-
ware Co," c1920 .... **70.00**
Punch Bowl, pedestal base, emb
grapes and leaves, dark brown
glaze, marked "Olympia J W
McCoy" **375.00**
Tureen, El Rancho Bar–B–Que
pattern, sombero cov, c1960 .. **50.00**
Urn, 6" h, onyx glaze, marked
"Nelson–McCoy" **35.00**
Vase
Grape, 9" h, high glaze **30.00**
Weeping Gold **30.00**
Wall Pocket, 4" l, women with bon-
net **20.00**

McKEE GLASS

History: The McKEE Glass Co. was established in 1843 in Pittsburgh, Pennsylvania. In 1852 they opened a factory to produce pattern glass. In 1888 the factory was
relocated to Jeannette, Pennsylvania, and
began to produce many types of glass kitch-
enwares, including several patterns of
Depression glass. The factory continued
until 1951 when it was sold to the Thatcher
Manufacturing Co.

McKEE named its colors Chalaine Blue,
Custard, Seville Yellow, and Skokie Green.
McKEE glass may also be found with
painted patterns, e.g., dots and ships. A few
items were decaled. Many of the canisters
and shakers were lettered in black to show
the purpose for which they were intended.

References: Gene Florence, *Kitchen*

*Glassware of the Depression Years, 5th
Edition,* Collector Books, 1994; Gene Florence, *Very Rare Glassware of the Depression Years, Third Series,* Collector Books,
1993; M'Kee and Brothers, *M'Kee Victorian
Glass,* Dover Publications, 1981 reprint.

Additional Listings: See *Warman's
Americana & Collectibles* for more examples.

**Children's Dishes, custard, red
trim, price for 10 pc set, $90.00.**

Animal Cov Dish
Dove, unsigned McKee **225.00**
Owl, split rib base, sgd "McKee" **225.00**
Squirrel, unsigned McKee **225.00**
Swan, unsigned McKee **225.00**
Basket, Queen pattern, apple
green **125.00**
Birdhouse, 5¼" d, Wren's Honey-
moon Hut, red roof, no closure **45.00**
Bowl, 4¾" d, Art Deco, black, ftd **15.00**
Box, cov, round, vaseline, sparrow
finial **100.00**
Candy Dish, cov, 8½" h, black, Art
Nouveau **90.00**
Casserole, cov, 10½" l, pearl finish **50.00**
Champagne, Eureka pattern,
heavy brilliant flint **85.00**
Cheese Dish, cov, Laurel, French
Ivory **36.00**
Clock, amber, marked "Tambour
Art" **350.00**
Compote, Autumn, oval, ftd, Sko-
kie green **42.00**
Creamer, Gothic **38.00**
Drawer Pull, Chalaine blue, me-
dium size, price for pair **25.00**

Eggcup, French Ivory	**5.00**
Goblet	
Gothic, flint	**37.50**
Puritan pattern, pink stem	**25.00**
Lamp, 11″ h, boudoir, Danse de Lumiere, green satin finish, price for pair	**450.00**
Punch Set, punch bowl, base, twelve cups, milk glass, relief grape ladle, plastic ladle, orig box, price for fifteen piece set	**85.00**
Salt and Pepper Shakers, pr, Roman Arch, black	**28.00**
Spooner, Gothic	**38.00**
Sugar, cov, Wiltec pattern, c1894	**25.00**
Toothpick Holder	
Aztec pattern, clear	**20.00**
Rock Crystal pattern, clear	**35.00**
Vase, 8½″ h, nude, Chalaine blue, hp clothes	**225.00**
Whiskey, Bottoms Up, caramel glass, coaster	**65.00**

MEDICAL AND PHARMACEUTICAL ITEMS

History: Medicine and medical instruments are well documented for the modern period. Some instruments are virtually unchanged since their invention. Others have changed drastically.

The concept of sterilization phased out decorative handles. Early handles of instruments were often carved and can be found in mother–of–pearl, ebony, and ivory. Today's sleekly designed instruments are not as desirable to collectors.

Pharmaceutical items include items commonly found in a drugstore and pertain to the items used to store or prepare medications.

References: A. Walker Bingham, *The Snake–Oil Syndrome: Patent Medicine Advertising,* Christopher Publishing House, 1994; Bill Carter, Bernard Butterworth, Joseph Carter, and John Carter, *Dental Collectibles & Antiques,* Dental Folklore Books of K.C., 1984; Douglas Congdon–Martin, *Drugstore and Soda Fountain Antiques,* Schiffer Publishing, 1991; Don Fredgant, *Medical, Dental & Pharmaceutical Collectibles,* Books Americana, 1981; Patricia McDaniel, *Drugstore Collectibles,* Wallace–Homestead, 1994; Lillian C. and Charles G. Richardson, *The Pill Rollers: Apothecary Antiques And Drug Store Collectibles, Second Edition,* Old Fort Press, 1992; Keith Wilbur, *Antique Medical Instruments: Revised Price Guide* Schiffer Publishing, 1987, 1993 value update.

Periodical: *Scientific, Medical & Mechanical Antiques,* 11824 Taneytown Pike, Taneytown, MD 21787.

Collectors' Clubs: Maryland Microscopical Society, 8621 Polk St., McLean, VA 22102; Medical Collectors Association, 1300 Morris Park Ave., Bronx, NY 10461.

Museums: Dittrick Museum of Medical History, Cleveland, OH; International Museum of Surgical Science & Hall of Fame, Chicago, IL; National Museum of Health & Medicine, Walter Reed Medical Center, Washington, DC; National Museum of History and Technology, Smithsonian Institution, Washington, DC; Schmidt Apothecary Shop, New England Fire & History Museum, Brewster, MA; Waring Historical Library, Medical University of South Carolina, Charleston, SC.

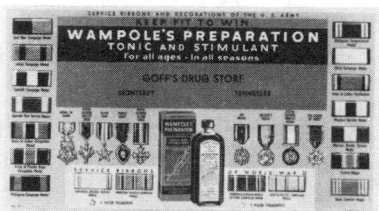

Blotter, Wampole's Preparation Tonic and Stimulant, printed color litho, WWII service ribbons illus, 6⅜ x 3½″, $8.00.

Amputation Kit, bone saws, knives, and instruments, fitted wood box, Civil War, c1860 . . .	**55.00**
Bedpan, 12 x 18″, metal, white porcelain finish	**12.00**
Blood Pressure Kit, 5¼ x 13¾″, stamped "Jarcho Pressometer," cased	**30.00**
Book	
An Inquiry Into The Nature, Causes and Cure of Hydro-	

thrax; Illustrated in Interesting Cases and Many Living Examples of the Success of the Mode of Treatment Recommended, Lachlan MacLean, Hale & Hosmer, Hartford, 1814, orig paper backed boards, badly deteriorating spine **80.00**

Currents and Counter–Currents in Medical Science, Oliver W Holmes, Ticknor and Fields, Boston, 1861, 1st ed, 12mo, orig cloth, ends worn, small blind stamp on title page **80.00**

Descriptive Anatomy of the Human Teeth, GV Black, Philadelphia, SS White Dental Manuf Co, 1902, 4th ed, cloth, worn edges **75.00**

Essentials of Medical Electricity, Edward R Morton, London, 1905, 12mo, cloth, worn **15.00**

History of Dentistry From The Most Ancient Times Until The End of The Eighteenth Century, Vincenzo Guerini, Philadelphia, Lea & Febiger, 1909, 4to, 355 pgs, cloth, slightly worn **80.00**

Life of Sir William Osler, Harvey Cushing, Oxford Univ Press, 1925, 2nd impression, 2 vols, cloth, light wear **30.00**

Practical Treatise On Operative Dentistry, J Taft, Philadelphia, 1868, 2nd ed, full calf, slight wear **85.00**

Principles and Practice of Medicine, Wm Osler, D Appleton, NY, 1896, 2nd ed, 8vo, half leather, worn, foxing **115.00**

Semi–Centennial Celebration of the Introduction of Homeopathy West of the Allegheny Mountains, Held at Pittsburgh, Penn'a, JC Burgher, Sept 20, 1887, 72 pgs, plates, orig cloth **50.00**

System of Practical Surgery, Wm Fergusson, Philadelphia, 1843, 32 pgs, full calf, ends worn, some foxing **30.00**

The Narcotic Drug Diseases and Allied Ailments, Pathol- *ogy, Pathogenesis, and Treatment,* Geo E Pettey, Philadelphia, 1913, 1st ed, 8vo, orig cloth, 516 pgs, faded spine .. **30.00**

Catalog
Bauer & Black, Chicago, IL, 1914, 73 pgs, illus, price list, medical and surgical plasters, dressings, cottons, ligatures, sutures, suspensories, athletic supporters, adhesive plaster tapes, court plasters, gauzes, and bandages, 4 x 6¾" **40.00**

L Manasse, Chicago, IL, 1895, 16 pgs, illus, supplementary circular to catalog #2, 4, and 5, descriptions, prices, optical, mathematical, and meteorological instruments, magic lanterns, spectacles, opera glasses, microscopes, compasses, thermometers, and medical batteries, 9 x 12" ... **90.00**

Dental Drill, cast iron, orig foot pedal, c1850 .... **650.00**

Doctor's Bag, leather, compartment int. with bottles, c1865 ... **100.00**

Eyecup
Green glass **10.00**
Milk glass **15.00**

First Aid Kit, A Friend in Need, Bauer & Black, Div of Kendall Co, gold and brown emb vinyl box **45.00**

Inhaler, Gilbertson's Perfect Inhaler, Eli Lilly & Co, ceramic tapered jar, cream, green, and black, information sheet **45.00**

Magazine, *The Dental Times,* James Truman, ed., 1869 ..... **12.00**

Medicine Cabinet, 12" w, 7" d, 13" h, Paidan, wood, glazed door with decal, three int. glass shelves **110.00**

Mortar and Pestle, 3¼" h, Renaissance style **50.00**

Ophthalmoscope, patent 1924 ... **45.00**

Poster, 38 x 25", Dr Meyers Foot Soap, 1920 .... **120.00**

Scale, 13 x 13 x 6", Rexall Drugs, metal, balance type, chains hold pans **165.00**

Stethoscope, monaural, SS, ivory earpiece, English, c1875 ...... **125.00**

Tooth Extractor **85.00**
Traveling Case, black leather, oak
   drawers **200.00**
Vaporizer, DeVilbiss, #145, 7 x
   5½", clear glass jar, green and
   yellow label **20.00**
Wrist Wrap, 5 x 2½ x 1", Fitsrite,
   leather, orig box **7.00**

MEDICINE BOTTLES

History: The local apothecary and his book of formulas played a major role in early America. In 1796 the first patent for a medicine was issued by the United States Patent Office. Anyone could apply for a patent. As long as the dosage was not poisonous, the patent was granted.

Patent medicines were advertised in newspapers and magazines and sold through the general store and by "medicine" shows. In 1907 the Pure Food and Drug Act, requiring an accurate description of contents of medicine on the label, put an end to the patent medicine industry. Not all medicines were patented.

Most medicines were sold in distinctive bottles, often with the name of the medicine and location in relief. Many early bottles were made in the glass manufacturing area of southern New Jersey. Later companies in western Pennsylvania and Ohio manufactured bottles.

References: Joseph K. Baldwin, *A Collector's Guide To Patent And Proprietary Medicine Bottles Of The Nineteenth Century,* Thomas Nelson, 1973; Ralph and Terry Kovel, *The Kovels' Bottles Price List, 9th Edition,* Crown Publishers, 1992; Carlo and Dot Sellari, *The Standard Old Bottle Price Guide,* Collector Books, 1989.

Periodicals: *Antique Bottle And Glass Collector,* PO Box 187, East Greenville, PA 18041; *Bottles & Extras Magazine,* PO Box 154, Happy Camp, CA 96039.

Ayer's Cherry Pectoral, 5¼" h,
   aqua **12.00**
Baker's Vegetable Blood & Liver
   Cure, TN, 9" h, amber **385.00**
Brown's Blood Cure, 6¼" h, yellow
   green **230.00**
Circassian/Lymph,   America,

J. R. Burdsell's Arnica Liniment, NY, aqua, open pontil, 5⅜" h, $25.00.

1830–60, 6⅝" h, violin shape,
   aquamarine, tooled mouth, pontil scar **160.00**
Davis Vegetable Pain Killer, 6⅝" h,
   rect **45.00**
Dixon's Dystemper Cure, 5" h,
   clear **25.00**
Dr Ira Warren's Blood & Bile Purifier, 8¾" h, aqua **225.00**
Dr Townsend's Sarsaparilla, 9¼"
   h, sq, emerald green, sloping
   collared mouth, iron pontil **225.00**
Faith Whitcomb's Balsam Cures
   Coughs, 9" h, aqua **150.00**
Gardiners Liniment, 4⅛" h, aqua,
   rolled lip **25.00**
Gibsborough Color Works, 3⅞" h,
   cylindrical, aquamarine, tooled
   mouth **80.00**
GWL Drug Co, 9⅞" h, amethyst . **165.00**
Hall's Balsam For The Lungs . . . **125.00**
Hart's Swedish Asthma Cure, amber **15.00**
Hunnewell's Universal Cough
   Remedy, 4½" h, aqua **45.00**
J L Leavitt, Boston, 8⅜" h, cylindrical, deep olive amber, sloping
   collared mouth with ring, iron
   pontil **155.00**
Kilmer's Cough Consumption Oil   **25.00**
Kurnitzki Swire Grall Liver & Kidney, oval, aqua **45.00**
Lindsey's Blood Searcher, 9¼" h,
   teal **1,000.00**
Mathewson's Infallible Remedy,
   aqua **150.00**

McMunn's Elixir of Opium, aqua, flared lip 25.00

Mrs S A Allen's Worlds Hair Restorer, America, 1860–80, 7¼" h, rect, beveled corners, light to medium pink amethyst, applied double collared mouth, smooth base, some ext. scratches, int. stain 160.00

Myers Rock Rose New Haven, America, 1845–60, 9⅛" h, sq, beveled corners, bright medium emerald green, applied sloping collared mouth, iron pontil mark **1,500.00**

Oldridge's Balm of Columbia, For Restoring Hair, America, 1840–60, 5⅛" h, rect, concave beveled corners, aquamarine, flared mouth, pontil scar 230.00

Park's Liver & Kidney Cure, 1870–80, 9¾" h, amber 75.00

Peptenzyme, 3" h, cobalt blue ... 10.00

Renne's Pain Killing Magic Oil, aqua 8.00

Rowand & Walton's Panacea, 6¼" h, rect, aquamarine, tooled mouth 95.00

R W Davis Drug Co, Chicago, USA, 1880–1900, 11" h, cylindrical, concentrically ringed shoulder and base, center body of sixteen panels, milk glass, sloping collared mouth with ring, smooth base 65.00

Spark's Kidney & Liver Cure, 9⅜" h, oval, amber 350.00

Thompsonian Appetizer, 9" h, sq, yellow amber, emb heavy man, sloping collared mouth, smooth base 275.00

Valentine Hassmer's Lung & Cough Syrup 100.00

Warner's Safe Diabetes Cure Melbourne, 9½" h, oval, golden amber, collared mouth, smooth base 355.00

MERCURY GLASS

History: Mercury glass is a light–bodied, double–walled glass that was "silvered" by applying a solution of silver nitrate to the inside of the object through a hole in the base of the formed object.

F. Hale Thomas, London, patented the method in 1849. In 1855 the New England Glass Co. filed a patent for the same type of process. Other American glassmakers soon followed. The glass reached the height of its popularity in the early 20th century.

Reference: Ellen T. Schroy, *Warman's Glass,* Wallace–Homestead, 1992.

Toothpick Holder, gold, pedestal base, 3½" h, $30.00.

Bowl, 4½" d, gold int. 50.00

Candlesticks, pr
  9½" h 80.00
  11" h, enameled floral dec 115.00

Candy Dish, cov, 4¼ x 8¼", pedestal base, clear glass domed cov 30.00

Carafe, 12" h, 5½" d, mushroom stopper, dated 1909 .... 50.00

Compote
  5¾ x 2¾", shallow, etched birds and leaves 45.00
  6½ x 7", enameled white floral dec, gold int. 65.00

Creamer
  6½" h, grapevine dec, etched, applied clear handle 125.00
  6¾" h, etched grapevine design, applied clear handle, Sandwich Glass Co 115.00

Curtain Tiebacks, 3" d, etched grape pattern, pewter shanks, price for pair 50.00

Darner, umbrella shape, enameled floral dec, brass trim 60.00

Pitcher
  6" h, etched ferns 135.00

6½" h, crimped handle, circular
base, 1855–70 .... **150.00**
Rolling Pin **60.00**
Salt, 3" d, urn shape, ftd **35.00**
Shaving Mug, fern dec **40.00**
Sweetmeat Dish, cov, 4" d, 7½" h,
clear glass cov, pedestal base . **40.00**
Toothpick Holder, white enameled
floral dec, gold int. **40.00**
Tumbler, 4½" h **20.00**
Urn
12" h, gold int., floral and foliage
dec **150.00**
13" h, baluster shape, marked
"Harnish & Co, London" **250.00**
Vase
7" h, ball shape, blue **35.00**
10½" h, baluster, spreading
mouth, etched floral dec,
spread circular foot, price for
pair **115.00**
12" h, ribbed, green, enameled
floral dec, birds, price for pair **125.00**
Wig Stand, 10½" h **210.00**

METTLACH

History: In 1809 Jean Francis Boch established a pottery at Mettlach in Germany's
Moselle Valley. His father had started a pottery at Septfontaines in 1767. Nicholas Villeroy began his pottery career at Wallerfan-
ger in 1789.

In 1841 these three factories merged.
They pioneered in underglaze printing on
earthenware, using transfers from copper
plates, and in using coal fired kilns. Other
factories were developed at Dresden, Wad-
gassen, and Danischburg.

The castle and Mercury emblems are the
two chief marks. Secondary marks are
known. The base also contains a shape
mark and usually a decor mark. Pieces are

found in relief, etched, printed under the
glaze, and cameo.

Prices are for print under glaze unless
otherwise specified.

References: Susan and Al Bagdade,
*Warman's English & Continental Pottery &
Porcelain, Second Edition,* Wallace–Home-
stead, 1991; Gary Kirsner, *The Mettlach
Book, Third Edition,* Glentiques, 1994; R.
H. Mohr, *Mettlach Steins, Ninth Edition,*
published by author, 1982.

Periodical: *The Beer Stein Journal,* PO
Box 8807, Coral Springs, FL 33075.

Collectors' Club: Stein Collectors International, 3530 Mimosa Court, New Orleans,
LA 70131.

Additional Listings: Villeroy & Boch.

Beaker, #3883/553, ¼ L, German
man leaning on rifle **70.00**
Butter Dish, cov, 18" d, shamrock
and rect dec, castle mark **125.00**
Cigar Holder, figural, boy with basket on back, wearing pointed hat **240.00**
Coaster
#1032, 4¾" d, price for set of 4 **400.00**
#2820, etched, college boy
holding stein **190.00**
Flagon, #2690, 13¾" h **750.00**
Mug, V & B Hires **150.00**
Plaque
#307, 12½" d, Dutch Scene ... **110.00**
#1044/354, 14" d, Oriental
woman in boat watching sun-
set **200.00**
#1607, 11" d, etched, ladies rep-
resenting summer and fall, sgd
"Warth, 1893" **500.00**

**Fruit Bowl, matching underplate,
open lattice work, creamware,
early 1800s, imp "VV," 7½" d x 3½"
h bowl, 10" d plate, $115.00.**

#2621, 7″ d, cavalier pouring
wine **175.00**
#2749, 20″ d, etched, church at
end of winding road **1,080.00**
#2875, 17½″ d, cameo, blue–
green, white classical woman
and man depicting industry . . **745.00**

Plate, #3096, octagonal, Art Deco
design, burnt gold, cream, and
royal blue **65.00**

Pokal, cov
#396, relief, crown top, pedestal
base, four scenes, German
text **450.00**
#2058, monkeys among
branches, monkey on lid **750.00**

Punch Bowl, #488, 8 qt, underplate and cov, relief grapes, lid
shows cherubs squeezing juice
from grapes into mouths **1,000.00**

Stein
#485, ½ L **250.00**
#1526, ½ L, Eisenbahn Regt,
Berlin, 1899–1901, roster, lo-
comotive scene **280.00**
#1642, ½ L **395.00**
#1786, 10¼″ h, mythical dragon
handle **635.00**
#2001C, ½ L, 4¼″ d, 5¾″ h,
book type, titled "The Scholar,"
etched pottery lids, owl on
pewter thumbpiece, blue, tan,
and brown **550.00**
#2180/955, 5 L, drinking scene,
sgd "Heinrich Schlitt" **1,300.00**
#2194, 3 L, relief, black whale
story, alligator handle, turtle on
lid **750.00**
#2691, 2¾ L, inlay, man with
guitar in cellar **1,100.00**
#2790/6147, ½ L, bearded man **380.00**
#2833, ½ L **575.00**
#2951, 1 L, 10¼″ h, 4″ d,
cameo, Prussian Eagle, white,
sage green ground, castle
mark, orig pewter top **815.00**
#2958, 3 L, etched, bowling
scene, sgd "F.Q." **600.00**
#3144, ½ L, etched, carved
clock in wreath above shield,
couple on each side, sgd "F.
Quidenus" **600.00**

Tureen, cov, 16½″ d, 15″ h, match-

ing underplate, imp "Mettlach
VB 2088" mark, artist's initials . **550.00**

Vase
#1537, 14″ h, etched four sea-
son panels with cherubs, pink
lining **350.00**
#1870, 14″ h, blue ground, geo-
metric dec, elephant handles,
castle mark **345.00**

Wine Pitcher, 13″ h, 3 L, six tan
relief friezes, center blue band of
Merry Dancing People, marked
"V & B, Mettlach" **450.00**

MILITARIA

History: Wars always have been part of
history. Until the mid–19th century, soldiers
often had to fill their own needs, including
weapons. Even in the 20th century a soldier's uniform and some of his gear are
viewed as his personal property, even
though issued by a military agency.

Conquering armed forces made a habit
of acquiring souvenirs from their van-
quished foes. They brought their own uniforms and accessories home as badges of
triumph and service.

Saving militaria may be one of the oldest
collecting traditions. Militaria collectors tend
to have their own special shows and view
themselves outside the normal antiques
channels. However, they haunt small indoor
shows and flea markets in hopes of finding
additional materials.

References: Thomas Berndt, *Standard
Catalog of U. S. Military Vehicles: 1940–
1965,* Krause Publications, 1993; Ray A.
Bows, *Vietnam Military Lore 1959–1973,*
Bows & Sons, 1988; Robert Fisch, *Field
Equipment of the Infantry 1914–1945,*
Greenberg Publications, 1989; Robin
Lumsden, *A Collector's Guide To Third
Reich Militaria,* Hippocrene Books, 1987;
Robin Lumsden, *A Collector's Guide To
Third Reich Militaria: Detecting The Fakes,*
Hippocrene Books, 1989; *North South
Trader's Civil War Collector's Price Guide,
5th Edition,* North South Trader's Civil War,
1991; Harry Rinker Jr. and Robert Heistand,
*World War II Collectibles: The Collector's
Guide To Selecting And Enjoying Military
And Home Front Items,* New Burlington

Books, 1993; Konrad F. Scheier, Jr., *Guide To U. S. Tanks & Artillery,* Krause Publications, 1994; Jack H. Smith, *Military Postcards 1870–1945,* Wallace–Homestead, 1988; Sydney B. Vernon, *Vernon's Collectors' Guide To Orders, Medals, and Decorations,* published by author, 1986; Richard Windrow and Tim Hawkins, *The World War II GI, U.S. Army Uniforms 1941–45,* Motorbooks International, 1993.

Periodicals: *Men at Arms,* 222 W. Exchange St., Providence, RI 02903; *Military Collector Magazine,* PO Box 245, Lyon Station, PA 19536; *Military Collector News,* PO Box 702073, Tulsa, OK 74170; *Military Trader,* PO Box 1050, Dubuque, IA 52004; *North South Trader's Civil War,* PO Drawer 631, Orange, VA 22960; *Wildcat Collectors Journal,* 15158 NE 6th Ave., Miami, FL 33162; *Wings & Things,* PO Box 17276, Sarasota, FL 34276.

Collectors' Clubs: American Society of Military Insignia Collectors, 526 Lafayette Ave., Palmerton, PA 18071; Association of American Military Uniform Collectors, PO Box 1876, Elyria, OH 44036; Company of Military Historians, North Main St., Westbrook, CT, 06498; Imperial German Military Collectors Association, 82 Atlantic St., Keyport, NJ 07735; Orders and Medals Society of America, PO Box 484, Glassboro, NJ 08028.

Reproduction Alert: Pay special attention to Civil War and Nazi material.

Additional Listings: Firearms, Nazi, and Swords. See World War I and World War II in *Warman's Americana & Collectibles* for more examples.

REVOLUTIONARY WAR

Book, *The Life of Nathanael Greene Major–General in the Army of the Revolution,* George Washington Greene, Hurd and Houghton, NY, 1871, 3 vols, 8vo, portfolio and four maps, ex–library set, wear, markings **110.00**

WAR OF 1812

Hat, leather, attached brass eagle, metallic rope twists **600.00**
Powder Horn, 24" l, cannon,

"Sacketts Harbor, May 12, 1813," naval battle scene, 3 large ships, several smaller ones **1,000.00**

CIVIL WAR

Belt Buckle, oval, CSA **45.00**
Blanket, course mixed tan wool, brown stripe, U.S. woven in center **500.00**
Book
A Prisoner of War In Virginia 1864–5, George H Putnam, NY, 1914, 12mo, orig cloth, 144 pgs **30.00**
History of the Civil War...Revised and Completed by Dr LP Brockett, Samuel M Schmucker, Philadelphia, c1865, 8vo, full calf, engraved plates, worn, some damp staining, foxing **40.00**
History of the Grand Army of the Republic, Robert B Beath, NY, 1889, large 8vo, orig bright blue pictorial cloth **70.00**
Personal Memoirs, US Grant, Charles L Webster, NY, 1885–86, 8vo, 2 vols, orig cloth, 1st ed, wear and rubbing **45.00**
Revised Register of the Soldiers and Sailors of New Hampshire in the War of the Rebellion 1861–1866, Augustus D Ayling, Concord, 1895, 1st ed, very thick 4to, orig leather backed boards, 1,347 pgs, modest scuffing **120.00**
Stonewall Jackson. A Military

Civil War, Pistol Box, marked "R Bingee New York Mfg," 1855, $150.00.

Biography, John Esten Cooke, Appleton, NY, 1876, 2nd ed, 8vo, orig sheep binding, maps, portraits, front cov detached, rubbing 30.00

The American Conflict: A History Of The Great Rebellion...With The Drift and Progress of American Opinion Respecting Human Slavery, Horace Greeley, OD Case & Co, Hartford, 1865–6, 4to, 2 vols, full calf, worn edges ... 40.00

Bugle, copper and brass, standard issue, pitched in key of C, manufacturer's mark 285.00

Button, officer, Alabama Volunteer Corps, 2 pcs, marked "A.V.C." between eagle wings 135.00

Cabinet Card, young soldier on front porch, full length, musket, bayonet, two left boots 65.00

Canteen, wood, drum shape, carved name and regiment of Confederate soldier 1,100.00

Cartridge Box Plate, oval, marked "US," dug Charleston, SC 30.00

Document
Envelope, 8th NH Regiment, engraving in upper left corner, unused 75.00
Journal, George B Gorden, Beverly MA, sailor, Aug 1864–Oct 1870, small 8vo, flexible leather, 74 pgs, describes naval service, Lee's surrender, Lincoln's death, weather entries 170.00
Records of Surgeon Luther Franklin Locke, Nashua, NH, lists of patients operated on and results, expenses ledger, other lists, military passes, family letters, books 450.00

Saddle, Confederate, C.S. saddle shield 500.00

Stirrups, artillery, brass, marked "U.S." on base 40.00

Uniform, frock coat
Confederate, double breasted, butternut color, lindsey–woolsey fabric 5,000.00
Federal, enlisted infantry, blue piping on collar and cuffs, 9

button front, maker and inspector marks in sleeve 1,900.00

Unit History, *History of Ram Fleet, Marine Brigade,* 1907 .... 400.00

INDIAN WAR

Belt Buckle, brass, US emb on front, marked "Anson Mills, patent 1881" 45.00

Powder Horn, 13" w, Jos Colton, Roxbury, 1764, map of Hudson River area, river scene 1,000.00

Textile, 23", multicolored print, Sitting Bull, Black Hawk, Oscela . 100.00

WORLD WAR I

Book
History of the 324th Field Artillery, United States Army, TQ Ashburn, George H Doran, NY, 1919, small 8vo, dj, 141 pgs . 30.00
The Price of Our Heritage. In Memory of the Heroic Dead of the 168 Infantry, Winfred E Robb, Des Moines, IA 1919, large 8vo, plates, 422 pgs ... 35.00

Buckle, US Balloon Corps, emb hot air balloon 25.00

Compass, marked "Made in France" 30.00

Gun Sling, soft leather, 1917, for 03 Springfield 25.00

Map Case, leather, strap, 9 orig tour maps of France 35.00

Medallion, 2½", bronze, soldier crossing battlefield, reverse marked "1917 France 1919," 79th Division map 50.00

Poster, They Are Giving All Will You Send Them Wheat?, 55 x 36", artist Harvey Dunn, 1918, litho by W F Power Co, NY, sponsored by US Food Adm, soldiers going over top in battle, minor edge tears 50.00

Trench Flashlight and Note Pad, German, black tin container, orig pad and pencil 40.00

Tunic and Trousers, gabardine, pinback, Air Corps and US discs 60.00

WORLD WAR II

Belt and Buckle, German Luftwaffe, silver wash on brass, 1942 .... 35.00
Bookends, pr, Iwo Jima, brass, hand crafted, 1940s 50.00
Cartograph, 1944 map depicting 42nd Inf. Rainbow Div, Mission of the Rainbow, colorful, folds, 25½ x 19½" 90.00
Flag, New Zealand PT boat, printed on blue cotton 35.00
Flask, 6" h, blown glass, amethyst, General MacArthur bust portrait, emb "Keep Them Flying," reverse with large "V," flags, script "God Bless America," 1942 ... 95.00
Medal, Order of the Rising Sun, 7th Class, red and green enameling on presentation case, lapel ribbon 60.00
Photograph, 76th Infantry, 1st Platoon, Camp Roberts 20.00
Pilot's Wings, breast badge, snap–on back 25.00
Range Indicator, 1944, US Navy AA, Bakelite paddle shaped viewer, AC Gilbert Co 225.00
Tunic, Marine Corps, dress blue, brass buttons, red piped shoulder boards 25.00
Wound Badge, German, silver, orig box, unissued 55.00

KOREA

Jacket, Sergeant's OD, Ike style, pile lined cap with ear flaps ... 15.00
Lead Soldiers, 1", models of American Army of Korean War period, flag bearer, trooper with tommy gun, rifleman, set of 18 .... 15.00
Photo Album, 11 x 15", inscribed "Soul Patrol, Co B 2nd BN 23rd Inf, APW," 2nd Division insignia, photos of troops, guard duty, USO 25.00

VIETNAM

Beret, black, S. Vietnam Special Forces, silvered device on plaque, sword and wreath, maker's tag 40.00
Helmet, Navy, patrol pilot's, lining, earphones, chin strap, white fiberglass body, decal on gold visor, dated 8–65 .... 20.00
Medal, US Service, bronze battle star, on ribbon 10.00

MILK GLASS

History: Opaque white glass attained its greatest popularity at the end of the 19th century. American glass manufacturers made opaque white tablewares as a substitute for costly European china and glass. Other opaque colors, e.g., blue and green, were made. As the Edwardian era began, milk glass expanded into the novelty field.

The surge of popularity in milk glass subsided after World War I. However, milk glass continues to be made in the 20th century. Some modern products are reissues and reproductions of early forms. This presents a significant problem for collectors, although it is partially obviated by patent dates or company markings on the originals and by the telltale signs of age.

Collectors favor milk glass from the pre–World War I era, especially animal covered dishes. The most prolific manufacturers of these animal covers were Atterbury, Challinor–Taylor, Flaccus, and McKee.

References: E. McCamley Belknap, *Milk Glass,* Crown Publishers, 1949, out–of–print; Regis F. and Mary F. Ferson, *Today's Prices For Yesterday's Milk Glass,* privately printed, 1985; Regis F. and Mary F. Ferson, *Yesterday's Milk Glass Today,* published by authors, 1981; Myrna and Bob Garrison, *Imperial's Vintage Milk Glass,* published by authors, 1992; Everett Grist, *Covered Animal Dishes,* Collector Books, 1988, 1993 value update; Lorraine Kovar, *Westmoreland Glass, 1950–1984,* Antique Publications, 1991; Lorraine Kovar, *Westmoreland Glass, 1950–1984, Volume II,* Antique Publications, 1991; S. T. Millard, *Opaque Glass,* Wallace–Homestead, 1975, 4th edition, out–of–print; Betty and Bill Newbound, *Collector's Encyclopedia of Milk Glass,* Collector Books, 1994.

Collectors' Club: National Milk Glass

Collectors Society, 46 Almond Dr., Hershey, PA 17033.

Museum: Houston Antique Museum, Chattanooga, TN.

Notes: There are many so–called McKee animal covered dishes. Caution must be exercised in evaluating pieces because some authentic covers were not signed. Further, many factories have made, and many still are making, split rib bases with McKee–like animal covers or with different animal covers. There also is disagreement among collectors on the issue of flared vs. unflared bases. The prices for McKee pieces as given are for authentic items with either the cover or base signed.

Bust, Lincoln, satinized, emb "Centennial Exhibition, Gillinder & Sons," 6″ h, $145.00.

Animal Cov Dish
Fish, entwined cov, dated	195.00
Owl, split rib base, sgd "McKee"	225.00

Berry Set, Fern, master bowl, five sauces 100.00

Bottle
Father's, 11½″ h, ⅘ quart, baby bottle shape	110.00
Octopus, 4½″ h, no closure . . .	375.00

Bust, Dewey, satinized, one button damaged 120.00

Butter Dish, cov
Ribs, blue	50.00
Versailles, orig fired–on flowers and scrolls	40.00

Candlestick, mermaid, Portlieux . 175.00

Celery Vase, 8⅝″ h, Jeweled pattern, blue 95.00

Compote
Atlas, open edge	75.00
C–Scroll	65.00
Jenny Lind	90.00
Open Hand, Atterbury	85.00
Rib and Scroll	60.00
Roses and Bows, 12″ d	140.00

Cracker Jar, cov, Forget–Me–Not pattern, chartreuse 200.00

Creamer, Roman Cross 40.00

Creamer and Sugar, C–Scroll . . . 65.00

Dresser Bottle
Fired–on coaching scene, price for pr	65.00
Medallion and Scroll, blue, swirl stopper	40.00

Easel, oval, souvenir of Allentown Fair 30.00

Eggcup
Basketweave, double side, patent date	25.00
Blackberry	25.00

Flask
Elk's Tooth	90.00

Eye Opener
Large	90.00
Small	75.00
Idaho Spud, 4¾″ h, dated 1893	200.00
Night Cap, 4″ h, no closure . . .	110.00

Fruit Jar, steer's head, screw lid, Flaccus 375.00

Goblet, Blackberry 30.00

Hatchet, souvenir, 6½″ l, price for pair 25.00

Honey Dish, Blackberry 20.00

Jar, cov, eagle 120.00

Lamp, Goddess of Liberty 325.00

Medication Lamp, Vapo Cresoline, milk glass hurricane globe 40.00

Miniature, mug, Liberty Bell, emb on front and back, dated 1771–1876 . . . . 110.00

Mug, Bird in Cattails, handle 45.00

Perfume Bottle, Gibson Girl, figural 100.00

Pitcher, 7½″ h, blown, applied handle, bird and flower fired–on dec, gold trim 225.00

Relish Scoop, Palmette 27.50

Salt and Pepper Shaker
Florette, blue, orig top	28.00
Medallion Sprig, white, orig top, price for pr	65.00

Salt, open, basket 30.00

Spooner, Melon with Leaf and Net,
decorated, patent date **85.00**
Syrup
    Alba Blossom **90.00**
    Fleur–de–Lis **115.00**
    Hobnail, applied handle **135.00**
    Iris, gold trim **135.00**
    Tree of Life, poor lid **90.00**
Table Set, Blackberry, price for
four piece set **150.00**
Tile, 5⅞" sq, owl, raised design,
fired–on **55.00**
Tumbler, Royal Oak, Northwood,
orig fired–on paint, green banding **45.00**
Tureen, 10½ x 6¾", Grape, three
feet **125.00**
Vase, horse's head, handles **25.00**
Water Set, C–Scroll, tankard
pitcher, six tumblers **225.00**

MILLEFIORI

History: Millefiori (thousand flowers) is
an ornamental glass composed of bundles
of colored glass rods fused to become
canes. The canes were pulled while still
ductile to the desired length, sliced, arranged in a pattern and again fused together. The Egyptians developed this technique in the first century B.C.; it was revived
in the 1880s.

Reproduction Alert: Millefiori items,
such as paperweights, cruets, toothpicks,
etc., are being made by many modern companies.

Bowl, 2" d, pink, green, and white
canes, applied handles **35.00**
Cup and Saucer, 2½" h, 2" d, multicolored, angular handle **45.00**
Cruet, faceted stopper, frosted
handle **70.00**
Goblet, 7½" h, clear stem and
base **175.00**
Lamp, 14" h, boudoir, 19th C, price
for pair **200.00**
Paperweight
    Baccarat, 3½" d, patterned,
    large red and white central
    cane, garland of green and
    white stardust canes, two dark
    blue trefoil garland canes,
    white and red stardust canes **240.00**

**Miniature Lamp, orange and
ochre canes, brass trim, electrified, 12" h, $600.00.**

    Clichy, 1½" d, concentric, central
    pink cane in blue, yellow, and
    white shaded circles, five large
    pink and white roses outer gar-
    land alternating with green and
    pink pairs of canes **120.00**
    New England, 3" d, eight colored
    center clustered canes, outer
    band of canes, white entwined
    threads **75.00**
Pitcher, 4⅞" h **55.00**
Sugar, cov, 3½" d, 4" h, cobalt
blue, white flowers **110.00**
Toothpick Holder, ruffled top,
c1890 .... **145.00**
Vase, 5½" h, purple bands, white
oval lines, white bands, red flowers with yellow centers **150.00**

MINIATURE LAMPS

History: Miniature oil and kerosene
lamps, often called "night lamps," are di-
minutive replicas of larger lamps. Simple
and utilitarian in design, miniature lamps
found a place in the parlor (as "courting"
lamps), hallway, children's rooms, and sick-
rooms.

    Miniature lamps are found in many glass
types from amberina to satin glass. Miniature lamps measure 2½ to 12 inches in
height with the principle parts being the

base, collar, burner, chimney, and shade. In 1877 both L. J. Atwood and L. H. Olmsted patented burners for miniature lamps. Their burners made the lamps into a popular household accessory.

Study a lamp carefully to make certain all parts are original; married pieces are common. Reproductions abound.

References: Frank R. & Ruth E. Smith, *Miniature Lamps,* Schiffer Publishing, 1981; Ruth E. Smith, *Miniature Lamps–II,* Schiffer Publishing, 1982; John F. Solverson, *Those Fascinating Little Lamps: Miniature Lamps and Their Values,* Antique Publications, 1988, includes prices for Smith numbers.

Collectors' Club: Night Light, 38619 Wakefield Ct., Northville, MI 48167.

Note: The numbers given below refer to the figure numbers found in the Smith books.

SI-214, milk glass, painted red, $125.00.

SI–II, milk glass, swirled pattern, green and blue floral dec, hornet burner, 8½" h **110.00**
SI–III, Artichoke, milk glass, yellow and green painted trim, nutmeg burner, 8" h **150.00**
SI–23, Time Lamp, clear, green beehive shade, 6¾" h **175.00**
SI–47, paneled, blue, acorn burner, 3½" h **150.00**
SI–50, Log Cabin, milk glass, hornet burner, emb patent date, 3¾" h **575.00**

SI–51, amber, figural, shoe, hornet burner, emb patent date, 3" h . . **800.00**
SI–52, blue, applied match holder, nutmeg burner, 7¾" h **750.00**
SI–166, clear, Greek Key pattern, acorn burner, 8½" h **65.00**
SI–240, Defender, milk glass, pale blue, nutmeg burner, 8½" h . . . **200.00**
SI–267, milk glass, blue Delft dec, nutmeg burner, Pairpoint Glass Co, 8½" h **500.00**
SI–287, Tulip, milk glass, pink and green painted dec, nutmeg burner, 8½" h **400.00**
SI–294, spatter glass, Swirl pattern, pale blue, off–white flecks, nutmeg burner, 6¾" h **400.00**
SI–374, pink cased, hornet burner, 8½" h **400.00**
SI–389, satin, pink cased, melon ribbed base, pansy dec shade, nutmeg burner, 6¾" h **400.00**
SI–398, satin, red, nutmeg burner, 8¾" h **450.00**
SI–432, Twinkle, bluish–green, acorn burner, 7" h **110.00**
SI–442, cranberry glass, hornet burner, 9" h **275.00**
SI–479, ribbed swirl pattern, amber, nutmeg burner, 8" h **450.00**
SI–482, Daisy & Cube pattern, emb, clear, nutmeg burner, 8" h **225.00**
SI–510, cranberry opalescent, clear base, nutmeg burner, 7½" h **3,400.00**
SI–524, blue opalescent, applied clear feet, foreign burner, 7" h . **4,000.00**
SI–529, cased, pink and white candy stripe, white lining, applied feet, foreign burner, 8" h . **3,750.00**
SI–531, satin, amber, cut velvet diamond pattern, clear feet, acorn burner, 7½" h **750.00**
SI–538, opalescent, pink, applied green leaves and feet, nutmeg burner, 8¼" h **2,250.00**
SI–543, amber and honey swirl pattern, amber pedestal, nutmeg burner, 9" h **3,750.00**
SI–567, light apple green **2,425.00**
SII–310, clear glass base, milk glass beehive shade, 8" h **175.00**
SII–403, pink cased, melon ribbed

base, rose petal shade, nutmeg
burner, 7" h **550.00**
SII–548, clear, swirled pattern,
ruby and white spatter, nutmeg
burner, 8¼" h **1,750.00**

MINIATURES

History: There are three sizes of miniatures: doll house scale (ranging from ½" to
1"), sample size, and child's size. Since
most earlier material is in museums or extremely expensive, the most common examples are 20th century.

Many mediums were used for miniatures:
silver, copper, tin, wood, glass, and ivory.
Even books were printed in miniature.
Prices are broad ranged, depending on
scarcity and quality of workmanship.

The collecting of miniatures dates back
to the 18th century. It remains one of the
world's leading hobbies.

References: Caroline Clifton–Mogg, *The
Dollhouse Sourcebook,* Abbeville Press,
1993; Nora Earnshaw, *Collecting Dolls'
Houses and Miniatures,* Pincushion Press,
1993; Caroline Hamilton, *Decorative Dollhouses,* Clarkson Potter, 1990; Flora Gill
Jacobs, *Dolls Houses in America: Historic
Preservation in Miniature,* Charles Scribner's Sons, 1974; Flora Gill Jacobs, *History
of Dolls Houses,* Charles Scribner's Sons;
Constance Eileen King, *Dolls and Doll
Houses,* Hamlyn, 1989; Eva Stille, *Doll
Kitchens, 1800–1980,* Schiffer Publishing,
1988; Margaret Towner, *Dollhouse Furniture,* Courage Books, Running Press, 1993;
Von Wilckens, *Mansions in Miniature,* Tuttle, out of print.

Periodicals: *Doll Castle News,* PO Box
247, Washington, NJ 07882; *Miniature Collector,* PO Box 631, Boiling Springs, PA
17007; *Miniature Collector,* Scott Publications, 30595 Eight Mile Rd., Livonia, MI
48152; *Miniature Industry Assoc. of America Member News,* 2270 Jacquelyn Dr.,
Madison, WI 53711; *Miniatures Showcase,*
21027 Crossroads Circle, PO Box 1612,
Waukesha, WI 53187; *Nutshell News,*
21027 Crossroads Circle, PO Box 1612,
Waukesha, WI 53187.

Collectors' Clubs: International Guild
Miniature Artisans, PO Box 71, Bridgeport,

NY 18080; National Association of Miniature Enthusiasts, PO Box 69, Carmel, IN
46032.

Museums: Margaret Woodbury Strong
Museum, Rochester, NY; Mildred Mahoney
Jubilee Doll House Museum, Fort Erie,
Canada; Museums at Stony Brook, Stony
Brook, NY; Toy and Miniature Museum of
Kansas City, Kansas City, MO; Toy Museum
of Atlanta, Atlanta, GA; Washington Dolls'
House and Toy Museum, Washington, DC.

Additional Listings: See Doll House
Furnishings in *Warman's Americana & Collectibles* for more examples.

**Clock, mantel type, cast metal,
painted gold, white clock face, Ty-
nietoy, 1¹⁄₁₆" h, 1" w, $25.00.**

CHILD'S SIZE

Bedroom Suite, Constructivist, Jan
Pieter, Dirk Van Gelder, painted
plywood, dressing table with mirror, bedside table, cradle, and
wardrobe, painted cream with
mustard and green details,
c1920–30, 9⅝" h wardrobe . . .**2,475.00**
Blanket Chest
Chippendale, PA, probably Lancaster or Chester County, figured walnut, molded rect top,
well with paper lined till, plain
case, ogee bracket feet,
1770–90, 19" w, 10½" d, 11½"
h **5,175.00**
New England, painted and dec,
rect top with applied moldings,

single compartment case, molded base, shaped skirt, bracket feet, sepia and mustard grain painted dec, c1825, 15" w, 7¾" d, 10" h **5,520.00**

Bureau, Federal, New England, mahogany, rect molded top, two small drawers over three long drawers, large wood knobs, brass escutcheons, rope turned columns, c1825, 16½" w, 8½" d, 18" h **1,500.00**

Chair, American, three molded vertical slats, turned stiles, shaped arm supports, rush seat, turned legs, double stretchers, painted and dec, 19th C, 11¼" h   **415.00**

Chaise Lounge, late Victorian, upholstered, 31" l **825.00**

Chest of Drawers
George II, walnut, rect top, scalloped front, two conforming drawers, ball feet, second quarter 18th C, 10½" w **1,035.00**
Hepplewhite, cherry, inlaid, four dovetailed drawers, 19¾" w, 11¾" d, 22½" h **250.00**
Regency, inlaid mahogany, bow front, three short over three long graduated drawers, turned feet, restored, c1810, 12¼" w, 5½" d, 8¼" h **925.00**
Sheraton, cherry and curly maple, five dovetailed drawers with applied edge beading, paneled ends, turned feet, refinished, replaced brass pulls   **775.00**

Chest on Chest, English, mahogany, four drawers, flush base, 14" h **230.00**

Chest on Stand, George I style, inlaid burl walnut, rect top, two short and three long graduated drawers, shaped skirt, cabriole legs, pad feet, 9" w, 5½" d, 12" h **3,165.00**

Commode, Louis XV style, brass mounted mahogany, serpentine marble top, two drawers, down curving feet, mounted with chutes and sabots, 12" w, 6½" d, 9½" h **635.00**

Cupboard, Victorian, maple, two glazed doors over two short and

two long drawers, 19th C, 18½" w, 9½" d, 32" h **450.00**

Desk
Hepplewhite, slant front, cherry, inlaid, dovetailed drawers, 21" w, 14" d, 28¾" h **440.00**
William and Mary, painted pine, rect molded top, int. pigeonholes and small drawers, single long molded drawer, molded base, ball feet, painted red, front foot loose, losses to paint, 13" w, 9¼" d, 14½" h ..**2,530.00**

Dressing Table, walnut, rect top, three hinged compartments, three drawers, tapered rect legs, bun feet, 19th C, 10" h **925.00**

Linen Press, Provincial Victorian, mahogany, two cupboard doors above projecting case with two frieze and three long graduated drawers, ogee bracket feet, 19th C, 24" w, 13" d, 39" h **1,550.00**

Mirror, oval, tilting, oval base with drawer, 6¼" w, 12¾" h **295.00**

Mug, gaudy Staffordshire, floral sprig design, red, green, blue, and black, minor damage, 1⅝" h   **12.00**

Stool, Landis Valley, PA, poplar, dec, rect top, ogee shaped apron, bootjack legs, red, green, and black foliage, flowers, baskets, and tendrils, yellow ground, mid 19th C, 8¾" w, 4" d, 3¾" h **1,725.00**

Swing Glider, wood, two facing bench seats, 24" w, 21" h **60.00**

Table, work, rosewood and fruitwood, rect hinged top, compartmented int., two sliding drawers, sq tapered legs, one handle missing, 10¾" h **490.00**

Tall Chest, Sheraton, American, walnut, rect top, four graduated long drawers, paneled ends, turned feet, c1820, 19¼" h **775.00**

Teapot, cloisonne enamel, globular form, floral design, black ground, 19th C, 2½" h **45.00**

Tea Set, English Staffordshire, teapot, open creamer, cov sugar, and two cups and saucers, floral dec **140.00**

Trunk, Southbridge, MA, area, dome top, rect box, paper lined int., top and sides painted with feathers and swags, red, yellow, and white, black ground, first half 19th C, 20″ w, 10″ d, 8″ h **575.00**

DOLLHOUSE SIZE

Bathroom Set, two toilets, tub, and sink, old china **50.00**
Dining Room Suite, Curtis, cast iron, white lacquer finish, two high backed benches, matching 4¾″ l table with openwork legs, 1936 .... **50.00**
Dresser, light mahogany, two drawers, mirror, 1″ scale **35.00**
Ice Cream Parlor Set, 3½″ round table with twisted wire legs, four matching chairs, heart shaped backs, blue blown glass pitcher with four matching lemonade glasses **100.00**
Living Room Suite, cast iron, sofa and chair, 1″ scale **75.00**
Refrigerator, Arcade, cast iron, white lacquer finish, gray trim, marked "Leonard," 5¾″ h **35.00**
Secretary Desk, Biedermeier, late 19th C, 1″ scale **150.00**
Wringer Washer, Sally Ann, cast iron, working rubber wringers, c1920 .... **50.00**

SALESMAN'S SAMPLES

Beer Cooler, Monarch, Washington, MO, wood, copper, and metal, working model, notched top, copper well with two spigots, small hinged refrigerator door, two hinged cooler doors, holds orig saleman's client cards, labeled "Washington Planing Mill, Store and Office Fixtures, Any Kinds of Woodwork, Washington, MO," early 20th C, 29¼″ w, 15½″ h **9,900.00**
Broom Rack, tin, three long handled brooms, two short brushes, worn green paint, bristles and brushes very worn, 8½″ h **55.00**
Bureau, Empire, mahogany, sleigh front, five drawer, 12″ w, 7″ d, 11″ h **265.00**

Casket, infant's, curly maple, possibly refinished, 5″ l **465.00**
Chair
Folding, wood, c1875 .... **50.00**
Victorian, walnut, spindle back, 9″ h **155.00**
Corset, lady's, 19th C, 8″ h **225.00**
Decoy, mallard
Cork body, unknown maker, price for pr **135.00**
Papier–Mache, J C Higgins Co **40.00**
Fire Bucket, English, emb coat of arms dec **110.00**
Fireplace, Batchelder, square tiles, blue, brown, and tan, some tiles with stylized birds, imp mark, 19 x 26 x 5½″ 1,325.00
Goblet, New England, engraved, demonstrates various script used on engraved pcs, faceted hollow stem, clear, 1860s, 6½″ h **470.00**
Ladder, painter's, wood, c1875 .. **40.00**
Manny Reaper, John Manny, Worcester, MA, working model, wood and brass, rect wood seat and arm blade control levers, turning paddle reaper, mower blades, one spoked and one solid wheel, with orig salesman's papers, c1850, 16″ l, 8½″ h, repair and restoration to frame ..**2,475.00**
Parka, fur, minor wear, price for pair, 10½″ and 14″ l **75.00**
Printing Press, cast iron, mounted on wood base, working model, operating gears, 4 x 4½ x 5″ .. **825.00**
Shoes, pr, three part leather, leather soles, wood heels, 4″ l . **175.00**
Table, Centennial style, drop leaf, walnut and pine, 1874 .... **65.00**

MINTON CHINA

History: In 1793 Thomas Minton and others formed a partnership and built a small pottery at Stoke–on–Trent, Staffordshire, England. Production began in 1798 with blue printed earthenware, mostly in the Willow pattern. In 1798 cream colored earthenware and bone china were introduced.

A wide range of styles and wares was produced. Minton introduced porcelain figures in 1826, Parian wares in 1846, encaustic tiles in the late 1840s, and Majolica wares in 1850. Many famous designers and artists in the English pottery industry worked for Minton.

Many early pieces are unmarked or have a Sevres–type marking. The "ermine" mark was used in the early 19th century. Date codes can be found on tableware and Majolica. Between 1873 and 1911 a small globe signed "Minton" with a crown on top was used.

In 1883 the modern company was formed and called Mintons Limited. The "s" was dropped in 1968. Minton still produces bone china tablewares and some ornamental pieces.

References: Paul Atterbury and Maureen Batkin, *The Dictionary of Minton,* Antique Collectors' Club; Susan and Al Bagdade, *Warman's English & Continental Pottery & Porcelain, Second Edition,* Wallace–Homestead, 1991; Joan Jones, *Minton: The First Two Hundred Years of Design and Production,* Swan Hill, 1993.

Bowl, 12½" d, floral reserves, cobalt blue ground, gold trim, c1810 ....1,400.00
Bulb Planter, 10¾" l, majolica, emb brown fence, green leaves, turquoise lining, marked 125.00
Candlestick, 9" h, majolica, figural, three monkeys, mustard green, yellow glaze 225.00
Compote, 8½" d, 3" h, white, red roses, marked 100.00
Demitasse Cup and Saucer, Indian Tree pattern, imp mark 35.00
Dessert Plate, blue and gold leaf borders, one plate repaired, price for set of 16 .... 55.00
Dinner Service
87 pcs, Dainty Sprays pattern, service for 12 and 3 serving pcs 650.00

101 pcs, Ancestral pattern, bread and butter, salad, and dinner plates, bowls, cups and saucers, platters, 3 pc tea service, and cov serving dish, 20th C 925.00
103 pcs, Gold Band, plates, tea cups, demitasse cups, bouillon cups, and other cups and saucers 685.00
Dresser Set, 12" l, 9" w tray, cov box, and ring tree, gold and green flowers, white ground, price for 3 pc set 200.00
Ewer, 8½" h, turquoise, raised putti holding swags leading to Neptune seated under spout, mermaid handle, c1868 .... 600.00
Figure
16" h, Ariadne on Panther, 1864 600.00
21½" h, magpies, majolica, printed marks, price for pr ... 520.00
Flask, 11" h, pate–sur–pate, moon shape, one with cow, frog, and pussy willows, other with rabbit, turtle, cherubs, and urns, gilt dec, price for pr 4,150.00
Jug, 6¼" h, applied hops and vine dec, 1848 .... 250.00
Marmalade Jar, butterflies, blue ground, c1920 .... 35.00
Pitcher, 12¾" h, majolica, molded

Tray, multicolored florals, gold and cobalt blue border, white center ground, gold accents, c1840, marked "Felspar Porcelain," 10" l, $135.00.

castle tower body, raised medieval figures, vine work border and handle, hinged lid with jester finial, imp mark, c1874 ...... **630.00**
Plate, dinner, Vermont pattern ... **25.00**
Pot, 6¾" h, majolica, frog form, grotesque, three legs, green glaze, imp mark, price for pr ... **1,100.00**
Service Plate
Set of 12, cream and gold band borders **350.00**
Set of 17, cobalt blue and gilt encrusted borders **2,100.00**
Set of 18, gold and mauve band borders **635.00**
Soup and Entree Plate, set of 16, floral borders and centers, gold edge **300.00**
Tea Set, teapot, creamer, and sugar, Cockatrice pattern **350.00**
Tile, 6" sq, Taming of the Shrew . **65.00**
Vase
5½" h, bulbous, green, white cameo, handled **90.00**
11" h, burnt amber, pink, and blue flowers, marked, c1875 . **150.00**
14¾" h, cov, elaborate gold trim, cream glaze, scroll feet and ends, openwork top and cov . **1,250.00**
Vegetable Tureen, cov, 11½" l, peach enamel, gilt trim, verse "All For The Best," 19th C **175.00**
Washbowl and Pitcher, amethyst, ruby, and yellow floral dec **150.00**

pink mug decorated with green ribbed bands. Most forms of mocha are hollow, e.g., mugs, jugs, bowls, and shakers.

English potters made the vast majority of the pieces. Marked pieces are extremely rare. Collectors group the ware into three chronological periods: 1780–1820, 1820–1840, and 1840–1880.

References: Susan and Al Bagdade, *Warman's English & Continental Pottery & Porcelain, Second Edition,* Wallace–Homestead, 1991; Dana G. Morykan and Harry L. Rinker, *Warman's Country Antiques & Collectibles, Second Edition* Wallace–Homestead, 1994.

Reproduction Alert.

Mug, worm and cat's eye, shades of brown, age crack, 6" h, $1,225.00.

MOCHA

History: Mocha decoration usually is found on utilitarian creamware and stoneware pieces and is produced through a simple chemical action. A color pigment of brown, blue, green, or black is made acidic by an infusion of tobacco or hops. When the acidic colorant is applied in blobs to an alkaline ground, it reacts by spreading in feathery, sea–plantlike designs. This type of decoration usually is supplemented with bands of light colored slip.

Types of decoration vary greatly, from those done in a combination of motifs, such as "Cat's Eye" and "Earthworm," to a plain

Bowl
6" d, earthworm dec, banded, some discoloration **550.00**
7¼" d, brown, tan, and white double spiral earthworm dec, bluish–gray band with blue stripe **425.00**
9¾" d, tan, white, and dark brown cat's–eye and earthworm dec, brown and blue bands, dark brown stripes ... **775.00**
Caster, 5½" h, early 19th C **435.00**
Creamer, 3¾" h, white, black stripes, wide blue bands **150.00**
Cup and Saucer, marbleized, black and white, geometric border, emb white ribbed band ... **425.00**

Mug
4½" h, seaweed dec, narrow
stripes, English, early 19th C,
imperfections 875.00
6¼" h, marbleized brown and
pumpkin ground, applied swag
design, England, early 19th C 750.00
Pitcher
6½" h, cat's–eye dec, banded,
imperfections 1,210.00
7" h, chocolate brown band with
white dec, blue, orange, and
brown stripes, emb leaf handle 350.00
8" h, milk, cat's–eye and earthworm dec 800.00
9¾" h, blue seaweed dec, white
slip band, East Liverpool, OH 450.00
Salt, 3" d, white, blue bands, gray–
green stripes 40.00
Salt and Pepper Shakers, pr
Blue and white, black stripes .. 140.00
Blue and white dec 85.00
Shaker
3¼" h, emb checkerboard dec,
brown, orange, and green ... 425.00
4¼" h, black and white wavy
lines on blue, dome top 175.00
4⅝" h, brown, white, and black
cat's–eye and earthworm dec,
emb black, white, and blue
stripes 450.00
Stein, 7⅞" h, domed pewter lid,
earthworm dec, blue ground,
dark brown bands, name in
script, dated 1854 .... 550.00
Tureen, cov, 8½" l, 7" w, earthworm dec, emb green rim, gray–
green band, dark brown stripes,
ring handles 1,225.00
Wastebowl, 4⅝ x 2⅔", emb green
rim, blue band, black stripes ... 135.00

MONART GLASS

History: Monart glass is a heavy, simple–
shaped art glass in which colored enamels
are suspended in the glass during the
glassmaking process. This technique was
originally developed by the Ysart family in
Spain in 1923. John Moncrief, a Scottish
glassmaker, discovered the glass while va-
cationing in Spain, recognized the beauty

and potential market, and began production
in his Perth glassworks in 1924.

The name "Monart" is derived from the
surnames Moncrief and Ysart. Two types of
Monart were manufactured: a "commercial"
line, which incorporated colored enamels
and a touch of aventurine in crystal, and the
"art" line in which the suspended enamels
formed designs such as feathers or scrolls.
Monart glass, in most instances, is not
marked. The factory used paper labels.

**Vase, green pedestal, brown
shading to clear to green rim, 8½"
h, $60.00.**

Bowl
9" d, Aventurine, blue, mottled
brown, and goldstone, pebbled 135.00
10½" d, 4¾" h, white, gray
crackle, yellow and green
flecks, oxblood red base and
rim 150.00
Candlesticks, pr, 3" h, mottled blue
shading to lavender 75.00
Urn, 7" h, clear, yellow lacy inclusions and bubbles 165.00
Vase
8½" h, goldstone shading to
clear, Scottish Cluthra 150.00
9" h, bulbous ovoid form, red
ground, white blue swirl dec,
orig paper label 125.00
9¼" h, brilliant opaque red, overlaid in clear crystal, crackled
black int. dec, circular label

"Moncrieff Scotland V.SA.91,"
1930s **385.00**

MONT JOYE GLASS

History: Mont Joye is a type of glass produced by Saint–Hilaire, Touvier, de Varreaux & Company at their glassworks in Pantin, France. Most pieces were lightly acid etched to give them a frosted appearance and decorated with enameled floral decorations. All pieces listed are frosted, unless otherwise noted.

Console Set, 3 pcs, two 11¾" h vases and matching 10" d center bowl, translucent red crystal, acid cut, enamel dec, cameo cut Art Nouveau scrolling borders with gilt embellishments, vases with columbine motif, bowl with poppy pods and blossoms, Mont Joye Pantin medallion mark on bowl **2,975.00**
Vase
   5½" h, open oval vessel, acid etched, bright green cameo cut border design with oak leaves, branches, and acorns, gold and silver enameled frieze, Mont Joye medallion mark on base **775.00**
   7¾" h, baluster shape, flowers and leaves dec, iced glass ground, Mont Joye shield mark **225.00**
   10" h, ribbed molded body, opalescent, polychrome enamel blossom and scrolling ribbon dec, stamp on base **220.00**
   10¼" h, pr, flared trumpet form, etched pale green, naturalistic applied twig handles, enameled pink and yellow snap dragons dec, gilt embellishments, minor chip **220.00**
   11½" h, conical trumpet form, aquamarine, rough textured etched surface, gilt and enameled long stemmed aster blossoms, Mont Joye shield mark on base **470.00**
   19" h, cameo, deep amethyst, green and gold carved and

enameled floral dec, gold cut floral top border, sgd **1,100.00**

MOORCROFT

History: William Moorcroft was first employed as a potter by James Macintyre & Co., Ltd. of Burslem in 1897. He established the Moorcroft pottery in 1913. The company initially used an impressed mark, "Moorcroft, Burslem"; a signature mark, "W. Moorcroft," followed.

The majority of the art pottery wares were hand thrown, resulting in a great variation among similarly styled pieces. Color and marks are keys to determining age.

Walker, William's son, continued the business upon his father's death and made the same style wares. Modern pieces are marked simply "Moorcroft" with export pieces also marked "Made in England."

References: Susan and Al Bagdade, *Warman's English & Continental Pottery & Porcelain, Second Edition,* Wallace–Homestead, 1991; Frances Salmon, *Collecting Moorcroft,* Kevin Francis Publishing, 1994.

Bowl
   7½" d, blue ground, florals **130.00**
   8½" d, Florian ware, yellow and green poppies, blue ground, printed mark, sgd "W Moorcroft, des," c1898 . . . . **675.00**
Bulb Bowl, 6½" d, white and purple Narcissus, dark blue and green ground, "Potter to the Queen" mark **130.00**
Candlesticks, pr, 6½" h, flambe, trees motif **475.00**
Compote, 7½ x 5½", Cornflower, mottled green ground, marked "W Moorcroft" **500.00**
Dish, 3¾" d, pink hibiscus dec, cobalt blue glaze **30.00**
Ginger Jar, 7" h, marked "Walter Moorcroft, 1960" **100.00**
Goblet, 5¾" h, multicolored

panels, white ground, gilt trim,
sgd "MacIntyre" **525.00**
Jardiniere, 7" h, cylindrical, ftd,
pink and purple poppies, blue
ground, imp and painted marks,
price for pair **275.00**
Lamp, 10½" h, fruit and leaves
flambe, 1928–34 . . . .**1,250.00**
Match Holder, 2¾" h, pink thistle
flowers, mottled green ground,
coat of arms, MacIntyre mark,
green painted initials "WM,"
printed "Redley Hall," c1897 . . **325.00**
Miniature, vase, 2" h, green
ground anemone dec **135.00**
Plate, 10" d, Reeds at Sunset,
1987 . . . . **50.00**
Teapot, 6¼" h, blue luster, individ-
ual size **95.00**

**Vase, Fresia pattern, blue, mus-
tard, and dark red florals, mustard
ground, blue int., c1935, signature
mark, 10½" h, $1,950.00.**

Vase
3½" h, 4" w, pansy dec, c1920 . **295.00**
5" h, pink and yellow hibiscus
dec, blue and green glaze . . . **100.00**
5½" h, flared, 18th C pattern . . **850.00**
6¼" h, blue, floral dec, imp mark,
c1945 . . . . **175.00**
8¾" h, waisted cylindrical, blos-
soming prunus, brilliant red
glaze, incised signature "W
Moorcroft" **750.00**

MORIAGE, JAPANESE

History: Moriage refers to applied clay
(slip) relief motifs and decorations used on
certain classes of Japanese pottery and
porcelain.

This decorating was done by three methods: 1) handrolling and shaping, which was
applied by hand to the biscuit in one or more
layers—the design and effect required determined thickness and shape; 2) tubing or
slip trailing, which applied decoration from
a tube, like decorating a cake; and 3) hak-
eme which is reducing the slip to a liquid
and decorating the object with a brush.
Color was applied either before or after the
process.

**Vase, green, rose coralene, all-
over raised gold dec, marked "Kin
& Am, U. S. Pat. Feb 9, 1909, Japan," 6½" h, $175.00.**

Bowl, 7½" d, green, floral center,
intricate white slip work, scal-
loped edge, ftd **145.00**
Floor Vase
44" h, satsuma, ovoid form, separate base, moriage figural
and floral dec, sgd, late 19th
C, rim ground, neck and base
cracks **550.00**
48" h, satsuma, baluster body,
scalloped rim, applied atten-
uated roosters and ribbons,
scenes of deities in reserve
ringed by multicolored enameled moriage floral designs,
20th C **1,100.00**

Hatpin Holder, 4¾" h, green beading, red flowers 60.00

Incense Burner, 3" h, gray, slip dragon, finial, gold foo dog handles 25.00

Jam Jar, cov, underplate, two panels, gold and magenta roses, green moriage, one bead missing on saucer 435.00

Pitcher, 6" h, pink on white, floral design, green slip netting 85.00

Rose Bowl, 5¾" h, turquoise and white slip work, jeweled, sgd . . 275.00

Box, clear green ground, enameled floral motif, gilded leaf banding, ftd, script sgd "Moser," 3" h, 4" d, $120.00.

MOSER GLASS

History: Ludwig Moser (1833–1916) founded his polishing and engraving workshop in 1857 in Karlsbad (Karlovy Vary), Czechoslovakia. He employed many famous glass designers, e.g., Johann Hoffmann, Josef Urban, and Rudolf Miller. In 1900 Moser and his sons, Rudolf and Gustav, incorporated Ludwig Moser & Söhne.

Moser art glass included clear pieces with inserted blobs of colored glass, cut colored glass with classical scenes, cameo glass, and intaglio cut. Many inexpensive enameled pieces also were made.

In 1922 Leo and Richard Moser bought Meyr's Neffe, their biggest Bohemian rival in art glass. Moser executed many pieces for the Wiener Werkstätte in the 1920s. The Moser glass factory continues to produce new items.

References: Gary Baldwin and Lee Carno, *Moser—Artistry In Glass: 1857–1938,* Antique Publications, 1988; Mural K. Charon and John Mareska, *Ludvik Moser, King of Glass: A Treasure Chest of Photographs And History,* published by author, 1984.

Basket, 5½" h, green malachite, molded cherubs dec, price for pair 800.00

Bowl, 7¼" d, pink opalescent, multicolored enameled oak leaves, applied luster acorns, sgd **1,100.00**

Cologne Bottle
6" h, 2½" d, amethyst to clear, gold garlands, scrolls, dots, and bands, matching dec amethyst bubble stopper 230.00

7¾" h, 3½" d, deep amethyst, deeply intaglio cut flowers and leaves, cut panels, matching bubble stopper with amethyst center and intaglio cut flowers, marked "Moser Karlsbad" on base 810.00

Condiment Set, salt, pepper, and mustard, Wilcox frame, figural swan feet and center handle . . 135.00

Cordial, 2¾" h, 1¼" d, deep cranberry, gold and enamel dec . . . 45.00

Cruet, 7¾" h, 4⅝" d, amethyst shading to clear, gold band with dot florals, flattened bulbous shape, applied clear handle, matching amethyst bubble stopper 215.00

Cup, 2¾" h, amber and clear, applied crimson wheel cut poppy cabochon, engraved leafy stems and flowers 255.00

Cup and Saucer, emerald green, gold and enamel dec 75.00

Decanter, 10½" h, elaborate gold and enameled floral dec 425.00

Jewel Box, 5" l, 5" h, cranberry, enamel birds and floral dec, brass mounts and handles, key **1,400.00**

Perfume Bottle
5" h, 2" d, amethyst to clear, gold

garlands, dots, and bands, matching dec amethyst bubble stopper, marked on base **230.00**

5½" h, cane cut, gold gilt highlights, orig stopper, sgd "Moser" **175.00**

Pitcher, 8¼" h, amber, multicolored pastel enameled flowers, leaves, and bird in flight, gold highlights, sapphire blue handle, trim, eight prunts, and four feet **275.00**

Pokal, 10½" h, amber, couple in costume **400.00**

Tazza, 4¾ x 5¾", deep cobalt blue, raised gold pattern and flower dec **400.00**

Tumbler, 5¼" h, lead crystal, gilded floral top band, Cut Diamond Nailhead pattern body, band of cut ovals, vertical notches, and ovals, sgd **145.00**

Vase

4⅞" h, green malachite, molded nude women under grapevine design **230.00**

5" h, crackle, enameled fish and seaweed **225.00**

5¾" h, pale aqua, enameled flowers and bird dec, sgd "Moser," artist sgd "Royo" ... **310.00**

6½" h, bud, green shaded to clear, gold vine and flowers .. **70.00**

7" h, clear and deep violet, incised oval "Moser Karlsbad" . **285.00**

9" h, cranberry ground, allover pastel enamel dec, large gold panels at center and sides .. **450.00**

10" h, bulbous base, ruffled flared top, clear, spattered gold edge, tiny gold encrusted flowers, petaled base, polished pontil, etched "722" ... **145.00**

12" h, bulbous, white cut back to light blue body, multicolored floral dec, gold trim **300.00**

16" h, stick, green, pink and blue enameled florals, gold trim .. **500.00**

MOSS ROSE PATTERN CHINA

History: Several English potteries manufactured china with a Moss Rose pattern in the mid–1800s. Knowles, Taylor and Knowles, an American firm, began production of a Moss Rose pattern in the 1880s.

The moss rose was a common garden flower grown in English gardens. When American consumers tired of English china with Oriental themes, they purchased the Moss Rose pattern as a substitute.

Plate, 10" d, $12.00.

Butter Dish, 6½" d, Meakin, missing insert, stained **12.50**

Butter Pat, 2½" sq, Meakin, price for set of 10 .... **25.00**

Cake Plate, ftd, Haviland **70.00**

Coffeepot, Meakin

8" h **20.00**

8½" h **35.00**

Creamer, 5¼" h, Meakin **30.00**

Cup and Saucer, 2¾" d, Haviland **35.00**

Dish, cov

8" sq, Meakin **85.00**

11" d, Meakin, stained **10.00**

Gravy Boat, 8" l, Meakin **20.00**

Pitcher, 6" h, sq, Meakin **40.00**

Plate

6¾" d, Meakin **4.00**

7" d, gold trim, Haviland **15.00**

10" d, Meakin, price for set of 3 **90.00**

Platter

13½" l, Haviland **35.00**

15½" l, Meakin **20.00**

Sauce Tureen, 8" d, underplate, Meakin **130.00**

Shaving Mug, 3½" h, Meakin, chip on base **90.00**

Sugar Bowl, 6½" h, Meakin **25.00**
Toothbrush Holder, 5¾" h, variant,
J W Pankhurst, stained **100.00**

MOUNT WASHINGTON GLASS COMPANY

History: In 1837 Deming Jarves, founder of the Boston and Sandwich Glass Company, established for George D. Jarves, his son, the Mount Washington Glass Company in Boston, Massachusetts. In the following years the leadership and the name of the company changed several times as George Jarves formed different associations.

In the 1860s the company was owned and operated by Timothy Howe and William L. Libbey. In 1869 Libbey bought a new factory in New Bedford, Massachusetts. The Mount Washington Glass Company began operating again there under its original name. Henry Libbey became associated with the company early in 1871. He resigned in 1874 during the general depression, and the glass works was closed. William Libbey had resigned in 1872 to work for the New England Glass Company.

The Mount Washington Glass Company opened again in the fall of 1874 under the presidency of A. H. Seabury and the management of Frederick S. Shirley. In 1894 the glass works became a part of the Pairpoint Manufacturing Company.

Throughout its history the Mount Washington Glass Company made a great variety of glass including pressed glass, blown glass and art glass, lava glass, Napoli, cameo, cut glass, Albertine, and Verona.

References: George C. Avila, *The Pairpoint Glass Story,* Reynolds–DeWalt Printing, 1968, out–of–print; Edward and Sheila Malakoff, *Pairpoint Lamps,* Schiffer Publishing, 1990; John A. Shuman III, *The Collector's Encyclopedia of American Art Glass,* Collector Books, 1988, 1994 value update.

Collectors' Club: Mount Washington Art Glass Society, 60 President Ave., Providence, RI 02906.

Museum: The New Bedford Glass Museum, New Bedford, MA.

Additional Listings: Burmese, Crown Milano, Peachblow, and Royal Flemish.

Biscuit Jar, 7" d, 8" h, lusterless white opal ground, raspberry and floral dec, orig metal frame, numbered, replaced cov **350.00**
Bowl, 10½" d, ruffled, blue satin int., chrysanthemums and leaves ext. **200.00**
Box, 6¾" w, 2½" h, poppies and bright blue bow dec, sgd "Patented April 10 1894," numbered **650.00**
Cologne Bottle, 10" h, bulbous mushroom body, long slender neck, extended flange, lusterless white opal ground, blown hollow stopper **250.00**
Creamer, 3¾" h, Burmese, Shape #78, subtle color, applied handle, tiny pointy spout **435.00**
Dresser Tray, free–form, lusterless white ground, enameled orchids, gold trim **85.00**
Ewer, 11½" h, 5½" w, satin, deep rose shading to light pink, MOP, DQ pattern, melon ribbed, applied frosted thorn handle, minor roughage on handle, discoloration in lining **175.00**
Mustard Jar, cov, ribbed barrel, lusterless white opal ground, pink floral dec, SP cov and bail handle **95.00**
Pin Bowl, 2" h, 3½" d, Burmese, rich salmon shaded to custard ground, collared top, leaves, vines, and berries dec **300.00**
Pitcher
8½" h, rainbow, IVT, reed handle **675.00**
8¾" h
6" w, satin, MOP, DQ, pink shading to orange to pink, white lining, applied frosted reeded shell handle **300.00**
7" w, satin, melon ribbed, Herringbone, shaded blue, white int., applied frosted handle **450.00**
Rose Bowl
3" h, 2⅝" d, star shaped rim, Burmese, salmon pink shaded to yellow, acid finish **180.00**
3¾" h, Burmese type shading from lemon to light peach, enameled blue and white forget–me–nots, tiny green

Salt Shaker, egg shape, painted and enamel floral dec, orig paper label, $125.00.

leaves, scalloped turned–in rim	**275.00**
Salt shaker, 3″ h, 2½″ w, fig, painted ground, floral dec	**110.00**
Sugar Shaker, 3″ h, 3½″ w, melon, ribbed, pale green ground, worn floral dec, base crack	**90.00**
Sweetmeat Jar, light green to white shaded ground, holly and berry dec, SP cov, sgd "MW" ..	**325.00**
Toothpick, 2½″ h, Burmese, soft blush pink shaded to soft yellow rim and base	**335.00**
Vase	
6″ h, satin, yellow shaded to white, diamond quilted design, MOP int.	**95.00**
8″ h	
Trumpet, Burmese, pale yellow shading to pink, ruffled rim	**145.00**
4½″ w, Alice Blue, Raindrop pattern, MOP, tightly crimped applied camphor edge, broken blister	**50.00**
6″ w, satin, bridal white, Raindrop pattern, MOP, applied camphor edge, modified petticoat, scalloped	**100.00**
9″ h, double gourd shape, Verona, crystal ground, raised white, yellow, and orange parrot tulips, green leaves, gold trim	**350.00**
10¾″ h, 4″ w, satin, deep rose shading to pink, Herringbone pattern, MOP, melon ribbed, applied frosted handle	**135.00**

MULBERRY CHINA

History: Mulberry china, made primarily in the Staffordshire district of England between 1830 and 1850, is porcelain whose transfer pattern is the color of mulberry juice. The potters that manufactured Flow Blue also made Mulberry china; the ware often has a flowing effect similar to Flow Blue.

References: Susan and Al Bagdade, *Warman's English & Continental Pottery & Porcelain, Second Edition,* Wallace–Homestead, 1991; Ellen R. Hill, *Mulberry Ironstone: Flow Blue's Best Kept Little Secret,* published by author, 1993; Petra Williams, *Flow Blue China and Mulberry Ware: Similarity and Value Guide,* Revised Edition, Fountain House East, 1993.

Bowl, Rhone, Thomas Furnival, 10¼″ d, fruit, handles, ftd	**45.00**
Butter Dish, cov, Coburg, John Edwards	**120.00**
Creamer, Cyprus, Davenport	**250.00**
Cup and Saucer, handleless	
Calcutta, E Challinor, small chips	**25.00**
Carrara, unknown maker	**50.00**
Corean, Podmore and Walker .	**60.00**
Cyprus, Davenport	**65.00**
Marble, A Shaw	**30.00**
Pelew, E Challinor	**45.00**
Washington Vase, Podmore and Walker	**60.00**

Plate, Athens pattern, Charles Meigh, 9¼″ d, $50.00.

Pitcher, Schnectady On The Mohawk, unknown maker, 8″ h ... **150.00**

Plate

Castle Scenery, unknown maker, 10½″ d **40.00**

Cyprus, Davenport, 10½″ d ... **50.00**

Jeddo, Adams and Son, 10½″ d **45.00**

Pelew, E Challinor **40.00**

Washington Vase, Podmore and Walker, 9¾″ h **48.00**

Platter

Castle Scenery, J Furnival, 15″ l **175.00**

Corean, Podmore and Walker, 14 x 16″ **250.00**

Tonquin, J Heath & Co, 12½″ w, 9½″ l **125.00**

Whampoa, Mellor Venables, 15″ l **245.00**

Shaving Mug, Washington Vase, Podmore and Walker **90.00**

Soup Plate, Peru, unknown maker, 10¾″ d **40.00**

Sugar, cov

Udina, J Clementson **80.00**

Washington Vase, Podmore and Walker, lion's head handles .. **240.00**

Teapot, cov, Jeddo, Adams **140.00**

Vegetable, cov

Corean, Podmore and Walker, 9″ l **435.00**

Wreath, T Furnival, 11″ l **425.00**

Washbowl and Pitcher Set, Cyprus, Davenport, pitcher, bowl, toothbrush holder, and cov soap dish with drain **675.00**

MUSIC BOXES

History: Music boxes were invented in Switzerland around 1825 and include a broad field of automatic musical instruments—from a small box to a huge circus calliope.

A cylinder box consists of a comb with teeth which vibrate when striking a pin in the cylinder and produce music from light tunes to opera and overtures.

The first disc music box was invented by Paul Lochmann of Leipzig, Germany, in 1886. It used an interchangeable steel disc with pierced holes bent to a point which hit the star–wheel as the disc revolved, and thus produced the tune. Discs were easily stamped out of metal, allowing a single music box to play an endless variety of tunes. It reached the height of its popularity from 1890 to 1910. The phonograph replaced it.

Music boxes also were put into many items, e.g., clocks, sewing and jewelry boxes, steins, plates, toys, perfume bottles, and furniture.

References: Gilbert Bahl, *Music Boxes: The Collector's Guide To Selecting, Restoring, and Enjoying New and Vintage Music Boxes,* Courage Books, Running Press, 1993; H. A. V. Bulleid, *Cylinder Musical Box Design and Repair,* Almar Press, 1987.

Collectors' Clubs: Musical Box Society International, 1062 Alber St., Wabash, IN 46992; Music Box Society of Great Britain, 102 High St., Landbeach, Cambridge CB4 4DT England.

Museums: Bells, Cars and Music of Yesterday, Sarasota, FL; Lockwood Matthews Mansion, Norwalk, CT; Miles Musical Museum, Eureka Springs, AR; The Musical Museum, Deansboro, NY; The Musical Wonder House Museum, Iscasset, ME.

Additional Listings: See *Warman's Americana & Collectibles* for more examples.

American, disc type, mahogany, domed cov, rect case, satinwood string inlay, cabinet stand, 23″ w, 21″ d, 39″ h **3,225.00**

Stella, disc type, mahogany case, beaded scrolled sides, matching mahogany stand, crank, 30 14″ d discs, marked "Pat. Sept 22 1885," 21½″ sq, $3,500.00.

Automaton, European, ormolu box, hinged lid, singing bird, key, damaged, 7⅛" w, 5¼" d, 4⅞" h, late 19th C 6,325.00

Celestina, coin–operated, paper roll, oak floor model, curved glass top cabinet with bells 4,200.00

Ducommon–Girod, Ducommon movement, highly carved case, allover carving of cherubs with musical instruments, peaked lid, good mechanism needs restoring, minor damage to case 5,500.00

Empress, disk type, parlor grand, mahogany, rect case, lion's paw feet, cabinet stand, 26" w, 21" d, 41" h 3,675.00

Gavioli, Artisan Factory, North Tonawanda, NY, 65 keys, Artisan pressure type double tracker bar system, 66 note Artisan rolls, heavily carved 10' h x 12' w facade, large carved moth at lower center, excess of 240 pipes, strong impressive sound, from Savin Rock Park Fairground .42,000.00

G. Baker Troll, 13" cylinder, Harp Harmonie Piccolo, great arrangements, lots of trills, orig condition 2,650.00

Imperial Symphonion, 17⅝" table model, mahogany case, carved front, double comb, fifteen discs, restored condition 6,500.00

Langdorf Longue Marche, interchangeable cylinders, 12½" playing length, Harmonie Concerto Piccolo format, four spring barrel arrangement, case with matching table, Queen Anne legs, cylinder storage drawer, governor and comb expertly repaired, repairs to 12 teeth, 7 cylinders 12,000.00

Lochmann, 24½" disc, tubular bells, single disc upright box, ten discs, replaced case, mechanism working but needs restoration 10,00.00

Mermod Freres Mandoline, 13" cylinder, needs restoration 1,800.00

Mills Violana Virtuoso, mahogany, orig unrestored condition, single roll 17,500.00

Mira, disk type, mahogany, shaped rect lid, case with cupboard door flanked by corner columns, 28" w, 22" d, 42" h 6,900.00

Olympia, 15½" single comb, pressed design case 3,000.00

Perfection, 14" single comb, felt dampering system, four discs, needs restoration 1,350.00

Regina

Automatic Changer, 27" dragon front, orig oak finish, solid wood lower front, home model, 18 discs 21,500.00

Casket, Style 6, 27" disc, small cabinet, twelve discs, orig fine condition 9,500.00

Curved Front Changer, 15½" d Home Model, all orig, needs mechanical restoration, some veneer replacement on door, no crown, not working 16,500.00

Style 36, oak front, coin–operated, new coil slide and selector, replaced dec brass trim, some repairs to case 16,500.00

Grandfather Clock, 15½" l bedplate, double comb movement, plain oak case, clock movement attributed to Seth Thomas 13,500.00

Stella, 9½" single comb, thirteen discs, unrestored condition 950.00

Swiss

4½" cylinder, 6 selections, inlaid box, single comb, 20th C 490.00

10¾" cylinder, 6 selections, No. 194, inlaid rosewood veneer box, single comb, 19th C 860.00

13" cylinder, 12 selections, inlaid walnut box, single comb, 19th C 1,600.00

18⅛" cylinder, 8 selections, inlaid rosewood box, single comb, late 19th C 1,150.00

Symphonion

13⅝" double comb, inlay case, inner glass lid and columns, eight discs, orig fine mechanism 3,250.00

17⅝" double comb, table model, mahogany case, fifteen discs, orig condition 5,800.00

MUSICAL INSTRUMENTS

History: From the first beat of the prehistoric drum to the very latest in electronic music makers, musical instruments have provided popular modes of communication and relaxation.

The most popular antique instruments are violins, flutes, oboes, and other instruments associated with the classical music period of 1650 to 1900. Many of the modern instruments, such as trumpets, guitars, drums, etc., have value on the "used" rather than antiques market.

The collecting of musical instruments is in its infancy. The field is growing very rapidly. Investors and speculators have played a role since the 1930s, especially in early string instruments. Skinner's, Sotheby's and Christie's hold annual auctions of fine musical instruments.

References: George Gruhn and Walter Carter, *Acoustic Guitars And Other Fretted Instruments: A Photographic History,* GPI Books, 1993; George Gruhn and Walter Carter, *Gruhn's Guide To Vintage Guitars,* GPI Books, 1991; Mike Longworth, *C. F. Martin & Co.: A History,* 4 Maples Press, 1994.

Periodicals: *Concertina & Squeezebox,* PO Box 6706, Ithaca, NY 14851; *Piano & Keyboard,* PO Box 767, San Anselmo, CA 94979–0767.

Collectors' Clubs: Automatic Musical Instrument Collectors Association, 919 Lantern Glow Trail, Dayton, OH 45431; Fretted Instrument Guild of America, 2344 S. Oakley Ave., Chicago, IL 60608; Musical Box Society International, 1062 Alber St., Wabash, IN 46992; Reed Organ Society, Inc., PO Box 901, Deansboro, NY 13328; The American Musical Instrument Society, 414 E. Clark St., Vermillion, SD 57069.

Museums: C. F. Martin Guitar Museum, Nazareth, PA; International Piano Archives at Maryland, Neil Ratliff Music Library, College Park, MD; Miles Musical Museum, Eureka Springs, AR; Streitwieser Foundation Trumpet Museum, Pottstown, PA; The Museum of the American Piano, New York, NY; The Musical Museum, Deansboro, NY; University of Michigan, Stearns Collection of Musical Instruments, Ann Arbor, MI; Yale University Collection of Musical Instruments, New Haven, CT.

Banjo
  Fairbanks, A C Company, Boston, model Whyte Laydie No 2, laminated maple, faux tortoiseshell binding, 27 bracket nickel plated rim, maple neck with pearl griffin and star peg head inlay, leather case, c1900 . . . .**2,750.00**
  Gibson Inc, Kalamazoo, Trapdoor Model, laminated maple, 24 bracket nickel plated rim, maple neck with pearl inlay, ebony fingerboard with pearl eyes, c1923 . . . . **325.00**
  Vega Company, Plectrum, electric, maple, black lacquer finish, white Bakelite pick plate and tone knobs, nickel hardware, rosewood fingerboard with pearl eyes, orig case and amplifier, stamped, 1930s . . . **650.00**
Bassoon, Heckel, Biebrich, 20th C **1,600.00**
Clavicord, John Challis, Detroit, fruitwood case, sq tapering legs, sgd "John Challis, Detroit, MI," 4' 9" l, 1' 4" w **1,900.00**
Dulcimer, 42½" l, grain painted case, 19th C **490.00**
Flute, T J Weygandt, Philadelphia, boxwood, ivory mounts, adjustable ivory stopper, four silver keys, stamped **250.00**
Guitar
  Gibson, acoustic, Style L5,

Piano, made by Bartolomeo Cristofari, Florence, Italy, 1720, $8,000.00.

arched top, label, stamped and sgd int., c1939 .... 2,750.00

Martin, Christian Frederick, model O–26, two piece back, Brazilian rosewood, marquetry center strip, wood and ivory binding on sides, stamped int., 1850–67 .... 1,875.00

Harpsicord, John Challis, Detroit, fruitwood case, sq tapering legs, 8' l, 4' w 2,800.00

Mandolin, 24" l, The New Washburn 1897 model, exotic wood, inlaid abalone, ivory, and tortoiseshell inlay, minor damage . 175.00

Piano, grand
Mason and Hamlin, Boston, 5' 8" l, 4' 8½" w, ebony finish, sq tapered legs 6,000.00
Steinway, Model M, 67" l, walnut case, sq tapered legs, bench, serial number 200430 ..... 8,250.00

Pianoforte, 70" l, classical, rosewood veneer, stenciled, gilt table inscribed "Loud Brothers–Philadelphia," gilt anthemion scrolls, striping and stamped brass in outline, minor surface imperfections, 1825–37 .... 2,075.00

Saxophone, Marceau, E–flat, alto, silver plated, satin finish 175.00

Trombone, Dupont, B–flat, tenor slide, burnished nickel plate ... 450.00

Trumpet, Concertone, nickel plated 225.00

Ukulele, tenor
C F Martin & Co, Nazareth, mahogany, celluloid binding, rosewood fingerboard, stamped "C F Martin & Co, Nazareth, PA," c1920 ..... 250.00
Gibson, Kalamazoo, mahogany, celluloid binding, bound rosewood fingerboard, pearly inlay, late 1920s 195.00

Viola
Erdesz, Otto Alexander, 16⅜" l, two piece medium curl back, similar ribs and scroll, red varnish, unlabeled 3,400.00
Postiglione, Vincenzo, 16⁹⁄₁₆" l, two piece medium curl back, light curl ribs and scroll, orange–brown varnish, label ... 3,400.00

Violin
Fred P Herson, Chelsea, 14 ³⁄₁₆" l, two piece back, medium curl, medium grain top, orange color varnish, 1907 .... 275.00
Heberlein, Heinrich T Jr, Markneukirchen, two piece medium curl back, similar ribs and scroll, red varnish 1,200.00
Kaplan, Ladislav, NY, 14" l, two piece medium curl back, similar ribs and scroll, red varnish, label, 1910 .... 2,100.00
Morse, John A, 14³⁄₁₆" l, two piece slight curl back, medium curl ribs and scroll, red–yellow varnish, label 450.00

Violin Bow
Castagneri, Andreas, Paris, France, 27¼" l, strong narrow curl top, broad curl ribs, fruitwood scroll with relief carved floral motif, yellow–gold varnish, c1940 .... 25,300.00
Milanese, 29¹⁵⁄₁₆" l, two piece back, red–brown varnish 9,900.00

MUSIC RELATED

Book, *The Classic Lines of Italian Violin Making, Piza,* Karel Jalovec, sgd by author, 1979 .... 150.00

Catalog
Howe Publishing Co, OH, 32 pgs, 5¼ x 8½" 15.00
Strich & Zeidler, Inc, NY, 12 pgs, pianos 18.00
W W Kimball Co, IL, c1920, pianos, 7½ x 9¾" 30.00

Music Stand
Wicker, 48½" h, ornate curlicue design, three wood shelves, late 19th C 925.00
Wood, 43" h, Regency, green and gilt painted, rect music rest pierced with lyre form splat, adjustable height, brass standard, downswept uncurvate tripod base with trailing ivy leaves dec 2,175.00

Piano Bench, 34" l, 17" h, French Provincial, fruitwood, pink floral upholstered seat, molded apron, cabriole legs 400.00

MUSTACHE CUPS AND SAUCERS

History: Mustache cups and saucers were popular in the late Victorian era, 1880–1900. They were made by many companies in porcelain and silver plate. The cups have a ledge across the top of the bowl of the cup to protect a gentleman's mustache from becoming soiled while drinking.

Reference: Susan and Al Bagdade, *Warman's English & Continental Pottery & Porcelain, Second Edition,* Wallace–Homestead, 1991.

Porcelain, Think of Me, green trim, gold lines, incised "Germany," $30.00.

PORCELAIN

German
Inscribed "A Present" in gold . . **50.00**
Lily of the valley and violets dec **45.00**
Roses, pink and yellow, green leaves **25.00**
Haviland, blue flowers, gold trim, pink scroll, marked "Haviland" . **125.00**
Sponge dec
Colonial couple, gold trim, ftd, large **90.00**
Portrait medallion, kettle shape, gold trim, ftd **65.00**
Unknown Maker
Forget–Me–Not dec, inscribed "From a Friend," bamboo handle **40.00**
Lilac and floral dec, white ground **40.00**
Wedding Band pattern, gold dec, white ground **65.00**

SILVER PLATED

Gorham, relief scroll work center band, monogram, 1896 . . . . **15.00**
Pairpoint, marked "Quadplate," engraved flowers **60.00**

NAILSEA TYPE GLASS

History: Nailsea type glass is characterized by swirls and loopings, usually white, on a clear or colored ground. One of the first areas where this glass was made was Nailsea, England, 1788–1873, hence the name. Several other glass houses, including American factories, made this type of glass.

Reference: Ellen T. Schroy, *Warman's Glass.* Wallace–Homestead, 1992.

Witch Ball, pale blue ground, white loopings, 4¼″ d, $95.00.

Bowl, 7⅝″ d, sapphire blue, opaque white looping, applied clear trim, feet and handles . . . **175.00**
Creamer, 4⅜″ h, opaque aquamarine, rose and blue looping, tooled rim **385.00**
Eggcup, 4⅝″ h, opaque white, pink looping, hollow stem **150.00**
Fairy Lamp, 4″ h, 4¾″ d base, blue shade, white looping, clear Clarke base **180.00**
Flask
4″ h, light green, white looping . **135.00**
7½″ h, clear, white looping **55.00**
8¾″ h, teardrop form, milk glass, blue looping, clear casing . . . **150.00**
Gemel Bottle, 7½″ h, clear, pink and white looping **65.00**
Pitcher, 9½″ h, deep greenish–

aqua, white looping, applied solid curled end handle and base, sheared mouth, ftd **600.00**

Rolling Pin, 17" l, clear, pink and white looping, knop ends, America, late 19th C **155.00**

Salt, clear, blue looping, ftd **60.00**

Whimsey, 11¼" h, bellows form, clear, amethyst looping, applied rigaree **75.00**

Witch Ball
3½" d, cobalt blue, white looping **825.00**
4⅜" d, milk glass, pink and blue looping **440.00**
4¾" d, clear, cranberry, blue, and white looping, ground mouth, smooth base **1,045.00**
5½" d, milk glass, red and gray looping **495.00**

Witch Ball and Stand, 13¼" h, clear, smokey tint, white looping, price for pair **330.00**

NANKING

History: Nanking is a type of Chinese porcelain made in Canton, China, from the early 1800s into the 20th century for export to America and England. It is often confused with the Canton pattern.

Three elements help distinguish Nanking from Canton. Nanking has a spear and post border, as opposed to the scalloped–line style of Canton, and the blues may tend to be darker on the Nanking ware. Second, in the water's edge or Willow pattern, Canton usually has no figures. Nanking features a standing figure with open umbrella on the bridge. Finally, Nanking wares often are embellished with gold.

Green and orange variations of Nanking survive, although they are scarce.

Reference: Gloria and Robert Mascarelli, *Warman's Oriental Antiques,* Wallace–Homestead, 1992.

Reproduction Alert: Copies of Nanking ware currently are being produced in China. They are of inferior quality and decorated in lighter rather than the darker blues.

Cider Jug, barrel shape
9¼" h, cov, gilt dec, imperfections, 19th C **975.00**

Plate, water's edge scene, 1780–1800, 9½" d, $375.00.

9½" h, imperfections, 19th C .. **575.00**

Coffeepot, cov, 9¾" h, lighthouse shape, gilt dec, mismatched cov, 19th C **865.00**

Cup and Saucer, loop handle ... **50.00**

Dish, 6" l, blue and white, leaf shape, twig handle **225.00**

Gravy Boat, 7½" l, blue and white, gilt trim, twisted handle **275.00**

Jug, cov, 9½" h, foo dog finial ... **285.00**

Plate, 9½" d, water's–edge scene, 1780–1800 .... **375.00**

Platter
14¾" l, oval, chips to underside of rim, 19th C **350.00**
15" l, cov, oval, 19th C **800.00**
15½" l, octagonal, pierced oval insert, imperfections, 19th C . **345.00**

Salad Bowl, pr, 9½" d, one repaired, 19th C **700.00**

Sauce Boat, 6½" l, undertray, chips, 19th C **315.00**

Soup Tureen, 13" l, 9" h, cracked cov, 19th C **500.00**

Teapot and Sugar Bowl, cov, 6" h teapot, imperfections, 19th C .. **450.00**

NAPKIN RINGS, FIGURAL

History: Gracious home dining during the Victorian era meant each household member had their personal napkin ring. Figural napkin rings were first patented in 1869. The remainder of the 19th century saw most plating companies, e.g., Cromwell, Eureka, Meriden, Reed and Barton, etc., manufacturing figural rings, many copying with slight variations the designs of other companies.

Values are determined today by the subject matter of the ring, the quality of the workmanship, and the condition.

Reference: Victor K. Schnadig, *American Victorian Figural Napkin Rings,* Wallace–Homestead, 1971, out–of–print.

Reproduction Alert: Quality reproductions do exist.

Additional Listings: See *Warman's Americana & Collectibles* for a listing of non–figural napkin rings.

Boy, standing behind ring, rect base, Simpson, Hall, Miller Co . **165.00**
Cat, standing beside ring, Eureka Silver Plate Co **175.00**
Cherub, pair supporting elaborate chased oval ring with wings, Wilcox Silver Plate Co **150.00**
Chick, standing guard over ring, oval base, ball feet, portion of orig label, Meriden, #222 . . . . . **200.00**
Dog, pulling cart, cherub riding on top of ring, movable wheels . . . **250.00**
Dragon, ivory, carved, black eyes **50.00**
Fox, standing on one side of ring, bunch of grapes on other, vintage dec, ornate base **195.00**
Girl with muff on one side, playful dog on other, Kate Greenaway type **215.00**
Horse
   Prancing, ring on back, sq base, ball feet **175.00**

Silverplated, cow standing by ring, leafy base, 2⅞" h, 3¼" l, $265.00.

Pulling cart, movable wheels . . **225.00**
Lady, leaning toward child, heavily draped attire, marked "Babcock" **260.00**
Little Red Riding Hood, holding basket, marked "Reed & Barton" **225.00**
Lily Pad, finger grip handle supports pedestal ring, shaped base **135.00**
Lion, standing, leaning against ring, rect base **175.00**
Owl, perched on leaf shaped base, Van Bergh Co, #99 . . . . **160.00**
Squirrel, sitting on pile of acorns, front paws on ring, Simpson, Hall, Miller Co **170.00**
Turtle Doves, spread wings support ring, Middletown Plate, #74 **130.00**

NASH GLASS

History: Nash glass is a type of art glass attributed to Arthur John Nash and his sons, Leslie H. and A. Douglas. Arthur John Nash, originally employed by Webb in Stourbridge, England, came to America and was employed in 1889 by Tiffany Furnaces at its Corona, Long Island, plant.

While managing the plant for Tiffany, Nash designed and produced iridescent glass. In 1928 A. Douglas Nash purchased the physical facilities of Tiffany Furnaces. The A. Douglas Nash Corporation remained in operation until 1931.

Reference: Ellen T. Schroy, *Warman's Glass,* Wallace–Homestead, 1992.

Bowl, 15½" d, Chintz pattern, amber, blue, and green opal, turned down rim **300.00**
Candlesticks, pr, 5" h, Chintz pattern, blood red, silver design . . **750.00**
Cocktail, 6½" h, clear stem, blue and black striped bowl, inscribed "Nash," price for set of 4 . . . . . **600.00**
Creamer, 4¼" h, clear, pale orchid and green design, clear handle **300.00**
Finger Bowl, 4¾" d, opal rays, cranberry rim, matching underplate, sgd **175.00**
Goblet, 6½" h, Chintz pattern, blue and green **60.00**
Perfume Bottle, 7⅞" h, rays of blue and lilac, pale blue foot, orig

Vase, irid blue, marked "B526 Nash," 5½" h, $600.00.

pointed amber stopper with silvery blue irid **700.00**
Vase
4¼" h, blown molded dec, irid gold, disk foot, inscribed "Nash 544" **750.00**
6½" h, bulbous, feathery blue strokes, bubbly lime green streaks, sgd **400.00**
9½" h, teal blue, silver striping, cupped platform base **500.00**
11" h, reddish brown, pulled feather design, green opal body, butterscotch striations, int. cased in white luster **1,850.00**

NAUTICAL ITEMS

History: The seas that surround us have fascinated man since time began. The artifacts of sailors have been collected and treasured for years. Because of their environment, merchant and naval items, whether factory or handmade, must be of quality construction and long lasting. Many of these items are aesthetically designed as well.

References: Jon Baddeley, *Nautical Antiques & Collectables,* Sotheby's Publications, 1993; Robert W. D. Ball, *Nautical Antiques,* Schiffer Publishing, 1994; Alan P. Major, *Maritime Antiques,* A. S. Barnes & Co, 1981; Jean Randier, *Nautical Antiques,* Doubleday and Co, 1977.

Periodicals: *Nautical Brass,* PO Box 3966, North Ft. Myers, FL 33918; *Nautical Collector,* PO Box 16734, Alexandria, VA 22302.

Collectors' Club: Nautical Research Guild, 62 Marlboro St., Newburyport, MA 01950.

Museums: Kittery Historical & Naval Museum, Kittery, ME; Lyons Maritime Museum, St. Augustine, FL; Museum of Science and Industry, Chicago, IL; Mystic Seaport Museum, Mystic, CT; National Maritime Museum, San Francisco, CA; Peabody Museum of Salem, Salem, MA; The Mariners' Museum, Newport News, VA; U.S. Naval Academy Museum, Naval Academy, MD.

Barometer/Thermometer, ship's, 7" d, Schatz & Shone, 20th C . **115.00**
Book, *The New American Practical Navigator,* Nathaniel Bowditch, Newburyport, MA, May 1897, second edition, orig foldout chart and leather binding . . **85.00**
Bowl, 5⅜" d, pewter, ship *HMS Champion* **200.00**
Catalog, Wilcox, Crittenden & Co, CT, c1910, 335 pgs, 7 x 10" . . . **38.00**
Clacker, marine, 10" l, wood, whale bone trim, dark patina . . **110.00**
Compass
Lifeboat, 14" h, brass, includes burners, drilled for lamp, minor dent, British, early 20th C . . . **230.00**

Souvenir Plank, book shape, incised "In Memory of the Eurydyce, Sunk March 24, 1878," 2³/₁₆ x 3¼ x¹¹/₁₆", $75.00.

Marine, 8″ d, cast brass, liquid, gimbal, 19th C **285.00**

Document Case, 9½″ l, ship *Reward,* metal, painted **125.00**

Lantern, ship's, 17½″ h, brass, Perkins, price for pair **275.00**

Model

Brig, 21½″ l, wood, painted, fully rigged, 25¾ x 29⅝ x 15¾″ case, 20th C **635.00**

Ship *Essex,* 35″ l, plank on frame, early 20th C **1,265.00**

Navigational Chart, George W Eldridge, Chart D, Massachusetts Bay **125.00**

Painting

14½ x 15½″, pr, "Lifting Fog, Provincetown" and "Morning Mist, Cape Cod," watercolor on paper, harbor scene with boats, matted and framed, sgd "John Hare" **600.00**

20 x 24″, "Star of France," oil on canvas, identified vessel, inscription on reverse, framed, 1908 .... **450.00**

22″ h, 26½″ w, harbor scene with sailboats, gilt frame, sgd "John Clymer" **965.00**

33½″ h, 29½″ w, sailboat with American flag, paper, opaque watercolor, matted and framed **135.00**

Quadrant, 17″ l, ebony, brass radial arm, ivory vernier scale ... **250.00**

Sea Chest

28¾″ l, pine, iron bound, end handles and strap hinges, old brown repaint **175.00**

34″ w, 18″ d, 19″ h, painted black, carved becket handles, New England, c1800 .... **410.00**

40″ l, pine, six board construction, base molding and till, iron heart escutcheon, replaced becket handles **175.00**

43″ l, poplar, six board construction, till, wrought iron lock and strap hinges, black paint, becket handles **210.00**

Sextant, silver vernier scale, orig box, Stanley, London **700.00**

Telescope

17″ l extended, three draw, wood and brass **75.00**

44⅛″ l, marine, wood and brass, adjustable two draw, missing tripod, 19th C **550.00**

Wheel, ship's, 30″ d, brass hub, inlay dec, label "American Engineering Co, Philadelphia" ... **350.00**

NAZI ITEMS

History: The National Socialist German Workers Party (NSDAP) was created on February 24, 1920, by Anton Drexler and Adolf Hitler. Its 25–point nationalist program was designed to renovate the depressed German economy and government.

In 1923, after the failed Beer Hall Putsch, Hitler was sentenced to a five–year term in Landsberg Prison. He spent only a year in prison, during which time he wrote the first volume of *Mein Kampf.*

In the late 1920s and early 1930s the NSDAP developed from a regional party into a major national party. In spring 1933 Hitler became Reich's chancellor. Shortly after the death of President von Hindenberg in 1934, Hitler combined the offices of president and chancellor into a single position, giving him full control over the German government as well as NSDAP. From that point until May 1945, the National Socialist German Worker's Party dominated all aspects of German life.

In the mid–1930s Hitler initiated a plan, from rearming to territorial acquisition, designed to unite the German speaking peoples of Europe in a single nation. Germany's invasion of Poland in 1939 triggered the hostilities that led to the Second World War. The war in Europe ended on VE Day, May 7, 1945.

References: John M. Kaduck, *World War II German Collectibles,* published by author, 1978, 1983 price update; Robin Lumsden, *A Collector's Guide To Third Reich Militaria,* Hippocrene Books, 1987; Robin Lumsden, *A Collector's Guide To Third Reich Militaria: Detecting The Fakes,* Hippocrene Books, 1989; Sydney B. Vernon, *Vernon's Collectors' Guide To Orders, Medals, and Decorations,* published by author, 1986.

Periodicals: *Der Gauleiter,* PO Box 721288, Houston, TX 77272; *Military Col-*

lector Magazine, PO Box 245, Lyon Station, PA 19536; *Military Collectors News,* PO Box 702073, Tulsa, OK 74170; *Military History,* 602 S. King St., Suite 300, Leesburg, VA 22075; *Military Trader,* PO Box 1050, Dubuque, IA 52004.

Note: The objects that appear below are associated with the NSDAP as a political party. See **Militaria** for objects associated with the German military prior to and during World War II.

Membership Pin, Hitler Hugend, red, white, and black enamel, 15/16" l, $5.00.

Banner, center swastika, 29 x 70"	65.00
Belt Buckle, DAF Labor Front, swastika in wheel	20.00
Book, *Mein Kampf,* A. Hitler, 1933, 407 pgs, orig dust cov	15.00
Breast Badge, Luftwaffe, pilot's, observer's, gold wreath, silver eagle holds swastika, orig blue case	250.00
Brooch, large floral swastika, rect back, gilt, 1936	15.00
Car Pennant, 1936 Berlin Olympics, eternal flame, Olympic symbol and date, tie ropes	75.00
Dagger, Army officer's, orange handle, silvered fittings, full eagle's breast, scabbard	140.00
Flag	
Army, Regimental Battle, 84 x 144", double sided, eagle, swastika, tricolor	75.00
Parade, NSDAP, 45½" l, hp black swastika on white, double sided, c1920	30.00
Flagpole Top, "Wird Waffe," Bakelite spearhead and oak leaves, cross guard dated 1940, iron cross dated 1939	40.00

Funeral Sash, SS, fabric and paper, silver lettering, white fringe, large silver SS Runes	125.00
Hat, R R Supervisor, red wool, black velvet band, two gold eagles, rosettes, black visor, orig maker's label	200.00
Medal, German Red Cross, 1937, black enameled eagle and red cross, red and white ribbon	80.00
Pillowcase, 15 x 18", NSDAP eagle and swastika, inscribed "Deutschland Erwacht"	50.00
Plaque, 6 x 8", bronze, Hitler's profile, dark brown patina	175.00
Plate, 7½" d, white porcelain, DAF insignia	12.00
Podium Pennant, NSDAP, white border and bottom fringe, large swastika	35.00
Ring, crossed swords, helmet, and swastika, silver	50.00
Wall Streamer, 43 x 7", NSDAP, two pc silk, light orange on red field, brass pole	35.00

NETSUKES

History: The traditional Japanese kimono has no pockets. Daily necessities such as money, tobacco supplies, etc., were carried in leather pouches or *inros* which hung from a cord with a netsuke toggle. The word netsuke comes from "ne" (to root) and "tsuke" (to fasten).

Netsukes originated in the 14th century and initially were associated with the middle class. By the mid–18th century all levels of Japanese society used them. Some of the most famous artists, e.g., Shuzan and Yamada Hojitsu, worked in the netsuke form.

Netsukes average 1 to 2 inches and are made from wood, ivory, bone, ceramics, metal, horn, nutshells, etc. The subject matter is broad based but always portrayed in a lighthearted, humorous manner. A netsuke must have no sharp edges and balance so it hangs correctly on the sash.

Value depends on artist, region, material, and skill of craftsmanship. Western collectors favor *katabori,* pieces which represent an identifiable object.

Reference: Gloria and Robert Mascarelli, *Warman's Oriental Antiques,* Wallace–Homestead, 1992.

Periodical: *Netsuke & Ivory Carving Newsletter,* 3203 Adams Way, Ambler, PA 19002.

Collectors' Club: Netsuke Kenkyukai Society, PO Box 31595, Oakland, CA 94604.

Reproduction Alert: Recent reproductions are on the market. Many are carved from African ivory.

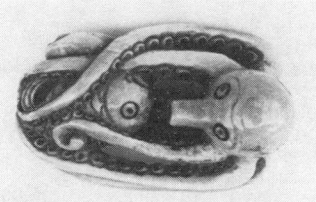

Carved ivory, 19th C, $85.00.

Black Lacquer, mermaid, gilt high-
  lights, 1½" l **315.00**
Boxwood, carved
  Daruma, sitting cross–legged,
    ivory and brass inlays, signed
    "Dosho," mid 18th C, 1¾" h . **1,100.00**
  Endo Morita, holding head of
    Kesa, signed "Meikei," orig
    box **2,875.00**
  Noh Mask, 19th C, 1¾" l **260.00**
  Shinzan Wood Urchin, 1½" h . . **1,035.00**
  Ship Captain, foreign, holding
    telescope, c1800, 2¾" h **700.00**
  Two Blind Men on Raft, signed
    "Sosui," So School, 2" l **1,500.00**
Bronze
  Actor's Mask, 1¼" l **315.00**
  Double Gourd, 3¼" l **230.00**
Bronze and Ivory, Kagamibuta,
  center bronze medallion relief
  dec with figures, ivory border,
  19th C, 1½" d **220.00**
Coral, carved, elder's profile, 19th
  C, 2" l **535.00**
Hardwood, carved, multiple
  masks, 2" d **230.00**

Ivory, carved
  Chokwaro's Horse, emerging
    from gourd, late 19th C, 3" l .   **400.00**
  Man and Child, playing horsey,
    signed, mid 19th C, 1¾" l . . .   **550.00**
  Octopus and Three Monkeys,
    Tokyo School, signed, 18th C,
    1¼" h **1,725.00**
  Oni, polishing large temple bell,
    signed "Tomahide," mid 19th
    C, 1½" h **925.00**
  Six Poets, signed "Ryukei," 19th
    C, 1¼" h **350.00**
  Skull, topped by black raven,
    signed "Meigyokusai," 1½" h   **4,825.00**
Lacquered Wood, brass mounted,
  miniature flintlock pistol, 19th C,
  2½" l **700.00**
Nut, carved, mask, late 19th C, 1"
  l **185.00**
Pottery
  Fox Mask, 2" l **185.00**
  Horned Demon Mask, 2" l **70.00**
Wood, carved
  Bird Mask, painted, 19th C, 2½"
    l **375.00**
  Gentleman's mask, late 19th/
    early 20th C, 1½" l **230.00**

NEWCOMB POTTERY

History: William and Ellsworth Woodward, two brothers, were the founders of a series of businesses which eventually merged into the Newcomb pottery effort. In 1885 Ellsworth Woodward, a proponent of vocational training for women, organized a school from which emerged the Ladies Decorative Art League. In 1886 the brothers founded the New Orleans Art Pottery Company with the ladies of the league serving as decorators. The first two potters were Joseph Meyer and George Ohr. The pottery closed in 1891.

William Woodward was on the faculty at Tulane. Ellsworth taught fine arts at the Sophie Newcomb College, a women's school which eventually merged with Tulane. In 1895 Newcomb College developed a pottery course in which the wares could be sold. Some of the equipment came from the old New Orleans Art Pottery.

Mary G. Sheerer joined the staff to teach decoration. In 1910 Paul E. Cox solved many of the technical problems connected with making pottery in a southern environment. Other leading figures were Sadie Irvine, Professor Lota Lee Troy, and Kathrine Choi. Pottery was made until the early 1950s.

Students painted a quality art pottery with a distinctive high glaze. Designs have a decidedly southern flavor, e.g., myrtle, jasmine, sugar cane, moss, cypress, dogwood, and magnolia motifs. Later matte–glazed pieces usually are decorated with carved–back floral designs. Pieces depicting murky, bayou scenes are most desirable.

References: Susan and Al Bagdade, *Warman's American Pottery and Porcelain,* Wallace–Homestead, 1994; Ralph and Terry Kovel, *Kovels' American Art Pottery: The Collector's Guide To Makers, Marks and Factory Histories,* Crown Publishers, 1993; Suzanne Ormond and Mary E. Irvine, *Louisiana's Art Nouveau: The Crafts Of The Newcomb Style,* Pelican Publishing, 1976; Jessie Poesch, *Newcomb Pottery: An Enterprise for Southern Women,* Schiffer Publishing, 1984.

Collectors' Club: American Art Pottery Association, 125 E. Rose Ave., St. Louis, MO 63119.

Museum: Newcomb College, Tulane University, New Orleans, LA.

Bowl
  5½" d, compressed form, low relief white narcissus border, blue ground, matte glaze, Sadie Irvine, c1821 . . . .   **715.00**
  5¾" d, sculpted low relief white honeysuckle blossoms, raised pierced rim, blue ground, matte glaze, Sadie Irvine and Joseph Meyer **950.00**
  8⅜" d, flared shape, incised beige rim bands, mauve ground **275.00**

Bowl, straight sides, incised floral dec, green and white ground, imp mark, $720.00.

Chamberstick, 4" h, blue, green, and cream stylized flowers, dark blue ground, marked "#TG37"   **1,100.00**
Chocolate Set, 10¼" h, chocolate pot, five 3¼" h cups, sculpted floral motif, blue–green, blue, green, and yellow underglaze, matte glaze, buff clay body, Sadie Irvine, c1915 . . . .**5,000.00**
Jar, cov, 7¾" h, carved light blue sweet peas band, glossy dark blue ground, center blossom and "Here are the sweet peas on the top toe of flint" on cov, marked "NC, MTR, W, JM SS64" **10,450.00**
Mug, 3" h, flared base, incised glossy stylized ivory flowers, green stems, cobalt blue band and handle, Leona Nicholson, 1906, marked **1,870.00**
Plaque, 6" d, blue and green trees with moss, pink sky, dark blue ground, Sadie Irvine, marked . .**1,210.00**
Plate, 12" d, carved and painted pink and cream pinecones, green foliage, dark blue ground, H Bailey, marked "#NS86" . . .**1,540.00**
Vase
  6" h, shouldered ovoid, subtle blue, green, and gray ethereal landscape, three full–length Southern pines, imp "NC J262 RM" and "HD11" **875.00**
  7" h, cylindrical, moonlit landscape, moss draped oak trees, dated 1925, marked "CN, JM, AFS 0266 318" **1,320.00**
  8½" h, carved purple swamp scene, moss, moon, and trees,

Sadie Irvine, dated 1927, hairline **3,960.00**
8¾" h, tapered, sloping shoulders, low relief flower bud,
pale blue, matte glaze, Cor-
inne Marie Chalaron, c1919 . **975.00**
10" h, white jonquils, green
stems, light blue ground, Anna
F Simpson, 1924 ....**3,800.00**
14" h, light green and blue
carved cypress trees, dark
blue top band, Sadie Irvine,
marked "FU49, B" in circle ..**7,700.00**

NILOAK POTTERY, MISSION WARE

History: Niloak pottery was made near
Benton, Arkansas. Charles Dean Hyten experimented with native clay, trying to preserve its natural colors. By 1911 he perfected Mission Ware, a marbleized pottery
in which the cream and brown colors predominate. The pieces were marked Niloak
(kaolin spelled backwards).

After a devastating fire, the pottery was
rebuilt and named Eagle Pottery. This factory included the space to add a novelty
pottery line which was introduced in 1929.
This line usually was marked "Hywood–Niloak" until 1934 when the name Hywood
was dropped from the mark. Mr. Hyten left
the pottery in 1941. In 1946 operations
ceased.

References: Susan and Al Bagdade,
Warman's American Pottery and Porcelain,
Wallace–Homestead, 1994; David Edwin
Gifford, *Collector's Encyclopedia of Niloak,*
Collector Books, 1993.

Collectors' Club: Arkansas Pottery Collectors Society, 12 Normandy Rd., Little
Rock, AR 72207.

Additional Listings: See *Warman's
Americana & Collectibles* for more examples, especially the novelty pieces.

Note: Prices listed below are for Mission
Ware pieces.

Bowl
4½" d **65.00**

**Vase, Mission Ware, wide flat rim,
glazed int., 3⅛" h, 5⅜" w, $75.00.**

10" d **200.00**
Candy Jar, cov, 8½" h, hand
thrown **2,550.00**
Clock, 4 x 5" **175.00**
Humidor, 5" h **750.00**
Mug, 4" h **50.00**
Pitcher, 10" h, strap handle **125.00**
Pot, 2¾" h **110.00**
Toothpick, 2½" h **60.00**
Tumbler, 4" h **60.00**
Umbrella Stand, 22" h **350.00**
Vase
4" h, 4" w, sgd **125.00**
5½" h, sgd **125.00**
7½" h, rolled rim, cream, blue,
and brown swirls **165.00**
9¼" h, multicolored **250.00**
10" h, dark brown, blue, and
cream **250.00**

NIPPON CHINA, 1891–1921

History: Nippon, Japanese hand–
painted porcelain, was made for export between 1891 and 1921. In 1891, when the
McKinley Tariff Act proclaimed that all items
of foreign manufacture be stamped with
their country of origin, Japan chose to use
"Nippon." In 1921 the United States decided the word "Nippon" no longer was acceptable and required that all Japanese
wares be marked with "Japan." The Nippon
era ended.

There are over 220 recorded Nippon
backstamps or marks. The three most popular are the wreath, maple leaf, and rising
sun marks. Wares with variations of all three

marks are being reproduced today. A knowledgeable collector can easily spot the reproductions by the mark variances.

The majority of the marks are found in three different colors: green, blue, and magenta. Colors indicate the quality of the porcelain used: green for first–grade porcelain, blue for second grade, and magenta for third grade. Marks were applied by two methods: decal stickers under glaze and imprinting directly on the porcelain.

References: Gene Loendorf, *Nippon Hand Painted China*, McGrew Color Graphics, 1975; Joan Van Patten, *The Collector's Encyclopedia Of Nippon Porcelain,* First Series (1979, 1994 value update), Second Series (1982, 1995 value update), Third Series (1986, 1994 value update), Collector Books; Kathy Wojciechowski, *The Wonderful World of Nippon Porcelain, 1891–1921,* Schiffer Publishing, 1992.

Collectors' Clubs: ARK–LA–TEX Nippon Club, 112 Ascot Drive, Southlake, TX 76092; Buckee Chapter, 700 E. High St., Hicksville, OH 43526; Dixieland Nippon Club, PO Box 1712, Centerville, VA 22020; International Nippon Collectors Club, 112 Ascot Drive, Southlake, TX 76092; Lakes & Plains Nippon Collectors Society, PO Box 230, Peotone, IL 60468; Long Island Nippon Collectors Club, 145 Andover Place, W. Hempstead, NY 11552; MD–PA Collectors' Club, 920 B Collings Ave., Collingswood, NJ 08107; New England Nippon Collectors Club, 64 Burt Rd., Springfield, MA 01118.

Additional Listings: See *Warman's Americana & Collectibles.*

Advisor: Kathy Wojciechowski.

Ashtray
   5¼" w, blown out horse's heads,
      green mark **350.00**
   6" d, scenic, beaded **200.00**
Asparagus Set, 12 x 7½" tray, six
   matching 7½" d plates, green M
   mark, price for 7 pc set **365.00**
Basket, 7" d, cobalt blue ground,
   gold trim, portrait medallion . . . **225.00**
Berry Set, cobalt blue rim, lavish
   gold, hp red and mocha roses,
   price for 7 pc set **170.00**
Biscuit jar, cov, English fox hunting
   scene **300.00**
Bottle, cov, 4½ x 6", hp, three feet,

   two ladies in courtyard, blue
   ground, flowers, beading **110.00**
Bowl
   7" d, molded in relief, peanuts,
      ftd **115.00**
   9½" l, oval, castle on lake scene,
      two handles, gold trim, green
      mark **100.00**
Cake Platter, butterflies **42.00**
Cake Set, sunset scene, price for
   7 pc set **175.00**
Candlestick, 8" h, woman walking
   dog on leash, purple and black,
   gold tracings **120.00**
Chocolate Set, 10" h chocolate
   pot, four cups and saucers,
   beige ground, scenic palm trees
   and mountains, beaded, China
   E–OH mark, price for 10 pc set **120.00**
Condensed Milk Jar, lid, liner, floral
   medallions, gold trim **150.00**
Cracker Jar, gold, flowers **225.00**
Creamer and Sugar, 4" h, 4" d
   creamer, 4¾" h, 7¾" d cov
   sugar, pedestal, pink roses, gold
   trim, ornate dec **120.00**
Demitasse Pot, gold, flowers **95.00**
Doll, 3¾" h, bisque, boy, blue
   swimsuit **120.00**
Ferner, 7½" d, 4⅝" h, four lobes,
   ftd, scalloped rim, large roses,
   relief scrolls, gold trim **150.00**

Vase, conical body, tapering straight neck, double scroll handles, abstract brown and pink, pinecones and needles, white Moriage type dec, olive ground, gold leaf sections, matte glaze, 8¼" h, $295.00.

Game Plate, 8½" d, deer on hill at sunset, 1½" cobalt blue trim, gold beaded floral overlay, maple leaf mark **150.00**

Hatpin Holder, hanging, cornucopia shape, apple blossoms, florals, and gooseberries dec, gold trim **275.00**

Humidor, Indian's head, peace pipe on side, applied Indian designs on lid, small int. chip **375.00**

Humidor, six sided, country scene **450.00**

Leaf Dish, 8" d, molded in relief acorns **95.00**

Mayonnaise Set, ftd bowl, underplate, ladle, cream ground, orange poppies, gold outlines, RC mark, price for 3 pc set **75.00**

Miniature, tea set, doll size, yellow birds, pink rose bouquets, teapot, sugar, creamer, two cups and saucers, two tea plates, blue rising sun mark **135.00**

Mug, moriage **225.00**

Mustard, cov, saucer, sunset scene band **65.00**

Pitcher, 5¾" h, 6½" d, scenic, Wedgwood blue, gold dec **75.00**

Plaque

8" d, ducks at water's edge, earth colors, green mark **125.00**

8¾" d, windmill, earth colors .. **190.00**

9" d, floral, matte **85.00**

9½" d

Floral, pink and orchid, wall type, matte finish **55.00**

Gooseberries **68.00**

10" d

Fall foliage scene **195.00**

Windmill scene **90.00**

10¼" d, landscape, tree, lake, and grass in browns, cream satin ground **200.00**

10½" d, blown out, bison, green M mark **595.00**

Plate, 9½" d, hp, pink castle, yellow trees and water, green M in wreath mark **95.00**

Punch Bowl and Stand, 10" d, cobalt blue and floral dec, ftd stand, green maple leaf mark .. **450.00**

Stamp Box, geometric black stripes, int. tray with two compartments, wreath mark **110.00**

Sugar Shaker, 5" h, bisque, boat scene, cobalt blue, gold handle **60.00**

Tankard, 12¼" h, poppies, scrolls **215.00**

Tea Set, Flying Geese, turquoise ground, jeweled gold borders, teapot, creamer, sugar, four each cups, saucers, cake plates, price for 16 pc set **400.00**

Toothpick, scenic, sailboats **90.00**

Urn, 14½" h, handles, Moriage, blue mark, lid missing, minor hairline int. rim **550.00**

Vase

5½" h, 4" d, ftd, handles, pink rose dec, green handles and feet **80.00**

6¼" h, 6¼" w, salmon flowers, cobalt band, gold beading and trim **145.00**

6½" h, relief molded, dogs pursuing stag, earth tones, two handles, green mark **795.00**

7½" h, matte, stylized trees, Art Deco design, earth tones, two handles **110.00**

8½" h, 4" w, 2¾" d, pillow, mountain and lake scene front and back, pagoda on front, delicate enameling, elephant handles **140.00**

11" h, bisque, pastel shaded ground, large lavender flowers gold outlines **155.00**

11½" h, large medallions, colored roses, flower clusters streaming down body, beaded gold **145.00**

11¾" h, 6" d, hexagonal, camel and oasis scene, floral and gold dec, marked "Royal Nishiki" **225.00**

12" h, 6" d, matte brown–black, relief falcon chained to wood perch **450.00**

Whiskey Jug, 8" l, moriage and scene **550.00**

NODDERS

History: Nodders are figurines with heads and/or arms attached to the body with wires to enable them to move. They are made in a variety of materials—bisque, celluloid, papier–mâché, porcelain, and wood.

Most nodders date from the late 19th century with Germany being the principal source of supply. Among the American–made nodders, those of Disney and cartoon characters are most eagerly sought.

Boy in tub, two pieces, marked "Patent/TT," 3¾ x 2½ x 3¼", $25.00.

Black Cat, composition, 5" h	**55.00**
Black Man, composition, painted, wood platform, 10½" h	**50.00**
Bowler, winkie eyes	**28.00**
Chinese Couple, standing, France, 15" h, price for pair ...	**1,250.00**
Couple, man juggling, woman playing drums and wearing gold and pink robe, price for pair ...	**250.00**
Dog, boxer, composition, brown flocking, gold paint, 7" l	**25.00**
Donkey, celluloid, 3" h	**30.00**
Elephant, composition, nodding head and tail, 12" l	**125.00**
Goose, celluloid, Germany, US Zone	**30.00**
Indian Man and Woman, salt-shaker type, drum base, price for pair	**20.00**
Indian Princess, bisque, pale blue robe, gold trim, 3¾" h	**120.00**
Jester, bisque, holding pipe, peach, white, and gold, 3½" h .	**70.00**
Kayo	**125.00**
Little Orphan Annie, bisque, Germany	**100.00**
Ma Winkle, bisque, Germany, 3" h	**175.00**
Man, comical, wood and composition, polychrome paint, top hat, 7½" h	**35.00**

Monkey, celluloid, jointed arms and legs, 6½" h	**65.00**
Oriental Lady, robe dec, 15" h ...	**100.00**
Oriental Man, bisque, holding knife and sheath, dressed in blue and white, skull cap, 5¾" h	**75.00**
Rabbit, papier–mache, glass eyes, 7" h	**65.00**
Turkey, papier–mache, male and female, orig black paint, polychrome trim, pewter feet, price for pair	**110.00**

NORITAKE CHINA

History: Morimura Brothers founded Noritake China in 1904 in Nagoya, Japan. They made high–quality chinaware for export to the United States and also produced a line of china blanks for hand painting. In 1910 the company perfected a technique for the production of high–quality dinnerware and introduced streamlined production.

During the 1920s the Larkin Company of Buffalo, New York, was a prime distributor of Noritake China. Larkin offered Azalea, Briarcliff, Linden, Modjeska, Savory, Sheridan, and Tree In The Meadow patterns as part of their premium line.

The factory was heavily damaged during World War II; production was reduced. Between 1946 and 1948 the company sold their china under the "Rose China" mark, since the quality of production did not match the earlier Noritake China. In 1948, expansion saw the resumption of quality production and the use of the Noritake name once again.

There are close to 100 different marks for Noritake, the careful study of which can determine the date of production. Most pieces are marked "Noritake" and have a wreath and "M," "N," or "Nippon." The use of the letter "N" was registered in 1953.

References: Joan Van Patten, *Collector's Encyclopedia of Noritake,* First Series (1984, 1994 value update), Second Series (1994), Collector Books.

Periodical: *Noritake News,* 1237 Federal Ave. East, Seattle, WA 98102.

Additional Listings: See *Warman's*

Americana & Collectibles for price listings of the Azalea pattern.

Basket
Acorns and Blossom 60.00
Magnolia Blossom, molded in relief, overhead handle, red mark 65.00
Bowl
7" w, scenic, windmill, red mark   45.00
7¾" d, scenic, ship 80.00
8½" d
Art Deco, blue luster, molded relief walnuts, figural red bird, Komaru mark #16 . . .   175.00
Chestnuts, earth tone colors, green mark 70.00
Bridge Set, playing cards, green mark 78.00
Cake Plate, ruffled, Art Deco parlor scene with two women 165.00
Cake Set, 10½" pierced handled plate, six 6¼" d plates, hp scene with windmill, green mark #27 .   100.00
Celery Set, figural, price for 7 pc set 120.00
Chamberstick 75.00
Children's Tea Set, hp floral, gold trim, creamer, four cups, saucers, and plates, cov sugar, cov teapot, red mark #50, price for 17 pc set 285.00
Chocolate Set, cov tankard pot, six cups and saucers, lavender shaded irises, gold trim, price for 7 pc set 245.00
Cigarette Holder, 5" h, bell shape, figural bird finial, #27 green mark 125.00

Cup and Saucer, white ground, pink and blue flowers, gold trim, 3" h cup, 5" d saucer, $30.00.

Compote, 6½" d, Art Deco scene   **150.00**
Condiment Set, green luster, Art Deco lady **175.00**
Creamer and Sugar
Art Deco, gray–green lusterware, MOP highlights, red mark #27 . . . .   **45.00**
Scenic, beaded **75.00**
Dessert Set, blue luster, googly eyed face in cup **110.00**
Dish, 8" l, divided, luster, figural bird **75.00**
Jam Jar, basket type, overhead handle, red molded cherries finial, notched lid, earth tone scenic dec **70.00**
Lemon Dish, figural **65.00**
Mint Dish, 7" d, open handle, hp, blue and yellow flowers, copper–brown twining leaves **35.00**
Napkin Ring, Art Deco man, green M mark **50.00**
Powder Puff Box, cov, painted floral **200.00**
Refreshment Set, Art Deco lady, orange **175.00**
Sandwich Plate **150.00**
Spoon Holder, pink rose dec, green M mark **20.00**
Teapot, 4¼" h, cream lusterware, blue and white border, red mark #50 . . . .   **40.00**
Tea Set, florals, hp, gold rim, four cups and saucers, cov teapot, red mark #50, price for 10 pc set **75.00**
Tete–A–Tete Set, orange and pearlized white, gold birds and flowers, round tray, demitasse pot, creamer, sugar, two cups and saucers, price for 8 pc set .   **140.00**
Urn, 10¼" h, scenic, magenta ground, fancy gold overlay, price for pair **275.00**
Vase, 9½" h, scenic, multicolored, hp, green mark **110.00**
Wall Pocket, scenic **85.00**

NORITAKE: TREE IN THE MEADOW PATTERN

History: Tree In The Meadow is one of the most popular patterns of Noritake china.

Since the design is hand painted, there are numerous variations of the scene. The basic scene features a large tree (usually in the foreground), a meandering stream or lake, and a peasant cottage in the distance. Principal colors are muted tones of brown and yellow.

The pattern is found with a variety of backstamps and appears to have been imported into the United States beginning in the early 1920s. The Larkin Company distributed this pattern through its catalog sales in the 1920-1930 period.

References: Joan Van Patten, *Collector's Encyclopedia of Noritake,* First Series (1984, 1994 value update), Second Series (1994), Collector Books.

Periodical: *Noritake News,* 1237 Federal Ave. East, Seattle, WA 98102.

Vegetable Dish, oval, Noritake mark, 9⅜" l, $40.00.

Bowl, 7" d	25.00
Bread Tray	45.00
Butter Dish, cov, insert	65.00
Cake Plate, 10" d	40.00
Celery Dish, 12" l	35.00
Coffeepot, cov	185.00
Compote	100.00
Condiment Set	40.00
Creamer and Sugar, cov	50.00
Cup and Saucer	18.00
Demitasse Pot, cov	160.00
Humidor, cov	375.00
Lemon Dish, 5½" d, handle	25.00
Mayonnaise, spoon and under-plate	30.00
Nappy	15.00

Plate	
6½" d	10.00
8½" d	15.00
Platter, 10" l	85.00
Salt and Pepper Shakers, pr	30.00
Shaving Mug	100.00
Sugar Shaker	30.00
Syrup	50.00
Teapot, cov	100.00
Toothpick, 2½" h	55.00
Vase, 5¾" h, fan shape	115.00
Vegetable Dish, 9¼" l, oval	30.00

NORTH DAKOTA SCHOOL OF MINES

History: The North Dakota School of Mines was established in 1890. Earle J. Babcock, an instructor in chemistry, was impressed with the high purity of North Dakota potter's clay. In 1898 Babcock received funds to develop his finds. He tried to interest commercial potteries in North Dakota clay, but had limited success.

In 1910 Babcock persuaded the school to establish a Ceramics Department. Margaret Cable, who studied under Charles Binns and Frederick H. Rhead, was appointed head. She remained until her retirement in 1949.

Decorative emphasis was placed on native themes, e.g., flowers and animals. Art Nouveau, Art Deco, and fairly plain pieces were made.

The pottery is marked in cobalt blue underglaze with "University of North Dakota/ Grand Forks, N.D./Made at School of Mines/N.D. Clay" in a circle. Some earlier pieces only are marked "U.N.D." or "U.N.D./Grand Forks, N.D." Most pieces are numbered (they can be dated with University records) and signed by both the instructor and student. Cable–signed pieces are most desirable.

References: Susan and Al Bagdade, *Warman's American Pottery and Porcelain,* Wallace–Homestead, 1994; *University Of North Dakota Pottery, The Cable Years,* Knight Publishing, 1977.

Collectors' Club: North Dakota Pottery Collectors Society, PO Box 14, Beach, ND 58621.

Bowl
  5" d, shaded blue glaze, sgd
  "Huck" **210.00**
  7" d, sky blue glaze, sgd "Mati-
  son" **85.00**
Ginger Jar, burgundy glaze, sgd
  "Middleton" **70.00**
Jar, 7½" h, bulbous, vertical neck,
  matte blue–gray excised stylized
  lamb and wreath of flowers,
  peach ground, Van Camp **950.00**
Lamp, 10½" h, tapered shape,
  shaded matte blue, green, and
  rust glaze, factory drilled base,
  die–stamped mark **330.00**
Paperweight, 3⅜" d, open flower
  head, lime green to yellow shading, marked **85.00**
Pitcher, 6¾" h, emb viking ship on
  sides, medium blue glaze,
  marked **1,495.00**

Vase, squatty bulbous, white shading to light green ground, imp circular dec separated by leaf shapes, stamp mark, inscribed mark "95A Huck" in circle, 4" h, 4½" d, $185.00.

Vase
  4" h, sgd "FLH" **135.00**
  6¾" h, imp rings on shoulder,
  matte green glaze **315.00**
  8½" h, cylindrical, small flared
  rim, apple blossom design,
  dark pink and green incised
  florals and leaves, gloss pink
  and cream ground, incised
  "Huck #5087 Apple Blos-
  soms" **1,045.00**

NUTTING, WALLACE

History: Wallace Nutting (1861–1941) was one of America's foremost photographers in the first third of the 20th century. Between 1897 and his death, he took over 50,000 pictures, kept approximately 10,000, destroyed the rest because they did not meet his standards, and commercially marketed over 2,500 of the 10,000 that he retained. Of the remaining 7,500 views, some were sold in limited numbers and the others used personally for lectures, research, or simply entertaining friends.

Millions of Nutting's hand–colored platinotype pictures were sold. Nutting opened his first studio in New York City in 1904. In 1905 he moved to a larger studio in Southbury, Connecticut. A Toronto branch office followed in 1907. In 1911–1912 Nutting sold his business and house, Nuttinghame, in Southbury. The person who purchased the business backed out, leaving Nutting without a home.

Nutting moved his entire operation, including 20 employees, to Framingham, Massachusetts. His business blossomed. At its peak, it provided employment for over 200 people in positions ranging from colorists and support staff to salesmen and framers.

Wallace Nutting began actively collecting antiques sometime around 1912. In 1917 he published his first book on furniture, *American Windsor*. In 1928 the first two volumes of *The Furniture Treasury* appeared. Volume 3 followed in 1933.

In 1917–1918 Wallace Nutting began offering reproduction furniture for sale. During the early 1920s the business prospered. However, by 1927–1928 the business was in decline. The Depression brought further decline. Nutting laid off employees, but refused to allow the business to fold. It was operating on a very limited basis at the time of his death.

During his lifetime Nutting had a close relationship with Berea College in Kentucky. Upon his wife's death, Berea was given the remains of the furniture business. After copying the blueprints and patterns at the Framingham factory for their records, Berea sold the business to Drexel Furniture Company.

References: Michael Ivankovich, *The Alphabetical & Numerical Index to Wallace Nutting Pictures*, Diamond Press, 1988; Michael Ivankovich, *The Guide To Wallace Nutting Furniture*, Diamond Press, 1990; Michael Ivankovich, *The Guide To Wallace–Nutting Like Photographers of the Early 20th Century*, Diamond Press, 1991; Michael Ivankovich, *The Price Guide To Wallace Nutting Pictures, Fourth Edition*, Diamond Press, 1989; Wallace Nutting, *Colonial Reproductions*, (reprint of 1921 catalog), Diamond Press, 1992; Wallace Nutting, *The Wallace Nutting Expansible Catalog* (reprint of 1915 catalog), Diamond Press, 1987; Wallace Nutting, *Wallace Nutting General Catalog, Supreme Edition* (reprint of 1930 catalog), Schiffer Publishing, 1977; Wallace Nutting, *Windsors*, (reprint of 1918 catalog), Diamond Press, 1992.

Collectors' Club: Wallace Nutting Collectors Club, 186 Mountain Ave., North Caldwell, NJ 07006.

Museum: Wadsworth Athenaeum, Hartford, CT.

Album, *Up At Vilas Farm,* 22 pgs, mounted, colored, and sgd pictures, leather bound, taken at Charles Nathaniel Vilas Estate in Alstead, NH, one of three known copies **2,850.00**

Book
Furniture Treasury, Volumes I
and II, 1948 edition **55.00**
Photographic Art Secrets, 1st
edition **135.00**
States Beautiful Series
  Maine Beautiful, 1st edition,
  green cover **50.00**
  Massachusetts Beautiful, 1st
  edition, green cover **50.00**

Picture, *On The Slope*, #312, Rhode Island, 11 x 17", $225.00.

New Hampshire Beautiful, 1st
edition, green cover **60.00**
New York Beautiful, 2nd edition, tan cover, dj **65.00**
Virginia Beautiful, 1st edition,
green cover, sgd by Wallace
Nutting **60.00**
Catalog, Furniture, 1926 . . . .   **70.00**
Furniture
Chair, ladderback, five back slats, bulbous turned front stretchers, sausage turned side stretchers, NE
  Arm **525.00**
  Side, maple finish, block brand   **325.00**
Library Table, maple, single drawer, paper label, light maple finish **750.00**
Windsor Chair
  Comb Back, arm **375.00**
  Slipper **625.00**
  Tenon, arm **700.00**
Greeting Card
  Easter **75.00**
  Silhouette **7.50**
Picture
Along The River, 14 x 17" **60.00**
Autumn Ripples, #5442, ext. VT river scene, 10 x 12" **85.00**
Car, black and white glossy . . .   **50.00**
Colorist's Coloring Instructions, #228, set of orig colorist's instructions, complete color specifications attached to model picture, 15 x 18" **200.00**
Comfort And A Cat, #545, girl sewing near Nuttinghame fireplace, cat sleeps in basket on Windsor chair, 13 x 15" **185.00**
Cottages On The Old Sod, #9850, Irish scene of two mothers and four young children, thatched roof cottages, 11 x 14" **675.00**
Cypress Heights, #2276, CA seascape, single cypress tree on rocky hilltop, 18 x 22" **725.00**
Dog–On–It, #2739, eight puppies sitting on green garden bench, 7 x 11" **1,150.00**
Drying Apples, #429, Uncle Sam and Granny core apples, fireplace, 10 x 12" **325.00**
Four O'Clock, #633, sixteen

cows standing in green field, blue stream, 14 x 17" **1,150.00**

Goose Chase Quilt, The, #2353, blue settle, girl sewing quilt by fireplace, 13 x 22" **250.00**

Grandmother's China, #2366, girl sitting beside corner cupboard filled with china, 11 x 17" **125.00**

Graves–Redfield House, Madison, CT, black and white, front view, brown clapboard house, snow scene, 13 x 16" **525.00**

Guardian Mother, The, #1043, little blond girl, standing to the left of her mother, flowing dresses, 9 x 14" **2,200.00**

Hollyhock Cottage, #6414, pink flowers, green garden border English cottage, 10 x 12" **85.00**

Honeymoon Cottage, 11 x 14" . **50.00**

Housatonic Blossoms, #980, blossoming trees by rushing Housatonic River, CT, 10 x 16" **170.00**

Ivy and Rose Cloister, #2197, ivy covered red brick CA mission, 13 x 16" **375.00**

June Joy, #6796, road with blossoming trees and bridge, 13 x 17" **50.00**

Litchfield Minister, #5845, English cathedral, 14 x 17" **150.00**

Sewing By The Fire, 11 x 14" . **60.00**

Sunshine and Music, #1340, girl playing piano, formal int. setting, orange dress, 10 x 16" . **210.00**

Sylvan Dell, #8129, tall elm tree by stream, 10 x 20" **115.00**

Where Trout Lie, #8645, rippling stream, 13 x 16" **120.00**

Winding The Tall Clock, #3302, girl, formal bedroom, winding tall case clock, 14 x 17" **165.00**

Silhouette
Girl
Looking into mirror, 5 x 5", round frame **60.00**
Sitting on garden bench, 7 x 8" **80.00**
With parasol, garden scene, 5 x 5", orig label on back, round frame **125.00**
George Washington, orig label on back, 4 x 5" **75.00**
Martha Washington, orig label on back, 4 x 5" **45.00**

OCCUPIED JAPAN

History: At the end of World War II, the Japanese economy was devastated. To secure needed hard currency, the Japanese pottery industry produced thousands of figurines and other knickknacks for export. From the beginning of the American occupation until April 28, 1952, these objects were marked "Japan," "Made in Japan," "Occupied Japan," and "Made in Occupied Japan." Only pieces marked with the last two designations are of strong interest to Occupied Japan collectors. The first two marks also were used during other time periods.

The variety of products is endless—ashtrays, dinnerware, lamps, planters, souvenir items, toys, vases, etc. Initially it was the figurines which attracted the largest number of collectors; today many collectors focus on non–figurine material.

References: Florence Archambault, *Occupied Japan For Collectors,* Schiffer Publishing, 1992; Gene Florence, *The Collector's Encyclopedia Of Occupied Japan Collectibles,* First Series (1976, 1992 value update), Second Series (1979, 1993 value update), Third Series (1987, 1994 value update), Fourth Series (1990, 1993 value update), Fifth Series (1992, 1994 value update), Collector Books; David C. Gould and Donna Crevar–Donaldson, *Occupied Japan Toys With Prices,* L–W Book Sales, 1993; Carole Bess White, *Collector's Guide To Made In Japan Ceramics: Identification & Values,* Collector Books, 1994.

Collectors' Club: The Occupied Japan Club, 29 Freeborn St., Newport, RI 02840.

Additional Listings: See *Warman's Americana & Collectibles* for more examples.

Ashtray
Bisque, cornucopia, 7 x 8", chariot, rearing horse, and two cherubs, multicolored beading, gold trim, unglazed **75.00**
Ceramic, elephants, stacking, set of four **25.00**
Metal, 3" d, baseball catcher's mitt **85.00**
Baby Rattle, celluloid, roly poly clown **15.00**

Figure, beetle, black top hat, green body, white violin, marked "Made in Occupied Japan," 3" h, $15.00.

Bell, 5" h, figural black boy **48.00**
Candy Dish, porcelain, black ground, green glaze, pr metal handles, pink flowers **15.00**
Cigarette Box, cov, metal, dog's head on red ground **10.00**
Creamer, 3¼" h, porcelain, bird on bamboo plant, colored flowers, brown and gold border **10.00**
Demitasse Cup and Saucer, bisque, imitation Royal Vienna . **20.00**
Dinner Service, white and green pagoda dec, marked "Narumi China Manchu 368," price for 89 pc set **1,450.00**
Figure
5" h, boy blowing horn **28.00**
10" h, Napoleon and Josephine, seated on chairs, sgd "Pauluk," price for pr **100.00**
Flower Frog, 6" l, bisque, figural, girl with bird on shoulder, pastel highlights, gold trim **45.00**
Lamp Base, bisque, colonial couple, oval, painted details **30.00**
Match Holder, 7 x 4½", bisque, colonial couple, each holding basket, striker on side **40.00**
Opera Glasses, metal and plastic **45.00**
Pencil Sharpener, figural bulldog head, metal **12.00**
Planter, 6" d, duck, bisque **25.00**
Salad Set, bowl, serving fork and spoon, lacquerware **20.00**
Salt and Pepper Shakers, porcelain

Frogs, tray, price for 3 pc set .. **13.00**
Windmill, moving blades, pr ... **25.00**
Shelf Sitter, porcelain, boy holding hat, blue pants, yellow coat ... **10.00**
Silent Butler, sq, metal, handled . **10.00**
Tape Measure, celluloid, pink pig **15.00**
Tea Set, teapot, creamer, and sugar, porcelain, figural tomato, price for 5 pc set **30.00**
Toy, celluloid, waltzing couple, orig box and key **65.00**
Toothpick Holder, bisque, young woman leaning against wall ... **20.00**
Tray, 8¼ x 5", papier–mache, hp, roses, marked "Alcohol Proof/ SS/Made in Occupied Japan" . **18.00**
Vase, 10½" h, Banko, scenic relief, beige and brown **75.00**
Wall Pocket, 4 x 2¾ x 1½", bisque, colonial woman on balcony ... **25.00**

G.E. OHR, BILOXI.

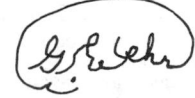

OHR POTTERY

History: Ohr pottery was produced by George E. Ohr in Biloxi, Mississippi. There is some discrepancy as to when he actually established his pottery. Some suggest 1878, but Ohr's autobiography indicates 1883. In 1884 Ohr exhibited 600 pieces of his work, indicating that he had been working for some time.

Ohr's techniques included twisting, crushing, folding, denting, and crinkling thin–walled clay into odd, grotesque, and sometimes graceful forms. Much of his early work is signed with an impressed stamp of his name and location in block letters. His later work, often marked with the flowing script designation "G E Ohr," was usually left unglazed.

In 1906 Ohr closed the pottery and stored over 6,000 pieces as his legacy to his family. He hoped it would be purchased by the U.S. Government, which never happened. The entire collection remained in storage until it was rediscovered in 1972.

Today Ohr is recognized as one of the

leading potters in the American Art Pottery movement. Some greedy individuals have taken the later unglazed pieces and covered them with poor–quality glazes in hopes of making them more valuable. These pieces, usually with the flowing script mark, do not have "stilt marks" on the bottom.

References: Susan and Al Bagdade, *Warman's American Pottery and Porcelain,* Wallace–Homestead, 1994; Garth Clark, Robert Ellison, Jr., and Eugene Hecht, *The Mad Potter of Biloxi: The Art & Life of George Ohr,* Abbeville Press, 1989.

Bowl
 3½" d, crimped body, streaked brown and gold gloss glaze, stamped "G E Ohr, Biloxi" ... **770.00**
 6" d, ovoid, folded form, mottled brown, high glaze, marked "G E Ohr, Biloxi, Miss" **2,000.00**
Figure, 3¼" h, ivory and brown speckled panther's head, dark ground plaque **650.00**
Goblet, 6¾" h, straight cylindrical bowl, flared foot, bisque finish, incised lines and script mark .. **115.00**
Inkwell, 2⅞" h, 3½" l, figural log cabin, green glaze, imp "G E Ohr, Biloxi" **1,035.00**
Jug, 7½" h, incised line at midpoint, loop handle, dark mottled green, glossy glaze, marked "Biloxi," 1891–1908 ....**1,100.00**
Mug, 5" h, G–clef handle, streaked gunmetal glaze, yellow–green glaze, incised "G E Ohr" **715.00**
Pitcher
 4¼" h, scalloped and folded rim, cutout handle, gunmetal gray glaze, mottled green base ...**1,760.00**
 6½" h, octagonal, concave sides, raised nude figures, cherub, and floral bouquet, mottled dark brown body, high glaze, inscribed "G E Ohr, Biloxi," 1891–1908 ....**1,200.00**
 7" h, paneled, molded design of children, women, and florals, dark red glaze, black accents, imp "George E Ohr, Biloxi, Miss" **3,080.00**
 7½" h, incised floral and foliate dec, loop handle, duck–billed

spout, green mottled body, high glaze, 1891–1908 .....**1,200.00**
Puzzle Mug
 3½" h, waisted body, D–form handle, brown mottled high glaze, imp "G E Ohr, Biloxi, Miss," 1891–1908 .... **650.00**
 4" h, cylindrical, pinched waist, ribbed handle, mottled dark brown, glossy glaze, marked "G E Ohr" in script, 1891–1908 ....**1,000.00**
Slop Jar, 2⅜" h, circular, speckled mustard dec, high glaze, 1891–1908 .... **650.00**
Teapot, 5¾" h, green, dark blue, and clear pigeon feathered glaze, orange clay body, reglazed cov **1,540.00**

Vase, bell-shaped body, extended neck, green, brown high glaze, marked, 4" h, $225.00.

Vase
 3" h, circular, dome shoulders, short neck, mottled dark green under high glaze, marked "Geo E Ohr, Biloxi, Miss," 1891–1908 .... **350.00**
 3½" h, deep blue, folded rim, high glaze, marked "G E Ohr, Biloxi, Miss," 1891–1908 .... **875.00**
 3¾" h, flaring bottom, black high glaze, marked "G E Ohr" in script **350.00**
 5" h, 7" w, twisted base, cylindrical neck, two shaped handles, gunmetal and brown glaze, marked "G E Ohr" **1,980.00**

6¾" h, pinched middle, rose–
pink gunmetal glaze, green
sponged and dripped glaze . . **3,300.00**
7¼" h, ruffled rim, dimpled base,
green gunmetal and mahog-
any glaze, clear drip glaze . . **1,870.00**

OLD IVORY
84

OLD IVORY CHINA

History: Old Ivory derives its name from
the background color of the china. It was
made in Silesia, Germany, during the second half of the 19th century. Marked pieces
usually have a pattern number (pattern
names are not common) and the crown Silesia mark.

Reference: Susan and Al Bagdade, *Warman's English & Continental Pottery & Porcelain, Second Edition,* Wallace–Homestead, 1991.

Periodical: *Old Ivory Newsletter,* PO Box
1004, Wilsonville, OR 97070.

Berry Set, #82, price for 7 pc set **300.00**
Bowl, 9½" d, #84 . . . . **90.00**

Nappy, #16 pattern, 6⅝" d, $68.00.

Cake Plate, 11¼" d, #84 . . . . **90.00**
Celery Tray, 9¼" l, #78 . . . . **65.00**
Chocolate Pot, #15 . . . . **275.00**
Chocolate Set, #73, marked "Si-
lesia," price for 13 pc set **700.00**
Cracker Jar, cov, #15, barrel
shape, flake lower edge **275.00**
Creamer and Sugar, Silesia, #75 **185.00**
Cup and Saucer
#15 . . . . **45.00**
#202 . . . . **35.00**
Dessert Plate, 6" d, Holly pattern,
sgd **65.00**
Plate, 8" d
#28 . . . . **35.00**
#84 . . . . **65.00**
Platter, 11½" l, Holly pattern, #22 **100.00**
Sugar, cov, #84 . . . . **50.00**
Toothpick, #75 . . . . **85.00**
Waste Bowl, #75 . . . . **110.00**

OLD PARIS CHINA

History: Old Paris china is fine–quality
porcelain made by various French factories
located in and about Paris during the 18th
and 19th centuries. Some pieces were
marked, but the majority was not. Characteristics of this type of china include fine
porcelain, beautiful decorations, and gilding. Favorite colors were dark maroon,
deep cobalt blue, and a deep green.

Reference: Susan and Al Bagdade, *Warman's English & Continental Pottery & Porcelain, Second Edition,* Wallace–Homestead, 1991.

Additional Listing: Continental China
and Porcelain (General).

Apothecary Jar, pr, 10½" h, cylindrical, drug name on gilt ground,
spherical finial **225.00**
Cachepot, attached stand **235.00**
Coffeepot, ovoid, landscape dec,
gold trim, lyre finial, 19th C **90.00**
Compote, pr, 8½" d, gold and
white, openwork, sq base **150.00**
Dinner Service
19 pcs, each painted with different bird, ornate gold borders,
soup tureen and underplate,
oval platters, chop dish, twelve

Tea and Coffee Service, coffeepot, teapot, cov sugar, creamer, 3 cov coffee canns, 3 cov teacups, gilt and cobalt blue banding, floral reserves, floral ground, bowknot and wreath handles, 3rd quarter 19th C, Vieux Paris, price for set, $990.00.

9¼" d plates, and mustard
  stand **8,525.00**
99 pcs, large tureen, three vegetable dishes, eleven cups and saucers, seven demitasse cups, eight saucers, five platters, one fish plate, eleven dinner plates, sixteen dessert bowls, ten soup bowls, two sauceboats and stands, two large serving bowls, one small serving bowl, and one compote, blue and white, mid 19th
  C **1,980.00**
Lamp, pr, 19" h, ormolu mounted, gray/blue ground, floral painted
  panels, c1850 .... **1,325.00**
Punch Bowl, 14¼" d, apple green sides, fruit reserves and gilt foliate scrollwork, mid 19th C **525.00**
Serving Dish, cov, 9" d, fruit knobbed finial, Anneau D'or,
  c1850 .... **90.00**
Vase
  9¼" h, ovoid notched rim, white body, gilt painted central grapevines motif, applied leaves, loop handles, mid 19th
    C **200.00**
  14" h, applied vining morning

glory dec, center painted floral bouquet, mid 19th C, price for
  pair **1,210.00**
14¼" h, mantel, floral and cobalt panels, gilt trim, price for pair **500.00**
16" h, mantel, flaring cornucopia form, gilt ground, one with maiden, other with suitor, 19th
  C, price for pair **825.00**

OLD SLEEPY EYE

History: Sleepy Eye, a Sioux Indian chief who reportedly had a droopy eye, gave his name to Sleepy Eye, Minnesota, and one of its leading flour mills. In the early 1900s Old Sleepy Eye Flour offered four Flemish gray, cobalt blue decorated heavy stoneware premiums: a straight–sided butter crock, curved salt bowl, stein, and vase. The premiums were made by Weir Pottery Company, later to become Monmouth Pottery Company, and finally to emerge as the present–day Western Stoneware Company of Monmouth, Illinois.

Additional pottery and stoneware pieces were issued. Forms included five sizes of pitchers (4, 5½, 6½, 8, and 9 inches), mugs, steins, sugar bowls, and tea tiles (hot plates). Most were cobalt blue on white, but other glaze hues, such as browns, golds, and greens, were used.

Old Sleepy Eye also issued many other items, including bakers' caps, lithographed barrel covers, beanies, fans, multicolored pillow tops, postcards, trade cards, etc. Production of Old Sleepy Eye stoneware ended in 1937.

In 1952 Western Stoneware Company made 22– and 40–ounce steins in chestnut brown glaze with a redesigned Indian head. From 1961 to 1972 gift editions, dated and signed with a maple leaf mark, were made for the Board of Directors and others within the company. Beginning in 1973, Western Stoneware Company issued an annual limited edition stein, marked and dated, for collectors.

References: Susan and Al Bagdade, *Warman's American Pottery and Porcelain*, Wallace–Homestead, 1994; Elinor Meugnoit, *Old Sleepy Eye*, published by author, 1979.

Collectors' Club: Old Sleepy Eye Collectors Club, PO Box 12, Monmouth, IL 61462.

Reproduction Alert: Blue and white pitchers, crazed, weighted, and often with a stamp or the word "Ironstone" are the most copied. The stein and salt bowl also have been made. Many reproductions come from Taiwan.

A line of fantasy items—new items which never existed as part of the original line—includes an advertising pocket mirror with miniature flour barrel label, small glass plates, fruit jars, toothpick holders, glass and pottery miniature pitchers, and salt and pepper shakers. One mill item has been made: a sack marked as though it were old but of a size that could not possibly hold the amount of flour indicated.

MILL ITEMS

Adv, pinback button, "Old Sleepy Eye For Me," Indian chief bust portrait	**150.00**
Cookbook	
"Sleepy Eye Flour Mills/Cookbook," Indian chief bust portrait, sq shape	**250.00**
"Sleepy Eye Milling Co," Indian chief portrait, bread loaf shape	**125.00**
Demitasse Spoon, roses in bowl .	**135.00**
Dough Scraper, wood handle with "Sleepy Eye Flour," tin blade ..	**250.00**
Letter Opener, bronze, Indian head on handle, marked "Sleepy Eye Milling Co, Sleepy Eye, Minn"	**750.00**
Label, barrel type, "Hummer Flour," two hummingbirds around flowers, lithograph, round	**250.00**
Sheet Music, "Sleepy Eye," lyrics by Mark Hawkins, music by Hall Parks	**200.00**
Teaspoon, silver plated, Indian on handle, Unity	**85.00**
Trade Cards, framed set of 10 ..	**1,500.00**

OLD SLEEPY EYE CLUB CONVENTION ITEMS

Barrel, 1982	**60.00**
Membership Pin, 1977	**60.00**

Tea Tile, cobalt blue and white stoneware, wood frame, $1,000.00.

Mug, 1976	**200.00**
Pitcher, 1983	**95.00**

POTTERY AND STONEWARE

Mug, 4¼" h, blue bands	**170.00**
Pitcher	
4" h, blue and white	**150.00**
5¼" h, blue on yellow, Indian head on handle	**700.00**
9" h, blue and white	**230.00**
Stein	
Blue on white, 7¾" h, 1907–37.	**260.00**
Brown on white, 7¾" h	**825.00**
Director's, blue on white, 1968 to 1973	**175.00**
Sugar Bowl, 4" h, cobalt blue on white, 1906–37	**360.00**

ONION MEISSEN

History: The blue onion or bulb pattern is of Chinese origin and depicts peaches and pomegranates, not onions. It was first made in the 18th century by Meissen, hence the name Onion Meissen.

Factories in Europe, Japan, and elsewhere copied the pattern. Many still have the pattern in production, including the Meissen factory in Germany.

Note: Prices given are for pieces produced between 1870 and 1930. Many pieces are marked with a company's logo; after 1891 the country of origin is indicated on imported pieces. Early Meissen examples bring a high premium.

Bowl, 11″ d, round, gold edge, pre–1900	**165.00**
Box, cov, 4 x 4¼″, round, rose finial	**70.00**
Candlesticks, pr, 7″ h	**75.00**
Creamer and Sugar, gold edge, c1900	**175.00**
Cup and Saucer	**65.00**
Demitasse Cup and Saucer, gold edge, c1900, price for set of 7	**55.00**
Dinner Service, service for six plus serving dishes, candlesticks, coffeepot, and teapot, price for 65 pc set	**3,000.00**
Dish, 7¾″ l, oval, marked	**70.00**
Fruit Knives, price for set of 6	**75.00**
Meat Pounder, large	**75.00**
Melon Mold, handled	**30.00**
Mustard Pot, 4¾″ h, ladle and underplate	**50.00**
Piecrust Crimper, wooden handle	**25.00**
Plate	
5½″ d, marked	**12.00**
8½″ d, marked	**25.00**
9″ l, leaf shape	**75.00**

Plate, scalloped edge, white ground, blue dec, marked, 14″ d, $85.00.

9¾″ d, blue crossed sword mark	**100.00**
10″ d	**75.00**
14″ d	**80.00**
Platter	
10″ l	**75.00**
12″ l, oval, marked	**65.00**
22″ l, Meissen crossed swords mark	**150.00**
Pot de Creme	**45.00**
Salt and Pepper Shakers, pr	**40.00**
Scoop, 9″ l	**35.00**
Serving Dish, butterfly shape, two sections, center handle	**225.00**
Shoe, 6″ l, c1860, Meissen crossed swords mark	**395.00**
Skimmer, reticulated, curved shape	**60.00**
Soup Tureen, marked	**170.00**
Teapot, 10″ h, mid 20th C	**325.00**
Tea Strainer, wooden handle	**20.00**
Tea Tile, 6″ d, 19th C, Meissen crossed swords mark	**198.00**
Tray, 15″ l, rect, flat, mid 20th C	**165.00**
Vase, bud, 6½″ h	**65.00**

OPALESCENT GLASS

History: Opalescent glass is a clear or colored glass with milky white decorations which shows a fiery or opalescent quality when held to light. The effect was achieved by applying bone ash chemicals to designated areas while a piece was still hot and then refiring it at tremendous heat.

There are three basic categories of opalescent glass: (1) Blown (or mold blown) patterns, e.g., Daisy & Fern and Spanish Lace; (2) Novelties, pressed glass patterns made in a limited number of pieces which often included unusual shapes such as Corn or Trough; and (3) Pattern (pressed) glass.

Opalescent glass was produced in England in the 1870s. Northwood began the American production in 1897 at its Indiana, Pennsylvania, plant. Jefferson, National Glass, Hobbs, and Fenton soon followed.

References: Gerry Baker, et al., *Wheeling Glass 1829-1939: Collection of the Oglebay Institute Glass Museum,* Oglebay Institute, 1994, distributed by Antique Publications; Bill Edwards, *The Standard Opalescent Glass Price Guide,* Collector

Books, 1992; William Heacock, *Encyclopedia of Victorian Colored Pattern Glass, Book II, Opalescent Glass from A to Z, Second Edition,* Antique Publications, 1977; William Heacock and William Gamble, *Encyclopedia of Victorian Colored Pattern Glass, Book 9, Cranberry Opalescent from A to Z,* Antique Publications, 1987; William Heacock, James Measell, and Berry Wiggins, *Dugan/Diamond: The Story of Indiana, Pennsylvania, Glass,* Antique Publications, 1993; William Heacock, James Measell, and Berry Wiggins, *Harry Northwood: The Early Years 1881–1900,* Antique Publications, 1990; William Heacock, James Measell, and Berry Wiggins, *Harry Northwood: The Wheeling Years, 1901–1925,* Antique Publications, 1991; Ellen T. Schroy, *Warman's Glass,* Wallace–Homestead, 1992; Ellen T. Schroy (ed.), *Warman's Pattern Glass,* Wallace–Homestead, 1993.

BLOWN

Barber Bottle, Swirl, cranberry, sq body, rolled lip **210.00**
Bowl
  Jewel & Fan, blue, ruffled **30.00**
  Ruffles & Rings, green **35.00**
Bride's Basket, Bubble Lattice, cranberry, hobnail, ruffled, and pleated rim, Northwood, ornate Wilcox holder of trailing six–pointed starflowers, two borders of relief flowers and coiled crustaceans with applied moths on feet **575.00**
Butter Dish, cov, Leaf and Basketweave, vaseline frosted **195.00**
Celery Vase, Chrysanthemum Base Swirl, satin ground, blue . **125.00**
Compote, Coin Spot, pleated edge, vaseline **35.00**
Cruet
  Daisy and Fern, blue, swirl **75.00**
  Seaweed, cranberry **850.00**
  Windows, cranberry, heat check **495.00**
Dish, Many Loops, green, trefoil . **30.00**
Jug, Windows, cranberry **600.00**
Lamp, Christmas Snowflake, cranberry, glass connector **550.00**
Pitcher
  Milk, Wide Stripe, cranberry . . . **500.00**

Water
  Albany Swirl, 10" h, 5½" w, blue, ruffled, modified tankard, applied blue handle . . **225.00**
  Blueberry, 9" h, 6½" w, deep cranberry, ruffled rim, applied crystal handle **425.00**
  Crisscross, Consolidated Glass Co, 9¼" h, 6½" w, deep cranberry, bright opal white, ruffled top, applied frosted clear handle **2,200.00**
  Daffodil, blue, heat check . . . **450.00**
  Daisy and Fern, vaseline, Fenton **185.00**
  Fern, 8¾" h, 7" w, deep cranberry, sq top, annealing line where handle meets body near top **450.00**
  Spanish Lace, 10" h, 6" w, deep cranberry, ruffled top, applied clear reeded shell handle **375.00**
  Stars and Stripes, 8½" h, 4½" w, tankard, deep cranberry, deep white opal **1,500.00**
  Swirl, white, blue handle **200.00**
Rose Bowl, Swirl, white **35.00**
Saltshaker, Spanish Lace, vaseline **95.00**
Sugar Shaker
  Bubble Lattice, cranberry **295.00**
  Coin Spot, blue, ring neck mold **250.00**
  Daisy and Fern, blue **275.00**
Syrup, Coin Spot, blue, bulbous **90.00**

Novelty, Pump and Trough, Northwood, vaseline, $160.00.

Water Set, pitcher and tumblers
  Beaumont Swirl, cranberry 375.00
  Blown Drapery, tankard shaped
    pitcher, blue 900.00

NOVELTIES

Bowl
  Keyholes, white 35.00
  Leaf and Diamonds, 3 ftd, white 35.00
  Winter Cabbage, white 35.00
Pump and Trough, blue, North-
  wood, small foot chip 110.00

PRESSED

Berry Bowl, master
  Beatty Rib, white 45.00
  Tokyo, green 55.00
Butter Dish, cov
  Idyll, green 200.00
  Palm Beach, vaseline 250.00
  Regal, blue 150.00
Celery Vase, Beatty Rib, blue ... 65.00
Compote, Everglades, ftd, yellow 95.00
Creamer
  Allover Hobnail 50.00
  Argonaut Shell, blue, sgd 175.00
  Intaglio, Northwood, blue 85.00
Creamer and Sugar, Hobnail,
  Northwood 50.00
Cruet, orig stopper
  Hobnail, white, pontil, stopper
    missing, Hobbs Brockunier,
    one bad hob 50.00
  Intaglio, white 115.00
  Iris with Meander, white 225.00
  Swag with Brackets, vaseline .. 300.00
  Wild Bouquet, white 175.00
Epergne, Jackson, blue 150.00
Finger Bowl, Beatty Rib, blue ... 40.00
Jelly Compote
  Intaglio, white 30.00
  Iris with Meander, blue 45.00
  Scroll with Acanthus 45.00
  Swag with Brackets, green 32.00
  Tokyo, blue 35.00
Plate, Iris with Meander, blue ... 30.00
Salt and Pepper Shakers, pr,
  Paneled Sprig, white lattice ... 125.00
Salt, individual, Beatty Rib, white 15.00
Sauce, Tokyo, low, white 35.00
Spooner
  Hobnail, blue 45.00

Idyll, green 90.00
Intaglio, white 23.00
Swag with Brackets, blue 32.00
Sugar, cov
  Daisy and Button, blue 45.00
  Idyll, green 150.00
Sugar Shaker
  Paneled Sprig, green and gold
    enamel 95.00
  Ribbed Opal Lattice, cranberry . 395.00
Toothpick
  Diamond Spearhead, green ... 65.00
  Ribbed Spiral, blue 110.00
  Wreath and Shell, vaseline,
    enamel dec 265.00
Tumbler, Regal, blue 50.00
Vase, Cherry Panels, ruffled, blue 48.00
Water Set, pitcher and tumblers,
  Beatty Rib, white, 6 pcs 175.00

OPALINE GLASS

History: Opaline glass was a popular mid
to late 19th century European glass. The
glass has a certain amount of translucency
and often is found decorated in enamel designs and trimmed in gold.

Reference: Ellen T. Schroy, *Warman's
Glass,* Wallace–Homestead, 1992.

**Box, hinged, pale green, gold
enameling, some cut design,
French, 4″ d, 2½″ h, $135.00.**

Basket, 8″ sq, ftd, French green . 45.00
Bowl, 9″ d, cov, enamel floral dec,
  ftd 60.00
Box, cov
  4″ d, French green, hinged lid,
    gilt metal mountings 60.00
  6½″ d, blue, floral enamel, tulip
    finial 50.00

Cologne Bottle, green, enamel beading, gilt scrolls, ftd, matching stopper 80.00

Creamer, green, Wheat and Rushes pattern 42.00

Cruet, 7″ h, pink, applied opaque handle, tulip shape stopper ... 200.00

Curtain Tiebacks, Victorian, brass calla lily dec, c1850, price for pair 280.00

Epergne, three trumpet vases, blue 200.00

Finger Bowl, blue, matching underplate 70.00

Goblet
5″ h, white 25.00
7″ h, blue 35.00

Hat, 3½″ d, fluted top, deep blue, white enamel dec 70.00

Inkwell, 3″ h, Louis XVI, gilt bronze mountings, broken column shape, periwinkle blue shaft and leaf tip molded base 200.00

Lantern, 30″ h, hall, blue, stamped brass mountings, cut glass prisms, French, minor imperfections 440.00

Mug, Bird and Wheat pattern ... 40.00

Perfume Bottle
4⅜″ h, gold bronze filigree overlay collar and hinged cap, French, price for pair 200.00
8½″ h, pink, price for pair 300.00

Pickle Castor, cov, green insert, silver plate ormolu frame, c1880 175.00

Pitcher, 7″ h, hp, cherubs, artist sgd, stamped 1873 Paris Exposition 275.00

Plate, 9¾″ d, white scalloped edge, gilt trim 30.00

Rose Bowl, 3″ d, hp dec 42.00

Soap Dish, cov, blue, hp, floral dec 75.00

Tumbler, 4½″ h, white, 18th C equestrian figure, gilt trim 40.00

Vase
5½″ h, globular, slender neck, pink and yellow flowers, green leaves 100.00
6¾″ h, mauve, gold trim, French, price for pair 170.00
9″ h, bulbous, slender neck, dark green enameled floral dec, mint green ground, price for pair 125.00

ORIENTAL RUGS

History: The history of Oriental rugs or carpets dates back to 3000 BC; but it was in the 16th century that they became prevalent. The rugs originated in the regions of Central Asia, Iran (Persia), Caucasus, and Anatolia. Early rugs can be classified into basic categories: Iranian, Caucasian, Turkoman, Turkish, and Chinese. Later India, Pakistan, and Iraq produced rugs in the Oriental style.

The pattern name is derived from the tribe which produced the rug, e.g., Iran is the source for Hamadan, Herez, Sarouk, Tabriz, and others.

When evaluating an Oriental rug, age, design, color, weave, knots per square inch, and condition determine the final value. Silk rugs and prayer rugs bring higher prices.

References: Murray Eiland, *Oriental Rugs: A New Comprehensive Guide,* Little, Brown and Company, 1981; Linda Kline, *Beginner's Guide To Oriental Rugs,* Ross Books, 1980; Ivan C. Neff and Carol V. Maggs, *Dictionary of Oriental Rugs,* Van Nostrand Reinhold, 1979; Joyce C. Ware, *The Official Price Guide to Oriental Rugs,* House of Collectibles, 1992.

Periodicals: *HALI,* PO Box 4312, Philadelphia, PA 19118; *Rug News,* 34 West 37th St., New York, NY 10018; *The Decorative Rug,* PO Box 709, Meredith, NH 03253.

Reproduction Alert: Beware! There are repainted rugs on the market.

Afshar, South Persia, last quarter 19th C, 6′ 2″ x 5′, midnight blue field, staggered rows of chuval guls, red, navy blue, brown, and pale blue–green, ivory meander border **1,265.00**

Aimaq, Northeast Persia, second half 19th C, 8′ 2″ x 3′ 8″, midnight blue field, diagonal rows with flower head motifs, red, aubergine, and light blue–green, red hooked diamond and cruciform motif border **3,110.00**

Baluch, Northeast Persia
4′ 9″ x 3′ 2″, late 19th C, camel field, tree of life design, light red, midnight blue, and brown,

Anatolia, Turkey, double prayer rug, mirhab border, c1910, 66" l, 44" w, $875.00.

midnight blue geometric border, elaborate weft float brocaded elems **1,500.00**

4' 10" x 3' 6", third quarter 19th C, midnight blue field, three columns, red, light rust, and royal blue serrated leaves, boteh hand dec panels, hexagon border **3,110.00**

6' 10" x 4', last quarter 19th C, black field, four elongated columns, red, sky blue, dull gold, and aubergine, red ribbon borders **870.00**

Bidjar, Northwest Persia
  10' 8" x 3' 10", late 19th/early 20th C, terra–cotta field, Herati variant design, sky blue, rose, brown, gold, and blue–green, turtle border **1,725.00**

  19' 8" x 15' 8", midnight blue field, palmettos, rosettes, birds, and arabesque leaves, red, royal blue, sky blue, rose, gold, camel, and blue–green, multiple floral borders **28,750.00**

Ersari Torba, West Turkestan, last quarter 19th C, 5' 2" x 1' 9", red field, rect medallion, midnight blue, ivory, apricot, and blue–green, dark blue–green border . **1,265.00**

Gendje, South Central Caucasus, last quarter 19th C, 5' x 3' 2", red field, hooked ivory and navy

blue medallion, small geometric motifs, sky blue, gold, aubergine, and blue–green, sky blue hooked shield motif border **4,315.00**

Hamadan, Northwest Persia, last quarter 19th C, 11' 7" x 3' 4", camel field, two open hexagonal medallions and octagon and geometric motifs, navy, sky blue, red, gold, apricot, and blue–green, ivory geometric border . **1,495.00**

Heriz, Northwest Persia
  11' 3" x 8' 8", last quarter 19th C, abrashed navy blue field, allover angular leaf and blossoming vines, red, rose, sky blue, tan–gold, and blue–green, terra–cotta rosette and serrated leaf border **4,600.00**

  11' 6" x 8' 8", early 20th C, terra–cotta field, sq medallion, midnight and royal blue, tan–gold, and green, palmetto pendants, stepped ivory spandrels, midnight blue turtle border **1,955.00**

Karabagh, South Caucasus, last quarter 19th C
  7' 9" x 4' 6", red field, ivory, sky blue, and pale blue–green diamond medallion, abrashed slate blue and ivory spandrels, gold geometric border **5,465.00**

  8' x 5', red field, sunburst medallions, navy and medium blue, ivory, gold, and light blue–green, ivory crab border **1,725.00**

Kashan, West Central Persia
  6' 4" x 4' 4", last quarter 19th C, light red field, ivory cartouche with inset red and tan floral motifs, calligraphic inscriptions, abrashed pale blue–green palmetto and rosette border **4,600.00**

  6' 6" x 4', second quarter 20th C, midnight blue field, oval medallion and dense floral motifs, red, gold, and pale blue–green, gold and rose spray border **1,955.00**

  12' 4" x 8' 4", early 20th C, midnight blue spandrels and floral dec field, red and sky blue lobed oval medallion, red palmetto and vine border **6,900.00**

Kazak, Southwest Caucasus, last quarter 19th C, 9' x 4' 2", geometric motifs, red, ivory, sky blue, gold, and blue–green, red rosette border **1,725.00**

Kerman, Southeast Persia, early 20th C, 16' 9" x 8' 9", scalloped diamond lattice and dense floral sprays, light and dark cochineal, royal blue, sky blue, brown, tan, and violet, ivory palmetto and rosette border **5,750.00**

Khamseh, Southwest Persia, late 19th C, 5' 5" x 4', ivory field, two midnight blue hooked hexagonal medallions, red, rust, sky blue, gold, and blue–green, rust rosette and boteh meander border **975.00**

Kuba, Northeast Caucasus, late 19th C, 4' 10" x 3' 4", black field, three stars, red, navy blue, gold, ivory, and blue–green, ivory crab border **1,100.00**

Malayer–Sarouk, West Persia, early 20th C, 13' x 9' 6", terra–cotta field, ivory arabesque lattice with palmettos, navy and sky blue, rose, camel, and abrashed blue–green, navy blue turtle border **26,450.00**

Melas, prayer, Southwest Anatolia, last quarter 19th C, 4' 10" x 3' 6", floral dec red field, ivory spandrels, gold border with red, blue, aubergine, and blue–green flower heads **1,150.00**

Moghan, Southeast Caucasus, last quarter 19th C, 5' x 3' 4", royal blue field, three stepped hexagonal medallions, red, apricot, aubergine, ivory, and blue–green, ivory meander border ..**1,150.00**

Mudjar, prayer, Central Anatolia, third quarter 19th C, red field, olive spandrels, red reciprocal arrowhead motif cross panel, gold rosette border **3,565.00**

Saryk Torba, West Turkestan, mid 19th C, 3' 8" x 1' 4", rust–red field, twelve guls and star type

motifs, midnight blue, gold, blue–green, and white, X motif border **21,850.00**

Seichour, Northeast Caucasus, third quarter 19th C, 9' x 3' 8", midnight blue field, four cross motifs, sky blue, red, gold, tan, dark brown, and blue–green, ivory Kufic border **3,450.00**

Senneh, Northwest Persia, last quarter 19th C, 6' 6" x 4' 2", midnight blue field, staggered elaborate boteh rows, red, sky blue, and blue–green, red turtle border **2,300.00**

Serab, runner, Northwest Persia, last quarter 19th C, 15' 7" x 3' 3", midnight and sky blue, red, rose, gold, camel, and blue–green tile motif field, five lobed ivory medallions, camel border .**1,500.00**

Shirvan, prayer, East Caucasus, last quarter 19th C, 4' 4" x 3' 4", midnight blue field, three Lesghi stars, red, ivory, sky blue, gold, and blue–green, ivory wine glass border **3,450.00**

Sultanabad, West Persia, third quarter 19th C, 11' 9" x 10' 2", camel field, palmettos, cloud bands, and animal motifs, red, sky blue, rose, and blue–green, red palmetto and serrated leaf border **16,100.00**

Tabriz, Northwest Persia, last quarter 19th C, 15' 2" x 11' 9", black field, gold floral design, wide gold border **27,600.00**

Talish, Southeast Caucasus, third quarter 19th C, 7' 8" x 3' 9", abrashed sky blue field, gold reciprocal border and ivory rosette border **12,650.00**

Tekke Torba, West Turkestan, third quarter 19th C, 3' 10" x 1' 7", rust–red field, six chuval guls, midnight blue, apricot, ivory, and blue–green, gotshak border ...**1,610.00**

Ushak, West Anatolia, late 19th C, 12' x 10', red field, two half–lobed circular medallions, orange, ivory, and pale green, orange spandrels, pale green palmetto and vine border **4,600.00**

Yuruk, Southeast Anatolia, late 19th/early 20th C, 5′ 10″ x 5′ 4″, red field, hooked diamond medallions, and two half–stepped medallions, red, tan–gold, royal blue, and aubergine, tan–gold spandrels, ivory star border . . . **5,175.00**

ORIENTALIA

History: Orientalia is a term applied to objects made in the Orient, which encompasses the Far East, Asia, China, and Japan. The diversity of cultures produced a variety of objects and styles.

References: Lea Baten, *Japanese Animal Art: Antique & Contemporary,* Charles Tuttle, 1989; Carl L. Crossman, *The Decorative Arts of The China Trade,* Antique Collectors Club, 1991; Christopher Dresser, *Traditional Arts and Crafts of Japan,* Dover Publications, 1994; John Esten (ed.), *Blue and White China,* Little, Brown and Company, 1987; Duncan Macintosh, *Chinese Blue and White Porcelain,* Antique Collectors Club, 1994; Gloria and Robert Mascarelli, *Warman's Oriental Antiques,* Wallace–Homestead, 1992.

Periodical: *The Orientalia Journal,* PO Box 94, Little Neck, NY 11363.

Museums: Art Institute of Chicago, Chicago, IL; Asian Art Museum of San Francisco, San Francisco, CA; George Walter Vincent Smith Art Museum, Springfield, MA; Pacific Asia Museum, Pasadena, CA.

Additional Listings: Canton, Celadon, Cloisonné, Fitzhugh, Nanking, Netsukes, Rose Medallion, Japanese Prints, and other categories.

Basin, 5½″ d, continuous mountain landscape scene, enameled aqua int., six character seal "Ta Ching Daoguang nien chih" . . . **260.00**
Bowl
  10″ d, blue and white landscape dec, Arita, Japanese **100.00**
  10½″ d, bronze, swan form . . . **115.00**
  12″ d, Kutani, hp, allover bird and floral motif, sgd, 19th C . **300.00**
Box
  5½″ l, lacquer, straw covered, detailed landscape scene on

lid with gold and silver inlay, Japanese **465.00**
7″ l, black lacquer, painted actors and musician scene on lid . . . **50.00**
15 x 8″, 7⅜″ h, pigskin, red, gold raised figural and floral dec, brass mounts, Chinese, 19th C **145.00**
23″ d, cov, red lacquer, lobed form, bats and scrolling lotus design, fitted int. with bats, plum, and prunus dec, four feet, Chinese, 19th C, price for pair **690.00**
Candlestick, pr, 34″ h, brass **410.00**
Charger, 15¾″ d, Imari, center bird and palm tree dec **55.00**
Dish, 8½″ d, blue and white, figures and garden setting dec, surrounded by diaper band, floral sprigs medallions, sprigs rim, Kangxi, Chinese **385.00**
Fan, 9¼″ l, peacocks motif, gilt lacquer, tasseled cords, guard sticks, Japanese **600.00**
Figure
  12½″ h, bronze, elephant, ivory tusks, sgd, Japanese, late 19th/early 20th C **400.00**
  19″ h, bronze, tiger, mid stride, cartouche with name, Japanese **385.00**
  24″ h, lions, cloisonne, price for pair **5,000.00**

Mug, Chinese Export, mauve, pink, and green floral, white ground, c1750–1800, 4½″ h, $265.00.

Furniture

Altar Table, Chinese

Mid 19th C, rect top scrolled under at each end, polychromed dec, red lacquer ground, 50½" l, 18¼" d, 32" h **435.00**

Late 19th C, Huang Huali, 36" l, 18¼" d, 34" h **525.00**

Bench, hardwood and marble, foliate carved splat, 41" l **550.00**

Cabinet, carved bird and floral dec, ivory and mother–of–pearl paneled doors, 43" w, 12" d, 62" h **525.00**

Chair, wood, carved, lacquer finish **345.00**

Cupboard, 22" w, 10¾" d, 30¾" h, lacquered, black, gilt and applied carved stone dec, two doors **235.00**

Curio Cabinet, 41½" w, 15¼" d, 77" h, teak, intricate carved fretwork and relief designs, two glazed doors top over, two bottom doors, Chinese **1,575.00**

Stand

13½ x 19½ x 19", teak, curved form, abalone inlay dec and rose medallion porcelain insert, Chinese **275.00**

16 x 18", hardwood, round lobed marble top, carved legs, ball and claw feet, Chinese **210.00**

Garden Ornament, 24½" h, cast concrete, horse **275.00**

Ginger Jar, 9" h, blue and white, wood lid **40.00**

Jacket, 34½" l, silk, coral, counted stitch dec on gauze with pavilion and landscape scenes, embroidered sleeve bands with garden and figure scene, Chinese, 19th C **825.00**

Jar, 12½" h, ovoid, porcelain, floral motif **350.00**

Kimona, 61" l, blue, green, and orange stitched bats and wave dec, black ground, Japanese .. **250.00**

Lamp, pr, 14" h, cinnabar, carved, baluster form **410.00**

Lantern, bronze, baluster form, relief dragon, flame finial, Japanese **325.00**

Letter Opener, 11½" l, ivory, wood box with jade lid, Chinese **60.00**

Mask, 9" h, iron, elderly man, beard, Japanese **90.00**

Plaque, 9½" w, 12¾" h, applied carved ivory woman, Japanese **75.00**

Robe

47" l, silk, apricot, embroidered peonies and butterflies, Peking knot, white sleeve bands, Chinese, 19th C **495.00**

72" w, 96" l, embroidered pagoda, characters, and dragon emblems, phoenix border, Chinese, 19th C **525.00**

Roof Tile, 14" h, warrior riding leaping horse, chestnut, green, and brown glaze, Chinese, 19th C **290.00**

Rug, 6' x 9', silk, dark green, floral dec, Chinese **355.00**

Sake Set, two vessels and five cups, blue lappet borders, sgd, Japanese, 20th C **250.00**

Screen, folding, two 33 x 72" sections, carved wood, red and black lacquer and applied ivory dec, birds on blossoming branches, Chinese **275.00**

Screen, four panels

15" w, 48" h panels, Chinese, 19th C, reticulated wood .. **825.00**

17" w, 77½" h panels, hardwood and porcelain, landscape scene flanked by dragon panels **2,530.00**

Scroll, ink and colored paper, silk backing, winter landscape scene with two foo dogs and birds, Chinese, 19th/20th C **115.00**

Tea Caddy, 8" l, lacquer and pewter, rect, serpentine shape, gilt and black lacquer dec, claw feet, lead lined int., 19th C **260.00**

Tea Set, 6½" h teapot, sugar, and creamer, silver, repousse, dragon handle, 28 oz, price for 3 piece set **975.00**

Tray, 15" l, marble and huali, fret border, Chinese, 19th C **1,045.00**

Urn, 15" h, conical body, buff clay, imp rope dec, three twisted peak grooved rims, four vertical carved grooves, Jomon period, Japanese **800.00**

Vase

25¼" h, bronze, relief foo lions chasing balls, flowering prunus branches extended to handles, wave ground, 19th/20th C **325.00**

30" h, ovoid, peacock blue, slightly flaring neck, turquoise glaze cov, mounted as lamp . **850.00**

OVERSHOT GLASS

History: Overshot glass was developed in the mid–1800s. A gather of molten glass was rolled over the marver upon which had been placed crushed glass to produce overshot glass. The piece then was blown into the desired shape. The finished effect was a glass that was frosted or iced in appearance.

Early pieces were mainly made in clear. As the demand for colored glass increased, color was added to the base piece and occasionally to the crushed glass.

Pieces of overshot generally are attributed to the Boston and Sandwich Glass Co., although many other companies also made it as it grew in popularity.

Reference: Ellen T. Schroy, *Warman's Glass,* Wallace–Homestead, 1992.

Museum: Sandwich Glass Museum, Sandwich, MA.

Bottle, 9½" h, 4½" d, cranberry, clear bubble stopper **135.00**

Celery Vase, 6" h, 3½" d, scalloped top, cranberry **90.00**

Cologne Bottle, 9½" h, Icicle, applied overshot icicles around neck extend down cranberry body, applied clear shell feet, orig overshot stopper, Sandwich **475.00**

Fairy Lamp

3¾" h, 3" d, pink, emb hobs, clear pressed glass "Clarke" base **125.00**

4¼" h, 3" d, opalescent, figural, crown shape, clear pressed glass "Clarke" base **175.00**

Pitcher

6" h, 4" w, deep cranberry, crys-

tal overshot, applied clear reeded shell handle, Sandwich **325.00**

7¼" h, cranberry, tankard, applied clear reeded handle ... **155.00**

8¼" h, green, amber shell handle, brown liquid carbon line near lip, Sandwich, c1875 ... **235.00**

9½" h, cranberry, tankard, thick handle, large ice bladder **800.00**

Toothpick, clear, flint, tab handles, gold trim, Portland **75.00**

Vase, 5½" h, pink, applied random amber threading **225.00**

OWENS POTTERY

History: J. B. Owens began making pottery in 1885 near Roseville, Ohio. In 1891 he built a plant in Zanesville and in 1897 began producing art pottery. Not much art pottery was produced by Owens after 1907, when most of their production centered on tiles.

Owens Pottery, employing many of the same artists and designs of its two crosstown rivals, Roseville and Weller, can appear very similar to that of its competitors (i.e., Utopian—brown glaze, Lotus—light glaze, Aqua Verde—green glaze, etc.).

There were a few techniques used exclusively at Owens. These included Red Flame ware (slip decoration under a high red glaze) and Mission (overglaze, slip decorations in mineral colors) depicting Spanish Mission scenes. Other specialties included Opalesce (semi-gloss designs in lustred gold and orange) and Coralene (small beads affixed to the surface of the decorated piece).

References: Susan and Al Bagdade, *Warman's American Pottery and Porcelain,* Wallace–Homestead, 1994; Paul Evans, *Art Pottery of the United States, 2nd Edition,* Feingold & Lewis Publishing, 1987; Ralph and Terry Kovel, *Kovels' American Art Pot-*

tery: *The Collector's Guide To Makers, Marks and Factory Histories,* Crown Publishers, 1993.

Bowl, 5½" d, Lotus, five color berry dec **225.00**
Ewer, 12¼" h, matte floral dec .. **175.00**
Jardiniere, 9" h, orange tulips, brown glaze **125.00**
Mug, 4½" h, Utopian, cherries, brown ground, artist sgd **150.00**
Plaque, 17 x 11¼", cloisonne dec, landscape, stucco cottage, aubergine and pink accents, brown roof, green trees, golden–yellow road, cobalt blue pond, contemporary golden oak frame **1,100.00**
Umbrella Stand, 20" h, Utopian, orange irises, brown glaze, sgd "Pillsbury" **525.00**

Vase, Aborigine, 6" h, $225.00.

Vase
4½" h, triangular, Utopian, yellow roses, dark brown ground **75.00**
5¼" h, Feroza, gold luster irid metallic oxides **395.00**
6" h, ovoid, slender neck, four buttresses at base, four small feet, bright green glaze, imp torch, banner, and "Owensart" **412.00**
8" h, emb enameled rose spray, matte pastel brown and blue ground, sgd "Tot Steele" **250.00**
10½" h, two handles at neck, brown and blue Art Nouveau carved bust of woman, matte ground, gold emb stylized band, Henri Deux, unmarked **660.00**
11¾" h, Utopia, slip dec thistles **230.00**

PAIRPOINT

History: The Pairpoint Manufacturing Co. was organized in 1880 as a silverplating firm in New Bedford, Massachusetts. The company merged with Mount Washington Glass Co. in 1894 and became the Pairpoint Corporation. The new company produced specialty glass items, often accented with metal frames.

Pairpoint Corp. was sold in 1938 and Robert Gunderson became manager. He operated it as the Gunderson Glass Works until his death in 1952. From 1952 until the plant closed in 1956, operations were maintained under the name Gunderson–Pairpoint. Robert Bryden reopened the glass manufacturing business in 1970, moving it back to the New Bedford area.

References: Edward and Sheila Malakoff, *Pairpoint Lamps,* Schiffer Publishing, 1990; Leonard E. Padgett, *Pairpoint Glass,* Wallace–Homestead, 1979, out–of–print; John A. Shumann III, *The Collector's Encyclopedia of American Art Glass,* Collector Books, 1988, 1994 value update.

Collectors' Club: Pairpoint Cup Plate Collectors, PO Box 890052, East Weymouth, MA 02189.

Museum: Pairpoint Museum, Sagamore, MA.

Beverage Set, 7 pcs, 10¼" h pitcher, six 4" h tumblers, clear, cut design, ftd pitcher **1,200.00**

Calling Card Receiver, etched swan in sq top, figural bird in center ring, round ftd base, 6" h, 5¾" w, $145.00.

Candlestick, pr, 11" h, silver and
brass wash, imp mark **210.00**
Centerpiece Bowl, 12" d, 3¼" h,
cut and engraved stylized floral
dec **50.00**
Dresser Box, scenic, brown **375.00**
Lamp
Boudoir
12½" h, reverse painted glass
shade with sailing boats, gilt
metal and marble base imp
"Pairpoint" and "E 3017" . . **1,840.00**
14" h
Puffy, silver plated candlestick base, Stratford shade
with red, pink, blue, and
yellow roses border, bas-
ket weave design ground **2,500.00**
9" d reverse painted ribbed
palm shade, fishing village
scene, green, yellow,
brown, blue, and orange,
brass paneled vasiform
base, spreading circular
foot **3,300.00**
15" h, 7" d puffy shade, rose
tree shade, black ground,
bright yellow, pink, and
green flowers, blue butterflies, molded brass candlestick base, circular foot,
base stamped "Pairpoint
C3064" **4,000.00**
16" h, 8" d puffy Stratford
shade, blown out dogwood
flowers, blue, yellow, pink,
and green, crystal and yellow latticino ground, vertically ribbed brass base, double stepped circular foot,
stamped "Pairpoint Mf'g Co
C3057" **2,600.00**
Desk, 12" h, 8½" d shade, four
ribbed reverse painted panels
with butterflies, brass fittings,
slender brass candlestick
base, circular foot, base
stamped "Pairpoint Mfg Co
C3020" **900.00**
Table
19" h, reverse painted glass
shade with red roses, silvered metal handled base,
imp "Pairpoint Mfg Co 3076" **9,200.00**

21" h, 14" d puffy reverse
painted
Oxford shade, blown out
deep pink and yellow
roses, leafy green foliage,
four brightly painted red,
yellow, blue, and green
flying butterflies, painted
white ground, gilt high-
lights on ext., glass
candlestick base, painted
rose dec, sq metal foot . **11,825.00**
Stratford shade, blown out
dogwood flowers and but-
terflies, alternating blue
and white vertical bands,
pastel blue, green, pink,
and yellow, SP molded tripod base, stamped "Pair-
point D3084" **6,250.00**
22" h, Exeter shade with re-
verse painted birds and
floral foliage, green ground,
silver plated trifid base **5,250.00**
23" h, Exeter shade with re-
verse painted whaling ships
and New Bedford harbor . . **5,000.00**
27" h, puffy shade with molded
relief apples, blossoms, butterflies, and bees, red, white,
green, yellow, and blue,
bronzed metal tree trunk
form base **24,000.00**
Lamp Shade, 15" d, beehive
shape, reverse painted fenced
cottage scene, artist sgd "H
Fisher" **1,265.00**
Mustache Cup and Saucer, quad-
ruplate, engraved flowers **60.00**
Perfume Bottle, 6" h, swirl mold,
enameled lily of the valley and
green scrolled dec **285.00**
Tray, 24¾" l, silver plated, chased
leaf and floral dec, angular cast
handles, 19th C **350.00**
Vase, trumpet, cobalt blue, sgd . . **190.00**

PAPER EPHEMERA

History: Maurice Rickards, author of *Collecting Paper Ephemera*, suggests that
ephemera are the "minor transient documents of everyday life," material destined

for the wastebasket but never quite making it. This definition is more fitting than traditional dictionary definitions that stress length of time, e.g., "lasting a very short time." A driver's license, which is used for a year or longer, is as much a piece of ephemera as is a ticket to a sporting event or music concert. The transient nature of the object is the key.

Collecting ephemera has a long and distinguished history. Among the English pioneers were John Seldon (1584–1654), Samuel Pepys (1633–1703), and John Bagford (1650–1716). Large American collections can be found at historical societies and libraries across the country, and museums, e.g., Wadsworth Antheneum, Hartford, CT, and the Museum of the City of New York.

When used by collectors, "ephemera" usually means paper objects, e.g., billheads and letterheads, bookplates, documents, labels, stocks and bonds, tickets, valentines, etc. However, more and more ephemera collectors are recognizing the transient nature of some three–dimensional material, e.g., advertising tins and pinback buttons. Today's specialized paper shows include dealers selling both two– and three–dimensional material.

References: Warren R. Anderson, *Owning Western History,* Mountain Press Publishing, 1993; Anne F. Clapp, *Curatorial Care of Works of Art on Paper,* Nick Lyons Books, 1987; Joseph Raymond LeFontaine, *Turning Paper To Gold,* Betterway Publications, 1988; John Lewis, *Printed Ephemera,* Antique Collectors' Club, 1990; Norman E. Martinus and Harry L. Rinker, *Warman's Paper,* Wallace–Homestead, 1994; Maurice Rickards, *Collecting Paper Ephemera,* Abbeville Press, 1988; Demaris C. Smith, *Preserving Your Paper Collectibles,* Betterway Publications, 1989; Gene Utz, *Collecting Paper: A Collector's Identification & Value Guide,* Books Americana, 1993.

Periodicals: *Paper & Advertising Collector,* PO Box 500, Mount Joy, PA 17552; *Paper Collectors' Marketplace,* PO Box 128, Scandinavia, WI 54977; *Paper Pile Quarterly,* PO Box 337, San Anselmo, CA 94979.

Collectors' Clubs: Ephemera Society, 12 Fitzroy Sq., London W1P 5HQ England;

The Ephemera Society of America, Inc., PO Box 37, Schoharie, NY 12157; The Ephemera Society of Canada, 36 Macauley Dr., Thornhill, Ontario L3T 5S5 Canada.

BLOTTERS

Blue Valley Butter	6.00
Eagle Pure White Lead, multicolored	6.00
Eastman's Extract Wild Roses, color litho	5.00
Fire Prevention Week, fireman, October calendar	5.00
Morton's Salt	10.00
Western Bank Note & Eng Co, Chicago, Lincoln's Gettysburg Speech, engraved to Thomas Jefferson, 1892	12.00

BOOKMARKS

Climax Catarrh Cure, woman with fur coat, multicolored	10.00
Hoyt's German Cologne, diecut, multicolored	6.00
James Annin Ag't Watches, Jewelry, Silver Ware, floral dec	5.00
Merry Christmas, cross–stitched on punched paper, red and green holly dec	20.00
Mr Peanut, diecut, black and white, orange stippled body, 1940s	25.00
So–Far, cross–stitched on punched paper, red and silver	10.00

BUSINESS CARDS

References: Kit Barry, *The Advertising Trade Card, Book 1,* privately printed, 1981; Robert Jay, *The Trade Card in Nineteenth–Century America,* University of Missouri Press, 1987; Avery Pitzak, *Business Cards,* privately printed, 1992; Avery N. Pitzak, *Make Your Business Card Incredibly Effective,* privately printed, 1990.

Collectors' Clubs: American Business Card Club, PO Box 460297, Aurora, CO 80046; Business Card Collectors International, PO Box 466, Hollywood, FL 33022.

Beck & Roda Fashionable Boot & Shoe Store, Rochester, NY, gold shoe	20.00

Bradley & Nash, Dealers in Hats, Caps, Boots, Shoes, Norwich, NY, blue with red, gold, and black printing **20.00**

Croul Bros Manufacturer Leather and Belting, Detroit, IL **20.00**

H C Frazer, Dealer in Shelf & Heavy Hardware, Iron, Nails & Glass, yellow with black printing **12.00**

Henry I Proctor, Manufacturer of Hand Hay Rakes, Ogdensburg, NY **10.00**

Mills & Perry Manufacturers & Dealers in Harness, Saddles, Trunks, yellow with black printing **12.00**

Royal Lace Manufacturers Boval Debeck, Bruxelles, pink with red and black printing **15.00**

The National Leather Co, Detroit, MI **40.00**

Watertown Fire Inc Co, Watertown, NY, red and black printing **25.00**

CALENDARS

1889, Youth's Companion, calendar on back **10.00**

1892, children litho, full pad, EP Dutton **40.00**

1904, Hoods Sarsaparilla, multicolored **35.00**

1905, Christmas, bell shape, adv on back **8.00**

1909, Roses to Greet You, metal hanging hook **15.00**

1916, Putnam Dyes **40.00**

CHECKS

1853, Illinois Central Railroad, vignettes **30.00**

1865, Charles Dickens' signature, March 21, twelve pounds, eight shillings **1,750.00**

1875, miners vignette, canceled . **20.00**

1884, I H Hershfield, vignette, slash cancel mark **25.00**

1887, Bank of CA, engraved **12.00**

LABELS

References: Jerry Chicone, Jr., *Florida's Classic Crates,* privately printed, 1985; Joe

Receipt for subscription to Drafted Men's Advocate, Dec 1, 1891 to Dec 1, 1892, sgd, $3.50.

Davidson, *Fruit Crate Art,* Wellfleet Press, 1990; Gordon T. McClelland and Jay T. Last, *Fruit Box Labels, A Collector's Guide,* Hillcrest Press, 1983; John Salkin and Lauri Gordon, *Orange Crate Art: The Story of Labels That Launched A Golden Era,* Warner Books, 1978.

Collectors' Clubs: Society of Antique Label Collectors, PO Box 24811, Tampa, FL 33623; The Citrus Label Society, 131 Miramonte Dr., Fullerton, CA 92365.

Cigar
Chief, Indian, emb, gold gilt dec **8.00**
Hotel Wenonah, gold gilt dec, 1903 .... **15.00**
Lemon
Cub, bear eating lemons, red ground, Upland, CA **4.00**
Galleon, sailing vessel, c1937 . **5.00**
Mission, Santa Barbara Mission **3.00**
Orange
Athlete, three runners, Claremont **5.00**
College Heights, packing house, orange blossoms, Claremont **3.00**
Kings Park, Kings Park scene, Ivanhoe **8.00**
Queen Esther, queen wearing crown and jewelry, Placentia . **4.00**
Sierra Vista, scenic design, Porterville **8.00**
Pear
Grand Coulee, dam illus **5.00**
Modoc, Indian chief, black ground **3.00**
Pirate's Cove, lake and country scene **2.00**
Swan, white swan, black ground **4.00**

LETTERHEADS AND BILLHEADS

Reference: Leslie Cabarga, *Letterheads: One Hundred Years of Design,* Chronicle Books, 1992.

Charles A Priest, Lumber Co, Fitchburg, MA, 1890	**12.00**
Daniel Warner, House and Sign Painter, blue paper, 1858	**12.00**
E B Badger & Son, Coppersmiths & Galvanized Iron Workers, Boston, 1887	**10.00**
Henry Shaw Horseshoeing, Carriage Ironing and General Jobbin, Millbrook, NY, 1890	**15.00**
The Bain Wagon Co, Kenosha, WI, 1917	**10.00**
Wm Wright, Builder of the Celebrated Wright Engine Newburgh, NY	**12.00**

POST CARDS

References: Diane Allmen, *The Official Price Guide to Postcards,* House of Collectibles, 1990; Janet Banneck, *The Antique Postcards of Rose O'Neill,* Greater Chicago Publications, 1992; Deborah Lengkeek (ed.), *The Postcard Collector Annual: Commemorating 100 Years Of The Postcard, Third Edition,* Jones Publishing, 1993; Joseph Lee Mashburn, *The Postcard Price Guide: A Comprehensive Listing, Second Edition,* Colonial House Production, 1995; Joseph Lee Mashburn, *The Super Rare Postcards of Harrison Fisher with Price Guide,* Colonial House Productions, 1992; Frederic and Mary Megson, *American Advertising Postcards—Set and Series: 1890–1920,* published by authors, 1985; Frederic and Mary Megson, *American Exposition Postcards, 1870–1920: A Catalog and Price Guide,* The Postcard Lovers, 1992; Ron Menchine, *A Picture Postcard History of Baseball,* Almar Press, 1992; Cynthia Rubin and Morgan Williams, *Larger Than Life; The American Tall–Tall Postcard 1905–1915,* Abbeville Press, 1990; Dorothy B. Ryan, *Picture Postcards In The United States, 1893–1918,* Clarkson N. Potter, 1982; Jack H. Smith, *Postcard Companion: The Collector's Reference,* Wallace–Homestead, 1989; Robert Ward, *Investment Guide To North American Real Photo Postcards,* Antique Paper Guide, 1991; Jane Wood, *The Collector's Guide To Post Cards,* L–W Promotions, 1984, 1993 value update.

Periodicals: *Barr's Postcard News,* 70 S. 6th St., Lansins, IA 52151; *Gloria's Corner,* PO Box 507, Denison, TX 75021; *Postcard Classics,* PO Box 8, Norwood, PA 19074; *Postcard Collector,* Joe Jones Publishing, 121 N. Main St., PO Box 337, Iola, WI 54945.

Special Note: An up–to–date listing of books about and featuring post cards can be obtained from Gotham Book Mart & Gallery, Inc., 41 West 47th Street, New York, NY 10036.

Collectors' Clubs: *Barr's Postcard News* and the *Postcard Collector* publish lists of over fifty regional clubs in the United States and Canada.

Advertising	
Banner Baking Co, Our Pony Team Delivery Wagon	**20.00**
Indian and Ceylon Tea	**8.00**
Majestic Stoves	**15.00**
Pope Toledo Motor Car Building, Toledo, OH	**10.00**
Sharples Tubular Cream Separator	**10.00**
Swift Pride Soap	**10.00**
White House Teas, children's tea party	**25.00**
Photographic	
Barnum & Bailey Circus, woman with horse, 1909	**12.00**
Boy, riding wire wheel pedal car	**12.00**
Fisherman, holding trout, hand tinted	**15.00**
Little Boy, holding drum by Christmas tree	**20.00**
Loon Lake Ice Co, horse pulled saws	**30.00**
Man in ice shanty	**10.00**
Supply Train, 6th Mass MNG, horse drawn National Guard Wagons and street scene	**10.00**
Political	
Admiral George Dewey, USN The Greatest Naval Hero of the War, portrait within purple wreath	**20.00**

American Undivided In The
Cause of Freedom, Wilson,
Lincoln, Washington, 1917 .. **10.00**
Where Women Vote, There Is
No Rest **8.00**
William McKinley, Late President
of the US **25.00**

SHEET MUSIC

References: Debbie Dillion, *Collectors Guide To Sheet Music,* L–W Promotions, 1988, 1993 value update; Anna Marie Guihenn and Marie Reine A. Pafik, *The Sheet Music Reference and Price Guide,* Collector Books, 1992.
Periodicals: *Sheet Music Magazine,* 352 Evelyn St., Paramus, NJ 07653; *Sonneck Society Bulletin,* PO Box 476, Canton, MA 02021.
Collectors' Clubs: City of Roses Sheet Music Collectors Club, 13447 Bush St. SE, Portland, OR 97236; National Sheet Music Society, 1597 Fair Park Ave., Los Angeles, CA 90041; New York Sheet Music Society, PO Box 1214, Great Neck, NY 11023; Ragtime Society, PO Box 520, Station A, Weston, Ontario, Canada M9N 3N3; Remember That Song (RTS), 5623 N 64th Ave., Glendale, AZ 85301; Sheet Music Exchange (SMX), 1202 12th St., Key West, FL 33040.
Museums: American Antiquarian Society, Worcester, MA; American Society of Composers, Authors & Publishers (ASCAP), New York, NY; Broadcast Music, Inc. (BMI), New York, NY.

Boys In Blue, Anthony L Maresch,
Schiebert Music Litho **8.00**
Coon, Coon, Coon, three blacks
on cov, 1900 .... **60.00**
Flag Of Our Union, O Ditson, 1862
copyright **20.00**
For You A Rose, Harrison Fisher,
1917 copyright **20.00**
Our Boys Are Marching Home,
Lee & Walker, 1865 copyright .. **30.00**
Sarah's Young Man, H DeMarsan,
Civil War scene **25.00**
Sidewalks of New York, 1926
copyright **15.00**
That Silver Haired Daddy of Mine,
Gene Autry, 1932 copyright ... **10.00**

STOCKS AND BONDS

Reference: Bill Yachtman, *The Stock & Bond Collectors Price Guide,* published by author, 1985.
Periodical: *Bank Note Reporter,* 700 East State St., Iola, WI 54990.
Collectors' Club: Bond and Share Society, 26 Broadway, New York, NY 10004.

Gerlach Barklow Company,
woman reading vignette, canceled **5.00**
Grants Hygienic Health Food Co,
emb and engraved, lady with
bear **12.00**
Honest Gold and Silver Mining
Company **35.00**
Lincoln Motor Company, orange,
sgd by W C Leland, 1920s **20.00**
Plumas Eureka Turnpike Road
Co, yellow, ornate, unused **35.00**
Real Estate Association, Petaluma, CA, black and white, issued, 1890s **25.00**
Woolworth Co, eagle over two
hemispheres vignette, brown .. **3.00**

TICKETS

Air France, 1952 .... **5.00**
American War Mothers Military
Ball, April 30, 1935 .... **12.00**
California Pacific International
Expo, San Diego, 1936 .... **6.00**
Toledo Cyclarma Building, purple,
black, and white, war scene ... **6.00**
World Columbian Expo, Manhattan Day October 21, 1893, blue
and beige **20.00**

PAPERWEIGHTS

History: Although paperweights had their origin in ancient Egypt, it was in the mid–19th century that this art form reached its zenith. The classic period for paperweights was 1845–55 in France where the Clichy, Baccarat, and Saint Louis factories produced the finest examples of this art. Other weights made in England, Italy, and Bohemia during this period rarely match the quality of the French weights.

In the early 1850s, the New England Glass Co. in Cambridge, Massachusetts, and the Boston and Sandwich Glass Co. in Sandwich, Massachusetts, became the first American factories to make paperweights.

Popularity peaked during the classic period and faded toward the end of the 19th century. Paperweights were rediscovered nearly a century later in the mid–1900s. Contemporary weights still are made by Baccarat, Saint Louis, Perthshire, and many studio craftsmen in the U.S. and Europe.

References: Monika Flemming and Peter Pommerencke, *Paperweights of the World,* Schiffer Publishing, 1994; Paul Hollister, Jr., *The Encyclopedia of Glass Paperweights,* Paperweight Press, 1969; Sibylle Jargstorf, *Paperweights,* Schiffer Publishing, 1991; Leo Kaplan, *Paperweights,* published by author, 1985; George N. Kulles, *Identifying Antique Paperweights–Lampwork,* Paperweight Press, 1987; James Mackay, *Glass Paperweights,* Facts on File, 1973; Edith Mannoni, *Classic French Paperweights,* Paperweight Press, 1984; Bonnie Pruitt, *St. Clair Glass Collectors Guide,* published by author, 1992; Pat Reilly, *Paperweights,* Courage Books, 1994; Sara Rossi, *A Collector's Guide To Paperweights,* Wellfleet Press, 1990; Lawrence H. Selman, *All About Paperweights,* Paperweight Press, 1992; L. H. Selman, *Collector's Paperweights: Price Guide and Catalogue,* Paperweight Press, 1986.

Periodical: *Paperweight News,* 761 Chestnut Street, Santa Cruz, CA 95060.

Collectors' Clubs: Caithness Collectors Club, 141 Lanza Ave., Building 12, Garfield, NJ 07026; International Paperweight Society, 761 Chestnut St., Santa Cruz, CA 95060; Paperweight Collectors Assoc. Inc., PO Box 1059, Easthampton, MA 01027; Paperweight Collectors Assoc. of Texas, 1631 Aguarena Springs Dr., #408, San Marcos, TX 78666.

Museums: Bergstrom–Mahler Museum, Neenah, WI; Corning Museum of Glass, Corning, NY; Degenhart Paperweight & Glass Museum, Inc., Cambridge, OH; Museum of American Glass at Wheaton Village, Millville, NJ.

Additional Listings: See *Warman's Americana & Collectibles* for examples of advertising paperweights.

ANTIQUE

Baccarat, garlanded buttercup, layer of cupped violet petals around layer of cupped white petals, center pale yellow stardust cane on stalk with red bud and variegated green leaves, garland of ruby, cadmium green, and pale yellow complex stardust/cog canes, star cut ground, six and faceting, 2¹³⁄₁₆″ d **3,300.00**

Bohemian, concentric millefiori, chartreuse, lavender, blue, yellow, pink, and white complex canes, green aventurine ground flecked with mica, minor scratches on dome, 3⅛″ d **495.00**

Clichy, mushroom, close concentric design, large central pink and green rose surrounded by pink, white, cobalt blue, and cadmium green complex millefiori, middle row of canes with ten green and white roses alternating with pink pastry mold canes, pink and white stem, 2¾″ d . . . **6,600.00**

Degenhart, John, amethyst flashed crystal cube with top window and four side windows, yellow and orange upright lily set in center, bubble in flower center, 2¹¹⁄₁₆″ h, 2¼″ d **990.00**

French, sulphide, side view cameo of woman with ivy in hair, wearing earrings and necklace, opaque blue ground translucent–to–clear in spots, 3⁷⁄₁₆″ d . **135.00**

Millville, pink fifteen petal crimp rose cupped in sheath of four green leaves, pedestal base, 4⁵⁄₁₆″ h, 3¹¹⁄₁₆″ d **3,025.00**

Mount Washington, magnum, 5 three–dimensional wild strawberries with emerald green leaves amid white blossoms with yellow centers, 3⅞″ d **11,000.00**

Nailsea, green bottle, large silvery foil flower growing from pot, three smaller flowers, 4⅝″ h . . . **155.00**

Clichy, Basket of Flowers, c1845–60, 4¼" w, 2½" h, $258,000.00. Photograph courtesy of L. H. Selman, Ltd.

New England Glass Company, blown pear, three dimensional yellow fruit with pink blush, clear cookie base, some hairline cracks in fruit, 2¾" d base **880.00**

Pantin Glass Factory, three–dimensional amber apple with leaf green star blossom, double cased amber and ruby over opaque white branch, opaline veined green leaves, 3" d **16,500.00**

Saint Louis, white pompon flower, white bud, green leaves, tomato red double swirl latticinio ground, 2⅞" d **5,225.00**

Sandwich Glass Company, cobalt blue poinsettia with double tier of petals around green, white, and red Lutz rose center, green stalk, variegated green leaves, 3" d **935.00**

Somerville, frit, central multi–tiered red flower with blue center surrounded by name "Pauline Imbescheid" in white, outer garland with pink, white, and blue flowers and green leaves, 3⁹⁄₁₆" d **135.00**

Val Saint Lambert, souvenir, sulphide plaque of hand holding floral bouquet, white torsade surrounding sulphide, translucent cranberry ground, 3⁷⁄₁₆" d **200.00**

Whitefriars, close concentric millefiori with pink, pale yellow, red, white, cobalt blue, and lavender cross canes, quatrefoil canes, and cog canes, ftd base, minor scratches on top, 3⅝" d **660.00**

COMMEMORATIVE

American Bicentennial, central US flag formed from millefiori canes and rods, resting on blue and white six–pointed star canes, sgd with blue and white date/signature cane with silhouette of robed friar and bicentennial commemorative dates, five and one faceting, Whitefriars, 1976, 3⅛" d **495.00**

Benjamin Franklin, sulphide, side view profile, translucent green over white ground, small crack in base near color ground, Clichy, 2¹³⁄₁₆" d **880.00**

Douglas MacArthur, sulphide, cameo sculpted by Gilbert Poillerat, star cut ground, lime green flash overlay cut with circular top facet and four circular side facets, fancy cutting on sides, limited edition of 300, D'Albret, 1968, 3¹⁄₁₆" d **175.00**

Louis Napoleon Bonaparte III, sulphide, side view cameo inscribed "L. N. Bonaparte" on bottom edge, surrounded by green lampwork crescent wreath tied with red ribbon, Saint Louis, 3" d **470.00**

Mount Rushmore, sulphide, monument cameo sculpted by Joseph Goy, floating inside red over white double overlay with circular top facet and eight oval side facets, translucent blue ground, limited edition of 1000, Baccarat, 1976, 3⁹⁄₁₆" w, 4¹⁄₁₆" l **525.00**

Prince Albert, miniature, clear, circular Prince Albert sulphide cameo inscribed "H.R.H Prince Albert, Born August 26, 1819, Married February 10, 1840," Apsley Pellatt, 2" d **385.00**

MODERN

Ayotte, Rick, purple finch on snow laden branch, surrounded by falling snow, sgd and dated, limited edition of 50, 1983, 2¹¹⁄₁₆″ d **550.00**

Baccarat, Gridel pelican cane surrounded by five concentric rings of yellow, pink, green, and white complex canes, pink canes contain eighteen Gridel silhouette canes, lace ground, date/signature cane, sgd and dated, limited edition of 350, 1973, 3¹⁄₁₆″ d ... **825.00**

Banford, Bob, blue clematis flower with double tier of pointed blue petals and yellow upright stamens, stalk with two blue buds and green leaves, red over white double overlay with six and one faceting and fancy cutting around base, signature cane, 2¹¹⁄₁₆″ d **770.00**

Banford, Ray, tightly furled pink rose blossom on stalk, green leaves, blue aventurine ground, gold foil bee on one leaf, signature cane, 2⅜″ d **300.00**

Buzzini, Chris, bouquet with two white flowers with upright yellow stamens, three yellow blossoms with upright stamens, spray of purple blossoms, buds, and green leaves, date/signature cane, sgd and dated, 1988, 3⅛″ d **550.00**

Kaziun, Charles, yellow crocus, six white tipped yellow petals around yellow stardust stamens, flower cupped inside three green leaves, K signature cane, pedestal base, 2¹⁵⁄₁₆″ h, 2″ d dome **880.00**

Kontes, three pears in various stages of ripeness, green stems with green leaves and single blossom with upright stamens, clear ground, K signature cane, 3¼″ d **1,870.00**

Parabelle Glass, moss ground patterned millefiori, chain of twelve alternating pink and green and white and green roses around central pink and green rose cane, outer edges dec with eight circlets of pink, ruby, forest green, aquamarine, royal blue, deep purple, and white complex canes, green moss ground, limited edition of 25, date/signature cane, 1992, 3″ d **605.00**

Rosenfeld, Ken, three ruby apples, white blossom with upright stamens, opening pink bud, and three closed buds on green branch, clear ground, sgd and dated, 1989, 3⁵⁄₁₆″ d **470.00**

Saint Louis, marbrie, pistachio, white, and blue swags emanating from central complex date/signature cane, limited edition of 250, 1971, 3⅛″ d **470.00**

Stankard, Paul, wild flax, five white petals with faint blue stripes, yellow stamens and pistil, slender stalk with two white buds and green leaves, dark green ground, S signature cane, 1977, 3³⁄₁₆″ d **1,050.00**

Tarsitano, Debbie, orange and purple bird–of–paradise flower on stalk, striped green leaves, star cut ground, DT signature cane, 2¹⁵⁄₁₆″ d **525.00**

Tarsitano, Delmo, two golden peaches with red blush hanging from brown branch, variegated green leaves, star cut ground, DT signature cane, 2¾″ d **880.00**

Trabucco, Victor, Nature in Ice, three dimensional red strawberry with yellow seeds on vine with white blossom with yellow upright stamens, one bud, and green leaves, crystal block weight cut and polished to resemble partially melted piece of ice, limited edition of 50, VT signature cane, sgd, 1982, 3″ h, 3⁷⁄₁₆″ w **660.00**

Whitefriars (Caithness), zodiac, scattered millefiori, silhouettes of twelve zodiac signs inside pink and green complex canes, upset muslin ground, arrangement rests inside swirling pink and white ext. with six and one faceting, date/signature cane, 1983, 2¾″ d **360.00**

Ysart, Paul, green fish with yellow eye and red lips and red fins, yellow and white jasper ground encircled by pink, green, and

white complex cane garland, PY
signature cane, 2¹⁵⁄₁₆" d **495.00**

PAPIER–MÂCHÉ

History: Papier–mâché is made from a mixture of wood pulp, glue, resin, and fine sand which is subject to great pressure and then dried. The finished product is tough, durable, and heat resistant. Various finishing treatments are used, such as enameling, japanning, lacquering, mother–of–pearl inlaying, and painting.

During the Victorian era papier–mâché articles such as boxes, trays, and tables were in high fashion. Papier–mâché also found use in the production of banks, candy containers, masks, toys, and other children's articles.

Halloween Decoration, jack–o–lantern, $20.00.

Box, 5¼" w, romantic scene on
cov, faux tortoiseshell finish ... **175.00**
Candy Container, 5" h, witch **100.00**
Coaster, black lacquered, gold leaf
and medallion dec, 19th C, price
for pair **250.00**
Desk, 12½" w, 9⅛" d, 3⅝" h, lap
type, battle scene, fitted int.,
Monitor and Merrimac cov, repainted **230.00**
Fan, troubadour scene, decou-
page, painted, reticulated, tassels, mid 19th C **120.00**

Figure, 32" h, man wearing over-
alls, carrying lunch pail **700.00**
Letter Holder, Oriental dec **130.00**
Marionette, 21" l, skeleton,
painted, black cloth robe with
hood **190.00**
Pip–Squeak, 6" h, rooster, orig
polychrome paint **145.00**
Roly Poly, 6½" h, German man,
wearing suit and bow tie **60.00**
Snuff Box, 3¹¹⁄₁₆" l, rect with cut
corners, woman in Empire costume examines her stockings in
cheval mirror, some wear and
chipping on cov, early 19th C .. **200.00**
Tray, Victorian
12½" l, oval, center floral spray
inside ribbon yield garland,
scalloped molded border
painted at intervals with gilt foliate lambrequins **400.00**
24 x 19½", painted hawks and
floral vignette center, inlaid
mother–of–pearl detail, 19th C **330.00**
29" l, oval, raised edges, gilded
geometric painting, black
ground **400.00**
30½" l, 23" w, oval, gilt diaper
border, late Regency style mahogany base, late 19th C ... **835.00**
31" l, 23" w, rect, bird, fruit, and
floral dec, later ebonized
stand, late 19th C **920.00**

PARIAN WARE

History: Parian ware is a creamy white, translucent, marble–like porcelain. It originated in England in 1842 and was first known as "Statuary Porcelain." Minton and Copeland have been credited with its development. Wedgwood also made it. In America, parian ware was manufactured by Chistopher Fenton in Bennington, Vermont.

At first parian ware was used only for figures and figural groups. By the 1850s it became so popular that a vast range of wares were manufactured.

References: Kathy Hughes, *A Collector's Guide to Nineteenth–Century Jugs,* Routledge & Kegan Paul, 1985; Kathy Hughes, *A Collector's Guide to Nine-*

teenth–Century Jugs, Volume II, Taylor Publishing, 1991.

Bust
Alexandra, 11¾" h, pedestal base, imp "Crystal Palace Art Union, F M Miller Sculpt, Pub'd Feb 11, 1863, Copeland" ... **225.00**
Maiden, 16" h, garland of flowers in hair, black pedestal base .. **150.00**
Man, 13" h, mustache, draped with sah, English, late 19th C **345.00**
Mendelssohn, 8" h, English ... **85.00**
Queen Victoria, 20¾" h, circular plinth, inscribed "To Commemorate the 60th year of Her Reign 1837–1897" **650.00**
Ulysses S Grant, 8" h, c1860 .. **60.00**
Compote, 10¼" h, low relief grapes and vines, English **275.00**
Ewer, raised scrollwork, glazed green and pink roping, c1853, Copeland, one handle damaged, price for pair **400.00**
Figure
Ariadne, reclining on panther ..**1,045.00**
Beatrice, 21½" h, standing female, classical style, imp mark "Copeland, Pub March 1, 1860, Edgar Papworth Jun SC" **400.00**
Clorinda, 13" l, wearing armor, imp marks "John Bell Feb 1848," "Minton," and ciphers . **500.00**
Dorothea, 13½" l, classical female seated on rock, modeler

Jug, Boy and Eagle, white, Keys and Mountford, c1850–59, 9½" h, $700.00.

John Bell, registry mark for 1847, imp "Minton" and cipher marks, chips, restoration **175.00**
Female, 16" h, peasant dress, scarf, barefoot, holding mandolin, shades of ivory, sgd "R & L" in lozenge, Robinson & Leadbeater, c1885 .... **550.00**
John Milton, 14" h, English, 19th C **285.00**
Medieval Warrior, 17" h, amidst classical ruins, English, late 19th C **345.00**
Mercury, 23¼" h, c1850 ......**1,495.00**
Nude female seated on panther, 14¼" h, rect base, imp "Minton" and 1857 year mark, ear chip **700.00**
Una, sitting on lion **880.00**
Victorian Lady, standing by column, holding garland of roses, 17¾" h **325.00**
Pitcher, 10½" h, deep relief witches and peasants, Jones and Wally, dated 1842 .... **225.00**

PATE–DE–VERRE

History: Pate–de–Verre can be translated simply as glass paste. It is manufactured by grinding lead glass into a powder or crystal form, making it into a paste by adding a 2% or 3% solution of sodium silicate, molding, firing, and carving. The Egyptians discovered the process as early as 1500 BC.

In the late 19th century, the process was rediscovered by a group of French glassmakers. Amalric Walter, Henri Cros, Georges Despret, and the Daum brothers were leading manufacturers.

Contemporary sculptors are creating a second renaissance, led by the technical research of Jacques Daum.

Belt Buckle, 4⅛" l, 2½" w, rect, rounded corners, gray, molded in low relief, faun masque amidst swirling foliage, red, blue, and purple, simple hammered silver mount, glass molded "G. A–R, G. Argy–Rousseau," silver imp "G. A–R France," c1925 ......**2,015.00**

Bowl, pedestal foot, purple grape relief, marked "G. Argy–Rousseau," 4" d, 1⅝" h, $850.00.

Bowl
3⅞" d, Etoiles, round, stepped, mottled blue and white ground, molded in high relief with overlapping deep indigo stars, sgd in mold "G. Argy–Rousseau" **6,050.00**

4¼" d, Papillons, white ground, molded with four violet and green butterflies, sgd in mold "G. Argy–Rousseau," c1915 . **9,775.00**

Box
3¼" d, 2" h, round, sloped sides, frosted blue, green, amethyst, and yellow, molded repeating flowering leaf and beetle design, inscribed "Daum Nancy" on base, missing cov **165.00**

3¾" d, 3¼" h, round, mottled all-over red poppy blossoms, domed cov, sgd in mold "G. Argy–Rousseau, 5997" **4,180.00**

Chandelier, 32" h, Grosse Fleur, 12" d deep violet shade molded as huge flower blossom with overlapping petals, sgd in mold "G. Argy–Rousseau France," suspended by three cords, all supported by gilt metal ceiling mount cast with rose clusters . **18,700.00**

Coupe, 3⅝" h, Chardons des Alpes, bulbous vessel, opal gray, molded with overlapping rondels enclosing thistle blossoms, shades of purple, yellow, green, cranberry, and charcoal gray, molded "G. Argy–Rousseau, France," c1922 . . . . **5,750.00**

Figure, 8" h, Tanagra, woman clothed in flowing classical drapery, shades of grass green streaked with emerald green and spring green, sgd "A Walter, Nancy," c1925, ground and polished **2,075.00**

Inkwell, cov, 4" h, bulbous base, slender neck, molded green slithering lizard and bee, moss green foliage, deep violet berries, circular cov molded with foliage and berries, sgd in mold "A. Walter, Berge SC" **6,050.00**

Lamp, 11⅜" h, 7¼" d domical shade, gray mottled with purple and violet, molded in low relief with diamonds enclosing red flower heads, suspended from raised netting, wrought iron base, three arm shade mount, shade and base molded "G. Argy–Rousseau," c1925 . . . . . **37,950.00**

Panel, 10 x 15⅛", rect, molded in medium and high relief, gourds pendent from leafy vines, gray with mottled lime green, emerald green, charcoal gray, ochre, and aubergine, molded "A Walter Nancy," c1920 . . . . **11,500.00**

Paperweight, 2" d, full relief green frog seated on mottled brown and green base, inscribed "A Walter, Nancy, Berge Sclt.," c1925 . . . . **3,450.00**

Pendant
1¼" d, Art Nouveau, molded amethyst, woman with flowing hair, fitted gilt metal mount . . **385.00**

1½" l, black and green insect, turquoise blue oval ground, A Walter, molded signature obscured **275.00**

Plafonnier, 6½" h, 15⅝" d, six tapering arched panels around central rondel, three panels depicting Leda and the swan, three with Bacchus, shades of turquoise, cobalt blue, and gold, white ground, central rondel with large flower head, metal banding painted blue with silver scrolling designs, Henri Cros, unsgd, c1900, damaged **2,300.00**

Plaque, 9¾ x 7⅝", figural, rect,

molded in low relief, Cupid and
Psyche, lavender, green, brown,
tan, and yellow, Henri Cros,
unsgd, c1910, chips to edges . **8,050.00**
Vase
8½" h, Feuillage Moderne, flaring cylindrical vessel, molded
with overlapping triangles, patterned rim and ft, gray mottled
and streaked with deep cobalt
blue and turquoise, molded
"G. Argy–Rousseau," c1925 . **8,625.00**
9" h, Le Jardin des Hesperides,
oviform, molded with Hesperides picking apples, red and
purple, molded "Argy–Rous-
seau," restored base **4,375.00**
Vide Poche, 8¼" l, lozenge
shaped, mottled mustard, green,
and blue, molded leaf and berries, back edge molded with nibbling brown mouse, engraved
"Daum Nancy" **3,075.00**

PATE–SUR–PATE

History: Pate–sur–pate, paste on paste,
is a 19th century porcelain form featuring
relief designs achieved by painting succes-
sive layers of thin pottery paste one on top
of the other.

About 1880 Marc Solon and other Sevres
artists, inspired by a Chinese celadon vase
in the Ceramic Museum at Sevres, experimented with this process of porcelain decoration. Solon migrated to England at the
outbreak of the Franco–Prussian War and
worked at Minton, where he perfected the
pate–sur–pate process.

Centerpiece, 11" l, putti cartouche,
ivory and gilt reserves, brown
ground, imp and printed Minton
factory marks, dec by H Hollins,
c1872 . . . . **1,400.00**
Cup, green, gold dragonflies,
white leaves **80.00**
Dish, 9½" d, brown, white slip
maiden design, gold key border,
gilt dentil rim, sgd "L Solon,"
c1880 . . . . **2,500.00**
Panel, pr, 7 x 4½", gilt metal frame,

**Plaque, blue ground, white pas-
toral setting of young courting
couple beneath tree, marked "F.
M./Limoges/France," wood frame,
4" d, $350.00.**

dancing maidens, sgd "Cre-
lerot," price for pair **660.00**
Plaque, 10¼ x 6¼", girl wearing
flowing gown, basket of flowers **275.00**
Plate
8⅞" d, white slip nymph seated
on branch, gilt floral border
and yellow band, Limoges,
c1885 . . . . **1,100.00**
9½" d, birds and branches, tur-
quoise, sgd "D Leroy, Minton" **450.00**
Vase
7¼" h, jade green, white flowers,
gold serpent skin twisted han-
dles, gold trim, price for pair . **995.00**
7½" h, cobalt blue, white cupids,
gold trim **160.00**
8¾" h, multicolored, two cherubs
over sea, gilt trim, marked
"Meissen" **1,000.00**
11¾" h, aqua, lavender panel
with white figures, gilt stand . **350.00**
Wall Pocket, 9" h, dark green,
white maiden and cupid **600.00**

PATTERN GLASS

History: Pattern glass is clear or colored
glass pressed into one of hundreds of patterns. Deming Jarves of the Boston and
Sandwich Glass Co. invented the first suc-

cessful pressing machine in 1828. By the 1860s glass pressing machinery had been improved, and mass production of good quality matched tableware sets began. The idea of a matched glassware table service (including goblets, tumblers, creamers, sugars, compotes, cruets, etc.) quickly caught on in America. Many pattern glass table services had numerous accessory pieces among which were banana stands, molasses cans, water bottles, etc.

Early pattern glass (flint) was made with a lead formula, giving it a ringing quality. During the Civil War lead became too valuable to be used in glass manufacturing. In 1864 Hobbs, Bruckunier & Co., West Virginia, developed a soda lime (non–flint) formula. Pattern glass also was produced in colors, milk glass, opalescent glass, slag glass, and custard glass.

The hundreds of companies which produced pattern glass experienced periods of development, expansions, personnel problems, material and supply demands, fires, and mergers. In 1899 the National Glass Co. was formed as a combine of 19 glass companies in Pennsylvania, Ohio, Indiana, West Virginia, and Maryland. U. S. Glass, another consortium, was founded in 1891. These combines resulted from attempts to save small companies by pooling talents, resources, and patterns. Because of this pooling, the same pattern can be attributed to several companies.

Sometimes the pattern name of a piece was changed from one company to the next to reflect current fashion trends. U. S. Glass created the States series by issuing patterns named for a particular state. Several of these patterns were new issues, others were former patterns renamed.

References: Gary Baker et al., *Wheeling Glass 1829-1939: Collection of the Oglebay Institute Glass Museum,* Oglebay Institute, 1994, distributed by Antique Publications; E. M. Belnap, *Milk Glass,* Crown Publishers, 1949; Bill Edwards, *Opalescent Glass,* Collector Books, 1992; Elaine Ezell and George Newhouse, *Cruets, Cruets, Cruets, Volume I,* Antique Publications, 1991; Regis F. and Mary F. Ferson, *Yesterday's Milk Glass Today,* published by authors, 1981; William Heacock, *Custard Glass From A to Z, Book 4,* Antique Publi-

cations, 1980; William Heacock, *More Ruby Stained Glass, Book 8,* Antique Publications, 1987; William Heacock, *Oil Cruets From A to Z, Book 6,* Antique Publications, 1981; William Heacock, *Old Pattern Glass,* Antique Publications, 1981; William Heacock, *1000 Toothpick Holders: A Collector's Guide,* Antique Publications, 1977; William Heacock, *Opalescent Glass from A to Z, Book 2,* Antique Publications, 1981; William Heacock, *Rare and Unlisted Toothpick Holders,* Antique Publications, 1984; William Heacock, *Ruby Stained Glass From A To Z, Book 7* Antique Publications, 1986; William Heacock, *Syrups, Sugar Shakers & Cruets, Book 3,* Antique Publications, 1981, 1991–92 value update; William Heacock, *Toothpick Holders from A to Z, Book 1, Encyclopedia of Victorian Colored Pattern Glass, Second Edition* Antique Publications, 1976, 1992 value update; William Heacock, *U. S. Glass From A to Z, Book 5,* Antique Publications, 1980; William Heacock and William Gamble, *Cranberry Opalescent From A to Z, Book 9,* Antique Publications, 1987; William Heacock, James Measell, and Berry Wiggins, *Harry Northwood: The Early Years 1881–1900,* Antique Publications, 1990; William Heacock, James Measell, and Berry Wiggins, *Harry Northwood: The Wheeling Years 1901–1925,* Antique Publications, 1991; Joyce Ann Hicks, *Just Jenkins,* printed by author, 1988; Kyle Husfloen, *Collector's Guide To American Pressed Glass, 1825–1915,* Wallace–Homestead, 1992.

Bill Jenks and Jerry Luna, *Early American Pattern Glass–1850 to 1910: Major Collectible Table Settings with Prices,* Wallace–Homestead, 1990; Bill Jenks, Jerry Luna, and Darryl Reilly, *Identifying Pattern Glass Reproductions,* Wallace–Homestead, 1993; Minnie Watson Kamm, *Pattern Glass Pitchers, Books 1 through 8,* published by author, 1970, 4th printing; Lorraine Kovar, *Westmoreland Glass: 1950–1984,* Volume I (1991), Volume II (1991), Antique Publications; Thelma Ladd and Laurence Ladd, *Portland Glass: Legacy of a Glass House Down East,* Collector Books, 1992; Ruth Webb Lee, *Early American Pressed Glass,* Lee Publications, 1966, 36th edition; Ruth Webb Lee, *Victorian Glass,* Lee Publications, 1944, 13th edition; Bessie M. Lindsey,

American Historical Glass, Charles E. Tuttle, 1967; Robert Irwin Lucas, *Tarentum Pattern Glass,* privately printed, 1981; Mollie H. McCain, *The Collector's Encyclopedia of Pattern Glass,* Collector Books, 1982, 1994 value update; George P. and Helen McKearin, *American Glass,* Crown Publishers, 1941; James Measell, *Greentown Glass,* Grand Rapids Public Museum Association, 1979, 1992–93 value update, distributed by Antique Publications; James Measell and Don E. Smith, *Findlay Glass: The Glass Tableware Manufacturers, 1886–1902,* Antique Publications, Inc, 1986; Alice Hulett Metz, *Early American Pattern Glass,* published by author, 1958; Alice Hulett Metz, *Much More Early American Pattern Glass,* published by author, 1965.

S. T. Millard, *Goblets I,* privately printed, 1938, reprinted Wallace–Homestead, 1975; S. T. Millard, *Goblets II,* privately printed, 1940, reprinted Wallace–Homestead, 1975; Arthur G. Peterson, *Glass Salt Shakers: 1,000 Patterns,* Wallace–Homestead, 1970; Ellen T. Schroy, *Warman's Glass,* Wallace–Homestead, 1992; Ellen T. Schroy (ed.), *Warman's Pattern Glass,* Wallace–Homestead, 1993; Jane Shadel Spillman, *American and European Pressed Glass in the Corning Museum of Glass,* Corning Museum of Glass, 1981; Jane Shadel Spillman, *The Knopf Collectors Guides to American Antiques, Glass,* Vol. 1 (1982), Vol. 2 (1983), Alfred A. Knopf; Doris and Peter Unitt, *American and Canadian Goblets,* Clock House, 1970; Doris and Peter Unitt, *Treasury of Canadian Glass, Second Edition,* Clock House, 1969; Peter Unitt and Anne Worrall, *Canadian Handbook, Pressed Glass Tableware,* Clock House Productions, 1983; Dina von Zweck, *The Woman's Day Dictionary of Glass,* Main Street Press, 1983.

Periodical: *Glass Collector's Digest,* Richardson Printing, PO Box 553, Marietta, OH 45750.

Collectors' Clubs: Early American Glass Traders, RD 5, Box 638, Milford, DE 19963; Early American Pattern Glass Society, PO Box 340023, Columbus, OH 43234; The National Early American Glass Club, PO Box 8489, Silver Spring, MD 20907.

Museums: Corning Museum of Glass, Corning, NY; National Museum of Man, Ottawa, Ontario, Canada; Sandwich Glass Museum, Sandwich, MA; Schminck Memorial Museum, Lakeview, OR.

Additional Listings: Bread Plates, Children's Toy Dishes, Cruets, Custard Glass, Milk Glass, Sugar Shakers, Toothpick Holders, and specific companies.

Abbreviations:
ah—applied handle
GUTDODB—Give Us This Day Our Daily Bread
hs—high standard
ls—low standard
os—original stopper

We continue to be fortunate in assembling a panel of prestigious pattern glass dealers to serve as advisors in reviewing the pattern glass listings found in this edition. Their dedication is symbolic of those dealers and collectors who view price guides as useful market tools and contribute their expertise and time to make them better.

Research in pattern glass is continuing. As in the past, we have tried to present patterns with correct names, histories, and pieces. Categories have been changed to reflect the most current thinking: all patterns are listed alphabetically. Colored, opalescent, and clear pieces now are included in one listing, avoiding duplication of patterns and colors.

Pattern glass has been widely reproduced. We have listed reproductions with an *. These markings are given only as a guide and clue to the collector that some reproductions may exist in a given pattern.

Advisors: John and Alice Ahlfeld, Mike Anderton.

ACTRESS

Made by Adams & Company, Pittsburgh, PA, c1880. All clear 20% less. Some items have been reproduced in clear and color by Imperial Glass Co., including amethyst pickle dish.

	Clear and Frosted		Clear and Frosted
Bowl		Dresser Tray	60.00
6", ftd	45.00	Goblet, Kate Claxton (2	
7", ftd	50.00	portraits)	85.00
8", Miss Neilson	85.00	Marmalade Jar, cov	125.00
9½", ftd.	85.00	Mug, HMS Pinafore	50.00
Bread Plate		*Pickle Dish, Love's Re-	
7 x 12", HMS Pinafore	90.00	quest is Pickles	45.00
9 x 13", Miss Neilson .	70.00	Pickle Relish, different ac-	
Butter, cov	90.00	tresses	
Cake Stand, 10"	150.00	4½ x 7".	35.00
Candlesticks, pr.	250.00	5 x 8"	35.00
Celery Vase		5½ x 9".	35.00
Actress Head.	130.00	Pitcher	
HMS Pinafore,		Milk, 6½", HMS	
pedestal	145.00	Pinafore	285.00
Cheese Dish, cov, The		Water, 9", Romeo &	
Lone Fisherman on		Juliet.	275.00
cov, Two Dromios on		Salt, master	70.00
base	250.00	Salt Shaker, orig pewter	
Compote		top.	42.50
Cov, hs, 12" d	300.00	Sauce	
Open, hs, 10" d	90.00	Flat	15.00
Open, hs, 12" d	120.00	Footed	20.00
Open, ls, 5" d.	45.00	Spooner	60.00
Creamer.	75.00	Sugar, cov	100.00

ADONIS (Pleat and Tuck, Washboard)

Pattern made by McKee & Bros. of Pittsburgh, PA, in 1897.

	Canary	Clear	Deep Blue
Bowl, 5", berry. . .	15.00	10.00	20.00
Butter, cov	70.00	48.00	80.00
Cake Plate, 11". .	25.00	20.00	32.00
Cake Stand,			
10½".	45.00	30.00	50.00
Celery Vase.	35.00	25.00	40.00
Compote			
Cov, hs	65.00	40.00	75.00
Open, hs, 8". . .	45.00	30.00	50.00
Open, jelly,			
4½".	28.00	18.00	32.00
Creamer.	28.00	22.50	32.00
Pitcher, water. . . .	55.00	35.00	60.00
Plate, 10".	25.00	18.00	32.00
Relish.	18.00	15.00	20.00

	Canary	Clear	Deep Blue
Salt & Pepper, pr.	40.00	35.00	45.00
Sauce, flat, 4" . . .	10.00	8.00	12.00
Spooner	35.00	20.00	40.00
Sugar, cov	40.00	35.00	45.00
Syrup	150.00	50.00	150.00
Tumbler	20.00	16.00	20.00

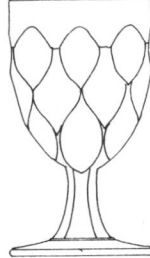

ALMOND THUMBPRINT (Pointed Thumbprint, Finger Print)

An early flint glass pattern with variants in flint and non-flint. Pattern has been attributed to Bryce, Bakewell, and U. S. Glass Co. Sometimes found in milk glass.

	Flint	Non-Flint		Flint	Non-Flint
Bowl, 4½" d, ftd. .	—	20.00	Decanter	75.00	—
Butter, cov	80.00	40.00	Egg Cup.	45.00	25.00
Celery Vase	50.00	25.00	Goblet	30.00	18.00
Champagne	60.00	35.00	Punch Bowl	—	75.00
Compote			Salt		
Cov, hs, 4¾", jelly	60.00	40.00	Flat, large	25.00	15.00
Cov, hs, 10" . . .	100.00	45.00	Ftd, cov	45.00	25.00
Cov, ls, 4¾" . . .	55.00	30.00	Ftd, open	25.00	10.00
Cov, ls, 7"	45.00	25.00	Spooner	20.00	15.00
Open, hs, 10½"	65.00	—	Sugar, cov	60.00	40.00
Cordial	40.00	30.00	Sweetmeat Jar, cov	65.00	45.00
Creamer	60.00	40.00	Tumbler	60.00	20.00
Cruet, ftd, os	55.00	—	Wine	25.00	10.00

APOLLO (Canadian Horseshoe, Shield Band)

Non-flint first made by Adams & Co., Pittsburgh, PA, c1890, and later by U. S. Glass Co. Frosted increases price 20%. Also found in ruby stained and engraved.

	Clear		Clear
Bowl		Butter, cov	40.00
4"	10.00	Cake Stand	
5"	10.00	8"	35.00
6"	12.00	9"	40.00
7"	15.00	10"	50.00
8"	20.00	Celery Tray, rect	20.00

	Clear		Clear
Celery Vase	35.00	Salt	20.00
Compote		Salt Shaker	25.00
Cov, hs	65.00	Sauce	
Open, hs	35.00	Flat	10.00
Open, ls, 7″	25.00	Ftd, 5″	12.00
Creamer	35.00	Spooner	30.00
Cruet	60.00	Sugar, cov	45.00
Egg Cup	30.00	Sugar Shaker	45.00
Goblet	35.00	Syrup	110.00
Lamp, 10″	125.00	Tray, water	45.00
Pickle Dish	15.00	Tumbler	30.00
Pitcher, water	65.00	Wine	35.00
Plate, 9½″, sq	25.00		

ARCHED GRAPE

Flint and non-flint made by Boston and Sandwich Glass Co., Sandwich, MA, c1880.

	Non-Flint		Non-Flint
Butter, cov	45.00	Pitcher, water, ah	60.00
Celery Vase	35.00	Sauce, flat	8.00
Champagne	35.00	Spooner	30.00
Compote, cov, hs	50.00	Sugar, cov	45.00
Creamer	40.00	Wine	25.00
Goblet	25.00		

ARGUS

Flint thumbprint type pattern made by Bakewell, Pears and Co. Pittsburgh, PA, in the early 1860s. Copiously reproduced, some by Fostoria Glass Co. with raised "H.F.M." trademark for Henry Ford Museum, Dearborn, MI. Reproduction colors include clear, red, green and cobalt blue.

	Clear		Clear
Ale Glass	75.00	* Creamer, applied handle	100.00
Bitters Bottle	60.00	Decanter, qt	70.00
Bowl, 5½″	30.00	Egg Cup	30.00
* Butter, cov	85.00	* Goblet	65.00
Celery Vase	85.00	Lamp, ftd	100.00
Champagne	65.00	Mug, ah	65.00
Compote, open, 6″ d, 4½″		Pitcher, water, ah	225.00
h	50.00	Salt, master, open	30.00

	Clear		Clear
*Spooner	45.00	Whiskey, ah	75.00
*Sugar, cov	65.00	*Wine	35.00
*Tumbler, bar	65.00		

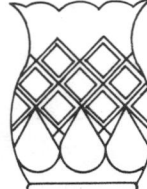

ART (Jacob's Tears, Job's Tears, Teardrop and Diamond Block)

Non-flint produced by Adams & Co., Pittsburgh, PA, in the 1880s. Reissued by U. S. Glass Co. in the early 1890s. A milk glass covered compote is known.

	Clear	Ruby Stained		Clear	Ruby Stained
Banana Stand	90.00	175.00	Creamer		
Biscuit Jar	135.00	175.00	Hotel, large,		
Bowl			round shape	45.00	90.00
6" d, 3¼" h, ftd	30.00	—	Regular	55.00	100.00
7", low, collar			Cruet, os	125.00	250.00
base	35.00	—	Goblet	55.00	—
8", berry, one			Pitcher		
end pointed	50.00	85.00	Milk	115.00	175.00
Butter, cov	60.00	125.00	Water, 2½ qt	100.00	—
Cake Stand			Plate, 10"	40.00	—
9"	75.00	—	Relish	20.00	65.00
10¼"	80.00	—	Sauce		
Celery Vase	40.00	100.00	Flat, round, 4"	15.00	—
*Compote			Pointed end	18.50	—
Cov, hs, 7"	100.00	185.00	Spooner	25.00	85.00
Open, hs, 9"	55.00	—	Sugar, cov	45.00	125.00
Open, hs, 9½" d	65.00	—	Tumbler	45.00	—
Open, hs, 10"	75.00	—	Vinegar Jug, 3 pt	75.00	—

ASHBURTON

A popular pattern produced by Boston and Sandwich Glass Co. and by McKee & Bros. Glass Co. from the 1850s to the late 1870s with many variations. Originally made in flint by New England Glass Co. and others and later in non-flint. Prices are for flint. Non-flint values 65% less. Also reported is an amber handled whiskey mug, flint canary celery vase ($750.00), and a scarce emerald green wine glass ($200.00). Some items known in fiery opalescent.

	Clear		Clear
Ale Glass, 5"	90.00	Quart	75.00
Bar Bottle		Bitters Bottle	55.00
Pint	55.00	*Bowl, 6½"	75.00

	Clear		Clear
Carafe	175.00	Lamp	75.00
Celery Vase, scalloped		*Lemonade Glass	55.00
top	125.00	Mug, 7"	100.00
Champagne, cut	75.00	*Pitcher, water	450.00
*Claret, 5¼" h	50.00	Plate, 6⅝"	75.00
*Compote, open, ls, 7½"	65.00	Sauce	10.00
Cordial, 4¼" h	75.00	*Sugar, cov	90.00
*Creamer, ah	250.00	Toddy Jar, cov	375.00
Decanter, qt, cut and		*Tumbler	
pressed, os	250.00	Bar	75.00
Egg Cup		Water	75.00
Double	95.00	Whiskey	60.00
Single	25.00	Whiskey, ah	125.00
Flip Glass, handled	140.00	Water Bottle, tumble up	95.00
*Goblet	55.00	*Wine	
Honey Dish	15.00	Cut	65.00
*Jug, qt	90.00	Pressed	40.00

ATLAS (Bullet, Cannon Ball, Crystal Ball)

Non-flint, occasionally ruby stained and etched, made by Adams & Co.; U. S. Glass Co. in 1891; and Bryce Bros., Mt. Pleasant, PA, in 1889.

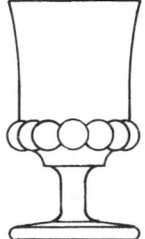

	Clear	Ruby Stained		Clear	Ruby Stained
Bowl, 9"	20.00	—	Marmalade Jar	45.00	—
Butter, cov,			Molasses Can	65.00	—
regular	45.00	75.00	Pitcher, water	65.00	—
Cake Stand			Salt		
8"	35.00	—	Master	20.00	—
9"	40.00	95.00	Individual	15.00	—
Celery Vase	28.00	—	Salt & Pepper, pr.	20.00	—
Champagne, 5½"			Sauce		
h	35.00	55.00	Flat	10.00	—
Compote			Footed	15.00	25.00
Cov, hs, 8"	65.00	—	Spooner	30.00	45.00
Cov, hs, 5",			Sugar, cov	40.00	65.00
jelly	50.00	80.00	Syrup	65.00	—
Open, ls, 7"	40.00	—	Toothpick	20.00	50.00
Cordial	35.00	—	Tray, water	75.00	—
Creamer			Tumbler	28.00	—
Table, ah	30.00	55.00	Whiskey	20.00	45.00
Tankard	25.00	—	Wine	25.00	—
Goblet	45.00	65.00			

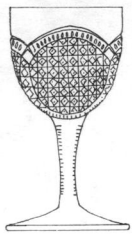

AUSTRIAN (Finecut Medallion)

Made by Indiana Tumbler and Goblet Co., Greentown, IN, 1897. Experimental pieces were made in cobalt blue, Nile green, and opaque colors.

	Amber	Canary	Clear	Emerald Green
Bowl				
8", round.....	—	150.00	50.00	—
8¼", rect.....	—	150.00	50.00	—
Butter, cov.....	185.00	300.00	90.00	—
Children's table set..........	—	550.00	325.00	—
Compote, open, ls............	—	150.00	75.00	—
Cordial........	145.00	150.00	50.00	150.00
Creamer.......	120.00	125.00	40.00	120.00
Goblet	—	150.00	40.00	—
Mug, child's.....	—	—	45.00	—
Nappy, cov......	—	135.00	55.00	—
Pitcher, water....	—	350.00	100.00	—
Plate, 10".......	—	—	40.00	—
Punch Cup......	150.00	150.00	18.00	125.00
Rose Bowl......	—	150.00	50.00	—
Sauce, 4⅝" d....	—	50.00	20.00	—
Spooner.......	—	100.00	40.00	—
Sugar, cov.....	—	175.00	45.00	—
Tumbler........	175.00	85.00	25.00	—
Wine..........	175.00	150.00	30.00	150.00

BALTIMORE PEAR (Double Pear, Fig, Gipsy, Maryland Pear, Twin Pear)

Non-flint originally made by Adams & Company, Pittsburgh, PA, in 1874. Also made by U. S. Glass Company in the 1890s. There are eighteen different size compotes. Given as premiums by different manufacturers and organizations. Heavily reproduced. Reproduced in clear and cobalt blue.

	Clear		Clear
Bowl		Cov, ls, 8½".........	45.00
6"................	30.00	Open, hs..........	30.00
9"................	35.00	Open, jelly.........	25.00
Bread Plate, 12½"......	70.00	*Creamer.............	30.00
*Butter, cov...........	75.00	*Goblet	35.00
*Cake Stand, 9"........	65.00	Pickle	20.00
*Celery Vase..........	50.00	*Pitcher	
Compote		Milk...............	80.00
Cov, hs, 7"..........	80.00	Water	95.00

	Clear		Clear
* Plate		Footed	**15.00**
8½"	**30.00**	Spooner	**40.00**
10"	**40.00**	* Sugar, cov	**50.00**
Relish	**25.00**	Tray, 10½"	**35.00**
* Sauce			
Flat	**10.00**		

BANDED PORTLAND (Virginia #1, Maiden's Blush)

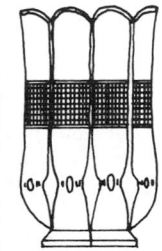

States pattern, originally named Virginia, by Portland Glass Co., Portland, ME. Painted and fired green, yellow, blue, and possibly pink; ruby stained, and rose-flashed (which Lee notes is Maiden's Blush, referring to the color rather than the pattern, as Metz lists it). Double-flashed refers to color above and below the band, single-flashed refers to color above or below the band only.

	Clear	Color- Flashed	Maiden's Blush Pink
Bowl			
4" d, open	**10.00**	—	**20.00**
6" d, cov	**40.00**	—	**55.00**
7½" d, shallow .	**30.00**	—	**55.00**
8" d, cov	**50.00**	—	**75.00**
Butter, cov	**50.00**	**165.00**	**85.00**
Cake Stand	**55.00**	—	**90.00**
Candlesticks, pr. .	**80.00**	—	**125.00**
Carafe	**80.00**	—	**90.00**
Celery Tray	**25.00**	—	**40.00**
Celery Vase	**35.00**	—	**45.00**
Cologne Bottle . . .	**50.00**	**65.00**	**85.00**
Compote			
Cov, hs, 7"	**65.00**	—	**125.00**
Cov, hs, 8"	**75.00**	—	**115.00**
Cov, jelly, 6" . . .	**40.00**	**65.00**	**90.00**
Creamer			
Individual, oval.	**25.00**	**35.00**	**38.00**
Regular, 6 oz. .	**35.00**	**45.00**	**50.00**
Cruet, os	**60.00**	**90.00**	**125.00**
Decanter,			
handled	**50.00**	—	**100.00**
Dresser Tray	**50.00**	—	**65.00**
Goblet	**40.00**	**55.00**	**65.00**
Lamp			
Flat	**45.00**	—	—
Tall	**50.00**	—	—
Nappy, sq.	**15.00**	**55.00**	**65.00**
Olive	**18.00**	—	**35.00**
Pin Tray	**16.00**	—	**25.00**

	Clear	Color-Flashed	Maiden's Blush Pink
Pitcher, tankard . .	75.00	95.00	240.00
Pomade Jar, cov .	35.00	45.00	65.00
Punch Bowl, hs . .	110.00	—	300.00
Punch Cup	20.00	—	30.00
Relish			
6½"	25.00	30.00	20.00
8¼"	20.00	35.00	40.00
Ring Holder	75.00	—	125.00
Salt & Pepper, pr.	65.00	95.00	95.00
Sardine Box	55.00	—	90.00
Sauce, round, flat,			
4 or 4½"	10.00	—	20.00
Spooner	28.00	—	45.00
Sugar, cov	48.00	75.00	75.00
Sugar Shaker, orig			
top.	45.00	—	85.00
Syrup	50.00	—	135.00
Toothpick	40.00	45.00	45.00
Tumbler	25.00	35.00	45.00
Vase			
6"	20.00	—	38.00
9"	35.00	—	50.00
Wine	35.00	—	75.00

BARBERRY (Berry, Olive, Pepper Berry)

Non-flint made by McKee & Bros. Glass Co. in the 1860s. The 6" plates are found in amber, canary, pale green, and pale blue; they are considered scarce. Pattern comes in "9 berry bunch" and "12 berry bunch" varieties.

	Clear		Clear
Bowl		Creamer	30.00
6", oval	20.00	Cup Plate	15.00
7", oval	25.00	Egg Cup	20.00
8", oval	25.00	Goblet	25.00
8", round, flat	25.00	Pickle	10.00
9", oval	30.00	Pitcher, water, ah	100.00
Butter		Plate, 6"	20.00
Cov	50.00	Salt, master, ftd	25.00
Cov, flange, pattern on		Sauce	
edge	80.00	Flat	10.00
Cake Stand	90.00	Footed	15.00
Celery Vase	55.00	Spooner, ftd	30.00
Compote		Sugar, cov	45.00
Cov, hs, 8", shell finial.	85.00	Syrup	150.00
Cov, ls, 8", shell finial .	75.00	Tumbler, ftd	25.00
Open, hs, 8"	35.00	Wine	30.00

BASKETWEAVE

Non-flint, c1880. Some covered pieces have a stippled cat's head finial.

	Amber or Canary	Apple Green	Blue	Clear	Vaseline
Bowl	20.00	—	25.00	15.00	—
Bread Plate, 11" .	35.00	—	35.00	10.00	—
Butter, cov	35.00	60.00	40.00	30.00	40.00
Compote, cov, 7".	—	—	—	40.00	—
Cordial	25.00	40.00	28.00	20.00	30.00
Creamer	30.00	50.00	35.00	28.00	36.00
Cup and Saucer .	35.00	60.00	35.00	30.00	38.00
Dish, oval	12.00	20.00	15.00	10.00	16.00
Egg Cup	20.00	30.00	25.00	15.00	25.00
*Goblet	28.00	50.00	35.00	20.00	30.00
Mug	25.00	40.00	25.00	15.00	30.00
Pickle	20.00	30.00	20.00	15.00	25.00
Pitcher					
Milk	40.00	60.00	45.00	35.00	50.00
*Water	60.00	75.00	80.00	45.00	85.00
Plate, 11",					
handled	25.00	35.00	25.00	20.00	30.00
Sauce	10.00	10.00	12.00	8.00	12.00
Spooner	30.00	36.00	30.00	20.00	30.00
Sugar, cov	35.00	60.00	35.00	30.00	40.00
Syrup	50.00	75.00	50.00	45.00	55.00
*Tray, water, scenic					
center	45.00	50.00	60.00	35.00	55.00
*Tumbler, ftd	18.00	30.00	20.00	15.00	20.00
Waste Bowl	20.00	35.00	25.00	18.00	25.00
Wine	30.00	50.00	30.00	20.00	30.00

BEADED GRAPE (Beaded Grape and Vine, California, Grape and Vine)

Non-flint made by U. S. Glass Co., Pittsburgh, PA, c1890. Also attributed to Burlington Glass Works, Hamilton, Ontario, and Sydenham Glass Co., Wallaceburg, Ontario, Canada, c1910. Made in clear and emerald green, sometimes with gilt trim. Reproduced in a variety of clear, milk glass, and several colors by many, including Westmoreland Glass Co.

	Clear	Emerald Green		Clear	Emerald Green
Bowl			8", round	28.00	35.00
5½", sq	20.00	25.00	Bread Plate	25.00	65.00
5½ x 8"	25.00	30.00	Butter, cov	65.00	85.00
6" sq	20.00	25.00	Cake Stand, 9" . .	65.00	85.00
7½", sq	25.00	35.00	Celery Tray	30.00	45.00

	Clear	Emerald Green		Clear	Emerald Green
Celery Vase.....	40.00	60.00	Pitcher		
*Compote			Milk..........	75.00	120.00
Cov, hs, 7"....	75.00	85.00	Water	85.00	150.00
Cov, hs, 8"....	80.00	90.00	*Plate, 8¼", sq ...	28.00	40.00
Cov, hs, 9"....	100.00	115.00	Salt & Pepper ...	45.00	65.00
Open, hs, 5",			*Sauce, 4".......	15.00	20.00
sq	55.00	75.00	Spooner........	35.00	45.00
Open, hs, 7"...	45.00	65.00	Sugar, cov		
Open, hs, 8"...	55.00	70.00	Large, ftd,		
Open, hs, 9"..	65.00	75.00	Australian...	60.00	75.00
Open, hs, jelly .	55.00	65.00	Table	45.00	55.00
Creamer........	40.00	50.00	Sugar Shaker ...	75.00	85.00
Cruet, os	65.00	125.00	Toothpick.......	40.00	65.00
*Goblet	35.00	50.00	*Tumbler	25.00	40.00
Olive, handle....	20.00	35.00	Vase, 6" h	25.00	40.00
Pickle..........	20.00	30.00	*Wine...........	35.00	65.00

BEADED LOOP (Oregon #1)

Non-flint made by U. S. Glass Co., Pittsburgh, PA, as Pattern Line No. 15,073. Reissued after the 1891 merger as one of the States series. Reproduced in clear and color by Imperial.

	Clear		Clear
Berry Set, master, 6 sauces	75.00	Open, hs, 5".........	25.00
Bowl		Open, hs, 6".........	30.00
3½"..............	10.00	Open, hs, 7".........	35.00
4"	10.00	Open, hs, 8".........	40.00
6"	12.00	Creamer	
7"	15.00	Flat................	30.00
8"	15.00	Footed	35.00
9", berry, cov	25.00	Cruet	50.00
Bread Plate	35.00	*Goblet	35.00
Butter, cov		Honey Dish	10.00
English	65.00	Mug	35.00
Flanged	50.00	Pickle Dish, boat shape .	15.00
Flat................	40.00	Pitcher	
Cake Stand		Milk................	40.00
8"	40.00	Water	60.00
9"	45.00	Relish...............	15.00
10"	55.00	Salt, master	20.00
Carafe, water..........	35.00	Salt & Pepper Shakers,	
Celery Vase...........	30.00	pr	40.00
Compote		Sauce	
Cov, hs, 5", jelly......	45.00	Flat, 3½ to 4"........	5.00
Cov, hs, 6"	50.00	Footed, 3½".........	10.00
Cov, hs, 7"	60.00	Spooner	
Cov, hs, 8"	65.00	Flat................	20.00

	Clear		Clear
Footed	25.00	Syrup	55.00
*Sugar, cov		Toothpick	55.00
Flat	25.00	Tumbler	25.00
Footed	30.00	Wine	50.00

BIGLER

Flint made by Boston and Sandwich Glass Co., Sandwich, MA, and by other early factories. A scarce pattern in which goblets are most common and vary in height, shape and flare. Rare in color. The goblet has been reproduced as a commemorative item for Biglerville, PA.

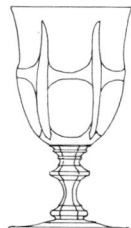

	Clear		Clear
Ale Glass	65.00	Goblet	
Bar Bottle, qt	95.00	Regular	48.00
Bowl, 10″ d	40.00	Short Stem	50.00
Butter, cov	125.00	Lamp, whale oil, monu-	
Celery Vase	100.00	ment base	155.00
Champagne	95.00	Mug, ah	60.00
Compote, open, 7″ d	40.00	Plate, 6″ d	30.00
Cordial	65.00	Salt, master	20.00
Creamer	75.00	Tumbler, water	65.00
Cup Plate	30.00	Whiskey, handled	100.00
Egg Cup, double	50.00	Wine	65.00

BIRD AND STRAWBERRY (Bluebird, Flying Bird and Strawberry, Strawberry and Bird)

Non-flint, c1914. Made by Indiana Glass Co., Dunkirk, IN. Pieces occasionally highlighted by coloring birds blue, strawberries pink, and leaves green, plus the addition of gilding.

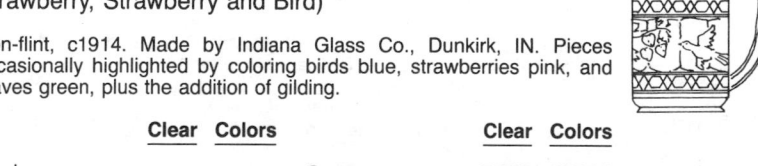

	Clear	Colors		Clear	Colors
Bowl			Creamer	55.00	135.00
5″	25.00	45.00	Cup	25.00	35.00
9½″, ftd	50.00	85.00	Goblet	200.00	300.00
10½″	55.00	95.00	Nappy	40.00	65.00
Butter, cov	100.00	175.00	Pitcher, water	235.00	350.00
Cake Stand	65.00	125.00	Plate, 12″	125.00	175.00
*Celery Vase	45.00	85.00	Punch Cup	25.00	35.00
Compote			Relish	20.00	45.00
*Cov, hs	125.00	200.00	Spooner	50.00	120.00
Open, ls,			Sugar, cov	65.00	125.00
ruffled	65.00	125.00	Tumbler	45.00	75.00
Jelly, cov, hs	150.00	225.00	Wine	65.00	100.00

BLEEDING HEART

Non-flint originally made by King Son & Co., Pittsburgh, PA, c1875, and by U. S. Glass Co. c1898. Also found in milk glass. Goblets are found in six variations. Note: A goblet with a tin lid, containing a condiment (mustard, jelly, or baking powder) was made. It is of inferior quality compared to the original goblet.

	Clear		Clear
Bowl		Molded Handle	30.00
7¼", oval	30.00	Dish, cov, 7"..........	55.00
8"	35.00	Egg Cup.............	45.00
9¼", oval, cov	65.00	Egg Rack, cov, 3 eggs ..	350.00
Butter, cov	75.00	Goblet, knob stem......	35.00
Cake Stand		Honey Dish	15.00
9"	75.00	Mug, 3¼"	40.00
10"	90.00	Pickle, 8¾" l, 5" w	30.00
11"	100.00	Pitcher, water, ah	150.00
Dessert slots	125.00	Plate.................	75.00
Compote		Platter, oval	65.00
Cov, hs, 8"	75.00	Relish, oval, 5½ x 3⅝"..	35.00
Cov, hs, 9"	95.00	Salt, master, ftd	60.00
Cov, ls, 7"..........	60.00	Salt, oval, flat.........	20.00
Cov, ls, 7½"	60.00	Sauce, flat	15.00
Cov, ls, 8"..........	75.00	Spooner..............	25.00
Open, ls, 8½"........	30.00	Sugar, cov	60.00
Creamer		Tumbler, ftd	80.00
Applied Handle	60.00	Wine................	175.00

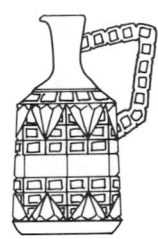

BLOCK AND FAN (Red Block and Fan, Romeo)

Non-flint made by Richard and Hartley Glass Co., Tarentum, PA, in the late 1880s. Continued by U. S. Glass Co. after 1891.

	Clear	Ruby Stained		Clear	Ruby Stained
Biscuit Jar, cov ..	65.00	150.00	salt, pepper &		
Bowl, 4", flat	20.00	—	cruet on tray ..	75.00	—
Butter, cov	50.00	85.00	Creamer		
Cake Stand			Individual	—	35.00
9"	35.00	—	Large	30.00	100.00
10"	42.00	—	Regular.......	25.00	45.00
Carafe	50.00	95.00	Small	35.00	75.00
Celery Tray	30.00	—	Cruet, os	35.00	—
Celery Vase.....	35.00	75.00	Dish, large, rect..	25.00	—
Compote, Open,			Finger Bowl	55.00	—
hs, 8"	40.00	165.00	Goblet	48.00	120.00
Condiment Set,			Ice Tub.........	45.00	50.00

	Clear	Ruby Stained		Clear	Ruby Stained
Orange Bowl	50.00	—	Ftd, 3¾"	12.00	25.00
Pickle Dish......	20.00	—	Spooner........	25.00	—
Pitcher			Sugar, cov	50.00	—
Milk..........	35.00	—	Sugar Shaker ...	40.00	—
Water	48.00	125.00	Syrup	75.00	95.00
Plate			Tray, ice cream,		
6"	15.00	—	rect..........	75.00	—
10"	18.00	—	Tumbler	30.00	40.00
Relish, rect......	25.00	—	Waste Bowl	30.00	—
Rose Bowl......	25.00	—	Wine...........	45.00	80.00
Salt & Pepper ...	30.00	—			
Sauce					
Flat, 5"	10.00	—			

BOW TIE (American Bow Tie)

Non-flint made by Thompson Glass Co., Uniontown, PA, c1889.

	Clear		Clear
Bowl		Pitcher	
8"	35.00	Milk...............	85.00
10¼" d, 5" h.........	65.00	Water	75.00
Butter, cov	65.00	Punch Bowl	100.00
Butter Pat...........	25.00	Relish, rect...........	25.00
Cake Stand, large, 9" d .	60.00	Salt	
Compote, open		Individual	20.00
hs, 5½"..............	60.00	Master	45.00
hs, 9¼"..............	65.00	Salt Shaker	40.00
ls, 6½"	45.00	Sauce, flat	15.00
ls, 8"	55.00	Spooner..............	35.00
Creamer..............	45.00	Sugar	
Goblet	60.00	Cov................	55.00
Honey cov	55.00	Open...............	40.00
Marmalade Jar	75.00	Tumbler	45.00
Orange Bowl, ftd, hs,			
10"	75.00		

BRIDAL ROSETTE (Checkerboard)

Made by Westmoreland Glass Co. in the early 1900s. Add 150% for ruby stained values. Reproduced since the 1950s in milk glass and in recent years, with pink stain. The Cambridge "Ribbon" pattern, usually marked "Nearcut," is similar.

	Clear		Clear
Bowl, 9", shallow	20.00	Water	35.00
Butter, cov	40.00	Plate	
Celery Tray	20.00	7"	15.00
Celery Vase	30.00	10"	20.00
Compote, open, ls, 8"	25.00	Punch Cup	5.00
Creamer	25.00	Salt & Pepper	40.00
Cruet, os	40.00	Sauce, flat	5.00
Cup	8.00	Spooner	20.00
Goblet	28.00	Sugar, cov	35.00
Honey Dish, cov, sq,		Tumbler	
pedestal	45.00	Iced Tea	25.00
Pitcher		Water	20.00
Milk	40.00	Wine	15.00

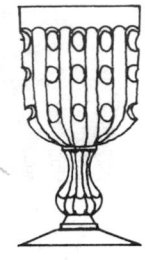

BROKEN COLUMN (Bamboo Irish Column, Notched Rib, Rattan, Ribbed Fingerprint)

Made in Findlay, OH, c1891, by Columbia Glass Co. c1892; and later by U. S. Glass Co. Notches may be ruby stained. A cobalt blue cup is known. The square covered compote has been reproduced. Some items have been reproduced for the Metropolitan Museum of Art. Some items are reproduced by the Smithsonian Institution with a raised "S.I." trademark.

	Clear	Ruby Stained		Clear	Ruby Stained
Banana Stand	185.00	—	Cruet, os	85.00	150.00
Basket, applied			Decanter	85.00	—
handle, 12" h,			Finger Bowl	30.00	—
15" l	125.00	—	*Goblet	55.00	100.00
Biscuit Jar	85.00	165.00	Marmalade Jar	85.00	—
Bowl			Pickle Castor, sp		
4", berry	15.00	20.00	frame	225.00	450.00
*8"	35.00	—	*Pitcher, water	90.00	230.00
9"	40.00	—	Plate		
Bread Plate	60.00	125.00	4"	25.00	40.00
Butter, cov	85.00	175.00	*7½"	40.00	95.00
Cake Stand, 9" or			Punch Cup	15.00	—
10"	75.00	225.00	Relish	25.00	—
Carafe, water	75.00	150.00	Salt Shaker	45.00	65.00
Celery Tray, oval	35.00	85.00	*Sauce, flat	10.00	20.00
Celery Vase	50.00	135.00	*Spooner	35.00	85.00
Champagne	100.00	—	*Sugar, cov	70.00	135.00
Claret	75.00	—	Sugar Shaker	85.00	200.00
Compote			Syrup	165.00	400.00
Cov, hs, 5¼" d,			Toothpick	150.00	—
10¼" h	90.00	200.00	Tumbler	45.00	55.00
Cov, hs, 10"	110.00	350.00	Vegetable, cov	90.00	—
Open, hs, 8" d	75.00	175.00	*Wine	80.00	125.00
*Creamer	42.50	125.00			

BUCKLE (Early Buckle)

Flint and non-flint pattern. The original maker is unknown. Shards have been found at the sites of the following glass houses: Boston and Sandwich Glass Co., Sandwich, MA; Union Glass Co., Somerville, MA; and Burlington Glass Works, Hamilton, Ontario, Canada. The non-flint production was made by Gillinder and Sons, Philadelphia, PA, in the late 1870s.

	Flint	Non-Flint		Flint	Non-Flint
Bowl			Goblet	40.00	25.00
8"	60.00	50.00	Pickle	40.00	15.00
10"	65.00	50.00	Pitcher, water, ah	500.00	85.00
Butter, cov	65.00	60.00	Salt		
Cake Stand, 9¾".	—	30.00	flat, oval	30.00	15.00
Champagne.....	60.00	—	footed	20.00	18.00
Compote			Sauce, flat	10.00	8.00
Cov, hs, 6" d ..	95.00	40.00	Spooner	35.00	27.50
Open, hs, 8½"	40.00	35.00	Sugar, cov	75.00	55.00
Open, ls	40.00	35.00	Tumbler	55.00	30.00
Creamer, ah.....	110.00	40.00	Wine...........	75.00	35.00
Egg Cup........	35.00	25.00			

BULL'S EYE

Flint made by the New England Glass Co. in the 1850s. Also found in colors and milk glass, which more than double the price.

	Clear		Clear
Bitters Bottle	80.00	Lamp	100.00
Butter, cov	150.00	Mug, 3½", ah..........	110.00
Carafe	45.00	Pitcher, water.........	285.00
Castor Bottle	35.00	Relish, oval	25.00
Celery Vase...........	85.00	Salt	
Champagne...........	95.00	Individual	40.00
Cologne Bottle........	85.00	Master, ftd	100.00
Cordial	75.00	Spill holder..........	85.00
Creamer, ah..........	125.00	Spooner	40.00
Cruet, os	125.00	Sugar, cov	125.00
Decanter, qt, bar lip	120.00	Tumbler	85.00
Egg Cup		Water Bottle, tumble up .	125.00
Cov................	165.00	Whiskey	70.00
Open...............	48.00	Wine................	50.00
* Goblet	65.00		

BULL'S EYE AND DAISY (Knobby Bull's Eye)

Made by U. S. Glass Co. in 1909. Also made with amethyst, blue, green, and pink stain in eyes.

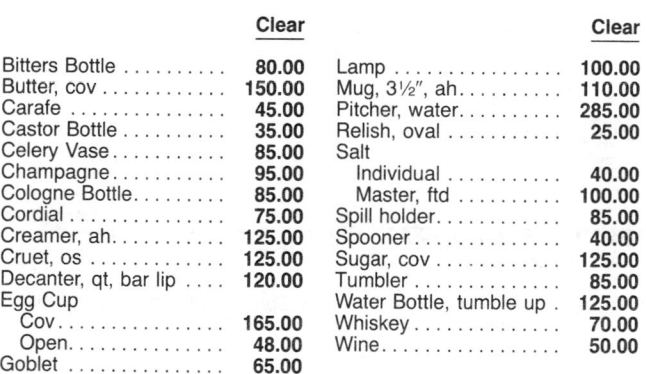

	Clear	Emerald Green	Ruby Stained
Bowl	15.00	20.00	30.00
Butter, cov	25.00	45.00	90.00
Celery Vase	20.00	25.00	40.00
Creamer	25.00	35.00	50.00
Decanter	—	110.00	—
Goblet	25.00	35.00	50.00
Pitcher, water	35.00	40.00	95.00
Salt Shaker	20.00	20.00	35.00
Sauce	7.50	10.00	20.00
Spooner	20.00	25.00	40.00
Sugar	22.00	30.00	45.00
Tumbler	15.00	20.00	35.00
Wine	20.00	25.00	40.00

BULL'S EYE WITH DIAMOND POINT (Owl, Union)

Flint made by New England Glass Co. c1869.

	Clear		Clear
Butter, cov	250.00	Salt, master, cov	100.00
Celery Vase	150.00	Sauce	20.00
Champagne	145.00	Spill	75.00
Cologne Bottle, os	90.00	Spooner	125.00
Creamer	200.00	Sugar, cov	175.00
Cruet, os	225.00	Syrup	175.00
Decanter, qt, os	200.00	Tumbler	145.00
Egg Cup	90.00	Tumble-Up	165.00
Goblet	120.00	Whiskey	150.00
Honey Dish, flat	25.00	Wine	135.00
Lamp, finger, ah	165.00		
Pitcher, water, 10¼", tankard	275.00		

BUTTERFLY AND FAN (Bird in Ring, Fan, Grace, Japanese)

Non-flint made by George Duncan & Sons, Pittsburgh, PA, c1880 and by Richards and Hartley Glass Co., Pittsburgh, PA, c1888.

	Clear		Clear
Bowl	30.00	Celery Vase	75.00
Bread Plate	50.00	Compote	
Butter, cov		Cov, hs, 8" d	95.00
Flat	100.00	Cov, hs, 7" d	95.00
Footed	75.00	Open, hs	30.00

	Clear		Clear
Creamer, ftd	**45.00**	Pitcher, water	**115.00**
Goblet	**65.00**	Sauce, ftd	**15.00**
Marmalade Jar	**75.00**	Spooner	**30.00**
Pickle Jar, SP frame and		Sugar cov, ftd	**50.00**
cov	**80.00**		

CABBAGE ROSE

Non-flint made by Central Glass Co., Wheeling, WV, c1870. Reproduced in clear and colors by Mosser Glass Co., Cambridge, OH, during the early 1960s.

	Clear		Clear
Basket, handled, 12"	**125.00**	Open, hs, 9½"	**100.00**
Bitters Bottle, 6½" h	**125.00**	Creamer, 5½", ah	**55.00**
Bowl, oval		Egg Cup	**45.00**
7½"	**30.00**	* Goblet	**40.00**
9½"	**40.00**	Mug	**60.00**
Bowl, round		Pickle Dish	**35.00**
6"	**25.00**	Pitcher	
7½", cov	**65.00**	Milk	**150.00**
Butter, cov	**60.00**	Water	**125.00**
Cake Stand		Relish, 8½" l, 5" w, rose-	
11"	**40.00**	filled horn of plenty	
12½"	**50.00**	center	**35.00**
Celery Vase	**48.00**	Salt, master, ftd	**25.00**
Champagne	**50.00**	* Sauce, 4"	**10.00**
Compote		Spooner	**25.00**
Cov, hs, 8½"	**120.00**	Sugar, cov	**55.00**
Cov, ls, 6"	**95.00**	Tumbler	**40.00**
Cov, ls, 7½"	**100.00**	Wine	**40.00**
Open, hs, 7½"	**75.00**		

CABLE (Cable with Ring)

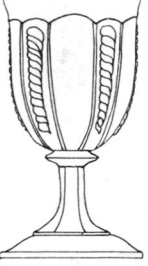

Flint, c1860. Made by Boston and Sandwich Glass Co. to commemorate the laying of the Atlantic Cable. Also found with amber stained panels and in opaque colors (rare).

	Clear		Clear
Bowl		Champagne	**250.00**
8", ftd	**45.00**	Compote, open	
9"	**70.00**	hs, 5½"	**70.00**
Butter, cov	**150.00**	ls, 7"	**60.00**
Cake Stand, 9"	**150.00**	ls, 9"	**65.00**
Celery Vase	**95.00**	ls, 11"	**85.00**

	Clear		Clear
Creamer..............	300.00	Plate, 6"...............	75.00
Decanter, qt, ground		Salt, individual, flat.....	35.00
stopper.............	295.00	Salt, master	
Egg Cup		Cov................	95.00
Cov................	225.00	Ftd	45.00
Open...............	60.00	Sauce, flat............	15.00
*Goblet	70.00	Spooner...............	45.00
Honey Dish	20.00	Sugar, cov	195.00
Lamp, 8¾"		Syrup	225.00
Glass Base	135.00	Tumbler, ftd	200.00
Marble Base	100.00	Wine.................	175.00
Pitcher, water, rare	500.00		

CANADIAN

Non-flint possibly made by Burlington Glass Works, Hamilton, Ontario, Canada, c1870.

	Clear		Clear
Bowl, 7" d, 4½" h, ftd ...	65.00	Goblet	45.00
Bread Plate, 10"	45.00	Mug, small............	45.00
Butter, cov	85.00	Pitcher	
Cake Stand, 9¼".......	85.00	Milk................	90.00
Celery Vase...........	65.00	Water	125.00
Compote		Plate, 6", handles	30.00
Cov, hs, 6"	90.00	Sauce	
Cov, hs, 7"	100.00	Flat................	15.00
Cov, hs, 8"	110.00	Footed	20.00
Cov, ls, 6"..........	50.00	Spooner.............	45.00
Cov, ls, 8"..........	75.00	Sugar, cov	90.00
Open, ls, 7"	35.00	Wine.................	45.00
Creamer.............	65.00		

CANE (Cane Insert, Hobnailed Diamond and Star)

Non-flint made by Gillinder and Sons Glass Co., Philadelphia, PA, and by McKee Bros. Glass Co., c1885. Goblets and toddy plates with inverted "buttons" are known.

	Amber	Apple Green	Blue	Clear	Vaseline
Butter, cov	45.00	60.00	75.00	40.00	60.00
Celery Vase.....	38.00	40.00	50.00	32.50	40.00
Compote, open, ls,					
5¾"..........	28.00	30.00	35.00	25.00	35.00
Cordial	—	—	—	25.00	—

	Amber	Apple Green	Blue	Clear	Vaseline
Creamer........	35.00	40.00	50.00	25.00	30.00
Finger Bowl.....	20.00	30.00	35.00	15.00	30.00
Goblet	25.00	40.00	35.00	20.00	40.00
Honey Dish.....	—	—	—	15.00	—
Match Holder, kettle.........	20.00	—	35.00	30.00	35.00
Pickle	25.00	20.00	25.00	15.00	20.00
Pitcher, milk.....	60.00	55.00	65.00	40.00	55.00
Pitcher, water....	80.00	85.00	80.00	48.00	85.00
Plate, toddy, 4½".	20.00	25.00	30.00	16.50	20.00
Relish..........	25.00	20.00	25.00	15.00	20.00
Salt & Pepper ...	60.00	50.00	80.00	30.00	70.00
Sauce, flat......	—	10.00	—	7.00	—
Slipper	30.00	—	25.00	15.00	30.00
Spooner........	42.00	35.00	30.00	20.00	30.00
Sugar, cov	45.00	45.00	45.00	25.00	45.00
Tray, water......	35.00	40.00	50.00	30.00	45.00
Tumbler	24.00	30.00	35.00	20.00	25.00
Waste Bowl, 7½".	32.50	30.00	35.00	20.00	30.00
Wine..........	35.00	40.00	35.00	20.00	35.00

CAROLINA (Inverness, Mayflower)

Made by Bryce Bros., Pittsburgh, PA, c1890 and later by U. S. Glass Co., as part of the States series, c1903. Ruby stained pieces often are souvenir marked. Some clear pieces found with gilt or purple stain.

	Clear	Ruby Stained		Clear	Ruby Stained
Bowl, berry......	15.00	—	Plate, 7½"	10.00	—
Butter, cov	35.00	—	Relish..........	10.00	—
Cake Stand	35.00	—	Salt Shaker	15.00	35.00
Compote			Sauce		
Open, hs, 8"...	38.50	—	Flat	8.00	—
Open, hs, 9½".	20.00	—	Footed	10.00	—
Open, jelly ...	10.00	—	Spooner........	20.00	—
Creamer........	20.00	—	Sugar, cov	25.00	—
Goblet	25.00	45.00	Tumbler	10.00	—
Mug	20.00	35.00	Wine..........	20.00	35.00
Pitcher, milk.....	45.00	—			

CATHEDRAL (Orion, Waffle and Fine Cut)

Non-flint pattern made by Bryce Bros. Pittsburgh, PA, in the 1880s and by U. S. Glass Co. in 1891. Also found in ruby stained (add 50%).

	Amber	Amethyst	Blue	Clear	Vaseline
Bowl, berry, 8"...	40.00	60.00	50.00	45.00	45.00
Butter, cov	60.00	110.00	40.00	45.00	60.00
Cake Stand	50.00	75.00	65.00	40.00	65.00
Celery Vase.....	35.00	60.00	40.00	30.00	40.00
Compote					
Cov, hs, 8"....	80.00	125.00	100.00	70.00	90.00
Open, hs, 9½".	50.00	85.00	65.00	55.00	—
Open, ls, 7"...	45.00	80.00	35.00	25.00	50.00
Open, jelly	—	—	—	25.00	
Creamer					
Flat, sq.......	50.00	85.00	—	35.00	50.00
Tall	45.00	80.00	50.00	30.00	45.00
Cruet, os	125.00	—	—	65.00	—
Goblet	50.00	70.00	50.00	40.00	60.00
Lamp, 12¾" h ...	—	—	185.00	—	—
Pitcher, water....	75.00	110.00	75.00	60.00	100.00
Relish, fish shape	40.00	50.00	50.00	—	45.00
Salt, boat shape .	20.00	30.00	25.00	15.00	25.00
Sauce					
Flat..........	15.00	30.00	20.00	15.00	20.00
Footed	15.00	35.00	20.00	15.00	20.00
Spooner........	40.00	65.00	50.00	35.00	45.00
Sugar, cov	70.00	100.00	60.00	50.00	60.00
Tumbler	40.00	40.00	35.00	25.00	40.00
Wine..........	40.00	60.00	55.00	30.00	50.00

COLORADO (Lacy Medallion)

Non-flint States pattern made by U. S. Glass Co. in 1898. Made in amethyst stained, ruby stained, and opaque white with enamel floral trim, all of which are scarce. Some pieces found with ornate silver frames or feet. Purists consider these two separate patterns, with the Lacy Medallion restricted to souvenir pieces. Reproductions have been made.

	Blue	Clear	Green
Banana Stand ...	65.00	35.00	50.00
Bowl			
6"	35.00	25.00	30.00
7½", ftd.......	40.00	25.00	35.00
8½", ftd.......	65.00	45.00	60.00
Butter, cov	175.00	60.00	100.00
Cake Stand	70.00	55.00	65.00
Celery Vase.....	65.00	35.00	75.00
Compote			
Open, ls, 5"...	35.00	20.00	30.00
Open, ls, 6"...	45.00	20.00	40.00
Open, ls, 9¼"..	85.00	35.00	65.00
Creamer			
Individual	35.00	30.00	25.00

	Blue	Clear	Green
Regular.......	95.00	45.00	70.00
Mug	40.00	20.00	30.00
Nappy..........	40.00	20.00	35.00
Pitcher			
Milk.........	250.00	—	100.00
Water	375.00	95.00	175.00
Plate			
6″	50.00	15.00	45.00
8″	65.00	20.00	60.00
Punch Cup......	30.00	18.00	25.00
Salt Shaker	65.00	30.00	40.00
Sauce, ruffled ...	30.00	15.00	25.00
Sherbet	50.00	25.00	45.00
Spooner........	65.00	40.00	70.00
Sugar			
Cov, regular ...	75.00	60.00	70.00
Open, indi-			
vidual	35.00	24.00	30.00
*Toothpick.......	55.00	30.00	35.00
Tray, calling card.	45.00	25.00	35.00
Tumbler	35.00	15.00	30.00
Vase, 12″	85.00	35.00	60.00
Violet Bowl......	60.00	—	—
Wine..........	—	25.00	40.00

COMET

Flint, possibly made by Boston and Sandwich Glass Co. in the early 1850s.

	Clear		Clear
Butter, cov	200.00	Pitcher, water..........	500.00
Compote, open, ls......	140.00	Spooner.............	95.00
Creamer.............	175.00	Sugar, cov	175.00
Goblet	135.00	Tumbler	110.00
Mug	135.00	Whiskey	165.00

CONNECTICUT

Non-flint, one of the States patterns made by U. S. Glass Co. c1900. Found in plain and engraved. Two varieties of ruby stained toothpicks ($90.00) have been identified.

	Clear		Clear
Biscuit Jar	25.00	8″	15.00
Bowl		Butter, cov	35.00
4″	10.00	Cake Stand	40.00

	Clear		Clear
Celery Tray	20.00	Pitcher, water.	40.00
Celery Vase.	25.00	Relish	15.00
Compote		Salt & Pepper	35.00
Cov, hs	40.00	Spooner	25.00
Open, hs, 7"	25.00	Sugar, cov	35.00
Creamer.	28.00	Sugar Shaker	35.00
Dish, 8", oblong.	20.00	Toothpick	50.00
Lamp, enamel dec	85.00	Tumbler, water.	20.00
Lemonade, handled	20.00	Wine	35.00

CRYSTAL WEDDING (Collins, Crystal Anniversary)

Non-flint made by Adams Glass Co., Pittsburgh, PA, c1890 and by U. S. Glass Co. in 1891. Also found in frosted, amber stained, and cobalt blue (rare). Heavily reproduced in clear, ruby stained, and milk with enamel trim.

	Clear	Ruby Stained		Clear	Ruby Stained
Banana Stand . . .	95.00	—	Pitcher		
Bowl			Milk, round	110.00	125.00
4½", individual			Milk, sq.	125.00	200.00
berry	15.00	—	Water, round . .	110.00	210.00
7", sq, cov	75.00	85.00	Water, sq	165.00	225.00
8", sq, berry . . .	50.00	85.00	Plate, 10"	25.00	40.00
8", sq, cov	60.00	95.00	Relish	20.00	40.00
Butter, cov	75.00	125.00	Salt		
Cake Plate, sq. . .	45.00	85.00	Individual	25.00	40.00
Cake Stand, 10" .	65.00	—	Master	35.00	65.00
Celery Vase	45.00	75.00	Salt Shaker	65.00	75.00
Compote			Sauce	15.00	20.00
*Cov, hs, 7 x			Spooner	30.00	60.00
13"	100.00	110.00	Sugar, cov	70.00	85.00
Open, ls, 5", sq	50.00	55.00	Syrup	150.00	200.00
Creamer.	50.00	75.00	Tumbler	35.00	45.00
Cruet	125.00	200.00	Vase		
*Goblet	55.00	85.00	Footed, twisted	25.00	—
Nappy, handle . . .	25.00	—	Swung	25.00	—
Pickle	25.00	40.00	Wine.	45.00	70.00

DAISY AND BUTTON

Non-flint made in the 1880s by several companies in many different forms. In continuous production since inception. Original manufacturers include: Bryce Brothers, Doyle & Co., Hobbs, Brockunier & Co., George Duncan & Sons, Boston & Sandwich Glass Co., Beatty & Sons, and U.S. Glass Co. Reproductions have existed since the early 1930s in original and new colors. Reproductions, too, have been made by several companies, including L. G. Wright, Imperial Glass Co., Fenton Art Glass Co., and Degenhart Glass Co. Also found in amberina, amber stain, and ruby stained.

	Amber	Apple Green	Blue	Clear	Vaseline
Bowl, triangular . .	45.00	45.00	45.00	25.00	65.00
Bread Plate, 13″ .	40.00	60.00	35.00	20.00	40.00
*Butter, cov					
Round.	70.00	90.00	70.00	65.00	95.00
Square	110.00	115.00	110.00	100.00	120.00
Butter Pat.	30.00	40.00	35.00	25.00	35.00
*Canoe					
4″	12.00	24.00	15.00	10.00	24.00
8½″.	35.00	35.00	35.00	25.00	50.00
12″	60.00	35.00	28.00	20.00	40.00
14″	30.00	40.00	35.00	25.00	40.00
*Castor Set					
4 bottle, glass std.	90.00	85.00	95.00	65.00	75.00
5 bottle, metal std.	100.00	100.00	110.00	100.00	95.00
Celery Vase	55.00	60.00	45.00	35.00	85.00
*Compote					
Cov, hs, 6″	35.00	50.00	45.00	25.00	50.00
Open, hs, 8″ . . .	75.00	65.00	60.00	40.00	65.00
*Creamer.	35.00	40.00	40.00	18.00	35.00
*Cruet, os	100.00	80.00	75.00	45.00	80.00
Egg Cup.	20.00	30.00	25.00	15.00	30.00
Finger Bowl	30.00	50.00	35.00	30.00	45.00
*Goblet	40.00	50.00	40.00	25.00	40.00
*Hat, 2½″.	30.00	35.00	40.00	20.00	40.00
Ice Cream Tray, 14 × 9 × 2″ . .	75.00	50.00	55.00	35.00	55.00
Inkwell	40.00	50.00	45.00	30.00	45.00
Parfait.	25.00	35.00	30.00	20.00	35.00
Pickle Castor	125.00	90.00	150.00	75.00	150.00
*Pitcher, water					
Bulbous, reed handle.	125.00	95.00	90.00	75.00	90.00
Tankard	65.00	65.00	65.00	60.00	70.00
*Plate					
5″, leaf shape. .	20.00	25.00	15.00	12.00	25.00
6″, round.	10.00	22.00	15.00	6.50	25.00
7″, square.	25.00	35.00	25.00	15.00	35.00
Punch Bowl, stand	90.00	100.00	95.00	85.00	100.00
*Salt & Pepper . . .	35.00	45.00	35.00	25.00	25.00
*Sauce, 4″	18.00	25.00	18.00	15.00	25.00
*Slipper					
5″	45.00	48.00	50.00	45.00	50.00
11½″.	40.00	50.00	30.00	35.00	50.00
*Spooner	40.00	40.00	45.00	35.00	45.00

	Amber	Apple Green	Blue	Clear	Vaseline
*Sugar, cov	45.00	50.00	45.00	35.00	50.00
Syrup	45.00	50.00	45.00	30.00	45.00
*Toothpick					
-Round.	40.00	55.00	35.00	40.00	45.00
Urn	25.00	30.00	35.00	15.00	30.00
*Tray	65.00	65.00	60.00	35.00	60.00
Tumbler	18.00	30.00	35.00	15.00	25.00
*Wine.	15.00	25.00	20.00	10.00	45.00

DAISY AND BUTTON WITH CROSSBARS (Daisy and Thumbprint Crossbar, Daisy and Button with Crossbar and Thumbprint Band, Daisy with Crossbar, Mikado)

Non-flint made by Richards and Hartley, Tarentum, PA, c1885. Reissued by U.S. Glass Co. after 1891. Shards have been found at Burlington Glass Works, Hamilton, Ontario, Canada.

	Amber	Blue	Clear	Vaseline
Bowl				
6"	25.00	30.00	15.00	25.00
9"	30.00	40.00	25.00	30.00
Bread Plate	30.00	45.00	25.00	35.00
Butter, cov				
Flat	55.00	55.00	45.00	55.00
Footed	—	75.00	25.00	60.00
Celery Vase	36.00	40.00	30.00	50.00
Compote				
Cov, hs, 8"	55.00	65.00	45.00	55.00
Open, hs, 8". . .	45.00	50.00	30.00	45.00
Open, ls, 7" . . .	30.00	—	20.00	45.00
Creamer				
Individual	30.00	30.00	20.00	30.00
Regular.	45.00	45.00	35.00	40.00
Cruet, os	75.00	85.00	35.00	100.00
Goblet	40.00	40.00	25.00	48.00
Mug, 3" h	15.00	18.00	12.50	20.00
Pitcher				
Milk.	90.00	95.00	45.00	90.00
Water	145.00	110.00	65.00	125.00
Salt & Pepper . . .	40.00	50.00	30.00	45.00
Sauce				
Flat	15.00	18.00	10.00	15.00
Footed	18.00	25.00	15.00	24.00
Spooner	35.00	35.00	25.00	35.00
Sugar, cov				
Individual	25.00	35.00	10.00	25.00
Regular.	50.00	60.00	25.00	55.00

	Amber	Blue	Clear	Vaseline
Syrup	125.00	125.00	65.00	125.00
Toothpick.	40.00	40.00	28.00	35.00
Tumbler	20.00	25.00	18.00	25.00
Wine.	30.00	35.00	25.00	30.00

DAKOTA (Baby Thumbprint, Thumbprint Band)

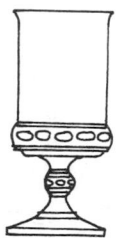

Non-flint made by Ripley and Co., Pittsburgh, PA, in the late 1880s and early 1890s. Later reissued by U. S. Glass Co. as one of the States patterns. Prices listed are for etched fern and berry pattern; also found with fern and no berry, and oak leaf etching, and scarcer grape etching. Other etchings known include fish, swan, peacock, bird and insect, bird and flowers, ivy and berry, stag, spider and insect in web, buzzard on dead tree, and crane catching fish. Sometimes ruby stained with or without souvenir markings. There is a four-piece table set available in a "hotel" variant, prices are about 20% more than the regular type.

	Clear Etched	Clear Plain	Ruby Stained
Basket, 10 x 2" . .	245.00	185.00	225.00
Bottle, 5½".	75.00	65.00	—
Bowl, berry.	45.00	35.00	—
Butter, cov	65.00	40.00	125.00
Cake Cover, 8" d.	300.00	200.00	—
Cake Stand			
9½".	60.00	35.00	—
10½".	65.00	45.00	—
Celery Tray	35.00	25.00	—
Celery Vase.	35.00	30.00	—
Compote			
Cov, hs, 5"	60.00	50.00	—
Cov, hs, 6"	65.00	50.00	—
Cov, hs, 7"	70.00	55.00	—
Cov, hs, 8"	75.00	60.00	—
Cov, hs, 9"	100.00	80.00	—
Cov, hs, 10" . . .	125.00	100.00	—
Open, ls, 5" . . .	40.00	30.00	—
Open, ls, 6" . . .	45.00	35.00	—
Open, ls, 7" . . .	45.00	35.00	—
Open, ls, 8" . . .	50.00	40.00	—
Open, ls, 9" . . .	65.00	55.00	—
Open, ls, 10" . .	75.00	65.00	—
Condiment Tray. .	—	75.00	—
Creamer.	55.00	30.00	60.00
Cruet	90.00	55.00	135.00
Goblet	35.00	25.00	85.00
Pitcher			
Milk.	120.00	80.00	200.00

	Clear Etched	Clear Plain	Ruby Stained
Tankard	125.00	95.00	225.00
Water	95.00	75.00	190.00
Plate, 10″	85.00	75.00	—
Salt Shaker	65.00	50.00	125.00
Sauce			
Flat, 4″ d.	20.00	15.00	25.00
Footed, 5″ d. . .	25.00	15.00	30.00
Spooner	30.00	25.00	65.00
Sugar, cov	65.00	55.00	85.00
Tray, water, 13″ d	100.00	75.00	—
Tumbler	35.00	30.00	55.00
Waste Bowl	65.00	50.00	75.00
Wine	30.00	20.00	55.00

DEER AND PINE TREE (Deer and Doe)

Non-flint made by Belmont Glass Co. and McKee & Bros. Glass Co. c1886. Souvenir mugs with gilt found in clear and olive green. Also made in canary (vaseline). The goblet has been reproduced since 1938. L. G. Wright Glass Co. has reproduced the goblet in clear glass using new molds.

	Amber	Apple Green	Blue	Clear
Bread Plate	90.00	100.00	100.00	65.00
Butter, cov	125.00	425.00	125.00	95.00
Cake Stand	—	—	—	75.00
Celery Vase	—	—	—	75.00
Compote				
Cov, hs, 8″, sq .	—	—	—	100.00
Open, hs, 7″ . . .	—	—	—	45.00
Open, hs, 9″ . . .	—	—	—	55.00
Creamer	95.00	85.00	90.00	65.00
Finger Bowl	—	—	—	55.00
* Goblet	—	—	—	55.00
Marmalade Jar . .	—	—	—	90.00
Mug	40.00	45.00	50.00	40.00
Pickle	—	—	—	30.00
Pitcher				
Milk	—	—	—	90.00
Water	125.00	125.00	125.00	125.00
Platter, 8 x 13″ . . .	75.00	—	80.00	60.00
Sauce				
Flat	—	—	—	20.00
Footed	—	—	—	25.00
Spooner	—	—	—	65.00
Sugar, cov	—	—	—	85.00
Tray, water	100.00	—	90.00	60.00

DELAWARE (American Beauty, Four Petal Flower)

Non-flint made by U. S. Glass Co., Pittsburgh, PA, 1899–1909. Also made by Diamond Glass Co., Montreal, Quebec, Canada, c1902. Also found in amethyst (scarce), clear with rose trim, custard, and milk glass. Prices are for pieces with perfect gold trim.

	Clear	Green w/Gold	Rose w/Gold
Banana Bowl. . . .	40.00	55.00	65.00
Bowl			
8″	30.00	40.00	50.00
9″	25.00	60.00	75.00
Bottle, os	80.00	150.00	185.00
Bride's Basket, SP frame	75.00	115.00	165.00
*Butter, cov	50.00	115.00	150.00
Claret Jug, tankard shape	110.00	195.00	200.00
Celery Vase, flat .	75.00	90.00	95.00
*Creamer.	45.00	65.00	70.00
Cruet, os	90.00	200.00	250.00
Finger Bowl	25.00	50.00	75.00
Lamp Shade, electric	85.00	—	100.00
Pin Tray	30.00	55.00	95.00
Pitcher, water. . . .	50.00	150.00	125.00
Pomade Box, jeweled.	100.00	250.00	350.00
Puff Box, bulbous, jeweled.	100.00	200.00	315.00
Punch Cup.	18.00	30.00	35.00
Salt and Pepper, pr	150.00	400.00	500.00
Sauce, 5½″, boat	15.00	35.00	30.00
Spooner	45.00	50.00	55.00
*Sugar, cov	65.00	85.00	100.00
Toothpick	35.00	115.00	125.00
Tumbler	20.00	40.00	45.00
Vase			
6″	25.00	60.00	70.00
8″	25.00	70.00	75.00
9½″	40.00	80.00	85.00

DIAMOND POINT (Diamond Point with Ribs, Pineapple, Sawtooth, Stepped Diamond Point)

Flint originally made by Boston and Sandwich Glass Co. c1850 and by the New England Glass Co., East Cambridge, MA, c1860. Many other companies manufactured this pattern throughout the 19th century. Rare in color.

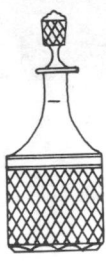

	Flint	Non-Flint		Flint	Non-Flint
Ale Glass, 6¼" h .	85.00	—	Egg Cup		
Bowl			Cov	75.00	50.00
7", cov	60.00	20.00	Open	40.00	20.00
8", cov	60.00	20.00	Goblet	45.00	35.00
8", open	45.00	15.00	Honey Dish	15.00	—
Butter, cov	95.00	50.00	Lemonade	55.00	—
Cake Stand, 14" .	185.00	—	Mustard, cov	25.00	—
Candlesticks, pr. .	145.00	—	Pitcher		
Castor Bottle	25.00	15.00	Pint	185.00	—
Celery Vase	75.00	30.00	Quart	275.00	—
Champagne	85.00	35.00	Plate		
Claret	90.00	—	6"	30.00	—
Compote			8"	50.00	—
Cov, hs, 8"	135.00	60.00	Salt, master, cov .	75.00	—
Open, hs 10½",			Sauce, flat	15.00	—
flared	100.00	—	Spill Holder	45.00	—
Open, hs, 11",			Spooner	45.00	30.00
scalloped rim	110.00	—	Sugar, cov	65.00	—
Open, ls, 7½" . .	50.00	40.00	Syrup	150.00	—
Cordial	165.00	—	Tumbler, bar	65.00	35.00
Creamer, ah	115.00	—	Whiskey, ah	85.00	—
Decanter, qt, os . .	165.00	—	Wine	75.00	30.00

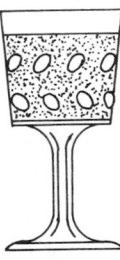

EGG IN SAND (Bean, Stippled Oval)

Non-flint, c1885. Has been reported in colors, but rare.

	Clear		Clear
Bread Plate, octagonal . .	25.00	Salt & Pepper	65.00
Butter, cov	40.00	Sauce	10.00
Compote, cov, jelly	45.00	Spooner, flat rim	30.00
Creamer	30.00	Sugar, cov	35.00
Dish, swan center	40.00	Tray, water	40.00
Goblet	30.00	Tumbler	30.00
Pitcher, water	45.00	Wine	35.00
Relish	15.00		

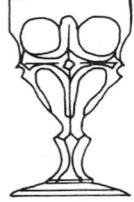

EXCELSIOR

Flint attributed to several firms, including Boston and Sandwich Glass Co., Sandwich, MA; McKee Bros., Pittsburgh, PA, and Ihmsen & Co., Pittsburgh, PA, 1850s–60s. Quality and design vary. Prices are for high quality flint. Very rare in color.

	Clear		Clear
Ale Glass	50.00	Bitters Bottle	95.00
Bar Bottle	85.00	Bowl, 10", open	125.00

	Clear		Clear
Butter, cov	100.00	Single	40.00
Candlestick, 9½" h	125.00	Goblet, Maltese Cross	50.00
Celery Vase, scalloped		Lamp, hand	95.00
top	85.00	Mug	30.00
Champagne	60.00	Pickle Jar, cov	45.00
Claret	45.00	Pitcher, water	350.00
Compote		Salt, master	30.00
Cov, ls	125.00	Spillholder	75.00
Open, hs	85.00	Spooner	60.00
Cordial	40.00	Sugar, cov	110.00
Creamer	85.00	Syrup	125.00
Decanter		Tumbler, bar	50.00
Pint	85.00	Whiskey, Maltese Cross	65.00
Quart	85.00	Wine	45.00
Egg Cup			
Double	45.00		

EYEWINKER (Cannon Ball, Crystal Ball, Winking Eye)

Non-flint made in Findlay, OH, in 1889. Reportedly made by Dalzell, Gilmore and Leighton Glass Co., which was organized in 1883 in West Virginia and moved to Findlay in 1888. Made only in clear glass; reproduced in color by several companies, including L. G. Wright Co. A goblet and toothpick were not originally made in this pattern.

	Clear		Clear
Banana Stand, hs	135.00	*Honey Dish	40.00
Bowl		Lamp, kerosene	125.00
6½"	25.00	Nappy, folded sides, 7¼"	30.00
9", cov	75.00	*Pitcher, water	95.00
*Butter, cov	70.00	Plate	
Cake Stand, 8"	55.00	7"	30.00
Celery Vase	45.00	9", sq, upturned sides	65.00
*Compote		10", upturned sides	85.00
Cov, hs, 6½"	85.00	Salt Shaker	35.00
Cov, hs, 9½"	150.00	Sauce	15.00
Open, 7¼", fluted	65.00	Spooner	35.00
Open, 4½", jelly	45.00	*Sugar, cov	55.00
Creamer	65.00	Syrup, pewter top	125.00
Cruet	65.00	*Tumbler	45.00

FEATHER (Cambridge Feather, Feather and Quill, Fine Cut and Feather, Indiana Feather, Indiana Swirl, Prince's Feather, Swirl, Swirl and Feather)

Non-flint made by McKee & Bros. Glass Co., Pittsburgh, PA, 1896–1901; Beatty-Brady Glass Co., Dunkirk, IN, c1903; and Cambridge Glass Co.,

Cambridge, OH, c1902–03. Later the pattern was reissued with variations and quality differences. Also found in amber stain (rare).

	Clear	Emerald Green		Clear	Emerald Green
Banana Boat, ftd	75.00	175.00	Open, ls, 7″	35.00	—
Bowl, oval			Open, ls, 8″	40.00	—
7 × 9″, ftd	35.00	—	Cordial	125.00	—
8½″	25.00	—	Creamer	40.00	85.00
9¼″	20.00	75.00	Cruet, os	45.00	250.00
Bowl, round			Dishes, nest of 3:		
6″	20.00	—	7″, 8″, and 9″	40.00	—
7″	25.00	75.00	Goblet	55.00	150.00
8″	30.00	85.00	Honey Dish	15.00	—
Bowl, sq			Marmalade Jar	125.00	—
4½″	15.00	—	Pickle Castor	145.00	—
8″	30.00	—	Pitcher		
Butter, cov	55.00	150.00	Milk	50.00	165.00
Cake Plate	65.00	—	Water	75.00	250.00
Cake Stand			Plate, 10″	50.00	75.00
8″	45.00	125.00	Relish	20.00	—
9½″	50.00	125.00	Salt Shaker	35.00	70.00
11″	70.00	175.00	Sauce	12.00	—
Celery Vase	45.00	80.00	Spooner	25.00	60.00
Champagne	65.00	—	Sugar, cov	50.00	85.00
Compote			Syrup	125.00	300.00
Cov, hs, 8½″	125.00	250.00	Toothpick	85.00	165.00
Cov, ls, 4¼″, jelly	100.00	150.00	Tumbler	50.00	85.00
Cov, ls, 8¼″	150.00	—	*Wine		
Open, ls, 4″	20.00	—	Scalloped border	40.00	—
Open, ls, 6″	25.00	—	Straight border	25.00	—

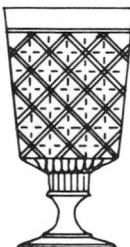

FINECUT (Flower in Square)

Non-flint made by Bryce Bros., Pittsburgh, PA, c1885, and by U. S. Glass Co. in 1891.

	Amber	Blue	Clear	Vaseline
Bowl, 8¼″	15.00	20.00	10.00	15.00
Bread Plate	50.00	60.00	25.00	50.00
Butter, cov	55.00	75.00	45.00	60.00
Cake Stand	—	—	35.00	—
Celery Tray	—	45.00	25.00	40.00
Celery Vase, SP holder	—	—	—	115.00
Creamer	60.00	40.00	35.00	75.00
Goblet	45.00	55.00	22.00	42.00
Pitcher, water	100.00	100.00	60.00	115.00

	Amber	Blue	Clear	Vaseline
Plate				
7″	25.00	40.00	15.00	20.00
10″	30.00	50.00	21.00	45.00
Relish..........	15.00	25.00	10.00	20.00
Sauce, flat	14.00	15.00	10.00	14.00
Spooner........	30.00	45.00	18.00	40.00
Sugar, cov	45.00	55.00	35.00	45.00
Tray, water......	50.00	55.00	25.00	50.00
Tumbler	—	—	18.00	28.00
Wine..........	—	—	24.00	30.00

FLAMINGO HABITAT

Non-flint, maker unknown, c1870, etched pattern.

	Clear		Clear
Bowl, 10″, oval	40.00	Open, 6″.............	40.00
Butter, cov	65.00	Creamer..............	40.00
Celery Vase...........	45.00	Goblet	45.00
Champagne...........	45.00	Sauce, ftd	15.00
Cheese Dish, blown	110.00	Spooner..............	25.00
Compote		Sugar, cov	50.00
Cov, 4½″............	75.00	Tumbler	30.00
Cov, 6½″............	95.00	Wine.................	45.00
Open, 5″, jelly	35.00		

FLORIDA (Emerald Green Herringbone, Paneled Herringbone)

Non-flint made by U. S. Glass Co., in the 1890s. One of the States patterns. Goblet reproduced in green and other colors.

	Clear	Emerald Green		Clear	Emerald Green
Berry Set	75.00	110.00	Mustard Pot, at-		
Bowl, 7¾″	10.00	15.00	tached under-		
Butter, cov	50.00	85.00	plate, cov	25.00	45.00
Cake Stand			Nappy..........	15.00	25.00
Large	60.00	75.00	Pitcher, water....	50.00	75.00
Small	30.00	40.00	Plate		
Celery Vase.....	30.00	35.00	7½″..........	10.00	15.00
Compote, open,			9¼″..........	15.00	25.00
hs, 6½″, sq....	—	40.00	Relish		
Creamer........	30.00	45.00	6″, sq	10.00	15.00
Cruet, os	40.00	110.00	8½″, sq.......	15.00	22.00
* Goblet, 5¾″ h ...	25.00	40.00	Salt Shaker	25.00	50.00

	Clear	Emerald Green		Clear	Emerald Green
Sauce	5.00	7.50	Syrup	60.00	175.00
Spooner	20.00	35.00	Tumbler	20.00	35.00
Sugar, cov	35.00	50.00	Wine	25.00	50.00

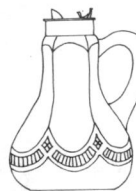

GALLOWAY (Mirror Plate, U.S. Mirror, Virginia, Woodrow)

Non-flint made by U. S. Glass Co., Pittsburgh, PA, c1904–19. Jefferson Glass Co., Toronto, Canada, produced it from 1900–25. Clear glass with and without gold trim; also known with rose stain and ruby stain.

	Clear w/ Gold	Rose Stained		Clear w/ Gold	Rose Stained
Basket, no gold	75.00	125.00	Pitcher		
Bowl			Milk	60.00	80.00
6½", belled	20.00	35.00	Tankard	75.00	125.00
8½", oval	35.00	45.00	Water, ice lip	65.00	175.00
8½", round	30.00	50.00	Plate, 8", round	40.00	65.00
9", rect	30.00	45.00	Punch Bowl	160.00	225.00
11" d, round	45.00	65.00	Punch Bowl Plate,		
Butter, cov	65.00	125.00	20"	80.00	125.00
Cake Stand	70.00	95.00	Punch Cup	10.00	15.00
Carafe, water	55.00	85.00	Relish	20.00	30.00
Celery Vase	35.00	75.00	Rose Bowl	25.00	60.00
Champagne	60.00	175.00	Salt, master	35.00	60.00
Compote			Salt & Pepper, pr.	40.00	75.00
Cov, hs, 6"	90.00	125.00	Sauce		
Open, hs, 5½"	25.00	40.00	Flat, 4"	10.00	20.00
Open, hs, 10",			Footed, 4½"	10.00	20.00
scalloped	55.00	75.00	Sherbet	25.00	30.00
Creamer	30.00	50.00	Spooner	30.00	80.00
Cruet	45.00	125.00	Sugar, cov	55.00	85.00
Egg Cup	40.00	60.00	Sugar Shaker	40.00	100.00
Finger Bowl	40.00	65.00	Syrup	65.00	135.00
Goblet	75.00	95.00	*Toothpick	30.00	55.00
Lemonade	35.00	45.00	Tumbler	35.00	45.00
Mug	40.00	50.00	Vase, swung	30.00	—
Nappy, tricorn	25.00	50.00	Waste Bowl	40.00	65.00
Olive, 6"	20.00	30.00	Water Bottle	40.00	85.00
Pickle Castor, sp			Wine	45.00	65.00
holder and lid	75.00	200.00			

GARFIELD DRAPE (Canadian Drape)

Non-flint issued in 1881 by Adams & Co., Pittsburgh, PA, after the assassination of President Garfield.

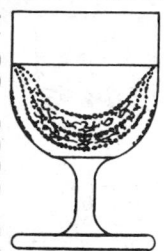

	Clear		Clear
Bread Plate		Goblet	40.00
Memorial, portrait of		Honey Dish	15.00
Garfield..........	65.00	Pitcher	
"We Mourn Our Nation's		Milk...............	70.00
Loss," portrait......	75.00	Water, ah	75.00
Butter, cov	70.00	Water, strap handle...	100.00
Cake Stand, 9½".......	75.00	Relish, oval	20.00
Celery Vase...........	55.00	Sauce	
Compote		Flat................	8.50
Cov, hs, 8"	100.00	Footed	12.00
Cov, ls, 6"..........	85.00	Spooner..............	35.00
Open, hs, 8½"	40.00	Sugar, cov	60.00
Creamer.............	40.00	Tumbler	35.00

GEORGIA (Peacock Feather)

Non-flint made by Richards and Hartley Glass Co., Tarentum, PA, and reissued by U. S. Glass Co. in 1902 as part of the States series. Rare in blue. (Chamber lamp, pedestal base, $275.00.) No goblet known in pattern.

	Clear		Clear
Bonbon, ftd	25.00	Creamer.............	35.00
Bowl, 8"	30.00	Cruet, os	45.00
Butter, cov	55.00	Decanter	70.00
Cake Stand, 10"	50.00	Lamp	
Castor Set, 2 bottles....	60.00	Chamber, pedestal ...	85.00
Celery Tray, 11¾"	35.00	Hand, oil, 7"	80.00
Children's		Mug	25.00
Cake Stand	35.00	Nappy................	25.00
Creamer............	35.00	Pitcher, water..........	65.00
Compote		Plate, 5¼"	15.00
Cov, hs, 5"	35.00	Relish................	15.00
Cov, hs, 6"	40.00	Salt Shaker	40.00
Cov, hs, 7"	45.00	Sauce................	10.00
Cov, hs, 8"	50.00	Spooner..............	35.00
Open, hs, 5".........	20.00	Sugar, cov	45.00
Open, hs, 6".........	25.00	Syrup, metal lid	65.00
Open, hs, 7".........	30.00	Tumbler	35.00
Open, hs, 8".........	35.00		
Condiment Set, tray, oil			
cruet, salt & pepper...	75.00		

HEART WITH THUMBPRINT (Bull's Eye in Heart, Columbia, Columbian, Heart and Thumbprint)

Non-flint made by Tarentum Glass Co. 1898–1906. Some emerald green pieces have gold trim. Made experimentally in custard, blue custard, opaque Nile green, and cobalt.

	Clear	Emerald Green	Ruby Stain
Banana Boat	75.00	—	125.00
Barber Bottle	115.00	—	—
Bowl			
7" sq	35.00	100.00	85.00
9½" sq	35.00	125.00	90.00
10" scalloped . .	45.00	100.00	80.00
Butter, cov	125.00	175.00	125.00
Cake Stand, 9" . .	150.00	—	175.00
Carafe, water. . . .	100.00	—	150.00
Card Tray.	20.00	55.00	80.00
Celery Vase	65.00	—	90.00
Compote, open, hs			
7½", scalloped .	150.00	—	175.00
8½"	100.00	—	185.00
Cordial, 3" h	125.00	175.00	150.00
Creamer			
Individual	30.00	45.00	35.00
Regular.	60.00	110.00	175.00
Cruet	75.00	—	—
Finger Bowl	45.00	85.00	65.00
Goblet	65.00	125.00	110.00
Hair Receiver, lid.	60.00	100.00	85.00
Ice Bucket	60.00	—	—
Lamp			
Finger.	95.00	150.00	—
Oil, 8"	125.00	225.00	—
Mustard, SP cov .	95.00	100.00	—
Nappy, triangular .	30.00	60.00	—
Pitcher, water. . . .	200.00	—	—
Plate			
6"	25.00	45.00	35.00
10"	45.00	85.00	75.00
Powder Jar, SP cov	65.00	—	—
Punch Cup.	20.00	35.00	30.00
Rose Bowl			
Large	60.00	—	90.00
Small	30.00	—	75.00
Salt & Pepper, pr.	95.00	—	—
Sauce, 5"	20.00	35.00	30.00
Spooner	50.00	85.00	75.00
Sugar			
Individual	25.00	35.00	35.00
Table, cov	85.00	90.00	—
Syrup	95.00	—	—
Tray, 8¼" l, 4¼" w	30.00	65.00	35.00
Tumbler	45.00	85.00	60.00
Vase			
6"	35.00	65.00	55.00
10"	65.00	100.00	85.00
Wine.	45.00	150.00	125.00

HOLLY

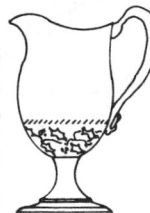

Non-flint, possibly made by Boston and Sandwich Glass Co. in the late 1860s and early 1870s.

	Clear		Clear
Bowl, cov, 8" d.	150.00	Pitcher, water, ah	225.00
Butter, cov	150.00	Salt	
Cake Stand, 11"	165.00	Flat, oval	65.00
Celery Vase	110.00	Ftd	60.00
Compote, cov, hs	165.00	Sauce, flat	20.00
Creamer, ah.	125.00	Spooner	60.00
Egg Cup.	65.00	Sugar, cov	125.00
Goblet	100.00	Tumbler	125.00
Pickle, oval	30.00	Wine	125.00

HONEYCOMB

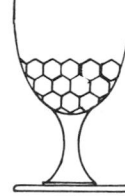

A popular pattern made in flint and non-flint glass by numerous firms, c1850–1900, resulting in many minor pattern variations. Found with copper wheel engraving. Rare in color.

	Flint	Non-Flint		Flint	Non-Flint
Ale Glass	50.00	25.00	Creamer, ah.	35.00	20.00
Barber Bottle	45.00	25.00	Decanter		
Bowl, cov, 7¼"			Pint	55.00	18.50
pat'd 1869,			Quart, os	70.00	65.00
acorn finial	100.00	45.00	Egg Cup.	20.00	15.00
Butter, cov	65.00	45.00	Finger Bowl	45.00	—
Cake Stand	55.00	35.00	Goblet	25.00	15.00
Castor Bottle	25.00	18.00	Honey Dish, cov.	15.00	25.00
Celery Vase	45.00	20.00	Lamp		
Champagne	50.00	25.00	All Glass	—	85.00
Claret	35.00	35.00	Marble base	—	90.00
Compote, cov, hs			Lemonade	40.00	20.00
6½" x 8½" h	100.00	50.00	Mug, half pint	25.00	15.00
9¼ x 11½" h	110.00	65.00	Pitcher, water, ah	165.00	60.00
Compote, open, hs			Plate, 6"	—	12.50
7 x 7" h.	60.00	40.00	Pomade Jar, cov.	50.00	20.00
7½", scalloped.	45.00	25.00	Relish	30.00	20.00
8 x 6¼" h	65.00	40.00	Salt, master, cov,		
Compote, open, ls			ftd	35.00	30.00
6" d, Saucer	35.00	25.00	Salt Shaker, orig		
Bowl	40.00	25.00	top.	—	35.00
7½", scalloped	40.00	25.00	Sauce	12.00	7.50
Cordial, 3½".	35.00	25.00	Spillholder	35.00	20.00
			Spooner	65.00	35.00

	Flint	Non-Flint		Flint	Non-Flint
Sugar			Footed	45.00	15.00
Frosted rose-			Vase		
bud finial....	—	50.00	7½"	45.00	—
Regular.......	75.00	45.00	10½".........	75.00	—
Tumbler			Whiskey, handled	125.00	—
Bar	35.00	—	Wine..........	35.00	15.00
Flat	40.00	12.50			

HORSESHOE (Good Luck, Prayer Rug)

Non-flint made by Adams & Co., Pittsburgh, PA, and others in the 1880s.

	Clear		Clear
Bowl, cov, oval		Marmalade Jar, cov	110.00
7"	150.00	Pitcher	
8"	195.00	Milk...............	165.00
Bread Plate, 14 x 10"		Water	135.00
Double horseshoe		Plate	
handles..........	65.00	7"	45.00
Single horseshoe han-		10"	55.00
dles..............	40.00	Relish	
Butter, cov	95.00	5 x 7"	20.00
Cake Plate............	40.00	8", Wheelbarrow, pew-	
Cake Stand		ter wheels.........	75.00
9"	70.00	Salt	
10"	80.00	Individual, horseshoe	
Celery Vase, knob stem .	40.00	shape	20.00
Cheese, cov, woman		Master, horseshoe	
churning	275.00	shape	100.00
Compote		Master, wheelbarrow,	
Cov, hs, 7", horseshoe		pewter wheels	75.00
finial	95.00	Sauce	
Cov, hs, 8 x 12¼"	125.00	Flat	10.00
Cov, hs, 11".........	135.00	Footed	15.00
Creamer, 6½"	55.00	Spooner	35.00
Doughnut Stand	75.00	Sugar, cov	65.00
Finger Bowl	80.00	Vegetable Dish, oblong..	35.00
Goblet		Waste Bowl	45.00
Knob Stem..........	40.00	Water Tray...........	125.00
Plain Stem	38.00	Wine................	150.00

ILLINOIS (Clarissa, Star of the East)

Non-flint. One of the States patterns made by U. S. Glass Co. c1897. Most forms are square. A few items are known in ruby stained, including a salt ($50.00) and a lidless straw holder with the stain on the inside ($95.00).

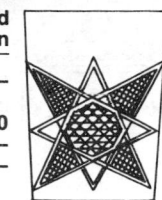

	Clear	Emerald Green		Clear	Emerald Green
Basket, ah, 11½".	100.00	—	Plate, 7", sq.	25.00	—
Bowl			Relish		
5", round	20.00	—	7½" x 4"	18.00	40.00
6", sq	25.00	—	8½ x 3"	18.00	—
8", round	25.00	—	9 × 3", canoe	40.00	—
9", sq	35.00	—	Salt		
*Butter, cov	60.00	—	Individual	20.00	—
Candlesticks, pr.	95.00	—	Master	35.00	—
Celery Tray, 11".	40.00	—	Salt & Pepper, pr	40.00	—
Cheese, cov	75.00	—	Sauce	15.00	—
Compote, open			Spooner	35.00	—
hs, 5"	40.00	—	Straw Holder, cov	175.00	400.00
hs, 9"	60.00	—	Sugar		
Creamer			Individual	30.00	—
Individual	30.00	—	Table, cov	55.00	—
Table	40.00	—	Sugar Shaker	65.00	—
Cruet	65.00	—	Syrup, pewter top	95.00	—
Finger Bowl	25.00	—	Toothpick		
Marmalade Jar	135.00	—	Adv emb in base	45.00	—
Olive	18.00	—	Plain	30.00	—
Pitcher, milk			Tray, 12 x 8",		
Round, SP rim.	175.00	—	turned up sides	50.00	—
Square	65.00	—	Tumbler	30.00	40.00
Pitcher, water			Vase, 6", sq	35.00	45.00
Square	70.00	—	Vase, 9½"	—	125.00
Tankard, round, SP rim	75.00	135.00			

IOWA (Paneled Zipper)

Non-flint made by U. S. Glass Co. c1902. Part of the States pattern series. Available in clear glass with gold trim (add 20%) and ruby or cranberry stained. Also found in amber (goblet, $65.00), green, canary, and blue. Add 50% to 100% for color.

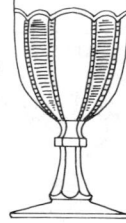

	Clear		Clear
Bowl, berry	15.00	Lamp	125.00
Bread Plate, motto	80.00	Olive	15.00
Butter, cov	40.00	Pitcher, water	50.00
Cake Stand	35.00	Punch Cup	15.00
Carafe	35.00	Salt Shaker, single	20.00
Compote, cov, 8"	40.00	Sauce, 4½"	6.50
Corn Liquor Jug, os	60.00	Spooner	30.00
Creamer	30.00	Sugar, cov	35.00
Cruet, os	30.00	Toothpick	20.00
Cup	15.00	Tumbler	25.00
Decanter, 1½ pts	40.00	Vase, 8" h	20.00
Goblet	25.00	Wine	30.00

JACOB'S LADDER (Maltese)

Non-flint made by Portland Glass Co., Portland, ME, and Bryce Bros, Pittsburgh, PA, in 1876 and by U. S. Glass Co. in 1891. A few pieces found in amber, yellow, blue, pale blue, and pale green.

	Clear		Clear
Bowl		Open, hs, 10″	40.00
6″ x 8¾″	15.00	Creamer	35.00
6¾″ x 9¾″	20.00	Cruet, os, ftd	85.00
7½″ x 10¾″	20.00	Goblet	65.00
9″, berry, ornate SP		Honey Dish, 3½″	10.00
holder, ftd	125.00	Marmalade Jar	75.00
Butter, cov	65.00	Mug	100.00
Cake Stand		Pitcher, water, ah	150.00
8″ or 9″	50.00	Plate, 6¼″	20.00
11″ or 12″	60.00	Relish, 9½ x 5½″	15.00
Castor Bottle	18.00	Salt, master, ftd	20.00
Castor Set, 4 bottles	100.00	Sauce	
Celery Vase	45.00	Flat, 4″ or 5″	8.00
Cologne Bottle, Maltese		Footed, 4″	12.00
cross stopper, ftd	85.00	Spooner	35.00
Compote		Sugar, cov	80.00
Cov, hs, 6″	80.00	Syrup	
Cov, hs 7½″	80.00	Knight's Head finial . . .	125.00
Cov, hs, 9½″	125.00	Plain top	100.00
Open, hs, 7½″	35.00	Tumbler, bar	85.00
Open, hs, 8½″, scal-		Wine	30.00
loped	30.00		
Open, hs, 9½″, scal-			
loped	38.00		

JERSEY SWIRL (Swirl)

Non-flint made by Windsor Glass Co., Pittsburgh, PA, c1887. Heavily reproduced in color by L. G. Wright Co. The clear goblet is also reproduced.

	Amber	Blue	Canary	Clear
Bowl, 9¼″	55.00	55.00	45.00	35.00
Butter, cov	55.00	55.00	50.00	40.00
Cake Stand, 9″ . .	75.00	70.00	45.00	30.00
*Celery Vase	42.00	42.00	35.00	30.00
*Compote, hs, 8″ .	50.00	50.00	45.00	35.00
Creamer	45.00	45.00	40.00	30.00
Cruet, os	—	—	—	25.00
*Goblet				
Buttermilk	40.00	40.00	35.00	30.00
Water	40.00	40.00	35.00	30.00
Marmalade Jar . .	—	—	—	50.00

	Amber	Blue	Canary	Clear
Pickle Castor, SP frame and lid . .	—	—	—	125.00
Pitcher, water. . . .	50.00	50.00	45.00	35.00
Plate, round				
6"	25.00	25.00	20.00	15.00
8"	30.00	30.00	25.00	20.00
10"	38.00	38.00	35.00	30.00
* Salt, ind	20.00	20.00	18.00	15.00
Sauce, 4½", flat. .	20.00	20.00	15.00	10.00
Spooner	30.00	30.00	25.00	20.00
Sugar, cov	40.00	40.00	35.00	30.00
Tumbler	30.00	30.00	25.00	20.00
* Wine.	50.00	50.00	40.00	15.00

KANSAS (Jewel with Dewdrop)

Non-flint originally produced by Co-Operative Flint Glass Co., Beaver Falls, PA. Later produced as part of the States pattern series by U. S. Glass Co. in 1901 and by Jenkins Glass Co, c1915–25. Also known with jewels stained in pink or gold. Mugs (smaller and inferior quality) have been reproduced in vaseline, amber, and blue.

	Clear		Clear
Banana Stand	90.00	Open, hs, 7"	35.00
Bowl		Open, hs, 8"	45.00
7", oval	35.00	Creamer	40.00
8"	40.00	* Goblet	55.00
Bread Plate, ODB	45.00	* Mug	
Butter, cov	65.00	Regular	45.00
Cake Plate	45.00	Tall	35.00
Cake Stand		* Pitcher	
7⅝"	45.00	Milk	50.00
9"	75.00	Water	60.00
10"	85.00	Relish, 8½", oval	20.00
Celery Vase	45.00	Salt Shaker	50.00
Compote		Sauce, flat, 4"	15.00
Cov, hs, 5"	45.00	Sugar, cov	65.00
Cov, hs, 6"	50.00	Syrup	125.00
Cov, hs, 7"	65.00	Toothpick	65.00
Cov, hs, 8"	85.00	Tumbler	45.00
Cov, ls, 5"	50.00	Whiskey, handle	45.00
Open, hs, 5"	25.00	Wine	65.00
Open, hs, 6"	30.00		

KENTUCKY

Non-flint made by U. S. Glass Co. c1897 as part of the States pattern series. The goblet is found in ruby stained ($50.00). A footed, square

sauce ($30.00) is known in cobalt blue with gold. A toothpick holder is also known in ruby stained ($150.00).

	Clear	Emerald Green		Clear	Emerald Green
Bowl, 8" d	20.00	—	Plate, 7", sq	15.00	—
Butter, cov	50.00	—	Punch Cup	10.00	15.00
Cake Stand, 9½"	40.00	—	Salt Shaker, orig		
Creamer	25.00	—	top	10.00	—
Cruet, os	45.00	—	Sauce, ftd, sq	5.00	10.00
Cup	10.00	20.00	Spooner	35.00	—
Goblet	20.00	50.00	Sugar, cov	30.00	—
Nappy	10.00	15.00	Toothpick, sq	35.00	75.00
Olive, handle	25.00	—	Tumbler	20.00	30.00
Pitcher, water	55.00	—	Wine	25.00	35.00

KING'S CROWN (Ruby Thumbprint, X.L.C.R.)

Non-flint made by Adams & Co. Pittsburgh, PA., in the 1890s and later. Known as Ruby Thumbprint when pieces are ruby stained. Made in clear and with the thumbprints stained amethyst, gold, green, and yellow, and in clear with etching and trimmed in gold. It became very popular after 1891 as ruby stained souvenir ware. Approximately 87 pieces documented. NOTE: Pattern has been copiously reproduced for the gift-trade market in milk glass, cobalt blue, and other colors. New pieces are easily distinguished: in the case of Ruby Thumbprint, the color is a very pale pinkish red. Available in amethyst stained goblet ($30.00) and wine ($10.00) and in green stained goblet ($25.00) and wine ($15.00). Add 30% for engraved pieces.

	Clear	Ruby Stained		Clear	Ruby Stained
Banana Stand,			Open, hs, 8¼"	75.00	95.00
ftd	85.00	135.00	Open, ls, 5¼"	30.00	45.00
* Bowl			* Cordial	45.00	—
9¼" d, pointed	35.00	90.00	* Creamer, ah		
10" d, scal-			Ind, tankard,		
loped	45.00	95.00	3¼" h	25.00	35.00
Butter, cov, 7½" d	50.00	90.00	Table, 4⅞" h	50.00	65.00
* Cake Stand			* Cup and Saucer	55.00	70.00
9" d	68.00	125.00	Custard Cup	15.00	25.00
10" d	75.00	125.00	* Goblet	35.00	45.00
Castor Set, glass			Honey Dish, cov,		
stand, 4 bottles	175.00	300.00	sq	100.00	175.00
Celery Vase	40.00	60.00	* Lamp, oil, 10"	135.00	—
* Champagne	25.00	35.00	Mustard, cov, 4"		
* Claret	35.00	50.00	h	35.00	75.00
* Compote			Preserve, 10" l	35.00	50.00
Cov, hs, 8"	65.00	245.00	* Pitcher		
Cov, ls, 12"	90.00	225.00	Milk, tankard	75.00	100.00

	Clear	Ruby Stained		Clear	Ruby Stained
Water, bulbous.	95.00	225.00	*Sauce, 4"	15.00	20.00
Water, tankard .	110.00	200.00	Spooner, 4¼" h . .	45.00	50.00
*Plate, 7"	20.00	45.00	*Sugar		
*Punch Bowl, ftd . .	275.00	300.00	Ind, open, 2¾"		
*Punch Cup	15.00	30.00	h	25.00	45.00
Salt			Table, cov, 6¾"		
Ind, rect	15.00	35.00	h	55.00	95.00
Master, sq	30.00	50.00	Toothpick, 2¾" h	20.00	35.00
Salt Shaker, 3⅛"			*Tumbler, 3¾" h . .	20.00	35.00
h	30.00	45.00	*Wine, 4⅜" h	25.00	40.00

KOKOMO (Bar and Diamond, R and H Swirl Band)

Non-flint made by Richards and Hartley, Tarentum, PA, c1885. Reissued by U. S. Glass Co., c1891 and Kokomo Glass Co., Kokomo, IN, c1901. Found in ruby stained and etched. Over 50 pieces manufactured.

	Clear	Ruby Stained		Clear	Ruby Stained
Bowl, 8½", ftd . . .	24.00	—	Finger Bowl	25.00	35.00
Bread Tray	30.00	45.00	Goblet	30.00	45.00
Butter, cov	35.00	—	Lamp, hand, atyp-		
Cake Stand	45.00	165.00	ical—has no		
Celery Vase	30.00	45.00	diamonds	50.00	100.00
Compote			Pitcher, tankard . .	55.00	100.00
Cov, hs, 7½" . .	35.00	165.00	Sauce, ftd, 5"	8.00	10.00
Open, hs, 6" . . .	25.00	—	Spooner	25.00	45.00
Open, hs, 8" . . .	35.00	—	Sugar, cov	45.00	65.00
Open, ls, 7½" . .	20.00	—	Sugar Shaker . . .	35.00	75.00
Condiment Set,			Syrup	45.00	130.00
oblong tray,			Tray, water	35.00	90.00
shakers, cruet .	80.00	195.00	Tumbler	25.00	35.00
Creamer, ah	35.00	50.00	Wine	25.00	35.00
Cruet	35.00	—			
Decanter, 9¾",					
wine	55.00	95.00			

LION (Frosted Lion)

Made by Gillinder and Sons, Philadelphia, PA, in 1876. Available in clear without frosting (20% less). Many reproductions.

	Frosted		Frosted
Bowl, oblong		8 x 5"	50.00
6½ x 4¼"	55.00	Bread Plate, 12"	90.00

	Frosted		Frosted
* Butter, cov		Cup and Saucer, child	
Lion's head finial	90.00	size	45.00
Rampant finial	125.00	* Egg Cup, 3½" h	65.00
Cake Stand	85.00	* Goblet	70.00
* Celery Vase	85.00	Marmalade Jar, rampant	
Champagne	175.00	finial	90.00
Cheese, cov, rampant		Pitcher	
lion's head finial.	400.00	Milk	375.00
Children's Table Set	500.00	Water	300.00
* Compote		Relish, lion handles.	35.00
Cov, hs, 7", rampant		* Salt, master, rect lid	250.00
finial	150.00	* Sauce, 4", ftd.	25.00
* Cov, hs, 9", rampant		* Spooner	75.00
finial, oval, collared		* Sugar, cov	
base	150.00	Lion's head finial	90.00
Cov, 9", hs	185.00	Rampant finial	110.00
Open, ls, 8"	75.00	Syrup, orig top.	350.00
Cordial	175.00	Wine.	200.00
* Creamer.	75.00		

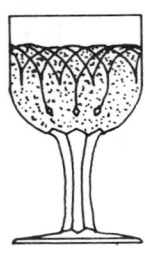

LOOP AND DART

Clear and stippled non-flint of the late 1860s and early 1870s. Made by Boston and Sandwich Glass Co., Sandwich, MA, and Richards and Hartley, Tarentum, PA. Pattern related to Loop and Dart with Diamond Ornament, and Loop and Dart with Round Ornament, which was made by Portland Glass Co., Portland, ME. Flint add 25%.

	Clear		Clear
Bowl, 9", oval.	30.00	Pitcher, water.	75.00
Butter, cov	45.00	Plate, 6"	35.00
Cake Stand, 10"	40.00	Relish.	20.00
Celery Vase	35.00	Salt, master	50.00
Compote		Sauce.	5.00
Cov, hs, 8"	85.00	Spooner	25.00
Cov, ls, 8".	65.00	Sugar, cov	50.00
Creamer.	35.00	Tumbler	
Cruet, os	95.00	Footed	30.00
Egg Cup.	25.00	Water	25.00
Goblet	25.00	Wine.	35.00
Lamp, oil	85.00		

LOUISIANA (Sharp Oval and Diamond, Granby)

Made by Bryce Bros., Pittsburgh, PA, in the 1870s. Reissued by U. S. Glass Co. c1898 as one of the States patterns. Also available with gold and also comes frosted.

	Clear			Clear	
Bowl, 9", berry	20.00		Match Holder	35.00	
Butter, cov	75.00		Mug, handled, gold top	25.00	
Cake Stand	65.00		Nappy, 4", cov	30.00	
Celery Vase	30.00		Pitcher, water	65.00	
Compote			Relish	15.00	
Cov, hs, 8"	75.00		Spooner	30.00	
Open, hs, 5", jelly	40.00		Sugar, cov	45.00	
Creamer	30.00		Tumbler	25.00	
Goblet	30.00		Wine	35.00	

MAINE (Paneled Stippled Flower, Stippled Primrose)

Non-flint made by U. S. Glass Co., Pittsburgh, PA, c1899. Researchers dispute if goblet was made originally. Sometimes found with enamel trim or overall turquoise stain.

	Clear	Emerald Green		Clear	Emerald Green
Bowl, 8"	30.00	40.00	Mug	35.00	—
Bread Plate, oval,			Pitcher		
10 × 7¾"	30.00	—	Milk	65.00	75.00
Butter, cov	45.00	—	Water	50.00	115.00
Cake Stand	40.00	60.00	Relish	15.00	—
Compote			Salt Shaker, single	30.00	—
Cov, jelly	50.00	75.00	Sauce	15.00	—
Open, hs, 7"	20.00	45.00	Sugar, cov	45.00	75.00
Open, ls, 8"	38.00	55.00	Syrup	75.00	225.00
Open, ls, 9"	30.00	65.00	Toothpick	125.00	—
Creamer	30.00	—	Tumbler	30.00	45.00
Cruet, os	80.00	—	Wine	50.00	75.00

MANHATTAN

Non-flint with gold made by U. S. Glass Co. c1902. A Depression glass pattern also has the "Manhattan" name. A table-sized creamer and covered sugar are known in true ruby stained, and a goblet is known in old marigold carnival glass. Heavily reproduced by Anchor Hocking Glass Co. and Tiffin Glass Co.

	Clear	Rose Stained		Clear	Rose Stained
Biscuit Jar, cov	60.00	85.00	10"	22.00	—
Bowl			12½"	25.00	—
6"	18.00	—	Butter, cov	55.00	—
8¼", scalloped	20.00	—	Cake Stand, 8"	45.00	55.00
*9½"	20.00	—	Carafe, water	40.00	65.00

	Clear	Rose Stained		Clear	Rose Stained
Celery Tray, 8"....	20.00	—	6"	10.00	30.00
Celery Vase......	25.00	—	8"	15.00	—
Cheese, cov, 8⅜"			10¾"........	20.00	—
d...........	—	115.00	Punch Bowl.....	125.00	—
Compote			Punch Cup......	10.00	—
Cov, hs, 9½" ..	60.00	—	Relish, 6"......	12.00	—
Open, hs, 9½".	45.00	—	Salt Shaker, single	20.00	35.00
Open, hs,			Sauce..........	14.00	20.00
10½".......	50.00	—	*Spooner........	20.00	—
*Creamer			Straw Holder, cov	95.00	
Individual	20.00	—	*Sugar		
Table	30.00	60.00	Individual,		
Cruet			open	15.00	—
Large	65.00	115.00	Table, cov	40.00	65.00
Small	50.00	—	Syrup..........	48.00	175.00
*Goblet	25.00	—	*Toothpick.......	30.00	—
Ice Bucket	—	65.00	Tumbler		
Olive, Gainsbor-			Iced Tea......	30.00	—
ough.........	30.00	—	Water	20.00	—
Pitcher, water, ½			Vase, 6"........	18.00	—
gal			Violet Bowl......	20.00	—
Bulbous, ah ...	70.00	—	Water Bottle.....	40.00	—
Tankard, ah ...	60.00	125.00	*Wine...........	15.00	—
Plate					
5"	10.00	—			

MARYLAND (Inverted Loop and Fan, Loop and Diamond)

Made originally by Bryce Bros., Pittsburgh, PA. Continued by U. S. Glass Co. as one of its States patterns.

	Clear w/ Gold	Ruby Stained		Clear w/ Gold	Ruby Stained
Banana Dish	35.00	85.00	Pitcher		
Bowl, berry......	15.00	35.00	Milk..........	42.50	135.00
Bread Plate	25.00	—	Water	50.00	100.00
Butter, cov	65.00	95.00	Plate, 7", round ..	25.00	—
Cake Stand, 8" ..	40.00	—	Relish, oval	15.00	55.00
Celery Tray	20.00	35.00	Salt Shaker, single	30.00	—
Celery Vase.....	30.00	65.00	Sauce, flat	10.00	15.00
Compote			Spooner........	30.00	55.00
Cov, hs.......	65.00	100.00	Sugar, cov	45.00	60.00
Open, jelly	25.00	45.00	Toothpick.......	125.00	175.00
Creamer.........	25.00	55.00	Tumbler	25.00	50.00
Goblet	30.00	45.00	Wine...........	40.00	75.00
Olive, handled...	15.00	—			

MASCOTTE (Dominion, Etched Fern and Waffle, Minor Block)

Non-flint made by Ripley and Co., Pittsburgh, PA, in the 1880s. Reissued by U. S. Glass Co. in 1891. The butter dish shown on Plate 77 of Ruth Webb Lee's *Victorian Glass* is said to go with this pattern. It has a horseshoe finial and was named for the famous "Maude S," "Queen of the Turf" trotting horse during the 1880s. Apothecary jar and pyramid jars made by Tiffin Glass Co. in the 1950s.

	Clear	Etched		Clear	Etched
Bowl			Pitcher, water. . . .	55.00	65.00
Cov, 5"	—	35.00	Plate, turned in		
Cov, 7"	—	45.00	sides	40.00	45.00
Open 9"	35.00	40.00	Pyramid Jar, 7" d,		
Butter Pat.	15.00	20.00	one fits into		
Butter, cov			other and forms		
"Maude S" . . . 100.00		110.00	tall jar-type con-		
Regular.	50.00	65.00	tainer with lid,		
Cake Basket,			three sizes with		
handle	80.00	95.00	flat separators .	50.00	55.00
Cake Stand	35.00	50.00	Salt Dip	25.00	—
Celery Vase	35.00	40.00	Salt Shaker, sin-		
Cheese, cov	70.00	80.00	gle.	25.00	25.00
Compote			Sauce		
Cov, hs, 5"	35.00	40.00	Flat	8.00	15.00
Cov, hs, 7"	45.00	55.00	Footed	12.00	15.00
Cov, hs, 9"	65.00	90.00	Spooner	30.00	35.00
Open, hs, 6". . .	20.00	25.00	Sugar, cov	40.00	45.00
Open, hs, 8". . .	30.00	35.00	Tray, water.	40.00	55.00
Open, ls, 8" . . .	30.00	45.00	Tumbler	20.00	35.00
Creamer.	30.00	45.00	Wine.	25.00	30.00
Goblet	40.00	45.00			

MASSACHUSETTS (Arched Diamond Points, Cane Variant, Geneva #2, M2-131, Star and Diamonds)

Made in the 1880s, unknown maker, reissued in 1898 by U. S. Glass Co. as one of the States series. The vase ($45.00) and wine ($45.00) are known in emerald green. Some pieces reported in cobalt blue and marigold carnival glass. Reproduced in clear and colors.

	Clear		Clear
Bar Bottle, metal shot		Celery Tray	30.00
glass for cover.	75.00	Champagne.	35.00
Basket, 4½", ah.	50.00	Cologne Bottle, os	37.50
Bowl		Compote, open	35.00
6", sq	20.00	Cordial	55.00
8", d	30.00	Creamer.	25.00
*Butter, cov	80.00	Cruet, os	45.00

	Clear		Clear
Goblet	45.00	Sherry	40.00
Gravy Boat	30.00	Spooner	20.00
Mug	20.00	Sugar, cov	40.00
Mustard Jar, cov	35.00	Syrup	65.00
Olive	8.50	Toothpick	40.00
Pitcher, water	65.00	Tumbler	30.00
Plate, 8″	30.00	Vase, trumpet	
Punch Cup	15.00	6½″ h	25.00
Relish, 8½″	25.00	7″ h	25.00
Rum Jug	90.00	9″ h	35.00
Salt Shaker, tall	25.00	Whiskey	25.00
Sauce, sq, 4″	15.00	Wine	40.00

MICHIGAN (Loop and Pillar)

Non-flint made by U. S. Glass Co. c1902 as one of the States pattern series. The 10¼″ bowl ($42.00) and punch cup ($12.00) are found with yellow or blue stain. Also found with painted carnations. Other colors include "Sunrise," gold, and ruby stained.

	Clear	Rose Stained		Clear	Rose Stained
Bowl			Olive, two		
7½″	15.00	30.00	handles	10.00	25.00
9″	35.00	60.00	Pickle	12.00	20.00
10¼″	35.00	62.00	Pitcher		
Butter, cov			8″	50.00	—
Large	60.00	125.00	12″, tankard	70.00	150.00
Small	65.00	—	Plate, 5½″ d	15.00	—
Celery Vase	40.00	85.00	Punch Bowl, 8″	50.00	—
Compote			Punch Cup	8.00	—
Jelly, 4½″	45.00	75.00	Relish	20.00	35.00
Open, hs, 9¼″	65.00	85.00	Salt Shaker, sin-		
Creamer			gle, 3 types	20.00	30.00
Ind, 6 oz,			Sauce	12.00	22.00
tankard	20.00	65.00	Sherbet cup,		
Table	30.00	70.00	handled	15.00	20.00
Cruet, os	60.00	225.00	Spooner	50.00	75.00
Crushed Fruit Bowl	75.00	—	Sugar, cov	50.00	85.00
Custard Cup	15.00	—	Syrup	95.00	175.00
Finger Bowl	15.00	—	*Toothpick	45.00	100.00
Goblet	45.00	65.00	Tumbler	30.00	40.00
Honey Dish	10.00	—	Vase		
Lemonade Mug	24.00	40.00	Bud	35.00	40.00
Nappy, Gainsbor-			Ftd, large	45.00	—
ough handle	35.00	—	Wine	35.00	50.00

MINERVA (Roman Medallion)

Non-flint made by Boston and Sandwich Glass Co., Sandwich, MA, c1870 as well as other American companies. Shards have been found at Burlington Glass Works, Hamilton, Ontario, Canada.

	Clear		Clear
Bowl		Creamer..............	45.00
Footed	40.00	Goblet	95.00
Rectangular		Marmalade Jar, cov	150.00
7"..............	25.00	Pickle	25.00
8 x 5"	30.00	Pitcher, Water	185.00
Bread Plate	65.00	Plate	
Butter, cov	75.00	8"	55.00
Cake Stand		10", handled........	60.00
9 x 6½".............	100.00	Platter, oval, 13"	65.00
10½"..............	120.00	Sauce	
13"	145.00	Flat	18.50
Champagne...........	85.00	Footed, 4"	20.00
Compote		Spooner	40.00
Cov, hs, 6"	85.00	Sugar, cov	65.00
Cov, hs, 8"	150.00	Waste Bowl	50.00
Cov, ls, 8"..........	125.00		
Open, hs, 10½", octagonal ftd	95.00		

MINNESOTA

Non-flint made by U. S. Glass Co. in the late 1890s as one of the States patterns. A two-piece flower frog has been found in emerald green ($45.00).

	Clear	Ruby Stained		Clear	Ruby Stained
Banana Stand ...	65.00	—	Cup............	18.00	—
Basket	65.00	—	Goblet	35.00	50.00
Biscuit Jar, cov ..	55.00	150.00	Hair Receiver. ...	30.00	—
Bonbon, 5"......	15.00	—	Juice Glass	20.00	—
Bowl, 8½", flared.	30.00	100.00	Match Safe	25.00	—
Butter, cov	50.00	—	Mug	25.00	—
Carafe	35.00	—	Olive...........	15.00	25.00
Celery Tray, 13"..	30.00	—	Pitcher, tankard..	85.00	200.00
Compote			Plate		
Open, hs, 10", flared.......	60.00	—	5", turned up edges	25.00	—
Open, ls, 9", sq	55.00	—	7⅜" d	15.00	—
Creamer			Pomade Jar, cov .	35.00	—
Individual	20.00	—	Relish..........	20.00	—
Table	30.00	—	Salt Shaker	25.00	—
Cruet	35.00	—	Sauce, boat shape	10.00	25.00

	Clear	Ruby Stained		Clear	Ruby Stained
Spooner	25.00	—	Tray, 8" l.	15.00	—
Sugar, cov	35.00	—	Tumbler	20.00	—
Syrup	65.00	—	Wine	40.00	—
Toothpick, 3 handles	30.00	150.00			

NEVADA

Non-flint made by U. S. Glass Co., Pittsburgh, PA, c1902 as a States pattern. Pieces are sometimes partly frosted and have enamel decoration. Add 20% for frosted.

	Clear		Clear
Biscuit Jar	45.00	Finger Bowl	25.00
Bowl		Jug	35.00
6" d, cov	35.00	Pickle, oval	10.00
7" d, open	20.00	Pitcher	
8" d, cov	45.00	Milk, tankard	45.00
Butter, cov	70.00	Water, bulbous	50.00
Cake Stand, 10"	35.00	Water, tankard	45.00
Celery Vase	25.00	Salt	
Compote		Individual	15.00
Cov, hs, 6"	40.00	Master	20.00
Cov, hs, 7"	45.00	Salt Shaker, table	15.00
Cov, hs, 8"	45.00	Sauce, 4" d	10.00
Open, hs, 6"	20.00	Spooner	35.00
Open, hs, 7"	30.00	Sugar, cov	35.00
Open, hs, 8"	35.00	Syrup, tin top	45.00
Creamer	30.00	Toothpick	35.00
Cruet	35.00	Tumbler	15.00
Cup, custard	12.00		

NEW HAMPSHIRE (Bent Buckle, Modiste)

Non-flint made by U. S. Glass Co., Pittsburgh, PA, c1903 in the States pattern series.

	Clear w/ Gold	Rose Stained	Ruby Stained
Biscuit Jar, cov	75.00	—	—
Bowl			
Flared, 5½"	10.00	—	25.00
Round, 8½"	18.00	30.00	—
Square, 8½"	25.00	35.00	—
Butter, cov	45.00	70.00	—
Cake Stand, 8¼"	30.00	—	—

	Clear w/ Gold	Rose Stained	Ruby Stained
Carafe	60.00	—	—
Celery Vase	35.00	50.00	—
Compote			
Cov, hs, 5"	50.00	—	—
Cov, hs, 7"	65.00	—	—
Open.	40.00	55.00	—
Creamer			
Individual	20.00	30.00	—
Table	30.00	45.00	—
Cruet	55.00	135.00	—
Goblet	25.00	45.00	—
Mug, large	20.00	45.00	50.00
Pitcher, water			
Bulbous, ah . . .	90.00	—	—
Straight Sides, molded			
handle.	60.00	90.00	—
Relish.	18.00	—	—
Salt & Pepper, pr.	35.00	—	—
Sauce.	10.00	—	—
Sugar			
Cov, table	45.00	60.00	—
Individual, open	20.00	25.00	—
Syrup	75.00	—	50.00
Toothpick	25.00	40.00	40.00
Tumbler	20.00	35.00	40.00
Vase.	35.00	50.00	—
Wine.	25.00	50.00	—

NEW JERSEY (Loops and Drops)

Non-flint made by U. S. Glass Co., Pittsburgh, PA, c1900–08 in States pattern series. Items with perfect gold are worth more than those with worn gold. An emerald green 11″ vase is known (value $75.00).

	Clear w/ Gold	Ruby Stained
Bowl		
8″, flared.	25.00	50.00
9″, saucer.	32.50	65.00
10″, oval	30.00	75.00
Bread Plate	30.00	—
Butter, cov		
Flat	75.00	100.00
Footed	125.00	—
Cake Stand, 8″ . .	65.00	—
Carafe	60.00	—

	Clear w/ Gold	Ruby Stained
Celery Tray, rect .	25.00	40.00
Compote		
Cov, hs, 5″, jelly	45.00	55.00
Open, hs, 6¾″ .	35.00	65.00
Open, hs, 8″. . .	60.00	75.00
Creamer.	35.00	60.00
Cruet	50.00	—
Goblet	40.00	65.00
Molasses Can . . .	90.00	—

	Clear w/ Gold	Ruby Stained		Clear w/ Gold	Ruby Stained
Olive	15.00	—	Small	35.00	55.00
Pickle, rect	15.00	—	Sauce	10.00	30.00
Pitcher			Spooner	27.00	75.00
Milk, ah	75.00	165.00	Sugar, cov	60.00	80.00
Water			Sweetmeat, 8"	70.00	90.00
Applied Handle	80.00	210.00	Syrup	90.00	—
Pressed			Toothpick	50.00	200.00
Handle	50.00	185.00	Tumbler	30.00	50.00
Plate, 8" d	30.00	45.00	Water Bottle	55.00	90.00
Salt & Pepper, pr			Wine	45.00	60.00
Hotel	50.00	115.00			

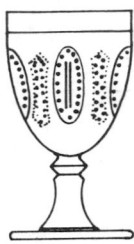

ONE HUNDRED ONE (Beaded 101)

Non-flint made by Bellaire Goblet Co., Findlay, OH, in the late 1880s.

	Clear		Clear
Bread Plate, 101 border, Farm implement center, 11"	75.00	Pickle	20.00
		Pitcher, water, ah	125.00
Butter, cov	40.00	Plate	
Cake Stand, 9"	65.00	6"	20.00
Celery Vase	50.00	8"	30.00
Compote		Relish	15.00
Cov, hs, 7"	60.00	Sauce	
Cov, ls	60.00	Flat	10.00
Creamer	45.00	Footed	15.00
* Goblet	50.00	Spooner	25.00
Lamp, hand, oil, 10"	80.00	Sugar, cov	45.00
		Wine	60.00

PALMETTE (Hearts and Spades, Spades)

Non-flint, unknown maker, late 1870s. Shards have been found at Burlington Glass Works, Hamilton, Ontario, Canada. Syrup known in milk glass.

	Clear		Clear
Bowl		Cake Stand, hs	100.00
8"	25.00	Castor Set, 5 bottles, sp	
9"	20.00	holder	125.00
Bread Plate, handled, 9"	30.00	Celery Vase	55.00
Butter Dish, cov	60.00	Champagne	75.00
Butter Pat	35.00	Compote	
Cake Plate, tab handles	35.00	Cov, hs, 8½"	75.00

	Clear			Clear
Cov, hs, 9¾"	85.00		Salt, master, ftd	22.00
Open, ls, 7"	30.00		Salt Shaker	55.00
Creamer, ah	65.00		Sauce, flat, 6"	10.00
Cup Plate	55.00		Shaker, saloon, oversize	80.00
Egg Cup	40.00		Spooner	35.00
Goblet	35.00		Sugar, cov	55.00
Lamp, 8½", all glass	95.00		Syrup, ah	125.00
Pickle, scoop shape	20.00		Tumbler	
Pitcher, bulbous, ah			Bar	75.00
Milk	135.00		Water, ftd	40.00
Water	125.00		Wine	110.00
Relish	18.00			

PANELED FORGET-ME-NOT (Regal)

Non-flint, made by Bryce Bros., Pittsburgh, PA, c1880. Reissued by U. S. Glass Co. c1891. Shards have been found at Burlington Glass Works, Hamilton, Ontario, Canada. Made in clear, blue, and amber with limited production in amethyst and green.

	Amber	Blue	Clear
Bread Plate	35.00	45.00	30.00
Butter, cov	50.00	60.00	45.00
Cake Stand, 10"	70.00	90.00	45.00
Celery Vase	45.00	70.00	36.00
Compote			
Cov, hs, 7"	90.00	110.00	65.00
Cov, hs, 8"	80.00	100.00	68.00
Open, hs, 8½"	60.00	75.00	50.00
Open, hs, 10"	60.00	80.00	40.00
Creamer	45.00	60.00	35.00
Cruet, os	—	—	45.00
Goblet	50.00	65.00	32.00
Marmalade Jar,			
cov	60.00	80.00	50.00
Pickle, boat			
shape	25.00	35.00	15.00
Pitcher			
Milk	90.00	110.00	50.00
Water	90.00	110.00	75.00
Relish, scoop			
shape	55.00	55.00	65.00
Salt & Pepper, pr.	—	—	65.00
Sauce, ftd	18.00	25.00	12.00
Spooner	40.00	50.00	25.00
Sugar, cov	60.00	75.00	40.00
Wine	55.00	65.00	60.00

PENNSYLVANIA (Balder)

Non-flint issued by U. S. Glass Co. in 1898. Also known in ruby stained. A ruffled jelly compote is documented in orange carnival.

	Clear w/ Gold	Emerald Green		Clear w/ Gold	Emerald Green
Biscuit Jar, cov ..	75.00	125.00	Goblet	24.00	—
Bowl			Juice Tumbler ...	10.00	20.00
4"	20.00	—	Molasses Can ...	75.00	—
8", berry	25.00	35.00	Pitcher, water....	60.00	—
8", sq	20.00	40.00	Punch Bowl	175.00	—
Butter, cov	60.00	85.00	Punch Cup......	10.00	—
Carafe	65.00	—	Salt Shaker	10.00	—
Celery Tray	30.00	—	Sauce.........	7.50	—
Celery Vase.....	45.00	—	*Spooner........	24.00	35.00
Champagne.....	25.00	—	Sugar, cov	40.00	55.00
Cheese Dish, cov	65.00	—	Syrup	50.00	—
Compote, hs,			Toothpick.......	35.00	90.00
jelly..........	50.00	—	Tumbler	28.00	40.00
Creamer........	25.00	50.00	Whiskey........	20.00	35.00
Cruet, os	45.00	—	Wine..........	10.00	35.00
Decanter, os	100.00	—			

PICKET (London, Picket Fence)

Non-flint made by the King, Son & Co., Pittsburgh, PA, c1890. Toothpick holders are known in apple green, vaseline, and purple slag.

	Clear		Clear
Bowl, 9½", sq	30.00	Salt	
Bread Plate	70.00	Individual	10.00
Butter, cov	65.00	Master	35.00
Celery Vase..........	40.00	Sauce	
Compote		Flat................	15.00
Cov, hs, 8"	85.00	Footed	20.00
Cov, ls, 8"...........	95.00	Spooner.............	30.00
Open, hs, 7", sq	35.00	Sugar, cov	50.00
Open, hs, 10", sq	70.00	Toothpick...........	35.00
Open, ls, 7"	50.00	Tray, water...........	65.00
Creamer.............	50.00	Waste Bowl	40.00
Goblet	50.00	Wine................	85.00
Pitcher, water.........	75.00		

QUEEN ANNE (Bearded Man)

Non-flint made by LaBelle Glass Co., Bridgeport, OH, c1879. Finials are Maltese cross. At least 28 pieces are documented. A table set and water pitcher are known in amber.

	Clear		Clear
Bowl, cov		Pitcher	
8", oval	45.00	Milk	75.00
9", oval	55.00	Water	85.00
Bread Plate	50.00	Salt Shaker	40.00
Butter, cov	65.00	Sauce	15.00
Celery Vase	35.00	Spooner	40.00
Compote, cov, ls, 9"	75.00	Sugar, cov	55.00
Creamer	45.00	Syrup	100.00
Egg Cup	45.00		

RED BLOCK (Late Block)

Non-flint with red stain made by Doyle and Co., Pittsburgh, PA. Later made by five companies, plus U. S. Glass Co. in 1892. Prices for clear 50% less.

	Ruby Stained		Ruby Stained
Banana Boat	75.00	Mustard, cov	55.00
Bowl, 8"	75.00	Pitcher, water, 8" h	150.00
Butter, cov	110.00	Relish Tray	25.00
Celery Vase, 6½"	85.00	Rose Bowl	75.00
Cheese Dish, cov	125.00	Salt Dip, individual	50.00
Creamer		Salt Shaker	75.00
Individual	45.00	Sauce, flat, 4½"	20.00
Table	70.00	Spooner	45.00
Decanter, 12", os,		Sugar, cov	90.00
variant	175.00	Tumbler	40.00
*Goblet	40.00	*Wine	35.00
Mug	50.00		

REVERSE TORPEDO (Bull's Eye Band, Bull's Eye with Diamond Point #2, Pointed Bull's Eye)

Non-flint made by Dalzell, Gilmore and Leighton Glass Co., Findlay, OH, c1888–90. Also attributed to Canadian factories. Sometimes found with copper wheel etching.

	Clear		Clear
Banana Stand, 9¾"	100.00	9", fruit, piecrust rim	70.00
Basket	175.00	10½", piecrust rim	75.00
Biscuit Jar, cov	135.00	Butter, cov, 7½" d	75.00
Bowl		Cake Stand, hs	85.00
8½", shallow	30.00	Celery Vase	55.00

	Clear		Clear
Compote		Honey Dish, sq, cov	145.00
Cov, hs, 7"	80.00	Jam Jar, cov	85.00
Cov, hs, 10"	125.00	Pitcher, tankard, 10¼" . .	160.00
Open, hs, 10½" d, V		Sauce, flat, 3¾"	10.00
shape bowl	90.00	Spooner	30.00
Open, hs, 7"	65.00	Sugar, cov	85.00
Open, ls, 9¼", ruffled .	85.00	Syrup	165.00
Doughnut Tray	90.00	Tumbler	30.00
Goblet	85.00		

ROMAN ROSETTE

Non-flint made by Bryce, Walker and Co., Pittsburgh, PA, c1890. Reissued by U. S. Glass Co. in 1892 and 1898. Attributed to Portland Glass Co. Also seen with English registry mark and known in amber stained.

	Clear	Ruby Stained		Clear	Ruby Stained
Bowl, 8½"	15.00	50.00	Pitcher		
Bread Plate	30.00	75.00	Milk	50.00	150.00
Butter, cov	50.00	125.00	Water	65.00	140.00
Cake Stand, 9" . .	45.00	—	Plate, 7½"	35.00	65.00
Celery Vase	30.00	95.00	Relish, oval, 9" . .	20.00	40.00
Compote			Salt & Pepper,		
Cov, hs, 4½",			glass tray	40.00	100.00
jelly	50.00	—	Sauce	15.00	20.00
Cov, hs, 6"	65.00	—	Spooner	25.00	45.00
Cordial	50.00	—	Sugar, cov	40.00	80.00
Creamer	32.00	45.00	Syrup	85.00	125.00
*Goblet	40.00	—	Wine	45.00	65.00
Mug	35.00	—			

ROSE-IN-SNOW (Rose)

Non-flint made by Bryce Bros., Pittsburgh, PA, in the square form c1880. Also made in the more common round form by Ohio Flint Glass Co. and after 1891 by U. S. Glass Co. Both styles reissued by Indiana Glass Co., Dunkirk, IN. Reproductions made by several companies, including Imperial Glass Co., as early as 1930 and continuing through the 1970s.

	Amber and Canary	Blue	Clear
Bowl, 8" sq.	40.00	50.00	30.00
Butter, cov			
Round	65.00	125.00	45.00

	Amber and Canary	Blue	Clear
Square	70.00	150.00	50.00
Cake Stand, 9" . .	125.00	175.00	90.00
Compote			
Cov, hs, 8"	125.00	175.00	80.00
Cov, ls, 7"	100.00	150.00	75.00
Open, ls, 5¾". .	65.00	120.00	35.00
Creamer			
Round.	60.00	100.00	45.00
Square	65.00	120.00	45.00
* Goblet	40.00	55.00	35.00
Marmalade Jar,			
cov	70.00	125.00	60.00
* Mug, "In Fond			
Remembrance"	65.00	125.00	35.00
* Pickle Dish			
Double, 8½" x 7"	85.00	110.00	100.00
Single, oval,			
handles at			
end	35.00	95.00	20.00
Pitcher, water, ah	175.00	200.00	125.00
Plate			
5"	40.00	40.00	35.00
6"	30.00	80.00	20.00
7"	30.00	80.00	20.00
* 9"	30.00	85.00	20.00
Platter, oval	—	—	125.00
Sauce			
Flat	15.00	20.00	12.00
Footed	8.00	45.00	18.00
Spooner			
Round.	30.00	80.00	25.00
Square	40.00	100.00	35.00
Sugar, cov			
Round.	55.00	120.00	50.00
* Square	50.00	140.00	45.00
Sweetmeat, cov,			
5¾" d	80.00	155.00	65.00
Toddy Jar, cov,			
underplate	150.00	155.00	125.00
Tumbler	60.00	100.00	50.00

SKILTON (Early Oregon)

Made by Richards and Hartley of Tarentum, PA, in 1888 and by U. S. Glass Co. after 1891. This is not one of the U. S. Glass States pattern series and should not be confused with Beaded Loop, which is Oregon #1, named by U. S. Glass Co. It is better known as Skilton (named by Millard) to avoid confusion with Beaded Loop.

	Clear	Ruby Stained		Clear	Ruby Stained
Bowl			Olive, handled . . .	20.00	—
5", round.	15.00	—	Pickle	15.00	—
7", rect	20.00	—	Pitcher		
9", rect	30.00	—	Milk	45.00	125.00
Butter, cov	45.00	110.00	Water	50.00	125.00
Cake Stand	35.00	—	Salt & Pepper, pr.	45.00	—
Celery Vase	35.00	95.00	Sauce, ftd	12.00	20.00
Compote			Spooner, flat	25.00	55.00
Cov, hs, 8"	45.00	—	Sugar, cov	35.00	85.00
Open, ls, 8"	30.00	75.00	Tray, water	45.00	—
Creamer	30.00	55.00	Tumbler	25.00	40.00
Dish, oblong, sq .	25.00	—	Wine	35.00	50.00
Goblet	35.00	50.00			

SPIREA BAND (Earl, Nailhead Variant, Spirea, Squared Dot)

Non-flint made by Bryce, Higbee and Co., Pittsburgh, PA, c1885.

	Amber	Blue	Clear	Vaseline
Bowl, 8"	25.00	40.00	20.00	30.00
Butter, cov	50.00	55.00	35.00	45.00
Cake Stand, 11" .	45.00	55.00	40.00	45.00
Celery Vase	40.00	50.00	25.00	40.00
Compote, cov, hs,				
7"	44.00	65.00	40.00	44.00
Cordial	38.00	42.00	20.00	38.00
Creamer	32.50	44.00	35.00	35.00
Goblet	30.00	35.00	25.00	35.00
Pitcher, water	65.00	80.00	35.00	60.00
Platter, 10½"	32.00	42.00	20.00	32.00
Relish	30.00	35.00	18.00	30.00
Sauce				
Flat	10.00	12.00	5.00	10.00
Ftd	15.00	15.00	8.00	15.00
Spooner	30.00	35.00	20.00	35.00
Sugar, open	32.00	40.00	25.00	32.00
Tumbler	24.00	35.00	20.00	30.00
Wine	30.00	35.00	20.00	30.00

STATES, THE (Cane and Star Medallion)

Non-flint made by U. S. Glass Co. Pittsburgh, PA, in 1905. Also found in emerald green (add 50%). Prices given for clear with good gold trim.

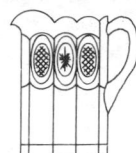

	Clear		Clear
Bowl		Punch Bowl, 13" d	75.00
7", round, 3 handles ..	25.00	Punch Cup............	10.00
9¼", round	30.00	Relish, diamond shape..	35.00
Butter, cov	65.00	Salt & Pepper	40.00
Celery Tray	20.00	Sauce, flat, 4", tub	
Celery Vase	20.00	shape	15.00
Cocktail	25.00	Spooner..............	25.00
Compote		Sugar	
Open, hs, 7".........	30.00	Individual, open......	15.00
Open, hs, 9".........	40.00	Regular, cov.........	40.00
Creamer		Syrup	65.00
Individual, oval.......	20.00	Toothpick, flat, rectangu-	
Regular, round.......	30.00	lar, curled lip	45.00
Goblet	35.00	Tray, 7¼" l, 5½" w......	20.00
Pickle Tray...........	15.00	Tumbler	25.00
Pitcher, water..........	45.00	Wine................	30.00
Plate, 10"............	25.00		

TENNESSEE (Jewel and Crescent, Jeweled Rosette)

Non-flint made by King, Son & Co., Pittsburgh, PA, and continued by U. S. Glass Co. in 1899 as part of the States series.

	Clear	Colored Jewels		Clear	Colored Jewels
Bowl			Open, hs, 8"...	40.00	—
Cov, 6"	35.00	—	Open, hs, 9"...	50.00	—
Cov, 7"	40.00	—	Open, hs, 10"..	65.00	—
Cov, 8"	50.00	—	Open, ls, 7" ...	35.00	—
Open, 8"......	35.00	40.00	Creamer........	30.00	—
Bread Plate	40.00	75.00	Cruet	65.00	—
Butter, cov	60.00	—	Goblet	40.00	—
Cake Stand			Mug	40.00	—
8"	35.00	—	Pitcher		
9½"..........	38.00	—	Milk..........	55.00	—
10½".........	45.00	—	Water	65.00	—
Celery Vase.....	35.00	—	Relish..........	20.00	—
Compote			Salt Shaker	30.00	—
Cov, hs, 5"....	40.00	55.00	Spooner........	35.00	—
Cov, hs, 6"....	45.00	—	Sugar, cov	45.00	—
Cov, hs, 7"....	50.00	—	Syrup	90.00	—
Cov, hs, 8"....	60.00	—	Toothpick.......	75.00	85.00
Open, hs, 5"....	25.00	—	Tumbler	35.00	—
Open, hs, 6"...	30.00	—	Wine...........	65.00	85.00
Open, hs, 7"...	35.00	—			

TEXAS (Loop with Stippled Panels)

Non-flint made by U. S. Glass Co., Pittsburgh, PA, c1900, in the States pattern series. Occasionally pieces are found in ruby stained. Reproduced in solid colors by Crystal Art Glass Co. and Boyd Glass Co., Cambridge, OH.

	Clear w/ Gold	Rose Stained		Clear w/ Gold	Rose Stained
Bowl			Pickle, 8½"......	25.00	50.00
7"	20.00	40.00	Pitcher, water....	145.00	400.00
9", scalloped ..	35.00	50.00	Plate, 9"........	35.00	60.00
Butter, cov	90.00	135.00	Salt Shaker	25.00	—
Cake Stand, 9½".	75.00	125.00	Sauce		
Celery Tray	30.00	50.00	Flat..........	10.00	20.00
Celery Vase.....	40.00	85.00	Footed	20.00	25.00
Compote			Spooner........	35.00	80.00
Cov, hs, 6"	80.00	200.00	Sugar		
Cov, hs, 7"	85.00	225.00	*Individual, cov .	45.00	—
Cov, hs, 8"	90.00	235.00	Table, cov	75.00	125.00
Open, hs, 5"...	65.00	100.00	Syrup	75.00	175.00
Creamer			Toothpick.......	25.00	95.00
*Individual	20.00	45.00	Tumbler	40.00	100.00
Table	45.00	85.00	Vase		
Cruet, os	60.00	165.00	6½"...........	25.00	—
Goblet	95.00	110.00	9"...........	35.00	—
Horseradish, cov .	50.00	—	*Wine...........	75.00	140.00

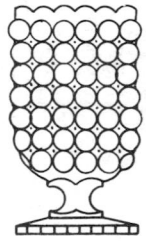

THOUSAND EYE

The original pattern was non-flint made by Adams & Co., Tarentum, PA, in 1875 and by Richards and Hartley in 1888 (pattern No. 103). It was made in two forms: Adams with a three-knob stem finial, and Richards and Hartley with a plain stem with a scalloped bottom. Several glass companies made variations of the original pattern and reproductions were made as late as 1981. Crystal Opalescent was produced by Richards and Hartley only in the original pattern. (Opalescent celery vase $70.00; open compote, 8", $115.00; 6" creamer, $85.00; ¼-gallon water pitcher, $140.00; ½-gallon water pitcher, $180.00; 4" footed sauce, $40.00; spooner, $60.00; and 5" covered sugar, $80.00.) Covered compotes are rare and would command 40% more than open compotes. A 2" mug in blue is known.

	Amber	Apple Green	Blue	Clear	Vaseline
ABC Plate, 6", clock center ...	55.00	60.00	55.00	45.00	55.00
Bowl, large, carriage shape ...	85.00	—	85.00	—	85.00
Butter, cov 6¼"..........	65.00	75.00	70.00	45.00	90.00

	Amber	Apple Green	Blue	Clear	Vaseline
7½″	65.00	75.00	70.00	45.00	90.00
Cake Stand					
10″	50.00	80.00	55.00	30.00	85.00
11″	50.00	80.00	55.00	30.00	85.00
Celery, hat shape	50.00	65.00	60.00	35.00	55.00
Celery Vase, 7″ . .	50.00	60.00	52.00	45.00	55.00
Christmas Light . .	30.00	45.00	35.00	25.00	40.00
Cologne Bottle. . .	25.00	45.00	35.00	20.00	45.00
Compote, cov, ls,					
8″, sq	—	100.00	100.00	—	—
Compote, open					
6″	35.00	40.00	40.00	25.00	40.00
7″	45.00	50.00	45.00	35.00	45.00
8″, round.	40.00	50.00	45.00	35.00	50.00
8″, sq, hs	40.00	50.00	50.00	40.00	55.00
9″	50.00	60.00	55.00	40.00	55.00
10″	55.00	65.00	60.00	45.00	60.00
Cordial	35.00	55.00	40.00	25.00	60.00
Creamer					
4″	35.00	40.00	40.00	25.00	40.00
6″	40.00	75.00	55.00	35.00	75.00
Creamer and					
Sugar Set.	—	150.00	—	100.00	—
*Cruet, 6″.	40.00	60.00	50.00	35.00	60.00
Egg Cup.	65.00	85.00	70.00	45.00	90.00
*Goblet	40.00	45.00	40.00	35.00	45.00
Honey Dish, cov,					
6 × 7¼″.	85.00	95.00	90.00	70.00	95.00
Inkwell, 2″ sq	45.00	—	75.00	35.00	80.00
Jelly Glass	25.00	30.00	25.00	15.00	25.00
Lamp, kerosene					
hs, 12″	120.00	150.00	130.00	100.00	140.00
hs, 15″	125.00	155.00	135.00	110.00	150.00
ls, handled	110.00	115.00	110.00	90.00	120.00
Mug					
2½″.	25.00	30.00	25.00	20.00	35.00
3½″.	25.00	30.00	25.00	20.00	35.00
Nappy					
5″	35.00	—	40.00	30.00	45.00
6″	40.00	—	45.00	35.00	55.00
8″	45.00	—	50.00	45.00	60.00
Pickle	25.00	30.00	30.00	20.00	30.00
Pitcher					
Milk, cov, 7″ . . .	85.00	110.00	115.00	70.00	105.00
Water, ¼ gal . .	70.00	85.00	80.00	55.00	80.00
Water, ½ gal . .	80.00	95.00	85.00	65.00	85.00
Water, 1 gal . . .	90.00	100.00	95.00	85.00	95.00
*Plate, sq, folded corners					
6″	25.00	30.00	30.00	25.00	30.00
8″	30.00	30.00	30.00	25.00	30.00

	Amber	Apple Green	Blue	Clear	Vaseline
10″	35.00	50.00	40.00	25.00	35.00
Platter					
8 × 11″, oblong	40.00	50.00	45.00	40.00	45.00
11″, oval	75.00	80.00	55.00	40.00	75.00
Salt Shaker, pr					
Banded	60.00	70.00	65.00	60.00	65.00
Plain	50.00	60.00	55.00	40.00	60.00
Salt, ind	80.00	95.00	90.00	50.00	90.00
Salt, open, carriage shape . . .	65.00	85.00	75.00	50.00	75.00
Sauce					
Flat, 4″	10.00	20.00	15.00	8.00	15.00
Footed, 4″	15.00	25.00	15.00	10.00	20.00
Spooner	35.00	50.00	40.00	30.00	45.00
*String Holder	35.00	60.00	45.00	30.00	45.00
Sugar, cov, 5″ . . .	55.00	75.00	60.00	50.00	60.00
Syrup, pewter top	80.00	100.00	70.00	55.00	70.00
Toothpick					
Hat	40.00	60.00	70.00	35.00	50.00
Plain	35.00	50.00	55.00	25.00	40.00
Thimble	55.00	—	—	—	—
Tray, water					
12½″, round . .	65.00	80.00	75.00	55.00	75.00
14″, oval	65.00	80.00	75.00	60.00	75.00
*Tumbler	30.00	65.00	35.00	25.00	30.00
*Wine	35.00	50.00	40.00	20.00	40.00

THREE-FACE

Non-flint made by George A. Duncan & Son, Pittsburgh, PA, c1878. Designed by John E. Miller, a designer with Duncan, who later became a member of the firm. It has been heavily reproduced by L. G. Wright Glass Co. and other companies as early as the 1930s. Imperial Glass Co. was commissioned by the Metropolitan Museum of Art, New York, to reproduce a series of Three-Face items, each marked with the "M.M.A." monogram.

	Clear		Clear
Biscuit Jar, cov	300.00	*Champagne	
*Butter, cov	165.00	Hollow stem	250.00
*Cake Stand		Saucer type	150.00
9″	175.00	*Claret	110.00
12½″	225.00	*Compote	
Celery Vase		Cov, hs, 8″	175.00
Plain	110.00	Cov, hs, 9″	190.00
Scalloped	110.00	Cov, hs, 10″	225.00

	Clear		Clear
Cov, ls, 6"..........	160.00	Pitcher, water.........	425.00
Open, hs, 9"........	135.00	* Salt Dip	35.00
Open, ls, 6"........	75.00	* Salt & Pepper	75.00
* Creamer.............	135.00	* Sauce, ftd	25.00
* Goblet	85.00	* Spooner.............	80.00
* Lamp, oil	150.00	* Sugar, cov	125.00
Marmalade Jar	275.00	* Wine................	150.00

TORPEDO (Pigmy)

Non-flint made by Thompson Glass Co., Uniontown, PA, c1889. A black amethyst master salt ($150.00) is also known.

	Clear	Ruby Stained		Clear	Ruby Stained
Banana Stand ...	75.00	—	Pickle Castor, sp		
Bowl			holder........	125.00	—
Cov, 7" d, 7¼" h	65.00	—	Pitcher		
Open, 7"......	18.00	—	Milk, 8½"	75.00	150.00
Open, 9"......	20.00	45.00	Water, 10½"...	85.00	175.00
Butter, cov	85.00	—	Punch Cup......	25.00	—
Cake Stand, 10" .	85.00	—	Salt		
Celery Vase, scal-			Individual	20.00	—
loped top	40.00		Master	35.00	—
Compote			Salt Shaker, sin-		
Cov, hs, 4",			gle, 2 types ...	50.00	—
jelly	65.00	—	Sauce, 4½", col-		
Cov, hs, 13¾" .	165.00	—	lared base	15.00	—
Creamer........	50.00	—	Spooner, scal-		
Cruet, os, ah	80.00	—	loped top	45.00	—
Cup and Saucer .	60.00	—	Sugar, cov	65.00	—
Decanter, os, 8"..	85.00	—	Syrup	95.00	175.00
Finger Bowl	55.00	—	Tray, water		
Goblet	45.00	85.00	10", round	85.00	—
Lamp			11¾", clover		
3", handled....	75.00	—	shaped	75.00	—
8", plain base,			Tumbler	45.00	60.00
pattern on			Wine...........	90.00	—
bowl	85.00	—			
Marmalade Jar,					
cov	85.00	—			

TRUNCATED CUBE (Thompson's #77)

Non-flint made by Thompson Glass Co., Uniontown, PA, c1894. Also found with copper wheel engraving.

	Clear	Ruby Stained		Clear	Ruby Stained
Bowl, 8″	—	40.00	Salt Shaker, single...........	15.00	30.00
Butter, cov	50.00	90.00	Sauce, 4″.......	30.00	50.00
Celery Vase.....	40.00	55.00	Spooner........	30.00	50.00
Creamer			Sugar, cov		
Individual	20.00	30.00	Individual	20.00	35.00
Regular........	35.00	65.00	Regular.......	30.00	65.00
Cruet, os, ph	35.00	90.00	Syrup	40.00	100.00
Decanter, os, 12″ h	60.00	150.00	Toothpick.......	30.00	45.00
Goblet	30.00	50.00	Tray, water......	20.00	40.00
Pitcher, ah			Tumbler	22.50	35.00
Milk, 1 qt	50.00	100.00	Wine...........	25.00	40.00
Water, ½ gal ..	60.00	115.00			

U. S. COIN

Non-flint frosted, clear, and gilted pattern made by U. S. Glass Co., Pittsburgh, PA, in 1892 for three or four months. Production was stopped by the U. S. Treasury because real coins, dated as early as 1878, were used in the molds. The 1892 coin date is the most common. Lamps with coins on font and stem would be 50% more.

	Clear	Frosted		Clear	Frosted
Ale Glass	250.00	350.00	* Creamer........	350.00	600.00
* Bowl			Cruet, os	375.00	500.00
6″	170.00	220.00	Epergne........	—	1,000.00
9″	215.00	325.00	Goblet	300.00	450.00
* Bread Plate	175.00	325.00	Goblet, dimes ...	—	550.00
Butter, cov, dollars and halves	250.00	450.00	Lamp		
Cake Stand, 10″.	225.00	400.00	Round font....	275.00	450.00
Celery Tray	200.00	—	Square font ...	300.00	—
Celery Vase, quarters	150.00	365.00	Mug, handled....	200.00	300.00
Champagne.....	—	400.00	Pickle	200.00	—
* Compote			Pitcher		
Cov, hs, 7″	300.00	500.00	Milk..........	600.00	600.00
Cov, hs, 8″, quarters and dimes	—	415.00	Water	400.00	800.00
			Sauce, ftd, 4″, quarters	100.00	185.00
Open, hs, 7″, quarters and dimes	200.00	300.00	* Spooner, quarters	225.00	325.00
Open, hs, 7″, quarters and halves......	225.00	350.00	* Sugar, cov	225.00	400.00
			Syrup, dated pewter lid	—	525.00
Open, 8⅜″ d, 6½″ h	—	240.00	* Toothpick.......	180.00	275.00
			Tray, water, 8″, round	275.00	—
			* Tumbler	140.00	250.00
			Waste Bowl	225.00	250.00
			Wine...........	225.00	375.00

U. S. SHERATON (Greek Key)

Made by U. S. Glass Co., Pittsburgh, PA, in 1912. This pattern was made only in clear, but can be found trimmed with gold or platinum. Some pieces are marked with the intertwined U. S. Glass trademark.

	Clear		Clear
Bowl		Squat, medium	**30.00**
6", ftd, sq	**15.00**	Tankard	**35.00**
8", flat.	**12.00**	Plate, sq	
Bureau Tray.	**30.00**	4½".	**8.00**
Butter, cov	**35.00**	9"	**12.00**
Celery Tray	**30.00**	Pomade Jar.	**14.00**
Compote		Puff Box.	**14.00**
Open, 4", jelly	**12.00**	Punch Bowl, cov, 14" . . .	**90.00**
Open, 6".	**14.00**	Ring Tree.	**25.00**
Creamer		Salt Shaker	
After dinner, tall, sq ft .	**12.00**	Squat	**12.00**
Berry, bulbous, sq ft . .	**15.00**	Tall	**15.00**
Large	**18.00**	Salt, individual	**17.00**
Cruet, os	**25.00**	Sardine Box.	**35.00**
Finger Bowl, underplate .	**24.00**	Spooner	
Goblet	**18.00**	Handled	**15.00**
Iced Tea.	**20.00**	Tray	**12.00**
Lamp, miniature	**50.00**	Sugar, cov	
Marmalade Jar	**35.00**	Individual	**15.00**
Mug	**15.00**	Regular.	**20.00**
Mustard Jar, cov	**30.00**	Sundae Dish	**10.00**
Pickle	**10.00**	Syrup, glass lid	**35.00**
Pin Tray	**12.00**	Toothpick	**35.00**
Pitcher, water		Tumbler	**15.00**
½ gallon	**30.00**		

VERMONT (Honeycomb with Flower Rim, Inverted Thumbprint with Daisy Band)

Non-flint made by U. S. Glass Co., Pittsburgh, PA, 1899–1903. Also made in custard (usually decorated), chocolate, caramel, novelty slag, milk glass, and blue. Toothpick holders have been reproduced by Crystal Art Glass Co., Mosser Glass Co., and Degenhart Glass (which marks its colored line).

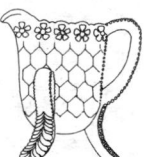

	Clear w/ Gold	Green w/ Gold		Clear w/ Gold	Green w/ Gold
Basket, handle .	**30.00**	**45.00**	Compote, hs		
Bowl, berry	**25.00**	**45.00**	Cov	**55.00**	**125.00**
Butter, cov.	**40.00**	**75.00**	Open	**35.00**	**65.00**
Card Tray	**20.00**	**35.00**	Creamer, 4¼" . .	**30.00**	**55.00**
Celery Tray. . . .	**30.00**	**35.00**	Goblet	**40.00**	**50.00**

	Clear w/ Gold	Green w/ Gold		Clear w/ Gold	Green w/ Gold
Pickle	20.00	30.00	Sugar, cov.....	35.00	80.00
Pitcher, water ..	50.00	125.00	*Toothpick	30.00	50.00
Salt Shaker....	20.00	35.00	Tumbler.......	20.00	40.00
Sauce	15.00	20.00	Vase	20.00	45.00
Spooner	25.00	75.00			

VIKING (Bearded Head, Bearded Prophet, Hobb's Centennial, Old Man of the Mountain)

Non-flint made by Hobbs, Brockunier, & Co., Wheeling, WV, in 1876 as its Centennial pattern. No tumbler or goblet originally made.

	Clear		Clear
Apothecary Jar, cov	60.00	Cup, ftd	35.00
Bowl		Egg Cup..............	40.00
Cov, 8″, oval.........	55.00	Marmalade Jar	85.00
Cov, 9″, oval.........	65.00	Mug, ah	50.00
Bread Plate	70.00	Pickle	20.00
Butter, cov	75.00	Pitcher, water.........	125.00
Celery Vase...........	45.00	Relish...............	20.00
Compote		Salt, master..........	40.00
Cov, hs, 9″	95.00	Sauce...............	15.00
Cov, ls, 8″, oval	75.00	Spooner	35.00
Open, hs	60.00	Sugar, cov	65.00
Creamer, 2 types.......	50.00		

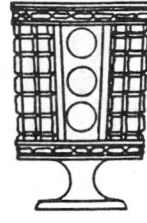

WAFFLE AND THUMBPRINT (Bull's Eye and Waffle, Palace, Triple Bull's Eye)

First made by the New England Glass Co., East Cambridge, MA, c1868 and by Curling, Robertson & Co., Pittsburgh, PA, c1856. Shards have been found at the Boston and Sandwich Glass Co., Sandwich, MA.

	Clear		Clear
Bottle, ftd	135.00	Decanter, os	
Bowl, 5 x 7″...........	30.00	Pint................	100.00
Butter, cov	95.00	Quart	145.00
Celery Vase...........	105.00	Egg Cup.............	45.00
Champagne...........	90.00	Goblet, knob stem......	65.00
Claret...............	110.00	Lamp	
Compote, cov, hs	150.00	9½″................	115.00
Cordial	100.00	11″, whale oil	175.00
Creamer.............	125.00	Pitcher, water.........	400.00

	Clear		Clear
Salt, master	45.00	Water, ftd	75.00
Spooner	45.00	Whiskey	75.00
Sugar, cov	125.00	Wine	70.00
Sweetmeat, cov, hs, 6" . .	150.00		
Tumbler			
Flip Glass	125.00		

WESTWARD HO! (Pioneer, Tippecanoe)

Non-flint, usually frosted, made by Gillinder and Sons, Philadelphia, PA, c1879. Molds made by Jacobus who also made Classic. Has been reproduced since the 1930s by L. G. Wright Glass Co., Westmoreland Glass Co., and several others. This pattern was originally made in milk glass (rare) and clear with acid finish as part of the design. Reproductions can be found in several colors and in clear.

	Clear		Clear
Bowl, 5", ftd	125.00	*Goblet	90.00
Bread Plate	175.00	Marmalade Jar, cov	200.00
*Butter, cov	185.00	Mug	
*Celery Vase	125.00	2"	225.00
*Compote		3½"	175.00
Cov, hs, 5"	225.00	*Pitcher, water.	250.00
Cov, hs, 9"	275.00	*Sauce, ftd, 4½"	35.00
Cov, ls, 5"	150.00	*Spooner	90.00
Open, hs, 8"	145.00	*Sugar, cov	185.00
*Creamer	95.00	*Wine	200.00

WHEAT AND BARLEY (Duquesne, Hops and Barley, Oats and Barley)

Non-flint made by Bryce Bros., Pittsburgh, PA, c1880. Later made by U. S. Glass Co., Pittsburgh PA, after 1891.

	Amber	Blue	Clear	Vaseline
Bowl, 8", cov	35.00	40.00	25.00	35.00
Butter, cov	45.00	60.00	35.00	55.00
Cake Stand				
8"	30.00	45.00	20.00	30.00
10"	40.00	50.00	30.00	40.00
Compote				
Cov, hs, 7"	45.00	55.00	40.00	45.00
Cov, hs, 8"	50.00	55.00	45.00	50.00
Open, hs, jelly .	32.50	40.00	30.00	35.00
*Creamer	30.00	40.00	28.00	35.00
*Goblet	40.00	55.00	25.00	40.00

	Amber	Blue	Clear	Vaseline
Mug	30.00	40.00	20.00	35.00
Pitcher				
Milk	70.00	85.00	40.00	95.00
Water	85.00	95.00	45.00	100.00
Plate				
7"	20.00	30.00	15.00	25.00
9", closed handles	25.00	35.00	20.00	40.00
Relish	20.00	30.00	15.00	25.00
Salt Shaker	25.00	30.00	20.00	25.00
Sauce				
Flat, handle . . .	15.00	15.00	10.00	15.00
Footed	15.00	15.00	10.00	15.00
Spooner	30.00	40.00	24.00	30.00
Sugar, cov	40.00	50.00	35.00	40.00
Syrup	175.00	195.00	85.00	—
Tumbler	35.00	40.00	20.00	35.00

WILLOW OAK (Acorn, Acorn and Oak Leaf, Bryce's Wreath, Stippled Daisy, Thistle and Sunflower)

Non-flint made by Bryce Bros. Pittsburgh, PA, c1885 and by U. S. Glass Company in 1891.

	Amber	Blue	Canary	Clear
Bowl, 8"	45.00	40.00	50.00	20.00
Butter, cov	65.00	65.00	80.00	40.00
Cake Stand, 8½".	55.00	65.00	70.00	45.00
Celery Vase	45.00	60.00	75.00	35.00
Compote				
Cov, hs, 7½" . .	50.00	65.00	80.00	40.00
Open, 7"	30.00	40.00	48.00	25.00
Creamer	45.00	50.00	60.00	40.00
Goblet	40.00	50.00	60.00	30.00
Mug	35.00	45.00	54.00	30.00
Pitcher				
Milk	50.00	60.00	70.00	45.00
Water	55.00	60.00	75.00	50.00
Plate				
7"	35.00	45.00	50.00	25.00
9"	35.00	35.00	40.00	25.00
Salt Shaker	25.00	40.00	55.00	20.00
Sauce				
Flat, handle, sq	15.00	20.00	24.00	10.00
Footed, 4"	20.00	25.00	30.00	15.00
Spooner	35.00	40.00	48.00	30.00
Sugar, cov	68.50	70.00	75.00	40.00
Tray, water, 10½"	35.00	50.00	60.00	30.00

	Amber	Blue	Canary	Clear
Tumbler	35.00	40.00	45.00	30.00
Waste Bowl	35.00	40.00	40.00	30.00

WISCONSIN (Beaded Dewdrop)

Non-flint made by U. S. Glass Co. in Gas City, IN, in 1903. One of the States patterns. Toothpick reproduced in colors.

	Clear		Clear
Banana Stand	75.00	Creamer.	50.00
Bowl		Cruet, os	80.00
4½ x 6½"	20.00	Cup and Saucer	50.00
6", oval, handled, cov .	40.00	*Goblet	65.00
7", round.	42.00	Marmalade Jar, straight	
8", oblong, preserve . .	42.00	sides, glass lid.	125.00
Butter, flat flange.	75.00	Mug	35.00
*Cake Stand		Pitcher	
8½"	45.00	Milk.	55.00
9½"	55.00	Water	70.00
Celery Tray	40.00	Plate, 6¾"	25.00
Celery Vase.	45.00	Punch Cup.	12.00
Compote		Relish.	25.00
Cov, hs, 5"	45.00	Salt Shaker	30.00
Cov, hs, 6"	50.00	Sauce, flat	10.00
Cov, hs, 7"	60.00	Spooner.	30.00
Cov, hs, 8"	75.00	Sugar, cov	55.00
Open, hs, 5".	30.00	Sugar Shaker	90.00
Open, hs, 6".	35.00	Sweetmeat, 5", ftd, cov. .	40.00
Open, hs, 7".	40.00	Syrup	110.00
Open, hs, 8".	50.00	*Toothpick, kettle.	55.00
Open, hs, 9".	60.00	Tumbler	40.00
Open, hs, 10".	75.00	Wine.	75.00
Condiment Set, salt &			
pepper, mustard,			
horseradish, tray	110.00		

X-RAY

Non-flint made by Riverside Glass Works, Wellsburgh, WV, 1896–98. Prices are for pieces with gold trim. A toothpick holder is known in amethyst ($125.00). Also a toothpick holder with marigold iridescence is known ($35.00).

	Clear	Emerald Green		Clear	Emerald Green
Bowl, berry, 8", beaded rim. . . .	25.00	45.00	Bread Plate	30.00	50.00
			Butter, cov	40.00	75.00

	Clear	Emerald Green		Clear	Emerald Green
Celery Vase.....	—	50.00	Salt Shaker	10.00	15.00
Compote			Sauce, flat, 4½″		
Cov, hs.......	40.00	65.00	d............	8.00	10.00
Jelly	—	40.00	Spooner........	25.00	40.00
Creamer			Sugar		
Individual	20.00	50.00	Individual,		
Regular.......	35.00	65.00	open	20.00	45.00
Cruet Set, 4-leaf			Regular, cov...	35.00	65.00
clover tray	125.00	350.00	Syrup..........	—	265.00
Goblet	20.00	35.00	Toothpick.......	25.00	50.00
Pitcher, water....	40.00	75.00	Tumbler	15.00	25.00

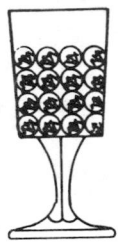

YALE (Crow-foot, Turkey Track)

Non-flint made by McKee & Bros. Glass Co., Jeannette, PA, patented in 1887.

	Clear		Clear
Bowl, berry, 10½″	20.00	Pitcher, water..........	65.00
Butter, cov	45.00	Relish, oval	10.00
Cake Stand	55.00	Salt Shaker	30.00
Celery Vase...........	40.00	Sauce, flat	10.00
Compote		Spooner..............	45.00
Cov, hs..............	50.00	Sugar, cov	35.00
Open, scalloped rim ..	25.00	Syrup	65.00
Creamer..............	60.00	Tumbler	25.00
Goblet	45.00		

ZIPPER (Cobb)

Non-flint made by Richards & Hartley, Tarentum, PA, c1888.

	Clear		Clear
Bowl, 7″ d	15.00	Pitcher water, ½ gal	40.00
Butter, cov	45.00	Relish, 10″ l...........	15.00
Celery Vase...........	25.00	Salt Dip	5.00
Cheese, cov	55.00	Sauce	
Compote, cov, ls, 8″ d...	40.00	Flat	7.50
Creamer..............	35.00	Footed	12.00
Cruet, os	45.00	Spooner..............	30.00
Goblet	20.00	Sugar, cov	45.00
Marmalade Jar, cov	45.00	Tumbler	20.00

S.E.G.

PAUL REVERE POTTERY

History: Paul Revere Pottery, Boston, Mass., was an outgrowth of a club known as "The Saturday Evening Girls." The S.E.G. was a group of young female immigrants who met on Saturday nights for reading and to work on crafts such as ceramics.

Regular production began in 1908. The name Paul Revere was adopted because the pottery was located near the Old North Church. In 1915 the firm moved to Brighton, Massachusetts. Known as the "Bowl Shop," the pottery grew steadily. In spite of popular acceptance and technical advancements, the pottery required continual subsidies. It finally closed in January 1942.

Items produced range from plain and decorated vases to tablewares to illustrated tiles. Many decorated wares were incised and glazed either in an Art Nouveau matte finish or an occasional high glaze.

In addition to the impressed mark, paper "Bowl Shop" labels were used prior to 1915. Pieces also can be found dated with "P.R.P." or "S.E.G." painted on the base.

References: Susan and Al Bagdade, *Warman's American Pottery and Porcelain,* Wallace–Homestead, 1994; Paul Evans, *Art Pottery of the United States, Second Edition,* Feingold & Lewis Publishing, 1987; Ralph and Terry Kovel, *Kovels' American Art Pottery: The Collector's Guide To Makers, Marks and Factory Histories,* Crown Publishers, 1993.

Collectors' Club: American Art Pottery Association, 125 E. Rose Ave., St. Louis, MO 63119.

Creamer, 2⅞" h, sgraffito, white wild rose border, blue and gray

ground, black matte outlines, white int., sgd "FR/255–6–09/SEG" **365.00**
Cup and Saucer, light blue band, narrow black band, medium blue ground **50.00**
Jar, cov, 5" d, 4½" h, white ground, purple moths border, blue and green stylized band, sgd by Sara Galner and Ida Goldstein, 1911 **1,540.00**
Jardiniere, 5½" d, 4¼" h, flared, yellow, repeating yellow, green, and blue tulip border, matte black outlines, sgd on back "11–26 PRP," X in circle artist's mark **375.00**
Pitcher, 7½" h, matte yellow glaze **375.00**
Planter, 9" d, 2⅝" h, shallow, yellow ground, brown and tan tree clusters on stylized border, white and yellow landscape, black matte outlines, marked "SEG/FL/1–23" **1,870.00**

Child's Bowl, blue tones, yellow and green center design and name "Johan," 5½" d, 2¼" h, $225.00.

Plate, 6¼" d, three color floral design **165.00**
Tankard, 5" h, snow capped mountains on rim, blue–green glaze **300.00**
Tea Tile, 5¾" d, green, brown, white, and orange center lake scene, black outlines, light blue ground **412.00**

Vase

3¾" h, high gloss, green, blue, and red blend, tiny silver crystals, pale green ground	95.00
4¾" h, high gloss, mottled shades of blue and black, tiny silver crystals	110.00
5" h, tapered base, wide, closed top, black glaze, SEG mark . .	120.00
7" h, bud, blue, marked "S.E.G."	135.00
9" h, stylized brown, green, and yellow flowers, matte yellow ground, hairlines, marked "9–26, S.E.G."	450.00

PEACHBLOW

History: Peachblow, an art glass which derives its name from a fine Chinese glazed porcelain, resembles a peach or crushed strawberries in color. Three American glass manufacturers and two English firms produced peachblow glass in the late 1880s. A fourth American firm renewed the process in the 1950s. The glass from each firm has its own identifying characteristics.

Hobbs, Brockunier & Co., Wheeling peachblow: Opalescent glass, plated or cased with a transparent amber glass; shading from yellow at the base to a deep red at top; glossy or satin finish.

Mt. Washington "Peach Blow": A homogeneous glass, shading from a pale gray–blue to a soft rose color. Pieces may be enhanced with glass appliqués, enameling, and gilting.

New England Glass Works, New England peachblow (advertised as "Wild Rose," but called "Peach Blow" at the plant): Translucent, shading from rose to white; acid or glossy finish. Some pieces enameled and gilted.

Thomas Webb & Sons and Stevens and Williams, England: Around 1888 these two firms made a peachblow–style art glass marked "Peach Blow" or "Peach Bloom." A cased glass, shading from yellow to red. Occasionally found with cameo–type designs in relief.

Gunderson Glass Co.: About 1950 produced peachblow–type art glass to order; shades from an opaque faint tint of pink, which is almost white, to a deep rose.

References: Gary E. Baker et al., *Wheeling Glass 1829–1939, Collection of the Oglebay Institute Glass Museum,* Oglebay Institute, 1994, distributed by Antique Publications; John A. Shuman III, *The Collector's Encyclopedia of American Glass,* Collector Books, 1988, 1994 value update.

GUNDERSON

Bowl, 4¾" d, shading from soft blue to pink	85.00
Compote, 4½" d, 3" h, glossy, orig paper label	150.00
Cup and Saucer	115.00
Decanter, 9½" h, deep rose shading to white, pedestal base, orig stopper	550.00
Plate, 8" d	175.00
Vase, 8½" h, classic shape, sq base, applied serpentine handles	165.00

NEW ENGLAND

Bowl, 5½" d, ruffled rim	375.00
Celery Vase, 6¼" h, ruffled top, glossy, belltone, thin walls	950.00
Creamer and Sugar, 2½" h, faint trace of 1893 World's Fair dec, deep blush, Libbey, price for pair	850.00
Darner, shiny finish, inscribed "World's Fair–1893"	175.00
Finger Bowl, 5¼" w	335.00
Punch Cup, 2¾" h, vivid color on ext. and int., white reeded handle	485.00
Rose Bowl, 3¾" d, crimp top, acid finish	350.00
Salt and Pepper Shakers, pr, shiny, bulbous, replaced tops . .	775.00
Toothpick Holder	
Satin finish, white shading to deep raspberry	
Cylinder shape, polished pontil, ornate high ftd handled holder	595.00
Tricorn	750.00
Shiny finish, pink blending to soft white, fine ribs, Libbey	425.00
Tumbler, 3⅝" h	350.00
Vase, 8" h, lily, satin finish, 3" deep crimson top	650.00

WEBB

Bowl, 4⅝" d, clear rigaree top
edge, applied clear branches,
leaves, and flowers, glossy finish, cream white lining, three
clear feet **400.00**
Butter Dish, cov **395.00**
Cologne Bottle, acid finish, metal
top **295.00**
Pitcher, 8¾" h, 7½" w, deep colored ext., cream int., applied
crystal handle, applied amber
and cranberry ruffled glass leaf,
ruffled heart shaped rim **1,020.00**
Scent Bottle, 3¾" h, blue enamel,
white and yellow forget–me–
nots, green leaf dec, creamy
white lining, acid finish, hallmarked silver dome top **650.00**
Vase
2½" h, 3" d, cylindrical bowl, recessed neck, plain vertical rim,
shiny finish, deep cherry red
turning to pink, ivory int., high
relief gilt dec, prunus blossoms and butterfly **300.00**
7½" d, cased, white int., deep
color, heavy enameled cher-
ries and leaves, price for pair **318.00**

WHEELING

Cream Pitcher, 4¼" h, applied amber handle **785.00**
Cruet, 6½" h, mahogany top shad-

**Pitcher, glossy, quatrefoil top, ap-
plied amber handle, Wheeling,
7½" h, $850.00.**

ing to cherry red to cream base,
white int., trefoil top **1,285.00**
Ewer, 10" h, 5" w, petticoat shape,
deep fuchsia–brown ruby to amber, white int., applied amber rigaree, applied amber reeded
shell handle, Hobbs, Brockunier
& Co **1,950.00**
Mustard, metal lid and handle ... **750.00**
Pitcher, water
8" h, 6½" w, matte finish, deep
red–fuchsia shading to amber,
applied amber handle, Hobbs,
Brockunier & Co **1,600.00**
8¼" h, 6½" w, glossy finish, deep
ruby red shading to amber, sq
top, applied deep amber han-
dle, Hobbs, Brockunier & Co . **1,250.00**
Sugar Shaker, 5½" h, petticoat
shape, deep color, orig metal
hardware, glossy finish **1,100.00**
Tumbler, 4" h, deep fuchsia shad-
ing to brilliant amber **350.00**
Vase, 8½" h, stick, bulbous base,
long narrow neck, acid finish,
oyster lining **850.00**

PEKING GLASS

History: Peking glass is a type of cameo
glass of Chinese origin. Its production began in the 1700s and continued well into
the 19th century. The background color of
Peking glass may be a delicate shade of
yellow, green, or white. One style of white
background is so delicate and transparent
that it often is referred to as the "snowflake"
ground. The overlay colors include a rich
garnet red, deep blue, and emerald green.
Reference: Gloria and Robert Mascarelli,
Oriental Antiques, Wallace–Homestead,
1992.

Bowl, 8" d, floriform, yellow, 19th
C **375.00**
Cocktail Shaker, 10" h, green, acid
etched dragon dec, 1920s **275.00**
Cup, 2¼" h, egg yolk yellow, flared
rim, 18th/19th C **385.00**
Cup and Saucer, blue overlay
dragons and clouds, white
ground, SS saucer **185.00**

Ginger Jar, 8" h, globular form, pink, relief crane and lotus design, mounted as lamp, 19th C ... 495.00

Jar, cov
3⅜" h, green, faceted, T'ung Chih mark 1,325.00
6¾" h, globular form, white floral design, red overlay 440.00

Plate, 10½" d, twelve sided, forest green, late 19th C 120.00

Saucer, 8" d, floriform, blue, 19th C 130.00

Snuff Bottle
Birds in landscape dec, nephrite stopper 225.00
Red, oval flask form, carnelian stopper, 20th C, 3⅜" h 55.00

Tumbler, 3½" h, cameo relief bird and flowers, jade green dec ... 95.00

Vase, white ground, red floral, 8" h, $200.00.

Vase
5¾" h, ruby, carved Chinese archaistic 625.00
8" h
Bottle shape, pr, turquoise, incised Qianlong six character mark, 19th C 3,300.00
Club form, cobalt blue, fitted case, Guangxu mark, c1900 ... 495.00
9¼" h, squat globular form, white ground, green and pink exotic bird and flower design, overlay dec 4,400.00
9½" h, blue and white overlay cut in honeycomb pattern ... 375.00
13½" h, club form, yellow, relief dragon dec, 19th C 1,265.00

PELOTON

History: Wilhelm Kralik of Bohemia patented Peloton art glass in 1880. Later it was also patented in America and England.

Peloton glass is found with both transparent and opaque grounds with opaque being more common. Opaque colored glass filaments (strings or threads) are applied by dipping or rolling the hot glass. Generally, the filaments are pink, blue, yellow, and white (rainbow colors) or a single color. Items also may have a satin finish and enamel decorations.

Reference: Ellen T. Schroy, *Warman's Glass,* Wallace–Homestead, 1992.

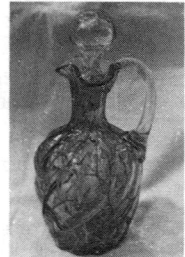

Cruet, light blue ground, multicolored strings, clear stopper, 7" h, $265.00.

Biscuit Jar, 5¾" d, 5¼" h, melon ribbed body, clear cased ground, multicolored filaments, white int., satin finish, SP rim, cov, and bail handle 600.00

Cruet, 6" h, amber body, multicolored filaments 350.00

Pitcher, 6½" h, bulbous ovoid body, cylindrical neck, pinched spout, applied clear handle, clear threads, pink, yellow, blue, and white filaments 140.00

Plate, 7¾" d, clear ground, blue filaments, enamel floral dec ... 120.00

Rose Bowl, 3¾" h, 3½" d, bulbous body, rim drawn up to four points, ftd, white opaque ground, deep pink, blue, yellow, and white filaments 295.00

Sweetmeat Jar, 5¼" d, cased, robin's–egg blue ground, pink, yellow, white, and blue filaments, white lining, SP rim, cov, and handle **595.00**

Vase

3½" h, 3" d, spherical body, ringed neck, flat ruffled rim, pink–lavender ground, white, pink, blue, and yellow filaments **200.00**

6¾" h, 5⅛" d, ovoid, emb ribs, flaring crimped rim, cased clear ground, royal blue filaments, white int. **225.00**

PERFUME, COLOGNE, AND SCENT BOTTLES

History: Decorative bottles to hold scents have been made in various shapes and sizes. They reached a "golden age" during the second half of the 19th century.

An atomizer is a perfume bottle with a spray mechanism. Cologne bottles usually are larger and have stoppers which also may be used as applicators. A perfume bottle has a stopper that often is elongated and designed as an applicator.

Scent bottles are small bottles used to hold a scent or smelling salts. A vinaigrette is an ornamental box or bottle with a perforated top used to hold aromatic vinegars or smelling salts. Fashionable women of the late 18th and 19th centuries carried them in purses or slipped them into gloves in case of a sudden fainting spell.

References: Joanne Dubbs Ball and Dorothy Hehl Torem, *Commercial Fragrance Bottles,* Schiffer Publishing, 1993; Glinda Bowman, *Miniature Perfume Bottles,* Schiffer Publishing, 1994; Jacquelyne Jones–North, *Commercial Perfume Bottles,* Schiffer Publishing, 1987; Jacquelyne Jones–North, *Czechoslovakian Perfume Bottles & Boudoir Accessories,* Antique Publications, 1990; Tirza True Latimer, *The Perfume Atomizer: An Object With Atmosphere,* Schiffer Publishing, 1991; Hazel Martin, *A Collection Of Figural Perfume & Scent Bottles,* published by author, 1982; Jacquelyne North, *Perfume, Cologne, and Scent Bottles,* Schiffer Publishing, 1987; Jean Sloan, *Perfume and Scent Bottle Collecting With Prices, Second Edition,* Wallace–Homestead, 1989.

Collectors' Clubs: International Perfume & Scent Bottle Collectors, 310 Maple Ave., Vienna, VA 22180; Mini–Scents, 1123 N. Flores St., Apt. 21, West Hollywood, CA 90069.

ATOMIZERS

Cambridge Glass, 6¼" h, gold stippled, opaque jade, silk lined box **135.00**

DeVilbiss, 8¾" h, gold–blue Aurene **795.00**

Frosted, 6" h, four molded panels of four seasons, Robj, Paris, c1925 .... **600.00**

Moser, octagonal, clear and deep violet, orig top and bulb, incised signature **285.00**

COLOGNE BOTTLES

Cranberry

5¾" h, 3⅛" d, white enameled flowers and leaves on front, orig cranberry bubble stopper **200.00**

8⅝" h, 2⅜" d, gold scrolls, small gold flowers, matching sq cranberry bubble stopper **175.00**

Depression Era, English Hobnail, 6⅝" h, orig stopper

Aqua **65.00**

Green, price for pr **115.00**

Mary Gregory, 9½" h, 3½" d, sapphire blue, white enameled young girl, blue bubble stopper **215.00**

Moser

6" h, 2½" d, amethyst to clear, gold garlands, scrolls, dots, and bands, matching dec amethyst bubble stopper **230.00**

7¾" h, 3½" d, deep amethyst, deeply intaglio cut flowers and leaves, cut panels, matching bubble stopper with amethyst center and intaglio cut flowers, marked "Moser Karlsbad" on base **810.00**

Overshot, 9½" h, Icicle, applied overshot icicles around neck extend down cranberry body, ap-

plied clear shell feet, orig over-
shot stopper, Sandwich **475.00**
Vaseline, 4½" h, flint, orig stopper,
attributed to New England Glass
Co **225.00**

PERFUMES

Baccarat
    5½" h, cylindrical, Lalique
    molded metalwork frame, Vi-
    olette D'orsey Baccarat, frame
    sgd "RL," c1912 . . . . **2,800.00**
    6⅜" h, molded and frosted, gray,
    acid stamped "Baccarat/
    France," mid 20th C **635.00**
Cameo Glass, 5½" h, transparent
    pale celadon, shaded brown,
    rose, cream, and white enam-
    eled sea grass and shells,
    enameled landscape scene on
    sides, enameled shell dec stop-
    per, sgd "Cristallerie d'Emile
    Galle/Nancy/Modele et decor
    deposes/EG" **13,800.00**
Cranberry, 5¼" w, 3" h, deep color,
    enameled blue and white forget–
    me–nots and green leaves,
    matching enameled orig stopper,
    four wheeled silver chariot
    holder, orange figural flowers,
    high fancy handle, marked "Mer-
    iden" **395.00**
Golliwog, clear, frosted, black face
    stopper, furry hair, orig box with
    pink satin int. **175.00**
Moser, 5" h, 2" d, amethyst to
    clear, gold garlands, dots, and
    bands, matching dec amethyst
    bubble stopper, marked on base **230.00**
Orrefors, 4⅛" h, triangular label,
    engraved marks and numbers . **85.00**
Rubina, 4½" h, 3½" d, squatty bul-
    bous, cranberry shading to clear,
    center cut bands of leaves, star
    cut base, clear stopper with cut-
    ting **115.00**
Webb, 10" l, cameo, carved floral
    design, frosted cranberry
    ground, orig silver plated cov
    and velvet and satin carrying
    case, stamped "Mappin & Webb,
    Silversmiths to the Queen, Lon-
    don and Sheffield" **3,850.00**

**Scent, glass, gold colored metal
casing, incised central tiled mosaic of bug, mosaic cap, Egyptian
motif, made in Italy, 2¾", $500.00.**

SCENTS

Cameo Glass, 3¾" h, gray opales-
    cent, teal blue overlay, cut ber-
    ries and leafage dec, pale amber
    floriform stopper, cameo sgd
    "Galle" **3,165.00**
Early American
    1¾" h, green, sunburst design . **310.00**
    1⅞" h, puce shaded to clear,
    scallop shell form **250.00**
    2" h, deep emerald green, con-
    centric ring **525.00**
    2¼" h, sapphire blue, concentric
    ring **470.00**
    2¾" h, amethyst, sunburst de-
    sign **330.00**
    2⅞" h, emerald green, sunburst
    design **495.00**
Northwood, 1⅛" d, 1¾" h, pull–up
    design, eight horizontal bands,
    alternating stripes of rust, char-
    treuse, and white, SS cap **385.00**

VINAIGRETTES

Cranberry, 2¼ x 1", rect, cut all
    around, enameled tiny pink
    roses, green leaves, gold dec
    hinged lid, stopper, finger chain **165.00**
Sterling Silver, 2 x 1½", engraved
    scrolling and scene, hinged lid,
    pierced gold lid int., Nathaniel
    Mills, Birmingham, 1849 . . . . . . **275.00**

PETERS AND REED POTTERY

History: J. D. Peters and Adam Reed founded their pottery company in South Zanesville, Ohio, in 1900. Common flowerpots, jardinieres, and cooking wares comprised the majority of their early output. Occasionally art pottery was attempted, but it was not until 1912 that their Moss Aztec line was introduced and widely accepted. Other art wares included Chromal, Landsun, Montene, Pereco, and Persian.

Peters retired in 1921 and Reed changed the name of the firm to Zane Pottery Company. Marked pieces of Peters and Reed Pottery are unknown.

Reference: Susan and Al Bagdade, *Warman's American Pottery and Porcelain,* Wallace–Homestead, 1994.

Vase, cylindrical, imp daisy design, green–red matte finish, sgd "Ferrell," 8″ h, $50.00.

Bookends, pr, 5″ h, Pereco, stylized dec, matte green glaze . . .	35.00
Bowl	
5″ d, 2″ h, brown, green accents	25.00
8½″ d, dark blue berries	50.00
Candlesticks, pr, 10¼″ h, speckled blue semi–matte glaze, marked "Zane Ware"	125.00
Jardiniere, 10″ w, Moss Aztec, emb flowers	75.00
Medallion, 2″ d, terra–cotta, 1915	145.00
Mug, 5¾″ h, high glaze, floral sprigs	35.00
Pitcher, 4″ h, green and yellow	

raised fern leaves, gloss dark brown ground	55.00
Spittoon, Moss Aztec, stylized rose dec	45.00
Umbrella Stand, 17″ h, marbleized finish	300.00
Vase	
5″ h, brown drip glaze, marked "Zane Ware"	35.00
6″ h, bud, Landsun	50.00
7″ h, Wilse blue	45.00
7¾″ h, Chromal, three color landscape scene	185.00
9″ h, Shadow Ware, white and green drip, tan ground	85.00

PEWTER

History: Pewter is a metal alloy consisting mostly of tin with small amounts of lead, copper, antimony, and bismuth added to improve formability and hardness. The metal can be cast, formed around a mold, spun, easily cut, and soldered to form a wide variety of utilitarian articles.

Pewter ware was known to the ancient Chinese, Egyptians, and Romans. English pewter supplied the major portion of the needs of the American colonies for nearly 150 years before the American Revolution. The Revolution ended the embargo on raw tin and allowed the small American pewter industry to flourish. This period lasted until the Civil War.

The listing concentrates on the American and English pewter forms most often encountered by the collector.

References: Donald L. Fennimore, *The Knopf Collectors' Guides to American Antiques: Silver & Pewter,* Alfred A. Knopf, 1984; Henry J. Kauffman, *The American Pewterer: His Techniques & His Products,* Astragal Press, 1994.

Collectors' Club: Pewter Collectors Club of America, 29 Chesterfield Road, Scarsdale, NY 10583.

Museum: The Currier Gallery of Art, Manchester, NH.

Advisor: Robert Limons.

Baptismal Bowl, 11¼″ d, unknown maker, 19th C	175.00

Barber Bowl, 9¼" d, engraved initials, late 18th C **410.00**

Basin

Boardman, Thomas Danforth, faint eagle touchmark, 8" d .. **300.00**

Eadem, Semper, Boston, faint touchmark, minor wear, polished, 8" d **440.00**

Ellis, Samuel, London, 18th C, 9⅛" d **200.00**

Lee, Richard, Springfield, VT, 1795–1815, 5¾" d **300.00**

Unknown Maker

6¼" d, pitted, sidewall crack, polished **165.00**

8" d, Love touchmark, wear, corroded **165.00**

13" d, Continental, angel touchmark, engraved initials on rim **335.00**

Beaker, Hiram Yale, Wallingford, CT, 1822–31, cast dec handle, 2¾" h **150.00**

Bowl, Liberty and Company, c1900, low bulbous, six dark blue glazed cabochons, three strapwork legs, imp "Made in England Tudric Pewter 01128 Made by Liberty & Co," 8¼" h . **575.00**

Candlestick

Buchrucher, Harald, c1930, hammered, shaped rect, domical base, three candle holders, imp marker's mark and numbers, 3" h, 10¼" l **175.00**

Dunham, Rufus, Westbrook, ME, c1840, straight line touch, 6" h, price for pair **750.00**

Gleason, Roswell, Dorchester, MA, c1840, 6½" h **275.00**

Hopper, Henry, NY, c1840, 10" h, price for pair **880.00**

Porter, F, Westbrook, ME, lightly battered, 5¾" h **165.00**

Unknown Maker, pr

7¼" h, old dark finish **325.00**

8¾" h, old finish, minor soldered repair **250.00**

9" h, pushups, 19th C **230.00**

9¾" h **100.00**

10" h, pushups, beaded rim, dec base **275.00**

10¼" h, baluster form, pushups, 19th C **255.00**

Charger

Austin, Nathaniel, Charleston, MA, 13½" d **450.00**

Cloudsley, T, pitted and scratched, 16¾" d **225.00**

Freeman, Duncumb, London, 14¾" d **335.00**

Hamlin, Samuel, polished, 15" d **925.00**

Langworthy, Lawrence, Exeter, base marked "COTOP 2839," 18½" d **690.00**

Roesler, I F, floral engraving, soldered hanger on back, 12⅜" d **165.00**

Unknown Maker

Continental, 19th C, base marked "IF" and fleur–de–lis, 18" d **435.00**

English, faint touchmarks, wear and pitting, 20" d **550.00**

Coffeepot

Boardman & Co, NY, marked "Thomas Connecticut Pewter & Pewterers 123B," minor imperfections, 12½" h **635.00**

Calder, William, Providence, RI, c1839, lighthouse shape, 11" h **650.00**

Graves, J B, incomplete finial, some battering and repair, 10" h **295.00**

Homan, H, cast flower finial, 9¾" h **100.00**

Porter, Freeman, Westbrook, ME, lighthouse shape, ear shape handle, battered, broken hinge, wafer missing on finial, 10⅝" h **150.00**

Richardson, George, Providence, RI, double bulbous, domed lid, "G Richardson, Warranted" touchmark, soldered, polished, 11" h **355.00**

Sellew & Co, Cincinnati, minor damage, 10½" h **250.00**

Trask, Israel, Beverly, MA, c1830, lighthouse shape, bright cut engraved band, 11" h **350.00**

Coffee Set, Sellew & Co, Cincinnati, OH, 12" h coffeepot, creamer, and sugar, price for 3 pc set **1,000.00**

Communion Chalice, Boardman, 7" h, price for pair **250.00**

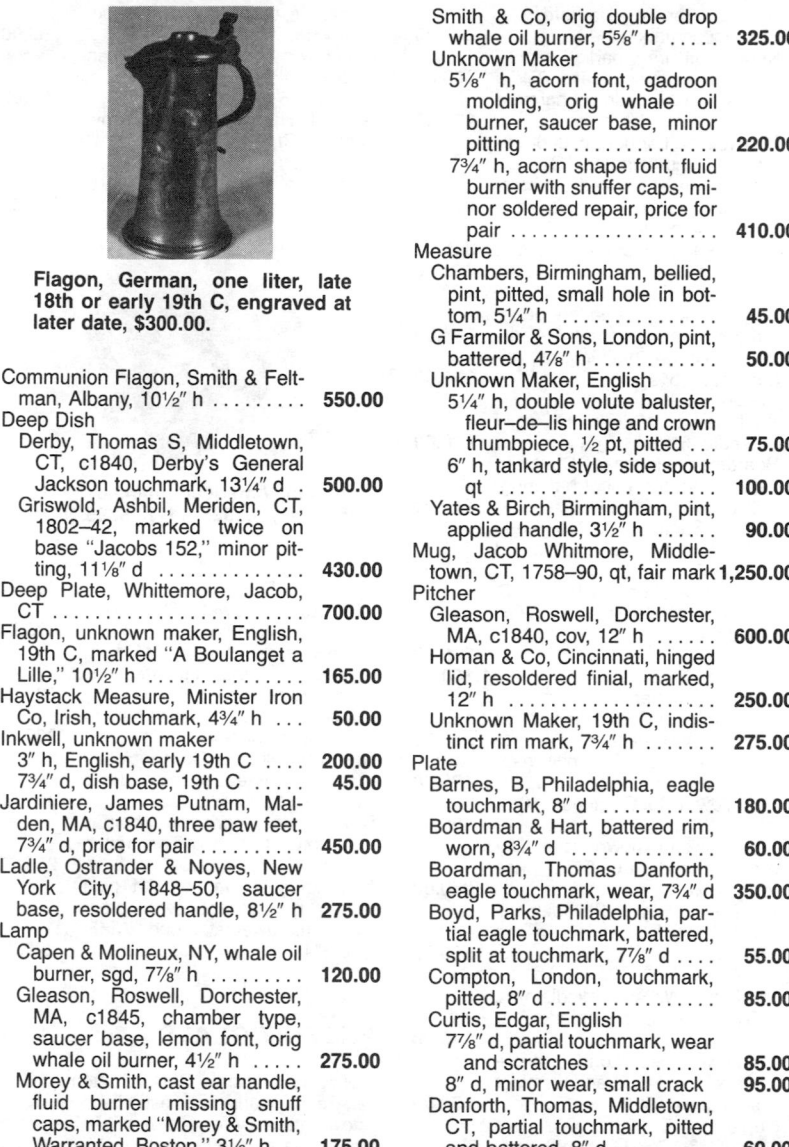

Flagon, German, one liter, late 18th or early 19th C, engraved at later date, $300.00.

Communion Flagon, Smith & Feltman, Albany, 10½" h 550.00
Deep Dish
  Derby, Thomas S, Middletown, CT, c1840, Derby's General Jackson touchmark, 13¼" d . 500.00
  Griswold, Ashbil, Meriden, CT, 1802–42, marked twice on base "Jacobs 152," minor pitting, 11⅛" d 430.00
Deep Plate, Whittemore, Jacob, CT 700.00
Flagon, unknown maker, English, 19th C, marked "A Boulanget a Lille," 10½" h 165.00
Haystack Measure, Minister Iron Co, Irish, touchmark, 4¾" h ... 50.00
Inkwell, unknown maker
  3" h, English, early 19th C 200.00
  7¾" d, dish base, 19th C 45.00
Jardiniere, James Putnam, Malden, MA, c1840, three paw feet, 7¾" d, price for pair 450.00
Ladle, Ostrander & Noyes, New York City, 1848–50, saucer base, resoldered handle, 8½" h 275.00
Lamp
  Capen & Molineux, NY, whale oil burner, sgd, 7⅞" h 120.00
  Gleason, Roswell, Dorchester, MA, c1845, chamber type, saucer base, lemon font, orig whale oil burner, 4½" h 275.00
  Morey & Smith, cast ear handle, fluid burner missing snuff caps, marked "Morey & Smith, Warranted, Boston," 3⅛" h .. 175.00

Smith & Co, orig double drop whale oil burner, 5⅝" h 325.00
Unknown Maker
  5⅛" h, acorn font, gadroon molding, orig whale oil burner, saucer base, minor pitting 220.00
  7¾" h, acorn shape font, fluid burner with snuffer caps, minor soldered repair, price for pair 410.00
Measure
  Chambers, Birmingham, bellied, pint, pitted, small hole in bottom, 5¼" h 45.00
  G Farmilor & Sons, London, pint, battered, 4⅞" h 50.00
  Unknown Maker, English
    5¼" h, double volute baluster, fleur–de–lis hinge and crown thumbpiece, ½ pt, pitted ... 75.00
    6" h, tankard style, side spout, qt 100.00
  Yates & Birch, Birmingham, pint, applied handle, 3½" h 90.00
Mug, Jacob Whitmore, Middletown, CT, 1758–90, qt, fair mark 1,250.00
Pitcher
  Gleason, Roswell, Dorchester, MA, c1840, cov, 12" h 600.00
  Homan & Co, Cincinnati, hinged lid, resoldered finial, marked, 12" h 250.00
  Unknown Maker, 19th C, indistinct rim mark, 7¾" h 275.00
Plate
  Barnes, B, Philadelphia, eagle touchmark, 8" d 180.00
  Boardman & Hart, battered rim, worn, 8¾" d 60.00
  Boardman, Thomas Danforth, eagle touchmark, wear, 7¾" d 350.00
  Boyd, Parks, Philadelphia, partial eagle touchmark, battered, split at touchmark, 7⅞" d 55.00
  Compton, London, touchmark, pitted, 8" d 85.00
  Curtis, Edgar, English
    7⅞" d, partial touchmark, wear and scratches 85.00
    8" d, minor wear, small crack 95.00
  Danforth, Thomas, Middletown, CT, partial touchmark, pitted and battered, 8" d 60.00

Havelin, Samuel, Hartford, CT,
int. touchmark, 8⅛" d 375.00
Kirby, William, partial touch-
marks, wear, scratches, 8⅞" d 660.00
Leeds, T W, London, engraved
initials "LR," 12" d 175.00
Maxwell, S, London, c1800, imperfections, marked "S Maxwell, Flourish, United States of
America," 8¾" d 235.00
Pierce, Samuel
8" d, eagle touchmark 385.00
11¾" d 495.00
Townsend, English, 9¼" d 100.00
Unknown Maker, London touchmark, wear, corroded, 9½" d . 85.00
Platter, unknown maker, oval, minor wear, 15⅞" l 60.00
Porringer
Attributed to Melville, RI, solid
handle, 5½" d 600.00
Boardman, Thomas Danforth,
crown handle, minor battering,
5" d 415.00
Green, Samuel, Boston, early
19th C, crown handle, marked
"SG," 5¼" d 275.00
Jones, Gershom, RI, c1775,
flower handle, marked "GI"
and lion
4¼" d 1,265.00
5½" d 1,100.00
Unknown Maker
3½" d, 19th C, includes spoon 145.00
5½" d, solid handle 965.00
8" l, early 19th C, crown handle marked "SC" 125.00
Pot, Sellew & Co, Cincinnati, 10½"
h 485.00
Pricket Stick, unknown maker, Baroque style, 19th C, 32" h, price
for pair 260.00
Salt, Parks Boyd, Philadelphia,
PA, 1795–1819, beaded rim and
base, ftd 950.00
Soup Plate
Danforth, William, Middletown,
CT, two eagle touchmarks, 11"
d...................... 210.00
Unknown Maker, London touchmark, wear and minor
scratches, 9⅝" d 90.00
Syrup
Homan & Co, Cincinnati, ear

handle, cast flower finial, hinge
and spout split, 6" h 55.00
Unknown Maker, cast ear handle, finial, handle with small
holes, 5¼" h 65.00
Tankard, Hamlin, Samuel, Providence, RI, first quarter 19th C,
tapered, molded base, serpentine strap handle, touch mark, 6"
h 2,300.00

**Teapot, American, marked "D. L.
Farnam," c1825, 11" h, $365.00.**

Teapot
Dunham, Rufus 100.00
Gleason, Roswell, Dorchester,
MA, marked base, 8½" h 175.00
Trask, Israel, Beverly, MA, lighthouse shape, imperfections,
marked base, 10½" h 330.00
Williams, L L, Philadelphia, resoldered handle, 8¼" h 300.00
Tea Set, Sellew & Co, Cincinnati,
3 pcs, 11" h teapot, minor dents,
battered handle 495.00
Toddy Plate, Boardman, Thomas,
Hartford, CT, two lion touchmarks, 6½" d 250.00
Tray, unknown maker, Art Nouveau, maiden squeezing grape
juice into ewer, stamped "WMF,"
10½" l 220.00

PHOENIX GLASS

History: Phoenix Glass Company, Beaver, Pennsylvania, was established in 1880.
Known primarily for commercial glassware,
the firm also produced a molded, sculp-

tured, cameo–type line from the 1930s until the 1950s.

References: Ellen T. Schroy, *Warman's Glass,* Wallace–Homestead, 1992; Jack D. Wilson, *Phoenix & Consolidated Art Glass, 1926–1980,* Antique Publications, 1989.

Collectors' Club: Phoenix & Consolidated Glass Collectors, PO Box 81974, Chicago, IL 60681.

Vase, Flying Geese, blue pastel ground, orig paper label, 9½" h, 11½" w, $200.00.

Berry Set, 6 pcs, 8" d master, five 4½" d individuals, clear and frosted, dancing nude women design 200.00
Bowl, Swallows, purple wash 145.00
Creamer and Sugar, Catalonia pattern, yellow 40.00
Lamp
  23" h, 16" d, reverse painted domical shade, lakeside mill scene, painted metal floral molded vasiform base, stepped circular foot 450.00
  24" h, reverse painted landscape scene shade 700.00
Planter, 8½" l, 3¼" h, sculptured green lion, white ground 50.00
Plate, 8¼" d, dancing nudes, yellow 50.00
Vase
  6¼" h, sculptured pink peonies, green leaves, white ground .. 80.00
  7" h, pale blue, clear and frosted flower dec, orig label 75.00
  7½" h, Philodendron, pink, paper sticker 95.00

8½" h, clear and frosted, floral design, orig label 100.00
8¾" h, clear and frosted, grasshoppers and reeds dec 125.00
9½" h, clear and frosted, goldfish design 100.00
11" h, Philodendron, cadet blue 125.00
12" h
  Dance of the Seven Veils design, clear and frosted 200.00
  Deep Sculpture, coral flowers, green vines, white matte ground 235.00

PHONOGRAPHS

History: Early phonographs were commonly called "talking machines." Thomas A. Edison invented the first successful phonograph in 1877. Other manufacturers followed with their variations.

References: Robert W. Baumbach, *Look For the Dog: An Illustrated Guide to Victor Talking Machines,* Stationery X–Press, 1990; Neil Maker, *Hand–Cranked Phonographs: It All Started With Edison...,* Promar Publishing, 1993; Arnold Schwartzman, *Phono–Graphics: The Visual Paraphernalia of the Talking Machine,* Chronicle Books, 1993.

Periodicals: *The Horn Speaker,* PO Box 1193, Mabank, TX 75147; *The New Amberola Graphic,* 37 Caledonia St., St. Johnsbury, VT 05819.

Collectors' Clubs: California Antique Phonograph Society, PO Box 67, Durate, CA 91010; Michigan Antique Phonograph Society, Inc., 2609 Devonshire, Lansing, MI 48910; Vintage Radio & Phonograph Society, Inc., PO Box 165345, Irving, TX 75016.

Museums: Edison National Historic Site, West Orange, NJ; Seven Acres Antique Village & Museum, Union, IL.

American Graphophone Co,
  Graphophone Type Q, c1897 .. 275.00
Brunswick, Parisiane, collapsible cardboard horn 400.00
Columbia
  Disc Graphophone, 1902 .....1,000.00
  Grafanola Baby Regent 400.00
  Graphophone, oak dome cov and cabinet 550.00

Edison
Amberola 30 . . . . 325.00
Diamond Disc Model No S19 . . 150.00
Gem, Model C 300.00
Model 50 . . . . 275.00
Triumph, Model H 500.00

Edison Amberola, Model 30, 4 main cylinders, built–in horn, hand crank, oak case, 11″ w, 14¼″ d, 12½″ h, $325.00.

Garrard, hand crafted snakeskin
horn, 1920 . . . . 1,250.00
Harmony, oak case, painted morn-
ing glory horn 400.00
Junophone, table model, oak
case, metal wood grain finish
horn 250.00
Kalamazoo Duplex 1,350.00
McDonald Graphophone, oak
case, open works 800.00
Regina Reginaphone Disc Musical
Box and Phonograph, oak case,
MOP inlay, five 15½″ discs,
c1904 . . . . 2,100.00
Sears Roebuck & Co, Silvertone,
1914 . . . . 150.00
Victor
Model 1050, record changer . . 450.00
V, oak horn, 1905–1914 . . . . . 1,375.00
V–II, wood horn 1,250.00
Victrola
Model VI, table type, oak 150.00
Model XI 100.00
Zonophone, Champion, table
model, oak case, ribbed brass
horn 750.00

PHOTOGRAPHS

History: A vintage print is a positive image developed from the original negative by the photographer or under the photographer's supervision at the time the negative is made. A non–vintage print is a print made from an original negative at a later date. It is quite common for a photographer to make prints from the same negative over several decades. Changes between the original printing and subsequent prints usually can be identified. Limited edition prints must be clearly labeled.

References: Stuart Bennett, *How To Buy Photographs,* Salem House, 1987; O. Henry Mace, *Collector's Guide To Early Photographs,* Wallace–Homestead, 1990; Norman E. Martinus and Harry L. Rinker, *Warman's Paper,* Wallace–Homestead, 1994; Lou W. McCulloch, *Card Photographs, A Guide to Their History And Value,* Schiffer Publishing, 1981; Floyd and Marion Rinhart, *American Miniature Case Art,* A. S. Barnes and Co, 1969; Susan Theran, *Prints, Posters & Photographs: Identification and Price Guide,* Avon Books, 1993; Susan Theran and Katheryn Acerbo (eds.), *Leonard's Annual Price Index of Prints, Posters & Photographs,* Auction Index, published annually; John Waldsmith, *Stereoviews: An Illustrated History and Price Guide,* Wallace–Homestead, 1991.

Periodicals: *CameraShopper,* 313 N. Quaker Lane, PO Box 37029, W. Hartford, CT 06137; *The Photograph Collector,* Photographic Arts Center, 163 Amsterdam Ave. #201, New York, NY 10023.

Collectors' Clubs: American Photographic Historical Society, Inc., 1150 Avenue of the Americas, New York, NY 10036; Association of International Photography Art Dealers, 1609 Connecticut Ave. NW #200, Washington, DC 20009; National Stereoscopic Association, PO Box 14801, Columbus, OH 43214; Photographic Historical Society of Canada, PO Box 54620, Toronto, Ontario M5M 4N5 Canada; Photographic Historical Society of New England, PO Box 189, Boston, MA 02165; The Daguerreian Society, PO Box 2129, Green Bay, WI 54306; The Photographic Historical Society, Inc., PO Box 39563, Rochester, NY 14604; Western Photographic Collectors

Assoc. Inc., PO Box 4294, Whittier, CA 90607.

Museums: Center for Creative Photography, Tucson, AZ; International Center of Photography, New York, NY; International Museum of Photography at George Eastman House, Rochester, NY; International Photographic Historical Association, San Francisco, CA; National Portrait Gallery, Washington, DC.

Additional Listings: See *Warman's Americana & Collectibles* for more examples.

Cabinet Card
Arizona Scenes Series, Mission int. view, Buehman, Tucson . **15.00**
Baby, wicker carriage **10.00**
Black Boy, fancy dress, large bow **10.00**
Captain Dreyfus and Mrs Alfred Dreyfus, parlor photo, black and white **15.00**
Girl, marked "Hamilton Studios" on skirt, flag on hat **20.00**
Queen Victoria, three–quarter length pose, holding crochet hook and material **17.00**
Cartes De Visite
Albino Girl, portrait, Charles Eisenmann photographer, NY . . **17.00**
Asylum for the Insane, Jacksonville, IL, c1869 .... **9.00**
Civil War Battle Scene **35.00**
Egyptian Woman, water jug on head **12.00**
Ku Klux Klan, in costume, c1878 **40.00**
Musician, holding instrument . . **7.00**
President Garfield, bust pose . . **9.00**
Prince of Wales and family **8.00**
Professional and Snapshot
American Girl in Italy, 1952, stamp signature beneath image lower right, titled and dated in pencil on reverse, photographer Ruth Orkin estate stamp on reverse, 11 x 14" **575.00**
Busch Stadium, St Louis, sgd "Jim Dow" on reverse, titled, dated, and numbered on reverse, three prints mounted together, matted, Kodacolor, 11 x 31½" **490.00**

Children, roller skating, black and white **8.00**
Circus Wagon, pulled by ponies, black and white **15.00**
Grocery Store, int. view, 5 x 7" . **20.00**
Seed Store, int. view, Ferry Seed Co display racks, sales people, 1920, 5 x 7" **10.00**
Sioux Indians—Braves and Beauties Rapid City, July 7th, 1884, group of nine Indians in fancy ceremonial dress, American flag, sgd in type "MS Fuller & Co, Rapid City, Dakota Territory" **125.00**
Tailor Shop, ext. view, bicycle in front **10.00**

PICKARD CHINA

History: The Pickard China Company was founded by Wilder Pickard in Chicago, Illinois, in 1897. Originally the company imported European china blanks, principally from the Havilands at Limoges, which they then hand painted. The firm presently is located in Antioch, Illinois.

Reference: Susan and Al Bagdade, *Warman's American Pottery and Porcelain*, Wallace–Homestead, 1994.

Collectors' Club: Pickard Collectors Club, 300 E. Grove St., Bloomington, IL 61701.

Advertising Sign, 4" w, 5" h, triangular, freestanding, gold lion with shield and banner, gold letters "Pickard China Made in USA" . **95.00**
Bowl
8¼" d, 8¾" w at handles, scalloped, pearlized irid, pastel highlights, orange poppies and buds, gold and red tracery, gold trim, c1898 .... **255.00**
13" d, 3" h, lemons and cherries

Vase, gold etched effect, blue bands, water lily dec, artist sgd "James," marked "Pickard," etched "China" in cartouche, blank marked "R. S. Tillowitz," $225.00.

dec, heavy gold, artist sgd
"Vokral" 495.00
Cake Plate, 11½" d, open handles,
artist sgd "Schoner" 395.00
Chocolate Pot, 11½" h, white MOP
ground, orchids and foliage dec 175.00
Claret Jug, hp, artist sgd "Vokral" 975.00
Creamer and Sugar
Floral band with plums and raspberries, gold ground, sgd
"Nessy" 175.00
Pilgrims and Mayflower, matte
finish, 1912–19 mark 225.00
Demitasse Pot, poinsettia dec, artist sgd, dated 1910 .... 200.00
Fruit Bowl, 10½ x 8½" w, 4" h, ext.
and int. dec with green leaves
and melons, gold border, four
gold feet, artist sgd 395.00
Marmalade, cov, cream ground,
orange water lilies, green lily
pads, scalloped gold trim and
outlines, artist sgd "Tolpin,"
1898 mark 175.00
Mustard Pot, cov, florals, gold,
1912–19 mark 85.00
Pitcher, tankard, cherries, sgd,
wear to gold 125.00
Plate
8¼" d, scenic, water, temple pillars, moon, trees, matte finish,

artist sgd, marked "Pickard,"
c1912 .... 200.00
8½" d
Daffodils, pink, artist sgd "Florence James" 125.00
Lilies, artist sgd "Marker" ... 140.00
Scenic, Yosemite, 1905 mark,
artist sgd "Marker" 175.00
Scotch Plaid border, three gold
shields with orange lions, allover pink thistles, blue bells,
gold oak leaves, gold trim,
artist sgd, c1910 .... 195.00
8¾" d, Wildwood pattern, artist
sgd 155.00
9" d
Gold plaid and lions dec, artist
sgd, 1910–12 mark 95.00
Poppies, artist sgd "Florence
James" 140.00
10" d, fruit and flowers in 5" d
medallion, sgd "Gasper" 170.00
Platter, 16" l, hp, artist sgd "Challinor" 575.00
Tea Set, teapot, creamer, and
sugar, hp, artist sgd "Klein" ... 595.00
Vase, 9¼" h, portrait, artist sgd .. 795.00

PICKLE CASTORS

History: A pickle castor is a table accessory used to serve pickles. It generally consists of a silver–plated frame fitted with a
glass insert, matching silver–plated lid, and
matching tongs. Pickle castors were very
popular during the Victorian era. Inserts are
found in pattern glass and colored art glass.
Reference: Ellen T. Schroy, *Warman's
Glass,* Wallace-Homestead, 1992.

Amber, Diamond Point, honey amber insert, ornate Forbes SP
frame, beaded pedestal base,
tongs 210.00
Clear
Cane pattern insert, resilvered
Oneida SP holder, lid, tongs,
fan finial, 12" h, 4" d 150.00
Cupid and Venus pattern insert,
SP holder 245.00
S pattern insert, resilvered
holder marked "CMS," 11½" h,
4" d 150.00

Amber Daisy and Button pattern glass insert, SP frame, tongs, made by Tufts, $185.00.

Stippled Panels pattern insert, clear, resilvered ftd Meriden SP holder, lid, claw tongs, 11" h, 5¼" d **150.00**

Cranberry, IVT pattern insert Resilvered frame, lid, claw tongs, 10½" h, 4⅜" d **270.00**

Silverplated frame, gold floral enameling **450.00**

Opalescent Stripes pattern insert, pink and white stripes, small breakfast size, orig SP frame and tongs **345.00**

Windows pattern insert, blue and white swirls, resilvered frame and tongs **345.00**

Pigeon Blood, Open Heart Arches pattern insert, satin finish, floral dec, fancy frame and tongs, Consolidated Glass Co **335.00**

Pink, Florette pattern insert, shiny finish, sgd frame **250.00**

Rubena Verde, Hobnail pattern insert, SP frame and tongs, breakfast size **265.00**

Satin, Heart Arches pattern insert, white ground, enameled maroon florals, green leaves, sgd frame **265.00**

PIGEON BLOOD GLASS

History: Pigeon blood refers to the deep orangish-red colored glassware produced around the turn of the century. Do not con-fuse it with the many other red glasswares of that period. Pigeon blood has a very definite orange glow.

Reference: Ellen T. Schroy, *Warman's Glass,* Wallace-Homestead, 1992.

Biscuit Jar, ribbed, silverplated fittings, 8½" h, $250.00.

Biscuit Jar, Beaded Drapery pattern, ornate SP rim, cov, and handle **200.00**

Bowl, 9" d, c1880 .... **155.00**

Bride's Basket, 9½" d, enamel floral dec, SP holder **220.00**

Creamer, Torquay pattern, SP rim and handle **125.00**

Pickle Castor, 8" h, Bulging Loops pattern, SP ftd frame, marked "Empire Mfg Co" **285.00**

Pitcher, Torquay pattern **320.00**

Salt and Pepper Shakers, pr, Bulging Loops pattern, orig tops ... **95.00**

Sugar, Torquay pattern, metal lid **100.00**

Syrup, Bulging Loops pattern ... **650.00**

Tumbler, Venicia pattern **85.00**

Vase, 10½" h, enameled flowers . **185.00**

PINK SLAG

History: True pink slag is found only in the molded Inverted Fan and Feather pattern. Quality pieces shade from pink at the top to white at the bottom.

Reference: Ellen T. Schroy, *Warman's Glass,* Wallace-Homestead, 1992.

Reproduction Alert: Recently, pieces of pink slag made from molds of the now defunct Cambridge Glass Company have been found in the Inverted Strawberry and Inverted Thistle pattern. This is not considered "true" pink slag and brings only a fraction of the Inverted Fan and Feather pattern prices.

Tumbler, 4″ h, $475.00.

Butter, cov	650.00
Creamer	450.00
Cruet, 6½″ h, orig stopper	1,300.00
Jelly Compote	375.00
Marmalade Jar, cov	875.00
Pitcher	775.00
Punch Cup, 2¼″ h	45.00
Sauce	225.00
Spooner	350.00
Toothpick Holder	825.00
Tumbler	475.00

PIPES

History: The history of pipe making dates as early as 1575. Almost all types of natural and man–made materials, some of which retained smoke and some that did not, were used to make pipes. Among the materials were amber, base metals, clay, cloisonné, glass, horn, ivory, jade, meerschaum, parian, porcelain, pottery, precious metals, precious stones, semi–precious stones, assorted woods, *inter alia*. Chronologically, the four most popular materials and their generally accepted introduction dates are: clay, c1575; woods, c1700; porcelain, c1710; and meerschaum, c1725.

National pipe styles exist around the globe, wherever tobacco smoking is custom or habit. Pipes reflect a broad range of themes and messages, e.g., figurals, important personages, commemoration of historical events, mythological characters, erotica and pornographica, the bucolic, the bizarre, the grotesque, and the graceful.

Pipe collecting began in the mid–1880s; William Bragge, F.S.A., Birmingham, England, was an early collector. Although firmly established through the efforts of freelance writers, auction houses, and museums (but not the tobacco industry), the collecting of antique pipes is an amorphous, maligned, and misunderstood hobby. It is amorphous because there are no defined collecting bounds; maligned because it is conceived as an extension of pipe smoking, now socially unacceptable (many pipe collectors are avid non–smokers); and misunderstood because of its association with the "collectibles" field.

References: R. Fresco–Corbu, *European Pipes*, Lutterworth Press, 1982; E. Ramazzotti and B. Mamy, *Pipes et Fumeurs des Pipes. Un Art, des Collections, Sous le Vent*, 1981; Benjamin Rapaport, *A Complete Guide To Collecting Antique Pipes*, Schiffer Publishing, 1979.

Periodicals: *The Complete Smoker Magazine*, PO Box 7036, Evanston, IL 60204; *The Pipe Smoker's Ephemeris*, 20–37 120th Street, College Point, NY 11356.

Collectors' Clubs: International Association of Pipe Smokers' Clubs, 47758 Hickory, Apt. 22305, Wixom, MI 48393; New York Pipe Club, PO Box 265, Gracie Station, New York, NY 10028; North Texas Pipe Club, 1624 East Cherry St., Sherman, TX 75090; Pipe Collectors Club of America, PO Box 5179, Woodbridge, VA 22194; Sherlock Holmes Pipe Club Ltd. USA, PO Box 221, Westborough, MA 01581; Society for Clay Pipe Research, PO Box 817, Bel Air, MD 21014; Southern California Pipe & Cigar Smokers' Association, 1532 South Bundy Dr., Apt. D, Los Angeles, CA 90025.

Museums: Museum of Tobacco Art and History, Nashville, TN; National Tobacco–Textile Museum, Danville, VA; Pipe Smoker's Hall of Fame, Galveston, IN; U.S. Tobacco Museum, Greenwich, CT.

Clay, 4¼″ l, blue and white bowl, brown stem, OH	170.00

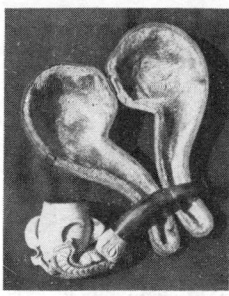

Meerschaum, orig leather case, $75.00.

Meerschaum, carved
> Bearded Male, wearing turban, fitted case, 20th C, 22¼" l ... **460.00**
> Cavalier, plumed hat **50.00**
> Horse's Head, agitated expression, gold ferrule, cheroot holder, amber stem, fitted case, 7¼" l **475.00**
> Indian Chief, full headdress, 14K ferrule marked "Shreve & Co," composition stem, fitted case marked "C P F," 8¼" l **650.00**
> Male, village landscape scene, brass fittings, similarly carved pr in fitted case, 20th C, 11" and 13" l **230.00**
> St George and the Dragon, cheroot holder, 6⅛" l **450.00**
> Tavern Scene, maid serving hunter, cheroot holder, amber stem, fitted case, 6⅞" l **425.00**

Porcelain
> Turkish Male Bust, jeweled and beaded turban, underglaze enamels, metal stem mount, hinged bowl cov, German, 19th C, 3½" h **1,500.00**
> Twig Stem, brass fittings, Bavarian, 19" l **50.00**

Sterling Silver, boatswain, macrame cord **40.00**

POCKET KNIVES

History: Alcas, Case, Colonial, Ka-Bar, Queen, and Schrade are the best of the modern pocket knife manufacturers, with top positions enjoyed by Case and Ka-Bar. Knives by Remington and Winchester, firms no longer in production, are eagerly sought.

Form is a critical collecting element. The most desirable forms are folding hunters (1 and 2 blades), trappers, peanuts, Barlows, elephant toes, canoes, Texas toothpicks, Coke bottles, gun stocks, and Daddy Barlows. The decorative aspect also heavily influences prices. Values are for pocket knives in mint condition.

References: Jacob N. Jarrett, *Price Guide To Pocket Knives, 1890–1970,* L-W Books, 1993; Bernard Levine, *Levine's Guide To Knives and Their Values, Third Edition* DBI Books, 1993; Bernard Levine, *Pocket Knives: The Collector's Guide To Identifying, Buying, and Enjoying Vintage Pocket Knives,* Apple Press, 1993; C. Houston Price, *The Official Price Guide To Collector Knives, Tenth Edition,* House of Collectibles, 1991; Jim Sargent, *Sargent's American Premium Guide To Pocket Knives & Razors, Identification and Values, 3rd Edition,* Books Americana, 1992; Ron Stewart and Roy Ritchie, *The Standard Knife Collector's Guide, 2nd Edition,* Collector Books, 1993.

Periodicals: *Knife World,* PO Box 3395, Knoxville, TN 37927; *The Blade,* 700 E. State St., Iola, WI 54990.

Collectors' Clubs: American Blade Collectors, PO Box 22007, Chattanooga, TN 37422; Canadian Knife Collectors Club, 3141 Jessuca Court, Mississauga, ON L5C1X7 Canada; Dare Blade Collectors' Society, 3938 Pineway Dr., Kitty Hawk, NC 27949; The National Knife Collectors Association, PO Box 21070, Chattanooga, TN 37421.

Museum: National Knife Collectors Museum, Chattanooga, TN.

Additional Listings: See *Warman's Americana & Collectibles* for more examples.

CASE

Case uses a numbering code for its knives. The first number (1–9) is the handle material; the second number (1–5) designates the number of blades; the third and fourth number (0–99) the knife pattern.

Stage (5), pearl (8 or 9), and bone (6) are most sought in handle materials. The most desirable patterns are 5165—folding hunters, 6185—doctors, 6445—scout, muskrat—marked muskrat with no number, and 6254—trappers.

In the Case XX series a symbol and dot code is used to designate a year.

1920–40
5111 ½ blade, lock	**600.00**
5452	**300.00**
6245, dog groomer	**200.00**
6261	**120.00**

1940–65
4200, melon taster, serrated blade	**150.00**
42507, "Office Knife" on handle	**100.00**
5265	**200.00**
61093	**175.00**
62009, Barlow	**100.00**
6214, with shield	**65.00**
640045R, scout	**25.00**
Muskrat	**90.00**

1965–70, XX series
5172, bulldog	**150.00**
5254	**85.00**
6111 ½	**100.00**
6143, Daddy Barlow	**40.00**
92042	**100.00**

1970–80 (number of dots indicates year)
2137, sod buster	**25.00**
52131, canoe	**100.00**
5375, stag	**70.00**
6246R, rigger	**45.00**
P13755, stag, Kentucky Bicentennial	**50.00**

KA-BAR (Union Cutlery Co, Olean, NY)

The company was founded by Wallace Brown at Tidioute, PA, in 1892. It was relocated in Olean, NY, in 1912. The products have many stampings including Union (inside shield), U–R Co, Tidioute (variations), Union Cutlery Co, Olean, NY, Alcut Olean, NY, Keenwell, Olean, NY, and Ka-Bar. The larger knives with a profile of a dog's head on the handle are most desirable. Pattern numbers rarely appear on a knife prior to the 1940s.

2217, rigger	**70.00**

61161, composition handle	**125.00**
6191, knife, fork, spoon	**625.00**
6250, elephant toe	**300.00**
6260, KF	**100.00**
Cigar Cutter	**150.00**

KEEN KUTTER (Simons Hardware, St. Louis, MO)

K1771 ¾, Daddy Barlow	**150.00**
K1898 ¾, toothpick	**100.00**
K8464 ¼, Kattle	**50.00**

REMINGTON, last made in 1940

R1273, bullet	**1,500.00**
R1535, florist	**80.00**
32373, cattle	**250.00**
R273, Texas Jack	**190.00**
3335, scout, red, white, and blue	**285.00**
4235, red, white, and blue	**200.00**
Bullet, authorized reproduction ..	**60.00**

WINCHESTER

1701, Barlow	**100.00**
1920, hunter	**1,100.00**
2070, office knife	**75.00**
2380, doctor's	**350.00**
3022, whittler	**250.00**
3376	**250.00**

OTHER MANUFACTURERS

Elephant Toe
Cattaraugus Cutlery Co	**300.00**
New York Knife Co	**350.00**

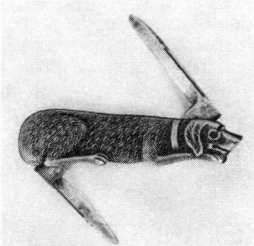

Figural, English, seated dog, $75.00.

Folding Hunter
  Bower, Atlanta, GA **85.00**
  C. Platts & Sons, Eldred, PA .. **100.00**
  Cattarangus Cutlery Co **350.00**
  Marbles Arms Co **350.00**
  New York Knife Co **500.00**
  Queen Cutlery Co, Titusville, PA **100.00**
  Schrade Walden, Walden, NY . **150.00**
  Union Razor Co, Titusville, PA . **100.00**
  Valley Forge Cutlery Co, NJ ... **200.00**
  Western States Cutlery Co,
    Boulder, CO, buffalo skull
    mark **300.00**

POISON BOTTLES

Cash Boots Chemist, emb "Not To Be Taken," green, 4⅛″ h, $15.00.

History: Poison bottles were designed to warn and prevent accidental intake or misuse of their poisonous contents, especially in the dark. Poison bottles generally were made of colored glass, embossed with "Poison" or a skull and crossbones, and sometimes were coffin-shaped.

John H. B. Howell of Newton, New Jersey, designed the first safety closure in 1866. The idea did not become popular until the 1930s when bottle designs became simpler and the user had to read the label to identify the contents.

References: Ralph and Terry Kovel, *The Kovels' Bottles Price List, 9th Edition,* Crown Publishers, 1992; Carlo and Dorothy Sellari, *The Standard Old Bottle Price Guide,* Collector Books, 1989.

Periodicals: *Antique Bottle and Glass Collector,* PO Box 187, East Greenville, PA 18041; *Bottles & Extras,* PO Box 154, Happy Camp, CA 90369.

Boyker's Pyrox Poison, clear **30.00**
Carbolic Acid Poison, 4⅜″ h, lattice design **45.00**
Coles Patent, Poison Ossidine, 7⅝″ h, cobalt blue **100.00**
Dutchers Dead Shot For Bed Bugs, 4⅞″ h, aqua **55.00**
Eccles–Chemist, 2⅝″ h, sq, cobalt blue **70.00**
Flask Form, 5½″ h, clear, acid etched skull and crossbones on one side, star on reverse **65.00**
Imperial Fluid Company Poison, embalming, clear **95.00**

Mercurous Iodide Yellow, 4″ h, black **25.00**
Norwich Coffin, 3⅜″ h, amber, emb, tooled lip **95.00**
P D & Co, 2½″ h, rect, amber, skull and crossbones **55.00**
Plumber Drug Co, 7½″ h, cobalt blue, lattice and diamond design **90.00**
Sharp & Dohme, 4⅝″ h, yellow amber, skull and crossbones .. **900.00**
Skull
  2⅞″ h, cobalt blue, emb "Poison," tooled mouth, smooth base **1,540.00**
  3⅜″ h, cobalt blue, tooled mouth, smooth base, emb "Poison" . **1,045.00**
Submarine, cobalt blue, emb "Poison," tooled mouth, smooth base, marked "Registered" ... **715.00**
Tinct Iodine, 2½″ h, cobalt blue, emb **130.00**
Vapo Cresolene, 4″ h, sq, clear .. **5.00**
Wm Radam's Microbe Killer, No 3, applied handle **85.00**

POLITICAL ITEMS

History: Since 1800 the American presidency has always been a contest between two or more candidates. Initially souvenirs were issued to celebrate victories. Items issued during a campaign to show support for a candidate were actively being distributed in the William Henry Harrison election of 1840.

Campaign items cover a wide variety of materials—buttons, bandannas, tokens, pins, etc. The only limiting factor has been the promoter's imagination. The advent of television campaigning has reduced the emphasis on individual items. Modern campaigns do not seem to have the variety of materials which were issued for earlier elections.

References: Herbert Collins, *Threads of History,* Smithsonian Institution Press, 1979; Stan Gores, *Presidential and Campaign Memorabilia With Prices, Second Edition,* Wallace-Homestead, 1988; Theodore L. Hake, *Encyclopedia of Political Buttons, United States, 1896-1972,* Americana & Collectibles Press, 1985; Ted Hake, *Hake's Guide to Presidential Campaign Collectibles,* Wallace-Homestead, 1992; Theodore L. Hake, *Political Buttons, Book II, 1920-1976,* Americana & Collectibles Press, 1977; Theodore L. Hake, *Political Buttons, Book III, 1789-1916,* Americana & Collectibles Press, 1978; Note: Theodore L. Hake issued a revised set of prices for his three books in 1991; Keith Melder, *Hail To The Candidate: Presidential Campaigns From Banners to Broadcasts,* Smithsonian Institution Press, 1992; Edmund B. Sullivan, *American Political Badges and Medalets, 1789-1892,* Quarterman Publications, 1981; Edmund B. Sullivan, *Collecting Political Americana,* Christopher Publishing House, 1991.

Collectors' Clubs: American Political Items Collectors, PO Box 134, Monmouth Junction, NJ 08852; Indiana Political Collectors Club, PO Box 11141, Indianapolis, IN 46201.

Periodicals: *Political Collector,* PO Box 5171, York, PA 17405; *The Political Bandwagon,* PO Box 348, Leola, PA 17540-0348.

Museums: National Museum of American History, Washington, DC; Smithsonian Museum, Washington, DC; Western Reserve Historical Society, Cleveland, OH.

Note: The abbreviation "h/s" is used to identify a head and shoulder photo or etching of a person.

Additional Listings: See *Warman's Americana & Collectibles* for more examples.

Advisor: Theodore L. Hake.

Hat, garrison style, "Vote Straight/Republican Conv., Chicago, '52," tan, blue letters, gold braiding, elephant and "Early Times" on back, $20.00.

Advertising Card
President and Mrs. Hayes, 3 x 4¼", green and cream, Mrs Hayes holding Mrs Potts' Cold Handle Sadirons, 1877–80 .. **50.00**
Theodore Roosevelt, 4 x 6", Fairbank's Fairy Soap adv on back, inscribed on front "Theodore Roosevelt, Colonel Volunteers (Rough Riders)," c1898 .... **55.00**
Tilden and Grant, 3½ x 4", Blackwell's Bull Durham Tobacco, metamorphic **30.00**
Arm Sash, 3 x 17", Roosevelt, fabric, glossy white, dark blue name, c1936 .... **25.00**
Ashtray, Dewey, 4" d, ¾" h, brass, "Dewey Headquarters/Hotel Walton/Phila 1940" **15.00**
Badge
Harrison, 1888, 1½ x 2½" diecut and emb brass shell, three prongs, log cabin, animal skin on front wall, barrel of hard cider **150.00**
National Republican Convention, Chicago, June 20, 1920, 4" h, brass segments joined by metal loops, eagle bar pin, red, white, and blue fabric ribbon holds Abraham Lincoln watch fob **75.00**
Bandanna
Carter/Mondale, 1980, 28" sq, bright green and white polyester **20.00**
Eisenhower, 26" sq, red, white,

and blue, shield and star design, "Win With Ike For President," inscription above large blue and white portrait **65.00**

Banner, 9 x 12", Franklin Roosevelt, red, white, and blue, FDR surrounded by red "V" symbol . **30.00**

Bookmark, 8¾" l, Lincoln, dark tan paper, black image and print, "Journal & Republican/Lowville NY Wednesday July 25, 1860" heading **275.00**

Bow Tie, 1960, 4¼ x 6½", clip–on, bright yellow, gold sparkles, hp, black and red design, "I'm For Kennedy" **65.00**

Bumper Sticker, 4 x 18", black, white, blue, and orange, inscribed "Kennedy For President," issued by "Massachusetts Committee For John F Kennedy For President" **18.00**

Cabinet Photo, 4 x 6½", Bryan, five photos, c1896 .... **25.00**

Calendar
FDR, 16 x 34", paper sheet for calendar, full color portrait surrounded by gold, green, blue, and brown Art Deco border, c1930 .... **20.00**

Wilkie/McNary, 12 x 15", cardboard, dark green and gold borders, color photo of US Capitol, inset black and white photos of Wilkie and McNary, inscribed "President Wendell Wilkie," "Vice–President Charles L McNary," and "Greetings And Good Wishes," c1940 .... **45.00**

Change Tray, Taft/Sherman, 4½", jugate, "Grand Old Party," tin, colored litho, names of Republican presidents from 1856 to 1908 printed around raised rim, color scene of candidates, American flags, and White House **70.00**

Cigar Band Set, twenty five 1 x 3" bands, emb color designs, color portraits of presidents Washington through T Roosevelt, c1904 **30.00**

Cigar Box, 8½ x 9½ x 1½", "True Yankee," portrait of T Roosevelt

surrounded by pair of eagles holding the constitution and a big stick, label inside lid, c1920 ... **50.00**

Clicker, Nixon, 2½" l, blue and white litho tin, "Click With Dick" **15.00**

Clock, 4 x 9 x 14", electric, white metal, gold, FDR at ship's wheel which surrounds clock dial, United Clock Corp, NY, c1930 . **125.00**

Cup, 3¼" h, Coffee With Kennedy, paper, red inscription, unused . **50.00**

Fan, Dewey, 10 x 10½", cardboard, diecut, white, dark blue . **30.00**

Feather, 6" l, Win with Landon, brown, yellow slogan, 1936 copyright Sport–A–Feather **20.00**

Flasher Ring
Kennedy, John, silver plastic base, color insert portrait of JFK and American flag, "35th President/John F Kennedy/1917–1963" **20.00**

Nixon, gold plastic base, light blue plastic disk inset, black and white picture of Nixon and Agnew, "President Nixon's Visit to Peking 21st Feb 1972" **15.00**

Flue Cover, 8" d, flat, "Hoover For President," litho tin, white and black, metal fastener riveted to reverse, c1928 .... **30.00**

Game, Meet The Presidents, 9½ x 19 x 2" box, unused, coin holder, presidential coins from Washington through Nixon, spinner, diecut circles for coins on game board, 1965, Selchow & Righter Co **20.00**

Glass, Bryan and Sewall, 3½", jugate, 1896 campaign, clear glass, frosted white portraits sur-

Pinback Button, I Like Ike, 1" d, red, white, and blue, $1.00.

rounded by stars, inscribed "Sixteen To One/Free Coinage Of Silver" 85.00

Harmonica, By Jiminy Peanut Harmonica, three–dimensional, peanut shape, raised dec, 6 x 7" card inscribed "The Big Happy Smile That Everybody Knows," Giftco, Inc, 1977 .... 8.00

Jug, miniature, ⅞" h, Harrison and Morton, brown pottery, small handle, black paper label 85.00

Key Ring
Democratic Convention, 1960, three–dimensional white metal donkey, painted brown, brass link chain, brass key ring holding large, heavy, brass key, one side of key shows smiling donkey standing on roof of jet plane, inscribed "Delegate Los Angeles 1960," reverse inscribed "Air Transport Association/Flying Donkey Club/National Democratic Convention" 10.00

Nixon, red, white, and blue plastic disk inscribed "President Nixon, Now More Than Ever," pair of pocket knife blades inside disk, brass key chain, orig gold box 15.00

Lapel Stud
Cox, lapel, small white metal rooster, name at center 25.00
Democratic 100 Club, brass, blue enamel circle, FDR at center 5.00

License Plate
Carter, 6 x 12", Inauguration, beige background, dark blue and red, set of 2 .... 25.00
Dewey, 6 x 10", fiberboard, dark blue ground, yellow inscription "Harrisburg Republican Club With Dewey–Bricker," 1944 .. 25.00
Hoover, 3½ x 12", red, white, and blue, embossed letters, c1928 .... 30.00

Magazine, 8½ x 11", *This Is Ike/A Picture Story Of The Man,* soft cover, 96 pgs, Holt & Co, 1952, 1st edition 5.00

Matchbook, 1½ x 2", New York/We Like Ike!, red, white, and blue,

unused, cardboard diecut of Ike inside cover, each individual match is lettered either "New York State" or "We Like Ike!" .. 15.00

Necktie, Dewey, full–size, rust color, silk screen, black, white, and yellow, image of Capitol dome above Dewey, Abraham & Strauss/Brooklyn, c1948 ...... 20.00

Newspaper
1797, March 15, *Columbian Sentinel,* Adams and Jefferson, 4 pgs, 12 x 19" 150.00
1865, April 16, *New York Herald,* Lincoln assassination, 8 pgs, 16 x 23" 450.00

Nodder
Kennedy For President, donkey, light brown head, yellow hat, red, white, and blue outfit, cardboard box with paper label inscribed "Donkey" 200.00
Nixon For President, 7½" h, elephant, composition, gray, red, white, and blue accents, stamped "Donkey" 125.00

Pen, 5" l, Goldwater, brass, black inscription, "Let's Win With Goldwater" 10.00

Pencil, 4" l, "Landon & Knox 1936," jugate, pencil stub in pull–out metal tube 175.00

Pennant, 29" l, Truman Inauguration, purple, yellow streamers, Truman portrait, caption "Our 33rd President" 75.00

Pinback Button
Bryan, ⅞" d, brown rooster, silver and gold tail feathers, stepping on gold thorn branch, 16 silver wheat stalks, inscribed "Bryan and Sewall" and "16 to 1," 1896 .... 85.00
Davis/Smith, ⅞" d, dark blue on white, John W Davis 1924 campaign 160.00
Dewey, 1944, 1¼", blue on white, inscribed "Dewey/The Racket Buster/New Deal Buster" 15.00
Eisenhower, 1956, 1⅛" d, red, white, and blue, inscribed "I Like Ike And Clyde" 24.00
McKinley, 1¼" d, In Memoriam

President Wm McKinley, closed back, St. Louis Button Company, 1901 . . . . 18.00

Nixon
1¼" d, Nixon/Agnew, 1968, jugate, black and white ovals, red, white, and blue designs, white ground 8.00
1¾ x 2¾", Nixon/Lodge, 1960, rect, red, white, and blue, light pink faces 10.00

Reagan/Bush, 1980, 1¾" d, jugate, black and white center, red, white, and blue edge, "Let's Make America Great Again" 5.00

Roosevelt/Wallace, 1940, 1¼" d, jugate, brown photos, bright red, white, and blue rim 40.00

TR/Lincoln, ⅞" d, brown and white photos, light blue ground, blue stars, gold eagle and rim, inscribed "50th Anniversary Of The Republican Party/1854 Lincoln/Roosevelt 1904" 35.00

Pipe, 6" l, Dewey, green and white sticker on bowl, Missouri Meerschaum Co, c1948 . . . . 50.00

Plate
Benjamin Harrison, 9" d, glazed, beige, dark brown portrait, leaf designs on rim, reverse imp mark "BM & Co Extra Quality," c1888 . . . . 30.00

Eisenhower, Presidential Inauguration 1953, 10" d, white, brown Capitol, list of past presidents, gold rim edge 40.00

For President William H Taft, 6" d, white china, center brown photo image, National China Co 20.00

Playing Cards, 2½ x 3½", Politicards, boxed deck, full color caricatures of Democrats, Republicans, and other political figures from 1980 . . . . 20.00

Pocket Knife, 3" l, McKinley, silver, flag design, McKinley portrait in wreath, "Our Martyred President" slogan, entwined ribbon and flower design with "God's Will, Not Ours, Be Done" slogan 25.00

Post Card, 3½ x 5½", Taft & Sherman A Winning Pair, black and white photos, ornate red, white and blue flag designs, emb gold details 45.00

Poster
For President Warren G Harding, 12½ x 18", large sepia photo, Edmonston Studio, Washington 70.00

Franklin D Roosevelt, 11 x 15", gray and white photo, bright red inscription, small caption "Photo August 1944" 25.00

Reagan, 18 x 27", satire, color, designed to resemble movie poster, Free Enterprise Films Presents Ronald Reagan In Bedtime For Brezhnev, two large scenes, six inset pictures, political figures in Western outfits, Oh Dawn, N.Y. distributors, copyright 1981 . . . . 25.00

Welcome President Nixon to Peking, 14 x 20", stiff cardboard, dark blue and orange, white ground, c1970 . . . . 20.00

Willkie–McNary, 10½ x 13½", red, white, and blue, imprinted "Pennsylvania Women's Committee, Philadelphia" 125.00

Program
Eisenhower
Inaugural Ball, 1953, 8½ x 11", dark blue cov, gold printing, gold cord spine, 16 pgs . . . 25.00
Republican Victory Kick–Off Dinner 1955–1956, football shape, brown, football design cov, gold inscription . . 55.00

Nixon Republican A Go Go, 9 x 12", 1966 fundraising event, Pittsburgh, 8 pgs, dark blue cov 75.00

Puppet
Johnson, 10" h, donkey, dark blue fabric, white mouth, dark maroon lettering, button eyes, 1964 . . . . 10.00

Nixon/Agnew, 12" h, caricature, fabric, large thick latex head, Nixon with blue fabric, white felt collar, light blue felt tie, Agnew with black and white check fabric, red collar and red felt bow tie, c1970, pr 80.00

Radio, Carter, 3 x 3 x 7½", figural, peanut, Carter's head at top, black plastic wrist strap, c1976 35.00

Ribbon

Harrison, 2½ x 5½", portrait, black signature, dark gold eagle design, red, white, and blue flags 150.00

Lincoln! Garfield! Grant!, Union Republican Ticket, 2 x 7", dark beige, red and blue design .. 125.00

President Truman, 2½ x 6", press, Philadelphia, Oct 6, 1948, red, white, and blue fabric, gold letters, 1½" metal stickpin 40.00

Republican National Convention, 9" l, dark olive green, silver lettering, diecut silvered brass eagle, Michigan state seal, "Alternate St Louis June 16, 1896" 75.00

Serving Tray, 10 x 13", Compliments of Cigar Makers' Union No 236 Reading, PA, litho metal, raised edge, dark green background, gold designs and lettering, black and light blue Union's paper stamp cigar box seal "Look For The Blue Label On Every Box" and "Smoke Only Union Made Cigars" inscriptions on edge, c1900 .... 135.00

Sheet Music, 8½ x 11", *Thomas E Dewey March,* 4 pgs, red, white, and blue, caption "Dedicated To A Great Governor Of New York State," includes photos of Dewey and the National Championship American Legion Band–Syracuse Post No 41, 1952 .... 10.00

Stickpin

Cleveland, ornate brass shell frame, sepia photo, c1888 ... 150.00

McKinley and Hobart, jugate, sepia photo 25.00

Ticket, 3 x 6", National Progressive Convention, Lincoln, Washington, and Jefferson pictures, "Good For First Day Only" 55.00

Tile, JFK, 6" d, white, full color illus

of Pres and Mrs. John F Kennedy, fabric covering and wall hanger on back 25.00

Tin Can, 2½" d x 4½" h, I Like Ike, elephant holding flag, red, white, and blue 25.00

Tintype, ⅞ x 1¹⁄₁₆", brass frame

George McClellan 125.00

Lincoln 300.00

Token

Blaine/Logan, 1" d, 1884 campaign, brass, jugate busts on front, "Union" and slogans on reverse 35.00

Garfield/Arthur, 1" d, 1880 campaign, brass, jugate busts on front, names and "Union" on reverse 25.00

Lincoln, ¾" d, 1864 campaign, copper, bust of Lincoln and "1864" on front, linked chain surrounding "O.K." on reverse 50.00

Watch Fob

Bryan/Stevenson, 7" l, brass clip holds two black fabric ribbons, oval silver metal slide holds two sepia photos 125.00

Taft, 1⅝" d, celluloid, portrait .. 50.00

POMONA GLASS

History: Pomona glass, produced only by the New England Glass Works and named for the Roman goddess of fruit and trees, was patented in 1885 by Joseph Locke. It is a delicate lead, blown art glass which has a pale, soft beige ground and a top one–inch band of honey amber.

There are two distinct types of backgrounds. First ground, made only from late 1884 to June 1886, was produced by fine cuttings through a wax coating followed by an acid bath. Second ground was made by rolling the piece in acid resisting particles and acid etching. Second ground was made in Cambridge until 1888 and until the early 1900s in Toledo where Libbey moved the firm after purchasing New England Glass works. Both methods produced a soft frosted appearance, with fine curlicue lines more visible on first ground pieces. Designs are used on some pieces, which were etched and then stained in color. The most familiar design is blue cornflowers.

Do not confuse Pomona with "Midwestern Pomona," a pressed glass with a frosted body and amber band.

References: Joseph and Jane Locke, *Locke Art Glass: A Guide For Collectors,* Dover Publications, 1987; Ellen T. Schroy, *Warman's Glass,* Wallace–Homestead, 1992.

Tumbler, first grind, enameled fern and daisy dec, $145.00.

Bowl, 5¼" d, second grind, fluted, Cornflower pattern **40.00**

Celery Vase, 6½" h, first grind, Cornflower pattern, blue dec .. **385.00**

Creamer, 3¾" h, enameled floral dec **50.00**

Lemonade Tumbler, first grind, leaf design, ring handle **75.00**

Nappy, 5¼" d, first grind, Cornflower pattern, blue dec, applied handle **125.00**

Pitcher, 7½" h, enameled floral dec **100.00**

Punch Cup, first grind, amber leaf design **45.00**

Rose Bowl, 4" d, 2⅝" h, second grind, three amber applied feet **160.00**

Spooner, 5" h, second grind, Blueberry pattern, red stemmed blueberry dec, crimped base **125.00**

Sugar, open, second grind, Cornflower pattern **150.00**

Toothpick, applied rigaree **235.00**

Tumbler, 3⅝" h, 2⅝" d, second grind, Cornflower pattern, diamond thumbprint, blue stain on flowers, straw color stain on top and leaves **150.00**

PORTRAIT WARE

History: Plates, vases, and other articles with portraits on them were popular in the second half of the 19th century. Although male subjects, such as Napoleon or Louis XVI, were used, the ware usually depicted a beautiful woman, often unidentified.

A large number of English and Continental china manufacturers made portrait ware. Because most ware was hand painted, an artist's signature often is found.

Dresser Tray, 12" l, two portrait medallions, four floral medallions, gold design, white ground, marked "Nippon" **225.00**

Plaque, pierced for hanging

4 x 5¾", waist–length portrait of young woman, wearing diaphanous gown, gilt gesso frame, sgd "Wagner," sgd on reverse "Marguerite Riesen," late 19th C **750.00**

9¾" d, cavalier, hp, artist sgd, marked "Coronet" **165.00**

10" d, Lund, hp, artist sgd "F Tenner," beehive mark **350.00**

Plate

8½" d, polychrome seated

Plate, Melle La Vallreie, blue mark "L. S. & S, Carlsbad, Austria," 8½" d, $35.00.

woman and floral design, blue rim, ormolu stand, artist sgd "Dillies," Sevres mark **250.00**

8¾" d, polychrome and gilt dec, artist sgd "G Perier," Sevres mark and "Mme de Cencin" . **115.00**

9½" d

Green and ivory, white reserves and polychrome floral dec, artist sgd "Morin," marked "Souise de Savoie, Sevres" **165.00**

Woman, gilt dec, artist sgd "O Brun," marked "Elisa Boneparte, M Imple de Sevres" . **125.00**

9¾" d

Marion, maroon luster, gold trim, raised turquoise beading, artist sgd, Royal Vienna **1,050.00**

Ruth, gold trim, sgd "Wagner," Royal Vienna mark **1,195.00**

Two mermaids and sailor, deep blue, gold design, artist sgd "Perges," Royal Vienna **1,000.00**

9⅞" d, pink, ivory reserves and polychrome floral dec, artist sgd "Morin," marked "Mme Elisabeth, Sevres" **200.00**

10" d

Scantily clad woman, dark green and gold ground, sgd "Royal Munich" and beehive mark **130.00**

Sowers, deep green, Royal Vienna, beehive mark **150.00**

10½" d, Konigin Louise, T Grassi, heavy gold rim, sgd "H. Wright," Dresden mark . . **1,295.00**

11½" d, dark haired woman, red, brown, and green dec, heavy gold, RS Prussia, Gaston mark 54 .... **200.00**

17½" d, Delft, hp, brown enameled minstrel portrait, mahogany frame, sgd and imp marks, late 19th C **500.00**

Ring Box, cov, green ground, marked "Nakara" **960.00**

Tray, 11¼" l, deep cobalt blue, couple dressed in 18th C clothing, gold and floral dec, artist sgd "Collier," Sevres **600.00**

Vase

6" h, enamel King Charles I and

James Graham Marquis of Montrose, blue ground, satyr mask handles, printed marks, Royal Worcester, c1862, price for pair **635.00**

8¾" h, Lady with Doves, maroon ground, turquoise jewels, marked "Prov. Saxe" **525.00**

9½" h, maiden portrait, gold framed cartouche, burgundy ground, artist sgd, Vienna shield mark, numbered **1,275.00**

15" h, cov, children and three young maidens, artist sgd "Nouck," Royal Vienna, imp beehive mark **1,450.00**

POSTERS

History: The poster was an extremely effective and critical means of mass communication, especially in the period before 1920. Enormous quantities were produced, helped in part by the propaganda role posters played in World War I.

Print runs of two million were not unknown. Posters were not meant to be saved. Once they served their purpose, they tended to be destroyed. The paradox of high production and low survival is one of the fascinating aspects of poster history.

The posters of the late 19th century and early 20th century represent the pinnacle of American lithographic printing. The advertising posters of firms such as Strobridge or Courier are true classics. Philadelphia was one center for the poster industry.

Europe pioneered in posters with high artistic and aesthetic content. Many major artists of the 20th century designed posters. Poster art still plays a key role throughout Europe today.

References: John Barnicoat, *A Concise History of Posters,* Harry Abrams, 1976; Tony Fusco, *Posters: Identification and Price Guide, Second Edition,* Avon Books, 1994; Walton Rawls, *Wake Up, America!: World War I and The American Poster,* Abbeville Press, 1988; Stephen Rebello and Richard Allen, *Reel Art: Great Posters From The Golden Age of The Silver Screen,* Abbeville Press, 1988; George Theofiles,

American Posters of World War I: A Price and Collector's Guide, Dafram House Publishers; Susan Theran, *Prints, Posters & Photographs: Identification and Price Guide*, Avon Books, 1993; Susan Theran and Katheryn Acerbo (eds.), *Leonard's Annual Price Index of Prints, Posters & Photographs*, Auction Index, published annually; Jon R. Warren, *Warren's Movie Poster Price Guide, 1993 Edition*, American Collector's Exchange, 1992; Bruce Lanier Wright, *Yesterday's Tomorrows: The Golden Age of Science Fiction Movie Posters, 1950–1964*, Taylor Publishing, 1993.

Periodical: *Hollywood Collectibles*, 2900 N. Meade St., Suite #4, Appleton, WI 54911.

Museum: Motion Picture Arts Gallery, New York, NY

Additional Listings: See *Warman's Americana & Collectibles* for more examples.

Advisor: George Theofiles.

ADVERTISING

Arrow Shirts, 22 x 28", c1925, litho, young couple in sailboat, blue water ground, orig frame . **450.00**
Chesterfield Cigarettes, cardboard **18.00**
Frigidaire, We Cool Our Milk With Frigidaire, 19 x 14", c1935, enameled dairy sign, white cow, blue ground, minor chipping . . . **110.00**
Heinz Baked Beans, 24 x 31", c1915, vivid colors **325.00**
Kodak, 17 x 26", c1920, monotone photo of young lady, beret, jacket, and necktie, self framed **200.00**
Lux Radio Theater, 15 x 23", c1930, full color, advertising Broadway hits broadcast through Columbia network, sponsored by Lux Toilet Soap . **40.00**
Moxie, Drink Moxie, 19 x 19", c1920, diecut head of soda fountain jockey **210.00**
Nivea, 44 x 60", Farago, 1938, bathing beauty, dark bronze suntan, gold and yellow background, floating tube holding bottle of Nivea suntan oil **550.00**
Prince Albert, The National Joy Smoke, 21 x 27", c1925, Chief Lean Wolf, bright colors **325.00**
Wrigleys Gum—Enjoy Daily—Chewing Helps You On The Job, 45 x 40", Otis Shepard, c1943, airbrushed design, workers welding, sparks flying in unison in front of repeated design of Wrigley's Gum, deep blues, greens, reds, and yellows **500.00**

MOVIE

One Sheet, silent
All Of A Sudden Norma, 41 x 81", BB Features, c1914, Bessie Barriscale, Ritchey stone litho, beautiful woman in front of moonlit window **550.00**
Charlie Chaplin In The Thief Catcher, 28 x 41", c1920, Chaplin with cigar leaning amid title, orange, brown, grays, red, and green, red borders **900.00**
Halfway To Heaven, 27 x 41", Paramount, c1925, Charles Buddy Rogers, Jean Arthur, bright blue and purple ground **275.00**
Story Seas, 27 x 41", Pathe, c1920, JP McGowan, Helen Holmes, litho of stars in front of burning and sinking steamship **350.00**
One Sheet, 27 x 41"
Adventure In Diamonds, Paramount, 1939, George Brent, Isa Miranda, starlet looking through jeweled facets, black ground **225.00**
Beyond Bengal, Showmen's Pictures, Harry Schenks, c1933, stone litho, boa constrictor attacking screaming native, lurid multicolor, cobalt blue ground **300.00**
Charlie's Aunt, Fox, 1941, Jack Benny, Kay Francis, Anne Baxter **275.00**
Daytime Wife, Fox, 1939, Tyrone Power, Linda Darnell, leggy secretary taking dictation at left, portrait close–ups of stars **475.00**
Gentlemen After Dark, United

Artists, 1942, Brian Donlevy, Miriam Hopkins, Preston Foster, looming portrait of Donlevy **150.00**

Invisible Menace, Warner Bros, 1937, Boris Karloff, Marie Wilson, litho, yellows, browns, and burnt oranges **425.00**

Madame X, MGM, 1937, Gladys George, John Beal, litho 1930's image **225.00**

Navy Spy, Grand National, 1937, Conrad Nagel, Eleanor Hunt, pulp cover like artwork of Nagel, flaming biplanes and dogfight **275.00**

Something For The Boys, 20th Century Fox, 1944, Carmen Miranda, Michael O'Shea, Phil Silvers, Earl Moran pin–up art of Vivian Blaine in leggy pose **325.00**

Two–Fisted Gentleman, Columbia, 1936, James Dunn, June Clayworth, boxing theme **225.00**

World And The Flesh, Paramount, 1932, George Bancroft, Miriam Hopkins, silk screen like design of Hopkins against black background, smiling Bancroft as Russian sailor **425.00**

Three Sheets, 41 x 81″

Abraham Lincoln, Feature Productions, 1930, Walter Huston, Una Merkel, D W Griffith production, image of Lincoln, white and blue foggy montage of other characters, Civil War battle **550.00**

Hoosier Schoolmaster, Monogram Pictures, 1935, Charlotte Henry, Norman Foster, litho portrait against book motif, full color, bright red ground **325.00**

Vertigo, Paramount, 1958, James Stewart, Kim Novak, Alfred Hitchcock film **650.00**

TRANSPORTATION

American–Hawaiian Steamship Company, 34 x 22″, Fred Pansing, c1900, chromolithograph, single stack steamer **975.00**

British Railways, 25 x 40″, The

Night Ferry, woodcut design, A N Wolstenholme, sleeping cars on ferry between London and Paris **280.00**

Fly To America By Clipper–Pan American World Airways, 28 x 42″, Von Arenburg, c1947, silk screen, Clipper in front of ghostly image of charging Indian chieftain, NY skyline **575.00**

In Old Kentucky, 27 x 40″, N C Wyeth, c1921, Modern Kentucky Is Served By The PA Railroad," Daniel Boone hunting **625.00**

Tahiti–Fly Teal, 24 x 38″, c1952, exotic, Australian, offset litho, stylized nude Tahitian maiden bathing, deep green ground, one of 7,000 copies **475.00**

United Air Lines–Colorado, 25 x 40″, c1953, Joseph Binder, fisherman, casting under shooting airliner **325.00**

United States Lines To America, 25 x 40″, c1935, US liner, unfurled American banner, reds, white, blues, black, yellows, upper right margin expertly rebuilt **675.00**

WORLD WAR I

America's Tribute to Britain, 20 x 30″, Fred G Cooper, woodcut design **350.00**

Columbia Calls, Enlist In The Army, 28 x 40″, Francis A Halstead, chromolithograph of Columbia with banner and sword, atop globe, sky blue ground ... **200.00**

Enlist Now And Go With Your Friends, 28 x 40″, Arthur N Edrop, issued by Mayor's Committee NYC, silhouettes of doughboys against American flag stripes ground **275.00**

Go Over The Top–US Marines, 21 x 28″, John A Coughlin, 1917, Marine leaps from trenches carrying Lewis gun **275.00**

Our American Boys In The European War, silent movie, Triangle Film, 27 x 41″, 1916, litho of wounded soldier being attended

to in front of American ambulance **375.00**
Pull Together Men—The Navy Needs Us, 14 x 22", Paul R Bloomhower, c1917, Boston Committee on Public Safety window card, sailors rowing lifeboat, dark green and orange sea ... **150.00**
The Salvation Army Lassie, 30 x 40", Keep Her on the Job **120.00**

World War II, WAAC, This Is My War Too!, $75.00.

WORLD WAR II

Arise Americans—Your Country And Your Liberty Are In Grave Danger, 28 x 41", McClelland Barclay, 1941, sailor preparing deck gun **150.00**
Become A Paratrooper—Jump Into The Fight, 17 x 25", Steve Savage, paratrooper and M–1 carbine **350.00**
Hit Back—Enlist In The Coast Guard—Remember Pearl Harbor, 22 x 28", 1943, silk screen, Coast Guard ensign, yellow ground **110.00**
If You Must Talk—Tell It To The Marines, 19 x 28", 1942, Marine talking to factory worker, bright orange ground **125.00**
Remember Dec 7th!, 28 x 40", tattered American flag flies at half

mast, grim background of fire and smoke **185.00**
United Nations Fight For Freedom, 29 x 40", Broder, 1942, flags of all nations, silver Statue of Liberty **100.00**

POT LIDS

History: Pot lids are the lids from pots or small containers which originally held ointments, pomades, or soap. Although a complete set of pot and lid is desirable to some collectors, lids are the most collectible. The lids frequently were decorated with multicolored underglaze transfers of rural and domestic scenes, portraits, florals, and landmarks.

The majority of the containers with lids were made between 1845–1920 by F. & R. Pratt, Fenton, Staffordshire, England. In 1920, F. & R. Pratt merged with Cauldon Ltd. Several lids were reissued by the firm using the original copper engraving plates. They were used for decoration and never served as actual lids. Reissues by Kirkhams Pottery, England, generally have two holes for hanging and often are marked as reissues. Cauldon, Coalport, and Wedgwood were other firms making reissues.

References: Susan and Al Bagdade, *Warman's English & Continental Pottery & Porcelain, 2nd Edition,* Wallace–Homestead, 1991; A. Ball, *The Price Guide to Pot–Lids And Other Underglaze Multicolor Prints On Ware, Second Edition,* Antique Collectors Club, 1991 value update; Ronald Dale, *The Price Guide To Black and White Pot Lids, 2nd Edition,* Antique Collectors Club, 1987; Barbara and Sonny Jackson, *American Pot Lids,* published by authors, 1987.

Note: Sizes are given for actual pot lids; size of any framing not included.

Areca Nut Tooth Paste
Cleansing Preserving And Beautifying The Teeth/Lewis and Burrows Ltd, London, roses, black on white, 2¾" d **80.00**
For Cleansing and Whitening The Teeth And Gums/Timothy White Company Chemists,

Burgess's Genuine Anchovy Paste, black transfer, c1890, 3¼" d, $35.00.

Portsmouth, geometric center, black on brown, 2¹⁵⁄₁₆" d 85.00

Bazin's Ambrosial Shaving Cream/X Bazin, Philadelphia/ Premium Perfumery, American eagle center, flower assortment below, blue on white, 3¹⁄₁₆" d .. 700.00

Cherry Tooth Paste, B & Co, cherry cluster on leafy branch, black on white, 2⁹⁄₁₆" d 300.00

Cold Cream/R Lemmon, Chemist, The Pharmacy Hythe, geometric border, gray on white, light rust stain, 2½" d 70.00

Huggin's Cherry Tooth Paste/For Cleansing Beautifying and Preserving The Teeth & Gums/ Trademark R Higgins, Chemist 235 Strand Next Temple Bar London, street scene, black on white, 2¾" d 180.00

Napoleon Price & Cos. Cherry Toothpaste/For Beautifying & Preserving The Teeth & Gums, 27 Bond St, London, bust of Queen Victoria and Prince Albert, shades of yellow, black on white, 3⅜" d 800.00

Rimmels, Cherry Tooth Paste, cherry bunch, deep yellow and pink cherries, green leaves, yellow–orange black band on white, 3" d 600.00

Senior's Carbolic Tooth Paste For Preserving & Beautifying The Teeth & Gums Trademark, kiwi feeding, outer geometric border, black on white, 2⁵⁄₁₆" d 145.00

Victoria Carbolic Toothpaste/For Preserving And Beautifying The Teeth/Perfumes The Breath, Strengthens The Gums/A B, warrior and shield lying against lion, black on white, sq, rounded corners, 2½" l 175.00

PRATT

PRATT
FENTON

PRATT WARE

History: The earliest Pratt earthenware was made in the late 18th century by William Pratt, Lane Delph, Staffordshire, England. From 1810–1818, Felix and Robert Pratt, William's sons, established their own firm, F. & R. Pratt, in Fenton in the Staffordshire district. Potters in Yorkshire, Liverpool, Sunderland, Tyneside, and Scotland copied the wares.

The wares consisted of relief molded jugs, commercial pots and tablewares with transfer decoration, commemorative pieces, and figure and animal groups.

Much of the early ware is unmarked. The mid–19th century wares bear several different marks in conjunction with the name Pratt, including "& Co."

References: Susan and Al Bagdade, *Warman's English & Continental Pottery & Porcelain, Second Edition,* Wallace–Homestead, 1991; John and Griselda Lewis, *Pratt Ware 1780–1840,* Antique Collectors' Club, 1984.

Additional Listing: Pot Lids.

Box, money, 5" h, house form, two children peering from windows, flanked by man and woman, blue, ochre, brown, and green, restored base and chimney, c1820 .... 600.00

Creamer, 4¾" h, children at play, heart shaped cartouche, underglaze blue, green, and brown .. **200.00**

Figure, 8½" h, mother with child, 19th C **475.00**

Jug, 8¾" h, Miser, hairline, repaired spout, 19th C **375.00**

Pipe

8" l, looped snakelike stem, bowl modeled as half figure of Admiral Nelson, military coat and tall hat, molded ribbons titled "Nelson" and "Forever," clasped hands, blue, yellow, orange, and brown underglazed enamels, c1800 .....**1,300.00**

8¼" l, coiled and twisted stem, bowl modeled with bust of woman's head, blue, yellow, and orange underglaze enamels, slight glaze wear, c1800 .**1,400.00**

8½" l, snake, coiled stem, molded scale body, head with open mouth holding bowl, allover brown, green, blue, and yellow underglazed enamel cross and line dec, stained mouthpiece, wear, c1800 .... **750.00**

10" l, snake, scaled body, head with open mouth holding bowl, double loop form and molded cottage figure to stem, blue, yellow, brown, and orange underglazed enamels, slight staining, nicks, c1800 ....**2,600.00**

12¾" l, elongated, molded fluted bowl, green, orange, and blue

underglazed enamel dot and dash dec, stem damage, c1800 ....**1,300.00**

Pitcher

7¼" h, relief scenes of children, heart shaped medallions, titled "Sportive Innocence" and "Mischievous Sport," rim hairlines, chip on base **250.00**

7½" h, relief busts and floral dec, multicolored, minor glaze wear and stains **400.00**

Platter, 12" l, Blind Fiddler **100.00**

Sugar, cov, 5¾" h, almond shaped relief medallion of woman and child, figural swan finial, stains, minor wear, and chips **400.00**

Teabowl and Saucer, 5¼" d, peafowl perched on leafy branch, blue, yellow, green, and ochre . **275.00**

Tea Caddy, 5¼" h, 19th C **275.00**

Vase, 7" h, finger, four colors, leaves and flowers, minor wear, slight hairline, price for pair ... **950.00**

PRINTS

History: Prints serve many purposes. They can be a reproduction of an artist's paintings, drawings, or designs. Prints themselves often are an original art form. Finally, prints can be developed for mass appeal as opposed to an aesthetic statement. Much of the production of Currier & Ives fits this latter category. Currier & Ives concentrated on genre, urban, patriotic, and nostalgia scenes.

Prints are beginning to attract a wide following. This is partially because prices have not matched the rapid rise in oil and other paintings.

References: William P. Carl, *Currier's Price Guide to American and European Prints at Auction, Third Edition,* Currier Publications, 1994; Clifford P. Catania, *Boudoir Art,* Schiffer Publishing, 1994; Karen Choppa and Paul Humphrey, *Maud Humphrey: Her Permanent Imprint On American Illustration,* Schiffer Publishing, 1993; Victor J. W. Christie, *Bessie Pease Gutmann: Her Life and Works,* Wallace-Homestead, 1990; Frederic A. Conningham and Colin Simkin, *Currier & Ives Prints, Revised Edition,*

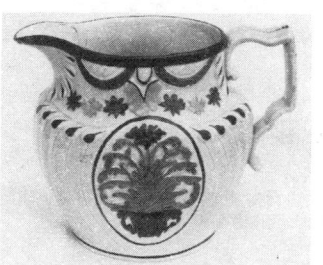

Pitcher, molded form, green, yellow, orange, and brown enamel, 5⅞" h, $165.00.

Crown Publishers, 1970; Erwin Flacks, *Maxfield Parrish Identification & Price Guide, Second Edition,* Collectors Press, 1994; Patricia L. Gibson, *R. Atkinson Fox & William M. Thompson Identification & Price Guide,* Collectors Press, 1994; William R. Holland, Clifford P. Catania, and Nathan D. Isen, *Louis Icart: The Complete Etchings,* Schiffer Publishing, 1994; William R. Holland and Douglas L. Congdon–Martin, *The Collectible Maxfield Parrish,* Schiffer Publishing, 1993; Denis C. Jackson, *The Price & Identification Guide to J. C. Leyendecker & F. X. Leyendecker,* published by author, 1983; Denis C. Jackson, *The Price & Identification Guide To: Maxfield Parrish, Eighth Edition,* published by author, 1992; M. June Keagy and Joan M. Rhoden, *More Wonderful Yard-Long Prints,* published by authors, 1992; William D. Keagy et al., *Those Wonderful Yard-Long Prints & More,* published by authors, 1989; Robert Kipp, *Currier's Price Guide to Currier & Ives Prints, Third Edition,* Currier Publications, 1994; Stephanie Lane, *Maxfield Parrish: A Price Guide,* L-W Book Sales, 1993; J. L. Locher (ed.), *M. C. Escher, His Life And Complete Graphic Work,* Harry N. Abrams, 1992; Coy Ludwig, *Maxfield Parrish,* Schiffer Publishing, 1973, 1993 reprint with value guide; Rita C. Mortenson, *R. Atkinson Fox, His Life and Work,* Volume 1 (1991, 1994 value update), Volume 2 (1992), L-W Book Sales; *Print Price Index '94: 1992–1993 Auction Season,* Gordon and Lawrence Art Reference, 1993; Susan Theran, *Prints, Posters & Photographs: Identification and Price Guide,* Avon Books, 1993; Susan Theran and Katheryn Acerbo (eds.), *Leonard's Annual Price Index of Prints, Posters & Photographs,* Auction Index, published annually.

Collectors' Clubs: American Antique Graphics Society, 5185 Windfall Rd., Medina, OH 44256; American Historical Print Collectors Society, PO Box 201, Fairfield, CT 06430; Gutmann Collector Club, PO Box 4743, Lancaster, PA 17604; Prang-Mark Society, PO Box 306, Watkins Glen, NY 14891.

Periodicals: *Audubon Newsletter,* 4700 N. Habana Ave., Tampa, FL 33614; *Journal of the Print World,* 1008 Winona Rd., Meredith, NH 03253; *The Illustrator Collector's News,* PO Box 1958, Sequim, WA 98382; *The Print Collector's Newsletter,* 119 East 79th St., New York, NY 10021.

Museums: Audubon Wildlife Sanctuary, Audubon, PA; John James Audubon State Park and Museum, Henderson, KY; National Portrait Gallery, Washington, DC.

Reproduction Alert: Reproductions are a problem, especially Currier & Ives prints. Check the dimensions before buying any print.

Additional Listing: See Wallace Nutting.

Appel, Karen, Two People Autumn Like, color serigraph, sgd in pencil, numbered 3/160, full sheet, 21½ x 29½" **345.00**

Baumann, Gustave, American, 1881–1971, color woodcut, laid paper, hand–in–heart watermark, sgd "Gustave Baumann" in pencil, hand–in–heart chop lower right, titled in pencil lower left, numbered in pencil lower right, framed
  Bound for Taos, edition of 120, 9½ x 11" image size **4,890.00**
  Ranchos de Taos, edition of 125, 9½ x 11¼" image size . **4,320.00**

Bellows, George, American, 1882–1925, The Irish Fair, litho, sgd "George Bellows" lower right and on stone lower left, sgd "Bolton Brown imp" in pencil lower left, pencil title lower center, edition of 84, framed, 18½ x 20½" image size **1,265.00**

Benson, Frank Weston, American, 1862–1951, etching, sgd "Frank W. Benson" in pencil lower left
  Baldpates, 1924, edition of 150, framed, 7¾ x 9¾" plate size . **490.00**
  Ducks Swimming, 1914, inscribed "To A. W. Elson" in pencil lower right, edition of 50, framed, 5 x 9⅞" plate size **1,380.00**

Benton, Thomas Hart, American, 1889–1975, litho, published by Associated American Artists, edition of 250
  Aaron, 1941, sgd "Benton" in pencil lower right and on the stone lower left, framed, 12¾ x 9½" image size **1,380.00**

J. C. Leyendecker, Cuchulain In Battle, color litho, 1907, $35.00.

Planting, 1939, sgd "Benton" in pencil and in the matrix lower right, matted, full sheet, deckled edges, 10 x 12⅝" image size **1,150.00**
Prodigal Son, 1939, sgd "Benton" in pencil lower right, on stone lower right, matted, 10¼ x 13¼" image size **1,380.00**
Calder, Alexander, American, 1898–1976, Flowers, litho, printed in black and red, sgd "Calder" in pencil lower right, inscribed "E. A." in pencil lower left, framed, 24½ x 18½" sight size **550.00**
Cassatt, Mary, drypoint etching, laid paper, watermark, c1904, posthumous printing
Looking into the Hand Mirror No. 3, 8⅛ x 5⅞" **550.00**
Sara Smiling, 9 x 6⅛" **490.00**

Chagall, Marc, Nude with Fan, drypoint etching, 1925, "Planche tiree pour le Portefeuille des Peintres Graveurs Independents, 31 Janvier 1925–Ch. Zervos" inscribed in plate, mat burn, 8½ x 11" **815.00**
Currier & Ives, hand colored litho
A Home On The Mississippi, matted, framed, 17½ x 21½" . **500.00**
American Fruit Piece, 13¾ x 16¾", molded walnut frame .. **175.00**
American Homestead Suite, Summer, Autumn, Winter, Spring, 1869, 1" margins, mat burn on verso of Summer and Autumn, price for set of four . **980.00**
Little Kitty, cross corner frame, white porcelain buttons, gilt liner, 14 x 16" **155.00**
The Darktown Fire Brigade To The Rescue, framed, 17¼ x 13¼" **385.00**
Dohanos, Stevan, American, b1907, The Mourner, 1932, litho, wove paper, "Kilmory Wove" watermark, sgd "Stevan Dohanos" in pencil lower right, titled in pencil lower left, matted, 8½ x 7½" image size **375.00**
Dow, Arthur Wesley, American, 1857–1922, Among the Sand Hills, Cow and Dunes, c1910, color woodblock, unsgd, matted, 6½ x 4⅜" image size **4,025.00**
Fiene, Ernest, American, 1894–1965, City Lights, etching, sgd "Ernest Fiene" in pencil lower right, Associated American Artists label on reverse, framed, 11¼ x 9" plate size **520.00**
Gorsline, Douglas Warner, American, 1939–85, Express Stop, etching, laid paper, partial figural watermark, 1948, sgd "Douglas W Gorsline" in pencil lower right, published by Society of American Etchers, matted, orig presentation folder, 6½ x 5¾" plate size **635.00**
Haden, Sir Francis Seymour, British, 1818–1910
Breaking Up the Agamemnon No. 1, etching with drypoint,

brown and black ink, sgd "Seymour Haden" in pencil lower right and date "...1870" in pencil lower left, annotated "proof of old English paper, date about 1800 (sic)..." along lower margin, framed, 7⅝ x 16⅛" **550.00**

On the Test, etching, laid paper, partial watermark, sgd "Seymour Haden" in the plate lower right, annotated along lower margin, matted, minor mat toning and soiling, 6 x 9" plate size **200.00**

Homer, Winslow, American, 1836–1910, Mending the Tears, etching, sgd "Winslow Homer N. A." in pencil next to anchor remarque lower left, signed in plate lower right, inscribed with publication information in the plate along upper edge, framed, sheet affixed to strainer, 17¼ x 23" plate size **8,050.00**

Icart, Louis, French, 1888–1950, color etching, aquatint, additional coloring

Don Juan, sgd "Louis Icart" in pencil lower right, inscribed "Copyright 1928 by L. Icart - Paris" in the plate upper right, "Editions d'Art...Paris" in plate upper left, annotated "A/413" next to artist's windmill drystamp lower left, framed, 21¼ x 14" plate size **1,150.00**

La Colombe Blessee (Wounded Dove), sgd "Louis Icart" in pencil lower right, inscribed "15" in pencil next to artist's windmill drystamp lower left, inscribed "Copyright 1929 by L. Icart, Paris," in plate upper left, oval format, framed, 21¼ x 16½" plate size **1,150.00**

La Glycine (Wisteria), sgd "Louis Icart" in pencil lower right, inscribed "© Copyright 1940 by L. Icart N. Y." in the plate upper right, artist's windmill drystamp lower left, framed, laid down, subtle creases, some defor-

mations to paper, 18 x 22" plate size **900.00**

L'Invitee (Guest), sgd "Louis Icart" in pencil lower right, inscribed "© Copyright 1940 by L. Icart N.Y." in the plate upper left, artist's windmill drystamp lower left, framed, several tiny abrasions/pin holes within image, 17½ x 11½" plate size . **1,265.00**

New Friends, sgd "Louis Icart" in pencil lower right, inscribed "109" in pencil lower left, inscribed "Copyright 1925 by les Graveurs Modernes...Paris" in plate upper left, oval format, framed, subtle toning and staining, 18 x 15" plate size . **805.00**

Spilled Milk, sgd "Louis Icart" in pencil lower right, inscribed "E/380" in pencil lower left, oval format, framed, laid down, subtle toning, losses to edges of margins, 17¼ x 21½" plate size **1,610.00**

Kent, Rockwell, American, 1882–1971, Girl on Cliff, 1930, wood engraving, sgd "Rockwell Kent" in pencil lower right, total edition of 1750, framed, 6½ x 4⅞" image size **635.00**

Kirmse, Marguerite, American, 1885–1954, Steady...Two Pointers in a Field, etching, sgd "Marguerite Kirmse" in pencil lower right, titled in pencil lower left, framed, 9 x 13½" plate size ... **345.00**

Lewis, Martin, American, 1881–1962, etching, laid paper, figural watermark, edition of 100

Chance Meeting, 1941, sgd "Martin Lewis" in pencil lower right, published by Society of American Etchers, matted, orig presentation folder, 10½ x 7½" plate size **3,220.00**

Quarter of Nine, Saturday's Children, 1929, sgd "Martin Lewis imp" in pencil lower right and in the plate lower left, label on reverse, framed, 10 x 12¾" plate size **7,475.00**

Lum, Bertha, American, 1868–1954, Parade of the Marionettes,

1927, raised ink hand–colored woodblock, sgd and inscribed "copyright 1927 by Bertha Lum" in pencil lower center, Doll & Richard label on reverse, framed, 17½ x 23½" image size **750.00**

Marsh, Reginald, American, 1898–1954, etching, Whitney Museum edition of 100, Whitney Museum drystamp lower right, numbered 2/100 in pencil lower left, matted

Star Burlesk, 1933, 12 x 8¾" plate size **520.00**

Steeplechase, 1932, 7¾ x 10¾" plate size **290.00**

Tenth Ave at 27th St, sgd and dated "Marsh 1931" in the plate lower right, 7¾ x 10¾" plate size **865.00**

Matisse, Henri, French, 1869–1954, Le repos du modele, litho, 1922, sgd "Henri Matisse" in pencil lower right, in reverse on stone upper right, publisher's drystamp lower right, published by Galerie des Peintres–Graveurs Paris, framed, 8¾ x 11½" image size **3,740.00**

Parrish, Maxfield, Twilight, 23½ x 19", orig ½" w frame **235.00**

Pennell, Joseph, American, 1857–1926, The River Front, Brooklyn, etching, plate tone on paper, sgd "J Pennell imp" lower center and lower right plate, reverse annotated in ink, 7⅞ x 9⅞" plate size **1,035.00**

Picasso, Pablo, Spanish, 1881–1973

Francoise, 1946, litho, sgd "Picasso" in pencil lower right, numbered "38/50" in pencil lower left, edition of 50, framed, full sheet, deckled edges, annotations and hinge tab on reverse, 25½ x 19½" sheet size **14,950.00**

Tete de femme, de profil, drypoint on heavy wove paper, unsgd, framed, mat burn, pale foxing, 11½ x 9¾" **6,325.00**

Ripley, Aiden Lassell, American, 1896–1969, Grouse and Vines, 1936, drypoint, wove paper,

"France" watermark, sgd "A. Lassell Ripley" in pencil lower right, matted, 6½ x 8¾" plate size **375.00**

Sloan, John, American, 1871–1951, Memory, 1906, etching, sgd "John Sloan" in pencil lower right, sgd and dated "John Sloan 1906" in plate lower right, edition of 110, framed, 7⅜ x 9" plate size **2,415.00**

Steinlen, Theophile Alexandre, Swiss/French, 1859–1923, Sleeping Tabby Cat, etching with aquatint, sgd "Steinlen" in pencil lower right, framed, 5¾ x 10" plate size **990.00**

Tissot, James Jacques Joseph, French, 1836–1902, Reverie, etching and drypoint, laid paper, sgd "J. Tissot" in pencil lower left and "J. J. Tissot 1889" in the plate upper right, artist's monogram stamp in red upper right, matted, unobtrusive soiling marks, annotations to margins and reverse, 9 x 4½" plate size **2,875.00**

Toulouse–Lautrec, Henri de, French, 1864–1901, litho, printed in color on paper, monogrammed and identified in matrix, unmatted, unframed

Babylone D'Allemagne, linen back, creases, abrasions, toning, paper losses at edges, 48 x 34" sheet size **4,900.00**

Troupe de Mlle Eglantine, Japan backing, unobtrusive creases, minute paper losses to edges, 24 x 31½" sheet size **7,475.00**

Wengenroth, Stow, American, 1906–1977, litho, sgd "Stow Wengenroth" in pencil lower right, numbered "Ed/40" in pencil lower left, annotated lower margin, edition of 40, matted

Brooklyn Bridge in Winter, 1959, 10⅝ x 16" image size **5,475.00**

Grand Central, 1949, 8¾ x 16" image size **2,990.00**

Lower Fifth Avenue, 1959, 10¼ x 15¾" image size **6,900.00**

Whistler, James Abbott McNeill, American, 1834–1903, Street at

Saverne, etching on fine paper, sgd "Whistler" in the plate lower left, identified on label from Frederick Keppel and Co, NY, on reverse, framed, laid down, annotated in margins, 8 x 6¼" plate size **865.00**

Wilson, John, American, b1922, Street Car Scene, 1945, litho on paper, sgd "John Wilson 1945" in pencil lower right, sgd "Wilson" on stone lower left, titled in pencil lower left, framed, mat toning, soiling to margin, 11¼ x 14¾" image size **2,070.00**

Wood, Grant, American, 1892–1942, February 1941, litho, "Rives" watermark, sgd "Grant Wood" in pencil lower right, Associated American Artists label on reverse, framed, 8⅞ x 12" image size **5,175.00**

Zorn, Anders, Swedish, 1860–1920

Guyilli II, etching, sgd "Zorn" in pencil lower right, monogrammed and dated "1918..." in plate lower left, framed, unobtrusive mat burn, several fox marks, 7¾ x 5¾" plate size . . **460.00**

Henri Marquand, etching, sgd "To my friend Ch. Nagel Zorn," in ink along lower edge, monogrammed and dated "...1893" in the plate lower center, matted, toning, soiling, glue residue in margins, 11 x 7¾" plate size **825.00**

The Hair Ribbon, etching, laid paper, figural watermark, sgd "Zorn" in pencil lower right, sgd and dated in the plate lower left, annotated along lower margin, matted, full sheet with deckled edges, 11⅞ x 8" plate size **1,035.00**

PRINTS—JAPANESE

History: Buying Japanese woodblock prints requires attention to detail and skilled knowledge of the subject. The quality of the impression (good, moderate, or weak), the

color, and condition are critical. Various states and strikes of the same print cause the price to fluctuate. Knowing the proper publisher and censor's seals is helpful in identifying an original print.

Most prints were recopied and issued in popular versions. These represent the vast majority of the prints found in the marketplace. These popular versions should be viewed solely as decorative since they have little value.

A novice buyer should seek expert advice before buying. Talk with a specialized dealer, museum curator, or auction division head.

The listings below concentrate on details to show the depth of data needed for adequate pricing. Condition and impression are good, unless indicated otherwise.

O = Oban, 10 x 15"	C = Chuban,
t = tat-e,	7 x 10"
large in width	H = Hosoban,
y = yoke-e,	5½ x 13"
large in length	T = Triptyck

Reference: Gloria and Robert Mascarelli, *Warman's Oriental Antiques,* Wallace-Homestead, 1992.

Collectors' Club: Ukiyo-E Society of America, Inc., FDR Station, PO Box 665, New York, NY 10150.

Museum: Honolulu Academy of Fine Arts, Honolulu, HI.

Chikanobu

Four Beautiful Women in a Garden on a Summer Evening, c1880, woodblock, excellent condition, OT **225.00**

Four ladies observing moon reflecting rice paddies, late 19th C, good condition, T **360.00**

Eisen, Keisai, 1790–1848, Aizuri–E snow scene, sgd and sealed "Keisai," Etsucho publisher's seal, kiwame seal **3,850.00**

Eizan, Kakemono–E, humorous tiger emerging from behind large stalk of bamboo, sgd "Kikugama Eizan hitsu," good impression, fair color, good condition **375.00**

Foujita, Tsugaharu, 1886–1968, Pekinese, litho with color on paper, sgd "Foujita" lower right, number "50/50" in ink lower left,

Rocky landscape with flowering tree, bird, printed on rice paper, 36 x 14½", $150.00.

sgd in plate upper right, framed, 9½ x 12" image size **1,380.00**
Gakutei, Yashima, courtier and dog, cartouche with poems, Uji shui monogatari series, sgd "Gakutei" **2,200.00**
Harunobo, courtesan showing the neck of her kamoro before a screen dec with farmers harvesting rice, entitled *Jin, Virtue,* from The Five Cardinal Virtues series, sgd "Suzuki Harunobo ga," Ct **7,750.00**
Hasui, Kawase
    Morning at Motoyoshiwara, dated 1940, first edition **220.00**
    Snow in Shiba Park—Tokyo, 1933, Watanabe publisher, first edition **1,155.00**
Hiroshige
    Lady cutting flowers, lady feed-

ing birds, and third lady cooking, minor worm holes, T **1,325.00**
The Landing Entry of the Seven Ri Ferry at Kuwana, from Fifty–three Stations of the Tokaido Road, Oy **1,210.00**
Two ladies playing board game, from 100 Poems by 100 Poets series, Ot **145.00**
Hiroshige II, Chuban Album, complete set of series Edo meisho yonju hakkei/Forty–eight famous Sights of Edo, each sgd "Hiroshige–ga," some margins with aratame/negetsu (c1860) and publisher Tsuta–ya Kichizo seals, good states, laid down, Ct **1,350.00**
Hokuji, Omocha–e with inset okubi–e portrait of IChimura Kakitsu next to eight depictions of various hair styles and hats, individual label cartouches, sgd "Shunkosai Hokushu–ga" with artist, carver, and publisher Toshijura–ya Shinbei seals, fair impression, Ot **325.00**
Hokusai, Kirifura Fall in Kurokawa Mountain, from Journey to Waterfalls of All the Provinces series, sgd, Kiwame seal **6,050.00**
Jun'ichiro, Sekino, titled Monjuro and Jihei, scene from bunraku love suicide, sgd "Jukichiro Sekino" in pencil, printed signature "Jun Sekino" and seal Jun on bottom, slightly soiled margin, reverse with masking tape **1,540.00**
Kawase Hasui
    Ebisu Harbor, Sado Island in Winter, from Tabi miyage dinishi series, sgd "Hasui," seated Kawase, dated Taishi 10 (1921), Watanabe publisher's seal, Oy **1,200.00**
    Okayamajo no Asahi/Dawn at Okayama Castle, dated Showa 30 (1955), misty view of castle, sgd "Hasui," circular Watanabe Shosaburo seal, good impression, color, and state, Ot **350.00**
Kikumaro, courtesan seated by hibachi, surrounded by female attendants, blossoming prunus

and sparrow, sgd "Kikumaro hitsu," fair impression, poor color, stained, Ot 275.00

Kotondo, Beauty In Sudden Shower, sgd "Genjin ga," dated Showa 4 (1929), numbered 84/200, published by Sakai–Kawaguchi, large Ot 1,000.00

Kunichika, Danjuro, samurai holding five pipes, Ot 140.00

Kunisada, woman washing face, cartouche ground of Shinto temple, Yamamoto–ya, Heikichi, Eikyudo, 1835 date mark, Ot 275.00

Kuniyoshi
Giyu hakken–den series, depicting Inyuama Dosetsu, sgd "Ichiyasi Kuniyoshi–ga," two naushi and publisher seals, fair impression and color, faded, fair state, Ot 100.00

Tanuki print showing four drunken badgers dancing and singing, illus text passage, sgd "Ichiyusai Kuniyoshi–giga," and one "Nanushi" and anonymous publisher's seal, fair impression and color, slightly faded, Ot 150.00

Oda Kazuma, entitled Matsue Ohashi/The Great Bridge of Matsue, group of figures crossing bridge in snowstorm, sgd "Kazuma hitsu," red artist's seal, right margin with title and dated Taisho 13 (1924), very good impression and color, Oy 850.00

Ohayagashi, Kuniyoshi, Fisherman, c1830, wood block, matted and unframed, 10½ x 15" w . . . 175.00

Saito, Kiyoshi, Aizu Yanaizu Fukushima, village rooftops, dated 1965, framed, 15½ x 21," Oy . . 610.00

Tadashi, Nakayama, girl wearing checkered patterned frock holding sunflower, sgd "T Nakayama," dated 1957, Nakayama seal on reverse 610.00

Tori Kyonagi, from Hinagata wakana no hatsumoyo series, sgd "Kiyonaga ga," fair impression and color, faded, rough margins, Ot 750.00

Toyokuni I, Utagawa, The Actor Matsumoto Koshire V and Another Actor in a Theatrical Scene, c1810, woodblock print, sgd "Toyokuni Ga," published by Eijudo 175.00

Toyokuni III, Utagawa, Night Scene: Two Actors Brandishing Torches, and a Woman Holding a Lantern, 1860, woodblock print, sgd "Toyokuni Gwa," OT . 275.00

Toyonari, Shanghai dancers, artist's brown seal, dated 1924, mica ground, good condition . . 4,675.00

Utamaro, attendant passing letter to dreaming courtesan, sgd "Utamaro hitsu," published Tsutaya Juzaburo, good impression, Ot 2,200.00

Yakamura Koko (Toyonari), three–quarter view of actor Matsumoto Koshiro as Sekibei, sgd "Koka–ga," publisher's seal and blind printed date Taisho 8 (1919), good impression and color, Ot . 900.00

Yoshida, Hiroshi, Soshu, dated 1940, jizuri seal, sgd in pencil, Oy 250.00

Yoshida, Toshi
Heirinji Temple Bell, sgd in pencil, dated 1951, fine impression, good color, Ot 125.00

Stone Lanterns, 1942, woodblock, pencil sgd, margin title, 6⅝ x 9⅜" 110.00

Yoshikawa Kampo, actor Nakamura Ganjiro as Kamiya Jihei (c1922), sgd, publisher Sato Shotaro, reverse with additional publisher cartouche, edition 51/200, good impression and color, foxed, slightly toned, Ot 375.00

Yoshitora, three ladies on balcony and cherry trees, OT 200.00

Yoshitoshi, from Yoshitoshi's Warriors Trembling with Courage series, 1883, Ot 250.00

PURPLE SLAG (MARBLE GLASS)

History: Challinor, Taylor & Co., Tarantum, Pennsylvania, c1870s–80s, was the largest producer of purple slag in the United

States. Since the quality of pieces varies considerably, there is no doubt other American firms made it as well.

Purple slag also was made in England. English pieces are marked with British Registry marks.

Other color combinations, such as blue, green, or orange, were made, but are rarely found.

Video: National Imperial Glass Collectors Society, *Glass of Yesteryears, The Renaissance of Slag Glass by Imperial,* RoCliff Communications, 1994.

Additional Listings: Greentown Glass (chocolate slag) and Pink Slag.

Reproduction Alert: Purple slag has been heavily reproduced over the years and is still being reproduced at the present time.

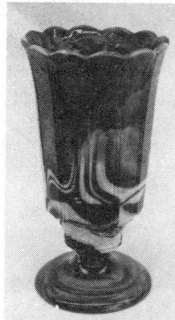

Celery Vase, Fluted Rib pattern, Challinor, 8¼″ h, 4¼″ d, $90.00.

Animal Cov Dish
  Hen
    Atterbury, Ferson #20
      Blue 475.00
      Lavender 600.00
    Blue marble, lacy base, Ferson #8 .... 275.00
  Rooster, Imperial 150.00
Bowl, 8″ d, Dart Bar pattern 50.00
Butter Dish, cov, 8″ h, paneled, waffle dome, ftd matching scalloped base 75.00
Celery Vase, Fluted pattern 80.00
Ccmpote, 4½″ h, 5″ d, Beaded Hearts pattern 75.00

Creamer, Scroll with Acanthus pattern 60.00
Goblet, 6½″ h, relief diamond below ridged fluting, knobbed stem, price for pair 50.00
Humidor, cov, 6″ d, 7″ h, vintage motif, marked "Fenton" 50.00
Match Holder, 5″ h, dolphin head 65.00
Plate, 10″ d, lattice edge 75.00
Spooner, Scroll with Acanthus pattern 120.00
Sugar, cov, Fluted pattern 165.00
Vase, 10″ h, wispy purple swirls, cloudy and clear body 100.00

PUZZLES

History: The jigsaw puzzle originated in mid–18th century Europe. John Silsbury, a London map maker, was selling dissected map jigsaw puzzles by the early 1760s. The first jigsaw puzzles in America were English and European imports aimed primarily at children.

Prior to the Civil War, several manufacturers, e.g., Samuel L. Hill, W. and S. B. Ives, and McLoughlin Brothers, included puzzle offerings as part of their line. However, it was the post–Civil War period that saw the jigsaw puzzle gain a strong foothold among the children of America.

In the late 1890s and first decade of the 20th century, puzzles designed specifically for adults first appeared. Both forms have existed side by side ever since. Adult puzzlers were responsible for two 20th century puzzle crazes: 1908–09 and 1932–33.

Prior to the mid–1920s the vast majority of jigsaw puzzles were cut using wood for the adult market and composition material for the children's market. In the 1920s the die–cut, cardboard jigsaw puzzle evolved. By the time of the puzzle craze of 1932–33, it was the dominant puzzle medium.

Jigsaw puzzle interest has cycled between peaks and valleys several times since 1933. Mini–revivals occurred during World War II and in the mid–1960s when Springbok entered the American market.

References: Linda Hannas, *The Jigsaw Book,* Dial Press, 1981, out of print; Harry L. Rinker, *Collector's Guide To Toys, Games and Puzzles,* Wallace–Homestead,

1991; Anne D. Williams, *Jigsaw Puzzles: An Illustrated History and Price Guide*, Wallace–Homestead, 1990.

Collectors' Clubs: American Game Collectors Association, 49 Brooks Ave., Lewiston, ME 04240; National Puzzler's League, PO Box 82289, Portland, OR 97282.

Additional Listings: See *Warman's Americana & Collectibles* for an expanded listing.

ADULT

Wood

Chad Valley Co., The Autocar Jig–Saw Puzzles, Meteors of Road and Track, by F. Gordon Crosby, No. 2 of series of 12, "Leyland (J. G. P. Thomas) and Fiat (E. A. D. Eldridge)," 10⅝ x 7⅛", 200 pcs, period box **80.00**

Fretts, Alden L., The Yankee Cut–ups, "Home Memories," English thatched roof cottage and garden scene, Thompson illus, 23 x 16", 676 pcs, 24 figural pcs, box missing, c1930s **45.00**

Gleason, H. A., Cheerio Jig Saw Puzzles, "A Scout Is Friendly," picture of Boy Scout assisting elderly couple to read time table, 16 x 20", 535 pcs, 12 figural, interlocking, orig cardboard box . **50.00**

Gencraft/Glendex, "Tree Island," New England landscape scene, 14 x 10", 304 pcs, interlocking, 1960s, orig cardboard box **25.00**

Macy's Jigsaw Puzzle, "On a Canal in Venice," canalboat at sunset in Venice, 10 x 12", 253 pcs, wood box with slide–top .. **25.00**

Par Company, Ltd., New York, NY, Par Picture Puzzle, "Full Honors," illustration of Japanese samurai riding through village, 15⅜ x 24⅜", about 750 pcs, numerous figural pieces of people, four medieval ladies each carrying a letter that spell "RUTH," two seahorses, some color line cutting, rounded edges, orig box .. **350.00**

Parker Brothers, Pastime Picture Puzzle

105 pcs, "The Jade Parure," Whitman Addett picture of woman seated at her vanity, curlicued interlocking cut, 7 x 9", 12 figural pcs, 1930, orig cardboard box **15.00**

350 pcs, "A Shady Pathway," lake country scene with shepherd and sheep, 17 x 11", 36 figural pcs, orig box, dated March 28, 1931 .... **40.00**

S & H Novelty Co., Atlantic City, NJ, Spare Time Jig Saw Puzzles, "Sulgrove Manor: Home of George Washington," 8 x 6", 75 pcs, some figural pcs, orig cardboard box **15.00**

Straus, Joseph K., "White Clipper," three–masted square rigger under full sail, D. Sherring illus, 16 x 12", 282 pcs, orig box, c1940s **18.00**

U–Nit Puzzles, West Caldwell, NJ, "Marina at Capri," fishing village, 21½ x 18", 600 pcs, orig cardboard box **50.00**

Unknown cutter
Jig–Sawed Picture Puzzle, No. 48–2108, untitled, image of

Cartoon Character, diecut, stiff board, "Blondie" Jigsaw Puzzle, uncut, 49 pieces, 1933, one of series of five cartoon theme puzzles used as supplements in Philadelphia Sunday Inquirer, 10 x 7⅞", $17.50.

Stuart painting Washington's portrait, 8 x 10", information from *The Literary Digest* inside box lid about the painting, cardboard box with plain red paper covering 20.00

200 pcs, "Old Glory Forever," John Arsdale's exploits at Fort George, November 25, 1783, Clyde D. DeLand illus, 14 x 10" 25.00

Diecut, Cardboard

Note: Cardboard puzzles from the post–1945 period sell for between twenty-five cents and four dollars depending on company and subject matter.

Consolidated Paper Box Company
Big Star, "The First Covey," 13¼ x 10⅛", 252 pcs, mid–1930s, orig box 4.00
Big Ten, "A Colonial Sweetheart," 10¼ x 15¼", 280 pcs, mid–1930s, orig box 3.00
Perfect Double, "Brookside Manor/Canal in Belgium," 10¼ x 15½", 280 pcs, orig box ... 7.50
Einson-Freeman Company, "Every Week" Jig–Saw Puzzle Series, No. 23, "The Warrior Prince," 10⅜ x 14¼", over 160 pcs, 1933, orig box 15.00
Harter Publishing Co., Teaser, "Village in the Hills," 15¾ x 11¾", mid–1930s, orig box 3.00
Milton Bradley, Chatham, No. 4730, "Santa Inez Valley," approx. 22 x 16", 468 pcs, mid–1930s, orig box 8.00
Once–a–Week Dime Jig–Saw Puzzle, Puzzle No. 3, "The Love Nest," 7⅜ x 9½", William Thompson illus., period envelope 12.00
Tichnor Brothers, Inc., See America First, "No. 39 Natural Bridge, Virginia," 10⅛ x 13¼", 315 pcs, mid–1930s, orig box 10.00
Tower Press, "Queen Elizabeth and Price Charles," 9½ x 14", 204 pieces, orig box, mid-1950s 20.00
TUCO (The Upson Company) ABC's Wide World of Sports, No.

8244, "Baseball," 15 x 11", 252 pcs, early 1970s, orig box 12.00
"Bell Airacobras," 14¾ x 19⅛", 320 pcs, "BELL AIRACOBRAS" printed on puzzle, Schieder illus., guide picture on box lid 20.00
Wilkie Picture Puzzle Company, Everybody, No. 24, "A Winter Day," G. Fleissner illus., 15¾ x 11⅞", 310 pcs, mid–1930s, orig box 5.00

CHILDREN

Pre–1940

Milton Bradley Co, Springfield, MA, "Dissected Outline Map of the United States of America," reversible map and US scenes, wood, wood box, c1880 ...... 75.00
McLoughlin Brothers, New York, NY, Locomotive Picture Puzzle, picture of engine at station, 24¾ x 18", composition board, 1887, orig box 250.00
Saalfield Publishing Co., No. 567, Kitty–Cat Picture Puzzle Box, six puzzle set, Fern Biesel Peat illus, each puzzle approx 7⅞ x 9⅞", guide picture for one puzzle on box lid 60.00

Post–1940

APC, No. 1245, "The Bionic Woman Jigsaw Puzzle," 17¼ x 11", 204 pcs, can format package 12.00
HG Toys, No. 465–02, "Happy Days Featuring 'The Fonz,'" approx 14 x 10", guide photograph on box 10.00
Milton Bradley, No. 4070, children's set, "Uncle Wiggily Picture Puzzles," Howard R. Garis, Elmer Rache illus., three puzzle set, each puzzle approx. 13 x 10", each puzzle 30 pcs, cover of box shows Uncle Wiggily and friends putting puzzle together . 50.00
Western Publishing Co., No. 4652,

UFO Shape Jigsaw Puzzle, 20 x 9", 48 pcs, orig box 20.00

Whitman, A Big Little Book, No. 4657-11, "Hanna-Barbera Frankenstein, Jr.," 10 x 13", 99 pcs, box with book format 15.00

Frame Tray

Jaymar Specialty Company, Rudolph the Red–Nosed Reindeer, Rudolph leads sled, 11 x 14", 1950 copyright 12.50

Thumbs–Up Enterprises, Inc., "One For The Thumb in 81," features image of Joe Greene in Steeler's uniform wearing four Super Bowl rings, 10 x 12½", 48 pcs 30.00

Whitman Publishing Company No. 4446, Captain Kangaroo Frame Tray Puzzle, shows Captain Kangaroo doing puzzle, 11¼ x 14⅜", 48 pcs 15.00

No. 4536, Tennessee Tuxedo, Tennessee and Walrus in diving helmets find a treasure chest at the bottom of the sea, 11⅜ x 14⁷⁄₁₆", 16 pcs, three figural pcs—telephone handle, bell, and flying bird 20.00

ADVERTISING

Burger Chef, "Dragon Wagon," part of Timetraveler Funmeal Fest, frame tray format, 9¼ x 6⅝", 16 pcs, 1980 .... 10.00

Camel Laird Picture Puzzles, Find the Camel, "CAM-BRU-MAC" Reversible Puzzle, No. 4, "Casting A Large Ingot, Sheffield and Birkenhead," wood, 6⅞ x 4⅞", 64 pcs, reverse side makes up into picture of camel on plain field, label mkd "Thos. Forman & Sons, Nottingham and London," orig box 75.00

Captain Crunch, cereal premium, hidden scene, Captain Crunch looking into ship's doorway, 4½ x 3", 10 pcs, orig wrap 10.00

Cocomalt, R. B. Davis Co., "The Windmill Jig–Saw Puzzle," windmill and harbor at low tide, 10 x 6½", 65 pcs, paper envelope .. 12.00

DeMartini Macaroni Co., Martini Brand Spaghetti, The Zoo in Puzzles, Series No. 1, "Giraffe," 5⅝ x 8" (includes label at top and bottom), complete 18.00

Hi–C Super Fruits, Coca-Cola Co, Zowie Powie Punch, 9¾ x 8", rounded corners, 28 pcs, orig packaging missing 30.00

Hood, C.J., Lowell, MA, "A Wedding in Catland and Hood's Bridge Puzzle," Louis Wain illus., 14½ x 9⅞", 35 pcs, orig box .. 200.00

Howard Clothes, 4¼ x 6½", 50 pcs, gentleman in modern suit superimposed over gentleman in early 19th century suit, dates "1833" to "1933," period packaging missing 25.00

Johnson Oil Refining Company, Chicago, "Johnson Jig–Saw Type Puzzle / Over 200 Pieces / Size 10 x 14" / All Masterpiece Productions ... Interesting ... Instructive," untitled, peasant scene of pair of horses pulling a manure wagon, logo for Johnson Grease, actual size 13⅞ x 9⅞", 1933, paper envelope 10.00

Johnston's Chocolates, "Garden No. 1," 7¹⁵⁄₁₆ x 5", 60 pcs, three couples in colonial costumes in formal garden setting, paper envelope 6½ x 9⅜", mid-1930s .. 35.00

Lucas Paints and Varnishes, "Giant Painter Puzzle," painter kneeling in miniature village, can of paint by right knee, holding house in left hand, 5½ x 7", orig box, guide picture on lid, c1920s 100.00

New Jersey Bell, "The Answer To Your Communication Puzzle: BELL," 8 x 8", 9 pcs, period packaging missing 8.00

Philadelphia Sunday Inquirer, "The Brinkley Girl" Jig–Saw Puzzle, 10 x 7⅞", uncut, complete border, issued as Sunday supplement, 1933 .... 15.00

Timken Silent Automatic Burner

Co., Canton, OH, 8 x 8½″, 87
pcs, paper envelope **22.50**

MULTIPURPOSE PUZZLES

Checkerboard, "The Famous Ban-
zee Island Checkerboard Puzzle," premium given away by
C.S.T. Co. (Wholesale / Collections and Adjustments), 12 pcs,
paper envelope **8.00**
Mystery, Jaymar Specialty Com-
pany, "Dick Tracy's 2 in 1 Mystery Puzzle," two puzzles, 10⅞ x
13⅞″ problem puzzle in vertical
format of 24 pcs, 10⅞ x 13⅞″
solution puzzle in horizontal format with 99 pcs, copyright 1948,
period box **45.00**

**World War II, Jaymar Specialty
Co., diecut, cardboard, Hobby Jig
Saw Series, Grumman "Avenger"
Navy Torpedo Bomber, over 300
pieces, guide picture on box lid,
c1943–45, 22 x 14″, $20.00.**

Skill, KLM, "Form a circle with
these 8 parts. You will be able to
read the words 'Fly KLM,' "
coated stiff cardboard, 8″ d, 8
pcs, 2⅛ x 3⅞″ envelope, instructions on back of envelope in En-
glish, Spanish, and Dutch **5.00**

JIGSAW PUZZLE EPHEMERA

Broadside, Advertising, Viking
Manufacturing Company, Picture Puzzle Weekly, Series D-3,
"The Chariot Race," 14¾ x 11″,
stiff board **35.00**
Comic Book, Golden Key,
10146607, The Man From
U.N.C.L.E., July 1966, story
"The Pizilated Puzzle Affair,"
opening page has jigsaw puzzle
theme, story focuses on jigsaw
puzzle **10.00**
Magazine
Jack and Jill, July 1947, center-
fold designed to be pasted to
cardboard and cut as puzzle,
pcs assemble into photo of
Statue of Liberty, 13¼ x 9⅞″
(page spread) **4.00**
People and Places, Vol. 13, No.
1, February 1956, published
by DeSoto-Plymouth, back
cover features jigsaw puzzle
theme advertisement for
DeSoto, "Easy way to solve
your new car puzzle," distributed by Ludwick Motors, Inc.,
Pottstown, PA **5.00**
Playboy, Vol. 7, No. 9, 1960, jig-
saw puzzle theme cover **20.00**

Quezal

QUEZAL

History: The Quezal Art Glass Decorating Company, named for the "quetzal," a
bird with brilliantly colored feathers, was organized in 1901 in Brooklyn, New York, by
two disgruntled Tiffany workers, Martin
Bach and Thomas Johnson. They soon
hired two more Tiffany workers, Percy Britton and William Wiedebine.

The first products, unmarked, were exact
Tiffany imitations. In 1902 the "Quezal"
trademark was first used. Quezal pieces differ from Tiffany pieces in that they are more
defined and the decorations are more visible and brightly colored. No new techniques
came from Quezal.

Johnson left in 1905. T. Conrad Vahlsing,
Bach's son–in–law, joined the firm in 1918,

but left with Paul Frank in 1920 to form Lustre Art Glass Company which copied Quezal pieces. Martin Bach died in 1924 and by 1925 Quezal ceased operations.

Wares are signed "Quezal" on the base of vases and bowls and on the rims of shades. The acid–etched or engraved letters vary in size and may be found in amber, black, or gold. A printed label of a quetzal bird was used briefly in 1907.

Reference: Ellen T. Schroy, *Warman's Glass,* Wallace–Homestead, 1992.

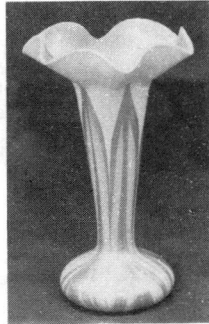

Vase, green feather leaf pattern, gold edges, orig irid int., ruffled edge, marked, 7½" h, $950.00.

Bowl, 12" d, peacock blue, hammered silver base, marked "Oscar B Bach NY" 500.00
Candlesticks, pr, 6½" h, flared bobeche rim, ringed hollow baluster opal body, overall orange–green King Tut irid dec, sgd . . . 975.00
Jack-In-The-Pulpit Vase, 11½" h, gold face, stem and back with gold and green leaf pulls, hooked waves, ivory ground, sgd "Quezal R 84" 6,000.00
Lamp Shade, 6½" d, 3¼" fitter ring, 8" h, irid green and gold hooked feather, sgd, rim chip . . 900.00
Miniature Lamp, 4¼" h, 4½" d shade, irid green and gold Hon-

eycomb pattern, brass candlestick type base 500.00
Nut Dish, triangular rim, gently rounded body, gold irid, inscribed "Quezal" 110.00
Vase
 2" h, 2½" w, deep bronze, deep blue and purple highlights . . . 425.00
 3" h, 4" d, bulbous, tapered shoulder, highly irid green hooked dec, purple highlights, opal and green ground, irid gold int., inscribed "Quezal B744" 700.00
 8" h, ovoid, flared rim, applied gold disk base, opal glass, gold int., broad random gold irid linear dec, sgd "Quezal" .1,150.00
 8¼" h, King Tut pattern, green, yellow, and silver, purple highlights, cased opal ground . . . 550.00
 9" h, Egyptian Revival design by Martin Bach, green zigzag shoulder dec, orig irid double hooked and pulled feathers, cream white oval body, ribbed and folded disk foot, inscribed "Quezal N.Y." 2,300.00

QUILTS

History: Quilts have been passed down as family heirlooms for many generations. Each is an individual expression. The same pattern may have hundreds of variations in both color and design.

The advent of the sewing machine increased, not decreased, the number of quilts which were made. Quilts are still being sewn today.

The key considerations for price are age, condition, aesthetic beauty, and design. Prices are now at a level position. Exceptions are the very finest examples which continue to bring record prices.

References: American Quilter's Society, *Gallery of American Quilts, 1849-1988,* Collector Books, 1988; Suzy McLennan Anderson, *Collector's Guide to Quilts,* Wallace-Homestead, 1991; Cuesta Benberry, *Always There: The African–American Pres-*

ence in *American Quilts*, Kentucky Quilt Project, 1992; Barbara Brackman, *Clues in the Calico: A Guide To Identifying and Dating Antique Quilts*, EPM Publications, 1989; Liz Greenbacker and Kathleen Barach, *Quilts: Identification and Price Guide*, Avon Books, 1992; Alda Leake Horner, *The Official Price Guide to Linens, Lace and Other Fabrics*, House of Collectibles, 1991; Carter Houck, *The Quilt Encyclopedia Illustrated*, Harry N. Abrams and Museum of American Folk Art, 1991; William C. Ketchum, Jr., *The Knopf Collectors' Guides to American Antiques: Quilts*, Alfred A. Knopf, 1982; Jean Ray Laury and California Heritage Quilt Project, *Ho For California: Pioneer Women and Their Quilts*, E. P. Dutton, 1990; Dana G. Morykan and Harry L. Rinker, *Warman's Country Antiques & Collectibles, Second Edition*, Wallace-Homestead, 1994; Patsy and Myron Orlofsky, *Quilts in America*, Abbeville Press, 1992; Lisa Turner Oshins, *Quilt Collections: A Directory For The United States And Canada*, Acropolis Books, 1987; Rachel and Kenneth Pellman, *The World of Amish Quilts*, Good Books, 1984; Schnuppe von Gwinner, *The History of the Patchwork Quilt*, Schiffer Publishing, 1988.

Periodicals: *Quilters Newsletter,* Box 394, Wheat Ridge, CO 80033; *Vintage Quilt Newsletter,* PO Box 744, Great Bend, TX 67530-0744.

Collectors' Club: American Quilt Study Group, Suite 400, 660 Mission St., San Francisco, CA 94105-4007; The American Quilter's Society, PO Box 3290, Paducah, KY 42001; The National Quilting Association, Inc., PO Box 393, Ellicott City, MD 21043.

Museums: Doll & Quilts Barn, Rocky Ridge, MD; Museum of the American Quilter's Society, Paducah, KY; National Museum of American History, Washington, DC; New England Quilt Museum, Lowell, MA.

Abstract Tree, cotton, lavender, blue, brown, and red diamonds against black ground, chestnut border, Amish, OH, c1910, 85 × 72″ **6,450.00**
Album, crazy quilt, silk and velvet, polychrome pieces embroidered

with flowers, fan, spider web, and other designs, Victorian, late 19th C, 64 × 64″ **1,275.00**
Bar
  Cotton Sateen, royal blue bars against black ground, black border, Amish, OH, c1910, 85 × 65″ **3,225.00**
  Wool, crimson and turquoise bars framed by rose bars, olive green border, embroidered initials on reverse, Amish, Lancaster County, PA, c1920, 85 × 76″ **8,750.00**
Basket
  Cotton, maroon and blue baskets on purple ground, maroon border, Amish, dated "Tuesday, February 11th, 1924," 85 × 72″ **3,450.00**
  Cotton and Chintz, purple, magenta, and mint green baskets, green ground, magenta border, Amish, OH, c1920, 82 × 80″ **1,500.00**
Bear Paw, red bear claws divided by zigzag calico bands, white ground, American, early 20th C, 82 × 72″ **375.00**
Blazing Star, cotton, four bands of lavender and yellow stars, green ground, lavender border, Amish, OH, c1920, 75 × 66″ **860.00**
Crazy Quilt, velvet patches surrounded by embroidery, Victorian, American, late 19th C, 86 × 70″ **860.00**
Delectable Mountain, red calico sawtooth triangles on white ground, American, third quarter 19th C, 95 × 90″ **800.00**
Double Irish Chain, red and yellow trellis on green ground, red sawtooth border, Mennonite, Pa, early 20th C, 86½ × 86½″ **975.00**
Double Wedding Ring, sateen and cotton, pink, red, lavender, purple, yellow, and green on black ground, Amish, OH, c1930 ....**5,750.00**
Feathered Star, cotton and calico, chestnut feathered stars, green ground, yellow calico border, Mennonite, third quarter 19th C, 72 × 72″ **925.00**

Kansas Troubles, calico, gray, blue, and black sawtooth triangles on red and black calico ground, American, late 19th C, 82 × 74" **500.00**

King David's Crown, polychrome calico elongated squares, yellow ground, American, c1930, 86 × 74" **350.00**

Lattice, each square contains four nine-patch squares, Amish, c1910, 67 × 53" **865.00**

Diamond, pieced, multicolored, 86 x 86", $250.00.

Lightning Streak, cotton sateen, black, purple, olive green, and maroon diagonal bands, royal blue frame, black border, Amish, c1920, 80 × 73" **2,300.00**

Log Cabin, calico, blue, red, and tan strips, American, 80 × 72" **400.00**

Log Cabin and Light and Dark Crosses, reversible, calico pieced squares one side, reverse with calico crosses, American, 79 × 66" **500.00**

Ocean Wave, polished cotton, multi–banded trellis in triangles

of blue, green, and lavender, black ground, cornflower blue border, Amish, OH, c1910, 73 × 73" **2,300.00**

Patchwork, wool, rose, red, turquoise, and brown star–filled blocks, American, c1930 ...... **500.00**

Pineapple, wool, brown, blue, and red strips, American, early 20th C, 74 × 71" **400.00**

Pinwheel, six bands of pink, green, yellow, and blue pinwheels, teal ground, Amish, OH, 88 × 78" . **1,150.00**

Prairie Star, star comprised of dark shading to light yellow diamonds, yellow ground, MO, c1920, 78½ × 76" **230.00**

Rose, appliqued, red and green roses within diamonds, American, third quarter 19th C, 72 × 72" **230.00**

Rose–Cross, appliqued, cotton, four red, yellow, and green roses, rosette and diamond pattern quilted ground, American, third quarter 19th C, 74 × 81" . **860.00**

Sawtooth Diamond in Square, wool, green diamond and square on crimson ground, Amish, Lancaster County, PA, c1900, 76 × 76" **3,900.00**

Schoolhouse, calico, four bands of red and blue schoolhouses, NY, late 19th C, 65 × 84" **800.00**

Star in Square, polished cotton, slate blue, rust, and rose star within maroon frame, blue ground, Amish, 20th C, 46 × 43" **300.00**

Swallow, red and black calico sawtooth blocks, white ground, IN, late 19th C, 72 × 70" **225.00**

Triple Irish Chain, wool, red and green trellis, slate blue ground, green corner squares, initialed "M.S.," Amish, Lancaster County, PA, late 19th C **3,500.00**

Wig Rose, appliqued, red and green roses, rose and vine border, American, third quarter 19th C, 86 × 82" **575.00**

Winged Square, lavender, yellow, and brown triangles on royal blue ground, yellow border, Amish, OH, c1930, 78 × 68" .. **1,375.00**

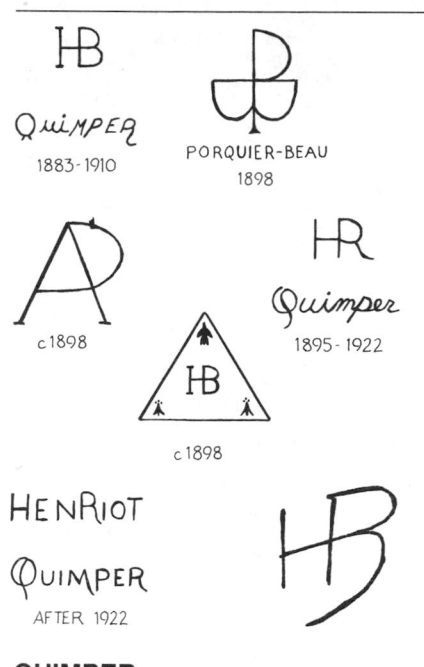

HB

$Q\mathcal{u}i\mathcal{M}PE\mathcal{R}$

1883-1910

PORQUIER-BEAU
1898

c1898

HR

$Q\mathcal{u}im\mathcal{per}$

1895-1922

HB

c1898

HENRIOT

QUIMPER

AFTER 1922

HB

QUIMPER

History: Quimper faience, dating back to the 17th century, is named for Quimper, a French town where numerous potteries were located. Several mergers resulted in the evolution of two major houses—the Jules Henriot and Hubaudiébre–Bousquet factories.

The peasant design first appeared in the 1860s, and many variations exist. Florals and geometrics, equally popular, also were produced in large quantities. During the 1920s the Hubaudiébre–Bousquet factory introduced the Odetta line which utilized a stone body and Art Deco decorations.

The two major houses merged in 1968, each retaining its individual characteristics and marks. The concern suffered from labor problems in the 1980s and recently was purchased by an American group.

Marks: The HR and HR Quimper marks are found on Henriot pieces prior to 1922. The Henriot Quimper mark was used after 1922. The HB mark covers a long span of time. The addition of numbers or dots and dashes refers to inventory numbers and are found on later pieces. Most marks are in blue or black. Pieces ordered by department stores, such as Macy's and Carson Pirie Scott, carry the store mark along with the factory mark, making them less desirable to collectors. A comprehensive list of marks is found in Bondhus's book.

References: Susan and Al Bagdade, *Warman's English & Continental Pottery & Porcelain, Second Edition,* Wallace–Homestead, 1991; Sandra V. Bondhus, *Quimper Pottery: A French Folk Art Faience,* published by author, 1981; Millicent Mali, *Quimper Faience,* Airon, 1979; Marjatta Taburet, *La Faience de Quimper,* Editions Sous le Vent, 1979, French text.

Museums: Musee des Faiences de Quimper, Quimper, France; Victoria and Albert Museum, French Ceramic Dept., London, England.

Advisors: Susan and Al Bagdade.

Bowl
8″ d, male peasant, blue jacket, rust breeches, blue line border with rust, yellow, blue, and green strokes, scalloped rim, two blue bands on ext., marked "HenRiot Quimper France 701" **220.00**
9½″ d, frontal view of male peasant, walking stick, flanked by florals, floral border with la touche yellow flowers, blue centers, blue outlined scalloped rim, marked "HenRiot Quimper" **175.00**
Candlesticks, pr, 8″ h
Figural, one blond male peasant, green shirt, blue pantaloons, other blond female peasant, green blouse, blue skirt, both with basket on head, marked "HenRiot Quimper France 138" **990.00**
Shaft, one with male peasant, other with female, raised yellow ribs on base, blue sponged collar with blue "X" and red dot design, marked "HB Quimper" **687.00**

Charger, 18" l, 14¼" w, central scene of blond female peasant, brown haired male peasant, seated at wooden table, window at left, door at right, stone wall at back, orange banded decor riche border, stippled blue scalloped rim, mistral blue glaze, artist sgd, marked "HenRiot Quimper" **450.00**

Cheese Dish, cov, 7½" d, 2½" h, female peasant, floral garland, four blue dot design, blue sponged butterfly knob, marked "HR Quimper" **258.00**

Cider Pitcher, 6½" h, male peasant on side with scattered flowers, top and side handles with blue stripes, blue and yellow banded base, marked "HenRiot Quimper France" under handle **187.00**

Compote, 5" h, 9¾" d, Modern Movement male peasant, ajonc sprays on border, green, yellow, blue, black, and brown, marked "HB Quimper" **210.00**

Creamer and Sugar, male or female peasant, scattered florals, blue forget–me–nots, blue outlined borders, gold handles with blue dashes, marked "HenRiot Quimper France" **125.00**

Cup and Saucer, band of red flowers and green leaves, blue sponged handle on cup, floral sprig, blue and yellow banded borders on saucer, marked "HenRiot Quimper France" **35.00**

Dish
6¼" d, frontal figure of male peasant, scattered green and red floral bunches, blue sponged and yellow outline pinched piecrust border, marked "HR Quimper" on front **175.00**

8" d, figure of woman, yellow jug on shoulder, red and blue flowers, green leaves, blue and red crisscross border, scalloped and half circle rim, "HR" mark **200.00**

11" l, 9¼" w, 3 section, male peasant in one, female in sec-

ond, florals in smaller section, blue striped center handle, marked "HB Quimper" **300.00**

Eggcup, 2¼" h, male or female peasant, blue, red, and green florals, marked "HB Quimper," price for pair **110.00**

Egg Set, 6½" h x 9¼" d base, shaped oval egg wells, male, female, or floral group, shaped indented rim, 3 sided center handle, six egg cups, male or female peasants, marked "HenRiot Quimper" **595.00**

Figure
6¼" h, 8" l, green eyed horned owl, holding mouse, brown and tan feathers, black accents, white breast, simulated log base, marked "HenRiot Quimper" **475.00**

7" h, St Yves, standing, brown hat, brown white–lined cloak, blue cassock, blue and yellow banded base, "ST YVES" on base, marked "HB Quimper" **60.00**

13" h, St Anne, light blue veil, cobalt blue mantle, yellow robe, figural Mary at side, "Ste ANNE" on base, marked "HenRiot Quimper France" .. **185.00**

Ginger Jar, 13" h, front panel with

Menu, multicolored pale peasant, yellow brick wall, blue lettering and outline, gold and yellow raised fleur-de-lis, Porquier–Beau, 6¼" h, 4½" w, $50.00.

seated female peasant knitting, male peasant with walking stick, blue raised ribbon outline, stylized blue chrysanthemum on reverse, raised seashell design, marked "HB Quimper 2" 575.00

Holy Water Font, 9¼" h, figural ermine tail, kneeling male peasant at shrine, 3 black ermine tails on front, blue sponged flowers, red centers, marked "HenRiot Quimper France 119" 250.00

Jug, 8¼" h, stoneware, dark brown oval bust of male peasant, irid green splashed body, dark green handle and spout, marked "HB Quimper, Odetta" 395.00

Menu, 7" h, 5" w, frontal view of female peasant with basket, blue forget–me–not spray above and "MENU," black and yellow outlined shaped rim, marked "HR Quimper" 240.00

Oyster Plate, 8¾" d, Art Deco style, male or female peasant, 6 wells, rose and yellow accents, tan ground, sponged circles, marked "HenRiot Quimper," price for pair 550.00

Pipe Rack, 10" h, 8½" w, figural molded shell, center with walking male peasant holding stick, floral sprays or blue or red crisscross design in side panels, small molded shell on base, blue outlined rim, c1890, marked "AP" .1,200.00

Pitcher
5¾" h, male peasant, blue coat, rust pantaloons, 4 blue dot design, blue striped handle, marked "HB Quimper France 911" 125.00

7½" h, male peasant with floral sprays, blue and yellow banded base, shaped rim, marked "HenRiot Quimper 82"   121.00

Planter
6" l, 5" w, oval, paneled sides, band of multicolored florals, shaped rim, marked "HB Quimper" 60.00

7¼" h, 5¾" l, figural, duck, blue and red stylized feathers,

green and red shaped body, yellow ground, c1930 . . . .   125.00

Plaque, 15½" l, 11¾" w, rect, relief molded figure of mother in white and blue bonnet, yellow banded vest, blue skirt, white apron, child in lap, beige dots with black accents on border, light brown glaze, Porquier–Beau mark . . .1,300.00

Plate
8¼" d, botanical, large pink and yellow blossoms, green stems and leaves, light blue glaze, yellow outlined scalloped rim, Porquier–Beau 800.00

9¼" d, standing male peasant, bagpipe, cottage, and fence, dark blue acanthus on yellow ground border, crest of Brittany at top, shaped rim, Porquier–Beau 590.00

9½" d
Dancing couple, multicolored costumes, orange crest of Brittany on border, dark blue decor riche design, inner orange border, scalloped rim, marked "HenRiot Quimper"   395.00

Female peasant, green top, blue skirt, rust apron, flanked by florals, a la touche border, large blue dots, blue outlined scalloped rim, marked "HR Quimper" on front 175.00

Platter, male peasant, multicolored flowers, border of three blue bands and wide yellow band, marked "HenRiot Quimper, France," pierced for hanging, 6½" l, 4¼" h, $190.00.

9⅝" d, multicolored "Mayflower" in center, French flags, single stroke border, marked "HenRiot Quimper France" .. 325.00

9¾" d, standing female peasant, wind blowing thru blue skirt and pink apron, purple vest, yellow blouse, small bouquets on border, shaped rim, marked "HB" 300.00

Platter

6½" l, 4¼" h, rect, cut corners, male with green jacket, rose pants, gold hose, female with green top, rose skirt, gold apron, green florals, rust with blue dots, dark blue border, marked "HenRiot Quimper 724," price for pair 350.00

14¼" l, 11" w, oval, center female peasant holding open umbrella over shoulder, band of red flowers, blue forget–me–nots on border, shaped rim, marked "HR" 525.00

Porringer, 7" w handle to handle, male peasant in bowl, flanked by florals, blue and yellow banded border, blue sponged handles, marked "HenRiot Quimper France" 50.00

Relish Dish, 7½" l, 4½" w, oval, frontal view of male peasant, arms folded, flanked by shrubs, blue flowers, blue rim, molded yellow bow on end, marked "HR Quimper" on front 145.00

Serving Dish, 10" d, female peasant in center flanked by green tree and florals, band on red and blue flowers, green leaves, blue sponged rim and handle, yellow ground, marked "HB Quimper" 125.00

Tea Set, 8¼" h teapot, 4" h creamer, 5½" cov sugar, seated male peasant with flute or seated female peasant, scattered hanging bellflowers, green and orange bands on rims, bases, spout, and handles, marked "HenRiot Quimper" 750.00

Tray, 11¾" l, 8" w, seated peasant woman in meadow, holding teacup, blue decor riche border outlined in orange, undulating rim, c1930, marked "HB Quimper" 250.00

Tulipiere, 7¼" h, 6 openings, front panel with female peasant holding distaff and floral sprays, stylized red daisy and blue flower on back panel, blue and red crisscross with green dots on side panels, spread base, scattered florals and crisscross design, marked "HenRiot Quimper France" 375.00

Tureen

5" h, 10½" w handle to handle, cov, female peasant and a la touche florals, finial with green leaves and apple, blue band on edge, base with male on one side, female on reverse, blue band, blue striped and 4 dot handles, three holes, marked "HB Quimper" 325.00

9¼" h, 11½" w handle to handle, male peasant on cov, band of orange, blue, and green florals on bowl, blue and yellow banded rims, blue sponged handles, marked "HenRiot Quimper" 545.00

Vase

5½" h, 6½" l, compressed oval shape, mother and child, sand sieves on front, yellow and pink rose on reverse, blue acanthus design on ends, Porquier Beau 875.00

7½" h, bud, bulbous base, scattered ajonc florals, tapered neck with male peasant holding walking stick and pipe, marked "HB Quimper" on front 135.00

10" h, Brodier Breton design, front panel of male peasant with basket on arm, standing female peasant, broken sunflowers in four panels, orange, red, and blue, marked "HB Quimper 11 510" 315.00

12½" h, bulbous base, cylinder neck, vertical handles, snail ends, female peasant with basket on one, male peasant with folded arms on other, band of rust florals, blue swirls on base, black "ST NAZARIE" on reverse, marked "HenRiot Quimper," price for pair **895.00**

13" h, bulbous, narrow top, male and female peasant on front, crest of Brittany on reverse, hanging ajonc and forget–me–not florals, panels on top and base, green trimmed rims, 2 yellow handles with orange lines, blue and green trim, marked "HenRiot Quimper 159" **1,275.00**

15" h, front panel of 2 male peasants, flute and bagpipe, back panel with blue and pink florals, blue acanthus design on body, 2 panels of yellow flowers on neck, marked "HB Quimper 128" **705.00**

Wall Pocket

7½" h, figural bellows, frontal view of male peasant with whip, red 4 dot border, red and blue stylized leaf handle, marked "HR Quimper" **275.00**

8" h, male peasant with hands in pocket, pipe in mouth, yellow and orange bow at top, brown pipes on sides, marked "HR Quimper" on front **220.00**

RADIOS

History: The radio was invented over 100 years ago. Marconi was the first to assemble and employ the transmission and reception instruments that permitted sending electric messages without the use of direct connections. Between 1905 and the end of World War I many technical advances were made to the "wireless," including the invention of the vacuum tube by DeForest. By 1920 technology progressed. Radios filled the entertainment needs of the average family.

Changes in design, style, and technology brought the radio from the black boxes of the 1920s to the stylish furniture pieces and console models of the 1930s and 1940s, to midget models of the 1950s, and finally to the high–tech radios of the 1980s.

References: Robert F. Breed, *Collecting Transistor Novelty Radios,* L–W Book Sales, 1990; Marty and Sue Bunis, *Collector's Guide To Antique Radios, Third Edition,* Collector Books, 1994; Marty and Sue Bunis, *Collector's Guide To Transistor Radios,* Collector Books, 1994; Marty Bunis and Robert Breed, *Collector's Guide To Novelty Radios,* Collector Books, 1994; Philip Collins, *Radio Redux: Listening In Style,* Chronicle Books, 1992; Philip Collins, *Radios: The Golden Age,* Chronicle Books, 1987; Alan Douglas, *Radio Manufacturers of the 1920s,* Vol. 1 (1988), Vol. 2 (1989), Vol. 3 (1991), Vestal Press; Roger Handy, Maureen Erbe, and Aileen Farnan Antonier, *Made In Japan: Transistor Radios of the 1950s and 1960s,* Chronicle Books, 1993; David Johnson, *Antique Radio Restoration Guide, 2nd Edition,* Wallace–Homestead, 1992; David and Betty Johnson, *Guide To Old Radios: Pointers, Pictures, And Prices,* Wallace–Homestead, 1989; David R. Lane and Robert A. Lane, *Transistor Radios: A Collector's Encyclopedia and Price Guide,* Wallace–Homestead, 1994; Harry Poster, *Poster's Radio & Television Price Guide: 1920–1990, Second Edition,* Wallace–Homestead, 1994; Ron Ramirez with Michael Prosise, *Philco Radio: 1928–1942,* Schiffer Publishing, 1993; John Sideli, *Classic Plastic Radios of the 1930s and 1940s: A Collector's Guide to Catalin Radios,* E. P. Dutton, 1990; Scott Wood (ed.), *Evolution of the Radio,* Vol. 1 (1991), Vol. 2 (1993), L–W Book Sales, 1991.

Periodicals: *Antique Radio Classified,* PO Box 2, Carlisle, MA 01741; *Radio Age,* 636 Cambridge Road, Augusta, GA 30909; *The Horn Speaker,* PO Box 1193, Mabank, TX 75147; *Transistor Network,* RR 1, Box 36, Bradford, NH 03221.

Collectors' Clubs: Antique Radio Club of America, 300 Washington Trails, Washington, PA 15301; Antique Wireless Association, 59 Main St., Bloomfield, NY 14469; New England Antique Radio Club, RR 1, Box 36, Bradford, NH 03221; Vintage Radio & Phonograph Society, Inc., PO Box 165345, Irving, TX 75016.

Museums: Antique Wireless Museum,

Bloomfield, NY; Caperton's Radio Museum, Louisville, KY; Muchow's Historical Radio Museum, Elgin, IL; Museum of Broadcast Communication, Chicago, IL; Museum of Wonderful Miracles, Minneapolis, MN; New England Wireless and Steam Museum, Inc., East Greenwich, RI; Voice of the Twenties, Orient, NY.

Advisor: Lewis S. Walters.

Additional Listings: See *Warman's Americana & Collectibles* for more examples.

Admiral, portable
#33–35–37, c1940	**25.00**
#218, leatherette, 1958	**40.00**
#909, All World, 1960	**85.00**

Air King, #1946, tombstone, Art Deco, plastic, 1935 ....**3,000.00**

Arvin
Character, Hopalong Cassidy, lariatenna	**450.00**
Table, #522A, ivory, metal, 1941	**60.00**
Tombstone, #617, Rhythm Maid, 1936	**215.00**

Atwater Kent
Breadboard
Model 9A	**550.00**
Model 10	**900.00**
Model 10C	**825.00**
Cathedral, #80, 1931	**380.00**
Table, #55 Kill	**225.00**

Crosley
Bandbox, #601, 1927	**75.00**
Gemchest, #609, 1928	**410.00**
Litfella, 1–N Cathedral	**175.00**
Pup, with orig box	**660.00**
Sheraton Cathedral, 1933	**290.00**
Showbox, #706, 1928	**100.00**
Super Buddy Boy, #122, 1930	**325.00**
"X" Table, 1922	**175.00**

Dumont, RA–346, table, scroll work, 1956 ....**110.00**

Emerson
AU–190, Catalin, tombstone, 1938	**1,000.00**
BT–235, Catalin, tombstone, scalloped dial, darker grill, 1939	**1,000.00**
#400	
Aristocrat, Catalin, 1940	**600.00**
Patriot, 1940	**750.00**
#409, Mickey Mouse, wood, metal, black and red, 1933	**1,300.00**

#411, Mickey Mouse, pressed wood, Mickey playing instrument, 1933	**1,400.00**
#570, Memento, place for pictures, 1945	**110.00**
#640, portable, plastic, flip up front, battery set, 1950	**30.00**

Fada
#43, cathedral, pressed wood	**240.00**
#60W, table, plastic	**75.00**
#136, table, Catalin, 1941	**1,000.00**
#252, table, Catalin, temple, 1941	**500.00**

Federal
#58DX, table, 1922	**500.00**
#100, table, 1924	**425.00**

General Electric
K–126, console, wood, 1933	**150.00**
#400, 410, 411, 414, table, all plastic	**30.00**
#515, 517, clock radio, 1950s	**30.00**

Grebe
CR–12, table, 1923	**600.00**
MU–1, table, with chain, 1925	**200.00**

Hallicrafters
TW–200, World Wide	**110.00**
TW–600, portable, map and whip antenna, AC/DC battery, 1954	**100.00**

Majestic
Charlie McCarthy, 1938	**1,000.00**
#92, console, 1929	**125.00**
#381, Treasure Chest, 1934	**225.00**

Motorola
Jewel Box, #5J1	**80.00**
Ranger, portable, leatherette trim	**40.00**

RCA Victor, Model 65XI, red plastic case, 11 x 7 x 6½", $95.00.

Table, plastic, 1950s	35.00
Olympic, radio with phonograph, lift top, wood	40.00
Paragon	
DA–2, table, 1921	450.00
RD–5, table, 1922	600.00
Philco	
17–20–38, cathedral	250.00
#37–62, table, two-tone	75.00
#37–602, table, Art Deco grill	90.00
#40–180, console, wood	130.00
#46–132, table	35.00
#49–506, Tranistone	35.00
Radiobar, complete console, glasses, decanter	1,200.00
Radio Corporation of America, RCA	
La Siesta, 1939	300.00
Radiola 18	55.00
Radiola 24	160.00
Radiola 28, console, highboy	200.00
Radiola 33	40.00
#40X56, 1939 World's Fair	975.00
Silvertone, Sears	
#1, table, 1950	75.00
1582, cathedral, wood	225.00
Sparton, #506, Bluebird, table, round blue or peach mirror	3,600.00
Stewart–Warner, table, slant, 1938	175.00
Zenith	
Table, 6D2615, boomerang dial, 1942	75.00
Trans–oceanic	80.00

RAILROAD ITEMS

History: Railroad collectors have existed for decades. The merger of rail systems and the end of passenger service made many objects available to private collectors. The Pennsylvania Railroad sold its archives at public sale.

Railroad enthusiasts have organized into regional and local clubs. Join one if interested. Your local hobby store can probably point you to the right person. The best pieces pass between collectors and rarely enter the general market.

References: Susan and Al Bagdade, *Warman's American Pottery and Porcelain,* Wallace–Homestead, 1994; Stanley L. Baker, *Railroad Collectibles: An Illustrated Value Guide, 4th Edition*, Collector Books, 1990, 1993 value update; Richard C. Barrett, *The Illustrated Encyclopedia of Railroad Lighting, Volume 1: The Railroad Lantern,* Railroad Research Publications, 1994; Phil Bollhagen (comp.), *The Great Book of Railroad Playing Cards, 1991 Version,* published by author, 1991; Arthur Dominy and Rudolph A. Morgenfruh, *Silver At Your Service,* published by authors, 1987; Richard Luckin, *Dining on Rails,* RK Publishing 1994; Richard Luckin, *Mimbres to Mimbreno: A Study of Santa Fe's Famous China Pattern,* RK Publishing, 1992; Richard Luckin, *Teapot Treasury and Related Items,* RK Publishing, 1987; Everett L. Maffet, *Silver Banquet II: A Compendium on Railroad Dining Car Silver Serving Pieces,* Silver Press, 1990; Douglas W. McIntrye, *The Official Guide To Railroad Dining Car China,* Walsworth Press, 1990, out–of–print; Larry R. Paul, *Sparkling Crystal: A Collector's Guide To Railroad Glassware,* Railroadiana Collectors Assoc., 1990; Don Stewart, *Railroad Switch Keys & Padlocks, 2nd Edition,* Key Collectors International, 1993.

Periodicals: *Key, Lock and Lantern,* 3 Berkeley Heights Park, Bloomfield, NJ 07003; *Main Line Journal,* PO Box 121, Streamwood, IL 60107.

Collectors' Clubs: Chesapeake & Ohio Historical Society, Inc., PO Box 79, Clifton Forge, VA 24422; Illinois Central Railroad Historical Society, 14818 Clifton Park, Midlothian, IL 60445; Railroad Enthusiasts, 102 Dean Rd., Brookline, MA 02146; Railroadiana Collectors Association, 795 Aspen Dr., Buffalo Grove, IL 60089; Railway and Locomotive Historical Society, PO Box 1418, Westford, MA 01886; Twentieth Century Railroad Club, 329 West 18th St., Suite 902, Chicago, IL 60616.

Museums: Baltimore and Ohio Railroad, Baltimore, MD; California State Railroad Museum, Sacramento, CA; Frisco Railroad Museum, Van Buren, AR; Museum of Transportation, Brookline, MA; National Railroad Museum, Green Bay, WI; New York Museum of Transportation, West Henrietta, NY; Old Depot Railroad Museum, Dassel, MN.

Additional Listings: See *Warman's Americana & Collectibles* for more examples.

Ticket Case, oak, tin ticket holders, 16″ l, 8½″ d, 17½″ h, $85.00.

Belt Buckle, Union Pacific, Smith
& Wesson insignia on reverse,
#J–36, 1866 .... 75.00
Blotter, Ozark Zephyr, Burlington
Route 9.00
China
  Ashtray, Great Northern, Mountains & Flowers, 4″ d, backstamp, Syracuse China 85.00
  Butter Pat, Atlantic Coast Line, Flora of the South, 3½″ d, backstamp, Syracuse China . 95.00
  Celery Tray, Grand Trunk Western, City of Grand Rapids, 11 x 6″, top logo, Rosenthal China 185.00
  Cereal Bowl, Baltimore & Ohio, Capitol, 6¼″ d, top logo, Shenango China 45.00
  Cup and Saucer
    Chessie, marked "Syracuse," tiny hairline above handle . 75.00
    Union Pacific, Desert Flower, backstamp, Syracuse China 95.00
  Gravy Boat, New York, New Haven & Hartford, Platinum Blue, side marked, backstamp, Buffalo China 125.00
  Mustard Pot, cov, Chesapeake & Ohio, Staffordshire, backstamp, Shenango China 175.00
  Pickle Tray, Northern Pacific, Monax, 7¾ x 3¾″, top logo, Shenango China 200.00
  Plate
    Minneapolis, St Paul & Sault

Saint Marie, Logan, 9¾″ d, backstamp, Mayer China .. 250.00
  Missouri Pacific, Eagle, 6¼″ d, top logo, backstamp, Syracuse China 38.00
  Platter
    Chicago, Milwaukee & Puget Sound, Puget, oval, 12¼ x 8½″, top logo, Maddock ... 200.00
    New York Central, Dewitt Clinton, rect, 8½ x 5¼″, top marked, backstamp, Syracuse China 48.00
  Sauce Dish, Reading, Stotesbury, 4¼″ sq, backstamp, Scammell China 165.00
  Soup Bowl, Norfolk & Western, Cavalier, 8¾″ d, top logo, Scammell China 75.00
Fire Grenades, Chicago & Northwestern RR, cast iron wall mount, emb "C&NW RR" 115.00
Glassware
  Highball, Pennsylvania, 4½″ h, maroon and white train, Washington, DC, and New York City skylines 25.00
  Water, Nickel Plate Road, 3¾″ h, white and blue logo, "NICKEL PLATE ROAD" inside 25.00
  Wine, Canadian National System, 4½″ h, 2½″ d, stemmed, etched logo 45.00
Hat, Sante Fe, conductor, 1925 .. 325.00
Headlight, 14″, marked "Imperial Incandescent Headlight" 250.00
Lantern
  Kansas City Southern Railway, Adams & Westlake Co, Adlake Reliable, single horiz wire guard bellbottom frame, 5⅜″ clear globe etched "KCSRY," patent date May 9, 1922, frame marked "KCSRY" 160.00
  New York, Philadelphia & Norfolk Railroad, Keystone Lantern Co, The Casey, single horiz wire guard, twist wick raiser, 5⅜″ amber globe, patent date Dec 30, 1902, frame marked "NYP&N R CO" 850.00
Lantern Globe
  Pennsylvania Lines, 5⅜″, red cast, extended base 150.00

Rutland, 6″, green, etched "Rutland RR Co," manufactured by Macbeth Pearl Glass 227 ... **200.00**

Santa Fe, 5⅜″, aqua, etched cross logo, "Santa Fe" logo . **325.00**

Western Maryland Railroad, 5⅜″, clear cast, extended base, rect panel marked "WMRR" **250.00**

Map, Ohio Railway, linen, 1902 .. **60.00**

Menu, Union Pacific RR, 1954, Bryce Canyon cov **9.00**

Oil Can, emb "NY, NH, & HRR," long spout **70.00**

Plaque, 9¼″, copper, builder s, "The Baldwin Locomotive Works/Philadelphia/USA/October 1912" **330.00**

Post Card

Hatfield Station, Fort Meyer, VA, divided back, photo, unused . **60.00**

Waiting for the Train, Egypt, MA depot, black and white, divided back, July 8, 1913 .... **7.00**

Silver

Coffeepot, New York Central, 8 oz, #070, incised side mark, backstamp, International Silver **85.00**

Corn Holder, Pennsylvania, incised PRR Keystone, logo on top, International Silver, pr ... **85.00**

Creamer, Southern, 10 oz, #1332, hinged lid, incised SR arrow on side, Reed & Barton **265.00**

Fork, cocktail, Louisville & Nashville, Cromwell, International Silver **22.00**

Knife

Atlantic Coast Line, Zephyr, small, International Silver .. **16.00**

Santa Fe #22, Priscilla, large, Rogers Brothers **22.00**

Spoon

Serving, Lehigh Valley, Rex, flag logo, Reed & Barton .. **85.00**

Tablespoon, Santa Fe, Albany, Gorham **12.00**

Teaspoon, Northern Pacific, Savoy, Victor **18.00**

Sugar Tongs, Frisco Lines, Dartmouth, 4¼″ l, backstamp, Wallace **125.00**

Tureen, cov, Atchison, Topeka &

Santa Fe, 6½″, double handles, side and top logo, Harrison Brothers **165.00**

Switch Key

L&N RR, 9639 .... **15.00**

MK&T RY, Slaymaker, football hallmark **25.00**

NPRR, Fraim, keystone hallmark **15.00**

Switch Lock

Boston & Maine Railroad, brass, early style, marked "B&M RR LS S, Sherburne & Co, Boston, MA" **125.00**

Erie Railroad Co, six lever, round **200.00**

Water Pail, Soo Line, 13 x 10″, emb metal, wide collar on bottom **45.00**

RAZORS

History: Razors date back several thousand years. Early man used sharpened stones. The Egyptians, Greeks, and Romans had metal razors.

Razors made prior to 1800 generally were crudely stamped WARRANTED or CAST STEEL, with the maker's mark on the tang. Until 1870 almost all razors for the American market were manufactured in Sheffield, England. Most blades were wedge shaped; many were etched with slogans or scenes. Handles were made of natural materials: various horns, tortoiseshell, bone, ivory, stag, silver, and pearl. All razors were handmade.

After 1870 razors were machine made with hollow ground blades and synthetic handle materials. Razors of this period usually were manufactured in Germany (Solingen) or in American cutlery factories. Hundreds of molded celluloid handle patterns were produced.

Cutlery firms produced boxed sets of two, four, and seven razors. Complete and undamaged sets are very desirable. Most popular are the 7–Day sets with each razor etched with a day of the week.

The fancier the handle or more intricately etched the blade, the higher the price. Rarest handle materials are pearl, stag, sterling silver, pressed horn, and carved ivory. Rarest blades are those with scenes etched across the entire front. Value is increased by certain manufacturer's names, e.g., H. Boker, Case, M. Price, Joseph Rogers, Simmons Hardware, Will & Finck, Winchester, and George Wostenholm.

Abbreviations:
hgb = hollow ground blade
wb = wedge blade
References: Ronald S. Barlow, *The Vanishing American Barber Shop,* Windmill Publishing, 1993; Robert A. Doyle, *Straight Razor Collecting, An Illustrated Price Guide,* Collector Books, 1980, out–of–print; Phillip L. Krumholz, *Value Guide For Barberiana & Shaving Collectibles,* Ad Libs Publishing, 1988; Jim Sargent, *Sargent's American Premium Guide To Pocket Knives & Razors, Identification and Values,* 3rd Edition, Books Americana, 1992.

Periodical: *Blade Magazine,* PO Box 22007, Chattanooga, TN 37422.

Additional Listings: See *Warman's Americana & Collectibles* for more examples.

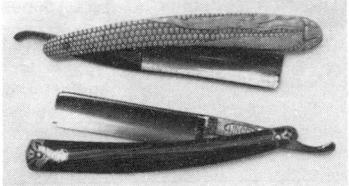

Top: Reliance Cutlery Co., ear of corn, two-colored celluloid handle, $65.00; bottom: J. P. Alamaiz, Schenectady, NY, marked "Lincoln," portrait bust of Lincoln on end, imitation celluloid wood grain handle, $75.00.

AMERICAN BLADES

Challenge Cutlery Co, Bridgeport, CT, blade etched "Rince," black peacock pattern 55.00
Novelty Cutlery Co, Canton, OH, USA, rounded point blade, handle with cow, horse, train, and owner's name and address, front dated "1921," German silver ends 80.00
Saffa, John J, St Louis, two gold camels and scroll scene on blade with "Silver Steel," ivory colored handle 25.00
Union Razor Cutlery Co, Union City, GA, banded tobacco pattern handle 40.00

ENGLISH BLADES, SHEFFIELD

Turniss Cutler & Stacey Sheffield, unusually shaped point blade, tang stamped "For Use," two pressed intertwined snakes on mottled horn handle 620.00
Wade & Butcher, hgb, engraved and ornate escutcheon plate with two inlaid engraved star shaped metal dec, mottled horn handle, blade etched "The Celebrated Hollow Ground Razor," c1850 . . . . 70.00

GERMAN BLADES

Boker, H & Co, etched blade with American Lines SS St Louis Ship scene, black celluloid handle 125.00
Eyre, B J, Germany, hgb, blade etched "Extra Hollow Ground" in gold, imitation ivory handle with light blue peacock feather pattern 75.00
Morley, W H & Co, hgb, blade etched "Real Hollow Ground," imitation ivory handle with raised orange flower and ribbon dec . . 55.00
Westfield Mfg Co, hgb, ivory handle with checkered raised shield 50.00

SETS OF RAZORS

7–Day Set, A J Jordan, Sheffield, England, blades engraved with days of week, tangs etched "Old Faithful," ivory handles with pointed ends, peeled perimeter and inlaid brass escutcheon plate on oak case, purple lining 245.00
7–Day Set, Sheffield Steel Warranted, rounded point hgb, imi-

tation ivory handles, tangs stamped "K" in a circle, leather cov wood case, burgundy velvet lined slotted int. **130.00**

7–Day Set, Taylor Eye–Witness Sheffield, semi–wedge blades with engraved days on top, ivory handle, leather cov wood case with German silver escutcheon plate, blue lining with gold adv, lock, and key **240.00**

RECORDS

History: With the advent of the more sophisticated recording materials, such as 33⅓ RPM long–playing records, 8–track tapes, cassettes, and compact discs, earlier phonograph records became collectors' items. Most have little value. The higher–priced examples are rare (limited production) recordings. Condition is critical.

References: Steven C. Barr, *The Almost Complete 78 RPM Record Dating Guide (II),* Yesterday Once Again, 1992; L. R. Docks, *1900–1965 American Premium Record Guide, 4th Edition,*, Books Americana, 1992; *Goldmine's 1995 Annual, 4th Edition,* Krause Publications, 1994; Anthony J. Gribin and Matthew M. Schiff, *Doo–Wop: The Forgotten Third of Rock 'n' Roll,* Krause Publications, 1992; Fred Heggeness, *Country Western Price Guide,* FH Publishing, 1990; Ron Lofman, *Goldmine's Celebrity Vocals,* Krause Publications, 1994; Vito R. Marino and Anthony C. Furfero, *The Official Price Guide To Frank Sinatra Records and CDs,* House of Collectibles, 1993; William M. Miller, *How To Buy & Sell Used Record Albums,* Loran Publishing, 1994; Jerry Osborne, *The Official Price Guide To Elvis Presley Records and Memorabilia,* House of Collectibles, 1994; Jerry Osborne, *The Official Price Guide To Movie/TV Soundtracks and Original Cast Albums,* House of Collectibles, 1991; Jerry Osborne, *The Official Price Guide To Records, 10th Edition,* House of Collectibles, 1993; Neal Umphred, *Goldmine's Price Guide To Collectible Jazz Albums, 1949–1969, 2nd Edition,* Krause Publications, 1994; Neal Umphred, *Gold-mine's Price Guide To Collectible Record Albums, 4th Edition,* Krause Publications, 1994; Neal Umphred, *Goldmine's Rock 'n Roll 45 RPM Record Price Guide, 3rd Edition,* Krause Publications, 1994.

Periodicals: *Cadence,* Cadence Building, Redwood, NY 13679; *DISCoveries Magazine,* PO Box 309, Fraser, MI 48026; *Goldmine,* 700 E. State St., Iola, WI 54990; *Jazz Beat Magazine,* 1206 Decatur St., New Orleans, LA 70116; *Joslin's Jazz Journal,* PO Box 213, Parsons, KS 67357; *Record Collectors Monthly,* PO Box 75, Mendham, NJ 07945; *Record Finder,* PO Box 1047, Glen Allen, VA 23060; *The New Amberola Graphic,* 37 Caledonia St., St. Johnsbury, VT 05819.

Collectors' Clubs: Association For Recorded Sound Collections, PO Box 453, Annapolis, MD 21404; International Association of Jazz Record Collectors, PO Box 75155, Tampa, FL 33605.

Additional Listings: See *Warman's Americana & Collectibles* for more examples.

Note: Most records, especially popular recordings, have a value of less than $3 per disc. The records listed here are classic recordings of their type and in demand by collectors.

Ames Brothers, In The Evening By
  The Moonlight, Coral, 56017 . . **12.00**
Annette, Songs From Annette,
  Mickey Mouse, 24 . . . . **40.00**

***Me and My Teddy Bear,* RCA Victor, Camden, NY, orig dust cov, 9⅞" d, $8.00.**

Bailey, Pearl, I'm With You, Coral,
56078 .... 16.00
Beach Boys, Surfin' Safari, Capitol, DT–1808 .... 30.00
Berry, Chuck, After School Session, Chess, 1426 .... 50.00
Calloway, Cab, Hi De Hi, Hi De Ho,
RCA Victor 16.00
Cole, Nat King, The King Cole
Trio, Volume 2, Capitol, H–29 . 20.00
Crosby, Bing, Jerome Kern Songs,
Decca, 5001 .... 20.00
Day, Doris, You're My Thrill, Columbia, 6071 .... 20.00
Domino, Fats, Rock and Rollin',
Imperial, 9009 .... 65.00
Ellington, Duke, Masterpieces By
Ellington, Columbia, 4418 .... 30.00
Fabian, Hold That Tiger, Chancellor, 5003 .... 20.00
Fisher, Eddie, I'm In The Mood For
Love, RCA Victor, 3058 ...... 16.00
Fitzgerald, Ella, Songs In A Mellow
Mood, Decca, 8068 .... 20.00
Gillespie, Dizzy, Dizzy Gillespie,
Volume 1, Atlantic, 138 ...... 150.00
Goodman, Benny, Carnegie Hall
Jazz Concert, Columbia, 160 .. 45.00
Haley, Bill & His Comets, Rock
With Bill Haley and The Comets,
Essex, 202 .... 75.00
Ink Spots, The Ink Spots, Volume
1, Decca, 5056 .... 20.00
Little Richard, Here's Little Richard, Specialty, 2100 .... 75.00
Mathis, Johnny, Warm, Columbia,
1078 .... 14.00
McGuire Sisters, By Request,
Coral, 56123 .... 20.00
Page, Patti, Tennessee Waltz,
Mercury, 25154 .... 16.00
Platters, The Platters, Mercury,
20146 .... 50.00
Righteous Brothers, Some Blue–
Eyed Soul, Moonglow, 1002 ... 8.00
Shirelles, Tonight's The Night,
Scepter, 501 .... 35.00
Sinatra, Frank, Songs By Sinatra,
Columbia, 124 .... 50.00
Torme, Mel, California Suite, Capitol, P–200 .... 30.00
Twitty, Conway, Conway Twitty
Songs, MGM, E–3744 .... 40.00

Williams, Hank, Hank Williams
Sings, MGM, E–107 .... **75.00**

REDWARE

History: The availability of clay, the same used to make bricks and roof tiles, accounted for the great production of red earthenware pottery in the American colonies. Redware pieces are mainly utilitarian—bowls, crocks, jugs, etc.

Lead–glazed redware retained its reddish color, but a variety of colored glazes were obtained by the addition of metals to the basic glaze. Streaks and mottled splotches in redware items resulted from impurities in the clay and/or uneven firing temperatures.

"Slipware" is a term used to describe redwares decorated by the application of slip, a semi–liquid paste made of clay. Slipwares were made in England, Germany, and elsewhere in Europe for decades before becoming popular in the Pennsylvania German region and elsewhere in colonial America.

References: Susan and Al Bagdade, *Warman's American Pottery and Porcelain,* Wallace–Homestead, 1994; William C. Ketchum, Jr., *American Pottery and Porcelain,* Avon Books, 1994; Kevin McConnell, *Redware: America's Folk Art Pottery,* Schiffer Publishing, 1988; Dana G. Morykan and Harry L. Rinker, *Warman's Country Antiques & Collectibles, Second Edition,* Wallace–Homestead, 1994.

Bank
5" h, ovoid, knob handle, twotone yellow slip, sgraffito inscription "A Present from Sod
Hill," clear glaze with brown
flecks **15.00**
6" h, mottled brown glaze, black
slashes, knob finial **145.00**
Bowl
6⅛" d, dark brown sponging, ftd **75.00**
7¼" d
Brown glaze, open rim handles **50.00**
Yellow slip dec, wavy lines and
dots, reddish glaze **325.00**
8½" d, yellow slip dec **30.00**
9½" d, tooled band, dark brown
sponging, deep orange

ground, rim spout, ribbed handle **175.00**
9¾" d, orange glazed int. **25.00**
10" d, yellow slip dec, brown wavy and straight lines **300.00**
10¼" d, glaze int. **45.00**
15½" d, wheel turned, lengthwise cut, glazed int. **50.00**
Charger
11¼" d, two line yellow slip dec, coggled rim **250.00**
12¾" d, slip dec, PA, wear and rim chips **750.00**
13" d, slip dec, PA, rim chips .. **350.00**
Coffeepot, 11¼" h, dome top, tooled dec, emb leaf handle, mismatched lid, English **150.00**
Cup, 2¾" h, brown splotches **50.00**
Dish
6¼" d, 3" h, applied rim handles, brown splotched glaze, edge chips **325.00**
7⅜" d, yellow slip wavy line dec **175.00**
Figure, 8¾" h, dog, seated, tooled coat and detail **450.00**
Flask, 6⅜" h, two-tone dark brown glaze **110.00**

Food Mold, turk's head, late, midwest, 10" d, $65.00.

Food Mold, turk's head
7" d, two–tone green glaze, emb ribs and handle, rim chips ... **65.00**
9" d, brown sponging, chips ... **25.00**
11¾" d, clear glaze, brown and green **75.00**
Jar
5" h, dark sponged dec, tooled line around middle **125.00**
6¾" h, ovoid, side spout, tooled line on shoulder, strap handle **225.00**
8¼" h, ovoid, glazed int. **85.00**

10" h, ovoid, brownish amber flecks, glazed **300.00**
Jug
6½" h, ovoid, clear glaze, strap handle **200.00**
7¾" h, mottled brown glaze, ribbed strap handle **155.00**
11" h, brown glaze **50.00**
Lamp, 3⅜" h, flared base, open font with wick support, clear glaze with running brown **1,000.00**
Loaf Pan, 12 x 14¾", white slip dec, dark glaze, chip and wear **40.00**
Milk Bowl, 15" d, dark brown int. glaze **200.00**
Mug
6" h, brown splotches, strap handle **250.00**
6¾" h, two-tone dark brown glaze **175.00**
8" h, two-tone dark brown glaze **200.00**
Pie Plate
7¾" d, coggled rim, three line yellow slip crow's foot design **100.00**
8" d, three line yellow slip dec, coggled rim, edge and surface chips **350.00**
8⅞" d, three line yellow slip dec, coggled rim, hairline crack ... **55.00**
9" d, coggled edge **65.00**
9½" d, yellow slip wavy line dec, coggled rim, old chips **625.00**
Pitcher
7½" h, ovoid, strap handle, hairline, chips, and wear **195.00**
8" h, brown fleck glaze, ribbed strap handle **90.00**
9½" h, ovoid, amber glaze, brown splotches, ribbed strap handle **45.00**
10¼" h, thick bluish-green mottled glaze **150.00**
10½" h, Shenandoah, white slip, clear glaze, running green and brown, strap handle, applied ornaments, minor edge chips **1,350.00**
Plate
8½" d, sponged dec, America, 19th C **145.00**
11" d, PA, slipware dec, initials "NP," upper edge chips **210.00**
14¼" d, PA, yellow slipware dec "St Justin the Apologist," scattered chips, rim flakes **800.00**

Salt, 11¾" h, white slip floral dec, "Salt" on rim opening, dark green glaze **65.00**
Sconce, 6½" h, candle type, wheel turned, socket in base **350.00**
Wash Bowl, 16" d, Shenandoah, white slip, clear glaze, running green and brown, applied handles and soap dish, glued repairs **800.00**

RED WING POTTERY

History: The Red Wing pottery category covers several potteries from Red Wing, Minnesota. In 1868 David Hallem started Red Wing Stoneware Co., the first pottery with stoneware as its primary product and with a red wing stamped under the glaze as its mark. The Minnesota Stoneware Co. started in 1883. The North Star Stoneware Co., 1892–1896, used a raised star and the words "Red Wing" as its mark.

The Red Wing Stoneware Co. and the Minnesota Stoneware Co. merged in 1892. The new company, the Red Wing Union Stoneware Co., made stoneware until 1920 when it introduced a pottery line which it continued until the 1940s. In 1936 the name was changed to Red Wing Potteries, Inc. During the 1930s it introduced several popular lines of hand–painted pattern dinnerware which were distributed through department stores, Sears, and gift stamp centers. Dinnerware production declined in the 1950s, being replaced with hotel and restaurant china in the early 1960s. The plant closed in 1967.

References: Susan and Al Bagdade, *Warman's American Pottery and Porcelain,* Wallace–Homestead, 1994; Stanley Bougie and David Newkirk, *Price Guide & Supplement for Red Wing Dinnerware (1990–1991 Edition),* published by authors, 1990; Dan and Gail DePasquale and Larry Peterson, *Red Wing Collectibles,* Collector Books, 1985, 1995 value update; Dan and Gail DePasquale and Larry Peterson, *Red Wing Stoneware,* Collector Books, 1983, 1994 value update; Dana G. Morykan and Harry L. Rinker, *Warman's Country Antiques & Collectibles, Second Edition,* Wallace–Homestead, 1994; David A. Newkirk, *A Guide To Red Wing Markings,* Monticello Printing, 1979; Gary and Bonnie Tefft, *Red Wing Potters and Their Wares, Second Edition,* Locust Enterprises, 1987.

Collectors' Club: Red Wing Collectors Society, Inc., PO Box 124, Neosho, WI 53059.

Additional Listings: See *Warman's Americana & Collectibles* for more examples.

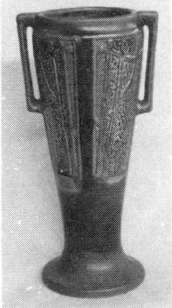

Vase, trumpet body, two handles, disc base, four relief panels of semiglaze brown trees, gray matte ground, marked "RED WING UNION/STONEWARE/CO./ RED WING/MINN," 9¾" h, $65.00.

Ashtray, wing shape, red glaze, 75th anniversary issue **35.00**
Bowl, 11" d, red and pink accented raised florals and dancing people, natural ground, imp "RED WING USA" **30.00**
Box, Magnolia Ware, matte ivory, imp "RED WING USA 1018" .. **25.00**

Butter Crock, gray line **175.00**
Casserole, cov, Saffron ware, brown sponged band on lid and bowl, handled, marked "Made In Red Wing" in circle on bottom . **185.00**
Churn, 8 gallon, cobalt blue "8" and double leaf design, unsgd . **325.00**
Compote, 7" h, paneled bowl, light brown ext., gloss yellow int., "RED WING USA M5008" **16.00**
Dish, center red apple, chartreuse ext. **10.00**
Ewer, 10½" h, serpent handle, serpents and face on base, ivory matte glaze **65.00**
Flowerpot, 4½" h, wide mouth, matte pink glaze **12.00**
Jug, 1 gallon, blue sponged dec, molded, wire bail with turned wood handle, incised "Minnesota Stoneware Co, Red Wing Minn" in bottom **875.00**
Milk Pan, 7" d, brown Albany glaze, incised "RWSCo" on bottom **45.00**
Pitcher, 10½" h, ewer shape, molded scroll design on base, fluted neck, figural animal's head handle, mint green ext., brown spatter, yellow int., imp "RED WING USA 220" **60.00**
Planter
  5" h, flared shape, flutes, ftd, semigloss black glaze, marked "RED WING USA M5004" .. **14.00**
  10" d, band of circles on rim, matte white glaze, raised "RED WING USA 445" **10.00**
Refrigerator Jar, cov, stacking, stoneware, cobalt blue bands and "Red Wing Refrigerator Jar" **135.00**
Spittoon, blue and white, sponged dec, unsgd **450.00**
Urn, ftd, Art Deco style, matte royal blue finish, #753 .... **75.00**
Vase
  4½" h, indented sides, gloss yellow glaze, blue "RED WING ART POTTERY 175" mark .. **40.00**
  6¼" h, fan shape, vertical ribbing, two small scroll handles on rim, aqua glaze, marked "950 RED WING USA" **25.00**

7" h, rect, center flutes, scroll handles, stippled golden brown glaze, imp "RED WING 751" **22.00**
8" h, ball shaped, gloss green glaze, #178 .... **85.00**

RELIGIOUS ITEMS

History: Objects for the worshipping of or the expression of man's belief in a superhuman power are collected by many people for many reasons.

Icons are included in this category since they are religious mementos, usually paintings with a brass encasement. Collecting icons dates from the earliest period of Christianity. Most antique icons in today's market were made in the late 19th century.

Collectors' Club: Foundation International for Restorers of Religious Medals, PO Box 2652, Worcester, MA 01608.

Museum: American Bible Society, New York, NY.

Reproduction Alert: Icons are heavily reproduced.

Textile, painted, embroidery highlights, possibly European, framed, 20¾ x 27", $350.00.

Altar Sticks, Louis Phillippe style, gilt bronze, fitted as table lamps, 37" h, pr **1,035.00**

Box, French, carved wood, Biblical figures flanking full figured lion clinging to box, winged figure on hinged cov, mirrored int., late 17th/early 18th C, 3¾" l **925.00**

Candelabra, gilt bronze, figural, thirteen light, associated marble top gilt bronze stand, 19th C, 39" h **750.00**

Casket, Italian Renaissance style, polychrome painted dec, Christ and saint, flaking, late 19th C, 40" l, 24" d, 39½" h **975.00**

Creche Figure, saint with sow, polychrome painted wood, lacking arms, flaking, worming, 27" h .. **375.00**

Figure
Angels with Censers, pr, Continental, Renaissance style, parcel gilt, bas-relief, polychrome dec, 40" h **3,325.00**

Buddha, carved giltwood, full standing figure, black plinth, Thai, 82" h **650.00**

Madonna and Child
Continental, carved boxwood, losses, 18th C, 6½" h **315.00**

Spanish, carved and painted wood, 17¾" h **115.00**

Saint, German, earthenware, polychrome dec tin glaze, 19th C, 18" h **630.00**

Icon, reverse painted glass, Virgin Mary and Child, framed, 17 x 13" **60.00**

Micro–Mosaic, St Peter's Square, Rome, 19th C, custom framed, 5⅛ x 7⅛" **1,600.00**

Needlework Picture, Baroque, religious scene, embroidered silk, watercolor accents, wood and stamped brass frame, fiber loss, 7½" w, 10½" h **525.00**

Painting
The Annunciation to the Virgin, Italian School, unsigned, oil on copper, minute scattered losses, surface grime, craquelure, unframed, 16th C style, 8¾ x 6¾" **750.00**

Virgin and Child with male saints, oil on panel, unsigned,

Italian school, losses, partially cleaned, minor retouch, craquelure, 16th C style, 25½ x 31½" **1,375.00**

Sculpture, carved wood, "Depiction of The Last Supper," 16" l .   **65.00**

Traveling Shrine, Japanese Rioro, lacquered, double petal doors opening to gilded and lacquered Amida Buddha figure, backed by pierced mandorla, single lotus blossom base and stepped throne, 19th C, 6¾" h **225.00**

REVERSE PAINTING ON GLASS

History: The earliest examples of reverse painting on glass were produced in 13th–century Italy. By the 17th century the technique had spread to Central and Eastern Europe. It spread westward as the glass industry center moved to Germany in the late 17th century.

The Alsace and Black Forest regions developed a unique portraiture style. The half and three-quarter portraits often were titled below the portrait. Women tend to have general names. Most males are of famous men.

The English used a mezzotint method, rather than free–style, to create their reverse paintings. Landscapes and allegorical figures were popular. The Chinese began working in the medium in the 17th century, eventually favoring marine and patriotic scenes.

Reverse painting was done in America. Most were unsigned by folk artists who favored portraits, patriotic and mourning scenes, floral compositions, landscapes, and buildings. Known American artists include Benjamin Greenleaf, A. Cranfield, and Rowley Jacobs.

In the late 19th century commercially produced reverse paintings, often decorated with mother-of-pearl, became popular. Themes included the Statue of Liberty, the capitol in Washington, D.C., and various world's fairs and expositions.

Reference: Shirley Mace, *Encyclopedia*

of Silhouette Collectibles On Glass, Shadow Enterprises, 1992.

PORTRAITS

9½ x 12", Emilie, balloon sleeve dress, large collar **500.00**
10 x 8", woman, plumed hat, seated by column, orig frame . . **375.00**
12¼ x 14¼", Napoleon, white uniform, green oval, black rect, gilt flowers in spandrels, beveled frame **1,000.00**
14½" x 11½", George Washington and family, Chinese Export, 19th C, molded wood frame **3,750.00**

Pastoral scene, dirt road, cottage in background, sgd "L. Ray," wood and plaster gilt frame, 16 x 20⅛", $70.00.

SCENES

9½ x 7½", Summer, maple frame, oval inner frame **350.00**
10 x 6½", *USS Maine* battleship . **90.00**
14¼ x 10¼", winter landscape, Currier and Ives type, inscribed "American Farm Scene," orig frame **135.00**
19 x 15", landscape, three Chinese figures with elephants, corner crack to glass, slight separation, 19th C, Chinese **810.00**
20 x 27", Blarney Castle, forest scene, mica and abalone highlights **150.00**

RIDGWAY

History: Throughout the 19th century the Ridgway family, through a series of partnerships, held a position of importance in Shelton and Hanley, Staffordshire, England. The connection began with Job and George, two brothers, and Job's two sons, John and William. In 1830 John and William separated with John retaining the Cauldon Place factory and William the Bell Works. By 1862 the porcelain division of Cauldon was carried on by Coalport China Ltd. William and his heirs continued at the Bell Works and the Church (Hanley) and Bedford (Shelton) works until the end of the 19th century.

Many early pieces are unmarked. Later marks include the initials of the many partnerships.

References: Susan and Al Bagdade, *Warman's English & Continental Pottery & Porcelain, Second Edition,* Wallace–Homestead, 1991; G. A. Godden, *Ridgway Porcelains,* Antique Collectors' Club, 1985.

Additional Listings: Staffordshire, Historical, and Staffordshire, Romantic.

Bowl, 9½" d, Coaching Days and Ways, Henry VIII and the Abbot, black and caramel brown **40.00**
Cake Stand, 9½" d, 2¼" h, Oriental floral design, butterflies, gilt trim, marked "Ridgway, Old Derby," stains, gilt wear, one has chip and hairline, price for pair . **125.00**
Cup and Saucer, scene of boy fishing on lake **25.00**
Pitcher, 4¼" h, red transfer, family scenes, cream ground in roundels, reserved on cobalt blue ground, c1890, marked "Humphrey's Clock and William Ridgway" **200.00**

Plate, blue transfer of bird in square, florals, banded design, gold rim, blue quiver mark, 9½" d, $48.00.

Plaque, 12" d, Coaching Days, In A Snow Drift, black transfer, yellow ground **130.00**
Plate, 8½" d, rust, rose, and purple Oriental type flowers with yellow centers, gray green branches, scalloped edge, No. 2004, c1830 .... **60.00**
Teapot, cov, Royal Vistas, black transfer, green yellow overglaze, copper luster trim **185.00**
Tray, 9½" l, 7½" w, Pickwick design, silver luster trim, scalloped rim, open handles **45.00**
Waste Pot, cov, 11" h, 10" d, Chester pattern, floral design, pink glaze **70.00**

RING TREES

History: A ring tree is a small, generally saucer–shaped object made of glass, porcelain, metal, or wood with a center post in the shape of a hand, branches, or cylinder for hanging or storing finger rings.

Bronze, 5" h, figural, parrot **45.00**
Glass
  Cameo, 3¼" h, acid cut, red flowers, leaves, and stems, leaf ground, St Louis **150.00**

Cranberry, 3¼" h, multicolored flowers, gold leaves **115.00**
Cut, 3" h, clear, flowers and leaves, black enamel bands . **55.00**
Lalique, 5" h, figural, Madonna, frosted, marked "R Lalique, France 288" **200.00**
Opaline
  2½" d, column center, round dish, blue, gold and white trim **50.00**
  3¼" h, hp, blue, orange and gold dec, ftd **45.00**

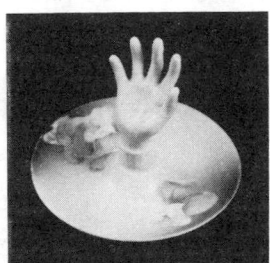

Porcelain, hand, hand painted, Germany, 3¾" d, $50.00.

Porcelain
  Hand Painted, hand and dish, rose dec, gilding, maple leaf mark, marked "Hand Painted" **50.00**
  Nippon, hand shape, floral dec, gold ground **45.00**
  Royal Worcester, maroon and yellow florals, beige satin finish, gold trim, c1912 .... **115.00**
  Wedgwood, Jasperware
    Cobalt blue, white relief figures, 2¾" h, marked **120.00**
    Dark blue, rose border, classical scenes, unmarked ... **175.00**
    Dark blue and white, classical figures **180.00**
  Scrimshaw, 5¾" h, bone, harp shape, Prisoner–of–War **100.00**
  Sterling Silver, figural, angel, Tiffany & Co **450.00**
  Wood, Tramp Art, fruitwood, hand shape, carved **25.00**

ROCKINGHAM AND ROCKINGHAM BROWN GLAZED WARES

History: Rockingham ware can be divided into two categories. The first consists of the fine china and porcelain pieces made between 1826 and 1842 by the Rockingham Company of Swinton, Yorkshire, England, and its predecessor firms: Swinton, Bingley, Don, Leeds, and Brameld. The Bramelds developed the cadogan, a lidless teapot. Between 1826 and 1842 a quality soft–paste body with a warm, silken feel was developed by the Bramelds. Elaborate specialty pieces were made. By 1830 the company employed 600 workers and listed 400 designs for dessert sets and 1,000 designs for tea and coffee services in their catalog. Unable to meet its payroll, the company closed in 1842.

The second category of Rockingham ware includes pieces produced in the famous Rockingham brown glaze that became an intense and vivid purple-brown when fired. It had a dark, tortoiseshell mottled appearance. The glaze was copied by many English and American potteries. American manufacturers who used Rockingham glaze include D. & J. Henderson of Jersey City, New Jersey; United States Pottery in Bennington, Vermont; potteries in East Liverpool, Ohio; and several potteries in Indiana and Illinois.

References: Susan and Al Bagdade, *Warman's American Pottery and Porcelain,* Wallace–Homestead, 1994; Susan and Al Bagdade, *Warman's English & Continental Pottery & Porcelain, Second Edition,* Wallace–Homestead, 1991; William C. Ketchum, Jr., *American Pottery and Porcelain,* Avon Books, 1994.

Museum: The Bennington Museum, Bennington, VT.

Additional Listings: Bennington and Bennington-Type Pottery.

Bowl	
9½" d	**75.00**
13" d, 5¾" h, small base flakes	**175.00**
Casserole, cov, 12" l, 10¼" h, oval,	
fruit finial	**265.00**
Creamer	
3⅞" h, glued handle	**25.00**
5⅝" h, figural, cow	**250.00**
Crock, 6½" d, 5" h, cov, emb peacocks	**65.00**
Cuspidor	
8¼" d, emb rib dec	**10.00**
18" d, shell shape	**25.00**
Dish	
8" sq, glazed	**125.00**
9" sq, emb rim	**45.00**
Figure	
9" h, dog, seated, pr	**330.00**
10" h, dog, seated, molded detail	**210.00**
Flask, 5⅝" h, potato shape	**80.00**
Foot Warmer, brown glaze	**70.00**
Frame, 8¼ x 9½", cherubs, naked	
ladies, and foliage scrolls dec .	**850.00**
Jar, 9¼" h, 8" d, cov	**150.00**
Mug, 3¾" h	**55.00**
Pie Plate	
9½" d	**50.00**
10" d	**65.00**
Pitcher	
7⅝" h, emb Cupid and Psyche	
scene	**75.00**
8½" h, boy and dog dec, hound	
handle, mid 19th C	**200.00**

Teapot, Rebekah at the Well, emb design, brown tobacco glaze, unmarked, 7¼" h, 8" w, $85.00.

8⅝" h, emb hunt scene, hairlines	45.00
9⅜" h, molded hunt scenes ...	85.00
9⅞", paneled, leaf design	65.00
10½" h, emb classical foliage, cov, chips and hairline	75.00
Plate, 8¾" w, octagonal shape, price for pair	130.00
Presentation Pitcher, 10" h, medallion portraits on sides, glazed frog figure on bottom int., marked "Mrs. John Webb"	225.00
Punch Pot, 7½" h, brown and yellow glaze, inset lid, knob finial, 2 qt	230.00
Salt, 6" d, emb peacocks, crest, hanging hole	45.00
Soap Dish, 4 x 5½", emb foliage dec, chip on base	175.00
Teapot, 7¾" h, paneled, "Rebekah at the Well"	85.00
Toby Bottle, 8½" h	150.00
Tray, 8½ x 11", scalloped rim ...	100.00

ROCK 'N' ROLL

History: Rock music can be traced back to early rhythm and blues music. It progressed and reached its golden age in the 1950s and 1960s. Attention and most of the memorabilia issued during that period focused on individual singers and groups. The two largest sources of collectibles are items associated with Elvis Presley and The Beatles.

In the 1980s two areas—clothing and guitars—associated with key Rock 'n' Roll personalities received special collector attention. Sotheby's and Christie's East regularly feature Rock 'n' Roll memorabilia as part of their collectibles sales. At the moment, the market is highly speculative and nostalgia driven.

It is important to identify memorabilia issued during the lifetime of an artist or performing group as opposed to material issued after they died or disbanded. This latter material is identified as "fantasy" items and will never achieve the same degree of collectibility as its period counterparts.

References: Jeff Augsburger, Marty Eck, and Rich Rann, *The Beatles Memorabilia Price Guide, Second Edition,* Wallace–Homestead, 1993; L. R. Docks, *1900-1965 American Premium Record Guide, Fourth Edition,* Books Americana, 1992; Barbara Fenick, *Collecting The Beatles: An Introduction and Price Guide To Fab Four Collectibles, Records and Memorabilia,* Vol. 1 (1984) and Vol. 2 (1985), Perian Press; Alison Fox, *Rock & Pop,* Boxtree (London), 1988; Anthony Gribin and Matthew Schiff, *Doo-Wop: The Forgotten Third of Rock 'n' Roll,* Krause Publications, 1992; Paul Grushkin, *The Art of Rock—Posters From Presley To Punk, Revised Edition,* Abbeville Press, 1991; David K. Henkel, *The Official Price Guide to Rock and Roll,* House of Collectibles, 1992; Karen and John Lesniewski, *Kiss Collectibles: Identification and Price Guide,* Avon Books, 1993; Stephen Maycock, *Miller's Rock & Pop Memorabilia,* Millers Publications, 1994; Greg Moore, *A Price Guide To Rock & Roll Collectibles,* published by author, 1993; Jerry Osborne, *The Official Price Guide To Elvis Presley Records and Memorabilia,* House of Collectibles, 1994; Jerry Osborne, *The Official Price Guide To Records, Tenth Edition,* House of Collectibles, 1993; Jerry Osborne, Perry Cox, and Joe Lindsay, *The Official Price Guide to Memorabilia of Elvis Presley And The Beatles,* House of Collectibles, 1988; Michael Stern, Barbara Crawford, and Hollis Lamon, *The Beatles: A Reference & Value Guide,* Collector Books, 1994; Neal Umphred, *Goldmine's Price Guide To Collectible Record Albums, 1949–1989, 4th Edition,* Krause Publications, 1994; Neal Umphred, *Goldmine's Rock 'n Roll 45 RPM Record Price Guide, 3rd Edition,* Krause Publications, 1994.

Periodicals: *Beatlefan,* PO Box 33515, Decatur, GA 30033; *Good Day Sunshine,* 397 Edgewood Avenue, New Haven, CT 06511; *Instant Karma,* PO Box 256, Sault Ste. Marie, MI 49783.

Collectors' Clubs: Beatles Connection, PO Box 1066, Pinellas Park, FL 34665; Beatles Fan Club of Great Britain, Superstore Productions, 123 Marina St., Leonards on Sea, East Sussex, TN38 OBN, England; Elvis Forever TCB Fan Club, PO Box 1066, Pinellas Park, FL 34665; Graceland News Fan Club, PO Box 452, Rutherford, NJ 07070; Working Class Hero Club, 3311 Niagara St., Pittsburgh, PA 15213.

Reproduction Alert: Records, picture sleeves, and album jackets, especially for The Beatles, have been counterfeited. Sound may be inferior. Printing on labels and picture jackets usually is inferior to the original. Many pieces of memorabilia also have been reproduced, often with some change in size, color, and design.

Additional Listings: See The Beatles, Elvis Presley, and Rock 'n' Roll in *Warman's Americana & Collectibles*.

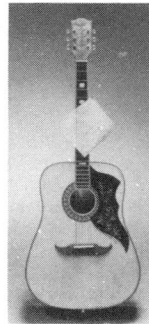

Acoustic Guitar, autographed "John Lennon, '71" on body, Japanese guitar, MOP inlay, decorative pick guard, $30,800.00. Photograph courtesy of Sotheby's.

Beatles
  Bicycle Seat, Yellow Submarine, 9 x 10", vinyl, connected to spring frame and post, off–white ground, yellow accents at top and bottom, 5" I yellow sub illus below two groups of tiny bubbles, Huffy, c1968 ...   150.00
  Coloring Book, 8½ x 11", 124 pgs, ten black and white photo pgs, Saalfield Publishing Co, copyright 1964 Nems Enterprises Ltd 50.00
  Doll, 15" h, Ringo Starr, plastic, inflatable, black hair, purple suit, black shoes, holding orange and white drum, facsimile signature on drum, copyright 1966 Nems Ltd 60.00

Figure, 4½" h, Paul McCartney, plastic body, soft vinyl head, life–like hair, black outfit, white shirt, black necktie, removable diecut plastic black guitar, gold trim and facsimile signature on guitar, orig box copyright 1964   150.00
Greeting Card, 3½ x 9 x 1", musical, unauthorized, plays "Happy Birthday To You," glued to red box with crank on side, card has full color illustration of four band members who resemble the Beatles, message inside is "Do I Wish You A Happy Birthday? Yea! Yea! Yea! Yea!," late 1960s 65.00
Pen, 5½" I, plastic, green, 2" clear plastic section with paper photo of band members, facsimile signatures, instrument illus, marked "The Beatles," c1960 ....   60.00
Puzzle, The Beatles Yellow Submarine, 650 pcs, 19 x 19" completed, titled "Sgt Pepper Band," unopened box, Jaymar copyright 1968 King Features Syndicate 90.00
Switchplate Cover, The Yellow Submarine, 6 x 12", cardboard, day–glo colored, copyright 1968 King Features Syndicate 35.00
Travel Case, 5 x 13 x 12", vinyl, zippered front, handle, group illus, facsimile signatures on front, Air Flite, copyright Nems Enterprises Ltd, c1960 ......   550.00
Wig, orig package 55.00
Bobby Sherman, lunch box, 7 x 9 x 4", metal, color photos and illus, 6½" h metal thermos with color photo and white plastic cup, King–Seeley, copyright 1972 Bobby Sherman Enterprises Inc 60.00
Boy George, doll, 15" h, plush body, molded vinyl head, red and white outfit, white shoes, red tie, black hat, red yarn hair with beads and bows, yellow and purple make–up, bright red lips,

LJN, copyright 1984 Sharpe-grade Ltd, orig box marked "The Huggable, Cute, Cuddly Doll" . **65.00**

Brenda Lee, necklace, gold chain with cultured pearl pendant, mounted on orig sealed card designed like a record, copyright Brenda Lee, 1950–60 . . . . **40.00**

Chubby Checker, record album, *Your Twist Party*, 12¼ x 12¼" cardboard cov, 33⅓ rpm, Parkway Records label, copyright 1961 . . . . **20.00**

Dave Clark, doll, 4½" h, hard plastic, soft vinyl head, black hair, small drum with facsimile signature, black base, Remco, copyright 1964 . . . . **70.00**

The Doors, songbook, 8½ x 11", copyright 1967 Nipper Music Co Inc, 32 pgs, eleven songs including "Light My Fire" and "Break On Through," black and white photos and text **20.00**

Elvis Presley
  Bust, 7" h, plaster, painted, thin glaze, facsimile signature on rect base, c1950 . . . . **600.00**
  Tab, 2" d, I Love Elvis, litho tin, blue and gold lettering, silver ground, c1970 . . . . **20.00**
  Tile, 6" sq, glazed ceramic, cork backing, cloth hanging loop, Elvis leaning back, marked "Best Wishes Elvis Presley," copyright 1956 Elvis Presley Enterprises **300.00**

Freddy and The Dreamers, pinback button, "I Love Freddy And The Dreamers," 3½" d, red and white lettering, black and white photo of five band members, copyright Premier Talent Associates Inc, c1960 . . . . **40.00**

Grateful Dead, record album, 33⅓ rpm, "Sampler For Deadheads" on both sides, one side with "Robert Hunter Tales Of The Great Rum Runners," photo of Garcia on label reverse, mailing address upper left corner orig mailing envelope, San Raphael, CA label, copyright 1974 . . . . . . **50.00**

James Dean
  Pinback Button, 2½" d, color photo, issued before his death, mid–1950 . . . . **65.00**
  Plate, 10" d, commemorative, white china, green illus and text, five portraits, biography sketch, birth and death dates, back with eulogy text, Kettlesprings Kilns signature, and registration number S846, c1955 . . . . **160.00**

James Gang, poster, 14 x 22", cardboard, Oct 2, 1971 at Curtis Hixon Hall, Tampa, FL, featuring James Gang and Country Joe McDonald, "Wanted" poster design **20.00**

Jimmi Hendrix, hanger, 15 x 17", cardboard, black and white photo on both sides, punch–out center, marked "Manufactured Exclusively By Sunders Enterprises/Jimmi Hendrix" **170.00**

Kingston Trio, book, *The Kingston Trio,* 8 x 11", hard cover, black and white and full color photos, published by Random House, copyright 1960 Highridge Music Inc, 36 pgs **20.00**

Kiss
  Lunch Box, 7 x 9 x 4", metal, color photos, King–Seeley, copyright 1977 Aucoin Management Inc **60.00**
  Stickers, Peter Criss, Kiss Rockstics, two–dimensional, puffy, orig card, unused, set of six, Dimension Weld, copyright 1978 Aucoin **40.00**
  View-Master Reels, 4½" envelope, full color photos, set of 3, copyright 1979 Aucoin Management **18.00**

Miscellaneous
  Bracelet, Tiger Beat, subscription premium, metallic gold, 1¼" d medallion with raised picture of tiger under Tiger Beat, c1968–70 . . . . **20.00**
  Magazine
    Life, 10½ x 13½", Vol 67, #9, Aug 29, 1969, ten page ar-

ticle on Woodstock, color
photos **20.00**
Rock N Roll Stars, 8½ x 11",
published by Fawcett Publications, copyright 1956 . . . . **70.00**
Necklace, Fave!, gold metal,
1¼" medallion with raised
flower surrounded by "Fave!
Peace And Love," subscription
premium, 1968–70 . . . . **20.00**
Photo Cards, Rock And Roll
Stars, 3¼ x 5¼", thirty–six unopened packages, three cards
per package, sepia photos, includes Everly Bros, Chuck
Berry, Frankie Avalon, Paul
Anka and sixty others, orig
box, Nu Trading Cards, late
1950s **90.00**
Poster, Family Dog, 14 x 20", pa-
per, June 1–4, 1967, Concert
at Avalon Ballroom, featuring
Miller Blues Band and The
Doors, #64–1, Victor Moscoso
artist, blue, red, and green . . **85.00**
Record Case, Dick Clark, 5 x 8
x 8", cardboard, red, white
plastic handle, full color photo,
white paper label with facsim-
ile signature, c1950 . . . . **75.00**
Monkees
Playing Cards, forty different
black and white photos, orig
full color box, copyright 1966
Rayburt Production Inc **35.00**
Model Kit, Monkeemobile, partially assembled body, instruction sheet, unused decals, orig
box, MPC copyright 1967 Ray-
burt Productions Inc **85.00**
Sheet Music, "Mary, Mary" and
"She," 8 x 11", paper, 3 pgs
with music, color photos on
front, copyright 1967 Screen
Gems–Columbia Music Inc . . **10.00**
Osmonds, lunch box, 7 x 9 x 4",
metal, full color illus, front with
name decal, Aladdin Industries,
copyright 1973 Osbro Produc-
tions **35.00**
Tiny Tim, record album, *God
Bless Tiny Tim,* includes "Tip–
Toe Thru' The Tulips With Me,"
12¼ x 12¼" cov with photos

front and back, paper sleeve
missing **20.00**
Yard Birds, poster, 14½ x 23½",
paper, 1967 concert at Civic Au-
ditorium, Santa Monica, featuring Yard Birds, Moby Grape, Iron
Butterfly, and Captain Beefheart,
red, white, and blue, R Tolmach
artist **65.00**

ROCKWELL, NORMAN

History: Norman Rockwell (February
1894–November 1978) was a famous
American artist and illustrator. During the
time he painted, from age 18 until his death,
he created over 2,000 works.

His first professional efforts were illustrations for a children's book. He next worked
for *Boy's Life,* the Boy Scout magazine. His
most famous works were used by *Saturday
Evening Post* for their cover illustrations.

Norman Rockwell painted everyday people in everyday situations, mixing a little
humor with sentiment. His paintings and illustrations are treasured because of this
sensitive approach. Rockwell painted people he knew and places with which he was
familiar. New England landscapes are found
in many of his illustrations.

References: Denis C. Jackson, *The Norman Rockwell Identification And Value
Guide To: Magazines, Posters, Calendars,
Books, 2nd Edition,* published by author,
1985; Mary Moline, *Norman Rockwell Collectibles, Sixth Edition,* Green Valley World,
1988.

Collectors' Club: Rockwell Society of
America, 597 Saw Mill River Rd., Ardsley,
NY 10502.

Museums: Museum of Norman Rockwell
Art, Reedsburg, WI; Norman Rockwell Mu-
seum, Stockbridge, MA; Norman Rockwell
Museum, Northbrook, IL; Norman Rockwell
Museum, Philadelphia, PA.

Reproduction Alert: Because of the
popularity of his works, they have been reproduced on many objects. These new collectibles should not be confused with original artwork and illustrations. However, they
do allow a collector more range in collecting
interests and prices.

Additiónal Listings: See *Warman's Americana & Collectibles* for more examples.

HISTORIC

Advertising Tray, Coca–Cola, Tom Sawyer Eating, 10½ x 13¼", 1931 .... **285.00**
Poster
  "Save Freedom Of Speech/Buy War Bonds," town meeting, 28 x 40", 1943 .... **125.00**
  "Let's Give Him Enough And On Time," machine gunner, 40 x 28", 1942 .... **950.00**
Window Card, Schmidt's Beer, 24 x 36", four men playing cards, 1935 .... **50.00**

Plate, Rediscovered Women Series, Dreaming in the Attic, Edwin M. Knowles, orig box, 8½" d, $25.00.

MODERN

Bell, Gorham Fine China, Snow Sculpturing, 1976 .... **45.00**
Christmas Ornament, Gorham Fine China, Tiny Tim, 1980 ... **24.00**
Coin, Hamilton Mint, The Four Seasons, 1½" d, price for set of four **95.00**
Figure
  Gorham Fine China
    Four Seasons, Grandpa and

Me, 1975, series No. 4, price for set of four **600.00**
  Saying Grace **120.00**
Grossman Designs, Inc.
  Leapfrog, 1979 .... **700.00**
  Schoolmaster, 1973 .... **150.00**
Ingot, Franklin Mint, Norman Rockwell's Fondest Memories, Playing Hookey, 1973 .... **35.00**
Plate
  Franklin Mint, etched crystal, American Sweethearts, 1977–78, price for set of 6 .... **165.00**
  Gorham Fine China, Four Seasons, A Boy and His Dog, 1971, Series No. 1, price for set of 4 .... **375.00**
  Rockwell Society of America, A Mother's Love, 1976 .... **95.00**
Puzzle, Parker Brothers 533, Happy Birthday Miss Jones, 11 x 14", 1973 .... **15.00**
Toby Mug, Grossman Designs, Inc, Merrie Christmas, 1979 ... **40.00**

ROGERS & SIMILAR STATUARY

History: John Rogers, born in America in 1829, studied sculpturing in Europe and produced the first plaster-of-paris statue, "The Checker Players," in 1859. It was followed by "The Slave Auction" in 1860.

His works were popular parlor pieces of the Victorian era. He produced at least 80 different subjects and the total number of groups made from the originals is estimated to be over 100,000.

Casper Hennecke, one of Rogers' contemporaries, operated C. Hennecke & Company from 1881 until 1896 in Milwaukee, Wisconsin. His statuary often is confused with Rogers' work since both are very similar.

It is difficult to find a statue in undamaged condition and with original paint. Use the following conversions: 10% minor flaking; 10% chips; 10-20% piece or pieces broken and reglued; 20% flaking; 50% repainting.

References: Paul and Meta Bieier, *John Rogers' Groups of Statuary*, published by authors, 1971; Betty C. Haverly, *Hennecke's Florentine Statuary*, published by author, 1972; David H. Wallace, *John Rogers: The People's Sculptor,* Wesleyan Univ., 1976.

Periodical: *The Rogers Group,* 4932 Prince George Avenue, Beltsville, MD 20705.

Museums: John Rogers Studio & Museum of the New Canaan Historical Society, New Canaan CT; Lightner Museum, Saint Augustine, FL.

Conquering Jealousy, $175.00.

ROGERS

Checkers At The Farm, c1875, 20″ h 440.00
Coming to the Parson, 21⅞″ h, 17⅜″ w, 10⅜″ d 450.00
Council of War, 25″ h 415.00
Elder's Daughter, 1887, 21½″ h . 750.00
Favored Scholar, 21⅛″ h, 15″ w, 11¼″ d 550.00
First Ride, 1888, 18″ h 750.00
Ha! I Like Not That!, 21⅞″ h, 21⅛″ w, 11½″ d 550.00
Is it So Nominated in the Bond?, 22 x 18″ 250.00
Neighboring Pews, terra-cotta glaze, 1889, 18½″ h 225.00
Rip Van Winkle On The Mountain, 1871, 21″ h 500.00
School Examination, 1867, 20″ h 500.00

ROGERS TYPE

Evening Devotion, 21″ h 250.00
Family Cares, 13″ h 95.00

First Love, 13½″ h 200.00
Lost & Found, 19″ h 100.00
Red Riding Hood, 11½″ h 350.00

ROOKWOOD POTTERY

History: Mrs. Marie Longworth Nicholas Storer, Cincinnati, Ohio, founded Rookwood Pottery in 1880. The name of this outstanding American art pottery came from her family estate "Rookwood," named for the rooks (crows) which inhabited the wooded grounds.

There are five elements to the Rookwood marking system—the clay or body mark, the size mark, the decorator mark, the date mark, and the factory mark. Rookwood art pottery can best be dated from factory marks.

From 1880–1882 the factory mark was the name "Rookwood" incised or painted on the base. Between 1881 and 1886 the firm name, address, and year appeared in an oval frame. Beginning in 1886, the impressed "RP" monogram appeared and a flame mark was added for each year until 1900. After 1900 a Roman numeral, indicating the last two digits of the year of production, was added at the bottom of the "RP" flame mark monogram. This last mark is the one most often found on Rookwood pottery today.

Though the Rookwood pottery filed for bankruptcy in 1941, it was soon reorganized under new management. Efforts at maintaining the pottery proved futile, and it again was sold in 1956 and in 1959. The pottery was moved to Starkville, Mississippi, in conjunction with the Herschede Clock Co. It finally ceased operation in 1967.

Rookwood wares changed with the times. The variety is endless, in part because of the great variations in glazes and designs due to the creativity of the many talented artists.

References: Susan and Al Bagdade, *Warman's American Pottery and Porcelain,* Wallace–Homestead, 1994; Anita J. Ellis, *Rookwood Pottery: The Glorious Gamble,* Rizzoli International and Cincinnati Art Museum, 1992; Ralph and Terry Kovel, *Kovels' American Art Pottery: The Collector's Guide To Makers, Marks and Factory Histories,* Crown Publishers, 1993; L–W Book Sales (ed.), *A Price Guide To Rookwood,* L–W Book Sales, 1993; Herbert Peck, *The Book of Rookwood Pottery,* Crown Publishers, 1968; Herbert Peck, *The Second Book of Rookwood Pottery,* published by author, 1985.

Video: Anita Ellis, *The Collectors Series: Rookwood Pottery,* distributed by Award Video and Film Distributors, Inc., 1994.

Collectors' Club: American Art Pottery Assoc., 125 E. Rose Ave., St. Louis, MO 63119.

Basket, 9" h, 20¼" l, folded bowl, two applied handles, four applied lion's-head feet, one side dec with alligators, palms, and Nile pyramids, other dec with spider and fly on spider web, copper luster highlights, imp "Rookwood, 1883" **5,000.00**
Bookends, pr
  Elephants, charcoal, 1925 .... **395.00**
  Rook against berried branches, semi–matte tan and dusky blue glaze, imp mark and artist's monogram of Helen McDonald, 1925 .... **335.00**
  Victorian Lady, yellow, 1919, #2185 .... **350.00**
Bowl, 8½" d, globular form, incised dec, rose shading to green glaze **460.00**
Box, cov, 5¼" h, triangular, ftd, abstract molded dec, triangular finial, high powder blue glaze, imp mark and artist's monogram of Louise Abel, 1931 .... **225.00**
Ewer
  8¼" h, rose jar form, mustard yellow, wax matte dec of fruiting branches, imp mark, "1342" above triangle, painted

artist's monogram for Catherine Covaleno, 1925 .... **600.00**
  10" h, standard glaze, bulbous body, long neck, trefoil mouth, paint and slip dec, flowering apple blossoms, yellow, peach, green, and brown, shaded brown and green ground, silver cased loop handle and lip, engraved monogram, silver overlay poppies, scrolling foliage, and latticework, marked "Gorham Mfg Co," incised artist's cipher of Emma D Foertmeyer, imp factory mark, 1893 date mark .. **1,200.00**
Figure
  Chinese Pheasant, 14" h, restoration to tail, shape 2832 .... **250.00**
  Radio Singers, paperweight shape, #6683 .... **295.00**
Flower Holder, 6½" h, rook on stump, #2710, blue, c1928 ... **75.00**
Inkwell, 8½" l, 8¼" w, 9" h, figural, sphinx, fitted with inkwell, molded pen tray, variegated straw colors, gray matte glaze, artist's mark of Louise Abel, imp pottery mark, 1920 .... **250.00**
Jar, cov, 5½" h, bulbous, sgd "B Cranch, #479W," 1889 .... **1,250.00**
Jardiniere, 8½" d, 7½" h, standard glaze, shape 180C, 3W, brown chrysanthemum branch dec, 1886, imp marks **520.00**
Lamp
  11¼" h, Aladdin's lamp shape,

Vase, aventurine glaze, 7¼" h, $225.00.

oblong, loop handle, small pewter cov, black floral and stork outlines, white ground, imp "Rookwood 1882, Hanna Plant, Box Tree," spout chip . **150.00**

14" h baluster base, ivory ground, underglaze dec of lavender and pink magnolias, orig fittings, orig medallion label . . **625.00**

Pitcher, 7" h, standard glaze, inverted baluster, painted and slip yellow and brown pansies dec, shaded brown ground, silver cased handle and rim, silver overlaid scrolling acanthus, flowers, and latticework, marked "Gorham Mfg Co," incised artist's cipher of Mary Nourse, imp factory mark, 1892 date mark . **1,800.00**

Plaque

4¼" h, 8½" w, incised rook perched on branch, incised name "Rookwood," green tones, imp mark, c1925 . . . . . **1,300.00**

6¼" h, 8¼" w, scenic vellum, Indian Summer, Edward Diers, 1915, artist initialed lower right, orig oak frame, paper label **2,300.00**

8" h, 6" w, woodland river scene, artist's monogram sgd on lower left, imp firm mark and "XXII," designed by Fred Rothenbusch, 1922 . . . . **2,650.00**

Rose Jar, 5½" h, powder pink, plum blossoms around shoulder, imp mark, "2831, V," and artist's monogram for ET Hurley, 1925 **350.00**

Tankard, 17½" h, cylinder, standard glaze, painted barn swallows in flight, imp mark, artist's monogram for Albert R Valentien, 1893, hairline **600.00**

Tile, three 11¾" woodland scenic tiles with raised outline details, blue, pale green, and dark green, twenty 6" surrounding matte green tiles, imp "Rookwood Faience" **3,850.00**

Vase

4¼" h, vellum glaze, band of stylized carp on water surface, blue and cream at shoulder, beige above and below, Lor-

inda Epply, 1908, shape 911E, imp marks, inscribed "V" and artist's mark, peppering, int. spider hairline **575.00**

4¾" h, baluster form, foliate and berry dec at neck, #2139 . . . **200.00**

5" h, sgd "L Fry, #415W" **650.00**

5¼" h, standard overglaze, bulbous, pinched sq walls and waisted neck, poppies in green and orange slip, dark brown ground, imp marks, designer Edward Diers monogram, c1898 . . . . **450.00**

5½" h, baluster, round foot, matte glazed multicolored dec, sgd on base, dated "1930" and numbered "2831," Jens Jensen **575.00**

6" h

Incised sea horse motif, mottled brown glaze **200.00**

Ovoid, molded water leaves, green shading to rose glaze **220.00**

6⅝" h, tiger's-eye glaze, shape 568C, middle band of gold and red highlights, imp borders, F D Koehler, 1896, imp and artist's marks **1,725.00**

6¾" h, vellum glaze, baluster, pale pink, blue, and green bleeding hearts, imp mark, incised "V" and artist's monogram for Edward Diers, 1931 **800.00**

7" h, ovoid, high glaze, geometric dec, Lorinda Epply **750.00**

7½" h

Blue porcelain glaze, cherry blossoms, sgd "Lorinda Epply," drilled **195.00**

Iris glaze, iris dec, shape 935D, Constance A Baker, 1903, imp and artist's marks **1,725.00**

7⅝" h, matte green glaze, incised vertical leaf blade pattern, Albert Munson, 1901, shape 299D Z, imp and artist's marks **865.00**

8" h

Swollen cylindrical form, sailing galleon in sunset silhouette, light blue, rose, and cream ground, artist sgd Edward Diers, number

"2032E," and other marks, 1918 .... 880.00

Tapering cylindrical form, matte glaze, floral dec, incised on base, dated "1915," numbered "9010," Lorinda Epply 550.00

8⅛" h, standard glaze, baluster, branch of orange nasturtiums, imp mark, artist's monogram for Lenore Asbury, 1903 .... 465.00

8¼" h, standard overglaze, ovoid form, tapered neck, earth tones, painted slip blossoms underglaze dec, imp marks, designer O Geneva Reed's initials, c1897 ...... 400.00

8½" h

Ovoid, standard glaze, dogwood dec, marked on base with Rookwood insignia "I, 927D" and artist's initials, c1901, Sallie Toohey 575.00

Slender baluster, pale green body, gray neck, shoulder painted with oak leaves and acorns, imp mark and artist's monogram for Lenore Asbury, 1911 .... 450.00

9" h, vellum glaze, scenic, wide mouth, cylindrical, flaring towards base, landscape band in green, blue, peach, and yellow, light gray–blue ground, imp marks and incised artist's signature Kataro Shirayamadani, 1912 .... 1,400.00

9⅛" h, matte glaze, wide mouth, angled shoulder and swollen cylindrical, shaded lavender glaze, rose and midnight blue floral dec, artist sgd Sara Sax, 1918 .... 750.00

9⅜" h, oviform, flaring mouth, roosters dec, tiger's-eye glaze, imp mark, artist's monogram of Harriet E Wilcox, c1894 ... 2,100.00

9½" h, vellum glaze, shouldered baluster body, everted rim, painted pink blossom border highlighted in blue below shoulder, medium blue ground within green borders, inscribed

Frederick Rothenbusch and other marks, 1924 .... 470.00

10½" h, matte glaze, pale red ground, green at shoulder and to one side, high relief buttress dec, shape 907DD, 1911, imp marks 635.00

11½" h, two handles, brown, portrait, sgd "G Young, #581D," 1902 .... 5,500.00

13" h, flared mouth, tapering toward foot, molded classical dancing women, deep mauve ext. glaze, turquoise int., artist sgd Louise Abel, c1920–32 .. 200.00

13½" h, matte glaze, swollen cylindrical body, incised and modeled low relief upright iris, dark red touched blossoms, artist sgd Charles Stewart Todd and other marks, c1914 330.00

13⅝" h, vellum glaze, scenic, cylindrical, flaring towards base, gray–blue landscape scene, shaded yellow to peach ground, imp marks, incised artist's initials ETH for Edward Timothy Hurley, 1913 ...... 2,000.00

ROSE BOWLS

History: A rose bowl, a decorative open bowl with a crimped, pinched, or petal top, held fragrant rose petals or potpourri which served as an air freshener in the late Victorian period. Practically every glass manufacturer made rose bowls in a variety of patterns and glass types, including fine art glass.

Reference: Ellen T. Schroy, *Warman's Glass*, Wallace-Homestead, 1992.

Additional Listings: See specific glass categories.

Cased Glass, 6" h, robin's-egg blue ext., white int., applied crystal swag trim, crystal rosettes and scroll feet 265.00

Mount Washington

4½" d, 4" h, Verona, clear, ribbed, English ivy and small purple flowers dec, gold rim trim 185.00

Opalescent Swirl, cranberry ground, $75.00.

5″ w, 4″ h, satin, bright yellow, enameled red berries, pale orange leaves and branches, eight large ribbed swirls **145.00**

Peachblow, 2½″ d, 2⅜″ h, DQ, MOP, eight crimp top, deep red shaded to amber pink, Webb . . **300.00**

Satin, 3⅞″ h, green shading to light green cabbage leaf form, crimped edge **100.00**

Smith Brothers
  3″ d, 2¼″ h, white and purple asters, blue stems and splashes, green leaves, cream ground **285.00**
  5½″ w, 4″ h, purple asters, green leaves, brown stems, salmon pink swirls, cream ground, white beaded top **295.00**

Spangle (Vasa Murrhina) Glass, 4¼″ d, 7¼″ h, overlay, deep rose, mica flakes, white lining, eight crimp top, applied clear thorny handle **215.00**

Stevens and Williams, 6″ d, 4½″ h, Pompeiian Swirl, large box-pleated top, deep gold shading to light gold, creamy white lining, small blister **225.00**

ROSE CANTON, ROSE MANDARIN, ROSE MEDALLION

History: The pink rose color has given its name to three related groups of Chinese export porcelain. Rose Mandarin was produced from the late 18th century to approximately 1840. Rose Canton production began somewhat later and extended through the first half of the 19th century. Rose Medallion originated in the early 19th century and was made through the early 20th century.

Rose Mandarin derives its name from the Mandarin figure(s) found in garden scenes with women and children. The women often feature gold decorations in their hair. Polychrome enamels and birds separate the scenes.

Rose Medallion has alternating panels of figures and birds and flowers. The elements are four in number, separated evenly around the center medallion. Peonies and foliage fill voids.

Rose Canton is similar to Rose Medallion except the figural panels are replaced by florals. People are present only if the medallion partitions are absent. Some patterns have been named—Butterfly and Cabbage, Rooster, etc. The category actually is a catchall for all pink enamel ware not fitting into the first two groups.

Reference: Gloria and Robert Mascarelli, *Warman's Oriental Antiques,* Wallace–Homestead, 1992.

Reproduction Alert: Rose Medallion is still made, although the quality does not match the earlier examples.

ROSE CANTON

Brush Pot, 4¾″ h, ladies in pavilion, reticulated, relief molded, gilt trim, c1850 . . . . **300.00**

Creamer, 4″ h, double twisted handle, gilt trim **200.00**

Demitasse Cup and Saucer, floral panels, c1860 . . . . **75.00**

Plate, 8½″ d, floral, insects on border **95.00**

Platter, 14¾″ l, thousand butterfly borders, China, 20th C, price for pair **690.00**

Vase, 10½″ h, medallions with flowers, butterflies, and birds, floral borders, mid 19th C **425.00**

ROSE MANDARIN

Bowl, 6" d, Canton, Chinese, 19th
C **50.00**
Dish, 11½" h, shaped, central
panels of courtyard figures, wide
floral and butterfly borders, one
restored, c1830, price for pair .   **950.00**
Mug, 4¾" h, molded spearhead
border, double twist handle,
c1840, rim nicks **350.00**
Pitcher, 8½" h, scalloped rim,
paneled, molded spearhead bor-
der, handle repair, c1840 . . . . .   **650.00**
Plate, 9¾" d, 19th C, price for pair **600.00**
Platter, 14⅜ x 17¾", oval, alter-
nating figural and ornaments
dec, border of ornaments, traces
of central monogram, orange
and brown enamel, gilt palette,
repair and wear, mid 19th C . . .   **200.00**
Shrimp Dish, 10" w, central courtyard figures panel, wide border
of flowers and precious orna-
ments, c1830 . . . .   **750.00**
Soup Plate, 9¾" d, armorial, arms
of Grand, ribbed motto "Craige-
lachie" and "Standfast," varying
central figural courtyard scenes,
wide floral and butterfly borders,
set of 6, c1810 . . . . **2,800.00**
Spill Vase, 4¾ h, allover molded
and enamel dec figural courtyard, pierced ground, gilt and
floral borders, hairline, restora-
tion, c1840 . . . .   **300.00**
Vase
10" h, 19th C, price for pair . . . **1,265.00**
23½" h, Temple, 19th C, chip . .   **865.00**
Vegetable Dish, cov, 8 x 9½", oblong, central courtyard and fig-

Cup and Saucer, Rose Medallion,
3" d cup, 5" d saucer, $85.00.

ural panels on cov and int., bird
and floral borders, simulated
bamboo handle on cov, slight gilt
wear, c1840 . . . . **1,200.00**

ROSE MEDALLION

Bowl
9" d, small edge chips **110.00**
13½" d, minor edge wear **550.00**
Box, 7" l, 3½" w, 3" h, cov, rect . .   **550.00**
Bouillon Cup and Saucer, cov . . . **115.00**
Brush Box, cov, 7½" l, rect, divided
int. **310.00**
Candlesticks, 9¼" h, marked
"China," c1900, price for pair . .   **900.00**
Chamber Bowl, 16¼" d, Canton,
flaring rim, Chinese, 19th C . . **1,000.00**
Cup and Saucer, set of 4 . . . .   **110.00**
Dish, 10 x 10¾", butterflies dec .   **440.00**
Fish Platter, 17¾" l, pierced
strainer, 19th C, hairline **750.00**
Mug, 4¾" h, 19th C **345.00**
Plate, 8" d, luncheon, exotic birds
and butterflies dec, price for pair   **95.00**
Platter
10½ x 13¼", oval **250.00**
16¾" l, tree and well dec **550.00**
Punch Bowl
11" d, rim chip **575.00**
11¾" d **865.00**
14¾" d, 19th C **1,035.00**
16" d, China, 19th C **925.00**
Shrimp Dish, 10¼" l, shaped rim,
rim nicks, mid 19th C **550.00**
Soap Dish, 6" l, 4½" w, 2½" h, cov,
insert **355.00**
Teapot
7" h, wicker cozy **225.00**
7½" h, domed lid, gold repainted
finial, small chips **110.00**
Tureen, 8¼" l, small **385.00**
Umbrella Stand, 23½" h, cylindri-
cal, hairlines, late 19th C **850.00**
Urn, cov, 15" h, low domed cov,
onion finial, int. rim chip **650.00**
Vase
15¼" h, bulbous, mid 19th C . .   **400.00**
15½" h, baluster, bulbous center,
flaring top and base, top rim
repair **450.00**
Vegetable Dish, cov
8½" sq, pineapple finial **225.00**
12 x 10" **275.00**

MARKE

ROSENTHAL

History: Rosenthal Porcelain Manufactory began operating at Selb, Bavaria in 1880. Specialties were tablewares and figurines. The firm is still in operation.

Reference: Susan and Al Bagdade, *Warman's English & Continental Pottery & Porcelain, Second Edition,* Wallace-Homestead, 1991.

Bonbon, 2½ x 5¼", Winifred pattern, pink Moss Rose dec, SS base **35.00**
Bouillon Cup and Saucer, Donatello, green leaves, blue–gray fuchsia type flowers, gold trim, marked "Selb Bavaria" **22.00**
Bowl, 9" d, hp, clusters of cherries, green ext., gold trim, double handles, artist sgd **85.00**
Cake Plate, 10" d, portrait of Mercury, violet ground, gold trim .. **60.00**
Coffeepot, cov, Grasses pattern . **40.00**
Coffee Set, Classic Rose pattern, price for five pc set **145.00**
Cup and Saucer
  Empress Flower pattern **25.00**
  Grasses pattern **15.00**
Figure
  4" l, 3½" h, deer, sitting **135.00**
  7" h, dachshund, standing on hind legs **165.00**
  8½" w, 7½" h, poodle, gray, sgd "Karner," #1211 .... **175.00**
  10½" l, Fairy Queen, Friedrich–Granau **325.00**
  18⅞" h, owl, natural colors, shaped stepped base, marked "Rosenthal Kunst–Abteilung" **250.00**
Gravy Boat, Aida pattern, gold trim, c1920, matching undertray, price for two pc set **35.00**

Vase, oval, flying mallard, marked "Germany Rosenthal Kunstabteilung Selb Handgewalt," 4⅝" h, $65.00.

Hatpin Holder, 5½" h, figural, stylized bust **40.00**
Plate, Grasses pattern, bread and butter **6.00**
Portrait Plate, 10" d, young woman, multicolored, cobalt blue rim, gold tracery **100.00**
Shaving Mug, rose dec, marked "RC," crossed lines, crown, "Madeleine," Bavaria **75.00**
Soup Plate, pink floral pattern, matching saucers, price for set of ten **75.00**
Tea Service, 10" h cov teapot, 5" h creamer, 5¼" h cov sugar, porcelain, silver overlay dec **300.00**
Urn, cov, 10½" h, portrait, woman in garden, multicolored **250.00**

ROSEVILLE POTTERY

History: In the late 1880s a group of investors purchased the J. B. Owens Pottery in Roseville, Ohio, and made utilitarian stoneware items. In 1892 the firm was incorporated and joined by George F. Young who became general manager. Four generations of Youngs controlled Roseville until the early 1950s.

A series of acquisitions began: Midland Pottery of Roseville in 1898, Clark Stoneware Plant in Zanesville (formerly used by Peters and Reed), and Muskingum Stoneware (Mosaic Tile Company) in Zanesville. In 1898 the offices also moved from Roseville to Zanesville.

In 1900 Roseville introduced its art pottery—Rozane. Rozane became a trade name to cover a large series of lines. The art lines were made in limited amounts after 1919.

The success of Roseville depended on its commercial lines, first developed by John J. Herald and Frederick Rhead in the first decades of the 1900s. In 1918 Frank Ferrell became art director and developed over 80 lines of pottery. The economic depression of the 1930s brought more lines, including Pine Cone.

In the 1940s a series of high gloss glazes were tried to revive certain lines. In 1952 Raymor dinnerware was produced. None of these changes brought economic success. In November 1954 Roseville was bought by the Mosaic Tile Company.

References: Susan and Al Bagdade, *Warman's American Pottery and Porcelain*, Wallace–Homestead, 1994; John W. Humphries, *A Price Guide To Roseville Pottery By The Numbers*, published by author, 1993; Sharon and Bob Huxford, *The Collectors Encyclopedia Of Roseville Pottery*, First Series (1976, 1995 value update), Second Series (1980, 1993 value update), Collector Books; Ralph and Terry Kovel, *Kovels' American Art Pottery: The Collector's Guide To Makers, Marks and Factory Histories*, Crown Publishers, 1993; Dana G. Morykan and Harry L. Rinker, *Warman's Country Antiques & Collectibles, Second Edition*, Wallace–Homestead, 1994; Leslie Pina, *Pottery: Modern Wares 1920-1960*, Schiffer Publishing, 1994.

Collectors' Clubs: American Art Pottery Association, 125 E. Rose Ave., St Louis, MO 63119; Roseville's of the Past, PO Box 681117, Orlando, FL 32868.

Additional Listings: See *Warman's Americana & Collectibles* for more examples.

Vase, Falline, 12¼" h, $395.00.

Bowl	
Ixia, yellow, 7" d	**45.00**
Pine Cone, blue, 11" d	**330.00**
Bud Vase, Pine Cone, brown	**195.00**
Candleholder, Florentine, 8" h . . .	**75.00**
Candlestick, pr, Foxglove, 1149–1½	**70.00**
Compote, Orian	**90.00**
Console Bowl	
Baneda, green, 232–6	**235.00**
Ming Tree, blue, 10" d	**70.00**
Console Set, Lotus, red and cream	**185.00**
Ewer, Poppy, pink, 10" h	**275.00**
Flower Frog, Moss, pink	**85.00**
Hanging Basket	
Lombardy, 5" h	**185.00**
Zephyr Lily, brown	**165.00**
Incense Burner, Donatello, two tiny nicks	**575.00**
Jardiniere, pedestal	
Blackberry, 28" h	**2,900.00**
Corinthian, 6" h	**350.00**
Snowberry, pink, 8" h	**425.00**
Lamp Base	
8½" h, bulbous, mottled blue and brown, trial glaze	**495.00**
19" h, Pauleo, solid blue, marbelized glaze at neck, dripped, price for pair	**275.00**
Pillow Vase, Pine Cone, gold and brown, 8" h, 845–8	**225.00**
Pitcher, Bleeding Heart	**395.00**
Planter, Bittersweet, yellow, 8" h .	**50.00**
Powder Jar, Donatello, two inside nicks	**350.00**
Basket	
Columbine, blue, 8" d	**135.00**
Wincraft, blue, 8" d	**55.00**
Bookends, pr, Thorn Apple, brown	**175.00**

Teapot, Della Robbia	**1,500.00**
Tray, Zephyr Lily, 14½" l	**175.00**
Umbrella Stand, Pine Cone, brown, 777–20	**1,500.00**

Urn
Sunflower	**485.00**
Tourmaline, turquoise, 1933, 4½" h	**125.00**

Vase
Carnelian II, two handles, purple over cranberry, 5" h	**165.00**
Cherry Blossom, brown, 8½"	**295.00**
Clematis, green, 764–8	**275.00**
Columbine, brown, floor type, 16" h	**375.00**
Dahlrose, bulbous	**175.00**
Florentine, blonde, 8" h	**65.00**
Futura, matte glaze, orange and brown, minor base glaze nicks, c1925, 12" h	**435.00**
Imperial I, 10" h	**135.00**
Iris, pink, 917–6	**100.00**
Magnolia, green, 15" h	**225.00**
Monticello, aqua, 4" h, 555–4	**155.00**
Orian, 7" h	**125.00**
Peony, 9" h, 64–9	**85.00**
Silhouette, fan shape, orange	**275.00**
Thorn Apple, blue, 6" h, 305–6	**120.00**
Wincraft, 7" h	**95.00**

Wall Pocket
Apple Blossom, brown	**165.00**

Carnelian
Blue	**120.00**
Green over tan	**120.00**
Clematis, green	**130.00**
Corinthian	**175.00**
Dogwood	**165.00**

Donatello
9¾" l	**150.00**
11½" l	**180.00**
Florentine, brown, 12½" l	**185.00**
Freesia, green	**140.00**
Gardenia, gray	**165.00**
Imperial	**110.00**
Iris, 6" h	**135.00**
Ming Tree, blue	**175.00**
Rosecraft Vintage	**200.00**
Silhouette, maroon	**130.00**

Snowberry
Green	**140.00**
Rose	**140.00**
Thorn Apple, brown	**310.00**
Tuscany, gray	**150.00**
White Rose, rose and green	**225.00**

Zephyr Lily, green	**170.00**
Window Box, Blue Cosmos	**450.00**

BAVARIA

ROYAL BAYREUTH

History: In 1794 the Royal Bayreuth factory was founded in Tettau, Bavaria. Royal Bayreuth introduced their figural patterns in 1885. Designs of animals, people, fruits, and vegetables decorated a wide array of tablewares and inexpensive souvenir items. Tapestry ware, in rose and other patterns, were made in the late 19th century. The surface of the ware feels and looks like woven cloth. Tapestry ware was made by covering the porcelain with a piece of fabric tightly stretched over the surface, decorating the fabric, glazing the piece, and firing.

The Royal Bayreuth crest mark varied in design and color. Many wares were unmarked. It is difficult to verify the chronological years of production due to the lack of records.

Royal Bayreuth still manufactures dinnerware. It has not maintained production of earlier wares, particularly the figural items.

References: Susan and Al Bagdade, *Warman's English & Continental Pottery & Porcelain, Second Edition,* Wallace-Homestead, 1991; Mary J. McCaslin, *Royal Bayreuth: A Collector's Guide,* Antique Publications, 1993.

Collectors' Club: Royal Bayreuth International Collectors' Society, PO Box 325, Orrville, OH 44667.

Art Nouveau
Dresser Tray, blue mark	**1,400.00**
Pitcher, water, blue mark	**1,350.00**

Devil and Cards
Ashtray	**200.00**
Candy Dish	**295.00**

Creamer and Sugar, green mark, lid damaged 300.00
Demitasse Cup and Saucer ... 85.00
Salt, master 165.00
Toothpick Holder 350.00

Elk
Creamer 110.00
Pincushion, insert missing, blue mark 300.00
Pitcher, water, blue mark 425.00
Toothpick Holder 225.00

Lobster
Ashtray 65.00
Creamer 95.00
Pitcher, milk 115.00
Salad Bowl 285.00

Miscellaneous Patterns
Biscuit jar, cov, figural, strawberry 135.00
Cake Plate, 10½" d, open handles, pink and green cherries, blossoms, and leaves, satin finish 50.00
Chocolate Pot, cov, boy seated on log 250.00
Creamer, figural
Apple 150.00
Butterfly, wide wings, orange, cerise, gray 395.00
Crow, red beak 110.00
Frog, unmarked 155.00
Lamplighter 250.00
Man in Mountain 50.00
Maple Leaf 250.00
Parakeet, unmarked 195.00
Pelican, unmarked 350.00
Robin 150.00
Shell and Sea horse 275.00
Creamer and Sugar
Apple 295.00
Pansy 235.00
Hair Receiver, green, storks dec 150.00
Hatpin Holder, farmer holding reins of two horses, farm house in background, scalloped saucer base, blue mark 250.00
Mug, 5¾" h, tavern scene 135.00
Pitcher
Alligator, milk pitcher 550.00
Coachman, water pitcher, small underside factory imperfection 450.00
Monk 525.00
Raven, 5" h 165.00

Plate, 9" d, girl with basket of flowers, gold scrolled edge .. 400.00
Slipper, man's, high top 225.00
Sugar, cov, lemon 175.00
Vase
3¼" h, baluster, lady carrying basket, boats, and water, blue and gray ground 50.00
7" h, bulbous, soccer scene, blue mark 300.00
Whiskey Jug, tall, orig stopper, blue mark 150.00

Nursery Rhyme
Basket, girl and dog playing ... 200.00
Box, cov, 5½" w, Little Jack Horner, shell shape 250.00
Bowl, 9½" d, Goose Girl 150.00
Creamer, Little Jack Horner, blue mark 110.00
Salt and Pepper Shakers, pr, Little Boy Blue 200.00

Red Poppy
Bowl, master, slight wear 195.00
Cake Plate, MOP, open handles 200.00
Creamer 175.00
Mustard, cov, green ladle 195.00
Nappy, four handles 125.00
Nut Dish 60.00
Salt and Pepper Shakers, pr, slight wear 195.00
Sugar, professional repair 150.00
Teapot 275.00

Scenic
Bell, Peacock 245.00
Ewer, 4½" h, hunter with dogs . 180.00
Match Holder, wall, The Tale of the Hunt 145.00
Vase
Babes in Woods, girl curtsying, handle 310.00
Dutch Children, double bud type 105.00

Shell
Ashtray, 4½ x 4½", blue mark . 45.00
Creamer
#365 .... 170.00
#510 .... 185.00
Match Holder, hanging 250.00

Snow Babies
Cereal Set, children on sled ... 165.00
Creamer, squatty 95.00
Inkwell, 4" w, sq base, children on sled 140.00
Vase, Ice Play, brown dec 105.00

Vase, white roses, ivory ground, blue mark, imp "Deponnert," 8½" h, $225.00.

Sunbonnet Babies
  Chamberstick, shield back, babies fishing, blue mark 500.00
  Creamer, 4" h, tankard, babies cleaning 215.00
  Cup and Saucer, babies sewing 150.00
  Mug, babies sewing 165.00
  Plate, 6½" d, babies washing .. 135.00
Tomato
  Biscuit Jar, cov 135.00
  Creamer 95.00
  Cup and Saucer 90.00
  Mustard Pot, leaf underplate .. 75.00
  Pitcher
    Milk 125.00
    Water 500.00
  Salt and Pepper Shakers, pr .. 60.00
  Sugar 95.00

ROSE TAPESTRY

Basket, 4¼ x 2½ x 4½" h, pink roses at rim, yellow roses each side and int., shadow green leaves, rope handle, blue mark 325.00
Creamer, pink roses 195.00
Cup, 3" h, three color roses 145.00
Dresser Tray, 11¼" l', 8" w, rect, blue mark 225.00
Match Safe, hanging 350.00
Mustard, cov, pink roses 445.00
Nappy, yellow roses, leaf shape, double handles, blue mark 175.00
Nut Set, price for 7 piece set 695.00
Plate
  6" d, raised foliate border design, blue mark, price for set of six 265.00

7⅛" d, raised foliate border design, green marks, price for set of six 285.00
Relish Dish, 8⅛" l, rose dec, blue mark 200.00
Tankard, 4" h, pink roses, yellow ferns, beaded, gold handle, blue mark 175.00

TAPESTRY, OTHER

Clock, Christmas cactus, blue mark 485.00
Creamer
  Colonial Curtsy scene, 4" h ... 265.00
  Highland Goats 355.00
  Highland Sheep 295.00
  The Bathers 285.00
Cup and Saucer, farmer with turkeys, blue mark 100.00
Dresser Tray, Japanese chrysanthemums, leaf shape 215.00
Hair Receiver, farmer with turkeys, blue mark 265.00
Miniature Pitcher, brown and white cows 185.00
String Holder, hanging, rooster .. 200.00
Toothpick Holder, lady with horse 410.00
Vase
  Stag in Stream 285.00
  Toaster Cavalier 220.00

1887-1920

Royal

1755

1920

Bonn

Bonn

Bonn

ROYAL BONN

History: In 1836 Franz Anton Mehlem founded a Rhineland factory that produced earthenware and porcelain, including household, decorative, technical, and sanitary items. In 1890 the name Royal was added to the mark. All items made after 1890 include the name "Royal Bonn." The firm reproduced Hochst figures between 1887 and 1903. These figures, produced in both porcelain and earthenware, were made from the original molds from the defunct Prince-Electoral Mayence Manufactory in Hochst. The factory was purchased by Villeroy and Boch in 1921 and closed in 1931.

Reference: Susan and Al Bagdade, *Warman's English & Continental Pottery & Porcelain, Second Edition,* Wallace-Homestead, 1991.

Vase, tapestry finish, steps and monument in garden setting, floral band, 8½" w, 8" h, $425.00.

Bowl, 9½" d, cream, floral dec, metal rim, c1760 . . . . 190.00
Charger, 20" d, center transfer with blue Rembrandt portrait, fruit border 165.00
Cheese Dish, cov, pink floral design 100.00
Cracker Jar, cov, 7½" h, ovoid, pink, blue, rose, and orange flower dec outlined with gold, beige and cream ground, emb swirls with gold trim, silver plated rim, cov, and bail handle 125.00
Ewer, 12½" h, hp, bird, orchids, and dragonfly, encircling gold lizard handle 175.00
Mug, 4" h, blackberries and flower dec, shaded green ground 50.00

Urn, cov, 24" h, Rococo style, elaborately painted and enameled, marked 650.00
Vase
9¼" h, bulbous, molded scalloped rim, shaped handles, enamel portraits of young woman, gilt trim, sgd "Dingendorf," printed marks, c1900, price for pair 700.00
11¼" h, pink and yellow roses, green and mustard yellow ground, gold trim, red crown mark of Franz Anton Mehlem Porcelain Factory, c1900 . . . . 250.00
12" h, hp, floral dec outlined in gold enamel 70.00
12¼" h, shaded green, gold trim, imp and stamped crown mark, price for pair 290.00
14" h, flaring form, oval portrait and landscape medallions, pink ground, gilt dec, No. 2835 175.00

c1889   c1923

ROYAL COPENHAGEN

History: Franz Mueller established a porcelain factory at Copenhagen in 1775. When bankruptcy threatened in 1779, the Danish king acquired ownership, appointing Mueller manager and adopting the name "Royal Copenhagen." The crown sold its interest in 1867; the company remains privately owned today.

Blue Fluted, Royal Copenhagen's most famous pattern, was created in 1780. It is of Chinese origin and comes in three styles: smooth edge, closed lace edge, and perforated lace edge (full lace). Many other factories copied it. Flora Danica, named for a famous botanical work, was introduced in 1789 and remained exclusive to Royal Copenhagen. Botanical illustrations were done freehand; all edges and perforations were cut by hand.

Royal Copenhagen porcelain is marked with three wavy lines (which signify ancient waterways) and a crown (added in 1889). Stoneware does not have the crown mark.

Reference: Susan and Al Bagdade, *Warman's English & Continental Pottery & Porcelain, Second Edition,* Wallace-Homestead, 1991.

Additional Listings: Limited Edition Collectors' Plates.

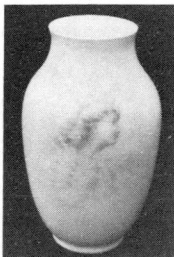

Vase, blue portrait on front, two children on reverse, white ground, 7½" h, $65.00.

Cup and Saucer, blue flower dec, basketweave border **40.00**
Dinner Service, 105 pcs, polychrome floral spray dec, molded basketweave, gilt borders, twelve dinner plates, salad plates, and bread and butter plates, ten soup plates **2,100.00**
Dinnerware, Flora Danica pattern, botanical specimen
 Demitasse Cup and Saucer, underglaze blue triple wave mark, green factory mark, #20/3618, set of 8 .... **3,300.00**
 Plate
  Bread and Butter, 5½" d, underglaze blue triple wave mark, green factory mark, #20/3552, black title, set of 8 .... **1,540.00**
  Dinner, 10¼" d, pink and gold molded beadwork border, gilt dentil rim, underglaze blue triple wave mark, #20/3519 and #20/3549, green factory mark and artist's initials, black botanical title, set of 8 .... **3,300.00**
  Fish, 10" d, reticulated, painted with different fish, green and gold molded beadwork borders, gilt dentil rims, underglaze blue triple wave mark, green factory mark, #19/3549, black title, set of 12 .... **8,800.00**
  Salad
   7½" d, paneled and molded beaded border, dentil rim, gilt and pink highlights, price for pair **550.00**
   7⅝" d, underglaze blue triple wave mark, green printed factory mark, #20/3573, black title, set of 8 ...... **2,200.00**
 Platter
  11½" l, reticulated, underglaze blue triple wave mark, #20/3574, green factory mark, black botanical inscription . **660.00**
  13" d, purple, puce, and green painted dec, gilt highlighted scalloped reticulated border, molded beading and dentil rim, #20/3528 .... **770.00**
 Soup Tureen, 9" h, 13¼" l, oval, pink and gold molded beadwork border, applied split twig handle with flower head terminals on cov, underglaze blue triple wave mark, #20/3559, painters marks and printed crown factory mark, green "Royal Copenhagen/Denmark," black botanical inscriptions **3,300.00**

Sugar, cov, 5½" h, 6" l, oval, molded pink and gilt border and edge, applied entwined twig form handle with flower head and leaf terminals on cov, underglaze blue triple wave and green crown factory mark, inscribed #20/3582 ... **935.00**

Wine Cooler, 4¾" h, cylindrical sides, painted, pink and gold molded beadwork border, applied split twig molded handles with flower head and leaf terminals, underglaze blue triple wave mark, green painter's and printed mark, #20/3570, black botanical inscription ... **935.00**

Figure
Cow and calf, 10½" h, No. 800 **245.00**
Young Pan, with goat, #1012/498 .... **190.00**
Gravy Boat, white, blue morning glories, underplate **50.00**
Jar, oval, silver coin set in lid surrounded by flowers **325.00**
Lamp, 25½" h, sphere held by three children, blue and white . **175.00**
Mug, 4½" h, Christmas, floral dec, c1905 .... **140.00**
Salt and Pepper Shakers, pr, 2½" h, Fluted Lace pattern, blue and white **70.00**
Vase, 8" h, narcissus dec, pale blue ground **85.00**

ROYAL CROWN DERBY

History: Derby Crown Porcelain Co., established in 1875 in Derby, England, had no connection with earlier Derby factories which operated in the late 18th and early 19th centuries. In 1890 the company was appointed "Manufacturers of Porcelain to Her Majesty" (Queen Victoria) and from that date has been known as "Royal Crown Derby."

Derby porcelains from 1878 to 1890 carry only the standard crown printed mark. After 1891 the mark carries the "Royal Crown Derby" wording. In the 20th century "Made in England" and "English Bone China" were added to the mark.

A majority of these porcelains, both tableware and figures, were hand decorated. A variety of printing processes were used for additional adornment. Today, Royal Crown Derby is a part of Royal Doulton Tableware, Ltd.

References: Susan and Al Bagdade, *Warman's English & Continental Pottery & Porcelain, Second Edition,* Wallace-Homestead, 1991; John Twitchett, *The Dictionary of Derby Porcelain 1748–1848,* Antique Collectors' Club; John Twitchett and Betty Bailey, *Royal Crown Derby,* Antique Collectors' Club, 1988.

Cup and Saucer, Oriental scene, blue transfers, gilt rim, $25.00.

Cabinet Urn, cov, double handled, floral reserves, gilt and cobalt field, lid repaired, 8¾" h **525.00**
Cup and Saucer, St George pattern **65.00**
Demitasse Cup and Saucer, St George pattern **50.00**
Dinner Service, 56 pcs, Imari dec, twelve dinner plates, twelve bouillon stands and saucers, and ten tea cups and saucers .**1,100.00**
Figure, porcelain, man with floral and gold cloak, standing beside vessel, damaged hand, 11¼" h **165.00**

Mug, grapes and vines dec, blue
and gold 130.00
Pitcher and Bowl, miniature, Japan pattern, Imari palette, octagonal, red painted marks, slight
gilt wear, minor chips, 1⅞" h
pitcher, 2⅞" d bowl, early 19th C 115.00
Plate
  Imari dec, service, gilt highlights,
  19th C, 10" d, set of eight ... 460.00
  St George pattern
    Bread and Butter 25.00
    Dinner 65.00
    Salad 35.00
Potpourri, urn form, mounted
masks, allover floral and gilt dec,
pierced top with finial, 6" h 75.00
Serving Dish, oval, Japan pattern,
Imari palette, painted red mark,
gilt edge wear, early 19th C,
10⅛" l 210.00
Soup, St George pattern, matching saucer, handles 75.00
Urn on Stand, miniature, Imari palette, double handles, standard
painted red marks, early 19th C,
1¼" h urn, 3½" h stand 435.00

ROYAL DOULTON

History: Doulton pottery began in 1815
under the direction of John Doulton at the
Doulton & Watts pottery in Lambeth, England. Early output was limited to salt-glazed industrial stoneware. John Watts retired in 1854. The firm became Doulton and
Company, and production was expanded to
include hand–decorated stoneware such as
figurines, vases, dinnerware, and flasks. In
1872 the firm began marking their ware
"Royal Doulton."

In 1878 John's son, Sir Henry Doulton,
purchased Pinder Bourne & Co. in Burslem

and the companies became Doulton & Co.,
Ltd. in 1882. Decorated porcelain was
added to Doulton's earthenware production
in 1884. The Royal Doulton mark was used
on both wares.

Most Doulton figurines were produced at
the Burslem plants from 1890 until 1978,
when they were discontinued. A new line of
Doulton figurines was introduced in 1979.

Beginning in 1913, an "HN" number was
assigned to each new Doulton figurine design. The HN numbers refer to Harry
Nixon, a Doulton artist. HN numbers were
chronological until 1940, after which blocks
of numbers were assigned to each modeler.
From 1928 until 1954, a small number appeared to the right of the crown mark; this
number added to 1927 gives the year of
manufacture of the figurines.

Dickens ware, in earthenware and porcelain, was introduced in 1908. The ware
was decorated with characters from Dickens' novels. The line was withdrawn in the
1940s, except for plates which continued
until 1974.

Character jugs, a 20th–century revival of
early Toby models, were designed by
Charles J. Noke for Doulton in the 1930s.
They come in four major sizes and feature
fictional characters from Dickens, Shakespeare, and other English and American
novelists, as well as historical heroes.

Doulton's Rouge Flambe (also Veined
Sung) is a highly glazed, strong–colored
ware noted most for fine modeling and exquisite colorings, especially in the animal
items. The process used to produce the
vibrant colors in this ware is a Doulton secret.

Production of stoneware at Lambeth
ceased in 1956; production of porcelain
continues today at Burslem.

References: Susan and Al Bagdade,
*Warman's English & Continental Pottery &
Porcelain, 2nd Edition,* Wallace–Homestead, 1991; Jean Dale, *The Charlton Standard Catalogue of Royal Doulton Animals,*
Charlton Press, 1994; Jean Dale, *The
Charlton Standard Catalogue of Royal
Doulton Beswick Storybook Figurines,*
Charlton Press, 1994; Jean Dale, *The
Charlton Standard Catalogue of Royal
Doulton Figurines, 4th Edition,* Charlton
Press, 1994; Jean Dale, *The Charlton Stan-*

dard Catalogue of Royal Doulton Jugs, Charlton Press, 1991; Louise Irvine, *Royal Doulton Bunnykins Figures,* UK International Ceramics, 1991; Jocelyn Lukins, *Collecting Royal Doulton Character & Toby Jugs,* Venta Books, 1985; Kevin Pearson, *The Character Jug Collectors Handbook, Fifth Edition,* Kevin Francis Publishing, 1991; Kevin Pearson, *The Doulton Figure Collectors Handbook, Third Edition,* Kevin Francis Publishing, 1993; Ruth M. Pollard, *The Official Price Guide To Royal Doulton, Sixth Edition,* House of Collectibles, 1988; Princess and Barry Weiss, *The Original Price Guide to Royal Doulton Discontinued Character Jugs, Sixth Edition,* Harmony Books, 1987.

Periodicals: *Collecting Doulton,* BBR Publishing, 2 Strattford Avenue, Elsecar, Nr. Barnsley, S. Yorkshire S74 8AA, England; *Doulton Divvy,* PO Box 2434, Joliet, IL 60434.

Collectors' Clubs: Heartland Doulton Collectors, PO Box 2434, Joliet, IL 60434; Mid–America Doulton Collectors, PO Box 483, McHenry, IL 60050; Royal Doulton International Collectors Club, PO Box 6705, Somerset, NJ 08873; Royal Doulton International Collectors Club, 850 Progress Ave, Scarborough, Ontario M1H 3C4 Canada.

Animal Mold
Airedale with Pheasant, HN1022	**400.00**
Cat, HN2539, 5" h, white	**135.00**
Mountain Sheep, HN2661	**175.00**

Biscuit Jar
6¾" h, 5" d, stoneware, cobalt blue borders, tan ground, emb blue flowers, brown leaves, hallmarked SS rim and handle, stoneware lid **175.00**
7¾" h, cream ribbed ground, band of turquoise with birds and animals, SP top, rim, and handle, marked "Doulton, Burslem Pottery" **200.00**

Bowl
3½" h, Chang, heavily crazed, dripping deep red, cream, and ochre glazes, marked "Chang, Royal Doulton, Noke" and Nixon mark, price for pair ...**1,900.00**
4¼" h, 8⅞" d, brown, brown geometric borders, grazing cows

and horses, sgd "Hannah Barlow, 1885" **650.00**

Character Jug, large, 5¼" to 7" h
'Arriet	**200.00**
Beau	**945.00**
Clown	**865.00**
Duchess	**400.00**
Groucho	**75.00**
Jocky Johnson	**300.00**
Pied Piper	**115.00**
Sairey Gamp	**60.00**
Sam Johnson	**325.00**
Scaramouche	**625.00**
St George	**310.00**
Yachtsman, factory second	**60.00**

Character Jug, miniature, 2¼" to 2½"
Bacchus, bone china	**45.00**
Fat Boy	**45.00**
Fortune Teller	**295.00**
Hook	**300.00**
Mikado	**300.00**
Old Charlie	**50.00**
Sairey Gamp	**50.00**
Sancho Panza	**60.00**
Teller	**300.00**

Character Jug, small, 3½" to 4" h
'Ard of 'Earing	**745.00**
Gondolier	**375.00**
Paddy	**45.00**

Figure
Artful Dodger	**55.00**

Autumn Breezes, HN1913, blue bodice, green skirt, blue hat and muff, 8" h, 5¼" d **230.00**
Ballerina, HN2116, lavender and white gown, 7½" h **300.00**
Cissie, HN1809, pink dress, blue hat, basket of yellow roses, 5" h, 3¼" d **110.00**
Cup of Tea **145.00**
Diana, HN1986, red dress and hat, flower bouquet, 5⅞" h, 2½" d **130.00**
Enchantment, HN2178, blue dress, yellow sleeves, 7¾" h, 4¼" d **170.00**
Fiona, HN2694 .... **125.00**
Karen, HN1994 .... **400.00**
Lady Anne Nevill, HN2006, blue gown, fur trim, 10¼" h **650.00**
Little Boy Blue, HN2062, blue outfit, 6" h, 2¼" d **100.00**
Lori **115.00**

Make Believe, HN2225 .... 125.00
Melanie, HN2271, deep blue
dress, gold collar and under-
skirt, yellow rose bouquet, 8"
h, 4½" d 150.00
Miss Muffet, HN1937 .... 235.00
Parisian 155.00
Pride and Joy, HN2945 .... 275.00
Royal Governor's Cook,
HN2233 .... 400.00
Sabbath Morn, HN1982, red
dress and hat, green shawl
and umbrella, 7¾" h, 4" d ... 310.00
Sam Weller, D2973, bottom rim
chip 95.00
Stiggins 55.00

**Pitcher, cobalt blue flower and
butterfly, gilt rim, off white
ground, cobalt blue handle and
panel under rim, Doulton Burslem
mark, 6⅝" h, $150.00.**

Sweet Anne, HN1496, lavender
and rose jacket, cream and
lavender skirt, lavender bonnet, 7⅜" h, 4⅜" d 245.00
Sweet Twenty, HN1298, red
dress, sitting on sofa, fan,
black hat, 6" h, 7½" w 275.00
Taking Things Easy 155.00
The Milkmaid, HN2057, brown
blouse, green skirt, blue bonnet and apron, 7" h, 2¾" d .. 180.00
The Shepherd, HN1975, tan outfit, brown hat, lantern, staff,
and lamb at side, 9" h, 3½" d 235.00
Tinkle Bell, HN1677, pink dress,
white bonnet, 5" h, 2¼" d ... 100.00

Top O' the Hill, HN1833, blue
and black hat, blue blouse,
green skirt, blue figured scarf,
7½" h, 4½" d 210.00
Victoria, HN2471 .... 175.00
Flambe
Bowl, 9¾" d, Oriental style 225.00
Vase, 9" h, bulbous, Veined
Sung 250.00
Jardiniere, 9" h, 10" d, Shake-
speare Ware, cream ground, for-
est scene, figures of Ophelia and
Hamlet, marked "Royal Doulton" 325.00
Lighter
Porthos 645.00
Winkle 585.00
Mug, large
Captain Ahab, D6500 .... 75.00
The Trapper, D6609 .... 75.00
Pitcher, 10½" h, iris front and back,
flowing cobalt blue, white
ground, gold flowers, scrolling,
and outlines, marked "Doulton
Burslem England" 415.00
Plate
Scottish castle ruins center, co-
balt blue borders, encrusted
gold dec, titled on back, price
for set of 12 ....3,400.00
Shylock 55.00
Story of Willow series, verse
printed on back of plate, center
multicolored scene of man
gardening, lady in robes sitting
and watching, willow birds in
sky, dated "December 1916,"
10½" d 140.00
Punch Bowl, 14¼" d, blue, flowers
and parrots dec, ftd 350.00
Tankard, 6" h, Queen Elizabeth,
Old Moreton Hall, c1920 ...... 45.00
Teapot, 9½" h, Gold Lace pattern,
H9989 .... 100.00
Toby, 5½" h, Happy John,
HN6070, c1939 .... 75.00
Vase
3¾" h, 5" w, Babes in the Woods,
pillow shaped, girl with basket
picking flowers 310.00
13¾" h, cobalt blue flared rim
and base with leafage dec,
blue floral dec, gold ground .. 180.00
20¼" h, bulbous, green and
blue, floral and gilt dec base . 425.00

ROYAL DUX

History: Royal Dux porcelain was made in Dux, Bohemia (Czechoslovakia), by E. Eichler at the Duxer Porzellan–Manufaktur, established in 1860. Many items were exported to the United States. By the turn of the century Royal Dux figurines, vases, and accessories—especially those with Art Nouveau designs—were captivating consumers.

A raised triangle with an acorn and the letter "E" plus "Dux, Bohemia," was used as a mark between 1900 and 1914.

Reference: Susan and Al Bagdade, *Warman's English & Continental Pottery & Porcelain, Second Edition,* Wallace–Homestead, 1991.

Bust, 14" h, woman, green scarf, open pink vest, green bodice, scrolled gold base, matte finish **365.00**

Figure
  6" h, peasant girl, hands folded at waist, matte green, pale pink clothes, pink triangle mark **200.00**
  8" h, Greek potter, seated, multicolored, c1900 .... **215.00**
  8⅛" h, 10⅜" l, Bohemia, ivory and brown highlights, triangle medallion, imp "0177 43" ... **175.00**
  12" h, troubadour holding mandolin and wine cup, other serving maiden, price for pair **300.00**
  18" h
    Man and woman, polychromed earthenware, biblical attire, price for pair **700.00**
    Michele, seated nude, polychrome glaze, green base, triangular wafer imp marks,

base damage, restoration, c1900 .... **625.00**
22¾" h, Pax Et Labor, group .. **210.00**
Jar, 9" h, Art Nouveau, woman's face, molded, multicolored **400.00**
Lamp, 9" h, Art Deco, woman spreading edges of cobalt blue gown, flesh tones, brass base . **400.00**
Powder Jar, 6½" d, cobalt and gold, seated lady figure on top, pink triangle mark **600.00**
Urn, cov, 12¼" h, baluster shape, three rams heads, three scroll and hoof feet, molded shaped trefoil base, royal blue and cream, gilt trim, ovoid finial, pink mark **325.00**

Vase, woman, figural outstretched arms, rising from sea, 15½" h, $95.00.

Vase
  8" h, flowers and cherries, orange and green, pr **90.00**
  10" h, Art Nouveau, matte colors, applied handles **125.00**
  14" h, heavy relief of leaves and open work, soft earth tone colors, c1900 .... **200.00**
  14½" h, figural, lady emerging from vase playing harp, pink triangle mark **450.00**
  14¾" h, Art Deco, woman draped over vase, cream, bronze, and gold, pink triangle mark **400.00**

ROYAL FLEMISH

History: Royal Flemish was produced by the Mount Washington Glass Co., New Bedford, Massachusetts. The process was patented by Albert Steffin in 1894.

Royal Flemish has heavy raised gold enamel lines on frosted transparent glass that separates areas into sections, often colored in russet tones. It gives the appearance of stained glass windows with elaborate floral or coin medallions in the design.

Collectors' Club: Mount Washington Art Glass Society, 60 President Ave., Providence, RI 02906.

Advisors: Clarence and Betty Maier.

Ewer, 12" h, gold and silver rampant lion and shield, raised gold borders, pastel blue cross with raised gold borders on reverse, applied twisted rope handle . . . **3,350.00**
Pickle Castor, frosted ground, gold wild rose dec, blown–out scrolls, purple enamel trim, fancy frame   **750.00**
Pitcher, 9" h, 6½" w, aquatic scene, fish swimming among sea plants and shellfish, shades of blue, green, and purple, gold highlights, applied rope handle, gold and lavender around helmet shaped spout, monogram, numbered "506" **6,800.00**
Sweetmeat Jar, cov, 5" h, 4½" w, white and yellow spider mums, leaves, and buds, frosted and gold ground, orig cov **450.00**
Vase, 7½" h, squatty round body, raised bulbed trefoil rim, frosted ground, gilt bordered panels of amber, brown, and rust, classical coin medallions, orig label on base "Mt W. G. Co. Royal Flemish" **3,500.00**

ROYAL RUDOLSTADT

History: Johann Fredrich von Schwarzburg–Rudolstadt was the patron of a faience factory located in Rudolstadt, Thuringen, Germany, from 1720 to c1790. The pottery's mark was a hayfork and later crossed two–prong hayforks in imitation of the Meissen mark.

In 1854 Ernst Bohne established a factory in Rudolstadt. His pieces are marked "EB."

The "Royal Rudolstadt" designation originated with wares imported by Lewis Straus and Sons (later Nathan Straus and Sons) of New York from the New York and Rudolstadt Pottery between 1887 and 1918. The factory's mark was a crown under which was a diamond enclosing the initials "RW." The factory manufactured several of the Rose O'Neill (Kewpie) items.

Reference: Susan and Al Bagdade, *Warman's English & Continental Pottery & Porcelain, Second Edition,* Wallace–Homestead, 1991.

Vase, Guba Duck dec, attributed to Frank Guba, raised gold sun, lead mallard, ten other ducks encircle perimeter, irregular panels of pastel tan and frosted clear, mauve and gold embellishments on upper 3" of crown-like top, 15¾" h, $6,500.00.

Vase, ivory ground, orange and pink flowers, green and brown leaves, gold details, blue mark, #6230 on base, 13½" h, $145.00.

Bowl, 10" d, pink, green, and white
flowers, gold band **75.00**
Celery Tray, 10" l, hp, large pink
and white flowers, white ground **48.00**
Creamer, feathered gold over dra-
pery, gold handle **48.00**
Cup and Saucer
Floral, pastel colors, gold trim . **35.00**
Kewpies, multicolored, sgd
"Rose O'Neill Wilson" **100.00**
Dresser Set, hair receiver, cov
powder jar, open handled tray,
pastel roses, white ground, price
for 3 pc set **60.00**
Ewer
11¾" h, hp, bird, butterfly, ferns,
and grass, ivory ground, gold
trim, green serpentine spout,
brown handle **150.00**
13¾" h, cream and light pink
shell body, pebbled ground,
brown worm type handle **175.00**
Figure, boy and girl, sitting on
bench, cream, beige, and gold . **200.00**
Hatpin Holder, hexagonal, roses
dec, pearl finish, sgd **145.00**
Mug, 3¾" h, Kewpies, decals, sgd
"O'Neill" **125.00**
Pitcher
9½" h, multicolored floral dec,
gilt trim, long thin neck, raised
mark **175.00**
15½" h, jeweled dec, inlaid gold
leaves **300.00**

Plate, water lily dec, Pickard style
painting **45.00**
Sweetmeat Jar, cov, 8" h, pink
floral dec, green and rust leaves,
cream ground, SP holder,
marked "Middletown" **135.00**
Urn, cov, 10" h, mythological
scene, Hector and Andro crown-
ing maiden, cobalt blue ground,
gold handles **125.00**
Vase
5¾" h, figural, peacock, open
wings, multicolored **65.00**
10½" h, multicolored flowers,
beige and yellow ground, han-
dled **125.00**

1749 -1864

ROYAL VIENNA

History: Production of hard–paste porcelain in Vienna began in 1720 with Claude
Innocentius du Paquier, a runaway employee of the Meissen factory. In 1744 Empress Maria Theresa brought the factory under royal patronage; subsequently the ware
became known as Royal Vienna. The firm
went through many administrative changes
until it closed in 1864. The quality of its
workmanship always was maintained.

Many other Austrian and German firms
copied the Royal Vienna products, including
the use of the "Beehive" mark. Many of the
pieces on today's market are from these
firms.

Reference: Susan and Al Bagdade, *Warman's English & Continental Pottery & Porcelain, Second Edition,* Wallace–Homestead, 1991.

Box, cov, 6¼" d, 4½" h, round, red
ground, center scene of lady on
lavender couch, cherub and
three attendants, alternating border panels of scenes and flow-
ers, beehive mark **350.00**

Candlestand, 30" h, 22¼" d, circular gilt wood frame top, painted doiley and angel with cupids, floral garland and cartouche frieze, reticulated pedestal with putti dec, four winged Amazon warriors, caryatid legs ... **3,200.00**

Charger, 12" d, portrait of three ladies holding globes in garden, artist sgd ... **175.00**

Creamer, 3⅛" h, landscape scenes, figures, harbor, gilt scroll rim band and handle, blue shield mark, c1770 ... **250.00**

Ewer, 15½" h, painted continuous scene of Hector and military, enameled panels, gilt ground, sgd "Bauer," blue beehive mark, late 19th C ... **1,760.00**

Figure
7" h, young boy, period costume, enameled, imp beehive mark ... **300.00**
9" h, soldier, wearing chapeau bras, reining in rearing horse ... **315.00**

Jardiniere, 12½" d, transfer printed, two classical maidens in oval panel, cobalt blue ground, gilt trim, multicolored paneled borders, blue shield mark ... **350.00**

Plate, mountainous scene with child and mother ... **150.00**

Urn, 11" h, scenes of Romans and ladies, molded heads and headdress, gold trim, cube base, beehive marks, price for pair ... **950.00**

Vase
11" h, oval reserve of maiden,

Figure, multicolored, blue beehive mark, 5" h, $165.00.

encrusted gilt dec handles, base, and lip ... **425.00**

11½" h, cov, goblet form, three musical nudes and two reserves of cupids and roses, red, green, and gold band, lid, and base, sgd "J Hubner," 19th C ... **575.00**

c.1876-1891   1891

ROYAL WORCESTER

History: In 1751 the Worcester Porcelain Company, led by Dr. John Wall and William Davis, acquired the Bristol pottery of Benjamin Lund and moved it to Worcester. The first wares were painted blue under the glaze, followed closely by painting on the glaze in enamel colors. Among the most famous 18th–century decorators were James Giles and Jefferys Hamet O'Neale. Transfer–print decoration was developed by the 1760s.

A series of partnerships took over upon Davis's death in 1783: Flight (1783–1793); Flight & Barr (1793–1807); Barr, Flight & Barr (1807–1813); and Flight, Barr & Barr (1813–1840). In 1840 the factory was moved to Chamberlain & Co. in Diglis. Decorative wares were discontinued. In 1852 W. H. Kerr and R. W. Binns formed a new company and revived the ornamental wares.

In 1862 the firm became the Royal Worcester Porcelain Co. Among the key modelers of the late 19th century were James Hadley, his three sons, and George Owen, an expert at pierced clay pieces. Royal Worcester absorbed the Grainger factory in 1889 and the James Hadley factory in 1905. Modern designers include Dorothy Doughty and Doris Lindner.

References: Susan and Al Bagdade, *Warman's English & Continental Pottery & Porcelain, Second Edition,* Wallace–Homestead, 1991; David, John, and Henry Sandon, *The Sandon Guide To Royal Worcester Figures, 1900–1970,* Alderman Press, 1987; John Sandon, *The Dictionary of Worcester Porcelain, Volume I: 1751–1851,* Antique Collectors' Club, 1993; Henry Sandon, *The Dictionary of Worcester Porcelain, Volume II: 1852 To The Present Day,* Antique Collectors' Club.

Museum: Charles William Dyson Perrins Museum, Worcester, England.

Plate, blue and orange Oriental florals, gilt trim, 7½" d, $95.00.

Biscuit Jar, cov, 7¾" h, enamel floral dec, ivory ground, raised gilt border, printed marks, 1890 ... **325.00**
Bowl, 4" h, reticulated border, floral with butterflies dec, pedestal, sgd "Hadley Faience, Worcester, England" ... **295.00**
Candleholder, 5" h, child leaning against large white dog, arms wrapped around turquoise candleholder, gold trim, turquoise base, c1876 ... **375.00**
Charger, 16½" d, brown sgraffito, buff ground, sgd, printed marks, price for pair ... **575.00**
Chop Plate, Engadine pattern, slight scratching ... **30.00**

Cologne Bottle, 3¾" h, lavender, rust, yellow, and green pansies and foliage, SP cap, 1887 date code ... **225.00**
Creamer, 6" h, yellow and gold dec, gold handle ... **75.00**
Cup and Saucer, 3⅞" d saucer, floral enamel and gilt dec, cobalt blue ground ... **200.00**
Dish, 7½" l, leaf form, pink daisies, gold outlined border ... **25.00**
Ewer, 8¾" h, blue flowers, tan leaves, gold outlines, cream satin ground, dragon twist handle, c1887 ... **450.00**
Figure, wood stand, Doris Lindner
  Aberdien Angus Bull ... **200.00**
  Hereford Bull ... **210.00**
  Jersey Cow ... **130.00**
  Santa Gertrudis Bull ... **145.00**
Fish Service, fish and seaweed centers en grisaille, includes sauceboat with tray, bowl, and twelve plates, 19th C, price for 15 pc set ... **550.00**
Fruit Plate
  Engadine pattern ... **12.00**
  Set of ten, varied fruit painted centers, cobalt blue and gold encrusted border, R Sebright ... **4,290.00**
Jam Pot, cov, tray, melon form, yellow ground, red veined leaves and vine on lid, sold by Tiffany and Co, 19th C ... **250.00**
Pitcher, 7¾" h, hp flowers and butterflies dec ... **165.00**
Plate
  9" d, Silver Chantilly ... **25.00**
  10" d, multicolored wildflowers center, etched light green border, purple mark ... **65.00**
Portrait Vase, 6" h, blue ground satyr mask handles, enamel dec portraits of King Charles I and James Graham Marquis of Montrose, printed marks, c1862, price for pair ... **635.00**
Rose Bowl, 2½" d, brown and orange bird, enameled gold branches, 1897 mark ... **195.00**
Sculpture, Crab Apple and Butterfly, modeled by Dorothy Doughty, leaf ends missing ... **55.00**
Soup Plate, Engadine pattern ... **15.00**

Tea Caddy, 4" h, gilded leaf and floral dec, ivory ground, green mark **100.00**

Teapot, cov, double spout, Imari pattern, compressed circular body, swirled alternating panels of flower chains and foliate scrolls, basketweave molded base, four compressed feet, arched handle, iron–red printed mark, date "N" letter, 1878 registry mark **335.00**

Urn, cov, 15¼" h, hp, flying fish shaped handles, rose dec, sgd "W E Jarman," c1910 ....**1,300.00**

Vase

8½" h, shell form, gilt seaweed support, circular base **325.00**

9½" h, bottle–form, ivory ground, hp enamel butterflies and gilt tall grass, late 19th C **230.00**

16½" h, gold lame-type parrot dec, pale green, cream, and rose ground, reticulated handles, imp mark **2,900.00**

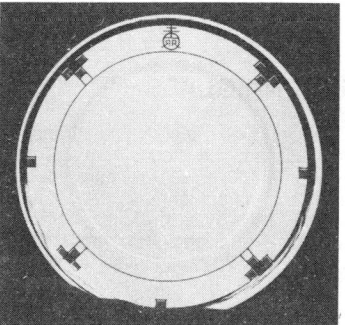

ROYCROFT

History: Elbert Hubbard founded the Roycrofters in East Aurora, New York, at the turn of the century. Considered a genius in his day, he was an author, lecturer, manufacturer, salesman, and philosopher.

Hubbard established a campus which included a printing plant where he published *The Philistine, The Fra,* and *The Roycrofter.* His most famous book was *A Message to Garcia,* published in 1899. His "community" also included a furniture manufacturing plant, a metal shop, and a leather shop.

References: Nancy Hubbard Brady, *The Book of The Roycrofters,* House of Hubbard, 1977; Nancy Hubbard Brady, *Roycroft Handmade Furniture,* House of Hubbard,

1973; Charles F. Hamilton, *Roycroft Collectibles,* A. S. Barnes & Company, 1980; Kevin McConnell, *Roycroft Art Metal, Second Edition,* Schiffer Publishing, 1994; Paul McKenna, *A New Pricing Guide For Materials Produced by The Roycroft Printing Shop, Second Edition,* Tona Graphics, 1982; The Roycrofters, *Roycroft Furniture Catalog, 1906,* Dover, 1994.

Collectors' Clubs: Foundation for the Study of Arts & Crafts Movement, Roycroft Campus, 31 S. Grove St., East Aurora, NY 14052; Roycrofters–At–Large Association, PO Box 417, East Aurora, NY 14052.

Museum: Elbert Hubbard Library–Museum, East Aurora, NY.

Additional Listing: Arts and Crafts Movement and Copper.

Bowl, matching handled serving plate, handles dec with stylized leaves, both pieces with Roycroft green and brick red geometric pattern and logo, sgd, some crackling, 11¼" w plate, 6" d x 2¼" h bowl **550.00**

Bracelet, 2³⁄₁₆" d, repousse floral medallion, hammered pattern band, imp marks **375.00**

Candlestick, 10" h, copper, U–shaped shaft, two candle cups above stepped rect base, four disk feet, dark gold wash, imp "R" in orb mark on base **200.00**

Plate, marked "Buffalo China," 9½" d, set of four, $470.00.

Chest of Drawers, oak, six stacked graduated locking drawers, black finished iron hardware, medium dark finish, carved "Roycroft," Aurora, NY, c1905, 29⅝" w, 25¾" d, 63" h, rear post crack **10,925.00**

Creamer and Sugar Bowl, Roycroft logo and green and brick red pattern, sgd "Buffalo Pottery 1926, Roycroft," hairline to creamer, chip to sugar underside, 2¾" h creamer, 3½" h sugar **385.00**

Library Table, No. 75, oak, rect overhanging top, two short drawers, base shelf, orig medium finish, copper hardware, carved orb mark, c1906, 52⅛" l, 33¼" w, 30" h **1,955.00**

Plate, dinner, set of four, Roycroft logo integrated in green and brick red geometric pattern, stamped "Buffalo Pottery, Semi–Vitreous," 9½" d **470.00**

Salt and Pepper Shakers, pr, 2¾" h, black Roycroft orb mark on ivory ground, green border around top, brick red and green geometric designs outlined in black, marked "Buffalo Pottery 1926, Roycroft," hairline in saltshaker base **275.00**

Serving Tray, No. 806, hammered copper, brass wash finish, imp mark, Aurora, NY, c1917, 15⅞" d, finish loss **260.00**

RUBENA GLASS

History: Rubena crystal is a transparent blown glass which shades from clear to red. It also is found as the background for frosted and overshot glass. It was made in the late 1800s by several glass companies, including Northwood and Hobbs, Brocunier & Co. of Wheeling, West Virginia.

Rubena was used for several patterns of pattern glass including Royal Ivy and Royal Oak.

Reference: Ellen T. Schroy, *Warman's Glass,* Wallace-Homestead, 1992.

Beverage Set, 7¼" h pitcher, three 3¾" h tumblers, white enamel dec of Whittier's Birthplace, Haverhill, MA, scene of early 19th C building, landscape painting ... **200.00**

Creamer
  Hobb's IVT **85.00**
  Royal Ivy **95.00**

Perfume Bottle, 4½" h, 3½" d, squatty bulbous, cranberry shading to clear, center cut bands of leaves, star cut base, clear stopper with cutting **115.00**

Vase, coralene dec, gold trim, 5" h, $375.00.

Salt **65.00**
Salt and Pepper Shakers, pr, Royal Oak, shiny tops **165.00**
Sugar, cov, 5" sq, Royal Oak, frosted, acorn finial **125.00**
Sugar Shaker, Hobb's Optic, acid etched florals, orig fancy lid ... **175.00**
Syrup, Hobb's Optic **235.00**
Water Set, 9½" h x 5½" d pitcher, six 3¾" h x 2¾" d tumblers, squatty bulbous pitcher shading from clear to cranberry, applied clear reeded handle, enameled yellow roses, white foliage, blue and gold flowers, price for set . **165.00**

RUBENA VERDE GLASS

History: Rubena Verde, a transparent glass that shades from red in the upper section to yellow-green in the lower, was made by Hobbs, Brockunier & Co., Wheeling, West Virginia, in the late 1880s. It often is found in the inverted thumbprint (IVT) pattern, termed "Polka Dot" by Hobbs.

Reference: Ellen T. Schroy, *Warman's Glass,* Wallace-Homestead, 1992.

Tumbler, Inverted Thumbprint pattern, 3⅞" h, $65.00.

Bowl, 9½" d, Hobnail pattern, crimped rim	**175.00**
Celery Dish, 6¼" l, IVT pattern	**225.00**
Cheese Dish, IVT pattern, orig vaseline Daisy and Button pattern base, Hobb's	**250.00**
Finger Bowl, IVT pattern, matching underplate	**75.00**
Pickle Castor, breakfast size, Hobnail pattern insert, SP frame and tongs	**265.00**
Pitcher	
7¼" h, bulbous, quatrefoil top, glossy, deep red shading to creamy pale green, white casing, ground pontil, applied amber handle, Hobbs Brockunier, c1870	**765.00**
8" h, Hobnail pattern, opalescent hobnails, applied vaseline handle	**790.00**
Saltshaker, 4¼" h, enameled floral dec, pewter top	**185.00**
Syrup, IVT pattern, applied handle, pewter lid, marked "Pat. March 29, 83"	**335.00**
Tumbler, 4" h, Hobnail pattern	**150.00**
Vase, 10" h, enameled florals, gold trim	**165.00**

RUBY STAINED GLASS, SOUVENIR TYPE

History: Ruby stained glass was produced in the late 1880s and 1890s by several glass manufacturers, primarily in the area of Pittsburgh, Pennsylvania.

Ruby stained items were made from pressed clear glass which was stained with a ruby red material. Pieces often were etched with the name of a person, place, date, or event and sold as souvenirs at fairs and expositions.

In many cases one company produced the pressed glass blanks and a second company stained and etched them. Many patterns were used, but the three most popular were Button Arches, Heart Band, and Thumbprint.

References: William Heacock, *Encyclopedia of Victorian Colored Pattern Glass, Book 7: Ruby-Stained Glass From A to Z,* Antique Publications, 1986; Ellen T. Schroy, *Warman's Glass,* Wallace-Homestead, 1992.

Reproduction Alert: Ruby staining is being added to many pieces through the use of modern stained glass coloring kits. A rash of fake souvenir ruby stained pieces was made in the 1960s, the best known example is the "bad" button arches toothpick.

Bell, etched holly and berries, clear handle and clapper	**85.00**
Butter Dish, cov, Button Arches, "Lancaster Fair, 1916"	**165.00**
Creamer, Star of David pattern, "St Louis World's Fair, 1904"	**125.00**

Salt Shaker, Button Arches, inscribed name, $25.00.

Goblet
  Ruby Thumbprint, "Mother" ... **30.00**
  Shriner Convention, Syria insig-
    nia and "Pittsburgh, PA" on
    front, "St Paul, MN, 1908" on
    back, words on sides, 5¼" h,
    3" d **100.00**
Mug, Button Band, 1900, etched
  leaf **35.00**
Napkin Ring, Diamond with Peg,
  "1907" **85.00**
Pitcher, tankard, Button Arches,
  "Pittsburgh" **125.00**
Sauce Dish, Cathedral, "Niagara
  Falls" **20.00**
Spooner, York Herringbone,
  "World's Fair, 1893" **45.00**
Toothpick Holder, "1908 Indiana
  State Fair" **40.00**
Wine, Thumbprint, etched holly
  and berries **40.00**

ВРАТЬЕВЪ

Baterin's factory
1812-1820

КорНИЛОВЬІХЪ

Korniloff's factory
c1835

RUSSIAN ITEMS

History: During the late 19th and early
20th centuries, Russia contained craftsmen
skilled in lacquer, silver, and enamel wares.
Located mainly in Moscow during the Czar-
ist era (1880–1917) was a group of master
craftsmen led by Fabergé, who created exquisite enamel pieces. Fabergé also had an
establishment in St. Petersburg and enjoyed the patronage of the Russian Imperial
family and royalty and nobility throughout
Europe.

Almost all enameling was done on silver.
Pieces are signed by the artist and the government assayer.

The Russian Revolution in 1917 brought
an abrupt end to the century of Russian
craftsmanship. The modern Soviet government has exported some inferior enamel
and lacquer work, usually lacking in artistic
merit. Modern pieces are not collectible.

References: Vladimir Guliayev, *The Fine
Art of Russian Lacquered Miniatures,*
Chronicle Books, 1993; A. Kenneth Snow-
man, *Fabergé: Lost and Found,* Harry N.
Abrams, 1993.

Museums: Cleveland Museum of Art,
Cleveland, OH; Forbes Magazine Collec-
tion, New York, NY; Hillwood, The Marjorie
Merriweather Post Collection, Washington,
DC; Virginia Museum of Fine Arts, Lillian
Thomas Pratt Collection, Richmond, VA;
Walters Art Gallery, Baltimore, MD.

Advisors: Barbara and Melvin Alpren.

**Cup, champleve enamel, shaded
multicolored enamel, marked, 5" l,
2¾" h, $3,500.00.**

Bookcase, Neoclassical style,
  brass mounted mahogany,
  shaped rect top with canted corners, cupboard door with diamond form dec, int. with two
  shelves flanked by brass pilasters raised on square tapering
  legs ending in brass sabots, 22"
  w, 13¾" d, 41½" h **805.00**
Box
  Oval, lacquer, painted scene of
    dancers in landscape, gilt
    floral highlights **60.00**
  Rect, Baroque style, Kholmo-
    gory, Arkhangelsk province,
    painted ivory, two parts, upper
    with shaped rect hinged top
    opening to well, tapered
    pierced frieze, lower with sec-

ond hinged top opening to well above pierced frieze, bracket feet, painted and etched with green trailing vines and blind fretwork, dated 1828, 9¼" w, 13" h **3,450.00**

Candelabra, Neoclassical, ormolu and patinated bronze, three light, center classically dressed winged female figure holding wreath supporting three scrolled candle branches, standing on orb raised on stepped socle fitted with flaming atheniennes and berried laurel wreaths with flamed torches, square base with leaf tip border, first quarter 19th C, 24" h, 11" w **8,050.00**

Chalice, high domed circular base chased with scrolling foliage, engraved biblical motif panels, baluster stem and bowl engraved with biblical text and motifs within scrolls, gilt int. calyx, Moscow, 1853, 12¼" h **1,895.00**

Cigarette Box, silver, rect form, hinged cov, match safe one end, diagonal ribbed pattern, 8 oz, 4" l **200.00**

Cup and Saucer, porcelain, burgundy band dec, gilt highlights, price for set of six **230.00**

Dressing Mirror, Neoclassical, birch, mahogany, and parcel gilt, hinged rect mirror plate, rosettes at corners, square tapering supports, concave fronted central drawer flanked by four short drawers, bone handles, first quarter 19th C **2,588.00**

Easter Egg, porcelain, painted portrait, young man holding candle, signed with initials, gilt rim dec with scrolls, reverse with gilt sunburst emanating from star, late 19th C, 4½" h **865.00**

Figure, bronze, horse pulling sled, sgd in Cyrillic by L P Grachev, founder's mark "C.F. Woerffel," 19th C, 4" h, 9½" l **825.00**

Icon

Christ on Cross, surrounded by saints, oil on wood panel, 14 x 12" **1,035.00**

St George and St Dimitri, early 18th C **865.00**

Virgin of Tenderness, silver gilt and enameled oklad, silver filigree robes, c1900, 7" h **1,265.00**

Nesting Dolls, lacquered **115.00**

Salt, silver, red, blue, and white enameled floral scrollwork, 19th C **265.00**

Salt Cellar, spoon, silver gilt and enamel, colorful stylized foliage, ring foot with cable border, 19th C, 1⅗" h **600.00**

Samovar

Brass, complete with kettle, tray missing, 19th C, 20¼" h **250.00**

Silver Plated, molded panel and column dec, two handles, hallmarked, 12½" d, 18¾" h **230.00**

Statue, cossack and gypsy woman on horseback, bronze, Alexei Gratcheff, Petersburg foundry, dark patina, imperfection on base, 1780–1850, 12" w, 13¾" h **3,450.00**

Sweetmeat Dishes, pr, silver and cut glass, swing handles, marked "84, Kakoshnick," 5" d, 2" h **525.00**

Teabowls, boxed set of six, porcelain, floral dec, Bulgarian silver frames, Kuznetsov, one cracked, some frame dents ... **200.00**

Tea Set, enameled silver, Pavel A Ovchinnikov, cov teapot, cov sugar, creamer, sugar tongs, and twelve teaspoons, flaring square form with domed and tube finial, enameled dec of exotic birds, fish, frogs amidst lily, water foliage, and flowers, late 19th C, 7" h teapot **11,000.00**

Troika

Bronze, grouping, three lively horses driven by winter clad bearded figure standing at front of sleigh, two figures seated behind wrapped in fur rug, naturalistically cast rect base, cast from model by Eugene Alexandrovich Lanceray, inscribed in Old Russian with artist's signature and "Made in Brest," 1848–86, 18" h **9,900.00**

Cast Iron, grouping, three peasants in cart, driver holding reins of three spirited horses, standing girl distracting driver with arm around his neck, second girl seated behind, holding her waist, rect base cast with rockwork and grasses, partial loss to one horse's forelegs, 19th C, 7½" h, 16" l **1,210.00**

Urn on Stand, floral and scenic dec, cobalt blue ground, 19th C, 16" h **2,185.00**

SABINO GLASS

History: Sabino glass, named for its creator Ernest Marius Sabino, originated in France in the 1920s and is an art glass which was produced in a wide range of decorative glassware: frosted, clear, opalescent, and colored glass. Both blown and pressed moldings were used. Hand–sculpted wooden molds that were cast in iron were used and are still in use at the present time.

In 1960 the company introduced a line of figurines, one to eight inches high, plus other items in a fiery opalescent glass in the Art Deco style. Gold was added to the batch to attain the fiery glow. These pieces are the Sabino that is most commonly found today. Sabino is marked with the name in the mold, an etched signature, or both.

Animal
  Dog
    Pekingese, small **20.00**
    Poodle, 1¾" **20.00**

Chicken, 7⅜" h, 6½" w, $400.00.

    Scottie **65.00**
    Elephant **25.00**
Ashtray, swallow, large **45.00**
Bird, feeding, small **20.00**
Bowl
  Fish **50.00**
  Shell **45.00**
Box, Petalia **90.00**
Chandelier, 24" d, 25" h, central shaft, flared chrome corona, eight downswept arms in two registers, cylindrical shades, relief molded overlapping leaves flanked by wings, c1925 . . . . . . **2,100.00**
Charger, 11¾" d, Art Deco, opalescent, molded spiral design and three nude swimming women, molded mark "Sabino Paris" **550.00**
Napkin Ring, birds, marked "Sabino" **35.00**
Scent Bottle, 5" h, Pineapple **165.00**
Statue, 6½" h, nude woman, long flowing hair **125.00**
Table Lamp, 7½" h, domed, three tiered shade, irregular edge, circular molded foot, fan shaped panels and triangles, shade molded "Sabino 4640 Paris Depose" **735.00**
Vase
  6" h, flared rim, opalescent, curvilinear Art Deco design, imp "Sabino Paris" **345.00**
  11" h, 7" w, six lobes, Art Deco geometric dec, royal blue, satin finished, polished highlights, sgd **575.00**

ℂ 𝒮 SALOPIAN

SALOPIAN WARE

History: Salopian ware was made at Caughley Pot Works, Salop, Shropshire, England, in the 18th century by Thomas Turner. The ware is polychrome on transfer. One time classified as Polychrome Transfer, it retains the more popular name of Salopian. Wares are marked with an "S" or

"Salopian" impressed or painted under the glaze. Much of it was sold through Turner's Salopian warehouse in London.

Bowl, 2½" h, Britannia, black transfer, polychrome enamel dec, emb ribs 115.00

Creamer, 6" h, black transfer, maiden with urn, yellow and burnt orange accents, black and white frieze, black, white, orange, and yellow florals around rim border, c1790 .... 225.00

Cup and Saucer, handleless, deer in foliage, green, amber, yellow, and blue 55.00

Dish, 10½" l, lozenge shape, lobed sides, scalloped rim, underglaze blue dec of Chantilly sprigs, blue rim, white ground, imp "Salopian," last quarter 18th C 350.00

Milk Jug, 5" h, black transfer, castle and cows, yellow–gold and blue accents, blue rim, int. with black and white geometric dec, c1790 .... 340.00

Plate, Oriental, 8¾" d, $185.00.

Plate, 8" d, scalloped, molded border, cavetto dec with scalloped radiating panels, underglaze blue dec, floral and geometric patterns, center flowering plants in a rock garden, butterfly above, powder blue ground, under border with three undulating vines,

two rim lines, imp "Salopian," last quarter 18th C 360.00

Posset Pot, 4" h, brown transfer, large and small flowers, light blue, orange, yellow, and green highlights 300.00

Teabowl and Saucer, brown transfer, farm scene, polychrome dec 150.00

SALT AND PEPPER SHAKERS

History: Collecting salt and pepper shakers, whether late 19th–century glass forms or the contemporary figural and souvenir types, is becoming more and more popular. The supply and variety is practically unlimited; the price for most sets is within the budget of cost–conscious young collectors. Finally, their size offers an opportunity to assemble a large collection in a small amount of space.

One can specialize in types, forms, or makers. Great art glass artisans such as Joseph Locke and Nicholas Kopp designed salt and pepper shakers in the normal course of their work. Arthur Goodwin Peterson's *Glass Salt Shakers: 1,000 Patterns* provides the reference numbers given below. Peterson made a beginning; there are hundreds, perhaps thousands, of patterns still to be cataloged.

The clear–colored and colored–opaque sets command the highest prices, clear and white sets the lowest. Although some shakers, e.g., the tomato or fig, have a special patented top and need it to hold value, it is usually not detrimental to the price to replace the top of a shaker.

The figural and souvenir type is often looked down upon by collectors. Sentiment and whimsy are prime collecting motivations. The large variety and current low prices indicate a potential for long–term price growth.

Generally, older shakers are priced by the piece, figural and souvenir types by the set. The pricing method is indicated at each division. All shakers are assumed to have original tops unless noted. Identification numbers are from Peterson's book.

References: Gideon Bosker, *Great Shakes: Salt and Peppers For All Tastes,*

Abbeville Press, 1986; Gideon Bosker, *Salt and Pepper Shakers: Identifications and Price Guide,* Avon Books, 1994; Larry Carey and Sylvia Tompkins, *Salt and Pepper: Over 1001 Shakers With Prices,* Schiffer Publishing, 1994; Melva Davern, *The Collector's Encyclopedia of Salt & Pepper Shakers: Figural And Novelty,* First Series (1985, 1991 value update), Second Series (1990, 1995 value update), Collector Books; Helene Guarnaccia, *Salt & Pepper Shakers,* Vol. I, (1985, 1993 value update), Vol. II (1989, 1993 value update), Vol. III (1991), Vol. IV (1993), Collector Books; Mildred and Ralph Lechner, *The World of Salt Shakers, 2nd Edition,* Collector Books, 1992; Arthur G. Peterson, *Glass Salt Shakers: 1000 Patterns,* Wallace–Homestead, 1970, out–of–print; Mike Schneider, *The Complete Salt and Pepper Shaker Book,* Schiffer Publishing, 1993.

Collectors' Clubs: Antique and Art Glass Salt Shaker Collectors Society, 2832 Rapidan Trail, Maitland, FL 32751; Novelty Salt & Pepper Shakers Club, 581 Joy Road, Battle Creek, MI 49017.

Museum: Judith Basin Museum, Stanford, MT.

Additional Listings: See *Warman's Americana & Collectibles* for more examples.

ART GLASS (PRICED INDIVIDUALLY)

Burmese, ribbed pillars, SP frame, matching napkin ring, price for 3 pc set 400.00

Figural, black cat, basket over arm, holding mustard pot basket, 4″ h, $25.00.

Cranberry, Inverted Thumbprint, matching enameled florals, bell shape, orig top 70.00
Mt Washington
  Egg, flat end 70.00
  Tomato 60.00
Peachblow, Wheeling, orig top .. 300.00
Pigeon Blood, Bulging Loop, orig top 45.00
Satin, Diamond Quilted, MOP, red shaded to pink 250.00
Wave Crest, tulip, house dec, orig top, worn dec 28.00

FIGURAL AND SOUVENIR TYPES (PRICED BY SET)

Dutch Boy and Girl, white metal figural top, clear base 90.00
Farmer Pig, gold trim, marked "Shawnee" 25.00
Poppy, orange, green leaves, marked "Royal Bayreuth" 40.00

OPALESCENT GLASS (PRICED INDIVIDUALLY)

Argonaut Shell, blue, 153–K 50.00
Beatty Honeycomb, white, 22–Q . 25.00
Paneled Sprig, white lattice 75.00
Ribbon Vertical 35.00

OPAQUE GLASS (PRICED INDIVIDUALLY)

Acorn, pink 40.00
Cone, Consolidated, pink 35.00
Double Deck, green opaque 30.00
Guttate, green 40.00
Florette, blue, orig top 28.00
Medallion Sprig, white, shiny, orig top 35.00
Scrolled Panel, green 35.00

PATTERN GLASS (PRICED INDIVIDUALLY)

Beaded Swag, ruby stained 65.00
Cane, apple green, 156–H 25.00
Eyewinker, orig top 65.00
Feather, 28–N 18.00
Maine, 22–M 20.00
National Eureka, ruby stained ... 75.00

Priscilla #2, emerald green, 169–G 30.00
Red Block, 169–R 60.00
Stars and Stripes, 173–S 15.00
Wheat and Barley, blue 35.00

SALTGLAZED WARES

History: Saltglazed wares have a distinctive "pitted" surface texture, made by throwing salt into the hot kiln during the final firing process. The salt vapors produce sodium oxide and hydrochloric acid which react on the glaze.

Many Staffordshire potters produced large quantities of this type of ware during the 18th and 19th centuries. A relatively small quantity was produced in the United States. Saltglazed wares still are made today.

Reference: Susan and Al Bagdade, *Warman's English & Continental Pottery & Porcelain, Second Edition,* Wallace–Homestead, 1991.

Dish, shaped rim, lattice work cartouche, basketweave border, c1760, 12″ d, $350.00.

Bottle, 6¾″ h, globular, polychrome enamel vignettes of Chinoiserie maidens among fruiting and flowering trees, short cylindrical neck with lattice and flowerhead border, English, c1750 . **7,200.00**
Dish, 10¼″ d, center molded herringbone sq, panels of star and dot diapering, tripod feet, upturned shaped rim, English, mid 18th C **900.00**
Figure, 4⅝″ h, lady, elaborate dress, braided hair hanging in ringlets at sides, wide brimmed hat, staff in one hand, nosegay in other, dog at feet, rect base, repair to bottom of skirt, English, mid 18th C **7,050.00**
Gravy Boat, 5¼″ l, molded grape leaves, loop handle, English, c1760 .... **330.00**
Mug, 5¼″ h, incised floral motif, blue highlights, England, c1750 **1,540.00**
Pepper Castor, 5⅛″ h, pear shaped body, molded seed pattern within panels, English, c1760, base rim nick **440.00**
Pitcher, allegorical, raised vignettes depicting evils of drinking, stamped "W Ridgway & Co, Oct 1, 1835" **150.00**
Plate, 9″ d, shaped and molded diaper, basketweave border, late 18th C, price for six piece set . **225.00**
Puzzle Jug, 7¾″ h, globular, brown glaze, neck pierced with wheel and leaf motifs, medallion molded in relief of ship in harbor, entitled "Porto Bello, 1741, Jos Puttock," florets applied to handle, triple nozzle rim, London . . **5,220.00**
Scent Flask, 2¾″ h, shield shape, hearts, flowerheads, and scattered asterisks, dark brown slip, imp zig–zag border, threaded aperture, English, c1725, repaired **750.00**

SALTS, OPEN

History: When salt was first mined, the supply was limited and expensive. The necessity for a receptacle in which to serve the salt resulted in the first open salt, a crude, hand–carved, wooden trencher.

As time passed salt receptacles were refined in style and materials. In the 1500s both master and individual salts existed. By the 1700s firms such as Meissen, Waterford, and Wedgwood were making glass, china, and porcelain salts. Leading manufacturers in the 1800s included Libbey Glass Co., Mount Washington, New England Glass Company, Smith Bros., Vallerysthal, Wavecrest, Webb, and many outstanding silversmiths in England, France, and Germany.

Open salts were used as the only means of serving salt until the appearance of the shaker in the late 1800s. The ease of procuring salt from a shaker greatly reduced the use and need for the open salts.

References: William Heacock and Patricia Johnson, *5,000 Open Salts: A Collectors Guide,* Richardson Printing Corporation, 1982, 1989 value update; L. W. and D. B. Neal, *Pressed Glass Dishes Of The Lacy Period 1825–1850,* published by author, 1962; Allan B. and Helen B. Smith have authored and published ten books on open salts beginning with *One Thousand Individual Open Salts Illustrated* (1972) and ending with *1,334 Open Salts Illustrated: The Tenth Book* (1984). Daniel Snyder did the master salt sections in Volumes 8 and 9. In 1987 Mimi Rudnick compiled a revised price list for the ten Smith Books.

Periodical: *Salty Comments,* 401 Nottingham Rd., Newark, DE 19711.

Collectors' Clubs: New England Society of Open Salt Collectors, PO Box 177, Sudbury, MA 01776; Open Salt Collectors of the Atlantic Region, PO Box 5112, Lancaster, PA 17604.

Note: The numbers in parentheses refer to plate numbers in the Smiths' publications.

CONDIMENT SETS WITH OPEN SALTS

Porcelain, light pink with gold trim on leaf shaped holder, marked "Made in Bavaria" (388) **125.00**
Silver Plated, 3 pcs, emb pattern around bowls, Oriental (461) .. **50.00**

INDIVIDUALS

Art Glass
Cameo, Webb, red ground, white lacy dec around bowl, sgd, matching spoon (137) .. **600.00**
Mt Washington, sgd **100.00**

Quezal, irid gold, sgd "Quezal" (92) **200.00**
Steuben, cobalt blue, pedestal, sgd "Steuben" (485) **225.00**
Tiffany, prunted **175.00**
Vallerysthal, hen **35.00**
Wave Crest **115.00**
China
Battersea, tiny **135.00**
Dresden Saxony, lily dec on one side (434) **45.00**
Majolica, flower shape, overlapping leaves, marked "No 35" (439) **60.00**
Royal Worcester, Leaf **45.00**
Wedgwood **100.00**
Cut Glass
Pedestal, faceted base (118) .. **52.00**
Round, alternating zippered and starred panels (361) **25.00**
Triangular, Star and Diamond, sgd "Hawkes" (466) **65.00**
Tub, tab handles, Diamond and Fan (361) **55.00**
Double Salts
China, Meissen, blue florals ... **70.00**
Glass
Blue, silver frames, four ribbed paw feet (460) **80.00**
Vaseline, ten panels, tall handle (460) **50.00**
In Metal Frames
Clear glass liner, ftd SS holder with four peacocks around outside, marked "Sterling" (411) **45.00**
Cobalt blue glass liner, basket, pierced ribbon handles, marked "E.P.N.S." (413) **35.00**

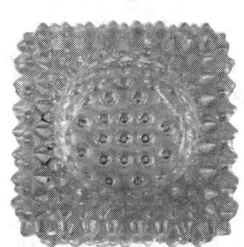

Master, Hobnail pattern, sapphire blue, 3″ sq, $5.00.

Metal, copper, heavy, pedestal,
deep maroon enamel (414) ... **25.00**
Pattern Glass
Acorn Band **25.00**
Morning Glory **110.00**
Tree of Life
Clear **35.00**
Green **85.00**
Wreath and Shell
Blue **80.00**
Vaseline **75.00**
Wood, Sandalwood, spoon (233) **25.00**

FIGURALS

Donkey, painted, pulling colorful
painted cart (458) **30.00**
Sleigh with Cupid driving reindeer,
SS, made in Germany (352) .. **400.00**

MASTERS

China
Belleek, shell shape (314) **40.00**
Leeds, boat shape, pedestal
(313) **65.00**
Minton, ftd, #57957 (314) **47.50**
Unknown Maker, round, subtly
ribbed, floral dec, gold and
green border (384) **45.00**
Colored Glass
Aventurine, narrow base (316) . **55.00**
Cranberry, horizontal colored
ribs (316) **65.00**
Fiery Opalescent, white, baskets
of fruit and floral designs, emb
on base "N. E. Glass Com-
pany Boston," 2⅞" l **275.00**
Vaseline, 101 Yacht Salt, Hobbs,
Brockunier & Co, Daisy and
Button, 4½" l, 1¼" h **235.00**
Cut Glass, round, diamond pattern
on top of bowl, ribbed base (404) **30.00**
Lacy
Clear
Horn of Plenty (329) **60.00**
Oval Diamond on Pedestal
(OP3:407) **150.00**
Colored
Basket of Flowers, opaque
blue (BF1C:324) **350.00**
Eagle, fiery milky opal, Ameri-
can eagle on corners, shield

center, Sandwich Glass-
works, c1840, 3" l **650.00**
Metal
Pewter, pedestal, cobalt blue
liner (349) **60.00**
Silver plated, Dolphin and Shell,
figural, clear glass insert,
marked "Pairpoint," 3½" d,
3¾" h **140.00**
Pressed Glass
Hobnail, round (407) **30.00**
Square Pillared (341) **25.00**
Vintage (340) **30.00**

SAMPLERS

History: Samplers served many purposes. For a young child they were a practice exercise and permanent reminder of
stitches and patterns. For a young woman
they demonstrated her skills in a "gentle"
art and preserved key elements of family
genealogy. For the mature woman they provided a useful occupation and functioned
as gifts or remembrances, e.g., mourning
pieces.

Schools for young ladies of the early 19th
century prided themselves on the needlework skills they taught. The Westtown
School in Chester County, Pennsylvania,
and the Young Ladies Seminary in Bethlehem, Pennsylvania, are two examples.
These schools changed their teaching as
styles changed. Berlin work was introduced
by the mid-19th century.

Examples of samplers date back to the
1700s. The earliest ones were long and narrow, usually done only with the alphabet and
numerals. Later examples were square. At
the end of the 19th century, the shape
tended to be rectangular.

The same motifs were used throughout
the country. The name is a key element in
determining the region. Samplers are assumed to be on linen unless otherwise indicated.

References: Ethel Stanwood Bolton and
Eva Johnston Coe, *American Samplers,*
Dover, 1987; Glee Krueger, *A Gallery of
American Samplers: The Theodore H.
Kapnek Collection,* Bonanza Books, 1984
edition; Dana G. Morykan and Harry L.
Rinker, *Warman's Country Antiques & Col-*

lectibles, Second Edition, Wallace–Homestead, 1994; Betty Ring, *American Needlework Treasures; Samplers and Silk Embroideries From The Collection of Betty Ring,* E. P. Dutton, 1987; Anne Sebba, *Samplers: Five Centuries of a Gentle Craft,* Thames and Hudson, 1979.

Museums: Cooper–Hewitt Museum, National Museum of Design, New York, NY; Smithsonian Institution, Washington, DC.

1770, linen homespun, alphabets, verse, landscape, stylized flowers, and "Christina Baldwin her work 1770," silk stitches, dark brown, blue, green, red, and beige, framed, 20" h, 12" w ... **500.00**

1791, linen homespun, alphabets, verse, and "Eliza Walker Katin of old York her sampler, born Nov 17, 1779 aged 12 years," silk stitches, black, brown, dark blue, white, and pink, framed, 10⅜" h, 8⅜" w **440.00**

1795, linen homespun, alphabets, stylized flowers, and "Mary McCloud, Her Work 1795," silk queen's stitch, green, blue, pink, brown, framed, 13¾" h, 11⅞" w **1,430.00**

"Elisheba Edwards Sampler, made in the 12 year of her age, Franklin, June 11, 1823," ivory, light green, and teal silk threads, linen ground, 16 x 17½", $475.00.

1798, linen homespun, alphabets, verse, and "Ann Lunn her sampler aged 6 years 1798," silk stitches, green, pink, mustard yellow, and white, framed, 12¾" h, 11" w **525.00**

1807, linen homespun, alphabets and "Ann Cornells Sampler 1807," silk stitches, black, blue, yellow, and white, framed, stained, 12¼" h, 18¼" w **775.00**

1811, homespun, verse, tree, windmill, castle tower, butterflies, and "Elizabeth Hatton's Work Aged 8 years, New York 1811," vining borders, silk stitches, light blue, olive, white, and black, framed, minor wear and stains, 16" h, 14" w **1,100.00**

1812, linen homespun, alphabets, and "Eliza Hand, Newton School, November 1812," green silk stitches, framed, minor stains, minor damage and holes, 14¼" h, 12½" w **715.00**

1821, linen homespun, alphabets, house, tree, and "Abigail Whiting, Franklin, September, AD 1821," vining floral border, silk stitches, green, brown, and yellow, framed, 18½" h, 11¾" w .. **1,100.00**

1824, linen homespun, stylized flowers, Adam and Eve, serpent in tree, and "Susan Parker her work anno Domini 1824, aged 11," strawberry border, green, white, pink, black, and yellow, framed, 10½" h, 8" w **1,760.00**

1826

17⅜" h, 18½" w, linen homespun, verse, house with trees and fence, and "Wrought by Diana Paine Stockbridge 1826, Mary Cooper, Instructress," silk stitches, green, beige, yellow, white, and black, framed, minor stains .. **9,795.00**

17¾" h, 13¾" w, natural brown linen homespun, alphabets, trees, house, fence, and "Sally Blish Her Sampler Age 13, 1826," vining border, silk stitches, yellow, white, and brown, framed **610.00**

1827, linen homespun, alphabets, flowers, house, trees, and "Wrought by Hannah Lewil aged 10 years born July 15, 1817," silk stitches, white, beige, blue–green, red, and black, gilt frame **1,540.00**

1829, greenish linen homespun, family records and "Wrought by Elizabeth A. Bryant Nelson, Aug 1829," silk stitches, pale blue, green, pink, white, and black, framed **2,695.00**

1830, homespun, alphabets, verse, flowers, buildings, and "Betsy Archer, Ivinghoe School May 26, 1830," vining border, silk stitches, green, blue, brown, and white, framed, stained, minor holes, edge damage, 16½" sq **880.00**

1836, alphabets, verse, and "Augusta Harriet Mather's, New Haven April 1836," Greek key border, silk stitches, green, blue, beige, and rust red, gilt frame, minor stains, 20½" h, 19½" w . **825.00**

1841
17 x 17", linen homespun, alphabets, stylized flowers, heart and scissors, "Mary A Morrison was born the fifth day of March, 1827 and has made this sampler in 1841," brown, blue, green, gold, and pink, unframed **450.00**

21¾" h, 22¼" w, homespun, alphabets and "Eliza Ann Green 1841," geometric border, silk stitches, blue, green, and beige, mahogany veneer frame **775.00**

1851, linen homespun, Adam and Eve, stylized trees, animals, house, and verse, "Emma Green Aged 16, 1851," strawberry border, silk stitches, green, brown, blue, and mustard yellow, framed, 17¼" h, 15" w **1,540.00**

1853, alphabets, stylized trees, birds, flowers, verse, and "Leah Cox, Milton, April 11, 1853, Oxfordshire," vining strawberry border, framed, minor stains, 15¼" h, 12" w **550.00**

1858, linen homespun, alphabets and "Fannie Cary's Sampler, Richfield, March 22, 1958, Aged 7 years," framed, 8" h, 14" w .. **225.00**

1862, wool on canvas, alphabets, house, animals, flowers, teakettle, and "Kunie G Hohmann, July 16, 1862," blue, red, green, and brown stitches, gilt frame, 13¼" h, 10¼" w **775.00**

Unknown Date
7¾" h, 9¼" w, linen homespun, alphabets, house, and trees, dog and strawberry border, silk stitches, tan, brown, green, pink, black, and white, framed, paper back marked "Made by Jane Butler" **650.00**

8⅜" h, 6⅞" w, linen homespun, alphabets, horizontal lines, and "Rebekah Chases Sampler age 9 years," silk stitches, blue, brown, and yellow, framed with orig Boston newspaper backing **660.00**

9½ x 9½", woven wool homespun, two figures, turkey, birds, butterfly, verse, and "Catherine Taylor," silk stitches, white, beige, blue, red, black, and gold, framed, stained, small holes and edge damage **550.00**

12¾" h, 10¾" w, linen homespun, alphabets and "Ann Gillingham," floral border design, silk stitches, blue, olive, tan, and white, gilt frame **525.00**

14" h, 18½" w, linen homespun, alphabets, landscape scene, stylized flowers, and "Death will dissolve" verse and "Hannah Bennett Hubbardston, born July 27th, 1800," satin stitch zigzag border, silk stitches, green, black, pinkish beige, blue, and white, framed **3,410.00**

16 x 16", linen homespun, silk stitches, alphabets, verse, and "Mary Smith," framed **275.00**

17" h
16" w, linen homespun, alphabets, verse, house, flowers, and "Elizabeth Myhill Aged

9 Years," vining floral border, precise and eyelet stitches, red, blue, green, yellow, black, and white, framed . . **1,650.00**

18½" w, linen homespun, alphabets, New England town buildings, and "Youthfull Genius here displayed, Portrays the....," geometric floral border, silk and wool stitches, blue, green, brown, white, yellow, pink, and black, framed **3,410.00**

17½" h, 18½" w, linen homespun, verse, red brick building, stylized trees, and "Eliza Wainwrights Work Aged 16," floral border, silk stitches, red, blue, olive green, and black, framed **990.00**

18" sq, natural cotton, yellow woven horizontal pinstripe, alphabets, flowers, butterflies, and mourning scene, vining floral border, silk and wool stitches, red, olive, yellow, pink, and black **1,210.00**

18¼" h
17½" w, linen homespun, alphabets, verse, buildings, trees, and "Wrought by Mary A. Lerned, Cambridge Aged 8," vining floral border, silk stitches, blue, green, beige, brown, and black, blue watercolor cloud sky, framed . **2,310.00**

17¾" w, linen homespun, alphabets, verse, and "Wrought by Roxanna Seward Aged 10," floral border, silk stitches, blue, green, blue–green, beige, white, and black, framed **2,750.00**

SANDWICH GLASS

History: In 1818 Deming Jarves was listed in the Boston Directory as a glass factor. The same year he was appointed general manager of the newly formed New England Glass Company. In 1824 Jarves toured the glassmaking factories in Pittsburgh, left New England Glass Company, and founded a glass factory in Sandwich.

Originally called the Sandwich Manufacturing Company, it was incorporated in April 1826 as the Boston & Sandwich Glass Company. From 1826 to 1858 Jarves served as general manager. The Boston & Sandwich Glass Company produced a wide variety and quality of wares. The factory used the free–blown, blown three–mold, and pressed glass manufacturing techniques. Both clear and colored glass were used.

Competition in the American glass industry in the mid–1850s forced a lowering of quality of the glasswares. Jarves left in 1858, founded the Cape Cod Glass Company, and tried to maintain the high quality of the earlier glass. At the Boston & Sandwich Glass Company emphasis was placed on mass production. The development of a lime glass (non–flint) led to lower costs for pressed glass. Some free–blown and blown–and–molded pieces, mostly in color, were made. Most of this Victorian–era glass was enameled, painted, or acid etched.

By the 1880s the Boston & Sandwich Glass Company was operating at a loss. Labor difficulties finally resulted in the closing of the factory on January 1, 1888.

References: Raymond E. Barlow and Joan E. Kaiser, *The Glass Industry In Sandwich*, Vol. 2, Vol. 3 and Vol. 4, distributed by Schiffer Publishing; Ruth Webb Lee, *Sandwich Glass: The History Of The Sandwich Glass Company*, Charles E. Tuttle, 1966; Ruth Webb Lee, *Sandwich Glass Handbook*, Charles E. Tuttle, 1966; George S. and Helen McKearin, *American Glass*, Crown Publishers, 1941 and 1948; L. W. and D. B. Neal, *Pressed Glass Dishes Of The Lacy Period 1825–1850*, published by author, 1962; Ellen T. Schroy, *Warman's Glass,* Wallace–Homestead, 1992; Catherine M. V. Thuro, *Oil Lamps II: Glass Kerosene Lamps*, Collector Books, 1994 value update.

Museum: Sandwich Glass Museum, Sandwich, MA.

Additional Listings: Blown Three Mold and Cup Plates.

Bowl, 7½" d, pressed, lacy, Tulip and Acanthus pattern **40.00**

Candlestick, pressed
  8½" h, crucifix, white opaque,
    flint, price for pair **175.00**
  10¼" h, 5" d base, flint, vaseline,
    c1890 .... **225.00**
Compote, 6" d, 5⅞" h, pressed,
  flint, Horn of Plenty pattern, Waffle pattern base, minor chips and
  roughage, price for pair **120.00**
Cup Plate, pressed
  3¾" d, heart border, light blue . **320.00**
  6⅛" d, Bigler pattern, dark ame-
    thyst, c1835–55, fine surface
    scratches **345.00**
Goblet, pressed, clear
  Bull's Eye and Fleur–de–Lis **75.00**
  Comet **75.00**

**Mustard, cov, Smith Bros. dec,
4½" h, $65.00.**

Lamp, oil
  8¾" h, pressed, Star and Punty,
    light blue, hexagonal base,
    very small chips to underside
    of base **2,875.00**
  12¼" h, overlay, star and quatre-
    foil cut white to red **865.00**
  13½" h, blown molded, opaque
    white globular font, ringed wa-
    fers, conical standard, pressed
    opalescent white lion head
    and basket of flowers base,
    one with glue repair, imperfec-
    tions, price for pair **4,315.00**

Miniature
  Chamber Set, 2½" h, pressed,
    cobalt blue, paneled pitcher,
    chips **420.00**
  Decanter, 3¾" h, blown molded,
    Sunburst pattern, c1825–35 . **300.00**
  Flatiron, 1⅜" l, ⅞" h, pressed,
    cobalt blue, c1850–70 ...... **260.00**
  Jug, blown mold, Diamond pat-
    tern, c1825–35 .... **300.00**
  Tumbler
    1½" h, yellow, amethyst, blue,
      and clear, c1830–50, few
      chips and hairline, price for
      set of four **115.00**
    1¾" h, lacy, opalescent, ame-
      thyst, and pr blue, pointed
      oval pattern, some base
      roughness, price for set of
      four **260.00**
Newel-post Ornament, 7½" h, one
  light blue, other light green, price
  for pair **175.00**
Salt, pressed
  3¼" l, Waffle, one amber, two
    amethyst, c1850, rim chips,
    price for set of three **230.00**
  3⅝" l, Lafayet Steamboat,
    marked "Lafayet" on paddle
    boxes, "B. & S. Glass Co." on
    stern, "Sandwich" on floor of
    boat, c1830–45, hairlines and
    chips **345.00**
Vase
  7⅛" h, trumpet, free blown, ame-
    thyst **750.00**
  9½" h, loop, pressed, amethyst,
    gauffered rim, hexagonal stan-
    dard, circular base **1,495.00**
  10" h
    Loop, pressed, green, gauf-
      fered rim, hexagonal
      standard, circular base, chip to
      underside of base **1,100.00**
    Tulip, pressed, emerald green,
      octagonal base, few small
      chips to underside of base,
      price for pair **4,887.00**
  10¼" h, tulip, pressed, dark
    amethyst, octagonal bases,
    few chips to underside of
    base, price for pair **2,415.00**
Whiskey Taster, cobalt blue, nine
  panels **125.00**

c1770

SARREGUEMINES

SARREGUEMINES CHINA

History: Sarreguemines ware is a faience porcelain, i.e., tin-glazed earthenware. The factory was established in Lorraine, France, in 1770, under the supervision of Utzcheider and Fabry. The factory was regarded as one of the three most prominent manufacturers of French faience. Most of the wares found today were made in the 19th century. Later wares are impressed "Sarreguemines" and "Germany" due to a change of boundaries and location of the factory.

Reference: Susan and Al Bagdade, *Warman's English & Continental Pottery & Porcelain, Second Edition,* Wallace-Homestead, 1991.

Basket, Rose and Leaf pattern, No. 4710 .... **245.00**

Bowl, 8" l, majolica, fish shape, multicolored **45.00**

Plate, black transfer of hunter, molded basketweave border, 7" d, $28.00.

Figure, 18" h, griffin with shell form bowl **200.00**

Oyster Plate, 9½" d, six gray and coral wells, marked "Sarreguemines France" **165.00**

Pitcher, crystalline blue–gray **295.00**

Plate
7½" d, majolica, leaves and fruit centers, olive green and mustard, scalloped leaf shaped edge, imp "Sarreguemines," price for set of six **275.00**

8¾" d, multicolored transfer of "De Walkure," bust of Wagner, music score, marked **25.00**

Platter, 12" d, majolica, fruits and leaves, multicolored **65.00**

Stein, 9" h, 4⅛" d, 1 L, cream pottery ground, multicolored tavern scene, hinged pewter lid, marked **200.00**

Teapot, 4¾" h, brown glaze, imp mark **25.00**

Toothpick Holder, figural, swan, multicolored **30.00**

Vase, 7½ x 13", triple, classic Art Nouveau form, oxblood, turquoise, and purple, gold trim, professional repair **250.00**

SARSAPARILLA BOTTLES

History: Sarsaparilla refers to a number of tropical American, spiny, woody vines of the lily family whose roots are fragrant. An extract was obtained from these dried roots and used for medicinal purposes. The first bottles containing the extract appeared in the 1840s. The earliest bottles were stoneware, later followed by glass.

Carbonated water often was added to sarsaparilla to make a soft drink or to make consuming it more pleasurable. For this reason, sarsaparilla and soda became synonymous even though they were two different entities.

References: Ralph and Terry Kovel, *The Kovels' Bottles Price List, 9th Edition,* Crown Publishers, 1992; Carlo and Dot Sellari, *The Standard Old Bottle Price Guide,* Collector Books, 1989.

Periodical: *Antique Bottle and Glass*

Collector, PO Box 187, East Greenville, PA 18041.

Additional Listings: See *Warman's Americana & Collectibles* for a list of soda bottles.

Dr Guysott's Compound Extract of Yellow Dock & Sarsaparilla, American, 1860–70, sq, beveled corners, brilliant blue-green, applied double collared mouth, smooth base, 1″ hairline crack in base corner, 9⅛″ h **550.00**

Dr Myer's Vegetable Extract, Sarsaparilla, Wild Cherry, Dandelion, Buffalo, NY, American, 1845–60, rect, beveled corners, aquamarine, applied sloping collared mouth, iron pontil mark, int. stain, 9¾″ h **230.00**

Dr Russell's Balsam of Horehound and Sarsaparilla, American, 1840–60, rect, beveled corners, aquamarine, applied sloping collared mouth with ring, pontil scar, some int. stain, ⅜″ chip at base, 9¼″ h **400.00**

Dr Townsend's Sarsaparilla, America, 1845–60, sq, beveled corners, bright blue-green, applied sloping collared mouth, iron pontil mouth, old ¹⁄₁₆″ flake at top of mouth, 9½″ h **200.00**

Dr Wynkoop's Katharismic Honduras Sarsaparilla, American, 1840–60, rect, beveled corners, sapphire blue, applied sloping collared mouth, pontil scar, dug bottle, overall ext. stain, two shallow chips on mouth, 10″ h .**1,200.00**

Turner's Sarsaparilla, America, 1860–80, oval, aquamarine, applied sloping collared mouth, smooth base, int. stain, 12½″ h **275.00**

SATIN GLASS

History: Satin glass, produced in the late 19th century, is an opaque art glass with a velvety matte (satin) finish which was achieved through treatment with hydrofluoric acid. A large majority of the pieces were cased or had a white lining.

While working at the Phoenix Glass Company, Beaver, Pennsylvania, Joseph Webb perfected Mother-of-Pearl (MOP) satin glass in 1885. Similar to plain satin glass in respect to casing, MOP satin glass has a distinctive surface finish and an integral or indented design, the most common being diamond quilted (DQ).

The most common colors are yellow, rose, or blue. Rainbow coloring is considered choice. Satin glass, both plain and MOP, has been widely reproduced.

Reference: Ellen T. Schroy, *Warman's Glass,* Wallace-Homestead, 1992.

Additional Listings: Cruets, Fairy Lamps, Miniature Lamps, and Rose Bowls.

Basket, 9½″ h, 5½″ w, tomato, leaf design, twisted frosted thorn handle, Victorian **200.00**

Bowl, 8½″ w, 2¾″ h, DQ, MOP, rainbow, pale pink, yellow, blue shading to white, three applied thorn feet, sgd "Patent," minor roughage on one foot **500.00**

Bride's Bowl, 10″ w, 4½″ h, deep rose int., brilliant green ext., applied frosted edge, enameled gold, white, and pink rose dec, silver plated Victorian holder with handle, Mt Washington ...**1,200.00**

Celery Vase, MOP, deep Alice blue, Muslin pattern, bulbous pouch shape, ruffled sq top, Mt Washington **275.00**

Fruit
Apple **125.00**
Pear, shaded amber to red **125.00**

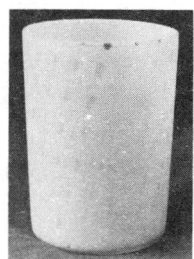

Tumbler, Raindrop pattern, MOP, white, 3¾″ h, $200.00.

Mug, 3½" h, white, pink and gold looping, applied frosted reeded handle **175.00**

Pitcher
6" h, 3" w, DQ, MOP, large loop frosted camphor shell handle, Mt Washington **325.00**
6½" h, 5" d, DQ, bright yellow shading to pale white, sq top, Mt Washington **375.00**

Punch Cup, 3" h, 2¾" w, DQ, MOP, seven color rainbow, sq top, applied frosted handle **200.00**

Tumbler, 4" h, Herringbone, shaded blue, Mt Washington .. **145.00**

Vase
5½" h, blue, MOP, hobnail, folded in sq top **620.00**
6½" h, rainbow, DQ, MOP, frosted clear rim, fan shaped crimped top, colors continue in intensity down shoulder and fade to white at base, satin finish, attributed to Mt Washington **975.00**
7" h, 5" d, basketweave, MOP, bulbous base, pale blue shading to deep blue base, creamy lining, Webb **750.00**
7½" h, blue, floral, and enamel dec, English **55.00**
10" h, shaded pink, white int., frosted ruffled rim **195.00**
10½" h, slender form, red narrow neck, white base, price for pair **110.00**
11½" h, Pompeiian Swirl, MOP, deep rose, pink–white lining, Stevens & Williams **950.00**

SATSUMA

History: Satsuma, named for a war lord who brought skilled Korean potters to Japan in the early 1600s, was a hand-crafted Japanese faience glazed pottery. It is finely crackled, has a cream, yellow-cream, or gray-cream color, and is decorated with raised enamels in floral geometric and figural motifs.

Figural satsuma was made specifically for export in the 19th century. Later satsuma, referred to as satsuma-style ware, is Japanese porcelain also hand decorated in raised enamels. From 1912 to the present, satsuma-style ware has been mass-produced. Much of the ware on today's market is of this later period.

Reference: Gloria and Robert Mascarelli, *Warman's Oriental Antiques,* Wallace-Homestead, 1992.

Box, cov, 2¾ x 3⅝", rect, gilt and enamel dec, bird, floral, and pagoda scene, Japan, early 20th C **110.00**

Charger, 12⅞" d, red and black flowers and birds, white ground, gold trim **120.00**

Dish, 9⅞" d, Kannon, arhats, and dragon, int. dec, scalloped, gilt ground, c1900 .... **265.00**

Jar
6½" h, octagonal, domed lid, figures in landscape dec, fitted on carved wood base, Meiji period **2,100.00**
16¼" h, cov, foo dog finial **300.00**

Miniature
Bowl, 3" d, green and gold dec, impressed signature **50.00**
Jar, 2¼" h, six panels, geisha and samurai warrior dec **100.00**

Vases, mountain, river, foliage, and peasant scene, Meiji period (1868–1912), wooden base, orig velvet lined case, price for pair, $700.00.

Teapot, cov, 2¾" h, shaped reserves around body 425.00
Vase
2¼" h, paneled, figure dec .. 100.00
3½" h, paneled, figure and
landscape dec 160.00
Napkin Ring, myriad butterflies
dec 285.00
Pitcher, 4½" h, warrior scene, gold
scrolled handle, c1920 .... 230.00
Planter, 11" w, rect, figural dec .. 250.00
Plate, 9¾" d, wisteria, peonies,
and waterfowl, c1900 .... ● 225.00
Tea Set
15 pcs, 7½" teapot, cov sugar
bowl, cov cream pitcher, and
six cups and saucers, tapered
baluster form, enameled figures and gilt geometric motifs,
Kyoto, late 19th C 550.00
21 pcs, teapot, covered creamer
and sugar, nine cups and saucers 610.00
Tile, 3¾ x 5½", women and children crossing bridge to crowded
country inn, polychrome and gilt
dec 300.00
Urn, 16" h, garden scene with arhats and scholars, raised handles, three children form legs,
foo dog finial, 19th C 810.00
Vase
7¼" h
Cylindrical, tapering, women
and children by river dec .. 80.00
Ovoid, children at play dec .. 95.00
9½" h, earthenware, gold and
enamel dec, five figures, butterflies, and flowers, late 19th/
early 20th C 225.00
15½" h, baluster form, geometric
patterned borders, dancing figures dec 350.00

SCALES

History: Prior to 1900 the simple balance
scale commonly was used for measuring
weights. Since then scales have become
more sophisticated in design and more accurate. A variety of styles and types include
beam, platform, postal, and pharmaceutical.

Collectors' Club: International Society of
Antique Scale Collectors, Suite 1706, 176
W. Adams St, Chicago, IL 60603.

C Porschiner, No. 2, balance, iron
ring and hook 22.00
Computing Scale Co, Dayton, OH,
computing, Coca–Cola adv, cast
metal and glass, restored, 19" w,
32" h 2,100.00
European, cast iron, brass pans,
six hexagonal form weights, late
19th C, 16" l base 115.00

**Chatillion Improved, NY, Pat. Dec
10, 1867, balance, $35.00.**

Miners Improved Gold Scale,
small brass scale, oval tole case
with red ground, black label with
eagle, and "Miners Improved
Gold Scale, Manufactured ex-
pressly for California, Germany,"
7¼" l 195.00
National Store Specialty, Pennsylvania, computing, brass pan,
weighs up to 3 lbs, restored, new
paint and decals, 16 x 16 x 6" . 350.00
Seederer–Kohlbusch, Englewood,
NJ, apothecary, walnut and
glass case, black glass damaged, drawer knob missing,
16¾" w, 9¾" d, 18⅛" h 175.00
Triner Scale, Chicago, 1941, balance, brass on black iron, 2 x 3"
pan, sealed 1972 .... 38.00
Watling, platform
Fortune Telling, 1¢, porcelain
top, mirrored front and marquee, 17" w, 66½" h, 25½" d 225.00

Lollipop style, porcelain and enameled, clear etched glass, see–thru penny back mechanism, side coat hooks, restored, 24" w, 72" h, 27" d . . . **1,700.00**

SCHLEGELMILCH PORCELAINS

History: Erdmann Schlegelmilch founded his porcelain factory in Suhl in the Thuringia region in 1861. Reinhold, his brother, established a porcelain factory at Tillowitz in Upper Silesia in 1869. In the 1860s Prussia controlled Thuringia and Upper Silesia, both rich in the natural ingredients needed for porcelain.

By the late 19th century an active export business was conducted with the United States and Canada due to a large supply of porcelain at reasonable costs achieved through industrialization and cheap labor. Both brothers marked their pieces with the RSP mark, a designation honoring Rudolph Schlegelmilch, their father. Over 30 mark variations have been discovered.

The Suhl factory ceased production in 1920, unable to recover from the effects of World War I. The Tillowitz plant, located in an area of changing international boundaries, finally came under Polish socialist government control in 1956.

References: Susan and Al Bagdade, *Warman's English & Continental Pottery & Porcelain, Second Edition*, Wallace–Homestead, 1991; Mary Frank Gaston, *The Collector's Encyclopedia Of R.S. Prussia and Other R.S. and E.S. Porcelain*, First Series (1982, 1993 value update), Second Series, (1986, 1994 value update), Third Series (1994), Fourth Series (1994), Collector Books; Clifford S. Schlegelmilch, *Handbook Of Erdmann And Reinhold Schlegelmilch, Prussia–Germany And Oscar Schlegelmilch, Germany, 3rd Edition*, published by author, 1973.

Collectors' Club: International Association of R. S. Prussia Collectors Inc., 22 Canterbury Dr., Danville, IN 46122.

Reproduction Alert: Many "fake" Schlegelmilch pieces are appearing on the market. These reproductions have new decal marks, transfers, or recently hand painted animals on old, authentic R.S. Prussia pieces.

R. S. GERMANY

c 1910 -1956

Berry Set, master and four serving bowls, roses, yellow, orange, and white, shaded brown to light green ground, blue mark **90.00**

Biscuit Jar, cov, poppies dec, gold trim **85.00**

Bonbon Dish, center handle, white poppies, shaded green ground . **35.00**

Bone Dish, gray, gold band, blue mark **30.00**

Bowl, 9" d, earth tones, white snowballs, gold **75.00**

Bread Tray, 14" l, shaded white to green ground, yellow and white roses in basket, open handles, blue mark **140.00**

Cake Plate, blown out carnations, gold flowers and trim, white ground, gold steeple mark **250.00**

Celery Tray, 12¼" l, 5⅜" w, cream to light gray ground, pink roses, green leaves **50.00**

Chocolate Cup and Saucer, 3" h,

R. S. Germany, cup and saucer, multicolored florals, cream ground, gold trim, marked, $25.00.

2¼" d, sweet peas dec, gold top band **50.00**

Chocolate Pot, cov, 10½" h, pale green, pink, yellow, and white roses, blue mark **150.00**

Creamer, corset shape, luster green, pink roses, four ftd **15.00**

Cup, 2½" h, pearlized ground, hp, chrysanthemum florals **20.00**

Dresser Set, tray, powder jar, hair receiver, and hatpin holder, violets dec, price for four piece set **225.00**

Dresser Tray, 11½" l, shaded green ground, red and pink roses **90.00**

Hair Receiver, 3½" d, hp, violets . **40.00**

Hatpin Holder, hexagonal, molded feet, white, delicate floral dec .. **45.00**

Inkwell, cov, lily of the valley dec **65.00**

Marmalade Jar, cov, floral **20.00**

Mustache Cup, peach dec, green leaves **55.00**

Mustard Jar, cov and ladle, hp, rose dec **45.00**

Nut Dish, floral, satin finish, price for six piece set **125.00**

Pitcher, 5¾" h, rose and chrysanthemums, blue mark **65.00**

Plate, 9½" d, red and yellow roses, lily of the valley dec, gold trim, marked "E. S. Germany, Prov. Saxe" **30.00**

Ramekin, satin finish, rose dec .. **30.00**

Tidbit Tray, 6½" d, center handle, berries dec **15.00**

Toothpick Holder, three gold handles **30.00**

Vase, 6" h, double handles, Nightwatch scene, gold and red trim **400.00**

R. S. Poland, berry dish, center pale green roses, light green ground, gold outlines, marked, 5″ d, $45.00.

Candlestick, 6" h, violets and lily of the valley dec, shiny finish .. **110.00**

Hair Receiver, violets and lily of the valley dec **100.00**

Planter, 6" w, 7" l, floral dec **215.00**

Powder Jar, cov, violets and lily of the valley dec **90.00**

Server, 11" d, 8" h, center handle, lavender and orange roses **515.00**

Vase, 8¾" h, 4½" d, cream ground, pink and white roses, gold band around top garlands of gold roses and leaves, marked "R. S. Poland" **185.00**

R. S. POLAND

Bowl, 10½" d, satin finish, heart mold, poppies **230.00**

c 1870s - 1880

c 1870s - 1914

R. S. PRUSSIA

Basket, oval, florals, gold trim, satin finish **175.00**

Bell, 3½" h, ruffled edge, white, small purple flowers, green leaves, twig handle **285.00**

Berry Set, master bowl, five serving dishes, blown out carnations, multicolored roses, turquoise trim, marked **500.00**

Bowl
10½" d, Swan and Gazebo ... **595.00**
11" d, 3" h, satin finish, four swans in lake scene, red mark **595.00**

Bread Plate, 13½" l, gold beading, pink flowers on water, open handles, red mark **125.00**

Cake Plate, 11" d, iris **215.00**

Celery, 13½" l, cobalt dec, daisies on rim, grape dec **290.00**

Chocolate Pot, cobalt blue, Carnation mold **1,200.00**

Clock, mantel, 7¼ x 6¾", hp, pink and yellow flowers, light blue and white ground, gold accents, unmarked **300.00**

Relish, 8½" l, Melon Eater, point and clover mold, green mark .. **695.00**

Tankard, 10¼" h, ftd, Fleur-de-Lis mold, baby blue dec, mixed lavender, pink, orange, and white flowers, unmarked **4,325.00**

Tea Set, child's, footed teapot, four cups and saucers, pink flowers, unmarked **595.00**

Toothpick, iris mold, pink poppies dec **310.00**

Vase
6½" h, cottage scene, brown tones, red mark **495.00**
7" h, pillow, Dice Players, jewels, red mark **2,300.00**

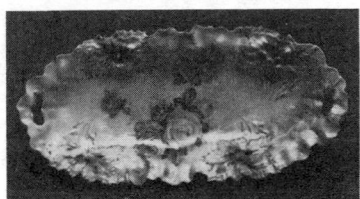

R. S. Prussia, celery tray, pink and white roses, green leaves, molded floral border, gilt trim, red and green mark, 13" l, $245.00.

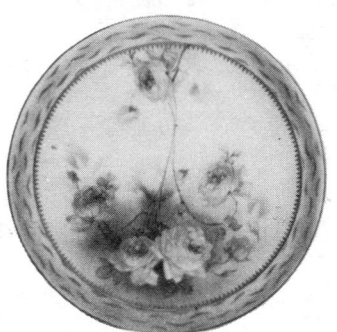

R. S. Suhl, plate, roses dec, beaded trim, marked "Erdmann Schlegelmilch Suhl Prussia," 8¾" d, $130.00.

Dessert Set, pink poppies, aqua, yellow, and purple highlights, plain mold, pedestal creamer and sugar, nine pedestal cups and saucers, two 9¾" d handled plates, eleven 7¼" d plates, price for 33 pieces **1,950.00**

Hatpin Holder, attached rect open trinket box, fancy emb shape, pink roses, powder blue and gold trim, red mark **125.00**

Pomander, roses dec **125.00**

Portrait Plate, 11½" d, dark haired woman, red, brown, and green dec, heavy gold, Gaston mark 54 .... **200.00**

R. S. SUHL

Bowl, 10" d, shepherd scene, cottage, red mark **500.00**

Coffee Set, 9" h cov coffeepot, creamer, sugar, six cups and saucers, figural scenes, gold trim, some marked "Angelica Kauffman," price for set **1,675.00**

Compote, 4½" h, ftd, creamy roses, gold stencil design, green mark **200.00**

Pitcher, 5½" h, white ground, red roses, unmarked **100.00**

Vase, 9½" h, Gibson Girl portrait, red mark **800.00**

R. S. TILLOWITZ

c1920-1930s

Bowl, 10" l, oval, hp, pheasant hen and cock, blue mark	275.00
Marmalade Jar, floral, underplate	50.00
Pitcher, lilies of the valley dec, matching underplate	40.00
Plate	
6" d, lilies of the valley dec, price for five pieces	35.00
7" d, stylized butterfly border, gold rim and handles, blue mark	45.00
Tray, five sided, roses	25.00

SCHNEIDER GLASS

History: Brothers Ernest and Charles Schneider founded a glassworks at Epiney-sur-Seine, France, in 1913. Charles, the artistic designer, previously had worked for Daum and Gallé.

Although Schneider art glass is best known, the firm also made table glass, stained glass, and lighting fixtures. The art glass exhibits simplicity of design; bubbles and streaking often are found in larger pieces. Other wares include cameo cut and hydrofluoric acid–etched designs.

Schneider signed their pieces with a variety of script and block signatures, "Le Verre Francais," or "Charder." Robert, son of Charles, assumed art direction in 1948. Schneider moved to Loris in 1962.

Bowl, 10" d, 4" h, cameo, orange cased to mottled tortoiseshell color glass, five stylized acid etched scarab beetles, engraved marks "Le Verre Francais, France, Ovington, New York" .. **750.00**

Dish, pedestal, orange to dark blue, amethyst with white ribbed base, etched "Schneider" on top of base, 13½" d, 5½" h, $275.00.

Box, rect, line cut, gilt metal frame, price for pr	785.00
Candlestick, 5½" h, paperweight base, coral and pink double clematis	200.00
Center Bowl, 12" d, clear, bubbled finish, pink mottling, pedestal foot, etched "Schneider" and "France"	345.00
Compote	
8½" d, opal lime green, amethyst base, sgd	650.00
14" d, 5⅛" h, clear orange, etched dec, mottled purple foot, etched "Schneider"	750.00
Ewer, 13" h, 7" w, handle, bright orange, cobalt blue mottling, three applied cobalt blue appliques, script sgd	700.00
Finger Bowl and Underplate, 4½" d bowl, 7¼" d underplate, mottled red, burnt umber, and colorless body, stamped mark on base	3,300.00
Lamp Base, 10" h, bulbous hollow glass shaft, cameo etched stylistic orange shaded to brown Art Deco designs, black metal shade holder and socket	260.00
Pitcher, 6½" h, elongated spout, layered glossy mottled purple to red, applied amethyst angled handle, side engraved "Schneider"	490.00
Vase	
5¼" h, flared rim, milky turquoise and green, maroon splotches, inscribed "Schneider" and "France"	285.00

10" h, mottled white and frosted ground, cased to orange, acid etched highly stylized foliate devices, two applied decorative purple handles, engraved "Charder, Le Verre Francais" **690.00**

11¾" h, heavy walled, oval, yellow cased to clear, mottled brown and blue splotches between, engraved "Schneider" **420.00**

12" h, Cluthra, flared ovoid, shaded and mottled pink, white, and colorless swirling dec, etched "Schneider" on foot, "France" on base **375.00**

20" h, bulbed, elongated slender neck, mottled pink cased to clear, yellow streaks, three applied nipple prunts, side engraved "Schneider" urn mark **575.00**

SCHOENHUT TOYS

History: Albert Schoenhut, son of a toymaker, was born in Germany in 1849. In 1866 he ventured to America to work as a repairman of toy pianos for Wanamaker's in Philadelphia, Pennsylvania. Finding the glass sounding bars inadequate, he perfected a toy piano with metal sounding bars. His piano was an instant success, and the A. Schoenhut Company had its beginning.

From that point, toys seemed to flow out of the factory. Each of his six sons entered the business. The business prospered until 1934 when misfortune forced the company into bankruptcy. In 1935 Otto and George Schoenhut contracted to produce the Pinn Family Dolls.

At the same time, the Schoenhut Manufacturing Company was formed by two other Schoenhuts. Both companies operated under a partnership agreement that eventually led to O. Schoenhut, Inc., which continues today.

Some dates of interest: 1872—toy piano invented; 1903—Humpty Dumpty Circus patented; 1911–1924—wooden doll production; 1928–1934—composition dolls manufactured.

References: Carol Corson, *Schoenhut Dolls,* Hobby House Press, 1993; Richard O'Brien, *Collecting Toys, 6th Edition,* Books Americana, 1993.

Collectors' Clubs: Schoenhut Collectors Club, 45 Louis Ave., West Seneca, NY 14224; Schoenhut Toy Collectors, 1916 Cleveland St., Evanston, IL 60202.

Animal
Bear, 4" h, brown, open mouth, glass eyes **385.00**
Elephant, glass eyes, painted, worn tusks **110.00**
Hippopotamus, 5" h, painted eyes, minor chipping and wear **220.00**
Zebra, 7" h, glass eyes, faded torso **410.00**

Circus
Accessories
4 pcs, ring, baton, gun, and bottle **385.00**
20 pcs, three white chairs, three platforms, three ladders, four pedestals, four multicolored barrels, two drums, and one ball, damage to ball **225.00**
Clown, 9½" h, orig clothes **90.00**
Ringmaster **75.00**

Doll, spring jointed
13½" h, painted blue eyes, open mouth, bald head, emb "H E Schoenhut 1918" and "Schoenhut Doll, patented January 17th '11 USA and Foreign Countries," chip on cheek, damaged left ear, worn fingers and toes **195.00**

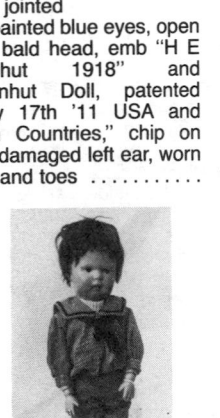

Doll, boy, pouty expression, wood spring jointed body, marked "75," $490.00.

15″ h, boy, painted blue intaglio eyes, closed mouth, carved hair, orig shoes, scuffed nose, minor wear **1,750.00**

16″ h, brown intaglio eyes, closed mouth, carved braided hair, emb mark, scuffed nose, paint loss, redressed **1,000.00**

16½″ h, boy, walker, marked "Schoenhut patent January 17, Welch USA and foreign countries" **160.00**

19″ h, brown intaglio eyes, closed pouty mouth, emb "Schoenhut Doll patented January 17th '11 USA and Foreign Countries," repainted face, nose and upper lip scuff **275.00**

21½″ h, painted intaglio eyes, closed pouty mouth, repainted body, replaced wig, shoes, and socks, emb "patented January 17th '11 USA and foreign countries" **550.00**

Piano, 19½ x 20 x 10″, upright, wood, eighteen keys, stool **155.00**

SCIENTIFIC INSTRUMENTS

History: Chemists, doctors, geologists, navigators, and surveyors used precision instruments as tools of their trade. Such objects are well designed and beautifully crafted. The principal medium is brass. Fancy hardwood cases also are common.

References: Florian Cajori, *A History of the Logarithmic Slide Rule and Allied Instruments,* Astragal Press, 1994; Gloria Clifton, *Directory of British Scientific Instrument Makers 1550–1851,* Zwemmer Books, distributed by Antique Collectors' Club; Crystal Payton, *Scientific Collectibles Identification & Price Guide,* published by author, 1978; Anthony Turner, *Early Scientific Instruments, Europe 1400–1780,* Sotheby's Publications, 1987.

Periodicals: *Rittenhouse,* American Scientific Instrument Enterprise, PO Box 151, Hastings–on–Hudson, NY 10706; *Scientific, Medical & Mechanical Antiques,* 11824 Taneytown Pike, Taneytown, MD 21787.

Collectors' Clubs: Maryland Microscopical Society, 8261 Polk St., McLean VA, 22102; The Oughtred Society, 8338 Colombard Court, San Jose, CA 95135; Zeiss Historical Society, PO Box 631, Clifton, NJ 07012.

Museum: Museum of American History, Smithsonian Institution, Washington, DC.

Barometer, stick type, mahogany, Abraham Optician, Exeter, England, mid 19th C, 37″ h **750.00**

Binoculars

Brass and Ivory, age cracks in ivory, 3¾″ h **135.00**

Gilt Brass, mother–of–pearl, worn black leather case, marked "Le Fils, Paris" **85.00**

Nickel Plated, gilt brass, and mother–of–pearl, marked "Le Moire, Paris, LM Prince, Cincinnati, O" **100.00**

Compass, convex glass lens, hand colored engraved paper face, turned wood case, 2″ d . . **150.00**

Gyroscope, lacquered, accessories, base sgd "T Cooke & Sons, York & London," late 19th C, 10½″ h **600.00**

Microscope, R & J Beck, London, brass, dual eyepieces, adjustable bed, assorted lenses, nine eyepieces, labeled slides, early brass-screwed wooden box, 5¼″ w, 15″ h, 7½″ d **425.00**

Microscope, cased brass, English, 19th C, two sets of lens, 10″ h, $290.00.

Octant, wood and brass, cased and labeled, Spencer Browning, Boston, 19th C **460.00**

Orrery, solar system model, marked "Trippensee Planetarium, Detroit, Michigan," early 20th C, 14 x 25½" **1,500.00**

Planisphere, Hammett's **175.00**

Quadrant, ebony, brass arm, sgd "Dollond of London" **600.00**

Sextant, brass, Japan, signed "Tamaya & Co. Ltd.," fitted brass-bound wood box, 20th C **400.00**

Slide Rule, cylindrical, brass and mahogany, drum covered with printed paper, Keuffel & Esser, 6½ x 23¾ x 6½" mahogany case **550.00**

Telescope
   Bardou & Son, Paris, brass, wood tripod stand, engraved marking, 38" l barrel, 60" h . . **990.00**
   Thomas Mason, Dublin **1,500.00**

Transit Level, brass, wood tripod stand, silvered face engraved "Henry Ware Maker, Cincinnati, OH," orig wood case with "Henry Ware" paper label, 66" h **915.00**

SCRIMSHAW

History: Norman Flayderman defined scrimshaw as "the art of carving or otherwise fashioning useful or decorative articles as practiced primarily by whalemen, sailors, or others associated with nautical pursuits." Many collectors expand this to include the work of Eskimos and War of 1812 French POWs.

Collecting scrimshaw was popularized during the presidency of John F. Kennedy.

References: E. Norman Flayderman, *Scrimshaw, Scrimshanders, Whales And Whalemen,* N. Flayderman & Co., 1972, out of print; Stuard M. Frank, *Dictionary of Scrimshaw Artists,* Mystic Seaport Museum, 1991; Nina Hellman and Norman Brouwer, *A Mariner's Fancy: The Whaleman's Art of Scrimshaw,* South Street Seaport Museum, Balsam Press, and the University of Washington Press, 1992; Martha Lawrence, *Scrimshaw: The Whaler's Legacy,* Schiffer Publishing, 1993; Richard C. Malley, *Graven By The Fishermen Themselves,* Mystic Seaport Museum, 1983.

Museums: Cold Spring Whaling Harbor Museum, Cold Spring Harbor, NY; Kendall Whaling Museum, Sharon, MA; Mystic Seaport Museum, Mystic, CT; National Maritime Museum, San Francisco, CA; New Bedford Whaling Museum, New Bedford, MA; Old Dartmouth Historical Society, New Bedford, MA; Pacific Whaling Museum, Waimanalo, HI; Sag Harbor Whaling & Historical Museum, Sag Harbor, NY; San Francisco Maritime National Historical Park, San Francisco, CA; South Street Seaport Museum, New York, NY; Whaling Museum, Nantucket, MA.

Reproduction Alert: The biggest problem in the field is fakes. A very hot needle will penetrate the common plastics used in reproductions. Ivory will not generate static electricity when rubbed, plastic will. Patina is not a good indicator; it has been faked using tea, or tobacco juice, burying in raw rabbit hide, and in other ingenious ways. Usually an old design will not be of consistent depth of cut as the ship rocked and tools dulled; however, skilled forgers have even copied these imperfections.

Cane
   32½" l, whalebone shaft, whale ivory knob carved with full-length portrait of lady, mid 19th C **600.00**
   34⅛" l, shark vertebrae shaft, whale's tooth handle, pinpoint engraving, third quarter 19th C **165.00**

Club, walrus tusk, engraved Liberty figure, American flag, shield, sea captain, three-quarter portrait of woman, eagle with American shield and crossed cannons, brig, star, and "Peacemaker," 19th C **880.00**

Corset Busk, whalebone
   13⅛" l, engraved and colored both sides, one side with Neptune in nautilus shell drawn by pair of sea horses, three ships in background, flanked with nesting bird on left and landscape with house, tower, and boat on right, other side with humorous primitive leopard flanked by flowers, mid 19th C **770.00**
   13½" l, engraved pot of flowers,

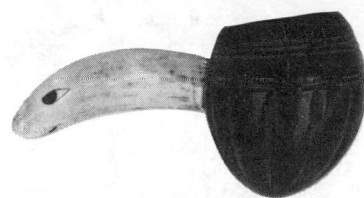

Dipper, sperm whale tooth handle carved as seal, incised dec coconut dipper, 8″ w, $375.00.

bust of woman, and monkey drinking from glass, practice drawing on back **275.00**

Cribbage Board, 16¾″ l, engraved whaling scenes and whaleship, ebony inlaid pins, four pegs, age crack and small chips around ebony pin **475.00**

Cup, 4⅝″ h, animal's leg bone, engraved seminude female figure in landscape, European, early 19th C, minor damage at base reglued **195.00**

Ditty Box, cov
   5¾″ d, round, baleen, engraved house and yard around sides, engraved geometric designs on lid sides, mirror set in floral engraved top, int. label reads "Mrs Ruth Remington 1838" followed by verse, second quarter 19th C, minor insect damage, mirror cracked and needs resilvering **600.00**

   6⅞″ l, oval, whalebone, mahogany bottom, sides engraved with panoramic American port scene with large urn containing ivy plant, large colonial house, four figures carrying sedan chair, and a second house, heavy whalebone cov engraved with finely detailed street scene with church and municipal buildings, cov engraving worn and missing side piece **1,050.00**

Medallion, whale ivory, engraved portrait of well-dressed young lady, mid 19th C, 3⅝″ h, 2¾″ w   **660.00**

Powder Horn
   15″ l, engraved man and Indian, sgd "Isaac Mead, Lake Gorg A.D. 1756" **2,100.00**

   17″ l, sailing ship *Alendale,* schoolhouse, church, and hunting scene **150.00**

Sewing Box, 10¼″ l, 6¼″ w, 3½″ h, light mahogany, whalebone inlays with colored geometric designs and engraved marine scene depicting sailor's farewell, top engraved "Lucy Francis," mid 19th C **4,125.00**

Tool, 5⅜″ l, bone, engraved ship scene **100.00**

Walrus Tusk
   15¼″ l, engraved and colored full figure portrait of lady wearing ball gown, saddled stallion by tower flying American flag, sailor on pedestal holding American flag, and flowering plant encircled by wreath, American, mid 19th C, few minor age cracks **2,750.00**

   18″ l, carved ladies and ships, signed "N G Phien," repaired **220.00**

   27″ l, carved arctic scene with ships, ice, and walrus, signed "Francisco Rapoza," damage to end **500.00**

Whale Tooth, carved
   6¼″ l, model, carved eagle head, mounted on oval wood base, 19th C **925.00**

   6¾″ h
     "Napoleon 1815" carved with portrait and gun crew **415.00**

     Whaling scene, blue enamel highlights **230.00**

   8″ h
     Ship and eagle **450.00**

     Two ladies and flowers **385.00**

SEBASTIAN MINIATURES

History: Sebastians are hand painted, lightly glazed figurines of characters from literature and history. They range in size from 3 to 4 inches. Each figurine is made in limited numbers. Other series include children and scenes from family life.

Prescott W. Baston, the originator and designer of Sebastian figures, began production in 1938 in Marblehead, Massachusetts. Sebastian Studios are located in Hudson, Massachusetts. Prescott Baston died on May 25, 1984.

Each year a Sebastian Auction is held in Boxborough, Massachusetts, at the Sebastian Collector's Society meeting. Prices are determined from this source plus the work of the Sebastian Exchange Board which develops a price list that is the standard reference for the field.

References: Dr. Glenn S. Johnson, *The Sebastian Miniature Collection & A Guide To Identifying, Understanding, and Enjoying Sebastian Miniatures,* Lance Corp., 1982; Paul J. Sebastian (comp.), *1991–92 Value Register Handbook For Sebastian Miniatures,* The Sebastian Exchange, 1990.

Collectors' Club: Sebastian Collector's Society, 321 Central Street, Hudson, MA 01749.

Aunt Betzy Trotwood, Marblehead label	50.00
Benjamin Franklin Printing Press	60.00
Cleopatra, version I, 1950–62	200.00
Colonial Lacemaker, blue label	25.00
Daniel Boone, 1940–45	140.00
Gathering Tulips	125.00
George Washington, cannon, sgd, 1947	80.00
Hey Diddle Diddle, Marblehead period	250.00
Howard Johnson Pie Man, Marblehead period	200.00
John and Priscilla Alden, green label	30.00

Priscilla, woman sitting at spinning wheel, $200.00.

John Smith and Pocahontas, orig Marblehead mark, pr	200.00
Lion, c1947	25.00
Lobster Man, Marblehead period	55.00
Mother, cooking at stove, Marblehead period	45.00
Parade Rest, green label	25.00
Pilgrims, Marblehead label, MIB	65.00
Santa Claus, 1980	80.00
Stagecoach	60.00
Swan Boat, Boston Public Garden, Marblehead period	150.00
Uncle Sam, green label	40.00
Victorian Couple, Marblehead label	50.00

SEVRES

History: The principal patron of the French porcelain industry in early 18th–century France was Jeanne Antoinette Poisson, Marquise de Pompadour. She supported the Vincennes factory of Gilles and Robert Dubois and their successors in their attempt to make soft–paste porcelain in the 1740s. In 1753 she moved the porcelain operations to Sevres near her home, Chateau de Bellevue.

The Sevres soft–past formula used sand from Fontainbleu, salt, and saltpeter, soda of alicante, powdered alabaster, clay, and soap. Many famous colors were developed, including a cobalt blue. The great scenic designs on the ware were painted by such famous decorators as Watteau, La Tour, and Boucher. Louis XV allowed the firm to use the "double L" insignia. In the 18th century Sevres porcelain was the world's foremost diplomatic gift.

In 1769 kaolin was discovered in France, and a hard–paste formula developed. The baroque gave way to rococo, a style favored by Jeanne du Barry, Louis XV's next mistress. Louis XVI took little interest in Sevres. Many factories began to turn out counterfeit copies. In 1876 the factory was moved to St. Cloud and was eventually nationalized.

Reference: Susan and Al Bagdade, *Warman's English & Continental Pottery & Porcelain, Second Edition,* Wallace–Homestead, 1991.

Reproduction Alert.

Bowl, 7″ h, ormolu mounted, painted and gilded cobalt bowl, supported by four Oriental figures sitting on chairs, shaped sq base, 18th C **3,675.00**

Box, cov
  8″ h, spherical form, ribbon and floral dec, rose finial, gilded bronze base, minor chip, late 19th C **145.00**
  8½″ l, oval, romantic couple in garden on lid, cobalt blue field **250.00**

Bread Basket, 10½″ l, painted and parcel gilt, reticulated, central foliate painted reserve, similar borders, mid 19th C **115.00**

Charger, 20″ d, hp, enamel dec, battle scene, gilt enhanced cobalt border, printed marks, c1844 . . . .**2,750.00**

Compote, 10″ h, ormolu mounted, ovoid form, floral and figural re-

Ewer, courting scene of couple walking, pastels, artist's initials, metal handles, rim, and base, 12″ h, $295.00.

serves on green ground, pedestal base mounted with acanthus form handles **750.00**

Cup and Saucer, 4¾″ d saucer, reticulated outer shell and rim, red circle mark, 1872–99 . . . . **865.00**

Demitasse Cup and Saucer, cobalt blue, oval reserve of couple on cup, two floral reserves on saucer **75.00**

Demitasse Set, 7⅝″ h pot, creamer, cov sugar, polychrome dec, reticulated outer shell, minor imperfections, red circle mark, 1872–99, price for three piece set **2,415.00**

Dish, hp, 12½″ d, central battle scene with cobalt grand border, enhanced with gilt and applied jeweling, mounted textile cov wood frame, painted mark, 19th C **1,375.00**

Inkstand, 10″ l, bronze mounted, rect, dark green enamel ground, gilt leaf borders, green feet, painted mark, mid 19th C **1,850.00**

Plate, 9½″ d, dinner, blue ground, central cartouches with putti flanking central gilt Louis–Phillipe monogram, printed marks, mid 19th C, price for set of twelve **925.00**

Platter, two handled, hp scene with lady and gentleman beside lake, cobalt border with gold detailing and floral medallions, mounted on gilt metal frame **515.00**

Tete–a–Tete, 11½″ l, cov teapot, cov sugar, creamer, two cups and saucers, and tray, blue ground with enamel dec putti flanking gilt monograms with cartouches, printed marks, c1846 . . . . **1,500.00**

Urn, cov, 14″ h, hp Georgian courting scene, artist sgd "P Roche" **300.00**

Vase

9½″ h, cylindrical, gilt metal mounted, rect reserves with romantic couples, cobalt blue and gold field, drilled for lamp, price for pair **800.00**

12¾″ h, baluster form, turquoise glaze, hp figural reserves, round red republic mark 1872–99, price for pair **865.00**

17″ h, cov, hp young girl with fishing pole and young boy playing flute, repaired cov . . . **355.00**

SEWING ITEMS

History: As recently as 50 years ago, a wide variety of sewing items were found in almost every home in America. Women of every economic and social status were skilled in sewing and dressmaking. Even the most elegant ladies practiced the art of embroidery with the aid of jeweled gold and silver thimbles. Sewing birds, an interesting convenience item, were used to hold cloth (in the bird's beak) while sewing. Made of iron or brass, they could be attached to table or shelf with a screw-type fixture. Later models featured a pincushion.

References: Carter Bays, *The Encyclopedia of Early American Sewing Machines,* published by author, 1993; Victor Houart, *Sewing Accessories: An Illustrated History,* Souvenir Press (London), 1984; Averil Mathias, *Antique and Collectible Thimbles and Accessories,* Collector Books, 1986, 1995 value update; Dana G. Morykan and Harry L. Rinker, *Warman's Country Antiques & Collectibles, Second Edition* Wallace-

Homestead, 1994; Gay Ann Rogers, *American Silver Thimbles,* Haggerston Press, 1989; Gay Ann Rogers, *An Illustrated History of Needlework Tools,* Needlework Unlimited, 1983, 1989 price guide; Gay Ann Rogers, *Price Guide Keyed To American Silver Thimbles,* Needlework Unlimited, 1989; James W. Slaten, *Antique American Sewing Machines: A Value Guide,* Singer Dealer Museum, 1992; Estelle Zalkin, *Zalkin's Handbook Of Thimbles & Sewing Implements,* Warman Publishing Co., 1988.

Periodical: *Thimbletter,* 93 Walnut Hill Rd., Newton Highlands, MA 02161.

Collectors' Clubs: International Sewing Machine Collectors Society, 1000E Charleston Blvd., Las Vegas, NV 89104; The Thimble Guild, PO Box 381807, Duncanville, TX 75138; Thimble Collectors International, 6411 Montego Bay Rd., Louisville, KY 40228.

Museums: Fabric Hall, Historic Deerfield, Deerfield, MA; Museum of American History, Smithsonian Institution, Washington, DC; Sewing Machine Museum, Oakland, CA; Shelburne Museum, Shelburne, VT.

Additional Listings: See Thimbles and *Warman's Americana & Collectibles* for more examples.

Pin Cushion, gilt embroidery scissors and thimble, 2″ d Limoges base, orig box, $45.00.

Box

12¾″ l, geometric and floral marquetry, cross banded trim, fitted int. **235.00**

13 x 19½ x 12″, beehive dec on front flanked by vines and

grape clusters, carved pear handle, old brown paint **1,150.00**
15" h, walnut, octagonal, revolving base, four drawers, applied and ring turned detail, acorn finial, old dark finish, wire nail construction **525.00**
Catalog
Montgomery Ward, Sewing Machines, 1910, 44 pgs **35.00**
Structo Weaving Looms, c1920, 42 pgs **25.00**
Darner, ebony, emb floral handle marked "Sterling" **40.00**
Dress Form, black velvet **35.00**
Embroidery Stamp, 1½ x 2 x 4", wood, hand carved semi-circles, 18th C, American **130.00**
Hem Gauge, ornate bands, dated "Oct 2, '94" **50.00**
Needle Case, 4" l, hand covered wood plug, knob finial **25.00**
Pin Cushion
Cast Iron, 4½" h, red wood covering **20.00**
Pewter, 7½" l, lady's shoe **20.00**
Scissors, Victorian, coin silver, hand wrought, emb grapes and vine handles, hallmarked "E L" **60.00**
Sewing Basket, 10" d, 9½" h, divided, polychrome painted floral dec, cloth lining, lid, Chinese .. **55.00**
Sewing Bird, 4½" l, brass, fabric covered pin cushion **195.00**
Table, 20" w, 16" d, 30½" h, Victorian, lift top, painted landscape scene and mother–of–pearl inlay dec, painted floral and gilt stenciled dec case, two drawers, stenciled cabriole legs, scalloped floral painted shelf, mid 19th C **660.00**
Tape Measure
Advertising
H. H. Babcock Co. Carriage & Auto Builders, Watertown, NY, pretty woman on front . **25.00**
Silks From Loom To You, Watertown NY, Syracuse, NY **20.00**
Figural
Fish, celluloid **30.00**
Hat, brass **145.00**
Thimble Holder, 3" l, Victorian,

ivory, acorn shaped, allover sinuous leaf carving **85.00**
Thread Caddy, 6" h, wood, turned stem, pincushion top, dark shiny finish **140.00**

SHAKER

History: The Shakers, so named because of a dance used in worship, are one of the oldest communal organizations in the United States. This religious group was founded by Mother Ann Lee who emigrated from England and established the first Shaker community near Albany, New York, in 1784. The Shakers reached their peak in 1850 with 6,000 members.

Shakers lived celibate and self-sufficient lives. Their philosophy stressed cleanliness, order, simplicity, and economy. Highly inventive and motivated, the Shakers created many utilitarian household forms and objects. Their furniture reflected a striving for quality and purity in design.

In the early 19th century, the Shakers produced many items for commercial purposes. Chairmaking and the packaged herb and seed business thrived. In every endeavor and enterprise, the members followed Mother Ann's advice: "Put your hands to work and give your heart to God."

References: Michael Horsham, *The Art of the Shakers,* Apple Press, 1989; Dana G. Morykan and Harry L. Rinker, *Warman's Country Antiques & Collectibles, Second Edition,* Wallace-Homestead, 1994; Charles R. Muller and Timothy D. Rieman, *The Shaker Chair,* Canal Press, 1984; Timothy D. Rieman and Jean M. Burks, *The Complete Book of Shaker Furniture,* Harry N. Abrams, 1993; June Sprigg and Jim Johnson, *Shaker Woodenware: A Field Guide,* Berkshire House, 1991; June Sprigg and David Larkin, *Shaker Life, Work, and Art,* Stewart, Tabori & Chang, 1987.

Periodical: *The Shaker Messenger,* PO Box 1645, Holland, MI 49422.

Museums: Hancock Shaker Village, Pittsfield, MA; Shaker Historical Museum, Shaker Heights, OH; Shaker Village of Pleasant Hill, Harrodsburg, KY 40330; The Shaker Museum and Library, Old Chatham, NY.

Books, pr, Richard McNemar, *The Kentucky Revival...*, NY, reprinted by Edward O Jenkins, 1846, paper boards, Richmond 933, spine tape repaired, and *Shaker Sermons: Scriptorational. Containing The Substance Of Shaker Theology*, South Union, KY, 1884, third edition, cloth, some damp staining and minor rubbing to binding .. **105.00**

Box
 Oval, cov
  3¾" l, two finger construction, 19th C **690.00**
  4⅝" l, underside of lid inscribed "Amanda Surman T.B. 1864," some wear to top **460.00**
  5¼" l, two finger construction, varnished, lid painted with skating scene, 20th C **1,135.00**
  13¼" l, four finger construction, painted deep orange, torn printed label "...the Canterbury Shakers...," lid painted with Christmas scene, 20th C **2,200.00**
  13½" l, four finger construction, painted salmon–brown **3,000.00**
 Rectangular, poplar, divided two tier int. above three short drawers in front with ring pulls, old salmon stained finish, two int. dividers missing, c1840, 34½" w, 9" d, 9½" h **1,150.00**
Carrier, cov, oval, three finger construction, bentwood bail handle, varnish, 20th C, 11¾" l **195.00**
Chair
 27½" h, #1, child's, arm, Mt Lebanon, NY, three arched splats, old red and black tape seat, old dark varnish surface, imperfections, 1880–1930 ..... **1,850.00**
 39½" h, side, maple, found in Harvard, MA, three arched splats, rush seat, box stretchers, old finish, marked "II," 19th C **375.00**
 40½" h, side, old red painted finish, tilters, tape seat, 19th C . **550.00**
Drawing, attributed to Joshua H Bussel (1816–1900), entitled "Poland Shakers," view of

Shaker Village at Poland Hills, pencil and watercolor on paper, titled in margin below image, verso with pencil sketch of barn and surrounding buildings, some staining, framed, 11⅞ x 14¾" **12,650.00**
Highchair, New England, maple, old red varnish finish, three arched splats, splint seat, box stretchers, 19th C, 42" h **925.00**
Hymnal, manuscript, Clarissa Jacobs book plate, Mt Lebanon, NY, leather, 8 vo, 118 pgs, dated 1892–1909 .... **920.00**

Work Table, projecting top, single drawer, square tapered legs, $3,750.00. Photograph courtesy of Garth's.

Journal, manuscript, Perry Place, New Lebanon, July 9, 1852–November 30, 1858, 118 pgs .. **3,100.00**
Manuscript, "Orders for the Church of Christ's Second Appearing Established by Ministry of Elders of the Church," Mt Lebanon, November 1887, 67 pgs . **230.00**
Pail, painted, blue ext., white int., wire bail with turned wood handle, small loss, 19th C, 4⅜" h . **575.00**
Rocker, child's, attributed to New Lebanon, maple, three shaped slats, splint seat, cheese cutter rockers, old finish, imperfections, 31" h, 11" h seat **1,300.00**

Sewing Desk
  Attributed to Enfield, NH, birch
  and pine, top section with six
  small drawers, pull–out work
  surface, bank of three narrow
  drawers in front, three wide
  drawers in side, refinished,
  c1860, 31″ w, 24″ d, 39½″ h . **575.00**
  Canterbury, NH, pine, shaped
  sides on open top, three graduated long drawers, bootleg
  ends, old refinish, imperfections, early 19th C, 22″ w, 17″
  d, 30½″ h **1,725.00**
  Swift, imperfections, 19th C, 23″ l **150.00**

c1908

SHAVING MUGS

History: Shaving mugs hold the soap, brush, and hot water used to prepare a beard for shaving. They come in a variety of materials including tin, silver, glass, and pottery. One style is the scuttle, so called because of its "coal scuttle" shape, with separate compartments for water and soap.

Shaving mugs were popular between 1880 and 1925, the period of the great immigration to the United States. At first barber shops used a common mug for all customers. This led to an epidemic of a type of eczema known as barber itch.

Laws were passed requiring each individual to have his own mug. Initially, names and numbers were used. This did not work well for those who could not read. The occupational mug developed because illiterate workers could identify a picture of their trade or an emblem of its tools. Fraternal emblems also were used and were the most popular of the decorative forms. Immigrants especially liked the heraldry of the fraternal emblems since it reminded them of what they knew in Europe.

European porcelain blanks were decorated by American barber supply houses. Prices ranged from 50¢ for a gold name mug to $2.50 for an elaborate occupational design. Most of the art work was done by German artists who had immigrated to America.

The invention of the safety razor by King C. Gillette, issued to 3.5 million servicemen during World War I, brought an end to the shaving mug era.

References: Susan and Al Bagdade, *Warman's English & Continental Pottery & Porcelain, 2nd Edition,* Wallace-Homestead, 1991; Ronald S. Barlow, *The Vanishing American Barber Shop,* Windmill Publishing, 1993; Phillip L. Krumholz, *Value Guide For Barberiana & Shaving Collectibles,* published by author, 1988; Robert Blake Powell, *Occupational & Fraternal Shaving Mugs of The United States,* published by author, 1978.

Collectors' Club: National Shaving Mug Collectors Association, 320 S. Glenwood St, Allentown, PA 18104.

Indian, hand painted, base marked "Daddy from Junior, Xmas, 1915," green mark "Hutschenreuther/Selb/Bavaria," $125.00.

BARBER SHOP: FRATERNAL

American Legion, star emblem,
  gold name and trim **420.00**
Civil War Sons Assoc, Veteran's
  Sons Commemorative Medal,
  hand marked "G.B.S. Co," worn
  lettering and gilt banding **120.00**

Grand Army of the Republic, American eagle spread over cannon and American flag above star shaped center medal, pink and blue floral design, gold highlights, marked "D & Co, France" **165.00**

Independent Order of Odd Fellows, three center loops, gold name and initials "FLT," marked "Royal China International" ... **50.00**

Knights of the Golden Eagle and Knights of the Mystic Chain, name in worn gold lettering, marked "TV" **150.00**

BARBER SHOP: OCCUPATIONAL

Bartender **425.00**

Black Jack **435.00**

Butcher, steer head surrounded by knives, cleaver, imprinted "Germany" **90.00**

Cabinetmaker, man working at large machine, circular saw, picture and name in gold, sgd "T & V Limoges" **325.00**

Cyclist, man riding bike, blue clothing **525.00**

Electrician, electric generator **275.00**

Farmer, man with plow, horse, house in background **450.00**

Fireman, two horses pulling steam engine, driver **650.00**

Horseman, horse head surrounded by horseshoe, stirrups, and flowers, stamped "TV Limoges France" **60.00**

Ice House, man driving one-horse ice wagon **425.00**

Lathe Operator, man working at lathe, stamped "TV France," worn lettering and gilt banding . **400.00**

Locomotive **395.00**

Minister, open Bible, stamped "C. A. Smith, Barber Supplies, Philadelphia" **1,600.00**

Musician, coronet player, gold instrument and name, blue asters, gold wheat ferns, and green leaves, blurred barber supply logo on base **425.00**

Painter, scaffold, painting building **550.00**

Piano Salesman, stamped "VD Austria," worn lettering **700.00**

Steamroller, transfer print, Aveling 1893 .... **65.00**

Trainman

Caboose, red, stamped "VD Austria," imprinted "62" **230.00**

Locomotive, 4–4–0, Odd Fellows symbol on cab, hand numbered "4787" **375.00**

Locomotive and Tender, 4–4–0, colorful flower bouquets, worn gilt banding and lettering **225.00**

BARBER SHOP: OTHER

Elk head, mountain background . **75.00**

Hunter, shooting bird, brown and white dog, sunset background, marked "Koken Barbers' Supply Co, St Louis, USA" **175.00**

Lilies, gold bands and name, marked "Vienna, Austria," red number **40.00**

Man in black carriage, derby, lap robe, brown trotting horse, "KPM Germany" stamped in green .. **95.00**

Patriotic, bald eagle supporting shield, surrounded by flags, gilt border details, blue back, imprinted "P/6241 Germany" **210.00**

Seashore scene, two gold highlighted pyramid shapes, two blue bands, purple mountains in background, c1885 .... **60.00**

St Bernard, pink rim, marked "Made in Germany" **45.00**

SCUTTLES

Dog's head, twisted handle, stamped "Bavaria" **125.00**

Eagle holding arrow, flag shield .. **85.00**

Floral spray **45.00**

Horses in field, white ground, gold trim **65.00**

SHAWNEE POTTERY

History: The Shawnee Pottery Co. was founded in 1937 in Zanesville, Ohio. The company acquired a 650,000–square–foot plant that formerly housed the American

Encaustic Tiling Company. Shawnee produced as many as 100,000 pieces of pottery per day until 1961, when the plant closed.

Shawnee limited its chief production to kitchenware, decorative art pottery, and dinnerware. Distribution was primarily through jobbers and chain stores.

Shawnee can be marked "Shawnee," "Shawnee U.S.A.," "USA #—," "Kenwood," or with character names, e.g., "Pat. Smiley," "Pat. Winnie," etc.

References: Susan and Al Bagdade, *Warman's American Pottery and Porcelain,* Wallace–Homestead, 1994; Jim and Bev Mangus, *Shawnee Pottery: An Identification and Value Guide,* Collector Books, 1994; Mark Supnick, *Collecting Shawnee Pottery: A Pictorial Reference And Price Guide,* L-W Book Sales, 1989, 1992 value update; Duane and Janice Vanderbilt, *The Collector's Guide To Shawnee Pottery,* Collector Books, 1992, 1994 value update.

Collectors' Club: Shawnee Pottery Collectors Club, PO Box 713, New Smyrna Beach, FL 32170.

Planter, puppy in shoe, burgundy, $8.00.

Ashtray, squirrel, marked "USA" .	10.00
Candlesticks, pr, 6½" h, hand dec gold trim	15.00
Cookie Jar	
Chef, caramel	110.00
Dutch Boy	65.00
Shamrock Winnie	300.00
Creamer, Corn King pattern, No. 70	12.00
Cup and Saucer, Corn King pattern, cup marked "90," saucer marked "91"	30.00

Darning Egg	20.00
Flower Frog, swan	32.50
Incense Burner	
Blue	65.00
Blue and gold	125.00
Pink	75.00
Planter	
Car, gold trim	26.50
Fawn, gold trim, marked "USA 535"	15.00
Windmill, gold trim, marked "Shawnee 715"	25.00
Platter, 12" l, Corn King pattern, marked "Shawnee 96"	20.00
Relish Tray, Corn King pattern, marked "Shawnee 79"	15.00
Salt and Pepper Shakers, pr	
Chanticleers, large	45.00
Dutch Kids, brown and green . .	55.00
Mugsey, large	150.00
Smiley and Winnie, heart, large	130.00
Sprinkler Bottle	20.00
Sugar, cov, Corn King pattern, white and green glaze	25.00
Teapot	
Granny Anne, gold trim and decals, marked "Granny Anne"	90.00
Rose	20.00
Vase	
Bow Knot, marked "USA 819" .	12.00
Cornucopia, 5" h, green	10.00
Fan, 4¼" h, yellow and green, blue flower, marked "USA" . .	8.00
Hand, marked "USA"	18.00
Vegetable Dish, 9" l, Corn King pattern, marked "Shawnee 95"	20.00
Wall Pocket, red feather	40.00

SILHOUETTES

History: Silhouettes (shades) are shadow profiles produced by hollow cutting, mechanical tracing, or painting. They were popular in the 18th and 19th centuries.

The name came from Etienne de Silhouette, a French Minister of Finance, who tended to be tight with money and cut "shades" as a pastime. In America the Peale family was one of the leading silhouette makers. An impressed stamp–marked "PEALE" or "Peale Museum" identifies their work.

Silhouette portraiture lost popularity with the introduction of daguerreotype prior to the Civil War. In the 1920s and 1930s a brief revival occurred when tourists to Atlantic City and Paris had their profiles cut as souvenirs.

References: Shirley Mace, *Encyclopedia of Silhouette Collectibles on Glass,* Shadow Enterprises, 1992; Dana G. Morykan and Harry L. Rinker, *Warman's Country Antiques & Collectibles, Second Edition,* Wallace–Homestead, 1994; Blume J. Rifken, *Silhouettes in America, 1790-1840, A Collectors' Guide,* Paradigm Press, 1987.

Museums: Essex Institute, Salem, MA; National Portrait Gallery, Washington, DC.

Gentleman, watercolor, sgd "Thomas Birch, Phila, Pa," oval frame, 4 x 3¼", $175.00.

Children
  5¼" h, 4⅜" w, girl, hollow cut, penciled detail, curly maple frame, gold and black painted liner **425.00**
  6¼" h, 5½" w, boy, hollow cut, laid paper, mahogany veneer frame **100.00**
  6½ x 3¾", boy, watercolor, "Henry, Age 9," one with hobbyhorse, other playing drum, mid 19th C, price for pair **650.00**
  7¾ x 5⅝", boy and cat, sgd "N. Champan," sitters identified as

"Louis Armitage" and "Chippy" the cat, framed **290.00**
Family, 11¾" h, 18¼" w, framed set, ten members of Dyson family, cut black paper, gilt detail, each identified on back with birth dates, orig mat and frame **910.00**
Gentleman
  5 x 3", stamped "Peale's Museum," framed, losses to eglomise mat, American School, 19th C, price for pair **975.00**
  5½" h, 4⅞" w, cutout, black ink and gilded detail, marked "Mr Minney, Butler to his Majesty George IV," black lacquer frame **385.00**
  5⅝" h, 4" w, cutout, white and red detail, framed **145.00**
  6 x 4", Richard Channing Moore, 1762, full figure, holding cane, name on back **200.00**
  6⅞" h, 6¼" w, hollow cut, mahogany veneer frame **125.00**
  8" h
    6½" w, black ink, gilt detail, bird's eye veneer frame ... **225.00**
    6¾" w, cutout, charcoal gouache, black ink and gilt detail, stenciled label "Herve, Miniature Painter 145 Strand, London," gilt frame **385.00**
  11¼ x 7⅜", litho int. view, sgd and dated "Aug Edouart fecit 1845 285 Broadway N.Y.," framed, water staining **400.00**
Man and Woman, 4⅞" h, 3⅞" w, each hollow cut, orig frames with broken glass, stained, price for pair **210.00**
Officer, 5⅜" h, 4½" w, cutout, charcoal gouache, black ink and gilt detail, black lacquer frame **250.00**
Woman
  4¾" h, 4⅛" w, hollow cut, penciled detail, gilt frame, minor stains **350.00**
  5" h, 4¼" w, red and gilt detail, black lacquer frame, dated 1826 .... **425.00**
  5⅝" h, 4¾" w, hollow cut, woodblock printed bodice, gilt frame with eglomise glass **550.00**

7" h, 5½" w, hollow cut, pencil detail, eglomise glass and gilded frame **1,025.00**

9½ x 7", lady in cloak, watercolor background, bronzed, framed **145.00**

11 x 7", lady offering a ring, bronzed, framed, scattered foxing, SPNEA label on back-board **115.00**

Young Man

6¼" h, 5" w, hollow cut, framed, minor stains **60.00**

6⅞" h, 5½" w, cutout, black ink and pencil detail, black lacquer frame **175.00**

Youth, 5" h, 4¼" w, hollow cut, ink detail, black cloth backing, framed, inscribed "Irving Phelps" **175.00**

SILVER

History: The natural beauty of silver lends itself to the designs of artists and craftsmen. It has been mined and worked into an endless variety of useful and decorative items. Pure silver is too soft to be fashioned into strong, durable, and serviceable utensils. Therefore, a way was found to give silver the required degree of hardness by adding alloys of copper and nickel.

Silversmithing in America goes back to the early 17th century in Boston and New York. It began in the early 18th century in Philadelphia. Boston was influenced by the English styles, New York by the Dutch.

References: Louise Bilden, *Marks Of American Silversmiths In the Ineson-Bissell Collection,* Univ. of Virginia Press, 1980; Frederick Bradbury, *Bradbury's Book of Hallmarks,* J. W. Northend, 1987; Maryanne Dolan, *1830's-1900's American Sterling Silver Flatware: A Collector's Identification & Value Guide,* Books Americana, 1993; Rachael Feild, *Macdonald Guide To Buying Antique Silver and Sheffield Plate,* Macdonald & Co., 1988; Donald L. Fennimore, *The Knopf Collectors' Guides To American Antiques: Silver & Pewter,* Alfred A. Knopf, 1984; Tere Hagan, *Silverplated Flatware: An Identification & Value Guide, Revised 4th Edition,* Collector Books, 1990; Kenneth Crisp Jones (ed.), *The Silversmiths of Bir-*

mingham and Their Marks, 1750-1980, N.A.G. Press, 1981, distributed by Antique Collectors Club; Joel Langford, *Silver: A Practical Guide To Collecting Silverware and Identifying Hallmarks,* Chartwell Books, 1991; Everett L. Maffett, *Silver Banquet II,* Silver Press, 1990; Penny Chittim Morrill and Carole A. Berk, *Mexican Silver 20th Century Handwrought Jewelry & Metalwork,* Schiffer Publishing, 1994; Richard Osterberg, *Sterling Silver Flatware,* Schiffer Publishing, 1994; Benton Rabinovitch, *Antique Silver Servers For The Dining Table,* Joslin Hall Publishing, 1991; Dorothy T. Rainwater, *Encyclopedia of American Silver Manufacturers, 3rd Edition,* Schiffer Publishing, 1986; Dorothy T. and H. Ivan Rainwater, *American Silverplate,* Schiffer Publishing, 1988; Jeri Schwartz, *The Official Identification And Price Guide To Silver and Silver-Plate, Sixth Edition,* House of Collectibles, 1989; *Sterling Silver, Silverplate, and Souvenir Spoons, Revised,* L–W Book Sales, 1987, 1994 value update; Peter Waldon, *The Price Guide To Antique Silver, 2nd Edition,* Antique Collectors' Club, 1982 (price revision list 1988); Joanna Wissinger, *Arts and Crafts Metalwork and Silver: The Details Series,* Chronicle Books, 1994; Seymour B. Wyler, *The Book Of Old Silver, English, American, Foreign,* Crown Publishers, 1937 (available in reprint).

Periodicals: *Silver,* PO Box 1243, Whittier, CA 90609; *The Silver Update,* 3366 Oak West Dr., Ellicott City, MD 21043.

Museums: Bayou Bend Collection, Houston, TX; Boston Museum of Fine Arts, Boston, MA; Currier Gallery of Art, Manchester, NH; Wadsworth Antheneum, Hartford, CT; Yale University Art Gallery, New Haven, CT.

Additional Listing: See Silver Flatware in *Warman's Americana & Collectibles* for more examples in this area.

SILVER, AMERICAN, 1790–1840
Mostly Coin

Coin silver is slightly less pure than sterling silver. Coin silver has 900 parts silver to 100 parts alloy. Sterling silver has 925 parts silver. American silversmiths followed the coin standards. Coin silver is also called Pure Coin, Dollar, Standard, or Premium.

Baldwin & Jones, Boston, c1815, coffeepot, 11¾" h, inverted pear form with gadroon rim and girdle, engraved with monogram "L.M.B.," leaf capped scroll handle, domed cov with foliate finial, spreading base raised on four winged paw feet, marked twice on base "BALDWIN & JONES" in scroll shaped punch, 45 oz, 6 dwts **900.00**

Ball, Black, and Company, 1851–76, compote, round form, mythical bird dec on stem, monogrammed, 26 troy oz **660.00**

Boyce, G, NY, mid 19th C, sugar, 9½" h, fluted urn form, domed cov, 28½ troy oz **330.00**

Buel, Abel, New Haven, CT, 1742–1825, ladle, marks worn from polishing, slight polishing scratches, 5 troy oz **150.00**

Edwards, John, Boston, c1730, pepper box, 3" h, cylindrical form with projecting molded borders and scroll handle, bun shaped cov pierced with concentric rows of dots, base engraved "IWR" and the weight "3 ozs," marked on body left of handle "IE" crowned above quatrefoil in shaped shield, 2 oz, 16 dwts ..**6,325.00**

Elliot, William H, Manchester, NH, c1840, spoon, 7½" to 9" l, 8 troy oz, set of six **115.00**

Fletcher & Gardiner, Philadelphia, c1820, flagon, chased, applied leaf and floral dec, 11¾" h, 55 troy oz **1,380.00**

Forbes, William, NY, 1935, mug, 5" h, chased, pear form, leaf, vine, and berry dec, cartouche erased, overstamped makers mark, 7½ troy oz **360.00**

Humphreys, Richard, Philadelphia, PA, 1775, cann, 5⅛" h, baluster form, engraved with contemporary foliate monogram "T.I.P.," leaf capped double scroll handle, molded spreading foot, base engraved with contemporary initials "E*M to TIP," marked "R Humphreys" italics in shaped punch on base, 13 oz, 16 dwts **6,250.00**

Jones, Ball and Company, 1882, coffeepot, 10⅜" h, ftd pear form, chased design on spout, oak branch finial, engraved initials, 29 troy oz **440.00**

Lincoln & Foss, Boston
Mug, c1850, engraved name, marked on base, 3½" h, 6 troy oz **260.00**
Sugar Urn, 1845, 8½" h, inverted pear form body, presentation inscriptions, marked "Lincoln & Reed, Pure Silver Coin, Boston," 16 troy oz **250.00**

Mood, John and Peter, Charleston, SC, c1835, fish slice, 12⅛" l, fiddle pattern, engraved with initial "B," blade pierced with scrolls, 6 oz **775.00**

Nichols, Basset, Providence, RI, 1815, sugar nips, etched floral dec, 1 oz **100.00**

Richardson, Joseph, Jr, Philadelphia, PA, 1777, sugar tongs, etched bellflower dec, 1 oz **425.00**

Shaver, Michael, Abington, VA, 1775–1859, luncheon fork, each marked, 6½" l, 4 troy oz, price for pair **345.00**

Stodder & Firobisher, Boston, c1823, coffee and tea service, coffeepot, creamer, cov sugar, matching Gorham teapot, c1885, monogrammed, 91 troy oz **1,610.00**

Syng, Phillip, Jr, Philadelphia,

Spoon Warmer, nautilus shell, seaweed base, c1840, hallmarked, 5½" h, 6" w, $165.00.

1703–89, sweetmeat basket, 4¾" l, 3¾" w, 6" h, reticulated, 3½ troy oz **550.00**
Tenney, William I, NY, c1830–40, mug, 3" h, repousse, 3 troy oz . **250.00**
Tyler, Andrew, Boston, c1730, caster, 6½" h, baluster form, pierced bayonet top, banded sphere finial, 6 oz **7,250.00**
Wilson, R. & W., Philadelphia, 1825–50, coffee and tea service, engraved dec, monogram, 9⅜" h coffeepot, teapot, creamer, cov sugar, 107 troy oz **2,415.00**
Wishart, Hugh, NY, 1815, teapot, engraved "J. B.," marked on base, 25 troy oz, price for pair **980.00**

SILVER, AMERICAN, 1840–1920
Mostly Sterling

There are two possible sources for the origin of the word sterling. The first is that it is a corruption of the name Easterling. Easterlings were German silversmiths who came to England in the Middle Ages. The second is that it is named for the starling (little star) used to mark much of the early English silver.

Sterling has 925/1,000 parts per silver. Copper comprises most of the remaining alloy. American manufacturers began to switch to the sterling standard about the time of the Civil War.

Alvin, flask, 7¼" l, 20th C, inscribed as yachting piece, enamel trim **250.00**
Bailey and Co, fish serving set, 1832–35, knife and fork, engraved dec, weighted handles, boxed, price for two pc set **525.00**
Black, Starr & Frost
    Centerpiece Bowl, early 20th C, paneled baluster, chased and engraved floral dec, engraved inscription, 10" h, 39 troy oz . **800.00**
    Serving Dish, late 19th C, Art Nouveau, shaped oval form, raised and chased floral design, convertible cov, monogram, 12¾" l, 36 troy oz **1,150.00**
Boardman and Son, J C, coffee set, mid 20th C, Colonial Revival

style, coffeepot, creamer, and open sugar, 30 troy oz, price for three piece set **420.00**
Caldwell, J E, Philadelphia, c1910, serving bowl, 14" w, ovoid, reticulated, elaborate pierced scroll work sides, lattice work handles, 17 troy oz **300.00**
Dominick & Haff, New York
    Bowl, 9¼" d, early 20th C, geometrically reticulated rim, 21 troy oz **330.00**
    Coffee and Tea Service, teapot, coffeepot, kettle, creamer, sugar, cov sugar, milk jug, waste bowl, 24" l serving tray, Virginia pattern, 180 oz, price for nine pc set **2,400.00**
    Coffee Service, early 20th C, coffeepot, kettle on stand, cov sugar, creamer, and waste bowl, chased scroll and floral dec, monogrammed, retailed by Shreve, Crump & Low Co, minor dents, 91 troy oz, price for five pc set **2,000.00**
    Pitcher, water, 13¾" h, late 19th C, chased vintage dec, retailed by Bigelow Kennard and Co, 44 troy oz **1,320.00**
    Salad Servers, c1905, blossom pattern spoon and fork, engraved, 6 troy oz **260.00**
Gale, William & Son, 19th C, basket, 6½" h, 5½" l, gold washed int., 6 troy oz **230.00**
Galt and Brothers, bell, 4" h, Arts and Crafts style, hammered and engraved, 4 troy oz **220.00**
Gorham
    Bowl, 1902, round, chased spiral pattern, 6⁷⁄₁₆" d, 11 troy oz . . **150.00**
    Candlesticks, pr, 1926, Colonial Revival style, weighted, 11¾" h **750.00**
    Coffee and Tea Service
        1890, repousse, coffeepot, teapot, creamer, cov sugar, waste bowl, monogram, dated on base, 85 troy oz .**5,175.00**
        20th C, Plymouth pattern, coffee and tea pots, creamer, cov sugar, waste bowl, waiter, 182 troy oz **2,760.00**

Demitasse Set, 1917, Colonial Revival style, chased floral dec, 12⅛″ d round tray, 9¾″ h pot, creamer, and open sugar, 48 troy oz **1,150.00**

Teapot, 1891, ribbed ovoid form, engraved date, monogram, 12″ h, 50 troy oz **815.00**

Guille, Peter, bowl, 7¾″ l, elongated octagonal form, 16 troy oz, price for pair **200.00**

Howard & Co, early 20th C

Compote, 12¼″ d, 5⅜″ h, shaped and reticulated applied floral rim and base, 23 troy oz **550.00**

Urn, cov, 14⅝″ h, cobalt blue liner, reticulated body, chased dec, 24 troy oz **690.00**

Jenkins & Jenkins, Baltimore, tray, 11½″ l, 1908–15, oval, repousse flower dec, undulating rim, 13 troy oz **500.00**

Kerr, W B, 9¾″ h, presentation cup, Art Nouveau, squat bowl, long baluster stem, engraved "Offered by A. Henry Higginson M.T.H. for the best pair of qualified hunter, The Country Club 1907," reverse "Won by Sinbad and Gloaming," 26 troy oz **375.00**

Kirk, S. & Son, 19th C, dessert knives, bright cut dec, engraved name and date, 27 troy oz, price for set of twelve **460.00**

Kohler, John P, 1910, bowl, 6¼″ d, 5⅜″ h, shaped reserve engraved "M. L. J. Oct 29, 1915," 12 troy oz **460.00**

Krider, tongs, 9″ l, bright cut dec, monogram, 4 troy oz **250.00**

Mayo & Co, serving bowl, 14″ d, c1900, foliate dec, raised shaped edge, 24 troy oz **360.00**

Mt Vernon, 1914, plate, 8⅞″ d, repousse, round, Colonial Revival rim, engraved central detail, monogram, 11 troy oz **115.00**

Poole, coffee and tea service, coffeepot, teapot, creamer, cov sugar, and tray, 159 oz, price for five piece set **1,500.00**

Reed & Barton

Mug, child's, 3¼″ h, repousse chrysanthemum dec, 3 troy oz **275.00**

Serving Spoon, 9¾″ l, Les Cinq Fleurs pattern, monogrammed, 6 troy oz **250.00**

Shiebler, c1900

Bowl, round, applied and chased poppy dec, 8⅝″ d, 15 troy oz **230.00**

Calling Card Case, 3⅛″ l, envelope form, postage and address, 2 troy oz **385.00**

Shreve and Co, San Francisco, cup, 3⅛″ h, 3⅛″ d, c1910, hammered finish, riveted strap handle, circular foot, imp marks ... **330.00**

Starr, Theodore B, loving cup, 10¼″ h, repousse, 82 troy oz . . **4,675.00**

Stieff

c1900, teapot, floral repousse, 7″ h, 29 troy oz **635.00**

Early 20th C, presentation vase, repousse, chased floral design, engraved inscription on rim "Mr. & Mrs. Albert Davidson from Baltimore Baseball Club 1914," 14⁵⁄₁₆″ h, 27 troy oz **1,495.00**

Stone, Arthur, tea set, 7½″ h teapot, creamer, and sugar, ivory finial, 20 oz, price for three pc set **600.00**

Sturgeon, W A, coffee and tea service, 9½″ h coffeepot, teapot, creamer, cov sugar, waste bowl, oval, scrolled foliate and fruit repousse dec, 80 oz, price for five pc set **1,600.00**

Tiffany

Compote, 1875–91, repousse, applied border, chased herbaceous border design, monogrammed, 7³⁄₁₆″ d, 20 troy oz, price for pair **1,380.00**

Fruit Bowl, 1907–38, round, applied scroll border, scroll feet, 9½″ d, 29 troy oz **1,955.00**

Porringer, 1917, Arts and Crafts, reticulated handle, 4½″ d, 7 troy oz **175.00**

Serving Bowl, 1891–1902, round, applied and reticulated clover border, monogram, 10⅛″ d, 14 troy oz **635.00**

Toilet Case, gentleman's traveling, early 20th C, int. fitted with engine turned sterling toilet articles, monogrammed, leather

case damaged, one piece
missing **750.00**
Towle
Coffee and Tea Service, hot
water kettle and stand, teapot,
coffeepot, creamer, sugar,
waste bowl, and tray, C–scroll
moldings, 270 troy oz, price for
seven piece set **4,400.00**
Compote, 10¼" d, 9" h, early
20th C, Neoclassical form,
monogrammed, 24 troy oz .. **475.00**
Watson, early 20th C, cake plate,
shaped edge, chased fruit de-
sign, 10¾" d, 14 troy oz **175.00**
Whiting
1889, water pitcher, raised and
chased design, acid etched inscription "Larchmont Special
Regatta, For Forty Footers,
Sept 28th 1889, won by Liris
against Mariquita, Gorillar and
Broncho," 9¾" h, 31 troy oz .**2,760.00**
Early 20th C, tray, rect, shaped
and chased poppy border, 16"
l, 28 troy oz **690.00**
Woodside, early 20th C
Basket, 12⅜" l, floral dec, articulated handle, 26 troy oz **620.00**
Compote, applied rose design,
reticulated rim and base, monogrammed, 9¼" d, 19 troy oz **520.00**

SILVER, CONTINENTAL

Continental silver does not have a strong
following in the United States. The strong
feeling of German silver cannot compare
with the lightness of the English examples.
In Canada, Russian silver finds a strong
market.

Austrian,
Candlesticks, 12" h, 19th C, Rococo Revival style, floral repousse baluster form standard, molded socle, cast
scrolls and wave work feet, 26
oz, price for pair **725.00**
Chalice, 7⅞" h, c1910, raised repeating geometric and medallion pattern, trumpet base with
raised repeating pyramid pat-

**Sugar Basket, red liner, Reed and
Barton, c1868, 4" h, 4¼" w, $85.00.**

tern, imp "WMFM," wear to finish **200.00**
Coffeepot and Ewer, VDC
maker, 1872, ovoid baluster,
carved ivory handles and finial, applied crest on side, 9⅝"
h, base of pot damaged, 36
troy oz **825.00**
Belgian, creamer, 1780, helmet
form, berry dec scroll handle, 10
oz **100.00**
Danish
Bowl, Georg Jensen, 1933,
Model #296A, oval, ftd, articulated grape cluster handles,
grape clusters around base,
inscription under base, 65 troy
oz **6,600.00**
Condiment, 5¼" h, Andress
Holm, Copenhagen, 1795,
hinged lid, cobalt blue glass
liner **275.00**
Flatware Service, Georg Jensen, Acorn pattern, twelve butter knives, dinner forks, dinner
knives, salad forks, and soup
spoons; twenty four tea-
spoons; salad servers, cake
server, sauce ladle, carving
set, 107 troy oz, price for set **5,255.00**
Salt and Pepper Shakers, pr, 5"
h, Andress Holm, Copen-
hagen, 1795, hinged lid, 4 troy
oz **350.00**
Tea Set, Christofle, Fjerdingstad
design, 12¼" w, 17" l rect tray,

6⅞" h teapot, creamer, and cov sugar, wooden handles with black finish, imp marks, price for four piece set **1,760.00**

Dutch

Box, 5¼" l, 19th C, fish form, hinged head with jeweled eyes, articulated body, fitted with clear glass flacon with stopper, 833 fine silver, 1 oz, 10 dwts **250.00**

Compote, 10¼" l, Sneek, Friesland, c1770, oval cross section, twin cast and pierced lug handles with mask and putti dec, deep repousse dished surface with shells and foliage dec, conforming molded foot, beaded punch work border, 7 oz **660.00**

Snuffbox, 1⅞" l, Amsterdam, c1740, cartouche form, molded rim, cov engraved with cipher, hinged lid **1,150.00**

Tankard, 6" h, cup form body, repousse vignettes with artistic cherubs, flattened cov with leaf form thumbpiece, claw and ball feet, 17 oz **1,320.00**

French

Cake Basket, 14⅜" l, Charles–Nicholas Odiot, Paris, 1819–38, rect, gadroon rim, border engraved with contemporary arms, wirework sides, pedestal base with gadroon borders, swing handle rising from leaves to fruit and flower high relief garland, detachable gilt–metal liner, marked on body and handle, 63 oz **3,575.00**

Ewer, Charles Odiot, Paris, mid 19th C, acanthus scrolls, shoulder relief band, band of cupids on center band, foliate and floral base border and foot, pr serpents entwined over handle, marked "Odiot A Paris" and "O" with fluid lamp in diamond shaped cartouche, 16" h, 120 troy oz, price for pair **16,100.00**

Pitcher, water, 12½" h, M Fray, mid 19th C, fluted baluster,

chased leafy Rococo scrolls, scroll handle with female figures, minor dents, 36 troy oz **1,980.00**

Salt, 2½" h, c1880, everted rim on bowl supported by cast openwork grapevine and mistletoe, marked "Veyrat" in lozenge, 950 fine, 14 troy oz, price for pair **690.00**

Snuffbox, oval, chased design, maker's mark "AD" on lozenge, 3 troy oz **200.00**

Teapot, 5" h, late 19th C, baluster, chased waves, flower and figural handle and spout, retailed by Tiffany, Paris, 950 fine, 23 troy oz **475.00**

Wine Taster, hallmarks

2⅝" d, late 18th C, serpent handle **150.00**

3" d, late 18th C, swirled design, reeded handle, incised on outer rim "M T Blandin" **450.00**

German

Beaker, 20" h, c1900, repousse body, hemispheres defined with cast foliage and roping bands, cap form lid, stepped molded foot, 62 oz **1,540.00**

Bun Warmer, 9½" h, 19th C, tripartite globular form, flutes and floral panels, Bacchic putti, 800 fine, 62 troy oz **2,420.00**

Cup, horn shape, 800 fine, chased tree trunk with ivy, gold washed accents, 8" l, 6 troy oz **260.00**

Figure, 9¾" l, goat with cart, chased, two wheeled cart with putti, 800 fine, 11 troy oz **770.00**

Goblet, 11" h, late 19th C, Renaissance style, weighted, cov **250.00**

Salt, Rococo style, boat form, putto and chased scrolls, 19th C Augsburg marks, 8 troy oz, price for pair **300.00**

Tankard

9¼" h, Altenberg, mid 19th C, engraved design, pierced apron, marked "AFB," 20 troy oz **525.00**

10¼" h, late 19th C, cylindrical, domed cov, scroll handle, allover relief of Renaissance foliage and moldings, stippled ground, base inscribed, marked 800M and maker "H. Man," 37 troy oz **1,650.00**

Indian, bowl, raised and chased, tiger and wild boar hunting scene, 7¾" h, 12" d, 58 troy oz **1,150.00**

Italian

Dessert Flatware, 20th C, silver–gilt, twelve pistol handled knives, twelve two prong forks, fitted 18th C tooled leather box **900.00**

Lamp, Sanctuary, 21" h, mid 19th C, baluster form, pierced and chased with floral reserves, borders of still leaves, hung by three chains from cherub heads, three matching smaller lamps, 149 oz **6,000.00**

Vase, 9¾" h, paneled ovoid body, fluted collar and spreading circular base, applied leaf scroll and floral trophies at "corners" of shoulder, modern, 800 fine silver, 19 oz **200.00**

Portuguese

Centerpiece, nine basket epergne with canopy, chinoiserie dec, bells hung from top, pineapple finial, Georgian style, retailed by Shreve, Crump & Low Co, Boston, 414 oz **18,700.00**

Ewer, 13¾" h, c1730, helmet form, partly fluted, engraved with contemporary arms, applied female mask within strapwork, raised female caryatid handle, detachable calyx chased with still leaves, strapwork, and shells, screw–on foot, modern base, unmarked, 54 oz, 10 dwts **2,875.00**

Tray, 24¾" long excluding handle, Oporto, c1886–1938, shaped oval form, border of chased and emb scrolls, shells, and flowers, scroll form bracket handles, unknown maker, 833 fine silver, 128 oz **800.00**

Russian

Candlesticks, 12" h, S Szkarlat, St Petersburg, 1870, knopped stem, chased foliage, 26 troy oz, price for pair **715.00**

Tray, 19¼" d, scroll center, outer edge in relief, 4 feet, 19¼" d, $500.00.

Flatware, C E Bolin, c1910, nine demitasse spoons, two spoons, fish knife, 14 troy oz, price for set **400.00**

SILVER, ENGLISH

From the 17th century to the mid-19th century, English silversmiths set the styles which American silversmiths copied. The work from the period exhibits the highest degree of craftsmanship. Active collection of English silver takes place in the American antiques marketplace.

Edwardian

Basket, London, 1904–05, GH maker, rect, 6 troy oz, price for pair **635.00**

Coffee and Tea Service, Sheffield, 1903–04, Atkins Bros, ribbed oval form, coffeepot, teapot, creamer, open sugar, some dents, 55 troy oz **815.00**

Creamer and Sugar, 1901–02, MM maker, hammered texture, twig form handles, chased floral accents, dents in creamer, 2⅜" and 2½" h, 11 troy oz . . **230.00**

Egg Stand, 8" h, London, 1909–10, barge form stand, wirework frame, four urn form cups, pierced and shaped loop handle, 20 troy oz **495.00**

Kettle On Stand, London, 1906–07, D. W. and J. W. makers, globular form, engraved dec and crest, 13⅜" h, burner missing, 45 troy oz **575.00**

Salver, Birmingham, 1905–06, W. A. maker, round, shaped rim, engraved center, 12⅝" d, 27 troy oz **350.00**

Stand, Dublin, Ireland, 1906–07, J. S. maker, chased and reticulated, flaring at base, animal and floral design, monogram, rim slightly bent, 8" d base, 4⅜" h, 11 troy oz **977.00**

Edward VII

Bowl, London, 1902, boat form, shaped rim, spreading foot, foliate piercing, marked "GJ DF" in shield, 30 troy oz **935.00**

Cup, 7" h, Comyns & Sons, London, 1911–12, made for Tiffany & Co, two handles, 24 troy oz **4,125.00**

Elizabeth II, sugar caster, C. & Co, 1953, baluster, gadrooned detail, 8⅜" h, 19 troy oz **415.00**

George II

Creamer, 4" h, London, 1753–54, shaped rim, hoop feet, engraved coat of arms, 9 troy oz **500.00**

Muffineer, 5½" h, London, 1736, baluster, pierced domed cov with knop finial, round foot with engraved crest, 4 troy oz **300.00**

Pen Tray, 7" l, London, 1743, rect, shaped border with C–scroll rim, engraved lion crest, acanthus and loop handle, scroll and shell feet, 10 troy oz **550.00**

Salver, 9⅜" d, London, 1735, unidentified maker's mark of "D.L.," incised crest with sea serpent, 18 troy oz **1,050.00**

Sauceboat, 5½" h, Philip Garden, 1753–54, inverted pear form, gadroon rim, dolphin handle, 13 troy oz **770.00**

Spoon, George Wicks, London, 1750, double drop handle, engraved on back "R Johnson," 1½ troy oz **100.00**

George III

Button, Susanna Barker, London, c1785, twelve large, twelve small, engraved hunt scenes, 4 troy oz, price for twenty-four piece set **1,980.00**

Cake Basket, 15" l, William Plummer, London, 1771–72, compressed oval cross section, pierced ogee body, fruit and floral swags dec, diapered ground gadrooned border, center dish with repousse leaves and engraved baron's crest, raked oval foot, arched swing handle, 36 troy oz **2,420.00**

Coffee and Tea Service, London, 1808–09, Charles Hougham, ribbed ovoid form, coffeepot, teapot, cov creamer, open sugar, crest, monogrammed, 69 troy oz ..**1,380.00**

Cup, London, 1800–01, Saml. Godbehere, Ed. Wigan, J. Bult makers, two handles, 5½" h, 10 troy oz **230.00**

Dish Cross, London, 1783–84, attributed to William Pitts, beaded detail, 12½" w, 17 troy oz **815.00**

Goblet, London, 1810–11, J. W. Story and W. Elliott, baluster form, vintage and ribbed bands, minor base dent, 6¼" h, 12 troy oz **435.00**

Hot Milk Jug, 8½" h, C Townsend, Dublin, 1776–77, plain baluster form, rattan cov handle, 22 troy oz **1,320.00**

Ladle, 7" l, attributed to Joseph Coles, London, 1817, thread and shell pattern, 4 troy oz .. **100.00**

Marrow Scoop, 9½" l, Hester Bateman, London, 1777–78, engraved crest, 1½ troy oz .. **350.00**

Salt

Edinburgh, third quarter 18th C, marked "RC," 3 troy oz, price for pair **150.00**

London, 1703–04, globular, floral chasing, hoof feet, maker rubbed, 4 troy oz, price for pair **110.00**

Salver, 13" d, London, 1769, piecrust C–scroll and acanthus

rim, raised scroll feet, 31 troy oz **1,700.00**

Sauceboat, 9¼" l, 7" h, Thomas Ellis, London, 1780, oval, engraved crest, beaded rim, loop handle, oval foot, 18 troy oz . **800.00**

Service Plate, 9½" d, Charles Wright, London, 1782, shaped gadrooned rim with engraved crest, 69 troy oz, price for four piece set **2,400.00**

Serving Spoon, 9" l, Paul Storr, London, 1813, Kings pattern, vermeil wash, 6 troy oz, price for pair **425.00**

Stuffing Spoon, 11½" l, David Peter, Dublin, Ireland, 1762, scallop shell terminal, 3 troy oz **165.00**

Sugar Bowl, 8½" l, London, 1801–02, tapering oval lobed form, two sq handles, maker rubbed, 10 troy oz **175.00**

Tea Caddy, 4½" h, William Vincent, London, 1777, reeded border, cut floral swags and gentleman crest dec, hinged oval cov, urn finial, 12 troy oz **1,200.00**

Teapot, 5" h, John Emes, London, 1802–03, compressed globular form, raked spout, repousse flower garlands, wave work borders, angular treen handle, reeded foot, 17 troy oz **330.00**

Wine Coaster, 5" d, Henry Chawner, London, 1787, pierced sides, serpentine rim, treen bottom, price for pair . . **400.00**

Wine Funnel, unmarked, leaf design, engraved crest, damage, 3 troy oz **175.00**

George III Style, sauceboat, 3½" h, scrolled rim, C–scroll handle, shell and pad feet, 6 troy oz . . . **175.00**

George IV

Grape Shears, 6½" l, Charles Rawlings, London, 1822, vermeil wash, grape and vine handles, 3 troy oz **650.00**

Inkstand, 8½" l, Joseph Angell, London, 1829–30, rect, scroll shaped rim, taperstick, two glass inkwells, tray, 19 troy oz **1,540.00**

Porringer, Edinburgh, 1826–27, J. H. maker, double handle,

engraved dec, initials, 4⅝" d, 7 troy oz **175.00**

Sauceboat, 9¼" l, Thomas Robins, London, 1825–26, oval bellied body, shaped everted rim, C–scroll spout, cast arched handle, three cast shells continue to scrolling legs, pad feet, 13½ troy oz . . **935.00**

George V

Candlestick, 10" h, London, 1833–34, Queen Anne style, knopped stem, weighted base, retailed by S Kirk & Son, price for set of four **1,760.00**

Coffee and Tea Service, Crichton & Co, Ltd, London, 1933–34, Queen Anne style, globular, molded handle, teapot, coffeepot, creamer, sugar, and waste bowl, 71 troy oz, price for five piece set **1,815.00**

Hot Water Kettle on Stand, 13" h, Hunt and Roshell Ltd, London, 1933–34, pear shape, engraved foliage, stand with shell feet, 44 troy oz **880.00**

Tray, 27½" l, London, c1928, rect cross section with molded cavetto corners, engraved foliage and medallions border, scrolling legs, stepped pad feet, marked "R C," 214 troy oz **4,400.00**

George VI, coffee and tea service, Ellis Silver Co, Birmingham, 1947–48, coffeepot, hot water kettle on stand, teapot, creamer, sugar, waste bowl, and plated tray, inverted pear form, engraved design, monogrammed, burner missing, dents, 116 troy oz, price for six piece set **2,310.00**

Regency

Bowl, 3½" d, Daniel Egan, Dublin, 1812, plain form, ring foot, slightly everted rim, 14 troy oz **770.00**

Teapot, 8" h, Solomon Hougham, London, 1817–18, ovoid, gadrooned, ball feet, 26 troy oz **990.00**

Victorian

Candlestick, 7½" h, Chippendale style, W Hutton & Sons, London, 1898, several small dents, price for pair **700.00**

Coffee and Tea Service, London, 1846–47, E. J. B. & W. Barnard, coffeepot, teapot, creamer, open sugar, engraved dec and crest, dents on pots, 75 troy oz **1,840.00**

Epergne, London, 1898, tapered cylindrical, scrolled rams suspending two baskets, acanthus pierced flaring rim, pierced round base, 41 troy oz **1,000.00**

Mirror Frame, London, 1896–97, William Comyns, Rococo style, scroll and cupid design, heart shaped beveled mirror, easel back, 17½" h **750.00**

Nutmeg Grater, 1½" l, George Unite, Birmingham, 1865, nut form, engraved dec **385.00**

Pitcher, Birmingham, 1888–89, J. G. & S. maker, hammer textured lid, spout, and handle, textured clear glass body, 6¾" h **290.00**

Salt, R Garrard, London, 1851–52, cast scallop shell, supported by waves, matching spoon, shell and branch design, 17 troy oz **2,310.00**

Salver, London, 8" d, piecrust border, scrolling feet, 13 troy oz, 1895–96 . . . . **600.00**

Serving Spoon, Joseph and Albert Savory, London, 1840–1901, King pattern, engraved arms, 13 troy oz, price for pair **500.00**

Stand, 7¼" h, London, 1897–98, dish surface with leaf tip borders, scrolling supports, columnar standard, circular dished and leaf tip embellished socle, ruffled shell and acanthus feet, marked "H W & Co," 44 troy oz, price for pair **1,650.00**

Tea Strainer, 5½" w, two handles, 1½ troy oz **150.00**

William IV

Bowl, 9" d, L Urouhart, Edinburgh, 1935–36, chased hunt scene, racing scene, floral scrolls, spreading foot, 29 troy oz **2,530.00**

Snuffbox, 1¼" w, 1⅞" l, Nathaniel Mills, Birmingham, 1831–32 **200.00**

SILVER, ENGLISH, SHEFFIELD

Sheffield Silver, or Old Sheffield Plate, was made by a fusion method of silver plating used from the mid-18th century until the mid-1880s, when the silver electroplating process was introduced.

Sheffield plate was discovered in 1734 when Thomas Boulsover of Sheffield, England, accidentally fused silver and copper. The process consisted of sandwiching a heavy sheet of copper between two thin sheets of silver. The result was a plated sheet of silver which could be pressed or rolled to a desired thickness. All Sheffield plate articles were worked from these plated sheets.

Most of the silver–plated items found today marked "Sheffield" are not early Sheffield plate. They are later wares made in Sheffield, England.

Argyle, 6⅜" h, c1830, cylindrical, beaded rim, raffia wrapped handle, shell terminal, faceted ovoid knob **275.00**

Cake Basket, 14⅞" l, c1820, rect, flower dec gadroon rim, sides chased scrolls and berried foliage, interlaced ribbonwork handle, satyr masks terminals, four paw feet **725.00**

Coffee Urn, c1780, two handled urn form, beaded rim, engraved crest and initial, bud finial, pedestal foot, four ball supports . . . **600.00**

Dish, cov, George IV, early 19th C, rect, floral relief corners, engraved crest, gadrooned borders, acanthus and foliate loop handle, price for pair **650.00**

Entree Dish, cov, shaped rect, 16½" l, c1810, ends scrolled to form handles, applied acanthus leaves, gadroon borders, detachable reeded and foliate ring finials, engraved mitre crests, price for pair **2,310.00**

Fish Knives and Forks, 1899, twelve each, bright cut blade,

bone handles, custom fitted case, price for twenty-four piece set **575.00**

Fruit Knives and Forks, c1876, six each, bright cut blade, ribbed pearl handles, custom fitted case, price for twelve piece set **715.00**

Hot Water Kettle, 12" h, William IV, c1835, reeded globular form, scrolled legs, paw feet, rosing . **425.00**

Jug, 15½" h, 1807, baluster, repousse clover thistle and rose dec, thistle finial, marked "Danels" **2,200.00**

Kettle On Stand, late 19th C, ribbed ovoid form, monogrammed, some wear, 11½" h . **145.00**

Muffineer, 1839, domical pierced lid, circular ftd base, custom case, 5 troy oz **60.00**

Salver, 24" d, c1825, circular, pierced border, relief dec of flowers, foliage, and scrolls, center engraved armorials, flat chased band of rococo ornaments, matted ground, three paneled feet .**2,350.00**

Sauce Tureen, cov, 8¼" l, c1820, oval bombe form, gadroon rims with flowerheads and leaves, acanthus handles, four paw feet with spreading acanthus, shaped rim cov, leafy scroll ring finial topped with shell, dense bed of leaves and flowerheads, price for pair **1,100.00**

Soup Tureen, cov, 18" l, Waterhouse, Hatfield & Co, c1835, circular bombe form, engraved armorials, reeded handles wrapped with grapevine, acanthus spray feet, molded rims with flowers, shells, and leaves, domed cov with silver heraldic finial by John Figg, London, 1842, detachable liner, matching stand **5,725.00**

Tea Set, Regency style, 19th C, 6" h teapot, creamer, and sugar, marked "TM," price for three piece set **220.00**

Tea Tray, 31¾" l, Matthew Boulton Plate Co, c1810, rect, undulating border, gadroon rim, leaf and double shells at intervals, match-

ing handles, center large engraved owl crest **3,325.00**

Venison Dish, cov, 24½" l, c1800, oval, gadroon rim, hot water compartment with pierced central cov and spigot, domed cov, foliate ring handle, engraved crest **2,425.00**

Wine Cooler, 7⅝" h, J Watson & Son, c1830, fluted circular form, vine branch handles, applied spreading grapevine, four shell feet flanked by acanthus, egg and dart borders, detachable fluted rim and liners, price for pair **4,125.00**

SILVER, PLATED

Plated silver production by an electrolytic method is credited to G. R. and H. Elkington, England, in 1838.

In electroplating silver, the article is completely shaped and formed from a base metal and then coated with a thin layer of silver. In the late 19th century, the base metal was Britannia, an alloy of tin, copper, and antimony. Other bases are copper and brass. Today the base is nickel silver.

In 1847 the electroplating process was introduced in America by Rogers Bros., Hartford, Connecticut. By 1855 a number of firms were using the method to produce silver–plated items in large quantities.

The quality of the plating is important. Extensive use or polishing can cause the base metal to show through. The prices for plated silver items are low, making it a popular item with younger collectors.

Argyle, 6½" h, Georgian, late 18th C, compressed urn form, cut engraved tapered body, raked spout, stepped oval cov with ball finial, treen loop handles, oval reeded socle **440.00**

Biscuit Box, 6½" h, oval, lift lid, ftd tray base **175.00**

Bowl, Elkington & Co, Birmingham, c1850, shaped oval form, stag head handles, scrolled feet, price for three piece set **750.00**

Candelabra, 29" h, William IV,

c1830, five scrolled foliate candle arms, fluted and acanthus column and base, central stem detached 660.00

Castor Set, 10¼" h, 9¾" l, 7" w, Colonial Revival style, six cut glass bottles, marked "Sheffield," edge roughness and chips to bottles 490.00

Coffee and Tea Service, Wallace, Baroque pattern, 11" h coffeepot, teapot, cov sugar, creamer, and 23½" l two handled waiter . 325.00

Collar Button Box, 2¼" d, emb sides, figural collar button on lid with engraving "HERE'S YOUR COLLAR BUTTON," marked "Holman Silver Co.," four SS buttons inside 40.00

Condensed Milk Can Holder, Rogers & Bros, cylindrical body, emb band at top and bottom, simple "C" handle, hole in lid for ladle 50.00

Dish, cov, 8" d, French, 19th C, circular, engraved noble crest, gadroon dec finial 200.00

Entree Dish, Elkington & Co, Birmingham, c1850, shaped oval form, stag head handles, scrolled feet, orig liner, price for set of seven 1,000.00

Hot Water Urn, Regency Style, late 19th C, tapered urn form, shaped base, ball feet, 21" h .. 330.00

Miniature, wine cooler, 3¼" d, 5½" h, Victorian, staved bucket shape, scalloped rim, figural lion head handles, classical figures form four feet 50.00

Muffin Basket, 13" l, oval, pierced ribbed sides, twin scrolled handles 75.00

Pitcher, water, 10" h, Classical style, c1920, large pouring lip, scroll handles, circular base, 28 troy ozs 380.00

Salver, 8" d, George III style, shell scallop rim, scroll feet 80.00

Sauce Tureen, 9" l, George III, late 18th C, Neoclassical compressed urn form, reeded finial, arched loop handles, oval gadrooned socle, price for pair ... 440.00

Serving Tray, 16½" w, 23½" l,

Mappin & Webb, London, oval, engraved noble crest 200.00

Spoon Warmer, English, nautilus shaped holder, flip lid opening on top for storage of large serving spoons at table, shell rests on mound of simulated rocks, shell shape thumb rest at one end .. 175.00

Sugar Bowl, cov, bird finial, twelve spoon hooks, marked "Quadplate" 190.00

Tea Tray, 24¼" l excluding handles, English, shaped oval tray with face hand engraved with scrolls and flowers, molded scroll and shell border, ftd, bracket handles, monogrammed 200.00

Tea Urn, 16½" h, Regency, rect tub form, two lion mask and ring handles, stepped molded cov, scrolled supports, raised on platform, urn form burner, ball feet . 880.00

Tray, 30" l, late Victorian, oval cross section with cast leaf entwined gadrooned border, engraved oval shields, two arched handles 1,100.00

Warming Stand, Victorian, shell form, two parts, branch form supports 200.00

SILVER DEPOSIT GLASS

History: Silver deposit glass, consisting of a thin coating of silver actually deposited on the glass by an electrical process, was popular at the turn of the century. The process was simple. The glass and a piece of silver were placed in a solution. An electric current was introduced which caused the silver to decompose, pass through the solution, and remain on those parts of the glass on which a pattern had been outlined.

Reference: Ellen T. Schroy, *Warman's Glass,* Wallace-Homestead, 1992.

Bowl, 10½" d, green, floral dec .. 40.00

Cabinet Vase, 3½" h, Art Nouveau, blue Favrile 500.00

Cologne Decanter, faceted knob stem 300.00

Compote, 7" d, floral dec 75.00

Vase, green ground, silver floral design, c1920, 16″ h, $85.00.

Decanter, 9″ h, emerald green, hollow stopper **60.00**

Pitcher, 7″ h, floral and leaf dec . **220.00**

Serving Plate, 12½″ d, black, Art Nouveau lily dec, pierced handles **55.00**

Toothpick, 2½″ h **40.00**

Tumbler, 4⅝″ h, flared top **20.00**

Vase, 11½″ h, rect urn shape, black glass, floral and line dec . **175.00**

SILVER OVERLAY

History: Silver overlay is silver applied directly to a finished glass or porcelain object. The overlay is cut and decorated, usually by engraving, prior to being molded around the object.

Glass usually is of high quality, either crystal or colored. Lenox used silver overlay on some porcelain pieces. The majority of design motifs are from the Art Nouveau and Art Deco periods.

Reference: Lillian F. Potter, *A Re-Introduction To Silver Overlay On Glass And Ceramics,* published by author, 1992.

Charger, 14″ d, floral dec **70.00**

Cruet, 8″ h, presentation, clear, scroll design, inscribed "Presented to the Honorable Samuel K. Robbins by Republican Friends of Morristown, NJ, January 12, 1904" **1,100.00**

Decanter, 7″ h, black–amethyst, animal and floral silver overlay, marked "Rockwell," stopper missing **300.00**

Flask, 2¼″ w, 4¼″ h, clear, scrolling overlay, hinged SS top **150.00**

Inkwell, 3″ w, triangular, green, marked "General Supply Co, Danielson, Conn, Pat #879470" **325.00**

Loving Cup, 7⅜″ h, three handles, sgd "Lenox" **1,650.00**

Perfume Bottle, floral scrollwork, matching stopper, 2¼″ d, 4½″ h, $225.00.

Perfume Bottle, 4″ h, ball shape, cranberry, SS floral and scrolling overlay, orig stopper **325.00**

Pitcher, 9⁵⁄₁₆″ h, green glass, vintage silver overlay, 20th C **1,380.00**

Vase
   5¾″ h, baluster, lime green, sgd "Lenox" **770.00**
   7½″ h, cobalt blue body, simulated mineral deposits, swirling silver dec, European lapis stone glass **440.00**
   8″ h, thick engraved silver, emb grapes and leaves, matte green crackle glaze, Roseville Chloron, marked "TRP Co & Chloron," "K" in script **8,500.00**
   12″ h, flute, green ground, intricate silver webb motif **375.00**
   13¾″ h, flared black amethyst ground, bubbled crystal ball stem, Art Deco silver overlay, Rockwell manner designs ... **550.00**

SILVER RESIST

History: Silver resist ware was first produced about 1805. It is similar to silver luster in respect to the silvering process and differs in that the pattern appears on the surface.

The outline of the pattern was drawn or stenciled on the ware's body. A glue or sugar-glycerin adhesive was brushed over the part not to be lustered, causing it to "resist" the lustering solution which was applied and allowed to dry. The glue or adhesive was washed off. When fired in the kiln, the luster glaze covered the entire surface except for the pattern.

**Cup and Saucer, Greek key dec,
2½" h cup, 5½" d saucer, $80.00.**

Bowl, 6" d, floral border 60.00
Creamer, 3¼" h, dark brown,
  flower each side, two handles . 75.00
Cup and Saucer, allover floral pattern 50.00
Jug, 4¼" h, band of flowering foliage, Staffordshire, 19th C 85.00
Mug, 3½", bird, flowers, line border, Leeds, c1815 . . . . 100.00
Pitcher
  4⅜" h, black transfer, enameled
    iron–red, blue, yellow, black,
    brown, and green robin on oak
    branch, c1815 . . . . 385.00
  4½" h, floral design, two white
    reserves with Oriental scenes 125.00
  5⅜" h, two hunters, one aiming
    rifle at bird, other seated on
    fallen tree, Staffordshire,
    c1815 . . . . 525.00

Wine, 4½" h, purple–pink luster,
  feathering above graduated
  dots, cream foot and int., iron–
  red rim, pedestal, and foot,
  c1810 . . . . 350.00

SMITH BROS. GLASS

History: After establishing a decorating department at the Mount Washington Glass Works in 1871, Alfred and Harry Smith struck out on their own in 1875. Their New Bedford, Massachusetts, firm soon became known worldwide for its fine opalescent decorated wares, similar in style to those of Mount Washington.

Their glass often is marked on the base with a red shield enclosing a rampant lion and the word "Trademark."

Reference: Ellen T. Schroy, *Warman's Glass,* Wallace-Homestead, 1992.

Reproduction Alert: Beware of examples marked "Smith Bros."

Bowl, 6" d, 2¾" h, melon ribbed,
  gold prunus dec, allover two
  shades of gold, beaded white
  rim, sgd 375.00
Humidor, 6¼" h, 4" w, pale beige
  ground, blue pansy dec, orig
  melon ribbed matching glass
  top, sgd 250.00
Pansy Bowl, 4" w, 2½" h, melon
  ribbed, blue pansies, blue
  ground, blue edge with white
  dots 225.00

**Rose Bowl, Shasta Daisy pattern,
gold rim, white beads, 3⅛" d, 4" h,
$150.00.**

Rose Bowl, 3″ d, 2½″ h, cream ground, jeweled gold prunus dec, gold beaded top, sgd **285.00**

Salt, open, 1¼″ h, 2¼″ d, three blue, one beige, two pink, gold prunus blossoms and leaves, sgd, price for set of six **650.00**

Salt and Pepper Shakers, pr, 4″ h, opal glass, pink and blue painted flowers, blue beads, price for pair **225.00**

Vase

6¼″ h, melon ribbed, daisy dec, rope rim, wear to dec **55.00**

6¾″ h, ten molded-in ribs swirl upward, two shiny gold neck rings, beaded rim, swags of daisy stalks, rampant lion mark **645.00**

7″ h, soft pink ground, white pond lily, blue–green/black leaves, brown stems, maroon trim, c1870, price for matching pair **375.00**

9¾″ h, 6¼″ w, pillow, purple and pink clematis dec, gold highlights, green leaves, gold beaded top **895.00**

SNOW BABIES

History: Snow babies, small bisque figurines spattered with glitter sand, were made originally in Germany and marketed in the early 1900s. There are several theories about their origin. One is that German doll makers copied the designs from the traditional Christmas candies. Another theory, the most accepted, is that they were made to honor Admiral Peary's daughter who was born in Greenland in 1893 and was called the "Snow Baby" by the Eskimos.

References: Ray and Eilene Early, *Snow Babies*, Collector Books, out of print; Mary Morrison, *Snow Babies, Santas, and Elves: Collecting Christmas Bisque Figures,* Schiffer Publishing, 1993.

Angel, sitting, outstretched arms, 1¾″ h **200.00**

Baby

Holding baton **115.00**

Baby sitting, 1⅛″ h, $195.00.

Holding hockey stick, 1½″ h ... **100.00**
Kneeling on one knee, 1″ h ... **75.00**
Lying on side, 1½″ h **90.00**
Lying on tummy, 1″ h **65.00**
Playing saxophone, marked "Germany" **80.00**
Sitting, 2¼″ h
  Outstretched arms and legs . **135.00**
  Snow cov cardboard box **125.00**
Sledding, marked "Germany" .. **85.00**
Carolers, three, standing in snow, lantern, marked "Germany," 2¼″ h **90.00**
Penguin, marked "Germany," 4″ l **70.00**
Polar Bear, 2½″ h **115.00**

SNUFF BOTTLES

History: Tobacco usage spread from America to Europe to China during the 17th century. Europeans and Chinese preferred to grind the dried leaves into a powder and sniff it into their nostrils. The elegant Europeans carried their snuff in boxes and took a pinch with their finger tips. The Chinese upper class, because of their lengthy fingernails, found this inconvenient and devised a bottle with a fitted stopper and attached spoon.

In the Chinese manner, these utilitarian objects soon became objets d'art. Snuff bottles were fashioned from precious and semi-precious stones, glass, porcelain and pottery, wood, metals, and ivory. Glass and transparent stone bottles often were enhanced further with delicate hand paintings, some done on the interior of the bottle.

Reference: Gloria and Robert Mascarelli, *Warman's Oriental Antiques,* Wallace-Homestead, 1992.

Collectors' Club: International Chinese Snuff Bottle Society, 2601 North Charles Street, Baltimore, MD 21218.

Agate
    Circular flask form, Chinese, 19th/20th C, 2" h **55.00**
    Oval flask form, carnelian stopper, Chinese, late 19th/early 20th C, 2¼" h **65.00**
Bone, conical shape, carved, brown top, Chinese, 3⅜" h **180.00**
Bronze, flask shape, chain **135.00**
Glass
    Clear
        Double carved handles, green stone stopper, 3" h **65.00**
        Painted int. with trees and mountains, green stone stopper, Chinese, 2¾" h . . .   **45.00**
        Mottled brown, black, and gray, bottle form, eye form stopper, Chinese, 20th C, 3" h **145.00**
        White, oval vase form, black stopper, Chinese, 2¾" h **40.00**
Hornbill, flattened pear shape, carved fruit and floral dec, painted character int., Chinese, 2⅛" h **750.00**
Ivory, floral and figural carved

Cloisonne, floral motif on one side, forest scene with deer on other, carved base, 3⅜" h, $250.00.

sides, brown stone stopper, signed, Chinese, late 19th/early 20th C, 2¼" h **130.00**
Jade
    Brown, ovoid form, paneled sides, gray jade stopper, Chinese, late 19th/early 20th C, 2½" h **130.00**
    White, ovoid form, cloud carved sides, metal and black cinnabar lacquer stopper, Chinese, late 19th/early 20th C, 2¼" h   **65.00**
Metal, jeweled, Asian **55.00**
Peking Glass
    Blue and white, dragon and symbols, metal and blue glass stopper, 2½" h **65.00**
    Clear and red, oval vase form, water lilies and ducks, red stone and glass stopper, 3¼" h **75.00**
Red
    Ovoid elephant form, white neck, rose quartz and red glass stopper, Chinese, 20th C, 3⅞" h **200.00**
    Tall ovoid form, black glass stopper, Chinese, 20th C, 2⅞" h **50.00**
Pewter, circular, gilt handles, Chinese **450.00**
Porcelain
    Bottle form
        Blue floral dec, coral stopper, Chinese, 3" h **30.00**
        Drunken monk and peddler dec, black stopper, Chinese, 3¼" h **90.00**
        Double gourd shape, blue figures, Chinese, 2¾" h **65.00**
        Flat circular flask shape
            Blue dragon dec, black stopper, Chinese, 3" h **40.00**
            Two reserves with red and blue figures, agate stopper, Chinese, 2¾" h **55.00**
    Rock Crystal, carved, rect shape, incised carved faces, paneled sides, ivory stopper, Chinese, 20th C, 2½" h **50.00**
Silver, figural, emb design on robe, head stopper, c1900 . . . .   **400.00**
Soapstone, carved, irregular shape, 3" h **50.00**

SOAPSTONE

History: The mineral steatite, known as soapstone because of its greasy feel, has been utilized for carving figural groups and designs by the Chinese and others. Utilitarian pieces also were made. Soapstone pieces were very popular during the Victorian era.

Vase, tan and brown, carved rodent, 2½″ h , $75.00.

Candlestick, 2½″ h, trapezoidal,
  gray 130.00
Carving, 11⅛″ h, mountain village,
  river and boat, greenish stone,
  dark brown soapstone base, minor edge damage 220.00
Figure
  Buddha, 11″ h, carved, 19th C,
    later teak stand, mounted as
    lamp, price for pair 550.00
  Dog, carved group of three 40.00
  Eskimo, holding child on back,
    carved and incised 3,750.00
  Guanyin, 5⅜″ h, seated, wearing
    headdress, hands resting on
    knee, ochre, shaped teak
    stand, China, 19th C 500.00
  Sage, 6″ h, carved black base,
    Oriental 100.00
Inkwell, geometric carved sides . . 140.00
Lamp, 7½″ l, spout 55.00
Paperweight, three monkeys 45.00
Toothpick Holder, figural, monkey 100.00
Urn, 7¼″ d, 10¼″ h, carved, figures, buildings, florals, and
  trees, elephant head handles,
  wood stand 150.00
Vase, rose color, double, joined by
  floral carving, Victorian 50.00
Wall Plaque, unicorn head 50.00

SOUVENIR AND COMMEMORATIVE CHINA AND GLASS

History: Souvenir, commemorative, and historical china and glass includes those items produced to celebrate special events, places, and people.

Among the china plates, those by Rowland and Marcellus and Wedgwood are most eagerly sought. Rowland and Marcellus, Staffordshire, England, made a series of blue and white historic plates that had a wide rolled edge and depicted scenes beginning with the Philadelphia Centennial in 1876 and continuing to the 1939 New York World's Fair. Wedgwood collaborated in 1910 with Jones, McDuffee and Stratton to produce a series of historic dessert–sized plates depicting scenes throughout the United States.

Many localities issued plates, mugs, glasses, etc., for anniversary celebrations or to honor a local historical event. These items seem to have greater value when sold in the region from which they originated.

Commemorative glass includes several patterns of pressed glass which celebrate persons or events. Historical glass includes campaign and memorial items.

References: Bessie M. Lindsey, *American Historical Glass,* Charles E. Tuttle Company, 1967; Ellen T. Schroy, *Warman's Glass,* Wallace-Homestead, 1992; Frank Stefano, Jr., *Wedgwood Old Blue Historical Plates And Other Views Of The United States Produced For Jones, McDuffee & Stratton Co., Boston, Importer: A Check–List with Illustrations,* published by author, 1975.

Collectors' Clubs: Antique Souvenir Collectors News, Box 562, Great Barrington, MA 01230; Statue of Liberty Collectors' Club, PO Box 535, Chautauqua, NY 14722.

Additional Listings: Cup Plates, Pressed Glass, Political Items, and Staffordshire, Historical. Also see *Warman's Americana & Collectibles* for more examples.

CHINA

Bread Plate, frosted FDR center,
  1904 . . . . **155.00**

Cup Plate, Henry Clay, Sandwich, LR566 B, 3⅝″ d, $80.00.

Cup and Saucer
Iowa State Capitol, white, gold trim 25.00
Waterfront Business Section, Seattle, WA, Nippon, SBN mark 40.00
Pitcher, General Andrew Jackson, copper luster, transfer print, 8″ h 125.00
Plate
FDR, Hyde Park, 7″ d 25.00
Panama Canal, Columbia, mermaid and Triton 85.00
Saratoga, NY, dark blue, rolled edges, vignette border, Rowland and Marcellus, 10½″ d . . 50.00
U.S. Capitol, 9″ d 25.00
Tray, George and Martha Washington portrait, "Washington's Home, Mt Vernon, VA" center, sq corners, enhanced enameling, gold trim, marked "Germany," 11 x 7½″ 80.00

GLASS

ABC Plate, Centennial Exposition 1876, clear, alphabet border, 6¾″ d 120.00
Bank, Independence Hall, 7¼″ h . 70.00
Bread Plate
Eagle and Constitution, "Give Us This Day" 100.00
Three Presidents, "In Remembrance" 100.00
Creamer and Sugar
Texas Centennial, clear 50.00

Vinton, IA, custard 70.00
Desk Stand, Memorial Hall form inkwell, Philadelphia Exposition 1876, clear, 6½″ l 180.00
Jar, Statue of Liberty, clear, worn gold dec, 12½″ h, 5″ d, price for pair 120.00
Mug, E Pluribus Unum, 5″ h, handled, clear 60.00
Plate
George Washington, 13 Star, 9¼″ d, milk glass 55.00
Heroes of Bunker Hill 50.00
Niagara Falls, 7″ d, milk glass . 25.00
Platter, clear
American Flag, rect, 48 stars, 9⅜ x 6¾″ 210.00
Bunker Hill, oval, 13¼″ l 50.00
Carpenters Hall, 12″ l 70.00
Salt and Pepper Shakers, pr, Columbian Exposition 1893, egg shape, raised lettering, Mt Washington 150.00
Toothpick, Button Arches, pink milk glass, inscribed "Christmas 1903" 25.00
Tray, Niagara Falls, clear, frosted, 16″ l 275.00
Whiskey, Bumper to the Flag, 3″ h 85.00

SOUVENIR AND COMMEMORATIVE SPOONS

History: Souvenir and commemorative spoons have been issued for hundreds of years. Early American silversmiths engraved presentation spoons to honor historical personages or mark key events.

In 1881 Myron Kinsley patented a Niagara Falls spoon, and in 1884 Michael Gibney patented a new flatware design. M. W. Galt, Washington, D.C., issued commemorative spoons for George and Martha Washington in 1889. From these beginnings a collecting craze for souvenir and commemorative spoons developed in the late 19th and first quarter of the 20th century.

References: Dorothy T. Rainwater and Donna H. Fegler, *A Collector's Guide To Spoons Around The World,* Everybodys Press, 1976; Dorothy T. Rainwater and Donna H. Fegler, *American Spoons, Souvenir and Historical,* Schiffer Publishing,

1990; Dorothy T. Rainwater and Donna H. Felger, *Spoons From Around the World,* Schiffer Publishing, 1992; *Sterling Silver, Silverplate, and Souvenir Spoons With Prices, Revised,* L-W Book Sales, 1987, 1994 value update.

Collectors' Clubs: American Spoon Collectors, 4922 State Line, Westwood Hills, KS 66205; Northeastern Spoon Collectors Guild, 52 Hillcrest Ave., Morristown, NJ 07960; The Scoop Club, 84 Oak Ave., Shelton, CT 06484.

Additional Listings: See *Warman's Americana & Collectibles* for more examples.

R.M.S. Adriatic, hallmarked, $20.00.

Boston Tea Party	25.00
Carlisle, KY	25.00
Cincinnati, OH	23.00
City Hall, New York, SS, engraved New York City bowl, bridal rose figural handle	22.00
Colorado, SS, state capitol scene on bowl	18.00
Fort Ticonderoga, 1775, Ethan Allen	30.00
Illinois, SS	
Gate To Union Stockyards, Chicago on bowl	40.00
Public Library, Danville on bowl	30.00
Indianapolis 500, 1915, SS, race cars, balloons, and biplane	100.00
Kaiser Wilhelm II, SP, bust handle, crest, flag, and Army and Navy figures, marked "Deutchland," plain bowl	45.00
Kansas City	35.00
Kentucky, state	28.00
Minnehaha Falls, Art Nouveau handle	46.00
Montana, cowboy	40.00
Mt Tom Railway, Holyoke, MA	45.00
Niagara, Indian Head	30.00
Old City Gates	35.00
Pennsylvania, Elk's Temple, SS, Erie on bowl	15.00
San Francisco–Eureka, SS, Golden Gate bowl, bear figure handle	50.00
Statue of Liberty, enamel bowl	42.00
Texas Centennial 1839–1936	60.00
Utah, SS	
Observatory Peak, Ogden in bowl	30.00
Salt Air Pavilion	18.00
Vassar College, Poughkeepsie, NY scene in bowl	35.00
Virginia, SS, engraved "Front Royal" in bowl	18.00
Wisconsin Dells, fish figural handle	25.00

SPANGLED GLASS

History: Spangled glass is a blown or blown molded variegated art glass, similar to spatter glass, with the addition of flakes of mica or metallic aventurine. Many pieces are cased with a white or clear layer of glass. Spangled glass was developed in the late 19th century and still is being manufactured.

Originally spangled glass was attributed only to the Vasa Murrhina Art Glass Company of Hartford, Connecticut, which distributed the glass for Dr. Flower of the Cape Cod Glassworks, Sandwich, Massachusetts. However, research has shown that many companies in Europe, England, and the United States made spangled glass, and attributing a piece to a specific source is very difficult.

Reference: Ellen T. Schroy, *Warman's Glass,* Wallace-Homestead, 1992.

Basket, 7¼" h, 4¼" d, eight crimps, rose bowl type, applied clear thorny handle, deep rose overlay with mica flakes, white lining **215.00**

Creamer, 5¾" h, swirled, pigeon blood red, green, yellow, opaque white, and green aventurine, applied clear reeded handle **165.00**

Fairy Lamp, 3¼" h, 2⅞" d, cranberry, mica flakes, emb swirl, green threaded pyramid, clear base, marked "Clarke" **150.00**

Pitcher, opalescent swirl, mica flecks, applied reeded clear handle, 6¾" h, $95.00.

Pitcher
7¼" h, 6" w, amberina, gold flecks, DQ, white int., applied amber shell handle, Hobbs, Brockunier & Co **450.00**

8" h
5½" d, six wide ribbed blown out panels, heart shaped pouring spout, silver mica with rose flecks, hp flowers and leaves, gold trim, white lining, applied clear handle, patented 1883, Hobbs, Brockunier & Co **550.00**

6" d, Leaf Mold, pink and white spatter, silver flecks, white lining, applied clear handle, Northwood **450.00**

8½" h, 4" w, Blue Nugget, deep cobalt blue, cased in clear with silver mica, beehive shape, applied clear handle, Hobbs, Brockunier & Co **275.00**

Vase, 8½" h, flattened oval, applied cranberry rigaree, copper aventurine flecks, scroll handles, c1880 .... **315.00**

SPATTER GLASS

History: Spatter glass is a variegated blown or blown molded art glass. It originally was called "End-of-Day" glass, based on the assumption that it was made from leftover batches of glass at the end of the day. However, spatter glass was found to be a standard production item for many glass factories.

Spatter glass was developed at the end of the 19th century and is still being produced in the United States and Europe.

References: William Heacock, James Measell and Berry Wiggins, *Harry Northwood: The Early Years 1881–1900*, Antique Publications, 1990; Ellen T. Schroy, *Warman's Glass,* Wallace-Homestead, 1992.

Reproduction Alert: Many modern examples come from Czechoslovakia.

Basket
5⅝" h, 6¼" d, pink, tan, and white spatter, white lining, ruffled edge, applied clear thorny handle **175.00**

6" h, 4¾ x 7", light green ground, light green spatter, ruffled edge, applied green thorny handle **175.00**

Berry Bowl, master, Leaf Mold, vaseline satin, white spatter ... **150.00**

Fairy Lamp, cased, satin finish, 3¾" d, 4⅝" h, $165.00.

Creamer, Royal Ivy, satin, cased, multicolored spatter 220.00

Darning Egg, red, yellow, and green, applied clear handle . . . 125.00

Hyacinth Vase, 6½″ h, 3½″ w, white, blue, and yellow spatter arranged in stripes, clear ground 25.00

Pitcher, water
8″ h, 6″ w, Leaf Mold, canary yellow ground, pink and yellow spatter, orig glossy finish, Northwood 275.00

8½″ h
Hobb's Spatter, ruffled top, c1890 . . . . 225.00
4″ w, tortoise shell, mottled amber and brown, applied amber handle 125.00
9″ h, cranberry and white, applied crystal handle, sq top, melon ribbed 215.00

Rose Bowl, Leaf Mold, vaseline satin ground, cranberry spatter, Northwood 160.00

Salt, Royal Ivy, cased, rainbow spatter 80.00

Sugar Shaker
Ribbed Pillar, cranberry satin ground, white spatter, pinhead rim flakes 70.00
Ring Neck, pink spatter 185.00

Tumbler, Reverse Swirl, white speckles, slight rim flakes 65.00

SPATTERWARE

History: Spatterware is made of common earthenware, although occasionally creamware was used. The earliest English examples were made about 1780. The peak period of production was 1810–1840. Marked pieces are rare. Firms known to have made spatterware are Adams, Barlow, and Harvey and Cotton.

The amount of spatter decoration varies from piece to piece. Some objects simply have decorated borders. These often are decorated with a brush, requiring several hundred touches per square inch to achieve the spatter effect. Other pieces have the entire surface covered with spatter. Aesthetics of the final product are a key to value.

Collectors today focus on the patterns—Cannon, Castle, Fort, Peafowl, Rainbow, Rose, Thistle, Schoolhouse, etc. On flatware the decoration is in the center. On hollow pieces it occurs on both sides.

Color of spatter is another price key. Blue and red are the most common. Green, purple, and brown are in a middle group. Black and yellow are scarce.

Like any soft paste, spatterware was easily broken or chipped. Prices are for pieces in very good to mint condition.

References: Susan and Al Bagdade, *Warman's English & Continental Pottery & Porcelain, Second Edition,* Wallace-Homestead, 1991; Kevin McConnell, *Spongeware and Spatterware,* Schiffer Publishing, 1990; Dana G. Morykan and Harry L. Rinker, *Warman's Country Antique & Collectibles, Second Edition,* Wallace-Homestead, 1994; Carl and Ada Robacker, *Spatterware and Sponge,* A. S. Barnes & Co., 1978.

Reproduction Alert: "Cybis" spatter is an increasing collectible ware made by Boleslaw Cybis of Poland. The design utilizes the Adams–type peafowl and was made in the 1940s. Many contemporary craftsmen also are reproducing spatterware.

Coffeepot, 9½″ h, Peafowl, England, 19th C 690.00

Creamer
5⅛″ h, blue spatter, red star . . . 270.00
5½″ h, paneled, blue spatter, red, green, and black Adams rose 275.00
5⅝″ h, paneled, multicolored spatter 275.00
6¼″ h, paneled, blue spatter, blue, green, red, and black peafowl 385.00

Cup and Saucer, handleless
Blue spatter, red, green, yellow, and black peafowl 220.00
Red and blue spatter 115.00
Red spatter, red, blue, black, and yellow ochre peafowl . . . 225.00

Jack-In-The-Pulpit Vase, 6¾″ h, tapered cylindrical body, green, white, and pink spatter int., green diamond quilted design ext. 100.00

Pitcher
7½" h, green spatter, blue, yellow, red, and black peafowl .. **660.00**
11¼" h, water, paneled, blue
spatter, red and green flower,
spout repair, hairline **330.00**
Plate
8" d, red, blue, and green spatter, red and green Adams
rose, imp "Adams" **330.00**
8¼" d, red, blue, and green
dahlia, blue spatter, edge chip
and stains **225.00**
8½" d, red, blue, and green
dahlia, blue spatter, glaze
flake **310.00**
9⅜" d, red spatter, red, blue, and
green dahlia, imp "Barber &
Till Opaque China" **385.00**
9½" d, purple spatter, peafowl
center **300.00**

**Sugar Bowl, blue spatter, gray
ground, 5" h, $265.00.**

Sugar Bowl
7¼" h, paneled, red spatter,
blue, red, green, and black
peafowl, repaired finial **355.00**
8¼" h, paneled, blue spatter
Adams Rose, red, green, and
black **275.00**
Peafowl, green, orange, red,
and black **385.00**
Teapot, 9" h, paneled, purple spatter, red, blue, green, and black
tulip **660.00**
Wash Bowl, 13¼" d, red and
white stick spatter, star center,
sawtooth rim **330.00**
Waste Bowl, 4⅞" d, 2¾" h, green
spatter, red and green balls ...**1,595.00**

SPONGEWARE

History: Spongeware is a specific type
of decoration, not a type of pottery or glaze.

Spongeware decoration is found on many
types of pottery bodies—ironstone, redware, stoneware, yellow ware, etc. It was
made in both England and the United
States. Marked pieces indicate a starting
date of 1815, with manufacturing extending
to the 1880s.

Decoration is varied. In some pieces the
sponging is minimal with the white underglaze dominant. Other pieces appear to be
sponged solidly on both sides. Pieces from
1840–1860 have sponging which appears
in either a circular movement or a streaked
horizontal technique.

Examples are found in blue and white,
the most common colors. Other prevalent
colors are browns, greens, ochres, and a
greenish-blue. The greenish-blue results
from blue sponging which has been over-
glazed in a pale yellow. A red overglaze
produces a black or navy color.

Other colors are blue and red (found on
English creamware and American earthenware of the 1880s), gray, grayish-green,
red, dark green on stark white, dark green
on mellow yellow, and purple.

References: Susan and Al Bagdade,
Warman's American Pottery and Porcelain,
Wallace–Homestead, 1994; Susan and Al
Bagdade, *Warman's English & Continental
Pottery & Porcelain, Second Edition,* Wal-
lace–Homestead, 1991; William C. Ket-
chum, Jr., *American Pottery and Porcelain,*
Avon Books, 1994; Kevin McConnell,
Spongeware and Spatterware, Schiffer
Publishing, 1990; Earl F. and Ada Ro-
backer, *Spatterware and Sponge,* A. S.
Barnes & Co., 1978.

Bank, 6" l, figural, pig **90.00**
Bowl, 10½" d, blue and tan **90.00**
Bread Plate, 10" l, blue sponging,
double open handles **100.00**
Cookie Jar, gold highlights, green,
brown, and ochre **300.00**
Cup Plate, 3⅛" d, blue sponging,
white ground **60.00**
Cuspidor, 7½" d, blue sponge dec
and bands, white ground **90.00**
Jardiniere, 11 x 8¼", blue dec,

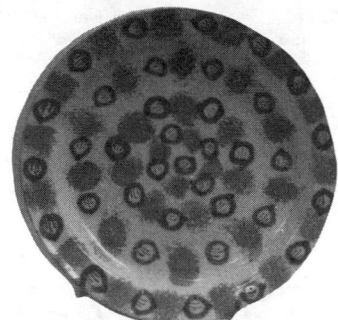

Plate, Delft, yellow, ochre, and blue sponged circles, early 18th C, England, 7½" d, $2,000.00.

gold flecked green rim, white
 ground **100.00**
Mixing Bowl, nested set of 3, 6¼
 to 8¼" d, blue and tan **250.00**
Pie Plate, 9" d, brown and green
 sponge, cream ground **50.00**
Pitcher
 4½" h, green and brown sponge,
  cream ground **65.00**
 8¾" h, blue and white, molded
  flower dec with blue highlights **475.00**
 9" h, blue and white dec **385.00**
Platter, 13¾" l, blue and white dec,
 minor crazing **190.00**
Salt and Pepper Shakers, pr, hand
 thrown, green and amber
 sponge, white ground **100.00**

SPORT CARDS

History: Baseball cards date from the late 19th century. By 1900 the most common cards, known as "T" cards, were those produced by tobacco companies such as American Tobacco Co., with the majority of the tobacco–related cards being produced between 1909 and 1915. During the 1920s American Caramel, National Caramel, and York Caramel candy companies issued cards identified in lists as "E" cards.

From 1933 to 1941 Goudey Gum Co. of Boston, and in 1939, Gum Inc., were the big producers of baseball cards. Following World War II, Bowman Gum of Philadelphia (B.G.H.L.I.), the successor to Gum, Inc., lead the way. Topps, Inc., (T.C.G.) of Brooklyn, New York, followed. Topps bought Bowman in 1956 and enjoyed almost a monopoly in card production until 1981.

In 1981 Topps was challenged by Fleer of Philadelphia and Donruss of Memphis. All three companies annually produce sets of cards numbering 600 cards or more.

Football cards have been produced since the 1890s. However, it was not until 1933 that the first bubble gum football card appeared in the Goudey Sport Kings set. In 1935 National Chickle of Cambridge, Massachusetts, produced the first full set of gum cards devoted exclusively to football.

Both Leaf Gum of Chicago and Bowman Gum of Philadelphia produced sets of football cards in 1948. Leaf discontinued production after their 1949 issue. Bowman Gum continued until 1955.

Topps Chewing Gum entered the market in 1950 with its college stars set. Topps became a fixture in the football card market with its 1955 All–American set. From 1956 through 1963 Topps printed a card set of National Football League players, combining them with the American Football League players in 1961.

Topps produced sets with only American Football League players from 1964 to 1967. The Philadelphia Gum Company made National Football League card sets during this period. Beginning in 1968 and continuing to the present, Topps has produced sets of National Football League cards, the name adopted by the merger of the two leagues.

References: James Beckett, *The Official 1995 Price Guide To Baseball Cards, 14th Edition*, House of Collectibles, 1994; James Beckett, *The Official 1994 Price Guide To Football Cards, 14th Edition*, House of Collectibles, 1994; James Beckett, *The Official 1994 Price Guide To Hockey Cards, 3rd Edition*, House of Collectibles, 1993; James Beckett, *The Sport Americana Baseball Card Alphabetical Checklist, No. 6*, Edgewater Book Co., 1994; James Beckett, *The Sport Americana Baseball Card Price Guide, No. 16*, Edgewater Book Co., 1994; James Beckett, *The Sport Americana Football Card Price Guide, No. 11*, Edgewater

Book Co, 1994; Tol Broome, *From Ruth to Ryan: Unbeatable Card Buys,* Krause Publications, 1994; Gene Florence, *Florence's Standard Baseball Card Price Guide, 6th Edition,* Collector Books, 1994; Jeff Fritsch, *The Sport Americana Team Baseball Card Checklist, No. 7,* Edgewater Book Co, 1994; Jeff Fritsch and Jane Fritsch–Gavin, *The Sport Americana Team Football and Basketball Card Checklist, Number 2,* Edgewater Book Co., 1993; Allan Kaye and Michael McKeever, *Baseball Card Price Guide 1995,* Avon Books, 1994; Allan Kaye and Michael McKeever, *Football Card Price Guide, 1995* Avon Books, 1994; Troy Kirk, *Collector's Guide To Baseball Cards,* Wallace–Homestead, 1990; Jeff Kurowski and Tony Prudom, *Sports Collectors Digest Pre–War Baseball Card Price Guide, 1887–1947,* Krause Publications, 1993; Mark Larson, *Sports Collectors Digest Minor League Baseball Card Price Guide,* Krause Publications, 1993; Mark Larson (ed.), *Sports Collectors Digest: The Sports Card Explosion,* Krause Publications, 1993; Bob Lemke (ed.), *Sports Collectors Digest Standard Catalog of Baseball Cards, 4th Edition,* Krause Publications, 1994; Bob Lemke and Sally Grace, *Sportscard Counterfeit Detector, 3rd Edition,* Krause Publications, 1994; Norman E. Martinus and Harry L. Rinker, *Warman's Paper,* Wallace–Homestead, 1994; Alan Rosen, *True Mint: Mr. Mint's Price & Investment Guide To True Mint Baseball Cards,* Krause Publications, 1994; Sports Collectors Digest, *Football, Basketball, & Hockey Price Guide, 2nd Edition,* Krause Publications, 1994; Sports Collectors Digest, *Getting Started In Card Collecting,* Krause Publications, 1993; Sports Collectors Digest, *101 Sports Card Investments,* Krause Publications, 1993; Sports Collectors Digest, *Sports Collectors Digest Baseball Card Price Guide, 8th Edition,* Krause Publications, 1994; *The Charlton Standard Catalogue of Canadian Baseball & Football Cards, 4th Edition,* The Charlton Press, 1995.

Periodicals: *Allan Kaye's Sports Cards News & Price Guides,* 10300 Watson Rd., St. Louis, MO 63127; *Baseball Update,* Suite 284, 220 Sunrise Highway, Rockville Centre, NY 11570; *Beckett Baseball Card Monthly,* Suite 200, 4887 Alpha Rd., Dallas, TX 75244; *Beckett Football Card Magazine,* Suite 200, 4887 Alpha Rd, Dallas, TX 75244; *Canadian Card News & Price Guide,* 700 E. State St., Iola, WI 54990; *Malloy's Sports Cards and Collectibles,* 17 Danbury Rd., Ridgefield, CT 06877; *Sport Card Economizer,* RFD 1 Box 350, Winthrop, ME 04364; *Sports Card Price Guide Monthly,* 700 E. State St., Iola, WI 54990; *Sports Cards,* 700 E. State St., Iola, WI 54990; *Sports Collectors Digest,* 700 E. State St., Iola, WI 54990; *The Old Judge,* PO Box 137, Centerbeach, NY 11720; *Tuff Stuff,* PO Box 1637, Glen Allen, VA 23060; *Your Season Ticket,* 106 Liberty Rd., Woodsboro, MD 21798.

Ty Cobb, Detroit, T-206, $4.00.

BASEBALL

Bowman
  1948 Bowman (black and white)

Complete set (48)	**525.00**
Common player (1–36)	**5.00**
Common player (37–48)	**7.50**
5 Bob Feller	**30.00**
17 Enos Slaughter	**18.00**
32 Bill Rigney	**6.00**

  1949 Bowman

Complete set (240)	**2,975.00**
Common player (1–36)	**5.00**
Common player (37–73)	**6.00**
Common player (74–144) . . .	**5.00**
Common player (145–240) . .	**20.00**

19 Bobby Brown 10.00
100 Gil Hodges 30.00
214 Richie Ashburn 85.00
1951 Bowman (color)
Complete set (324) 3,850.00
Common player (1–36) 5.00
Common player (37–252) . . . 5.00
Common player (253–324) . . 15.00
26 Phil Rizzuto 20.00
122 Joe Garagiola 20.00
314 Johnny Sain 18.00
1953 Bowman (black and white)
Complete set (160) 1,200.00
Common player (1–112) 10.00
Common player (113–128) . . 16.00
Common player (129–160) . . 12.00
59 Mickey Mantle 500.00
118 Billy Martin 70.00
148 Billy Goodman 15.00
1955 Bowman (color)
Complete set (320) 1,150.00
Common player (1–224) 2.50
Common player (225–320) . . 4.00
22 Roy Campanella 22.00
179 Hank Aaron 20.00
242 Ernie Banks 80.00
Topps Era
1951, red backs
Complete set (52) 250.00
Common player (1–52) 3.00
1 Yogi Berra 25.00
31 Gil Hodges 10.00
38 Duke Snider 20.00
1953 Topps
Complete set (280) 2,800.00
Common player (1–165) 4.50
Common player (166–220) . . 3.50
Common player (221–280) . . 16.00
27 Roy Campanella 45.00
76 Pee Wee Reese 30.00
82 Mickey Mantle 420.00
147 Warren Spahn 25.00
258 Jim Gilliam 70.00
280 Milt Bolling 25.00
1955 Topps
Complete set (210) 1,225.00
Common player (1–150) 2.50
Common player (151–160) . . 3.50
Common player (161–210) . . 4.50
28 Ernie Banks 6.00
123 Sandy Koufax 100.00
124 Harmon Killebrew 35.00
164 Roberto Clemente 130.00
194 Willie Mays 110.00

1957 Topps
Complete set (407) 1,575.00
Common player (1–264) 1.25
Common player (265–352) . . 5.00
Common player (353–407) . . 1.25
18 Don Drysdale 32.00
25 Whitey Ford 15.00
35 Frank Robinson 15.00
328 Brooks Robinson 80.00
1959 Topps
Complete set (572) 975.00
Common player (1–110) 1.00
Common player (111–506) . . .70
Common player (507–572) . . 2.50
50 Willie Mays 27.00
150 Stan Musial 20.00
202 Roger Maris 20.00
380 Hank Aaron 25.00
514 Bob Gibson 10.00

FOOTBALL

Bowman Gum Company
1948
Common card 2.25
Sammy Baugh 20.00
Sid Luckman 18.00
1951
Common card 1.50
Norm Van Brocklin 12.00
1952
Common card, large 2.50
Tom Landry, small 30.00
1955
Common card 1.00
Doak Walker 5.00
Frank Gifford 7.50
Fleer Gum Company
1960
Common card 35
George Blanda 3.00
Ron Mix 2.00
1961
Common card 30
Jim Brown 12.00
Leaf Gum
1948
Common card 3.00
Bobby Layne 2.00
Jackie Jensen 18.00
1949
Common card 3.00
John Lujack 10.00

Topps Chewing Gum Inc
1950
    Common card **1.25**
    Darryl Royal **12.00**
    Joe Paterno **18.00**
1951
    Common card . . . .   **.40**
    Bill Wade **2.00**
1955
    Common card . . . .   **.75**
    Four Horsemen **20.00**
    Jim Thorpe **15.00**
    Sid Luckman **10.00**
1956
    Common card . . . .   **.50**
    Chuck Bednarik **5.00**
    Lenny Moore **5.00**
1958
    Common card . . . .   **.40**
    John Unitas **7.50**
1959
    Common card . . . .   **.30**
    Jim Brown **12.00**
    Ollie Spencer **5.00**

SPORTS COLLECTIBLES

History: Individuals have been saving sports–related equipment since the inception of sports. Some was passed down from generation to generation for reuse. The balance occupied dark spaces in closets, attics, and basements.

In the 1980s two key trends brought collectors' attention to sports collectibles. First, decorators began using old sports items, especially in restaurant decor. Second, card collectors began to discover the thrill of owning the "real" thing. Although the principal thrust was on baseball material, by the beginning of the 1990s all sport categories were collectible, with golf and football especially strong.

References: Gwen Aldridge, *Baseball Archaeology: Artifacts From The Great American Pastime,* Chronicle Books, 1993; Sarah Baddiel, *Miller's Golf Memorabilia,* Millers Publications, 1994; Sarah Baddiel, *The World of Golf Collectibles,* Wellfleet Press, 1992; Mark Allen Baker, *All-Sport Autograph Guide,* Krause Publications, 1994; Mark Baker, *Sport Collectors Digest Baseball Autograph Handbook, 2nd Edition,* Krause Publications, 1991; Mark Baker, *Team Baseballs: The Complete Guide to Autographed Team Baseballs,* Krause Publications, 1992; Don Bevans and Ron Menchine, *Baseball Team Collectibles,* Wallace-Homestead, 1994; David Bushing, *Guide To Spalding Bats 1908–1938,* published by author; Dave Bushing and Joe Phillips, *Vintage Baseball Glove Pocket Price Guide,* published by authors, 1994; Peter Capano, *Baseball Collectibles,* Schiffer Publishing, 1989; Bruce Chadwick, *Baseball's Hometown Teams: The Story of the Minor Leagues,* Abbeville Press, 1994; Bruce Chadwick, *Reds: Memories and Memorabilia of the Big Red Machine,* Abbeville Press, 1994; Bruce Chadwick and David M. Spindel, *The Baltimore Orioles,* Abbeville Press, 1995; Bruce Chadwick and David M. Spindel, *The Chicago Cubs: Memories and Memorabilia of the Wrigley Wonders,* Abbeville Press, 1994; Bruce Chadwick and David M. Spindel, *The Dodgers: Memories and Memorabilia from Brooklyn to L. A.,* Abbeville Press, 1993; Bruce Chadwick and David M. Spindel, *The Giants: Memories and Memorabilia from a Century of Baseball,* Abbeville Press, 1993; Bruce Chadwick and David M. Spindel, *The Saint Louis Cardinals,* Abbeville Press, 1995; Duncan Chilcott, *Miller's Soccer Memorabilia,* Miller's Publications, 1994; Douglas Congdon–Martin and John Kashmanian, *Baseball Treasures: Memorabilia From The National Pastime,* Schiffer Publishing, 1993; Ralf Coykendall, Jr., *Coykendall's Second Sporting Collectibles Price Guide,* Lyons & Burford, 1992; Ralf Coykendall, Jr., *Coykendall's Sporting Collectibles Price Guide,* Lyons & Burford, 1991; Ted Hake and Roger Steckler, *An Illustrated Price Guide To Non–Paper Sports Collectibles,* Hake's Americana & Collectibles Press, 1986; Buck Kronnick, *The Baseball Fan's Complete Guide To Collecting Autographs,* Betterway Publications, 1990; Mark Larson, *Sports Collectors Digest Complete Guide To Baseball Memorabilia, 2nd Edition,* Krause Publications, 1994; Mark Larson, Rick Hines, and David Platta (eds.), *Mickey Mantle Memorabilia,* Krause Publications, 1993; Norman E. Martinus and Harry L. Rinker, *Warman's Paper,* Wallace–Homestead, 1994; Roderick A. Malloy, *Malloy's Sports Collectibles Value Guide: Up–To–Date Prices For Noncard Sports Memorabilia,* Attic Books Ltd., Wallace–Homestead, 1993; Ron Menchine, *A Picture Postcard History of Baseball,* Almar Press, 1992; John M. and Morton W. Olman, *Golf Antiques & Other Treasures of the Game, Expanded Edition,* Market Street Press, 1993; Joe Phillips and Dave Bushing, *Vintage Baseball Glove Price Guide: A Comprehensive Guide To Valuation of Vintage Baseball Gloves,* published by authors, 1992; Donald M. and R. Craig Raycraft, *Value Guide To Baseball Collectibles,* Collector Books, 1992; Beverly Robb, *Collectible Golfing Novelties,* Schiffer Publishing, 1992; George Sanders, Helen Sanders, and Ralph Roberts, *The Sanders Price Guide To Sports Autographs, 1994 Edition,* Scott Publishing, 1993; Shirley and Jerry Sprung, *Decorative Golf Collectibles: Collector's Information, Current Prices,* Glentiques, 1991; Mark Wilson (ed.), *The Golf Club Identification and Price Guide III,* Ralph Maltby Enterprises, 1993.

Periodicals: *Baseball Hobby News,* 4540 Kearney Villa Rd., San Diego, CA 92123; *Beckett Focus on Future Stars,* Suite 200, 4887 Alpha Rd., Dallas, TX 75244; *Boxing Collectors Newsletter,* 59 Boston St., Revere, MA 02151; *Fantasy Baseball,* 700 E. State St., Iola, WI 54990; *Golfiana Magazine,* PO Box 688, Edwardsville, IL 62025; *Malloy's Sports Cards and Collectibles,* 15 Danbury Rd., Ridgefield, CT 06877; *Old Tyme Baseball News,* PO Box 833, Petroskey, MI 49770; *Sporting Collector's Monthly,* PO Box 305, Camden, DE 19934; *Sports Collectors Digest,* 700 E. State St., Iola, WI 54990; *The Diamond Angle,* PO Box 409, Kaunakakai, HI 97648; *Tuff Stuff,* PO Box 1637, Glen Allen, VA 23060; *U.S. Golf Classics & Heritage Hickories,* 5407 Pennock Point Rd., Jupiter, FL 33458.

Collectors' Club: Boxiana & Pugilistica Collectors International, PO Box 83135, Portland, OR 97203; Golf Club Collectors Association, 640 E Liberty St, Girard, OH 44420-2308; Golf Collectors Society, PO Box 491, Shawnee Mission, KS 66202; Society for American Baseball Research, PO Box 93183, Cleveland, OH 44101; The

(Baseball) Glove Collector, 14507 Rolling Hills Lane, Dallas, TX 75240.

Museums: Aiken Thoroughbred Racing Hall of Fame & Museum, Aiken, SC; International Boxing Hall of Fame, Canastota, NY; Metropolitan Museum of Art, The Jefferson Burdich Collection, New York, NY; Naismith Memorial Basketball Hall of Fame, Springfield, MA; National Baseball Hall of Fame & Museum, Inc., Cooperstown, NY; National Bowling Hall of Fame & Museum, St. Louis, MO; New England Sports Museum, Boston, MA; PGA/World Golf Hall of Fame, Pinehurst, NC; The Kentucky Derby Museum, Louisville, KY.

Figure, young boy, standing, holding tennis racket and ball, red tie, light green pants, high glaze, marked "Made in Germany, 2672," 6⅛" h, $60.00.

BASEBALL

Bank, baseball shape, plastic
American League All–Stars, black base, blue signatures, early 1950s **75.00**
New York Yankees, removable black base, blue signatures, incised coin slot, early 1950s **125.00**
Baseball, autographed
Babe Ruth, Lou Gehrig, Jimmie Foxx, Hank Gowdy, and Rube Walberg signatures, dated "Boston 1929" **1,430.00**
New York Giants, twenty signatures, 1957 .... **440.00**
Bat, 38" l, Ty Cobb, 125 Louisville Slugger, Hillerich and Bradsby

Co, marked in pencil "Ty Cobb 6–29–25" **3,740.00**

Coaster, 4¼" d, cardboard, Ballantine Ale & Beer adv, black and white portrait illus of Bob Klinger and Virgil Davis, late 1930s ...　**40.00**

Cy Young Award, ebonized plaque, mounted cast metal banner with raised letters "Cy Young Awards," baseball diamond and hand clutching baseball framed by "V" symbol, "Presented to Early Wynn Most Valuable Pitcher 1959," includes photo of Wynn receiving award **12,100.00**

Document, autographed, "Shoeless" Joe Jackson, 4 x 1½" cut from legal document, printed, written, and typed information on back, sgd on April 1936 .....**23,100.00**

Jacket

Boston Red Sox, Hall of Fame, wool, black, red collar, cuffs, and waistband, button front, red "B" motif, A G Spalding & Bros tag and stitched "1048" canvas tag, c1940 ....**4,180.00**

Don Newcombe, Brooklyn Dodgers, blue faded to purple, zippered, Dodgers across front, leather sleeves with cuffs, fold felt label stitched "Newcombe 36" inside left pocket, "Butwin the Champion of Jackets" and "Dick Fisher Athletic Goods" labels **4,620.00**

Medallion, 1½" d, Babe Ruth Shrine, Ruth at bat on one side, Baltimore birthplace on other ..　**55.00**

Money Clip, 1962 San Francisco Giants National League Champions, 14k, baseball and two bats, back engraved "Edgar Feeley 1944" **1,760.00**

Nodder

Mickey Mantle, 7½" h, composition, white and blue Yankee uniform, emb "NY" symbol on cap and chest, sq base, decal with signature, base stamped "Patent Pending, Japan," 1961–62 ....　**200.00**

Willie Mays, 7" h, composition, holding baseball in one hand,

decal on cap and chest, 1961–62 ....　**250.00**

Painting, 18 x 12", Casey Stengel, oil on canvas, matted and framed ....　**460.00**

Pennant, 28½" l, Yankees American League Winners 1922, fourteen bust profile lineups **1,100.00**

Photo Card, Al Bridwell, 5 x 7½", "New York National" and "Bridwell" in margin, 1911 copyright　**150.00**

Photograph, 13 x 10½", Babe Ruth, black and white, inscribed black ink "To my friend Jack Lawton from Babe Ruth Dec 15th 1931" **1,870.00**

Plaque, 6 x 8", Chicago Cubs, plaster, raised portraits of three players, Charley Grimm, Lon Warneke, Woody English, gold wash, dark brown shadowing, two hanging hooks, early 1930s　**250.00**

Press Pin

Chicago Cubs 1938 World Series, bear cub clutching enameled baseball marked "Chicago Press 1938" ....　**825.00**

New York Yankees 1938 World Series, two crossed bats, raised baseball, Press 1938, red, white and blue border marked "World Series Yankee Stadium" ....　**825.00**

Program, 11 x 9", Yankee Stadium Opening Day, April 18, 1923, portraits on cov ....　**770.00**

Ring, Jose Canseco Rookie of the Year, 10K gold, green glass set with simulated diamond, marked "American League Rookie of the Year Jose Canseco Oakland A's Athletics 33 and 1986, 117 RBI, 33 HR All Star," sgd inside band "HJ–10K" **4,400.00**

Whiskey Bottle, 5" h, clear amber, center label with Pittsburgh ball player illus, late 1800s ....　**150.00**

BOXING

Photograph, autographed

Jack Dempsey, 13 x 11", Dempsey with bulldog and mug of Bulldog beer, inscribed "Hi

Rich, Swell Job, Pal Jack
Dempsey" **120.00**
Jess Willard, 6½ x 8½", black
and white glossy, pencil inscription on reverse "Jess Wil-
lard," early 1900s **15.00**
Playing Cards, James J Jeffries
Championship, 52 cards, photo
boxer portrait on each card,
1909 copyright **100.00**

FOOTBALL

Bookends, pr, Knute Rockne, cast
iron, raised portrait of Rockne,
incised inscription "The Rock Of
Notre Dame," early 1930s **150.00**
Pennant
New York Giants, 29" l, felt,
white inscription and stadium
design, dark blue background,
red trim, National Football
League insignia lower left, late
1960s **20.00**
New York Jets, 30" l, felt, white
design and inscriptions, green
background, late 1960s **20.00**
San Diego Chargers, 29½" l, felt,
yellow–gold and white lettering
and helmet design, blue background, American Football
League insignia, late 1960s .   **15.00**
Program, 5½ x 8", Harvard and
Yale first football match, Hamil-
ton Park, Saturday Nov 13, 1875   **770.00**
Puzzle, Roman Gabriel, 300 pcs,
full color photo action scene,
5½" h cardboard canister, American Publishing Corp, 1972
copyright **15.00**

GOLF

Magazine
Saturday Evening Post
Golf driving range at night illus
cov, 1952 . . . .   **30.00**
Woman golfer cov, 1903 . . . .   **50.00**
Sports Illustrated, Palmer/Ven-
turi/Finsterwald cover, 1960 . .   **27.00**
Print, Temper, A B Frost, 18 x 15"
overall, oak frame **75.00**
Sheet Music, *The Caddy,* Dean
Martin and Jerry Lewis, 1953 . .   **20.00**

RACING

Glass, souvenir, 1964 Kentucky
Derby, 5¼" h, frosted, brown
horse's head, gold inscription
"Kentucky   Derby/Churchill
Downs," reverse with white let-
tering listing winners from 1875
to 1963 . . . .   **25.00**
Nodder, 6½" h, Shenandoah
Downs jockey, composition, gold
paper sticker, 1962 copyright,
Japan **50.00**
Plate, Kentucky Derby Series,
Nearing Finish, Reed and Bar-
ton, 1972 . . . .   **100.00**

STAFFORDSHIRE, HISTORICAL

History: The Staffordshire district of England is the center of the English pottery
industry. There were 80 different potteries
operating there in 1786, with the number
increasing to 179 by 1802. The district includes Burslem, Cobridge, Eturia, Fenton,
Foley, Hanley, Lane Delph, Lane End,
Longport, Shelton, Stoke, and Tunstall.
Among the many famous potters were Adams, Davenport, Spode, Stevenson, Wedgwood, and Wood.

In historical Staffordshire the view is the
most critical element. American collectors
pay much less for non-American views.
Dark blue pieces are favored. Light views
continue to remain undervalued. Among the
forms, soup tureens have shown the highest price increases.

References: David and Linda Arman,
*First Supplement, Historical Staffordshire:
An Illustrated Check List,* published by au-
thors, 1977, out-of-print; David and Linda
Arman, *Historical Staffordshire: An Illus-
trated Check List,* published by authors,
1974, out-of-print; Susan and Al Bagdade,
*Warman's English & Continental Pottery &
Porcelain, Second Edition,* Wallace-Home-
stead, 1991; Ada Walker Camehl, *The Blue
China Book,* Tudor Publishing Co., 1946,
(Dover, reprint); A.W. Coysh and R. K. Hen-
rywood, *The Dictionary Of Blue And White
Printed Pottery, 1780–1880,* (1982) and *The
Dictionary of Blue and White Printed Pot-*

tery, Vol. II (1989), Antique Collectors' Club; Ellouise Larsen, *American Historical Views On Staffordshire China, 3rd Edition,* Dover Publications, 1975.

Museum: Hershey Museum, Hershey, PA.

Notes: Prices are for proof examples. Adjust prices by 20% for a slight chip, a faint hairline, or an undetectable professional repair; by 35% for knife marks through the glaze and a visible professional repair; by 50% for worn glaze and major repairs.

The numbers in parentheses refer to items in the books by Linda and David Arman, which constitute the most detailed list of American historical views and their forms.

W.ADAMS&SONS ADAMS

ADAMS

The Adams family has been associated with ceramics since the mid-17th century. In 1802 William Adams of Stoke–upon–Trent produced American views.

In 1819 a fourth William Adams, son of William of Stoke, became a partner with his father and was later joined by his three brothers. The firm became William Adams & Sons. The father died in 1829 and William, the eldest son, became manager.

The company operated four potteries at Stoke and one at Tunstall. American views were produced at Tunstall in black, light blue, sepia, pink, and green in the 1830–40 period. William Adams died in 1865. All operations were moved to Tunstall. The firm continues today under the name of Wm. Adams & Sons, Ltd.

Hudson River Series
  Fair Mount, 4″ cup plate, pink
    (459) **80.00**
  Fort Edwards, Hudson River,
    5¼″ plate, pink (460) **60.00**
  Log Cabin, Gen. Harrison medallions on border, waste bowl, brown (458) **250.00**
  U. S. Views, Catskill Mountain House, 10¼″ soup plate, light blue (445) **75.00**

CLEWS

From sketchy historical accounts that are available, it appears that James Clews took over the closed plant of A. Stevenson in 1819. His brother Ralph entered the business later. The firm continued until about 1836 when James Clews came to America to enter the pottery business at Troy, Indiana. The American venture was a failure because of the lack of skilled workmen and the proper type of clay. Clews returned to England but did not re-enter the pottery business.

Clews, plate, Don Quixote, $150.00.

Cities Series, dark and medium blue
  Philadelphia, 5½″ plate (26) . . .   **425.00**
  Quebec, 9″ plate (28) **225.00**
  Sandusky, 17″ platter, dark blue
    (B-29) **4,700.00**
Doctor Syntax, dark blue
  Doctor Syntax, advertisement for a wife, 16″ platter (64) . . .   **550.00**
  Doctor Syntax disputing his bill with landlady, 10″ plate (38) .   **225.00**

Doctor Syntax mistakes a gentleman's house for an inn, 10"
soup (42) 150.00
Doctor Syntax with the dairy
maid, 3⅞" cup plate (46) 500.00
Don Quixote Series, dark blue
Don Quixote, repose in woods,
6" plate (71) 150.00
Mambrino's Helmet, 10" d, plate
(74) 150.00
Sancho Panza and the priest
and barber, 7½" plate (75) .. 150.00
Landing of Lafayette at Castle
Garden, dark blue (1)
Mug, 4¾" h, cracks 865.00
Plate
5½" 250.00
10" 225.00
Platter, 15" 450.00
Soup Plate, 9" 275.00
Vegetable Dish, 10" square ... 900.00
Peace and Plenty, dark blue, plate
9" (A-34a) 250.00
10" (34) 225.00
Picturesque Views Series
Hudson, Hudson River, 10½"
soup plate, brown (107) 60.00
Near Hudson, Hudson River,
brown, 7" plate (113) 60.00
Pittsfield Elm, dark blue (33)
Plate, 8" 425.00
Platter, 15" 600.00
Soup Plate, 10½" d, Winter View
of Pittsfield, MA 325.00
States or American and Independence Series, dark blue
Building, Deer on Lawn, 10½"
soup plate (A-2) 500.00
Building, Sheep on Lawn, 8⅞"
plate (5) 225.00
Mansion, circular drive, vegetable dish (14) 800.00
Mansion, winding drive, 4⅞" h
creamer, unrecorded form ...1,500.00
Three Story Mansion, 4½" cup
plate, three small rim roughages (7) 400.00
Two Story Building, curved
drive, 8" plate (9) 225.00
University Building with six chimneys, two people and eight
sheep, 8¾" plate 250.00
Wilkie, Christmas Eve, 8⅞" plate,
dark blue (87) 150.00

J&J. JACKSON

J. & J. JACKSON

Job and John Jackson began operations at the Churchyard Works, Burslem, about 1830. The works formerly were owned by the Wedgwood family. The firm produced transfer scenes in a variety of colors, such as black, light blue, pink, sepia, green, maroon and mulberry. Over 40 different American views of Connecticut, Massachusetts, Pennsylvania, New York, and Ohio were issued. The firm is believed to have closed about 1844.

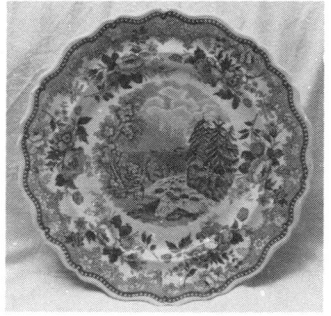

Jackson, plate, View of the Canal, Little Falls, Mohawk River, American Scenery Series, (490), 10½" d, $125.00.

American Scenery Series, all colors
Deaf & Dumb Asylum, Phila, 7"
plate (471) 70.00
Fort Ticonderoga, New York,
gravy tureen with cover (473) 250.00
State House, Boston, 10½" plate
(484) 60.00
View of the Canal, Little Falls,
Mohawk River, 10½" plate
(490) 125.00
Miscellaneous
New York, Select Sketches series, 17" platter (496) 400.00
Schenectady on Mohawk River,
8" pitcher (494) 275.00

THOMAS MAYER

In 1829, Thomas Mayer and his brothers, John and Joshua, purchased Stubbs' Dale Hall Works of Burslem. They continued to produce a superior grade of ceramics.

Arms of the American States, dark blue
GA, 11¾" vegetable dish (500) **3,000.00**
MA, 9½" platter (502) **3,500.00**
MD, ftd scalloped rim punch bowl, 4⅞" h, 11½" d, unlisted form, brilliant, high glaze, soft blue, crisp transfer **8,700.00**
NY
9¾" plate **650.00**
10" plate **600.00**
RI, c1829, 8½" plate **460.00**
Lafayette
At Washington's Tomb, dark blue, sugar bowl (511) **700.00**
At Franklin's Tomb, dark blue, waste bowl (512) **600.00**

J.W. R.

JOHN & WILLIAM RIDGWAY - c.1814-1830

Stone China

W. RIDGWAY

J. & W. RIDGWAY AND WILLIAM RIDGWAY & CO.

John and William Ridgway, sons of Job Ridgway and nephews of George Ridgway who owned Bell Bank Works and Couldon Place Works, produced the popular Beauties of America series at the Couldon plant. The partnership between the two brothers was dissolved in 1830. John remained at Couldon.

William managed the Bell Bank works until 1854. Two additional series were produced based upon the etchings of Bartlett's American Scenery. The first series had various borders including narrow lace. The second series is known as Catskill Moss.

Beauties of America is in dark blue. The other series are found in the light transfer colors of light blue, pink, brown, black, and green.

Ridgway, platter, Syndey Sussex College, Cambridge, light blue, lattice edge, 9½ x 11¾", $450.00.

American Scenery
Columbia Bridge on the Susquehanna, pitcher (281) **275.00**
Peekskill Landing, Hudson River, vegetable dish (287) .. **200.00**
Beauties of America, dark blue
Almshouse, New York, 16" platter (255) **600.00**
Boston State House, custard cup, 2¾" h, very minor rim chip **145.00**
City Hall, New York, 10" plate, medium dark blue (A-260) ... **190.00**
Court House, Boston, 10½" platter, medium dark blue **1,100.00**

Exchange
Baltimore, cup plate (264) . . .	**450.00**
Charleston, 8½″ gravy tureen undertray	**600.00**
Hospital, Boston, 12″ platter, medium dark blue	**950.00**
Library, Phila, 8″ plate (268) . . .	**175.00**
Octagon Church, Boston, 10″ soup plate, medium dark blue (A-271)	**265.00**
Pennsylvania Hospital, Philadelphia, 19″ platter, medium dark blue (B-272)	**1,100.00**

Catskill Moss
Kosciusko's Tomb, 10″ soup (305)	**70.00**
Meredith, 9½″ plate (307)	**60.00**
President's House, tray (311) . .	**100.00**

Columbia Star, Harrison's Log Cabin
End View, soup (276)	**90.00**
Side View	
Plate, 10¼″, plowing, (277) . .	**90.00**
Sugar Bowl (277)	**275.00**

ROGERS

ROGERS

John Rogers and his brother George established a pottery near Longport in 1782. After George's death in 1815, John's son Spencer became a partner and the firm operated under the name of John Rogers & Sons. John died in 1816. His son continued the use of the name until he dissolved the pottery in 1842.

Boston Harbor, dark blue (441)
Cup and Saucer	**600.00**
Sugar Bowl	**600.00**

Boston State House, dark blue (442)
Plate, 10″	**125.00**
Platter, 14″	**475.00**
Sauce Tureen, cov, 8″ l, cov repaired	**350.00**

Zebra, medium dark blue
Basket, openwork, scalloped rim, emb handles, underglaze eagle and imp marks	**575.00**
Cup and Saucer	**175.00**

c 1816 -1830

R. S. W.

STEVENSON

As early as the 17th century the name Stevenson was associated with the pottery industry. Andrew Stevenson of Cobridge introduced American scenes with the flower and scroll border. Ralph Stevenson, also of Cobridge, used a vine and leaf border on his dark blue historical views and a lace border on his series in light transfers.

The initials R. S. & W. indicate Ralph Stevenson and Williams are associated with the acorn and leaf border. It has been reported that Williams was Ralph's New York agent and the wares were produced by Ralph alone.

Acorn and Oak Leaves Border, dark blue
Baltimore Exchange, 5½″ plate (348)	**750.00**
Harvard College, 8⅜″ d, plate, dark blue	**275.00**
Octagon Church, Boston, 4½″ cup plate (356)	**750.00**
Park Theater, New York, 10″ plate (357)	**175.00**
St Paul's Chapel, New York, medium blue, 6¼″ plate (359) . .	**800.00**

Floral and Scroll Border, dark blue
City Hall, New York, 7″ plate (397)	**1,100.00**
Columbia College, New York, 6½″ soup (398)	**900.00**

New York
  From Brooklyn Heights, medium blue 10¼" plate **950.00**
  From Heights near Brooklyn, medium dark blue 16¼" platter 1,600.00
Lace Border
  Erie Canal at Buffalo, 10" soup (386) **150.00**
  New Orleans
    Cup and Saucer (387) **100.00**
    Teapot (387) **225.00**
Vine Border
  Almshouse, Boston, 14" platter (365) **700.00**
  Capitol, Washington, 10" soup (370) **400.00**

Spread Eagle Border, dark blue
  Church in the City of New York, 6⅛" plate (322) **750.00**
  City Hall, New York, 6½" plate, (A-323) **200.00**
  Fair Mount Near Philadelphia, 10" plate (A-324a) **200.00**
  Upper Ferry Bridge over the River Schuykill 8¾" plate (332) **150.00**

WOOD

Enoch Wood, sometimes referred to as the Father of English Pottery, began operating a pottery at Fountain Place, Burslem, in 1783. A cousin, Ralph Wood, was associated with him. In 1790 James Caldwell became a partner and the firm was known as Wood and Caldwell. In 1819 Wood and his sons took full control.

Enoch died in 1840. His sons continued under the name of Enoch Wood & Sons. The American views were first made in the mid-1820s and continued through the 1840s.

It is reported that the pottery produced more signed historical views than any other Staffordshire firm. Many of the views attributed to unknown makers probably came from the Woods.

Marks vary, although always include the name Wood. The establishment was sold to Messrs. Pinder, Bourne & Hope in 1846.

Celtic China, light transfer colors
  Buffalo on Lake Erie, vegetable dish (236) **275.00**
  Harvard College, 10" plate (240) **100.00**
  Natural Bridge, VA, 9¼" plate (244) **75.00**
  Pass in the Catskill Mountains, 7" plate (247) **75.00**
  Trenton Falls, 8" plate (251) ... **60.00**
Floral Border, irregular, dark blue

c1828-1830

STUBBS

In 1790 Stubbs established a pottery works at Burslem, England. He operated it until 1829 when he retired and sold the pottery to the Mayer brothers. He probably produced his American views about 1825. Many of his scenes were from Boston, New York, New Jersey and Philadelphia.

Rose Border, dark blue
  Bank of the United States, Philadelphia, 10" d plate, small chips to foot rim **345.00**
  City Hall, NY
    Pitcher, 6" h (335) **375.00**
    Sugar Bowl (336) **350.00**
    Teapot (336) **500.00**

Commodore   MacDonnough's
Victory (154)
Cream Pitcher, 3½" h, barrel
shaped **1,750.00**
Plate
9¼", some glaze wear 230.00
10", small rim chip 345.00
Erie Canal, View of the Aque-
duct Bridge at Little Falls (158)
Pitcher, 6½" **1,250.00**
Soup Plate, 10¼" 850.00
Sugar Bowl 750.00
Landing of the Pilgrims, Landing
of the Fathers, medium blue, 10"
plate, pr (218) 250.00
Shell Border, circular center, dark
blue
Baltimore and Ohio Railroad,
10⅛" soup plate (183) 700.00
Chief Justice Marshall Troy, 8⅛"
plate (127) 450.00
Chiswick on the Thames, gravy
tureen, orig lid, undertray, and
ladle **2,000.00**
City of Albany, 10¼" plate (163) 425.00
Highlands, Hudson River, 5¾"
plate (167) 875.00
Mount Vernon, 7½" plate (173) 500.00
Railroad, Baltimore and Ohio,
10" plate (183) 600.00
Union Line, 10" plate (144) 575.00
Shell Border, irregular center, dark
blue
Commodore   MacDonnough's
Victory (130)
Plate, 9" 375.00
Teapot 750.00
Cowes Harbor, 6½" plate (B-
132) 215.00
Eddistone Lighthouse, 8½" open
vegetable dish 700.00
Union Line, 9¼" plate (144) . . . 375.00
Wadsworth Tower, 4½" pitcher
(147) 550.00

UNKNOWN MAKERS

American Naval Heroes, pitcher,
6" h 700.00
Anti-Slavery (608)
Cup Plate, 4", light blue 450.00
Plate, 6", light blue 200.00
Basket of Flowers, 4½" cup plate,
dark blue 100.00

Batahla, 11 x 8½" oval bowl, dark
blue **900.00**
Erie Canal inscription
Pitcher, 5¾", dark blue (598) . . **1,400.00**
Plate, 10" (597) 450.00
Maypole, 6¾" pitcher, medium
dark blue, floral border, village
scene with livestock in fore-
ground, people dancing 200.00
Mount Vernon, the Seat of the late
Gen'l Washington, sugar bowl,
cov, 7" l, imperfections 175.00

STAFFORDSHIRE ITEMS

History: A wide variety of ornamental
pottery items originated in England's Staffordshire district, beginning in the 17th century and extending to the present. The
height of production was from 1820 to 1890.
These naive pieces are considered folk
art by many collectors. Most items were not
made carefully; some were even made and
decorated by children.
The types of objects are varied, e.g., animals, cottages, and figurines (chimney ornaments). The key to price is age and condition. The older the piece, the higher the
price is a general rule.

References: Susan and Al Bagdade,
*Warman's English & Continental Pottery &
Porcelain, Second Edition,* Wallace-Home-
stead, 1991; Pat Halfpenny, *English Earth-
enware Figures, 1740–1840,* Antique Col-
lectors' Club, 1992; Charles Kenyon Kies,
*Collecting Victorian Staffordshire Pottery
Figures,* Antique Publications, 1989; P. D.
Gordon Pugh, *Staffordshire Portrait Figures
Of The Victorian Era,* Antique Collectors'
Club, 1987; Dennis G. Rice, *English Por-
celain Animals Of The 19th Century,* An-
tique Collectors' Club, 1989.

Animal Dish, cov, hen, black and
white, light brown basketweave
base, 8" l 250.00
Bank, cottage, white snow cov
roof, two chimneys, black out-
line, c1885, 5" h 200.00
Chimney Ornament, two girls at
dog house, one on roof, other
petting dog at door, 6" h 100.00

Teabowl, hounds surrounded by scrolling foliage, c1858, unmarked, 3¼" h, $45.00.

Figure
Girl, holding basket, mottled yellow and brown glaze, early 19th C, 4⅜" h **115.00**
King and Queen of Prussia, 19th C, 16½" h, price for pair **450.00**
King Edward VII and Queen Alexandra, 14¾" h, pr **250.00**
Lion, open mouth, curled tail, front leg resting on globe, rect base with acanthus leaf border, 11" l, 9" h, pr **5,525.00**
Queen of England, 19th C, 17¾" h **325.00**
Recumbent Lion, oval plinth, chip to one ear, 19th C, 11¼" h **165.00**
Spaniel, seated, gold luster detail, 19th C, pr
9⅛" h **175.00**
12⅜" h, painted face, hairlines **430.00**
Victor and Moses, 19th C, 9¾" h **350.00**
Village Maid, young woman seated on tree stump reading book, glaze chips, early 19th C, 10⅜" h **400.00**
Whieldon, man wearing hat, draped with scarf, riding horse, cream and green glaze, mid 18th C, 8¼" h **865.00**
Whippet, holding hare, 19th C, 7½" h **165.00**
Figural Group, hunter with dead tiger atop elephant, loss to tusks and enamel, 19th C, 8¾" h ... **415.00**
Fruit Basket, undertray, Zebra pattern, imp "John Rogers & Son, England," blue, c1814–36, 8¾" l **925.00**
Inkwell, man, black hat and breeches, green jacket, blue scarf, red shirt, holding fish, seated on tan mound, basket form inkwell, mid 19th C, 4⅞" h **150.00**
Jug, commemorative, canary yellow and silver luster, iron–red transfer portrait of Sir Francis Burdett, inscription below, obverse with additional text within foliage wreath, silver luster neck, iron–red band at rim, handle, and spout, c1810, 6½" h **600.00**
Mug, child's, maxim transfer **140.00**
Pastille Burner, house, yellow sides, gray windows, arched ochre door, olive green roof, two yellow chimneys with brown edging, green grassy mound base, c1790, 4⅝" h **675.00**
Plate
4½" d, child's, octagonal, multicolored transfers, raised flower dec borders, price for pair **135.00**
10" d
Joseph Stubbs, blue, minor imperfections, set of nine .. **1,500.00**
R Hall & Son, Pains Hill Survey, blue, marked on base, minor imperfections, second quarter 19th C, set of twelve **1,150.00**
Platter
16¾" l, polar bear hunt, blue, imp "Enoch Wood & Sons Burslem," imperfections, second quarter 19th C **865.00**
17" l, Gyrn, Flintshire Wales, R Hall & Son, blue, second quarter 19th C **700.00**
23" l, pastoral scene enclosed by floral border, blue, imperfections, 19th C **575.00**
Sauce Tureen, cov, undertray, fruit pattern, blue, chips, second quarter 19th C, 8¼" l tureen ... **635.00**
Stirrup Cup, fox head, grape and leaf base, 19th C, 5" h **200.00**
Supper Set, blue and white, dog handles, four fans form cov serving dishes dec with rabbits in garden, mahogany oval tray, second quarter 19th C, 23" l .. **1,725.00**
Toby, begging spaniel, 19th C, 10" h **165.00**

Vase, figural
  Couple with dog beside tree
  trunk, sheep below, 19th C .. **300.00**
  Squirrel holding nuts, 19th C,
  6¼" h, pr **1,020.00**

STAFFORDSHIRE, ROMANTIC

History: In the 1830s two factors transformed the blue and white printed wares of the Staffordshire potters into what is now called "Romantic Staffordshire." Technical innovations expanded the range of transfer–printed colors to light blue, pink, purple, black, green, and brown. There was also a shift from historical to imaginary scenes. These patterns had less printed detail and more white space, adding to the pastel effect.

Shapes in the 1830s were predominately rococo with rounded forms, scroll handles, and floral finials. With time, patterns and shapes became simpler and the earthenware bodies coarser. The late 1840s and 1850s saw angular gothic shapes and the weight and texture of ironstone.

The most dramatic post–1870 change was the impact of the Japanese design craze with zig–zag border elements and such motifs as bamboo, fans, and cranes. Brown printing dominated this style, sometimes with polychrome enamel highlights.

Wares are often marked with pattern or potter's names, but marking was inconsistent and many authentic unmarked examples exist. The addition of "England" as a country of origin mark in 1891 helps to distinguish 20th–century wares made in the romantic style.

References: Susan and Al Bagdade, *Warman's English & Continental Pottery & Porcelain, Second Edition,* Wallace-Homestead, 1991; Petra Williams, *Staffordshire: Romantic Transfer Patterns,* Fountain House East, 1978; Petra Williams, *Staffordshire II,* Fountain House East, 1986.

Advisors: Mark R. Brown and Tim M. Sublette.

Caledonia, William Adams, 1830s
  Plate
    7½" d **90.00**
    10½" d **135.00**

Plate, Tuscan Rose, dark brown transfer, marked "JWR," 9¼" d, $30.00.

Platter, 17" l **500.00**
Soup Plate, two color **165.00**
Canova, Thomas Mayer, c1835; G
  Phillips, c1840
  Plate, 10½" d **95.00**
  Pudding Bowl, two color **225.00**
  Vegetable, cov **350.00**
Columbia, W Adams & Sons, 1850
  Creamer **110.00**
  Cup and Saucer **55.00**
  Cup Plate **55.00**
  Plate, 10" d **55.00**
  Relish **65.00**
Coral Border, Thomas Dimmock,
  1830s, chestnut basket, without
  tray **275.00**
Dado, Ridgways, 1880s
  Creamer, brown **75.00**
  Cup and Saucer, polychrome .. **75.00**
  Plate
    7½" d, brown **35.00**
    8½" d, polychrome **55.00**
    10½" d, polychrome **70.00**
  Platter, 11½" l, polychrome **150.00**
  Sugar, brown **85.00**
Japonica, maker unknown, 1830s
  Creamer **125.00**
  Sugar **135.00**
Marmora, William Ridgway & Co,
  1830s
  Platter, 16½" l **325.00**
  Sauce Tureen, matching tray .. **350.00**
  Soup Plate **90.00**
Melbourne, Gildea & Walker, 1881
  Sauce Tureen, matching tray .. **165.00**

Soup Plate	50.00
Vegetable, cov	150.00
Millenium, Ralph Stevenson & Son, 1830s, plate, 10½" d	135.00
Palestine, William Adams, 1836	
Creamer	135.00
Cup and Saucer	
Single color	55.00
Two color	135.00
Cup Plate	55.00
Plate	
5" d	45.00
6" d	45.00
7" d	45.00
8½" d	50.00
9½" d	
Single color	55.00
Two color	110.00
10" d	100.00
Platter	
13" l	325.00
15" l	350.00
17" l	375.00
Sugar	165.00
Tall Pot	600.00
Teapot	350.00
Vegetable, open	
10" l	135.00
12" l	200.00
Union, William Ridgway Son & Co, 1840s	
Plate, 10½" d	65.00
Platter, 15" l	175.00
Venus, Podmore, Walker & Co, 1850s	
Plate	
7½" d	45.00
10" d	55.00
Sugar	110.00

STAINED AND/OR LEADED GLASS PANELS

History: American architects in the second half of the 19th century and the early 20th century used stained and leaded glass panels as a chief decorative element. The designs were assembled by skilled glass craftsmen, the best known being Louis C. Tiffany.

The panels are held together with soft lead cames or copper wraps. When pur-

chasing a panel, check the lead and have any repairs made to protect your investment.

Periodicals: *Glass Art Magazine,* PO Box 260377, Highlands Ranch, CO 80126; *Glass Patterns Quarterly,* PO Box 131, Westport, NY 40077.

Collectors' Club: Stained Glass Association of America, PO Box 22462, Kansas City, MO 64113.

Museum: Corning Museum of Glass, Corning, NY.

Panel, arched, Star of David center motif, American, c1900, 55½ x 24", $1,250.00.

Leaded
Fire Screen, 29" w, 25½" h, three panel, central red bull's eye, side panel blue bull's eyes centered by pale yellow, amethyst, pale green and amber geometric pattern, scrolling brass frame, unsigned, Boston, c1910 ....**2,185.00**
Window
36" w, 100" h, cathedral arched panel, multicolored and textured glass segments, copy of waterfall window designed by Tiffany Studios for the First Reformed Church of Albany, some segments damaged .**5,750.00**
38½" w, 37⅞" l, Prairie School, designed by Purcell and Elmslie for Woodbury County Courthouse, Sioux City, IA, amber ripple arrowheads topped by orange glass over horizontal green ripple bar, blue ripple bar highlighted in yellow, opales-

cent ground, light blue int. border highlighted by orange, green and blue, opalescent caramel slag border, c1915 .... **2,990.00**

Stained

30″ l, 17″ h, hunt scent, primarily shades of dark green and blue, later mounted in pink cabinet, illuminated from within **225.00**

39″ l, 24½″ h, blue shield crest, yellow faceted circular center surrounded by floral vines, flanked by elongated pointed panels, squared diamond motif, light pink reserve, orig frame **285.00**

STANGL POTTERY BIRDS

History: Stangl ceramic birds were produced from 1940 until the Stangl factory closed in 1972. The birds were produced at Stangl's Trenton plant and shipped to their Flemington, New Jersey, plant for hand painting.

During World War II the demand for these birds and Stangl pottery was so great that 40 to 60 decorators could not keep up with it. Orders were contracted out to private homes. These orders then were returned for firing and finishing. Colors used to decorate these birds varied according to the artist.

As many as ten different trademarks were used. Almost every bird is numbered; many are artist signed. However, the signatures are used only for dating purposes and add very little to the value of the birds.

Several birds were reissued between 1972 and 1977. These reissues are dated on the bottom and valued at approximately one half of the older birds.

References: Susan and Al Bagdade, *Warman's American Pottery and Porcelain,* Wallace–Homestead, 1994; Harvey Duke, *Stangl Pottery,* Wallace-Homestead, 1992; Harvey Duke, *The Official Identification And Price Guide To Pottery And Porcelain, Eighth Edition,* House of Collectibles, 1994; Joan Dworkin and Martha Horman, *A Guide To Stangl Pottery Birds,* Willow Pond Books, 1973; Norma Rehl, *The Collectors Handbook of Stangl Pottery,* Democrat Press, 1982; Mike Schneider, *Stangl and Pennsbury Birds,* Schiffer Publishing, 1994.

Collectors' Club: Stangl Bird Collectors Association, PO Box 419, Ringoes, NJ 08551.

Additional Listings: See *Warman's Americana & Collectibles* for more examples.

#3276, blue, yellow ground, $85.00.

3250E, Drinking duck, 3¾″ h	**60.00**
3400, Lovebird	**55.00**
3401, Wren, 3½″ h	**50.00**
3401D, Wren, pr, 8″ h	**90.00**
3402S, Oriole, 3¼″ h, orig tag ...	**40.00**
3405S, Cockatoo	**45.00**
3406S, Kingfisher, 3½″ h	**50.00**
3408, Bird of Paradise	**125.00**
3444, Cardinal, 6½″ h	**55.00**
3447, Prothonatary Warbler	**100.00**
3454, Key West Quail Dove, small crazing hairline on leaf	**225.00**
3456, Creulean Warbler	**68.00**
3484, Cockatoo, 11⅜″ h	**190.00**
3491, Hen Pheasant, 6¼ x 11″ ..	**140.00**
3492, Cock Pheasant, 6¼ x 11″ .	**140.00**
3580, Cockatoo, sgd "D C F" ...	**65.00**
3581, Chickadees	**225.00**
3582D, Parakeets	**300.00**
3583, Parula Warbler, 4¼″ h, orig tag	**50.00**
3585, Rufous Hummingbird, 3″ h	**50.00**
3589, Indigo Bunting, 3¼″ h	**85.00**
3590, Chat, 4¼″ h	**100.00**
3592, Titmouse	**68.00**
3594, Red–Faced Warbler, 3″ h .	**55.00**
3595, Bobolink, 4¾″ h	**125.00**

3597, Wilson Warbler, 3½" h	65,00
3598, Kentucky Warbler, 3" h, orig tag	40.00
3599D, Hummingbird, pr, 8 x 10½"	240.00
3626, Broadtail Hummingbird ...	130.00
3627, Hummingbird	40.00
3628, Rieffers Hummingbird, 4½" h	125.00
3629, Hummingbird	125.00
3634, Allen Hummingbird, 3½" h .	40.00
3813, Evening Grossbeak	95.00
3853, Group of Kinglets	375.00

STEIFF

History: Margarete Steiff, GmbH, established in Germany in 1880, is known for very fine-quality stuffed animals and dolls as well as other beautifully made collectible toys. It is still in business, and its products are highly respected.

The company's first products were woolfelt elephants made by Margaret Steiff. In a few years the elephant line was expanded to include a donkey, horse, pig, and camel.

By 1903 the company also was producing a jointed mohair Teddy Bear, whose production dramatically increased to over 970,000 units in 1907. Margarete's nephews took over the company at this point. The bear's head became the symbol for its label, and the famous "Button in the Ear" round, metal trademark was added.

Newly designed animals were added: Molly and Bully, the dogs, and Fluffy, the cat. Pull toys and kites also were produced, as well as larger animals on which children could ride or play.

Become familiar with genuine Steiff products before purchasing an antique stuffed animal. Plush in old Steiff animals was mohair; trimmings usually were felt or velvet. Unscrupulous individuals have attached the familiar Steiff metal button to animals that are not Steiff.

References: Peggy and Alan Bialosky, *The Teddy Bear Catalog,* Workman Publishing, Revised Edition, 1984; Jurgen & Marianne Cieslik, *Button In Ear: The History of Teddy Bear and His Friends,* distributed by Theriault's, 1989; Margaret Fox Mandel, *Teddy Bears And Steiff Animals,* First Series (1984, 1993 value update), Second Series (1987), Collector Books; Margaret Fox Mandel, *Teddy Bears, Annalee Animals & Steiff Animals, Third Series,* Collector Books, 1990; Dana G. Morykan and Harry L. Rinker, *Warman's Country Antiques & Collectibles, Second Edition,* Wallace–Homestead, 1994; Linda Mullins, *Teddy Bear & Friends Price Guide, Fourth Edition,* Hobby House Press, 1993; Christel & Rolf Pistorius, *Steiff: Sensational Teddy Bear, Animals & Dolls,* Hobby House Press, 1991; Jean Wilson, *Steiff Toys Revisited,* Wallace–Homestead, 1989.

Collectors' Club: Steiff Collectors Club, PO Box 798, Holland, OH 43528.

Additional Listings: Teddy Bears. See Stuffed Toys in *Warman's Americana & Collectibles* for more examples.

Bambi, deer, 1939, 32" to top of head, $400.00.

Boy, 27" h, Souvenir of Berchtesgaden, felt, blond mohair hair, black button eyes, traditional costume, black leather shoes, green knapsack, shovel and hoe, early 1930s	**1,035.00**
Camel, 11" h, raised script button, 1950s	190.00
Cat, 3" h, Tapsy, raised script button, orig ribbon and bell	110.00
Dachshund, 14" l, button and yellow tag in ear	55.00
Donkey, 4½" h, mohair, gray, black mane, red leather bridle, chest tag	135.00

Elephant, 7″ h, mohair, gray, standing, plastic tusks, red felt blanket and bells, 1950–60 . . . . **125.00**
Fox Terrier, 6½″ h, mohair, white, standing, black and brown markings **65.00**
Goat, 6″ h, mohair, frosted, brown, black felt horns, 1950–60 . . . . . **75.00**
Koala Bear, 8″ h, mohair, gray, beige, and cream, fully jointed, chest tag **500.00**
Leopard, 8½″ l, baby, paper label **150.00**
Mickey Mouse, 6″ h, velvet, leather applied eyes, metal button in left ear, orig cardboard tag, early 1930s **1,955.00**
Rabbit, 8″ h, mohair, beige, tan, and white, jointed neck, brown glass eyes, pink stitched nose and mouth, blue ribbon around neck, chrome button **150.00**
Teddy Bear, 14″ h, voicebox, felt pads, black eyes, button in ear **600.00**
Tiger, 4¼″ h, baby, seated **225.00**

Porcelain, Second Edition, Wallace-Homestead, 1991; John L. Hairell, *Regimental Steins,* published by author, 1984; Gary Kirsner, *German Military Steins, Revised Edition,* Glentiques, 1995; Gary Kirsner, *The Mettlach Book, Third Edition,* Glentiques, 1994; Gary Kirsner and Jim Gruhl, *The Stein Book,* Glentiques, 1984; Eugene Manusov, *Encyclopedia of Character Steins,* Wallace-Homestead, 1976, out-of-print; Eugene V. Manusov and Mike Wald, *Character Steins: A Collector's Guide,* Cornwall Books, 1987; James R. Stevenson, *Antique Steins: A Collectors' Guide, Second Edition,* Cornwall Books, 1989; Mike Wald, *HR Steins,* SCI Publications, 1980.

Collectors' Club: Stein Collectors International, 3530 Mimosa Court, New Orleans, LA 70131.

Periodicals: *Stein Line,* PO Box 48716, Chicago, IL 60648-0716; *The Beer Stein Journal,* PO Box 8807, Coral Springs, FL 33075.

1892-1921

STEINS

History: A stein is a mug especially made to hold beer or ale, ranging in size from the smaller ³⁄₁₀ liters and ¼ liters to the larger 1, 1½, 2, 3, 4, and 5 liters, and in rare cases to 8 liters. (A liter is 1.05 liquid quarts.)

Master steins or pouring steins hold 3 to 5 liters and are called krugs. Most steins are fitted with a metal hinged lid with thumblift. The earthenware character-type steins usually are German in origin.

References: Susan and Al Bagdade, *Warman's English & Continental Pottery &*

Regimental, ½ L, porcelain, Bruder Stolst Die Glaseran Reserve, 1910–12, officer lithophane, $950.00.

China, 4¾″ h, 3⅞″ d, hinged pewter top, monk with stein, large keg in background, rust brown dec, marked "C. P. & Co," and "Manning Bowman & Co, Meriden, Conn" on base **100.00**

Glass

    6" h, pressed, applied glass handle, pewter top with porcelain inlay of dancing couple wearing Bavarian costume, house in background **60.00**

    7½" h, pewter lid with dwarf in relief, eagle thumbrest, enameled hops, barley, and goat dec, dated 1888 . . . .   **130.00**

    9¼" h, 4" d, irid honey colored ground, applied glass handle, hinged pewter lid, lacy white enameled leaves and scrolls dec around middle **260.00**

Mosaic, 7" h, ½ L, panels with gentleman, maiden holding steins, and wandering man wearing lederhosen, marked "L 1266," base chip **45.00**

Pewter, 8" h, ¼ L, Bonn relief scenes, Besetzlich Geschutz, F M & N Company **40.00**

Porcelain

    5" h, brown and white, golfer in knickers ready to hit ball, lid with porcelain inlay scene of Brooklyn Bridge, bottom marked "Paris, France O'Hara Dial Co., Waltham Massachusetts U.S.A." **550.00**

    7" h, Delft style, blue and white, windmills and sailing ships, porcelain lid in pewter ring, c1950 . . . .   **200.00**

Pottery

    4½" h, ½ L, occupational, beekeeper and beehive emblem, light blue ground, Mettlach, sgd "H.D.," #1526, 663 Geschutz **100.00**

    7½" h, relief dec of man with scale weighing beer keg and mugs, base imp with "328" on relief banner, jeweled pewter top, Villeroy & Boch **325.00**

Stoneware, 7¾" h, Old Sleepy Eye, blue–gray, Flemish **450.00**

Wood, 11" h, 1" w banding, two quadruple plated ribbons with Art Nouveau blossoms wrapped around top and bottom, St Louis Silver Co, c1905 . . . .   **300.00**

1903–32

STEUBEN GLASS

History: Frederick Carder, an Englishman, and Thomas G. Hawkes of Corning, New York, established the Steuben Glass Works in 1904. In 1918 the Corning Glass Company purchased the Steuben company. Carder remained with the firm and designed many of the pieces bearing the Steuben mark. Probably the most widely recognized wares are "Aurene," "Verre De Soie," and "Rosaline," but many other types were produced.

The firm continues operating, producing glass of exceptional quality.

References: Paul Gardner, *The Glass of Frederick Carder,* Crown Publishers, 1971; Paul Perrot, Paul Gardner, and James S. Plaut, *Steuben: Seventy Years Of American Glassmaking,* Praeger Publishers, 1974; Ellen T. Schroy, *Warman's Glass,* Wallace-Homestead, 1992.

Museums: Corning Museum of Glass, Corning, NY; Rockwell Museum, Corning, NY.

AURENE

AURENE

Bowl

    3¾" d, 1¾" h, gold, satin finish, #818 . . . .   **220.00**

    8" d, platinum blue irid, low bowl, three applied feet, inscribed "Aurene 2586," three prong base, marked "Steuben/Aurene 2744," price for pair **920.00**

Candlesticks, pr, 10" h, blue, twisted stems, inscribed "Steuben/Aurene 686," some variation in silvery luster **1,380.00**

Center Bowl, 12" d, 4¾" h, gold, brilliant stretched irid, inscribed "Aurene 2852" **750.00**

Vase, green swirl pattern, scalloped edge, sgd, 7½" h, $210.00

Compote, 6½" d, 6" h, blue, stretched silver blue irid, six crimps, bright blue twist stem and base, inscribed "Steuben/Aurene 367" **815.00**

Jack-in-the-Pulpit Vase, 6" h, floriform, gold, irid luster, inscribed "Aurene 2699" **1,610.00**

Lampshade
4¾" h, 7" d, 3⅞" collet edge, bulbous, ten–rib, white calcite ext., gold aurene int., fleur-de-lis mark, some chips at collet edge **290.00**
5" h, 2¼" collet edge, gold, ten–rib, trumpet shape, fleur-de-lis mark, price for set of three . . **345.00**

Lamp, table, 21" h, gold, ruffled edge 14" d dome shade, matching base, shade inscribed "F. Carder–Aurene" under gilt metal cap and finial **2,415.00**

Perfume, 6¾" h, gold, tapered cones, conforming stopper, inscribed "Aurene 3294," one dauber damaged, price for pair **1,035.00**

Planter Bowl, 10" d, flat round, fine color, irid, inscribed "Aurene 2586," some int. scratches **520.00**

Salt, blue/gold irid, marked "Aurene #564" **265.00**

Vase
5" h, archetypical flared oval, faint ten–rib molding, blue, inscribed "Steuben" **635.00**
6½" h, triparite, gold, three prong flower holder, inscribed "Steuben/Aurene 2744" . . . . :. **750.00**

8" h, shouldered classic form, blue, silvered luster shading to mirror bright base, inscribed "Steuben/Aurene 2144" **865.00**

8½" h, 8" d, flared top, blue, eight tooled crimps, fine lustrous irid, 1952 variant, inscribed "Steuben" on base . . **1,100.00**

10½" h, broad classic shape, blue, silvery irid, inscribed "Steuben Aurene 2683," minor surface wear **1,035.00**

14" h, classic oval flared body, cupped disk base, gold, satiny irid allover luster **1,150.00**

CRYSTAL

Animal, pigeon
6½" l, 6" h, #6824, cut, inscribed "Steuben," minor chips at wing tips, price for pair **1,725.00**
7¼" l, 6" h, #7729, pouter, Sidney Waugh design, molded, uncut model **425.00**

Center Bowl, 10¼" l, 7¾" w, 7½" h, ovoid, designed by Donald Pollard **320.00**

Decanter, 17" h, three applied neck rings, solid bull's eye stopper, Frederick Carder design #7712, price for pair **980.00**

Goblet, 7¼" h, bulbed teardrop stem, Sidney Waugh design, #7737, orig Fifth Ave box, price for set of twelve **1,150.00**

Luminor, 9¾" h, pineapple, spiral controlled bubble paperweight crystal, central teardrop, orig black glass light box **690.00**

Vase
7" h, flared ribbed clear ground, irregular applied Rosa reeded, faint fleur-de-lis mark on base **230.00**
13¾" h, Lotus, eight applied petals below flared trumpet form, inscribed "Steuben" **375.00**

JADE

Beverage Set, 9½" h pitcher, four 6" h lemonade tumblers, deep green, applied alabaster handles, price for five pc set **690.00**

Bowl, 8" d, 7" h, green, layered in alabaster, acid etched Art Deco style Matzu dec, Japaneseque trees and clouds, #6078 ...... **805.00**

Center Bowl, 12" d, 4⅜" h, green, flared, applied alabaster disk base, #5022 .... **320.00**

Compote, 10" d, 4" h, yellow, translucent butterscotch coloring, #3234 ....**1,265.00**

Vase, oval body, alabaster casing, acid etched dec, repeating elements of exotic birds, blossoming trees, #938 ....**2,185.00**

MISCELLANEOUS

Bowl, 11" d, Pomona Green, sgd **135.00**

Center Bowl, 11¾" d, 5" h, swirled topaz bowl, celeste blue, cupped pedestal foot, mica inclusions, folded edge **345.00**

Dessert Bowl, ftd, Bristol Yellow, #7724, sgd **60.00**

Disk, 16" d, Tyrian, leaf and vine dec, raised irid threading applied over green–purple surface, Frederick Carder **16,100.00**

Lampshade, green and gold on calcite, pulled feather dec **150.00**

Perfume, 5⅞" h, Verre de Soie, eight bulb base, four bulb teardrop stopper, full-length dauber, #2183 .... **445.00**

Vase

6¾" h, Intarsia, flared oval crystal, internal midnight blue/ black dec, applied double wafer stem, sq black foot, inscribed "Fred'k Carder" at side **7,475.00**

7" h, Cintra, green, white, and gray, sgd **550.00**

8" h, baluster, ruffled top, blue . **600.00**

11" h, 8" d, topaz and blue, brilliant applied Flemish blue rim wrap, solid disk foot, #938 variant **230.00**

12" h, 7" w, Rosaline, threading, #6812, sgd **250.00**

13¼" h, flattened oval, mottled green cintra overlaid with alabaster, acid etched Carder's sculptured chrysanthemum

pattern, Art Deco border, #6589, large fleur-de-lis mark etched at lower side **5,475.00**

STEVENGRAPHS

History: Thomas Stevens of Coventry, England, first manufactured woven silk designs in 1854. His first bookmark was produced in 1862, followed by the first Stevengraphs, perhaps in 1874, but definitely by 1879 at the York Exhibition. The first "portrait" Stevengraphs (of Disraeli and Gladstone) were produced in 1886, and the first post cards incorporating the silk woven panels in 1904. Stevens offered many other items with silk panels, including valentines, fans, pincushions, needle cases, etc.

Stevengraphs are miniature silk pictures, matted in cardboard, and usually having a trade announcement, or "label," affixed to the reverse. Of the early Stevengraphs Thomas Stevens' name appears on the mat directly under the silk panel. Many of the later "portraits" and the larger silks (produced initially for calendars) have no identification on the front of the mat other than the phrase "woven in pure silk" and have no label on the back. Other companies, notably W. H. Grant of Coventry, copied this technique. Their efforts should not be confused with Stevengraphs.

American collectors favor the Stevengraphs of American interest, such as "Signing of the Declaration of Independence," "Columbus Leaving Spain," and "Landing of Columbus." Sports-related Stevengraphs such as "The First Innings" (baseball) and "The First Set" (tennis) are also popular, as well as portraits of Buffalo Bill, President and Mrs. Cleveland, George Washington, and President Harrison.

The bookmarks are longer than they are wide, have mitered corners at the bottom, and are finished with a tassel. Originally, Stevens' name was woven into the foldover at the top of the silk, but soon the identification was woven into the fold-under mitered corners. Almost every Stevens bookmark has such identification, except the ones woven at the World's Columbian Exposition in Chicago, 1892–93.

Post cards with very fancy embossing around the aperture in the mount almost always have Stevens' name printed on them. Embossed cards from the "Ships" and "Hands Across The Sea" series generally are not printed with Stevens' name. The most popular post card series in the United States are "Ships" and "Hands Across the Sea," the latter incorporating two crossed flags and two hands shaking. Seventeen flag combinations have been found, but only seven are common. Stevens produced silks that were used in the "Alpha" Publishing Co. cards. Many times the silks were the top or bottom half of regular bookmarks.

References: Geoffrey A. Godden, *Stevengraphs and Other Victorian Silk Pictures,* Associated University Presses, 1971; Chris Radley, *The Woven Silk Postcard,* privately printed, 1978; Austin Sprake, *The Price Guide to Stevengraphs,* The Antique Collectors' Club, Baron Publishing, 1972.

Collectors' Club: Stevengraph Collectors' Association, 2103-2829 Arbutus Road, #2103, Victoria, British Columbia V8N 5X5 Canada.

Museums: Herbert Art Gallery and Museum, Coventry, England; Paterson Museum, Paterson, NJ.

Note: Prices are based on pieces in mint or close-to-mint condition.

Advisor: John High.

BOOKMARK

Babes in the Wood	**70.00**
Charles Dickens	**100.00**
God Speed the Plough, gilt frame	**100.00**
Home Sweet Home	**135.00**
I Love Little Pussy, 1874	**75.00**
Lady Godiva Procession, framed	**225.00**
Merry Christmas And A Happy New Year, pointed on both ends	**100.00**
Morning Hymn–Awake My Soul . .	**75.00**
New Year's Auld Lang Syne	**70.00**
Prince of Wales Anthem, 1863 . .	**100.00**

STEVENSGRAPH

Are You Ready, 6⅞" h, 9⅞" w, orig mat, framed	**225.00**
Crystal Palace, orig mat, framed .	**385.00**
Declaration of Independence	**350.00**
First Touch, orig mat, framed . . .	**330.00**
Good Old Days, 7½" h, 10½" w, framed	**195.00**
Jubilee 1837–1887	**55.00**
Landing of Columbus	**350.00**
Park In Coventry, 7 x 13"	**150.00**
Rescue at Sea, 6¼" h, 9¼" w, orig mat, framed	**220.00**
Victoria, Queen of an Empire on which The Sun Never Sets, 7" h, 5" w, orig mat	**195.00**
Water Jump, 6⅞" h, 9¾" w, orig mat, framed	**225.00**

THE LADY GODIVA PROCESSION.

Lady Godiva's
Procession #2,
$65.00.

19th C

STEVENS AND WILLIAMS

History: In 1824 Joseph Silvers and Joseph Stevens leased the Moor Lane Glass House at "Briar Lea Hill" (Brierley Hill), England, from the Honey-Borne family. In 1847 William Stevens and Samuel Cox Williams took over, giving the firm its present name. In 1870 the firm moved to its Stourbridge plant. In the 1880s the firm employed such renowned glass artisans as Frederick C. Carder, John Northwood, other Northwood family members, James Hill, and Joshua Hodgetts.

Stevens and Williams made cameo glass. Hodgets developed a more commercial version using thinner-walled blanks, acid etching, and the engraving wheel. Hodgetts, an amateur botantist, was noted for his brilliant floral designs.

Other glass products and designs manufactured by Stevens and Williams include intaglio ware, Peach Bloom (a form of peachblow), moss agate, threaded ware, "jewell" ware, tapestry ware, and Silveria. Stevens and Williams made glass pieces covering the full range of late Victorian fashion.

After WWI the firm concentrated on refining the production of lead crystal and achieving new glass colors. In 1932 Keith Murray came to Stevens and Williams as a designer. His work stressed the pure nature of the glass form. Murray stayed with Stevens and Williams until WWII and later followed a career in architecture.

References: Ellen T. Schroy, *Warman's Glass,* Wallace-Homestead, 1992; R.S. Williams-Thomas, *The Crystal Years,* Stevens and Williams Limited, England, Boerum Hill Books, 1983.

Additional Listing: Cameo Glass.

Basket, 9" l, 6" h, applied crimped amber glass rim, transparent

Sauce, cut glass, red strawberries, gold leaves, 5½" d, $165.00.

blue handle, blue folded pedestal bowl, enameled florals, sgd "S & W Stourbridge" **250.00**
Biscuit Jar, cov, 8" h, blue swirls, metal lid and handle **425.00**
Bowl, 6¾" d, pink, MOP, satin, Swirl pattern, cream lining, box pleated top **500.00**
Jack-in-the-Pulpit Vase, 15¼" h, slender lily form vase, wide crimped down folded rim, pink and white stripes, crystal casing, round foot **300.00**
Pitcher
  6" h, 5" w, ribbed, yellow–opal vertical stripe, clear ground, shell reeded handle **225.00**
  10½" h, cranberry overlay, blue int., applied amber feet and rim, green handle form green leaves, yellow flower **625.00**
Rose Bowl
  3½" d, 4" h, rose–pink swirled pattern ext., white cased int., attached leaf shaped, light green base **450.00**
  6" d, 4½" h, Pompeiian Swirl, box pleated top, deep gold shading to light gold, creamy white lining, small blister **225.00**
Sweetmeat Jar, cov, 6" h, opaque cream ground, pink lining, three applied amber and green leaves, SP rim, lid, and handle **275.00**
Toothpick, green cut to clear, hallmarked sterling silver rim **350.00**

Vase

5" h, bulbous, spiral and vertical ribbing, four loped lip, peach, cased butterscotch 465.00

7½" h, 5" w, vertical ribs, striped swirl, frosted deep pink and yellow stripes, frosted ground 425.00

11" h, 4½" d, MOP satin, Swirl pattern, orange shading to white, white lining 275.00

13½" h, horn shape, milky opal ground, crimped amber rim, applied amber stems, green leaves, cherries, plums, apple, and pear, applied amber knop on tip, two large amber applied feet 2,275.00

STICKLEYS

History: There were several Stickley brothers: Albert, Gustav, Leopold, George, and John George. Gustav often is credited with creating the Mission style, a variant of the Arts and Crafts style. Gustav headed Craftsman Furniture, a New York firm, much of whose actual production took place near Syracuse. A characteristic of Gustav's furniture is exposed tenon ends. Gustav published *The Craftsman*, a magazine supporting his anti-machine points of view.

Originally Leopold and Gustav worked together. In 1902 Leopold and John George formed the L. and J. G. Stickley Furniture Company. This firm made Mission-style furniture and cherry and maple early American style pieces.

George and Albert organized the Stickley Brothers Company, located in Grand Rapids, Michigan.

References: David M. Cathers, *Furniture Of The American Arts and Crafts Movement*, New American Library, 1981; Donald A. Davidoff and Robert L. Zarrow, *Early L. & J. G. Stickley Furniture: From Onondaga Shops to Handcraft,* Dover Publications, 1992; Bruce Johnson, *The Official Identification And Price Guide To Arts And Crafts, Second Edition,* House of Collectibles, 1992; L-W Book Sales (ed.), *Furniture Of The Arts & Crafts Period,* L-W Book Sales, 1992; Mary Ann Smith, *Gustav Stickley: The Craftsman,* Dover Publications, 1983, 1992 reprint.

Periodical: *Arts and Crafts Quarterly,* 9 Main St., Lambertville, NJ 08530.

Collectors' Club: Foundation for the Study of Arts & Crafts Movement, Roycroft Campus, 31 S. Grove St., East Aurora, NY 14052.

Museum: Craftsman Farms Foundation, Inc., Morris Plains, NJ.

Armchair, No. 660, orig medium finish, green Naugahyde upholstered cushion seat, stenciled model no., L and JG Stickley Onondaga Shops, c1905, 27¾" w, 39" h 635.00

Arm Rocker, No. 423, orig medium finish, spring cushion, Handcraft Furniture decal, L and JG Stickley, c1910, 28" w, 36" h 700.00

Bed, twin size, orig medium finish, vertical slat headboard and footboard, branded mark, Gustav Stickley, c1912, 46⅜" w, 79" l, 46¼" h 1,725.00

Bookcase, No. 510, orig medium finish, overhanging top above two twelve–pane doors with mitered mullions, six adjustable shelves int., platform base with reverse corbels at each corner, Gustav Stickley, c1901, 58½" w, 14½" d, 53½" h, top reinforced, missing escutcheons 15,000.00

Book Stand, No. 4702, orig dark finish, three shelves, spindle sides, Quaint Furniture, metal tag and stenciled number, Stickley Bros, c1907, 26" w, 12¼" d, 31¼" h 800.00

Candlestick, No. 74, hammered copper, bronze patina, riveted strap handle with incised border, imp mark, Gustav Stickley, 9" h 350.00

Chest, cedar–lined, orig dark finish, black finished iron strap hardware, recessed panels, unsgd, Gustav Stickley, c1901, 40¾" l, 20½" w, 25⅛" h, later paint dec 7,475.00

China Cabinet, No. 8250, orig medium finish, hammered copper hardware, pair glazed doors, three adjustable shelves, stenciled model no., Stickley Bros, c1907, 36¾" w, 14½" d, 56¼" h **1,375.00**

Dining Table, orig medium finish, round fixed top, "The Work of..." decal, L & JG Stickley, 42" d, 29⅛" h **1,500.00**

Library Table, No. 659, orig medium–light finish, iron hardware with black finish, three short drawers, vertical side spindles, base shelf, black stamp mark, Gustav Stickley, c1910, 54" w, 32" d, 29" h **5,465.00**

Morris Chair, No. 336, bow arm, adjustable back, pyramidal pegs, rope seat, unsgd, Gustav Stickley, c1904, 31" w, 39⅜" h, missing one peg, edge roughness **8,050.00**

Prairie Settle, No. 234, even–arm, orig medium finish, box spring cushion, broad even crest rail over seven elongated corbels, thirty–five vertical back spindles, eleven vertical side spindles below each arm, branded mark "The Work of...," L and JG Stickley, c1912, 85¾" w, 33⅞" d, 25¼" h, unupholstered **37,375.00**

Rocker, No. 817, orig medium finish, spring cushion, Handcraft Furniture decal, L and JG Stickley, c1910, 26¾" w, 35" h, minor imperfections **315.00**

Settle, No. 232, even–arm, single wide vertical slat under each arm, orig medium finish, reupholstered spring cushion, "The Work of..." decal, L and JG Stickley, c1910, 72" w, 27" d, 28⅛" h, rear post crack **2,645.00**

Sideboard, No. 804, designed by Harvey Ellis, six short drawers, two cupboard doors, single long drawer, arched apron, hammered iron hardware, orig medium finish, red decal and remnants of Craftsman paper label, Gustav Stickley, c1907, 54¼" w, 22⅛" d, 42½" h **7,475.00**

Smoker's Cabinet, No. 522, single cupboard door, orig medium finish, fitted drawer and compartments int., red decal, Gustav

Stickley, c1902, 17" w, 15" d, 27" h **3,735.00**

Stamp Box, hammered copper, orig deep bronze patina, imp mark, Gustav Stickley, 4¼" l, 2¼" w, 2⅛" h **400.00**

Table Lamp, No. 506, oak and hammered copper, orig medium finish, bronze patina, triangular peaked shade with glass panels, amber ext. glass backed with white int. glass, oak trestle base, imp and branded mark, Gustav Stickley, c1912, 10¼" w, 8½" d, 16¼" h, replaced glass **4,600.00**

Tea Table, orig medium finish, top set with twelve Grueby matte green glazed tiles, red decal, Gustav Stickley, c1903, 24" w, 20¼" d, 25" h, top water stains and light toning **29,900.00**

Tray, No. 355, hammered copper, oval, slightly dished, two handles, imp mark, Gustav Stickley, 23" l, 11½" w, cleaned **430.00**

Umbrella Stand, No. 100, ten slats riveted to three hammered iron hoops, orig medium finish, red decal, Gustav Stickley, c1907, 12⅛" d, 24" h, missing pan ... **1,275.00**

Window Bench, No. 178, horizontal slat arms, no back, flat stretcher, upholstered seat, red decal, Gustav Stickley, 36" w, 18" d, 27" h, painted green **2,425.00**

STIEGEL TYPE GLASS

History: Baron Henry Stiegel founded America's first flint glass factory at Manheim, Pennsylvania, in the 1760s. Although clear glass was the most common color made, amethyst, blue (cobalt), and fiery opalescent are found. Products included bottles, creamers, flasks, flips, perfumes, salts, tumblers, and whiskeys. Prosperity was short lived. Stiegel's extravagant living forced the factory to close.

It is very difficult to identify a Stiegel-made item. As a result, the term "Stiegel type" is used to identify glass made at that time period in the same shapes and colors.

Enamel decorated ware also is attributed

to Stiegel. True Stiegel pieces are rare. An overwhelming majority is of European origin.

References: Frederick W. Hunter, *Stiegel Glass*, 1950, available in Dover reprint; Ellen T. Schroy, *Warman's Glass,* Wallace-Homestead, 1992.

Reproduction Alert: Beware of modern reproductions, especially in enamel wares.

Creamer, ftd, expanded diamond pattern, fiery opalescent, 3½″ h, $800.00.

Creamer, 3¾″ h, pear shaped body, cobalt blue, diamond pattern, applied foot and handle .. **1,045.00**
Decanter, blown three mold, ½ pint, GII-18 .... **350.00**
Flask, Europe, 1775–1825, swirled, half-post construction, 6¼″ h
  Bright sapphire blue, tooled mouth, pontil scar **1,100.00**
  Deep sapphire blue, sheared mouth, applied pewter collar and cap, pontil scar **400.00**
Flip Glass
  3½″ h, enameled flowers, berries, and running rabbit **325.00**
  5″ h, clear, engraved swag motifs, sheared rim **145.00**
  7½″ h, engraved rim and squiggle dec, matching lid, blown panel molded **575.00**
  7⅞″ h, engraved tulips, c1770 . **350.00**
Mug, 6⅜″ h, clear, blown, large engraved tulip plant, applied strap handle **250.00**
Nursing Bottle, 3⅜″ h, blown half–

post type, clear, pontil, engraved bow and leaf dec **175.00**
Salt, 2⅛″ d, 3″ h, cobalt blue, diamond pattern, double ogee bowl, short stem, applied foot **935.00**
Scent Bottle, 2¾″ l, swirled, deep cobalt blue **150.00**
Spirits Bottle, enameled, Europe, 1750–1850, rect, beveled corners, colorless, sheared mouth, applied pewter collar, pontil scar, closure missing
  5½″ h, red, white, blue, and yellow floral dec, man walking, holding drinking glass, small loss to enamel, some int. haze **300.00**
  6½″ h, red, white, blue, yellow and green enameled woman, inscription on reverse, some faint int. haze **325.00**
Whiskey Tumbler, 3⅛″ h, clear, blown, engraved sunburst with two birds **575.00**

STONEWARE

History: Made from dense kaolin clay and commonly saltglazed, stonewares were hand-thrown and high-fired to produce a simple, bold vitreous pottery. Stoneware crocks, jugs, and jars were produced for storage and utility purposes. This use dictated shape and design—solid, thick-walled forms with heavy rims, necks, and handles with little or no embellishment. When decorated, the designs were simple: brushed cobalt oxide, incised, slip trailed, stamped, or tooled.

Stoneware has been made for centuries. Early American settlers imported stoneware items at first. As English and European potters refined their earthenware, colonists began to produce their own wares. Two major North American traditions emerged based only on the location or type of clay. North Jersey and parts of New York comprise the first area; the second was eastern Pennsylvania spreading westward and into Maryland, Virginia, and West Virginia. These two distinct locations, style of decoration, and shape are discernible factors in classifying and dating early stoneware.

By the late 18th century, stoneware was

manufactured in all sections of the country. During the 19th century, this vigorous industry flourished until glass "fruit jars" appeared and refrigeration became widespread. By 1910, commercial production of saltglazed stoneware came to an end.

References: Susan and Al Bagdade, *Warman's American Pottery and Porcelain,* Wallace–Homestead, 1994; Georgeanna H. Greer, *American Stoneware: The Art and Craft of Utilitarian Potters,* Schiffer Publishing, 1981; William C. Ketchum, Jr., *American Pottery and Porcelain,* 1994; Jim Martin and Bette Cooper, *Monmouth-Western Stoneware,* published by authors, 1983, 1993 value update; Dana G. Morykan and Harry L. Rinker, *Warman's Country Antiques & Collectibles, Second Edition,* Wallace-Homestead Book Co., 1994; Don and Carol Raycraft, *Collector's Guide to Country Stoneware & Pottery,* First Series (1985, 1992 value update), Second Series (1990, 1992 value update), Collector Books; Don and Carol Raycraft, *Country Stoneware and Pottery,* Collector Books, 1985, 1992 value update; George Sullivan, *The Official Price Guide To American Stoneware,* House of Collectibles, 1993.

Periodical: *Bottles & Extras,* PO Box 154, Happy Camp, CA 96039.

Collectors' Club: American Stoneware Association, 930 Country Lane, Indiana, PA 15701.

Museum: Museum of Ceramics at East Liverpool, East Liverpool, OH.

Bottle, 9⅜" h, cylindrical, gray, cobalt blue glazed dots, sloping shoulder **165.00**
Butter Crock, 9½" d, 5" h, cobalt blue floral rim, imp "1" **25.00**
Churn, 12½" h, cobalt blue brushed foliage design and "3," applied handles, imp label "F Fowler, Beaver, PA" **610.00**
Cooler
 16¾" h, emb blue and white woman and wishing well scene **150.00**
 18" h, keg shape, gray salt glaze, greenish highlights, emb bands **50.00**
Crock
 8½" h, cobalt blue stenciled and

Crock, 4 gallon, unknown maker, cobalt blue pecking chicken dec, $575.00. Photograph courtesy Arthur Auctioneering.

 freehand label "Williams & Reppert, Greensboro, PA 2" . **350.00**
 9" h, 10½" d, cobalt blue quill work tulip and "2," imp "Burger & Co Rochester, NY" **110.00**
 9¼" h, cobalt blue quill bow design, imp "A K Ballard, Burlington, VT 2" **110.00**
 9½" h, cobalt blue brushed flower and "2" **55.00**
 10" h, cobalt floral motif, 2 gal, imp "Lyons," second quarter 19th C **210.00**
 10½" h, cobalt floral motif, 2 gal, imp "John Burger, Rochester" **255.00**
 10¾" h, cobalt blue slip flower dec, imp "Whites Utica NY 3" **145.00**
 13" h, cobalt blue floral motif, 4 gal, imp "N Clark & Co Lyons," 1825–52 .... **255.00**
Cuspidor, 13¾" d, molded beading and Greek Key bands, blue stripes, Albany slip int. **1,155.00**
Funnel, 5" h, brown Albany slip .. **155.00**
Jar
 7¾" h, cobalt blue brushed dec **250.00**
 8" h, ovoid, cobalt blue stripes and "Hamilton & Jones, Greensboro, Green Co, PA" . **140.00**
 8½" h
  Cobalt blue dec, ½ gal, 19th C **465.00**
  Cobalt blue stenciled and freehand label, "Hamilton & Jones, Greensboro, PA" ... **355.00**
 8¾" h, ovoid, cobalt blue quill work design, imp "Fort Edward NY" **85.00**

9" h, ovoid, cobalt blue stenciled and freehand label, "Hamilton & Jones, Greensboro, PA 1½" **325.00**

9¼" h, ovoid, brushed cobalt blue floral design, incised "1," applied handles **165.00**

9½" h, ovoid, gray salt glaze, Albany slip dec, cobalt blue label, imp "Purdy" **200.00**

10¼" h, ovoid, cobalt blue brushed lines and dashes and "2" **125.00**

10¾" h, cobalt blue floral dec, T Stetzenmeyer, Rochester, NY, 2 gal **165.00**

11" h, cobalt blue slip floral design, imp "White Utica 2" . . . **330.00**

11¾" h, ovoid, floral design and "2," brushed cobalt blue slip dec, stained and hairlines . . . **75.00**

12¾" h, ovoid, brushed cobalt blue flower dec, imp "Sipe & Sons, W'msport, PA 4," applied handles **245.00**

13½" h, ovoid, cobalt blue brushed floral design and "5," brown pebbly highlights, gray salt glaze **195.00**

14" h
Cobalt blue brushed stripes, wavy lines, and "3," stenciled label "RT Williams, New Geneva, Pa" **195.00**

Cobalt blue quill work stylized polka dot floral design, imp "CL & AK Ballard, Burlington, Vt 2" **275.00**

15" h
Brushed cobalt blue double row of foliage, imp label "McCarel & Burns, Richmond, O 6" **365.00**

Brushed cobalt blue stripes, vining foliage, and "4," applied shoulder handles, imp "Poughner Greensboro, PA" **1,430.00**

15½" h, ovoid, cobalt blue brushed tulips, applied handles, imp label **250.00**

17" h, ovoid, cobalt blue brushed vine, applied handles, imp "6" **245.00**

Jug
10⅞" h, brushed cobalt blue flower, imp "Gerity Bros Elmira, NY" **110.00**

11" h, brown Albany slip, heron with beak in bottle, sgraffito work banner "Timothy McCarty" **610.00**

11½" h, cobalt blue quill floral design, imp "Troy NY Pottery" **180.00**

12" h, ovoid, brushed cobalt blue floral design and "2," imp label "S Hart Fulton" **330.00**

13½" h, ovoid, cobalt blue highlights and imp "Charlestown 2" **225.00**

14" h, cobalt blue quill work "Lyons 2" and flourish, imp "Fisher, Lyons, NY" **220.00**

Match Holder, 3¼" h, figural, tree stump and mouse, glazed finish **145.00**

Milk Bowl, 17" d, brown glazed ext. with imp floral design, gray glazed int. with cobalt dec, 19th C **550.00**

Pitcher
8½" h, light tan and ivory glaze, hound handles **50.00**

9" h, cobalt blue slip flower dec, imp "1/2" **465.00**

11¾" h, brown Albany slip **45.00**

13½" h, cobalt blue brushed floral dec, strap handle, imp "2" **825.00**

Preserving Jar
8¼" h, cobalt blue stenciled label with shield, "Wilton & Jones, Greensboro, PA" **200.00**

9" h, brushed cobalt blue foliage design **160.00**

9½" h, cobalt blue fruit and long stem **330.00**

10" h, stenciled and freehand cobalt blue label "Hamilton & Jones, Greensboro, PA" **175.00**

Salt, 2⅝" h, cobalt blue dec, two rim chips **500.00**

STONEWARE, BLUE AND WHITE

History: Blue and white stoneware refers to molded, salt glazed, domestic, utilitarian earthenware with a blue glaze produced in the late 19th and early 20th centuries. Earlier stoneware was usually hand thrown and either undecorated, hand decorated in Spencerian script floral and other motifs, or stenciled. The stoneware of the blue and white period is molded with a design impressed, embossed, stenciled, or printed.

Although known as blue and white, the base color is generally grayish in tone. The blue cobalt glaze may coat the entire piece, appear as a series of bands, or accent the decorative elements.

All types of household products were available in blue and white stoneware. Bowls, crocks, jars, pitchers, mugs, and salts are just a few examples. The ware reached its height of popularity between 1870 and 1890. The advent of glass jars, tin containers, and chilled transportation brought its end. The last blue and white stoneware was manufactured in the 1920s.

Reference: Kathyrn McNerney, *Blue & White Stoneware,* Collector Books, 1981, 1993 value update.

Collectors' Club: Blue & White Pottery Club, 224 12th St. NW, Cedar Rapids, IA 52405.

Reproduction Alert: The vast majority of blue and white stoneware pieces found in antiques shops and flea markets are unmarked reproductions from Rushville Pottery, Rushville, Ohio.

Bowl, 10½" d, feathers, double ring 100.00
Butter Dish, cov
  Apple Blossom 250.00
  Good Luck 125.00
Cookie Jar, 9" h, Turkey Eye, diffused bands, acorn finial 140.00
Cooler
  11" l, barrel shape, cobalt blue dec, three short feet 150.00
  16¾" h, emb blue and white woman at wishing well scene, lid 150.00
Creamer, 4½" h, Arc and Leaf, paneled 70.00
Custard Cup, 4" d, 3½" h, blue and orange brush dec, wide blue band 65.00
Match Holder, 5½" d, 5" h, Duck . 65.00
Mixing Bowl, 7½" d, Flying Bird .. 175.00
Mug, 5" h, bulbous, Basketweave

and Flower, rolled rim, rope handle 60.00
Pie Plate, 10½" d, blue on blue, raised grooved base 100.00
Pitcher
  8" h, molded bark design, portrait, rose, and leaves dec ... 195.00
  10" h, two molded busts design, dog's head spout, dolphin handle 110.00
  11" h, molded stippled detail, portrait medallions, German inscription 165.00
Wash Bowl and Pitcher Set, Rose and Fishscales 250.00

STRETCH GLASS

History: Stretch glass was produced by many glass manufacturers in the United States between the early 1900s and the 1920s. The most prominent makers were Cambridge, Fenton (which probably manufactured more stretch glass than any of the others), Imperial, Northwood, and Steuben. Stretch glass can be identified by its iridescent, onionskin-like effect. Look for mold marks. Imported pieces are blown and show a pontil mark.

References: Ellen T. Schroy, *Warman's Glass,* Wallace-Homestead, 1992; Berry Wiggins, *Stretch Glass,* Antique Publications, 1972, 1987 value update.

Collectors' Club: Stretch Glass Society, PO Box 770643, Lakewood, OH 44107.

Bonbon, Florentine green, dolphin handle, Fenton 45.00

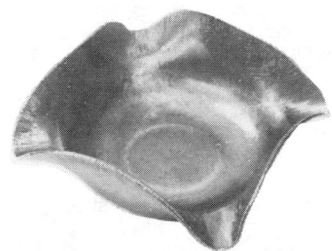

Dish, scalloped at corners, Imperial, 6½" w, 3" h, $125.00.

Bowl
   8½" d, 1¾" h, gold, stretched
      edge **40.00**
   9¾" d, orange, ftd **50.00**
   10" d, blue, sq ftd base, North-
      wood **32.00**
Candlesticks, pr, 8½" h, vaseline **70.00**
Candy Dish, 9½" d, cov, pink **30.00**
Compote
   7⅝" d, 4½" h, green irid, clear
      stem, amber base **65.00**
   9½" d, 5½" h, vaseline, bark pat-
      terned stem, sgd "Northwood" **135.00**
Plate
   6" d, octagonal, vaseline **10.00**
   8¼" d, Aurene, gold **70.00**
Powder Jar, cov, ice blue **40.00**
Sherbet, liner, vaseline **20.00**
Vase
   5" h, white irid, fluted top **325.00**
   6" h, hp florals and leaves, rolled
      rim, clear ribbed int. **30.00**

Court Jester, chalkware **35.00**
Dutch Girl, cast iron, hanging type **20.00**
Girl, wearing blue bonnet, chalk-
   ware **45.00**
Leaf design, emb, cast iron, 9¾" h **75.00**
Old Lady, sitting in rocking chair,
   chalkware **25.00**

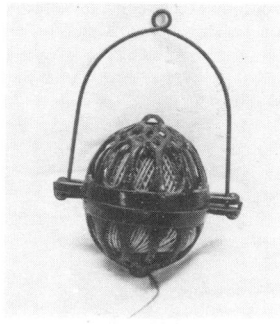

Cast Iron, hanging type, $40.00.

STRING HOLDERS

History: The string holder was developed as a utilitarian tool to assist the merchant or manufacturer who needed tangle-
free string or twine to tie packages. The
early holders were made of cast iron, some
patents dating to the 1860s.

When the string holder moved to the
household, lighter and more attractive
forms developed, many made of chalkware.
The string holder remained a key kitchen
element until the early 1950s.

Advertising, Jaxon Soap, cast iron **70.00**
Apple
   Chalkware, red, on branch with
      blackberries **15.00**
   Tin, marked "Shenandoah Val-
      ley Apple Candy, Winchester,
      VA," 4 x 4" **150.00**
Beehive, cast iron, dated "Apr
   1865," 6" h **50.00**
Blown Glass, clear, applied cobalt
   blue base and finial, 4¾" d, 4½"
   h, Pittsburgh **125.00**
Cat, yarn holder **25.00**
Chef, chalkware **45.00**

Pear, chalkware, purple plums and
   leaves
      Yellow **20.00**
      Red **15.00**
Rooster, ceramic, Royal Bayreuth **225.00**
Teapot, wood, chef decal **25.00**
Victorian, oval, cast lattice pattern,
   recessed ball and spout, ceiling
   mount, 10" d **125.00**

SUGAR SHAKERS

History: Sugar shakers, sugar castors,
or muffineers all served the same purpose:
to "sugar" muffins, scones, or toast. They
are larger than salt and pepper shakers,
were produced in a variety of materials, and
were in vogue in the late Victorian era.

Reference: William Heacock, *Encyclopedia of Victorian Colored Pattern Glass,
Book III, Syrups, Sugar Shakers & Cruets,
From A to Z,* Antique Publications, 1976,
1991–92 value update.

CHINA

Meissen, 6½" h, baluster, hp, multicolored floral spray, ozier band, pierced cov edged in puce, c1750, chip on finial 450.00
Schlegelmilch, R S Prussia, 4¾" h, luster finish, rose dec, scalloped base, red mark 235.00
Wedgwood, blue, white classical figures 48.00

Milk Glass, blue, ribbed, metal top, 4½" h , $75.00.

GLASS

Amberina, 5¼" h, DQ, MOP, pewter top 650.00
Cone, shiny pink, white int. 85.00
Cranberry, IVT, tapered shape ... 110.00
Crown Milano, ribbed, wild rose dec 475.00
Cut Glass, 3¾" h, Block and Fan, stars, rayed base, SS chased top and rim 175.00
Forget–Me–Not, opaque, pink, Challinor 110.00
Hobb's
  Bulbous base, cranberry 160.00
  Optic Rubina, acid etched, florals 175.00
Ribbed Lattice, opalescent
  Blue 235.00
  Cranberry 385.00
Rubena, Royal Ivy, orig top 110.00
Satin, 3¼" h, Fleurette pattern, pink, squatty, brass top 125.00
Spanish Lace, vaseline opal 200.00

CAMBRIAN POTTERY
c1783-1810

DILLWYN & CO.
SWANSEA
c1811-1817

BEVINGTON & CO.
c1817-1824

SWANSEA

History: This superb pottery and porcelain was made at Swansea (Glamorganshire, Wales) as early as the 1760s with production continuing until 1870.

Marks on Swansea vary. The earliest marks were "SWANSEA" impressed under glaze and "DILLWAN" under glaze after 1805. "CAMBRIAN POTTERY" was stamped in red under glaze from 1803–1805. Many fine examples, including the Botanical series in pearlware, are not marked but may have the botanical name stamped under glaze.

Fine examples of Swansea often may show imperfections, such as firing cracks. These pieces are considered mint because they left the factory in this condition.

Reference: Susan and Al Bagdade, *Warman's English & Continental Pottery & Porcelain, Second Edition,* Wallace-Homestead, 1991.

Reproduction Alert: Swansea porcelain has been copied for many decades in Europe and England. Marks should be studied carefully.

Dessert Tray, 9½" l, hp, creamware, gilding, polychrome, under glaze mark "Swansea," c1780 . 275.00
Dish, 11½" d, botanical series, c1805 .... 325.00
Plate
  7¾" d, hp, creamware, flowers, reticulated, marked "Dillwyn," c1805 .... 190.00
  8½" d, center floral, molded foliate scroll rim 230.00

Cup and Saucer, c1815, 3⅝" d, cup, 6" d saucer, $115.00.

Punch Bowl, earthenware, Oriental dec, marked "Cambrian Pottery," c1803 . . . . **1,000.00**
Serving Dish
   8" sq, sweet peas, botanical, c1805 . . . . **175.00**
   11½" l, oblong, lily, pink, botanical, c1805 . . . . **350.00**

SWORDS

History: The first swords in America came from Europe. The chief cities for sword manufacturing were Solingen in Germany, Klingenthal in France, and Hounslow and Shotley Bridge in England. Among the American importers of these foreign blades was "Horstmann" whose mark is found on many military weapons.

New England and Philadelphia were the early centers for American sword manufacturing. By the Franco-Prussian War, the Ames Manufacturing Company of Chicopee, Massachusetts, was exporting American swords to Europe.

Sword collectors concentrate on a variety of styles: commission vs. non-commission officers' swords, presentation swords, naval weapons, and swords from a specific military branch such as cavalry or infantry. The type of sword helped identify a person's military rank and, depending on how he had it customized, his personality as well.

Following the invention of repeating firearms in the mid-19th century, the sword lost its functional importance as a combat weapon and became a military dress accessory. Condition is a key criterion determining value.

References: Harold L. Peterson, *The American Sword 1775–1945,* Ray Riling Arms Books Co., 1965; Gerald Welond, *A Collector's Guide to Swords, Daggers & Cutlasses,* Chartwell Books, 1991.

Collectors' Club: The Association of American Sword Collectors, PO Box 288, Parsonburg, MD 21849.

Museum: Fort Ticonderoga Museum, Ticonderoga, NY.

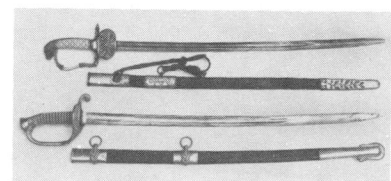

Top: Civil War, Naval officer, made by Tiffany, New York City, eagle engraved 29" blade, $300.00; bottom: Model 1837, officer, eagle hilted, 29" blade, $650.00.

AMERICAN

Artillery, Foot, 1832, 25" l, Roman type short sword, brass eagle pommel, "Ames Mfg Co, Chicopee, MA," leather scabbard . . . **350.00**
Cavalry, saber
   Contract of 1816, Starr, cast iron hilt, wood grip with leather, "N Starr and US/P/LS," iron japanned scabbard **300.00**
   Model 1860, Deluxe, 41" l overall, 35" blade, 21" etched pattern on both sides, obverse with foliage, an American eagle, a trophy of arms, and scrolls with "Ames Mfg Co/Chicopee/Mass" at ricasso, reverse with scrolls, a trophy of arms and "US" in script letters, gilt brass hilt with sharkskin wrapped grip cast with light relief work at top of pommel and rear of knuckle guard, bright finished steel scabbard **3,250.00**
Fraternal, Ames, regular, 29½" l blade, 19" etched design, ob-

verse with profuse foliage, "Charles S. Tanner," and a standing knight in armor and "Ames Sword Co/Chicopee, Mass," gilt brass hilt with anchor on langet over "HOPE," fitted with black grip with gilt cross, orig black leather scabbard with engraved gilt brass mounts, the throat with "IN HOC SIGNO/ VINCES" with a snake and cross **45.00**

Infantry, Officer, 1820–50, 35" l, brass hilt and Indian head pommel, mother–of–pearl or ivory grip with brass wire, back etched with eagle and military motif, brass scabbard **650.00**

Musician's Sword, Model 1840, stamped at obverse ricasso "US/1863/FSS," reverse stamped "C ROBY W CHELMS-FORD.MS," orig issue scabbard **400.00**

Naval, Cutlass, 1841, 26¼" l, brass hilt and grip, half basket, guard, "N P Ames/Springfield" and "USN/1843/RC," leather scabbard **600.00**

EUROPEAN

Continental, Cavalry, saber, 38" l, 32½" slightly curved blade, iron hilt with two branches stamped "GA/III," wooden grips covered with black leather, iron scabbard **200.00**

English

Naval, Officer, 35¼" l, 30" single edged blade with rounded back, etched "PROSSER/ Maker To The/Queen & Royal Family, London," and with naval themes, brass hilt with large gilt brass guard with crown and naval anchor, lion's head pommel, sharkskin over wood grip **200.00**

Officer, saber, 30⅜" l, curved single edged 25¼" blade, brass hilt cast in one piece with lion's head pommel, black leather scabbard with brass mounts **175.00**

French, Officer, saber, 40½" l, 35¼" slightly curved blade, ob-

verse engraved and gilt dec against blue ground and marked "Gendarmerie du Roi," reverse with military motifs and Sun King emblem, blade sgd "Coulaux Freres Klingenthal," gilded brass hilt with three branches with relief floral work, pommel emb fleur–de–lis, black leather and wire grip, steel scabbard with gilded brass carrying ring mounts **800.00**

Halbert Head, 24½" head, 42½" l, orig straps for attaching to pole, pole partially broken and cut off just beyond end of straps, large deep anchor shaped maker's stamp **425.00**

TEA CADDIES

History: Tea once was a precious commodity. Special boxes or caddies were used as containers to accommodate different teas, including a special cup for blending.

Around 1700 silver caddies appeared in England. Other materials, such as Sheffield plate, tin, wood, china, and pottery, also were used. Some tea caddies were very ornate.

Pewter, Japanese, 5" h, $115.00.

Burl Walnut, English, dome top, brass fittings, two compartments, ivory finials, 19th C, 8¼" w, 4¾" d, 5⅜" h **230.00**

Lacquered Wood, Chinese
Black and gold, rect, floral design, four paw ft **200.00**

Gilded, ext. dec with panels depicting figures pursuing scholarly activities against background with dragons, bats, and Buddhist emblems, fitted pewter box int. with ivory finial, late 19th C, 11" w, 7¾" d, 6½" h **690.00**

Mahogany, English
Cubical, inlaid shell design on lid, lion head handles **275.00**
Regency, crossbanded top, rect case, c1810, 5" h **260.00**

Porcelain, French, faience, polychrome, marked "Rouen," missing lid, 4¼" h **125.00**

Rosewood, English
Inlaid mother–of–pearl dec **95.00**
Regency, tapered sides, domed cover, c1820, 9" w, 4¾" d, 4½" h **285.00**

Rosewood Veneer, floral inlay and "Tea," fitted int. with two glass jars and mixing bowl, 13" h ... **140.00**

Silver, Continental, domed cov, rect body, incised with village reserve, 19th C, 12 oz, 4" w, 2¾" d, 3½" h **315.00**

Tole
Floral dec, red, yellow, white, and green, orig black paint, 5½" h **85.00**
Stenciled "Crown Stores, Pure Teas," round, numbered 1 through 4, 19th C, 17½" h, price for set of four **1,950.00**

Walnut and Ebonized, Continental, bombe form, 19th C, 16½" w, 8" h **460.00**

Wood and Rolled Paper, George III, English, diamond shaped, floral dec **120.00**

Wood Veneer, English, rect, seashell inlay, repaired, reproduction paper on int., 19th C, 7½" w, 4½" d, 4¾" h **460.00**

TEA LEAF IRONSTONE CHINA

History: Tea Leaf Ironstone china flowed into America from England in great quantities in the 1860 to 1910 period and graced the tables of working-class America. It traveled to California and Texas in wagons and by boat down the Mississippi River to Kentucky and Missouri. It was too plain for the rich homes; its simplicity and strength appealed to wives forced to watch pennies. Tea Leaf found its way into the kitchen of Lincoln's Springfield home; sailors ate from it aboard the *Star of India*, now moored in San Diego and still displaying Tea Leaf.

Tea Leaf was not manufactured exclusively by English potters in Staffordshire, contrary to popular opinion. Although there were more than 35 English potters producing Tea Leaf, at least 26 American potters helped satisfy the demand. However, American potters perpetuated the myth by using backstamps bearing an English coat of arms and the marking "Warrented." The American housewife favored imported ware to that made by Americans.

Anthony Shaw (1850–1900) first registered the pattern in 1856 as Luster Band and Sprig. Edward Walley (1845–56) already was decorating ironstone with luster trefoil leaf, a detached bud, and trailing green vine. Walley's products are designated Pre-Tea Leaf and are sought by eclectic collectors. Other early variants include Morning Glory and Pepper Leaf or Tobacco Leaf by Elsmore & Forster (Foster) (1853–57) and Teaberry by Clementson Bros. (1832–1916). Cloverleaf, Cinquefoil, and Pinwheel all may be found in a collection specializing in early ware.

The most prolific Tea Leaf makers were Anthony Shaw and Alfred Meakin (c1875). Johnson Bros. (c1883), Henry Burgess (1864–92) and Arthur J. Wilkinson (c1897), all of whom shipped much of their ware to America, followed close behind Shaw and Meakin.

Although most of the English Tea Leaf is copper luster, Powell and Bishop (1868–78) and their successors, Bishop and Stonier (1891–1936), worked exclusively in gold luster. Beautiful examples of gold luster by H. Burgess still are being found. Mellor, Taylor & Co. (1880–1904) used gold luster on their children's tea sets. Other English potters also used gold lustre. Recently discovered are gold lustre pieces by W. & E. Corn, Thomas Elsmore, and Thomas Hughes.

J. & E. Mayer, Beaver Falls, Pennsylvania, were English potters who immigrated to America and produced a large amount of copper luster Tea Leaf. The majority of the American potters decorated with gold luster, with no brown underglaze like that found under the copper luster.

East Liverpool, Ohio, potters such as Cartwright Bros. (1864–1924), East End Pottery (1894–1909), Knowles, Taylor & Knowles (1870–1934), and others decorated only in gold luster. This is also true of Trenton, New Jersey, potters such as Glasgow Pottery, American Crockery Co., and Fell & Thropp Co. Since no underglazing was used with the gold, much of it has been washed away.

By the 1900s Tea Leaf's popularity had waned. The sturdy ironstone did not disappear. It was stored in barns and relegated to attics and basements. Much of it was disposed of in dumps, from which one enterprising collector has dug up some beautiful pieces.

A frequent myth about Tea Leaf is that pieces marked "Wedgwood" are *the* Wedgwood, Josiah. This is not true! Dealers and collectors who perpetuate this myth should be confronted. Enoch Wedgwood was the only potter of that name to produce Tea Leaf. Enoch Wedgwood's product is beautiful with large showy leaves. He deserves full credit for his work.

References: Susan and Al Bagdade, *Warman's English & Continental Pottery & Porcelain, Second Edition,* Wallace-Homestead, 1991; Annise Doring Heaivilin, *Grandma's Tea Leaf Ironstone,* Wallace-Homestead, 1981; Jean Wetherbee, *A Look At White Ironstone,* Wallace-Homestead, 1980, out of print; Jean Wetherbee, *A Second Look At White Ironstone,* Wallace-Homestead, 1985, out of print.

Collectors' Club: Tea Leaf Club International, PO Box 14133, Columbus, OH 43214.

Museums: Lincoln Home, Springfield, IL; Ox Barn Museum, Aurora, OR; Sherman Davidson House, Newark OH.

Reproduction Alert: There are reproductions that are collectible, and there are *reproductions*! Avoid the latter. Collectible reproductions were made by Cumbow China Decorating Co. of Abington, Virginia, from 1932 to 1980. Wm. Adams & Sons, an old English firm which made Tea Leaf in the 1960s, made reproduction Tea Leaf from 1960 to 1972. Red Cliff, which decorated Hall China blanks with Tea Leaf and clearly marked them, worked in the late 1960s and early 1970s.

Ruth Sayer started making Tea Leaf reproductions in 1981. Although her early pieces were not marked, all of it now is marked with a leaf and the initials "RS" on the bottom. In 1968 Blakeney Pottery, a Staffordshire firm, manufactured a poor-quality reproduction of Meakin's Bamboo pattern and marked it "Victoria." It was distributed through a Pennsylvania antiques reproduction outlet.

Tray, marked "Anthony Shaw Opaque Stone China England," 12″ w handle to handle, $95.00.

Bone Dish, 6⅝″ l, 3⅛″ w, crescent shape, Meakin	**50.00**
Bowl	
5″ d, unsigned	**12.00**
8″ w, sq, Alfred Meakin	**55.00**
Butter Dish, cov, sq, orig sq Tea Leaf drainer, Meakin	**165.00**
Butter Pat, round, unsigned	**8.00**
Compote, Shaw, 9″ d, 3½″ h	**400.00**

Creamer, 5⅛" h, Bamboo pattern,
V–shaped lip, Meakin, 1883 ... **115.00**
Cup and Saucer
  Bishop & Powell **50.00**
  Shaw **35.00**
  Unsigned **25.00**
Cup Plate, Chinese shape, An-
thony Shaw, dated 1846, 4½" d **55.00**
Gravy Boat, Mayer **45.00**
Nappy, Meakin, price for pair **25.00**
Pitcher
  7" h, Lily of the Valley pattern,
  Anthony Shaw, 1860s **300.00**
  8" h, sq, Shaw **150.00**
Plate
  6⅞" d, Meakin **7.50**
  7" d, unsigned **10.00**
  8" d, Meakin **10.00**
  9" d
    Shaw **15.00**
    Unsigned **10.00**
  10" d, Shaw **15.00**
Platter
  10 x 6", copper luster, sgd
  "Meakin" **35.00**
  12" l, handle, Shaw **35.00**
  13" l, oval, Meakin **60.00**
  13 x 9½", rect, Meakin **45.00**
  14" l, rect, Shaw **50.00**
Relish Dish, Pepper Leaf variant,
unmarked **125.00**
Sauce Dish, 4¾" w, eight sided,
Anthony Shaw **15.00**
Sauce Tureen, cov, underplate,
6¾" h, oval, Lily of the Valley
pattern, Shaw, repaired lid,
1860s **350.00**
Saucer, Meakin **14.00**
Shaving Mug, copper luster, lily of
the valley mold, sgd "Shaw" .. **155.00**
Soap Dish, cov, liner, 3⅞" h, Cable
and Ring pattern, Anthony Shaw **195.00**
Soup Bowl, 9" d, flanged rim,
marked "Meakin," price for set of
five **145.00**
Sugar Bowl, cov, Meakin **75.00**
Toothbrush Holder, Mellor, Taylor
& Co **165.00**
Tureen, cov, 5½" h, oblong, six
sided, Sunburst pattern, 1880s,
Shaw **175.00**
Vegetable Tureen, cov, Mayer ... **85.00**

1859-97

TEPLITZ CHINA

History: Around 1900, 26 ceramic manufacturers were located in Teplitz, a town in
the Bohemian province of Czechoslovakia.
Other potteries were located in the nearby
town of Turn. Wares from these factories
were molded, cast, and hand decorated.
Most are in the Art Nouveau and Art Deco
styles. Most pieces do not carry a specific
manufacturer's mark. They are simply
marked "Teplitz," "Turn-Teplitz," or "Turn."
Reference: Susan and Al Bagdade, *Warman's English & Continental Pottery & Porcelain, Second Edition,* Wallace-Homestead, 1991.

Bust, Art Nouveau style woman,
white rose in hair, green–gold
finish, marked "E.W.," 10" h ... **750.00**
Candlestick, 5¼" h, figural, woman
wearing flowing gown **150.00**
Creamer, 3¾" h, drummer boy,
house, fence, and trees, hp,
marked "Stellmacher" **70.00**

**Cornucopia, ecru to beige to pink,
marked "6207/58," 11" max. width,
6½" h, $325.00.**

Dish, cov, 5½" w, 6¾" h, Jugendstil ceramic, white with black line dots, paneled gilt rims, sgd "E. Wahliss," red "Vienna Turn Austria" crown mark 900.00

Ewer, 9" h, poppies, molded, shades of purple, gold trim, cream ground, applied handle, marked "RS & K" 90.00

Vase
6 x 9", bombe shape, pierced rim, gold Japanese style flowering branches, cobalt ground, ornate upswept handles, Wahliss, professionally restored int. flake 550.00

6¾" h, irregular gold ground, portrait of girl with long hair holding flowers, cobalt blue, white enamel, "R St K" mark 495.00

11" h, wolfhound, applied, bronze finish, Amphora, "Turn Teplitz" mark 700.00

15" h, cobalt blue, white enameled flowers, gold tracery, butterflies in flight, sgd "E Wahliss" 575.00

18" h, pale green Art Nouveau, raised woman's profile, gold lilies and leaves in relief, professionally restored 650.00

TERRA-COTTA WARE

History: Terra-cotta is ware made of a hard, semi-fired ceramic clay. The color of the pottery ranges from a light orange-brown to a deep brownish red. It is usually unglazed, but some pieces can be found partially glazed or decorated with slip designs, incised, or carved. Examples include utilitarian objects as well as statuettes and large architectural pieces. Fine early Chinese terra-cotta pieces recently have brought substantial prices.

Brackets, pr, Rococo style, fruiting grape leaves in relief, chips, late 19th/early 20th C, 11" h 290.00

Figural Group, Madonna and Child, losses, 19th C, 14" h . . . 100.00

Figure, Baccanalian Boy, French, brown overglaze, 18th C, 8" h . 315.00

Figures, Chinese, c1830–40, seal sgd, 9¼" w, 9¾" h, $750.00.

Model, Sphinx, Louis XVI style, 7" l 1,265.00

Olive Jar, bulbous, French, 19th C, 42" h 650.00

Plaque
8⅜" d, portrait, possibly Joseph II, with verse surrounding border, France, 19th C, 8⅜" d . . 225.00

19⅜" w, 36" h, Madonna and Child, bas-relief, pedimented, off–white, blue ground, damaged, 19th C 635.00

Sculpture, Rubin Nakian, American, entitled "Nymph and Satyr," signed, 9" h 575.00

Spill Vase, Royal Worcester, figural, boy gathering wood, holding hollowed wood bundle, gilt highlights, circular turquoise glazed base, imp mark, restored chip to back feet, c1870, 4¾" h 110.00

Umbrella Stand, raised dragons and gilt dec, 24" h 80.00

TEXTILES

History: Textiles are cloth or fabric items, especially anything woven or knitted. Those that survive usually represent the best since these were the objects that were used carefully and stored by the housewife.

Textiles are collected for many reasons— to study fabrics, understand the elegance of an historical period, and for decorative and modern use. The renewed interest in clothing has sparked a revived interest in textiles of all forms.

References: Gideon Bosker, Michele Mancini, John Gramstad, *Fabulous Fabrics of the 50s, 30s, and 40s, and Other Terrific Textiles of the 20s, 30s, and 40s,* Chronicle Books, 1992; William C. Ketchum, Jr., *The Knopf Collectors' Guides to American Antiques: Quilts,* Alfred A. Knopf, 1982; Dana G. Morykan and Harry L. Rinker, *Warman's Country Antiques & Collectibles, Second Edition,* Wallace-Homestead, 1994; Betty Ring, *Needlework: An Historical Survey, Revised Edition,* Main Street Press, 1984; Carleton L. Safford and Robert Bishop, *America's Quilts And Coverlets,* Bonanza Books, 1985; Jessie A. Turbayne, *Hooked Rugs: History and the Continuing Tradition,* Schiffer Publishing, 1991; Jessie A. Turbayne, *The Hookers' Art: Evolving Designs In Hooked Rugs,* Schiffer Publishing, 1993; Helene Von Rosenstiel, *American Rugs And Carpets: From The Seventeenth Century To Modern Times,* William Morrow and Company, 1978; Sigrid Wortmann Weltge, *Women's Work: Textile Art From The Bauhaus,* Chronicle Press, 1993.

Periodicals: *International Old Lacers Bulletin,* PO Box 481223, Denver, CO 80248; *The Lace Collector,* PO Box 222, Plainwell, MI 49080; *The Textile Museum Newsletter,* The Textile Museum, 2320 S St. NW, Washington, DC 20008.

Collectors' Clubs: Costume Society of America, 55 Edgewater Dr., PO Box 73, Earleville, MD 21919; Stumpwork Society, PO Box 122, Bogota, NJ 07603.

Museums: Cooper-Hewitt Museum, New York, NY; Currier Gallery of Art, Manchester, NH; Ipswich Historical Society, Ipswich, MA; Museum of American Textile History, North Andover, MA; Museum of Art, Rhode Island School of Design, Providence, RI; Philadelphia College of Textiles & Science, Philadelphia, PA; The Lace Museum, Mountain View, CA; The Textile Museum, Washington, DC; Valentine Museum, Richmond, VA.

Additional Listings: See Clothing, Linens, Quilts, and Samplers.

Comforter, knotted, log cabin pattern, dark prints and solids, 67 x 77″ **410.00**

Bed Covering, Yo–Yo pattern, mixed cottons, peach predominate color, 84″ sq bed cover, two matching pillow shams, c1920, price for set, $200.00.

Coverlet
  Jacquard
    1824, one piece, four large floral medallions, eagle borders, navy and white, signed "Jacob Northrop New York, July 4, 1824, Gen'l Lafayette," American, 77 x 90″ .. **225.00**
    1830, two piece, allover floral design with scrolling flower and vine motif and eagles on two sides, signed "M.S. Taber 1830," American, 71 x 84″ **140.00**
    1847, two piece, three rows of four octagonal medallions surrounded by floral border on three sides, indigo and madder, dated, LaTourette, IN, 90 x 74″ **500.00**
    1848, one piece, lattice design with alternating floral and geometric medallions, floral border, courthouse corners, blue and white, dated, Decatur County, IN, 74½ x 86″ **925.00**
  Overshot
    c1830
      Three piece, yellow grid design on pink, blue, and white, American, 63 x 85″ **115.00**

Two piece, rose pattern, four large and four small roses in each wheel, blue and navy, American, 76 x 84" **60.00**

c1834, three piece, allover starburst and floral design with floral border and peacock corners, red and blue, inscribed "Manufactured by Henry Oberly Homelsdorf, Penn.," 75 x 76" **80.00**

c1850, one piece, allover interlocking circle pattern, rust and white, Goodwin Guild tag, American, 75 x 97" ... **115.00**

Doily, quatrefoil shape, formed filet crochet with roses, white, late 19th C, 24 x 24" **35.00**

Mattress Cover, two pc, blue and white plaid, machine sewn center seam, 66 x 105" **105.00**

Needlework

Family Register, 1824, Maria Barnard, silk threads, linen ground, "Worked by Maria Barnard, Oct. 1824," some losses to threads and ground, unframed, 22½" sq **490.00**

Memorial

1806, silk threads, linen ground, "sacred to the mem-

ory of John G. Hillhouse, died October 9, 1806," some losses to silk, threads, and ground, framed, 16 x 10" .. **460.00**

1836, Mary A Fairbairn, polychrome silk threads, linen ground, verse and basket with flowers within vining floral and vintage border, "Mary A. Fairbairn age 12 years New York 1836," some discoloration, framed, 17¾ x 17¼" **2,300.00**

Picture, 1818, Ann Rofs, lady and child, outdoor setting, silk ground, silk threads and paint, eglomise mat, some restoration to painted areas, loss to ground fabric, framed, 15½ x 18½", price for pair **800.00**

Rug

Amish, wool, pieced hexagons and appliqued felt trefoils, minor damage **135.00**

Crewelwork, vining floral design in pale and dark blue, green, and rose, ivory field, floral border, 108 x 72" **345.00**

Drugget, Nile pattern, beige, red, black, and mustard, holes, wear, stains, 11' 8" x 9' 8" .. **600.00**

Hooked, pictorial, American

Black and White Cat, floral ground, early 20th C, some fiber loss, rebacked, 21½ x 40½" **1,500.00**

Butterfly and Scroll Motif, ivory field, green border, 112 x 72" **115.00**

Dog and Cat, field of hearts, early 20th C, some fiber loss, rebacked, 21½ x 40½" **2,500.00**

Pineapple Motif, beige field, yellow and green border, 102 x 70" **115.00**

Two Yawls Racing, striped border, early 20th C, bound edge, fiber loss, rebacked, 37 x 67" **6,325.00**

Needlepoint, alternating columns of stepped geometric variations, pink, green, yellow, and mustard, bleeding, 14' 7" x 10' 3" **600.00**

Show Towel, white homespun

Shadow Box, black ground, blue, red, and white chenille flowers, cherry stained frame, 23½" d, $265.00.

linen, blue, pink, and green embroidery, "F R Enimardin 1802," 80" l, 16½" w **60.00**

Table Cover, European, maize field with three cruciform medallions within multiple dec borders, brick red, green, blue, and ochre, 96 x 57" **350.00**

THIMBLES

History: Thimbles often are thought of as common household sewing tools. Many are. However, others are miniature works of art, souvenirs of places, people, and events, or gadgets (thimbles with expanded uses such as attached threaders, cutters, or magnets).

There were many thimble manufacturers in the United States prior to 1930. Before we became a "throwaway" society, hand sewing was a never-ending chore for the housewife. Garments were mended and altered. When they were beyond repair, pieces were salvaged to make a patchwork quilt. Thimble manufacturers tried to create a new thimble to convince the home sewer that "one was not enough."

By the early 1930s only one manufacturer of gold and silver thimbles remained in business in the United States—the Simons Brothers Company of Philadelphia, which was founded by George Washington Simons in 1839. Simons Brothers thimbles from the 1904 St. Louis World's Fair and the 1893 Columbian Exposition are prized acquisitions for any collector. The Liberty Bell thimble, in the shape of the bell, is one of the most novel.

Today, the company is owned by Nelson Keyser and continues to produce silver and gold thimbles. The Simons Brothers Company designed a special thimble for Nancy Reagan as a gift for diplomats' wives who visited the White House. The thimble has a picture of the White House and the initials "N. D. R."

Thimbles have been produced in a variety of materials: gold, silver, steel, aluminum, brass, china, glass, vegetable ivory, ivory, bone, celluloid, plastics, leather, hard rubber, and silk. Common metal thimbles usually are bought by the intended user, who makes sure the size is a comfortable fit. Precious-metal thimbles often were received as gifts. Many of these do not show signs of wear from constant use, either because it did not fit well or was simply too elegant for mundane work.

During the 20th century thimbles were used as advertising promotions. It is not unusual to find a thimble that says "You'll Never Get Stuck Using Our Product" or a political promotion stating "Sew It Up—Vote for John Doe for Senator."

References: Helmut Greif, *Talks About Thimbles,* Fingerhut museum, Cregligen, Germany, 1983 (English edition available from Dine-American, Wilmington, DE); Edwin F. Holmes, *A History Of Thimbles,* Cornwall Books, 1985; Mrytle Lundquist, *The Book Of A Thousand Thimbles,* Wallace-Homestead, 1970, out of print; Myrtle Lundquist, *Thimble Americana,* Wallace-Homestead, 1981, out of print; Myrtle Lundquist, *Thimble Treasury,* Wallace-Homestead, 1975, out of print; Averil Mathis, *Antique and Collectible Thimbles and Accessories,* Collector Books, 1986, 1995 value update; Bridget McConnel, *A Collector's Guide To Thimbles,* Wellfleet Press, 1990; Gay Ann Rogers, *American Silver Thimbles,* Haggerston Press, 1989; Gay Ann Rogers, *Price Guide Keyed To American Silver Thimbles,* Needlework Unlimited, 1989; John Von Hoelle, *Thimble Collectors Encyclopedia,* Wallace-Homestead, 1986, out of print; Estelle Zalkin, *Zalkin's Handbook Of Thimbles & Sewing Implements,* Warman Publishing, 1988.

Periodical: *Thimbletter,* 93 Walnut Hill Road, Newton Highlands, MA 02161.

Collectors' Clubs: Empire State Thimble Collectors, 8289 Northgate Dr., Rome, NY 13440; The Thimble Guild, PO Box 381807, Duncanville, TX 75138; Thimble Collectors International, 6411 Montego Bay Rd., Louisville, KY 40228.

Advisor: Estelle Zalkin.

Reproduction Alert: Reproductions can be made by restrikes from an original die or cast from a mold made from an antique thimble. Many reproductions are sold as such and priced accordingly. Among the reproduced thimbles are a pre-revolution Russian enamel thimble and the Salem

Witch thimble (the repro has no cap, and the seam is visible).

Advertising
Clark's O.N.T., brass 20.00
Domestic Sewing Machine, silver, early 20th C 50.00
Brass, ornate band, scalloped rim 38.00
Celluloid, floral decal 5.00
Commemorative, coronation, King George and Queen Mary, gold . 900.00
Dorcas, Daisy pattern, silver, steel lined 50.00
Enameled, floral dec, South Staffordshire, enamel on brass, 19th C 1,200.00

Sterling silver, American, 19th C, $35.00.

Gold
American, scenic band, late 19th/early 20th C 100.00
Continental, band with scenic vignettes, 19th C 135.00
English, alternating pearls and rubies on rim, 19th C 175.00
Scandinavian, semi–precious stone cap 125.00
Ivory, carved foliate band, 19th C 80.00
Political
Dewey–Brinker, plastic 2.50
Hoover, "Home Happiness," aluminum 20.00
Porcelain
American, hp floral dec, late 19th/early 20th C 40.00
English, bird and flowers dec, Royal Worcester, 19th C 650.00
Silver, steel capped, engraved initials, 19th C 30.00

Souvenir
Louisiana Purchase Expo, St Louis, MO, The Golden Spike, gold, scenic band, 1904 . . . . . 575.00
New Orleans, silver, applied enamel shield 18.00
St Peters, Rome, enamel on silver, semi–precious stone cap 95.00
Steel, damascene dec band, India, 19th C 80.00
Tortoiseshell, gold medallion, silver cap 1,350.00

THREADED GLASS

History: Threaded glass is glass decorated with applied threads of glass. Before the English invention of a glass threading machine in 1876, threads were applied by hand. After this invention, threaded glass was produced in quantity by practically every major glass factory.

Threaded glass was revived by the art glass manufacturers, such as Durand and Steuben, and continues to be made today.

Compote, clear, light green threads, controlled bubble, 8⅛" d top, 7" h, $130.00.

Bowl, 12" d, 4" w, clear, pink threaded bands around ruffled rim, three applied feet, cut starburst on base, Lutz–type, attributed to Boston & Sandwich Glassworks, 1870–85 . . . . 385.00

Epergne, four purple lilies, white
threading **375.00**
Finger Bowl, 5" d, fluted edge,
chartreuse threads **60.00**
Honey Pot, cov, 5¾" h, 6½" w,
clear, satin finished, pulled and
twisted pattern of blue and white
threads, twig finial, twig–like
metal frame **450.00**
Mug, 5⅜" h, clear, cranberry
threading, Sandwich **125.00**
Rose Bowl, 6" h, 5" d, clear, pink
threading **50.00**
Salt, 2¾" d, cranberry, white
threading, applied clear petal
feet **75.00**
Tumbler, ftd, clear, mulberry
threading, sgd "Libbey" **175.00**
Vase, 5½" h, pink overshot body,
applied random amber threading **225.00**

TIFFANY

History: Louis Comfort Tiffany (1849–
1934) established a glass house in 1878
primarily to make stained glass windows.
There he developed a unique type of colored iridescent glass called Favrile. His Favrile glass differed from other art glass in
manufacture as it was a composition of colored glass worked together while hot. The
essential characteristic is that ornamentation is found within the glass. Favrile was
never further decorated. Different effects
were achieved by varying the amount and
position of colors which project movement
in form and shape.

In 1890, in order to utilize surplus materials at the plant, Tiffany began to design
and produce "small glass" such as iridescent glass lamp shades, vases, stemware,
and tableware in the Art Nouveau manner.
Commercial production began in 1896.
Most Tiffany wares are signed with the
name "L. C. Tiffany" or the initials "L.C.T."
Some pieces also carry the word "Favrile"
as well as a number. A number of other
marks can be found, e.g., "Tiffany Studios"
and "Louis C. Tiffany Furnaces."

Louis Tiffany and the artists in his studio
also are well known for their fine work in
other areas—bronzes, pottery, jewelry, silver and enamels.

References: Victor Arwas, *Glass, Art
Nouveau and Art Deco,* Rizzoli International Publications, 1977; Vivienne Could-
rey, *Tiffany: The Art of Louis Comfort,* Wellfleet Press, 1989; *The Art Work of Louis C.
Tiffany,* Apollo Books, 1987; Alastair Duncan, *Louis Comfort Tiffany,* Harry N.
Abrams, 1992; Robert Koch, *Louis C. Tiffany, Rebel In Glass,* Crown Publishers,
1966; Ellen T. Schroy, *Warman's Glass,*
Wallace-Homestead, 1992; John A. Shuman III, *The Collector's Encyclopedia of
American Art Glass,* Collector Books, 1988,
1994 value update.

Museums: Chrysler Museum, Norfolk,
VA; Corning Glass Museum, Corning, NY;
University of Connecticut, The William Ben-
ton Museum of Art, Storrs, CT.

BRONZE

Bowl, low, crimped edge, raised
low pedestal base, imp "Tiffany
Studios New York 1713," gilt finish worn, price for pair **225.00**
Box, 6" l, Pine Needle pattern,
glass panels **600.00**
Candelabrum, gilt bronze, blown
out, three branch candleholders

**Vase, Favrile, irid gold, sgd
"1067–9673 L. L.C. Tiffany, Favrile," $800.00.**

with green Favrile glass liners centering candle snuffer on chain, smooth shaft and foot, imp label "Tiffany Studios New York 7361," paint worn, wire plug on foot, bobeche lacking, 12½" h **1,750.00**

Chamberstick, gilt bronze, adjustable candle lamp, orig pressed mesh metal shade of blue pansy enameled design, base imp "Louis C. Tiffany Furnaces Inc. Favrile 82," 14½" h **875.00**

Clock, enameled, pyramidal frame, blue, amethyst, and yellow dec, circular "Tiffany & Co. New York" Chelsea clock mechanism, base imp "Louis C. Tiffany Furnaces, Inc. 360," 5¾" h **2,750.00**

Desk Set, gilt bronze

Pine Needle pattern, #845 inkwell, #941 calendar, #961 hooked bill file, #995 blotter rocker, #1004 pen and pencil tray, #1060 holder, blotter ends, green slag and beading, each imp "Tiffany Studios New York," price for set **1,610.00**

Venetian pattern, #1644 letter holder, #1645 stamp box, #1646 pen tray, #1694 blotter ends, each imp "Tiffany Studios New York," price for set . **885.00**

Lamp Base, 23" h, gilt bronze, simulated jewels and turtleback tiles on shaft and platform base, three socket wheel and heat cap, inscribed "Tiffany Studios New York 587" **2,530.00**

Picture Frame, gilt bronze, inlaid floral swag border centering dragon and urn cartouche, imp "Tiffany Studios New York 1611," 9¾" w, 12" h **1,250.00**

GLASS

Bonbon, 6¼" d, 1¾" h, gold, stretched irid, flared bowl, inscribed "L. C. Tiffany Favrile 1561," orig foil and paper label **550.00**

Bowl

6" d, 2" h, gold irid, sgd "L. C. Tiffany, Favrile, 1401, F299 K" **395.00**

6¼" d, 2¾" h, gold, crimped edge, ribbed, engraved leaf and vine border on int., base marked "L. C. Tiffany Favrile" **920.00**

7" d, optic blue **1,050.00**

8¼" d, 3½" h, gold, ten prominent ribs, scalloped rim, strong irid, base inscribed "L.C.T. Favrile" **865.00**

Candlesticks, pr, 9" h, gold Favrile, ten rib twisted stem, fine gold irid luster, each inscribed "L. C. T." **1,955.00**

Center Bowl, 11½" d, 4½" h, engraved leaf and vine dec, gold irid Favrile glass bowl, heavy gilt metal foliate molded base, inscribed "Louis C. Tiffany Furnaces Favrile 500" **1,495.00**

Compote

4" h, gold irid, two engraved butterflies on int., folded pedestal foot, inscribed "L. C. Tiffany Favrile 1149" **1,380.00**

5" d, gold, stretched edge **600.00**

5½" d, 11¼" h, gold, tall stemmed irid dish, cupped pedestal foot, inscribed "L. C. T." **815.00**

Lampshade

4¼" h, lily, gold, eight scalloped edge design, fine luster, inscribed "L.C.T." **375.00**

7" d, feather dec **1,800.00**

Tazza, 6½" d, Venetian Optic ... **600.00**

Vase

3" h, four green pulled feather elements, opal white shoulder, base inscribed "L. C. T. Y9494" **920.00**

3½" h, gold, eight applied glass pads trailing threads to base, marked "L. C. T." **345.00**

5¾" h, trumpet, flared, lustrous gold irid, disk foot inscribed "L. C. Tiffany Favrile 3493H" ... **575.00**

6" h, gold, smooth irid, inscribed "L. C. Tiffany Favrile 62" and "63 P1812," price for pair ... **750.00**

6½" h, dimpled shoulder, conforming gold and opal heart shaped dec elements, base inscribed "L. C. T. Q 1105" ...**1,725.00**

7" h, floriform, morning glory, pastel, yellow and white, opal-

escent stem, foot inscribed "L.
C. Tiffany Favrile 1918" **815.00**
9¾" h, trumpet, gold, ribbed design, applied decorative ring,
flared base inscribed "L. C.
Tiffany Inc. Favrile 1554–
5574N," int. stain on foot **750.00**
10" h, floriform, pastel, bright
pink and opal morning glory
blossom, striped stem, clear
foot, engraved wreath of flowers, inscribed "L. C. T. Favrile
1832" **1,100.00**
17½" h, gold irid trumpet base
sgd "L.C.T. Favrile," inserted
into dark bronze holder inscribed "Louis C. Tiffany Furnaces Inc. 158," glass top chip **460.00**

LAMPS

Candle, 12½" h, 7" d shade, gold
Favrile, twisted ten rib candlestick, metal spring operated
holder, ruffled edged shade with
fine stretched irid, metal insert
resoldered, base and shade sgd
"L.C.T." **1,150.00**
Chandelier, globe, Favrile glass
ball shade of opal glass, glossy
gold irid allover lily pad and vine
motif surface dec, rim marked
"L.C.T.," bronze collar and three
scrolled arms fixed to three suspension chains, ceiling fixture,
12" d globe **3,850.00**
Desk
Arabian, gilt bronze ten ribbed
base imp "Louis Comfort Tiffany Furnaces, Inc. 16," amber
Favrile glass vertically dec
conical shade cased with opal
white and dec with three darkly
irid prunts, sgd "L.C.T. Fa-
vrile," 13¾" h, 7" d shade ...**2,200.00**
Counterbalance, dark patina on
bronze cantilever base, imp
"Tiffany Studios New York
417," amber cased to opal
glass shade with green irid
damascene swirls, sgd at top
rim "L.C.T. Favrile," adjustable
to 17" h, 7" d shade **4,075.00**

Floor
Counterbalance, bronze, dark
brown–green patina, adjustable cantilever base, smooth
shaft, five curved legs, pad
feet, imp "Tiffany Studios New
York 468" on one foot, 56" h .**1,550.00**
Harp Bridge, dark green–brown
patina on harp, smooth shaft,
three splayed legs, pad feet,
imp cap between legs "Tiffany
Studios New York 423,"
socket, shade, and shade
holder replaced, 55" h **1,000.00**
Hanging, 19" h, six sided teardrop
lantern shade, broad bronze partitions housing rect green Favrile
glass segmented panels, reticulated bronze border, hook and
chain hanging devices, electrified socket **8,100.00**
Table, 22" h, 20" d conical shade,
Favrile glass segments leaded
as green and opal white lily pads
floating on water's surface, rim
edge with green Favrile jewel
necklace, imp "Tiffany Studios
New York 1502–10," 20" bronze
ring support, sgd oil canister, integrated water lily base molded
as lily pads, buds, and naturalistic grasses **68,500.00**

SILVER

Child's Feeding Set, 3⅝" h mug,
5" d bowl, and 7½" d plate, wide
repousse border, chased farm
landscape, each marked "Tiffany & Co," c1926, 22 oz, 10
dwt, price for 3 pc set **2,100.00**
Demitasse Service, 8¼" h cov
demitasse pot, creamer, cov
sugar, austere paneled design,
imp "Tiffany & Co. 180 Makers/
Silver Soldered E.D. Douple,"
monogrammed, price for three
pc set **650.00**
Pitcher, globular, curved flat
chased acanthus leaf handle,
circular foot, wide repousse
Olympian pattern band, neck
band of repousse scrolled acanthus, marked "Tiffany & Co, New

York," c1880, 28 oz, 10 dwt, 7"
h **7,700.00**
Vase, sterling silver and metal,
ovoid body, dragonfly dec, figural dragonfly handles, raised
feet, 6½" h **10,500.00**

Lemonade Set, pitcher, four matching cups, green, threaded, black handle, $115.00.

c1960

TIFFIN GLASS

History: A. J. Beatty & Sons built a glass manufacturing plant in Tiffin, Ohio, in 1888. On January 1, 1892, the firm joined the U. S. Glass Co. and was known as factory "R." Quality and production at this factory were very high and resulted in fine Depression-era glass.

Beginning in 1916 wares were marked with a paper label. From 1923 to 1936, Tiffin produced a line of black glassware, called Black Satin. The company discontinued operation in 1980.

References: Fred Bickenheuser, *Tiffin Glassmasters, Book I,* Glassmasters Publications, 1979; Fred Bickenheuser, *Tiffin Glassmasters, Book II,* Glassmasters Publications, 1981; Fred W. Bickenheuser, *Tiffin Glassmasters, Book III,* Glassmasters Publications, 1985; Bob Page and Dale Fredericksen, *Tiffin Is Forever: A Stemware Identification Guide,* Page-Fredericksen, 1994; Ellen T. Schroy, *Warman's Glass,* Wallace-Homestead, 1992.

Collectors' Club: Tiffin Glass Collectors Club, PO Box 554, Tiffin, OH 44883.

Animal, pheasants ....**150.00**
Aster Bowl, 5" d, black, #16273 .   **35.00**
Bell
    Cerice **75.00**
    Palois Versailles **95.00**
Candlesticks, pr
    #5831, crystal, double **35.00**
    #15328, black, satin, 8" h **45.00**

Champagne
    Fontaine, pink **30.00**
    June Night **18.00**
Cheese Compote, Sylvan, green   **15.00**
Claret
    Canterbury, citron **17.50**
    June Night **32.00**
Cocktail
    June Night **22.00**
    Leige, #17467 ....   **14.00**
Compote, 10" d, 5¾" h, black
    satin, twisted stem, two colorful
    hp cockatoos, sprays of green
    leaves, white enamel dots **165.00**
Creamer and Sugar, matching
    tray, Cerice, crystal **95.00**
Cup and Saucer, blown
    Flanders, yellow **65.00**
    Rosalind, yellow **35.00**
Dish, cov, heart shaped, black ...   **65.00**
Goblet
    Fontaine, pink **40.00**
    June Night, 8" h **26.00**
    Rambling Rose **23.00**
Iced Tea Tumbler, ftd
    Canterbury, citron **15.00**
    June Night **30.00**
Juice Tumbler
    Classic, 3½" h **35.00**
    Cordelia, yellow **15.00**
Lamp, figural
    Owl, brown **350.00**
    Parrot, multicolored **375.00**
Mayonnaise Set, 3 pc set
    Cerice **30.00**
    Cherokee Rose **40.00**
Plate, 8" d
    Cerice **12.50**
    Empire, twilight **17.50**

Sherbet
  Canterbury, citron **12.50**
  Rambling Rose **16.00**
Sugar, Chinese Modern **12.00**
Sundae
  Cerice **18.00**
  Fontaine, green **25.00**
Tumbler, ftd, Cerice, 4⅞" h **20.00**
Vase, fan, black, heavy sterling
  overlay floral dec, enameled
  jewels **175.00**

c1875

c1880

c1872-1951

TILES

History: The use of decorated tiles peaked during the latter part of the 19th century. Over 100 companies in England alone were producing tiles by 1880. By 1890 companies had opened in Belgium, France, Australia, Germany, and the United States.

Tiles were not limited to adorning fireplaces. Many were installed into furniture, such as washstands, hall stands, and folding screens. Since tiles were easily cleaned and, hence, hygienic, they readily were used on the floors and walls of entry halls, hospitals, butcher shops, or any place where sanitation was a concern. Many public buildings and subways also employed tiles to add interest and beauty.

Condition is an important fact in determining price. A cracked, badly scuffed and scratched, or heavily chipped tile has very little value. Slight chipping around the outer edges of a tile is, at times, considered acceptable by collectors, especially if these chips can be covered by a frame.

It is not uncommon for the highly glazed surface of some tiles to have become crazed. Crazing is not considered a deterrent as long as it does not detract from the overall appearance of the tile.

References: J. & B. Austwick, *The Decorated Tile,* Pitman House, 1980; Susan and Al Bagdade, *Warman's American Pottery and Porcelain,* Wallace–Homestead, 1994; Susan and Al Bagdade, *Warman's English & Continental Pottery & Porcelain, Second Edition,* Wallace–Homestead, 1991; Julian Barnard, *Victorian Ceramic Tiles,* N. Y. Graphic Society, 1972; Ralph and Terry Kovel, *Kovels' American Art Pottery: The Collector's Guide To Makers, Marks and Factory Histories,* Crown Publishers, 1993; Terence A. Lockett, *Collecting Victorian Tiles,* Antique Collectors Club, 1979; Ralph Moore and Dinah Tanner, *Porcelain & Pottery Tea Tiles,* Antique Publications, 1994; Noel Riley, *Tile Art: A History of Decorative Ceramic Tiles,* Chartwell Books, 1987; Ronald L. Rindge et al., *Ceramic Art of the Malibu Potteries: 1926–1932,* Malibu Lagoon Museum, 1994; Hans Van Lemmen, *Tiles: A Collectors' Guide,* Seven Hills Books, 1985.

Periodical: *Flash Point,* PO Box 1850, Healdsburg, CA 95448.

Collectors' Club: Tiles & Architectural Ceramics Society, Ironbridge Gorge Museum, Ironbridge, Telford, Shropshire TF8 7AW, England.

American Encaustic Tiling Co, Zanesville, OH
  3" sq, William Jennings Bryan, 1896 election **145.00**
  6¼ x 10½", hp, birds, wooden frames, price for pair **350.00**
Beaver Falls Art Tile Co, Beaver Falls, PA, 12 x 12", molded, George Washington profile portrait, allover stars background, sgd and dated "Broome 1892" . **825.00**
Byrdcliffe Pottery, Woodstock, NY,

J. & J. G. Low Patent Art Tile Works, abstract iris, beige and brown, 6" sq, $60.00.

5⅝" sq, potted wildflowers, blue, yellow, burgundy, and green, neutral ground, some corner roughness **225.00**

California Faience Co, Berkeley, CA, 5½" d, round, stylized green dandelion leaves, red blossoms, sky blue ground, incised, mark . **275.00**

Chelsea Keramic Art Works, Chelsea, MA, 5⅞ x 11¾", rect, raised double handled vase dec, glossy brown glaze, imp "Chelsea Keramic Art Works, Robertson and Sons," rough corner, late 19th C **175.00**

Creil & Montereau, Creil, France, 8" sq, polychrome dec, coastal city scene, sgd on face, marked on back, wood frame, c1870 .. **325.00**

Flint Faience Tile, Flint, MI, 6" sq, fruit compote, multicolored, Grueby style **135.00**

Grueby Faience and Tile Co, Boston, MA

4" sq, allegorical, molded motif, Love, Music, Beauty, and Industry, one imp "Grueby Boston," price for set of four **475.00**

6" sq, white water lily blossoms and buds, green leaf pads, dark green ground, imp "Grueby Boston," price for set of three **1,100.00**

J & J G Low, 6" sq, Boy Reading Book, 1881 .... **250.00**

Limoges, 8 x 12", rect, hp, European peasant couple with child, seated on bench, house in background, scroll–molded frame, c1900 .... **650.00**

Marblehead Pottery, Marblehead, MA

4¾" sq, sailing ship dec, blue, green, and brown, metal ftd frame, imp mark on back, early 20th C **495.00**

6" sq, marsh landscape, row of oak trees reflected in tidal pools, brown, tan, green, and yellow, incised mark **375.00**

Minton China Works, Stoke–on–Trent, Staffordshire, England, 6" sq, transfer printed, ten different titled allegorical scenes, four seasons, stylized borders, sepia, ochre, and sage green, raised relief mark, some edge chipping, price for set of ten **495.00**

Pardee Works, Perth Amboy, NJ

4" w, sailing ship, crystalline glaze, black, rust, cream, and green, low relief dec **80.00**

4⅜" sq, incised and painted design, duck and frog at pond edge, blue, green, and yellow, raised mark, early 20th C ... **250.00**

Paul Revere Pottery, Boston, MA, 5⅝" d, round, central landscape dec, green, yellow, and blue, navy blue ground, imp and painted marks, paper label, Fanny Levine, c1925 .... **275.00**

Pewabic Pottery, Detroit, MI

2¾" sq, incised floral dec **165.00**

4" sq, incised sailing ship dec . **275.00**

7½" sq, United States seal dec, copper reduction glaze, incised circle mark **325.00**

TINWARE

History: Beginning in the 1700s many utilitarian household objects were made of tin. Tin is nontoxic, rust resistant, and fairly durable, so it can be used for storing food. It often was plated to iron to provide strength. Because it was cheap, tinware and tin-plated wares were in the price range of most people.

An early center of tinware manufacture in the United States was Berlin, Connecticut. Almost every small town and hamlet had its own tinsmith, tinner, or whitesmith. Tinsmiths used patterns from which to make items. They cut out the pieces, hammered and shaped them, and soldered the parts. If a piece was to be used with heat, a copper bottom was added because of the low melting point of tin. The Industrial Revolution brought about machine-made, mass-produced tinware pieces. The handmade era ended by the late 19th century.

This category is a catchall for tin objects which do not fit into other categories in our book.

References: Dover Stamping Co, *1869 Illustrated Catalog,* Astragal Press, 1994 reprint; Dana G. Morykan and Harry L. Rinker, *Warman's Country Antiques & Collectibles, Second Edition* Wallace-Homestead, 1994.

Museum: Cooper-Hewitt Museum National Museum of Design, New York, NY; Smithsonian Institution, Washington, DC.

Additional Listings: See Advertising, Kitchen Collectibles, Lanterns, Lamps and Lighting, and Tinware: Decorated.

Fish Pan, oval, two wire handles, 13 x 11⅞ x 2½", $15.00.

Biscuit Cutter, fluted edge, strap
   handle **8.00**
Candle Mold
   9" h, thirty six tube **330.00**
   10¼" h, six tube **55.00**
   10½" h, twelve tube, round,
     crimped top, flanged bottom . **450.00**
   10¾" h, six tube **75.00**
   11" h, twelve tube, old black re-
     paint **85.00**
   11½" h, twelve tube **90.00**
Candle Sconce, 16" h, hooded
   semi–circular crests with
   crimped edge, semi–circular
   base pans, single candle socket,
   price for pair **2,310.00**
Chamberstick, 9" d, 4½" h, deep
   pan, pushup conical snuffer, re-
   pair **60.00**
Chandelier, 33½" h, baluster form
   body, sixteen arms **4,025.00**
Coffee Urn, 23½" h, handled, pol-
   ished brass fittings, label "The
   Eclipse Copper Co Sole Makers,
   York" **125.00**
Colander, 18¾" d, old black traces **75.00**
Condiment Set, 6½" d, six cylin-
   drical shakers, holder **140.00**
Cookie Cutter
   3⅞" l, spaniel, American, 19th C **75.00**
   4¼" l, razorback pig **45.00**
   6¼" l, full-length silhouette of
     man **70.00**
   6¾" l, stylized animal, long ears **215.00**
   7" l, dancing Dutch man, dark
     patina **225.00**
Food Mold, cov
   5½" d, round, fruit design **75.00**
   6" l, oval, cornucopia design . . **35.00**
   7¼" l, oval, thistle design **85.00**
   8½" l, comet **50.00**
Grater, 15½" h, semi–circular . . . **15.00**
Lamp
   Betty, 12½" h, crimped detailed
     stand **650.00**
   Skater's, 6¼" h, clear globe . . . **55.00**
Lantern, blackout, 9½" h, spring
   loaded candle tube, copper
   band, old dark patina **200.00**
Lighting Fixture and Stand, primi-
   tive **195.00**
Megaphone, 30" h, worn red paint **100.00**
Nutmeg Grater, 6¼" l, marked
   "Edgar" **50.00**
Roly Poly, 6½" h, rabbit, orange,
   tan, white, yellow, and black,
   marked "J Chein" **175.00**
Rum Warmer, 7¼" h, pewter finial,
   turned curly maple handle **385.00**

Shorebird
    11½" l, folding, worn orig paint,
      label "Pat Oct 27, 1874" **175.00**
    14½" h, folding, rod and drift-
      wood base, old worn paint .. **165.00**
Snuff Box, 3¼" l, oval, primitive,
    hinged lid **95.00**
Tinder Box, 3¼" h, candleholder,
    int. with flint, steel, flax tinder,
    and damper **275.00**
Tube Pan, 6½" d, round, swirl de-
    sign **10.00**

TINWARE: DECORATED

History: The art of decorating sheet iron, tin, and tin-coated sheet iron dates back to the mid-18th century. The Welsh called the practice pontipool, the French To'le Peinte. In America the center for tin-decorated ware was in the late 1700s was Berlin, Connecticut.

Several styles of decorating techniques were used: painting, japanning, and stenciling. Designs were done by both professionals and itinerants. English and Oriental motifs strongly influenced both form and design.

A special type of decoration on unpainted tin was the punch work practiced by the Pennsylvania tinsmiths. Forms included coffeepots, spice boxes, and grease lamps.

Reference: Dana G. Morykan and Harry L. Rinker, *Warman's Country Antiques & Collectibles, 2nd Edition* Wallace-Homestead, 1994.

ABC Plate, 8" d, Mary Had A Little
    Lamb **110.00**
Architectural Panel, 23 x 47",
    pressed, classical bow and ar-
    row motif, polychrome paint ... **575.00**
Box
    3½ x 6 x 9", red and yellow strip-
      ing, bronze powder stenciled
      floral dec, orig brown japan-
      ning, minor wear, edge dam-
      age **75.00**
    8" w, orig black paint, red floral
      dec **185.00**
Bread Box, 16" l, metallic stenciled
    label, orig worn black paint, red
    accents **115.00**
Cache Pot, 7¼" h, shaped oval

Match Safe, wall type, yellow, orig dec, $135.00.

    well, chinoiserie dec body, land-
    scape and figures scene,
    pierced everted lip, flared base
    with brown and black tones and
    gilt highlights **1,495.00**
Candle Box, 10½" l, hanging, cy-
    lindrical, old black paint **135.00**
Candle Sconce, 13½" h, circular
    crimped crest, worn patina and
    yellow silver paint, imp "J S
    Grose" near hanging hole **145.00**
Chestnut Urn, pr, Regency style,
    black, gold vintage dec, lion
    head and ring handles, pedestal
    foot, paint loss, 19th C **375.00**
Deed Box, 8" l, white and blue
    stripes, orig brown japanning .. **65.00**
Footwarmer
    7½ x 9", 5¾" h, mortised walnut
      frame with turned posts,
      punched heart and circle de-
      sign **330.00**
    7¾ x 9", mortised hardwood,
      turned corner posts, punched
      circle design **135.00**
Jardiniere, pr, 14¾" h, Empire,
    flared form, gold toned Neo-
    classical motifs, red ground, sq
    plinth with painted faux marble
    design, claw feet, first quarter
    19th C **4,025.00**
Lamp, pr, 3¾" h, conical font,
    hinged snuffer, saucer pan,
    brass and tin whale oil burner,
    worn blue japanning **245.00**
Lantern, 11¼" h plus ring handle,

round, conical top, six glass sides, hinged door, old black paint 225.00

Plaque, 10¼" d, hp portrait of noblewoman wearing blue and white cap 40.00

Tea Set, child's, 19 pcs, tray, eight plates and cup and saucers, and two creamers, chromolithography of Mother Goose, one creamer missing handle, Ohio Art, price for set 50.00

Tea Tray, 29" l, oval serpentine shape, peacock and flowers dec, black and gold border, 19th C . 550.00

Tray
12½" w, octagonal, orig brown japanning, yellow striping, white band with floral dec ... 75.00

16½" l, 16½" h, two tiers, oval, reticulated galleries, black repaint, landscape scene with classical ruins 275.00

23½ x 18½", Victorian, painted castle scene 135.00

30 x 21¾", Victorian, gilt dec, high raised lip, stenciled dec with birds perched in flowering branches, mid 19th C 750.00

TOBACCO CUTTERS

History: Before pre-packaging, tobacco was delivered to merchants in bulk form. Tobacco cutters were used to cut the tobacco into desired sizes.

Enterprise Manufacturing Co, Philadelphia, PA, cast iron, emb "E. W. Venables Tobaccos" adv, patented April 15, 1875, 16½" l, 7" h 135.00

John Finzer & Brothers, Louisville, KY, cast iron, emb adv, 17" l, 7" h 125.00

P J Sorg Co, spearhead, cast iron, red, black lettering, 16½" l 150.00

R J Reynolds Co, black japanned finish 90.00

Unmarked
Battle axe shaped blade, cast iron, wood handle and base, 18" l, 7½" h 225.00

Wooden base, cast iron cutter, 11½" l, 6¼ x 7¼" graduated width, $40.00.

Fancy mark on blade and hinge, wrought iron, wood base with dark patina, dated "1773," European, some insect damage to base, 35" l 225.00

Horse model, cast iron, wood base, 11½" l, 6" h 450.00

TOBACCO JARS

History: A tobacco jar is a container for storing tobacco. Tobacco humidors were made of various materials and in many shapes, including figurals. The earliest jars date to the early 17th century. However, most examples in today's market were made in the late 19th or early 20th centuries.

Reference: Deborah Gage and Madeleine Marsh, *Tobacco Containers & Accessories,* Gage Bluett & Company, 1988.

Collectors' Club: Society of Tobacco Jar Collectors, 3021 Courtland Blvd., Shaker Heights, OH 44122.

Delft, 10⅝" h, Indian, smoking pipe, seated beside cargo including tobacco jar inscribed "TONKA" and package inscribed "VOC," blue and white, two Dutch ships in background, blue "BP" mark, Dutch, late 18th C 600.00

Glass, 7½" h, opaque opaline

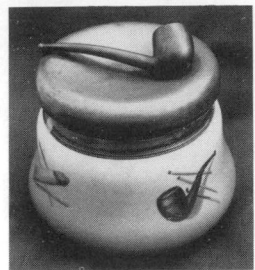

Porcelain, multicolored dec, 6¼″ h, $85.00.

ground, oviform, ext. painted with half-length portrait of Indian brave, buckskin, shaded green, russet, and tan ground, knopped, hinged cov inscribed "Tobacco" in brown and white enamel, florette patterned metal mount, ornate frontal thumbpiece, stamped "Decorated by P. J. Handel, Meriden, CT, #89/130" **1,000.00**

Porcelain

5¾″ h, Schafer and Vater, cartouche with raised female figure outlined in gold, pink luster bottom, raised cartouche on cov with child, tan ground, imp mark, c1900 .... **90.00**

5⅞″ h, KPM, rect, molded dec, scrolls enclosing groups of figures in landscape vignettes on front and back, sides with flower garlands, floral finial, ormolu mounted keyhole, gilt metal mounted, scroll feet and handles, underglaze blue "G" mark, restoration to handles and finial, c1760 ....**6,100.00**

Stoneware

4½″ h, Quimper, relief floral dec, rim and base with beaded band, brown glaze **150.00**

5″ h, Dresden, round, raised white dec, windmill, figures, animals, and trees, tan ground, dark brown neck and lid, tamper, imp "Royal Doulton" **450.00**

5¾″ h, salt glazed, six sided, figural tollhouse, trees around door and windows, brown ... **325.00**

Terra-Cotta, 6″ h, Torquay, inscribed "Tobacco You Are Welcome," amber **115.00**

TOBY JUGS

History: A toby jug is a drinking vessel usually depicting a full-figured, robust, genial, drinking man. They originated in England in the late 18th century. The term "Toby" probably related to the character Uncle Toby from *Tristam Shandy* by Laurence Sterne.

References: Susan and Al Bagdade, *Warman's English & Continental Pottery & Porcelain, Second Edition,* Wallace-Homestead, 1991; Vic Schuler, *Collecting British Toby Jugs, Second Edition,* Kevin Francis Publishing, 1994, distributed by Wallace-Homestead.

Additional Listing: Royal Doulton.

Reproduction Alert: Within the last 100 years or more, tobies have been reproduced copiously by many potteries in the United States and England.

Bennington, 10⅜″ h, Coachman, Rockingham glaze, honey colored, 1849 mark **475.00**

Pearlware, 10¾″ h, standing man, wearing green hat and jacket, brown flowered waistcoat, ochre breeches, and brown gloves,

J. Bull, 4¾″ h, $30.00.

rocky base, tree trunk forming handle, hat restored, attributed to Yorkshire, c1790 .... **550.00**

Pratt

9" h, Martha Gunn, seated woman, holding flask and beaker, canted square base, wearing green, blue, and orange floral dec dress with yellow and brown trim, rim and beaker restored, c1800 ..... **2,225.00**

11¼" h, Hearty Good Fellow, walking man, wearing blue jacket, ochre waistcoat, and yellow breeches, green glazed base extending to form handle, restoration to hat and shoulders, c1800 .... **1,000.00**

Royal Doulton, 5½" h, Happy John, #6070, c1939 .... **75.00**

Staffordshire

6½" h, seated man, smoking, holding ale jug on knee, wearing blue jacket and gray breeches, pipe repaired, late 18th C **750.00**

9⅝" h, Admiral Lord Howe, seated on barrel, dog and pipe at feet, green jacket, manganese waistcoat and breeches, foaming globular ale jug, hat restored, late 18th C **3,185.00**

10" h, Tax Collector, seated man, rust trousers, gold vest, blue jacket, black boots and hat **400.00**

10¼" h, Punch, wearing green hat and white and rust striped clothing, c1890 .... **265.00**

TOOLS

History: Before the advent of assembly line and mass production, practically everything required for living was handmade at home or by a local tradesman or craftsman. The cooper, the blacksmith, the cabinet maker, and the carpenter all had their special tools.

Early examples of these hand tools are collected for their workmanship, ingenuity, place of manufacture, or design. Modern-day craftsmen often search out old hand tools for use to authentically recreate the manufacture of an object.

References: *A Price Guide To Keen Kutter Tools,* L-W Books, 1993; Ronald S. Barlow, *The Antique Tool Collector's Guide to Value, Third Edition,* Windmill Publishing, 1991; Terri Clemens, *American Family Farm Antiques,* Wallace-Homestead, 1994; Kenneth L. Cope, *American Machinist's Tools: An Illustrated Directory of Patents,* Astragal Press, 1993; Kenneth L. Cope, *Makers of American Machinist Tools,* Astragal Press, 1994; Herbert P. Kean and Emil S. Pollak, *A Price Guide To Antique Tools,* Astragal Press, 1992; Herbert P. Kean and Emil S. Pollak, *Collecting Antique Tools,* Astragal Press, 1990; Kathryn Mc-Nerney, *Antique Tools, Our American Heritage,* Collector Books, 1979, 1995 value update; Dana G. Morykan and Harry L. Rinker, *Warman's Country Antiques & Collectibles, Second Edition* Wallace-Homestead, 1994; Emil and Martyl Pollak, *A Guide To American Wooden Planes and Their Makers, Third Edition,* The Astragal Press, 1994; Emil and Martyl Pollak, *Prices Realized on Rare Imprinted American Wood Planes, 1979–1992,* Astragal Press, 1993; R. A. Salaman, *Dictionary of Tools,* Charles Scribner's Sons, 1974; John Walter, *Antique & Collectible Stanley Tools: A Guide To Identity and Value,* Tool Merchants, 1990; John M. Whelan, *The Wooden Plane: Its History, Form, and Function,* Astragal Press, 1993; Jack P. Wood, *Early 20th Century Stanley Tools: A Price Guide,* L-W Book Sales, n.d.; Jack P. Wood, *Town-Country Old Tools and Locks Keys and Closures,* L-W Books, 1990.

Periodicals: *Fine Tool Journal,* PO Box 4001, Pittsford, VT 05763; *Plumb Line* 10023 St. Clair's Retreat, Fort Wayne, IN 46825; *Stanley Tool Collector News,* 208 Front St., PO Box 227, Marietta, OH 45750; *Tool Ads,* PO Box 33, Hamilton, MT 59840.

Collectors' Clubs: Collectors of Rare & Familiar Tools Society, 38 Colony Ct., Murray Hill, NJ 07974; Early American Industries Assoc., PO Box 2128, Empire State Plaza Station, Albany, NY 12220; Early American Industries-West, 8476 West Way Dr., La Jolla, CA 92038; Mid-West Tool Collectors Assoc., 808 Fairway Dr., Columbia,

MO 65201; Missouri Valley Wrench Club, 613 N. Long St., Shelbyville, IL 62565; New England Tool Collectors Assoc., 303 Fisher Rd., Fitchburg, MA 01420; Ohio Tool Collectors Assoc., PO Box 261, London, OH 43140; Pacific Northwest Tool Collectors, 2132 NE 81st St., Seattle, WA 98115; Potomac Antique Tools & Industries Assoc., 6802 Newbitt Pl., McLean, VA 22101; Rocky Mountain Tool Collectors, 2024 Owens Ct., Denver, CO 80227; Society of Workers in Early Arts & Trades, 606 Lake Lena Blvd., Auburndale, FL 33823; Southwest Tool Collectors Assoc., 7032 Oak Bluff Dr., Dallas, TX 75240; Three Rivers Tool Collectors, 39 S. Rolling Hills, Irwin, PA 15642; Tool Group of Canada, 7 Tottenham Rd., Ontario MC3 2J3 Canada.

Museums: American Precision Museum Association, Windsor, VT; Mercer Museum, Doylestown, PA; Shelburne Museum, Shelburne, VT; World of Tools Museum, Waverly, TN.

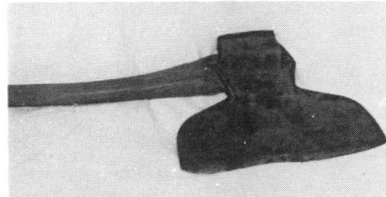

Broad Axe, marked "Wm Beatty & Son, Cast Steel, Chester," 23½" w, $45.00.

Adze, house carpenter's, Douglas Axe Mfg, MA, c1864, 4" w cutter, hickory handle	30.00
Axe, mortising, 9½" head	40.00
Brace, ratchet, Peck, Stow & Wilcox, Sampson No. 8008A, nickel plated frame, rosewood pad and wrist	25.00
Caliper, Brown & Sharp, No. 826, ice tong shape, 24" l	20.00
Draw Knife, A J Wilkinson, patented 1895, folding handle	38.00
Gauge, mortise, Stanley No. 198, oval head, rosewood, twin nickel plated stems	40.00
Hammer, roofer's, hand forged square faced extended claw, separate strap handle, 2 lb	80.00
Level, G. S. Crosby, Brooklyn, NY, Boss, mahogany, heavy brass plates, orig box, 12" l	150.00
Plane, Stanley	
Block, No. 65, low angle, nickel plated metal, knuckle joint lever cap	30.00
Cabinet Maker's Edge, No. 97, 1905–40, 10" l	250.00
Jack, Bailey No. 27, wood bottom, 1870–1917, 15" l, 2½" w cutter	25.00
Rule, Chapin Stephens Co, No. 36½, one foot, two fold, boxwood, caliper, brass square joint, tips, and slide	30.00
Saw, hand, Keen Kutter No. KK88, applewood handle, 26" l	30.00
Spoke Shave, W Johnson, Newark, NJ, wood, 9" l	20.00
Square, steel rafter, Ideal Tool Co, patented 1914, triangle with hinged arm at apex	30.00
Vise, bench top, handwrought, ram's horn wing nut clamp, 2½" jaws	45.00
Wrench, buggy wheel, A. P. Joy, Rockingham, NH, No. 1, patented Feb 1, 1898, nickel plated frame, wood side handle, lever on back of head	25.00

TOOTHPICK HOLDERS

History: Toothpick holders, indispensable table accessories of the Victorian era, are small containers used to hold toothpicks.

They were made in a wide range of materials: china (bisque and porcelain), glass (art, blown, cut, opalescent, pattern, etc.), and metals, especially silver plate. Makers include both American and European firms.

Toothpick holders were used as souvenir items by applying decals or transfers. The same blank may contain several different location labels.

References: William Heacock, *Encyclopedia Of Victorian Colored Pattern Glass,*

Book I, Toothpick Holders From A To Z, Second Edition, Antique Publications, 1976, 1992 value update; William Heacock, *1,000 Toothpick Holders: A Collector's Guide,* Antique Publications, 1977; William Heacock, *Rare & Unlisted Toothpick Holders,* Antique Publications, 1984; National Toothpick Holders Collectors Society, *Toothpick Holders: China, Glass, and Metal,* Antique Publications, 1992.

Collectors' Club: National Toothpick Holders Collectors Society, 1224 Spring Valley Lane, West Chester, PA 19380.

Additional Listings: See *Warman's Americana & Collectibles* for more examples.

Advisor: Judy Knauer.

GLASS

Amberina, IVT, bulging base, NTHCS #88	195.00
Burmese, tricorner	395.00
Cameo, gold cut back to chipped ice frosted peach ground, Thistle and Leaf pattern, gold rim and base, sgd "Daum Nancy" with cross of Lorraine	495.00
Custard	
Bees on basket	48.00
Vermont, green trim	95.00
Hat	
Amber, ribbed	24.00
Brown, rolled up rim, crude broken pontil	24.00
Clear, blown, 1⅛" d, 2" rim	30.00
Opaque Glass, Shell & Seaweed, pink, canary blush dec	90.00
Pattern Glass	
Brittanic, amber flashed	135.00
Daisy and Button	
Amberina, Hobb's	350.00
Blue, 3" d base, 4¾" d rim	40.00
Canary, flared rim	35.00
Fine Cut, amber	40.00
Libbey's Little Lobe, dec	130.00
Opalescent	
Ribbed Spiral, blue	110.00
Wreath and Shell, vaseline, enamel dec	265.00
Opaline, blue, ruffled piecrust rim, polished pontil, NTHCS #123	95.00
Pattern Glass	
Delaware, green, gold trim	110.00
Hobb's Hobnail, vaseline	35.00
Josephine's Fan	62.50
Wellington, gold trim	65.00
Winsome	37.50
Peachblow, satin finish, white shading to deep raspberry, cylinder shape, polished pontil, ornate high ftd handled holder, New England	595.00
Spatter, Royal Ivory, cranberry spatter, crackle finish	275.00

PORCELAIN

Coalport, cream ground, gold trim, marked "Coalport Porcelain Works, Coalport, England," English registry number, NTHCS #548	50.00
Majolica, three faced gargoyle, blue, green, and brown, NTHCS #682	40.00
Occupied Japan, 4½" h, bisque, figural, little girl holding cookie, leaning against barrel, NTHCS #668	40.00
Royal Bayreuth	
Blue, ship at sea dec, green mark	130.00
Yellow and green turkeys and farmer, blue mark	110.00
RS Prussia, NTHCS #429	375.00

SILVERPLATED

Cat, seated beside bucket, marked "Babcock & Co., Quad-

Silver plated, "Take Your Pick," ruffled, marked "Osborn & Co, Lancaster, PA," 2¼" h, $45.00.

ruple Plate," c1890, NTHCS
#707 .... 50.00
Dog, holding bone, sitting in front
of basket, openwork top, marked
"James Tufts" 170.00
Porcupine, Meridan 95.00
Rabbit, nibbling leaf, inscribed
"Good Morning," marked "Mid-
dletown Plate Co., Quadruple
Plate, 37, Hard White Metal,
B.C.," c1890, NTHCS #742 ... 95.00
Violin on one side, top hat on
other, marked "Wilcox Silver
Plate Co," c1900, NTHCS #709 125.00

TORTOISESHELL ITEMS

History: For many years amber and mottled colored tortoiseshell has been used in
the manufacture of small items such as
boxes, combs, dresser sets, and trinkets.

Note: Anyone dealing in the sale of tortoiseshell objects should be familiar with the
Endangered Species Act and Amendment
in its entirety. As of November 1978, antique
tortoiseshell objects can be legally imported
and sold with some restrictions.

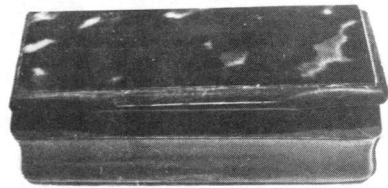

**Box, hinged lid, 1½ x 3½",
$125.00.**

Box, cov
3" d, circular, ivory trim 95.00
7½" w, Colonial, octagonal, tortoiseshell veneer over sandalwood, ornate carved ivory inlaid panels and trim, eight
carved ivory paw feet 300.00
Card Case
3½" h, rect, rounded edges,
ivory trim, frame–type border 225.00

4" h, mother–of–pearl inlaid flowers, ivory trim 90.00
Cigar Case, 5" h, 3" w, rect, serpentine shaped front and back . 220.00
Cigarette Box, 5½" w, rect, slightly
domed lid with monogrammed
initials 550.00
Fan, 17" w, gold inlaid cresting, tortoiseshell loop, brown ribbon .. 285.00
Glove Box, 3½" h, Colonial,
domed lid, ornate ivory strap-
ping, sandalwood int. 375.00
Model, 8" l, rickshaw, hinged hood,
spoked wheels, metal poles ... 105.00
Patch Box, 2" w, rect, slightly
domed lid, ivory trim 210.00
Picture Frame, 9 x 7", rect,
rounded corners, inlaid ivory
trim 285.00
Pin
Guitar, 5" l, ivory and mother–of–
pearl trim 65.00
Violin and Bow, 4½" l, ivory and
mother–of–pearl trim 165.00
Scent Bottle Case, 2½" h, Georgian, arched cov, convex front
and back 110.00
Sewing Box, 10" w, 7½" d, 4" h,
William IV, sarcophagus form,
molded lid, padded int., ball feet,
first half 19th C 1,850.00
Snuff Bottle, 4" w, rect 75.00
Tea Caddy, English
4½" h, blond colored, rect,
rounded corners, inlaid ivory
stringing forms paneled design, ivory escutcheon, three
compartments 1,100.00
6" w, 4" d, 6" h, Regency, ball
finial above rect body, two int.
lidded compartments, ball feet,
first quarter 19th C 1,850.00
7" w, 4¼" d, 7" h, Regency,
domed lid, bowed front with
sunburst design, two cov tea
bins int., early 19th C 1,100.00
10½" w, 5½" d, 6" h, George III,
rect, arched silver plated bail
handle, int. with twin lidded
wells centering mixing bowl,
plain conforming case, late
18th C 1,275.00
Thimble Case, slanted top, ivory
trim 182.00

TOYS

History: In America the first cast iron toys began to appear shortly after the Civil War. Leading 19th century manufacturers included Hubley, Dent, Kenton, and Schoenhut. In the first decades of the 20th century, Arcade, Buddy L, Marx, and Tootsietoy joined these earlier firms. Wooden toys were made by George Brown and other manufacturers who did not sign or label their work.

In Europe, Nuremberg, Germany, was the center for the toy industry from the late 18th through the mid-20th century. Companies such as Lehmann and Marklin produced high-quality toys.

Every toy is collectible. The key is the condition and working order if mechanical. Examples listed are considered to be in good to very good condition to mint condition unless otherwise specified.

References: Linda Baker, *Modern Toys, American Toys, 1930–1980,* Collector Books, 1985, 1993 value update; William M. Bean and Al M. Sternagle, *Greenberg's Guide To Gilbert Erector Sets Volume One, 1913–1932,* Greenberg Publishing, 1993; Raymond V. Brandes, *Big Bang Cannons,* Ray-Vin Publishing, 1993; Bill Bruegman, *Toys of the Sixties,* Cap'n Penny Productions, 1991; Steve Butler and Clarence Young, *Autoquotes, The Complete Reference For: Promotions, Pot Metal & Plastic with Prices,* Autohobby Publication, 1993; Robert Carter and Eddy Rubinstein, *Yesterday's Yesteryears: Lesney "Matchbox" Models,* Haynes Publishing Group (London), 1986; Roger Case and Tom Hammel (eds.), *1995 Toys & Prices, 2nd Edition,* Krause Publications, 1994; Wallace M. Chrouch, *Mego Toys: An Illustrated Value Guide,* Collector Books, 1995; Jurgen and Marianne Cieslik, *Lehmann Toys,* New Cavendish Books, 1982; Gael de Courtivron, *Collectible Coca-Cola Toy Trucks,* Collector Books, 1994; Don Cranmer, *Collectors Encyclopedia, Toys-Banks,* L-W Books, 1986, 1993 value update; Edward Force, *Corgi Toys,* Schiffer Publishing, 1984, 1991 value update; Edward Force, *Dinky Toys,* Schiffer Publishing, 1988, 1992 value update; Edward Force, *Matchbox and Lledo Toys,* Schiffer Publishing, 1988; Edward Force, *Solido Toys,* Schiffer Publishing, 1993; Tom Frey, *Toy Bop: Kid Classics of the 50's & 60's,* Fuzzy Dice Productions, 1994; Richard Friz, *The Official Identification And Price Guide To Collectible Toys, 5th Edition,* House of Collectibles, 1990; Gordon Gardiner and Alistair Morris, *The Illustrated Encyclopedia of Metal Toys,* Harmony Books, 1984; Christine Gentry and Sally Gibson-Downs, *Motorcycle Toys: Antique and Contemporary,* Collector Books, 1994; Lillian Gottschalk, *American Toy Cars & Trucks,* Abbeville Press, 1985; David C. Gould and Donna Crevar-Donaldson, *Occupied Japan Toys With Prices,* L-W Book Sales, 1993; Bill Hanlon, *Plastic Toys: Dimestore Dreams of the '40s & '50s,* Schiffer Publishing, 1993; Michael V. Harwood, *The Hess Toy Collector,* F.S.B.O. Books, 1991; Jay Horowitz, *Marx Western Playsets: The Authorized Guide,* Greenberg Publishing, 1992; Don Hultzman, *Collecting Battery Toys: A Reference, Rarity, and Value Guide,* Books Americana, 1994; Dana Johnson, *Matchbox Toys 1948 to 1933: Identification and Value Guide,* Collector Books, 1994; Joe Johnson and Dana McGuinn, *Toys That Talk: Over 300 Pullstring Dolls & Toys–1960s To Today,* Firefly Publishing, 1992; Dale Kelley, *Collecting The Tin Toy Car, 1950–1970,* Schiffer Publishing, 1984; Constance King, *Metal Toys & Automata,* Chartwell Books, 1989; Raymond R. Klein, *Greenberg's Guide To Tootsietoys 1945–1969,* Greenberg Publishing, 1993; Samuel H. Logan and Charles W. Best, *Cast Iron Toy Guns and Capshooters,* published by authors, 1990; Ernest and Ida Long, *Dictionary of Toys Sold in America,* 2 vols, published by authors; David Longest, *Antique & Collectible Toys 1870–1950,* Collector Books, 1994; David Longest, *Character Toys and Collectibles,* Collector Books, 1984, 1992 value update; David Longest, *Character Toys and Collectibles, Second Series,* Collector Books, 1987, 1990 value update; David Longest, *Toys: Antique & Collectible,* Collector Books, 1990, 1994 value update; Charlie Mack, *Lesney's Matchbox Toys: Regular Wheel Years, 1947–1969,* Schiffer Publishing, 1992; Charlie Mack, *Lesney's Matchbox Toys: The Superfast Years, 1969–1982,* Schiffer Publishing, 1993; Charlie Mack,

Matchbox Toys: The Universal Years, 1982–1992, Schiffer Publishing, 1993; Albert W. McCollough, The New Book of Buddy L Toys, Vol. I (1991), Vol. II (1991), Greenberg Publishing; Neil McElwee, McElwee's Collector's Guide #1: Smith-Miller 1944–1955, published by author, 1994; Neil McElwee, McElwee's Collector's Guide #3: Tonka Toys 1947–1961, published by author, 1992; Neil McElwee, McElwee's Collector's Guide #5: Postwar Buddy "L," 1945–1970, published by author, 1992; Neil McElwee, McElwee's Collector's Guide #6: Ny-Lint 1946–1970, published by author, 1993; Neil McElwee, McElwee's Collector's Guide #7: Big Ertl, Cast Commercial Trucks & Construction Vehicles, 1950's–1990, published by author, 1993; Neil McElwee, McElwee's Collector's Guide #8: Gasoline Company Toys...Trucks & Automotive, 1930's–1990's, published by author, 1994; Neil McElwee, McElwee's Collector's Guide #9: Structo 1912–1976, published by author, 1993; Neil McElwee, McElwee's Collector's Guide #10: Postwar Big Metal Classics, published by author, 1994; Neil McElwee, McElwee's Small Motor News Annual 1995, published by author, 1994; Kevin McGimpsey and Stewart Orr, Collecting Matchbox Diecast Toys: The First Forty Years, Major Productions Limited (England), 1989; Brian Moran, Battery Toys, Schiffer Publishing, 1984; Richard O'Brien, Collecting Toy Cars & Trucks: Identification And Value Guide, Books Americana, 1994; Richard O'Brien, Collecting Toys: A Collectors Identification and Value Guide, 6th Edition, Books Americana, 1993; Richard O'Brien, The Story of American Toys, Abbeville Press, 1990; Bob Parker, Hot Wheels: A Collector's Guide, Schiffer Publishing, 1993; Maxine A. Pinsky, Greenberg's Guide To Marx Toys, Vol. I (1988), Vol. II (1990), Greenberg Publishing Co; David Pressland, The Art of the Tin Toy, New Cavendish Books, 1976; David Pressland, The Book of Penny Toys, New Cavendish Books, 1991; David Richter, Collector's Guide To Tootsietoys, Collector Books, 1991; Harry L. Rinker, Collector's Guide To Toys, Games, And Puzzles, Wallace-Homestead, 1991; Nancy Schiffer, Matchbox Toys, Schiffer Publishing, 1983; Martyn L.

Schorr, The Guide To Mechanical Toy Collecting, Performance Media, 1979; Schroeder's Collectible Toys: Antique to Modern, Collector Books, 1994; Robin Langley Sommer, I Had One Of Those: Toys Of Our Generation, Crescent Books, 1992; Bruce and Diane Stoneback, Matchbox Toys: A Guide To Selecting, Collecting, and Enjoying New and Vintage Models, Chartwell Books, 1993; Jack Tempest, Post-War Tin Toys: A Collector's Guide, Wallace-Homestead, 1991; Glenda Thomas, Toy Sewing Machines, Collector Books, 1994; Toyshop Magazine, Toyshop 1995 Annual, 3rd Edition, Krause Publications, 1994; Tom Tumbusch, Tomart's Price Guide To Hot Wheels, Tomart Publications, 1993; Carol Turpen, Baby Boomer Toys and Collectibles, Schiffer Publishing, 1993; Peter Viemeister, Micro Cars, Hamilton's, 1982; Gerhard G. Walter, Metal Toys from Nuremberg: The Unique Mechanical Toys of the Firm of Georg Kellerman & Co. of Nuremberg 1910–1979, Schiffer Publishing, 1992; Blair Whitton, Paper Toys of The World, Hobby House Press, 1986; Blair Whitton, The Knopf Collector's Guide to American Antiques: Toys, Alfred A. Knopf, 1984.

Periodicals: Antique Toy World, PO Box 34509, Chicago, IL 60634; Canadian Toy Mania, PO Box 489, Rocanville, Saskatchewan SOA 3LO Canada; Collectible Toys & Values, Attic Books, 15 Danbury Rd., Ridgefield, CT 06877; Die Cast & Tin Toy Report, 559 North Park Ave., Easton, CT 06612; Model & Toy Collector Magazine, 137 Casterton Ave., Akron, OH 44303; Plastic Figure & Playset Collector, PO Box 1335, La Crosse, WI 54602; Plastic Warrior, 905 Harrison St., Allentown, PA 18103; Robot World & Price Guide, PO Box 184, Lenox Hill Station, New York, NY 10021; The Plane News, PO Box 845, Greenwich, CT 06836; Toybox Magazine, 8393 E. Holly Rd., Holly, MI 48442; Toy Cannon News, PO Box 2052-N, Norcross, GA 30071; Toy Collector & Price Guide, 700 E. State St., Iola, WI 54990; Toy Collector Marketplace, 1550 Territorial Rd., Benton Harbor, MI 49022; Toy Gun Collectors of America Newsletter, 312 Starling Way, Anaheim, CA 92807; Toy Shop, 700 E. State St., Iola, WI 54990; Toy Trader, 100 Bryant St., Dubuque, IA 52003; *Toy Trucker & Contractor,* HC 2, Box 5, LaMoure, ND 58458; *U.S. Toy Collector Magazine,* PO Box 4244, Missoula, MT 59806; *Yo-Yo Times,* PO Box 1519, Herndon, VA 22070.

Collectors' Clubs: A.C. Gilbert Heritage Society, 594 Front St., Marion, MA 02738; American Game Collectors Assoc., 49 Brooks Ave., Lewiston, ME 04240; American International Matchbox Collectors & Exchange Club, 532 Chestnut St., Lynn, MA 01904; Antique Engine, Tractor & Toy Club, Inc., 5731 Paradise Rd., Slatington, PA 18080; Antique Toy Collectors of America, 13th Floor, Two Wall Street, New York, NY 10005; Capitol Miniature Auto Collectors Club, 10207 Greenacres Dr., Silver Spring, MD 20903; Diecast Exchange Club, PO Box 1066, Pineallas Park, FL 34665; Ertl Collectors Club, Highways 136 & 120, Dyersville, IA 52040; Farm Toy Collectors Club, PO Box 38, Boxholm, IA 50040; Majorette Diecast Toy Collectors Assoc., 13447 NW Albany Ave., Bend, OR 97701; Matchbox Collectors Club, PO Box 278, Durham, CT 06422; Matchbox International Collectors Assoc., 574 Canewood Crescent, Waterloo, Ontario N2L 5P6 Canada; Matchbox U.S.A., 62 Saw Mill Rd., Durham, CT 06422; San Francisco Bay Brooklin Club, PO Box 61018, Palo Alto, CA 94306; Schoenhut Collectors Club, 45 Louis Ave., West Seneca, NY 14224; Southern California Toy Collectors Club, Suite 300, 1760 Termino, Long Beach, CA 90804.

Museums: American Museum of Automobile Miniatures, Andover, MA; Eugene Field House & Toy Museum, St. Louis, MO; Evanston Historical Society, Evanston, IL 60201; Forbes Magazine Collection, New York, NY; Hobby City Doll & Toy Museum, Anaheim, CA; Margaret Woodbury Strong Museum, Rochester, NY; Matchbox & Lesney Toy Museum, Durham, CT; Matchbox Road Museum, Newfield, NJ; Museum of the City of New York, New York, NY; Smithsonian Institution, Washington, DC; Spinning Top Exploratory Museum, Burlington, WI; Toy & Miniature Museum of Kansas City, Kansas City, MO; Toy Museum of Atlanta, Atlanta, GA; Washington Dolls' House & Toy Museum; Western Reserve Historical Society, Cleveland, OH.

Additional Listings: Characters, Disneyana, Dolls, and Schoenhut. Also see *Warman's Americana & Collectibles* for more examples.

Alps, Japanese
Bell Ringing Santa, windup, cloth dressed, vinyl face, orig box, 16½" h **270.00**
Butterfield Stage Coach, litho tin windup, articulated horses, scratches, 13" l **50.00**
Arcade, Freeport, IL, 1893–1946, painted cast iron
Bell Telephone Truck, pole trailer, green truck, blue trailer with winch, ditch digger, two ladders, two shovels, 9" l truck, 8" l trailer **700.00**
Buick Sedan, light bluish–green, black top, hood, and running boards, nickel plated wheels, spare tire imp "Buick," nickel plated driver, few chips and scratches, 8¼" l, 3¾" h **5,450.00**
Car Transport, green tractor, steel trailer, green car, blue car, green truck, red wrecker, mint condition, 4" l tractor, 11⅛" trailer **675.00**
Double Decker Bus, Fifth Ave type, rear stair platform, six lead passengers, very little wear to paint, rubber tires, Arcade sticker, orig driver, c1927, 8" l, 4" h **700.00**

Unknown Maker, cowboy riding horse, litho tin windup, $235.00.

Dump Truck, International Harvester, red, nickel plated driver and hoist, played–with condition, 10½″ l, 4½″ h **350.00**

Ford

Roadster, rumble seat, red, nickel plated grill, rubber tires, chips to top paint, c1934, 6½″ l, 2½″ h **600.00**

Sedan, yellow, nickel plated grill, Arcade sticker, paint chips and scratches, c1934, 6½″ l, 2½″ h **1,200.00**

Ice Truck, red, gold trim, nickel plated grill, glass ice block and tongs, 6¾″ l **475.00**

Model T Coupe, red, nickel plated wheels, 7″ l, 3½″ h ... **425.00**

Pontiac Sedan, blue, nickel plated grill, rubber tires, 6½″ l, 2″ h **1,200.00**

Touring Car, red, nickel plated wheels, wear and chipping to paint, 6¼″ l, 4″ h **250.00**

Yellow Cab Coupe, restored, replaced figure, 9″ l, 4½″ h **800.00**

American National, Mack van, painted pressed steel, green and red, allover crazing, paint loss, rear doors missing, 26″ l **450.00**

Bing, Gebruder, Nurnberg, Germany

Battleship, tin, clockwork, black and gray hull, ram front, two smoke stacks, six cannons, minor damage, 16″ l, 5½″ h .. **700.00**

Touring Car, litho tin windup, red, gold striping, driver, brown seats, 9½″ l, 4″ h **550.00**

Bliss, Pawtucket, RI

Firehouse, litho on wood, clanging bell, brick litho building, marked "Bliss" over front doors, 10″ l, 12½″ h, 3½″ w . **775.00**

Noah's Ark, bright litho, wood roof, wood hull, cardboard building, marked "The Wonder," various animals looking out window, animals missing, some paper loss, 22″ l, 9¾″ h **400.00**

Buddy L, East Moline, IL, 1921–Present, painted pressed steel

Auto Wrecker, boom missing .. **75.00**

Bonnet Bus, olive green, gold

trim, opening doors, pitting, paint chips, and wear, 29″ l ..**2,200.00**

Buddy "L" Ranch pickup truck, 1960s **80.00**

Concrete Mixer, gray, working cranks, brass spigot on water tank, paint loss, extensive rust, 14½″ h **450.00**

Derrick, small, red and black, paint chips, 25″ l **400.00**

Dredge on Treads, black and red, minor rust and scratches, 33″ l **3,800.00**

Dump Truck

Chain type dump lift, black, red chassis, scratches, paint chips, 24″ l **500.00**

Hydraulic dump mechanism, dual rear wheels, pitting, dents, wheels repainted, 24″ l **850.00**

Fire Truck, red, rust, 23″ l **600.00**

Ice Truck, yellow and black, ice, tongs, and tarpaulin cov, some paint blistering and chips, 26″ l **1,050.00**

Ladder Truck, swinging wrecker boom, four ladders, overall paint loss, rust, 25″ l **825.00**

Lumber Truck, black and red, missing two side panels and tailgate rail, paint chips, 24″ l **2,500.00**

Pile Driver Car, black, red roof, paint loss, rust, 18″ l **2,300.00**

Richmond Dump Truck, near mint **125.00**

Road Roller, green and red, nickel plated parts, rust, steering mechanism missing, 18½″ l **2,000.00**

Sand and Gravel, portable loader **225.00**

Shell Oil Truck **95.00**

Steam Shovel, "Improved," treads, black and red, roof scuffed, slight chips, 21″ l ...**3,700.00**

Studebaker Truck, High Lift Scoop N Dump **150.00**

Trench Digger, yellow and red, working cranks, repainted treads, replaced gears, 19″ h **3,200.00**

Trestle Bridge, three piers, new condition, 48″ l **325.00**

Carpenter, Port Chester, NY, dump

cart, painted cast iron, red cart, white horse, paint loss, missing rear gate, 13" l **225.00**

Chein, A. J., Harrison, NJ, c1930 Busy Mike, litho tin, sand toy, articulated monkey, red base, edge wear, slight scratches, 7" h **55.00**

Disneyland Rollercoaster, litho tin windup, side panels with Disney characters, minor wear, missing cars, 20" l **180.00**

Music Maker, litho tin, crank operated plinker, frog graphics, scratches, 3½" h **40.00**

Popeye Puncher, litho tin windup, overhead punching bag, copyright 1932 King Features Syndicate, wear on platform, fading to top, 9½" h, 4½" l, 4¼" w **1,525.00**

Cor–Cor, Corcoran Manufacturing Co, Washington, IN, c1935, painted pressed steel Airflow Sedan, red, four-door, rubber tires, electric headlights, paint chips, 17" l **1,400.00**

Graham Sedan, blue, electric lights, scratches and wear, 19½" l **1,200.00**

Crandall, Charles M., Montrose, PA, 1870–80, acrobats, orig box, dated 1867, 10" l, 6" w, 2" h ... **250.00**

De Camp, tiger, clockwork, hide covered, glass eyes, whiskers, leaps forward, moves head, 14" l, 6" h, 4" w **300.00**

E.T.C.O., Japanese, comet jetliner, litho tin friction, sparking action, paint chips and wear, 16" l **110.00**

Fisher-Price, East Aurora, NY, 1930–Present Jumbo Rollo, elephant, riding tricycle, c1951 .... **25.00**

Looky Push Car, 20" handle, plastic steering wheel, #875 . **30.00**

Xylophone Pull Toy, Donald Duck, #177, 11" h **85.00**

Hess, Germany, flotilla, painted tin, windup, battle cruiser pulls four small training ships, fair orig box, illustrated label, 8" l lead ship .. **900.00**

Hiller Industries, American, Hiller Comet, painted pressed steel,

Arcade, Hathaway's Bakery truck, cast iron, black hood, cream sides, 9¼" l, 3½" h, together with magazine tear sheet showing real truck (not shown), $17,600.00. Photograph courtesy of James D. Julia, Inc.

blue race car, ignition type gas engine, orig illus box, warranty, parts list, instructions, 18¼" l .. **1,350.00**

Hoge Mfg Co, New York City, 1935–45, fire chief car, painted pressed steel, red and black, battery operated headlights, windup with siren, 13½" l **400.00**

Hubley, Lancaster, PA, 1894–1965, painted cast iron Airflow Sedan, pale plum colored auto, nickel trim, battery operated headlights, rubber tires, wood hubs, paint chips, 8" l **1,300.00**

Automotive Pumper, red, nickel parts, 5" l **170.00**

Coupe, two door, black, silver grill, headlights, and wheels, 7" l, 3½" h **200.00**

Patrol Wagon, blue, yellow wheels, molded driver, three patrolmen, 6½" l, 3" h **110.00**

Royal Circus Calliope Wagon, two white horses, head harness, red and gold saddles, driver and passenger, blue wagon, gold highlights, red hitch, gold trim on wheels, two figures repainted, 16" l, 8" h, 4½" w ... **2,500.00**

Issmayer, Germany, swimmer man, hand painted tin windup, moves arms and legs while laying on stomach in swimming position, paint loss to back, 7" l, 2" h, 1½" w **125.00**

Ives, Bridgeport, CT, tin, clockwork
General Butler, walks, red and
blue cloth uniform, brass buttons, hand painted face, 10" h **3,000.00**
Gun Boat, gray, two stacker, two
masts, one cannon, stamped
"Ives Toys" on deck, clockwork not working, 12½" l, 6½"
h **125.00**
Ocean Liner, gray hull, cream
colored deck, one stacker, two
masts, clockwork not working,
10½" l, 5½" h **200.00**
K, Japanese, covered wagon, litho
tin friction, wagon and horses,
Indian graphics on cov, tin driver,
scratches, 9" l **60.00**
Kenton, Kenton, OH, painted cast
iron
Buckeye Ditch Digger, rusty
buckets and chain, played with
condition, 12½" l, 6½" h **325.00**
Jaeger Cement Mixer, red truck,
molded driver, nickel plated
mixing drum, rubber tires, 9¼"
l, 4" h **725.00**
Nash Sedan, four-door, six windows, spare tire, blue body,
black fenders and running
boards, 8" l, 3½" h **5,200.00**
Keystone Mfg Co, Boston, painted
pressed steel
Army Truck, khaki, canvas cov,
paint flaking, 26½" l **375.00**
Dump Truck, green and orange,
metal wheels, scratches, paint
loss, 23½" l **210.00**
Railway Express Truck, two
piece wheels, repainted, 26" l **500.00**
Riding Locomotive, steam type
locomotive, added electric
lights, paint chips, wear, 26½"
l **210.00**
US Mail Plane, yellow and orange, clicker, belt driven propeller, extensive paint loss,
scratches, belt missing, 24" l . **425.00**
Kingsbury, Keene, NH
Fire Pumper, painted pressed
steel, windup
Motor pumper, red, silver and
gold boiler, overpainted boiler,
repainted driver, minor
scratches, 11½" l **500.00**

Truck mounted pumper, hoses
missing, paint loss, 24" l **900.00**
Stake Truck, motor driven,
painted pressed steel, red and
black, minor touch-up, chips,
and rust, windup not working,
25" l **1,400.00**
Lehmann, Nurmberg, Germany,
1881–Present, litho tin windup
Bulky Mule, kicking mule rearing
against two-wheel chariot,
clown driver, 7" l **225.00**
Motor Ambulance, uniformed
driver, some bends, scratches,
discoloration, rear doors retouched, 5½" l **500.00**
Uhu, land and sea racer, streamlined, wheel fins, orig driver
with rotating head, 9½" l **2,500.00**
Lindstrom, Bridgeport, CT, 1913–
40s, Johnny, litho tin windup, red
and yellow costume, 8" h **110.00**
Linemar
Donald Acrobat, windup, celluloid Donald swings on wire trapeze, paint chips, 7½" h **160.00**
Old Jalopy, litho tin friction, red
car, black fenders, allover
printed slogans, scratches, 9"
l **145.00**
Olive Oyl on Tricycle, windup
mechanical, working order, repainted arms and feet, 3½" l,
4" h **250.00**
Marklin, Goppingen, Germany,
1859–Present
Racer, tinplate, painted red,
driver, four rubber tires, c1935,
11" l **675.00**
Sand Dumper Cart, four cast
iron wheels, tin cart, wood
frame chasis, c1895, 15½" l,
8¼" h, 8" w **450.00**
Train Station, tin, telegraph
room, waiting room, bright
painted colors, c1915, 10¾" l,
7½" h, 5" w **1,000.00**
Marx, Louis, & Co., NY, 1921–
Present
Acrobat Marvel, litho tin windup,
rocking action, monkey,
scratches, 13½" h **95.00**
Airplane
Gyroplane, 7½" wingspan ... **125.00**

P35
13½″ wingspan **125.00**
16″ wingspan, two engine
bomber **150.00**
Stratojet, friction, MIB **95.00**
Amos and Andy Taxi, litho tin
windup, cowl lights, horseshoe
missing, discolored figures,
scratches, 7½″ l **350.00**
Automobile, Convertible, wind-
up, 11″ l, near mint **250.00**
Buck Rogers Rocketship, MIB . **2,500.00**
Fix All Tractor, orange plastic
tractor, plastic tools, driver
missing, orig box, 9¼″ l **65.00**
Lone Ranger, rearing Silver, rotating lasso, dated 1938 . . . . **375.00**
Pathenews, 1930s type car . . . **175.00**
Pinocchio the Acrobat, litho tin
windup, figure faded, rocking
tin base, scratches, 16½″ h . . **270.00**
Police Cycle, litho tin windup,
cop, orange cycle, paint
scratches **210.00**
Race Car, painted pressed steel,
red, rubber wheels, electric
lights, scratches, old battery
stuck on box, 8½″ l **150.00**
Rocket Racer, windup, 16½″ l . **395.00**
Rocking Cowboy with Lasso,
litho tin windup, brown and
white horse, light scuffing, 7½″
l **160.00**
Roy Rogers Silver Rifle Gun . . **175.00**
Sam The Gardener, pushing
wheelbarrow with tools, MIB . **350.00**
Siren Sparkling Fire Engine,
9″ l **125.00**
Tank, turn over, #5 . . . . **175.00**
Tricky Fire Chief **125.00**
Tricky Taxi **125.00**
Walking Tiger, windup, 8″ l **175.00**
Zeppelin, Trans Atlantic, windup,
10″ l **190.00**
Metalcraft, St Louis, MO, 1928,
wrecker truck, painted pressed
steel, red and white, three
spares, promotes Goodrich
Tires, paint chips, scratches, 12″
l **250.00**
Ohio Art, Bryan, OH, 1908–Pres-
ent, circus shooting gallery, rotating disk, moving ducks, orig
guns and darts, MIB **225.00**

Salco, England
Disney Hurdy–Gurdy, Mickey,
Minnie, and Donald, cast
metal, paint scratches and
wear, 3½″ h **85.00**
Disney Wheelbarrow, Donald
pushes Mickey, cast metal, red
wheelbarrow, paint chips and
wear, 2½″ h **120.00**
Donald Duck's Dairy, Donald
pulled in milk cart by Pluto,
cast metal, minor paint chips,
good orig box, 4½″ l **170.00**
Mickey and Minnie on the River,
cast metal, figures in rowboat
on wheels, orig oars, paint
chips on boat, good orig box,
5¼″ h **275.00**
Schieble Toy and Novelty Co,
Dayton, OH, painted pressed
steel
Four-Door Sedan, friction, orig
dark blue, repainted black,
paint chips, missing one head-
light, 17½″ l **325.00**
Right Plane, monoplane, light
blue, red, and yellow, belt
driven propeller, scratches, mi-
nor bends, 29″ l **525.00**
Schuco, trademark of Schreyer
and Co, Germany, 1912–Present
Clown with Mouse, litho tin
windup, fabric covering, red
and black, 4½″ h **180.00**
Donald Duck, litho tin windup,
orig blue felt sailor shirt and
hat, 6″ h **420.00**
Drummer, litho tin windup, fabric
covering, red and green, moth
damaged hat, chipped paint,
4½″ h **100.00**
Mouse in Convertible, litho tin
windup, blue car, gray fabric
covered mouse, 5¾″ l **220.00**
Sonny, painted pressed steel
Army Truck, khaki, canvas cov,
division insignia on cab,
crazed paint, slight rust, 27″ l **320.00**
Parcel Post Truck, green and
black, orange wheels, under-
carriage and roof with paint
blemishes, paint loss to cab
int., 26″ l **625.00**

Railway Express Truck, maroon and black, orange wheels, wear on roof, rust, overall paint loss, 26" l **500.00**

Steelcraft, scout plane, painted pressed steel, red and white, belt driven propeller, numerous scratches, belt missing, 22" l .. **290.00**

Strauss, Ferdinand, Corp., NY City, 20th C, Ham and Sam the Minstrel Team, litho tin windup, banjo players, arms need reattaching, figure not orig to toy, numerous scratches and dents, 6½" l **300.00**

Sturditoy, Pressed Metal Co., Pawtucket, RI, painted pressed steel

Coal Truck, orange and black, surface scratches, slight rust, minor repairs, 27" l **1,300.00**

Dump Truck, narrow bed, dark green, black, and red, paint chips, rust, 25" l **400.00**

Fire Truck

Engine, American–La France, overall paint loss, fading, hoses and front bumper missing, 26" l **575.00**

Water Tower, frame repainted, paint loss, replaced hoses, rust, hole in reservoir, 34" l **475.00**

Open Truck, olive green, black frame and fenders, major paint loss, 22½" l **120.00**

Railway Express Truck, green, black, and red, paint loss, dents, rear door latch missing, 26" l **775.00**

Tractor Trailer, gasoline tanker, red, detached headlights, paint loss and blemishes, 33" l **1,900.00**

TM, Japanese, Capsule 7, litho tin battery operated, circling astronaut, orig box, 10½" l **135.00**

Toledo Metal Wheel Co, Toledo, OH, 1920s, dump truck, painted pressed steel, Mack type, black, red bed, lift mechanism, large areas of paint loss and rust, 27" l **725.00**

Unique Art, Newark, NJ

GI Joe Jeep, litho tin windup, soldier, red jeep, not working, 7" l **90.00**

Kiddy Cyclist, litho tin windup, light rust, discoloration, 7½" l **150.00**

Unknown Makers

American

Airflow Car

Convertible, painted cast iron, yellow, black fenders, nickel trim, white tires on wood hubs, 6½" l **1,500.00**

Sedan, painted cast iron, salmon colored, nickel trim, white tires, wood hubs, paint chips and scratches, 4½" l **170.00**

Billiard Player, litho tin windup, age discoloration, pool balls missing, 6" l **70.00**

Early tin, hand painted

Rocking Toy, jockey on horse, emb tin rocking base, 7" l, 7" h **950.00**

Train

Clockwork, Boss, 7¾" l, 5½" h, 3" w **500.00**

Pull toy, normal paint loss, nice window stenciling on cab and frame, 12" l, 7" h, 3¾" w **550.00**

Sightseeing Bus, painted cast iron, blue and white, "Atlantic City N.J." printed on top, rubber wheels, scratches, 7½" l **575.00**

Toledo Racer, polished cast aluminum, red steel wheels, rubber tires, scratches, discoloration, 13" l **180.00**

German

Ladder Truck, litho tin windup, red truck, extension ladder, six firemen, scratches, faded areas, 12½" l **400.00**

Toonerville Trolley, painted tin, paint chips, scratches, spring broken, 5" l **350.00**

Japanese

Cheery Cook, painted, windup, celluloid boy, erratically moving plate, orig box, 4½" h **40.00**

Indians in Canoe, litho tin friction, two drumming and pad-

dling Indians, scratches, 9½"
h **70.00**
Police Patrol, litho tin battery
operated, tin cop, three
wheel cycle, left arm loose,
scratches, rust, not working,
7" h **75.00**
Wolverine Supply & Mfg Co,
1903–Present
Dump Truck, "White 3000 Mus-
tang" **195.00**
Merry-Go-Round, four flags, four
planes, 1930s **450.00**
Speedway Bus, "5 Via Main
Street" **150.00**
Wyandotte, American
Moving Van, "Wyandotte Van
Lines, Coast to Coast," 8" l .. **75.00**
Ride 'em Cowboy, litho tin
windup, red and white horse,
Red Ranger, slight scratches,
6½" l **150.00**
Sedan with Trailer, painted
pressed steel, green auto,
travel trailer, scratches, 17½" l **450.00**
Stake Truck, painted pressed
steel, red and green truck,
wooden wheels, scratches,
12½" l **85.00**

TRAINS, TOY

History: Railroading has always been an
important part of childhood, largely because
of the romance associated with the railroad
and the emphasis on toy trains.

The first toy trains were cast iron and tin;
windup motors added movement. The
Golden Age of toy trains was 1920–1955
when electric powered units were available
and names such as Ives, American Flyer,
and Lionel were household words. The construction of the rolling stock was of high
quality. The advent of plastic in the late
1950s lessened this quality considerably.

Toy trains were designated by a model
scale or gauge. The most popular are HO,
N, O and standard. Narrow gauge was a
response to the modern capacity to minia-
turize. Its popularity has lessened in the last
few years.

Condition of trains is critical. Items in fair
condition (scratched, chipped, dented,

rusted or warped) and below generally have
little value to a collector. Restoration is acceptable, provided it is done accurately. It
may enhance the price one or two grades.
Prices listed below are for very good to mint
condition unless noted.

References: Paul V. Ambrose, *Green-
berg's Guide To Lionel Trains, 1945–1969,
Vol. III,* Greenberg Publishing, 1990; Paul
V. Ambrose and Joseph P. Algozzini,
*Greenberg's Guide To Lionel Trains 1945–
1969, Vol. IV, Uncatalogued Sets,* Green-
berg Publishing, 1992; Paul V. Ambrose and
Joseph P. Algozzini, *Greenberg's Guide To
Lionel Trains 1945–1969, Vol. V, Rare and
Unusual,* Greenberg Publishing, 1993; Su-
san and Al Bagdade, *Collector's Guide To
American Toy Trains,* Wallace-Homestead,
1990; John O. Bradshaw, *Greenberg's
Guide To Kusan Trains,* Greenberg Publish-
ing, 1987; Pierce Carlson, *Collecting Toy
Trains,* Pincushion Press, 1993; W. G. Clay-
tor, Jr., P. Doyle, and C. McKenney, *Green-
berg's Guide To Early American Toy Trains,*
Greenberg Publishing, 1993; Joe Deger,
*Greenberg's Guide To American Flyer S
Gauge* Vol. I, 4th Ed. (1991), Vol. II (1991),
Vol. III (1992), Greenberg Publishing; Cindy
Lee Floyd (comp.), *Greenberg's Marx Train
Catalogues,* Greenberg Publishing, 1993;
Richard Friz, *The Official Identification And
Price Guide To Toy Trains,* House of Col-
lectibles, 1990; John Glaab, *The Brown
Book of Brass Locomotives, Third Edition,*
Chilton, 1993; Bruce Greenberg, *Green-
berg's Guide to Ives Trains, 1901–1932,*
Vol. I: L and Wide Gauge (1991) and Vol.
II: O Gauge (1992), Greenberg Publishing;
Bruce Greenberg (edited by Christian F.
Rohlfing), *Greenberg's Guide To Lionel
Trains: 1901–1942,* Vol. 1 (1988), Vol. 2
(1988), Greenberg Publishing; Bruce
Greenberg, *Greenberg's Guide To Lionel
Trains: 1945–1969,* Vol. 1: 8th Edition
(1992), Vol. 2: 2nd Edition (1993), Green-
berg Publishing; Greenberg Publishing,
*Greenberg's Lionel Catalogues, Vol. V:
1955–1960,* Greenberg Publishing, 1992;
Greenberg Publishing, *Greenberg's Marx
Train Catalogues: 1938–1975,* Greenberg
Publishing, 1992; George Horan and Vin-
cent Rosa, *Greenberg's Guide To Lionel
HO Vol. I, 1957–1966, 2nd Edition,* Green-
berg Publishing, 1993; George Horan,

Greenberg's Guide to Lionel HO Vol. II 1974–1977, Greenberg Publishing, 1993; John Hubbard, *The Story of Williams Electric Trains,* Greenberg Publishing, 1987; Steven H. Kimball, *Greenberg's Guide To American Flyer Prewar O Gauge,* Greenberg Publishing, 1987; Roland La Voie, *Greenberg's Guide To Lionel Trains, 1970–1991, Vol. I* (1991), *Vol. II* (1992), Greenberg Publishing; Lionel Book Committee, *Lionel Trains: Standard Of The World, 1900–1943,* Train Collectors Assoc., 1989; Dallas J. Mallerich III, *Greenberg's American Toy Trains: From 1900 With Current Values,* Greenberg Publishing, 1990; Dallas J. Mallerich III, *Greenberg's Guide to Athearn Trains,* Greenberg Publishing, 1987; Eric J. Matzke, *Greenberg's Guide To Marx Trains, Vol. 1* (1989), *Vol. II* (1990), Greenberg Publishing; Tom McComas and James Tuohy, *Lionel: A Collector's Guide & History,* 6 vols., Chilton, 1993; Robert P. Monaghan, *Greenberg's Guide to Markin O/HO,* Greenberg Publishing, 1989; Richard O'Brien, *Collecting Toy Trains: An Identification and Value Guide, No. 3,* Books Americana, 1991; John R. Ottley, *Greenberg's Guide To LGB Trains,* Greenberg Publishing, 1989; Alan R. Schuweiler, *Greenberg's Guide to American Flyer, Wide Gauge,* Greenberg Publishing, 1989; John D. Spanagel, *Greenberg's Guide to Varney Trains,* Greenberg Publishing, 1991; Robert C. Whitacre, *Greenberg's Guide To Marx Trains Sets, Vol. III,* Greenberg Publishing, 1992.

Periodicals: *Classic Toy Trains,* 21027 Crossroads Cr., Waukesha, WI 53187; *Lionel Collector Series Marketmaker,* Trainmaster, PO Box 1499, Gainesville, FL 32602.

Collectors' Clubs: American Flyer Collectors Club, PO Box 13269, Pittsburgh, PA 15234; Lionel Collectors Club of America, PO Box 479, LaSalle, IL 61301; Lionel Operating Train Society, 18 Eland Ct., Fairfield, OH 45014; Marklin Club–North America, PO Box 51559, New Berlin, WI 53151; Marklin Digital Special Interest Group, PO Box 51319, New Berlin, WI 53151; The National Model Railroad Assoc., 4121 Cromwell Road, Chattanooga, TN 37421; The Toy Train Operating Society, Inc., Suite 308, 25 West Walnut St., Pasadena, CA

91103; Train Collector's Assoc., PO Box 248, Strasburg, PA 17579.

Museum: Toy Train Museum of the Train Collectors Assoc., Strasburg, PA 17579.

Additional Listings: See *Warman's Americana & Collectibles* for more examples.

American Flyer
Car
    1202, baggage, eight wheel, litho, blue **75.00**
    9912, observation, aluminum, black lettering, 10½″ l **50.00**
Locomotive
    356, Silver Bullet, streamlined, chrome, yellow and blue decals, 1953 .... **125.00**
    1218, steeple cab, black, 1920–21 .... **125.00**
Set, Burlington Zephyr, litho sheet metal, three unit, power car with electric motor, coach, observation, 1935 .... **125.00**
Ives
Car
    72, parlor, NY and Chicago, litho steel, brown sides, 1914–20, 12″ l **350.00**
    550, baggage, litho, four wheel, emerald green, black roof, 1913–30, 6½″ l **35.00**

Lionel, 8E locomotive, red, re-wheeled, one reproduction light, #337 pullman, #338 observation car, olive and maroon, standard gauge, price for set, $115.00.

Locomotive
5, cast iron, black, 1917–22 . **75.00**
1122, steam, diecast boiler,
black boiler and tender,
brass trim, 1929–30 ...... **300.00**
Lionel
Car
802, stock, green, Union Stock
Line, 1915–26 .... **35.00**
3651, operating lumber car,
black, silver lettering, 1939–
42 .... **20.00**
3830, flatcar with submarine,
blue car, gray submarine,
1960–63 .... **75.00**
6672, Santa Fe, refrigerator,
white, brown roof, blue lettering, 1954–56 .... **45.00**
Locomotive
250, electric, terra-cotta body,
maroon frame, 1934 ...... **225.00**
1681E, steam, red, red frame,
1934–35 .... **90.00**
2328, Burlington, GP–7, silver,
black lettering, red frame,
1955–56 .... **325.00**
Set, 636W, diesel locomotive,
two coach cars, and observation car, yellow and brown,
1936–41 .... **400.00**
Marx
Car
550, New York Central,
wrecker crane, orange cab,
1934–36 .... **35.00**
558A, passenger, scarlet red,
red and white frame, "Bo-
gota," illuminated **25.00**
Locomotive, 500, Army Supply
Train, streamlined, sheet
metal, electric motor, olive
drab, 1938–42 .... **50.00**

TRAMP ART

History: Tramp art was prevalent in the United States from 1875 to the 1930s. Items were made by itinerant artists who left no record of their identity. They used old cigar boxes and fruit and vegetable crates. The edges of items were chip-carved and lay-ered, creating the "Tramp Art" effect. Fin-ished items usually were given an overall stain. Today they are collected primarily as folk art.

Reference: Helaine Fendelman, *Tramp Art: An Itinerant's Folk Art Guide,* E. P. Dut-ton & Co, 1975.

Sewing Box, painted pink, rose velvet pin cushion, one drawer, 5½ x 6¼ x 7", $75.00.

Box
11" w, 8½" d, 10½" h, alternating
painted red and green dec,
hinged lid, diamond motif on
lid and sides, till and deep well
int., bracket feet, early 20th C **450.00**
13½" w, 10½" d, 9" h, inlaid top
with "Edith Amy," wear, early
20th C **250.00**
Frame
11¾ x 14", old patina **55.00**
18½ x 31½", old dark finish, minor edge damage **85.00**
25½ x 32½", decorative crest,
good detail **440.00**
Jewelry Box, 9" l, paper label,
marked "Dec 24, 1932" **145.00**
Sign, 101" h, parade type, double
sided, pictorial needlework,
"Feed My Lambs" and "Evan-
gelical Sunday School Hatfield,"
elaborate frame surmounted
with two birds, applied leaves
and flowers on corners, late 19th
C **825.00**
Stand, 24½" h, pedestal, chip
carved, octagonal top, elongated
eight sided column with two centered blocks, sq stepped base,
late 19th/early 20th C **55.00**

TRANSPORTATION MEMORABILIA

History: The first airlines in the United States depended on subsidies from the government for carrying mail for most of their income. The first non-Post Office Department flight for mail carrying was in 1926 between Detroit and Chicago. By 1930 there were 38 domestic and 5 international airlines operating in the United States. A typical passenger load was 10. After World War II, 4-engine planes with a capacity of 100 or more passengers were introduced.

The jet age was launched in the 1950s. In 1955 Capitol Airlines used British-made turboprop airliners in domestic service. In 1958 National Airlines began domestic jet passenger service. The giant Boeing 747 went into operation in 1970 as part of the Pan American fleet. The Civil Aeronautics Board, which regulates the airline industry, ended control of routes in 1982 and fares in 1983.

Transoceanic travel falls into two distinct periods—the era of the great clipper ships and the era of the diesel powered ocean liners. The later craft reached their "Golden Age" in the period between 1900 and 1940.

An ocean liner was a city unto itself. Many had their own printing rooms to produce a wealth of daily memorabilia. Companies such as Cunard, Holland-America, and others encouraged passengers to acquire souvenirs with the company logo and ship name.

Certain ships acquired a unique mystic. The *Queen Elizabeth, Queen Mary,* and *United States* became symbols of elegance and style. Today the cruise ship dominates the world of the ocean liner.

References: Aeronautica & Air Label Collectors Club of Aerophilatelic Federation of America, *Air Transport Label Catalog,* published by club; Stan Baumwald, *Junior Crew Member Wings,* published by author; Trev Davis and Fred Chan, *Airline Playing Cards: Illustrated Reference Guide, 2nd Edition,* published by authors, 1987; Lynn Johnson and Michael O'Leary, *En Route: Label Art From The Golden Age of Air Travel,* Chronicle Books, 1993; Karl D. Spence, *How To Identify and Price Ocean Liner Collectibles,* published by author,

1991; Karl D. Spence, *Oceanliner Collectibles,* published by author, 1992; Richard R. Wallin, *Commercial Aviation Collectibles: An Illustrated Price Guide,* Wallace-Homestead, 1990.

Periodical: *Airliners,* PO Box 52-1238, Miami, FL 33152.

Collectors' Clubs: Aeronautic & Air Label Collectors Club, PO Box 1239, Elgin, IL 60121; National Assoc. of Timetable Collectors, 125 American Inn Rd., Villa Ridge, MO 63089; Oceanic Navigation Research Society, PO Box 8005, Studio City, CA 91608-0005; Steamship Historical Society of America, Inc., Suite #4, 300 Ray Drive, Providence, RI 02906; The Gay Airline Club, PO Box 69A04, West Hollywood, CA 90069; Titanic Historical Society, PO Box 51053, Indian Orchard, MA 01151; Titanic International, PO Box 7007, Freehold, NJ 07728; Transport Ticket Society, 4 Gladridge Close, Earley, Reading Berks RG6 2DL England; World Airline Historical Society, 3381 Apple Tree Lane, Erlanger, KY 41018.

Museums: Owls Head Transportation Museum, Owls Head, ME; South Street Seaport Museum, New York, NY; University of Baltimore, Steamship Historical Society Collection, Baltimore, MD.

Additional Listings: See Automobilia and Railroad Items in *Warman's Antiques And Collectibles Price Guide* and Aviation Collectibles, Ocean Liner Collectibles, and Railroad Items in *Warman's Americana & Collectibles.*

AIR

Baggage Label, United Air Lines, oval, plane flying above clouds, "Coast–To–Coast Border–To–Border"	**10.00**
Casserole, Australian Airlines, oblong, white, gold flying kangaroo logo, Wedgwood	**20.00**
Certificate, Japan Air Lines, International Dateline Crossing, 1966	**12.00**
Coffee Pitcher, Pan Am, gooseneck, International Silver Co, 1940s	**200.00**
Knife, American Airlines, Flagship pattern, silver plate, DC–3 nose stamped on solid handle, 1930s	**20.00**

Plate, Pan Am, white, dark blue
band and logo, Walker China,
mid 1940s **100.00**
Poster, Colonial Airlines, DC–4
over island of Bermuda, 1950s,
27 x 41″ **350.00**
Salt and Pepper Shakers, pr, British Airways, white, gold trim and
dec, Royal Doulton **30.00**
Timetable, United Air Lines, bi–
plane and map of US, 1930s .. **40.00**
Vase, Delta Air Lines, clear, gold
logo, ftd **20.00**

LAND

Bond, Arkansas Highway Bond,
$10,000, State House vignette,
green border, 1931 .... **10.00**
Book, *Trolley Car Treasury,* Frank
Rowsome, 1946, 200 pgs, over
300 photos, dj **30.00**
Catalog, H A Moyer Carriage Co,
Syracuse, NY, 1900, 82 pgs, 7 x
8¼″ **150.00**
Envelope, Yellow Cab, taxi image,
c1910, 2 x 4½″ **5.00**
Trolley Sign, Wrigley's Gum,
trademark arrow, people and
jesters surrounding king on
throne, various product pkgs,
20½ x 10½″ **110.00**
Waybill, Holbrook & Fort Apache
Stage Line, 1904, 7 x 17″ **35.00**

SEA

Book, *The Steam Engine, Its Origin and Gradual Improvement,*
New York, D Appleton & Co,
1841, minor edge damage,
some water staining, 14 x 19″ . **250.00**
Cup and Saucer, presentation
piece, Old Paris porcelain,
painted and dec by R T Lux,
New Orleans, 6¼″ d saucer with
steamer *Dexter* painted on border with gold on rim and center,
3¼″ h cup with gold lettered
"Sam Montgomery, Master"
painted around steamer *Dexter* **2,700.00**
Decanter, cut glass, orig stopper,
engraved with anchor and "Line"
from St Louis and New Orleans

**Advertising Mirror, celluloid, mul-
ticolored, American Line, Phila-
delphia-Liverpool-Queenstown,
1¾″ d, $75.00.**

Anchor Line, c1880, lip chip, 9½″
h **100.00**
Envelope, postmarked "Louisville
and Cincinnati Mailboat, 1874" **45.00**
Ledger, from steamer *J.C. Kerr,*
details wharf boat charges on
upper Ohio River 1884–87, edge
damage, 9 x 14″ **55.00**
Lithograph, entitled "Steamer
Messenger No. 2, Capt. J. C.
Woodward," C#5735, bird's-eye
maple frame, 19½ x 15½″ ... **500.00**
Model, steam engine, brass, 10¾
x 3½″ **250.00**
Photograph
Albumen photo on cardboard,
steamer *City of Owensboro*
new at Howard Yards, Jeffer-
sonville, IN, minor foxing, 18 x
15″ **250.00**
Sepia, steamer *Jewel* at Rockport, IN, by LM John, stains,
matted and framed, 16½ x
13½″ **80.00**
Pickaroon, log rafting, cast iron
head, wooden handle, 35½″ l .. **165.00**
Pilot Wheel, painted wood, metal
reinforcing ring on outside circle,
45″ d including handles **140.00**
Pitcher, ice water, silver plated, engraved "Presented to Capt. A.B.
Conkey by passengers of
Steamer *Idaho* June 20, 63,"

patterned handle and finial, base marked "Meridan Brit'a double wall pitcher," some wear, 12" h ... **415.00**

Poster, White Star line, 1920, floor plan of *Olympic,* British **125.00**

Reverse Painting on Glass, 7½ x 9½", *RMS Titanic,* mother–of–pearl inlay **185.00**

Sign, Hamburg–American Packet Co, New York–Hamburg, paper, sailing steamship illus, Chas Shields Litho, 25½ x 20" **20.00**

Steam Whistle, Lunkenheimer, cast iron and copper, acorn finial, from steamer *Gold Dust* (built 1900, burned 1901), mounted on stand, 8" d, 42" h . **385.00**

TRUNKS

History: Trunks are portable containers that clasp shut for the storage or transportation of personal possessions. Normally "trunk" means the ribbed flat- or dome-top models of the second half of the 19th century. Unrestored they sell for between $50 and $150. Refinished and relined the price rises to $200 to $400, with decorators being a principal market.

Early trunks frequently were painted, stenciled, grained, or covered with wallpaper. These are collected for their folk art qualities and, as such, experience high prices.

Reference: Martin and Maryann Labuda, *Price & Identification Guide to Antique Trunks,* published by authors, 1980.

Hump back, metal, curved slats, c1890, $150.00.

11¼" l, flat top, black leather, brass tack and red trim, iron bail handles and lock, fabric lined int., pen and ink signature **140.00**

15" l, 7" h, dome top, sponge painted dec, black and brown, plain simulated burl int., early 19th C **145.00**

18 x 36 x 22", dome top, immigrant's **80.00**

24" l, dome top, rawhide cov, leather trim, brass studs, wrought iron lock with hasp, lined with newspaper, worn and damaged **75.00**

24½" l
- 10" h, dome top, painted swag dec, green ground, America, 19th C **1,100.00**
- 12½" h, dome top, black painted dec, red–brown ground, America, 19th C **575.00**

30" l, 13½" h, dome top, vinegar grained, green striping dec, light ochre ground, America, 19th C **320.00**

31" l, dome top, pine, wrought iron banding, brown graining, red painted label, bear trap lock and key, white painted int. **110.00**

37½" l, dome top, pine, dovetailed, orig reddish–brown paint, black painted stripes, iron strap hinges, handles, and lock, initialed and dated "1846" **220.00**

41" l, pine, wrought iron banding, strap hinges, floral dec on lid int., weathered finish **355.00**

43" l, 23" d, 23" h, Louis Vuitton, late 19th/early 20th C, scuffs, losses **980.00**

46¼" w, 17½" d, 19" h, flat top, oak, handmade, chamfered panels, recessed brass combination lock, NY, late 19th C ... **400.00**

VALENTINES

History: Early cards were handmade, often containing both handwritten verses and hand-drawn pictures. Many cards also were hand colored and contained cutwork.

Mass production of machine-made cards featuring chromolithography began after

1840. In 1847 Esther Howland of Worcester, Massachusetts, established a company to make valentines which were hand decorated with paper lace and other materials imported from England. They had a small "H" stamped in red in the top left corner. Howland's company eventually became the New England Valentine Company (N.E.V. Co.).

After the Civil War George C. Whitney and his brother founded a company which dominated the market from the 1870s through the first decades of the 20th century. They bought out several competitors, one of which was the New England Valentine Company.

Lace paper was invented in 1834. The 1835 to 1860 period is known as the "golden age" of lacy cards.

Embossed paper was used in England after 1800. Embossed lithographs and woodcuts developed between 1825–40, with early examples being hand colored.

References: Roberta B. Etter, *Tokens Of Love,* Abbeville Press, 1990; Ruth Webb Lee, *A History of Valentines*; Frank Staff, *The Valentine And Its Origins*, out-of-print.

Collectors' Club: National Valentine Collectors Association, Box 1404, Santa Ana, CA 92702.

Additional Listings: See *Warman's Americana & Collectibles* for more examples.

Advisor: Evalene Pulati.

Post Card, "To My Valentine,"
bluetone, cupid in center heart,
floral bouquet, emb, divided back,
marked "TRCo," $2.00.

Easel Back, 8½" h, girl carrying red honeycomb paper parasol .	50.00
Foldout	
5" h, cupid, c1920	10.00
13 x 10", diecut, lady, lacy border, c1890	25.00
Layered, 5" h, hearts and flowers, c1860	15.00
Mechanical, black boy and girl, chicken and duck pop out of watermelon with cards in beaks ..	25.00
Sailor's	
9" d, double, To A Lover 1,150.00	
12" d, single, I'm Yours/Be Mine	600.00
Stand-Up, diecut	
6¾" h, girl holding doves, German	8.00
9" h, Woods adv, "If You Love Your Wife, Give Her A Woods," girl riding in Woods car	20.00
Tuck, Raphel, 12½" h, Irish boy, green jacket, top hat, string moves jointed arms, legs	75.00

VALLERYSTHAL GLASS

History: Vallerysthal (Lorraine), France, has been a glass-producing center for centuries. In 1872 two major factories, Vallerysthal glassworks and Portieux glassworks, merged and produced art glass until 1898. Later, pressed glass covered animal dishes were introduced. The factory continues in operation today.

Reference: Ellen T. Schroy, *Warman's Glass,* Wallace-Homestead, 1992.

Animal Dish, cov	
Hen on nest, blue	85.00
Robin	110.00
Box	
3½ x 4", cov, blue milk glass ..	70.00
5 x 3", cameo, dark green, applied and cut dec, sgd	950.00
Butter Dish, figural, radish	75.00

Salt, cov, hen on nest, pale pink, 2½ x 1¾ x 2″, $42.50.

Candlestick, Grecian Girl, frosted ... **50.00**
Candy Dish, 4⅛″ d, white milk
glass, basketweave, rope handles and finial **90.00**
Goblet, blue, ftd **60.00**
Lemon Dish, cov, figural, lemon,
opaque yellow **50.00**
Plate
7½″ d, floral dec, blue **35.00**
8″ d, Thistle pattern, green **70.00**
Tumbler, 4″ h, cobalt blue **45.00**
Vase, 9¾″ h, swelled cylinder, inverted, scalloped rim, opalescent blue ground, cased in burgundy, intaglio carved crocus, engraved "Vallerysthal" **950.00**

VAL SAINT-LAMBERT

History: Val Saint-Lambert, a 12th-century Cistercian abbey, was located during different historical periods in France, Netherlands, and Belgium (1930 to present). In 1822 Francois Kemlin and Auguste Lelievre, along with a group of financiers, bought the abbey and opened a glassworks. In 1846 Val Saint-Lambert merged with the Société Anonyme des Manufactures de Glaces, Verres à Vitre, Cristaux et Gobeletaries. The company bought many other glassworks.

Val Saint-Lambert developed a reputation for technological progress in the glass industry. In 1879 Val Saint-Lambert became an independent company employing 4,000 workers. Val Saint-Lambert concentrated on the export market making table glass, cut, engraved, etched, and molded pieces, and chandeliers. Some pieces were finished in other countries, e.g., silver mounts added in the United States.

Val Saint-Lambert executed many special commissions for the artists of the Art Nouveau and Art Deco periods. The tradition continues. The company also made cameo-etched vases, covered boxes, and bowls. The firm celebrated its 150th anniversary in 1975.

Reference: Ellen T. Schroy, *Warman's Glass,* Wallace-Homestead, 1992.

Powder Box, cameo glass, cupids, green and gold mums and leaves, emb silver lid, 7″ d, 4″ h, $950.00.

Bottle, 6⅞″ h, green vines and flowers dec, clear acid finished ground, green cut to clear overlay edge, sgd "Val/St Lambert" **100.00**
Chess Set, clear crystal half, green and clear crystal remaining half, each piece labeled and sgd, tallest piece 6½″ h **300.00**
Fruit Bowl, 10″ d, crystal, scalloped edges, fruit design, Brussell's pattern on bottom, matching 13″ platter **118.00**
Goblet, 5⅜″ h, clear, blown mold, applied foot and stem **50.00**
Punch Bowl, 12″ d, 7¼″ h, heavy walled, brilliant red overlay, faceted circle and panel dec **435.00**
Tray, 8½ x 11½″, ribbed, Fort Mon-

tago Hotel and ship in center, frosted mark **37.50**
Vase, 9″ h, cameo, red cut to yellow cut to clear, florals, sgd . . . **850.00**

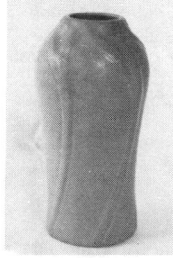

VAN BRIGGLE POTTERY

History: Artus Van Briggle, born in 1869, was a talented Ohio artist. He joined Rookwood in 1887 and studied in Paris under Rookwood's sponsorship from 1893 until 1896. In 1899 he moved to Colorado for his health and established his own pottery in Colorado Springs in 1901.

Van Briggle's work was influenced heavily by the Art Nouveau "school" he saw in France. He produced a great variety of matte-glazed wares in this style. Colors varied.

The "AA" mark, a date, and "Van Briggle" were incised on all pieces prior to 1907 and sometimes into the 1910s and 1920s. After 1920, "Colorado Springs, Colorado" or an abbreviation was added. Dated pieces are the most desirable.

Artus died in 1904. Anne Van Briggle continued the pottery until 1912.

References: Barbara Arnest (ed.), *Van Briggle Pottery: The Early Years,* The Colorado Springs Fine Arts Center, 1975; Susan and Al Bagdade, *Warman's American Pottery and Porcelain,* Wallace–Homestead, 1994; Carol and Jim Carlton, *Colorado Pottery,* Collector Books, 1994; Ralph and Terry Kovel, *Kovels' American Art Pottery: The Collector's Guide To Makers, Marks and Factory Histories,* Crown Publishers, 1993; Scott N. Nelson, Lois Crouch, Euphemia Demmin, and Robert Newton, *Collector's Guide To Van Briggle Pottery,* Halldin Publishing, 1986; Richard Sasicki and Josie Fania, *Collector's Encyclopedia of Van Briggle Art Pottery,* Collector Books, 1993.

Collectors' Club: American Art Pottery Association, 125 E. Rose Ave., St. Louis, MO 63119.

Museum: Pioneer Museum, Colorado Springs, CO.

Reproduction Alert: Van Briggle pottery still is made today. These modern pieces often are mistaken for older examples. Among the glazes used are Moonglo (offwhite), Turquoise Ming, Russet, and Midnight (black).

Vase, Design #836, stylized flowers, turquoise matte glaze, c1916, $390.00.

Bowl
  5¼″ d, 3½″ h, emb oak leaves and acorns, blue–green crystalline glaze, marked "AA VAN BRIGGLE, Colo. Spgs, 670" . **385.00**
  6″ d, 3″ h, raised leaves and pods, matte blue ground, c1920 . . . . **235.00**
  8½″ d, 4¾″ h, Persian rose leaf pattern **125.00**
Cowboy Hat, 5½″ w, turquoise and dark blue **100.00**
Creamer, 4″ h, Sweetheart, two-tone blue **40.00**
Cup and Saucer, Ming Turquoise **140.00**
Flower Frog, 10″ d, duck, blue, old mark **50.00**
Lamp Base, 12″ h, Indian Chief, matte rust brown, black streaking, green/blue highlights, unsigned, remnant of paper label, hairline, two chips **420.00**
Mug, 4½″ h
  Sgd "Artus Van Briggle" **1,950.00**
  Sgd "H Wilcox" **950.00**
Night-Light, 6″ h, mulberry, overlapping leaves, orig fittings, 1914 **395.00**

Pitcher, 5¾" h, tapered shape, buttress handle, matte blue glaze . 82.00
Planter, 9" l, figural, conch shell, turquoise glaze, sq "AA Van Briggle Colo. Springs" mark ... 55.00
Plate, 8½" d, large poppy, leaves, apple green glaze, #20, c1908–11 .... 975.00
Vase
  5" h, hand thrown, trial glaze, heavy turquoise flambe with fine crystals over pale blue green, beige bleeding through, early 1920s 220.00
  5¼" h, molded floral heads on shoulder, incised stems to base, matte green glaze, incised "AA VAN BRIGGLE 392 1906" 385.00
  6" h, two-tone blue, Design #859, 1922, USA mark 100.00
  7" h, molded poppies, whiplash stems, blue and green matte glaze, c1908–12 .... 770.00
  8" h
    Mulberry/blue, late teens 180.00
    Mulberry, green leaves, Design #742, date obscured . 850.00
  12" h, defined blue matte and maroon peacock feathers, suspended blue matte glaze, Design #386, 1905 .... 990.00
  18" h, floor, blue, Design #157, center flowers, long pointed leaves, c1903 .... 400.00

VENETIAN GLASS

History: Venetian glass has been made on the island of Murano, near Venice, since the 13th century. Most of the wares are thin walled. Many types of decoration have been used: embedded gold dust, lace work, and applied fruits or flowers.
  Reference: Ellen T. Schroy, *Warman's Glass,* Wallace-Homestead, 1992.
  Reproduction Alert: Venetian glass continues to be made today.

Animal, rooster, 10" h, multicolored, gold speckled tail and beak, clear casing 95.00
Beverage Set, 10½" h pitcher, ap-

plied striped handle, eight flared tumblers, six spherical glasses, each striped with opaque orange, transparent yellow–amber, and clear crystal, design attributed to Fulvio Bianconi, price for 15 pc set **1,800.00**
Bottle, 9" h, flattened oval, transparent amber, submerged opaque black glass dec, acid stamp on base "Venni Murano Italia," some surface scratches .**1,210.00**
Candlesticks, pr, 12¼" h, vasiform shaft, pink, gold washed base . 255.00
Decanter, 9¼" h, candlestick shape, floral stopper, price for pair 110.00
Flower Holder, 20½" h, pink, four trumpet shaped holders 295.00
Fruit, two pears, two apples, pepper, and lemon 185.00
Tray, 16" d, price for pair **2,000.00**
Vase
  5¾" h, Vaso a Canne, irregular rim, flared cylinder, repeating sequence of red, green, gray, blue, amethyst, and amber stripes 675.00
  10" h, bulbous, flaring neck, circular plinth, jeweled dec 175.00
  19¾" h, goblet form, green, price for pair **2,000.00**

VERLYS GLASS

History: Originally made by Verlys France, 1931–1960, this Lalique-influenced art glass was produced in America by The Holophane Co., 1935–1951, and select pieces by the A. H. Heisey Co., 1955–1957. Holophane acquired molds and glass formulas from Verlys France and began making the art glass in 1935 at their Newark, Ohio, facility. They later leased molds to the Heisey Co. and in 1966 finally sold all molds and rights to the Fenton Art Glass Co.
  The art glass was made in crystal, topaz, amber, rose, opalescent, and Directorie Blue. Heisey added turquoise. Most pieces have the relief designs etched (frosted).

Verlys France signed the glass with mold impressed "Verlys France" and "A Verlys France." Holophane (also known as Verlys of America) signed with the mold impressed "Verlys" and a scratched script signature of "Verlys." The A. H. Heisey Co. used only a paper label which reads "Verlys by Heisey."

Reference: Carole and Wayne McPeek, *Verlys of America Decorative Glass, 1935–1951,* published by authors, 1972, Revised Edition 1992.

Advisor: Wayne McPeek.

Bowl
    6" d, 2" h, Cupidon, clear frosted, cupid with bow and arrow, script sgd **125.00**
    11½" d, Tassels, sgd "Verlys" . **125.00**
    12" d, Tassels, blue, sgd "Verlys" **350.00**
    14" d, 1⅝" h, Orchid, opalescent frosted, three orchids, mold sgd "Verlys" **460.00**
Candlesticks, pr, 3½" h, Americana, three eagles form stick, script sgd **550.00**
Console Bowl, 14" d, Poppy pattern, marked "Verlys France" .. **250.00**
Plaque, 5¼ x 3¼ x ⅞", St Theresa, clear frosted, profile of saint holding roses and crucifix, script sgd **500.00**
Vase
    9⅞" h, 6¼" d, high relief thistle flower, six clear arched panels in lower section, mold sgd "Verlys" **650.00**
    11¼" h, 6" d, Fleur de Chine, clear frosted, intaglio Chinese

Vase, fan shape, Love Birds, script sgd, 6½" w, 4½" h, $145.00.

man, woman, tree, and bush, script sgd "Verlys," artist sgd "Carl Schmitz" **650.00**

1874 - PRESENT

1885 - PRESENT

VILLEROY & BOCH

History: Pierre Joseph Boch established a pottery near Luxemburg, Germany, in 1767. Jean Francis, his son, introduced the first coal-fired kiln in Europe and perfected a water-power-driven potter's wheel. Pierre's grandson, Eugene Boch, managed a pottery at Mettlach; Nicholas Villeroy also had a pottery nearby.

In 1841 the three potteries were merged into the firm of Villeroy & Boch. Early production included a hard-paste earthenware comparable to English ironstone. The factory continues to use this hard-paste formula for its modern tablewares.

References: Susan and Al Bagdade, *Warman's English & Continental Pottery & Porcelain, Second Edition,* Wallace-Homestead, 1991; Gary Kirsner, *The Mettlach Book, Third Edition,* Glentiques, 1994.

Additional Listings: Mettlach.

Candlestick, 8¼" h, pottery, open circular base, brick and beige geometric dec, cream ground, imp mark **180.00**
Charger, 15" d, flow blue, scene with deer **175.00**
Ewer, 10" h, heavy earthenware,

Platter, marked "Villeroy & Boch/ Mettlach/Gesehutzt," Remagen Dec 158, imp "1044," 12¾" d, $250.00.

three color geometric dec, incised VBM 150.00
Mug, 3½" h, tan, leaf and twig dec, twig handle 50.00
Pitcher, 10⅝" h, six sided, white int., dark gray raised scrolls, leaves, pods, and birds, gray ground, beige crest mark 250.00
Plaque
  13" d, Rheinstein castle 45.00
  16" d, horse race, P.U.G., Dresden 150.00
Plate, 9" h, polychrome floral dec, gaudy stick spatter 65.00
Stein, ½ liter, five white figures, blue ground, 6½" h, #171, Mercury mark 225.00
Teapot, 6¼" h, blue and white dec 130.00
Tray
  5 x 7½", Mettlach Abbey 70.00
  11 x 16", cavalier, P.U.G. 155.00
Vase, 7" h, white relief floral dec, yellow ground 100.00

WARWICK
CHINA

WARWICK

History: Warwick China Manufacturing Co., Wheeling, West Virginia, was incorpo-

rated in 1887 and continued until 1951. The company was one of the first manufacturers of vitreous glazed wares in the United States. Production was extensive and included tableware, garden ornaments, and decorative and utilitarian items.

Pieces were hand painted or decorated by decals. Collectors seek portrait items and fraternal pieces for groups such as the Elks, Eagles, and Knights of Pythias.

Some experimental, eggshell–type porcelain was made before 1887. A few examples are in the market.

Reference: Susan and Al Bagdade, *Warman's American Pottery and Porcelain,* Wallace–Homestead, 1994.

Pitcher, brown ground, rose motif, marked "IOGA," 10½" h, $120.00.

Bowl, 4" d, flower and stems 70.00
Chocolate Pot, 10½" h, orange thorn apple branches, brown to creamy yellow shading, ivory ground, twig handle, marked "Warwick China" 175.00
Cream Soup, white, gold trim, underplate 10.00
Creamer, speckled blue and white, raised leaves with gold trim on rim, marked "Warwick China" . 35.00
Humidor, cov, portrait of woman, brown ground, marked "IOGA" 200.00
Mug
  Monk drinking from mug 50.00
  Monk pointing to wine glass ... 45.00

Pitcher
Cider, fruit dec, brown glaze . . . **100.00**
Lemonade, portrait dec, brown
glaze, marked **165.00**
Plate, monk **80.00**
Portrait Plate, 10″ d, Indian, yellow
shading to brown ground **65.00**
Tankard, 13″ h, BPOE, elk and
clock, marked "IOGA" **110.00**
Vase
8″ h, portrait of woman, large hat
with peacock feathers, holding
rose to lips, ·shaded brown to
cream ground, ftd, marked
"IOGA" **100.00**
10½″ h, brown, portrait with or-
chid **225.00**
11½″ h, red, portrait, sgd "IOGA" **185.00**

WATCHES, POCKET

History: Pocket watches can be found
from flea markets to the specialized jewelry
sales at Butterfield & Butterfield, William
Doyle Galleries, and Skinners. Condition of
movement is first priority; design and detailing of case is second.

In pocket watches, listing aids are size
(18/0 to 20), number of jewels in the movement, open or closed (hunter) face, and
whether the case is gold, gold filled, or
some other metal. The movement is the
critical element since cases often were
switched. However, an elaborate case, especially of gold, adds significantly to value.

Pocket watches designed to railroad
specifications are desirable. They are 16 to
18 in size, have a minimum of 17 jewels,
adjust to at least five positions, and conform
to many other specifications. All are open
faced.

Study the field thoroughly before buying.
There is a vast amount of literature, including books and newsletters from clubs and
collectors. Abbreviations: S = size; gf =
gold filled; yg = yellow gold; j = jewels.

References: August C. Bolino, *The
Watchmakers of Massachusetts,* Kensing-
ton Historical Press, 1987; Howard Brenner,
*Collecting Comic Character Clocks and
Watches,* Books Americana, 1987; Roy Ehr-
hardt and Joe Demsey, *Cartier Wrist &
Pocket Watches, Clocks: Identification &
Price Guide 1992,* Heart of America Press,
1992; Roy Ehrhardt and Joe Demsey, *Patek
Phillipe,* Heart of America Press, 1992; Roy
Ehrhardt and William Meggers, *American
Pocket Watches Identification And Price
Guide: Beginning To End...1830–1980,*
Heart of America Press, 1987; Roy Ehr-
hardt and William Meggers, *American
Pocket Watch Serial Number Grade Book,
1993 Prices,* Heart of America Press, 1993;
The Ehrhardts, *European Pocket Watches,
Book 2: Identification and Price Guide,*
Heart of America Press, 1993; Cedric Jag-
ger, *The Artistry Of The English Watch,*
Charles E. Tuttle Co., 1988; Reinhard Meis,
*Pocket Watches: From the Pendant Watch
To The Tourbillon,* Schiffer Publishing,
1987, orig published in German; Cooksey
Shugart and Richard E. Gilbert, *Complete
Price Guide To Watches, Thirteenth Edition,*
Cooksey Shugart Publications, 1993.

Periodical: *Watch & Clock Review,*
2403 Champa St., Denver, CO 80205.

Collectors' Clubs: American Watchmakers Institute Chapter 102, 3 Washington
Sq., Apt. 3C, Larchmont, NY 10538; Early
American Watch Club Chapter 149, PO Box
5499, Beverly Hills, CA 90210; National Association of Watch & Clock Collectors, 514
Poplar Street, Columbia, PA 17512. *Bulletin*
(bi-monthly) and *Mart* (bi-monthly).

Museums: American Clock & Watch Museum, Bristol, CT; Hoffman Clock Museum,
Newark, NY; National Association of Watch
and Clock Collectors Museum, Columbia,
PA; The Time Museum, Rockford, IL.

Lady's, gold filled case, $170.00.

Character

Donald Duck, Mickey on reverse, Ingersoll, c1939 . . . . . . **450.00**

Hopalong Cassidy, rawhide strap and fob, US Time, c1950 **275.00**

Lone Ranger, 2″ d, color portrait on reverse, New Haven Time Co, c1939 . . . . **200.00**

Popeye, friends on dial, New Haven Time Co, c1935 . . . . **350.00**

Enameled

52mm, gold enamel portrait, ¾ plate lever movement, c1910 **1,700.00**

56mm, transfer painted lovers, gilt case, c1761 . . . . **600.00**

Railroad

Elgin, Father Time, 16 S, 21j, 12K gf case **140.00**

Hamilton, 16 S, 23j, dial marked "23 Jewels–Railway Special," 10K ygf case **450.00**

Illinois, 16 S, 21j, Sangamo Special, ygf case, engraved design **250.00**

South Bend, 16 S, 21j, Studebaker, star nickel case **185.00**

Waltham, 16 S, 23j, Vanguard, Canadian dial, Keystone base metal case, train engraving on reverse **200.00**

Regular

American Watch Co, hunter, 10 S, 11–15j, 14K, #1874 . . . . . **325.00**

Aurora, open face, 18 S, 11j, key wind, key set, gilded, ... **165.00**

Double dial hunter, 14K yg, calendar, engine turned cov, white enamel dial, black Roman numerals, moon phases, gold arrow hands, reverse dial with chapter ring calibrated in Russian, exposed movement, c1900 . . . . **2,200.00**

Elgin, 18 S, 11j, open face, lever set, stem wind **70.00**

Frodsham, hunter, 18K yg, #05406, engraved banderole and monogram, gold stopwatch hand **1,900.00**

Hamilton, The Banner, hunter, 18 S, 17j, #927 . . . . **150.00**

Illinois, open face, 14 S, 21j, #1–2–3, stem wind **110.00**

Keystone Standard, hunter, 6 S, 7–10j **125.00**

Longines, 14K yg, white matte face, Arabic numerals, leather case **200.00**

New Haven, 16 S, Angelus, two rotating dials **55.00**

Rockford, 16 S, 21j, bridge plate design movement, stem wind, silveroid **100.00**

Seth Thomas, open face, 0 S, 15j, gold jewel settings, No 3 **70.00**

Waltham Riverside A Model, 19j, 14K white gold, open face, engine turned bezel, silver matte dial, Arabic numerals, five adjustments **175.00**

WATCHES, WRIST

History: The definition of a wristwatch is simple: "a small watch that is attached to a bracelet or strap and is worn around the wrist." However, a watch on a bracelet is not necessarily a wristwatch. The key is the ability to read the time. A true wristwatch allows you to read the time at a glance, without making any other motions. Early watches on a bracelet worn on the arm had the axis of their dials, from 6 to 12, perpendicular to the band. Reading them required some extensive arm movement.

The first true wristwatch appeared about 1850. However, the key date is 1880 when the stylish decorative wristwatch appeared and almost universal acceptance occurred. The technology to create the wristwatch existed in the early 19th century with Brequet's shock-absorbing "Parachute System" for automatic watches and Ardien Philipe's winding stem.

The wristwatch was a response to the needs of the entrepreneurial age with its emphasis on punctuality and planned free time. By approximately 1930 the sales of wristwatches surpassed that of pocket watches. Swiss and German manufacturers were quickly joined by American makers.

The wristwatch has undergone many technical advances during the 20th century including self-winding (automatic), shock-resistance, electric operation, etc. It truly is the most significant and dominant clock of the century.

References: Howard S. Brenner, *Identification and Value Guide Collecting Comic Character Clocks and Watches,* Books Americana, 1987; Hy Brown with Nancy Thomas, *Comic Character Timepieces: Seven Decades of Memories,* Schiffer Publishing, 1992; Gisbert L. Brunner and Christian Pfeiffer–Belli, *Wristwatches,* Schiffer Publishing, 1993; *The Classic Watch: The Great Watches and Their Makers From The First Wrist Watch To Present Day,* The Wellfleet Press, 1989; Roy Ehrhardt and Joe Demsey, *Cartier Wrist & Pocket Watches, Clocks: Identification & Price Guide 1992,* Heart of America Press, 1992; Roy Ehrhardt and Joe Demsey, *Patek Phillipe,* Heart of America Press, 1992; Roy Ehrhardt and Joe Demsey, *Rolex Identification and Price Guide, 1993,* Heart of America Press, 1993; Sherry and Roy Ehrhardt and Joe Demsey, *Vintage American & European Wrist Watch Price Guide, Book 6,* Heart of America Press, 1993; Heinz Hampel, *Automatic Wristwatches from Switzerland,* Schiffer Publishing, 1994; Helmut Kahlert, Richard Mühee, and Gisbert L. Brunner, *Wristwatches: History of a Century's Development,* Schiffer Publishing, 1986; Gerd J. Lang and Reinhard Meis, *Chronograph Wristwatches: To Stop Time,* Schiffer Publishing, 1993; Isabella de Lisle Selby, *Wrist Watches,* Courage Books, 1994; Cooksey Shugart and Richard E. Gilbert, *Complete Price Guide To Watches, Thirteenth Edition,* Cooksey Shugart Publications, 1993.

Periodical: *International Wrist Watch* 242 West Ave., Darien, CT 06820.

Collectors' Clubs: International Wrist Watch Collectors Chapter 146, 5901C Westheimer, Houston, TX 77057; National Association of Watch & Clock Collectors, 514 Poplar Street, Columbia, PA 17512; The Swatch Collectors Club, PO Box 7400, Melville, NY 11747.

Museums: American Clock & Watch Museum, Bristol, CT; Hoffman Clock Museum, Newark, NY; National Association of Watch and Clock Collectors Museum, Columbia, PA; The Time Museum, Rockford, IL.

Character
Captain Marvel, small size, plastic box, New Haven, c1948 .. **175.00**
Dick Tracy, six shooter arm action, New Haven, c1952 .... **275.00**
Goofy, backward, Helbros, 1972 **700.00**
Snow White, plastic, US Time, c1962 .... **50.00**
Superman, 1¼" d dial, full color illustration, yellow hands and border, Dabs and Co, copyright 1977 DC Comics **150.00**
Tom Mix, Ingersoll, c1936 .... **500.00**
Woody Woodpecker, round dial, Ingraham, c1952 .... **150.00**
Gentleman's
American Waltham, 21j, 14K, Albright **125.00**
Bulova, 23j, 14K, waterproof .. **120.00**
Cartier, 18j, 14K, date chapter, Le Coultre **1,200.00**
Elgin, 15j, silver, enamel dial, wire lugs, c1915 .... **175.00**
Longines, 21j, stainless steel, Grand Prize, c1946 .... **125.00**
Rolex, 17j, silver, graduated bezel, c1928 .... **950.00**
Lady's
Cartier, 18j, 18K, European Watch Co **900.00**
Hamilton, 14K white gold, asymmetrical case with conforming hinged cover set with fifty–five round diamonds and eleven baguettes, white round face, blued hands, attached double box-link chain bracelet, c1950 .... **950.00**
Mathey Tissot, platinum and 14K white gold, rect case, scrolling lugs, band of single and baguette–cut diamonds, attached full–cut diamond line bracelet, c1930 .... **2,000.00**
Movado, 18K red, white and yg, round gold face, baton numerals and hands, diamond set bezel, two heart shaped lugs, flat brushed three-tone gold flexible band, 40 dwt **650.00**
Universal Geneve, 14K red and yg, sq, gold face, baton hands, flexible two-tone gold hollow link bracelet **350.00**

WATERFORD

History: Waterford crystal is quality flint glass commonly decorated with cuttings. The original factory was established at Waterford, Ireland, in 1729. Glass made before 1830 is darker than the brilliantly clear glass of later production. The factory closed in 1852. After 100 years it reopened and continues in production.

Compote, 4¼″ h, 4⅞″ d, $160.00.

Carving Set, 2 pcs, crystal handles, orig box and labels	20.00
Decanter	
Alana, sgd, ships	175.00
Lismore, sgd	150.00
Ships, 10½″ h, 7½″ w base, sgd	190.00
Goblet	
Cameragh	30.00
Glengarett	35.00
Jar, cov, 7″ h, fan and diamond cuts	125.00
Pitcher, 10″ h, diamond cuts, applied handle	200.00
Plate, 8″ d, diamond cut center . .	90.00
Salt, 3⅞″ d, master, oval, diamond cut	65.00
Tableware, Tramore pattern, 11	

juice glasses, 11 liqueur stands, 11 sherbet stands, 6 medium tumblers, 11 large tumblers, 19 red wines, 6 white wines **1,050.00**
Vase, 7¼″ h, bulbous, top to bottom vertical cuts separated by horizontal slash cuts, sgd **100.00**

WAVE CREST WARE

c1892

WAVE CREST

History: The C. F. Monroe Company of Meriden, Connecticut, produced the opal glassware known as Wave Crest from 1898 until World War I. The company bought the opaque, blown molded glass blanks for decoration from the Pairpoint Manufacturing Co. of New Bedford, Massachusetts, and other glass makers including European factories. Florals were the most common decorative motif. Trade names used were "Wave Crest Ware," "Kelva," and "Nakara."

References: Wilfred R. Cohen, *Wave Crest: The Glass of C. F. Monroe,* Collector Books, 1987, out-of-print; Elsa H. Grimmer, *Wave Crest Ware,* Wallace-Homestead, 1979, out-of-print.

Bonbon, 6″ w, 6¾″ h, painted Burmese ground, allover beaded white enamel dots, four hp gray and white wild roses, ornate brass trim and handle, painted int., sgd "Nakara"	575.00
Bowl, 1½″ h, two handles	175.00
Box, cov	
5″ w, 5¾″ h, hp floral dec, on sides, robin dec, metal fittings, extra metal embellishments on shoulder and base	1,850.00
6″ d	
3½″ h, round mold, bright blue, pink flowers, marked "Kelva"	700.00
4½″ h, hinged, round, courting scene	950.00
6½″ d, 5″ h, Helmschmidt Swirl, hinged, allover hp floral dec, soft green ground, pale beige	

under frosted surface, beaded
rim, Belle Ware **480.00**
9¾" h, blown out design, pale
yellow ground, purple and blue
iris dec, white enamel beaded
top **595.00**

WEATHER VANES

History: A weather vane indicates wind
direction. The earliest known examples
were found on late 17th century structures
in the Boston area. The vanes were hand-
crafted of wood, copper, or tin. By the last
half of the 19th century, weather vanes
adorned farms and houses throughout the
nation. Mass-produced vanes of cast iron,
copper, and sheet metal were sold through
mail-order catalogs or at country stores.

The champion vane is the rooster. In fact,
the name weathercock is synonymous with
weather vane. The styles and patterns are
endless. Weathering can affect the same
vane differently. For this reason, patina is a
critical element in collecting vanes.

Whirligigs are a variation of the weather
vane. Constructed of wood and metal, often
by unskilled craftsmen, whirligigs not only
indicate the direction of the wind and its
velocity, but their unique movements also
served as entertainment for children, neigh-
bors, and passersby.

References: Robert Bishop and Patricia
Coblentz, *A Gallery of American Weather-
vanes and Whirligigs,* E. P. Dutton, 1981;
Ken Fitzgerald, *Weathervanes and Whirli-
gigs,* Clarkson N. Potter, 1967; Dana G.
Morykan and Harry L. Rinker, *Warman's
Country Antiques & Collectibles, Second
Edition,* Wallace–Homestead, 1994.

Reproduction Alert: Reproductions of
early models exist. They are being aged
and sold as originals.

**Box, cov, hinged, blue floral, 7" d,
4" h, $425.00.**

foreground, pond lily dec, pink
and purple highlights **1,100.00**
Celery Vase, yellow shaded to
white ground, wild rose dec ... **275.00**
Cigar Humidor, 5½" h, 4" d, dark
rust ground, white daisies, white
beading, "Cigars" in gold script
across front **650.00**
Cologne Bottle, white opaque
ground, gold garland, blue flowers, mushroom stopper **350.00**
Compote, 3" d, two handles **225.00**
Cracker Jar, cov
7½" h, hp florals, acorn finial,
beaded handle **425.00**
8" h, 5½" w, egg crate, pale blue
shading to cream background,
hp deep pink and rose daisy
like flowers, white and yellow
enameled highlights, fancy
floral emb lid and handle **650.00**
Dresser Box, 4¼" d, 3¼" h, opalescent, molded shell type design, pink and blue floral dec, gilt
metal hinged rims and clasp,
satin int., red banner mark **210.00**
Hair Receiver, 2¾" h, 4" w, painted
Burmese ground, hp violet dec,
white enamel beads, ornate
brass cov and rim, sgd "Nakara" **495.00**
Jam Jar, 3½" d, 3½" h, floral transfer, SP rim, top, and handle ... **400.00**
Jardiniere, 8½" d, pink ground, hp
flowers in cartouches, ftd **895.00**
Ring Box, cov, green, portrait,
marked "Nakara" **960.00**
Sugar Shaker, Helmschmidt Swirl,
pale yellow ground, pink and
gold scrolls, pale gray traceries,
ornate cov **525.00**
Vase
6" h, multicolored orchids dec

Arrow, 58" l, 23" h, copper, early
20th C **435.00**
Cow
26½" l, molded copper, 20th C . **550.00**
49" h, zinc, cast iron and copper
arrow, lightning rod base, bullet holes **195.00**
Eagle, 26" l, 46" wingspan, copper **2,150.00**
Fire Chief, 52½" h, 22½" w, iron,

Cow, silhouette, sheet metal, rod standard mounting, directionals, 16″ l, $550.00.

painted, running with speaking trumpet in one hand, grappling hook in other, wrought iron reinforcing rod, c1850 . . . . **35,200.00**
Fish, 23¼″ h, 15¼″ l, pine, carved, pearl button eyes, cut sheet metal fin, harpoon projecting from mouth, orig gilding, mounted on rod on turned baluster form base, 19th C **1,100.00**
Fox, 30″ l, 23″ h, steel, running, weathered green, brown, and gray paint **550.00**
Gabriel, 48″ h, sheet metal, blowing horn, paint traces, early 20th C **3,335.00**
Grasshopper, 16¼″ h, 41½″ l, copper, molded, orig gilding, 19th C **4,675.00**
Horse
  28″ l, running, sheet iron, riveted, black and green repaint **725.00**
  29″ l, running, molded copper, painted black, A J Harris & Co, Boston, 19th C **575.00**
  31″ l, running, copper, hollow, cast zinc head, patina, gilt traces **660.00**
  33″ l, 27″ h, molded copper, cast zinc head **8,250.00**
  64″ l, running, sheet metal **880.00**
Horse and Sulky, copper
  33″ l, rod and directional **110.00**
  34″ l, includes rider, bronze paint over orig gilt, 19th C **1,600.00**
Hunter, 29½″ h, 47″ l, copper,

molded, holding rifle, wearing cap and jacket, standing on island shape base, 19th C **8,250.00**
Indian Chief, 49½″ h, 44″ l, pine and tin, painted, carved, wearing feathered headdress, kneeling position, drawing bow and arrow, painted grassy base, 19th C . . **10,450.00**
Locomotive, wrought iron **465.00**
Miss Liberty, 36″ h, 28″ w, copper, molded, gilded, holding American flag in one hand, pointing with other, wearing Phrygian cap, standing on octagonal shape base, mounted on two tier green painted wood base, 19th C **104,500.00**
Pheasant, 9″ h, 16″ l, copper, molded, cut crown feathers and split tail feathers, yellow double neck ring, brown paint traces, mounted on wrought iron rod, 19th C **2,750.00**
Quill Pen, 33″ l, copper, molded, yellow polychrome paint, repousse feathers, mounted on rod on black metal base, 19th C **9,900.00**
Rooster, 20½″ h, sheet iron, riveted, wrought iron bracing, old black paint **880.00**
Ship, 39″ l, wood, carved and painted, 20th C **115.00**

WEBB, THOMAS & SONS

History: Thomas Webb & Sons was established in 1837 in Stourbridge, England. The company probably is best known for its very beautiful English cameo glass. However, many other types of colored glass were produced including enameled glass, iridescent glass, pieces with heavy glass ornamentation, cased glass, and other art glass besides cameo.

References: Charles R. Hajdamach, *British Glass, 1800–1914,* Antique Collectors' Club, 1991; Ellen T. Schroy, *Warman's Glass,* Wallace-Homestead, 1992.

Additional Listings: Burmese, Cameo, and Peachblow.

Bowl
  5″ d, 1¾″ h, Alexandrite, twenty-

four ruffles, shaded citron yellow to rose to blue **1,200.00**
9⅞" d, satin, yellow, white base, frosted ruffled rim **85.00**
10" d, 3¾" w, satin, MOP, DQ, deep rose shaded to pink to white, box pleated top, applied solid frosted base **750.00**
Bride's Bowl, 6" h, satin, MOP, Herringbone, green to white ext., chartreuse int., gold foliage dec **1,350.00**
Cologne Bottle, 6" h, cameo, spherical, clear frosted glass, overlaid white and red, carved blossoms, buds, leafy stems, and butterfly, linear borders, hallmarked silver cov, molded and chased blossom dec **3,200.00**
Custard Cup and Underplate, cameo, moire pattern clear ground, delicate blue foliage and flowers with butterfly, underplate with imp Webb mark, minor rim chip on cup **650.00**
Fairy Lamp
4½" h, 5" w, Burmese, pleated skirt, marked "Thos Webb & Sons Queens Burmeseware Patent" and "S Clark Fairy Patent Trade Mark," clear candle cup marked "S Clark Pyramid Fairy Trade Mark" **1,150.00**
4¾" h, 4" d base, Burmese, vines, leaves, and red berries dec shade, clear Clark base . **475.00**
Goblet, 4½" h, Alexandrite, minute honeycomb pattern, reactive glass, blue–purple to pink to amber, amber stem **450.00**
Perfume Bottle, 3¼" h, cameo, pale cornflower blue ball shaped base, white overlay, carved apple blossom and leaves, circular mark "Thomas Webb & Sons Cameo," threaded rim, hallmarked silver monogrammed cap **1,200.00**
Pitcher and Tumbler, 8¾" h, opaline, internal red striping, gold enamel floral dec, price for pair **345.00**
Sweetmeat Jar, cov, satin, MOP, Flower and Acorn pattern, deep brilliant blue ground, painted green, brown, and maroon berry,

Vase, Peachblow, multicolored dec, 6¼" h, $175.00.

leaf, and branch dec, SP top, bamboo handle **1,250.00**
Vase
2¾" h, 3½" d, Burmese, squatty, flower form, crimped edge, autumn leaves dec, berries **625.00**
5" h, 6" w, blue shading from sky blue to pale white, applied crystal edge, enameled gold and yellow flowers, leaves, and buds, full butterfly, acid–cut basketweave surface **425.00**
7" h
Queen's Burmese, gourd shape, bright red and orange nasturtium flowers, red and gray leaves, scroll design at rim **1,200.00**
5½" w, satin, MOP, basketweave, deep brown shading to tan to gold to cream, creamy white lining **850.00**
8" h
Burmese, gourd, bright orange nasturtium dec, gray–green leaves, sgd "Thomas Webb & Sons" **1,250.00**
Cameo, ovoid, tricolor, white over red, cameo cut floral spray, butterfly, marked in semicircle "Thomas Webb & Sons," ½" side fracture **1,265.00**
Satin, 4" d bulbous base, pink and white stripes, frilly top, c1885 .... **425.00**
8¼" h, bud, Burmese, floral dec, SP handled frame **515.00**

8¾" h, dark green lines bordering areas of pink cov with
white dots, winding over blue
forget–me–nots background,
metal feet **670.00**
10½" h, gourd, satin, bright yellow shading to paler yellow,
creamy white int., bleed thru
pontil **285.00**

WEDGWOOD

c1759-1769

WEDGWOOD
c1900

WEDGWOOD

History: In 1754 Josiah Wedgwood entered into a partnership with Thomas Whieldon of Fenton Vivian, Staffordshire, England. Products included marbled, agate,
tortoiseshell, green glaze, and Egyptian
black wares. In 1759 Wedgwood opened
his own pottery at the Ivy House works,
Burslem. In 1764 he moved to the Brick
House (Bell Works) at Burslem. The pottery
concentrated on utilitarian pieces.

Between 1766 and 1769 Wedgwood built
the famous works at Etruria. Among the
most renowned products of this plant were
the Empress Catherina of Russia dinner
service (1774) and the Portland Vase
(1790s). Product lines were caneware, unglazed earthenwares (drabwares), piecrust
wares, variegated and marbled wares,
black basalt (developed in 1768), Queen's
or creamware, Jasperware (perfected in
1774), and others.

Bone china was produced under the direction of Josiah Wedgwood II between
1812 and 1822 and revived in 1878. Moonlight luster was made from 1805 to 1815.

Fairyland luster began in 1920. All luster
production ended in 1932.

A museum was established at the Etruria
pottery in 1906. When Wedgwood moved
to its modern plant at Barlaston, North Staffordshire, the museum was continued and
expanded.

References: Susan and Al Bagdade,
*Warman's English & Continental Pottery &
Porcelain, Second Edition,* Wallace-Home-
stead, 1991; David Buten and Jane Clancy,
*Eighteenth-Century Wedgwood: A Guide
For Collectors And Connoisseurs,* Main
Street Press, 1980; Diana Edwards, *Black
Basalt: Wedgwood and Contemporary
Manufacturers,* Antique Collectors' Club,
1994; Robin Reilly, *The Collector's Wedg-
wood,* Portfolio Press/A Robert Campbell
Rowe Book, 1980; Robin Reilly, *Wedg-
wood: The New Illustrated Dictionary,* An-
tique Collectors' Club, 1994; Peter Williams,
Wedgwood: A Collector's Guide, Wallace-
Homestead, 1992; Geoffrey Wills, *Wedg-
wood,* Chartwell Books, 1989.

Periodical: *ARS Ceramica,* 5 Dogwood
Court, Glen Head, NY 11545.

Collectors' Clubs: The Wedgwood Society, The Roman Villa, Rockbourne, For-
dingbridge, Hants, SP6 3PG, England;
Wedgwood Collectors Society, PO Box
14013, Newark, NJ 07198.

Museums: Art Institute of Chicago, Chi-
cago, IL; Birmingham Museum of Art, Bir-
mingham, AL; Cincinnati Museum of Art,
Cincinnati, OH; Cleveland Museum of Art,
Cleveland, OH; Henry E. Huntington Library
and Art Gallery, San Marino, CA; Nassau
County Museum System, Long Island, NY;
Nelson-Atkins Museum of Art, Kansas City,
MO; Potsdam Public Museum, Potsdam,
NY; Rose Museum, Brandeis University,
Waltham, MA; Wadsworth Atheneum, Hart-
ford, CT.

BASALT

Cufflinks, pr, 1⅛ x 1", intaglio, oval
framed in 14K gold, imp marks,
late 18th/early 19th C **375.00**
Ewer, 8" h, oenochoe shape, encaustic dec, iron red, white and
black classical figure, leaf and
berry banding, handle terminating at satyr mask, imp mark,

early 19th C, hairline at handle,
slight nicks to enamel **1,725.00**
Figure
Innocence, 12¼" h, one hand
holding bird, shell in other, imp
mark, late 19th C, arm and bird
repair **230.00**
Scotland, 12½" h, standing atop
circular base, modeled by W
Beattie, imp title and mark,
c1859 .... **690.00**
Inkstand
3¾" h, molded double well tray
with central handled vase, removable engine turned inkpot
and sander, imp marks, firing
line on inkpot, sander and tray
restored, early 19th C **489.00**
5¾ x 8", cut corner rect form,
enamel dec flowers in famille
rose manner, imp mark, manufactured inserts and covers,
c1820 .... **690.00**
Inkwell, 2" h, 2¾" d, drum shape,
rib patterned sides, center hole
in top, five smaller holes around,
unmarked **90.00**

BISCUITWARE

Bowl, cov, underdish, 5⅞" d,
molded leaf body with berries,
entwined twig handle, glazed insert liner, imp mark, rim chips,
c1862 .... **230.00**
Urn, 7⅞" h, oenochoe shape with
loop handles terminating in satyr
head masks, white body, imp
mark, c1830, handle hairline .. **460.00**

CANEWARE

Creamer, 3½" h, brown applied
classical relief, imp mark, c1800 **430.00**
Cup and Saucer, child's, 3¼" d
saucer, engine turned body, red
enamel trim, imp mark, late 18th
C **435.00**
Game Pie Dish, cov, 9¼" l, molded
game and fruiting grape vines,
hare finial cov, glazed insert, imp
marks, insert restored, c1870 .. **260.00**

Potpourri Basket, cov, 4" l, miniature, white applied grapevine relief, molded basketweave body,
entwined handles, pierced
cover, imp mark, c1800 .... **460.00**

CREAMWARE

Bowl, 9½" d, black transfer, nautical and military subjects, imp
mark, c1800, foot rim chips, hairline, int. wear **315.00**
Inkstand, 10¼" l, boat shaped, Viking head and swan ends, two
cov cylindrical inkpots with inserts, enameled leaf and floral
dec, imp marks, early 19th C .. **805.00**
Lobster Bowl, 10" d, enamel dec
transfer print of ocean foliage,
three molded lobster feet, silver
plated rim, imp marks, c1864 .. **290.00**
Oil Lamp, 5⅞" l, Emile Lessore,
circular body, crescent–shaped
handle, enamel dec woman and
cherub subjects, artist sgd, imp
marks, c1869, rim nick, cov
damaged **490.00**
Potpourri Vase, cov, 11½" h,
molded and rouletted body with
ormolu mounts, pierced and
scrolled leaf molded cov, imp
mark, repaired cov, early 19th C **750.00**
Teapot, cov
8" w, black transfer printed, foliate framed cartouches with
sailing ship on one side, verse
"When this you see remember
me, Tho' many leagues we
distant be" on other side, low-
ercase mark, restored spout,
cov rim chip, rim nicks and
wear, late 18th C **520.00**
11½" w, Masonic, black transfer
printed arms of the Society of
Free and Accepted Masons on
either side, imp mark, chips,
small hairline, cov chips restored, c1790 ....**1,725.00**
Vase, 5¼" h, Emile Lessore dec,
bottle form, enamel figural landscape subjects, stylized leaf borders, artist sgd, imp "Wedg-
wood," c1865, chips restored .. **175.00**

DRABWARE

Crater Urn, cov, 9½" h, 13¼" l, insert disc lid, pierced cov, white applied fruiting grapevine border, imp mark, one handle with hairline, restored cov, insert married, early 19th C 230.00
Tea Canister, cov, 4" h, glazed, imp mark 200.00

JASPER

Biscuit Jar, cov, 5" h, three color dip, central dark blue ground with white classical relief, light blue banding at top and bottom, silver plated cov, rim, and handle, imp mark, 19th C 200.00
Bough Pot, cov, 11¼" l, oval form, light blue dip, white classical relief, pierced cov, eight amorini, acanthus leaf borders, imp marks, restored hairlines, late 18th C, price for pair 2,185.00
Box, cov, 3" d, crimson dip, white classical relief, vine border, imp mark, early 20th C 575.00
Brooch, 1⅝ x 1⅜", three color dip, oval shape framed in 9K gold, lilac ground, green central medallion, white classical relief, imp mark, mid 19th C 350.00
Candelabra, 16" h, dark blue dip, white classical relief to drum—form bases, imp marks, each capped and fitted with two arm sconces, floral glass finial, late 19th C, wood base damage, price for pair 520.00
Candlestick, 8" h, dark blue dip, white classical relief, silver plated rims, imp marks, nicks, c1900, price for pair 290.00
Ceiling Fixture, 11" d, light blue dip, white classical relief within leafy panels, 19th C 230.00
Claret Jug, cov, 10½" h, dark blue dip, white classical relief, silver plated handle, spout, and hinged cov, imp marks, c1900 . . . . 400.00
Jardiniere, 9" h, dark blue dip, white classical relief, imp mark, c1840 . . . . 315.00

Mug, 5" h, 3¾" d, dark blue dip, raised white classical women and cupids, small white medallion at front with two soldiers, marked "Wedgwood" 130.00
Perfume, 5¼" l, cut corner rectangular form, pale blue dip, white classical relief, brass screw cov, unmarked, late 18th C 690.00
Pitcher
Crimson dip, 5¼" h, white classical relief, rope twist handle, imp marks, early 20th C 520.00
Light Blue dip, 2¾" h, white classical relief, satyr head below spout, miniature, imp mark, c1895 . . . . 345.00
Three Color dip, 4¼" h, white body, applied lilac bellflowers alternating between green acanthus leaves, imp mark, minor staining, mid 19th C . . 520.00
Plaque
4 x 5", three color dip, white relief of Apollo with central light blue ground, outer green trim, imp mark, mid 19th C, wood frame 575.00
5¾ x 18¼", light blue dip, white applied relief of "Hercules in the Garden of the Hesperides," imp mark, early 19th C, wood frame 1,725.00
Portland Vase
10¼" h, dark blue dip, white classical relief with half—length figure wearing Phrygian cap under base, unmarked, 19th C, slight relief loss 575.00
10½" h, dark blue dip, white classical relief, half—length figure wearing Phrygian cap under base, imp mark, relief crazed, mid 19th C 1,725.00
Portrait Medallion, 2⅝ x 3¼", blue dip, Lord Camden, oval form, white relief, imp mark, late 18th C, backside rim chips 315.00
Potpourri, cov, 3½" l, miniature, dark blue dip, white classical relief, two handled, pierced cov, imp marks, c1886 . . . . 460.00
Salad Bowl, 7½" h, yellow dip, black classical relief, rope twist handle, imp mark, early 20th C 430.00

Salad Set, 3 pcs
Dark Blue dip, white classical relief, two handled bowl with tapered sides, small nicks on
servers, imp mark on bowl,
late 19th C 315.00
Yellow dip, 8½" d, black relief
grapevine festoons terminating in lion masks, silver plated
rim and utensils, imp mark on
bowl, 19th C 635.00
Spill Vase, 5¾" h, three color dip,
white ground, green and lilac relief acanthus and bellflowers,
imp mark, c1860 .... 690.00
Stilton Cheese Dish, cov, 10¼" d,
crimson dip, white classical relief, acorn finial cov, spurious
factory mark, early 20th C 690.00
Tankard
5½" h, 3⅜" d, dark blue dip,
raised white classical ladies,
cupid, grapes border, marked
"Wedgwood" 125.00
6⅜" h, 3¾" d, sage green, white
classical ladies and cupids,
grape border, marked "Wedgwood, England" 165.00
Tea Set, yellow dip, applied black
classical relief, 8" l cov teapot,
cov sugar, and creamer, imp
marks, staining, early 20th C,
price for 3 pc set 490.00
Urns, 14¼" h, dark blue dip,
mounted atop drum bases, white
classical relief, imp marks, mid
19th C, price for pair 1,265.00
Vase
3⅛" h, miniature, green dip,
white classical relief, trophies
at collar, imp marks, mid 19th
C, price for pair 750.00
5" h, three color dip, light blue
body, white and lilac relief
medallions between floral festoons and lion mask and paw
columns, 19th C, price for pair1,725.00
6½" h, light blue dip, white classical relief, two handled,
mounted to flat solid white
plinth atop cylindrical drum
pedestal, imp marks, missing
cov, c1865 .... 290.00
13¾" h, light blue dip, white

body, green and lilac applied
relief, trophy subjects, and
classical medallions, cov, imp
mark, 19th C 3,105.00

LUSTERS

Cup and Saucer, Moonlight, 2⅜" d
cup, imp mark, c1810 .... 200.00
Vase, Fairyland
7⅞" h, Butterfly Woman, black,
trumpet shape #2810, Z4968,
int. Floating Fairies border,
printed mark, very slight gilt
wear 3,000.00
8" h, Willow pattern, shape
#2410, Z4968, printed and
imp marks, gilded initials "KR"
within horseshoe, c1925, very
slight gilt wear 1,600.00

MAJOLICA

Dish, 12" l, molded body, albino
ground, polychrome leaves and
berries, imp marks, c1880 .... 375.00
Sardine Box, cov, 7¼ x 8", molded
wave base with shells and seaweed surrounding wood-simu-
lated box, rope finial, imp mark,
c1868, rim flakes to glaze 1,100.00

MISCELLANEOUS

Artware, Vase, 11" h, Marsden,
painted and raised slip leaf dec
in colored glazes, dark brown
ground, imp mark, c1885 ..... 630.00
Earthenware
Dinner Service, child's, partial,
red floral transfers, yellow,
green, and blue enamels, six
3½" d plates, six 3½" d soup
plates, 4½" l oval cov soup tureen, 2⅜" d cov tureen with
underdish, 4" h oval cov vegetable bowl, 2¾ x 3¾" oval
platter, printed marks, early
20th C, price for 16 pcs 690.00
Doric Jug, 8¼" h, brown glazed,
surface agate ground with
gilded trim and mask head below spout, hinged pewter lid,

imp mark, c1866, glaze scratches **115.00**

Inkstand, 4¼" h, cream glazed, removable inkpot, fluted and gilt dec bowl supported by three dolphin feet, imp mark, c1850, restored chips on stand, pot stained **230.00**

Luncheon Service, partial, blue–gray transfer borders and central scenes from Thomas Allen's Ivanhoe series, nine 9⅞" d plates, five 9⅛" d plates, ten 9⅛" d soup plates, four 8⅛" d plates, six 3¼" d teacups, two 11¼" w handle to handle sq cut–corner cov vegetable dishes, two 16¾" l oval platters, ten 5½" d saucers, eight 6¼" d saucers, 7½" l handle to handle cov sauce tureen with underdish, 7½" l gravy with underdish, and 12½" l handle to handle cov soup tureen with underdish, imp and printed marks, c1883, chips, hairlines, staining, price for 59 pcs **1,100.00**

Motto Tankard, 4" h, Harry Barnard, raised slip floral dec and verse "Here's to Thee My Honest Friend, Wishing These Hard Times to Mend," imp mark and artist signature, late 19th C **700.00**

Pedestal, 35" h, blue transfer dec, hexagonal form, continuous bands of Greek musicians and classical subjects designed by Thomas Allen between wide floral borders, imp mark and date letters, c1882, restorations **750.00**

Plate, 8⅜" d, black transfer, green, yellow, and tan enamel and gilt dec, imp "Wedgwood," price for pair **60.00**

Tile, 7½ x 12", yellow glazed, relief of tritons and Nereids riding sea creatures, framed, imp mark, third quarter 19th C, rim chips, glaze crazed **375.00**

Ivory Vellum, vase, 9⅞" h, molded elephant handles, gilded and polychrome enameled leaf and

floral dec, printed mark, c1890, gilt rim slightly retouched **230.00**

Rhodian Ware, vases, 9¾" h, hand painted in Islamic style with silver lustre and colored enamels, printed marks, c1926, base rim repairs to one vase, price for pair **800.00**

Stoneware, mortar and pestle, vitreous, 4¼" d mortar with imp mark and "Best Composition," 7½" l pestle with wood handle imp with "2," c1800 .... **260.00**

PEARLWARE

Egg Standish, 10¼" h, tray with six pierced cups surrounding central salt cellar, blue enamel trim, imp mark, early 19th C, rim chips .. **460.00**

Vase, cov, 9¾" h, underglazed blue ribbed banding, pierced cov, imp mark, c1800, rim nicks on cov **635.00**

Terra-Cotta, sucrier, black Egyptian motif, alligator finish, 5½" w, $825.00.

QUEEN'S WARE

Bowl, 8½" d, ram's head handles, imp mark **40.00**

Vase, 5½" h, bulbous, everted rim, circular base, molded floral and leaf dec, hp dot and floral fields, printed "Wedgwood Etruria England, Ovington Bros" **715.00**

ROSSO ANTICO

Inkstand, 6" d, black basalt relief with hieroglyphics banded to three int. compartments, Greek key and stylized floral borders, ext. meandering banding, imp mark, c1810, minor relief loss, hairlines, restoration **690.00**

Teapot, cov, 7¾" w, oval, black basalt trim, molded foliate design, imp "Wedgwood," early 19th C, chips to spout **385.00**

WELLER POTTERY

History: In 1872 Samuel A. Weller opened a small factory in Fultonham, near Zanesville, Ohio, to produce utilitarian stoneware, such as milk pans and sewer tile. In 1882 he moved his facilities to Zanesville. In 1890 Weller built a new plant in the Putnam section of Zanesville along the tracks of the Cincinnati and Muskingum Railway. Additions followed in 1892 and 1894.

In 1894 Weller entered into an agreement with William A. Long to purchase the Lonhuda Faience Company, which had developed an art pottery line under the guidance of Laura A. Fry, formerly of Rookwood. Long left in 1895, but Weller continued to produce Lonhuda under a new name, Louwelsa. Replacing Long as art director was Charles Babcock Upjohn. He, along with Jacques Sicard, Frederick Hurten Rhead, and Gazo Fudji, developed Weller's art pottery lines.

At the end of World War I, many prestige lines were discontinued and Weller concentrated on commercial wares. Rudolph Lorber joined the staff and designed lines such as Roma, Forest, and Knifewood. In 1920 Weller purchased the plant of the Zanesville Art Pottery and claimed to be the largest pottery in the country.

Art pottery enjoyed a revival when the Hudson Line was introduced in the early 1920s. The 1930s saw Coppertone and Graystone Garden ware added. However, the Depression forced the closing of the Putnam plant and one on Marietta Street in Zanesville. After World War II, cheap Japanese imports took over Weller's market. In 1947 Essex Wire Company of Detroit bought the controlling stock. Early in 1948 operations ceased.

References: Susan and Al Bagdade, *Warman's American Pottery and Porcelain*, Wallace–Homestead, 1994; Sharon and Bob Huxford, *The Collectors Encyclopedia Of Weller Pottery*, Collector Books, 1979, 1994 value update; Ralph and Terry Kovel, *Kovels' American Art Pottery: The Collector's Guide To Makers, Marks and Factory Histories*, Crown Publishers, 1993; Ann Gilbert McDonald, *All About Weller: A History And Collectors Guide To Weller Pottery, Zanesville, OH*, Antique Publications, 1989.

Collectors' Club: American Art Pottery Association, 125 E. Rose Ave., St. Louis, MO 63119.

Additional Listings: See *Warman's Americana & Collectibles* for more examples.

Basket, 13" h, Silvertone **75.00**
Batter Bowl, Mammy **995.00**
Bowl, blue drapery, 5½" d **60.00**
Bulb Bowl, 10¼" d, shallow round bowl, sq rose and white line dec, black ground, imp mark **100.00**
Center Bowl, 6" d, 4½" h, lobes, irid green clover and dots, irid copper ground **660.00**
Cornucopia, Lido, 7¼" h, turquoise **25.00**
Creamer, Mammy **495.00**
Ewer, 7" h, Louwelsa, brown glaze, yellow daffodil, artist sgd, half circle mark **225.00**
Figure
    7½" h, Parrot, Brighton, natural colors **600.00**
    15½" l, 4½" w, 8" h, Roaring Panther, irid green, red, and copper glaze, inscribed in

glaze "Weller/Sicard," restoration to ear **2,530.00**
Flower Frog
2" d, Coppertone **175.00**
4" d, Coppertone **275.00**
8½" h, Hobart, standing nude, ivory **125.00**
Ginger Jar, 12" h, Chengtu **150.00**
Jardiniere, 10¾" h, 13½" d, matte green glaze, low relief foliate dec, unsgd, c1915 .... **350.00**
Jug, 5½" h, three feet, gold open rose, branches, green leaves, orange accents, dark brown glossy ground **245.00**
Mug
4½" h, Dickens Ware, brown, molded white lily of the valley dec **350.00**
5¾" h, Eocean, mushrooms dec **145.00**
Pitcher
5" h, Dickens Ware II, grotesque fish **325.00**
5½" h, Forest **165.00**
7¾" h, Kingfisher, paneled, foliage, and cattails, leaf spout, floral rim, limb handle, marked "Weller Ware" **300.00**
12" h, Souevo **350.00**
Place Card and Bud Vase, butterfly **300.00**
Planter
Dog, three noses **65.00**
Duck **55.00**
Rabbit **55.00**
Platter, 8" d, circular, crimped rim, floral dec, brown field **220.00**

Vase, Marvo pattern, brown tones, stamped mark, 6½" h, $25.00.

Syrup, Mammy **595.00**
Umbrella Stand, 22½" h, Denton . **1,100.00**
Vase
5" h, Silvertone, iris dec, nick on bottom **235.00**
5¾" h, Cretone, black antelopes, flowers, and leaves, ivory ground **260.00**
7" h
Bulbous cylindrical form, relief dec, owls, squirrels, and oak trees, sgd "Weller" **185.00**
Irregular three sided form, irid glaze in shades of red with green and gold, floral design, inscribed on two sides "Weller" and "Sicard," imp "18," minor glaze burst at foot, c1905 .... **1,150.00**
7⅝" h, irid metallic glaze, landscape dec, gold, red, and green-gold, mark inscribed in glaze, c1922 .... **400.00**
9¼" h, Bonita, orange tiger lily . **160.00**
10" h, Pearl **225.00**
Wall Pocket
9" h, Glendale **250.00**
10" h, Silvertone **350.00**

WHALING

History: Whaling items are a specialized part of nautical collecting. Provenance is of prime importance since whaling collectors want assurances that their pieces are from a whaling voyage. Since ships' equipment seldom carries the ship's identification, some individuals have falsely attributed a whaling provenance to general nautical items. Know the dealer, auction house, or collector from whom you buy.

Special tools, e.g., knives, harpoons, lances, spades, etc., do not overlap the general nautical line. Makers' marks and condition determine value for these items.

References: Nina Hellman and Norman Brouwer, *A Mariner's Fancy: The Whaleman's Art of Scrimshaw,* South Street Seaport Museum, Balsam Press, and University of Washington Press, 1992; Martha Lawrence, *Scrimshaw: The Whaler's Legacy,*

Schiffer Publishing, 1993; Thomas G. Lytle, *Harpoons And Other Whalecraft,* Old Dartmouth Historical Society, 1984.

Museums: Cold Spring Harbor Whaling Museum, Cold Spring Harbor, NY; Kendall Whaling Museum, Sharon, MA; Mystic Seaport Museum, Mystic, CT; National Maritime Museum Library, San Francisco, CA; New Bedford Whaling Museum, New Bedford, MA; Pacific Whaling Museum, Waimanalo, HI; Sag Harbor Whaling & Historical Museum, Sag Harbor, NY; South Street Seaport Museum, New York, NY.

Additional Listings: Nautical Items and Scrimshaw.

Carving Set, knife and fork, metal inlaid sheathes with whaling motifs, Faeroe Islands **330.00**

Engraving, aquatint, baleen whaling, Dutch, early 18th C, unframed **550.00**

Journal, whaling master's, last Pacific Ocean voyage of Nantucket ship *Clarkson,* daily record from Sept 15, 1842, through Jan 5, 1846, by Joseph C Chase, sperm whaling voyage account, with shale stamps, large folio, orig buckram, 173 pgs **2,640.00**

Lithograph, "Sperm Whaling With Its Varieties," from painting by Benjamin Russell, large folio, foxed, white spotting in sky area, modern frame and matting **650.00**

Log Book, ship *Splendid* of Cold Spring Harbor, NY, daily entries at sea and port by First Officer Elihu M Pierson of Bridge Hampton during North Pacific voyage to Okhotsk Sea, Arctic Ocean, Northwest Coast, and Sandwich Islands from Oct 27, 1848, through Mar 15, 1851, with whale stamps, large folio, orig half calf binding, some oil stains on cov, 175 pgs **2,640.00**

Model, 25½ x 33", whaling ship *Charles W Morgan,* planked and framed, masts, spars, rigging, and deck including anchors with bound wooden stocks, catheads, windlass, companionship, hatches, boiling pans and fires, belaying rails and pins, deck light, ship's wheel, and two carvel built whaling boats with bottom boards, thwarts, oars, and sails, built by R M Walker, Bearsden, varnish finish **450.00**

Painting
Brown, Paul (1893–1958), "Whaling Scene," oil on canvas, sgd lower left, dated 1871, 24 x 47" **1,100.00**

Nye, William, American, 19th C, "The Capture," oil on artist's panel, old copy of famous whaling scene by William John Huggins, sgd lower right "Wm. Nye/1880," orig frame, 8½ x 21" **600.00**

Post Cards, whaling theme, 64 views of Nantucket, 11 watercolors from log ship *Iris,* 48 miscellaneous including photo card of whaleboat in New Bedford Museum, 1908 comic card "Feeling Down in the Mouth," three men seated in mouth of "Giant Whale Caught off the Coast of Washington," and Hutchinson and Detroit whaler cards, price for 124 cards **80.00**

Silhouette, 8 x 10", portrait of whale and whaling tools, hand painted, purchased from estate of Captain James Tilton of New Bedford, MA, framed **110.00**

Spyglass, opens to 41" l, English, marked "C.A. Saxe Philada" on sunshade, old paper label indicates glass used by Captain Alexander Russell of Nantucket ship *Sea Lion* whaling off South American coast, mid 19th C, working optics, leather cov poor, repair on objective lens holder, missing eyecup and objective lens dust cap, leather wrap in poor condition **250.00**

Walrus Tusk, 26" l, engraved sperm whaling scene, ship *Nabob,* portrait of *Yankee Tar, Ship Matchless,* and *Sail Ho,* Eskimos, and scrollwork, late 19th C, cleanly broken and refastened five inches from top **200.00**

WHIELDON

WHIELDON

History: The Staffordshire potter, Thomas Whieldon, established his shop in 1740. He is best known for his mottled ware, molded in forms of vegetables, fruits, and leaves. Josiah Spode and Josiah Wedgwood, in different capacities, had connections with Whieldon.

Whieldon ware is a generic term. His wares were never marked and other potters made similar items. Whieldon ware is agate–tortoiseshell earthenware, in limited shades of green, brown, blue and yellow. Most pieces are utilitarian items, e.g., dinnerware and plates, but figurines and other decorative pieces are found.

Reference: Susan and Al Bagdade, *Warman's English & Continental Pottery & Porcelain, Second Edition,* Wallace-Homestead, 1991.

Plate, brown tortoiseshell glaze, ribbed rim, c1760, 9″ d, $450.00.

Creamer, 7½″ l, 5″ h, cow, gilt dec	110.00
Figure, 3¼″ h, pug dog, seated, ochre, brown, and gray glaze . .	450.00
Miniature, pitcher, scalloped rim, green, orange, ochre, brown and buff tortoiseshell glaze	150.00
Plate, octagonal	
9″ d, emb rim, brown tortoiseshell glaze	450.00
9⅛″ d, tortoiseshell glaze, black, brown, blue, and green spots	550.00
9⅜″ d, emb rim, brown tortoiseshell glaze	400.00
9¾″ d, tortoiseshell glaze, black, brown, blue, and green spots	475.00
Porringer, 4¾ x 2¾″, creamware, sponged manganese, green and ochre brushed glaze, c1770 . . .	600.00
Stirrup Cup, 4¹⁵⁄₁₆″ h, stag's head, creamware head, brown and green stripes, brown and ochre dots highlights, brown ears, incised eyelashes, dimpled nose, ochre whorl–molded crest, c1780, minor repairs	4,125.00
Sugar Castor, 4¼″ h, translucent colors	200.00
Teapot, cov, 7″ h, relief grapevine and leaf dec, molded crabstock handle and spout, brown glaze	400.00

WHIMSIES, GLASS

History: Glassworkers occasionally spent time during lunch or after completing their regular work schedule creating unusual glass objects, known as whimsies, e.g. candy-striped canes, darners, hats, paperweights, pipes, witch balls, etc. Whimsies were taken home and given as gifts to family and friends.

Because of their uniqueness and infinite variety, whimsies can rarely be attributed to a specific glass house or glassworker. Whimsies occurred wherever glass was made, from New Jersey to Ohio and westward. Some have suggested that style and color can be used to pinpoint region or factory, but no one has yet developed an identification key that is adequate.

One of the most collectible types of whimsies is glass canes. Glass canes range from very short, under one foot, to lengths of ten feet and beyond. They come in both hollow and solid form. Hollow canes can have a bulb-type handle or the rarer "C-" or "L-" shaped handle. Canes are found in many fascinating colors, with the candy striped being a regular favorite with collectors. Many canes are also filled with various colored powders, gold and white being the most common and silver being harder to find. Sometimes they were even used as candy containers.

References: Gary Baker et al., *Wheeling Glass 1829–1939: Collection of the Oglebay Institute Glass Museum,* Oglebay Institute, 1994, distributed by Antique Publications; Joyce E. Blake, *Glasshouse Whimsies,* published by author, 1984; Joyce E. Blake and Dale Murschell, *Glasshouse Whimsies: An Enhanced Reference,* published by authors, 1989.

Collectors' Club: The Whimsey Club, 4544 Cairo Drive, Whitehall, PA 18052.

Advisors: Joyce E. Blake and Lon Knickerbocker.

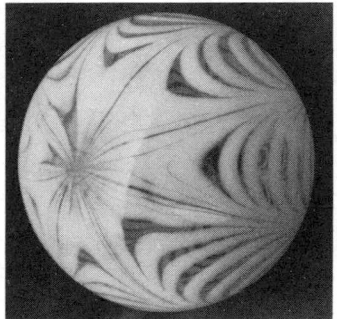

Witch Ball, Nailsea type, pale blue ground, white loopings, 4¼″ d, $115.00.

Bellows Bottle, 16½″ h, ftd, clear neck threading, clear quilled rigaree on each corner, cranberry body, clear applied standard and foot, pontil scar 115.00

Bird Fountain, 6¼″ h, pattern molded, eight rib, colorless, cobalt blue ball finial, tooled mouth, pontil scar, American, 1830–70   275.00

Cane
   31½″ l, cased, cranberry, swirled ribbed ext., mid 19th C 175.00
   45½″ h, clear, hollow body, bulbous end, sq shaft tapering to twisted bottom half, mid 19th C 145.00

Garden Dome, 1½ to 5″ h, free blown, pale aquamarine, tooled rim, pontil scar, American, 1850–1900, price for pair **170.00**

Hat, 2½″ h, 6½″ d, free blown, aquamarine, tooled rim, pontil scar, American, 1840–60 ..... **80.00**

Kugel, 7½″ d, golden bronze, sheared mouth fitted with metal hanging device, Germany, c1900 .... **120.00**

Pipe, 26½″ l, Nailsea type, opaque white, pink loopings, three separate pcs, bowl, stem, and connector, c1870 .... **165.00**

Target Ball, 2¾″ d
   Bright light amethyst, sheared mouth, smooth base, emb "WW Greeners St. Marys Works Birmm & 68 Haymarket London," English, c1880 .... **425.00**
   Deep sapphire blue, sheared mouth, smooth base, attributed to France, 1880–90, price for pair **200.00**
   Sapphire blue, three part mold, crudely sheared mouth, smooth base, American, 1880–90 .... **85.00**

Witch Ball, 3″ d, free blown, milk glass, red and blue splotches, tooled mouth, smooth base, American, 1850–80 .... **110.00**

WHISKEY BOTTLES, EARLY

History: The earliest American whiskey bottles were generic-form bottles blown by pioneer glassmakers in the 18th century. The Biningers (1820–1880s) were the first bottles specifically designed for whiskey. After the 1860s distillers favored the cylindrical "fifth" form.

The first embossed brand-name bottle was the amber E. G. Booz Old Cabin Whiskey bottle which was issued in 1860. Many stories have been told about this classic bottle. Unfortunately, most are not true. Research has proved that "booze" was a corruption of the words "bouse" and "boosy" from the 16th and 17th centuries. It was only a coincidence that the Philadelphia distributor also was named Booz. This bottle has been reproduced extensively.

Prohibition (1920–1933) brought the legal whiskey industry to a standstill. Whiskey was marked "medicinal purposes only" and distributed by private distillers in unmarked or paper label bottles.

The size and shape of whiskey bottles are standard. Colors are limited to amber, amethyst, clear, green, and cobalt blue (rare). Corks were the common closure in the early period, with the inside screw top being used in the 1880–1910 period.

Bottles made prior to 1880 are the most desirable. In purchasing a bottle with a label, condition is a critical factor. In the 1950s distillers began to issue collectors' special edition bottles to help increase sales.

References: Ralph & Terry Kovel, *The Kovels' Bottles Price List, 9th Edition,* Crown Publishers, 1992; Carlo and Dorothy Sellari, *The Standard Old Bottles Price Guide,* Collector Books, 1989.

Periodicals: *Antique Bottle and Glass Collector,* PO Box 187, East Greenville, PA 18041; *Bottles & Extras,* PO Box 154, Happy Camp, CA 96039.

Museum: The Seagram Museum, Waterloo, Ontario, Canada.

Additional Listing: See *Warman's Americana & Collectibles* for a listing of Collectors' Special Editions Whiskey Bottles.

Bininger's Knickerbocker Whiskey, brilliant yellow amber, bulbous, applied handle, applied sloping collared mouth, pontil scar, 6⅜" h, c1840–60, stress crack around lower handle attachment	550.00
Casper's Whiskey Made By Honest North Carolina People, blue, round, tooled tapered lip, 12" h, c1870–80	425.00
Diamond Club, round, medium blue–green, applied tapered ring lip, iron pontil, 9⁷⁄₁₆" h, 1850–60	200.00
Flora Temple Harness Trot, horse, topaz–olive, applied ring lip and handle, smooth base, 8½" h, c1880	80.00
Griffith Hyatt & Co, Baltimore, yellow olive, bulbous, applied handle, applied sq collared mouth,	

pontil scar, 7" h, c1840–60, handle rigaree chipped	470.00
Louis Weber, Louisville, KY, round, olive–green, applied tapered lip, smooth base, emb "W McCully & Co, Pittsburgh" on base, 10" h, c1870	240.00
Nathans Bros 1863, Philadelphia, amber emb	125.00
Osceola Exchange, Tavares, Fla, bright yellow amber, strap sided, double collared mouth, smooth base, half pint, 1880–1900, dug, overall haze, small chips at strap edge	420.00
Phoenix Old Bourbon, honey amber, bird and coffin, pt	115.00
Pride of Kentucky, yellow amber	750.00
Sour Mash 1867, amber, barrel shape, 8¼" h	20.00
Spruance Stanley & Co, San Francisco, tooled top, 1869	25.00
Theodore Netter, barrel, clear	25.00
Turner Brothers, sq, olive green, 9¾" h, 1860–1900	65.00
Wharton's Whiskey 1850 Chestnut Grove, oval pocket flask form, cobalt blue, double collared mouth, smooth base, 5⅜" h, 1860–80	275.00

WHITE PATTERNED IRONSTONE

History: White patterned ironstone is a heavy earthenware, first patented in 1813 by Charles Mason, Staffordshire, England, using the name "Patent Ironstone China." Other English potters soon began copying this opaque, feldspathic, white china.

All-white ironstone dishes first became available in the American market in the early 1840s. The first patterns had simple Gothic lines similar to the shapes used in transfer wares. Pattern shapes, such as New York, Union, and Atlantic, were designed to appeal to the American housewife. Motifs, such as wheat, corn, oats, and poppies, were embossed on the forms as the American western prairie influenced design. Eventually, over 200 shapes and patterns, with variations of finials and handles, were made.

White patterned ironstone is identified by shape names and pattern names. Many potters only named the shape in their catalogs. Pattern names usually refer to the decoration motif.

References: Dana G. Morykan and Harry L. Rinker, *Warman's Country Antiques & Collectibles, Second Edition,* Wallace–Homestead, 1994; Jean Wetherbee, *A Look At White Ironstone,* Wallace-Homestead, 1980, out-of-print; Jean Wetherbee, *A Second Look At White Ironstone,* Wallace-Homestead, 1985, out-of-print.

Butter Pat, emb scrolled rims, price for set of 6	**40.00**
Cake Plate, 12" l, Cable and Ring, reticulated handles, Anthony Shaw and Son, England	**10.00**
Coffeepot, Wheat and Blackberry, Clementson Bros	**100.00**
Compote, Pearl Sydenham, ftd, Meakin	**175.00**
Creamer, Wheat and Clover, Turner & Tomkinson	**60.00**
Cup and Saucer	
Acorn and Tiny Oak, Pankhurst	**25.00**
Grape and Medallion, Challinor	**35.00**
Ewer, 12¾" h, Corn and Oats, Wedgwood	**150.00**
Gravy Boat, Vintage	**25.00**
Nappy, Prairie Flowers, Livesley Powell	**15.00**

Pancake Server, octagonal, Boote, 1851	**40.00**
Pitcher	
8½" h, Wheat, ribbed	**30.00**
10¾" h, Ceres, Elsmore & Forster	**130.00**
Plate	
7" d, Wheat and Clover, Turner & Tomkinson	**18.00**
8¾" d, Corn and Oats, Wedgwood, 1863	**20.00**
9" d, Ceres Wheat, Elsmore & Forster	**20.00**
10½" d, Corn, Davenport	**20.00**
Platter	
14½" l, Lily Of The Valley, Alfred Meakin	**40.00**
16" l, Ceres, Elsmore & Forster	**55.00**
Relish Dish, parish shape, Alcock	**20.00**
Sauce Tureen and Undertray, Fluted Pearl, J Wedgwood	**100.00**
Soup Plate, 9" d, Wheat and Clover, Turner & Tomkinson	**25.00**
Sugar, Fuchsia, Meakin	**40.00**
Syllabub Cup, Trumpet Vine	**20.00**
Teapot, 8⅞" h, forget–me–not, Wood, Rathbone and Co, Cobridge, Staffordshire	**80.00**
Toothbrush Holder, cov, Hyacinth, Wedgwood	**60.00**
Tureen, cov, underplate, orig ladle, Wheat	**325.00**

Tureen, cov, ladle, underplate, marked "Richard Alcock," 9 x 6½", $70.00.

WILLOW PATTERN CHINA

History: Josiah Spode developed the first "traditional" willow pattern in 1810. The components, all motifs taken from Chinese export china, are: a willow tree, "apple" tree, two pagodas, fence, two birds, and three figures crossing a bridge. The legend, in its many versions, is an English invention based on the design components.

By 1830, there were over 200 makers of willow pattern china in England. The pattern has remained in continuous production. Some of the English firms that still produce willow pattern china are Burleigh, Johnson Bros. (Wedgwood Group), Royal Doulton's continuation of the Booths pattern, and Wedgwood.

By the end of the 19th century, pattern

production spread to France, Germany, Holland, Ireland, Sweden, and the United States. In the United States, Buffalo Pottery made the first willow pattern beginning in 1902. Many other companies followed, developing willow variants using rubber-stamp simplified patterns as well as overglaze decals. The largest American manufacturers of the traditional willow pattern were Royal China and Homer Laughlin, usually preferred because it is dated. Shenango pieces are most desired among restaurant-quality ware.

Japan began producing large quantities of willow pattern china in the early 20th century. Noritake began about 1902. Its early pieces used a Nippon "Royal Sometuke" mark. Most Japanese pieces are porous earthenware with a dark blue pattern using the traditional willow design, usually with no inner border. Noritake did put the pattern on china bodies. Unusual forms include salt and pepper shakers, one-quarter pound butter dishes, and canisters. "Occupied Japan" may add a small percentage to the value of common tablewares. Maruta and Moriyama marked pieces are especially valued. The most sought after Japanese willow is the fine quality NKT Co. ironstone with a copy of the old Booths pattern. Recent Japanese willow is a paler shade of blue on a porcelain body.

The most common dinnerware color is blue. However, pieces can also be found in black (with clear glaze or mustard-color glaze by Royal Doulton), brown, green, mulberry, pink (red), and polychrome. Although colors other than blue are hard to find, there is less demand; thus, prices may not necessarily be higher.

The popularity of the willow design has resulted in a large variety of willow-decorated products: candles, fabric, glass, graniteware, linens, needlepoint, plastic, tinware, stationery, watches, and wall coverings. All this material has collectible value.

References: Robert Copeland, *Spode's Willow Pattern and Other Designs After The Chinese,* Studio Vista, 1980, 1990 reprint; Mary Frank Gaston, *Blue Willow: An Identification & Value Guide, Revised Second Edition,* Collector Books, 1990, 1994 value update; Veryl Marie Worth and Louise M.

Loehr, *Willow Pattern China: Collector's Guide, 3rd Edition,* H. S. Worth Co, 1986.

Periodicals: *American Willow Report,* PO Box 900, Oakridge, OR 97463; *The Willow Word,* PO Box 13382, Arlington, TX 76094.

Collectors' Clubs: International Willow Collectors, 2903 Blackbird Rd., Petroskey, MI 49770; Willow Society, 39 Medhurst Rd., Toronto Ontario M4B 1B2 Canada.

Reproduction Alert: The Scio Pottery, Scio, Ohio, currently manufactures a willow pattern set sold in variety stores. The pieces have no marks or back stamps, and the transfer is of poor quality. The plates are flatter in shape than those of other manufacturers.

Vegetable Bowl, blue, marked "Venton/Stevenson," 9½" l, 7½" w, 2" h, $35.00.

Bowl, 9" d, marked "Royal"	5.00
Children's Dishes, dinner service, four plates, four cups and saucers, creamer, cov sugar, teapot, platter, cov casserole, and gravy boat, large size, marked "Japan," price for 23 pc set	225.00
Cookie Canister, round	150.00
Creamer, 2⅜" h, handle, pitcher shape, marked "Shenango"	12.50
Eggcup, 2¼" h, border on base, marked "England"	15.00
Gravy Boat, light blue, underplate, marked "Copeland"	45.00
Juice Pitcher, 10" h, Japan	70.00
Kitchen Stack Set, Japan, price for 4 pc set	110.00

Plate
9" d, Royal China Co 7.00
10" d, pink, marked "Allerton" . 6.00
Platter, 8 x 11", marked "Buffalo
 Pottery," c1908 .... 46.00
Salad Bowl, 9¾" d, fork and spoon 35.00
Salt and Pepper Shakers, pr, 4" h,
 bulbous 18.00
Snack Plate and Cup Set, sq ... 20.00
Soup Plate, flanged, marked "Al-
 lerton" 20.00
Teapot, pink, marked "Royal" ... 25.00
Toby Mug, Japan 300.00
Tureen, cov, large 140.00

**Box, cov, turned urn shape, ped-
estal base, 2⅝" d, 6¼" h, $85.00.**

WOODENWARE

History: Many utilitarian household objects and farm implements were made of
wood. Although they were used heavily,
these implements were made of the strongest woods and were well taken care of by
their owners.

This category serves as a catchall for
wood objects which do not fit into other categories.

References: Dana G. Morykan and
Harry L. Rinker, *Warman's Country Antiques & Collectibles, Second Edition*, Wallace–Homestead, 1994; George C. Neumann, *Early American Antique Country
Furnishings: Northeastern America, 1650–
1880's*, L–W Book Sales, 1984, 1993 reprint; June Sprigg and Jim Johnson, *Shaker
Woodenware: A Field Guide*, Berkshire
House, 1991.

Additional Listings: See *Warman's
Americana & Collectibles* for more examples.

Artist's Model, articulated, late
 19th/early 20th C 490.00
Bowl
 9⅝" d, burl, vestiges of blue
 paint, Northeast Woodland Indians, early 19th C 750.00
 12 x 19½", oblong, refinished .. 145.00
 19 x 19¾", poplar, turned, worn
 finish 165.00
 21½" d, burl, dark patina 825.00
Box
 9½" l, burl veneer, dome top,

tooled brass fittings, abalone
 shell inlay 100.00
13¾" l, pine, dovetailed, slant
 top lift lid with diamond inlay,
 fitted int., red stain finish 220.00
18" l, bentwood, oblong, spring
 clip lid, old blue and green
 paint, handle with red repaint 225.00
20¾" l, pine, dovetailed, base
 molding, wrought iron strap
 hinges, worn red paint 310.00
Butter Paddle, 9½" l, burl ash, old
 patina 385.00
Candle Box
 10" l, pine, dovetailed, old refinish 145.00
 11½" l, pine and poplar, old dark
 paint 110.00
 15" l, pine, canted sides, old red
 paint 350.00
 16" l, butternut, dovetailed
 drawer, hinged lid, old finish . 385.00
 19" l, hanging, oak, dovetailed,
 old dark finish, lid with beveled
 edge 310.00
Cigarette Box, 7" l, inlaid dec, fitted
 int. 115.00
Clothes Pins, set of 24, handmade, tin bands 125.00
Columns, pr, 83" h, carved walnut,
 fluted spiraled form, bases
 carved in deep relief with grapes
 and leaves, French, 18th/19th C 2,750.00
Corner Brackets, pr, 13" h, Rococo
 Revival, giltwood, fern frond supports, quarter round shelf, mid
 19th C 1,600.00

Decanter Case, 5½" h, rosewood veneer, silver and nacre inlay, fitted int. with four clear bottles .. **180.00**

Dough Trough, 38¼" w, 20½" d, 27½" h, Federal, pine, rect plank top, canted sides, ring turned round splayed legs, 19th C **225.00**

Drying Rack, 18 x 10½", 4¾" h, wood frame, woven splint, old blue repaint **130.00**

Figure
8¾" h, carved, polychrome paint **250.00**
14" h, Continental, carved walnut, putto on rockery **315.00**

Foot Warmer, 11½ x 11¾", 9½" h, cherry, dovetailed, hinged round door, wire bale handle, blue paint traces, missing pan **355.00**

Game Board
17¾ x 18¾", checkers and backgammon, red, black, gray, and brown, painted, raised button edge **485.00**
18" sq, pine, checkers on side, Parcheesi on reverse, breadboard ends, painted **550.00**

Knife Box, 13¾" l, dovetailed, old dark finish **95.00**

Letter Box, 12" w, 8½" d, 5" h, rect, rosewood, inlaid mother–of–pearl dec, scrolling inlaid brass border centering cartouche enriched with abalone, mid 19th C 1,050.00

Model, 30" l, steamship *Normandie*, primitive, mahogany and glass case **715.00**

Mortar and Pestle, 8" h, burl, refinished **145.00**

Salt Box, 12" w, 13¼" h, hanging, pine, brown stain, shaped crest **110.00**

Shelf, 10" w, 13" h, walnut, carved eagle bracket with glass eyes, worn black paint **275.00**

Silent Butler, 32" h, figural, man, carved, orig polychrome paint .1,000.00

Smoothing Board, 29½" l, poplar, relief carved tulip, heart, and compass star, dated "1798" ... **575.00**

Sugar Bucket, 10" h, stave constructed, refinished **255.00**

Tray, butler's, 30" w, 22" d, 23" h, Georgian, rect, mahogany, pierced shaped gallery, handled,

later addition custom stand with molded legs and base shelf ...**1,275.00**

Vase, 7½" h, cylindrical, treenware, ring turned, 19th C **85.00**

Wall Plaque, pr, 20½" h, carved and gilded, cornucopia with fruit dec **550.00**

Weather vane Finial, 17¾" h, rooster, carved, good detail, worn and weathered polychrome paint **660.00**

Whirligig, 12" h, carved, polychrome paint **135.00**

Work Box, 9⅝" l, rosewood, tooled brass inlay, engraved medallion "Susan L Bell," fitted int. **110.00**

WORLD'S FAIRS AND EXPOSITIONS

History: The Great Exhibition of 1851 in London marked the beginning of the World's Fair and Exposition movement. The fairs generally feature exhibitions from nations around the world displaying the best of their industrial and scientific achievements.

Many important technological advances have been introduced at world's fairs. Examples include the airplane, telephone, and electric lights. The ice cream cone, hot dog, and iced tea were products of vendors at fairs. Art movements often were closely connected to fairs with the Paris Exhibition of 1900 generally considered to have assembled the best of the works of the Art Nouveau artists.

References: Carl Abbott, *The Great Extravaganza: Portland and the Lewis and Clark Exposition,* Oregon Historical Society, 1981; *American Art, New York World's Fair 1939,* Apollo Books, 1987; Stanley Appelbaum, *The New York World's Fair, 1939/1940,* Dover Publications, 1971; Patricia F. Carpenter and Paul Totah, *The San Francisco Fair, Treasure Island, 1939–1940,* Scottwall Associates, 1989; Robert L. Hendershot, *1904 St. Louis World's Fair Mementos and Memorabilia,* Kurt R. Krueger Publishing, 1994; Kurt Krueger, *Meet Me In St. Louis—The Exonumia Of The 1904 World's Fair,* Krause Publications, 1979; Frederick and Mary Megson, *American Ex-*

position Postcards, 1870–1920: A Catalog and Price Guide, The Postcard Lovers, 1992; Howard Rossen and John Kaduck, *Columbia World's Fair Collectibles,* Wallace-Homestead, 1976, revised price list 1982, out-of-print; Larry Zim, Mel Lerner and Herbert Rolfes, *The World of Tomorrow: The 1939 New York World's Fair,* Harper & Row Publishers, 1988.

Periodical: *World's Fair,* PO Box 339, Corte Madera, CA 94925.

Collectors' Clubs: 1904 World's Fair Society, 529 Barcia Dr., St. Louis, MO 63119; World's Fair Collectors' Society, Inc., PO Box 20806, Sarasota, FL 34276.

Museums: Atwater Kent Museum, Philadelphia, PA; Buffalo & Erie County Historical Society, Buffalo, NY; California State University, Madden Library, Fresno, CA; 1898 Chicago World's Fair Columbian Exposition Museum, Columbus, WI; Museum of Science & Industry, Chicago, IL; Presidio Army Museum, San Francisco, CA; The Queens Museum, Flushing, NY.

1876, Philadelphia, Centennial
    Advertising Trade Card, Boschee's German Syrup, multicolored Agricultural Hall image   **15.00**

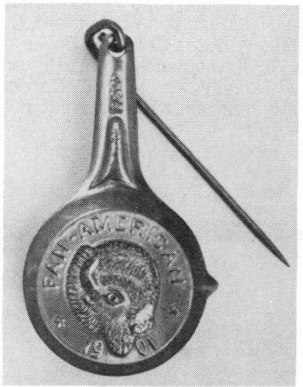

Stickpin, 1901 Pan American Expo, buffalo in frying pan, stamped, copper plated, 1½" l, $15.00.

    Label, Merrimac Woolen Mills, Columbia bestowing wreath, Washington, Lincoln, Jackson, and Grant vignettes, "Highest Award of the Exhibition 1876," needle holes **40.00**
    Memo Pad, Memorial Hall on cov, 6¼ x 3⅝", some pgs used **25.00**
    Plate, Memorial Hall transfer, red border, Prattware, 8½" d **125.00**
1893, Chicago, Columbian Exposition
    Booklet, Lanoline and Personal Beauty, Souvenir of the World's Fair, 16 pgs **30.00**
    Picture Book, Pictorial Chicago and Illustrated World's Columbian Exhibition, Rand, McNally & Co, Chicago photos, Fair drawings, unpaginated **25.00**
    Ribbon, hand painted "Greetings from the World's Fair" and two pansies, 16" l **30.00**
1901, Buffalo, Pan–American Exposition
    Beer Mug, miniature, ruby flash, marked "Pan–American," 2" h **20.00**
    Bucket, wood, bail handle, "Pan–American 1901," buffalo image **25.00**
    Map, Prescott's 20th Century Map of Buffalo the Pan–American Exposition and Niagara Falls 1901, foldout, brown pebbled paper cover **10.00**
    Miniature Lamp, opal globe and base, painted blue, inscribed "Pan–American Exposition 1901, Buffalo, N.Y., USA," orig burner and chimney **550.00**
    Paperweight, oval, Manufacturers & Liberal Arts buildings, slight staining, 7" l **40.00**
1904, St. Louis, Louisiana Purchase Exposition
    Change Purse, Liberal Arts Building, metal top **35.00**
    Pinback Button, celluloid, multicolored, Columbia and eagle studying US map, "Louisiana Purchase Exposition, St Louis USA 1904," Baltimore Badge & Novelty Co **35.00**
    Post Card, Blanke's Coffee,

General Grant's log cabin, purple 20.00

Watch Fob, "St Louis Through the Pike 1904" 40.00

1926, Philadelphia, Sesquicentennial International Exposition

Choral Book, Sesqui–Centennial Festival Chorus and Chorus of the States, 68 pgs 8.00

Paperweight, figural Liberty Bell, pot metal, hollow, 3¼" h 20.00

Pin, brass, "Treasure Island Doubloon 1776–1926 Philadelphia," Liberty Bell, skull and crossbones 10.00

1933, Chicago, Century of Progress

Booklet, North American Indians, from Indian Trading Post, illus, 12 pgs 25.00

Cocktail Shaker, green Depression glass, aluminum top, copper wheel engraved "World's Fair 1933 Bobby and Johnny," 11½" h 45.00

Handkerchief, silk, "1933 Japanese Silk" logo, pink border, orig paper label 20.00

Vase, ceramic, shades of green, wheel cut "World's Fair 1934," 8" h 75.00

1939, New York, New York World's Fair

Ashtray, Bakelite, Trylon and Perisphere center, 5¾" d 35.00

Bracelet, brass plated, openwork center with Trylon and Perisphere locket 30.00

Menu, Finnish Pavilion, 1940 .. 15.00

Pillow, silk, applied ribbon border, Trylon and Perisphere, Statue of Liberty, and Empire State Building, 7" w 15.00

1939, San Francisco, Golden Gate International Exposition

Glass, clear, blue Expo logo beneath seafood illus, red "Castagnola Bros/Fisherman's Wharf/San Francisco," 4¾" h 25.00

Plate, Homer Laughlin, 10" d .. 65.00

1964, New York, New York World's Fair

Pennant, 26" l, dark blue, orange and white inscription, orange band, blue streamers, 26" l .. 25.00

Tray, composition, syroco wood style finish, high relief exhibit buildings, raised beige letters, 12" l 25.00

YELLOW WARE

History: Yellow ware is a heavy earthenware of differing weight and strength which varies in color from a rich pumpkin to lighter shades which are more tan than yellow. Although plates, nappies, and custard cups are found, kitchen bowls and other cooking utensils are most prevalent.

The first American yellow ware was produced at Bennington, Vermont. English yellow ware has additional ingredients which make its body much harder. Derbyshire and Sharp's were foremost among the English manufacturers.

References: Susan and Al Bagdade, *Warman's American Pottery and Porcelain,* Wallace–Homestead, 1994; John Gallo, *Nineteenth and Twentieth Century Yellow Ware,* Heritage Press, 1985; William C. Ketchum, Jr., *American Pottery and Porcelain,* Avon Books, 1994; Joan Leibowitz, *Yellow Ware: The Transitional Ceramic,* Schiffer Publishing, 1985, 1993 value update; Lisa S. McAllister and John L. Michael, *Collecting Yellow Ware,* Collector Books, 1993; Dana G. Morykan and Harry L. Rinker, *Warman's Country Antiques & Collectibles, Second Edition,* Wallace–Homestead, 1994.

Bowl, blue band, incised dec, 10¾" d, 5¾" h, $35.00.

Bedpan, 8¼" d, white band, blue seaweed dec **110.00**
Bowl
  8¾" d, white band, blue seaweed dec, Liverpool, OH **275.00**
  11¾" d, white band, black stripes, blue seaweed dec ... **110.00**
Creamer, 4½" h, green and brown sponging **75.00**
Cuspidor, 7½" d, 5" h, green, blue, and tan sponging **60.00**
Food Mold, 9" d, Turk's head, brown sponging **110.00**
Mixing Bowl
  13½" d, white band, blue seaweed dec, brown stripes, Liverpool, OH **275.00**
  14¾" d, white band, blue seaweed dec, Liverpool, OH **175.00**
  22½" d, molded rim, blue band **75.00**
Mug
  2¼" h, white and dark brown stripes **125.00**
  3¼" h, brown polka dot dec ... **675.00**
Pitcher, 6¾" h, brown, black, and green sponging **225.00**
Rolling Pin, wood handles **175.00**

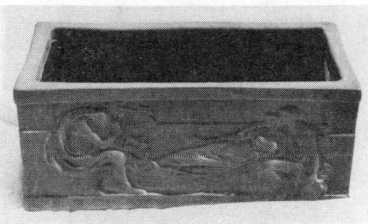

Window Box, Moss Aztec, sgd "Ferrell," 12½" l, 5" w, 6" h, $125.00.

Jardiniere, 14½" h, variegated green semi–matte glaze, two handles, Montene **125.00**
Vase
  3½" h, sq, geometric design, rich green **65.00**
  7" h, flowing medium green, dark forest green ground, marked . **90.00**
  8" h, mint green and cream drip over light and dark brown speckled ground **135.00**
Window Box, 12½" l, 5" w, 6" h, Moss Aztec, sgd "Ferrell" **125.00**

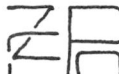

ZANE WARE
MADE IN U.S.A.

ZANE POTTERY

History: In 1921 Adam Reed and Harry McClelland bought the Peters and Reed Pottery in Zanesville, Ohio. The firm continued production of garden wares and introduced several new art lines: "Sheen," "Powder Blue," "Crystalline," and "Drip." The factory was sold in 1941 to Lawton Gonder.

Reference: Jeffery, Sherrie, and Barry Hersone, *The Peters and Reed and Zane Pottery Experience,* published by authors, 1990.

Additonal Listings: Gonder and Peters and Reed.

Bowl, 5" d, blue and brown **40.00**
Figure, 10⅛" h, black cat, green eyes **500.00**

LA MORO

ZANESVILLE POTTERY

History: Zanesville Art Pottery, one of several potteries located in Zanesville, Ohio, began production in 1900. A line of utilitarian products was first produced. Art pottery was introduced shortly thereafter. The major line was La Moro which was hand painted and decorated under glaze. The impressed block-print mark "La Moro" appears on the high-glazed and matte-glazed decorated ware. The firm was bought by S. A. Weller in 1920 and became known as Weller Plant No. 3.

References: Louise and Evan Purviance and Norris F. Schneider, *Zanesville Art Pottery In Color,* Mid-America Book Company, 1968; Evan and Louise Purviance, *Zanesville Art Tile In Color,* Wallace-Homestead, 1972, out-of-print.

Vase, bulbous, handle, pansy dec, olive to brown left to right glaze, marked "LAMORO," numbered, $140.00.

Bowl, 6½" d, mottled blue, fluted edge	**40.00**
Jardiniere, 9" h, brown and gold glaze	**125.00**
Paperweight, A. E. Tiling Co. Ltd, 1896 calendar on back	**25.00**
Pitcher, tankard shape, floral dec, artist sgd	**300.00**
Tile, 24", sq, sixteen tiles, elk, needlepoint style dec, "Mosaic" in oval and round circle mark	**90.00**
Vase, 8¾" h, cone shape top, bulbous base, two handles, La Moro, marked "2/802/4"	**350.00**

ZSOLNAY POTTERY

History: Vilmos Zsolnay (1828–1900) assumed control of his brother's factory in Pécs, Hungary, in the mid-19th century. In 1899 Miklos, Vilmos's son, became manager. The firm still produces ceramic ware.

The early wares are highly ornamental, glazed, and have a cream color ground.

"Eosin" glaze, a deep rich play of colors reminiscent of Tiffany's iridescent wares, received a gold medal at the 1900 Paris Exhibition. Zsolnay Art Nouveau pieces show great creativity.

Originally no trademark was used. Beginning in 1878 a blue mark depicting the five towers of the cathedral at Pécs was used. The initials "TJM" represent the names of Miklos's three children.

Zsolnay's recent series of iridescent glazed figurines, which initially were inexpensive, now are being sought by collectors and show a steady increase in value.

Reference: Susan and Al Bagdade, *Warman's English & Continental Pottery & Porcelain, Second Edition,* Wallace-Homestead, 1991.

Vase, enameled rust and iron–red flowers and butterflies, chocolate Oriental bark ground, dated 1896, marked "Millenium Zsolnay," 16" h, $25,000.00.

Bowl, 9⅛" d, irid brick red ext., irid green, red, and ivory int., imp "Zsolnay 24C 17"	**410.00**
Compote, pierced, pink roses, c1890	**95.00**
Ewer	
4½" h, green and beige, ornate handle, medallions alternating with reticulated panels, gold spires, imp "198 Zsolnay Pecs"	**90.00**
17¾" h, baluster form, irregular	

rim, modeled with partially draped maiden and satyr around rim, purple luster glaze, imp "Zsolnay Pecs 6129 23 1" **4,025.00**

Figure

3½" h, seated man, after Henry Moore, green luster finish . . . **330.00**

13" h, wrestling bears, high relief, irid green and blue glaze, incised name and date "1911," stamped "Zsolnay/Hungary," five towers mark **1,265.00**

Jug, 5¾" h, reticulated, double walled, bulbous, openwork on handle **200.00**

Stein, baluster form, figural and floral bas-relief dec, cream glazed, glaze imperfections, patinated metal cov, late 19th C, 11¾" h **225.00**

Vase

4" h, bulbous, irid red, gold, and green bubbles on red, purple and gold ground, marked . . . **400.00**

6½" h, reticulated, double walled, cobalt blue, gold, and beige **350.00**

6⅞" h, double gourd shape, four handles, red and mustard irid glaze, four mice dec on upper section, imp factory mark and "6020" **990.00**

8½" h, double gourd form, forest landscape with leafy trees in foreground, irid purple, green, red, blue, and amber glaze,

raised and incised factory marks, c1900 . . . . **2,475.00**

8⅞" h, earthenware, ovoid body splitting at lower body with four three–scrolling tendrils continuing to open circular foot, trefoil lip, white, cream, cinnamon, and deep green pendent wisteria blossoms and leafage, irid amber–green ground, raised factory mark, c1920 . . **495.00**

9½" h, double gourd shape, three scrolled handles, textured yellow glazed body, three applied openwork medallions in yellow, black, and red, imp "Zsolnay" **115.00**

10" h, baluster form, cylindrical neck, peacock irid glaze, five tower circular mark **660.00**

10½" h, ovoid, incurvate rim, low ftd base, stylized foliage in geometric patterns, green, gold, gray, silver, and burgundy lusters, black ground, printed factory mark, c1900 . . **2,300.00**

14¾" h, baluster form, flowering peony, butterflies, and leaves, spotted ground, rich colors, gilded highlights, stamped trademark and "872" **1,725.00**

19½" h, globular body, flared base and rim, large foliate pierced handles, polychrome underglaze and overglaze Islamic style dec, 20th C, price for pair **1,650.00**

INDEX

See *Warman's Americana & Collectibles, 6th Edition* (1993)
for expanded listings of categories preceded by †.

- A -

ABC Plates, 1–2, 712, 766
Abino Ware, 82
Acorn and Oak Leaf, 565–565
Acorn, 105
Acorn, 565–565
Acorn Burrs, 105
Actress, 498–499
Adams & Co., 2, 77, 256, 449, 715, 724, 731
Adams, John Quincy, 38, 588
Adams Rose, 2
Adonis, 499–500
† Advertising, 2–8, 16, 42, 46, 49, 62, 71, 83, 114, 130, 131, 137, 152, 166, 200, 233, 421, 422, 474, 485, 579, 585, 593, 608, 636, 689, 747, 758, 767, 815
Advertising Trade Cards, 8–12, 64
Agata Glass, 12
Alcock, 256–258, 810–811
Alice in Wonderland, 200–201
Alexandra, 77–80
Allen, Jimmie, 118
Almond Thumbprint, 500
Alps, 775
Alt Beck Gottschalk, 207
Amberina Glass, 13–14, 110, 175, 758, 771
Amberina Glass, Plated, 14–15
Amelung, 328–329
American Beauty, 525
American Belleek, 56, 399–400
American Bisque, 166
American Blades, 622
American Bow Tie, 511
American Brilliant Period, 179–183
American Encaustic, 763
American Flint Glass Works, 329
American Flyer, 781–782
American National, 776
American Silver, 695–699
American Sweetheart, 191
American Swords, 749–750
Amos N Andy, 64–65, 779
Amphora, 15–16, 25–28, 779
Anchor Hocking Glass, 190–200
Andy Gump, 115
† Animal Collectibles, 16–17, 46, 49, 80, 212, 213, 326, 424, 652, 682
APC, 607
Apollo, 500
April Showers, 105
Arcade, 154, 155, 439, 775–776

Arched Diamond Points, 543–544
Arched Grape, 501
Architectural Elements, 16, 20–23, 25, 110–112, 252, 356, 362–363, 390, 482, 673, 797–798, 813
Arequipa Pottery, 29–30
Argand, 391
Argus, 501–502
Armstrong, Jack, 118
Arsall, 92
Art, Pattern Glass, 502
Art Deco, 23–25, 132, 138, 160, 220, 267, 273, 330, 340, 343, 371, 372, 392, 399, 422, 463, 465, 707, 738
Art Nouveau, 25–28, 35, 161, 189, 273, 340, 343, 372, 399, 412, 423, 424, 495, 645, 706, 736, 753
Art Pewter, 28–29
Art Pottery, 29–32, 459, 461, 466, 470, 483, 567, 637, 789
Arts and Crafts Movement, 32, 273, 372, 396, 420, 659, 741
Ashburton, 502–503
Ashworth, G. L., 256–258
Astral, 391
Atlas, 503
Atlases, 68–72, 418–419
Atomizers, 180, 571
Aurene, 736–737
Austrian, 504
Austrian Ware, 25–27, 34, 80, 141, 343, 365, 591, 753
† Autographs, 35–39, 114, 721, 722
Automobiles, 39–42
† Automobilia, 2, 42–44, 99, 110, 320, 585
Autry, Gene, 118–119
Autumn Leaf, 340–341
† Aviation Collectibles, 321, 784–785
Ayotte, Rick, 491

- B -

Baby Thumbprint, 523–524
Baccarat Glass, 13, 44–46, 85, 219, 227, 326, 392, 435, 490, 492, 572
Bahr & Proschild, 207
† Bakelite, 339–340, 360, 816
Balder, 550
Baltimore Pear, 504–505
Bambi, 201
Bamboo Irish Column, 512
Banded Portland, 505–506
Banford, 492

Banks, Mechanical, 46–49
† Banks, Still, 17, 43, 49–51, 114, 200, 268, 329, 624, 712, 716, 721, 729
Bar and Diamond, 539
Barber Bottles, 51–52, 420, 476
Barberry, 506
† Barber Shop, 51, 621, 691
Bareuther, 401
Barometers, 52–53, 456, 683
Basalt, 800–801
Baseball Cards, 717–720
Baseball Collectibles, 4, 38, 99, 721–722
Baskets, 53–54
Basketweave, Carn Glass, 105
Basketweave, Pat Glass, 507
Batman, 115, 159
Battersea Enamels, 54–55, 668
Bavarian China, 55, 668, 692
Beaded Dewdrop, 565
Beaded Grape, 337–338, 507–508
Beaded Grape and Vine, 507–508
Beaded Loop, 508–509
Beaded 101, 548
Bean, 526
Bearded Head, 562
Bearded Man, 550–551
Bearded Prophet, 562
Beatles, 633
Beaver Falls Art Tile Co., 763
Beds, 275, 437, 741
Belleek, 55–57, 344, 399, 669
Bells, 57–58, 74, 89, 180, 250, 351, 470, 679, 695, 762, 775
Benches, 277, 317, 452, 742
Benevolent & Protective Order of Elks, 269
Bennett, Dunn, 258
Bennington and Bennington-Type Pottery, 58–60, 240, 360, 768
Bent Buckle, 546–545
Benton, Thomas Hart, 598–599
Bentwood, 53–54, 278
Berlin, 401–402
Berry, 507
Betty Boop, 115
Bierschenk, Fritz, 207
Big Fish, 105
Bigler, 509
Billheads, 488
Bing, 776
Bing & Grondahl, 402–403
Bird and Strawberry, 509
Bird Collectibles, 16, 66, 86, 733, 809
Bird in Ring, 514–515
Biscuit Jars, 60, 84, 92, 174, 180, 334, 370, 434, 447, 462, 570, 581, 646, 652, 658, 678, 740, 802
Biscuitware, 801

Bisque, 60–61, 85, 227, 462, 463–464, 469
Bitters Bottles, 61–62
† Black Memorabilia, 2, 8, 46, 50, 61, 62–65, 114, 213, 464, 470, 805
Blanket Chests, 278–279, 437
Bleeding Heart, 510
Bliss, 204–205, 320, 776
Block and Fan, 510–511
Block Optic, 191–192
Blondie and Dagwood, 606
Blotters, 486, 620
Blown Three Mold, 65–66, 109, 254, 328, 360
Blue and White Stoneware, 745–746
Bluebird, 509
Boehm Porcelains, 66–67, 404
Bogart, Humphrey, 119
Bohemian Glass, 67–68, 109, 490
Bone Stem, 538–539
Bookcases, 279, 662, 741
† Books, 16, 21, 43, 63, 68, 200–204, 242, 337, 382, 425, 430, 452, 456, 458, 468, 785
Bootjacks, 71
† Bookmarks, 486, 587, 739
Boston and Sandwich, 98, 394, 483, 672–673
† Bottle Openers, 19
† Bottles, 51, 61, 71–73, 239, 260, 427, 571, 585, 667, 674, 709, 809
Bouquet, 105
Bovine, 17, 48, 59, 86, 797
Bow, 222
Bowman Gum Co., 717–720
Bow Tie, 511
Boyd, William, 38, 116, 794
Boxes, 281–282
Boxing Collectibles, 722–723
Bradley and Hubbard, 213–216, 394
Brass Items, 48, 72–74, 98, 227, 242, 251, 326, 343, 371, 382, 386, 391, 397, 422, 423, 481, 662
Bread Plates, 74–75, 180, 332, 466, 678, 680, 687, 711, 716, 758
Breakfronts, 279–281
Bridal Rosette, 511–512
Bride's Baskets, 13, 75–76, 91, 180, 476, 581, 675, 799
Bristol Glass, 51, 76–77, 109
† British Royalty Commemoratives, 77–80, 491, 593, 758
Broken Column, 512
Bronze Items, 16, 23, 25, 80–81, 85, 88, 98, 136, 252, 326, 371, 391, 459, 630, 662, 710, 759
Bru, 208
Brush, 166
Bryce's Wreath, 565–565

Buckle, 513
Buddy L, 776
Buffalo Pottery, 81–84, 88, 659, 811
Bullet, 503
Bull's Eye, 513
Bull's Eye and Daisy, 513–514
Bull's Eye and Waffle, 562–563
Bull's Eye Band, 551–552
Bull's Eye in Heart, 531–532
Bull's Eye with Diamond Point, 514
Bull's Eye with Diamond Point #2, 551–552
Burgess & Leigh, 256–258, 358
Burmese Glass, 84–85, 227, 396, 447, 666, 771, 798
Bushel Basket, 105
Bush, George, 589
Business Cards, 87–88, 486
Buster Brown, 50, 115, 320
Busts, 15, 61, 78, 85–86, 167, 172, 259, 331, 399, 434, 494, 654, 753
Butterfly and Berry, 105
Butterfly and Fan, 514
Butter Prints, 86–87, 262, 387
Byrdcliffe Pottery, 763

- C -

Cabbage Rose, 515
Cabinet Card, 579, 587
Cabinets, 4, 282, 741
Cable, 515–516
Cactus, 337–338
Calendar Plates, 87
† Calendars, 4, 43, 114–120, 153, 487, 587
California, 507–508
California Faience, 30, 764
California Originals, 166
Calling Card Cases and Receivers, 25, 87–88, 484
Cambridge Feather, 527–528
Cambridge Glass, 88–90, 99, 328, 571
Cambridge Pottery, 90–91
Cameo Doll Co., 75
Cameo Glass, 91–95, 396, 569, 572, 630, 668, 771, 787, 798
Cameras, 47, 95–97, 114, 593
Campaign Items, 585–590
Camphor Glass, 97
Canadian, 516
Canadian Drape, 530–531
Canadian Horseshoe, 500
Candlestands, 283–284, 362, 657
Candlesticks, 97–98
† Candy Containers, 18, 99–101, 120, 493
Cane and Star Medallion, 554–555

Cane, 516–517, 747
Canes, 101–102, 684, 809
Cane Variant, 543–544
Caneware, 801
Cannon Ball, 503, 527
Canton China, 102–103, 642
Cantor, Eddie, 119
Capo-Di-Monte, 103–104
Captain America, 115, 159
Captain Kangaroo, 115
Captain Marvel, 795
Captain Midnight, 115
Carlsbad China, 104–105
Carnival Glass, 105–107, 344, 396
Carolina, 517
Carousel Figures, 21, 107–108
Carpenter, 776–777
Carter, James, 585–590
Cartes De Visite, 579
Case Knives, 583–584
Cash Registers, 7, 155–156
Cast Iron Items, 1, 16, 20, 46, 49, 71, 212, 213, 252, 273, 360, 361, 362, 371, 386, 422, 423, 437, 663, 689, 747, 767, 773, 797
Castleford, 108–109
Castor Sets, 65, 67, 109–110, 441, 442, 667, 706
† Catalogs, 4, 20, 21, 43, 110, 129, 250, 426, 452, 468, 689
† Cat Collectibles, 17, 47, 49, 108, 113, 213, 227, 239, 259, 321, 327, 455, 456, 464, 608, 734, 747, 771, 785
Caughley, 222
Celadon, 112
† Celluloid Items, 6, 19, 112, 114, 339, 464, 469, 758
Chad Valley Co., 606
Chairs, 4, 23, 33, 125, 126, 284, 317, 438, 690, 741
Chalkware, 18, 50, 113–114, 747
Challinor, E., 177, 256–258, 448
Chan, Charlie, 119
Chandeliers, 45, 392–394, 495, 761, 765
Chaplin, Charlie, 100, 593
† Character and Personality Items, 114–120, 592, 606, 794, 795
Character Jugs, 652
Charles (Prince of Wales), 77–80
Checkerboard, 511
Checks, 487
Chein, 777
Chelsea, 120–122
Chelsea, Grandmother's Ware, 122
Chelsea Keramic Art Works, 187–189, 764
Cherries, 106
Cherryberry, 192–193

Cherry, 106
Chests of Drawers, 51, 288, 438, 660
Chests, Other, 291, 438, 457
† Children's Books, 122–124
† Children's Feeding Dishes, 124–125
Children's Nursery Items, 110, 114, 125–
   127, 149, 150, 204, 273, 469, 690
† Children's Toy Dishes, 127–128, 163, 185,
   200, 325, 338, 465, 680, 767, 812
Chinese Ceramics, 366–370, 481–483
Chinese Export, 165, 228, 253, 366, 481,
   629
† Christmas Items, 1, 2, 17, 25, 46, 110, 128–
   130, 132, 320, 387, 486, 650, 709, 809
† Christmas Plates, 400–406
Cigar Cutters, 130–131
Cigar Store Figures, 131–132
Cinderella, 201, 387
Cinnabar, 132, 371
Cisco Kid, 116, 159
Civil War, 37, 431–432, 691, 749
Clambroth Glass, 132–133
Clarice Cliff, 133–134
Clarissa, 534–535
Clark, 179–183
Clewell Pottery, 134–135
Clews, 724, 177
Clichy, 490–491
Clifton Pottery, 135–136
† Clocks, 5, 23, 26, 28, 33, 80, 136, 153, 200,
   267, 351, 370, 385, 424, 437, 361, 587,
   647, 680, 760
Cloisonne, 147–148, 481, 710
† Clothing, 148–150
† Clothing Accessories, 150–151
Coalport, 151–152, 358, 629, 771
Cobb, 566
Cobb, Ty, 38, 718, 721
† Coca-Cola Items, 79, 152–154, 636
Coffee Mills, 154
† Coin-Operated Items, 155–157
Coin Silver, 88, 695–697
Collins, 520
Cologne Bottles, 13, 45, 173, 181, 354, 445,
   447, 478, 483, 569, 571, 658, 706, 797,
   799
Colonial Panel, 106
Colorado, 518–519
Columbia, 531–532
Columbian, 531–532
Comet, 519
† Comic Books, 157–160, 200–204, 609
† Commemorative Items, 711–712
Compacts, 160–162
Connecticut, 519–520
Consolidated Glass Co., 162–163, 476, 666
Consolidated Paper Box, 607

Continental China and Porcelain, General,
   127, 141, 163–165
Continental Silver, 699–701
Coogan, Jackie, 119
† Cookie Jars, 17, 165–167, 423, 693, 746
Copeland and Spode, 167–168, 494
Copper Items, 25, 27, 32, 168–169, 242,
   397, 797
Copper Luster, 414
Coralene, 169–170
Corbett, Tom, 118
Corkscrews, 170–171
Cor-Cor, 777
Cosmetic Bottles, 72
Cosmos & Cane, 106
Coventry Glass Works, 329, 360
Coverlets, 755–756
Cowan Pottery, 171–172
Cradles, 125, 293
Cranberry Glass, 172–174
Crandall, 777
Creamware, 398, 411, 413, 748, 801
Creil & Montereau, 764
Crested Wares, 333–334
Crosby, Bing, 119, 624
Crow-foot, 566
Crown Milano, 60, 76, 174–175, 748
Cruets, 76
Crystal Anniversary, 520
Crystal Ball, 503, 527
Crystal Wedding, 520
Cuno & Otto, 208
Cupboards, 293–295, 438
Cup Plates, 176–177, 673, 712, 716, 753
Currier and Ives, 599
Custard Glass, 177–179, 396, 422, 771
Cut Glass, American, 60, 109, 143, 179–
   183, 326, 353, 360, 400, 630, 668, 745,
   785, 796
Cut Velvet, 183
Czechoslovakian Items, 15–16, 25, 34,
   183–184

- D -

Dagwood, 116
Daisy and Button, 520–522
Daisy and Thumbprint Crossbar, 522–523
Daisy with Crossbar, 522–523
Daisy and Button with Crossbars, 522–523
Dakota, 523–524
Dalzell, Gilmore, and Leighton, 240
D'Argental, 92
Daum Nancy, 93, 393, 395, 494
Davenport, 177, 184, 256–258, 324, 448,
   811

Davis, Bette, 119
Davy Crockett, 116, 201
Daybeds, 295–296
Day, Doris, 119
DeCamp, 777
Decoys, 185–187, 259, 766
Dedham Pottery, 187–189
Deer and Doe, 524
Deer and Pine Tree, 524
Degenhart, John, 490
Delatte, 93
Delaware, 525
Deldare, 83
Delftware, 189–190, 393, 411, 767
Dennis The Menace, 159
† Depression Glass, 190–200, 571
Derby, 223
Desks, 296, 438, 493
Design Spatterware, 224–225
Devez, 93
De Vilbiss, 571
Dewey, 585–590, 758
Diamond Glass Co., 106
Diamond Point, 525–526
Diamond Point with Ribs, 525–526
Diana (Princess of Wales), 77–80
Dick Tracy, 116, 795
Dimmock, Thomas, 256–258, 731
† Dionne Quintuplets, 119
† Disneyana, 122, 157, 200, 623, 773, 795
Disneyland, 201
Display Cabinets, 4, 282
† Dog Collectibles, 4, 18, 47, 50, 59, 87, 100,
    113, 124, 214, 227, 399, 455, 464, 631,
    692, 730, 734, 772
Dogwood, 193
Doll Houses, 204–206, 437–439
† Dolls, 64, 112, 114, 125, 203, 206–212, 358,
    462, 632, 663, 683
Dominion, 543
Donald Duck, 113, 159, 201–202, 794
Door Knockers, 17, 212–213
† Doorstops, 17, 213–216, 363
Dorflinger, 179–183
Double Pear, 504–505
Dough Troughs, 298, 387, 814
Doulton & Co., 258
Drabware, 802
Dragon and Lotus, 106
Dresden/Meissen, 216–218, 668, 768
Dry Sinks, 299
Dugan, 105–107
Dumbo, 202
Duncan and Miller, 218–219, 326, 558
Duquesne, 563–564
Durand, 91, 219–221, 396
Durante, Jimmy, 119

- E -

Earl, 554
Early American Glass, 176, 254, 328, 572,
    669, 672, 747
Early Buckle, 513
Early Oregon, 553–554
Eastern Star, 269
Eastman Kodak, 96
Edwards, James, 177, 256–258, 448
Edward VII, 77–80
Edward VIII, 77–80
Effanbee, 208
Eggington, 179–183
Egg In Sand, 526
Einson-Freeman, 607
Eisenhower, Ike, 66, 585–590
† Elephant Collectibles, 18, 47, 49, 100, 108,
    156, 214, 327, 388, 417, 422, 464, 638,
    682, 735
Ellenville, 329
Elizabeth (Queen Mother), 77–80
Elizabeth II (Queen of England), 77–80
Elsmore & Forster, 811
Elvis, 634
Emerald Deldare, 83
Emerald Green Herringbone, 529–530
English Cameo Glass, 91–95
English China and Porcelain (General),
    221, 224, 226, 322, 398
English Hobnail, 193–194, 571
English Silver, 701–705
Eskimo, 355–356
Etched Fern and Waffle, 543
E.T.C.O., 777
Excelsior, 526–527
Expositions, 814–816
Eyewinker, 527

- F -

Fairings, Match-Strikers, and Trinket
    Boxes, 226–227
Fairy Lamps, 61, 173, 227, 410, 453, 482,
    714, 799
Famille Rose, 228–229
Fan, 514–515
Fanciful, 106
Fans, 153, 156, 229, 481, 493, 587, 772
Fantasia, 202
Favrile Glass, 91, 706, 759
Feather, 527–528
Feather and Quill, 527–528
Federal Glass, 326–328
Felix The Cat, 18, 100, 116
Fell, Thomas, 257
Fentonia, 106
† Fenton Glass, 105, 109, 235–237, 746

Ferdinand, 202
Fields, W. C., 119
† Fiesta, 237–239
Fig, 504–505
Figural Bottles, 19, 59, 117, 239–240
Findlay Onyx Glass, 240
Fine Arts, 240–241, 260, 365, 457
Finecut, 528–529
Fine Cut and Feather, 527–528
Fine Cut and Roses, 106
Finecut Medallion, 504
Finger Print, 500
Firearm Accessories, 2–8, 241–243
Firearms, 101, 110–112, 243–250
† Firehouse Collectibles, 100, 250–251, 620, 776, 797
Fireplace Equipment, 16, 22, 26, 32, 73, 251–252, 362, 729, 809
Fischer China, 252–253
Fish Collectibles, 19, 798
Fisher-Price, 777
Fishnet, 106
Fish Sets, 28, 35
Fitzhugh, 253–254
Flamingo Habitat, 529
Flask, Powder, 242–243
Flasks, 59, 91, 254–256, 329, 434, 440, 453, 707, 743
Fleer Gum Co., 717–720
Flint Faience Tile Co., 764
Flintlock Long Arms, 248
Flintlock Pistols, 244–245
Florentine #1, 194–195
Florida, 529–530
Flow Blue, 256–258
Flower in Square, 528–529
Flute, 106
Flying Bird and Strawberry, 509
Flynn, Errol, 119
Folk Art, 101, 185, 259, 264, 273, 437, 610, 628, 669, 689, 693, 754
Food Bottles, 260–261
Food Molds, 19, 169, 261–262, 336, 387, 625, 765
Football Cards, 717–720
Football Collectibles, 47, 723
Fostoria Glass, 263–264, 326, 396
Four Petal Flower, 525
Foxy Grandpa, 116
Fraktur, 264–266, 690
Frankart, 267
† Fraternal Organizations, 269–270, 691, 749
French Cameo Glass, 91–95
French China and Porcelain, 127, 163–165, 613–617
Frog Collectibles, 19, 51
Frosted Lion, 539–540

Fruit Jars, 270–271
Fruits & Flowers, 106
Fry Glass, 271–272
Fulper Pottery, 272–273
Furniture, 23, 25, 32, 110, 125, 273–318, 437, 468, 482, 659, 689, 741
Furnival, Jacob & Thos., 256–258, 448

- G -

Galle, 94, 395
Galloway, 530
Game Plates, 83, 318–319, 345, 406, 416, 463, 642, 649, 648
† Games, 64, 114, 204, 281, 313, 319–321, 587, 685, 788, 814
Garden Furniture, 22
Garfield Drape, 530–531
Garland, Judy, 119
Gaudy Dutch, 322–323
Gaudy Ironstone, 323
Gaudy Welsh, 324
Gaultier, Francois, 208
Geisha Girl Porcelain, 324–326
Geneva, 338
Geneva #2, 543–544
George V, 77–80
George VI, 77–80, 758
Georgia, 531
German Toys, 773–780
German China and Porcelain, 163–165, 383
Gildea & Walker, 731
Gipsy, 504–505
Girandoles and Mantel Lustres, 326
Glass Animals, 219, 326–328, 346, 354, 664, 737, 762, 790
Glass, Early American, 328–330, 808
Gleason, Jackie, 119
Goldscheider, 330–331
Goldwater, Barry, 588
† Golf Collectibles, 214, 239, 723
† Gonder Pottery, 337–332
Goofus Glass, 332
Goofy, 202
Good Luck, 106
Good Luck, 534
Gordon, Flash, 116
Gorham, 320, 697–698
Goss and Crested Ware, 333–334
Gouda Pottery, 334–335
Grable, Betty, 119
Grace, 514–515
Granby, 540–541
† Graniteware, 335–336
Grant, Ulysses, 494, 586
Grape, 106
Grape and Cable, 106

Grape and Gothic Arches, 106
Grape and Vine, 507–508
Greek Key, 561
Greenaway, Kate, 336–337
Green Hornet, 116
Greentown Glass, 337–338, 347–348
Grindley, W. H., 256–258
Grueby Pottery, 338–339, 764
Gunderson, 568–569

- H -

Hacker, Christian, 205
Hair Ornaments, 339–340
† Hall China Company, 340–341
Hampshire Pottery, 341–342
Hancock, Sampson, 258
Handel, 391–396, 396
Hand-Painted China, 342–343, 406, 412, 630
Handwerck, Heinrich, 208
Harrison, Benjamin, 589
Hatpins and Hatpin Holders, 20, 334, 343–344, 445, 463, 643, 646, 656, 679, 680
Hat Racks and Hall Trees, 299, 348
Haviland & Parlon, 403
Haviland China, 344–345, 446, 453
Hawkes, 179–183
Hayes, Gabby, 119
Hayes, Rutherford, 586
Hazel Atlas Glass, 190–200
Heart and Thumbprint, 531–532
Hearts and Flowers, 106
Hearts and Spades, 548–549
Heart with Thumbprint, 531–532
Heath, 256–258
Heather Rose, 341
Heisey Glass, 326, 345–347, 422
Hess, 777
Heubach, Gebruder, 208–209
Hickok, Wild Bill, 118
Hiller Industries, 777
Historical Flasks, 254–256
Historical Glass Cup Plates, 176–177
Historical Staffordshire, 723–729
Hobb's Centennial, 562
Hobnail, 195
Hobnailed Diamond and Star, 516
Hocking Glass, 190–200
Hoge Mfg Co., 777
Holly Amber, 347–348
Holly, Carn Glass, 106
Holly, Pat Glass, 533
Honeycomb, 533–534
Honeycomb with Flower Rim, 561–562
Hoover, Herbert, 588, 758
Hopalong Cassidy, 38, 116, 794
Hope, Bob, 119

Hops and Barley, 563–564
Horn, 102, 229–236, 243, 348
† Horse Collectibles, 19, 22, 47, 50, 87, 108, 327, 432, 455, 798
Horse Racing Collectibles, 47, 321, 723, 773
Horseshoe, 534
Household Bottles, 72
Howdy Doody, 116, 159, 261
Hubley, 213–216, 777
Hughes, Thomas, 256–258
Hull Pottery, 348–350
Hummel Items, 350–352

- I -

Icart, Louis, 600
Ice Cream Molds, 262
Illinois, 534–535
Imari, 352–353
Imperial Glass, 105, 326, 332, 353–354
Independent Order of Odd Fellows, 269–270, 692
Indiana Feather, 527–528
Indiana Glass, 190–200
Indiana Swirl, 527–528
Indian Artifacts, American, 53, 354–358, 798
Indian Tree Pattern, 358–359
Indian War, 432
Ink Bottles, 359–360
Inkwells, 66, 74, 91, 93, 329–330, 335, 360–361, 471, 478, 495, 575, 639, 646, 679, 687, 707, 711, 730, 800
Inverness, 517
Inverted Loop and Fan, 542–543
Iowa, 535
Iris, 195
Irish Belleek, 56–57
Irons, 361–362
Ironware, 362–363, 386–388
Issmayer, 777
Italian China and Porcelain, 163–165
Ives, 319, 778, 781
Ivory, 101, 109, 229, 344, 363, 382, 458, 684, 710, 758

- J -

Jackfield, 223
Jack In The Pulpit Vases, 13, 84, 365, 412, 610, 737, 740
Jackson, J. & J., 725
Jacobi & Jenkins, 182
Jacob's Ladder, 536
Jacob's Tears, 502
Jade, 102, 365–366, 710
Jade Glass, 737–738

Japanese and Chinese Ceramics, 352, 366, 388, 481
Japanese, 514–515
Japanese Prints, 602–604
Japanese Toys, 773–780
Jasperware, 370–371, 802–803
Jaymar Specialty Co., 608–609
Jeannette Glass, 190–200
Jefferson, Thomas, 588
Jensen, Georg, 161
Jersey Swirl, 536–537
Jervis Pottery, 30
Jewel and Crescent, 555
Jewel Boxes, 175, 371, 421, 445, 783
Jeweled Rosette, 555
Jewelry, 23, 30, 33, 44, 111, 114, 132, 200, 268, 269, 343, 354, 365, 372–381, 458, 494, 585, 620, 632, 659, 793, 794, 800
Jewel with Dewdrop, 537
Job's Tears, 502
Johnson Bros., 256–258, 359
Johnson, Lyndon, 589
Judaica, 381–383
Jugendstil, 754
Jugtown Pottery, 383
Jumeau, 209

- K -

Ka-Bar Knives, 584
Kammer & Reinhardt, 209–210
Kansas, 537
Kauffmann, Angelica, 385
Kayo, 117, 464
Kayserzinn, 28
Kaziun, Charles, 492
Keen Kutter Knives, 584
Kelly, Grace, 119
Kennedy, John, 45, 585–590
Kenton Hills, 30
Kenton Toys, 778
Kentucky, 537–538
Kestner, 210
Kew Blas, 385–386
Kewpie, 51, 113, 124, 130, 656
Keystone Mfg Co., 778
King, Martin Luther, Jr., 65
Kingsbury, 778
King's Crown, 538–539
King's Rose, 224–226
† Kitchen Collectibles, 2, 168, 237, 261, 270, 271, 273, 335, 386, 429, 454, 474, 475, 573, 624, 626, 743, 745, 764, 766, 812, 813
K, Japanese Toys, 778
Kley and Hahn, 210
Knives, 153
Knobby Bull's Eye, 513–514

Knowles, Taylor, and Knowles, 413, 446
Kokomo, 539
Koppelsdorf, Heubach, 210
Korean Ceramics, 369–370
Korean Conflict, 433
KPM, 383–385, 768
Kutani, 388–389

- L -

Labels, 5, 17, 20, 474, 487, 784, 815
Lacy Glass, 328–330
Lacy Medallion, 518–519
Lafayette, 36, 255, 414
Lalique, 389–391, 403, 630
Lamps and Lighting, 14, 24, 26, 31, 33, 66, 74, 77, 81, 92, 114, 133, 162, 173, 178, 227, 267, 330, 334, 352, 363, 389, 391, 410, 425, 434, 435, 444, 467, 470, 473, 476, 482, 485, 495, 575, 577, 625, 638, 644, 650, 654, 664, 673, 711, 737, 742, 761, 762, 765, 766, 789, 801
Lamp Shades, 182, 354, 396–397, 410, 485, 610, 737, 760
Lancaster Glass Co., 190–200
Landon, Alfred, 585–590
Land Transportation Collectibles, 784–785
Lanterns, 45, 397–398, 457, 478, 482, 620, 765, 766
Late Block, 551
Laurel & Hardy, 119
Laurel Cut Glass, 179–183
Leaded Glass, 396–397
Leaf & Beads, 106
Leaf Bracket, 338
Leaf Gum Co., 717–720
Leaf Rays, 106
Leeds China, 177, 203, 398–399, 669
Lefton, 166
Legras, 95
Lehmann, 778
Lennon Sisters, 119
Lenox China, 399–400, 404, 707
Letterheads, 5, 488
Le Verre Francais, 95
Leyendecker, J. C., 599
Libbey Glass, 13, 179, 400, 771
Liberty, 28–29
Li'l Abner, 117
Limited Edition Collectors Plates, 400–406, 636
Limoges, 24, 344, 406–407, 692, 764
Lincoln, Abraham, 39, 487, 586, 594
Lindstrom, 778
Linemar, 78
Linens, 407–410, 458, 610, 754
Lion, 539–540
Lionel, 781–783

Lithophanes, 78, 410–411
Little Lulu, 117
Little Orphan Annie, 117, 464
Liverpool China, 411–412
Loetz Glass, 365, 396, 412–413
London, 550
Lone Ranger, 117, 779, 794
Loop and Dart, 540
Loop and Diamond, 542
Loop and Pillar, 544
Loops and Drops, 547–548
Loop with Stippled Panels, 556
Louisiana, 540–541
Lorenze Freres, 95
Lotus and Grape, 106
Lotus Ware China, 413
Lowestoft, 223
Low, J. & J. G., 764
Luster Wares, 414–415, 803
Lustres, Mantel, 68, 168, 326
Lutz-Type Glass, 415

- M -

Maastricht Ware, 415–416
MacBeth Evans, 190–200
Madame Alexander, 210
Maddock, John & Co., 256–258
Maddox & Sons, 359
†Magazines, 44, 64, 114, 130, 202, 426, 588,
    609, 634, 723
Magazine Racks, 300
Maiden's Blush, 505–506
Maine, 541
Majolica, 17, 34, 416–418, 439, 668, 674,
    771, 803
Maltese, 536
Manhattan, 541–542
Mansfield, Jayne, 119–120
Mantel Lustres, 68, 168, 326
Mantua, 329
Maps, 68–72, 418–419, 432, 621, 815
Marblehead Pottery, 419–420, 764
Marbles, 59
Marble Slag Glass, 604–605
Margaret (Princess), 77–80
Marklin, 778
Marlboro Street Glassworks, 329
Marseille, Armand, 210–211
Marx Toys, 778–779
Marx Trains, 781–783
Mary Gregory Type Glass, 51, 175, 371,
    420–421, 571
Maryland, 542
Maryland Pear, 504–505
Mascotte, 543
Mason Jars, 270–271
Masonic, 255, 269

Massachusetts, 543–544
Master Salts, 669
Match Holders, 59, 61, 337, 370, 421, 421–
    422, 444, 470, 745, 746
Match Safes, 5, 270, 422, 766
Match-Strikers, 226–227
Mayer, T. J. & J., 177, 728, 731
Mayflower, 517
McCarthy, Charlie, 50, 115–116
McCoy Pottery, 166, 423–424
McKee Glass, 424–425
McKinley, William, 102, 588
McLoughlin Brothers, 319, 607
Meakin, J. G., 1, 256, 446, 751, 810
Mechanical Banks, 46–49
Medical and Pharmaceutical Items, 425–
    427, 674–675
Medicine Bottles, 427–428
Meerschaum, 583
Meigh, Charles, 256–258
Meissen, 99, 216–218, 474–475, 668, 748
Mellor, Venebles & Co., 256–258, 449, 751–
    753
Mercury Glass, 428–429
Merrimac Pottery, 30
Metalcraft, 778
Metlox, 166
Mettlach, 429–430, 736
Michigan, 544
Mickey Mouse, 48, 113, 123, 159, 202–203,
    623
Midwestern Glass, 176–177, 329
Mikado, 106
Mikado, 522–523
Militaria, 37, 243, 321, 430–433
Milk Bottles, 261
Milk Glass, 75, 388, 433–435, 436, 712, 787
Millefiori, 435
Millersburg, 105–107
Milton Bradley, 319–321, 607
Mineral Bottles, 72
Minerva, 545
Minnesota, 545
Miniature Lamps, 77, 104, 162, 435–437,
    610, 815
Miniatures, 78, 127, 142, 152, 182, 222,
    260, 324, 362, 371, 388, 434, 437–439,
    444, 463, 647, 673, 678, 693, 706, 803,
    808, 815
Minor Block, 543
Minton China, 359, 439–440, 493, 496, 669,
    764
Mirror, 530
Mirrors, 6, 24, 74, 153, 300–301, 348, 363,
    438, 663, 704
Mix, Tom, 120
Mocha, 441–442

Modern Paperweights, 489–493
Modiste, 546–547
Molds, 86
Monart Glass, 442–443
Monroe, Marilyn, 120
Mont Joye Glass, 443
Moondrops, 196–197
Moorcroft, 443–444
Moriage, Japanese, 444–445, 461
Morley, Francis, 256–258
Morning Glory, 106
Moser Glass, 327, 445–446, 571, 572
Moss Rose Pattern China, 446–447
Mother's Day Plates, 400–406
Mount Washington, 13, 60, 84, 91, 109, 174, 365, 447–448, 490, 640, 666, 668, 675
Movie Posters, 114, 203, 593
Mulberry China, 448–449
Muller Croismare, 95
Musical Instruments, 317, 451–452, 683
Music Boxes, 18, 48, 273, 449–450
Mustache Cups and Saucers, 453
Mutt and Jeff, 118
Mystery Peacock, 106

- N -

Nailhead Variant, 554
Nailsea Type Glass, 453–454, 490, 809
Nanking, 454
Napkin Rings, 18, 454–455, 465, 662, 664, 677
Nash Glass, 455–456
Nautical Items, 101, 456–457, 683, 684, 787, 798, 806
Nazi Items, 457–458
Netsukes, 458–459
Neuman, Alfred, 115
Nevada, 546
Newcomb Pottery, 459–461
New England Glass, 13, 14, 176, 329, 435, 491, 568, 669
New Hall, 223–224
New Hampshire, 546–547
New Jersey, 547–548
† New Martinsville Glass Co., 190–200, 326–328
New York, 329–330
New Wharf, 256–258
Niloak Pottery, Mission Ware, 461
† Nippon China, 75, 461–463, 591, 630, 712
Nixon, Richard, 585–590
Nodders, 18, 61, 114–120, 722
† Noritake China, 75, 464–465
Noritake: Tree In The Meadow, 465–466
Norse, 30
North Dakota School of Mines, 466–467

Northeast and Woodlands Indians, 356
Northwest Coast Indians, 356
Northwood, 105, 177, 396, 496, 572, 714, 747
Notched Rib, 512
Nursing Bottles, 72–73, 743
Nutting, Wallace, 467–469
Nymphenburg, 99

- O -

Oats and Barley, 563–564
Ocean Liner Collectibles, 784–785
Occupational Shaving Mugs, 692
Occupied Japan, 469–470, 771
Ohio Art, 779
Ohr Pottery, 470–472
Old English, 197
Old Ivory China, 472
Old Man of the Mountain, 562
Old Paris China, 472–473
Old Sleepy Eye, 473–475, 736
Olive, 506
One Hundred One, 548
Onion Meissen, 474–475
Onyx Glass, 240
Opalescent Glass, 51, 175, 328, 365, 389, 436, 475, 581, 666, 669
Opaline Glass, 60, 477–478, 630, 767, 771
Orange Poppy, 341
Orange Tree, 106
Orchid, 197–198
Oregon #1, 508–509
Orientalia, 112, 273, 366, 395, 444, 464, 481, 569, 628, 629, 641, 676, 711, 750, 754
Oriental Fans, 234–235
Oriental Rugs, 478–481
Orion, 517–518
Ornaments, 130
Orvit, 29
Ottman, 319–321
Overbeck Pottery, 30
Overshot Glass, 228, 483, 571
Owens Pottery, 483–484
Owl, 514

- P -

Paden City Glass Co., 190–200
Paintings, 240, 384, 628, 629, 722, 807
Pairpoint, 60, 84, 109, 179, 392, 395, 436, 484
Palace, 562–563
Palmette, 548–549
Paneled Forget-Me-Not, 549
Paneled Herringbone, 529–530
Paneled Stippled Flower, 541
Paneled Zipper, 535

Pantin, 95
Paper Ephemera, 2, 35, 42, 62, 111, 114, 128, 153, 200, 229, 250, 264, 269, 485, 585, 592, 632, 690, 721, 784, 786, 806, 814
Paperweights, 6, 19, 45, 78, 153, 182, 338, 390, 435, 467, 487, 495, 711, 815
Papier Mache, 50, 464, 470, 493
Par Co., 606
Pardee, C, 764
Parian Ware, 78, 85–86, 493–494
Paris China, 163–165
Parker Brothers, 37, 319–321, 606
Parrish, Maxfield, 601
Pate-De-Verre, 494–496
Pate-Sur-Pate, 496
Patrick, 198
Pattern Glass, 1, 75, 109, 128, 176, 496, 580, 666, 667, 672, 712, 771
Pattern Molded Glass, 328–330
Paul Revere Pottery, 567–568, 764
Peachblow, 76, 228, 400, 568, 641, 666, 771, 799
Peacock, 106
Peacock and Dahlia, 106
Peacock and Urn, 107
Peacock at the Fountain, 107
Peacock at the Urn, 107
Peacock Feather, 531
Pearlware, 398–399, 768, 804
Peking Glass, 569–570, 710
Peloton, 570–571
Pennsylvania, 550
Pepper Berry, 506
Percussion Long Arms, 248–249
Percussion Pistols, 245–247
Perfume Bottles, 27, 92, 114, 182, 184, 371, 421, 434, 445, 455, 478, 485, 571, 660, 707, 737, 799, 802
Persian Gardens, 107
Personality Items, 114–120
Peter Pan, 203
Peters and Reed Pottery, 573
Pewabic Pottery, 30–31, 764
Pewter, 27, 28, 110, 391, 573, 669, 710, 735, 750
Phillips, G., 256–258
Phoenix Glass, 576–577
Phonographs, 577–578
Photographs, 64, 114, 433, 578, 585, 635, 722, 785
Pickard China, 579–580, 656
Picket, 550
Pickle Castors, 14, 174, 478, 580, 581, 655, 661
Pictorial Flasks, 254–256
Pigeon Blood Glass, 581, 666

Pigmy, 559
†Pinback Buttons, 7, 19, 44, 64, 114, 251, 585, 634, 815
Pineapple, 525–526
Pink Luster, 414
Pink Slag, 581–582
Pinky Lee, 120
Pinocchio, 203
Pioneer, 563
Pipes, 355–358, 582–583, 589, 597, 809
Pisgah Forest, 31
Pittsburgh Glass, 330
Plains Indians, 356–357
Plated Silver Items, 25, 99, 109, 422, 453, 454, 484, 580, 667, 705, 771
Pleat and Tuck, 499–500
Pluto, 203
Pocket Cigar Cutters, 131
Pocket Knives, 583–585, 589
Pocket Watches, 793–794
Podmore, Walker & Co., 177, 256, 448, 732
Pointed Bull's Eye, 551–552
Pointed Thumbprint, 500
Poison Bottles, 239, 585
Political Items, 38, 321, 488, 585–590, 758
Pomona Glass, 60, 590–591
Popeye, 118, 215, 794
Poppins, Mary, 202
Poppy Show, 107
Portrait Ware, 27, 87, 164, 175, 384, 407, 410, 417, 591–592, 643, 658, 680, 754, 793, 802
†Post Cards, 17, 44, 114, 130, 251, 488, 589, 621, 807, 815
†Posters, 6, 64, 114–120, 426, 432, 589, 592, 609, 635, 636, 785
Pot Lids, 595–596
Powder Horns, 243, 430–433, 685
Pratt Ware, 596–597, 769
Prayer Rug, 534
Presidential, 585–590
Presley, Elvis, 37, 120, 634
Prince's Feather, 527–528
Prints, 19, 22, 34, 337, 467, 597–602, 723, 785, 807
Prints, Japanese, 602–604
Purple Slag Glass, 604–605
†Puzzles, 64, 114, 130, 200, 605, 633, 636, 723
Pyrex, 387

- Q -

Queen Anne, 550–551
Queen Mary, 198
Queen Victoria, 48, 77, 177, 494, 739
Queen's Ware, 804
Quezal, 219, 396, 609–610, 668

Quilts, 126, 610–612
Quimper, 109, 422, 613–617, 768

- R -

Racing Collectibles, 723
Radios, 50, 111, 153, 156, 590, 593, 617–619
† Railroad Collectibles, 619–621, 692, 794
Raindrop, 107
R and H Swirl Band, 539
Rattan, 512
Razors, 621–623
Reagan, Ronald, 38, 589
Reco International, 404
Records, 200–204, 623–624, 632–635
Red Block and Fan, 510–511
Red Block, 551
Red Ryder, 118
Reddy Kilowatt, 118
Redware, 361, 624–626
Red Wing Pottery, 626–627
Reed, 205
Reed & Barton, 404
Regal China, 166
Regal, 549
Regout, Petrus, 256–258
Religious Items, 351, 381, 410, 573, 615, 627, 662, 711, 754, 783
Remington Knives, 584
Reverse Painting on Glass, 628–629, 786
Reverse Torpedo, 551–552
Revolutionary War, 431
Revolvers, 247–248
Ribbed Fingerprint, 512
Richard, 95
Ridgway, 629, 726–727, 731
Ridgway, Wm, 726–727, 731
Rifles, 249
Ring Trees, 630
Ripple, 107
Rockers, 126, 301–302, 317, 741
Rockingham and Rockingham Brown Glazed Wares, 19, 631–632
Rock 'N' Roll, 632–635
Rockwell, Norman, 635–636
Rogers & Similar Statuary, 636–637
Rogers, John, 727
Rogers, Roy, 120, 779
Roman Medallion, 545
Roman Rosette, 552
Romantic Staffordshire, 177, 731–732
Romeo, 510–511
Rookwood Pottery, 637–640
Roosevelt, Franklin, 38, 585–590, 711
Roosevelt, Theodore, 64, 585–590
Rosaline, 738
Rose Bowls, 14, 84, 134, 175, 179, 182, 183, 220, 237, 273, 326, 354, 386, 412, 413, 445, 447, 476, 478, 568, 570, 591, 639, 658, 670, 708, 715, 740
Rose Canton, Rose Mandarin, Rose Medallion, 641–642
Rose-In-Snow, 552
Rosenthal, 404, 643
Rose, 552
Rose Show, 107
Rose Tapestry, 647
Roseville Pottery, 125, 643–645, 707
Rosso Antico, 805
Round Up, 107
Royal Bayreuth, 125, 344, 422, 645–647, 747, 771
Royal Bonn, 60, 647–648
Royal Copenhagen, 404–405, 648–650
Royal Crown Derby, 650–651
Royal Doulton, 125, 344, 405, 651–653, 768, 769
Royal Dux, 654
Royal Flemish, 655
Royal Ivy, 715, 748
Royal Lace, 198–199
Royal Ruby, 199
Royal Rudolstadt, 655–656
Royal Vienna, 592, 656–657
Royal Worcester, 60, 592, 630, 657–658, 668, 754, 758
Roycroft, 32, 83, 659–660
R. S. Germany, 678–679
R. S. Poland, 679
R. S. Prussia, 592, 679–670, 748, 771
R. S. Suhl, 680
R. S. Tillowitz, 681
Rubena Glass, 572, 660
Rubena Verde Glass, 581, 660–661
Ruby Stained Glass, Souvenir Type, 661–662, 666
Ruby Thumbprint, 538–539
Rugs, 25, 126, 260, 269, 281, 358, 478–481, 482, 756
Russian Items, 163, 232, 382, 662–664
Ruth, Babe, 721

- S -

Saalfield Publishing, 607
Sabino Glass, 664
Saint Louis, 95, 491, 492
Salco, 779
Salopian Ware, 664–665
Salt and Pepper Shakers, 665–666
Saltglazed Wares, 667, 743–746
Salts, Open, 667–669
Samplers, 260, 669–672
Samson, 163–165

Sandwich Glass, 13, 65, 110, 491, 669, 672–673
Sarreguemines China, 674
Sarsaparilla Bottles, 674–675
Satin Glass, 76, 109, 193, 228, 447, 581, 641, 666, 675, 748, 798
Satsuma, 676–677
Saturday Evening Girls, 567–568
Sawtooth, 525–526
Scales, 677–678
Scent Bottles, 94, 97, 328–330, 569, 572, 664, 743
Schieble Toy Co., 779
Schlegelmilch, 344, 678–681, 748
Schmidt, Bruno, 210
Schneider Glass, 681–682
Schoenhut Toys, 111, 205, 682–683
Schuco, 779
Schwab, Hertel, 211
Scientific Instruments, 52, 74, 456, 683
Scrimshaw, 102, 630, 806–807
Scroll Embossed, 107
Sculptures, 22, 45, 628, 658, 754
Scuttles, 692
Sea Transportation Collectibles, 784–785
Sebastian Miniatures, 685–686
Secretaries, 302–304, 439
Selchow & Righter, 319–321, 587
Settees, 304–305, 318, 742
Sevres, 165, 592, 686–688
† Sewing Items, 2, 11, 19, 33, 111, 113, 120, 203, 281, 337, 355, 470, 685, 688, 691, 693, 715, 754, 757, 772, 783
Shaker, 273–318, 689–691
Sharp Ovals and Diamond, 540–541
Shaving Mugs, 79, 407, 414, 429, 466, 643, 691–692, 753
Shaw, Anthony, 751–753, 810–811
† Shawnee Pottery, 166, 388, 666, 692–693
Sheffield Silver, 99, 704–705
Shelf Clocks, 138–143
† Sheet Music, 19, 114, 130, 200–204, 474, 489, 590, 635, 723
Shield Band, 500–501
Shotguns, 249–250
Shreve and Co., 698
Shuttle, 338
Sideboards, 25, 305, 742
Signs, 6, 19, 44, 114, 153, 202, 783
Silhouettes, 469, 693–695, 807
Silver Deposit Glass, 706–707
Silver Items, 695–706. See also Plated Silver Items; Sterling Silver Items, 27, 76, 87, 99, 102, 110, 111, 160, 340, 343, 372, 381, 422, 423, 454, 484, 572, 583, 621, 630, 710, 712, 751, 758, 761
Silver Luster, 415

Silver Overlay, 400, 707
Silver Resist, 708
Simon & Halbig, 211
Sinatra, Frank, 37, 120, 624
Sinclaire, 179–183
Singing Birds, 107
Skeezix, 118
Skilton, 553–554
Smith Brothers Glass, 60, 641, 673, 708–709
Snapshots, 579
Snow Babies, 125, 648, 709
Snow White, 124, 201–203
Snuff Bottles, 132, 367, 493, 570, 709–710, 766
Soapstone, 710, 711
Societe Francaise de Bebes et Jouets, 211–212
Sofas, 306–307
Sonny, 779
Souvenir and Commemorative China and Glass, 1, 48, 74, 77, 83, 102, 177, 254, 263, 344, 345, 346, 399, 423, 456, 491, 711, 723, 758, 788, 815
Souvenir and Commemorative Fans, 233–234
Souvenir and Commemorative Spoons, 474, 712–713
Spades, 548–549
Spangled Glass, 228, 713–714
Spatter Glass, 365, 714–715, 771
Spatterware, 224–226, 715–716
Spirea, 554
Spirea Band, 554
Spongeware, 716–717
Sports Cards, 717–720
Spode, Josiah, 167, 256, 359, 811
Sports Collectibles, 1, 38, 717, 720–723
Springtime, 107
Springtime, Hall China, 341
Spring Water Bottles, 72
Squared Dot, 554
Staffordshire, Historical, 723–729
Staffordshire Items, 729–730, 769
Staffordshire Pottery, 1, 2, 125, 126, 177, 184, 224, 723, 769, 808
Stained and/or Leaded Glass Panels, 732–733
Stands, 308–309, 318, 452, 783
Stangl Pottery Birds, 733–734
Stankard, Paul, 492
Stanley Pottery, 256–258
Star and Diamonds, 543–544
Star of David, 107
Star of the East, 534–535
States, The, 554–555
Statues, 663, 664

Steelcraft, 780
Steiff, 734–735
Steiner, Jules, 212
Steins, 165, 410, 421, 430, 442, 474, 735–736, 792
Stepped Diamond Point, 525–526
Steps, 309
Sterling Silver Items, 695–706. See also Silver
Steuben Glass, 365, 393, 396, 668, 736–738
Stevens and Williams, 92, 641, 740–741
Stevensgraphs, 738–739
Stevenson, 727–728, 732
Stickleys, 32–34, 273–318, 741–742
Stiegel-Type Glass, 742–743
Still Banks, 17, 43, 49, 114, 200, 268, 329, 624, 712, 716, 721, 729
Stippled Daisy, 564–565
Stippled Oval, 526
Stippled Primrose, 541
Stippled Rays, 107
Stock and Bond Certificates, 489, 785
Stockton Art Pottery, 31
Stoddard, 330
Stoneware, 743–745, 768, 804
Stoneware, Blue and White, 387, 745–746
Stools, 309–310, 348, 438
Straight Shooter, 118
Straus, Joseph, 606
Strauss, 130, 780
Strawberry and Bird, 509
Strawberry, 107
Strawberry China, 224–226
Stretch Glass, 746–747
String Holders, 19, 153, 647, 747
Stubbs, 728
Sturditoy, 780
Sugar Shakers, 170, 174, 337, 448, 463, 466, 476, 477, 569, 702, 715, 747, 797, 808
Sunbonnet Babies, 647
Sunderland Luster, 415
Swansea, 748–749
Swirl and Feather, 527–528
Swirl, 527–528
Swirl Hobnail, 107
Swords, 102, 663, 749–750

- T -

Tables, 24, 26, 33, 310, 318, 438, 660, 689, 690, 742, 761
Taft, William, 587
Tall-Case Clocks, 143–146
Tapestry Ware, 647, 648
Tarzan, 118

Tea Caddies, 229, 334, 399, 482, 597, 659, 703, 750, 772, 802
Tea Leaf Ironstone, 751–753
Teardrop and Diamond Block, 502
Teco Pottery, 31
Teddy Bears, 48
Temple, Shirley, 120
Ten Mums, 107
Tennessee, 555
Teplitz China, 15–16, 753–754
Terra Cotta, 754, 768
Texas, 556
Textiles, 114, 260, 355, 407, 432, 458, 610, 628, 669, 738, 754–757, 815
Thermometers, 7, 65, 153
Thimbles, 689, 757–758, 772
Thistle and Sunflower, 564–565
Thistle, 107
Thompson's #77, 559–560
Thousand Eye, 556–558
Threaded Glass, 483, 738, 758, 759
Three Face, 558
Three Fruits, 107
Three Little Pigs, 204
Thumbprint Band, 523–524
Tickets, 489
Tiffany, 91, 161, 182, 281, 365, 379, 394, 396, 609, 668, 759–762
Tiffin Glass, 326–328, 762–763
Tiles, 29, 34, 82, 337, 339, 435, 441, 475, 482, 567, 590, 639, 677, 763, 804
Tinware, 2, 46, 99, 128, 262, 391, 394, 397, 423, 764, 773
Tinware: Decorated, 397–398, 766–767
† Tins, 7, 79
Tippecanoe, 563
TM, Japanese Toys, 780
Tobacco Cutters, 767
Tobacco Jars, 18, 83, 136, 147, 175, 181, 270, 335, 385, 418, 463, 466, 708, 767–768
Toby Jugs, 59, 632, 636, 653, 768, 813
Tole, 751
Toledo Metal Wheel Co., 780
Tools, 366, 685, 769–770
Toothpick Holders, 12, 14, 85, 97, 179, 264, 415, 425, 435, 448, 568, 582, 591, 647, 662, 679, 680, 707, 711, 712, 740, 770–772
Topps Chewing Gum Co., 717–720
Torpedo, 559
Tortoise Shell Items, 88, 141, 339–340, 758–773
Town Pump, 107, 476
Toys, 19, 65, 113, 114, 126, 127, 130, 200, 363, 470, 493, 682, 734, 765, 773–781
Tracy, Dick, 116, 160

Trains, Toy, 259, 781–783
Tramp Art, 630, 783
Transportation Memorabilia, 129, 268, 320, 489, 594, 609, 773, 784
Trinket Boxes, 226–227
Triple Bull's Eye, 562–563
Truman, Harry, 38, 588
Truncated Cube, 559–560
Trunks, 438, 786
Tuco, 607
Turkey Track, 566
Tuthill, 179–183
Twin Pear, 504–505
Twin Winton, 166

- U -

Union, 514
Union Glass, 385–386
Unique Art, 780
University City, 31
U. S. Coin, 560
U. S. Glass, 105–107, 190–200, 496–566
U. S. Mirror, 530
U. S. Sheraton, 561

- V -

Valentines, 786–787
Valentino, Rudy, 120
Vallerystahl, 668, 787–788
Vallona Star, 166
Val Saint Lambert, 491, 788–789
Van Briggle Pottery, 789–790
Vandor, 167
Vasa Murrhina, 714–715
Vauxhall, 224
Vending Machines, 155–157
Venetian Glass, 790
Verlys Glass, 790–791
Vermont, 561–562
Verre De Soie, 738
Vessiere, 95
Victrola, 577–578
Vietnam War, 433
Viking, 562
Villeroy & Boch, 736, 791–792
Vinaigrettes, 572
Vintage, 107
Virginia, 530
Virginia #1, 505–506
Volkmar, 31

- W -

Waffle and Fine Cut, 517–518
Waffle and Thumbprint, 562–563
Walker, Thomas, 256–258
Walking Sticks, 101–102

Wall Clocks, 146–147
Walley Pottery, 31
Walrath Pottery, 31–32
Wannopee Pottery, 32
War of 1812, 431
Warwick China, 258
Washboard, 499–500
Washington, George, 255, 258, 411, 469, 489, 585, 629, 712, 729
Watches, Pocket, 793–794
Watches, Wrist, 65, 114, 203, 794–795
Watch Fobs, 20, 251, 590, 816
Waterford, 796
Water Lily, 107
Water Lily and Cattail, 338
Wave Crest, 60, 371, 592, 666, 668, 796–797
Weather Vanes, 19, 169, 260, 797–798, 814
Webb, Thomas & Sons, 84, 92, 569, 572, 668, 798–800
Wedgwood, 60, 124, 127, 324, 370, 405, 417, 630, 668, 748, 800–804, 811
Wedgwood, John, 256–258
Weller, 805–806
West and Southwest Indians, 357–358
Western Publishing, 607
Westford, 330
Westward Ho!, 563
Whaling, 102, 684, 806
Wheat and Barley, 563–564
Wheatley Pottery, 32
Wheeling, 256–258, 569
Whieldon, 808
Whimsies, Glass, 237, 415, 454, 808–809
Whirligigs, 260
Whiskey Bottles, Early, 809–810
Whitefraiers, 491, 492
White Patterned Ironstone, 810–811
Whitman, 608
Wicker, 125–126, 317–318
Wild Rose and Bowknot, 338
Wilkie, Wendel, 587, 607
Wilkinson, Arthur, 258
Willow Oak, 564–565
Willow Pattern China, 82, 152, 811–813
Wilson, Woodrow, 38, 489
Winchester Knives, 584
Windflower, 107
Windsor, 199–200
Winking Eye, 527
Winnie the Pooh, 204
Wisconsin, 565
Witch Balls, 330, 453–454, 809
Withers, Jane, 120
Wizard of Oz, 118, 122–124
Wolverine, 781
†Woodenware, 20, 46, 71, 86, 101, 259, 273,

361, 371, 382, 386, 397, 459, 630, 688, 689, 736, 813
Wood, Enoch, 728–729
Woodrow, 530
†World's Fairs and Expositions, 7, 13, 233, 268, 400, 489, 568, 662, 711, 712, 739, 814–816
†World War I, 432, 594–595
†World War II, 433, 457–458, 595
Wreath of Roses, 107
Wyandotte, 781

- X, Y, Z -

X.L.C.R., 538–539
X-Ray, 565–566

Yale, 566
Yellow Glazed, 224–226
Yellow Kid, 118
Yellow Ware, 816–817
Ysart, Paul, 492
Zane Pottery, 573, 817
Zanesville Glass, 330
Zanesville Pottery, 805–806, 817–818
Zark Pottery, 32
Zenith, 619
Zig Zag, 107
Zipper, 566
Zorn, Anders, 602
Zorro, 204
Zsolnay, 818–819

Harry and the Rinkettes. *Left to right:* Nancy M. Butt, Jocelyn C. Mousley, Harry L. Rinker, Jr., Terese J. Oswald, Harry L. Rinker, Ellen T. Schroy, and Dana Gehman Morykan.

HARRY L. RINKER, nationally recognized antiques and collectibles author, teacher, and collector, is editor of *Warman's Americana and Collectibles* and *Warman's Furniture;* author of *Collector's Guide to Toys, Games, and Puzzles, How to Make the Most of Your Investments in Antiques and Collectibles,* and *Rinker on Collectibles;* co-author with Frank Hill of *The Joy of Collecting with Craven Moore,* with Norman E. Martinus of *Warman's Paper,* and with Dana Gehman Morykan of *Warman's Country Antiques & Collectibles, Second Edition;* syndicated columnist of "Rinker on Collectibles," and executive director of The Institute for the Study of Antiques and Collectibles.